Benchmark Series

Levels 1 & 2

Microsoft®

Access®

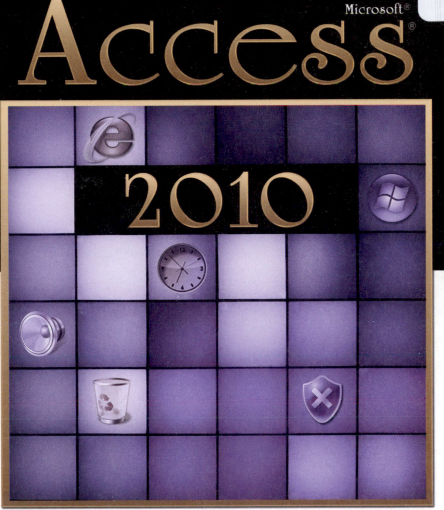

Nita Rutkosky
Pierce College at Puyallup
Puyallup, Washington

Denise Seguin
Fanshawe College
London, Ontario

Audrey Rutkosky Roggenkamp
Pierce College at Puyallup
Puyallup, Washington

Paradigm Publishing
St. Paul • Indianapolis

Managing Editor Sonja Brown
Senior Developmental Editor Christine Hurney
Production Editor Donna Mears
Copy Editor Susan Capecchi
Cover and Text Designer Leslie Anderson
Desktop Production Ryan Hamner, Julie Johnston, Jack Ross
Proofreader Laura Nelson
Indexer Sandi Schroeder

Acknowledgements: The authors, editors, and publisher thank the following instructors for their helpful suggestions during the planning and development of the books in the Benchmark Office 2010 Series: Somasheker Akkaladevi, Virginia State University, Petersburg, VA; Ed Baker, Community College of Philadelphia, Philadelphia, PA; Lynn Baldwin, Madison Area Technical College, Madison, WI; Letty Barnes, Lake Washington Technical College, Kirkland, WA; Richard Bell, Coastal Carolina Community College, Jacksonville, NC; Perry Callas, Clatsop Community College, Astoria, OR; Carol DesJardins, St. Clair County Community College, Port Huron, MI; Stacy Gee Hollins, St. Louis Community College--Florissant Valley, St. Louis, MO Sally Haywood, Prairie State College, Chicago Heights, IL; Dr. Penny Johnson, Madison Technical College, Madison, WI; Jan Kehm, Spartanburg Community College, Spartanburg, SC; Jacqueline Larsen, Asheville Buncombe Tech, Asheville, NC; Sherry Lenhart, Terra Community College, Fremont, OH; Andrea Robinson Hinsey, Ivy Tech Community College NE, Fort Wayne, IN; Bari Siddique, University of Texas at Brownsville, Brownsville, TX; Joan Splawski, Northeast Wisconsin Technical College, Green Bay, WI; Diane Stark, Phoenix College, Phoenix, AZ; Mary Van Haute, Northeast Wisconsin Technical College, Green Bay, WI; Rosalie Westerberg, Clover Park Technical College, Lakewood, WA.

The publishing team also thanks the following individuals for their contributions to this project: checking the accuracy of the instruction and exercises—Robertt (Rob) W. Neilly, Traci Post, and Lindsay Ryan; developing lesson plans, supplemental assessments, and supplemental case studies—Jan Davidson, Lambton College, Sarnia, Ontario; writing rubrics to support end-of-chapter and end-of-unit activities—Robertt (Rob) W. Neilly, Seneca College, Toronto, Ontario; writing test item banks—Jeff Johnson; writing online quiz item banks—Trudy Muller; and developing PowerPoint presentations—Janet Blum, Fanshawe College, London, Ontario.

ISBN 978-0-76384-302-1 (Text)
ISBN 978-0-76384-305-2 (Text + CD)

875 Montreal Way
St. Paul, MN 55102
Email: educate@emcp.com
Website: www.emcp.com

Printed in the United States of America

19 18 17 16 15 14 13 12 11 2 3 4 5 6 7 8 9 10

Contents

Microsoft Access 2010 Level 2

Preface

Benchmark Microsoft Access 2010 is designed for students who want to learn how to use this feature-rich data management tool to track, report, and share information. No prior knowledge of database management systems is required. After successfully completing a course using this textbook, students will be able to

- Create database tables to organize business or personal records
- Modify and manage tables to ensure that data is accurate and up to date
- Perform queries to assist with decision making
- Plan, research, create, revise, and publish database information to meet specific communication needs
- Given a workplace scenario requiring the reporting and analysis of data, assess the information requirements and then prepare the materials that achieve the goal efficiently and effectively

In addition to mastering Access skills, students will learn the essential features and functions of computer hardware, the Windows 7 operating system, and Internet Explorer 8.0. Upon completing the text, they can expect to be proficient in using Access to organize, analyze, and present information.

Achieving Proficiency in Access 2010

Since its inception several Office versions ago, the Benchmark Series has served as a standard of excellence in software instruction. Elements of the book function individually and collectively to create an inviting, comprehensive learning environment that produces successful computer users. The following visual tour highlights the text's features.

UNIT OPENERS display the unit's four chapter titles. Each level has two units, which conclude with a comprehensive unit performance assessment.

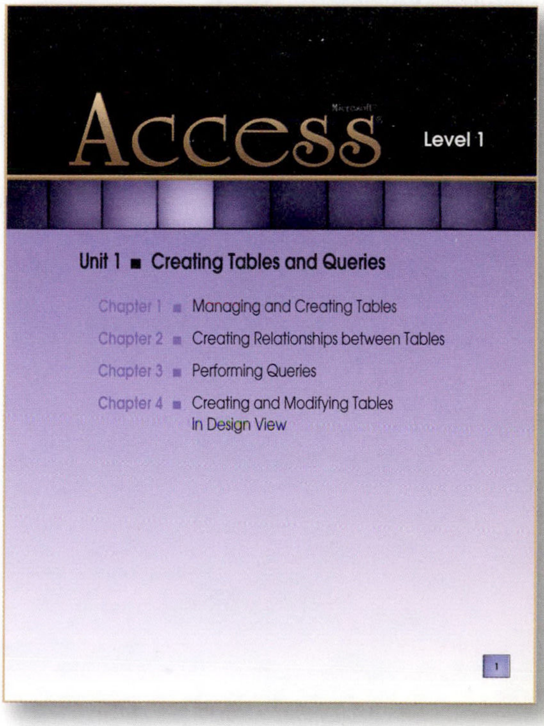
Access Level 1

Unit 1 ■ Creating Tables and Queries

Chapter 1 ■ Managing and Creating Tables
Chapter 2 ■ Creating Relationships between Tables
Chapter 3 ■ Performing Queries
Chapter 4 ■ Creating and Modifying Tables In Design View

1

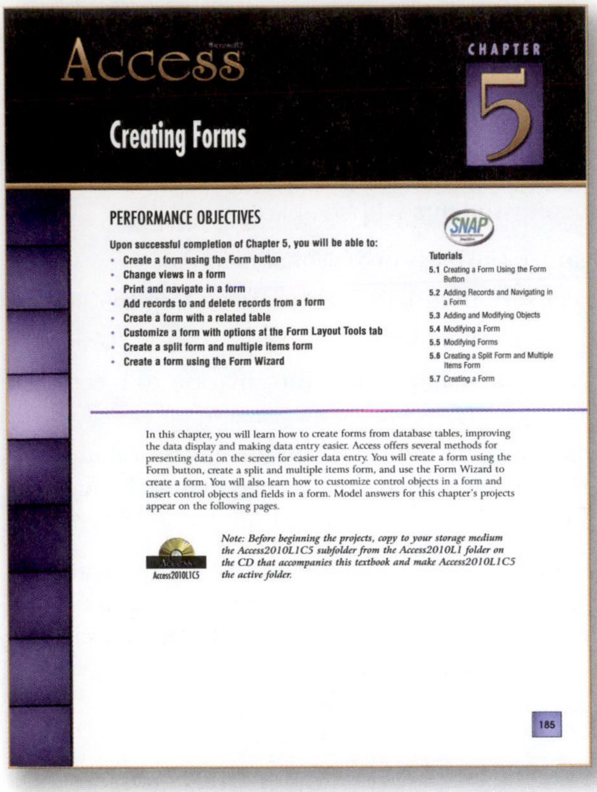
Access

Creating Forms

CHAPTER 5

PERFORMANCE OBJECTIVES

Upon successful completion of Chapter 5, you will be able to:

- Create a form using the Form button
- Change views in a form
- Print and navigate in a form
- Add records to and delete records from a form
- Create a form with a related table
- Customize a form with options at the Form Layout Tools tab
- Create a split form and multiple items form
- Create a form using the Form Wizard

SNAP

Tutorials

5.1 Creating a Form Using the Form Button
5.2 Adding Records and Navigating in a Form
5.3 Adding and Modifying Objects
5.4 Modifying a Form
5.5 Modifying Forms
5.6 Creating a Split Form and Multiple Items Form
5.7 Creating a Form

In this chapter, you will learn how to create forms from database tables, improving the data display and making data entry easier. Access offers several methods for presenting data on the screen for easier data entry. You will create a form using the Form button, create a split and multiple items form, and use the Form Wizard to create a form. You will also learn how to customize control objects in a form and insert control objects and fields in a form. Model answers for this chapter's projects appear on the following pages.

Access2010L1C5

Note: Before beginning the projects, copy to your storage medium the Access2010L1C5 subfolder from the Access2010L1 folder on the CD that accompanies this textbook and make Access2010L1C5 the active folder.

185

CHAPTER OPENERS present the performance objectives and an overview of the skills taught.

SNAP interactive tutorials are available to support chapter-specific skills at www.snap2010.emcp.com.

DATA FILES are provided for each chapter. A prominent note reminds students to copy the appropriate chapter data folder and make it active.

PROJECT APPROACH: Builds Skill Mastery within Realistic Context

MODEL ANSWERS provide a preview of the finished chapter projects and allow students to confirm they have created the materials accurately.

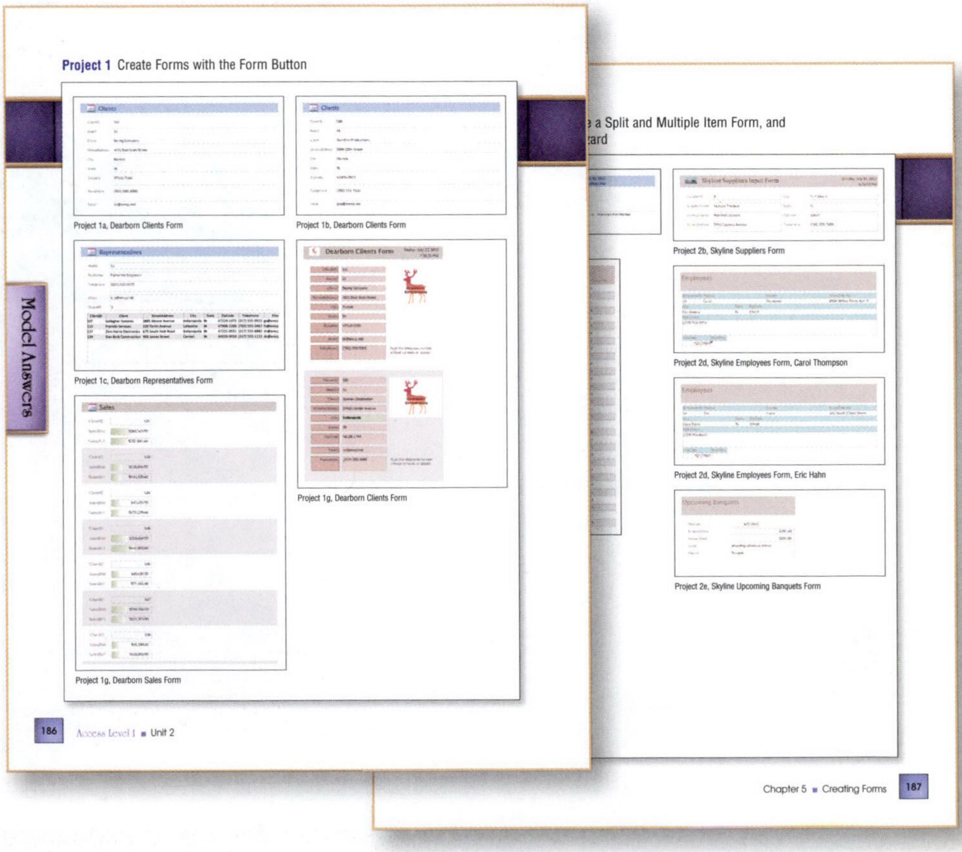
Project 1 Create Forms with the Form Button

Project 1a, Dearborn Clients Form

Project 1b, Dearborn Clients Form

Project 1c, Dearborn Representatives Form

Project 1g, Dearborn Clients Form

Project 1g, Dearborn Sales Form

Model Answers

186 Access Level 1 ■ Unit 2

...a Split and Multiple Item Form, and ...ard

Project 2b, Skyline Suppliers Form

Project 2d, Skyline Employees Form, Carol Thompson

Project 2d, Skyline Employees Form, Eric Hahn

Project 2e, Skyline Upcoming Banquets Form

Chapter 5 ■ Creating Forms 187

MULTIPART PROJECTS provide a framework for the instruction and practice on software features. A project overview identifies tasks to accomplish and key features to use in completing the work.

Project 1 Create Forms with the Form Button — 7 Parts

You will use the Form button to create forms with fields in the Clients, Representatives, and Sales tables. You will also add, delete, and print records and use buttons in the Form Layout Tools Format tab to apply formatting to control objects in the forms.

Quick Steps
Create a Form with Form Button
1. Click desired table.
2. Click Create tab.
3. Click Form button.

HINT A form allows you to focus on a single record at a time.

HINT Save a form before making changes or applying formatting to the form.

Creating a Form

Access offers a variety of options for presenting data in a more easily read and attractive format. When entering data in a table in Datasheet view, multiple records display at the same time. If a record contains several fields, you may not be able to view all fields within a record at the same time. If you create a form, generally all fields for a record are visible on the screen. Several methods are available for creating a form. In this section, you will learn how to create a form using the Form, Split Form, and Multiple Items buttons as well as the Form Wizard.

Creating a Form with the Form Button

You can view, add, or edit data in a table in Datasheet view. You can also perform these functions on data inserted in a form. A ***form*** is an object you can use to enter and edit data in a table or query and is a user-friendly interface for viewing, adding, editing, and deleting records. A form is also useful in helping prevent incorrect data from being entered and it can be used to control access to specific data.

You can use a variety of methods to create a form. The simplest method to create a form is to click the Create tab and then click the Form button in the Forms groups. Figure 5.1 displays the form you will create in Project 1a with the

Form

Figure 5.1 Form Created from Data in the Clients Table

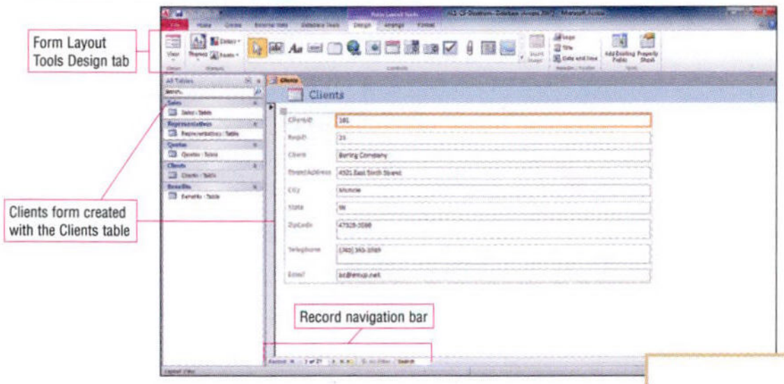

188 Access Level 1 ■ Unit 2

Between project parts, the text presents instruction on the features and skills necessary to accomplish the next section of the project.

STEP-BY-STEP INSTRUCTIONS guide students to the desired outcome for each project part. Screen captures illustrate what the student's screen should look like at key points.

Adding and Deleting Records

Add a new record to the form by clicking the New (blank) record button (contains a right arrow followed by a yellow asterisk) that displays in the Record navigation bar along the bottom of the form. You can also add a new record to a form by clicking the Home tab and then clicking the New button in the Records group. To delete a record, display the record, click the Home tab, click the Delete button arrow in the Records group, and then click *Delete Record* at the drop-down list. At the message telling you that the record will be deleted permanently, click Yes.

Quick Steps
Add a Record
Click New (blank) record button in Record navigation bar.
OR
1. Click Home tab.
2. Click New button.
Delete a Record
1. Click Home tab.
2. Click Delete button arrow.
3. Click *Delete Record.*
4. Click Yes.

New Record

Delete

Sorting Records

You can sort data in a form by clicking in the field containing data on which you want to sort and then clicking the Ascending button or Descending button in the Sort & Filter group in the Home tab. Click the Ascending button to sort text in alphabetic order from A to Z or numbers from lowest to highest or click the Descending button to sort text in alphabetic order from Z to A or numbers from highest to lowest.

Project 1b **Adding and Deleting Records in a Form** — Part 2 of 7

1. With the Clients form open and the first record displayed, add a new record by completing the following steps:
   a. Click the New (blank) record button located in the Record navigation bar.
   b. At the new blank record, type the following information in the specified fields (move to the next field by pressing Tab or Enter; move to the previous field by pressing Shift + Tab):

ClientID	=	128
RepID	=	14
Client	=	Gen-Erin Productions
StreetAddress	=	1099 15th Street
City	=	Muncie
State	=	IN
ZipCode	=	473067963
Telephone	=	7655553120
Email	=	gep@emcp.net

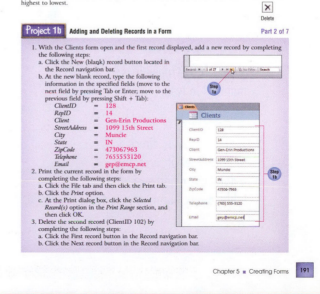

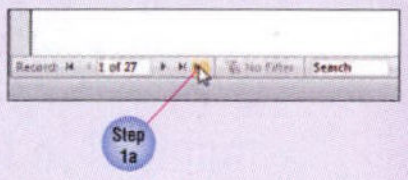

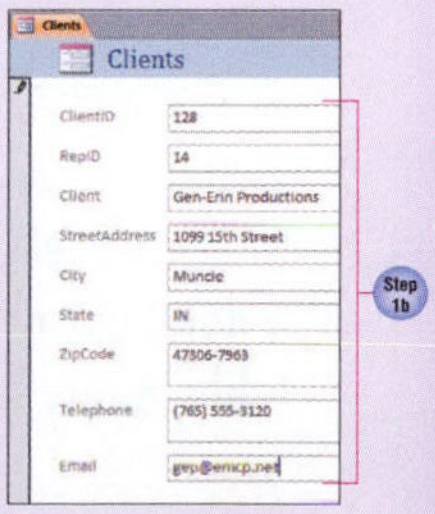

2. Print the current record in the form by completing the following steps:
   a. Click the File tab and then click the Print tab.
   b. Click the *Print* option.
   c. At the Print dialog box, click the *Selected Record(s)* option in the *Print Range* section, and then click OK.
3. Delete the second record (ClientID 102) by completing the following steps:
   a. Click the First record button in the Record navigation bar.
   b. Click the Next record button in the Record navigation bar.

Chapter 5 ■ Creating Forms 191

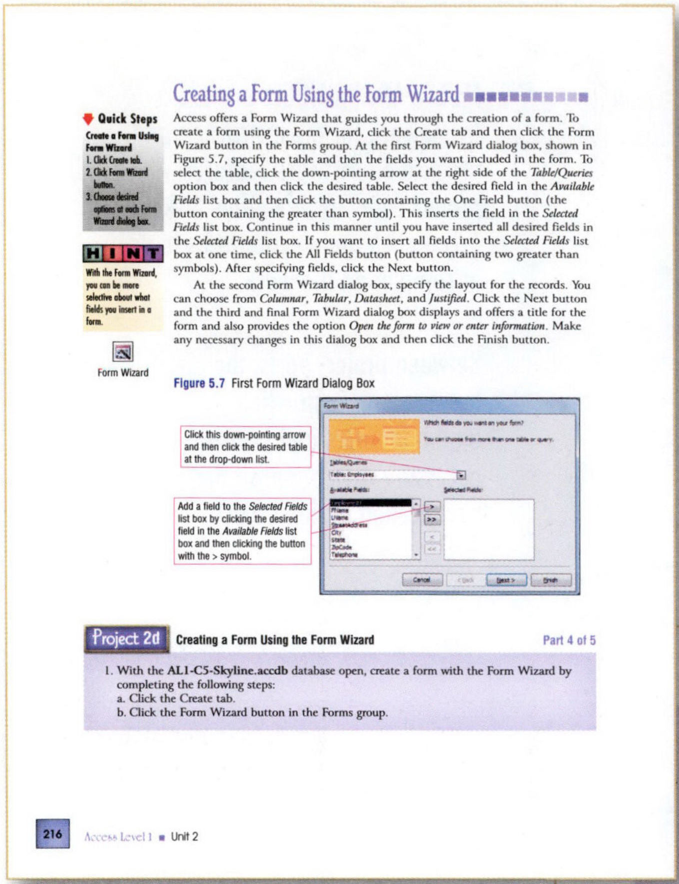

Creating a Form Using the Form Wizard

Quick Steps
Create a Form Using Form Wizard
1. Click Create tab.
2. Click Form Wizard button.
3. Choose desired options at each Form Wizard dialog box.

HINT
With the Form Wizard, you can be more selective about what fields you insert in a form.

Form Wizard

Access offers a Form Wizard that guides you through the creation of a form. To create a form using the Form Wizard, click the Create tab and then click the Form Wizard button in the Forms group. At the first Form Wizard dialog box, shown in Figure 5.7, specify the table and then the fields you want included in the form. To select the table, click the down-pointing arrow at the right side of the *Table/Queries* option box and then click the desired table. Select the desired field in the *Available Fields* list box and then click the button containing the One Field button (the button containing the greater than symbol). This inserts the field in the *Selected Fields* list box. Continue in this manner until you have inserted all desired fields in the *Selected Fields* list box. If you want to insert all fields into the *Selected Fields* list box at one time, click the All Fields button (button containing two greater than symbols). After specifying fields, click the Next button.

At the second Form Wizard dialog box, specify the layout for the records. You can choose from *Columnar*, *Tabular*, *Datasheet*, and *Justified*. Click the Next button and the third and final Form Wizard dialog box displays and offers a title for the form and also provides the option *Open the form to view or enter information*. Make any necessary changes in this dialog box and then click the Finish button.

Figure 5.7 First Form Wizard Dialog Box

Click this down-pointing arrow and then click the desired table at the drop-down list.

Add a field to the *Selected Fields* list box by clicking the desired field in the *Available Fields* list box and then clicking the button with the > symbol.

Project 2d Creating a Form Using the Form Wizard — Part 4 of 5

1. With the **AL1-C5-Skyline.accdb** database open, create a form with the Form Wizard by completing the following steps:
   a. Click the Create tab.
   b. Click the Form Wizard button in the Forms group.

216 Access Level 1 ■ Unit 2

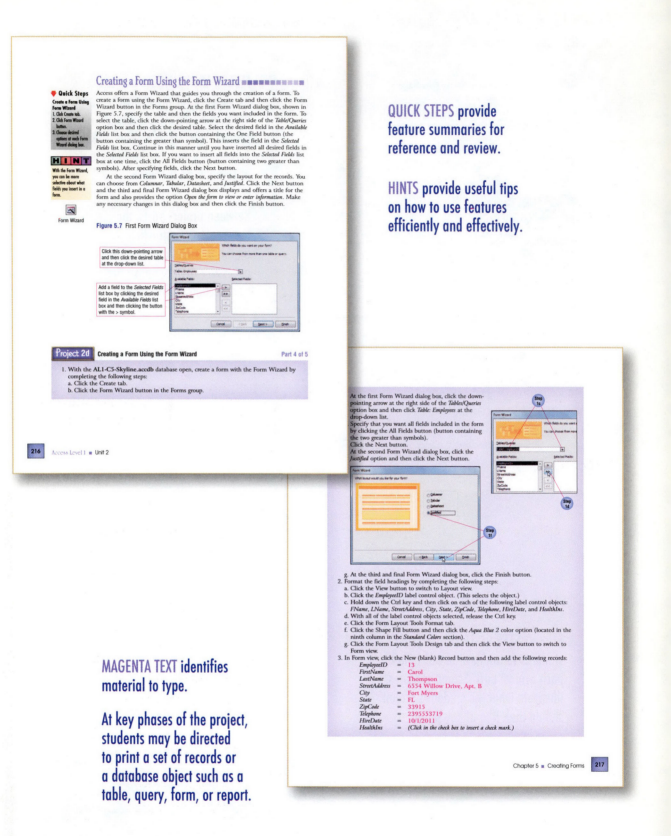

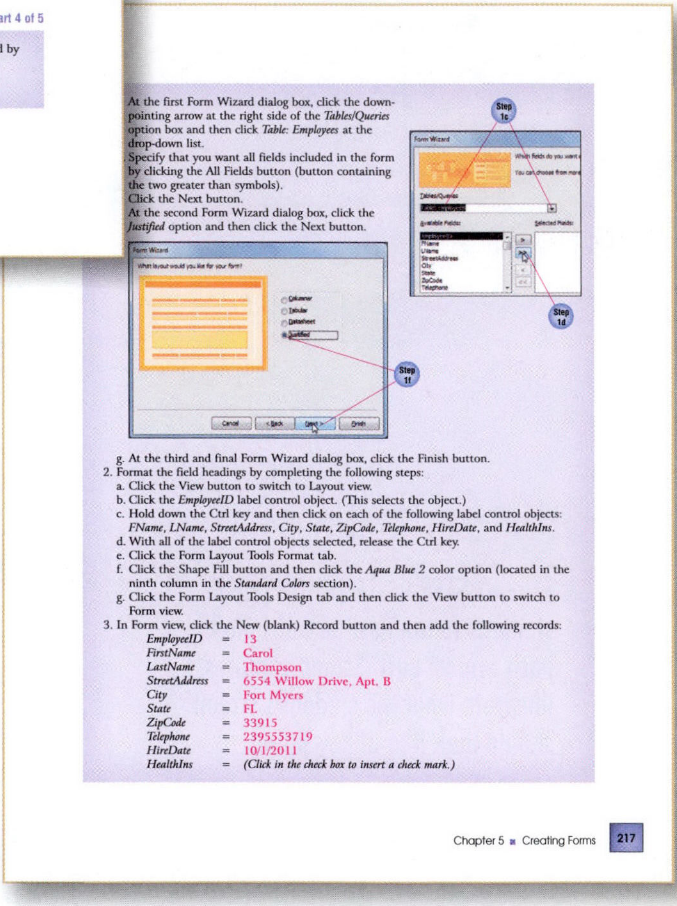

At the first Form Wizard dialog box, click the down-pointing arrow at the right side of the *Tables/Queries* option box and then click *Table: Employees* at the drop-down list.
Specify that you want all fields included in the form by clicking the All Fields button (button containing the two greater than symbols).
Click the Next button.
At the second Form Wizard dialog box, click the *Justified* option and then click the Next button.

g. At the third and final Form Wizard dialog box, click the Finish button.
2. Format the field headings by completing the following steps:
   a. Click the View button to switch to Layout view.
   b. Click the *EmployeeID* label control object. (This selects the object.)
   c. Hold down the Ctrl key and then click on each of the following label control objects: *FName*, *LName*, *StreetAddress*, *City*, *State*, *ZipCode*, *Telephone*, *HireDate*, and *HealthIns*.
   d. With all of the label control objects selected, release the Ctrl key.
   e. Click the Form Layout Tools Format tab.
   f. Click the Shape Fill button and then click the *Aqua Blue 2* color option (located in the ninth column in the *Standard Colors* section).
   g. Click the Form Layout Tools Design tab and then click the View button to switch to Form view.
3. In Form view, click the New (blank) Record button and then add the following records:

EmployeeID	=	13
FirstName	=	Carol
LastName	=	Thompson
StreetAddress	=	6554 Willow Drive, Apt. B
City	=	Fort Myers
State	=	FL
ZipCode	=	33915
Telephone	=	2395553719
HireDate	=	10/1/2011
HealthIns	=	*(Click in the check box to insert a check mark.)*

Chapter 5 ■ Creating Forms 217

QUICK STEPS provide feature summaries for reference and review.

HINTS provide useful tips on how to use features efficiently and effectively.

MAGENTA TEXT identifies material to type.

At key phases of the project, students may be directed to print a set of records or a database object such as a table, query, form, or report.

CHAPTER REVIEW ACTIVITIES: A Hierarchy of Learning Assessments

Chapter Summary

- Microsoft Access is a database management system software program that will organize, store, maintain, retrieve, sort, and print all types of business data.
- In Access, open an existing database by clicking the Open button at the New tab Backstage view. At the open dialog box, navigate to the location where the database is located, and then double-click the desired database.
- Only one database can be open at a time.
- Some common objects found in a database include tables, queries, forms, and reports.
- The Navigation pane displays at the left side of the Access screen and displays the objects that are contained in the database.
- Open a database object by double-clicking the object in the Navigation pane. Close an object by clicking the Close button that displays in the upper right corner of the work area.
- When a table is open, the Record Navigation bar displays at the bottom of the screen and contains a button for displaying records in the table.
- Insert a new record in a table by clicking the [...] in the Home tab or by clicking the New [...] Navigation bar. Delete a record by clickin[...] to delete, clicking the Delete button arro[...] *Delete Record* at the drop-down list.
- To add a column to a table, click the first [...] heading and then type the desired data. T[...] and then use the mouse to drag a thick, b[...] column) to the desired location. To delete [...] click the Delete button arrow, and then cl[...]
- Data you enter in a table is automatically [...] a table are not automatically saved.
- You can hide, unhide, freeze, and unfreez[...] button drop-down list. Display this list b[...] Records group in the Home tab.
- Adjust the width of a column (or selected [...] longest entry by double-clicking the colu[...] width of a column by dragging the colum[...]
- Print a table by clicking the File tab, click[...] the *Quick Print* option. You can also previ[...] the *Print Preview* option at the Print tab B[...]
- With buttons and option on the Print Pr[...] size, orientation, and margins.
- The first principle in database design is t[...] redundant data increases the amount of [...] chances for errors, and takes up additiona[...]
- A data type defines the type of data Acce[...] type to a field with buttons in the Add & [...] tab, by clicking an option from the colum[...] options at the More button drop-down li[...]

CHAPTER SUMMARY captures the purpose and execution of key features.

- Rename a column heading by right-clicking the heading, clicking *Rename Field* at the shortcut menu, and then typing the new name.
- Type a name, a caption, and a description for a column with options at the Enter Field Properties dialog box.
- Use options in the *Quick Start* category in the More Fields button drop-down list to define a data type and assign a field name to a group of related fields.
- Insert a default value in a column with the Default Value button and assign a field size with the *Field Size* text box in the Properties group in the Table Tools Fields tab.
- Use the *Data Type* option box in the Formatting group to change the AutoNumber data type for the first column in a table.

Commands Review

COMMANDS REVIEW summarizes visually the major features and command options.

FEATURE	RIBBON TAB, GROUP	BUTTON, OPTION	KEYBOARD SHORTCUT
Open dialog box	File	Open	Ctrl + O
Close database	File	Close Database	
New record	Home, Records	[icon]	Ctrl + +
Next field			Tab
Previous field			Shift + Tab
Delete record	Home, Records	[X] Delete Record	
Delete column	Home, Records	[X] Delete Column	
Hide column	Home, Records		
Unhide column	Home, Records		
Freeze column	Home, Records		
Unfreeze column	Home, Records		
Print tab Backstage view	File		
Print Preview	File		
Print dialog box	File		
Page size	File		
Page margins	File		

Concepts Check Test Your Knowledge

Completion: In the space provided at the right, indicate the correct term, symbol, or command.

1. The Query Design button is located in the Queries group in this tab.

2. Click the Query Design button and the query window displays with this dialog box open.

3. To establish a criterion for the query, click in this row in the column containing the desired field name and then type the criterion.

4. This is the term used for the results of the query.

5. This is the symbol Access automatically inserts around a date when writing a criterion for the query.

6. Use this symbol to indicate a wildcard character when writing a query criterion.

7. This is the criterion you would type to return field values greater than $500.

8. This is the criterion you would type to return field values that begin with the letter *L*.

9. This is the criterion you would type to return field values that are not in Oregon.

10. You can sort a field in a query in ascending order or this order.

11. Enter a criterion in this row in the query design grid to instruct Access to display records that match either of the two criteria.

12. This wizard guides you through the steps for preparing a query.

13. This type of query calculates aggregate functions in which field values are grouped by two fields.

14. Use this type of query to compare two tables and produce a list of the records in one table that have no matching record in the other related table.

CONCEPTS CHECK questions assess knowledge recall.

SKILLS CHECK exercises ask students to develop both standard and customized kinds of database elements.

VISUAL BENCHMARK assessments test students' problem-solving skills and mastery of program features.

CASE STUDY requires analyzing a workplace scenario and then planning and executing multipart projects.

Students strengthen their analytical and writing skills by using Microsoft Word to describe best uses of Access features or to explain the decisions they made in completing the Case Study.

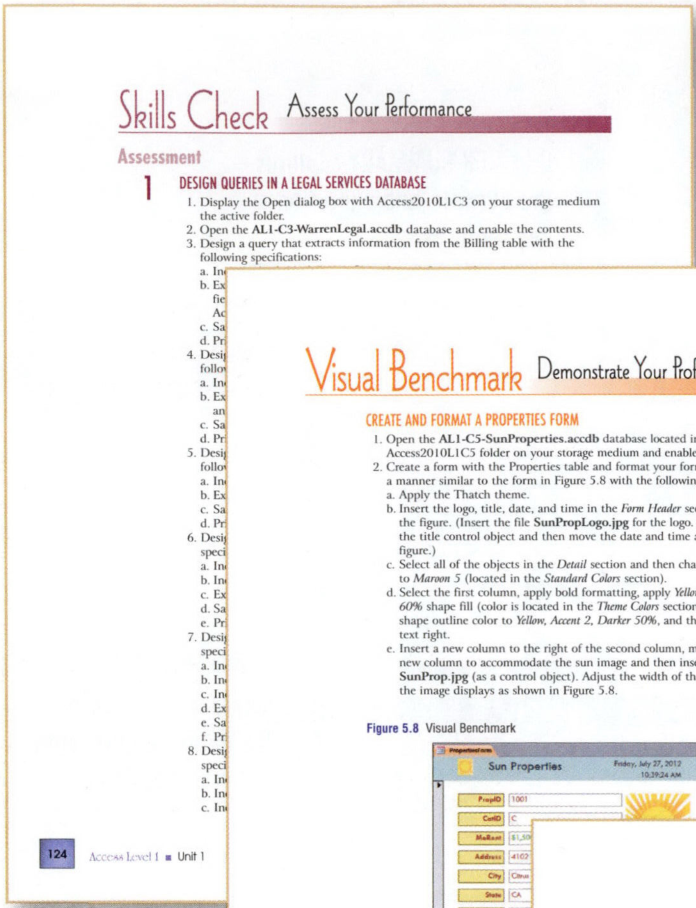

Skills Check Assess Your Performance

Assessment

1 DESIGN QUERIES IN A LEGAL SERVICES DATABASE

1. Display the Open dialog box with Access2010L1C3 on your storage medium the active folder.
2. Open the **AL1-C3-WarrenLegal.accdb** database and enable the contents.
3. Design a query that extracts information from the Billing table with the following specifications:
 a. In
 b. Ex
 fie
 Ac
 c. Sa
 d. Pr
4. Desi
 follo
 a. In
 b. Ex
 an
 c. Sa
 d. Pr
5. Desi
 follo
 a. In
 b. Ex
 c. Sa
 d. Pr
6. Desi
 spec
 a. In
 b. In
 c. Ex
 d. Sa
 e. Pr
7. Desi
 spec
 a. In
 b. In
 c. In
 d. Ex
 e. Sa
 f. Pr
8. Desi
 spec
 a. In
 b. In
 c. In

124 Access Level 1 ■ Unit 1

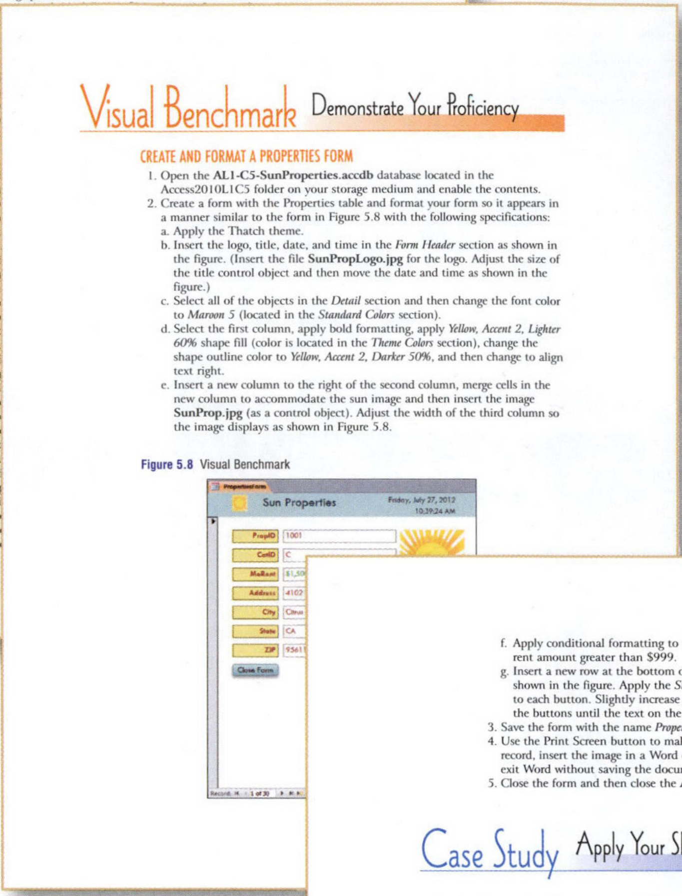

Visual Benchmark Demonstrate Your Proficiency

CREATE AND FORMAT A PROPERTIES FORM

1. Open the **AL1-C5-SunProperties.accdb** database located in the Access2010L1C5 folder on your storage medium and enable the contents.
2. Create a form with the Properties table and format your form so it appears in a manner similar to the form in Figure 5.8 with the following specifications:
 a. Apply the Thatch theme.
 b. Insert the logo, title, date, and time in the *Form Header* section as shown in the figure. (Insert the file **SunPropLogo.jpg** for the logo. Adjust the size of the title control object and then move the date and time as shown in the figure.)
 c. Select all of the objects in the *Detail* section and then change the font color to *Maroon 5* (located in the *Standard Colors* section).
 d. Select the first column, apply bold formatting, apply *Yellow, Accent 2, Lighter 60%* shape fill (color is located in the *Theme Colors* section), change the shape outline color to *Yellow, Accent 2, Darker 50%*, and then change to align text right.
 e. Insert a new column to the right of the second column, merge cells in the new column to accommodate the sun image and then insert the image **SunProp.jpg** (as a control object). Adjust the width of the third column so the image displays as shown in Figure 5.8.

Figure 5.8 Visual Benchmark

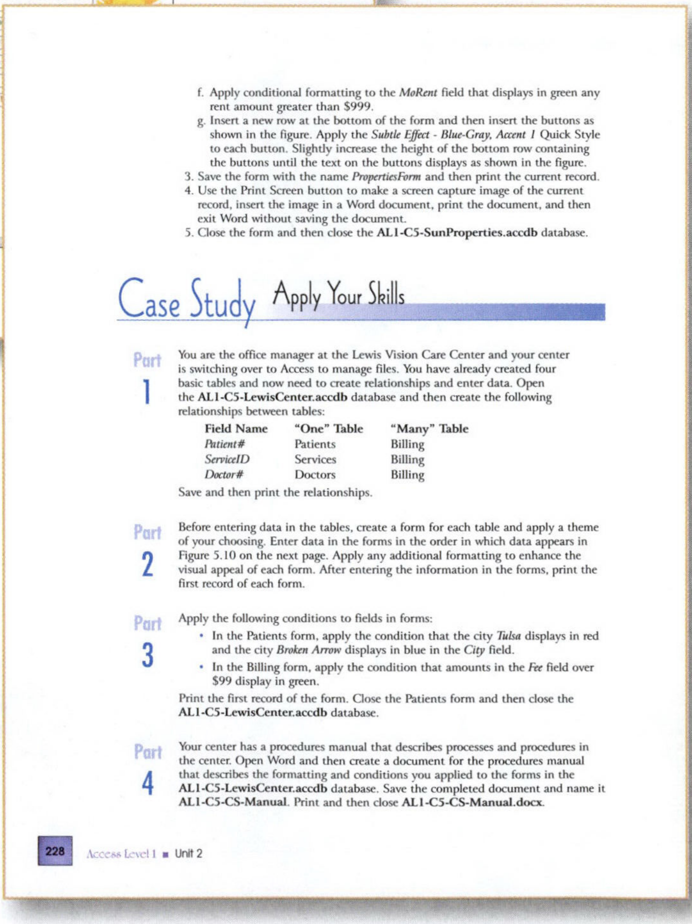

 f. Apply conditional formatting to the *MoRent* field that displays in green any rent amount greater than $999.
 g. Insert a new row at the bottom of the form and then insert the buttons as shown in the figure. Apply the *Subtle Effect - Blue-Gray, Accent 1* Quick Style to each button. Slightly increase the height of the bottom row containing the buttons until the text on the buttons displays as shown in the figure.
3. Save the form with the name *PropertiesForm* and then print the current record.
4. Use the Print Screen button to make a screen capture image of the current record, insert the image in a Word document, print the document, and then exit Word without saving the document.
5. Close the form and then close the **AL1-C5-SunProperties.accdb** database.

Case Study Apply Your Skills

Part 1

You are the office manager at the Lewis Vision Care Center and your center is switching over to Access to manage files. You have already created four basic tables and now need to create relationships and enter data. Open the **AL1-C5-LewisCenter.accdb** database and then create the following relationships between tables:

Field Name	"One" Table	"Many" Table
Patient#	Patients	Billing
ServiceID	Services	Billing
Doctor#	Doctors	Billing

Save and then print the relationships.

Part 2

Before entering data in the tables, create a form for each table and apply a theme of your choosing. Enter data in the forms in the order in which data appears in Figure 5.10 on the next page. Apply any additional formatting to enhance the visual appeal of each form. After entering the information in the forms, print the first record of each form.

Part 3

Apply the following conditions to fields in forms:
 • In the Patients form, apply the condition that the city *Tulsa* displays in red and the city *Broken Arrow* displays in blue in the *City* field.
 • In the Billing form, apply the condition that amounts in the *Fee* field over $99 display in green.
Print the first record of the form. Close the Patients form and then close the **AL1-C5-LewisCenter.accdb** database.

Part 4

Your center has a procedures manual that describes processes and procedures in the center. Open Word and then create a document for the procedures manual that describes the formatting and conditions you applied to the forms in the **AL1-C5-LewisCenter.accdb** database. Save the completed document and name it **AL1-C5-CS-Manual**. Print and then close **AL1-C5-CS-Manual.docx**.

228 Access Level 1 ■ Unit 2

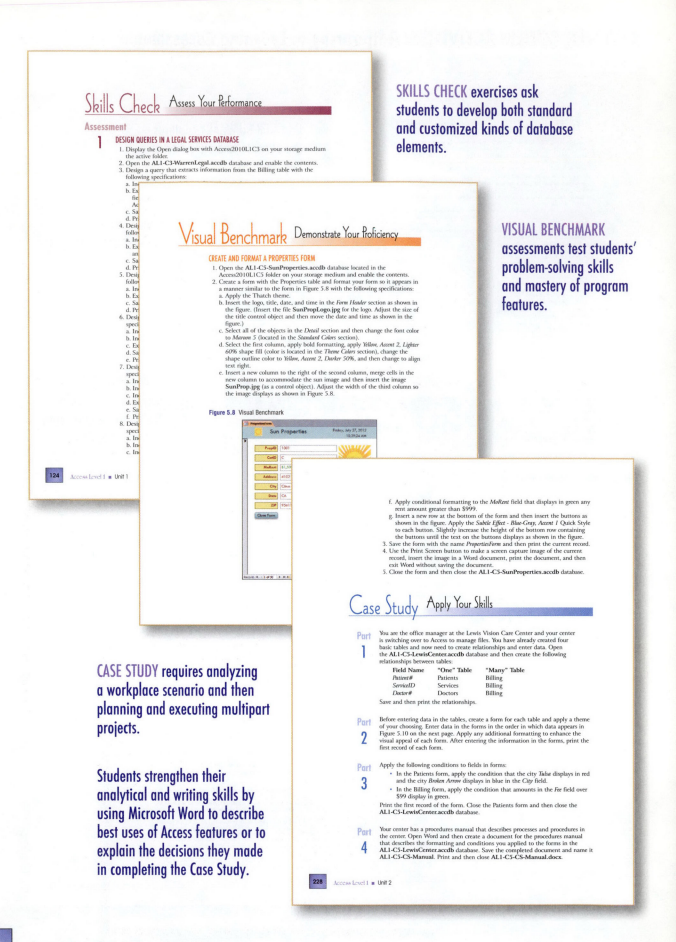

UNIT PERFORMANCE ASSESSMENT: Cross-Disciplinary, Comprehensive Evaluation

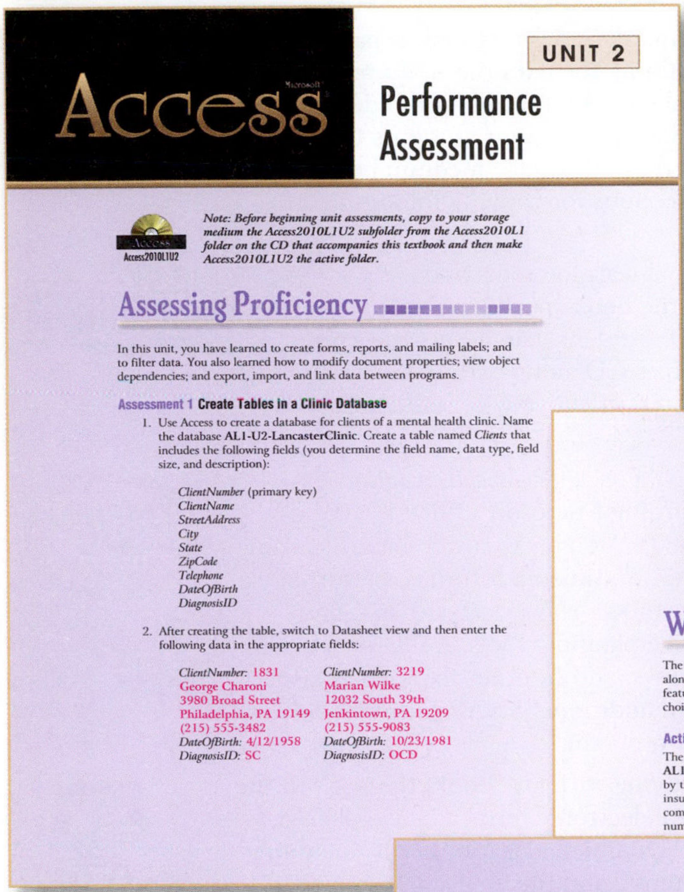

UNIT 2

Access

Performance Assessment

Note: Before beginning unit assessments, copy to your storage medium the Access2010L1U2 subfolder from the Access2010L1 folder on the CD that accompanies this textbook and then make Access2010L1U2 the active folder.

Access2010L1U2

Assessing Proficiency

In this unit, you have learned to create forms, reports, and mailing labels; and to filter data. You also learned how to modify document properties; view object dependencies; and export, import, and link data between programs.

Assessment 1 Create Tables in a Clinic Database

1. Use Access to create a database for clients of a mental health clinic. Name the database **AL1-U2-LancasterClinic**. Create a table named *Clients* that includes the following fields (you determine the field name, data type, field size, and description):

   ClientNumber (primary key)
   ClientName
   StreetAddress
   City
   State
   ZipCode
   Telephone
   DateOfBirth
   DiagnosisID

2. After creating the table, switch to Datasheet view and then enter the following data in the appropriate fields:

ClientNumber: 1831	*ClientNumber:* 3219
George Charoni	Marian Wilke
3980 Broad Street	12032 South 39th
Philadelphia, PA 19149	Jenkintown, PA 19209
(215) 555-3482	(215) 555-9083
DateOfBirth: 4/12/1958	*DateOfBirth:* 10/23/1981
DiagnosisID: SC	*DiagnosisID:* OCD

ASSESSING PROFICIENCY checks mastery of features.

WRITING ACTIVITIES involve applying program skills in a communication context.

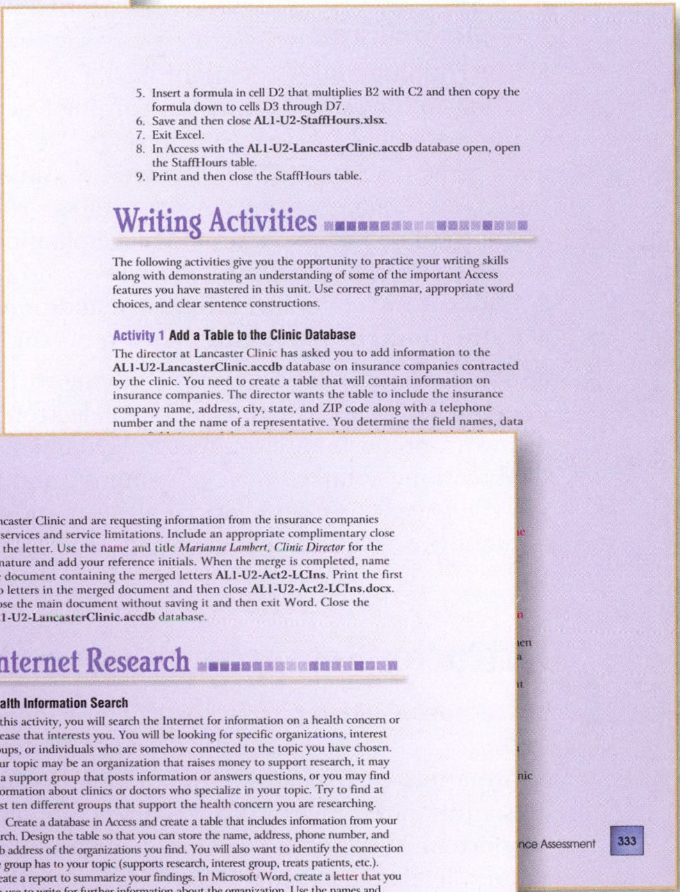

5. Insert a formula in cell D2 that multiplies B2 with C2 and then copy the formula down to cells D3 through D7.
6. Save and then close **AL1-U2-StaffHours.xlsx**.
7. Exit Excel.
8. In Access with the **AL1-U2-LancasterClinic.accdb** database open, open the StaffHours table.
9. Print and then close the StaffHours table.

Writing Activities

The following activities give you the opportunity to practice your writing skills along with demonstrating an understanding of some of the important Access features you have mastered in this unit. Use correct grammar, appropriate word choices, and clear sentence constructions.

Activity 1 Add a Table to the Clinic Database

The director at Lancaster Clinic has asked you to add information to the **AL1-U2-LancasterClinic.accdb** database on insurance companies contracted by the clinic. You need to create a table that will contain information on insurance companies. The director wants the table to include the insurance company name, address, city, state, and ZIP code along with a telephone number and the name of a representative. You determine the field names, data

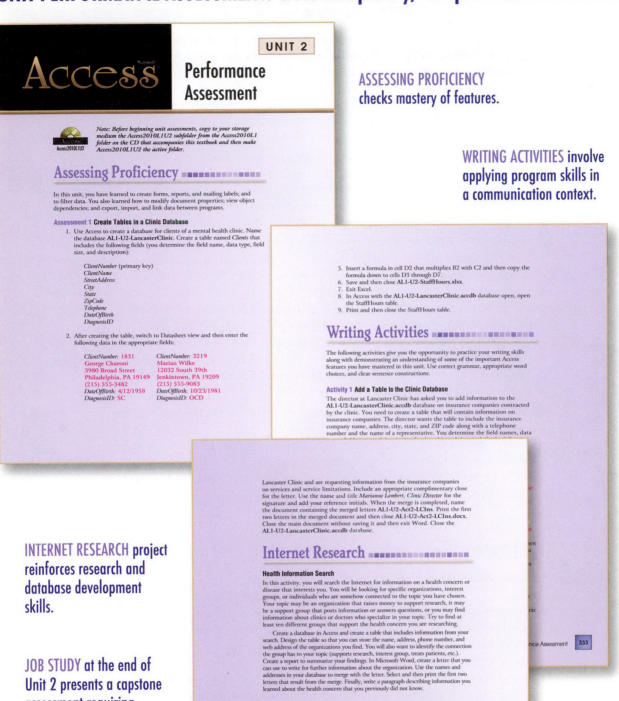

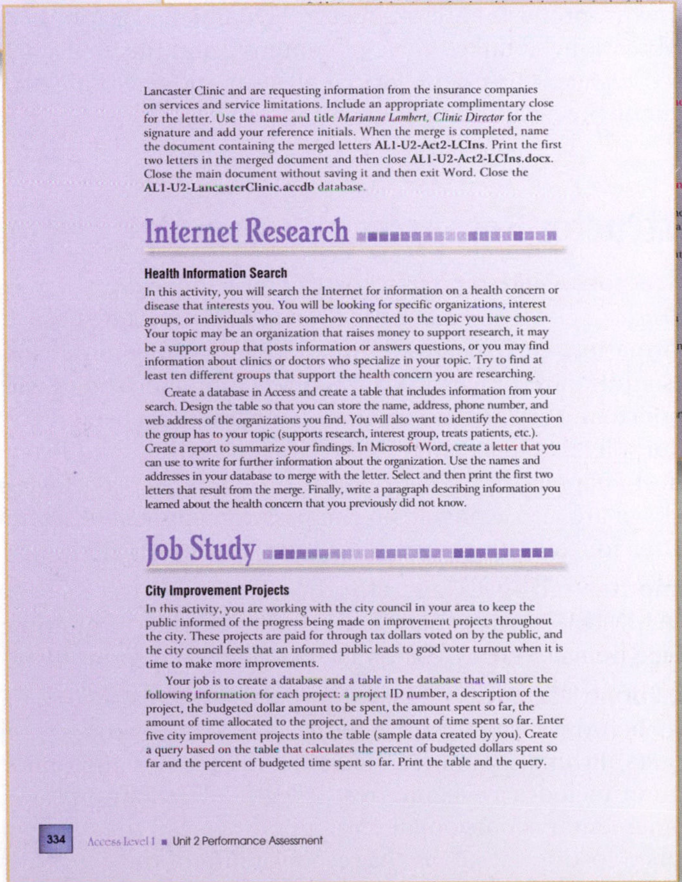

Lancaster Clinic and are requesting information from the insurance companies on services and service limitations. Include an appropriate complimentary close for the letter. Use the name and title *Marianne Lambert, Clinic Director* for the signature and add your reference initials. When the merge is completed, name the document containing the merged letters **AL1-U2-Act2-LCIns**. Print the first two letters in the merged document and then close **AL1-U2-Act2-LCIns.docx**. Close the main document without saving it and then exit Word. Close the **AL1-U2-LancasterClinic.accdb** database.

Internet Research

Health Information Search

In this activity, you will search the Internet for information on a health concern or disease that interests you. You will be looking for specific organizations, interest groups, or individuals who are somehow connected to the topic you have chosen. Your topic may be an organization that raises money to support research, it may be a support group that posts information or answers questions, or you may find information about clinics or doctors who specialize in your topic. Try to find at least ten different groups that support the health concern you are researching.

Create a database in Access and create a table that includes information from your search. Design the table so that you can store the name, address, phone number, and web address of the organizations you find. You will also want to identify the connection the group has to your topic (supports research, interest group, treats patients, etc.). Create a report to summarize your findings. In Microsoft Word, create a letter that you can use to write for further information about the organization. Use the names and addresses in your database to merge with the letter. Select and then print the first two letters that result from the merge. Finally, write a paragraph describing information you learned about the health concern that you previously did not know.

Job Study

City Improvement Projects

In this activity, you are working with the city council in your area to keep the public informed of the progress being made on improvement projects throughout the city. These projects are paid for through tax dollars voted on by the public, and the city council feels that an informed public leads to good voter turnout when it is time to make more improvements.

Your job is to create a database and a table in the database that will store the following information for each project: a project ID number, a description of the project, the budgeted dollar amount to be spent, the amount spent so far, the amount of time allocated to the project, and the amount of time spent so far. Enter five city improvement projects into the table (sample data created by you). Create a query based on the table that calculates the percent of budgeted dollars spent so far and the percent of budgeted time spent so far. Print the table and the query.

INTERNET RESEARCH project reinforces research and database development skills.

JOB STUDY at the end of Unit 2 presents a capstone assessment requiring critical thinking and problem solving.

Student Courseware

Student Resources CD Each Benchmark Series textbook is packaged with a Student Resources CD containing the data files required for completing the projects and assessments. A CD icon and folder name displayed on the opening page of chapters reminds students to copy a folder of files from the CD to the desired storage medium before beginning the project exercises. Directions for copying folders are printed on the inside back cover.

Internet Resource Center Additional learning tools and reference materials are available at the book-specific website at www.emcp.net/BenchmarkAccess10. Students can access the same files that are on the Student Resources CD along with study aids, web links, and tips for using computers effectively in academic and workplace settings.

SNAP Training and Assessment SNAP is a web-based program offering an interactive venue for learning Microsoft Office 2010, Windows 7, and Internet Explorer 8.0. Along with a web-based learning management system, SNAP provides multimedia tutorials, performance skill items, document-based assessments, a concepts test bank, an online grade book, and a set of course planning tools. A CD of tutorials teaching the basics of Office, Windows, and Internet Explorer is also available if instructors wish to assign additional SNAP tutorial work without using the web-based SNAP program.

eBook For students who prefer studying with an eBook, the texts in the Benchmark Series are available in an electronic form. The web-based, password-protected eBooks feature dynamic navigation tools, including bookmarking, a linked table of contents, and the ability to jump to a specific page. The eBook format also supports helpful study tools, such as highlighting and note taking.

Instructor Resources

Instructor's Guide and Disc Instructor support for the Benchmark Series includes an *Instructor's Guide and Instructor Resources Disc* package. This resource includes planning information, such as Lesson Blueprints, teaching hints, and sample course syllabi; presentation resources, such as PowerPoint slide shows with lecture notes and audio support; and assessment resources, including an overview of available assessment venues, live model answers for chapter activities, and live and PDF model answers for end-of-chapter exercises. Contents of the *Instructor's Guide and Instructor Resources Disc* package are also available on the password-protected section of the Internet Resource Center for this title at www.emcp.net/BenchmarkAccess10.

Computerized Test Generator Instructors can use the EXAMVIEW® Assessment Suite and test banks of multiple-choice items to create customized web-based or print tests.

Blackboard Cartridge This set of files allows instructors to create a personalized Blackboard website for their course and provides course content, tests, and the mechanisms for establishing communication via e-discussions and online group conferences. Available content includes a syllabus, test banks, PowerPoint presentations with audio support, and supplementary course materials. Upon request, the files can be available within 24–48 hours. Hosting the site is the responsibility of the educational institution.

System Requirements

This text is designed for the student to complete projects and assessments on a computer running a standard installation of Microsoft Office 2010, Professional Edition, and the Microsoft Windows 7 operating system. To effectively run this suite and operating system, your computer should be outfitted with the following:

- 1 gigahertz (GHz) processor or higher; 1 gigabyte (GB) of RAM
- DVD drive
- 15 GB of available hard-disk space
- Computer mouse or compatible pointing device

Office 2010 will also operate on computers running the Windows XP Service Pack 3 or the Windows Vista operating system.

Screen captures in this book were created using a screen resolution display setting of 1280 × 800. Refer to the *Customizing Settings* section of *Getting Started in Office 2010* following this preface for instructions on changing your monitor's resolution. Figure G.10 on page 10 shows the Microsoft Office Word ribbon at three resolutions for comparison purposes. Choose the resolution that best matches your computer; however, be aware that using a resolution other than 1280 × 800 means that your screens may not match the illustrations in this book.

About the Authors

Nita Rutkosky began teaching business education courses at Pierce College in Puyallup, Washington, in 1978. Since then she has taught a variety of software applications to students in postsecondary Information Technology certificate and degree programs. In addition to *Benchmark Office 2010,* she has co-authored *Marquee Series: Microsoft Office 2010, 2007,* and *2003; Signature Series: Microsoft Word 2010, 2007,* and *2003;* and *Using Computers in the Medical Office: Microsoft Word, Excel, and PowerPoint 2007* and *2003*. She has also authored textbooks on keyboarding, WordPerfect, desktop publishing, and voice recognition for Paradigm Publishing, Inc.

Denise Seguin has been teaching at Fanshawe College in London, Ontario, since 1986. She has taught a variety of software applications to learners in postsecondary Information Technology diploma programs and in Continuing Education courses. In addition to co-authoring books in the *Benchmark Office 2010* series, she has authored *Microsoft Outlook 2010, 2007, 2003, 2002,* and *2000*. She has also co-authored *Our Digital World*; *Marquee Series: Microsoft Office 2010, 2007,* and *2003*; *Office 2003*; *Office XP*; and *Using Computers in the Medical Office 2007* and *2003* for Paradigm Publishing, Inc.

Audrey Rutkosky Roggenkamp has been teaching courses in the Business Information Technology department at Pierce College in Puyallup since 2005. Her courses have included keyboarding, skill building, and Microsoft Office programs. In addition to this title, she has co-authored *Marquee Series: Microsoft Office 2010* and *2007; Signature Series: Microsoft Word 2010* and *2007;* and *Using Computers in the Medical Office 2007* and *2003* for Paradigm Publishing, Inc.

What is the Microsoft® Office Specialist Program?

The Microsoft Office Specialist Program enables candidates to show that they have something exceptional to offer—proven expertise in certain Microsoft programs. Recognized by businesses and schools around the world, over 4 million certifications have been obtained in over 100 different countries. The Microsoft Office Specialist Program is the only Microsoft-approved certification program of its kind.

What is the Microsoft Office Specialist Certification?

The Microsoft Office Specialist certification validates through the use of exams that you have obtained specific skill sets within the applicable Microsoft Office programs and other Microsoft programs included in the Microsoft Office Specialist Program. Candidates can choose which exam(s) they want to take according to which skills they want to validate.

The available Microsoft Office Specialist Program exams* include:

- Using Windows Vista®
- Using Microsoft® Office Word 2007
- Using Microsoft® Office Word 2007 - Expert
- Using Microsoft® Office Excel® 2007
- Using Microsoft® Office Excel® 2007 - Expert
- Using Microsoft® Office PowerPoint® 2007
- Using Microsoft® Office Access® 2007
- Using Microsoft® Office Outlook® 2007
- Using Microsoft SharePoint® 2007

The Microsoft Office Specialist Program 2010 exams* include:

- Microsoft Word 2010
- Microsoft Word 2010 Expert
- Microsoft Excel® 2010
- Microsoft Excel® 2010 Expert
- Microsoft PowerPoint® 2010
- Microsoft Access® 2010
- Microsoft Outlook® 2010
- Microsoft SharePoint® 2010

What does the Microsoft Office Specialist Approved Courseware logo represent?

The logo indicates that this courseware has been approved by Microsoft to cover the course objectives that will be included in the relevant exam. It also means that after utilizing this courseware, you may be better prepared to pass the exams required to become a certified Microsoft Office Specialist.

For more information:

To learn more about Microsoft Office Specialist exams, visit www.microsoft.com/learning/msbc. To learn about other Microsoft approved courseware from Paradigm Publishing, Inc., visit www.ParadigmCollege.com.

*The availability of Microsoft Office Specialist certification exams varies by Microsoft program, program version, and language. Visit www.microsoft.com/learning for exam availability.

Getting Started in Office 2010

In this textbook, you will learn to operate several computer application programs that combine to make an application "suite." This suite of programs is called Microsoft Office 2010. The programs you will learn to operate are the software, which includes instructions telling the computer what to do. Some of the application programs in the suite include a word processing program named Word, a spreadsheet program named Excel, a database program named Access, and a presentation program named PowerPoint.

Identifying Computer Hardware

The computer equipment you will use to operate the suite of programs is referred to as hardware. You will need access to a microcomputer system that should consist of the CPU, monitor, keyboard, printer, drives, and mouse. If you are not sure what equipment you will be operating, check with your instructor. The computer system shown in Figure G.1 consists of six components. Each component is discussed separately in the material that follows.

Figure G.1 Microcomputer System

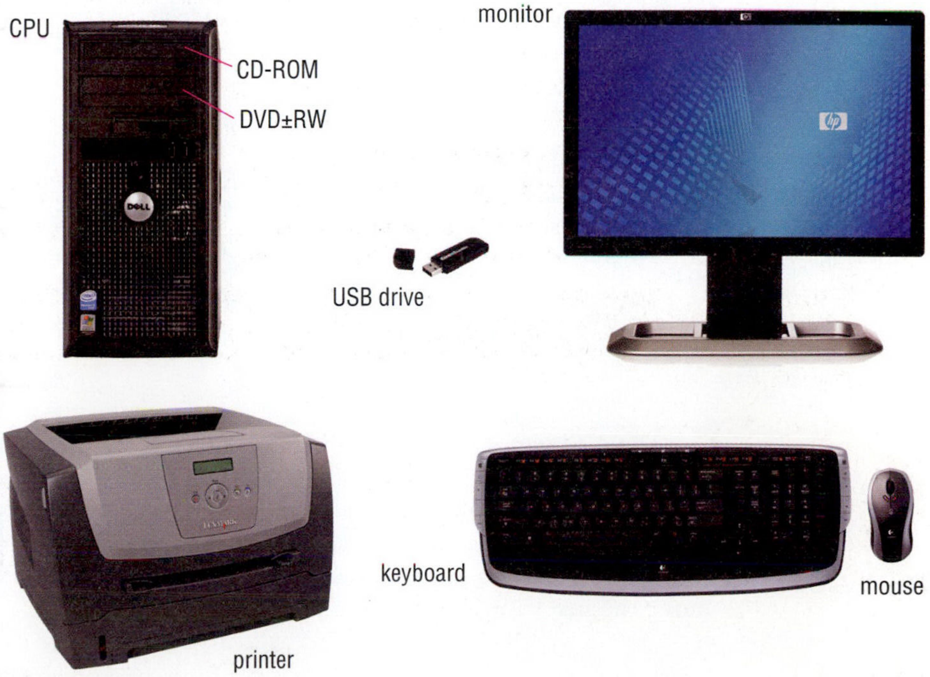

CPU

CPU stands for Central Processing Unit and it is the intelligence of the computer. All the processing occurs in the CPU. Silicon chips, which contain miniaturized circuitry, are placed on boards that are plugged into slots within the CPU. Whenever an instruction is given to the computer, that instruction is processed through circuitry in the CPU.

Monitor

The monitor is a piece of equipment that looks like a television screen. It displays the information of a program and the text being input at the keyboard. The quality of display for monitors varies depending on the type of monitor and the level of resolution. Monitors can also vary in size—generally from 15-inch size up to 26-inch size or larger.

Keyboard

The keyboard is used to input information into the computer. Keyboards for microcomputers vary in the number and location of the keys. Microcomputers have the alphabetic and numeric keys in the same location as the keys on a typewriter. The symbol keys, however, may be placed in a variety of locations, depending on the manufacturer. In addition to letters, numbers, and symbols, most microcomputer keyboards contain function keys, arrow keys, and a numeric keypad. Figure G.2 shows an enhanced keyboard.

Figure G.2 Keyboard

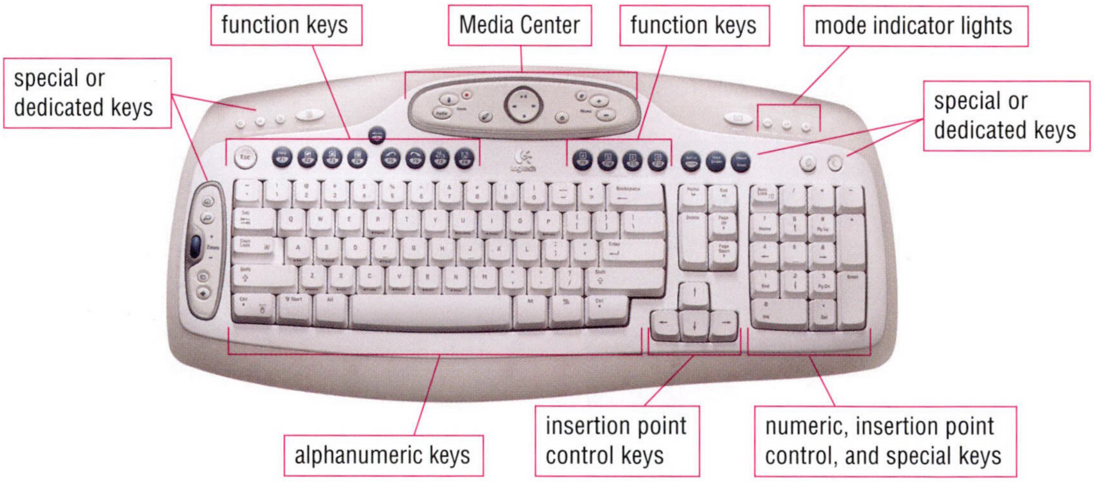

The 12 keys at the top of the keyboard, labeled with the letter F followed by a number, are called ***function keys***. Use these keys to perform functions within each of the suite programs. To the right of the regular keys is a group of ***special*** or ***dedicated keys***. These keys are labeled with specific functions that will be performed when you press the key. Below the special keys are arrow keys. Use these keys to move the insertion point in the document screen.

A keyboard generally includes three mode indicator lights. When you select certain modes, a light appears on the keyboard. For example, if you press the Caps Lock key, which disables the lowercase alphabet, a light appears next to Caps Lock. Similarly, pressing the Num Lock key will disable the special functions on the numeric keypad, which is located at the right side of the keyboard.

Disk Drives

Depending on the computer system you are using, Microsoft Office 2010 is installed on a hard drive or as part of a network system. Whether you are using Office on a hard drive or network system, you will need to have available a DVD or CD drive and a USB drive or other storage medium. You will insert the CD (compact disc) that accompanies this textbook in the DVD or CD drive and then copy folders from the CD to your storage medium. You will also save documents you complete at the computer to folders on your storage medium.

Printer

A document you create in Word is considered soft copy. If you want a hard copy of a document, you need to print it. To print documents you will need to access a printer, which will probably be either a laser printer or an ink-jet printer. A laser printer uses a laser beam combined with heat and pressure to print documents, while an ink-jet printer prints a document by spraying a fine mist of ink on the page.

Mouse

Many functions in the suite of programs are designed to operate more efficiently with a mouse. A mouse is an input device that sits on a flat surface next to the computer. You can operate a mouse with the left or the right hand. Moving the mouse on the flat surface causes a corresponding mouse pointer to move on the screen. Figure G.1 shows an illustration of a mouse.

Using the Mouse

The programs in the Microsoft Office suite can be operated with the keyboard and a mouse. The mouse may have two or three buttons on top, which are tapped to execute specific functions and commands. To use the mouse, rest it on a flat surface or a mouse pad. Put your hand over it with your palm resting on top of the mouse and your wrist resting on the table surface. As you move the mouse on the flat surface, a corresponding pointer moves on the screen.

When using the mouse, you should understand four terms — point, click, double-click, and drag. When operating the mouse, you may need to point to a specific command, button, or icon. Point means to position the mouse pointer on the desired item. With the mouse pointer positioned on the desired item, you may need to click a button on the mouse. Click means quickly tapping a button on the mouse once. To complete two steps at one time, such as choosing and then executing a function, double-click a mouse button. Double-click means to tap the left mouse button twice in quick succession. The term drag means to press and hold the left mouse button, move the mouse pointer to a specific location, and then release the button.

Using the Mouse Pointer

The mouse pointer will change appearance depending on the function being performed or where the pointer is positioned. The mouse pointer may appear as one of the following images:

- The mouse pointer appears as an I-beam (called the I-beam pointer) in the document screen and can be used to move the insertion point or select text.

- The mouse pointer appears as an arrow pointing up and to the left (called the arrow pointer) when it is moved to the Title bar, Quick Access toolbar, ribbon, or an option in a dialog box.

- The mouse pointer becomes a double-headed arrow (either pointing left and right, pointing up and down, or pointing diagonally) when performing certain functions such as changing the size of an object.

- In certain situations, such as moving an object or image, the mouse pointer displays with a four-headed arrow attached. The four-headed arrow means that you can move the object left, right, up, or down.

- When a request is being processed or when a program is being loaded, the mouse pointer may appear with a circle beside it. The moving circle means "please wait." When the process is completed, the circle is removed.

- The mouse pointer displays as a hand with a pointing index finger in certain functions such as Help and indicates that more information is available about the item. The mouse pointer also displays as a hand when you hover the mouse over a hyperlink.

Choosing Commands

Once a program is open, you can use several methods in the program to choose commands. A command is an instruction that tells the program to do something. You can choose a command using the mouse or the keyboard. When a program such as Word or PowerPoint is open, the ribbon contains buttons for completing tasks and contains tabs you click to display additional buttons. To choose a button on the Quick Access toolbar or in the ribbon, position the tip of the mouse arrow pointer on a button and then click the left mouse button.

The Office suite provides access keys you can press to use a command in a program. Press the Alt key on the keyboard to display KeyTips that identify the access key you need to press to execute a command. For example, press the Alt key in a Word document with the Home tab active and KeyTips display as shown in Figure G.3. Continue pressing access keys until you execute the desired command. For example, if you want to begin spell checking a document, you would press the Alt key, press the R key on the keyboard to display the Review tab, and then press the letter S on the keyboard.

Choosing Commands from Drop-Down Lists

To choose a command from a drop-down list with the mouse, position the mouse pointer on the desired option and then click the left mouse button. To make a selection from a drop-down list with the keyboard, type the underlined letter in the desired option.

Figure G.3 Word Home Tab KeyTips

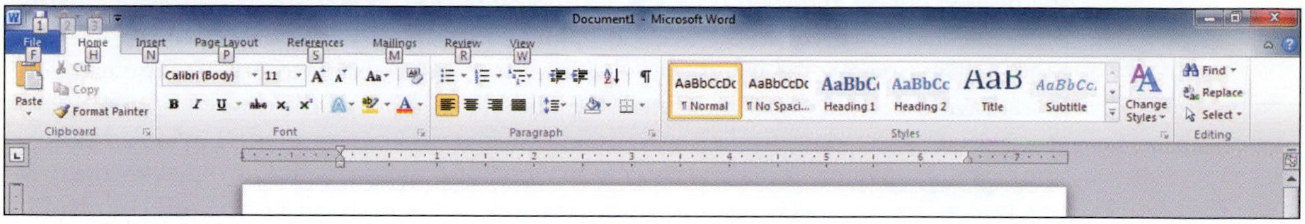

Some options at a drop-down list may be gray-shaded (dimmed), indicating that the option is currently unavailable. If an option at a drop-down list displays preceded by a check mark, that indicates that the option is currently active. If an option at a drop-down list displays followed by an ellipsis (...), a dialog box will display when that option is chosen.

Choosing Options from a Dialog Box

A dialog box contains options for applying formatting to a file or data within a file. Some dialog boxes display with tabs along the top providing additional options. For example, the Font dialog box shown in Figure G.4 contains two tabs — the Font tab and the Advanced tab. The tab that displays in the front is the active tab. To make a tab active using the mouse, position the arrow pointer on the desired tab and then click the left mouse button. If you are using the keyboard, press Ctrl + Tab or press Alt + the underlined letter on the desired tab.

Figure G.4 Word Font Dialog Box

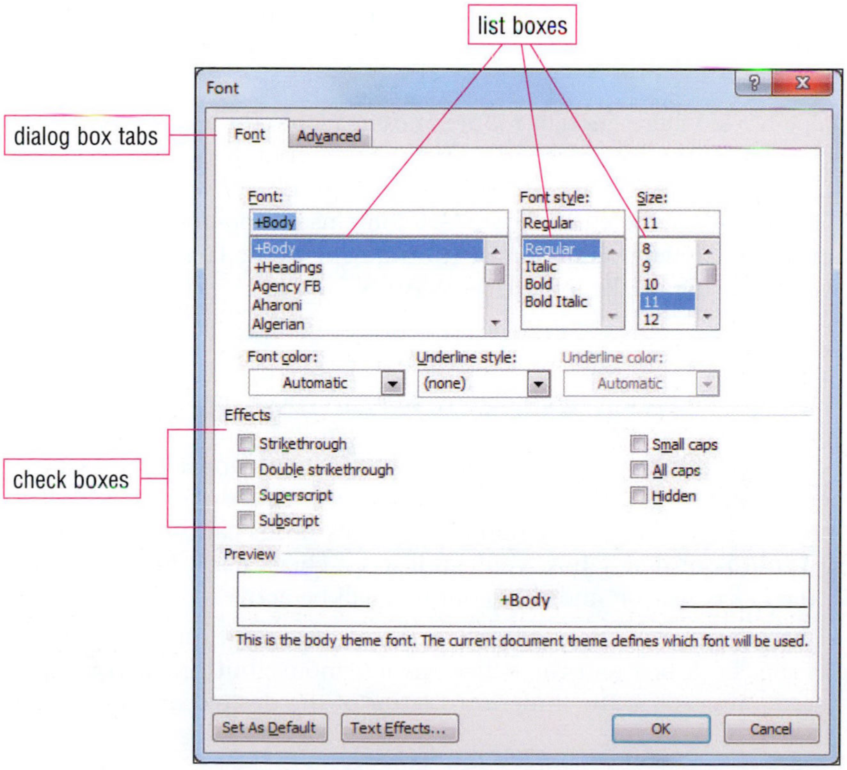

To choose options from a dialog box with the mouse, position the arrow pointer on the desired option and then click the left mouse button. If you are using the keyboard, press the Tab key to move the insertion point forward from option to option. Press Shift + Tab to move the insertion point backward from option to option. You can also hold down the Alt key and then press the underlined letter of the desired option. When an option is selected, it displays with a blue background or surrounded by a dashed box called a marquee. A dialog box contains one or more of the following elements: text boxes, list boxes, check boxes, option buttons, measurement boxes, and command buttons.

List Boxes

Some dialog boxes such as the Word Font dialog box shown in Figure G.4 may contain a list box. The list of fonts below the *Font* option is contained in a list box. To make a selection from a list box with the mouse, move the arrow pointer to the desired option and then click the left mouse button.

Some list boxes may contain a scroll bar. This scroll bar will display at the right side of the list box (a vertical scroll bar) or at the bottom of the list box (a horizontal scroll bar). You can use a vertical scroll bar or a horizontal scroll bar to move through the list if the list is longer than the box. To move down through a list on a vertical scroll bar, position the arrow pointer on the down-pointing arrow and hold down the left mouse button. To scroll up through the list in a vertical scroll bar, position the arrow pointer on the up-pointing arrow and hold down the left mouse button. You can also move the arrow pointer above the scroll box and click the left mouse button to scroll up the list or move the arrow pointer below the scroll box and click the left mouse button to move down the list. To move through a list with a horizontal scroll bar, click the left-pointing arrow to scroll to the left of the list or click the right-pointing arrow to scroll to the right of the list.

To make a selection from a list using the keyboard, move the insertion point into the box by holding down the Alt key and pressing the underlined letter of the desired option. Press the Up and/or Down Arrow keys on the keyboard to move through the list.

In some dialog boxes where enough room is not available for a list box, lists of options are inserted in a drop-down list box. Options that contain a drop-down list box display with a down-pointing arrow. For example, the *Underline style* option at the Word Font dialog box shown in Figure G.4 contains a drop-down list. To display the list, click the down-pointing arrow to the right of the *Underline style* option box. If you are using the keyboard, press Alt + U.

Check Boxes

Some dialog boxes contain options preceded by a box. A check mark may or may not appear in the box. The Word Font dialog box shown in Figure G.4 displays a variety of check boxes within the *Effects* section. If a check mark appears in the box, the option is active (turned on). If the check box does not contain a check mark, the option is inactive (turned off). Any number of check boxes can be active. For example, in the Word Font dialog box, you can insert a check mark in any or all of the boxes in the *Effects* section and these options will be active.

To make a check box active or inactive with the mouse, position the tip of the arrow pointer in the check box and then click the left mouse button. If you are using the keyboard, press Alt + the underlined letter of the desired option.

Text Boxes

Some options in a dialog box require you to enter text. For example, the boxes below the *Find what* and *Replace with* options at the Excel Find and Replace dialog box shown in Figure G.5 are text boxes. In a text box, you type text or edit existing text. Edit text in a text box in the same manner as normal text. Use the Left and Right Arrow keys on the keyboard to move the insertion point without deleting text and use the Delete key or Backspace key to delete text.

Option Buttons

The Word Insert Table dialog box shown in Figure G.6 contains options in the *AutoFit behavior* section preceded by option buttons. Only one option button can be selected at any time. When an option button is selected, a blue circle displays in the button. To select an option button with the mouse, position the tip of the arrow pointer inside the option button and then click the left mouse button. To make a selection with the keyboard, hold down the Alt key and then press the underlined letter of the desired option.

Measurement Boxes

Some options in a dialog box contain measurements or numbers you can increase or decrease. These options are generally located in a measurement box. For example, the Word Paragraph dialog box shown in Figure G.7 contains the *Left*, *Right*, *Before*, and *After* measurement boxes. To increase a number in a measurement box, position the tip of the arrow pointer on the up-pointing arrow to the right of the desired option and then click the left mouse button. To decrease the number, click the down-pointing arrow. If you are using the keyboard, press Alt + the underlined letter of the desired option and then press the Up Arrow key to increase the number or the Down Arrow key to decrease the number.

Command Buttons

In the Excel Find and Replace dialog box shown in Figure G.5, the boxes along the bottom of the dialog box are called command buttons. Use a command button to execute or cancel a command. Some command buttons display with an ellipsis (...). A command button that displays with an ellipsis will open another dialog box. To choose a command button with the mouse, position the arrow pointer on the desired button and then click the left mouse button. To choose a command button with the keyboard, press the Tab key until the desired command button contains the marquee and then press the Enter key.

Figure G.5 Excel Find and Replace Dialog Box

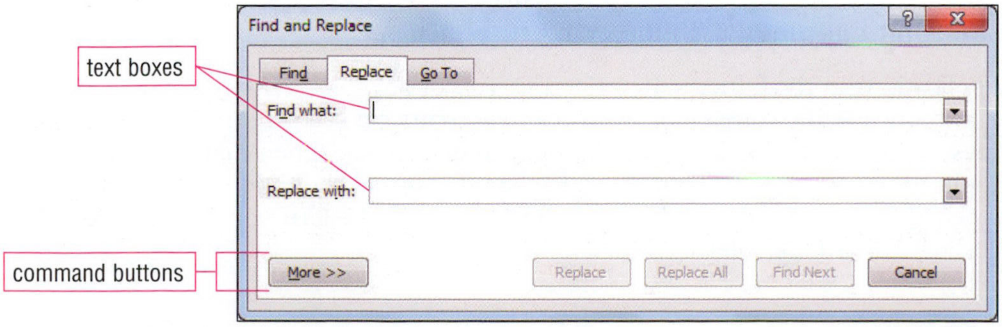

Figure G.6 Word Insert Table Dialog Box

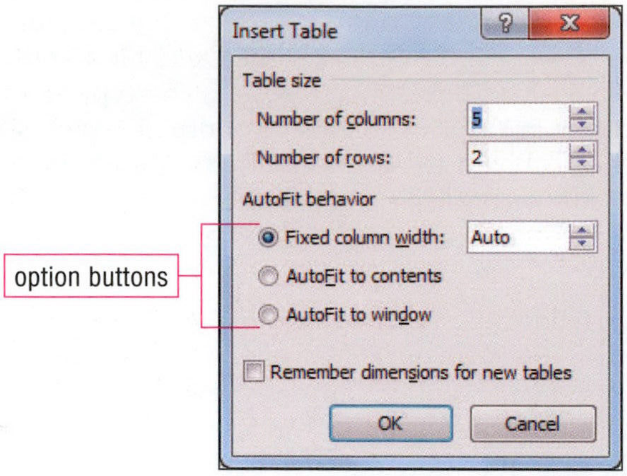

Figure G.7 Word Paragraph Dialog Box

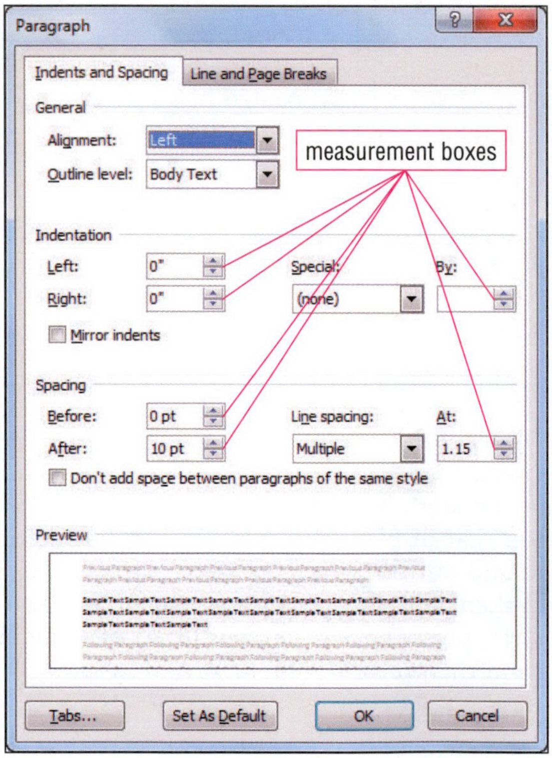

Choosing Commands with Keyboard Shortcuts

Applications in the Office suite offer a variety of keyboard shortcuts you can use to execute specific commands. Keyboard shortcuts generally require two or more keys. For example, the keyboard shortcut to display the Open dialog box in an application is Ctrl + O. To use this keyboard shortcut, hold down the Ctrl key, type the letter O on the keyboard, and then release the Ctrl key. For a list of keyboard shortcuts, refer to the Help files.

Choosing Commands with Shortcut Menus

The software programs in the suite include menus that contain commands related to the item with which you are working. A shortcut menu appears in the file in the location where you are working. To display a shortcut menu, click the right mouse button or press Shift + F10. For example, if the insertion point is positioned in a paragraph of text in a Word document, clicking the right mouse button or pressing Shift + F10 will cause the shortcut menu shown in Figure G.8 to display in the document screen (along with the Mini toolbar).

To select an option from a shortcut menu with the mouse, click the desired option. If you are using the keyboard, press the Up or Down Arrow key until the desired option is selected and then press the Enter key. To close a shortcut menu without choosing an option, click anywhere outside the shortcut menu or press the Esc key.

Working with Multiple Programs

As you learn the various programs in the Microsoft Office suite, you will notice how executing commands in each is very similar. For example, the steps to save, close, and print are virtually the same whether you are working in Word, Excel, or PowerPoint. This consistency between programs greatly enhances a user's ability to transfer knowledge learned in one program to another within the suite. Another appeal of Microsoft Office is the ability to have more than one program open at the same time. For example, you can open Word, create a document, and then open Excel, create a spreadsheet, and copy the spreadsheet into Word.

Figure G.8 Word Shortcut Menu

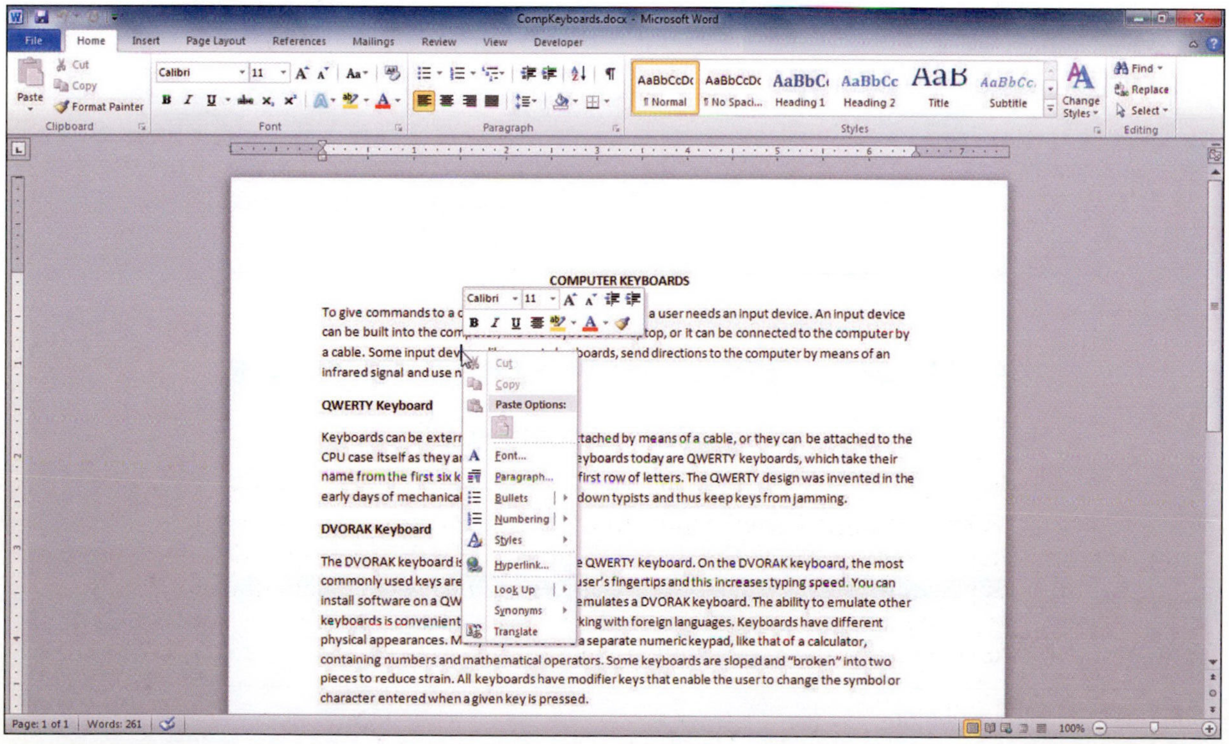

Figure G.9 Taskbar with Word, Excel, and PowerPoint Open

When you open a program, a button displays on the Taskbar containing an icon representing the program. If you open another program, a button containing an icon representing the program displays to the right of the first program button. Figure G.9 shows the Taskbar with Word, Excel, and PowerPoint open. To move from one program to another, click the button on the Taskbar representing the desired program file.

Customizing Settings

Before beginning computer projects in this textbook, you may need to customize the monitor settings and turn on the display of file extensions. Projects in the chapters in this textbook assume that the monitor display is set at 1280 by 800 pixels and that the display of file extensions is turned on.

Changing Monitor Resolutions

Before you begin learning the applications in the Microsoft Office 2010 suite, take a moment to check the display settings on the computer you are using. The ribbon in the Microsoft Office suite adjusts to the screen resolution setting of your computer monitor. Computer monitors set at a high resolution will have the ability to show more buttons in the ribbon than will a monitor set to a low resolution. The illustrations in this textbook were created with a screen resolution display set at 1280 × 800 pixels. In Figure G.10 the Word ribbon is shown three ways: at a lower screen resolution (1024 × 768 pixels), at the screen resolution featured

Figure G.10 Monitor Resolution

1024 × 768 screen resolution

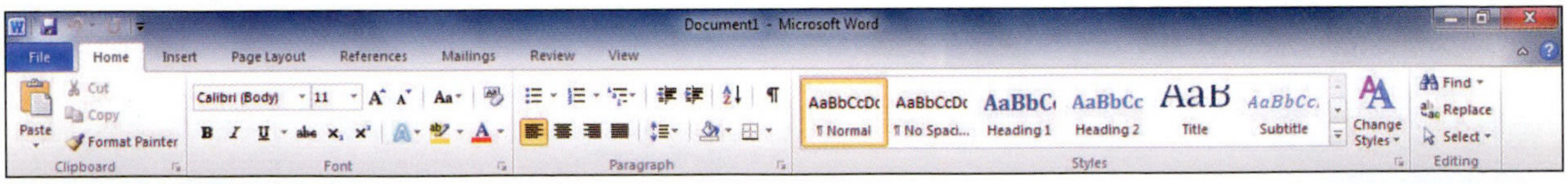

1280 × 800 screen resolution

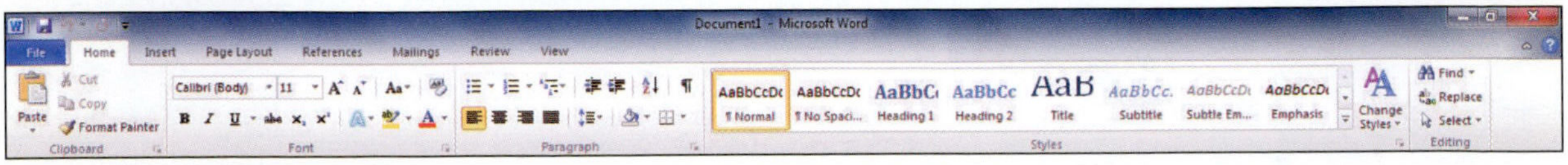

1440 × 900 screen resolution

throughout this textbook, and at a higher screen resolution (1440 × 900 pixels). Note the variances in the ribbon in all three examples. If possible, set your display to 1280 × 800 pixels to match the illustrations you will see in this textbook.

Project 1 Setting Monitor Display to 1280 by 800

1. At the Windows 7 desktop, click the Start button and then click *Control Panel*.
2. At the Control Panel dialog box, click the *Adjust screen resolution* option in the Appearance and Personalization category.
3. At the Control Panel Screen Resolution window, click the Resolution option button. (This displays a drop-down slider bar. Your drop-down slider bar may display differently than what you see in the image at the right.)
4. Drag the slider bar button on the slider bar until *1280 × 800* displays to the right of the slider button.
5. Click in the Control Panel Screen Resolution window to remove the slider bar.
6. Click the Apply button.
7. Click the Keep Changes button.
8. Click the OK button.
9. Close the Control Panel window.

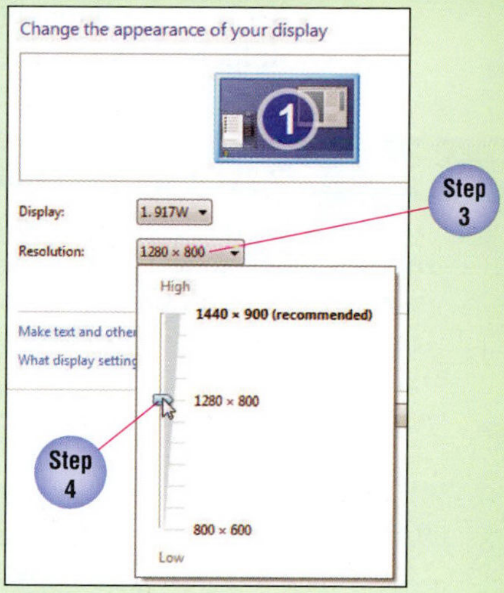

Project 2 Displaying File Extensions

1. At the Windows 7 desktop, click the Start button and then click *Computer*.
2. At the Computer window, click the Organize button on the toolbar and then click *Folder and search options* at the drop-down list.
3. At the Folder Options dialog box, click the View tab.
4. Click the *Hide extensions for known file types* check box to remove the check mark.
5. Click the Apply button.
6. Click the OK button.
7. Close the Computer window.

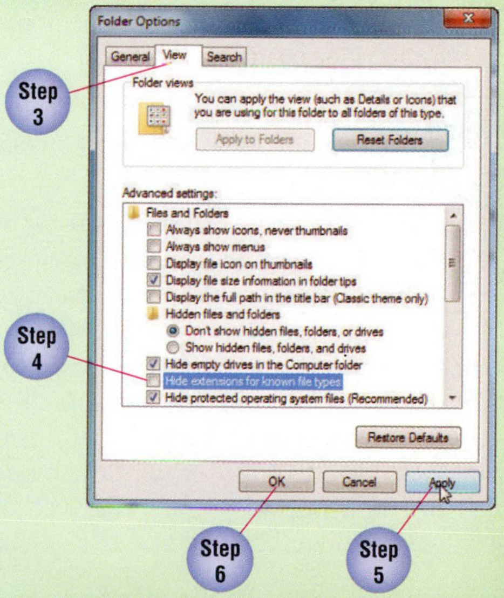

Completing Computer Projects

Some computer projects in this textbook require that you open an existing file. Project files are saved on the Student Resources CD that accompanies this textbook. The files you need for each chapter are saved in individual folders. Before beginning a chapter, copy the necessary folder from the CD to your storage medium (such as a USB flash drive) using the Computer window. If storage capacity is an issue with your storage medium, delete any previous chapter folders before copying a chapter folder onto your storage medium.

Project 3 Copying a Folder from the Student Resources CD

1. Insert the CD that accompanies this textbook in the CD drive. At the AutoPlay window that displays, click the Close button located in the upper right corner of the window.
2. Insert your USB flash drive in an available USB port. If an AutoPlay window displays, click the Close button.
3. At the Windows desktop, open the Computer window by clicking the Start button and then clicking *Computer* at the Start menu.
4. Double-click the CD drive in the Content pane (displays with the name *BM10StudentResources* preceded by the drive letter).
5. Double-click the desired program folder name in the Content pane.
6. Click once on the desired chapter subfolder name to select it.
7. Click the Organize button on the toolbar and then click *Copy* at the drop-down list.
8. In the Computer window Content pane, click the drive containing your storage medium.
9. Click the Organize button on the toolbar and then click *Paste* at the drop-down list.
10. Close the Computer window by clicking the Close button located in the upper right corner of the window.

Project 4 Deleting a Folder

Note: Check with your instructor before deleting a folder.

1. Insert your storage medium (such as a USB flash drive) in the USB port.
2. At the Windows desktop, open the Computer window by clicking the Start button and then clicking *Computer* at the Start menu.
3. Double-click the drive letter for your storage medium (drive containing your USB flash drive such as *Removable Disk (F:)*).
4. Click the chapter folder in the Content pane.
5. Click the Organize button on the toolbar and then click *Delete* at the drop-down list.
6. At the message asking if you want to delete the folder, click the Yes button.
7. Close the Computer window by clicking the Close button located in the upper right corner of the window.

Using Windows 7

A computer requires an operating system to provide necessary instructions on a multitude of processes including loading programs, managing data, directing the flow of information to peripheral equipment, and displaying information. Windows 7 is an operating system that provides functions of this type (along with much more) in a graphical environment. Windows is referred to as a ***graphical user interface*** (GUI—pronounced *gooey*) that provides a visual display of information with features such as icons (pictures) and buttons. In this introduction, you will learn these basic features of Windows 7:

- Use desktop icons and the Taskbar to launch programs and open files or folders
- Add and remove gadgets
- Organize and manage data, including copying, moving, creating, and deleting files and folders; and create a shortcut
- Explore the Control Panel and personalize the desktop
- Use the Windows Help and Support features
- Use search tools
- Customize monitor settings

Before using one of the software programs in the Microsoft Office suite, you will need to start the Windows 7 operating system. To do this, turn on the computer. Depending on your computer equipment configuration, you may also need to turn on the monitor and printer. If you are using a computer that is part of a network system or if your computer is set up for multiple users, a screen will display showing the user accounts defined for your computer system. At this screen, click your user account name and, if necessary, type your password and then press the Enter key. The Windows 7 operating system will start and, after a few moments, the desktop will display as shown in Figure W.1. (Your desktop may vary from what you see in Figure W.1.)

Exploring the Desktop

When Windows is loaded, the main portion of the screen is called the ***desktop***. Think of the desktop in Windows as the top of a desk in an office. A business person places necessary tools—such as pencils, pens, paper, files, calculator—on the desktop to perform functions. Like the tools that are located on a desk, the desktop contains tools for operating the computer. These tools are logically grouped and placed in dialog boxes or panels that you can display using icons on the desktop. The desktop contains a variety of features for using your computer and software programs installed on the computer. The features available on the desktop are represented by icons and buttons.

Figure W.1 Windows 7 Desktop

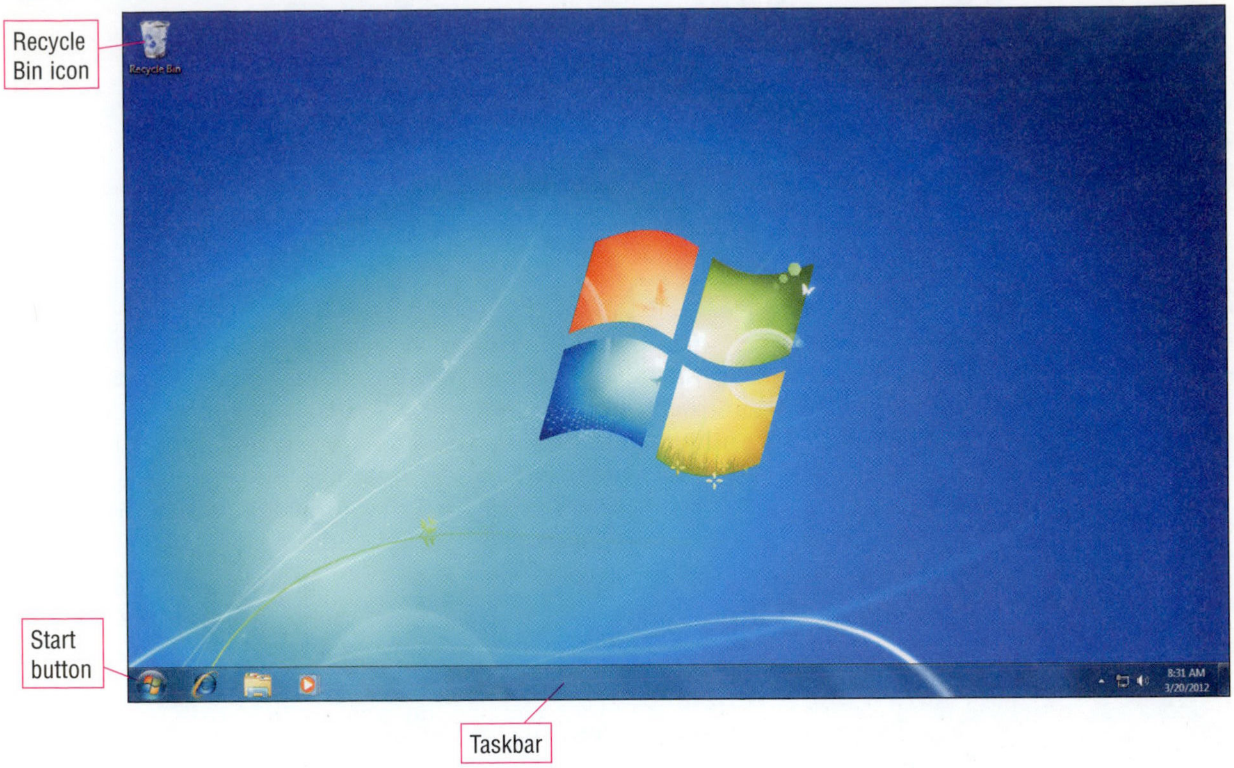

Using Icons

Icons are visual symbols that represent programs, files, or folders. Figure W.1 identifies the Recycle Bin icon located on the Windows desktop. The Windows desktop on your computer may contain additional icons. Programs that have been installed on your computer may be represented by an icon on the desktop. Also, icons may display on your desktop representing files or folders. Double-click an icon and the program, file, or folder it represents opens on the desktop.

Using the Taskbar

The bar that displays at the bottom of the desktop (see Figure W.1) is called the Taskbar. The Taskbar, shown in Figure W.2, contains the Start button, pinned items, a section that displays task buttons representing active tasks, the notification area, and the Show Desktop button.

Figure W.2 Windows 7 Taskbar

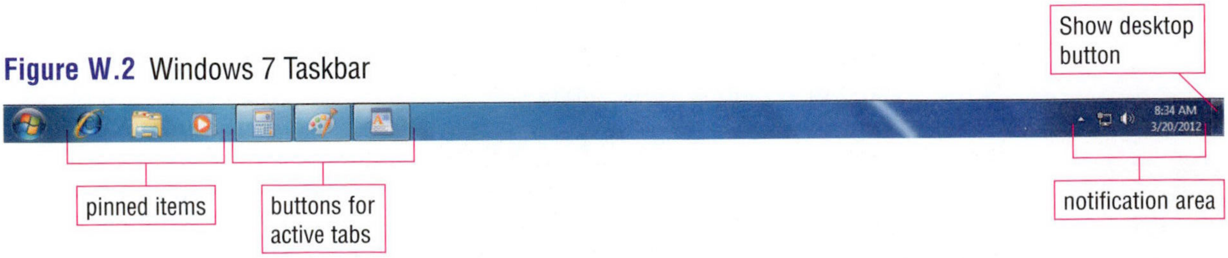

Click the Start button, located at the left side of the Taskbar, and the Start menu displays as shown in Figure W.3 (your Start menu may vary). You can also display the Start menu by pressing the Windows key on your keyboard or by pressing Ctrl + Esc. The left side of the Start menu contains links to the most recently and frequently used programs. The name of the currently logged on user displays at the top of the darker right portion of the menu followed by the user's libraries. The two sections below the personal libraries provide links to other Windows features, such as games, the Control Panel, and Windows Help and Support. Use the Shut down button to put the system in a power-conserving state or into a locked, shut down, or sleep mode.

To choose an option from the Start menu, drag the arrow pointer to the desired option (referred to as ***pointing***) and then click the left mouse button. Pointing to options at the Start menu that are followed by a right-pointing arrow will cause a side menu to display with additional options. When a program is open, a task button representing the program appears on the Taskbar. If multiple programs are open, each program will appear as a task button on the Taskbar (a few specialized tools may not).

Manipulating Windows

When you open a program, a defined work area displays on the screen, which is referred to as a ***window***. A Title bar displays at the top of a window and contains buttons at the right side for closing the window and minimizing, maximizing, and restoring the size of the window. You can open more than one window at a time and the open windows can be cascaded or stacked. Windows 7 contains a Snap feature that causes a window to "stick" to the edge of the screen when the window

Figure W.3 Start Menu

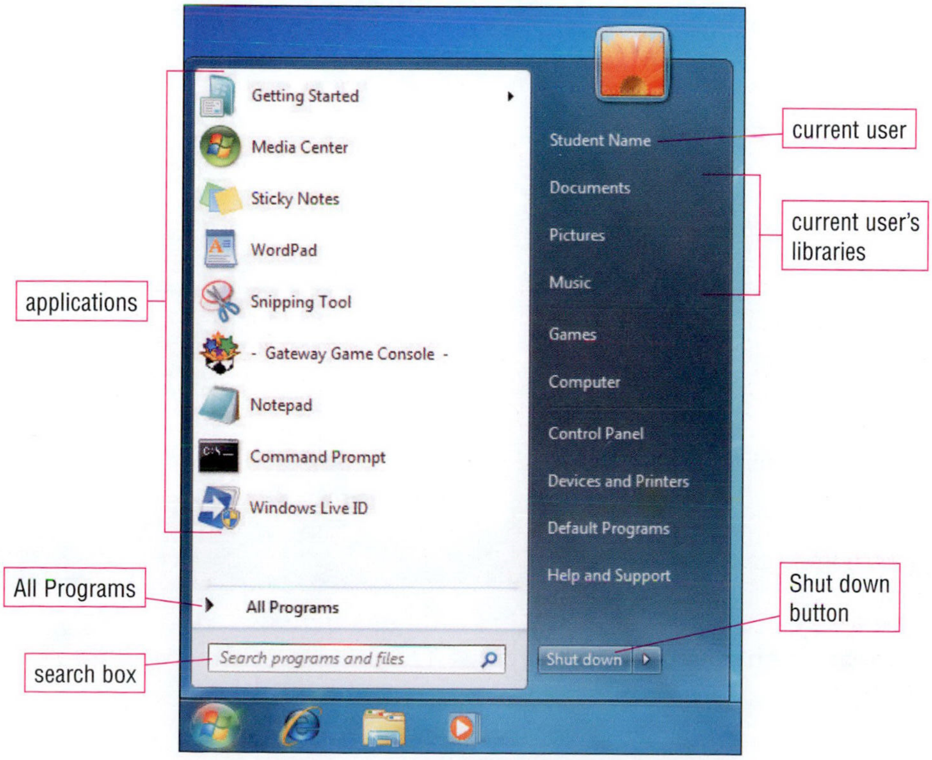

is moved to the left or right side of the screen. Move a window to the top of the screen and the window is automatically maximized. If you drag down a maximized window, the window is automatically restored down.

In addition to moving and sizing a window, you can change the display of all open windows. To do this, position the mouse pointer on the Taskbar and then click the right mouse button and a pop-up list displays with options for displaying multiple open windows. You can cascade the windows, stack the windows, and display the windows side by side.

Project 1 Opening Programs, Switching between Programs, and Manipulating Windows

1. Open Windows 7. (To do this, turn on the computer and, if necessary, turn on the monitor and/or printer. If you are using a computer that is part of a network system or if your computer is set up for multiple users, you may need to click your user account name and, if necessary, type your password and then press the Enter key. Check with your instructor to determine if you need to complete any additional steps.)
2. When the Windows 7 desktop displays, open Microsoft Word by completing the following steps:
   a. Position the arrow pointer on the Start button on the Taskbar and then click the left mouse button.
   b. At the Start menu, click *All Programs* and then click *Microsoft Office* (this displays programs in the Office suite below Microsoft Office).
   c. Drag the arrow pointer down to *Microsoft Word 2010* and then click the left mouse button.
   d. When the Microsoft Word program is open, notice that a task button representing Word displays on the Taskbar.

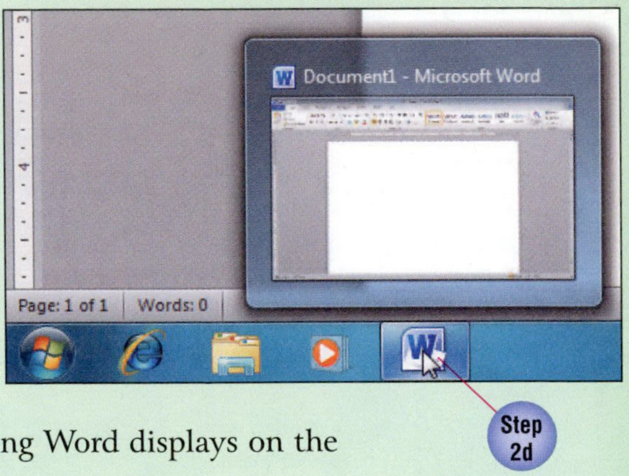

3. Open Microsoft Excel by completing the following steps:
   a. Position the arrow pointer on the Start button on the Taskbar and then click the left mouse button.
   b. At the Start menu, click *All Programs* and then click *Microsoft Office*.
   c. Drag the arrow pointer down to *Microsoft Excel 2010* and then click the left mouse button.
   d. When the Microsoft Excel program is open, notice that a task button representing Excel displays on the Taskbar to the right of the task button representing Word.
4. Switch to the Word program by clicking the task button on the Taskbar representing Word.
5. Switch to the Excel program by clicking the task button on the Taskbar representing Excel.

6. Restore down the Excel window by clicking the Restore Down button that displays immediately left of the Close button in the upper right corner of the screen. (This reduces the Excel window so it displays along the bottom half of the screen.)

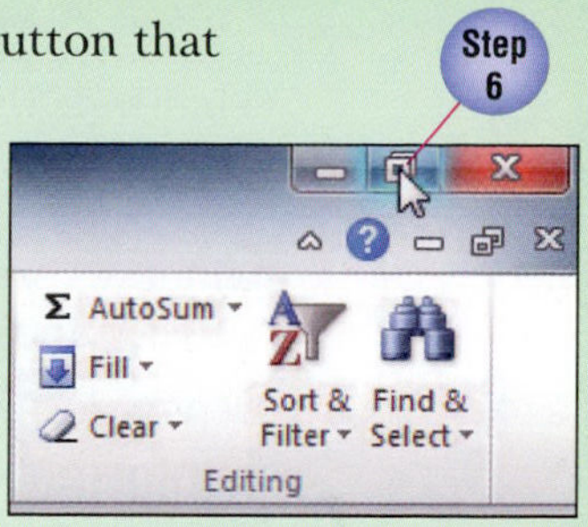

7. Restore down the Word window by clicking the Restore Down button located immediately left of the Close button in the upper right corner of the screen.
8. Position the mouse pointer on the Word window Title bar, hold down the left mouse button, drag to the left side of the screen until an outline of the window displays in the left half of the screen, and then release the mouse button. (This "sticks" the window to the left side of the screen.)

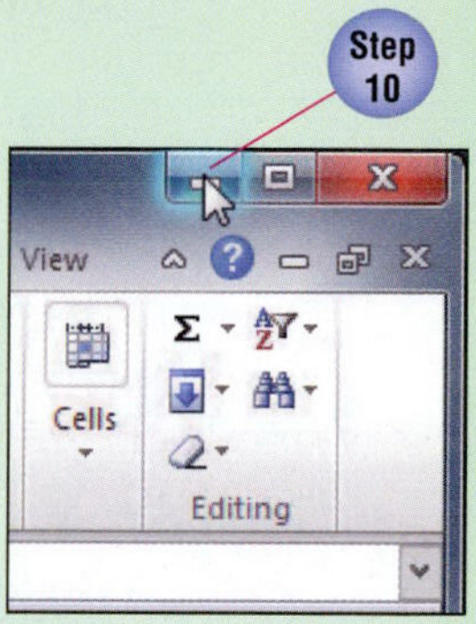

9. Position the mouse pointer on the Excel window Title bar, hold down the left mouse button, drag to the right until an outline of the window displays in the right half of the screen, and then release the mouse button.
10. Minimize the Excel window by clicking the Minimize button that displays in the upper right corner of the Excel window Title bar.
11. Hover your mouse over the Excel button on the Taskbar and notice the Excel window thumbnail that displays above the button and then click the thumbnail. (This displays the Excel window at the right side of the screen.)

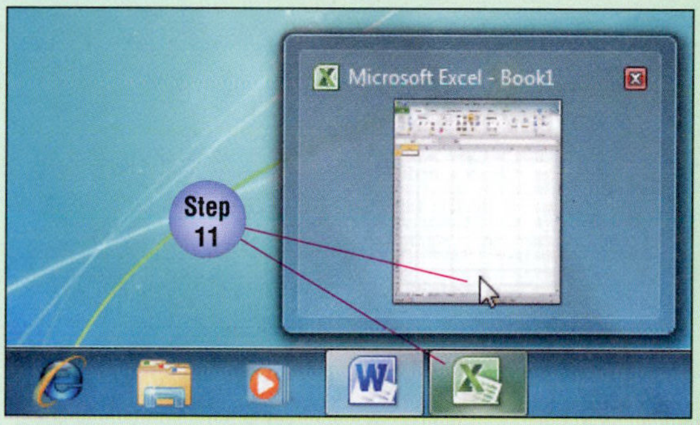

12. Cascade the Word and Excel windows by positioning the arrow pointer on an empty area on the Taskbar, clicking the right mouse button, and then clicking *Cascade windows* at the pop-up list.
13. After viewing the windows cascaded, display them stacked by right-clicking an empty area on the Taskbar and then clicking *Show windows stacked* at the pop-up list.
14. Display the desktop by right-clicking an empty area on the Taskbar and then clicking *Show the desktop* at the pop-up list.

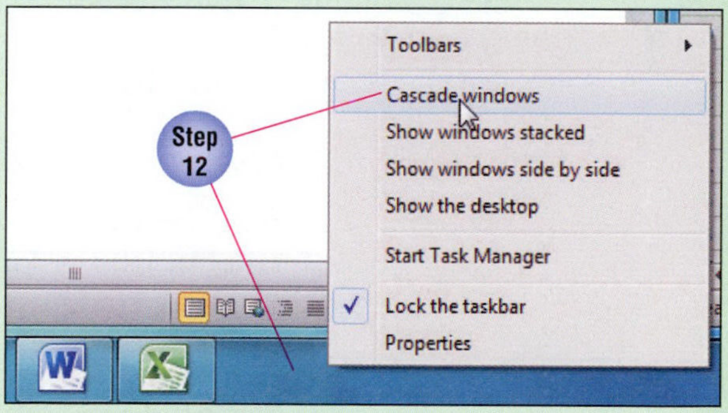

15. Display the windows stacked by right-clicking an empty area on the Taskbar and then clicking *Show open windows* at the pop-up list.
16. Position the mouse pointer on the Word window Title bar, hold down the left mouse button, drag the window to the top of the screen, and then release the mouse button. This maximizes the Word window so it fills the screen.
17. Close the Word window by clicking the Close button located in the upper right corner of the window.
18. At the Excel window, click the Maximize button located immediately left of the Close button in the upper right corner of the Excel window.
19. Close the Excel window by clicking the Close button located in the upper right corner of the window.

Using the Pinned Area

The icons that display immediately right of the Start button are pinned programs. Clicking an icon opens the program associated with the icon. Click the first icon to open the Internet Explorer web browser, click the second icon to open a window containing Libraries, and click the third icon to open the Windows media player window.

Exploring the Notification Area

The notification area is located at the right side of the Taskbar and contains icons that show the status of certain system functions such as a network connection or battery power. It also contains icons you can use to manage certain programs and Windows 7 features. The notification area also contains the system clock and date. Click the time or date in the notification area and a window displays with a clock and a calendar of the current month. Click the Change date and time settings hyperlink that displays at the bottom of the window and the Date and Time dialog box displays. To change the date and/or time, click the Change date and time button and the Date and Time Settings dialog box displays similar to the dialog box shown in Figure W.4. (If a dialog box displays telling you that Windows needs your permission to continue, click the Continue button.)

Change the month and year by clicking the left-pointing or right-pointing arrow at the top of the calendar in the *Date* section. Click the left-pointing arrow to display the previous month(s) and click the right-pointing arrow to display the next month(s).

To change the day, click the desired day in the monthly calendar that displays in the dialog box. To change the time, double-click either the hour, minute, or seconds and then type the appropriate time or use the up- and down-pointing arrows in the spin boxes to adjust the time.

Some programs, when installed, will add an icon to the notification area of the Taskbar. Display the name of the icon by positioning the mouse pointer on the icon and, after approximately one second, the icon label displays. If more icons have been inserted in the notification area than can be viewed at one time, an up-pointing arrow button displays at the left side of the notification area. Click this up-pointing arrow button and the remaining icons display.

Setting Taskbar Properties

You can customize the Taskbar with options from the Taskbar shortcut menu. Display this menu by right-clicking on an empty portion of the Taskbar. The Taskbar shortcut menu contains options for turning on or off the display of specific toolbars, specifying the display of multiple windows, displaying the Start Task Manager dialog box, locking or unlocking the Taskbar, and displaying the Taskbar and Start Menu Properties dialog box.

With options in the Taskbar and Start Menu Properties dialog box shown in Figure W.5, you can change settings for the Taskbar as well as the Start menu. Display this dialog box by right-clicking on an empty area on the Taskbar and then clicking *Properties* at the shortcut menu.

Each property is controlled by a check box. Property options containing a check mark are active. Click the option to remove the check mark and make the option inactive. If an option is inactive, clicking the option will insert a check mark in the check box and turn on the option (make it active).

Figure W.4 Date and Time Settings Dialog Box

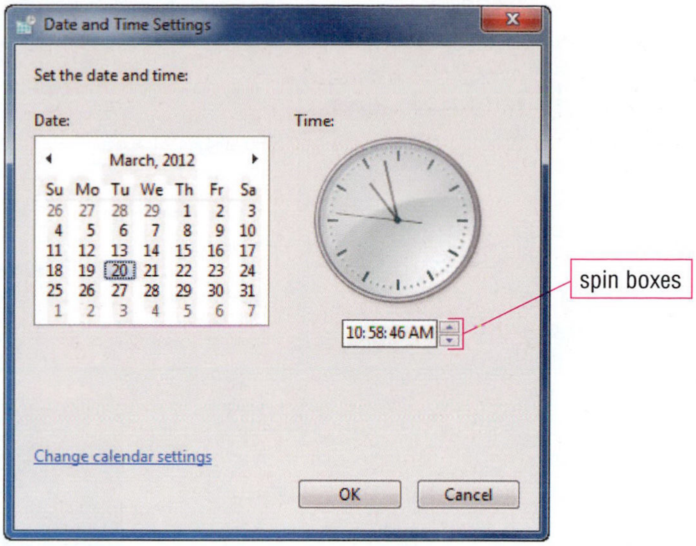

Figure W.5 Taskbar and Start Menu Properties Dialog Box

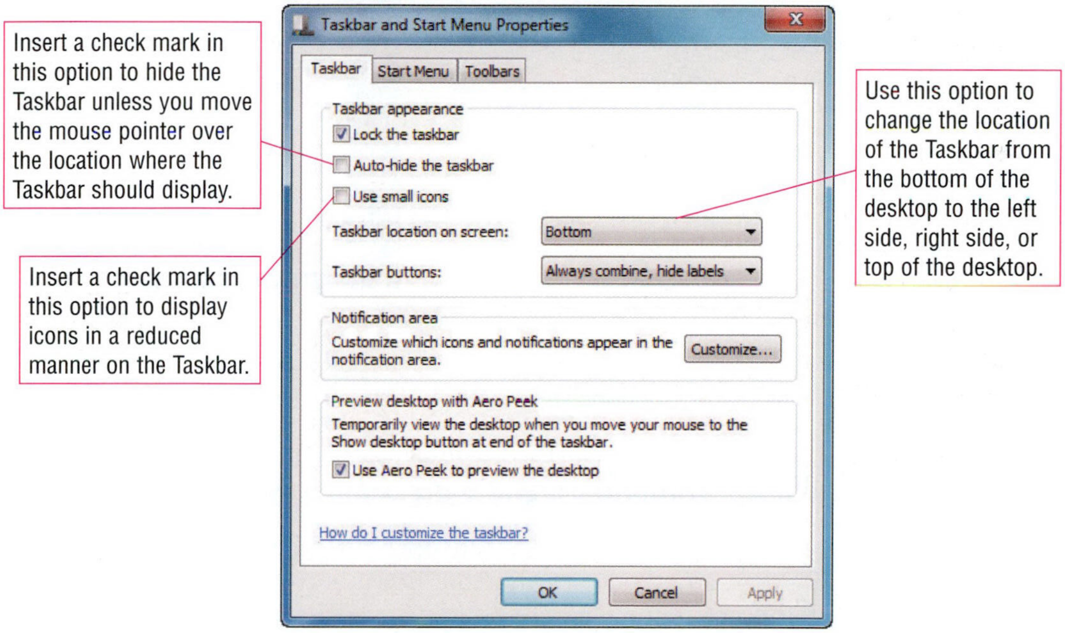

Project 2 Changing Taskbar Properties

1. Make sure the Windows 7 desktop displays.
2. Change Taskbar properties by completing the following steps:
   a. Position the arrow pointer on any empty area on the Taskbar and then click the right mouse button.
   b. At the shortcut menu that displays, click *Properties*.

c. At the Taskbar and Start Menu Properties dialog box, click the *Auto-hide the taskbar* check box to insert a check mark.

d. Click the *Use small icons* check box to insert a check mark.

e. Click the button (displays with the word *Bottom*) that displays at the right side of the *Taskbar location on screen* option and then click *Right* at the drop-down list.

f. Click OK to close the dialog box.

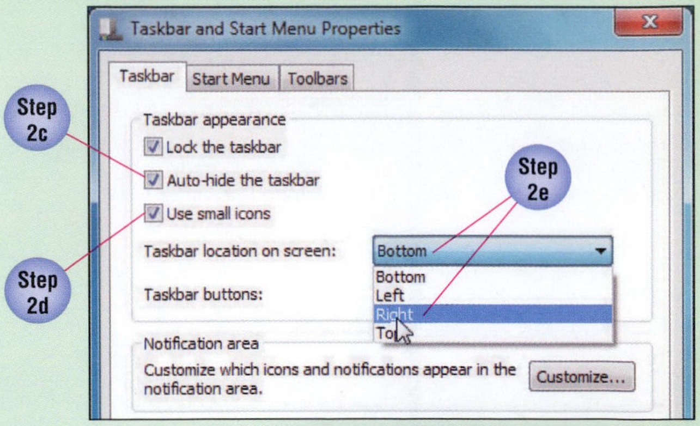

3. Since the *Auto-hide the taskbar* check box contains a check mark, the Taskbar does not display. Display the Taskbar by moving the mouse pointer to the right side of the screen. Notice that the icons on the Taskbar are smaller.
4. Return to the default settings for the Taskbar by completing the following steps:

   a. Move the mouse pointer to the right side of the screen to display the Taskbar.

   b. Right-click any empty area on the Taskbar and then click *Properties* at the shortcut menu.

   c. Click the *Auto-hide the taskbar* check box to remove the check mark.

   d. Click the *Use small icons* check box to remove the check mark.

   e. Click the button (displays with the word *Right*) that displays at the right side of the *Taskbar location on screen* option and then click *Bottom* at the drop-down list.

   f. Click OK to close the dialog box.

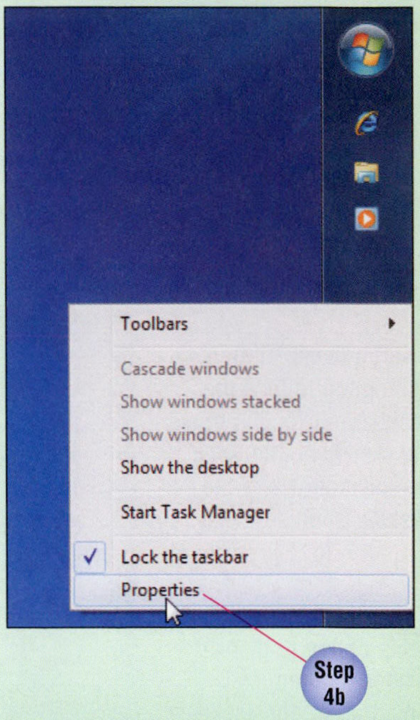

Powering Down the Computer

If you want to shut down Windows, close any open programs, click the Start button on the Taskbar, and then click the Shut down button as shown in Figure W.6. Click the button containing a right-pointing triangle that displays at the right side of the Shut down button and a drop-down list displays with options for powering down the computer.

In a multi-user environment, click the *Switch user* option to change users or click the *Log off* option to log off your computer, which shuts down your applications and files and makes system resources available to other users logged on to the system. If you need to walk away from your computer and you want to protect your work, consider locking the computer by clicking the *Lock* option. When you lock the computer, the desktop is hidden but the system is not shut down and the power is not conserved. To unlock the computer, click the icon on the desktop representing your account, type your password, and then press Enter. Click the *Restart* option to shut down and then restart the computer and click

Figure W.6 Shut Down Button and Power Options Button

Click this button to shut down your computer.

Click this button arrow to display a list of options for switching the user, logging off or locking the computer, restarting the computer, or putting the computer in sleep mode.

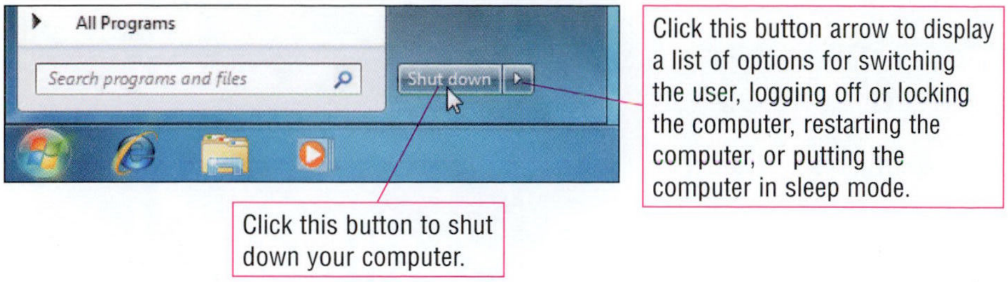

the *Sleep* option to save power without having to close all files and applications. In sleep mode, Windows saves files and information about programs and then powers down the computer to a low-power state. To "wake" the computer back up, quickly press the computer's power button.

Using Gadgets ▪▪▪▪▪▪▪▪▪▪▪▪▪▪▪▪▪▪▪▪▪▪▪▪▪▪▪

You can add gadgets to your desktop. A gadget is a mini program providing information at a glance and easy access to frequently used tools. For example, you can add a Clock gadget to your desktop that shows the current time, a Weather gadget that displays the current temperature where you live, or a Calendar gadget that displays the current date. Gadgets are added to the Sidebar, which is a location at the right side of the Windows 7 desktop.

To view available gadgets, right-click in a blank area on the desktop and then click *Gadgets* at the shortcut menu. This displays the gadget gallery similar to what you see in Figure W.7. To add a gadget to the Sidebar, double-click the desired gadget. To remove a gadget from the Sidebar, hover the mouse pointer over the gadget and then click the Close button that displays at the upper right side of the gadget. *Note: The Gadget option on the shortcut menu may be missing if the computer you are using is located in a school setting where customization options have been disabled. If you do not see **Gadget** on the shortcut menu, please skip Project 3.*

Figure W.7 Gadget Gallery

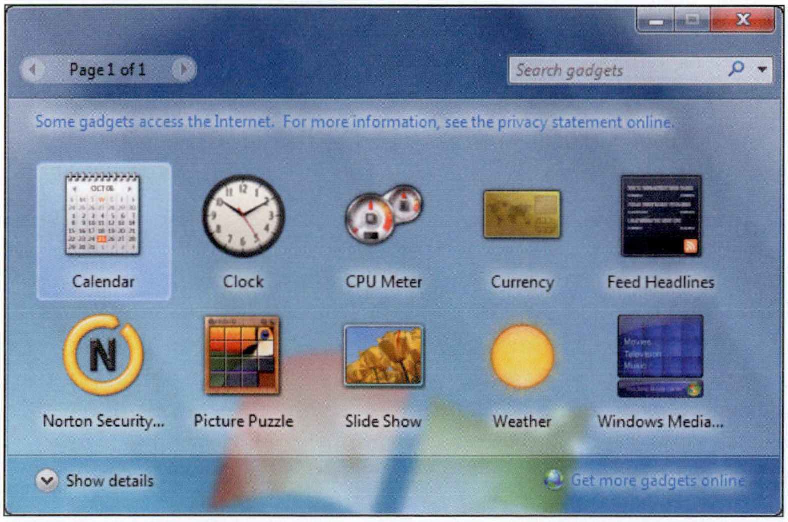

Project 3 Adding and Removing Gadgets

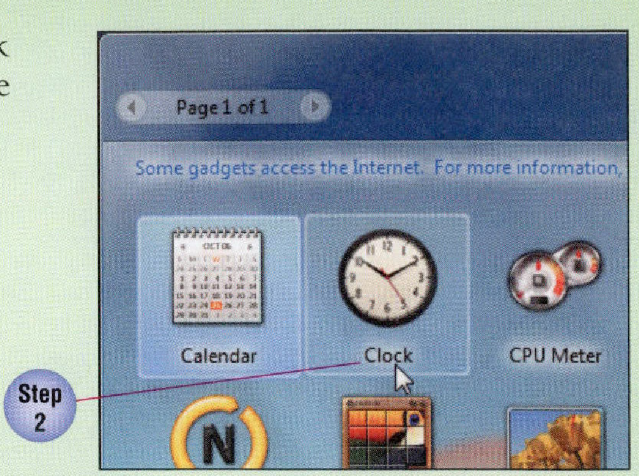

1. At the Windows 7 desktop, right-click in a blank area on the desktop and then click *Gadgets* at the shortcut menu.
2. At the Gadgets Gallery, double-click the *Clock* gadget.
3. Double-click the *Weather* gadget.
4. Double-click the *Calendar* gadget.
5. Close the Gadget Gallery by clicking the Close button located in the upper right corner of the gallery.
6. Hover your mouse over the Calendar gadget until buttons display at the right side of the gadget and then click the Larger size button. (This expands the calendar to display the days of the month.)
7. Hover your mouse over the Weather gadget and then click the Options button.
8. At the Weather dialog box that displays, type in the *Select current location* text box the name of your city followed by your state (or province) and then press Enter.
9. If a drop-down list displays with city names, scroll down the list to display your city and then click your city and state (or province).
10. Click OK to close the Weather dialog box.
11. After viewing the gadgets, remove the Clock gadget by hovering the mouse over the clock and then clicking the Close button that displays at the upper right side of the clock.
12. Close the Weather gadget by hovering the mouse over the gadget and then clicking the Close button that displays.
13. Close the Calendar gadget by hovering the mouse over the gadget and then clicking the Close button that displays.

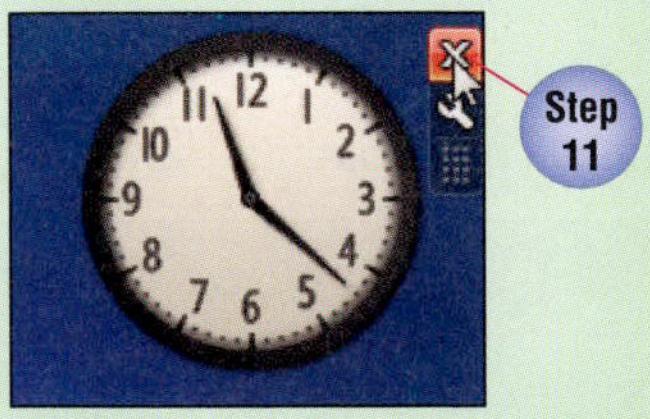

Managing Files and Folders

As you begin working with programs in Windows 7, you will create files in which data (information) is saved. A file might contain a Word document, an Excel workbook, or a PowerPoint presentation. As you begin creating files, consider creating folders into which those files will be stored. You can complete file management tasks such as creating a folder and copying and moving files and folders at the Computer window. To display the Computer window shown in Figure W.8, click the Start button on the Taskbar and then click *Computer*. The various components of the Computer window are identified in Figure W.8.

Figure W.8 Computer Window

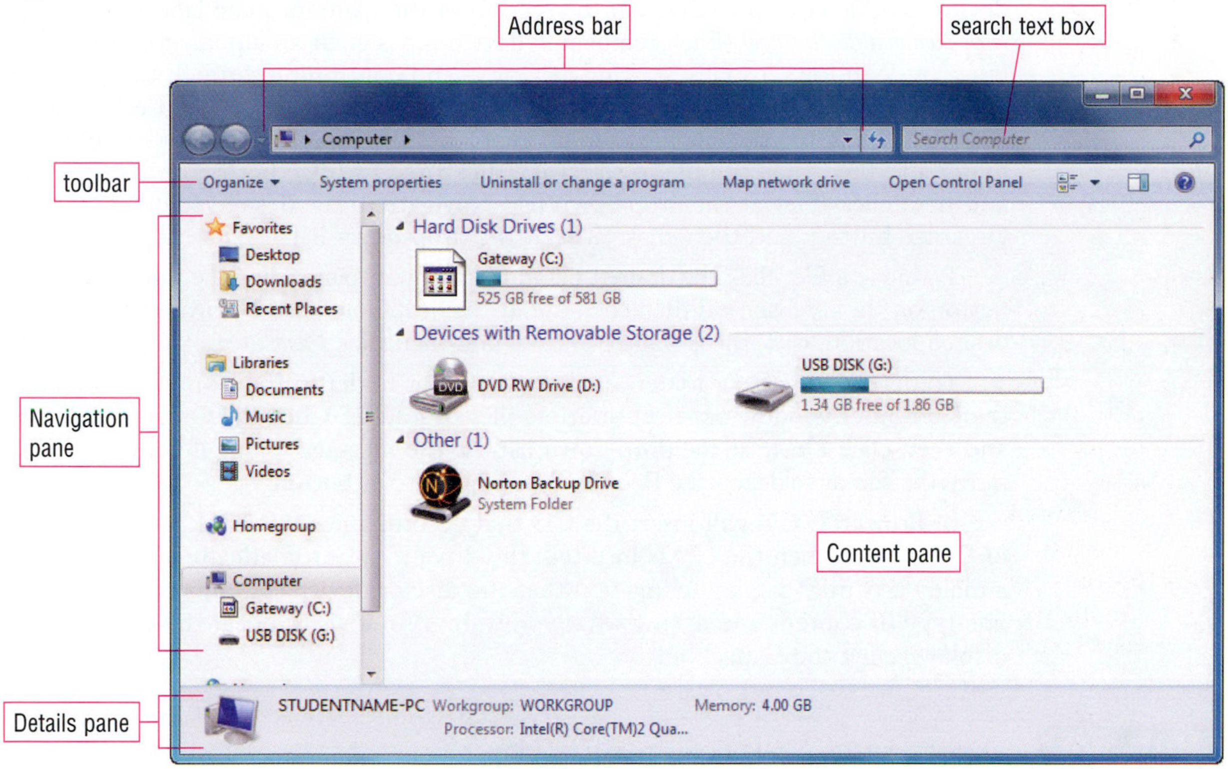

In the Content pane of the Computer window, icons display representing each hard disk drive and removable storage medium such as a CD, DVD, or USB device connected to your computer. Next to each storage device icon, Windows provides the amount of storage space available as well as a bar with the amount of used space shaded with color. This visual cue allows you to see at a glance the proportion of space available relative to the capacity of the device. Double-click a device icon in the Content pane to change the display to show the contents stored on the device. You can display contents from another device or folder using the Navigation pane or the Address bar on the Computer window.

Copying, Moving, and Deleting Files and Folders

File and folder management activities might include copying and moving files or folders from one folder or drive to another, or deleting files or folders. The Computer window offers a variety of methods for copying, moving, and deleting files and folders. This section will provide you with steps for copying, moving, and deleting files and folders using options from the Organize button on the toolbar and the shortcut menu.

To copy a file to another folder or drive, first display the file in the Content pane by identifying the location of the file. If the file is located in the Documents folder, click the *Documents* folder in the *Libraries* section in the Navigation pane and then click the file name in the Content pane that you want to copy. Click the Organize button on the toolbar and then click *Copy* at the drop-down list. In the Navigation pane, click the location where you want to copy the file. Click the Organize button and then click *Paste* at the drop-down list. You would complete similar steps to copy and paste a folder to another location.

If the desired file is located on a storage medium such as a CD, DVD, or USB device, double-click the device in the section of the Content pane labeled *Devices with Removable Storage*. (Each removable device is assigned an alphabetic drive letter by Windows, usually starting at F or G and continuing through the alphabet depending on the number of removable devices that are currently in use.) After double-clicking the storage medium in the Content pane, navigate to the desired folder and then click the file to select it. Click the Organize button on the toolbar and then click *Copy* at the drop-down list. Navigate to the desired folder, click the Organize button, and then click *Paste* at the drop-down list.

To move a file, click the desired file in the Content pane, click the Organize button on the toolbar, and then click *Cut* at the drop-down list. Navigate to the desired location, click the Organize button, and then click *Paste* at the drop-down list.

To delete a file(s) or folder(s), click the file or folder in the Content pane in the Computer window or select multiple files or folders. Click the Organize button and then click *Delete* at the drop-down list. At the message asking if you want to move the file or folder to the Recycle Bin, click the Yes button.

In Project 4, you will insert the CD that accompanies this book into the DVD or CD drive. When the CD is inserted, the drive may automatically activate and a dialog box may display telling you that the disc or device contains more than one type of content and asking what you want Windows to do. If this dialog box displays, click the Cancel button.

Project 4 Copying a File and Folder and Deleting a File

1. Insert the CD that accompanies this textbook into the appropriate drive. If a dialog box displays telling you that the disc or device contains more than one type of content and asking what you want Windows to do, click the Cancel button.
2. Insert your storage medium (such as a USB flash drive) in the USB port (or other drive). If an AutoPlay window displays, click the Close button.
3. At the Windows 7 desktop, click the Start button and then click *Computer* located at the right side of the Start menu.
4. Copy a file from the CD that accompanies this textbook to the drive containing your storage medium by completing the following steps:
   a. Double-click the CD drive in the Content pane containing the CD from the book.
   b. Double-click the *StudentDataFiles* folder in the Content pane.
   c. Double-click the *Windows7* folder in the Content pane.
   d. Click ***WordDocument01.docx*** in the Content pane.
   e. Click the Organize button on the toolbar and then click *Copy* at the drop-down list.

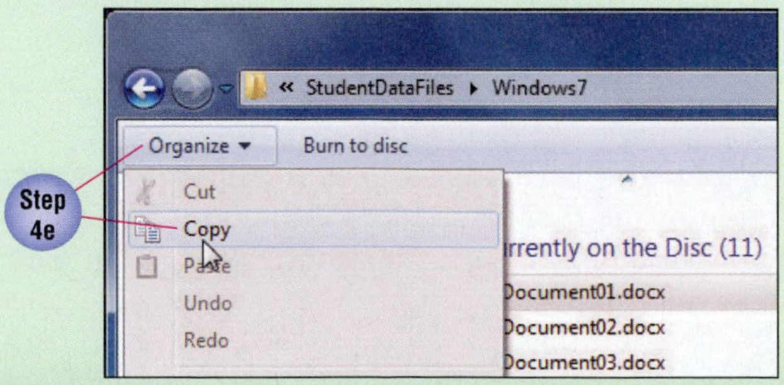

f. In the Computer section in the Navigation pane, click the drive containing your storage medium. (You may need to scroll down the Navigation pane.)
g. Click the Organize button and then click *Paste* at the drop-down list.

5. Delete ***WordDocument01.docx*** from your storage medium by completing the following steps:
   a. Make sure the contents of your storage medium display in the Content pane in the Computer window.
   b. Click ***WordDocument01.docx*** in the Content pane to select it.
   c. Click the Organize button and then click *Delete* at the drop-down list.
   d. At the message asking if you want to permanently delete the file, click the Yes button.
6. Copy the Windows7 folder from the CD to your storage medium by completing the following steps:
   a. With the Computer window open, click the drive in the *Computer* section in the Navigation pane that contains the CD that accompanies this book.
   b. Double-click *StudentDataFiles* in the Content pane.
   c. Click the *Windows7* folder in the Content pane.
   d. Click the Organize button and then click *Copy* at the drop-down list.
   e. In the *Computer* section in the Navigation pane, click the drive containing your storage medium.
   f. Click the Organize button and then click *Paste* at the drop-down list.
7. Close the Computer window by clicking the Close button located in the upper right corner of the window.

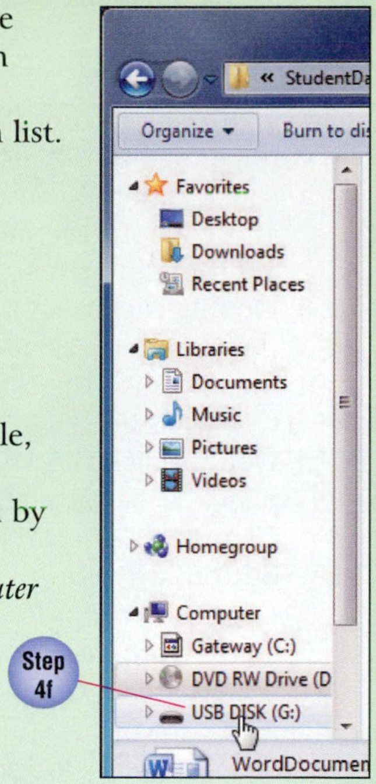

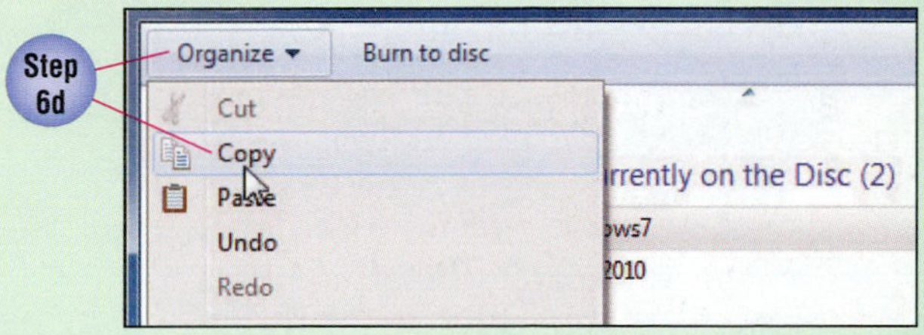

In addition to options in the Organize button drop-down list, you can use options in a shortcut menu to copy, move, and delete files or folders. To use a shortcut menu, select the desired file(s) or folder(s), position the mouse pointer on the selected item, and then click the right mouse button. At the shortcut menu that displays, click the desired option such as Copy, Cut, or Delete.

Selecting Files and Folders

You can move, copy, or delete more than one file or folder at the same time. Before moving, copying, or deleting files or folders, select the desired files or folders. To make selecting easier, consider changing the display in the Content pane to List or Details. To change the display, click the Views button arrow on the toolbar in the Computer window and then click *List* or *Details* at the drop-down list. You can also cycle through the various views by clicking the Views button. Hover your mouse over the Views button and the ScreenTip *Change your view* displays.

To select adjacent files or folders, click the first file or folder, hold down the Shift key, and then click the last file or folder. To select nonadjacent files or folders, click the first file or folder, hold down the Ctrl key, and then click any other files or folders.

Project 5 Copying and Deleting Files

1. At the Windows 7 desktop, click the Start button and then click *Computer*.
2. Copy files from the CD that accompanies this textbook to the drive containing your storage medium by completing the following steps:

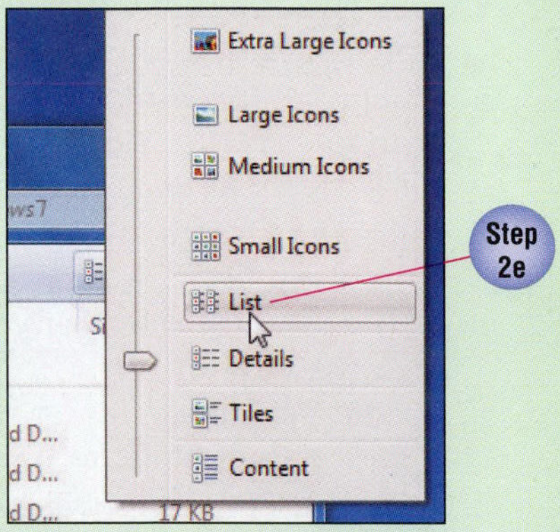

   a. Make sure the CD that accompanies this textbook and your storage medium are inserted in the appropriate drives.
   b. Double-click the CD drive in the Content pane in the Computer window.
   c. Double-click the *StudentDataFiles* folder in the Content pane.
   d. Double-click the *Windows7* folder in the Content pane.
   e. Change the display to List by clicking the Views button arrow on the toolbar and then clicking *List* at the drop-down list.

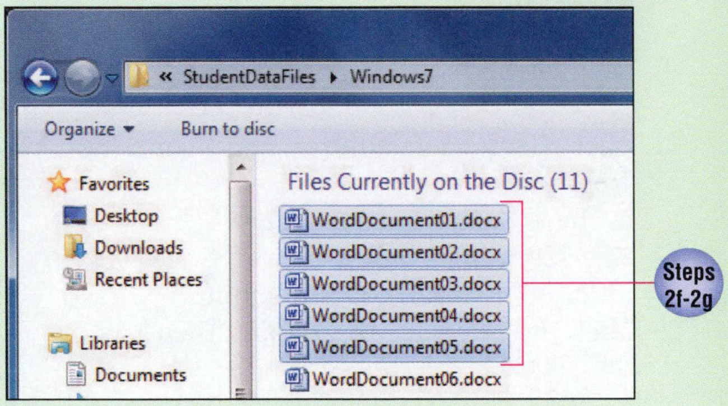

   f. Click ***WordDocument01.docx*** in the Content pane.
   g. Hold down the Shift key, click ***WordDocument05.docx***, and then release the Shift key. (This selects five documents.)
   h. Click the Organize button and then click *Copy* at the drop-down list.
   i. In the *Computer* section in the Navigation pane, click the drive containing your storage medium.
   j. Click the Organize button and then click *Paste* at the drop-down list.
3. Delete the files from your storage medium that you just copied by completing the following steps:

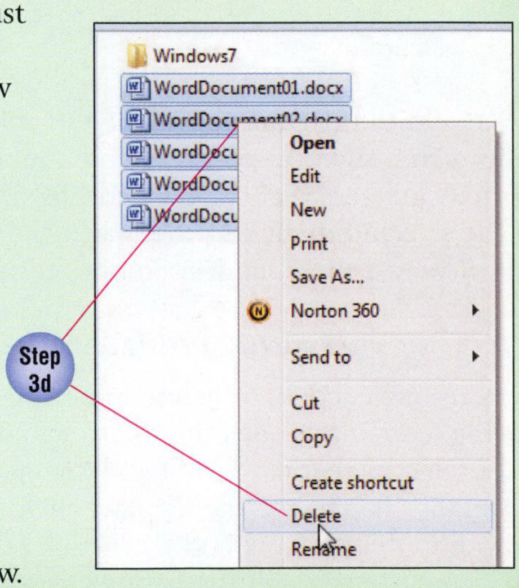

   a. Change the view by clicking the Views button arrow bar and then clicking *List* at the drop-down list.
   b. Click ***WordDocument01.docx*** in the Content pane.
   c. Hold down the Shift key, click ***WordDocument05.docx***, and then release the Shift key.
   d. Position the mouse pointer on any selected file, click the right mouse button, and then click *Delete* at the shortcut menu.
   e. At the message asking if you are sure you want to permanently delete the files, click Yes.
4. Close the Computer window by clicking the Close button located in the upper right corner of the window.

Manipulating and Creating Folders

As you begin working with and creating a number of files, consider creating folders in which you can logically group the files. To create a folder, display the Computer window and then display in the Content pane the drive or folder where you want to create the folder. Position the mouse pointer in a blank area in the Content pane, click the right mouse button, point to *New* in the shortcut menu, and then click *Folder* at the side menu. This inserts a folder icon in the Content pane and names the folder *New folder*. Type the desired name for the new folder and then press Enter.

Project 6 Creating a New Folder

1. At the Windows 7 desktop, open the Computer window.
2. Create a new folder by completing the following steps:
   a. Double-click in the Content pane the drive that contains your storage medium.
   b. Double-click the *Windows7* folder in the Content pane. (This opens the folder.)
   c. Click the Views button arrow and then click *List* at the drop-down list.
   d. Position the mouse pointer in a blank area in the Content pane and then click the right mouse button.
   e. Point to *New* in the shortcut menu and then click *Folder* at the side menu.

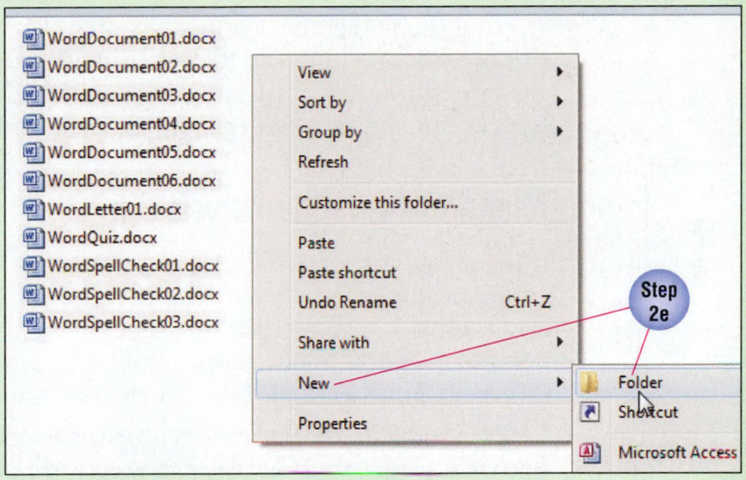

   f. Type **SpellCheckFiles** and then press Enter. (This changes the name from *New folder* to *SpellCheckFiles*.)

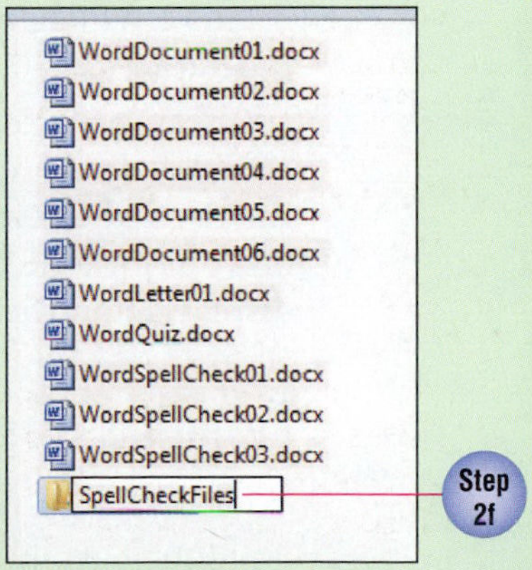

3. Copy **WordSpellCheck01.docx**, **WordSpellCheck02.docx**, and **WordSpellCheck03.docx** into the SpellCheckFiles folder you just created by completing the following steps:
   a. Click the Views button arrow and then click *List* at the drop-down list. (Skip this step if *List* is already selected.)
   b. Click once on the file named **WordSpellCheck01.docx** located in the Content pane.
   c. Hold down the Shift key, click once on the file named **WordSpellCheck03.docx**, and then release the Shift key. (This selects three documents.)
   d. Click the Organize button and then click *Copy* at the drop-down list.
   e. Double-click the *SpellCheckFiles* folder in the Content pane.
   f. Click the Organize button and then click *Paste* at the drop-down list.

4. Delete the SpellCheckFiles folder and its contents by completing the following steps:
   a. Click the Back button (contains a left-pointing arrow) located at the left side of the Address bar.
   b. With the SpellCheckFiles folder selected in the Content pane, click the Organize button and then click *Delete* at the drop-down list.
   c. At the message asking you to confirm the deletion, click Yes.

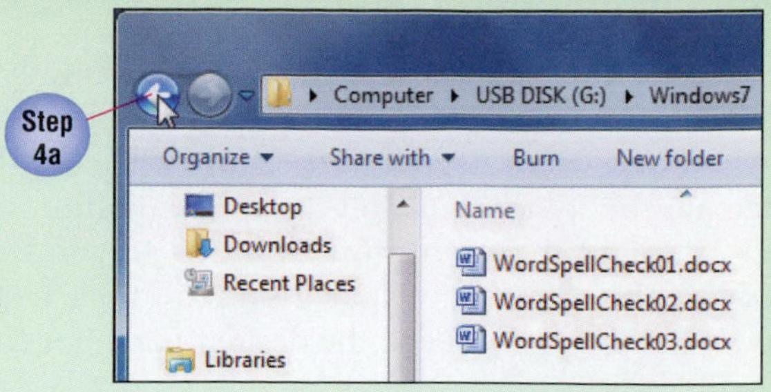

5. Close the window by clicking the Close button located in the upper right corner of the window.

Using the Recycle Bin

Deleting the wrong file can be a disaster but Windows 7 helps protect your work with the Recycle Bin. The Recycle Bin acts just like an office wastepaper basket; you can "throw away" (delete) unwanted files, but you can "reach in" to the Recycle Bin and take out (restore) a file if you threw it away by accident.

Deleting Files to the Recycle Bin

A file or folder or selected files or folders you delete from the hard drive are sent automatically to the Recycle Bin. If you want to permanently delete files or folders from the hard drive without first sending them to the Recycle Bin, select the desired file(s) or folder(s), right click on one of the selected files or folders, hold down the Shift key, and then click *Delete* at the shortcut menu.

Files and folders deleted from a USB flash drive or disc are deleted permanently. (Recovery programs are available, however, that will help you recover deleted files or folders. If you accidentally delete a file or folder from a USB flash drive or disc, do not do anything more with the USB flash drive or disc until you can run a recovery program.)

You can delete files in the manner described earlier in this section and you can also delete a file by dragging the file icon to the Recycle Bin. To do this, click the desired file in the Content pane in the Computer window, drag the file icon on top of the Recycle Bin icon on the desktop until the text *Move to Recycle Bin* displays, and then release the mouse button.

Restoring Files from the Recycle Bin

To restore a file from the Recycle Bin, double-click the Recycle Bin icon on the desktop. This opens the Recycle Bin window shown in Figure W.9. (The contents of the Recycle Bin will vary.) To restore a file, click the file you want restored and then click the Restore this item button on the toolbar. This removes the file from the Recycle Bin and returns it to its original location. You can also restore a file by positioning the mouse pointer on the file, clicking the right mouse button, and then clicking *Restore* at the shortcut menu.

Figure W.9 Recycle Bin Window

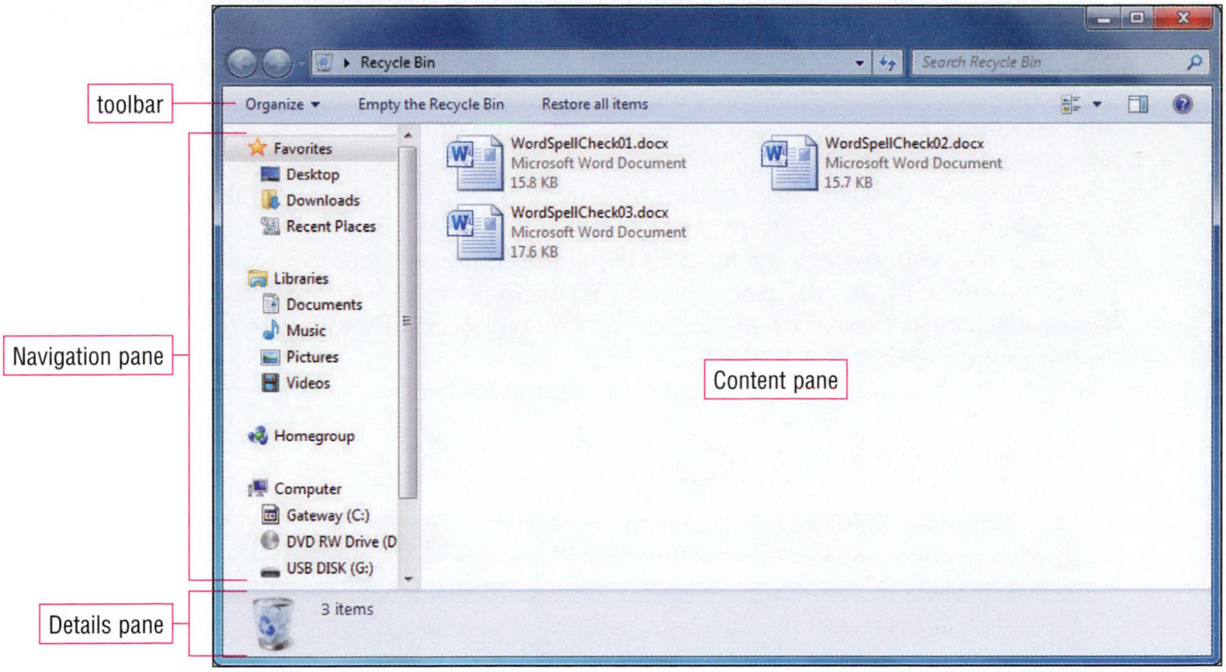

Project 7 Deleting Files to and Restoring Files from the Recycle Bin

Before beginning this project, check with your instructor to determine if you can copy files to the hard drive.

1. At the Windows 7 desktop, open the Computer window.
2. Copy files from your storage medium to the Documents folder on your hard drive by completing the following steps:
   a. Double-click in the Content pane the drive containing your storage medium.
   b. Double-click the *Windows7* folder in the Content pane.
   c. Click the Views button arrow and then click *List* at the drop-down list. (Skip this step if *List* is already selected.)
   d. Click ***WordSpellCheck01.docx*** in the Content pane.
   e. Hold down the Shift key, click ***WordSpellCheck03.docx***, and then release the Shift key.
   f. Click the Organize button and then click *Copy* at the drop-down list.
   g. Click the *Documents* folder in the *Libraries* section in the Navigation pane.
   h. Click the Organize button and then click *Paste* at the drop-down list.

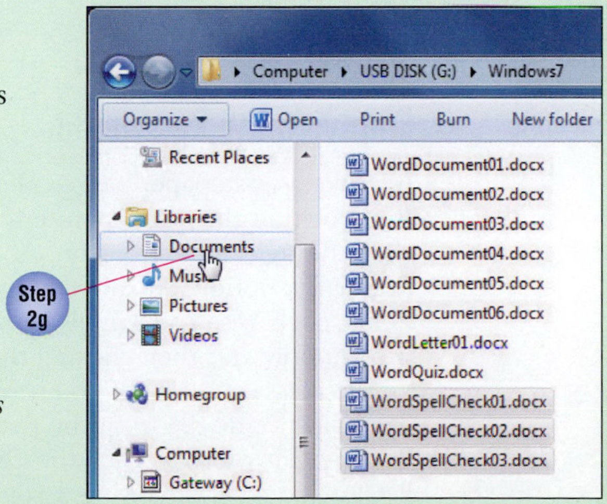

3. Delete to the Recycle Bin the files you just copied by completing the following steps:
   a. With **WordSpellCheck01.docx** through **WordSpellCheck03.docx** selected in the Content pane, click the Organize button and then click *Delete* at the drop-down list.
   b. At the message asking you if you are sure you want to move the items to the Recycle Bin, click Yes.
4. Close the Computer window.
5. At the Windows 7 desktop, display the contents of the Recycle Bin by double-clicking the Recycle Bin icon.
6. Restore the files you just deleted by completing the following steps:
   a. Select **WordSpellCheck01.docx** through **WordSpellCheck03.docx** in the Recycle Bin Content pane. (If these files are not visible, you will need to scroll down the list of files in the Content pane.)
   b. Click the Restore the selected items button on the toolbar.

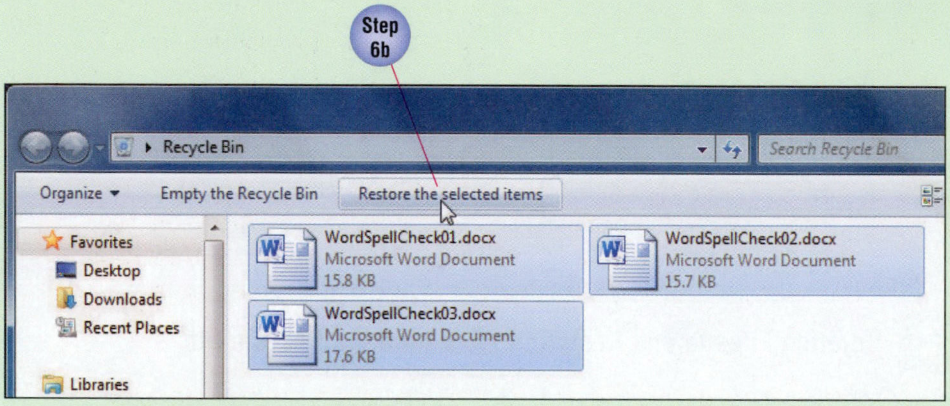

7. Close the Recycle Bin by clicking the Close button located in the upper right corner of the window.
8. Display the Computer window.
9. Click the *Documents* folder in the *Libraries* section in the Navigation pane.
10. Delete the files you restored.
11. Close the Computer window.

Emptying the Recycle Bin

Just like a wastepaper basket, the Recycle Bin can get full. To empty the Recycle Bin, position the arrow pointer on the Recycle Bin icon on the desktop and then click the right mouse button. At the shortcut menu that displays, click the *Empty Recycle Bin* option. At the message asking if you want to permanently delete the items, click Yes. You can also empty the Recycle Bin by displaying the Recycle Bin window and then clicking the Empty the Recycle Bin button on the toolbar. At the message asking if you want to permanently delete the items, click Yes. To delete a specific file from the Recycle Bin window, click the desired file in the Recycle Bin window, click the Organize button, and then *Delete* at the drop-down list. At the message asking if you want to permanently delete the file, click Yes. When you empty the Recycle Bin, the files cannot be recovered by the Recycle Bin or by Windows 7. If you have to recover a file, you will need to use a file recovery program.

Project 8 Emptying the Recycle Bin

Before beginning this project, check with your instructor to determine if you can delete files/folders from the Recycle Bin.

1. At the Windows 7 desktop, double-click the Recycle Bin icon.
2. At the Recycle Bin window, empty the contents by clicking the Empty the Recycle Bin button on the toolbar.
3. At the message asking you if you want to permanently delete the items, click Yes.
4. Close the Recycle Bin by clicking the Close button located in the upper right corner of the window.

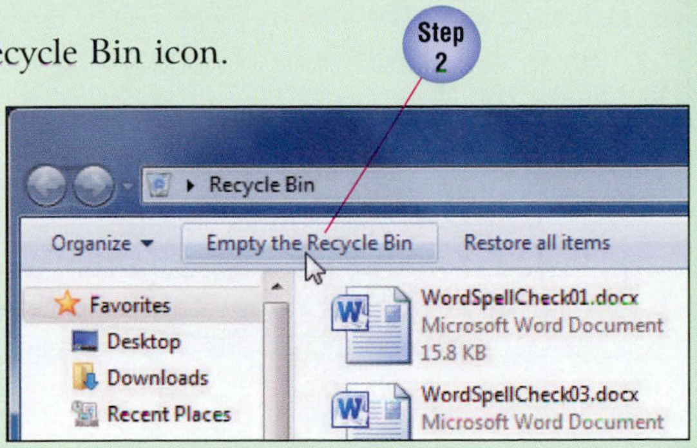

Creating a Shortcut

If you use a file or program on a consistent basis, consider creating a shortcut to the file or program. A shortcut is a specialized icon that represents very small files that point the operating system to the actual item, whether it is a file, a folder, or an application. If you create a shortcut to a Word document, the shortcut icon is not the actual document but a path to the document. Double-click the shortcut icon and Windows 7 opens the document in Word.

One method for creating a shortcut is to display the Computer window and then make active the drive or folder where the file is located. Right-click the desired file, point to *Send To*, and then click *Desktop (create shortcut)*. You can easily delete a shortcut icon from the desktop by dragging the shortcut icon to the Recycle Bin icon. This deletes the shortcut icon but does not delete the file to which the shortcut pointed.

Project 9 Creating a Shortcut

1. At the Windows 7 desktop, display the Computer window.
2. Double-click the drive containing your storage medium.
3. Double-click the *Windows7* folder in the Content pane.
4. Change the display of files to a list by clicking the Views button arrow and then clicking *List* at the drop-down list. (Skip this step if *List* is already selected.)
5. Create a shortcut to the file named **WordLetter01.docx** by right-clicking ***WordLetter01.docx***, pointing to *Send to*, and then clicking *Desktop (create shortcut)*.

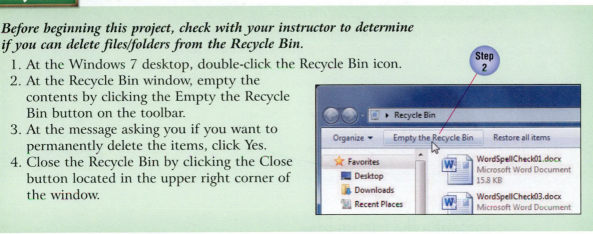

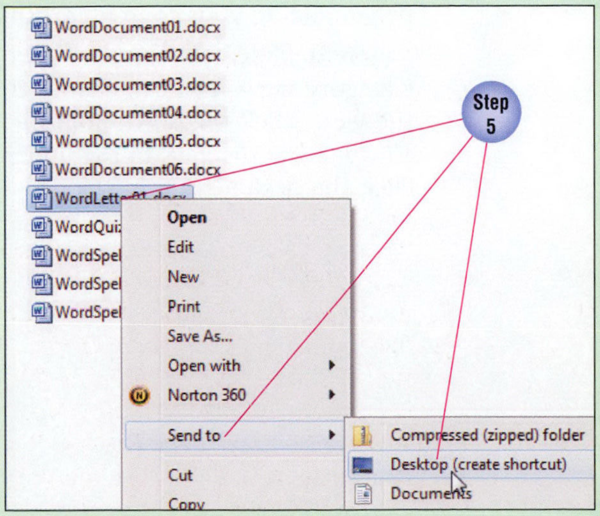

6. Close the Computer window.
7. Open Word and the file named **WordLetter01.docx** by double-clicking the *WordLetter01.docx* shortcut icon on the desktop.
8. After viewing the file in Word, exit Word by clicking the Close button that displays in the upper right corner of the window.
9. Delete the *WordLetter01.docx* shortcut icon by completing the following steps:
   a. At the desktop, position the mouse pointer on the *WordLetter01.docx* shortcut icon.
   b. Hold down the left mouse button, drag the icon on top of the Recycle Bin icon, and then release the mouse button.

Exploring the Control Panel

The Control Panel, shown in Figure W.10, contains a variety of icons you can use to customize the appearance and functionality of your computer as well as access and change system settings. Display the Control Panel by clicking the Start button on the Taskbar and then clicking *Control Panel* at the Start menu. The Control Panel organizes settings into categories to make them easier to find. Click a category icon and the Control Panel displays lower-level categories and tasks within each of them.

Hover your mouse over a category icon in the Control Panel and a ScreenTip displays with an explanation of what options are available. For example, if you hover the mouse over the Appearance and Personalization icon, a ScreenTip displays with information about the tasks available in the category such as changing the appearance of desktop items, applying a theme or screen saver to your computer, or customizing the Start menu and Taskbar.

If you click a category icon in the Control Panel, the Control Panel displays all of the available subcategories and tasks in the category. Also, the categories display in text form at the left side of the Control Panel. For example, if you click the Appearance and Personalization category icon, the Control Panel displays as shown in Figure W.11. Notice how the Control Panel categories display at the left side of the Control Panel and options for changing the appearance and personalizing your computer display in the middle of the Control Panel.

By default, the Control Panel displays categories of tasks in what is called Category view. You can change this view to *Large icons* or *Small icons*. To change the view, click the down-pointing arrow that displays at the right side of the text *View by* that displays in the upper right corner of the Control Panel, and then click the desired view at the drop-down list (see Figure W.10).

Figure W.10 The Control Panel

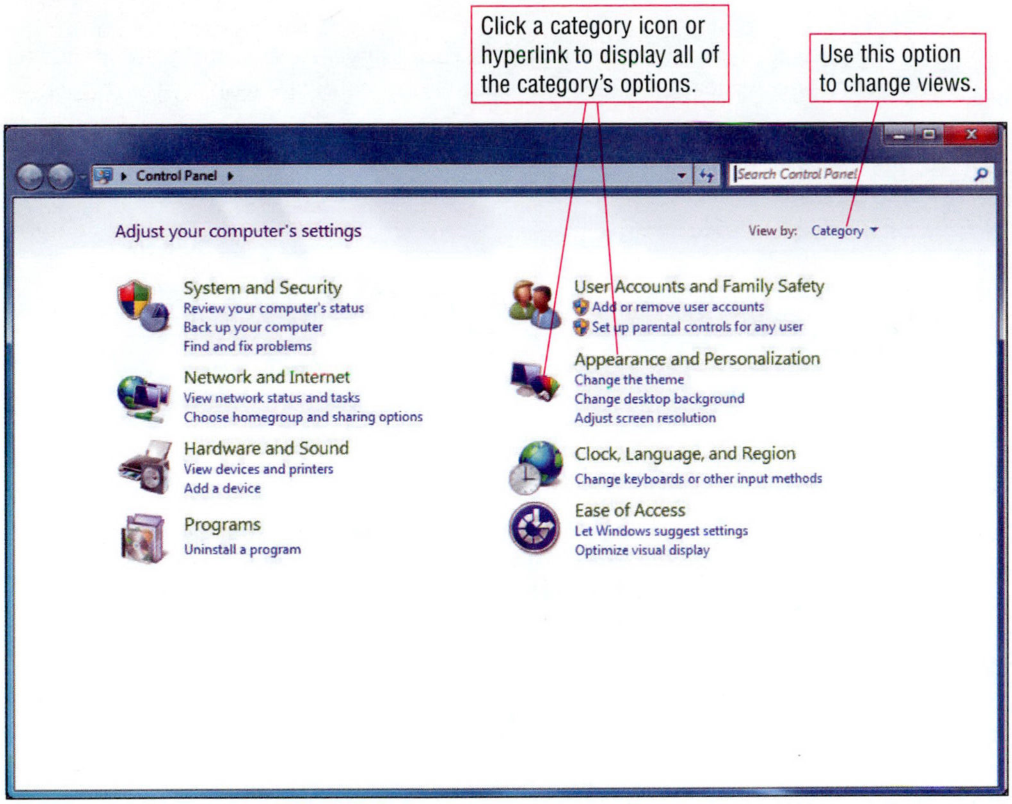

Figure W.11 Appearance and Personalization Window

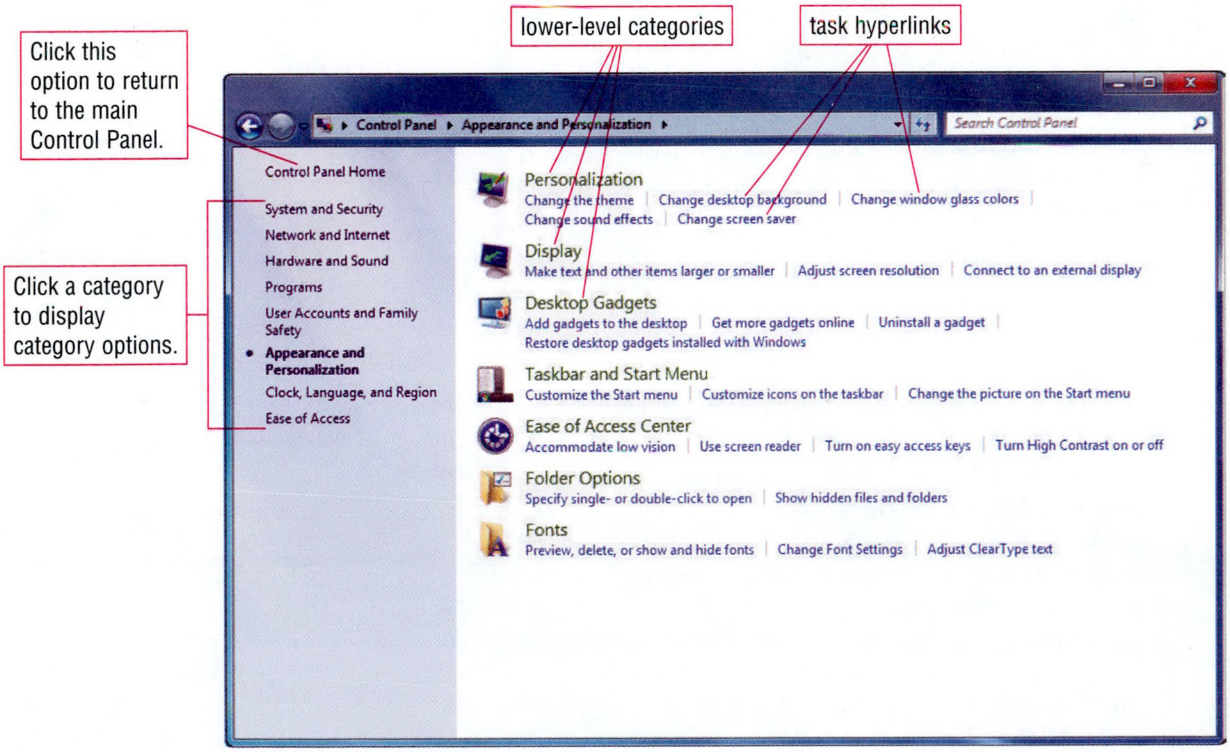

Project 10 Changing the Desktop Theme

1. At the Windows 7 desktop, click the Start button and then click *Control Panel* at the Start menu.
2. At the Control Panel, click the Appearance and Personalization category icon.

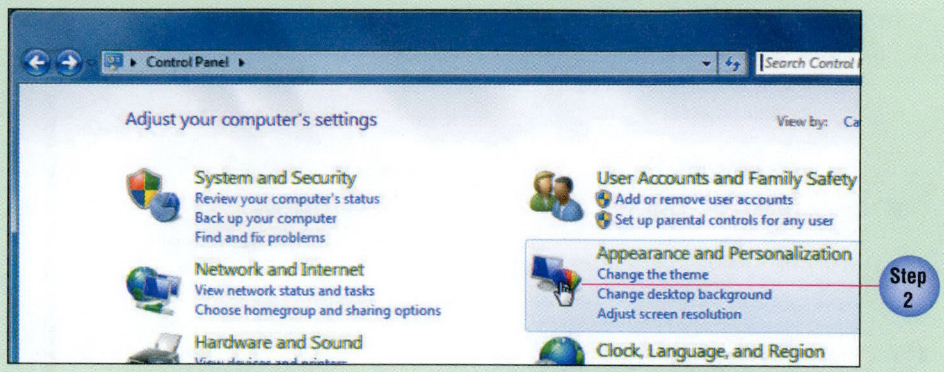

3. Click the Change the theme hyperlink that displays below the Personalization category in the panel at the right in the Control Panel.
4. At the window that displays with options for changing visuals and sounds on your computer, click the *Landscapes* theme.

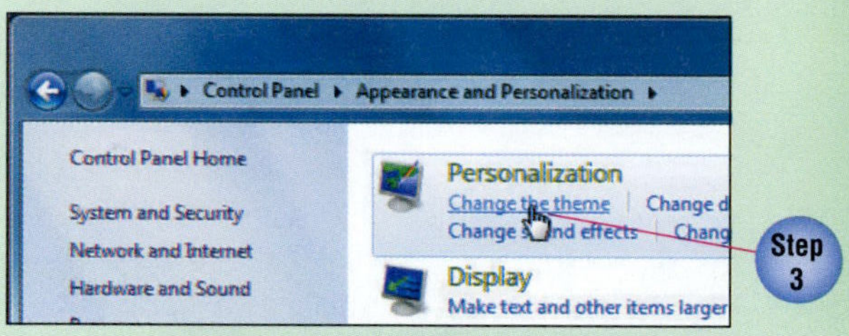

5. Click the Desktop Background hyperlink that displays in the lower left corner of the panel at the right.
6. Click the button that displays below the text *Change picture every* and then click *10 Seconds* at the drop-down list. (This tells Windows to change the picture on your desktop every 10 seconds.)
7. Click the Save changes button that displays in the lower right corner of the Control Panel.
8. Click the Close button located in the upper right corner to close the Control Panel.
9. Look at the picture that displays as the background at the desktop. Wait for 10 seconds and then look at the second picture that displays.
10. Click the Start button and then click *Control Panel* at the Start menu.
11. At the Control Panel, click the Appearance and Personalization category icon.
12. Click the Change the theme hyperlink that displays below the Personalization category in the panel at the right.

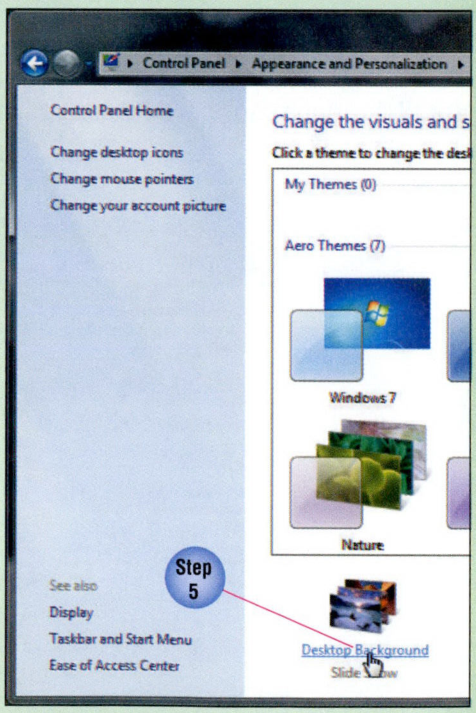

13. At the window that displays with options for changing visuals and sounds on your computer, click the *Windows 7* theme in the *Aero Themes* section. (This is the default theme.)
14. Click the Close button located in the upper right corner of the Control Panel.

Searching in the Control Panel

The Control Panel contains a large number of options for customizing the appearance and functionality of your computer. If you want to customize a feature and are not sure where the options for the feature are located, search for the feature. To do this, display the Control Panel and then type the name of the desired feature. By default, the insertion point is positioned in the *Search Control Panel* text box. When you type the feature name in the Search Control Panel, options related to the feature display in the Control Panel.

Project 11 **Customizing the Mouse**

1. Click the Start button and then click *Control Panel*.
2. At the Control Panel, type **mouse**. (The insertion point is automatically located in the *Search Control Panel* text box when you open the Control Panel. When you type *mouse*, features for customizing the mouse display in the Control Panel.)

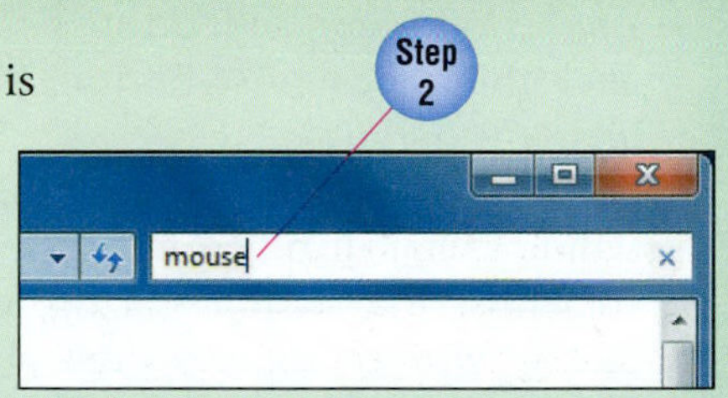

3. Click the Mouse icon that displays in the Control Panel.
4. At the Mouse Properties dialog box, notice the options that display. (The *Switch primary and secondary buttons* option might be useful, for example, if you are left-handed and want to switch the buttons on the mouse.)
5. Click the Cancel button to remove the dialog box.
6. At the Control Panel, click the Change the mouse pointer display or speed hyperlink.

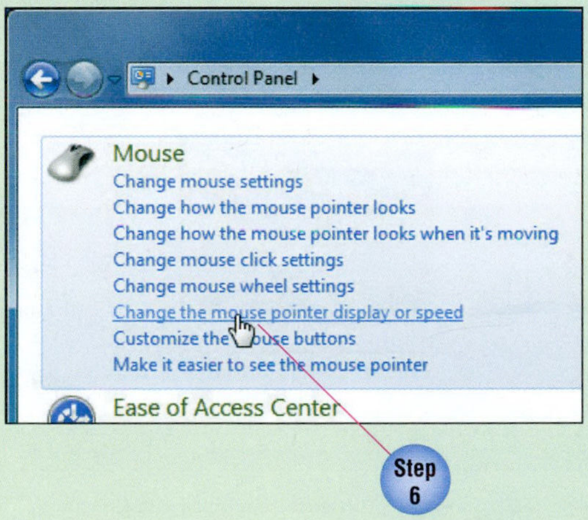

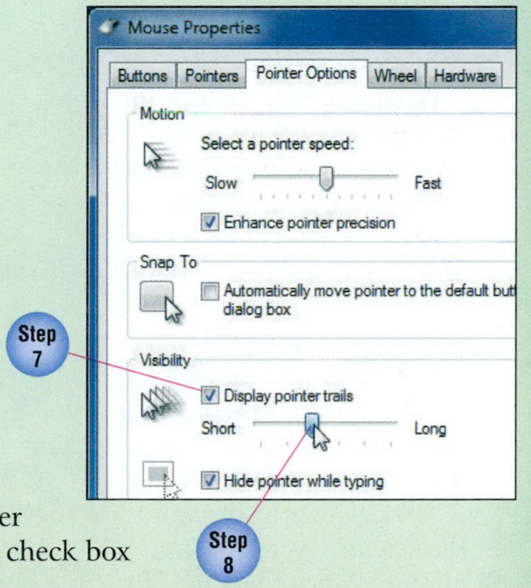

7. At the Mouse Properties dialog box with the Pointer Options tab selected, click the *Display pointer trails* check box in the *Visibility* section to insert a check mark.
8. Drag the button on the slider bar (located below the *Display pointer trails* check box) approximately to the middle of the bar.
9. Click OK to close the dialog box.
10. Close the Control Panel.
11. Move the mouse pointer around the screen to see the pointer trails as well as the speed at which the mouse moves.

Displaying Personalize Options with a Shortcut Command

In addition to the Control Panel, you can display customization options with a command from a shortcut menu. Display a shortcut menu by positioning the mouse pointer in the desired position and then clicking the right mouse button. For example, display a shortcut menu with options for customizing the desktop by positioning the mouse pointer in an empty area on the desktop and then clicking the right mouse button. At the shortcut menu that displays, click the desired shortcut command.

Project 12 Customizing with a Shortcut Command

1. At the Windows 7 desktop, position the mouse pointer in an empty area on the desktop, click the right mouse button, and then click *Personalize* at the shortcut menu.
2. At the Control Panel Appearance and Personalization window that displays, click the Change mouse pointers hyperlink that displays at the left side of the window.
3. At the Mouse Properties dialog box, click the Pointer Options tab.
4. Click in the *Display pointer trails* check box to remove the check mark.
5. Click OK to close the dialog box.
6. At the Control Panel Appearance and Personalization window, click the Screen Saver hyperlink that displays in the lower right corner of the window.
7. At the Screen Saver Settings dialog box, click the option button below the *Screen saver* option and then click *Ribbons* at the drop-down list.
8. Check the number in the *Wait* text box. If a number other than *1* displays, click the down-pointing arrow in the spin box at the right side of the text box until *1* displays. (This tells Windows to display the screen saver after one minute of inactivity.)
9. Click OK to close the dialog box.
10. Close the Control Panel by clicking the Close button located in the upper right corner of the window.

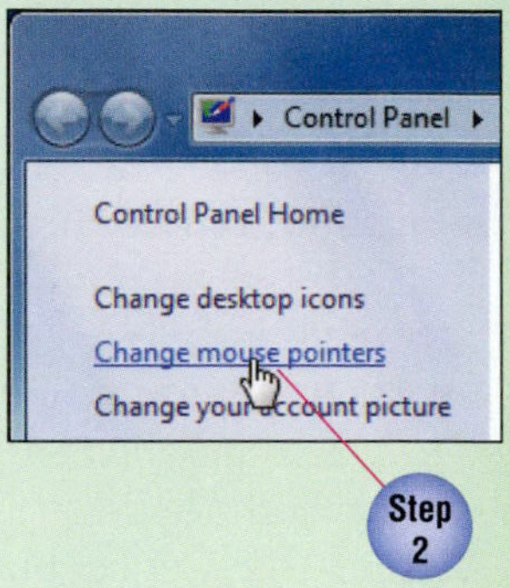

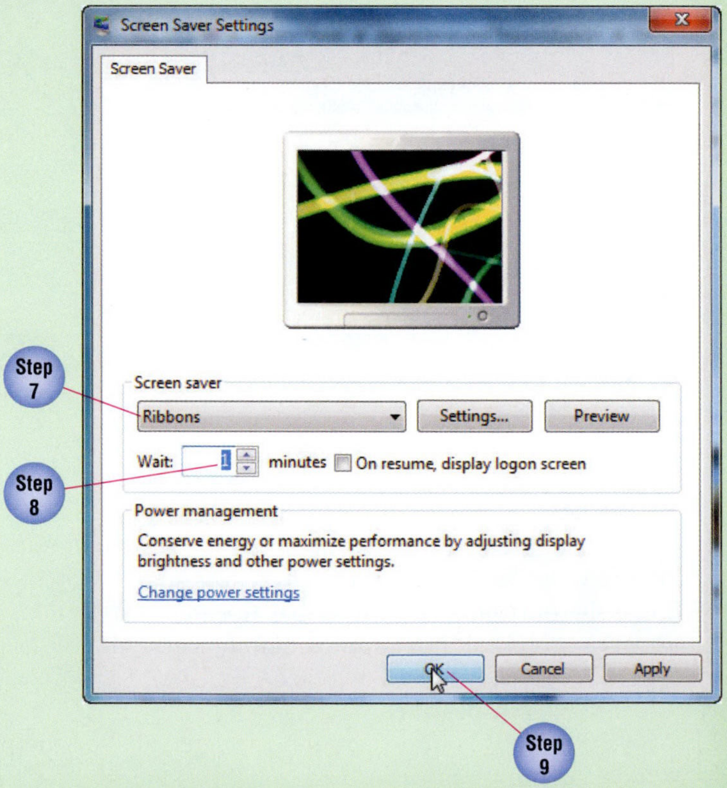

11. Do not touch the mouse or keyboard and wait over one minute for the screen saver to display. After watching the screen saver, move the mouse. (This redisplays the desktop.)
12. Right-click in an empty area on the desktop and then click *Personalize* at the shortcut menu.
13. At the Control Panel Appearance and Personalization window, click the <u>Screen Saver</u> hyperlink.
14. At the Screen Saver Settings dialog box, click the option button below the *Screen saver* option and then click *(None)* at the drop-down list.
15. Click OK to close the dialog box.
16. Close the Control Panel Appearance and Personalization window.

Exploring Windows Help and Support ■■■■■■■■■■■■■■■■

Windows 7 includes an on-screen reference guide providing information, explanations, and interactive help on learning Windows features. Get help at the Windows Help and Support window shown in Figure W.12. Display this window by clicking the Start button and then clicking *Help and Support* at the Start menu. Use buttons in the window toolbar to display the opening Windows Help and Support window, print the current information, display a list of contents, get customer support or other types of services, and display a list of Help options.

Figure W.12 Windows Help and Support Window

Type search text in this text box.

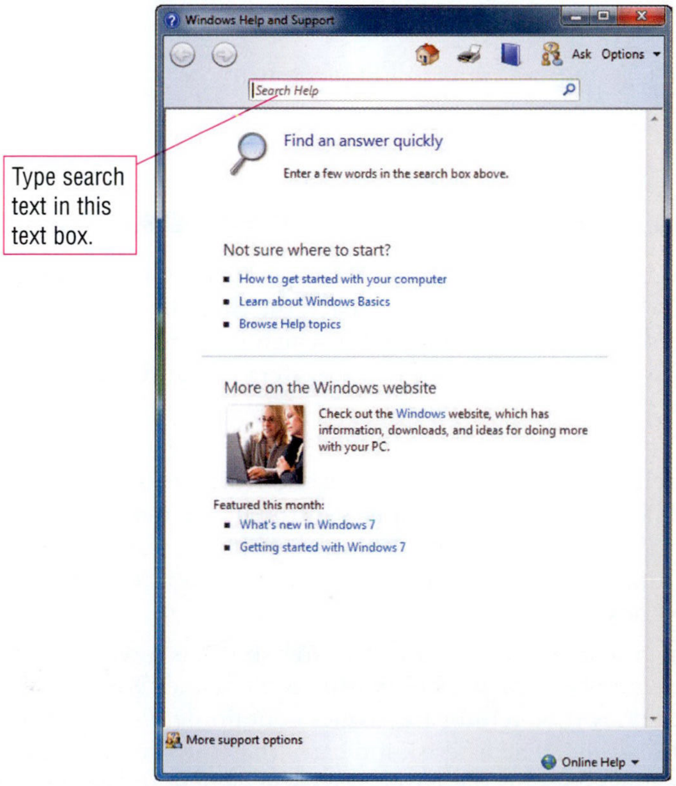

Project 13 Getting Help

1. At the Windows 7 desktop, click the Start button and then click *Help and Support* at the Start menu.
2. At the Windows Help and Support window, click the Learn about Windows Basics hyperlink.
3. Click a hyperlink that interests you, read the information, and then click the Back button on the Windows Help and Support window toolbar. (The Back button is located in the upper left corner of the window.)
4. Click another hyperlink that interests you and then read the information.
5. Click the Help and Support home button that displays on the window toolbar. (This returns you to the opening Windows Help and Support window.)
6. Click in the *Search Help* text box, type **delete files**, and then press Enter.
7. Click the Delete a file or folder hyperlink that displays in the window.
8. Read the information that displays about deleting files or folders and then click the Print button on the window toolbar.
9. At the Print dialog box, click the Print button.
10. Click the Close button to close the Windows Help and Support window.

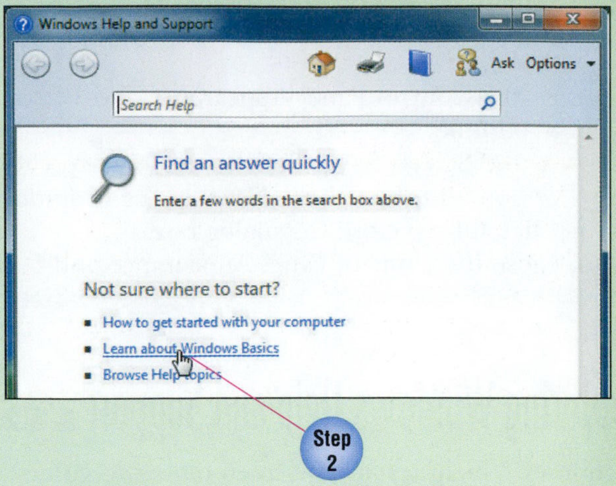

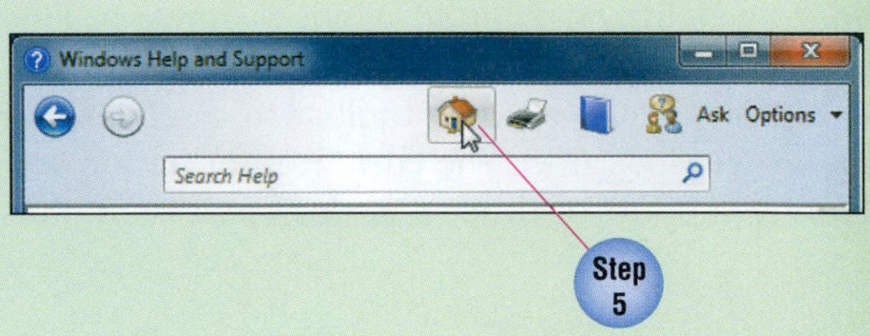

Using Search Tools

The Start menu contains a search tool you can use to quickly find a program or file on your computer. To use the search tool, click the Start button and then type the first few characters of the program or file for which you are searching in the *Search programs and files* text box. As you type characters in the text box, a pop-up list displays with program names or file names that begin with the characters. As you continue typing characters, the search tool refines the list.

You can also search for programs or files with the search text box in the Computer window. The search text box displays in the upper right corner of the Computer window at the right side of the Address bar. If you want to search a specific folder, make that folder active in the Content pane and then type the search text in the text box.

When conducting a search, you can use the asterisk (*) as a wildcard character in place of any letters, numbers, or symbols within a file name. For example, in the following project you will search for file names containing *check* by typing ***check** in the search text box. The asterisk indicates that the file name can start with any letter but it must contain the letters *check* somewhere in the file name.

Project 14 Searching for Programs and Files

1. At the Windows 7 desktop, click the Start button.
2. With the insertion point positioned in the *Search programs and files* text box, type paint. (Notice as you type the letters that Windows displays programs and/or files that begin with the same letters you are typing or that are associated with the same letters in a keyword. Notice that the Paint program displays below the heading *Programs* at the top of the list. Depending on the contents stored in the computer you are using, additional items may display below Paint.)

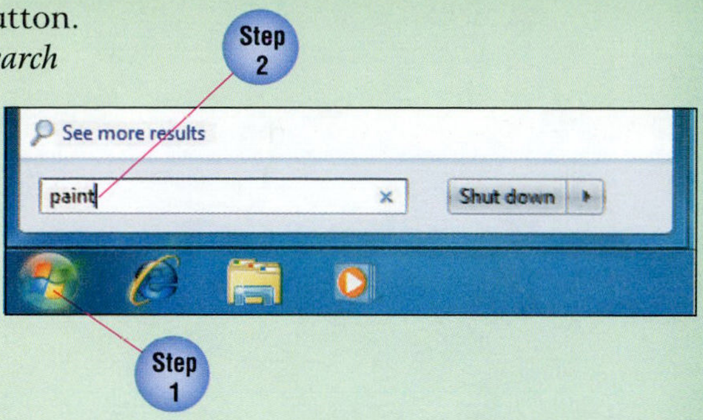

3. Click *Paint* that displays below the *Programs* heading.
4. Close the Paint window.
5. Click the Start button and then click *Computer*.
6. At the Computer window, double-click the icon representing your storage medium.
7. Double-click the *Windows7* folder.
8. Click in the search text box located at the right of the Address bar and then type document. (As you begin typing the letters, Windows filters the list of files in the Content pane to those that contain the letters you type. Notice that the Address bar displays *Search Results in Windows7* to indicate that the files that display matching your criteria were limited to the current folder.)

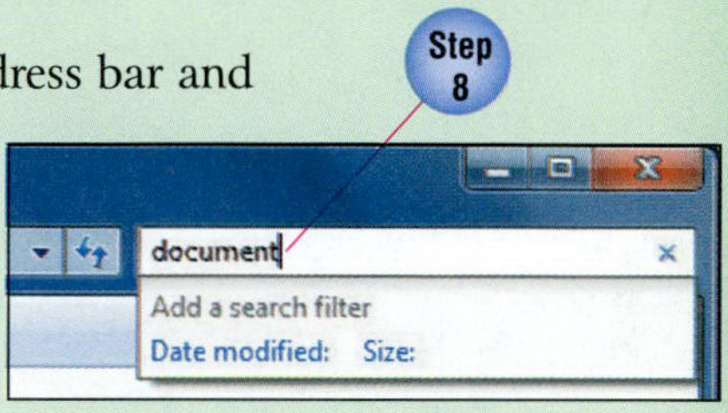

9. Select the text *document* that displays in the search text box and then type *check. (Notice that the Content pane displays file names containing the letters *check* no matter how the file name begins.)
10. Double-click ***WordSpellCheck02.docx*** to open the document in Word.
11. Close the document and exit Word by clicking the Close button located in the upper right corner of the window.
12. Close the Computer window.

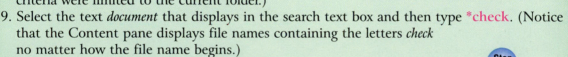

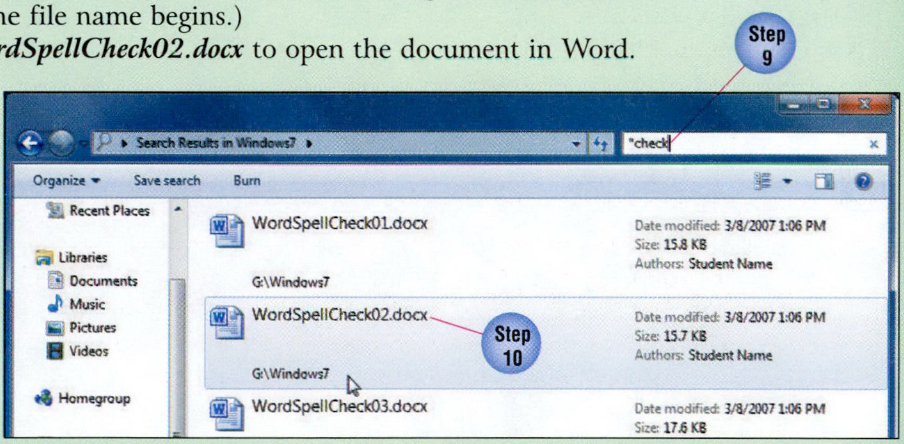

Browsing the Internet Using Internet Explorer 8.0

Microsoft Internet Explorer 8.0 is a web browser program with options and features for displaying sites as well as navigating and searching for information on the Internet. The ***Internet*** is a network of computers connected around the world. Users access the Internet for several purposes: to communicate using instant messaging and/or email, to subscribe to newsgroups, to transfer files, to socialize with other users around the globe in chat rooms, and also to access virtually any kind of information imaginable.

Using the Internet, people can find a phenomenal amount of information for private or public use. To use the Internet, three things are generally required: an Internet Service Provider (ISP), a program to browse the Web (called a ***web browser***), and a ***search engine***. In this section, you will learn how to:

- Navigate the Internet using URLs and hyperlinks
- Use search engines to locate information
- Download web pages and images

You will use the Microsoft Internet Explorer web browser to locate information on the Internet. Uniform Resource Locators, referred to as URLs, are the method used to identify locations on the Internet. The steps for browsing the Internet vary but generally include: opening Internet Explorer, typing the URL for the desired site, navigating the various pages of the site, navigating to other sites using links, and then closing Internet Explorer.

To launch Internet Explorer 8.0, click the Internet Explorer icon on the Taskbar at the Windows desktop. Figure IE.1 identifies the elements of the Internet Explorer, version 8.0, window. The web page that displays in your Internet Explorer window may vary from what you see in Figure IE.1.

If you know the URL for the desired website, click in the Address bar, type the URL, and then press Enter. The website's home page displays in a tab within the Internet Explorer window. URLs (Uniform Resource Locators) are the method used to identify locations on the Internet. The format of a URL is *http://server-name.path*. The first part of the URL, *http*, stands for HyperText Transfer Protocol, which is the protocol or language used to transfer data within the World Wide Web. The colon and slashes separate the protocol from the server name. The server name is the second component of the URL. For example, in the URL http://www.microsoft.com, the server name is *microsoft*. The last part of the URL specifies the domain to which the server belongs. For example, *.com* refers to "commercial" and establishes that the URL is a commercial company. Examples of other domains include *.edu* for "educational," *.gov* for "government," and *.mil* for "military."

Figure IE.1 Internet Explorer Window

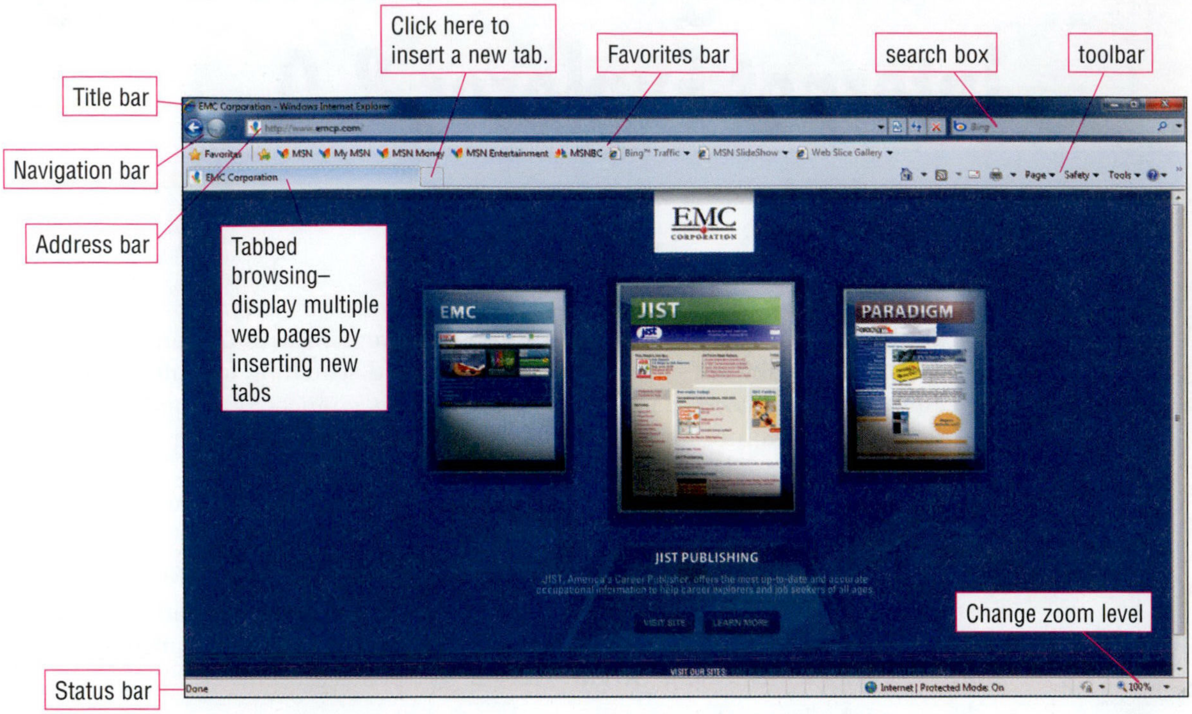

Project 1 Browsing the Internet Using URLs

1. Make sure you are connected to the Internet through an Internet Service Provider and that the Windows desktop displays. (Check with your instructor to determine if you need to complete steps for accessing the Internet such as typing a user name and password to log on.)
2. Launch Microsoft Internet Explorer by clicking the Internet Explorer icon located on the Taskbar located at the bottom of the Windows desktop.
3. At the Internet Explorer window, explore the website for Yosemite National Park by completing the following steps:
   a. Click in the Address bar, type **www.nps.gov/yose**, and then press Enter.
   b. Scroll down the home page for Yosemite National Park by clicking the down-pointing arrow on the vertical scroll bar located at the right side of the Internet Explorer window.
   c. Print the home page by clicking the Print button located on the Internet Explorer toolbar. (Some websites have a printer friendly button you can click to print the page.)

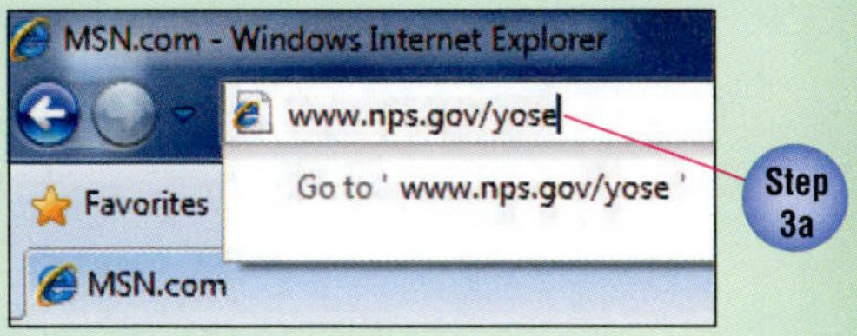

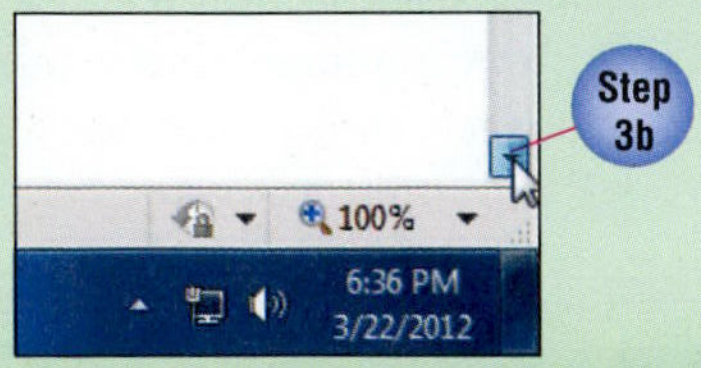

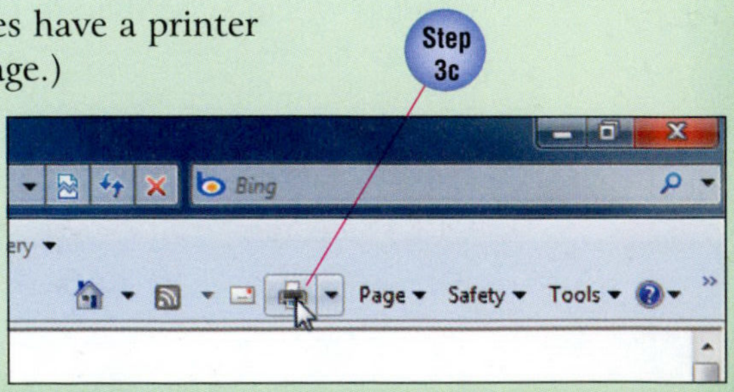

4. Explore the website for Glacier National Park by completing the following steps:
   a. Click in the Address bar, type www.nps.gov/glac, and then press Enter.
   b. Print the home page by clicking the Print button located on the Internet Explorer toolbar.
5. Close Internet Explorer by clicking the Close button (contains an X) located in the upper right corner of the Internet Explorer window.

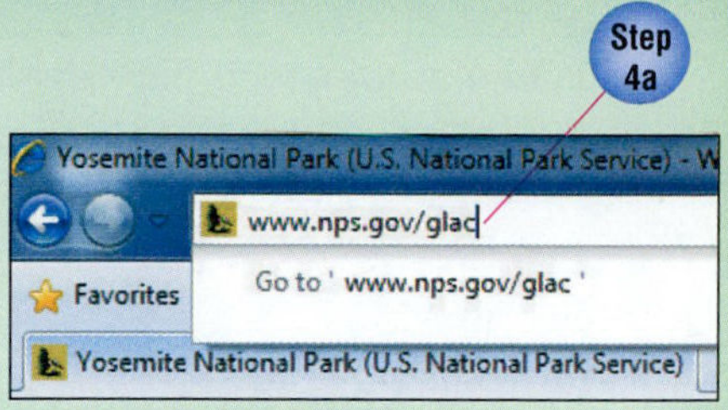

Navigating Using Hyperlinks

Most web pages contain "hyperlinks" that you click to connect to another page within the website or to another site on the Internet. Hyperlinks may display in a web page as underlined text in a specific color or as images or icons. To use a hyperlink, position the mouse pointer on the desired hyperlink until the mouse pointer turns into a hand, and then click the left mouse button. Use hyperlinks to navigate within and between sites on the Internet. The navigation bar in the Internet Explorer window contains a Back button that, when clicked, takes you to the previous web page viewed. If you click the Back button and then want to return to the previous page, click the Forward button. You can continue clicking the Back button to back your way out of several linked pages in reverse order since Internet Explorer maintains a history of the websites you visit.

Project 2 Navigating Using Hyperlinks

1. Make sure you are connected to the Internet and then click the Internet Explorer icon on the Taskbar.
2. At the Internet Explorer window, display the White House web page and navigate in the page by completing the following steps:
   a. Click in the Address bar, type whitehouse.gov, and then press Enter.
   b. At the White House home page, position the mouse pointer on a hyperlink that interests you until the pointer turns into a hand, and then click the left mouse button.
   c. At the linked web page, click the Back button. (This returns you to the White House home page.)
   d. At the White House home page, click the Forward button to return to the previous web page viewed.
   e. Print the web page by clicking the Print button on the Internet Explorer toolbar.

3. Display the website for Amazon.com and navigate in the site by completing the following steps:
   a. Click in the Address bar, type www.amazon.com, and then press Enter.

b. At the Amazon.com home page, click a hyperlink related to books.
c. When a book web page displays, click the Print button on the Internet Explorer toolbar.
4. Close Internet Explorer by clicking the Close button (contains an X) located in the upper right corner of the Internet Explorer window.

Searching for Specific Sites

If you do not know the URL for a specific site or you want to find information on the Internet but do not know what site to visit, complete a search with a search engine. A search engine is a software program created to search quickly and easily for desired information. A variety of search engines are available on the Internet, each offering the opportunity to search for specific information. One method for searching for information is to click in the search box located to the right of the Address bar, type a keyword or phrase related to your search, and then click the Search button or press Enter. Another method for completing a search is to visit the website for a search engine and use options at the site.

Bing is Microsoft's online search portal and is the default search engine used by Internet Explorer. Bing organizes search results by topic category and provides related search suggestions.

Project 3 Searching for Information by Topic

1. Start Internet Explorer.
2. At the Internet Explorer window, search for sites on bluegrass music by completing the following steps:
   a. Click in the search box (may display *Bing*) located at the right side of the Address bar.
   b. Type **bluegrass music** and then press Enter.
   c. When a list of sites displays in the Bing results window, click a site that interests you.
   d. When the page displays, click the Print button.

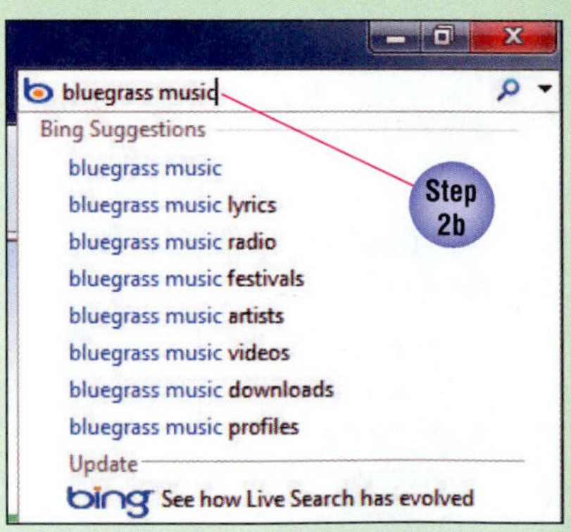

3. Use the Yahoo! search engine to find sites on bluegrass music by completing the following steps:
   a. Click in the Address bar, type **www.yahoo.com**, and then press Enter.
   b. At the Yahoo! website, with the insertion point positioned in the search text box, type **bluegrass music** and then press Enter. (Notice that the sites displayed vary from sites displayed in the earlier search.)
   c. Click hyperlinks until a website displays that interests you.
   d. Print the page.

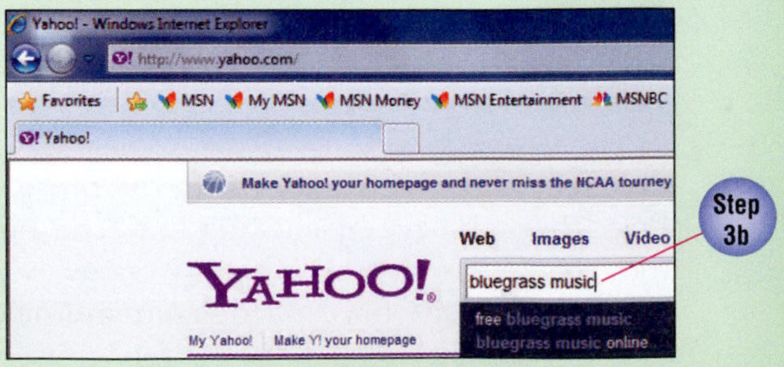

4. Use the Google search engine to find sites on jazz music by completing the following steps:
   a. Click in the Address bar, type www.google.com, and then press Enter.
   b. At the Google website, with the insertion point positioned in the search text box, type jazz music and then press Enter.
   c. Click a site that interests you.
   d. Print the page.
5. Close Internet Explorer.

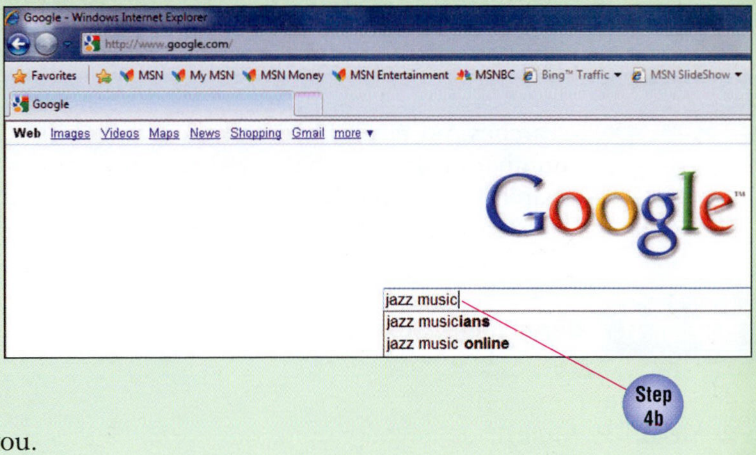

Using a Metasearch Engine

Bing, Yahoo!, and Google are search engines that search the Web for content and display search results. In addition to individual search engines, you can use a metasearch engine, such as Dogpile, that sends your search text to other search engines and then compiles the results in one list. With a metasearch engine, you type the search text once and then access results from a wider group of search engines. The Dogpile metasearch engine provides search results from Google, Yahoo!, Bing, and Ask.

Project 4 Searching with a Metasearch Search Engine

1. At the Windows desktop, click the Internet Explorer icon on the Taskbar.
2. Click in the Address bar.
3. Type www.dogpile.com and then press Enter.
4. At the Dogpile website, type jazz music in the search text box and then press Enter.
5. Click a hyperlink that interests you.
6. Close the Internet Explorer window.

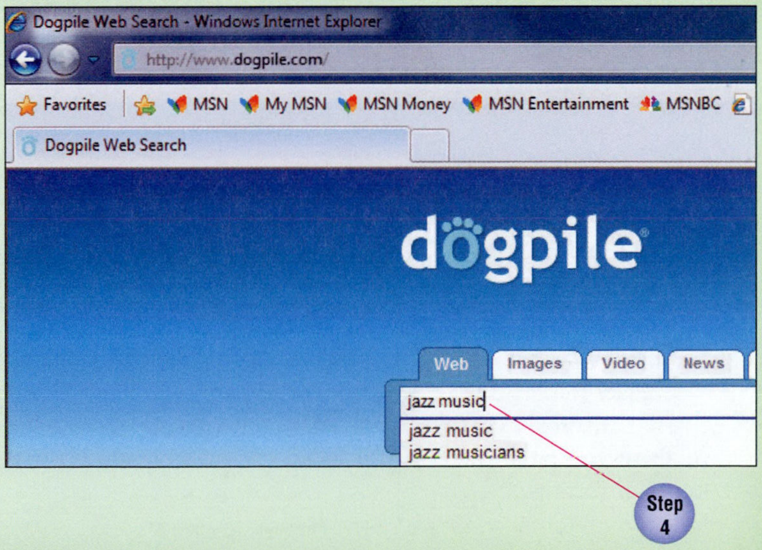

Completing Advanced Searches for Specific Sites

Web Search

The Internet contains an enormous amount of information. Depending on what you are searching for on the Internet and the search engine you use, some searches can result in several thousand "hits" (sites). Wading through a large number of sites can be very time-consuming and counterproductive. Narrowing a search to very specific criteria can greatly reduce the number of hits for a search. To narrow a search, use the advanced search options offered by the search engine.

Project 5 Narrowing a Search

1. Start Internet Explorer.
2. Search for sites on skydiving in Oregon by completing the following steps:
   a. Click in the Address bar, type **www.yahoo.com**, and then press Enter.
   b. At the Yahoo! home page, click the Web Search button next to the search text box.
   c. Click the <u>more</u> hyperlink located above the search text box and then click Advanced Search at the drop-down list.
   d. At the Advanced Web Search page, click in the search text box next to *all of these words*.
   e. Type **skydiving Oregon tandem static line**. (This limits the search to web pages containing all of the words typed in the search text box.)
   f. Click the Yahoo! Search button.
   g. When the list of websites displays, click a hyperlink that interests you.
   h. Click the Back button until the Yahoo! Advanced Web Search page displays.
   i. Click in the *the exact phrase* text box and then type **skydiving in Oregon**.
   j. Click the *Only .com domains* in the *Site/Domain* section.
   k. Click the Yahoo! Search button.
   l. When the list of websites displays, click a hyperlink that interests you.
   m. Print the page.
3. Close Internet Explorer.

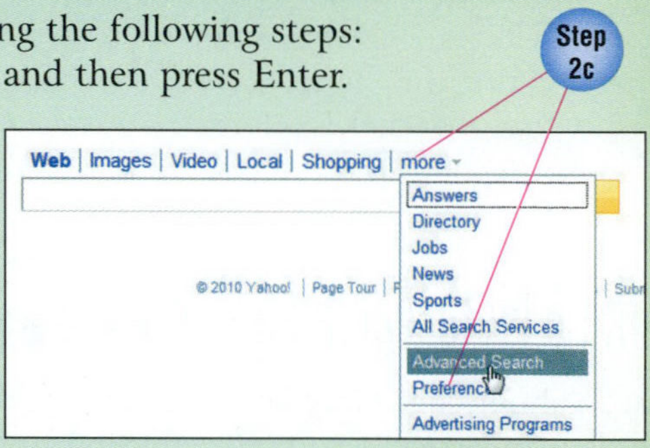

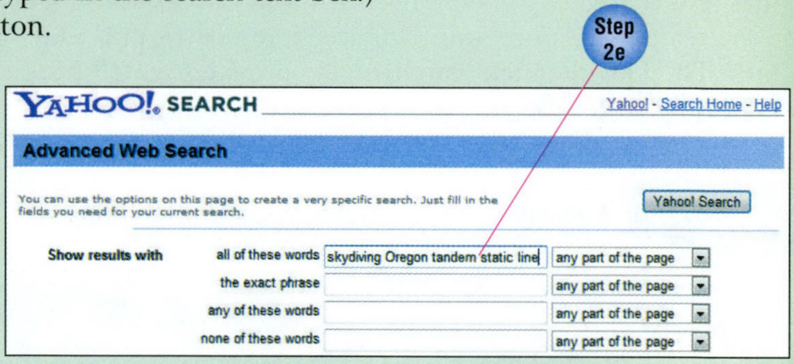

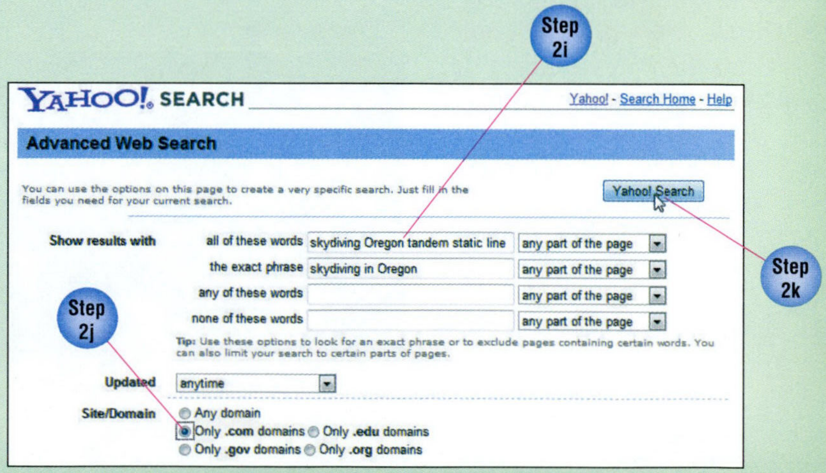

Downloading Images, Text, and Web Pages from the Internet

The image(s) and/or text that display when you open a web page as well as the web page itself can be saved as a separate file. This separate file can be viewed, printed, or inserted in another file. The information you want to save in a separate file is downloaded from the Internet by Internet Explorer and saved in a folder of your choosing with the name you specify. Copyright laws protect much of the information on the Internet. Before using information downloaded from the Internet, check the site for restrictions. If you do use information, make sure you properly cite the source.

Project 6 Downloading Images and Web Pages

1. Start Internet Explorer.
2. Download a web page and image from Banff National Park by completing the following steps:
   a. Search for sites on the Internet for Banff National Park.
   b. From the list of sites that displays, choose a site that contains information about Banff National Park and at least one image of the park.
   c. Save the web page as a separate file by clicking the Page button on the Internet Explorer toolbar and then clicking *Save As* at the drop-down list.
   d. At the Save Webpage dialog box, type **BanffWebPage**.
   e. Navigate to the drive containing your storage medium and then click the Save button.

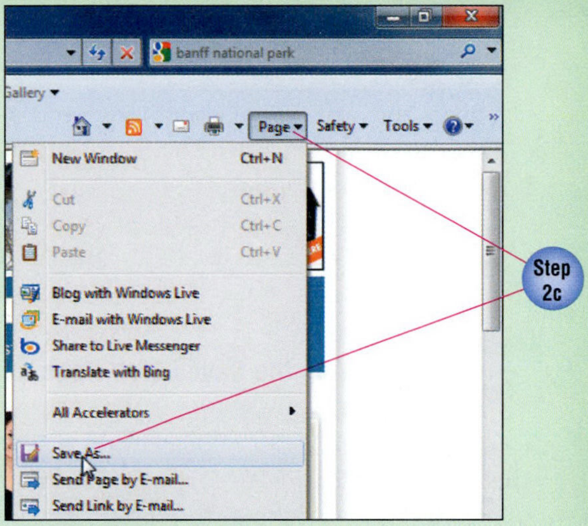

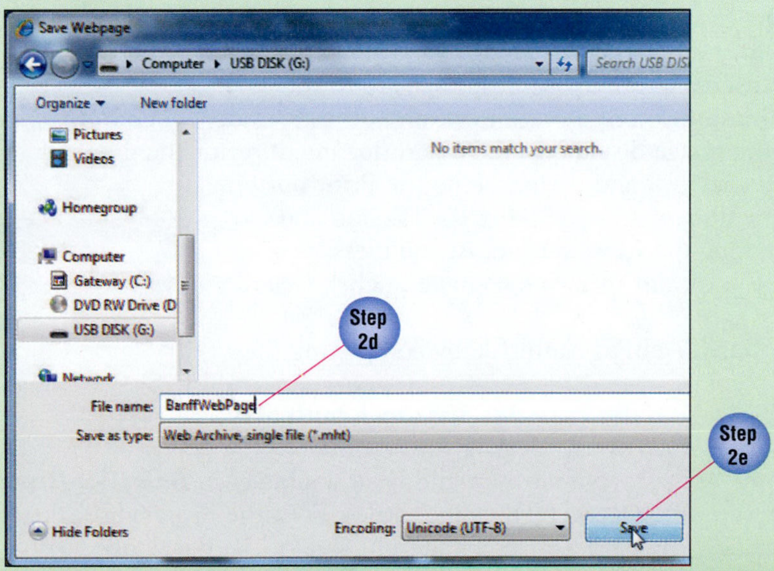

3. Save an image file by completing the following steps:
   a. Right-click an image that displays at the website. (The image that displays may vary from what you see below.)
   b. At the shortcut menu that displays, click *Save Picture As*.
   c. At the Save Picture dialog box, type **BanffImage** in the *File name* text box.

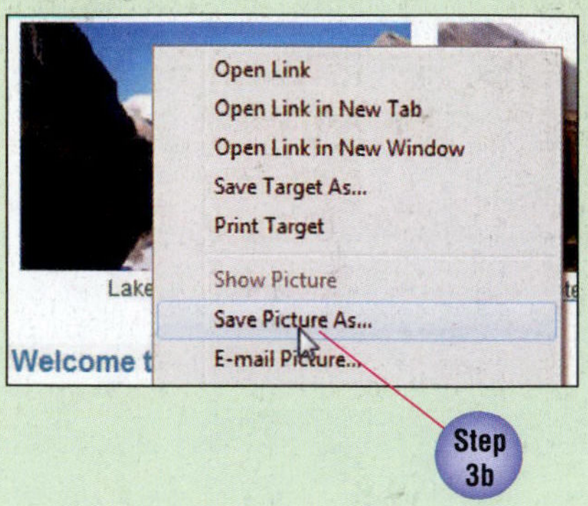

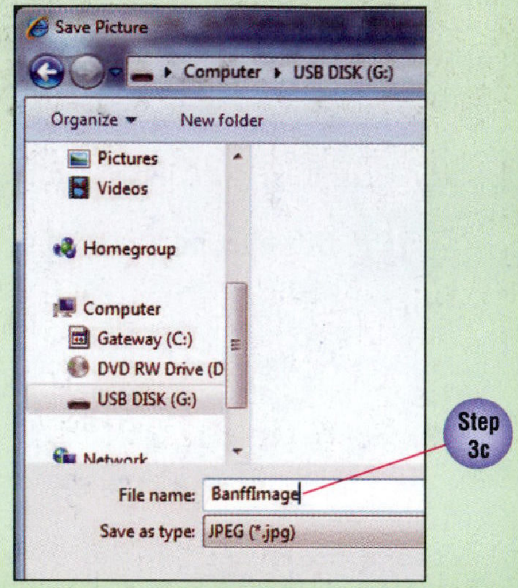

   d. Navigate to the drive containing your storage medium and then click the Save button.
4. Close Internet Explorer.

Project 7 Opening the Saved Web Page and Image in a Word Document

1. Open Microsoft Word by clicking the Start button on the Taskbar, clicking *All Programs*, clicking *Microsoft Office*, and then clicking *Microsoft Word 2010*.
2. With Microsoft Word open, insert the image in a document by completing the following steps:
   a. Click the Insert tab and then click the Picture button in the Illustrations group.
   b. At the Insert Picture dialog box, navigate to the drive containing your storage medium and then double-click ***BanffImage.jpg***.

   c. When the image displays in the Word document, print the document by pressing Ctrl + P and then clicking the Print button.
   d. Close the document by clicking the File tab and then clicking the Close button. At the message asking if you want to save the changes, click *Don't Save*.
3. Open the **BanffWebPage.mht** file by completing the following steps:
   a. Click the File tab and then click the Open button.
   b. At the Open dialog box, navigate to the drive containing your storage medium and then double-click ***BanffWebPage.mht***.

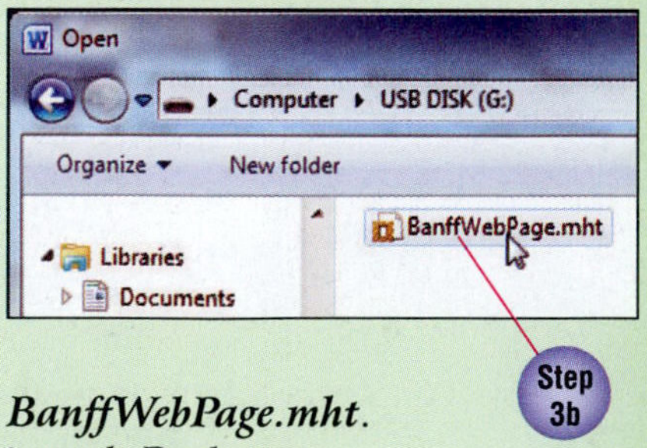

   c. Preview the web page(s) by pressing Ctrl + P. At the Print tab Backstage view, preview the page shown at the right side of the Backstage view.
4. Close Word by clicking the Close button (contains an X) that displays in the upper right corner of the screen.

Microsoft®

Access® Level 1

Unit 1 ■ Creating Tables and Queries

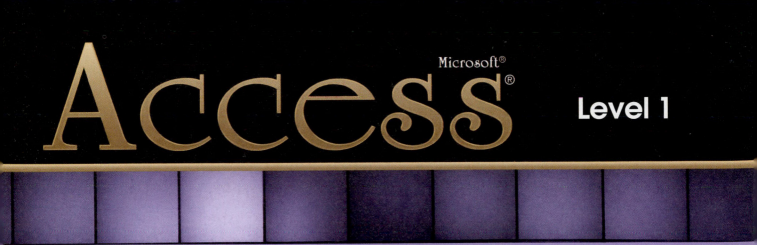

Microsoft® Access®

CHAPTER 1

Managing and Creating Tables

PERFORMANCE OBJECTIVES

Upon successful completion of Chapter 1, you will be able to:

- **Open and close objects in a database**
- **Insert, delete, and move rows and columns in a table**
- **Hide, unhide, freeze, and unfreeze columns**
- **Adjust table column width**
- **Preview and print a table**
- **Design and create a table**
- **Rename column headings**
- **Insert a column name, caption, and description**
- **Insert Quick Start fields**
- **Assign a default value and field size**

SNAP Training and Assessment. Simplified.

Tutorials

1.1 Opening Access, Navigating and Printing a Table

1.2 Adding Records in Datasheet View

1.3 Creating a New Database

1.4 Creating a Table Using Quick Start Fields

Managing information in a company is an integral part of operating a business. Information can come in a variety of forms, such as data about customers, including names, addresses, and telephone numbers; product data; purchasing and buying data; and much more. Most companies today manage data using a database management system software program. Microsoft Office Professional includes a database management system software program named *Access*. With Access, you can organize, store, maintain, retrieve, sort, and print all types of business data. For example, the manager of a bookstore could use Access to maintain data on customers, such as names, addresses, types of books purchased, and types of books ordered.

This chapter contains just a few ideas on how to manage data with Access. With a properly designed and maintained database management system, a company can operate smoothly with logical, organized, and useful information. Model answers for this chapter's projects appear on the following pages.

Access

Access2010L1C1

Note: Before beginning the projects, copy to your storage medium the Access2010L1C1 subfolder from the Access2010L1 folder on the CD that accompanies this textbook. Make sure you have copied the files from the CD to your storage medium. Open all database files from your removable storage device and not directly from the CD since Access database files on the CD are read-only. Steps on how to copy a folder are presented on the inside of the back cover of this textbook. Do this every time you start a chapter's projects.

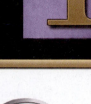

Suppliers 7/6/2012

Supplier#	SupplierName	StreetAddress	City	Prov/State	PostalCode	Field1	EmailAddress
10	Hopewell, Inc.	5600 Carver Road	Port Moody	BC	V3H 1A4	(604) 555-3843	hopewell@emcp.net
25	Langley Corporation	805 First Avenue	Burnaby	BC	V3J 1C9	(604) 555-1200	langley@emcp.net
31	Sound Supplies	2104 Union Street	Seattle	WA	98105	(206) 555-4855	ssupplies@emcp.net
35	Emerald City Products	1059 Pike Street	Seattle	WA	98102	(206) 555-7728	ecproducts@emcp.net
38	Hadley Company	5845 Jefferson Street	Seattle	WA	98107	(206) 555-8003	hcompany@emcp.net
42	Fraser Valley Products	3894 Old Yale Road	Abbotsford	BC	V2S 1A9	(604) 555-1455	fvproducts@emcp.net
54	Manning, Inc.	1039 South 22nd	Vancouver	BC	V5K 1R1	(604) 555-0087	manning@emcp.net
68	Freedom Corporation	14 Fourth Avenue	Vancouver	BC	V5K 2C7	(604) 555-2155	freedom@emcp.net
70	Rosewood, Inc.	998 North 42nd Street	Vancouver	BC	V5K 2N8	(778) 555-6643	rosewood@emcp.net
84	Macadam, Inc.	675 Third Street	Vancouver	BC	V5K 2R9	(604) 555-5522	macadam@emcp.net
99	KL Distributions	402 Yukon Drive	Bellingham	WA	98435	(360) 555-3711	kldist@emcp.net

Page 1

Suppliers Table

Products 7/6/2012

Product#	Product	Supplier#	UnitsInStock	UnitsOnOrder	ReorderLevel
101-S1B	SL 0-degrees down sleeping bag, black	54	16	0	15
101-S1R	SL 0-degrees down sleeping bag, red	54	17	0	15
101-S2B	SL 15-degrees synthetic sleeping bag, black	54	21	0	15
101-S2R	SL 15-degrees synthetic sleeping bag, red	54	12	15	15
101-S3B	SL 20-degrees synthetic sleeping bag, black	54	8	15	15
101-S3R	SL 20-degrees synthetic sleeping bag, red	54	4	10	10
209-L	Gordon wool ski hat, L	68	21	25	25
209-XL	Gordon wool ski hat, XL	68	14	25	25
209-XXL	Gordon wool ski hat, XXL	68	10	20	20
210-L	Tech-lite ski hat, L	68	17	25	25
210-M	Tech-lite ski hat, M	68	6	15	15
210-XL	Tech-lite ski hat, XL	68	22	0	20
299-M1	HT waterproof hiking boots, MS13	31	8	0	10
299-M2	HT waterproof hiking boots, MS12	31	2	10	10
299-M3	HT waterproof hiking boots, MS11	31	6	10	10
299-M4	HT waterproof hiking boots, MS10	31	7	0	10
299-M5	HT waterproof hiking boots, MS9	31	9	10	10
299-W1	HT waterproof hiking boots, WS11	31	5	8	8
299-W2	HT waterproof hiking boots, WS10	31	9	0	8
299-W3	HT waterproof hiking boots, WS9	31	3	10	10
299-W4	HT waterproof hiking boots, WS8	31	2	10	10
299-W5	HT waterproof hiking boots, WS7	31	3	10	10
299-W6	HT waterproof hiking boots, WS6	31	11	0	10
371-L	Lite-tech ski gloves, ML	68	3	10	10
371-M	Lite-tech ski gloves, MM	68	5	0	15
371-XL	Lite-tech ski gloves, MXL	68	3	10	10
371-XXL	Lite-tech ski gloves, MXXL	68	12	0	10
375-L	Lite-tech ski gloves, WL	68	22	0	20
375-M	Lite-tech ski gloves, WM	68	3	20	20
375-S	Lite-tech ski gloves, WS	68	6	20	20
442-1A	Polar backpack, 150BR	42	12	0	10
442-1B	Polar backpack, 150RW	42	9	10	10
443-1A	Polar backpack, 250BR	42	14	0	15
443-1B	Polar backpack, 250RW	42	6	15	15

Page 1

Products Table, Page 1

Project 2 Manage Tables in a Database

AL1-C1-PacTrek.accdb

Products 7/6/2012

Product#	Product	Supplier#	UnitsInStock	UnitsOnOrder	ReorderLevel
558-C	ICE snow goggles, clear	68	18	0	15
559-B	ICE snow goggles, bronze	68	22	0	20
602-XR	Binoculars, 8 x 42	35	3	5	5
602-XT	Binoculars, 10.5 x 45	35	5	0	4
602-XX	Binoculars, 10 x 50	35	7	0	5
647-1	Two-person dome tent	99	10	15	15
648-2	Three-person dome tent	99	5	0	10
651-1	K-2 one-person tent	99	8	0	10
652-2	K-2 two-person tent	99	12	0	10
804-50	AG freestyle snowboard, X50	70	7	0	10
804-60	AG freestyle snowboard, X60	70	8	0	5
897-L	Lang blunt snowboard	70	8	0	7
897-W	Lang blunt snowboard, wide	70	4	0	3
901-S	Solar battery pack	38	16	0	15
917-S	Silo portable power pack	38	8	0	10

Page 2

Products Table, Page 2

Orders 7/6/2012

Order#	Supplier Number	Product Number	UnitsOrdered	Order Amount	OrderDate
1	54	101-S3	10	$1,137.50	1/2/2012
2	68	209-L	25	$173.75	1/2/2012
3	68	209-XL	25	$180.00	1/2/2010
4	68	209-XXL	20	$145.80	1/2/2010
5	68	210-M	15	$97.35	1/2/2010
6	68	210-L	25	$162.25	1/2/2010
7	31	299-M2	10	$887.90	1/16/2012
8	31	299-M3	10	$887.90	1/16/2012
9	31	299-M5	10	$887.90	1/16/2012
10	31	299-W1	8	$602.32	1/16/2012
11	31	299-W3	10	$752.90	1/16/2012
12	31	299-W4	10	$752.90	1/16/2012
13	31	299-W5	10	$752.90	1/16/2012
14	35	602-XR	5	$2,145.00	1/16/2012

Page 1

Orders Table

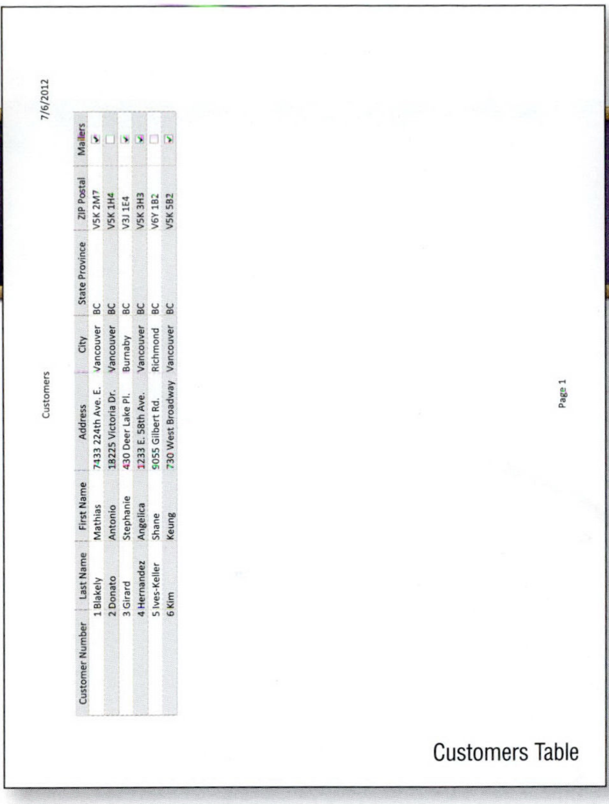

7/6/2012

Customers

Customer Number	Last Name	First Name	Address	City	State Province	ZIP Postal	Mailers
1	Blakely	Mathias	7433 224th Ave. E.	Vancouver	BC	V5K 2M7	☑
2	Donato	Antonio	18225 Victoria Dr.	Vancouver	BC	V5K 1H4	☐
3	Girard	Stephanie	430 Deer Lake Pl.	Burnaby	BC	V3J 1E4	☑
4	Hernandez	Angelica	1233 E. 58th Ave.	Vancouver	BC	V5K 3H3	☑
5	Ives-Keller	Shane	9055 Gilbert Rd.	Richmond	BC	V6Y 1B2	☐
6	Kim	Keung	730 West Broadway	Vancouver	BC	V5K 5B2	☑

Page 1

Customers Table

Project 1 Explore an Access Database — 1 Part

You will open a database and open and close objects in the database including tables, queries, forms, and reports.

Exploring a Database

A ***database*** is comprised of a series of objects such as tables, queries, forms, and reports that you use to enter, manage, view, and print data. Data in a database is organized into tables, which contain information for related items such as customers, employees, orders, and products. To view the various objects in a database, you will open a previously created database and then navigate in the database and open objects.

To create a new database or open a previously created database, click the Start button on the Taskbar, point to *All Programs*, click *Microsoft Office*, and then click *Microsoft Access 2010*. (These steps may vary depending on your system configuration.) This displays the Access New tab Backstage view as shown in Figure 1.1. The Backstage view organizes database management tasks into tabs. Quick Command buttons such as Save, Save Object As, Save Database As, Open, and Close Database are located at the top left pane in the view. Below the Quick Command buttons the view is organized into tabs such as Info, Recent, New, Print, Save & Publish, and Help.

Start

To create a new database, click the folder icon that displays to the right of the file name at the right side of the screen, navigate to the location where you want to save your database, and then click the Create button.

Create

Figure 1.1 New Tab Backstage View

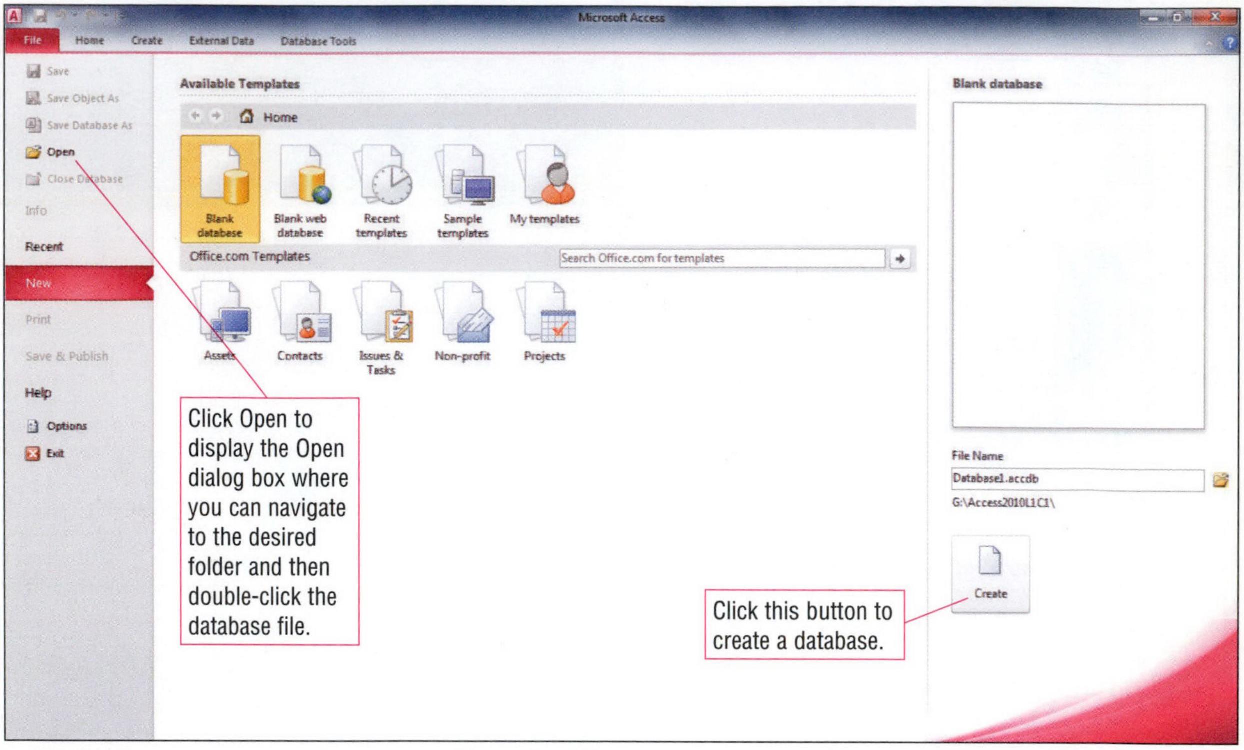

Opening and Closing a Database

Quick Steps

Open a Database

1. Open Access.
2. Click Open button.
3. Navigate to desired location.
4. Double-click database.

HINT

Only one database can be open at a time.

HINT

The active database is saved automatically on a periodic basis and also when you make another record active, close the table, or close the database.

Close

To open an existing Access database, click the Open button located at the left side of the New tab Backstage view. At the Open dialog box, navigate to the location where the database is located and then double-click the database name. You can also open a database that you previously opened by clicking the Recent tab at the New tab Backstage view. This displays the Recent tab Backstage view and a list of the most recently opened databases displays in the *Recent Databases* list box. To open a database, click the desired database in the list box.

When you open a database, the Access screen displays as shown in Figure 1.2. Refer to Table 1.1 for a description of the Access screen elements. To close a database, click the File tab and then click the Close Database button. To exit Access, click the Close button that displays in the upper right corner of the screen, or click the File tab and then click the Exit button that displays below the Help tab.

Only one Access database can be open at a time. If you open a new database in the current Access window, the existing database is closed. (You can however open multiple instances of Access and open a database in each.) In other applications in the Microsoft Office suite, you have to save a revised file after you edit data in the file. In an Access database, changes you make to data are saved automatically when you move to the next record.

Figure 1.2 Access Screen

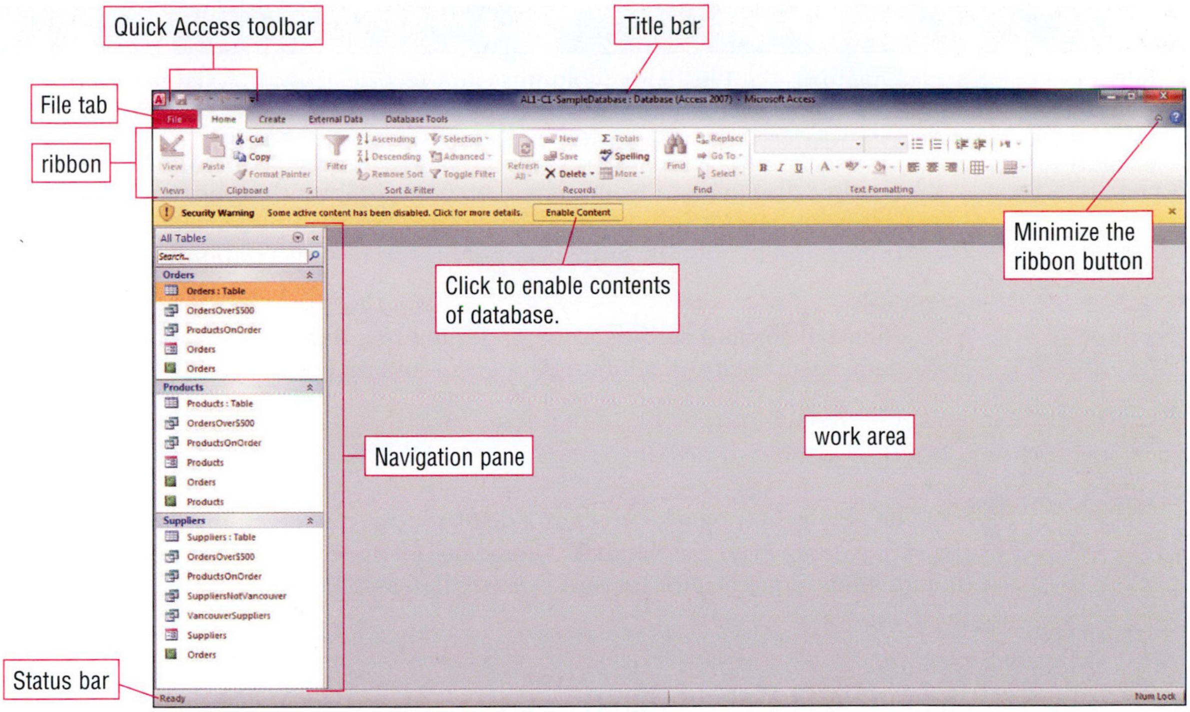

Table 1.1 Access Screen Elements

Feature	*Description*
Quick Access toolbar	Contains buttons for commonly used commands.
File tab	Click this tab and the Backstage view displays containing buttons and tabs for working with and managing databases.
Title bar	Displays database name followed by program name.
Tabs	Contain commands and features organized into groups.
Ribbon	Area containing the tabs and commands divided into groups.
Message bar	Displays security alerts if the database you open contains potentially unsafe content.
Navigation pane	Displays names of objects within database grouped by categories.
Work area	Area in screen where opened objects display.
Status bar	Displays number of pages and words, View buttons, and the Zoom slider bar.

A security warning message bar may appear below the ribbon if Access determines the file you are opening did not originate from a trusted location on your computer and may have viruses or other security hazards. This often occurs when you copy a file from another medium (such as a CD or the Web). Active content in the file is disabled until you click the Enable Content button. The message bar closes when you identify the database as a trusted source. Before making any changes to the database, you must click the Enable Content button.

Table 1.2 Database Objects

Object	*Description*
Table	Organizes data in fields (columns) and records (rows). A database must contain at least one table. The table is the base upon which other objects are created.
Query	Used to display data from a table or related tables that meets a conditional statement and/or to perform calculations. For example, display all records from a specific month or display only those records containing a specific city.
Form	Allows fields and records to be presented in a different layout than the datasheet. Used to facilitate data entry and maintenance.
Report	Prints data from tables or queries.

The Navigation pane at the left side of the Access screen displays the objects that are contained in the database. Some common objects found in a database include tables, queries, forms, and reports. Refer to Table 1.2 for a description of these four types of objects.

Opening and Closing Objects

HINT

Hide the Navigation pane by clicking the button in the upper right corner of the pane (called the Shutter Bar Open/Close Button) or by pressing F11.

Shutter

Database objects display in the Navigation pane. Control what displays in the pane by clicking the Menu bar at the top of the Navigation pane and then clicking the desired option at the drop-down list. For example, to display a list of all saved objects in the database, click the *Object Type* option at the drop-down list. This view displays the objects grouped by type—Tables, Queries, Forms, and Reports. To open an object, double-click the object in the Navigation pane. The object opens in the work area and a tab displays with the object name at the left side of the object.

To view more of an object, consider closing the Navigation pane by clicking the Shutter Bar Open/Close Button located in the upper right corner of the pane. Click the button again to open the Navigation pane. You can open more than one object in the work area. Each object opens with a visible tab. You can navigate to objects by clicking the object tab. To close an object, click the Close button that displays in the upper right corner of the work area.

Project 1 **Opening and Closing a Database and Objects in a Database** **Part 1 of 1**

1. Open Access by clicking the Start button on the Taskbar, pointing to *All Programs*, clicking *Microsoft Office*, and then clicking *Microsoft Access 2010*. (These steps may vary.)
2. At the New tab Backstage view, click the Open button that displays at the left side of the screen.
3. At the Open dialog box, navigate to the Access2010L1C1 folder on your storage medium and then double-click the database ***AL1-C1-SampleDatabase.accdb***. (This database contains data on orders, products, and suppliers for a specialty hiking and backpacking outfitters store named Pacific Trek.)

4. Click the Enable Content button in the message bar if the security warning message appears. (The message bar will display immediately below the ribbon.)
5. With the database open, click the All Access Objects button (displays as a down-pointing arrow at the top of the Navigation pane) and then click *Object Type* at the drop-down list. (This option displays the objects grouped by type—Tables, Queries, Forms, and Reports.)
6. Double-click *Suppliers* in the *Tables* section of the Navigation pane. This opens the Suppliers table in the work area as shown in Figure 1.3.
7. Close the Suppliers table by clicking the Close button in the upper right corner of the work area.

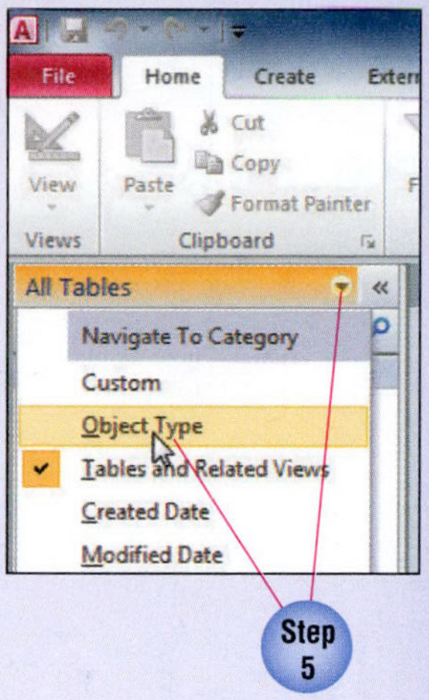

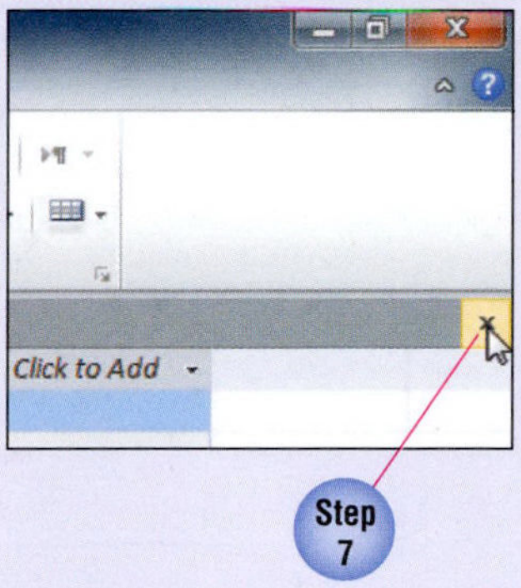

8. Double-click *OrdersOver$500* in the *Queries* section of the Navigation pane. A query displays data that meets a conditional statement and this query displays orders that meet the criterion of being more than $500.
9. Close the query by clicking the Close button in the upper right corner of the work area.
10. Double-click the *SuppliersNotVancouver* query in the Navigation pane and notice that the query displays information about suppliers except those located in Vancouver.
11. Click the Close button in the work area.
12. Double-click *Orders* in the *Forms* section of the Navigation pane. This displays an order form. A form is used to view and edit data in a table one record at a time.
13. Click the Close button in the work area.
14. Double-click *Orders* in the *Reports* section of the Navigation pane. This displays a report with information about orders and order amounts.
15. Close the Navigation pane by clicking the Shutter Bar Open/Close Button located in the upper right corner of the pane.
16. After viewing the report, click the button again to open the Navigation pane.
17. Click the Close button in the work area.
18. Close the database by clicking the File tab and then clicking the Close Database button.
19. Exit Access by clicking the Close button (contains an X) that displays in the upper right corner of the screen.

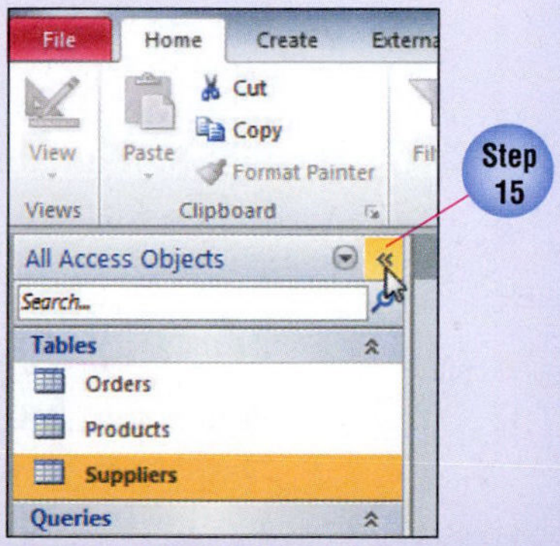

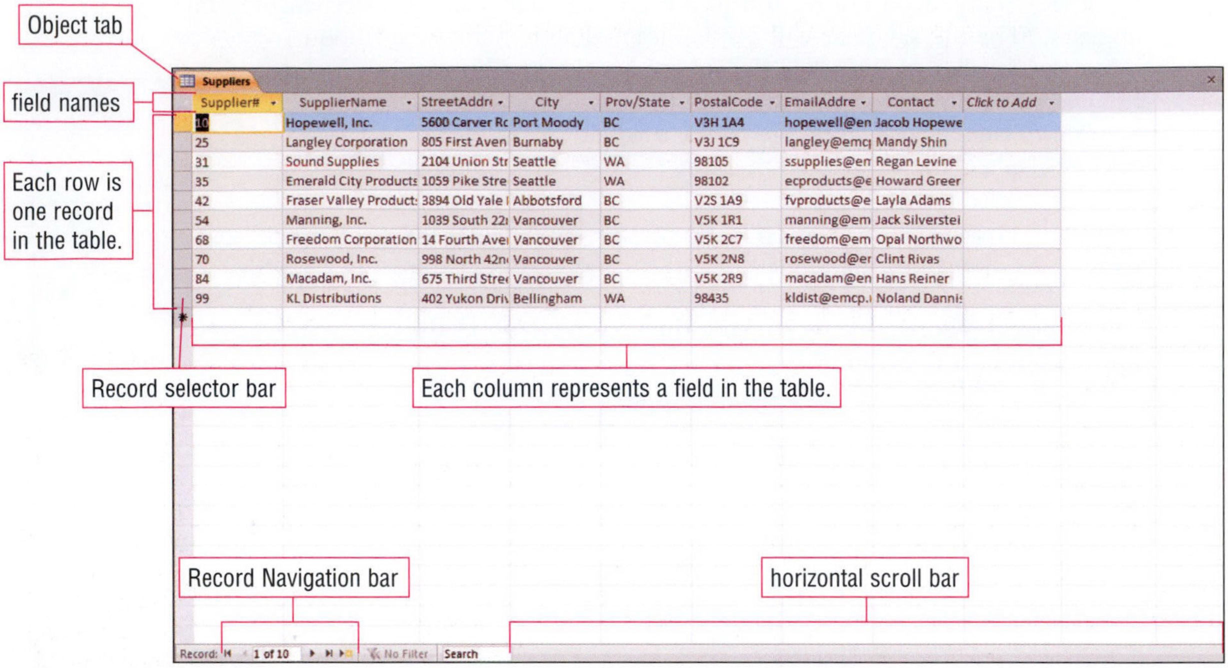

Object tab
field names
Each row is one record in the table.
Suppliers
Supplier# SupplierName StreetAddr City Prov/State PostalCode EmailAddre Contact Click to Add
10 Hopewell, Inc. 5600 Carver Rc Port Moody BC V3H 1A4 hopewell@en Jacob Hopewe
25 Langley Corporation 805 First Aven Burnaby BC V3J 1C9 langley@emc Mandy Shin
31 Sound Supplies 2104 Union Str Seattle WA 98105 ssupplies@en Regan Levine
35 Emerald City Products 1059 Pike Stre Seattle WA 98102 ecproducts@e Howard Greer
42 Fraser Valley Product: 3894 Old Yale Abbotsford BC V2S 1A9 fvproducts@e Layla Adams
54 Manning, Inc. 1039 South 22 Vancouver BC V5K 1R1 manning@em Jack Silverstei
68 Freedom Corporation 14 Fourth Ave Vancouver BC V5K 2C7 freedom@em Opal Northwo
70 Rosewood, Inc. 998 North 42n Vancouver BC V5K 2N8 rosewood@er Clint Rivas
84 Macadam, Inc. 675 Third Stre Vancouver BC V5K 2R9 macadam@en Hans Reiner
99 KL Distributions 402 Yukon Driv Bellingham WA 98435 kldist@emcp. Noland Dannis
Record selector bar
Each column represents a field in the table.
Record Navigation bar
horizontal scroll bar
Record: 1 of 10
No Filter
Search

Figure 1.3 Open Suppliers Table

Project 2 Manage Tables in a Database — 7 Parts

Pacific Trek is an outfitting store specializing in hiking and backpacking gear. Information about the store including suppliers and products are contained in a database. You will open the database and then insert and delete records; insert, move, and delete fields; preview and print tables; and create two new tables for the database.

Managing Tables

In a new database, tables are the first objects created since all other database objects rely on a table for the source of the data. Maintenance of the database and tables in the database is important to keep the database up to date. Managing tables in a database may include inserting or deleting records, inserting or deleting fields, renaming fields, and creating a hard copy of the table by printing the table.

Inserting and Deleting Records

When you open a table, it displays in Datasheet view in the work area. The Datasheet view displays the contents of a table in a column and row format similar to an Excel worksheet. Columns contain the field data, with the field names in the header row at the top of the table, and records are represented as rows. A Record Navigation bar displays at the bottom of the screen just above the Status bar and contains buttons to navigate in the table. Figure 1.4 identifies the buttons on the Record Navigation bar.

Figure 1.4 Record Navigation Bar

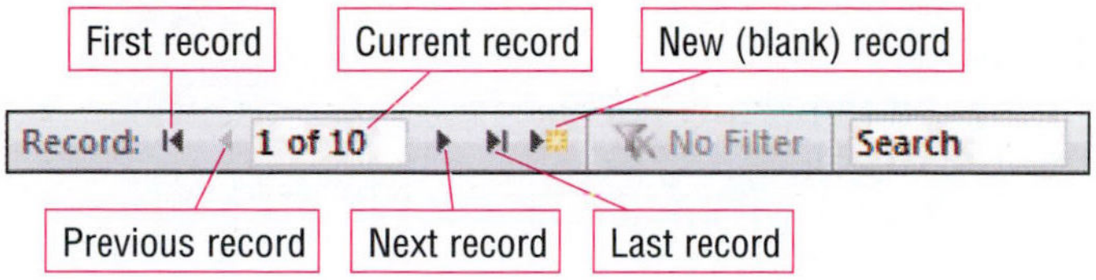

To add a new record to the open table, make sure the Home tab is selected and then click the New button in the Records group. This moves the insertion point to the first field in the blank row at the bottom of the table and the *Current Record* box on the Record Navigation bar indicates what record you are creating (or editing). In addition to clicking the New button in the Records group in the Home tab, you can create a new record by clicking the New (blank) record button on the Record Navigation bar.

When working in a table, press the Tab key to make the next field active or press Shift + Tab to make the previous field active. You can also click in the desired field using the mouse. When you begin typing data for the first field in the record, another row of cells is automatically inserted below the current row and a pencil icon displays in the record selector bar at the beginning of the current record. The pencil icon indicates that the record is being edited and that the changes to the data have not been saved. When you enter the data in the last field in the record and then move the insertion point out of the field, the pencil icon is removed, indicating that the data is saved.

When maintaining a table, you may need to delete a record when you no longer want the data in the record. One method for deleting a record is to click in one of the fields in the record, make sure the Home tab is selected, click the Delete button arrow, and then click *Delete Record* at the drop-down list. At the message that displays asking if you want to delete the record, click the Yes button. When you click in a field in a record, the Delete button displays in a dimmed manner unless specific data is selected.

When you are finished entering data in a record in a table, the data is automatically saved. Changes to the layout of a table, however, are not automatically saved. For example, if you delete a record in a table, when you close the table you will be asked if you are sure you want to delete the record.

Quick Steps

Add New Record
1. Open table.
2. Click New button in Home tab.
3. Type data.

OR

1. Open table.
2. Click New (blank) Record button on Record Navigation bar.
3. Type data.

Delete Record
1. Open table.
2. Click Delete button arrow in Home tab.
3. Click *Delete Record*.
4. Click Yes button.

New

Delete

Project 2a Inserting and Deleting Records in a Table

Part 1 of 7

1. Open Access.
2. At the New tab Backstage view, click the Open button that displays at the left side of the screen.
3. At the Open dialog box, navigate to the Access2010L1C1 folder on your storage medium and then double-click the database ***AL1-C1-PacTrek.accdb***.
4. Click the Enable Content button in the message bar if the security warning message appears. (The message bar will display immediately below the ribbon.)
5. With the database open, make sure the Navigation pane displays object types. (If it does not, click the All Access Objects button at the top of the Navigation pane and then click *Object Type* at the drop-down list.)

6. Double-click the *Suppliers* table in the Navigation pane. (This opens the table in Datasheet view.)
7. With the Suppliers table open and the Home tab active, type a new record by completing the following steps:
   a. Click the New button in the Records group in the Home tab. (This moves the insertion point to the first field in the blank record at the bottom of the table and the *Current Record* box in the Record Navigation bar indicates what record you are creating (or editing).
   b. Type **38**. (This inserts *38* in the field immediately below *99*.)
   c. Press the Tab key (this makes the next field active) and then type **Hadley Company**.
   d. Press the Tab key and then type **5845 Jefferson Street**.
   e. Press the Tab key and then type **Seattle**.
   f. Press the Tab key and then type **WA**.
   g. Press the Tab key and then type **98107**.
   h. Press the Tab key and then type **hcompany@emcp.net**.
   i. Press the Tab key and then type **Jurene Miller**.

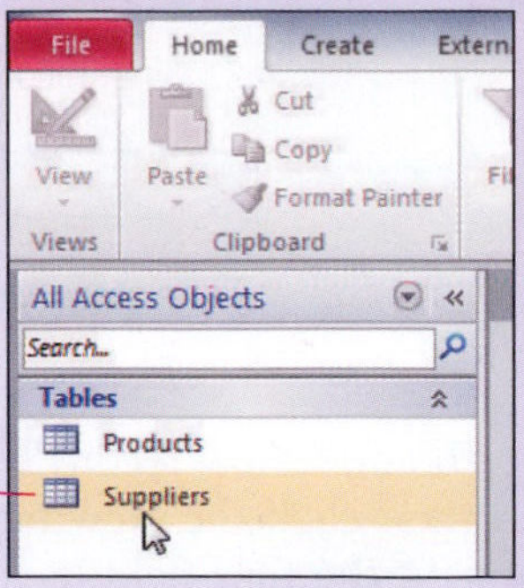

Step 6

Step 7a

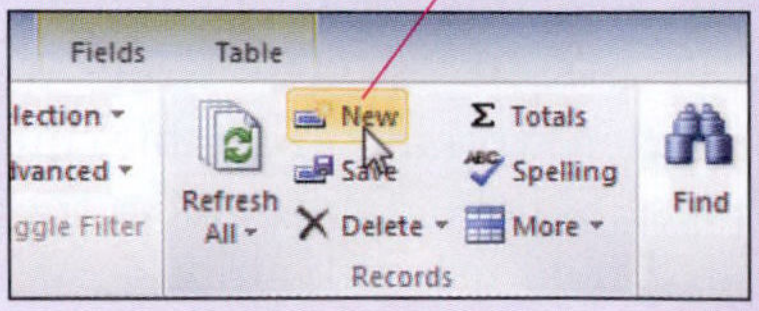

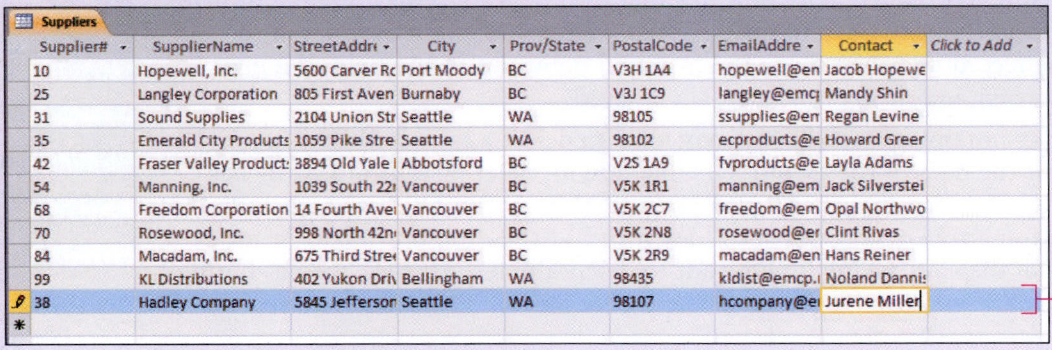
Suppliers

Supplier#	SupplierName	StreetAddre	City	Prov/State	PostalCode	EmailAddre	Contact	Click to Add
10	Hopewell, Inc.	5600 Carver Rc	Port Moody	BC	V3H 1A4	hopewell@en	Jacob Hopewe	
25	Langley Corporation	805 First Aven	Burnaby	BC	V3J 1C9	langley@emcp	Mandy Shin	
31	Sound Supplies	2104 Union Str	Seattle	WA	98105	ssupplies@em	Regan Levine	
35	Emerald City Products	1059 Pike Stre	Seattle	WA	98102	ecproducts@e	Howard Greer	
42	Fraser Valley Product	3894 Old Yale I	Abbotsford	BC	V2S 1A9	fvproducts@e	Layla Adams	
54	Manning, Inc.	1039 South 22	Vancouver	BC	V5K 1R1	manning@em	Jack Silverstei	
68	Freedom Corporation	14 Fourth Ave	Vancouver	BC	V5K 2C7	freedom@em	Opal Northwo	
70	Rosewood, Inc.	998 North 42n	Vancouver	BC	V5K 2N8	rosewood@er	Clint Rivas	
84	Macadam, Inc.	675 Third Stre	Vancouver	BC	V5K 2R9	macadam@en	Hans Reiner	
99	KL Distributions	402 Yukon Driv	Bellingham	WA	98435	kldist@emcp.i	Noland Dannis	
38	Hadley Company	5845 Jefferson	Seattle	WA	98107	hcompany@e	Jurene Miller	
*								

Steps 7b-7i

8. Close the Suppliers table by clicking the Close button in the work area.
9. Open the Products table by double-clicking *Products* in the *Tables* section of the Navigation pane. (This opens the table in Datasheet view.)
10. Insert two new records by completing the following steps:
    a. Click the New button in the Records group and then type data for a new record as shown in Figure 1.5 (the record that begins with *901-S*).
    b. When you type the last field entry in the record for product number 901-S, press the Tab key. This moves the insertion point to the blank field below *901-S*.
    c. Type the new record as shown in Figure 1.5 (the record that begins *917-S*).

11. With the Products table open, delete a record by completing the following steps:
    a. Click in the field containing the data *780-2*.
    b. Click the Delete button arrow in the Records group (the button will display in a dimmed manner) and then click *Delete Record* at the drop-down list.
    c. At the message asking if you want to delete the record, click the Yes button.
12. Click the Save button on the Quick Access toolbar.
13. Close the Products table by clicking the Close button in the work area.

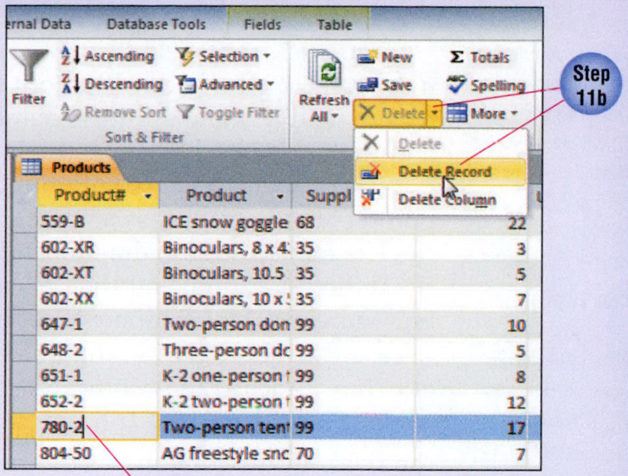

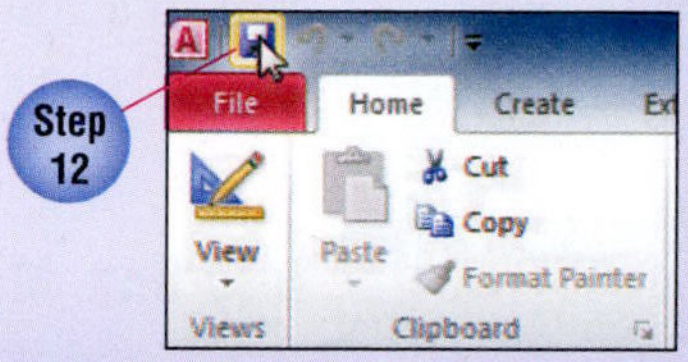

Figure 1.5 Project 2a, Step 10

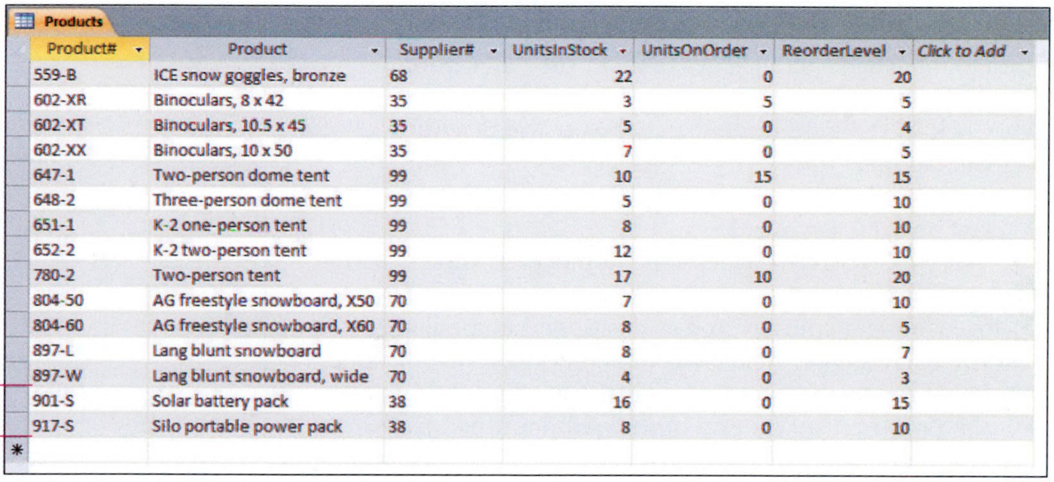

Products

Product#	Product	Supplier#	UnitsInStock	UnitsOnOrder	ReorderLevel	Click to Add
559-B	ICE snow goggles, bronze	68	22	0	20	
602-XR	Binoculars, 8 x 42	35	3	5	5	
602-XT	Binoculars, 10.5 x 45	35	5	0	4	
602-XX	Binoculars, 10 x 50	35	7	0	5	
647-1	Two-person dome tent	99	10	15	15	
648-2	Three-person dome tent	99	5	0	10	
651-1	K-2 one-person tent	99	8	0	10	
652-2	K-2 two-person tent	99	12	0	10	
780-2	Two-person tent	99	17	10	20	
804-50	AG freestyle snowboard, X50	70	7	0	10	
804-60	AG freestyle snowboard, X60	70	8	0	5	
897-L	Lang blunt snowboard	70	8	0	7	
897-W	Lang blunt snowboard, wide	70	4	0	3	
901-S	Solar battery pack	38	16	0	15	
917-S	Silo portable power pack	38	8	0	10	

Step 10

Inserting, Moving, and Deleting Fields

When managing a database, you may determine that you need to add additional information to a table. For example, you might decide that you want to insert a field for contact information, a field for cell phone numbers, or a field for the number of items in stock. To insert a new field in a table, open the table in Datasheet view and then click in the first field below the *Click to Add* heading. Type the desired data in the field for the first record, press the Down Arrow key to make the field below active, and then type the desired data for the second record. Continue in this manner until you have entered data in the new field for all records in the table. In addition to pressing the Down Arrow key to move the

Quick Steps

Insert New Field
1. Open table.
2. Click in first field below *Click to Add* heading.
3. Type desired data.

Quick Steps

Move Field Column
1. Select column.
2. Position mouse pointer on heading.
3. Hold down left mouse button.
4. Drag to desired location.
5. Release mouse button.

Delete Field
1. Click in field.
2. Click Delete button arrow in Home tab.
3. Click *Delete Column*.
4. Click Yes button.

insertion point down to the next field, you can click in the desired field using the mouse. Or, you can press the Tab key until the desired field is active.

You add a new field to the right of the existing fields. In some situations you may want to change this location. Move a field by positioning the mouse pointer on the field heading until the pointer displays as a downward-pointing black arrow and then clicking the left mouse button. This selects the entire column. With the field column selected, position the mouse pointer on the heading (the mouse pointer should display as a white arrow pointing up and to the left), hold down the left mouse button, drag to the left until a thick, black vertical line displays in the desired location, and then release the mouse button. The thick, black vertical line indicates the position where the field column will be positioned when you release the mouse button. In addition, the pointer displays with the outline of a gray box attached to it, indicating that you are performing a move operation.

Delete a field column in a manner similar to deleting a row. Click in one of the fields in the column, make sure the Home tab is selected, click the Delete button arrow, and then click *Delete Column* at the drop-down list. At the message that displays asking if you want to delete the column, click the Yes button.

Project 2b Inserting, Moving, and Deleting Fields

Part 2 of 7

1. With the **AL1-C1-PacTrek.accdb** database open, you decide that contacting suppliers by telephone is important so you decide to add a new field to the Suppliers table. Do this by completing the following steps:
   a. Double-click the *Suppliers* table in the Navigation pane.
   b. Click in the field immediately below the heading *Click to Add*.
   c. Type (604) 555-3843 and then press the Down Arrow key on your keyboard.
   d. Type the remaining telephone numbers as shown at the right.

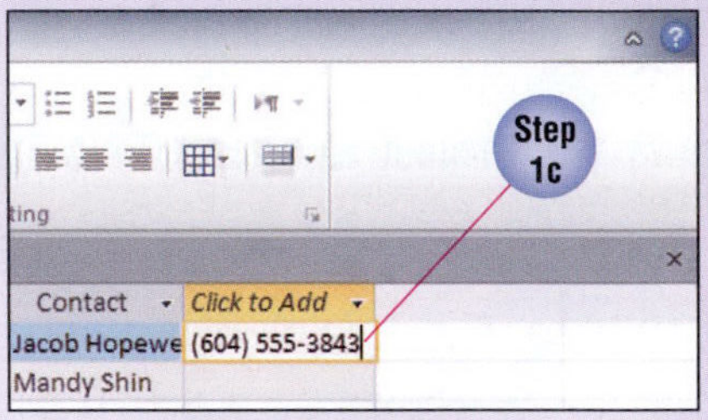

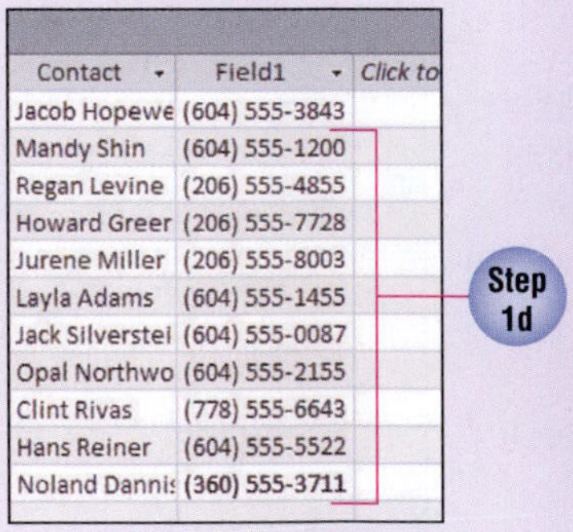

2. Move the field column so it is positioned immediately left of the *EmailAddress* field by completing the following steps:
   a. Position the mouse pointer on the heading *Field 1* until the pointer displays as a downward-pointing black arrow and then click the left mouse button. (This selects the column.)
   b. Position the mouse pointer on the heading (the pointer displays as the normal white arrow pointer), hold down the left mouse button, drag to the left until the thick, black vertical line displays immediately left of the *EmailAddress* field, and then release the mouse button.

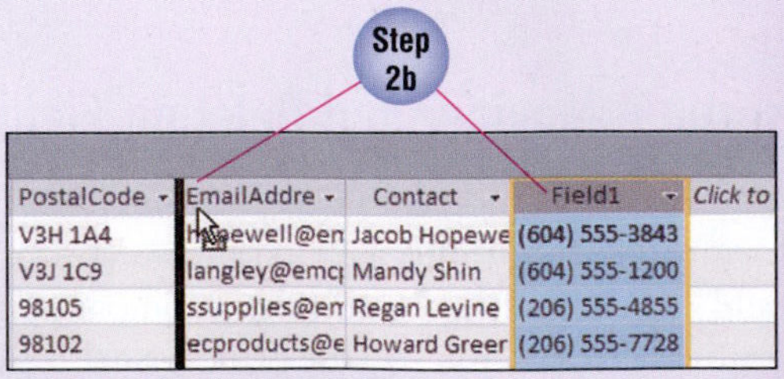

3. You realize that you no longer need the supplier contact information so you decide to delete the field. Do this by completing the following steps:
   a. Position the mouse pointer on the heading *Contact* until the pointer displays as a downward-pointing black arrow and then click the left mouse button. (This selects the column.)

b. Click the Delete button arrow in the Records group and then click *Delete Column* at the drop-down list.
c. At the message asking if you want to permanently delete the selected fields, click the Yes button.

4. Close the Suppliers table. At the message that displays asking if you want to save the changes to the layout of the table, click the Yes button.

Hiding, Unhiding, Freezing, and Unfreezing Column Fields

You can hide columns of data in a table if you do not want the data visible or you want to hide columns between two columns containing data you want to compare. To hide a column, click in any field in the column you want to hide, click the More button in the Records group in the Home tab, and then click *Hide Fields* at the drop-down list. You can hide adjacent columns by selecting the columns, clicking the More button in the Records group, and then clicking *Hide Fields* at the drop-down list. To unhide columns, click the More button and then click *Unhide Fields*. At the Unhide Columns dialog box that displays, insert a check mark in the check box for those columns you want visible.

Another method for comparing column fields side by side is to freeze a column. Freezing a column is also helpful when not all of the columns of data are visible at one time. To freeze a column, click in any field in the column you want to freeze, click the More button, and then click *Freeze Fields* at the drop-down list. To freeze adjacent columns, select the columns first, click the More button, and then click *Freeze Fields* at the drop-down list. To unfreeze all columns in a table, click the More table and then click *Unfreeze All Fields* at the drop-down list.

Changing Column Width

When entering data in the Suppliers and Products table, did you notice that not all of the data was visible? To remedy this, you can adjust the widths of columns so that all data is visible. You can adjust the width of one column in a table to accommodate the longest entry in the column by positioning the arrow pointer on the column boundary at the right side of the column until it turns into a double-headed arrow pointing left and right with a line between and then double-clicking the left mouse button.

You can adjust the width of adjacent columns by selecting the columns first and then double-clicking on one of the selected column boundaries. To select adjacent columns, position the arrow pointer on the first column heading until the pointer turns into a down-pointing black arrow, hold down the left mouse button, drag to the last column you want to adjust, and then release the mouse button. With the columns selected, double-click one of the column boundaries.

You can also adjust the width of a column by dragging the boundary to the desired position. To do this, position the arrow pointer on the column boundary until it turns into a double-headed arrow pointing left and right with a line between, hold down the left mouse button, drag until the column is the desired width, and then release the mouse button.

Quick Steps

Change Table Column Width
Double-click column boundary.
OR
Select columns, then double-click column boundary.
OR
Drag column boundary to desired position.

HINT

Automatically adjust column widths in an Access table in the same manner as adjusting column widths in an Excel worksheet.

Project 2c Hiding, Unhiding, Freezing, and Unfreezing Columns; Changing Column Widths

Part 3 of 7

1. With **AL1-C1-PacTrek.accdb** open, open the Suppliers table.
2. Hide the *PostalCode* column by clicking in any field in the *PostalCode* column, clicking the More button in the Records group in the Home tab, and then clicking *Hide Fields* at the drop-down list.
3. Unhide the column by clicking the More button and then clicking *Unhide Fields* at the drop-down list. At the Unhide Columns dialog box, click in the *PostalCode* check box to insert a check mark, and then click the Close button.

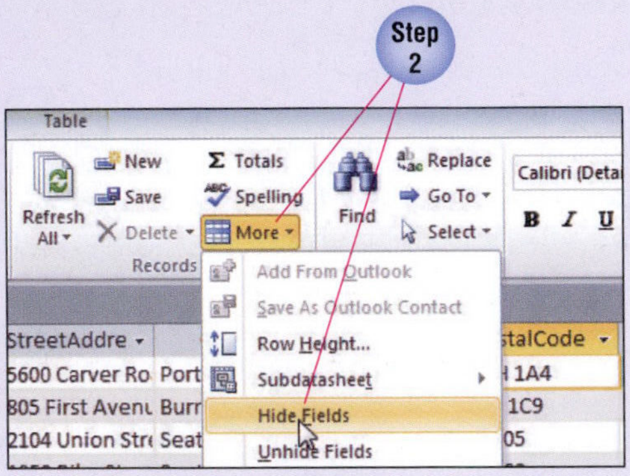

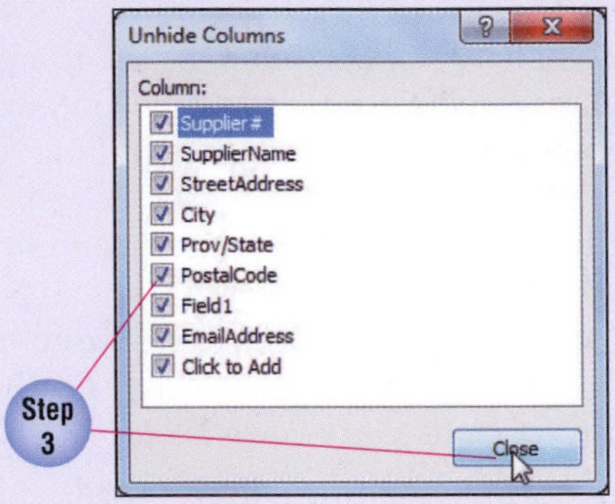

4. Adjust the width of the *Supplier#* column by positioning the arrow pointer on the column boundary at the right side of the *Supplier#* column until it turns into a double-headed arrow pointing left and right with a line between and then double-clicking the left mouse button.

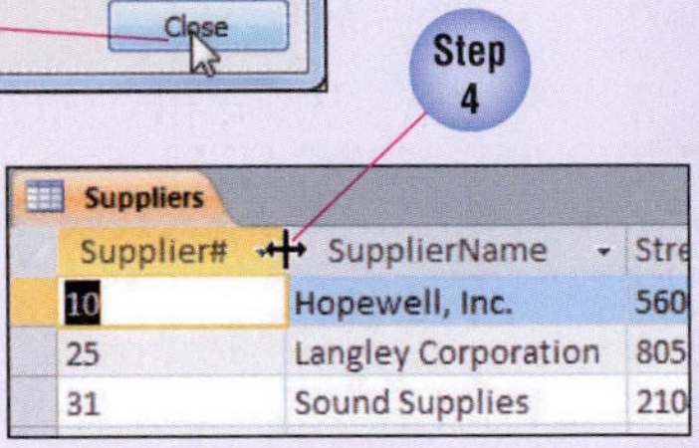

5. Adjust the width of the remaining columns by completing the following steps:
   a. Position the arrow pointer on the *SupplierName* heading until the pointer turns into a down-pointing black arrow, hold down the left mouse button, drag to the *EmailAddress* heading, and then release the mouse button.
   b. With the columns selected, double-click one of the column boundaries.
   c. Click in any field in the table to deselect the columns.
6. Increase the width of the *EmailAddress* column by positioning the arrow pointer on the column boundary at the right side of the *EmailAddress* column until it turns into a double-headed arrow, holding down the left mouse button while dragging all of the way to the right side of the screen, and then releasing the mouse button. (Check the horizontal scroll bar located toward the bottom of the table and notice that the scroll bar contains a scroll box.)
7. Position the mouse pointer on the scroll box on the horizontal scroll bar and then drag to the left until the *Supplier#* field is visible.
8. Freeze the *Supplier#* column by clicking in any field in the *Supplier#* column, clicking the More button in the Records group, and then clicking *Freeze Fields* at the drop-down list.

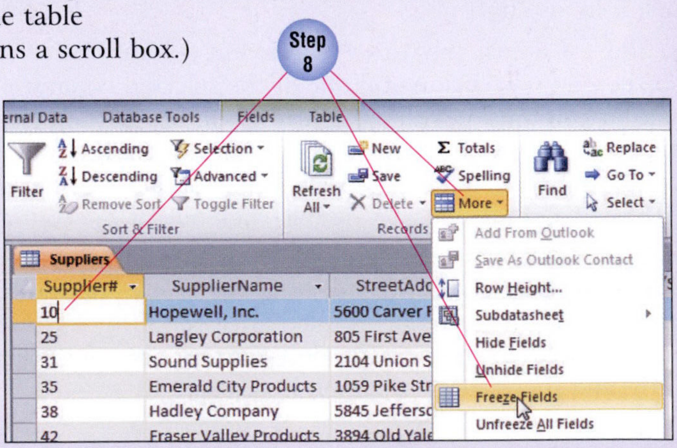

9. Using the mouse, drag the scroll box along the horizontal scroll to the right and then to the left and notice that the *Supplier#* column remains visible on the screen.
10. Unfreeze the column by clicking the More button in the Records group and then clicking *Unfreeze All Fields* at the drop-down list.
11. Double-click on the column boundary at the right side of the *EmailAddress* column.
12. Close the Suppliers table and click the Yes button at the message that asks if you want to save the changes to the layout.
13. Open the Products table and then complete steps similar to those in Step 5 to select and then adjust the column widths.
14. Close the Products table and click the Yes button at the message that asks if you want to save the changes to the layout.

Printing a Table

In some situations, you may want to print the data in a table. To do this, open the table, click the File tab, and then click the Print tab. This displays the Print tab Backstage view as shown in Figure 1.6. Click the *Quick Print* option to send the table directly to the printer without any changes to the printer setup or the table formatting. Click the *Print* option to display the Print dialog box where you can specify the printer, the page range, and specific records. Click OK to close the dialog box and send the table to the printer. By default, Access prints a table on letter-size paper in portrait orientation.

Quick Steps

Print a Table
1. Click File tab.
2. Click Print tab.
3. Click *Quick Print* option.

OR

1. Click File tab.
2. Click Print tab.
3. Click *Print* option.
4. Click OK.

Figure 1.6 Print Tab Backstage View

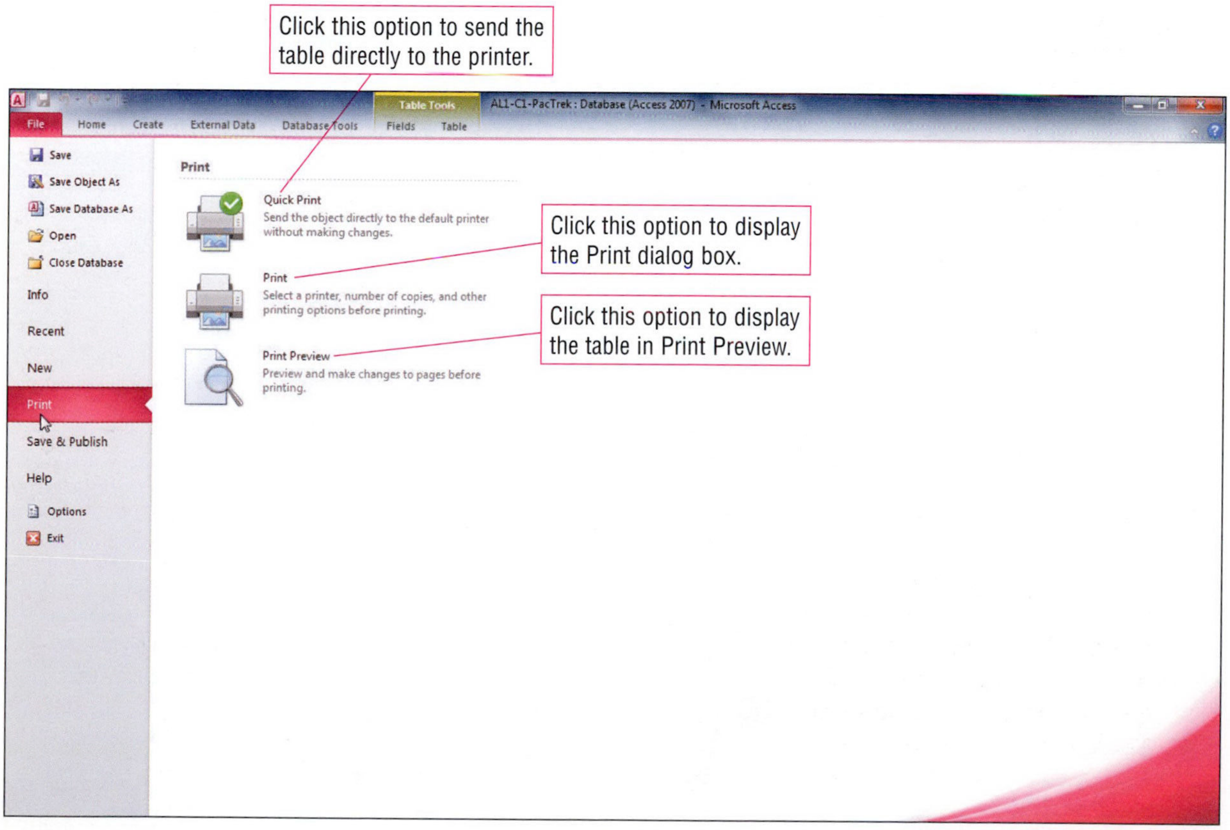

Previewing a Table

> **Quick Steps**
> **Preview a Table**
> 1. Click File tab.
> 2. Click Print tab.
> 3. Click *Print Preview* option.

Print Preview

Before printing a table, you may want to display the table in Print Preview to determine how the table will print on the page. To display a table in Print Preview, as shown in Figure 1.7, click the *Print Preview* option at the Print tab Backstage view.

Use options in the Zoom group in the Print Preview tab to increase or decrease the size of the table display. You can also change the size of the table display using the Zoom slider bar located at the right side of the Status bar. If your table spans more than one page, you can use buttons on the Navigation bar to display the next or previous page in the table.

In Print Preview you can print the table by clicking the Print button located at the left side of the Print Preview tab. Click the Close Print Preview button if you want to close Print Preview and return to the table without printing the table.

Changing Page Size and Margins

Size

Margins

By default, Access prints a table in standard page size that is 8.5 inches wide and 11 inches tall. Click the Size button in the Page Size group in the Print Preview tab and a drop-down list displays with options for changing the page size to legal size, executive size, envelope size, and so on. Access uses default top, bottom, left, and right margins of 1 inch. Change these default margins by clicking the Margins button in the Page Size group and then clicking one of the predesigned margin options.

Figure 1.7 Print Preview

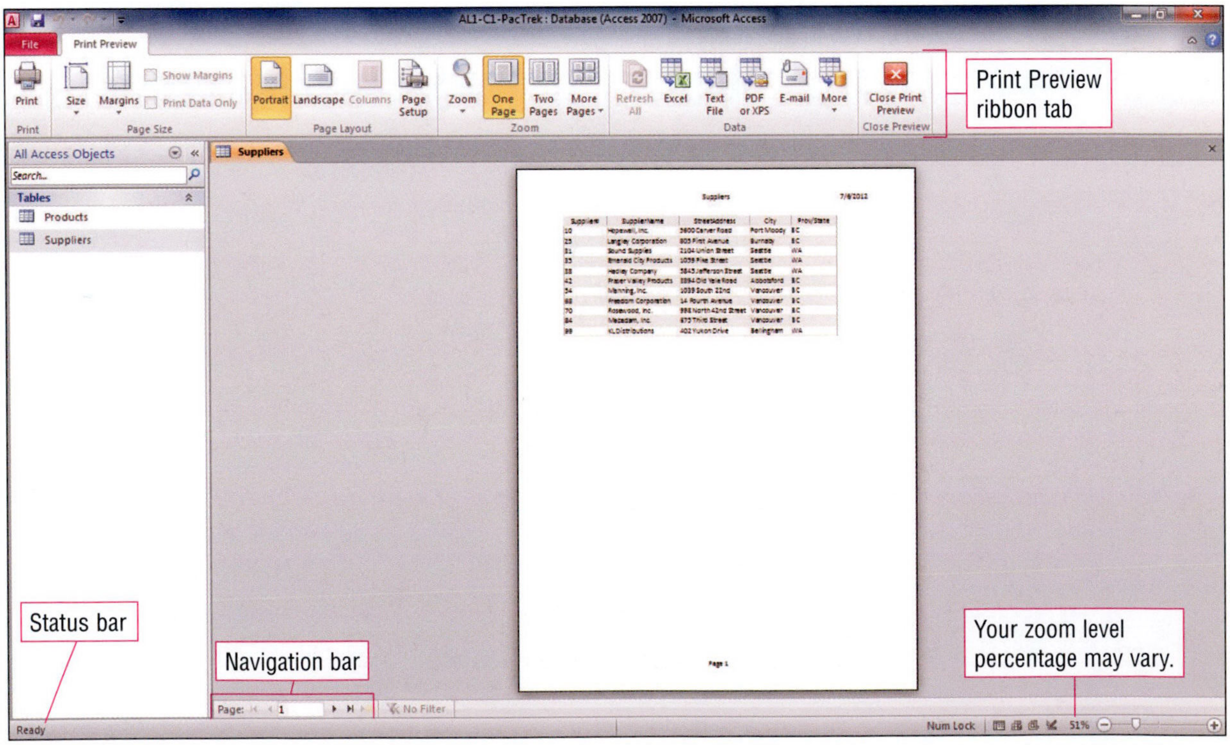

Changing Page Layout

The Print Preview tab contains the Page Layout group with buttons for controlling how data is printed on the page. By default, Access prints a table in portrait orientation which prints the text on the page with the height taller than the width (like a page in this textbook). If a table contains a number of columns, changing to landscape orientation allows more columns to fit on a page. Landscape orientation rotates the printout to print wider than it is tall. To change from the default portrait orientation to landscape, click the Landscape button in the Page Layout group in the Print Preview tab.

Click the Page Setup button in the Page Layout group and the Page Setup dialog box displays as shown in Figure 1.8. At the Page Setup dialog box with the Print Options tab selected, notice that the default margins are 1 inch. Change these defaults by typing a different number in the desired margin text box. By default, the table name prints at the top center of the page along with the current date printed in the upper right side of the page. In addition, the word *Page* followed by the page number prints at the bottom of the page. If you do not want the name of the table and the date as well as the page number printed, remove the check mark from the *Print Headings* option at the Page Setup dialog box with the Print Options tab selected.

Quick Steps

Display Page Setup Dialog Box
1. Click File tab.
2. Click Print tab.
3. Click *Print Preview* option.
4. Click Page Setup button.

Landscape

Page Setup

Click the Page tab at the Page Setup dialog box and the dialog box displays as shown in Figure 1.9. Change the orientation with options in the *Orientation* section, and change the paper size with options in the *Paper* section. Click the *Size* option button and a drop-down list displays with paper sizes similar to the options available at the *Size* button drop-down list in the Page Size group in the Print Preview tab. Specify the printer with options in the *Printer for (table name)* section of the dialog box.

Figure 1.8 Page Setup Dialog Box with Print Options Tab Selected

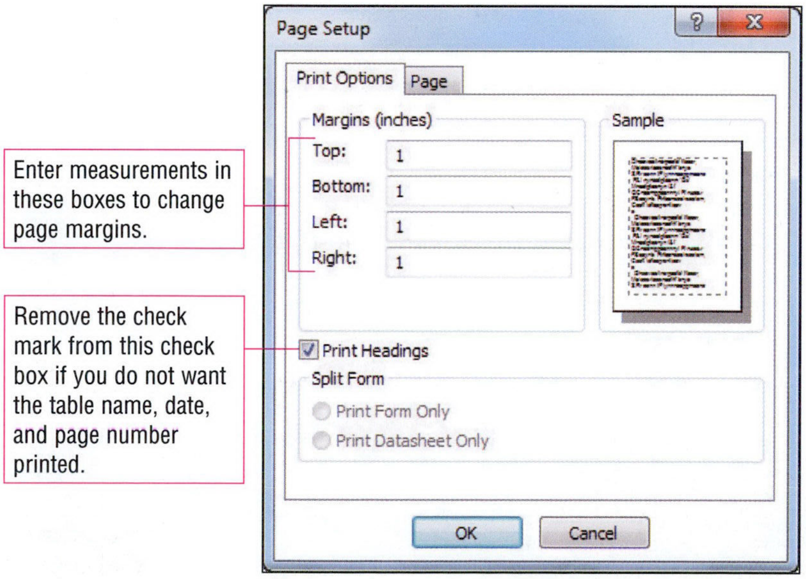

Figure 1.9 Page Setup Dialog Box with Page Tab Selected

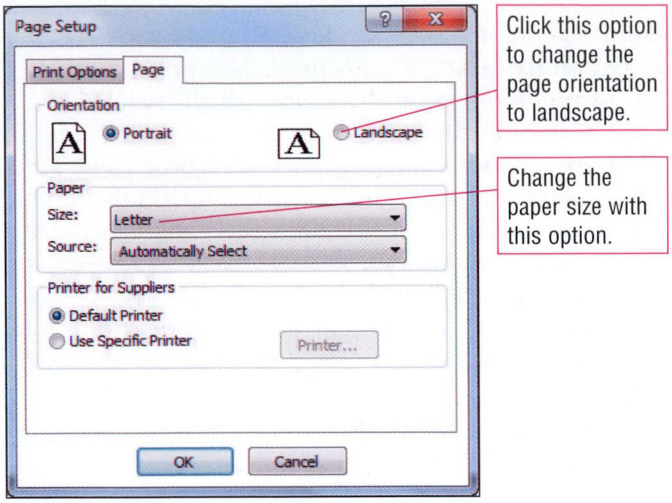

Project 2d Previewing, Changing Page Layout, and Printing Tables

Part 4 of 7

1. With **AL1-C1-PacTrek.accdb** open, open the Suppliers table.
2. Preview and then print the Suppliers table in landscape orientation by completing the following steps:
   a. Click the File tab and then click the Print tab.
   b. At the Print tab Backstage view, click the *Print Preview* option.
   c. In Print Preview, click the Two Pages button in the Zoom group in the Print Preview tab. (This displays two pages of the table.)
   d. Click the Zoom button arrow in the Zoom group in the Print Preview tab and then click *75%* at the drop-down list.

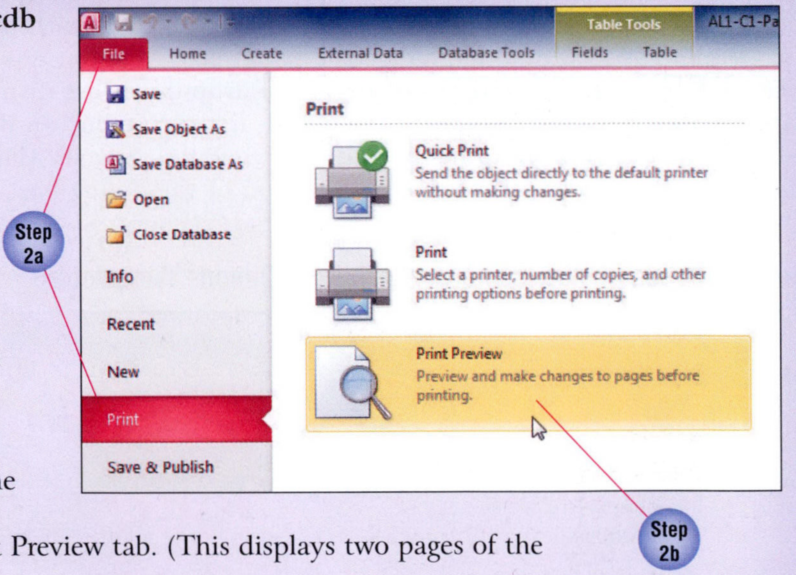

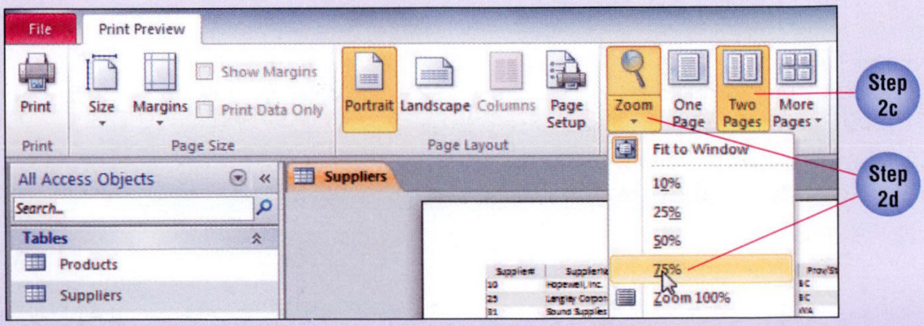

e. Position the arrow pointer on the Zoom slider bar button that displays at the right side of the Status bar, hold down the left mouse button, drag to the right until *100%* displays immediately left of the Zoom slider bar, and then release the mouse button.

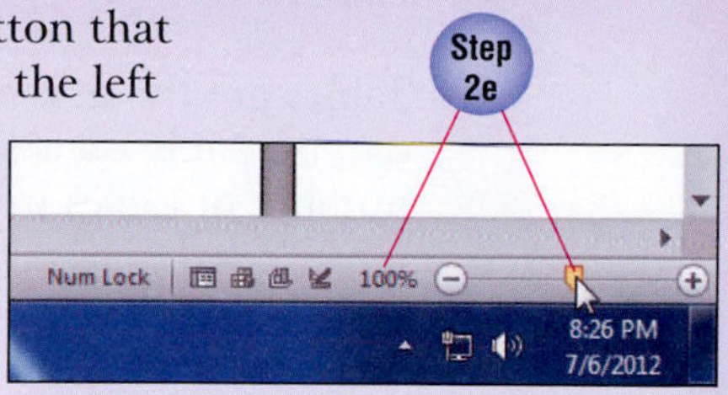

f. Return the display to a full page by clicking the One Page button in the Zoom group in the Print Preview tab.

g. Click the Margins button in the Page Size group in the Print Preview tab and then click the *Narrow* option at the drop-down list. (Notice how the data will print on the page with the narrow margins.)

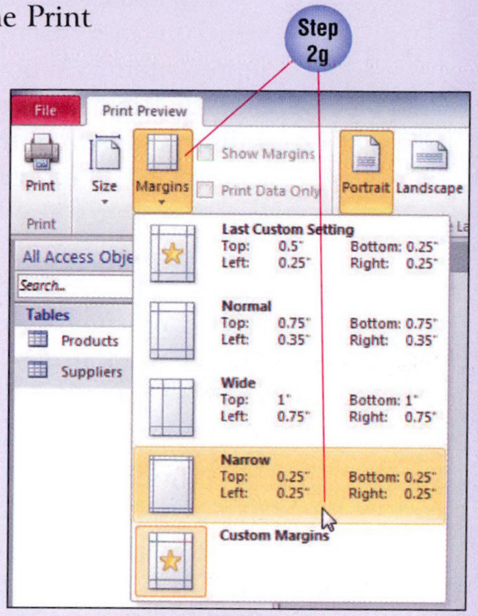

h. Change the margins back to the default by clicking the Margins button in the Page Size group and then clicking the *Normal* option at the drop-down list.

i. Change to landscape orientation by clicking the Landscape button in the Page Layout group. (Check the Next Page button on the Navigation pane and notice that it is dimmed. This indicates that the table will print on only one page.)

j. Print the table by clicking the Print button located at the left side of the Print Preview tab and then clicking the OK button at the Print dialog box.

3. Close the Suppliers table.
4. Open the Products table and then print the table by completing the following steps:
   a. Click the File tab and then click the Print tab.
   b. At the Print tab Backstage view, click the *Print Preview* option.
   c. Click the Page Setup button in the Page Layout group in the Print Preview tab. (This displays the Page Setup dialog box with the Print Options tab selected.)

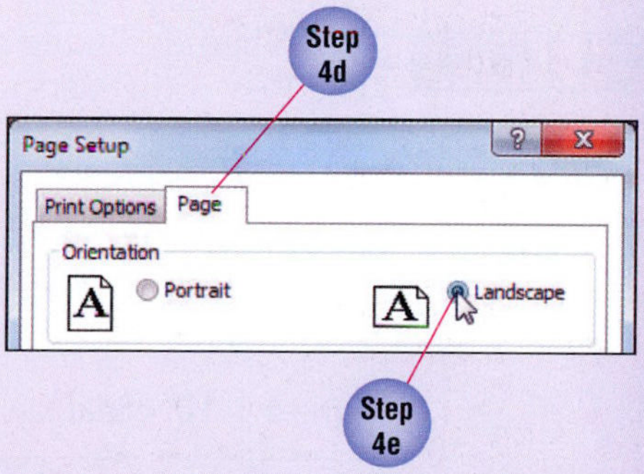

   d. At the Page Setup dialog box, click the Page tab.
   e. Click the *Landscape* option.
   f. Click the Print Options tab.
   g. Select the current measurement in the *Top* measurement box and then type **0.5**.
   h. Select the current measurement in the *Bottom* measurement box and then type **0.5**.
   i. Select the current measurement in the *Left* measurement box and then type **1.5**.
   j. Click OK to close the dialog box.
   k. Click the Print button at the Print Preview tab and then click the OK button at the Print dialog box. (This table will print on two pages.)

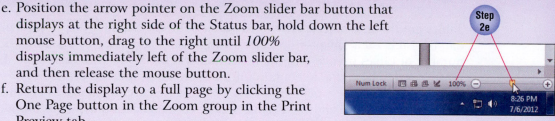

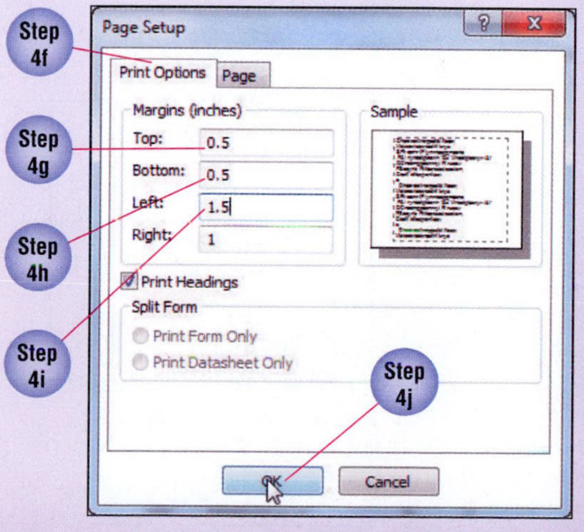

5. Close the Products table.

Designing a Table

Tables are the first objects created in a new database and all other objects in a database rely on a table for data. Designing a database involves planning the number of tables needed and the fields that will be included in each table. Each table in a database should contain information about one subject only. For example, the Suppliers table in the AL1-C1-PacTrek.accdb database contains data only about suppliers and the Products table contains data only about products.

Database designers often create a visual representation of the database's structure in a diagram similar to the one shown in Figure 1.10. Each table is represented by a box with the table name at the top of the box. Within each box, the fields that will be stored in the table are listed with the field names that will be used when the table is created. Notice that one field in each table has an asterisk next to the field name. The field with the asterisk is called a ***primary key***. A primary key holds data that uniquely identifies each record in a table and is usually an identification number. The lines drawn between each table in Figure 1.10 are called ***join lines*** and represent links established between tables (called ***relationships***) so that data can be extracted from one or more tables. Notice the join lines point to a common field name included in each table that is to be linked. (You will learn how to join [relate] tables in Chapter 2.) A database with related tables is called a ***relational database***.

Notice the join line in the database diagram that connects the *Supplier#* field in the Suppliers table with the *Supplier#* field in the Products table and another join line that connects the *Supplier#* field in the Suppliers table with the *Supplier#* field in the Orders table. In the database diagram, a join line connects the *Product#* field in the Products table with the *Product#* field in the Orders table.

HINT
Organize data in tables to minimize or eliminate duplication.

When designing a database, you need to consider certain design principles. The first principle is to reduce redundant (duplicate) data because redundant data increases the amount of data entry required, increases the chances for errors and inconsistencies, and takes up additional storage space. The Products table contains a *Supplier#* field and that field reduces the redundant data needed in the table. For example, rather than typing the supplier information in the Suppliers

Figure 1.10 Database Diagram

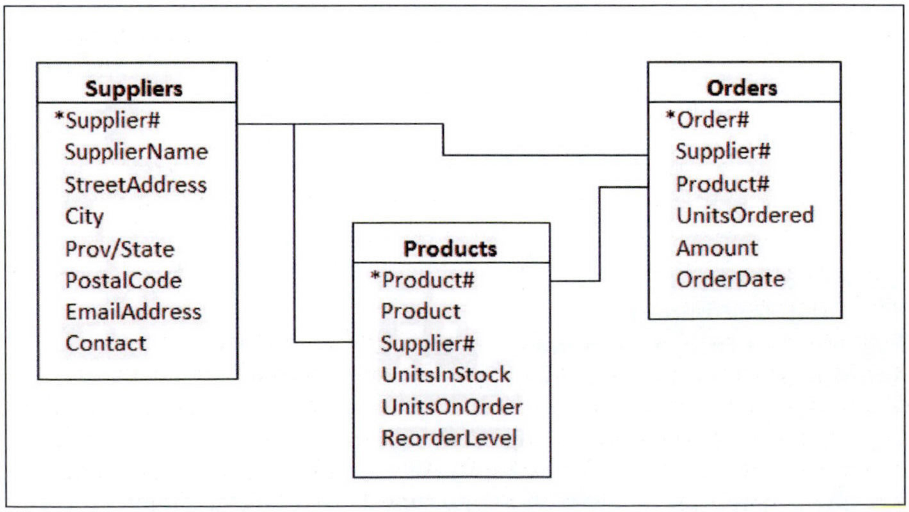

table AND the Products table, you type the information once in the Suppliers table and then "join" the tables with the connecting field *Supplier#*. If you need information on suppliers as well as specific information about products, you can draw the information into one object such as a query or report using data from both tables. When you create the Orders table, you will use the *Supplier#* field and the *Product#* field rather than typing all of the information for the suppliers and the product description. Typing a two-letter unique identifier number for a supplier greatly reduces the amount of typing required to create the Orders table. Inserting the *Product#* field in the Orders table eliminates the need to type the product description for each order; instead, you type a unique five-, six-, or seven-digit identifier number.

Creating a Table

Creating a new table generally involves determining fields, assigning a data type to each field, modifying properties, designating the primary key, and naming the table. This process is referred to as ***defining the table structure***.

The first step in creating a table is to determine the fields. A ***field***, commonly called a column, is one piece of information about a person, a place, or an item. Each field contains data about one aspect of the table subject such as a company name or product number. All fields for one unit, such as a customer or product, are considered a ***record***. For example, in the Suppliers table in the AL1-C1-PacTrek.accdb database, a record is all of the information pertaining to one supplier. A collection of records becomes a ***table***.

When designing a table, determine fields for information to be included on the basis of how you plan to use the data. When organizing fields, be sure to consider not only current needs for the data but also any future needs. For example, a company may need to keep track of customer names, addresses, and telephone numbers for current mailing lists. In the future, the company may want to promote a new product to customers who purchase a specific type of product. For this situation, a field that identifies product type must be included in the database. When organizing fields, consider all potential needs for the data but also try to keep the fields logical and manageable.

HINT

A database table contains fields that describe a person, customer, client, object, place, idea, or event.

You can create a table in Access in Datasheet view or in Design view. To create a table in Datasheet view, open the desired database (or create a new database), click the Create tab, and then click the Table button in the Tables group. This inserts a blank table in the work area with the tab labeled *Table1* as shown in Figure 1.11. Notice the column with the field name *ID* has been created automatically. Access creates *ID* as an AutoNumber field in which the field value is assigned automatically by Access as you enter each record. In many tables, you can use this AutoNumber field to create the unique identifier for the table. For example, in Project 2e you will create an Orders table and you will use the ID AutoNumber field to assign automatically a number to each order since each order must contain a unique number.

Table

When creating a new field (column), determine the type of data you will insert in the field. For example, one field might contain text such as a name or product description, another field might contain an amount of money, and another might contain a date. The data type defines the type of information Access will allow to be entered into the field. For example, Access will not allow alphabetic characters to be entered into a field with a data type set to Date & Time.

HINT

Assign a data type for each field that determines the values that can be entered for the field.

Figure 1.11 Blank Table

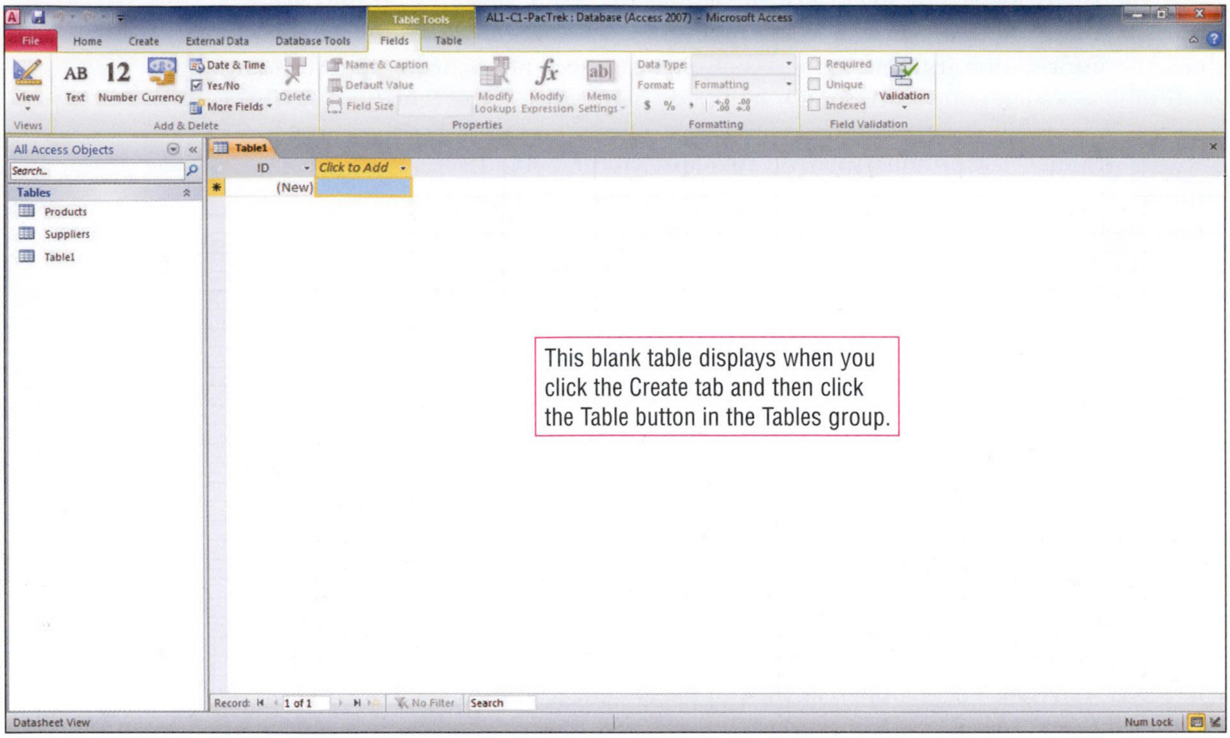

This blank table displays when you click the Create tab and then click the Table button in the Tables group.

More Fields

The Add & Delete group in the Table Tools Fields tab contains five buttons for assigning data types plus a More Fields button. A description of the five data types assigned by the buttons is shown in Table 1.3.

Table 1.3 Data Types

Data Type Button	*Description*
Text	Alphanumeric data up to 255 characters in length, such as a name, address, or value such as a telephone number or social security number that is used as an identifier and not for calculating.
Number	Positive or negative values that can be used in calculations; do not use for values that will calculate monetary amounts (see Currency).
Currency	Values that involve money; Access will not round off during calculations.
Date & Time	Use this data type to ensure dates and times are entered and sorted properly.
Yes/No	Data in the field will be either *Yes* or *No*; *True* or *False*, *On* or *Off*.

In Project 2e, you will create the Orders table as shown in Figure 1.10. Looking at the diagram in Figure 1.10, you will assign the following data types to the columns:

Order#	=	AutoNumber (Access automatically assigns this data type to the first column)
Supplier#	=	Text (the supplier numbers are identifiers, not numbers for calculating)
Product#	=	Text (the product numbers are identifiers, not numbers for calculating)
UnitsOrdered	=	Number (the unit numbers are values for calculating)
Amount	=	Currency
OrderDate	=	Date & Time

When you click a data type button, Access inserts a field to the right of the *ID* field and selects the field heading *Field1*. Type a name for the field, press the Enter key, and Access selects the next field column name *Click to Add* and inserts a drop-down list of data types. This drop-down list contains the same five data types as the buttons in the Add & Delete group as well as additional data types. Click the desired data type at the drop-down list, type the desired field name, and then press Enter. Continue in this manner until you have entered all field names for the table. When naming a field, consider the following naming guidelines:

- Each field must contain a unique name.
- The name should describe the contents of the field.
- A field name can contain up to 64 characters.
- A field name can contain letters and numbers. Some symbols are permitted but others are excluded, so you should avoid using symbols other than the underscore character that is used as a word separator and the number symbol to indicate an identifier number.
- Do not use a space in a field name. Although a space is an accepted character, most database designers avoid using spaces in field names and object names. Use field compound words for field names or the underscore character as a word separator. For example, a field name for a person's last name could be named *LastName*, *Last_Name*, or *LName*.
- Abbreviate field names so that the names are as short as possible but easily understood. For example, a field such as *CompanyName* could be shortened to *CoName* and a field such as *EmailAddress* could be shortened to *Email*.

HINT

Avoid using spaces in field names.

Project 2e **Creating a Table and Entering Data** Part 5 of 7

1. With **AL1-C1-PacTrek.accdb** open, create a new table and specify data types and column headings by completing the following steps:
   a. Click the Create tab.
   b. Click the Table button in the Tables group.
   c. Click the Text button in the Add & Delete group.

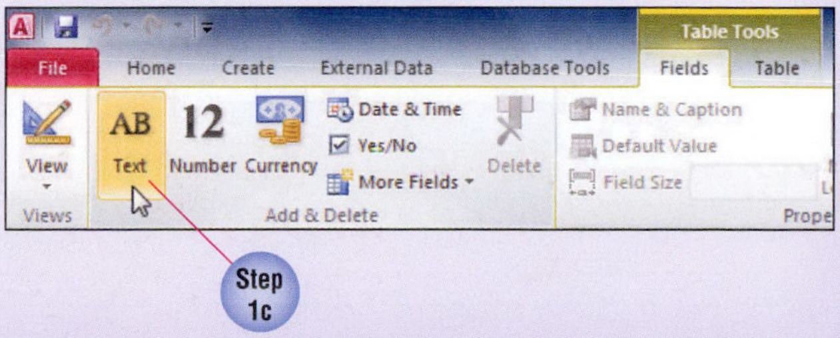

d. With the *Field1* column heading selected, type **Supplier#**, and then press the Enter key. (This displays a drop-down list of data types below the *Click to Add* heading.)
e. Click the *Text* option at the drop-down list.
f. Type **Product#** and then press Enter.
g. Click *Number* at the drop-down list, type **UnitsOrdered**, and then press Enter.
h. Click *Currency* at the drop-down list, type **Amount**, and then press Enter.
i. Click *Date & Time* at the drop-down list and then type **OrderDate**. (Do not press the Enter key since this is the last column in the table.)

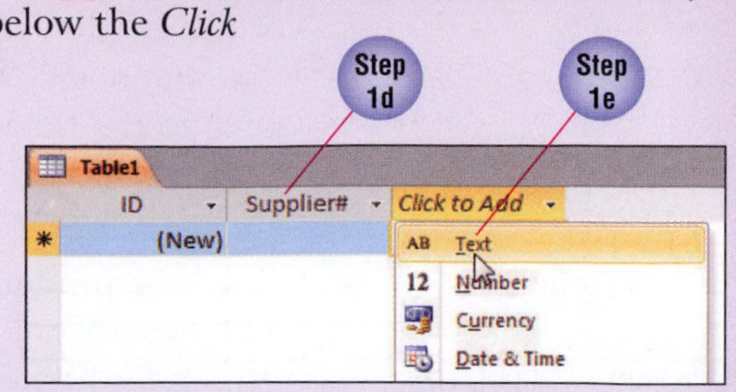

2. Enter the first record in the table as shown in Figure 1.12 by completing the following steps:
   a. Click twice in the first field below the *Supplier#* column heading. (The first time you click the mouse button, the row is selected. Clicking the second time makes active only the field below *Supplier#*.)
   b. Type the data in the fields as shown in Figure 1.12. Press the Tab key to move to the next field or press Shift + Tab to move to the previous field. Access will automatically insert the next number in the sequence in the first column (the *ID* column). When typing the money amounts in the *Amount* column, you do not need to type the dollar sign or the comma. Access will automatically insert them when you make the next field active.
3. When the 14 records have been entered, click the Save button on the Quick Access toolbar.
4. At the Save As dialog box, type **Orders** and then press the Enter key. (This saves the table with the name *Orders*.)
5. Close the Orders table by clicking the Close button located in the upper right corner of the work area.

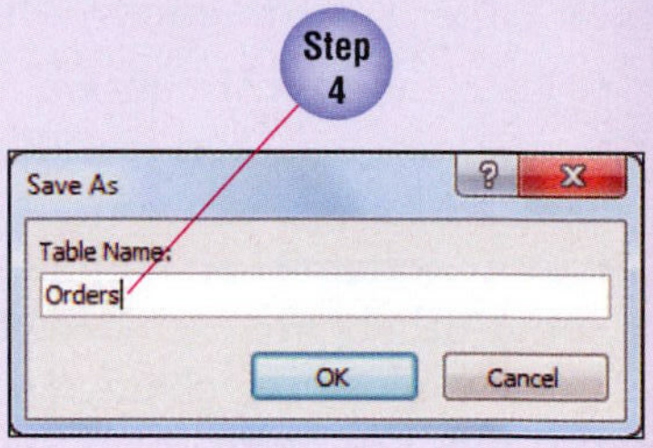

Figure 1.12 Project 2e

Orders

ID	Supplier#	Product#	UnitsOrdere	Amount	OrderDate	Click to Add
1	54	101-S3	10	$1,137.50	1/2/2012	
2	68	209-L	25	$173.75	1/2/2012	
3	68	209-XL	25	$180.00	1/2/2010	
4	68	209-XXL	20	$145.80	1/2/2010	
5	68	210-M	15	$97.35	1/2/2010	
6	68	210-L	25	$162.25	1/2/2010	
7	31	299-M2	10	$887.90	1/16/2012	
8	31	299-M3	10	$887.90	1/16/2012	
9	31	299-M5	10	$887.90	1/16/2012	
10	31	299-W1	8	$602.32	1/16/2012	
11	31	299-W3	10	$752.90	1/16/2012	
12	31	299-W4	10	$752.90	1/16/2012	
13	31	299-W5	10	$752.90	1/16/2012	
14	35	602-XR	5	$2,145.00	1/16/2012	
(New)						

Renaming a Field Heading

When you click a data type button or click a data type at the data type drop-down list, the default heading such as *Field1* is automatically selected. You can type a name for the field heading that takes the place of the selected text. If you create a field heading and then decide to change the name, right-click the heading, click *Rename Field* at the shortcut menu (this selects the current column heading), and then type the new name.

Inserting a Name, Caption, and Description

Name & Caption

When you create a table that others will use, consider providing additional information so the user understands the fields in the table and what should be entered in each field in the table. Along with the field heading name, you can provide a caption and description for each field with options at the Enter Field Properties dialog box shown in Figure 1.13. Display this dialog by clicking the Name & Caption button in the Properties group in the Table Tools Fields tab.

At the Enter Field Properties dialog box, type the desired name for the field heading in the *Name* text box. If you want a more descriptive name for the field heading, type the heading in the *Caption* text box. The text you type will display as the field heading but the actual field name will still be part of the table structure. Creating a caption is useful if you abbreviate a field name or want to show spaces between words in a field name and a caption provides more information for others using the database. The name is what Access uses for the table and the caption is what displays to users.

The *Description* text box is another source for providing information about the field to someone using the database. Type information in the text box that specifies what should be entered in the field. The text you type in the *Description* text box displays at the left side of the Status bar when a field in the column is active. For example, if you type *Enter the total amount of the order* in the *Description* text box for the *Amount* field column, that text will display at the left side of the Status bar when a field in the column is active.

Figure 1.13 Enter Field Properties Dialog Box

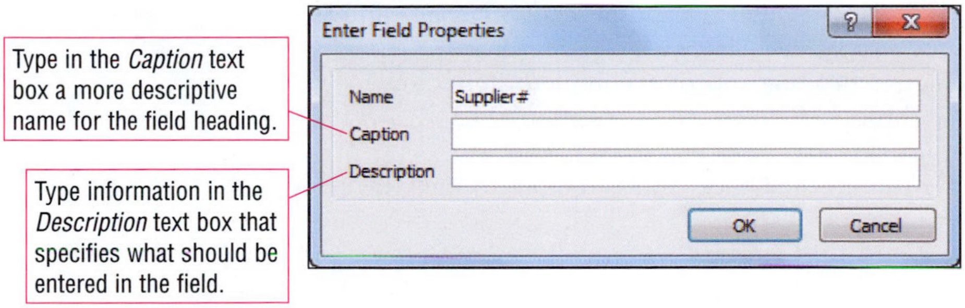
Type in the *Caption* text box a more descriptive name for the field heading.
Type information in the *Description* text box that specifies what should be entered in the field.
Enter Field Properties
Name
Supplier#
Caption
Description
OK
Cancel

Project 2f Inserting a Name, Caption, and Description Part 6 of 7

1. With **AL1-C1-PacTrek.accdb** open, open the Orders table.
2. Access automatically named the first field *ID*. You want to make the heading more descriptive so you decide to rename the heading. To do this, right-click the *ID* heading and then click *Rename Field* at the drop-down list.

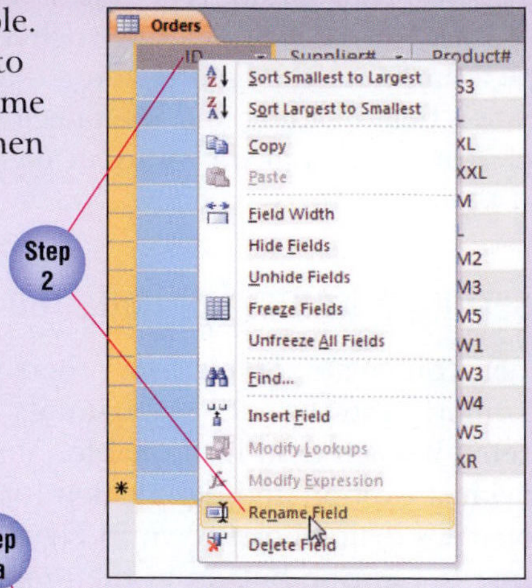

3. Type **Order#**.
4. To provide more information for someone using the table, you decide to add information for the *Supplier#* field by creating a caption and a description. To do this, complete the following steps:
   a. Click the *Supplier#* field heading. (This selects the entire column.)
   b. Click the Table Tools Fields tab.
   c. Click the Name & Caption button in the Properties group. (At the Enter Field Properties dialog box, notice that *Supplier#* is already inserted in the *Name* text box.)

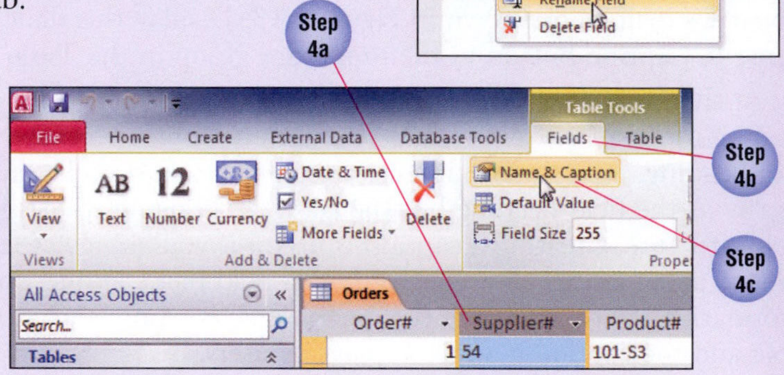

   d. At the Enter Field Properties dialog box, click in the *Caption* text box and then type **Supplier Number**.
   e. Click in the *Description* text box and then type **Supplier identification number**.
   f. Click OK to close the dialog box. (Notice that the field name now displays as *Supplier Number*. The field name is still *Supplier#* but what displays is *Supplier Number*.)

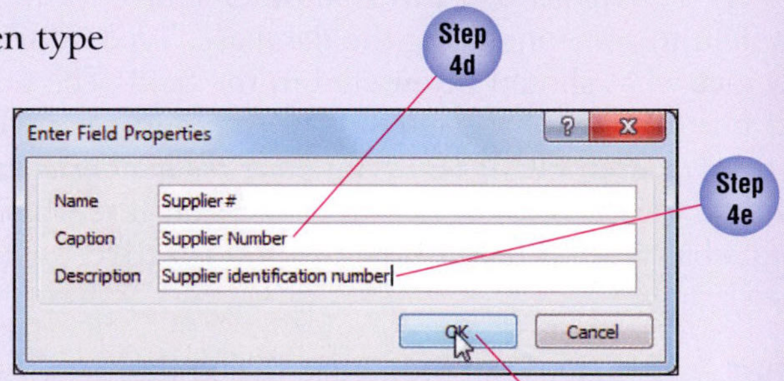

5. Click the *Product#* field heading and then complete steps similar to those in Steps 4c through 4f to create the caption *Product Number* and the description *Product identification number*.
6. Click the *Amount* field heading and then complete steps similar to those in Steps 4c through 4f to create the caption *Order Amount* and the description *Total amount of order*.
7. Click the Save button on the Quick Access toolbar to save the changes to the Orders table.
8. Close the Orders table.

Inserting Quick Start Fields

Text

The Add & Delete group in the Table Tools Fields tab contains buttons for specifying a data type. You used the Text button to specify the data type for the *Supplier#* field when you created the Orders table. You also used the field heading drop-down list to choose a data type. In addition to these two methods, you can specify a data type by clicking the More Fields button in the Add & Delete group in the Table Tools Fields tab. When you click this button, a drop-down list displays with data types grouped into categories such as *Basic Types*, *Number*, *Date and Time*, *Yes/No*, and *Quick Start*.

The options in the *Quick Start* category not only define a data type but also assign a field name. Additionally, with options in the *Quick Start* category, you can add a group of related fields in one step. For example, if you click the *Name* option in the *Quick Start* category, Access inserts the *LastName* field in one column and the *FirstName* field in the next column. Both fields are automatically assigned a text data type. If you click the *Address* option in the *Quick Start* category, Access inserts five fields including *Address*, *City*, *StateProvince*, *ZIPPostal*, and *CountryRegion*, all with the text data type assigned.

Assigning a Default Value

Default Value

The Properties group in the Table Tools Fields tab contains additional buttons for defining field properties in a table. If most records in a table are likely to contain the same field value in a column, consider inserting that value by default. You can do this by clicking the Default Value button in the Properties group. At the Expression Builder dialog box that displays, type the default value you want to appear in the fields, and then click OK. For example, in Project 2g, you will create a new table in the AL1-C1-PacTrek.accdb database containing information on customers and most of the customers live in Vancouver, British Columbia. You will create a default value of *Vancouver* that is automatically inserted in the *City* field and *BC* that is automatically inserted in the *Prov/State* field. You can type different text over the value so if a customer lives in Abbotsford instead of Vancouver, you can type *Abbotsford* in the field.

Assigning a Field Size

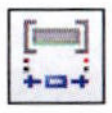
Field Size

The default field size property varies depending on the data type. For example, if you assign a text data type to a field, the maximum length of the data you can enter in the field is 255 characters. You can decrease this number depending on what data will be entered in the field. You can also change the field size number to control how much data is entered and help reduce errors. For example, if you have a field for states and you want the two-letter state abbreviation inserted in each field in the column, you can assign a field size of 2. If someone entering data into the table tries to type more than two letters, Access will not accept the additional text. To change field size, click in the *Field Size* text box in the Properties group in the Table Tools Fields tab and then type the desired number.

Changing the AutoNumber Field

Access automatically applies the AutoNumber data type to the first field in a table and assigns a unique number to each record in the table. In many cases, letting Access automatically assign a number to a record is a good idea. Some situations may arise, however, where you want the first field to contain a unique value for each record other than a number.

If you try to change the AutoNumber data type in the first column by clicking one of the data type buttons in the Add & Delete group in the Table Tools Fields tab, Access creates another field. To change the AutoNumber data type for the first field, you need to click the down-pointing arrow at the right side of the *Data*

Type option box in the Formatting group in the Table Tools Fields tab and then click the desired data type at the drop-down list.

Project 2g Creating a Customers Table Part 7 of 7

1. The owners of Pacific Trek have decided to publish a semiannual product catalog and have asked customers who want to receive the catalog to fill out a form and include on the form whether or not they want to receive notices of upcoming sales as well as the catalog. Create a table to store the data for customers by completing the following steps:
   a. With the **AL1-C1-PacTrek.accdb** database open, click the Create tab.
   b. Click the Table button in the Tables group.
   c. With the *Click to Add* field heading active, click the More Fields button in the Add & Delete group in the Table Tools Fields tab.
   d. Scroll down the drop-down list and then click *Name* located in the *Quick Start* category. (This inserts the *Last Name* and *First Name* field headings in the table.)
   e. Click the *Click to Add* field heading that displays immediately right of the *First Name* field heading. (The data type drop-down list displays. You are going to use the More Fields button rather than the drop-down list to create the next fields.)

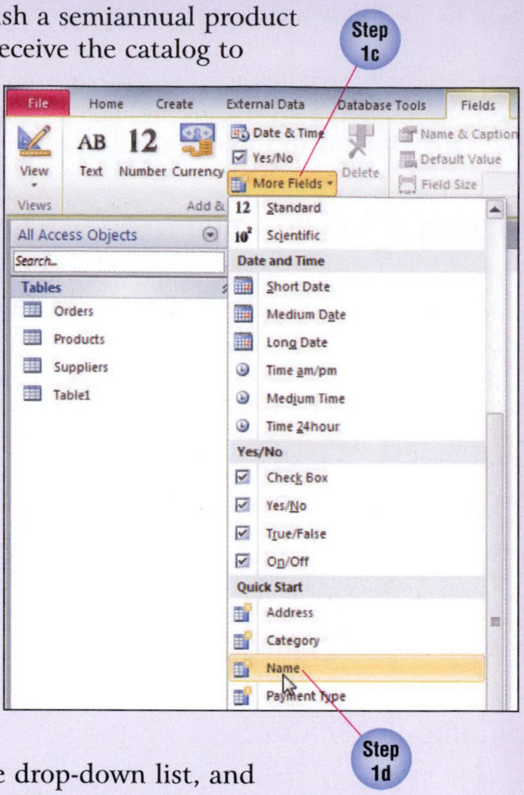

   f. Click the More Fields button, scroll down the drop-down list, and then click *Address* in the *Quick Start* category. (This inserts five more fields in the table.)
   g. Scroll to the right in the table to display the *Click to Add* field heading that follows the *Country Region* column heading. (You can scroll in the table using the horizontal scroll bar that displays to the right of the Navigation bar.)
   h. Click the *Click to Add* field heading and then click *Yes/No* at the drop-down list.

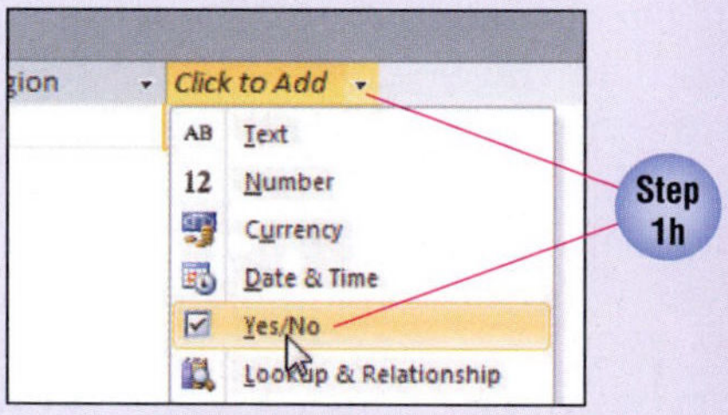

   i. With the name *Field1* selected, type **Mailers**. (When you enter records in the table, you will insert a check mark in the field check box if a customer wants to receive sales promotion mailers. If a customer does not want to receive the mailers, you will leave the check box blank.)

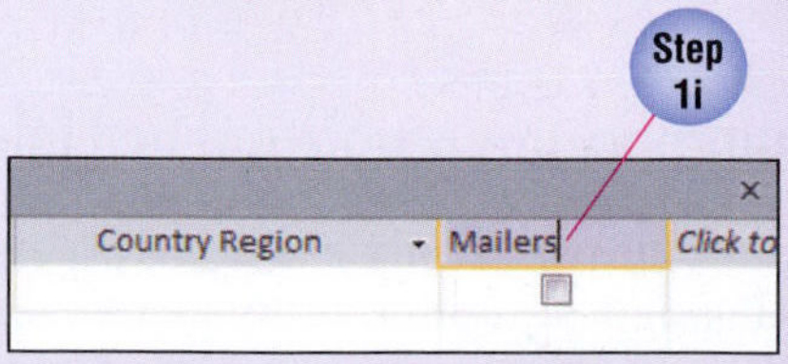

2. Rename and create a caption and description for the *ID* column heading by completing the following steps:
   a. Scroll to the beginning of the table and then click the *ID* column heading. (You can scroll in the table using the horizontal scroll bar that displays to the right of the Navigation bar.)
   b. Click the Name & Caption button in the Properties group in the Table Tools Fields tab.

c. At the Enter Field Properties dialog box, select the text *ID* that displays in the *Name* text box and then type **Customer#**.
d. Press the Tab key and then type **Customer Number** in the *Caption* text box.
e. Press the Tab key and then type **Access will automatically assign the record the next number in the sequence.**

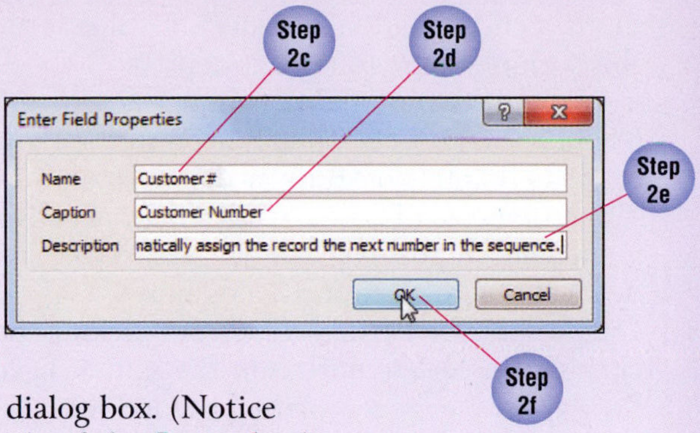

f. Click OK to close the Name & Caption dialog box. (Notice the description that displays at the left side of the Status bar.)

3. Add a description to the *Last Name* column by completing the following steps:
   a. Click the *Last Name* column heading.
   b. Click the Name & Caption button in the Properties group.
   c. At the Enter Field Properties dialog box notice that Access named the field *LastName* but provided the caption *Last Name*. You do not want to change the name and caption so press the Tab key twice to make the *Description* text box active and then type **Customer last name**.
   d. Click OK to close the dialog box.
4. You know that more than likely a customer's last name will not exceed 30 characters, so you decide to limit the field size. To do this, click in the *Field Size* text box in the Properties group (this selects *255*), type **30**, and then press the Enter key.

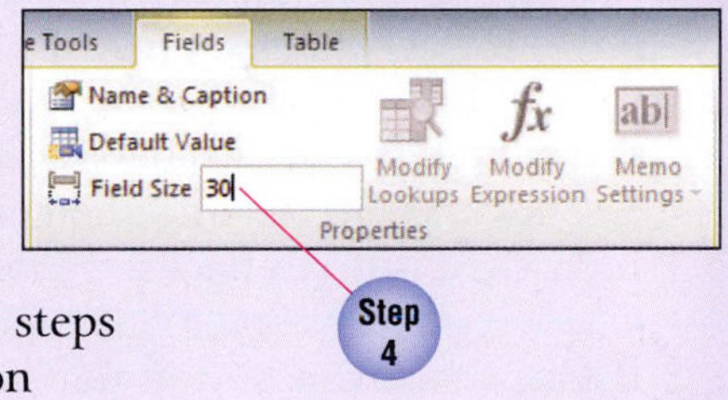

5. Click the *First Name* column heading and then complete steps similar to those in Steps 3 and 4 to create the description *Customer first name* and change the field size to *30*.
6. Since most of Pacific Trek's customers live in the city of Vancouver, you decide to make it the default field value. To do this, complete the following steps:
   a. Click the *City* column heading.
   b. Click the Default Value button in the Properties group.
   c. At the Expression Builder dialog box, type **Vancouver**.
   d. Click the OK button to close the dialog box.

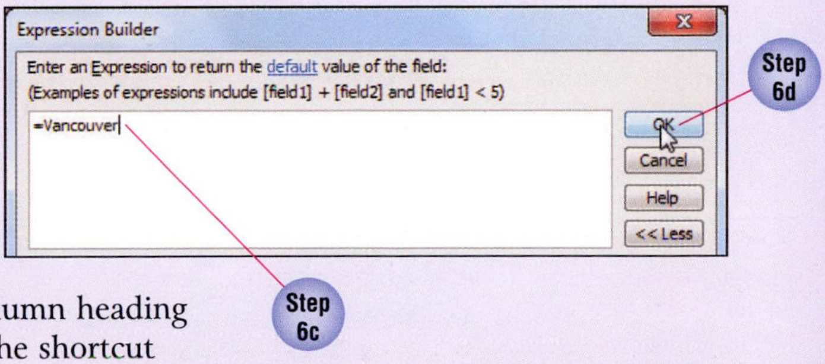

7. Change the name of the *State Province* field name and insert a default value by completing the following steps:
   a. Right-click the *State Province* column heading and then click *Rename Field* at the shortcut menu.
   b. Type **Province**.
   c. Click the Default Value button in the Properties group.
   d. Type **BC** in the Expression Builder dialog box and then click the OK button.
8. Click the *ZIP Postal* column heading and then limit the field size to 7 by clicking in the *Field Size* text box (this selects *255*), typing **7**, and then pressing the Enter key.

9. Since most of the customers want to be sent the sales promotional mailers, you decide to insert a check mark as the default value in the check boxes in the *Yes/No* column. To do this, complete the following steps:
   a. Click the *Mailers* field heading.
   b. Click the Default Value button in the Properties group.
   c. At the Expression Builder dialog box, press the Backspace key to delete the 0 and then type **1**. (The zero indicates a negative such as "no," "false," or "off" and the one indicates a positive such as "yes," "true," or "on.")
   d. Click OK to close the dialog box.
10. Delete the *Country Region* field by clicking the *Country Region* field heading and then clicking the Delete button in the Add & Delete group.
11. Save the table by completing the following steps:
   a. Click the Save button on the Quick Access toolbar.
   b. At the Save As dialog box, type **Customers**, and then press Enter.
12. Enter the six records in the table as shown in Figure 1.14. To remove a check mark in the *Mailers* column, press the spacebar.
13. Adjust the column widths to accommodate the longest entry in each column by completing the following steps:
   a. Position the arrow pointer on the *Customer Number* field heading until the pointer turns into a down-pointing black arrow, hold down the left mouse button, drag to the *Mailers* field heading, and then release the mouse button.
   b. With the columns selected, double-click one of the column boundaries.
14. Click the Save button to save the Customers table.
15. Print the Customers table by completing the following steps:
   a. Click the File tab and then click the Print tab.
   b. At the Print tab Backstage view, click the *Print Preview* option.
   c. Click the Landscape button in the Page Layout group in the Print Preview tab.
   d. Click the Print button that displays at the left side of the Print Preview tab.
   e. At the Print dialog box, click OK.
16. Close the Customers table.
17. Open the Orders table.
18. Automatically adjust the column widths to accommodate the longest entry in each column.
19. Click the Save button to save the Orders table.
20. Print the table in landscape orientation (refer to Step 15) and then close the table.
21. Close the **AL1-C1-PacTrek.accdb** database.

Figure 1.14 Project 2g

Customers

Customer Number	Last Name	First Name	Address	City	State Province	ZIP Postal	Mailers
1	Blakely	Mathias	7433 224th Ave. E.	Vancouver	BC	V5K 2M7	☑
2	Donato	Antonio	18225 Victoria Dr.	Vancouver	BC	V5K 1H4	☐
3	Girard	Stephanie	430 Deer Lake Pl.	Burnaby	BC	V3J 1E4	☑
4	Hernandez	Angelica	1233 E. 58th Ave.	Vancouver	BC	V5K 3H3	☑
5	Ives-Keller	Shane	9055 Gilbert Rd.	Richmond	BC	V6Y 1B2	☐
6	Kim	Keung	730 West Broadway	Vancouver	BC	V5K 5B2	☑
(New)				Vancouver	BC		☑

Chapter Summary

- Microsoft Access is a database management system software program that will organize, store, maintain, retrieve, sort, and print all types of business data.
- In Access, open an existing database by clicking the Open button at the New tab Backstage view. At the open dialog box, navigate to the location where the database is located, and then double-click the desired database.
- Only one database can be open at a time.
- Some common objects found in a database include tables, queries, forms, and reports.
- The Navigation pane displays at the left side of the Access screen and displays the objects that are contained in the database.
- Open a database object by double-clicking the object in the Navigation pane. Close an object by clicking the Close button that displays in the upper right corner of the work area.
- When a table is open, the Record Navigation bar displays at the bottom of the screen and contains a button for displaying records in the table.
- Insert a new record in a table by clicking the New button in the Records group in the Home tab or by clicking the New (blank) record button in the Record Navigation bar. Delete a record by clicking in a field in the record you want to delete, clicking the Delete button arrow in the Home tab, and then clicking *Delete Record* at the drop-down list.
- To add a column to a table, click the first field below the *Click to Add* column heading and then type the desired data. To move a column, select the column and then use the mouse to drag a thick, back vertical line (representing the column) to the desired location. To delete a column, click the column heading, click the Delete button arrow, and then click *Delete Column* at the drop-down list.
- Data you enter in a table is automatically saved while changes to the layout of a table are not automatically saved.
- You can hide, unhide, freeze, and unfreeze columns with options at the More button drop-down list. Display this list by clicking the More button in the Records group in the Home tab.
- Adjust the width of a column (or selected columns) to accommodate the longest entry by double-clicking the column boundary. You can also adjust the width of a column by dragging the column boundary.
- Print a table by clicking the File tab, clicking the Print tab, and then clicking the *Quick Print* option. You can also preview a table before printing by clicking the *Print Preview* option at the Print tab Backstage view.
- With buttons and option on the Print Preview tab, you can change the page size, orientation, and margins.
- The first principle in database design is to reduce redundant data because redundant data increases the amount of data entry required, increases the chances for errors, and takes up additional storage space.
- A data type defines the type of data Access will allow in the field. Assign a data type to a field with buttons in the Add & Delete group in the Table Tools Fields tab, by clicking an option from the column heading drop-down list, or with options at the More button drop-down list.

- Rename a column heading by right-clicking the heading, clicking *Rename Field* at the shortcut menu, and then typing the new name.
- Type a name, a caption, and a description for a column with options at the Enter Field Properties dialog box.
- Use options in the *Quick Start* category in the More Fields button drop-down list to define a data type and assign a field name to a group of related fields.
- Insert a default value in a column with the Default Value button and assign a field size with the *Field Size* text box in the Properties group in the Table Tools Fields tab.
- Use the *Data Type* option box in the Formatting group to change the AutoNumber data type for the first column in a table.

Commands Review

FEATURE	RIBBON TAB, GROUP	BUTTON, OPTION	KEYBOARD SHORTCUT
Open dialog box	File	Open	Ctrl + O
Close database	File	Close Database	
New record	Home, Records		Ctrl + +
Next field			Tab
Previous field			Shift + Tab
Delete record	Home, Records	, Delete Record	
Delete column	Home, Records	, Delete Column	
Hide column	Home, Records	, Hide Fields	
Unhide column	Home, Records	, Unhide Fields	
Freeze column	Home, Records	, Freeze Fields	
Unfreeze column	Home, Records	, Unfreeze Fields	
Print tab Backstage view	File	Print	
Print Preview	File	Print, Print Preview	
Print dialog box	File	Print, Print	Ctrl + P
Page size	File	Print, Print Preview, 	
Page margins	File	Print, Print Preview, 	

FEATURE	RIBBON TAB, GROUP	BUTTON, OPTION	KEYBOARD SHORTCUT
Page Setup dialog box	File	Print, Print Preview,	
Landscape orientation	File	Print, Print Preview,	
Portrait orientation	File	Print, Print Preview,	
Create table	Create, Tables		
Text data type	Table Tools Fields, Add & Delete	AB	
Number data type	Table Tools Fields, Add & Delete	12	
Currency data type	Table Tools Fields, Add & Delete		
Date & Time data type	Table Tools Fields, Add & Delete		
Yes/No data type	Table Tools Fields, Add & Delete		
Enter Field Properties dialog box	Table Tools Fields, Properties		
Expression Builder dialog box	Table Tools Fields, Properties		

Concepts Check Test Your Knowledge

Completion: In the space provided at the right, indicate the correct term, symbol, or command.

1. This view displays when you open Access. ____________________
2. This toolbar contains buttons for commonly used commands. ____________________
3. This displays the names of objects within a database grouped by categories. ____________________
4. When you open a table, it displays in this view. ____________________
5. Use buttons on this bar to navigate in the table. ____________________
6. To add a new record, click the New button in this group in the Home tab. ____________________
7. At the Print tab Backstage view, click this option to send the table directly to the printer. ____________________
8. The Landscape button is located in this group in the Print Preview tab. ____________________

9. All fields for one unit, such as an employee or customer, are considered to be this. ____________

10. Assign this data type to values that involve money. ____________

11. Click this button in the Properties group in the Table Tools Fields tab to display the Enter Field Properties dialog box. ____________

12. With options in this category in the More Fields button drop-down list, you can define a data type and also assign a field name. ____________

13. If you want to assign the same field value to a column, click this button to display the Expression Builder dialog box and then type the desired value. ____________

Skills Check Assess Your Performance

The database designer for Griffin Technologies has created the database diagram, shown in Figure 1.15, to manage data about company employees. You will open the Griffin database and maintain and create tables that follow the diagram.

Figure 1.15 Griffin Technologies Database Diagram

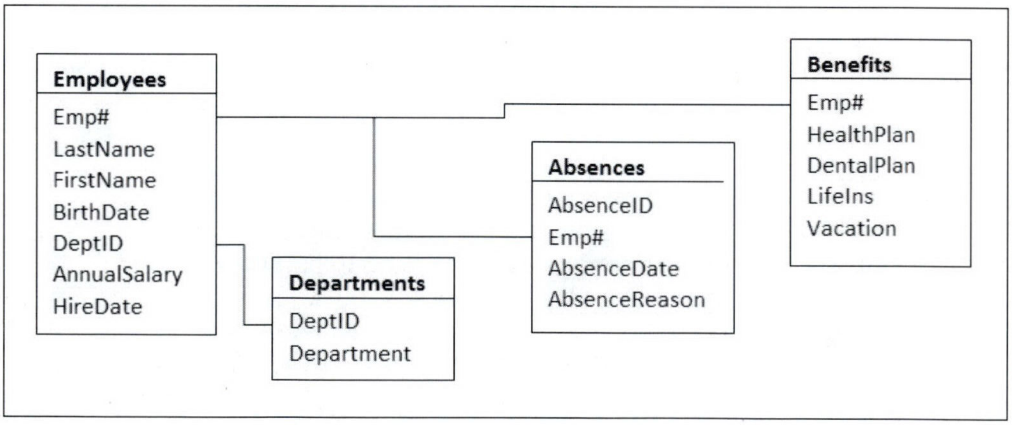

Assessment 1

INSERTING AND DELETING ROWS AND COLUMNS

1. In Access, open the database named **AL1-C1-Griffin.accdb** located in the Access2010L1C1 folder on your storage medium and enable the contents.
2. Double-click the *Employees* table in the Navigation pane.
3. Delete the record for Scott Jorgensen (employee number 1025).
4. Delete the record for Leanne Taylor (employee number 1060).

5. Insert the following records:

Emp#: **1010**	Birthdate: **9/7/1976**
LastName: **Harrington**	AnnualSalary: **$53,350**
FirstName: **Tyler**	HireDate: **10/1/2005**
Emp#: **1052**	Birthdate: **12/4/1978**
LastName: **Reeves**	AnnualSalary: **$38,550**
FirstName: **Carrie**	HireDate: **10/1/2008**

6. Close the Employees table.
7. Looking at the database diagram in Figure 1.15, you realize that the Employees table includes a *DeptID* field. Open the Employees table, insert the new field in the Employees table and name it *DeptID*. Change the field size to 2 (since department abbreviations are only one or two letters in length). At the message telling you that some data may be lost, click the Yes button. Type the department identification for each record as shown below (the records are listed from left to right):

1001: HR	1002: RD	1003: IT	1005: DP	1010: DP
1013: RD	1015: HR	1020: A	1023: IT	1030: PR
1033: A	1040: DP	1043: HR	1045: RD	1050: IT
1052: PR	1053: HR	1063: DP	1065: DP	1080: IT
1083: HR	1085: PR	1090: RD	1093: A	1095: RD

8. Move the *DeptID* column so it is positioned between the *BirthDate* column and the *AnnualSalary* column.
9. Automatically adjust the widths of the columns.
10. Save the table.
11. Display the table in Print Preview, change the top margin to 1.5 inches, the left margin to 1.25 inches, and then print the table.
12. Close the Employees table.

Assessment 2

CREATE A DEPARTMENTS TABLE

1. You entered a one- or two-letter abbreviation representing a department within the company. Creating the abbreviations saved you from having to type the entire department name for each record. You need to create the Departments table that will provide the department names for each abbreviation. Create a new table in the **AL1-C1-Griffin.accdb** database with the column headings and data as shown in Figure 1.16 by completing the following steps:
   a. Click the Create tab and then click the Table button.
   b. Click the *ID* column heading, click the down-pointing arrow at the right side of the *Data Type* option box in the Formatting group, and then click *Text* at the drop-down list.
   c. Limit the field size to 2 and rename the heading to *DeptID*.
   d. Click the *Click to Add* column heading, click *Text* at the drop-down list, and then type **Department**.
   e. Type the data in the fields as shown in Figure 1.16.
   f. Automatically adjust the widths of the columns.
2. Save the table and name it *Departments*.
3. Print and then close the table.

Figure 1.16 Departments Table

Departments

DeptID	Department	Click to Add
A	Accounting	
DP	Design and Production	
HR	Human Resources	
IT	Information Technology Services	
PR	Public Relations	
RD	Research Development	
*		

Assessment

3 CREATE A BENEFITS TABLE

1. Create a new table in the **AL1-C1-Griffin.accdb** database with the data shown in Figure 1.17 with the following specifications:
   a. Name the fields as shown in the Benefits table in the diagram in Figure 1.15 and create the caption names for the fields as shown in Figure 1.17. (For example, name the life insurance field *LifeIns* and create the caption *Life Insurance*.)
   b. For the first column (Emp#), click the *ID* column heading, click the down-pointing arrow at the right side of the *Data Type* option box in the Formatting group, and then click *Text* at the drop-down list. Limit the field size to 4 and rename the field to *Emp#*.
   c. Apply the Yes/No data type to the second column, make the default value a check mark (type a 1 at the Expression Builder dialog box), and provide the description *A check mark indicates the employee is signed up for the health plan.*

Figure 1.17 Benefits Table

Benefits

Emp#	Health Plan	Dental Plan	Life Insurance	Vacation	Click to Add
1001	☑	☑	$100,000.00	4 weeks	
1002	☑	☑	$200,000.00	4 weeks	
1003	☐	☑	$150,000.00	3 weeks	
1005	☑	☑	$200,000.00	3 weeks	
1010	☑	☑	$185,000.00	4 weeks	
1013	☐	☑	$200,000.00	3 weeks	
1015	☐	☐	$100,000.00	3 weeks	
1020	☑	☑	$200,000.00	4 weeks	
1023	☐	☐	$75,000.00	2 weeks	
1030	☑	☑	$125,000.00	3 weeks	
1033	☑	☑	$200,000.00	3 weeks	
1040	☑	☑	$200,000.00	3 weeks	
1043	☐	☐	$50,000.00	2 weeks	
1045	☑	☐	$125,000.00	2 weeks	
1050	☑	☑	$85,000.00	3 weeks	
1052	☑	☑	$175,000.00	3 weeks	
1053	☑	☐	$100,000.00	2 weeks	
1063	☑	☑	$150,000.00	2 weeks	
1065	☑	☑	$200,000.00	2 weeks	
1080	☐	☑	$150,000.00	1 week	
1083	☑	☐	$75,000.00	1 week	
1085	☑	☑	$125,000.00	1 week	
1090	☑	☐	$150,000.00	1 week	
1093	☐	☑	$185,000.00	1 week	
1095	☐	☐	$200,000.00	1 week	
*	☑	☑			

d. Apply the Yes/No data type to the third column, make the default value a check mark (type a 1 at the Expression Builder dialog box), and provide the description *A check mark indicates the employee is signed up for the dental plan*.
e. Apply the Currency data type to the fourth column.
f. Apply the Text data type to the fifth column and limit the field size to 8.
g. Type the data in each record as shown in Figure 1.17.
h. Automatically adjust the column widths.
i. Save the table and name it *Benefits*.

2. Display the table in Print Preview, change the top and left margins to 1.5 inches, and then print the table.
3. Close the Benefits table.

Assessment 4

SORT DATA

1. With **AL1-C1-Griffin.accdb** open, open the Employees table.
2. Experiment with the buttons in the Sort & Filter group in the Home tab and figure out how to sort columns of data in ascending and descending order.
3. Sort the records in the Employees table in ascending order by last name.
4. Save, print, and then close the Employees table.
5. Open the Benefits table and then sort the records in descending order by life insurance amounts.
6. Save, print, and then close the Benefits table.

Visual Benchmark Demonstrate Your Proficiency

CREATE AN ABSENCES TABLE

Note: The starting file for this activity is the file created after completing the previous Skills Check assessments.

1. With the **AL1-C1-Griffin.accdb** database open, create the Absences table shown in Figure 1.18 (using the field names as shown in Figure 1.15 on page 36) with the following specifications:
   a. Use the default AutoNumber data type for column 1. Apply the appropriate data type to the other columns.
   b. Create an appropriate caption and description for the *Emp#*, *AbsenceDate*, and *AbsenceReason* columns.
   c. Apply the default value of *Sick Day* to the *AbsenceReason* column. (You will need to type "Sick Day" in the Expression Builder dialog box.)
2. Save the table and name it *Absences*.
3. Print the table in landscape orientation with 1.5 inch top and left margins.
4. Close the Absences table and then close the **AL1-C1-Griffin.accdb** database.

Figure 1.18 Visual Benchmark

Absences

AbsenceID	Emp#	Absence Date	Absence Reason	Click to Add
1	1065	1/2/2012	Sick Day	
2	1065	1/3/2012	Sick Day	
3	1023	1/5/2012	Sick Day	
4	1023	1/6/2012	Sick Day	
5	1019	1/6/2012	Jury Duty	
6	1019	1/9/2012	Jury Duty	
7	1030	1/9/2012	Sick Day	
8	1052	1/20/2012	Bereavement	
9	1052	1/23/2012	Bereavement	
10	1013	1/23/2012	Sick Day	
11	1095	1/25/2012	Sick Day	
12	1095	1/26/2012	Sick Day	
13	1040	1/27/2012	Sick Day	
14	1083	1/27/2012	Sick Day	
15	1045	1/30/2012	Sick Day	
16	1010	1/30/2012	Sick Day	
17	1093	1/31/2012	Sick Day	
18	1007	1/31/2012	Sick Day	
* (New)			Sick Day	

Case Study Apply Your Skills

You are the office manager for Elite Limousines and your company is switching over to Access for managing company data. The database designer has provided you with the database diagram in Figure 1.19. She wants you to follow the diagram when creating the database.

Figure 1.19 Elite Limousines Database Diagram

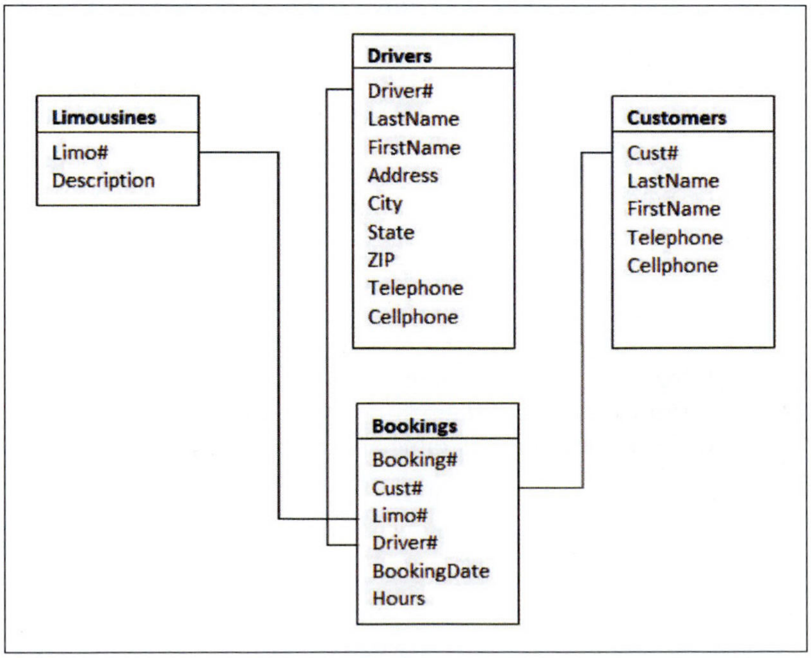

Part 1

Create a new database named **AL1-C1-Elite.accdb** and then create the Limousines table shown in the database diagram in Figure 1.19. The database designer has asked you to include an appropriate caption and description for both fields and change the field size for the *Limo#* field. Type the following records in the table:

Limo#: **01**
Description: **2008 White stretch**

Limo#: **02**
Description: **2008 Black stretch**

Limo#: **04**
Description: **2009 Black minibus**

Limo#: **06**
Description: **2009 Black standard**

Limo#: **08**
Description: **2011 Black SUV stretch**

Limo#: **10**
Description: **2011 Black stretch**

Part 2

With **AL1-C1-Elite.accdb** open, create the Drivers table shown in the database diagram shown in Figure 1.19 and include an appropriate caption and description for the fields and change the field size where appropriate. Type the following records in the table:

Driver#: **101**
LastName: **Brennan**
FirstName: **Andrea**
Address: **4438 Gowan Rd.**
City: **Las Vegas**
State: **NV**
ZIP: **89115**
Telephone: **(702) 555-3481**
Cellphone: **(702) 555-1322**

Driver#: **114**
LastName: **Gould**
FirstName: **Randall**
Address: **330 Aura Ave.**
City: **Las Vegas**
State: **NV**
ZIP: **89052**
Telephone: **(702) 555-1239**
Cellphone: **(702) 555-7474**

Driver#: **120**
LastName: **Martinelli**
FirstName: **Albert**
Address: **107 Cameo Dr.**
City: **Las Vegas**
State: **NV**
ZIP: **89138**
Telephone: **(702) 555-0349**
Cellphone: **(702) 555-6649**

Driver#: **125**
LastName: **Nunez**
FirstName: **Frank**
Address: **4832 Helena St.**
City: **Las Vegas**
State: **NV**
ZIP: **89129**
Telephone: **(702) 555-3748**
Cellphone: **(702) 555-2210**

Part 3

With **AL1-C1-Elite.accdb** open, create the Customers table shown in the database diagram shown in Figure 1.19 and include an appropriate caption and description for the fields and change the field size where appropriate. Type the following records in the table:

Cust#: 1001
LastName: Spencer
FirstName: Maureen
Telephone: (513) 555-3943
Cellphone: (513) 555-4884

Cust#: 1002
LastName: Tsang
FirstName: Lee
Telephone: (702) 555-4775
Cellphone: (702) 555-42116

Cust#: 1028
LastName: Gabriel
FirstName: Nicholas
Telephone: (612) 555-7885
Cellphone: (612) 555-7230

Cust#: 1031
LastName: Marshall
FirstName: Patricia
Telephone: (702) 555-6410
Cellphone: (702) 555-0137

Cust#: 1010
LastName: Chavez
FirstName: Blake
Telephone: (206) 555-3774
Cellphone: (206) 555-3006

Cust#: 1044
LastName: Vanderhage
FirstName: Vernon
Telephone: (213) 555-8846
Cellphone: (213) 555-4635

Part 4

With **AL1-C1-Elite.accdb** open, create the Bookings table shown in the database diagram and include an appropriate caption and description for the fields and change the field size where appropriate. Type the following records in the table:

Booking#: (AutoNumber)
Cust#: 1044
Limo#: 02
Driver#: 114
BookingDate: 07/01/2012
Hours: 6

Booking#: (AutoNumber)
Cust#: 1001
Limo#: 10
Driver#: 120
BookingDate: 07/01/2012
Hours: 8

Booking#: (AutoNumber)
Cust#: 1002
Limo#: 04
Driver#: 101
BookingDate: 07/06/2012
Hours: 8

Booking#: (AutoNumber)
Cust#: 1028
Limo#: 02
Driver#: 125
BookingDate: 07/06/2012
Hours: 4

Booking#: (AutoNumber)
Cust#: 1010
Limo#: 06
Driver#: 125
BookingDate: 07/03/2012
Hours: 3

Booking#: (AutoNumber)
Cust#: 1031
Limo#: 08
Driver#: 120
BookingDate: 07/07/2012
Hours: 5

Automatically adjust the column widths of each table to accommodate the longest entry in each column. Print each of the tables so all records fit on one page.

Microsoft® Access®

CHAPTER 2

Creating Relationships between Tables

PERFORMANCE OBJECTIVES

Upon successful completion of Chapter 2, you will be able to:

- **Define a primary key in a table**
- **Create a one-to-many relationship**
- **Specify referential integrity**
- **Print, edit, and delete relationships**
- **Create a one-to-one relationship**
- **View and edit a subdatasheet**

SNAP Training and Assessment. Simplified.

Tutorials

2.1 Creating a Relationship between Two Tables in a Database

2.2 Printing, Editing, and Deleting Relationships

Access is a relational database program you can use to create tables that have a relation or connection to each other within the same database. When a relationship is established between tables, you can view and edit records in related tables with a subdatasheet. In this chapter, you will learn how to identify a primary key in a table that is unique to that table, how to join tables by creating a relationship between tables, and how to view and edit subdatasheets. Model answers for this chapter's projects appear on the following pages.

Access

Access2010L1C2

Note: Before beginning the projects, copy the Access2010L1C2 subfolder from the Access2010L1 folder on the CD that accompanies this textbook to your storage medium and make Access2010L1C2 the active folder.

Project 1 Establish Relationships between Tables

Orders 7/9/2012

Order#	OrderDate	Supplier#	Product#	UnitsOrdered	Amount
1001	1/2/2012	54	101-S2R	15	$1,945.25
1002	1/2/2012	33	202-CW	5	$124.25
1003	1/2/2012	33	201-CW	5	$99.75
1004	1/2/2012	84	100-05	5	$129.75
1005	1/2/2012	54	101-S3R	10	$1,199.50
1006	1/2/2012	54	101-S3B	10	$1,137.50
1007	1/2/2012	84	100-02	10	$45.95
1008	1/16/2012	25	590-TL	5	$196.25
1009	1/16/2012	35	602-XR	5	$2,145.00
1010	1/16/2012	31	299-W5	10	$752.90
1011	1/16/2012	31	299-W4	10	$752.90
1012	1/16/2012	31	299-W3	10	$752.90
1013	1/16/2012	31	299-W1	8	$602.32
1014	1/16/2012	25	560-TL	20	$397.00
1015	2/1/2012	31	299-M5	10	$887.90
1016	2/1/2012	31	299-M3	10	$887.90
1017	2/1/2012	51	442-1B	10	$1,495.00
1018	2/1/2012	51	443-1B	15	$2,397.75
1019	2/1/2012	99	780-2	10	$1,288.50
1020	2/1/2012	31	299-M2	10	$887.90
1021	2/1/2012	99	647-1	15	$2,999.85
1022	2/15/2012	68	209-XXL	20	$145.80
1023	2/15/2012	10	152-H	15	$44.85
1024	2/15/2012	68	210-L	25	$162.25
1025	2/15/2012	68	210-M	15	$97.35
1026	2/15/2012	68	375-S	20	$199.00
1027	2/15/2012	68	375-M	20	$199.00
1028	2/15/2012	68	371-L	10	$129.50
1029	2/15/2012	68	209-L	25	$173.75
1030	2/15/2012	68	209-XL	25	$180.00
1031	2/15/2012	10	155-35	10	$199.50
1032	2/15/2012	10	155-20	15	$104.25
1033	2/15/2012	51	185-10	10	$310.90

Page 1

Project 1, Orders Table

Products 7/9/2012

Product#	Product	Supplier#	UnitsInStock	UnitsOnOrder	ReorderLevel
100-01	Wrist compass	84	12	0	10
100-02	Multi-function compass	84	8	10	5
100-03	Lenspro plastic compass	84	6	0	5
100-04	Lenspro metal compass	84	8	0	5
100-05	Deluxe map compass	84	2	5	5
101-S1B	SL 0-degrees down sleeping bag, black	54	16	0	15
101-S1R	SL 0-degrees down sleeping bag, red	54	17	0	15
101-S2B	SL 15-degrees synthetic sleeping bag, blac	54	21	0	15
101-S2R	SL 15-degrees synthetic sleeping bag, red	54	12	15	15
101-S3B	SL 20-degrees synthetic sleeping bag, blac	54	8	15	15
101-S3R	SL 20-degrees synthetic sleeping bag, red	54	4	10	10
152-H	Lantern hanger	10	12	15	15
155-20	Shursite angle-head flashlight	10	14	20	20
155-30	Shursite aluminum flashlight	10	8	0	5
155-35	Shursite portable camp light	10	7	10	10
155-45	Shursite propane lantern	10	12	0	10
155-55	Shursite waterproof headlamp	10	7	0	5
200-CW	Four-piece titanium cookware	33	6	0	5
201-CW	Eight-piece stainless steel cookware	33	3	5	5
202-CW	Ten-piece hiker cookware	33	2	5	5
209-L	Gordon wool ski hat, L	68	21	25	25
209-XL	Gordon wool ski hat, XL	68	14	25	25
209-XXL	Gordon wool ski hat, XXL	68	10	20	20
210-L	Tech-lite ski hat, L	68	17	25	25
210-M	Tech-lite ski hat, M	68	6	15	15
210-XL	Tech-lite ski hat, XL	68	22	0	20
299-M1	HT waterproof hiking boots, MS13	31	8	0	10
299-M2	HT waterproof hiking boots, MS12	31	2	10	10
299-M3	HT waterproof hiking boots, MS11	31	6	10	10
299-M4	HT waterproof hiking boots, MS10	31	7	0	10
299-M5	HT waterproof hiking boots, MS9	31	9	10	10
299-W1	HT waterproof hiking boots, WS11	31	5	8	8
299-W2	HT waterproof hiking boots, WS10	31	9	0	8
299-W3	HT waterproof hiking boots, WS9	31	3	10	10
299-W4	HT waterproof hiking boots, WS8	31	2	10	10

Page 1

Project 1, Products Table, Page 1

Products 7/9/2012

Product#	Product	Supplier#	UnitsInStock	UnitsOnOrder	ReorderLevel
299-W5	HT waterproof hiking boots, WS7	31	3	10	10
299-W6	HT waterproof hiking boots, WS6	31	11	0	10
371-L	Lite-tech ski gloves, ML	68	3	10	10
371-M	Lite-tech ski gloves, MM	68	5	0	15
371-XL	Lite-tech ski gloves, MXL	68	3	10	10
371-XXL	Lite-tech ski gloves, MXXL	68	12	0	10
375-L	Lite-tech ski gloves, WL	68	22	0	20
375-M	Lite-tech ski gloves, WM	68	3	20	20
375-S	Lite-tech ski gloves, WS	68	6	20	20
442-1A	Polar backpack, 150BR	51	12	0	10
442-1B	Polar backpack, 150RW	51	9	10	10
443-1A	Polar backpack, 250BR	51	14	0	15
443-1B	Polar backpack, 250RW	51	6	15	15
558-C	ICE snow goggles, clear	68	18	0	15
559-B	ICE snow goggles, bronze	68	22	0	20
560-TL	Thermaline sleeping pad	25	13	20	20
570-TL	Thermaline lightweight cot	25	8	0	5
580-TL	Thermaline camp seat	25	12	0	10
590-TL	Thermaline roll-top table	25	4	5	5
602-XR	Binoculars, 8 x 42	35	3	5	5
602-XT	Binoculars, 10.5 x 45	35	5	0	4
602-XX	Binoculars, 10 x 50	35	7	0	5
647-1	Two-person dome tent	99	10	15	15
648-2	Three-person dome tent	99	5	0	10
651-1	K-2 one-person tent	99	8	0	10
652-2	K-2 two-person tent	99	12	0	10
780-2	Two-person tent	99	17	10	20
804-50	AG freestyle snowboard, X50	70	7	0	10
804-60	AG freestyle snowboard, X60	70	8	0	5
897-L	Lang blunt snowboard	70	8	0	7
897-W	Lang blunt snowboard, wide	70	4	0	3
701-BK	Basic first aid kit	33	8	0	5
703-SP	Medical survival pack	33	8	0	5
185-10	Trail water filter	51	4	10	10
185-50	Trail filter replacement cartridge	51	14	0	10

Page 2

Project 1, Products Table, Page 2

Suppliers 7/9/2012

Supplier#	SupplierName	StreetAddress	City	Prov/State	PostalCode	Telephone	EmailAddress
10	Hopewell, Inc.	5600 Carver Road	Port Moody	BC	V3H 1A4	(604) 555-3843	hopewell@emcp.net
25	Langley Corporatio	805 First Avenue	Burnaby	BC	V3J 1C9	(604) 555-1200	langley@emcp.net
31	Sound Supplies	2104 Union Street	Seattle	WA	98105	(206) 555-4855	ssupplies@emcp.net
33	Bayside Supplies	6705 North Street	Bellingham	WA	98432	(360) 555-6005	bside@emcp.net
35	Emerald City Produ	1059 Pike Street	Seattle	WA	98102	(206) 555-7728	ecproducts@emcp.n
51	Fraser Valley Prod	3894 Old Yale Roa	Abbotsford	BC	V2S 1A9	(604) 555-1455	fvproducts@emcp.n
54	Manning, Inc.	1039 South 22nd	Vancouver	BC	V5K 1R1	(604) 555-0087	manning@emcp.net
68	Freedom Corporati	14 Fourth Avenue	Vancouver	BC	V5K 2C7	(604) 555-2155	freedom@emcp.net
70	Rosewood, Inc.	998 North 42nd St	Vancouver	BC	V5K 2N8	(778) 555-6643	rosewood@emcp.ne
84	Macadam, Inc.	675 Third Street	Vancouver	BC	V5K 2R9	(604) 555-5522	macadam@emcp.ne
99	KL Distributions	402 Yukon Drive	Bellingham	WA	98435	(360) 555-3711	kldist@emcp.net
16	Olympic Suppliers	1773 50th Avenue	Seattle	WA	98101	(206) 555-9488	olysuppliers@emcp.
28	Gorman Company	543 26th Street	Vancouver	BC	V5K 3C5	(778) 555-4550	gormanco@emcp.ne

Project 1, Suppliers Table

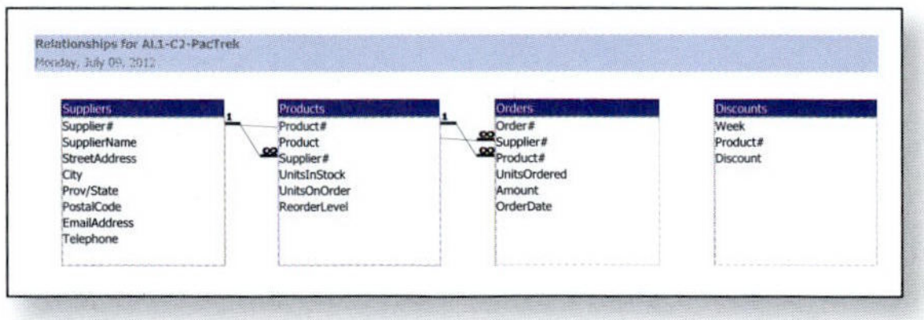

Project 1, Relationships Table

Model Answers

Project 2 Create Relationships and Display Subdatasheets in a Database

Benefits 7/9/2012

Emp#	Health Plan	Dental Plan	Life Insurance	Vacation
1001	☑	☑	$100,000.00	4 weeks
1002	☑	☑	$200,000.00	4 weeks
1003	☐	☑	$150,000.00	3 weeks
1006	☑	☑	$175,000.00	3 weeks
1007	☑	☑	$200,000.00	4 weeks
1010	☑	☑	$185,000.00	4 weeks
1013	☐	☑	$200,000.00	3 weeks
1015	☐	☐	$100,000.00	3 weeks
1019	☑	☑	$75,000.00	3 weeks
1020	☑	☑	$200,000.00	4 weeks
1023	☐	☐	$75,000.00	2 weeks
1025	☐	☐	$100,000.00	3 weeks
1030	☑	☑	$125,000.00	3 weeks
1033	☑	☑	$200,000.00	3 weeks
1040	☑	☑	$200,000.00	3 weeks
1043	☐	☐	$50,000.00	2 weeks
1045	☑	☐	$125,000.00	2 weeks
1050	☑	☑	$85,000.00	3 weeks
1052	☑	☑	$175,000.00	3 weeks
1053	☑	☐	$100,000.00	2 weeks
1063	☑	☑	$150,000.00	2 weeks
1065	☑	☑	$200,000.00	2 weeks
1080	☐	☑	$150,000.00	1 week
1083	☑	☐	$75,000.00	1 week
1085	☑	☑	$125,000.00	1 week
1090	☑	☐	$150,000.00	1 week
1093	☐	☑	$185,000.00	1 week
1095	☑	☑	$200,000.00	1 week
1096	☑	☐	$100,000.00	2 weeks

Page 1

Project 2, Benefits Table

Employees 7/9/2012

Emp#	LastName	FirstName	BirthDate	DeptID	AnnualSalary	HireDate
1001	Navarro	Kate	1/4/1958	HR	$74,500.00	6/1/2004
1002	Sorenson	Lorraine	12/13/1970	RD	$67,700.00	2/1/2005
1003	Zamora	Deanna	7/23/1975	IT	$51,350.00	6/1/2005
1006	Tannenbaum	Sylvia	1/15/1977	HR	$52,455.00	9/1/2005
1007	Michaud	Diane	12/20/1980	A	$57,500.00	10/1/2005
1010	Harrington	Tyler	9/7/1976	DP	$53,350.00	10/1/2005
1013	Frye	Stacy	10/17/1978	RD	$48,800.00	10/1/2005
1015	Brummel	Janelle	2/26/1979	HR	$51,000.00	2/15/2006
1019	Reynolds	Sylvester	3/30/1978	A	$49,750.00	4/1/2006
1020	Alvarado	Melissa	6/22/1977	A	$58,575.00	4/1/2006
1023	Chovanak	Peter	9/23/1980	IT	$40,150.00	5/15/2006
1025	Singh	Jason	8/3/1980	PR	$45,000.00	6/1/2006
1030	Marshall	Charlene	4/7/1980	PR	$42,450.00	7/15/2006
1033	Rowe	Edward	9/12/1976	A	$55,730.00	10/15/2006
1040	Spencer	Christina	5/5/1980	DP	$42,500.00	2/1/2007
1043	Sadler	Daniel	4/20/1971	HR	$68,525.00	10/1/2007
1045	Tanner	Helen	7/23/1981	RD	$38,500.00	4/1/2008
1050	Weatherhill	Kevin	1/4/1981	IT	$39,750.00	9/1/2008
1052	Reeves	Carrie	12/4/1978	PR	$38,550.00	10/1/2008
1053	Yoshimoto	David	10/8/1981	HR	$38,425.00	11/15/2008
1063	Wakefield	Patricia	6/23/1980	DP	$32,600.00	4/1/2009
1065	Quinones	Santos	7/20/1981	DP	$38,750.00	11/15/2009
1080	Vignola	John	8/3/1975	IT	$65,250.00	7/1/2009
1083	Lincoln	William	1/5/1978	HR	$59,750.00	10/15/2010
1085	Hollinger	Eleanor	5/13/1968	PR	$58,000.00	11/15/2010
1090	Koenig	Wesley	9/19/1965	RD	$57,525.00	2/1/2011
1093	McLeod	Yolanda	8/4/1979	A	$61,500.00	6/15/2011
1095	Weyland	Richard	3/8/1980	RD	$45,250.00	7/1/2011
1096	Schwartz	Bryan	5/21/1980	IT	$45,000.00	1/15/2007

Page 1

Project 2, Employees Table

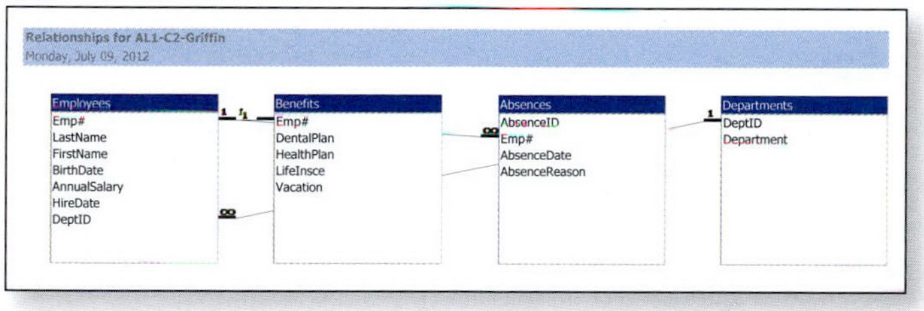

Project 2, Relationships

Project 1 Establish Relationships between Tables — 4 Parts

You will specify primary keys in tables, establish one-to-many relationship between tables, specify referential integrity, and print the relationships. You will also edit and delete a relationship.

Creating Related Tables

Generally, a database management system fits into one of two categories—either a file management system (also sometimes referred to as a ***flat file database***) or a relational database management system. A flat file management system stores all data in a single directory and cannot contain multiple tables. This type of management system is a simple way to store data but it becomes more inefficient as more data is added.

In a ***relational database management system***, like Access, relationships are defined between sets of data allowing greater flexibility in manipulating data and eliminating data redundancy (entering the same data in more than one place).

HINT
Defining a relationship between tables is one of the most powerful features of a relational database management system.

In Project 1, you will define relationships between tables in the AL1-C2-PacTrek.accdb database. Because the tables in the database will be related, information on a product does not need to be repeated in a table on orders. If you used a flat file management system to maintain product information, you would need to repeat the product description for each order.

Determining Relationships

Taking time to plan a database is extremely important. Creating a database with related tables takes even more consideration. You need to determine how to break down the required data and what tables to create to eliminate redundancies. One idea to help you determine the necessary tables in a database is to think of the word "about." For example, the Pacific Trek store needs a table "about" products, another "about" suppliers, and another "about" orders. A table should be only about one subject such as products, suppliers, or orders.

HINT
Use the Table Analyzer Wizard to analyze your tables and restructure them to better conform to relational theory. Start the wizard by clicking the Database Tools tab and then clicking the Analyze Table button.

Along with deciding on the necessary tables for a database, you also need to determine the relationship between tables. The ability to relate, or "join," tables is what makes Access a relational database system. As you learned in Chapter 1, database designers often create a visual representation of the database's structure in a diagram. Figure 2.1 displays the database diagram for the AL1-C2-PacTrek.accdb database. (Some of the fields in the tables have been slightly modified from the database you used in Chapter 1.)

Defining the Primary Key

A database table can contain two different types of keys—a primary key and a foreign key. In the database diagram in Figure 2.1, notice that one field in each table contains an asterisk. The asterisk indicates a ***primary key field***, which is a field that holds data that uniquely identifies each record in a table. For example,

Figure 2.1 AL1-C2-PacTrek.accdb Database Diagram

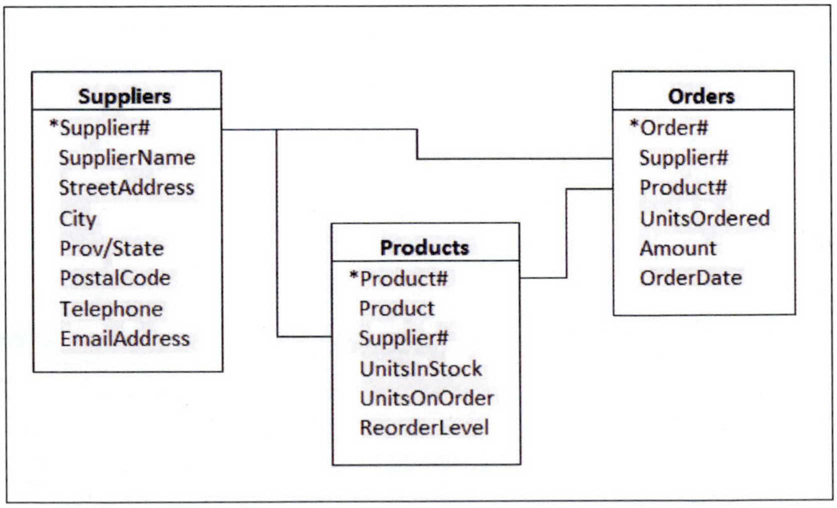

the *Supplier#* field in the Suppliers table contains a unique supplier number for each record in the table, and the *Product#* field in the Products table contains a unique product number for each product. A table can have only one primary key field and it is the field by which the table is sorted whenever the table is opened.

When a new record is added to a table, Access checks to ensure that there is no existing record with the same data in the primary key. If there is, Access displays an error message indicating there are duplicate values and will not allow the record to be saved. When adding a new record to a table, the primary key field cannot be left blank. Access expects a value in each record in the table and this is referred to as ***entity integrity***. If a value is not entered in a field, Access actually enters a null value. A null value cannot be given to a primary key field. Access will not let you close a database containing a primary key field with a null value.

Quick Steps

Define a Primary Key

1. Open table.
2. Click View button.
3. Click desired field.
4. Click Primary Key button.
5. Click Save button.

Primary Key

By default, Access includes the *ID* field as the first field in a table, assigns the AutoNumber data type, and identifies the field as the primary key. The AutoNumber data type assigns the first record a field value of *1* and each new record is assigned the next sequential number. You can use this default field as the primary key or define your own. To determine what field is the primary key or to define a primary key field, you must display the table in Design view. To do this, open the table and then click the View button located at the left side of the Home tab. You can also display the table in Design view by clicking the View button arrow and then clicking *Design View* at the drop-down list. To add or remove a primary key from a field, click the desired field in the *Field Name* column and then click the Primary Key button in the Tools group in the Table Tools Design tab. A key icon is inserted in the field selector bar (blank column to the left of the field names) for the desired field. Figure 2.2 displays the Products table in Design view with the *Product#* field identified as the primary key.

Figure 2.2 Products Table in Design View

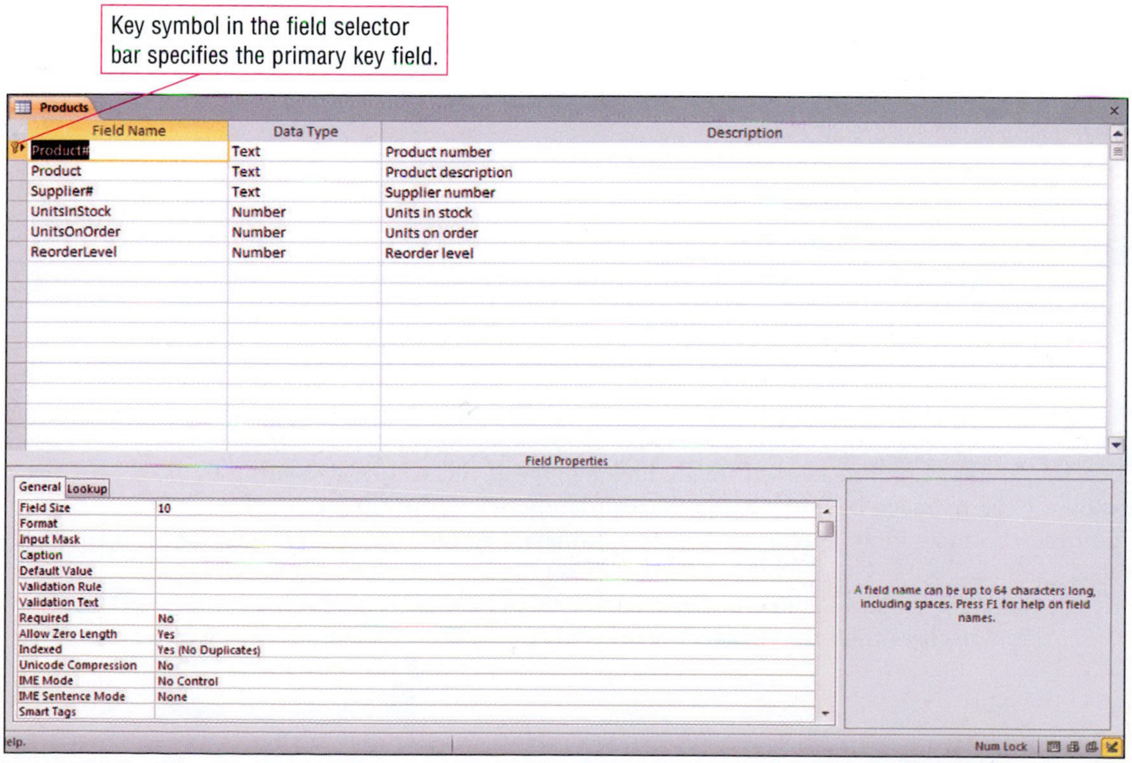

Typically, a primary key field in one table becomes the ***foreign key field*** in a related table. For example, the primary key field *Supplier#* in the Suppliers table is considered the foreign key field in the Orders table. In the Suppliers table, each entry in the *Supplier#* field must be unique since it is the primary key field, but the same supplier number may appear more than once in the *Supplier#* field in the Orders table (such as a situation where more than one product is ordered from the same supplier).

HINT

Access uses a primary key to associate data from multiple tables.

Data in the foreign key field must match data in the primary key field of the related table. For example, any supplier number you enter in the *Supplier#* field in the Orders table must be contained in the Suppliers table. In other words, you would not be making an order to a supplier that does not exist in the Suppliers table. Figure 2.3 identifies the primary and foreign keys in the tables in the AL1-C2-PacTrek.accdb database. Primary keys are identified with *(PK)* and the foreign keys are identified with *(FK)* in the figure.

HINT

You must enter a value in the primary key in every record.

Figure 2.3 AL1-C2-PacTrek.accdb Database Diagram with Primary and Foreign Keys Identified

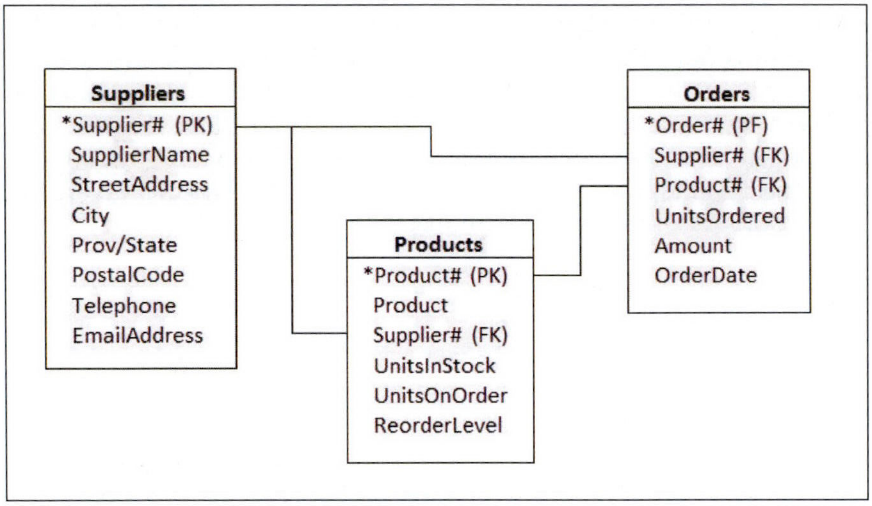

Project 1a Defining a Primary Key Field

Part 1 of 4

1. Open Access.
2. At the New tab Backstage view, click the Open button that displays at the left side of the screen.
3. At the Open dialog box, navigate to the Access2010L1C2 folder on your storage medium and then double-click the database ***AL1-C2-PacTrek.accdb***.
4. Click the Enable Content button in the message bar if the security warning message appears. (The message bar will display immediately below the ribbon.)
5. Open the Products table and then view the primary key field by completing the following steps:
   a. Click the View button located at the left side of the Home tab. (This displays the table in Design view.)

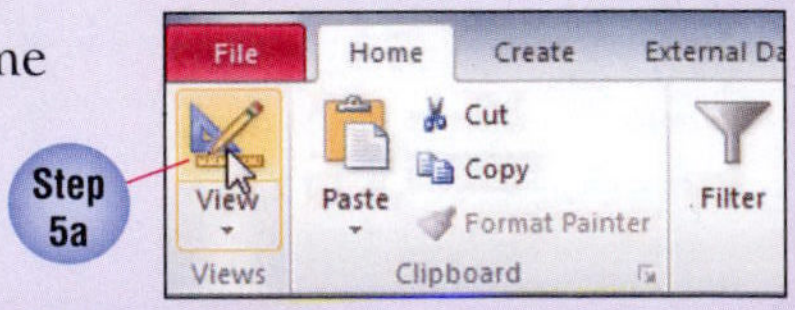

b. In Design view, notice the *Field Name*, *Data Type*, and *Description* columns and notice the information that displays for each field. The first field, *Product#*, is the primary key field and is identified by the key icon that displays in the field selector bar.
c. Click the View button to return to the Datasheet view.
d. Close the Products table.

6. Open the Suppliers table, click the View button to display the table in Design view, and then notice the *Supplier#* field is defined as the primary key field.
7. Click the View button to return to Datasheet view and then close the table.
8. Open the Orders table. (The first field in the Orders table has been changed from the AutoNumber field automatically assigned by Access in the AL1-C2-PacTrek.accdb database to a Text data type field.)
9. Define the *Order#* field as the primary key field by completing the following steps:
   a. Click the View button located at the left side of the Home tab.
   b. With the table in Design view and the *Order#* field selected in the *Field Name* column, click the Primary Key button located in the Tools group in the Table Tools Design tab.

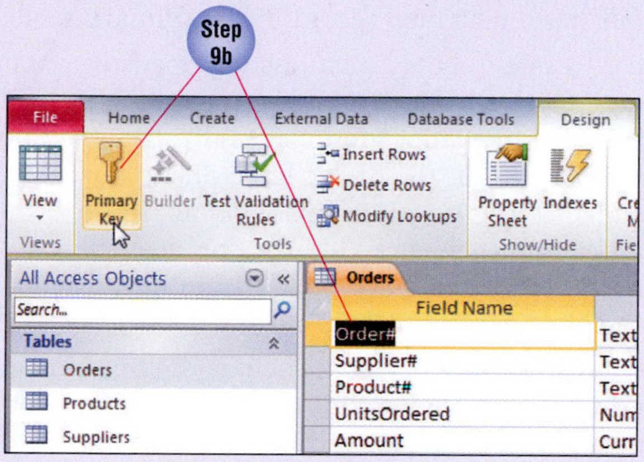

   c. Click the Save button on the Quick Access toolbar.
   d. Click the View button to return the table to Datasheet view.
10. Move the *OrderDate* field by completing the following steps:
   a. Click the *OrderDate* field heading. (This selects the column.)
   b. Position the mouse pointer on the heading, hold down the left mouse button, and then drag to the left until the thick, black vertical line displays immediately left of the *Supplier#* field, and then release the mouse button.

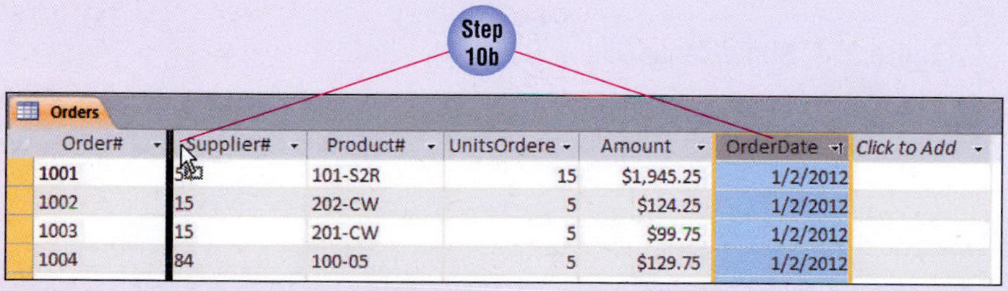

11. Automatically adjust the column widths.
12. Save and then close the Orders table.

Relating Tables in a One-to-Many Relationship

In Access, one table can be related to another, which is generally referred to as performing a ***join***. When tables with a common field are joined, data can be extracted from both tables as if they were one large table. Relate tables to ensure the integrity of the data. For example, in Project 1b, you will create a relationship between the Suppliers table and the Products table. The relationship you establish will ensure that a supplier number cannot be entered in the Products table without first being entered in the Suppliers table. This type of relationship is called a ***one-to-many relationship***, which means that one record in the Suppliers table will match zero, one, or many records in the Products table.

In a one-to-many relationship, the table containing the "one" is referred to as the ***primary table*** and the table containing the "many" is referred to as the ***related table***. Access follows a set of rules known as ***referential integrity***, which enforces consistency between related tables. These rules are enforced when data is updated in related tables. The referential integrity rules ensure that a record added to a related table has a matching record in the primary table.

Relationships

To create a one-to-many relationship, open the database containing the tables to be related. Click the Database Tools tab and then click the Relationships button in the Relationships group. This displays the Show Table dialog box, as shown in Figure 2.4. At the Show Table dialog box, each table that will be related must be added to the Relationships window. To do this, click the first table name to be included and then click Add (or double-click the desired table). Continue in this manner until all necessary table names have been added to the Relationships window and then click the Close button.

At the Relationships window, such as the one shown in Figure 2.5, use the mouse to drag the common field from the primary table (the "one") to the related table (the "many"). This causes the Edit Relationships dialog box to display as shown in Figure 2.6. At the Edit Relationships dialog box, check to make sure the correct field name displays in the *Table/Query* and *Related Table/Query* list boxes and the relationship type at the bottom of the dialog box displays as *One-To-Many*.

Specify the relationship options by choosing *Enforce Referential Integrity*, as well as *Cascade Update Related Fields* and/or *Cascade Delete Related Records*, and then click the Create button. This causes the Edit Relationships dialog box to close and the Relationships window to display showing the relationship between the tables.

Figure 2.4 Show Table Dialog Box

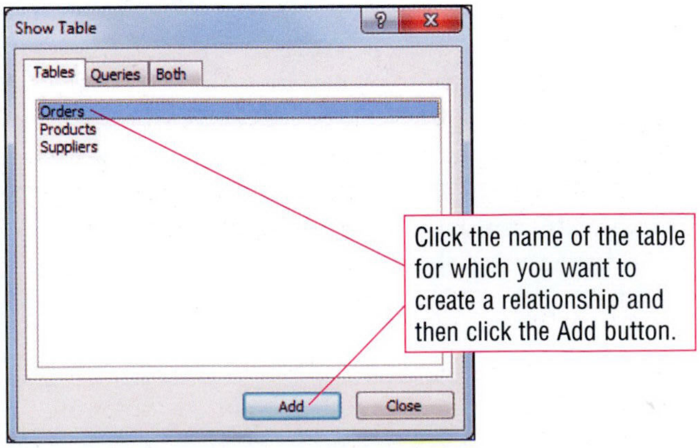

Figure 2.5 Relationships Window

Insert in the Relationships window those tables for which you will create a relationship.

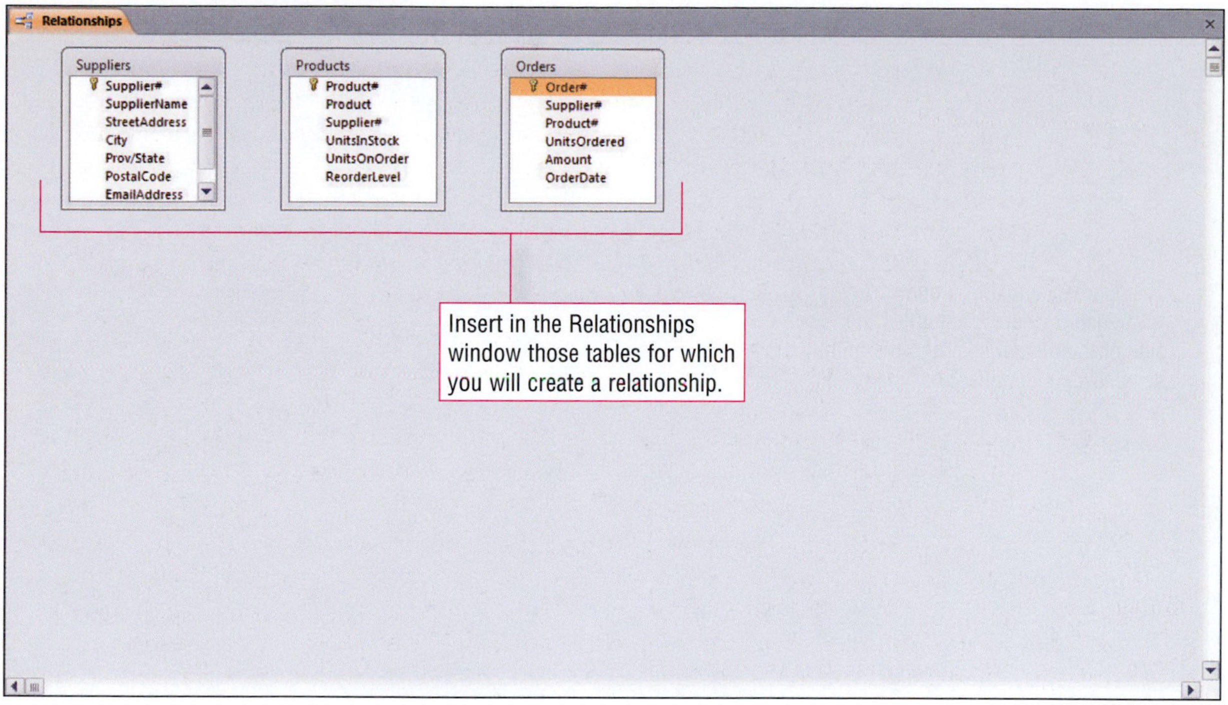

Figure 2.6 Edit Relationships Dialog Box

Make sure the correct field names display here.

Make sure the relationship type is *One-To-Many*.

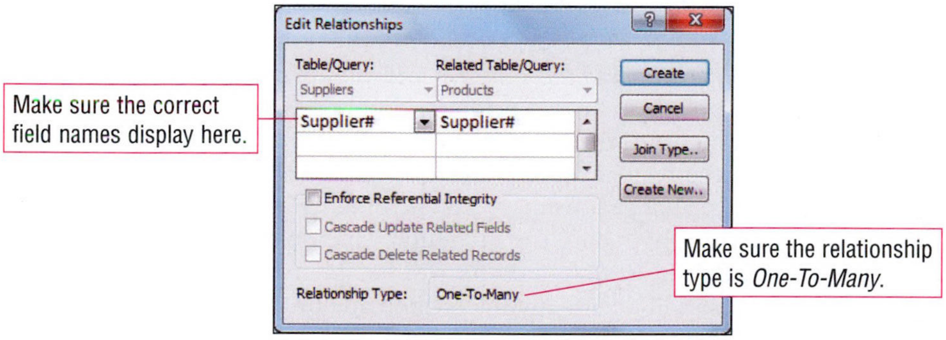

In Figure 2.7, the Suppliers table displays with a black line attached along with the number *1* (signifying the "one" side of the relationship). The black line is connected to the Products table along with the infinity symbol ∞ (signifying the "many" side of the relationship). The black line, called the *join line*, is thick at both ends if the enforce referential integrity option has been chosen. If this option is not chosen, the line is thin at both ends. Click the Save button on the Quick Access toolbar to save the relationship. Close the Relationships window by clicking the Close button located in the upper right corner of the window.

Specifying Referential Integrity

Choose *Enforce Referential Integrity* at the Edit Relationships dialog box to ensure that the relationships between records in related tables are valid. Referential integrity can be set if the field from the primary table is a primary key and the

▼ Quick Steps

Create a One-to-Many Relationship
1. Click Database Tools tab.
2. Click Relationships button.
3. At Show Table dialog box, add tables.
4. In Relationships window, drag "one" field from primary table to "many" field in related table.
5. At Edit Relationships dialog box, enforce referential integrity.
6. Click Create button.
7. Click Save button.

Figure 2.7 One-to-Many Relationship

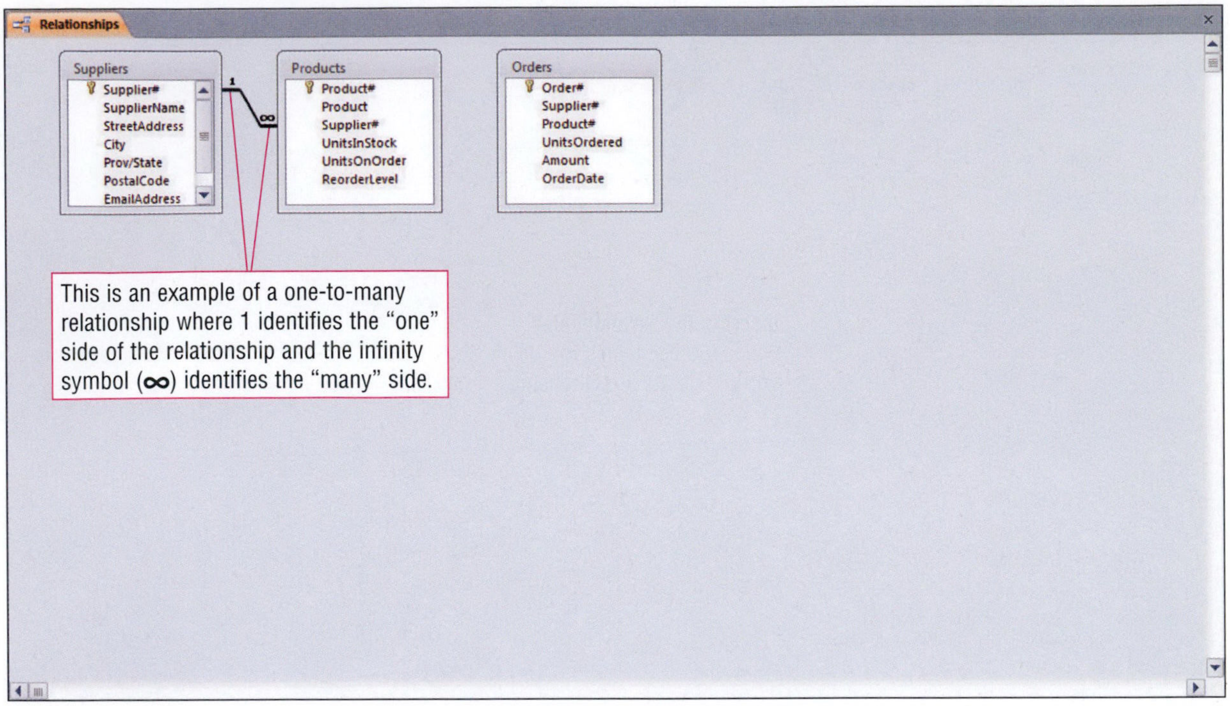

HINT

Referential integrity ensures that a record exists in the "one" table before the record can be entered in the "many" table.

related fields have the same data type. When referential integrity is established, a value for the primary key must first be entered in the primary table before it can be entered in the related table.

If you select only *Enforce Referential Integrity* and the related table contains a record, you will not be able to change a primary key field value in the primary table. You will not be able to delete a record in the primary table if its key value equals a foreign key in the related table. If you choose *Cascade Update Related Fields*, you will be able to change a primary key field value in the primary table and Access will automatically update the matching value in the related table. Choose *Cascade Delete Related Records* and you will be able to delete a record in the primary table and Access will delete any related records in the related table.

In Project 1b, you will be creating a one-to-many relationship between tables in the AL1-C2-PacTrek.accdb database. Figure 2.8 displays the Relationships window with the relationships identified that you will create in the project.

Quick Steps

Print Relationships
1. Click Database Tools tab.
2. Click Relationships button.
3. Click Relationships Report button.
4. Click Print button.
5. Click OK.
6. Click Close button.

Relationship Report

Printing a Relationship

You can print a report displaying the relationships between tables. To do this, display the Relationships window and then click the Relationship Report button in the Tools group. This displays the Relationships report in Print Preview. Click the Print button in the Print group in the Print Preview tab and then click OK at the Print dialog box. After printing the relationships report, click the Close button to close the relationships report.

Figure 2.8 Relationships in the AL1-C2-PacTrek.accdb Database

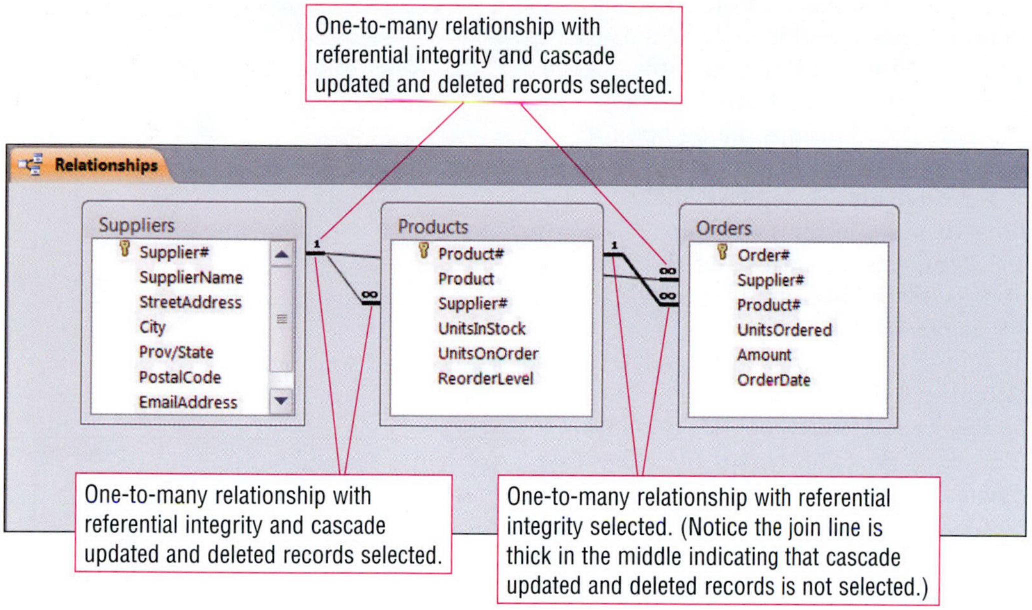

Project 1b Creating Relationships between Tables

Part 2 of 4

1. With the **AL1-C2-PacTrek.accdb** database open, click the Database Tools tab and then click the Relationships button in the Relationships group.
2. If the Show Table dialog box does not display, click the Show Table button in the Relationships group in the Relationship Tools Design tab. At the Show Table dialog box, add the Suppliers, Products, and Orders tables to the Relationships window by completing the following steps:
   a. Click *Suppliers* in the Show Table dialog box list box and then click the Add button.
   b. Click *Products* in the list box and then click the Add button.
   c. Click *Orders* in the list box and then click the Add button.
3. Click the Close button to close the Show Table dialog box.
4. At the Relationships window, drag the *Supplier#* field from the Suppliers table to the Products table by completing the following steps:
   a. Position the arrow pointer on the *Supplier#* field that displays in the Suppliers table.

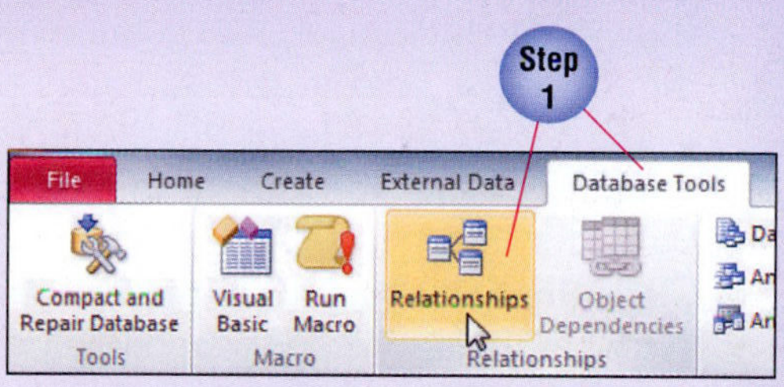

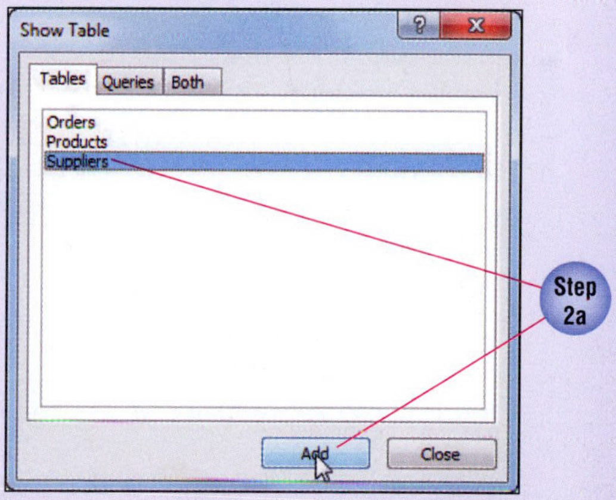

b. Hold down the left mouse button, drag the arrow pointer (with a field icon attached) to the *Supplier#* field in the Products table, and then release the mouse button. (This causes the Edit Relationships dialog box to display.)

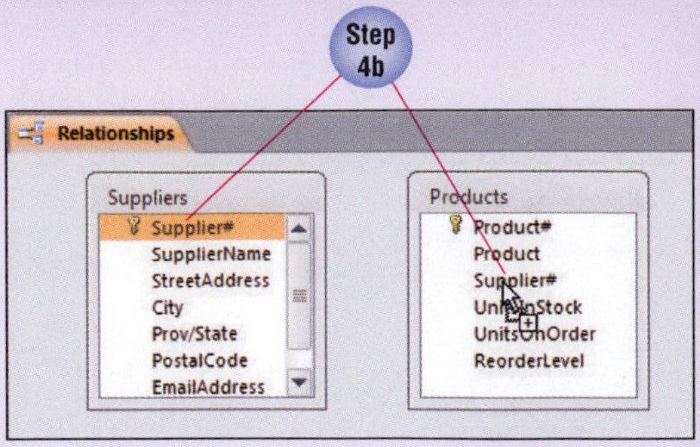

5. At the Edit Relationships dialog box, make sure *Supplier#* displays in the *Table/Query* and *Related Table/Query* list boxes and the relationship type at the bottom of the dialog box displays as *One-To-Many*.
6. Enforce the referential integrity of the relationship by completing the following steps:
   a. Click the *Enforce Referential Integrity* check box to insert a check mark. (This makes the other two options available.)
   b. Click the *Cascade Update Related Fields* check box.
   c. Click the *Cascade Delete Related Records* check box.
7. Click the Create button. (This causes the Edit Relationships dialog box to close and the Relationships window to display showing a thick black line connecting the *Supplier#* field in the Suppliers table to the *Supplier#* field in the Products table. A *1* appears at the Suppliers table side and an infinity symbol ∞ appears at the Products table side of the thick, black line.)

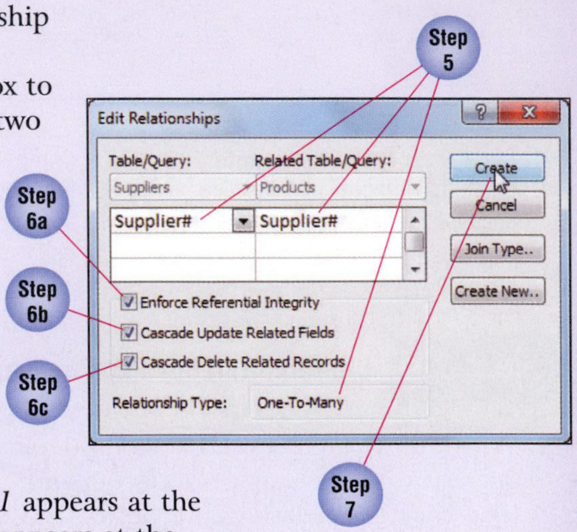

8. Click the Save button on the Quick Access toolbar to save the relationship.
9. With the Relationships window still open, create a one-to-many relationship between the Suppliers table and the Orders table with the *Supplier#* field by completing the following steps:
   a. Position the arrow pointer on the *Supplier#* field that displays in the Suppliers table.
   b. Hold down the left mouse button, drag the arrow pointer (with a field icon attached) to the *Supplier#* field in the Orders table, and then release the mouse button.

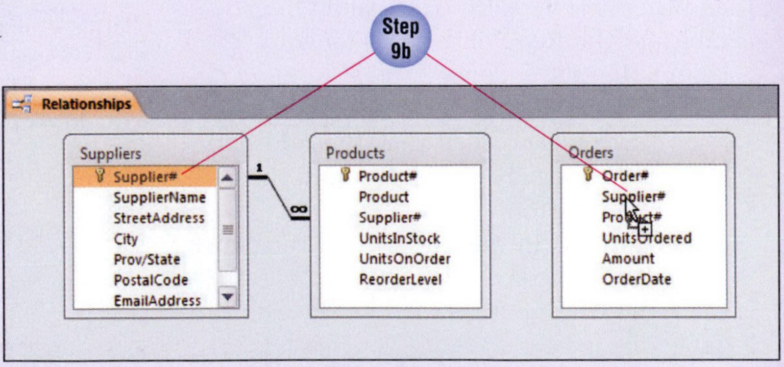

   c. At the Edit Relationships dialog box, make sure *Supplier#* displays in the *Table/Query* and *Related Table/Query* list boxes and the relationship type displays as *One-To-Many*.

d. Click the *Enforce Referential Integrity* check box. (This makes the other two options available.)

e. Click the *Cascade Update Related Fields* check box.

f. Click the *Cascade Delete Related Records* check box.

g. Click the Create button.

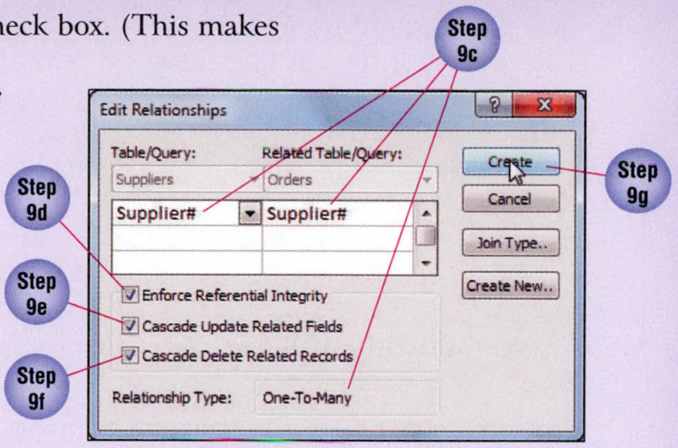

10. Create a one-to-many relationship between the Products table and the Orders table with the *Product#* field by completing the following steps:
    a. Position the arrow pointer on the *Product#* field that displays in the Products table.
    b. Hold down the left mouse button, drag the arrow pointer (with a field icon attached) to the *Product#* field in the Orders table, and then release the mouse button.
    c. At the Edit Relationships dialog box, make sure *Product#* displays in the *Table/Query* and *Related Table/Query* list boxes and the relationship type displays as *One-To-Many*.
    d. Click the *Enforce Referential Integrity* check box. (Do not insert check marks in the other two check boxes.)
    e. Click the Create button.
11. Click the Save button on the Quick Access toolbar to save the relationships.
12. Print the relationships by completing the following steps:
    a. At the Relationships window, click the Relationship Report button in the Tools group. This displays the Relationships report in Print Preview. (If a security notice displays, click the Open button.)
    b. Click the Print button in the Print group at the left side of the Print Preview tab.

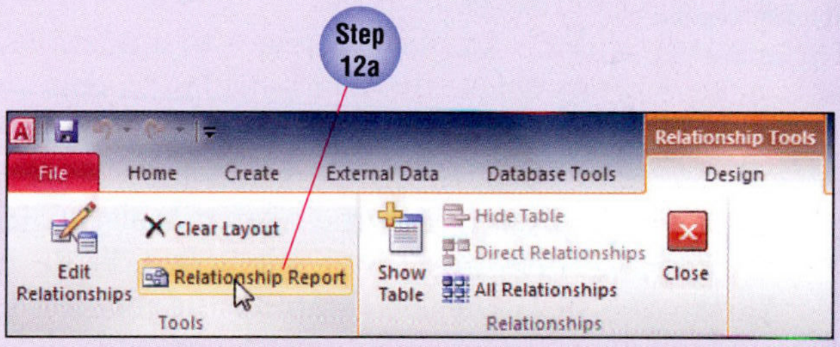

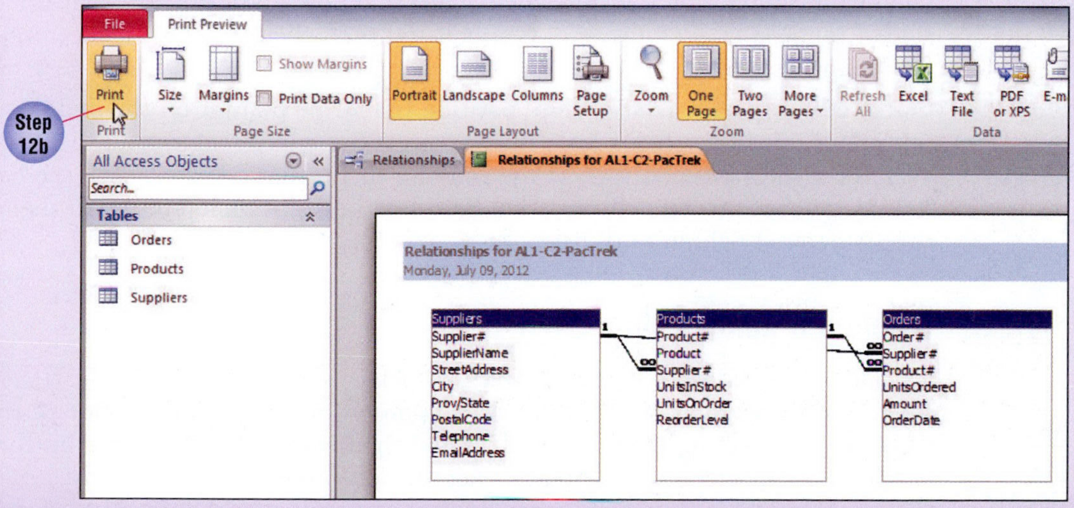

c. Click OK at the Print dialog box.
d. Close the report by clicking the Close button that displays in the upper right corner of the work area.
e. At the message asking if you want to save changes to the design of the report, click No.

13. Close the Relationships window by clicking the Close button that displays in the upper right corner of the work area.

Showing Tables

Show Table

Once a relationship has been established between tables and the Relationships window is closed, clicking the Relationships button causes the Relationships window to display without the Show Table dialog box. To display the Show Table dialog box, click the Show Table button in the Relationships group.

Pacific Trek offers a discount on one product each week. You want to keep track of this information so you decide to create a Discounts table that includes the discount item for each week of the first three months of the year. (You would add a new record to this field each week when the discount item is chosen.) In Project 1c, you will create the Discounts table shown in Figure 2.9 on page 59 and then relate the Products table with the Discounts table using the *Product#* field.

Quick Steps

Edit a Relationship
1. Click Database Tools tab.
2. Click Relationships button.
3. Click Edit Relationships button.
4. Make desired changes at Edit Relationships dialog box.
5. Click OK.

Delete a Relationship
1. Click Database Tools tab.
2. Click Relationships button.
3. Right-click on black line connecting related tables.
4. Click *Delete*.
5. Click Yes.

Edit Relationships

Editing a Relationship

You can make changes to a relationship that has been established between tables or delete the relationship. To edit a relationship, open the database containing the tables with the relationship, click the Database Tools tab, and then click the Relationships button in the Relationships group. This displays the Relationships window with the related tables. Click the Edit Relationships button located in the Tools group to display the Edit Relationships dialog box similar to the one shown in Figure 2.5. Identify the relationship you want to edit by clicking the down-pointing arrow at the right side of the *Table/Query* option box and then clicking the table name containing the "one" field. Click the down-pointing arrow at the right side of the *Related Table/Query* option box and then click the table name containing the "many" field.

To edit a specific relationship, position the arrow pointer on the middle portion of one of the black lines that connects the related tables and then click the right mouse button. At the shortcut menu that displays, click the *Edit Relationship* option. This displays the Edit Relationships dialog box with the specific related field in both list boxes.

Deleting a Relationship

To delete a relationship between tables, display the related tables in the Relationships window. Position the arrow pointer on the middle portion of the black line connecting the related tables and then click the right mouse button. At the shortcut menu that displays, click the left mouse button on *Delete*. At the message asking if you are sure you want to permanently delete the selected relationship from your database, click Yes.

Project 1c Creating a Table and Creating and Editing Relationships

Part 3 of 4

1. With **AL1-C2-PacTrek.accdb** open, create the Discounts table shown in Figure 2.9 by completing the following steps:
   a. Click the Create tab.
   b. Click the Table button in Tables group.
   c. Click the Text button in the Add & Delete group. (This creates and then selects the *Field1* heading that displays to the right of the *ID* column.)
   d. Type **Product#** and then press Enter.
   e. Click the *Text* option at the drop-down list and then type **Discount**.
   f. Click the *ID* heading (the first column), click the down-pointing arrow at the right side of the *Data Type* option box in the Formatting group, and then click *Text* at the drop-down list.
   g. Click in the *Field Size* text box in the Properties group (this selects *255*), type **5**, and then press the Enter key.
   h. Right-click the *ID* heading, click *Rename Field* at the shortcut menu, type **Week**, and then press Enter.
   i. Type the twelve records in the Discounts table as shown in Figure 2.9 on page 59.

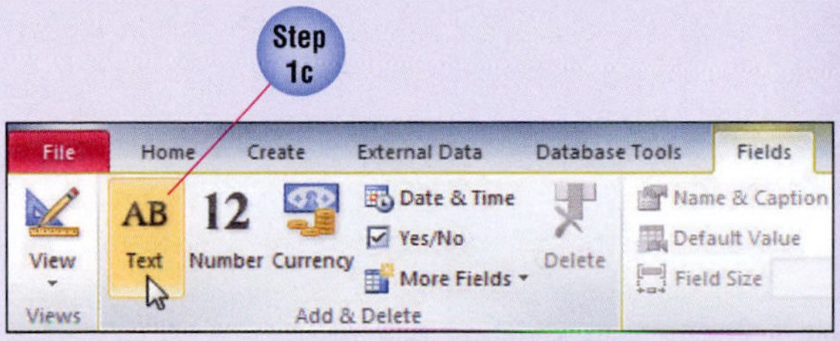

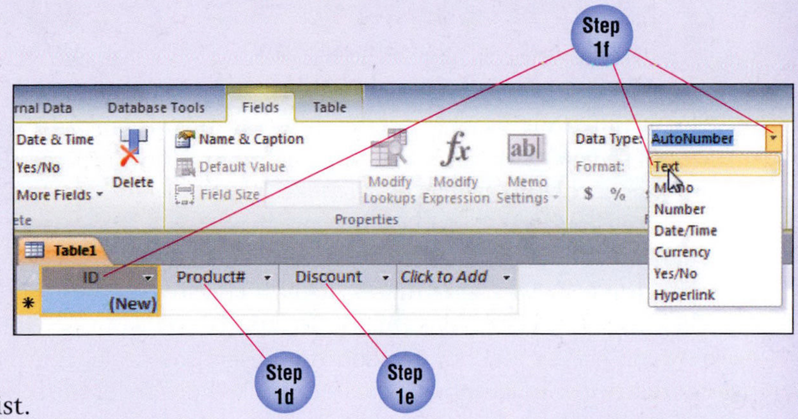

2. After typing the records, save the table by completing the following steps:
   a. Click the Save button on the Quick Access toolbar.
   b. At the Save As dialog box, type **Discounts** and then press Enter.
3. Close the Discounts table.
4. Create a relationship from the Products table to the Discounts table by completing the following steps:
   a. Click the Database Tools tab and then click the Relationships button in the Relationships group.
   b. Display the Show Table dialog box by clicking the Show Table button in the Relationships group.
   c. At the Show Table dialog box, double-click the Discounts table.
   d. Click the Close button to close the Show Table dialog box.

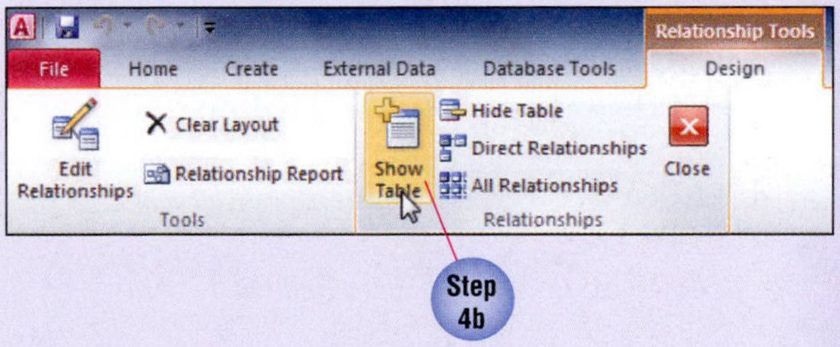

5. At the Relationships window, create a one-to-many relationship between the Products table and the Discounts table with the *Product#* field by completing the following steps:
   a. Drag the *Product#* field from the Products table to the *Product#* field in the Discounts table.

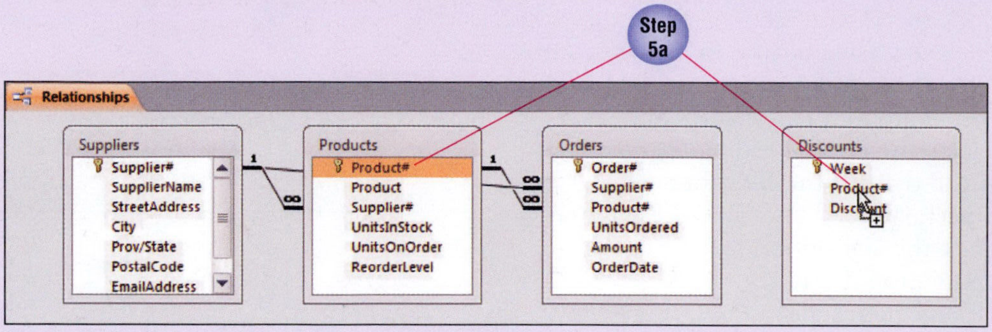

   b. At the Edit Relationships dialog box, make sure *Product#* displays in the *Table/Query* and *Related Table/Query* list boxes and the relationship type at the bottom of the dialog box displays as *One-To-Many*.
   c. Click the *Enforce Referential Integrity* check box.
   d. Click the *Cascade Update Related Fields* check box.
   e. Click the *Cascade Delete Related Records* check box.
   f. Click the Create button. (At the Relationships window, notice the join line that displays between the Products table and the Discounts table. If a message occurs telling you that the relationship cannot be created, click the Cancel button. Open the Discounts table, check to make sure the product numbers are entered correctly in the *Product#* field, and then close the Discounts table. Try again to create the relationship.)
6. Edit the one-to-many relationship between the *Product#* field in the Products table and the Orders table and specify that you want to cascade updated and related fields and cascade and delete related records by completing the following steps:
   a. Click the Edit Relationships button located in the Tools group in the Relationship Tools Design tab.
   b. At the Edit Relationships dialog box, click the down-pointing arrow at the right side of the *Table/Query* option box and then click *Products* at the drop-down list.
   c. Click the down-pointing arrow at the right side of the *Related Table/Query* option box and then click *Orders* at the drop-down list.
   d. Click the *Cascade Update Related Fields* check box.
   e. Click the *Cascade Delete Related Records* check box.
   f. Click the OK button.

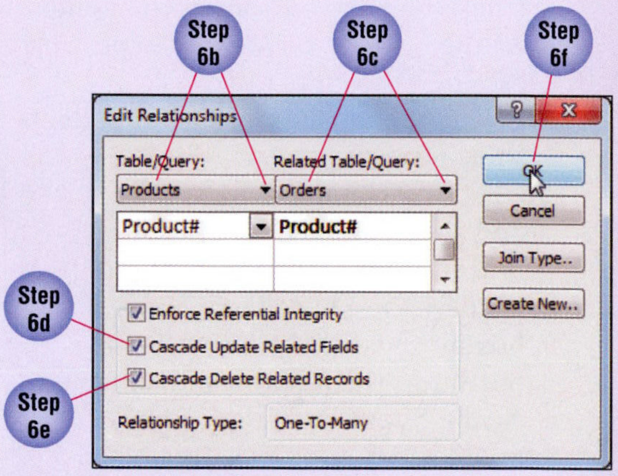

7. Click the Save button on the Quick Access toolbar to save the relationship.
8. Print the relationships by completing the following steps:
   a. Click the Relationship Report button in the Tools group.
   b. Click the Print button in the Print group.
   c. Click OK at the Print dialog box.
   d. Close the report by clicking the Close button that displays in the upper right corner of the work area.

e. At the message asking if you want to save changes to the design of the report, click No.
9. Delete the relationship between the Products table and the Discounts table by completing the following steps:
   a. Position the arrow pointer on the thin portion of the black line connecting the *Product#* field in the Products table with the *Product#* field in the Discounts table and then click the right mouse button.
   b. Click the *Delete* option at the shortcut menu.

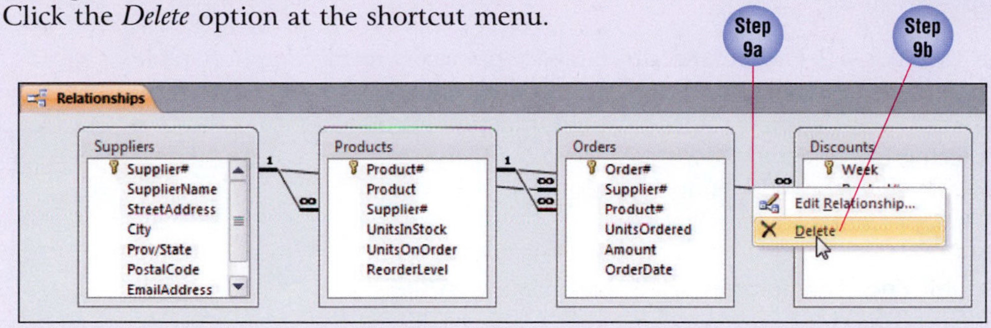

   c. At the message asking if you are sure you want to permanently delete the selected relationship from your database, click Yes.
10. Click the Save button on the Quick Access toolbar to save the relationship.
11. Print the relationships by completing the following steps:
   a. Click the Relationship Report button in the Tools group.
   b. Click the Print button in the Print group.
   c. Click OK at the Print dialog box.
   d. Close the report by clicking the Close button that displays in the upper right corner of the work area.
   e. At the message asking if you want to save changes to the design of the report, click No.
12. Close the Relationships window by clicking the Close button that displays in the upper right corner of the work area.

Figure 2.9 Discounts Table

Discounts

Week	Product#	Discount	Click to Add
01-01	652-2	15%	
01-02	155-45	20%	
01-03	443-1A	20%	
01-04	202-CW	15%	
02-01	804-60	10%	
02-02	652-2	15%	
02-03	101-S1B	5%	
02-04	560-TL	20%	
03-01	652-2	20%	
03-02	602-XX	15%	
03-03	100-05	10%	
03-04	652-2	15%	
*			

Inserting and Deleting Records in Related Tables

In the relationship established in Project 1b, a record must first be added to the Suppliers table before a related record can be added to the Products table. This is because you chose the *Enforce Referential Integrity* option at the Edit Relationships dialog box. Because you chose the two options *Cascade Update Related Fields* and *Cascade Delete Related Records*, records in the Suppliers table (the primary table) can be updated and/or deleted and related records in the Products table (related table) will be automatically updated or deleted.

Project 1d Editing and Updating Records — Part 4 of 4

1. With the **AL1-C2-PacTrek.accdb** database open, open the Suppliers table.
2. Change two supplier numbers in the Suppliers table (Access will automatically change the numbers in the Products table and the Orders table) by completing the following steps:
   a. Double-click the field value *15* that displays in the *Supplier#* field.
   b. Type **33**.
   c. Double-click the field value *42* that displays in the *Supplier#* field.
   d. Type **51**.
   e. Click the Save button on the Quick Access toolbar.
   f. Close the Suppliers table.
   g. Open the Products table and notice that the supplier number *15* changed to *33* and supplier number *42* changed to *51*.
   h. Close the Products table.

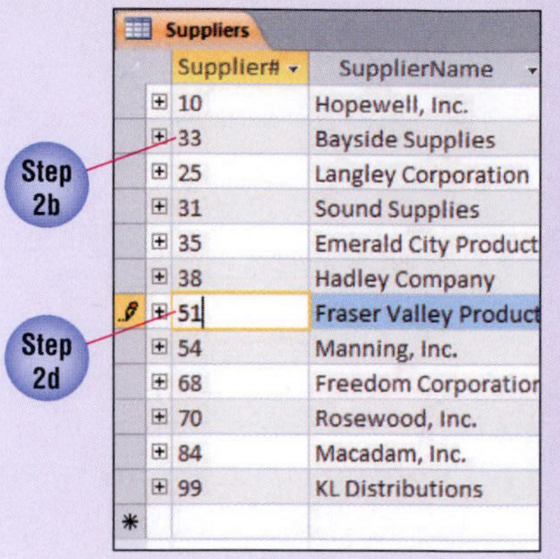

Supplier#	SupplierName
10	Hopewell, Inc.
33	Bayside Supplies
25	Langley Corporation
31	Sound Supplies
35	Emerald City Product
38	Hadley Company
51	Fraser Valley Product
54	Manning, Inc.
68	Freedom Corporatior
70	Rosewood, Inc.
84	Macadam, Inc.
99	KL Distributions

3. Open the Suppliers table and then add the following records:

   Supplier#: **16**
   SupplierName: **Olympic Suppliers**
   StreetAddress: **1773 50th Avenue**
   City: **Seattle**
   Prov/State: **WA**
   PostalCode: **98101**
   Telephone: **(206) 555-9488**
   EmailAddress: **olysuppliers@emcp.net**

   Supplier#: **28**
   SupplierName: **Gorman Company**
   StreetAddress: **543 26th Street**
   City: **Vancouver**
   Prov/State: **BC**
   PostalCode: **V5K 3C5**
   Telephone: **(778) 555-4550**
   EmailAddress: **gormanco@emcp.net**

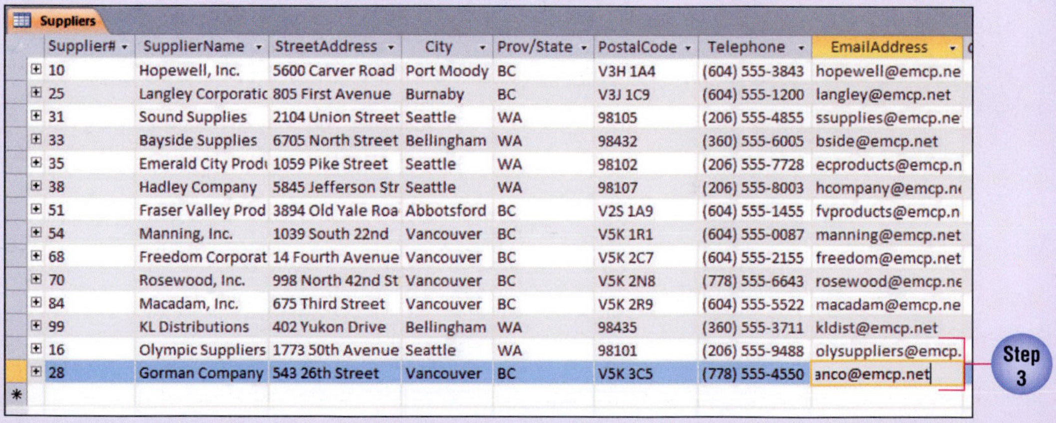

Supplier#	SupplierName	StreetAddress	City	Prov/State	PostalCode	Telephone	EmailAddress
10	Hopewell, Inc.	5600 Carver Road	Port Moody	BC	V3H 1A4	(604) 555-3843	hopewell@emcp.ne
25	Langley Corporatic	805 First Avenue	Burnaby	BC	V3J 1C9	(604) 555-1200	langley@emcp.net
31	Sound Supplies	2104 Union Street	Seattle	WA	98105	(206) 555-4855	ssupplies@emcp.ne
33	Bayside Supplies	6705 North Street	Bellingham	WA	98432	(360) 555-6005	bside@emcp.net
35	Emerald City Prodı	1059 Pike Street	Seattle	WA	98102	(206) 555-7728	ecproducts@emcp.n
38	Hadley Company	5845 Jefferson Str	Seattle	WA	98107	(206) 555-8003	hcompany@emcp.n
51	Fraser Valley Prod	3894 Old Yale Roa	Abbotsford	BC	V2S 1A9	(604) 555-1455	fvproducts@emcp.n
54	Manning, Inc.	1039 South 22nd	Vancouver	BC	V5K 1R1	(604) 555-0087	manning@emcp.net
68	Freedom Corporat	14 Fourth Avenue	Vancouver	BC	V5K 2C7	(604) 555-2155	freedom@emcp.net
70	Rosewood, Inc.	998 North 42nd St	Vancouver	BC	V5K 2N8	(778) 555-6643	rosewood@emcp.ne
84	Macadam, Inc.	675 Third Street	Vancouver	BC	V5K 2R9	(604) 555-5522	macadam@emcp.ne
99	KL Distributions	402 Yukon Drive	Bellingham	WA	98435	(360) 555-3711	kldist@emcp.net
16	Olympic Suppliers	1773 50th Avenue	Seattle	WA	98101	(206) 555-9488	olysuppliers@emcp.
28	Gorman Company	543 26th Street	Vancouver	BC	V5K 3C5	(778) 555-4550	anco@emcp.net

4. Delete the record for supplier number *38* (*Hadley Company*). At the message telling you that relationships that specify cascading deletes are about to cause records in this table and related tables to be deleted, click Yes.
5. Display the table in Print Preview, change to landscape orientation, and then print the table.

6. Close the Suppliers table.
7. Open the Products table and then add the following records to the table:

Product#: **701-BK**
Product: **Basic first aid kit**
Supplier#: **33**
UnitsInStock: **8**
UnitsOnOrder: **0**
ReorderLevel: **5**

Product#: **703-SP**
Product: **Medical survival pack**
Supplier#: **33**
UnitsInStock: **8**
UnitsOnOrder: **0**
ReorderLevel: **5**

Product#: **185-10**
Product: **Trail water filter**
Supplier#: **51**
UnitsInStock: **4**
UnitsOnOrder: **10**
ReorderLevel: **10**

Product#: **185-50**
Product: **Trail filter replacement cartridge**
Supplier#: **51**
UnitsInStock: **14**
UnitsOnOrder: **0**
ReorderLevel: **10**

8. Display the Products table in Print Preview, change to landscape orientation, change the top and bottom margins to 0.4 inches and then print the table. (The table will print on two pages.)
9. Close the Products table.
10. Open the Orders table and then add the following record:

Order#: **1033**
OrderDate: **2/15/2012**
Supplier#: **51**
Product#: **185-10**
UnitsOrdered: **10**
Amount: **$310.90**

11. Print and then close the Orders table.
12. Close the **AL1-C2-PacTrek.accdb** database.

Project 2 Create Relationships and Display Subdatasheets in a Database

2 Parts

You will open a company database and then create one-to-many relationships between tables as well as a one-to-one relationship. You will also display and edit subdatasheets.

Creating a One-to-One Relationship

You can create a ***one-to-one relationship*** between tables in which each record in the first table matches only one record in the second table and one record in the second table matches only one record in the first table. A one-to-one relationship is not as common as a one-to-many relationship since the type of information used to create the relationship can be stored in one table. A one-to-one relationship is generally used when you want to break a large table with many fields into two smaller tables.

HINT
The Relationships window displays any relationship you have defined between tables.

In Project 2a, you will create a one-to-one relationship between the Employees table and the Benefits table. Each record in the Employees table and each record in the Benefits table pertains to one employee. These two tables could be merged into one but the data in each table is easier to manage when separated. Figure 2.10 shows the relationships you will define between the tables in the AL1-C2-Griffin.accdb database. The Benefits table and the Departments table have been moved down so you can more easily see the relationships.

Figure 2.10 AL1-C2-Griffin.accdb Table Relationships

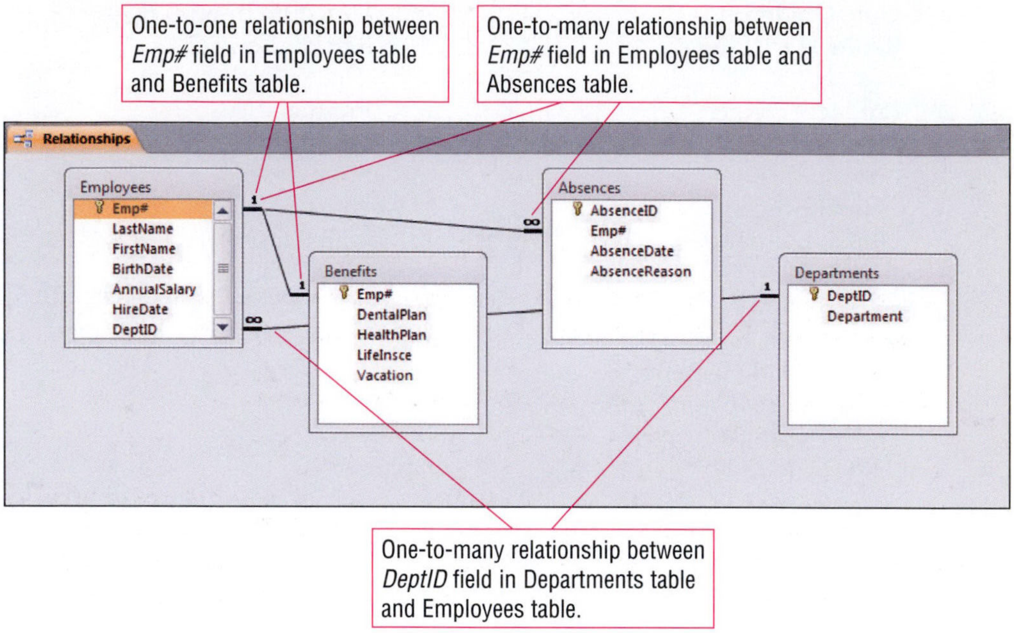

Project 2a Creating One-to-Many and One-to-One Relationships

Part 1 of 2

1. Open **AL1-C2-Griffin.accdb** and enable the contents.
2. Click the Database Tools tab.
3. Click the Relationships button in the Relationships group.
4. At the Show Table dialog box, add all of the tables to the Relationships window by completing the following steps:
   a. Double-click *Employees* in the Show Table dialog box list box. (This inserts the table in the Relationships window.)
   b. Double-click *Benefits* in the list box.
   c. Double-click *Absences* in the list box.
   d. Double-click *Departments* in the list box.
   e. Click the Close button to close the Show Table dialog box.
5. At the Relationships window, create a one-to-many relationship with the *Emp#* field in the Employees table as the "one" and the *Emp#* field in the Absences table the "many" by completing the following steps:
   a. Position the arrow pointer on the *Emp#* field that displays in the Employees table.

b. Hold down the left mouse button, drag the arrow pointer (with a field icon attached) to the *Emp#* field in the Absences table, and then release the mouse button. (This causes the Edit Relationships dialog box to display.)

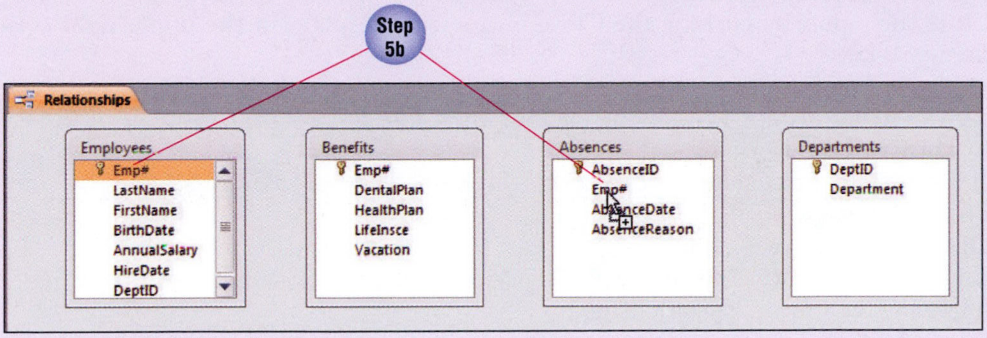

c. At the Edit Relationships dialog box, make sure *Emp#* displays in the *Table/Query* and *Related Table/Query* list boxes and the relationship type at the bottom of the dialog box displays as *One-To-Many*.
d. Click the *Enforce Referential Integrity* check box to insert a check mark.
e. Click the *Cascade Update Related Fields* check box.
f. Click the *Cascade Delete Related Records* check box.
g. Click the Create button. (A *1* appears at the Employees table side and an infinity symbol ∞ appears at the Absences table side of the thick, black line.)

6. Complete steps similar to those in Step 5 to create a one-to-many relationship with the *DeptID* field in the Departments table the "one" and the *DeptID* field in the Employees table the "many."
7. Create a one-to-one relationship with the *Emp#* field in the Employees table and the *Emp#* field in the Benefits table by completing the following steps:
   a. Position the arrow pointer on the *Emp#* field in the Employees table.
   b. Hold down the left mouse button, drag the arrow pointer to the *Emp#* field in the Benefits table, and then release the mouse button. (This displays the Edit Relationships dialog box; notice at the bottom of the dialog box that the relationship type displays as *One-To-One*.)
   c. Click the *Enforce Referential Integrity* check box to insert a check mark.
   d. Click the *Cascade Update Related Fields* check box.
   e. Click the *Cascade Delete Related Records* check box.
   f. Click the Create button. (Notice that a *1* appears at the side of the Employees table and at the side of the Benefits table, indicating a one-to-one relationship.)
8. Click the Save button on the Quick Access toolbar to save the relationships.

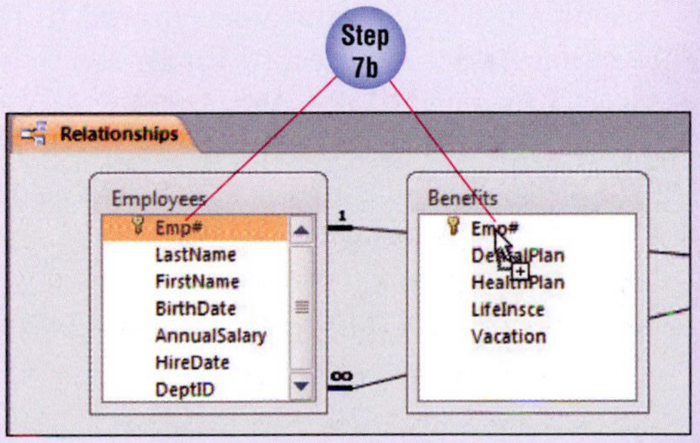

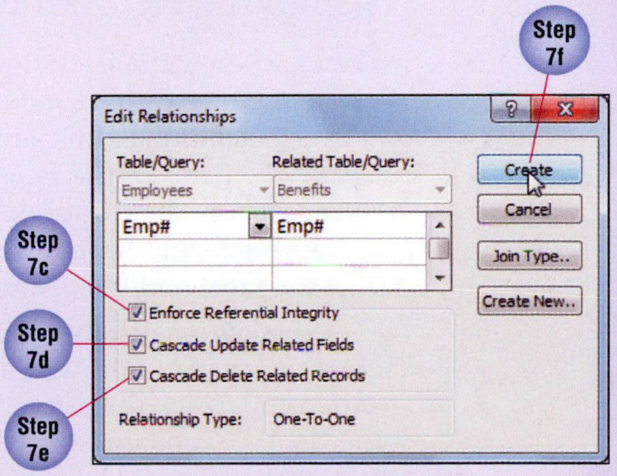

9. Print the relationships by completing the following steps:
   a. Click the Relationship Report button in the Tools group.
   b. Click the Print button in the Print group.
   c. Click OK at the Print dialog box.
   d. Close the report by clicking the Close button that displays in the upper right corner of the work area.
   e. At the message asking if you want to save changes to the design of the report, click No.
10. Close the Relationships window by clicking the Close button that displays in the upper right corner of the work area.
11. Add a record to and delete a record from the Employees and Benefits tables by completing the following steps:
   a. Open the Employees table.
   b. Click the New button in the Records group in the Home tab and then type the following data in the specified field:
      Emp#: **1096**
      LastName: **Schwartz**
      FirstName: **Bryan**
      BirthDate: **5/21/1980**
      DeptID: **IT**
      AnnualSalary: **$45,000.00**
      HireDate: **1/15/2007**
   c. Delete the record for Trevor Sargent (employee number 1005). At the message telling you that relationships that specify cascading deletes are about to cause records in this table and related tables to be deleted, click Yes.
   d. Save, print, and then close the Employees table.
12. Open the Benefits table and notice that the record for Trevor Sargent was deleted but the new employee record you entered in the Employees table is not reflected in the Benefits table. Add a new record for Bryan Schwartz with the following information:
      Emp#: **1096**
      Health Plan: (Leave check mark.)
      Dental Plan: (Press spacebar to remove check mark.)
      Life Insurance: **$100,000.00**
      Vacation: **2 weeks**
13. Print and then close the Benefits table.

Displaying Related Records in a Subdatasheet

When a relationship is established between tables, you can view and edit records in related tables with a ***subdatasheet***. Figure 2.11 displays the Employees table with the subdatasheet displayed for the employee Kate Navarro. The subdatasheet displays the fields in the Benefits table related to Kate Navarro. Use this subdatasheet to view information and also to edit information in the Employees table as well as the Absences table. Changes made to fields in a subdatasheet affect the table and any related table.

Access automatically inserts plus symbols (referred to as ***expand indicators***) before each record in a table that is joined to another table by a one-to-many relationship. Click the expand indicator and, if the table is related to only one other table, a subdatasheet containing fields from the related table displays below the record as shown in Figure 2.11. To remove the subdatasheet, click the minus sign (referred to as the ***collapse indicator***) preceding the record. (The plus symbol turns into the minus symbol when a subdatasheet displays.)

Figure 2.11 Table with Subdatasheet Displayed

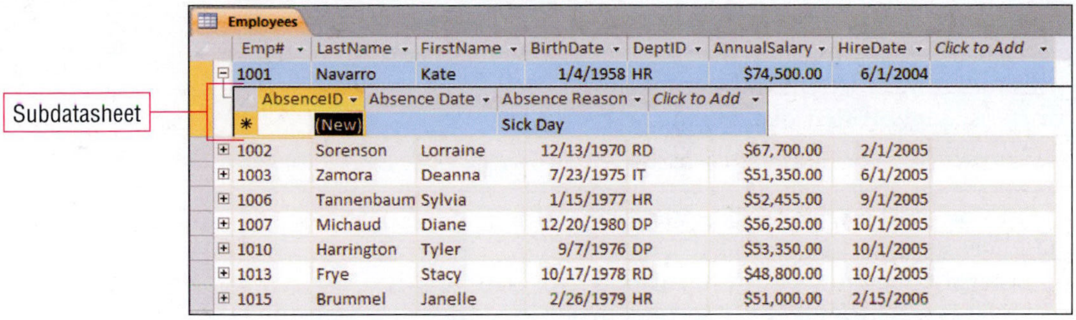

Emp#	LastName	FirstName	BirthDate	DeptID	AnnualSalary	HireDate	Click to Add
1001	Navarro	Kate	1/4/1958	HR	$74,500.00	6/1/2004	
1002	Sorenson	Lorraine	12/13/1970	RD	$67,700.00	2/1/2005	
1003	Zamora	Deanna	7/23/1975	IT	$51,350.00	6/1/2005	
1006	Tannenbaum	Sylvia	1/15/1977	HR	$52,455.00	9/1/2005	
1007	Michaud	Diane	12/20/1980	DP	$56,250.00	10/1/2005	
1010	Harrington	Tyler	9/7/1976	DP	$53,350.00	10/1/2005	
1013	Frye	Stacy	10/17/1978	RD	$48,800.00	10/1/2005	
1015	Brummel	Janelle	2/26/1979	HR	$51,000.00	2/15/2006	

Subdatasheet for 1001:

AbsenceID	Absence Date	Absence Reason	Click to Add
(New)		Sick Day	

If a table has more than one relationship defined, clicking the expand indicator will display the Insert Subdatasheet dialog box shown in Figure 2.12. At this dialog box, click the desired table in the Tables list box and then click OK. You can also display the Insert Subdatasheet dialog box by clicking the More button in the Records group in the Home tab, pointing to *Subdatasheet*, and then clicking *Subdatasheet*. You can display subdatasheets for all records by clicking the More button, pointing to *Subdatasheet*, and then clicking *Expand All*. Remove all subdatasheets by clicking the More button, pointing to *Subdatasheet*, and then clicking *Collapse All*.

If a table is related to two or more tables, specify the desired subdatasheet at the Subdatasheet dialog box. If you decide to display a different subdatasheet, remove the subdatasheet first before selecting the next subdatasheet. Do this by clicking the More button, pointing to *Subdatasheet*, and then clicking *Remove*.

Quick Steps

Display Subdatasheet

1. Open table.
2. Click expand indicator at left side of desired record.
3. Click desired table at Insert Subdatasheet dialog box.
4. Click OK.

Figure 2.12 Insert Subdatasheet Dialog Box

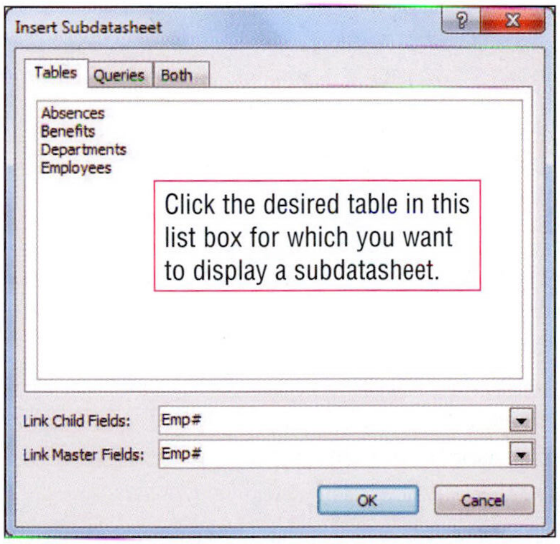

Project 2b Viewing and Editing a Subdatasheet Part 2 of 2

1. With the **AL1-C2-Griffin.accdb** database open, open the Employees table.
2. Display a subdatasheet by clicking the expand indicator (plus symbol) that displays at the left side of the first row (the row for Kate Navarro).

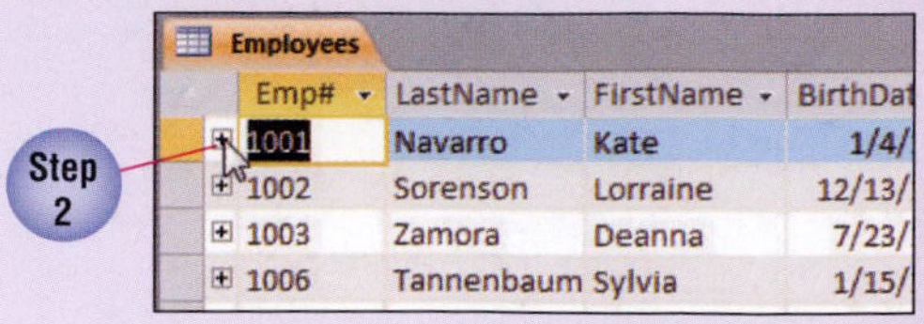

3. Remove the subdatasheet by clicking the collapse indicator (minus sign) that displays at the left side of the record for Kate Navarro.
4. Display subdatasheets for all of the records by clicking the More button in the Records group, pointing to *Subdatasheet*, and then clicking *Expand All*.

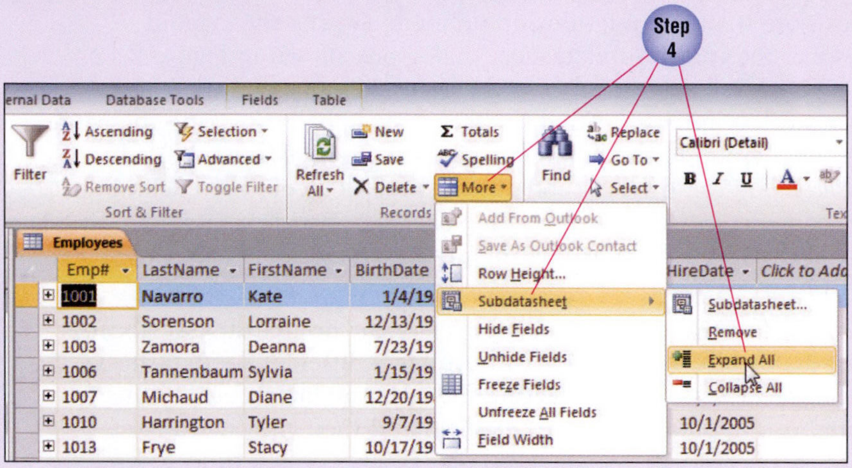

5. Remove the display of all subdatasheets by clicking the More button, pointing to *Subdatasheet*, and then clicking *Collapse All*.
6. Remove the connection between the Employees and Absences table by clicking the More button, pointing to *Subdatasheet*, and then clicking *Remove*. (Notice that the expand indicators [plus symbols] no longer display before each record.)

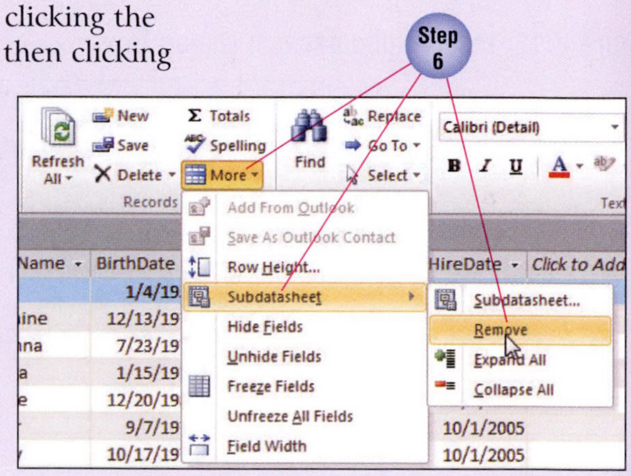

7. Suppose that the employee, Diane Michaud, has moved to a different department and has had an increase in salary. Display the Benefits subdatasheet and make changes to fields in the Employees table and the Benefits table by completing the following steps:
   a. Click the More button in the Records group, point to *Subdatasheet*, and then click *Subdatasheet* at the side menu.

b. At the Insert Subdatasheet dialog box, click *Benefits* in the list box and then click OK.
c. Change the department ID for the *Diane Michaud* record from *DP* to *A*.
d. Change the salary from *$56,250.00* to *$57,500.00*.
e. Click the expand indicator (plus symbol) that displays at the left side of the *Diane Michaud* record.
f. Insert a check mark in the *Dental Plan* check box and change her vacation from 3 weeks to 4 weeks.

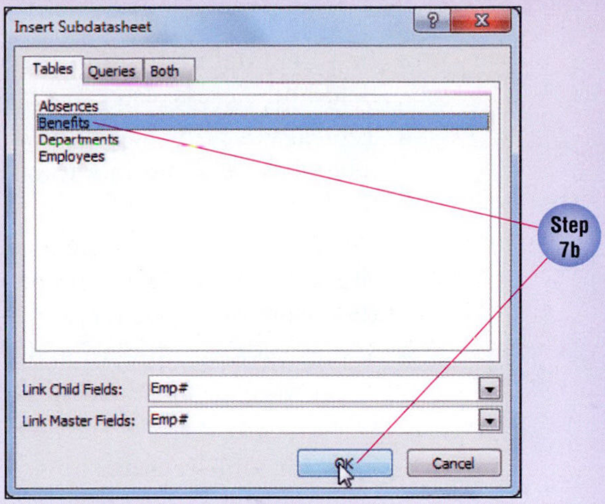

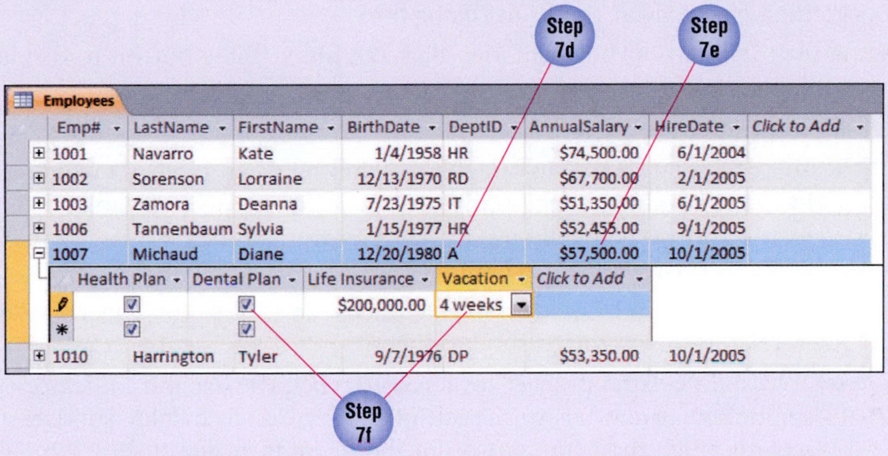

g. Click the collapse indicator (minus symbol) that displays at the left side of the *Diane Michaud* record.

8. Click the Save button on the Quick Access toolbar.
9. Print and then close the Employees table.
10. Open, print, and then close the Benefits table.
11. Close the **AL1-C2-Griffin.accdb** database.

Chapter Summary

- Access is a relational database software program in which you can create tables that have a relation or connection to one another.
- When planning a table, take time to determine how to break down the required data and what relationships will need to be defined to eliminate data redundancies.
- Generally, one field in a table must be unique so that one record can be distinguished from another. A field with a unique value is considered a primary key field.

- A table can have only one primary key field and it is the field by which the table is sorted whenever the table is opened.
- In a field defined as a primary key field, duplicate values are not allowed in the field and Access also expects a value in each record in the primary key field.
- Typically, a primary key field in one table becomes the foreign key field in a related table. Data in a foreign key field must match data in the primary key field of the related tables.
- In Access, you can relate a table to another by performing a join. When tables that have a common field are joined, you can extract data from both tables as if they were one large table.
- You can create a one-to-many relationship between tables. In this relationship, a record must be added to the "one" table before it can be added to the "many" table.
- To print table relationships, display the Relationships window, click the Relationship Report button, click the Print button in the Print Preview tab, and then click OK at the Print dialog box.
- At the Relationships window, click the Show Table button to display the Show Table dialog box.
- You can edit or delete a relationship between tables.
- You can create a one-to-one relationship between tables in which each record in the first table matches only one record in the related table. This type of relationship is generally used when you want to break a large table with many fields into two smaller tables.
- When a relationship is established between tables, you can view and edit fields in related tables with a subdatasheet.
- To display a subdatasheet for a record, click the expand indicator (plus symbol) that displays to the left of the record. To display subdatasheets for all records, click the More button in the Records group in the Home tab, point to *Subdatasheet*, and then click *Expand All*.
- Display the Insert Subdatasheet dialog box by clicking the More button in the Reports group in the Home tab, pointing to *Subdatasheet*, and then clicking *Subdatasheet*.
- Turn off the display of a subdatasheet by clicking the collapse indicator (minus symbol) at the beginning of the record. To turn off the display of subdatasheets for all records, click the More button, point to *Subdatasheet*, and then click *Collapse All*.

Commands Review

FEATURE	RIBBON, GROUP	BUTTON	OPTION
Primary key	Table Tools Design, Tools		
Relationships window	Database Tools, Relationships		
Relationships report window	Relationship Tools Design, Relationships		
Show Table dialog box	Relationship Tools Design, Relationships		
Edit Relationships dialog box	Relationship Tools Design, Tools		
Insert Subdatasheet dialog box	Home, Records		Subdatasheet, Subdatasheet

Concepts Check Test Your Knowledge

Completion: In the space provided at the right, indicate the correct term, symbol, or command.

1. A database table can contain a foreign key field and this type of key field. ____________________
2. In Access, one table can be related to another, which is generally referred to as performing this. ____________________
3. Open a table, click the View button in the Home tab, and the table displays in this view. ____________________
4. In a one-to-many relationship, the table containing the "one" is referred to as this. ____________________
5. In a one-to-many relationship, the table containing the "many" is referred to as this. ____________________
6. In a one-to-many relationship, Access follows a set of rules that enforces consistency between related tables and is referred to as this. ____________________
7. In related tables, this symbol displays near the black line next to the related table. ____________________
8. The black line that connects related tables is referred to as this. ____________________

9. Establish this type of relationship between tables in which each record in the first table matches only one record in the second table and one record in the second table matches only one record in the first table. ____________

10. The plus symbol that displays at the beginning of a record in a related table is referred to as this. ____________

11. The minus symbol that displays at the beginning of a record in a related table with a subdatasheet displayed is referred to as this. ____________

12. Display subdatasheets for all records by clicking the More button, pointing to *Subdatasheet*, and then clicking this option. ____________

Skills Check Assess Your Performance

The database designer for Copper State Insurance has created the database diagram, shown in Figure 2.13, to manage company data. You will open the Copper State Insurance database and maintain and create tables that follow the diagram.

Figure 2.13 Copper State Insurance Database Design

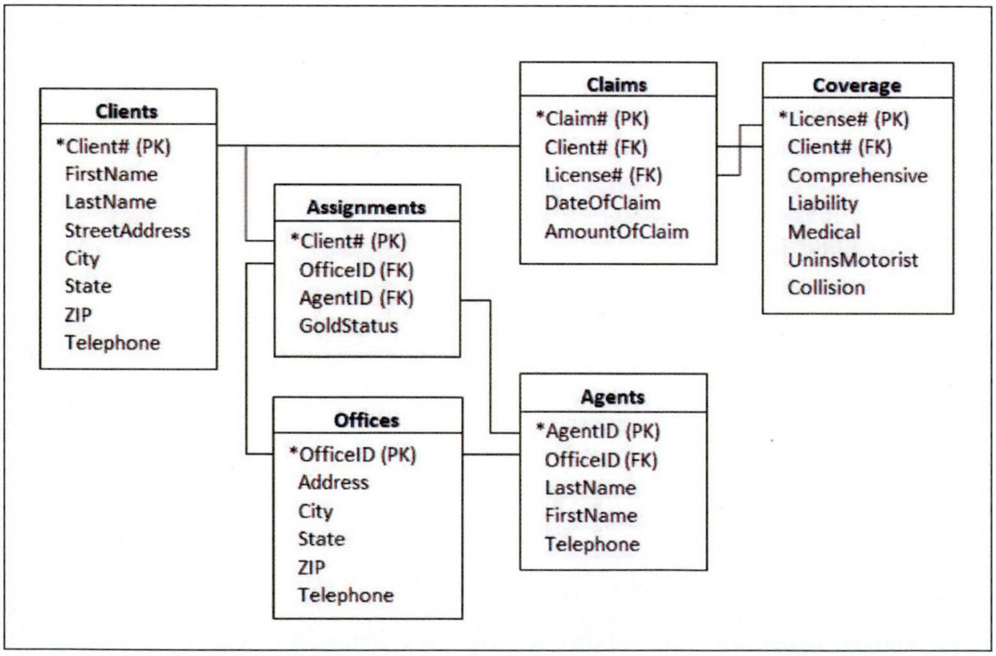

Assessment 1

CREATE RELATIONSHIPS IN AN INSURANCE COMPANY DATABASE

1. Open the **AL1-C2-CopperState.accdb** database and enable the contents.
2. Open the Claims table.
3. Display the table in Design view, define the *Claim#* field as the primary key field, click the Save button on the Quick Access toolbar, and then close the Claims table.
4. Display the Relationships window and then insert the Clients, Claims, and Coverage tables.
5. Create a one-to-many relationship with the *Client#* field in the Clients table the "one" and the *Client#* field in the Claims table the "many." Enforce referential integrity and cascade fields and records.
6. Create a one-to-many relationship with the *Client#* field in the Clients table the "one" and the *Client#* field in the Coverage table the "many." Enforce referential integrity and cascade fields and records.
7. Create a one-to-many relationship with the *License#* field in the Coverage table the "one" and the *License#* field in the Claims table the "many." Enforce referential integrity and cascade fields and records.
8. Save and then print the relationships.
9. Close the relationships report without saving it and close the Relationships window.

Assessment 2

CREATE A NEW TABLE AND RELATE THE TABLE

1. With **AL-C2-CopperState.accdb** open, create the Offices table shown in Figure 2.14. Change the data type of the first column to *Text*. (Do this with the *Data Type* option box in the Formatting group in the Table Tools Fields tab.) Change the field size to *2*. Change the default value for the *State* field to *AZ*.
2. After typing the records, adjust the column widths to accommodate the longest entry in each column and then save the Offices table.
3. Print and then close the Offices table.
4. Display the Relationships window and then add the Offices table and the Assignments table to the window.
5. Create a one-to-many relationship with the *OfficeID* field in the Offices table the "one" and the *OfficeID* field in the Assignments table the "many." Enforce referential integrity and cascade fields and records.
6. Create a one-to-one relationship with the *Client#* field in the Clients table and the *Client#* field in the Assignments table. Enforce referential integrity and cascade fields and records.
7. Save and then print the relationships in landscape orientation. To do this, click the Landscape button in the Page Layout group in Print Preview.
8. Close the relationships report without saving it and then close the Relationships window.

Figure 2.14 Assessment 2 Offices Table

Offices

	OfficeID	Address	City	State	ZIP	Telephone	Click to Add
	GN	North 51st Avenue	Glendale	AZ	85305	(623) 555-8800	
	GW	West Bell Road	Glendale	AZ	85312	(623) 555-4300	
	PG	Grant Street West	Phoenix	AZ	85003	(602) 555-6200	
	PM	McDowell Road	Phoenix	AZ	85012	(602) 555-3800	
	SE	East Thomas Road	Scottsdale	AZ	85251	(480) 555-5500	
	SN	North 68th Street	Scottsdale	AZ	85257	(480) 555-9000	
*				AZ			

Assessment 3

DELETE AND EDIT RECORDS IN TABLES

1. With **AL1-C2-CopperState.accdb** open, open the Clients table.
2. Delete the record for Harold McDougal (client number 9879). (At the message telling you that relationships that specify cascading deletes are about to cause records in this table and related tables to be deleted, click Yes.)
3. Delete the record for Vernon Cook (client number 7335). (At the message telling you that relationships that specify cascading deletes are about to cause records in this table and related tables to be deleted, click Yes.)
4. Change the client number for Paul Vuong from *4300* to *2560*.
5. Print the Clients table in landscape orientation and then close the table.
6. Open the Claims table, print the table, and then close the table. (The Claims table initially contained two entries for client number 9879 and one entry for 7335. These entries were deleted automatically when you deleted the records in the Clients table.)

Assessment 4

DISPLAY AND EDIT RECORDS IN A SUBDATASHEET

1. With the **AL1-C2-CopperState.accdb** database open, open the Clients table.
2. Click the expand indicator (plus symbol) that displays at the left side of the record for Erin Hagedorn. At the Insert Subdatasheet dialog box, click *Claims* in the list box, and then click OK.
3. Change the amount of the claim from *$1,450.00* to *$1,797.00*, change Erin's street address from *4818 Oakes Boulevard* to *763 51st Avenue*, and change her ZIP code from *85018* to *85014*.
4. Click the collapse indicator (minus symbol) that displays at the left side of the record for Erin Hagedorn.
5. Remove the connection between the Clients and Claims tables by clicking the More button in the Records group in the Home tab, pointing to *Subdatasheet*, and then clicking *Remove*.
6. Click the More button in the Records group, point to *Subdatasheet*, and then click *Subdatasheet*.
7. At the Insert Subdatasheet dialog box, click *Coverage* in the list box and then click OK.
8. Expand all records by clicking the More button, pointing to *Subdatasheet*, and then clicking *Expand All*.
9. Change the telephone number for Claire Azevedo (client number 1379) from *480-555-2154* to *480-555-2143* and insert check marks in the *Medical* field and the *UninsMotorist* field.
10. Change the last name of Joanne Donnelly (client number 1574) to *Marquez* and remove the check mark from the *Collision* field.
11. Display the record for Brenda Lazzuri (client number 3156) and then insert a check mark in the *UninsMotorist* field and the *Collision* field for both vehicles.
12. Click in any field heading and then collapse all records.
13. Remove the connection between the Clients and Coverage tables.
14. Save, print, and then close the Clients table. (Make sure the table displays in landscape orientation.)
15. Open the Coverage table, print the table, and then close the table.

Visual Benchmark Demonstrate Your Proficiency

CREATE AN AGENTS TABLE

Note: The starting file for this activity is the file created after completing the previous Skills Check assessments.

1. With the **AL1-C2-CopperState.accdb** database open, create the Agents table shown in Figure 2.15. You determine the data types and field sizes. Create a more descriptive caption for each field name and create a description for each field.
2. Save, print, and then close the Agents table.
3. Display the Relationships window, add the Agents table to the window, and then create the two additional relationships shown in the diagram in Figure 2.16. (You determine what table contains the "one" and what table contains the "many.")
4. Save and then print the relationships in landscape orientation and then close the Relationships window.
5. Open the Agents table.
6. Change the AgentID for Troy Bajema from *04* to *05*.
7. Change Joanna Logan's last name from *Logan* to *Janowski*.
8. Print and then close the Agents table.
9. Open the Assignments table, print the table, and then close the table. (Notice that the *04* AgentID in the Assignments table was changed to *05*. This is because the tables are related and the changes you make in the primary table are made automatically in the related table.)
10. Close the **AL1-C2-CopperState.accdb** database.

Figure 2.15 Visual Benchmark Agents Table

Agents

AgentID	OfficeID	FirstName	LastName	Telephone	Click to Add
02	PM	Marsha	Brundage	(602) 555-3805	
03	PM	Greg	Dunlap	(602) 555-3811	
04	PM	Troy	Bajema	(602) 555-3815	
11	PG	Joanna	Logan	(480) 555-6255	
12	PG	Dana	Rosario	(480) 555-6243	
14	PG	Dennis	Stansbury	(480) 555-6218	
21	GW	Kerri	Watanabe	(623) 555-4300	
23	GW	Roland	Linderman	(623) 555-4328	
25	GW	Marian	Monaghan	(623) 555-4317	
32	GN	Eugene	Kessler	(623) 555-8803	
34	GN	Bruce	Neville	(623) 555-8823	
35	GN	Cheryl	Rhoades	(623) 555-8811	
41	SE	Nina	Chesheva	(480) 555-5502	
42	SE	Steven	Gabrielson	(480) 555-5510	
45	SE	Laura	Mellema	(480) 555-5528	
51	SN	Michael	Tan	(480) 555-9002	
52	SN	Angie	Santagelo	(480) 555-9006	
53	SN	Martin	Osborne	(480) 555-9010	
*					

Figure 2.16 Visual Benchmark Table Relationships Diagram

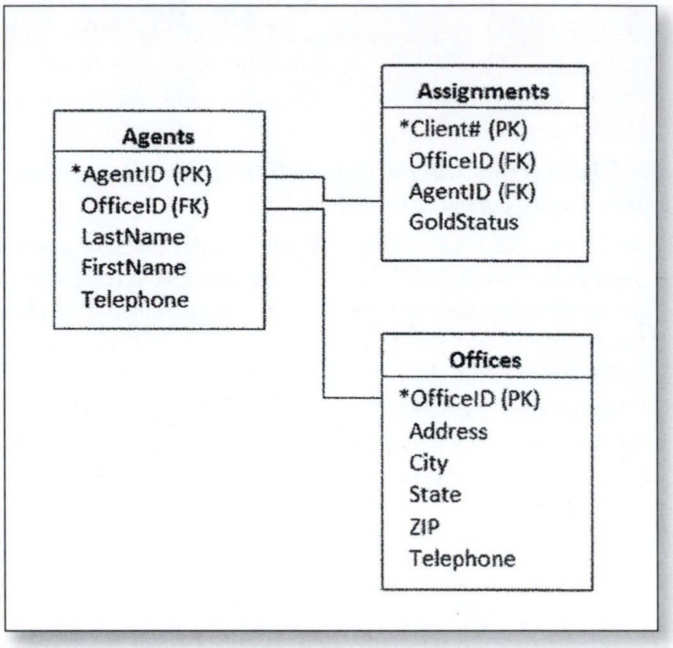

Case Study Apply Your Skills

You are the manager for Gold Star Cleaning Services and your company is switching over to Access for managing company data. The database designer has provided you with the database diagram in Figure 2.17. He wants you to follow the diagram when creating the database.

Figure 2.17 Gold Star Cleaning Services Database Diagram

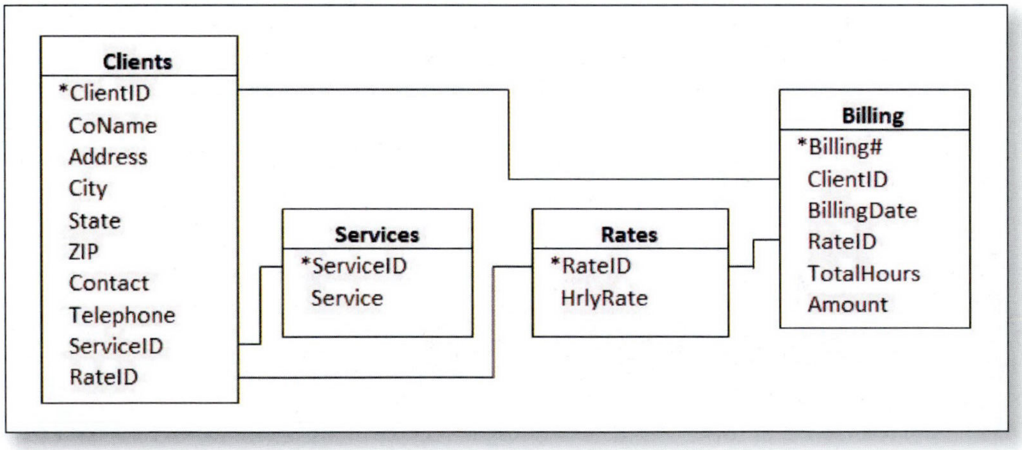

Part 1

Create a new database named **AL1-C2-GoldStar.accdb** and then create the Clients table shown in the database diagram. The database designer has asked you to include an appropriate caption and description for the fields. Specify a field size of *3* for the *ClientID* field, *4* for the *ServiceID* field, and *1* for the *RateID* field. You determine the field size for the *State*, *ZIP*, and *Telephone* fields. He also wants you to set the default value for the *City* field to *St. Louis* and the *State* field to *MO*. Type the following records in the table:

ClientID: **101**
CoName: **Smithson Realty**
Address: **492 Papin Street**
City: (default value)
State: (default value)
ZIP: **63108**
Contact: **Danielle Snowden**
Telephone: **(314) 555-3588**
ServiceID: **GS-1**
RateID: **B**

ClientID:**102**
CoName: **Air-Flow Systems**
Address: **1058 Pine Street**
City: (default value)
State: (default value)
ZIP: **63186**
Contact: **Nick Cline**
Telephone: **(314) 555-9452**
ServiceID: **GS-3**
RateID: **A**

ClientID: **107**
CoName: **Mainstreet Mortgage**
Address: **North 22nd Street**
City: (default value)
State: (default value)
ZIP: **63134**
Contact: **Ted Farrell**
Telephone: **(314) 555-7744**
ServiceID: **GS-1**
RateID: **D**

ClientID: **110**
CoName: **Firstline Finances**
Address: **104 Scott Avenue**
City: (default value)
State: (default value
ZIP: **63126**
Contact: **Robert Styer**
Telephone: **(314) 555-8343**
ServiceID: **GS-2**
RateID: **A**

ClientID:**112**
CoName: **GB Construction**
Address: **988 Lucas Avenue**
City: (default value)
State: (default value)
ZIP: **63175**
Contact: **Joy Ewing**
Telephone: **(314) 555-0036**
ServiceID: **GS-1**
RateID: **C**

ClientID: **115**
CoName: **Simko Equipment**
Address: **1200 Market Street**
City: (default value)
State: (default value)
ZIP: **63140**
ZIP: **Dale Aldrich**
Telephone: **(314) 555-3315**
ServiceID: **GS-3**
RateID: **C**

Create the Services table shown in the database diagram. Change the *ServiceID* field size to 4. Type the following records in the table:

ServiceID: **GS-1**
Service: **Deep cleaning all rooms and surfaces, garbage removal, recycling, carpet cleaning, disinfecting**

ServiceID: **GS-2**
Service: **Deep cleaning all rooms, all surfaces, garbage removal, disinfecting**

ServiceID: **GS-3**
Service: **Deep cleaning all rooms and surfaces, disinfecting**

Create the Rates table shown in the database diagram. Change the *RateID* field size to 1. Type the following records in the table:

RateID: A HrlyRate: $75.50	RateID: B HrlyRate: $65.00
RateID: C HrlyRate: $59.75	RateID: D HrlyRate: $50.50

Create the Billing table shown in the database diagram. Change the *Billing#* field size to 2, the *ClientID* field size to 3, and the *RateID* field size to 1. Apply the appropriate data types to the fields. Type the following records in the table:

Billing#: 40 ClientID: 101 BillingDate: 4/2/2012 RateID: B TotalHours: 26 Amount: $1,690.00	Billing#: 41 ClientID: 102 BillingDate: 4/2/2012 RateID: A TotalHours: 32 Amount: $2,416.00	Billing#: 42 ClientID: 107 BillingDate: 4/2/2012 RateID: D TotalHours: 15 Amount: $747.50
Billing#: 43 ClientID: 110 BillingDate: 4/2/2012 RateID: A TotalHours: 30 Amount: $2,265.00	Billing#: 44 ClientID: 112 BillingDate: 4/2/2012 RateID: C TotalHours: 20 Amount: $1,195.00	Billing#: 45 ClientID: 115 BillingDate: 4/2/2012 RateID: C TotalHours: 22 Amount: $1,314.50

Automatically adjust the column widths of each table to accommodate the longest entry in each column and then print each table on one page. ***Hint: Check the table in Print Preview and, if necessary, change to landscape orientation and change the margins.***

Part 2

With **AL1-C2-GoldStar.accdb** open, create the one-to-many relationships required to connect the tables. (Refer to Figure 2.17 as a guide.) You will need to increase the size of the Clients table to view all of the fields. To do this, position the mouse pointer on the bottom border of the Clients table in the Relationships window until the pointer turns into a white arrow pointing up and down. Hold down the left mouse button, drag down to the desired position, and then release the mouse button. Print the relationships report.

Part 3

Open the Services table and then make the following changes to the field values in the *ServiceID* field:

Change *GS-1* to *GS-A*
Change *GS-2* to *GS-B*
Change *GS-3* to *GS-C*

Save, print, and then close the Services table. Open the Clients table, delete the record for client number 112 and then insert the following record:

ClientID: **108**
Name: **Cedar Ridge Products**
Address: **6400 Olive Street**
City: (default value)
State: (default value
ZIP: **63114**
Contact: **Penny Childers**
Telephone: **(314) 555-7660**
ServiceID: **GS-B**
RateID: **B**

Save, print, and then close the Clients table. Open the Billing table, print the table, and then close the table. Close the **AL1-C2-GoldStar.accdb** database.

Microsoft®
Access®

CHAPTER 3

Performing Queries

PERFORMANCE OBJECTIVES

Upon successful completion of Chapter 3, you will be able to:

- **Design queries to extract specific data from tables**
- **Use the Simple Query Wizard to create queries**
- **Modify queries**
- **Design queries with *Or* and *And* criteria**
- **Create a calculated field**
- **Use aggregate functions in queries**
- **Create crosstab, duplicate, and unmatched queries**

SNAP Training and Assessment. Simplified.

Tutorials

3.1 Creating Queries in Design View
3.2 Using Criteria Statements in Queries
3.3 Using And/Or Criteria in Queries
3.4 Creating Queries Using the Simple Query Wizard
3.5 Performing Calculations in a Query
3.6 Using Aggregate Functions
3.7 Using Advanced Queries
3.8 Creating Duplicate and Unmatched Queries

One of the primary uses of a database is to extract specific information from the database. A company might need to know such information as: How much inventory is currently on hand? What products have been ordered? What accounts are past due? What customers live in a particular city? You can extract this type of information from a table or multiple tables by completing a query. You will learn how to perform a variety of queries on information in tables in this chapter. Model answers for this chapter's projects appear on the following pages.

Access
Access2010L1C3

Note: Before beginning the projects, copy the Access2010L1C3 subfolder from the Access2010L1 folder on the CD that accompanies this textbook to your storage medium and make Access2010L1C3 the active folder.

Project 1 Design Queries

Project 1a

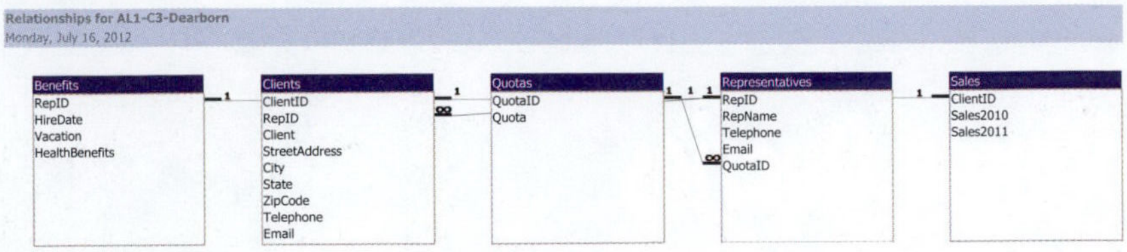

Dearnborn_Relationships

RepName	Telephone
Lee Hutchinson	(765) 555-4277
Isabelle Marshall	(765) 555-8822
Lydia Alvarado	(765) 555-4996

RepsWith765AreaCodeQuery

Client	StreetAddress	City	State	ZipCode
Fairhaven Developers	574 East Raymond Street	Indianapolis	IN	46219-3005
Landower Company	1299 Arlington Avenue	Indianapolis	IN	46236-1299
Harford Systems	9654 Jackson Street	Indianapolis	IN	46247-9654
Gallagher Systems	3885 Moore Avenue	Indianapolis	IN	47229-1075
Blue Ridge, Inc.	29 South 25th Street	Indianapolis	IN	46227-1355
Alderton Metals	103 South Parker Avenue	Indianapolis	IN	47220-1450
DV Corporation	210 West Michigan Stree	Indianapolis	IN	46251-4503
Wheeling Products	5567 Washburn Avenue	Indianapolis	IN	46247-5567
Martin Manufacturing	422 West Morris Street	Indianapolis	IN	46238-4220
Valley Construction	123 46th Street	Indianapolis	IN	46242-1230
AeroTech	9905 West 16th Street	Indianapolis	IN	46241-9905
Miles & Harrisburg	11029 47th Street East	Indianapolis	IN	46238-1120
Haute Contractors	422 Kessler Boulevard	Indianapolis	IN	46218-4220
Eagleton Industries	544 Eastridge Drive	Indianapolis	IN	47230-5440
Zinn-Harris Electronics	675 South Holt Road	Indianapolis	IN	47221-0551

ClientsIndianapolisQuery

RepName	QuotaID
Catherine Singleton	3
Isabelle Marshall	3
Maureen Pascual	3
Linda Foster	3
Kwan Im	4
William Ludlow	4
Lydia Alvarado	4
Alfred Silva	5
Gina Tapparo	5

QuotaIDGreaterThanTwoQuery

ClientID	Sales2011
101	$327,541.00
103	$144,328.00
104	$130,239.00
105	$441,000.00
107	$221,379.00
108	$105,000.00
109	$721,923.00
112	$200,540.00
115	$103,400.00
118	$175,011.00
119	$222,133.00
121	$103,435.00
122	$125,900.00
123	$265,439.00
125	$120,890.00
127	$176,420.00

2011SalesOver$99999Query

Project 1b

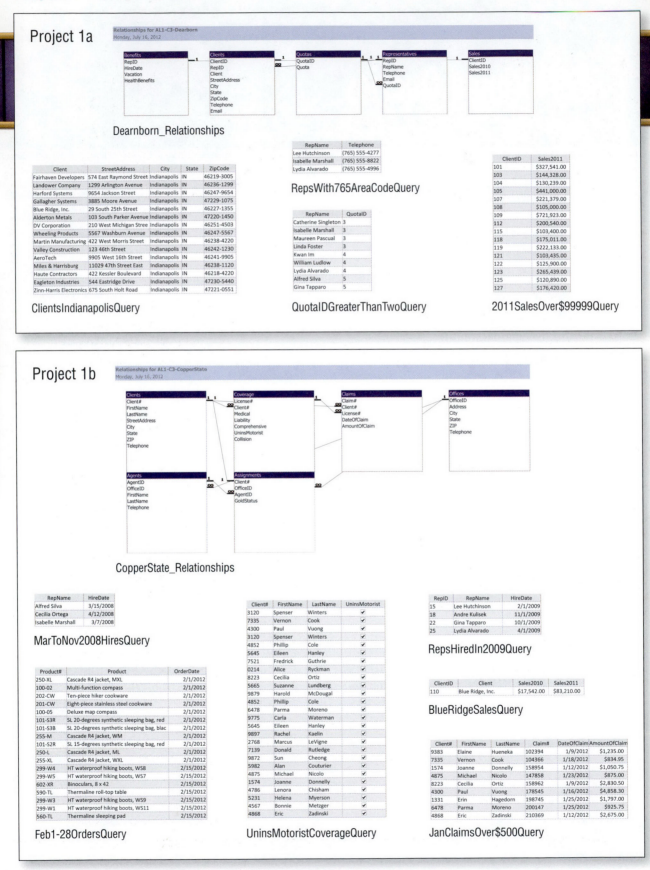

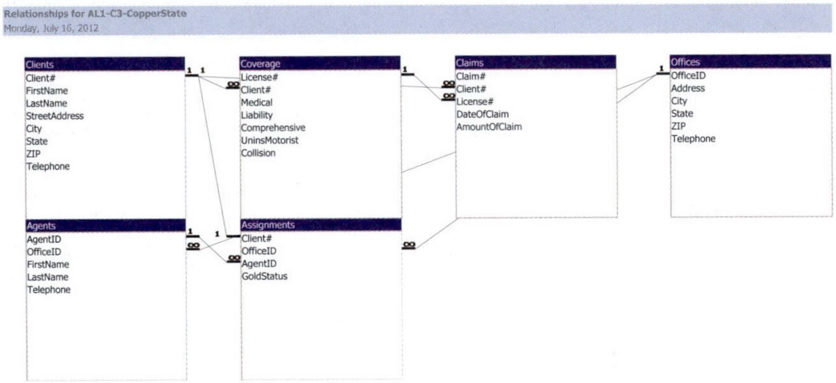

CopperState_Relationships

RepName	HireDate
Alfred Silva	3/15/2008
Cecilia Ortega	4/12/2008
Isabelle Marshall	3/7/2008

MarToNov2008HiresQuery

Product#	Product	OrderDate
250-XL	Cascade R4 jacket, MXL	2/1/2012
100-02	Multi-function compass	2/1/2012
202-CW	Ten-piece hiker cookware	2/1/2012
201-CW	Eight-piece stainless steel cookware	2/1/2012
100-05	Deluxe map compass	2/1/2012
101-S3R	SL 20-degrees synthetic sleeping bag, red	2/1/2012
101-S3B	SL 20-degrees synthetic sleeping bag, blac	2/1/2012
255-M	Cascade R4 jacket, WM	2/1/2012
101-S2R	SL 15-degrees synthetic sleeping bag, red	2/1/2012
250-L	Cascade R4 jacket, ML	2/1/2012
255-XL	Cascade R4 jacket, WXL	2/1/2012
299-W4	HT waterproof hiking boots, WS8	2/15/2012
299-W5	HT waterproof hiking boots, WS7	2/15/2012
602-XR	Binoculars, 8 x 42	2/15/2012
590-TL	Thermaline roll-top table	2/15/2012
299-W3	HT waterproof hiking boots, WS9	2/15/2012
299-W1	HT waterproof hiking boots, WS11	2/15/2012
560-TL	Thermaline sleeping pad	2/15/2012

Feb1-28OrdersQuery

Client#	FirstName	LastName	UninsMotorist
3120	Spenser	Winters	✔
7335	Vernon	Cook	✔
4300	Paul	Vuong	✔
3120	Spenser	Winters	✔
4852	Phillip	Cole	✔
5645	Eileen	Hanley	✔
7521	Fredrick	Guthrie	✔
0214	Alice	Ryckman	✔
8223	Cecilia	Ortiz	✔
5665	Suzanne	Lundberg	✔
9879	Harold	McDougal	✔
4852	Phillip	Cole	✔
6478	Parma	Moreno	✔
9775	Carla	Waterman	✔
5645	Eileen	Hanley	✔
9897	Rachel	Kaelin	✔
2768	Marcus	LeVigne	✔
7139	Donald	Rutledge	✔
9872	Sun	Cheong	✔
5982	Alan	Couturier	✔
4875	Michael	Nicolo	✔
1574	Joanne	Donnelly	✔
4786	Lenora	Chisham	✔
5231	Helena	Myerson	✔
4567	Bonnie	Metzger	✔
4868	Eric	Zadinski	✔

UninsMotoristCoverageQuery

RepID	RepName	HireDate
15	Lee Hutchinson	2/1/2009
18	Andre Kulisek	11/1/2009
22	Gina Tapparo	10/1/2009
25	Lydia Alvarado	4/1/2009

RepsHiredIn2009Query

ClientID	Client	Sales2010	Sales2011
110	Blue Ridge, Inc.	$17,542.00	$83,210.00

BlueRidgeSalesQuery

Client#	FirstName	LastName	Claim#	DateOfClaim	AmountOfClaim
9383	Elaine	Hueneka	102394	1/9/2012	$1,235.00
7335	Vernon	Cook	104366	1/18/2012	$834.95
1574	Joanne	Donnelly	158954	1/12/2012	$1,050.75
4875	Michael	Nicolo	147858	1/23/2012	$875.00
8223	Cecilia	Ortiz	158962	1/9/2012	$2,830.50
4300	Paul	Vuong	178545	1/16/2012	$4,858.30
1331	Erin	Hagedorn	198745	1/25/2012	$1,797.00
6478	Parma	Moreno	200147	1/25/2012	$925.75
4868	Eric	Zadinski	210369	1/12/2012	$2,675.00

JanClaimsOver$500Query

Project 1c

Product#	Supplier#	UnitsOrdered	Amount
442-1B	42	10	$1,495.00
780-2	99	10	$1,288.50
250-L	60	10	$1,285.00
250-XL	60	10	$1,285.00
101-S3R	54	10	$1,199.50
101-S3B	54	10	$1,137.50
299-M3	31	10	$887.90
299-M5	31	10	$887.90
299-M2	31	10	$887.90
299-W5	31	10	$752.90
299-W4	31	10	$752.90
299-W3	31	10	$752.90
299-W1	31	8	$602.32
255-M	60	5	$599.50
255-XL	60	5	$599.50
560-TL	25	20	$397.00
155-35	10	10	$199.50
375-S	68	20	$199.00
375-M	68	20	$199.00
590-TL	25	5	$196.25
209-XL	68	25	$180.00
209-L	68	25	$173.75
210-L	68	25	$162.25
209-XXL	68	20	$145.80
100-05	84	5	$129.75
371-L	68	10	$129.50
202-CW	15	5	$124.25
155-20	10	15	$104.25
201-CW	15	5	$99.75
210-M	68	15	$97.35
100-02	84	10	$45.95
152-H	10	15	$44.85

OrdersLessThan$1500Query

OfficeID	FirstName	LastName
GW	Carlos	Alvarez
GW	Joanne	Donnelly
GW	Cecilia	Ortiz
GW	Donald	Rutledge
GW	Paul	Vuong

GWClientsQuery

Client	Sales2010	RepName
Madison Electrics	$99,450.00	William Ludlow
Landower Company	$97,653.00	Robin Rehberg
Providence, Inc.	$85,628.00	Isabelle Marshall
Karris Supplies	$61,349.00	Edward Harris
Paragon Corporation	$51,237.00	Jaren Newman
Martin Manufacturing	$35,679.00	Lydia Alvarado
Hoosier Corporation	$24,880.00	Craig Johnson
Blue Ridge, Inc.	$17,542.00	Maureen Pascual
Valley Construction	$15,248.00	Lee Hutchinson
Alderton Metals	$9,547.00	Alfred Silva
Northstar Services	$9,457.00	Alfred Silva
Milltown Contractors	$2,356.00	Kwan Im

2010SalesLessThan$100000Query

Project 1d

Client	Sales2011	RepName
Fairhaven Developers	$95,630.00	Kwan Im
Blue Ridge, Inc.	$83,210.00	Maureen Pascual
Providence, Inc.	$75,462.00	Isabelle Marshall
Franklin Services	$65,411.00	Catherine Singleton
Martin Manufacturing	$61,539.00	Lydia Alvarado
Alderton Metals	$45,230.00	Alfred Silva
Hoosier Corporation	$31,935.00	Craig Johnson
Milltown Contractors	$31,230.00	Kwan Im
Valley Construction	$22,478.00	Lee Hutchinson
Paragon Corporation	$20,137.00	Jaren Newman
Northstar Services	$15,094.00	Alfred Silva

2011SalesLessThan$100000Query

RepName	Vacation
Alfred Silva	3 weeks
Cecilia Ortega	3 weeks
Isabelle Marshall	3 weeks
Craig Johnson	3 weeks
Gina Tapparo	3 weeks
Edward Harris	3 weeks

RepsWith3WeekVacationsQuery

Project 1e

RepName	Vacation
William Ludlow	4 weeks
Alfred Silva	3 weeks
Cecilia Ortega	3 weeks
Robin Rehberg	4 weeks
Isabelle Marshall	3 weeks
Craig Johnson	3 weeks
Gina Tapparo	3 weeks
Edward Harris	3 weeks

RepsWith3Or4WeekVacationsQuery

Client	City	Sales2010	Sales2011
Harford Systems	Indianapolis	$215,420.00	$441,000.00
Gallagher Systems	Indianapolis	$199,346.00	$221,379.00
DV Corporation	Indianapolis	$138,560.00	$200,540.00
Wheeling Products	Indianapolis	$115,423.00	$103,400.00
AeroTech	Indianapolis	$156,439.00	$175,011.00
Miles & Harrisburg	Indianapolis	$201,430.00	$222,133.00
Haute Contractors	Indianapolis	$174,319.00	$125,900.00
Eagleton Industries	Indianapolis	$300,137.00	$265,439.00
Zinn-Harris Electronics	Indianapolis	$214,000.00	$176,420.00

SalesOver$100000IndianapolisQuery

Supplier#	SupplierName	Product
25	Langley Corporation	Thermaline sleeping pad
25	Langley Corporation	Thermaline light-weight cot
25	Langley Corporation	Thermaline camp seat
25	Langley Corporation	Thermaline roll-top table
31	Sound Supplies	HT waterproof hiking boots, MS13
31	Sound Supplies	HT waterproof hiking boots, MS12
31	Sound Supplies	HT waterproof hiking boots, MS11
31	Sound Supplies	HT waterproof hiking boots, MS10
31	Sound Supplies	HT waterproof hiking boots, MS9
31	Sound Supplies	HT waterproof hiking boots, WS11
31	Sound Supplies	HT waterproof hiking boots, WS10
31	Sound Supplies	HT waterproof hiking boots, WS9
31	Sound Supplies	HT waterproof hiking boots, WS8
31	Sound Supplies	HT waterproof hiking boots, WS7
31	Sound Supplies	HT waterproof hiking boots, WS6
42	Fraser Valley Product	Polar backpack, 250RW
42	Fraser Valley Product	Polar backpack, 150BR
42	Fraser Valley Product	Polar backpack, 150RW
42	Fraser Valley Product	Polar backpack, 250BR

Suppliers25-31-42Query

Order#	SupplierName	Product	UnitsOrdered
1017	Freedom Corporation	Gordon wool ski hat, L	25
1009	Freedom Corporation	Gordon wool ski hat, XL	25
1008	Freedom Corporation	Gordon wool ski hat, XXL	20
1012	Freedom Corporation	Tech-lite ski hat, L	25
1013	Freedom Corporation	Tech-lite ski hat, M	15
1016	Freedom Corporation	Lite-tech ski gloves, ML	10
1015	Freedom Corporation	Lite-tech ski gloves, WM	20
1014	Freedom Corporation	Lite-tech ski gloves, WS	20

SkiHatsGlovesOnOrderQuery

Product#	Product	SupplierName
443-1B	Polar backpack, 250RW	Fraser Valley Product
101-S1B	SL 0-degrees down sleeping bag, black	Manning, Inc.
101-S1R	SL 0-degrees down sleeping bag, red	Manning, Inc.
101-S2B	SL 15-degrees synthetic sleeping bag, blac	Manning, Inc.
101-S2R	SL 15-degrees synthetic sleeping bag, red	Manning, Inc.
101-S3B	SL 20-degrees synthetic sleeping bag, blac	Manning, Inc.
101-S3R	SL 20-degrees synthetic sleeping bag, red	Manning, Inc.
299-M1	HT waterproof hiking boots, MS13	Sound Supplies
299-M2	HT waterproof hiking boots, MS12	Sound Supplies
299-M3	HT waterproof hiking boots, MS11	Sound Supplies
299-M4	HT waterproof hiking boots, MS10	Sound Supplies
299-M5	HT waterproof hiking boots, MS9	Sound Supplies
299-W1	HT waterproof hiking boots, WS11	Sound Supplies
299-W2	HT waterproof hiking boots, WS10	Sound Supplies
299-W3	HT waterproof hiking boots, WS9	Sound Supplies
299-W4	HT waterproof hiking boots, WS8	Sound Supplies
299-W5	HT waterproof hiking boots, WS7	Sound Supplies
299-W6	HT waterproof hiking boots, WS6	Sound Supplies
442-1A	Polar backpack, 150BR	Fraser Valley Product
442-1B	Polar backpack, 150RW	Fraser Valley Product
443-1A	Polar backpack, 250BR	Fraser Valley Product

BootsSleepingBagsBackpacksQuery

Client#	FirstName	LastName	Medical	Liability	Comprehensive	UninsMotorist	Collision
3156	Brenda	Lazzuri	☐	✔	☐	☐	☐
8854	Edward	Bakalarski	☐	✔	☐	☐	☐
3156	Brenda	Lazzuri	☐	✔	☐	☐	☐
3164	Bret	Mardock	☐	✔	☐	☐	☐
9746	Carlos	Alvarez	☐	✔	☐	☐	☐

ClientsWithOnlyLiabilityQuery

Model Answers

Project 1f

ClientID	Client	Sales2010	Sales2011
101	Bering Company	$289,563.00	$327,541.00
102	Fairhaven Developers	$101,210.00	$95,630.00
103	Clearwater Service	$125,436.00	$144,328.00
104	Landower Company	$97,653.00	$130,239.00
105	Harford Systems	$215,420.00	$441,000.00
106	Providence, Inc.	$85,628.00	$75,462.00
107	Gallagher Systems	$199,346.00	$221,379.00
108	Karris Supplies	$61,349.00	$105,000.00
109	HE Systems	$554,120.00	$721,923.00
110	Blue Ridge, Inc.	$17,542.00	$83,210.00
111	Alderton Metals	$9,547.00	$45,230.00
112	DV Corporation	$138,560.00	$200,540.00
113	Franklin Services	$141,670.00	$65,411.00
114	Milltown Contractors	$2,356.00	$31,230.00
115	Wheeling Products	$115,423.00	$103,400.00
116	Martin Manufacturing	$35,679.00	$61,539.00
117	Valley Construction	$15,248.00	$22,478.00
118	AeroTech	$156,439.00	$175,011.00
119	Miles & Harrisburg	$201,430.00	$222,133.00
120	Paragon Corporation	$51,237.00	$20,137.00
121	Madison Electrics	$99,450.00	$103,435.00
122	Haute Contractors	$174,319.00	$125,900.00
123	Eagleton Industries	$300,137.00	$265,439.00
124	Hoosier Corporation	$24,880.00	$31,935.00
125	Dover Industries	$151,003.00	$120,890.00
126	Northstar Services	$9,457.00	$15,094.00
127	Zinn-Harris Electronics	$214,000.00	$176,420.00

Client2010-2011SalesQuery

Supplier#	SupplierName	Product#	Amount
10	Hopewell, Inc.	155-35	$199.50
10	Hopewell, Inc.	152-H	$44.85
10	Hopewell, Inc.	155-20	$104.25
15	Bayside Supplies	202-CW	$124.25
15	Bayside Supplies	201-CW	$99.75
25	Langley Corporation	590-TL	$196.25
25	Langley Corporation	560-TL	$397.00
31	Sound Supplies	299-M5	$887.90
31	Sound Supplies	299-M3	$887.90
31	Sound Supplies	299-M2	$887.90
31	Sound Supplies	299-W4	$752.90
31	Sound Supplies	299-W5	$752.90
31	Sound Supplies	299-W3	$752.90
31	Sound Supplies	299-W1	$602.32
35	Emerald City Products	602-XR	$2,145.00
42	Fraser Valley Product	443-1B	$2,397.75
42	Fraser Valley Product	442-1B	$1,495.00
54	Manning, Inc.	101-S3R	$1,199.50
54	Manning, Inc.	101-S3B	$1,137.50
54	Manning, Inc.	101-S2R	$1,945.25
60	Cascade Gear	250-XL	$1,285.00
60	Cascade Gear	255-M	$599.50
60	Cascade Gear	250-L	$1,285.00
60	Cascade Gear	255-XL	$599.50
68	Freedom Corporation	209-XXL	$145.80
68	Freedom Corporation	209-XL	$180.00
68	Freedom Corporation	210-L	$162.25
68	Freedom Corporation	210-M	$97.35
68	Freedom Corporation	375-S	$199.00
68	Freedom Corporation	375-M	$199.00
68	Freedom Corporation	371-L	$129.50
68	Freedom Corporation	209-L	$173.75
84	Macadam, Inc.	100-02	$45.95
84	Macadam, Inc.	100-05	$129.75
99	KL Distributions	780-2	$1,288.50
99	KL Distributions	647-1	$2,999.85

ProductOrderAmountsQuery

Project 1g

SupplierName	StreetAddress	City	Prov/State	PostalCode
Bayside Supplies	6705 North Street	Bellingham	WA	98432
Hadley Company	5845 Jefferson Street	Seattle	WA	98107
Cascade Gear	540 Broadway	Seattle	WA	98106
Sound Supplies	2104 Union Street	Seattle	WA	98105
Emerald City Products	1059 Pike Street	Seattle	WA	98102
KL Distributions	402 Yukon Drive	Bellingham	WA	96435

SuppliersNotBCQuery

Client	StreetAddress	City	State	ZipCode
Bering Company	4521 East Sixth Street	Muncie	IN	47310-5500
Clearwater Service	10385 North Gavin Stree	Muncie	IN	47308-1236
Providence, Inc.	12490 141st Street	Muncie	IN	47306-3410
Paragon Corporation	4500 Meridian Street	Muncie	IN	47302-4338
Dover Industries	4839 Huchins Road	Muncie	IN	47306-4839
Northstar Services	5135 West Second Street	Muncie	IN	47301-7774

ClientsMuncieQuery

Client#	FirstName	LastName	StreetAddress	City	State	ZIP	Claim#	AmountOfClaim
7335	Vernon	Cook	1230 South Mesa	Phoenix	AZ	85018	104366	$834.95
1331	Erin	Hagedorn	4818 Oakes Boulevard	Phoenix	AZ	85018	198745	$1,797.00
9879	Harold	McDougal	7115 Elizabeth Lane	Phoenix	AZ	85009	174589	$752.45
9775	Carla	Waterman	3979 19th Avenue	Phoenix	AZ	85031	241485	$4,500.00
6478	Parma	Moreno	610 Sheridan Avenue	Phoenix	AZ	85031	200147	$925.75
4868	Eric	Zadinski	1301 North Meridian	Phoenix	AZ	85031	210369	$2,675.00
9879	Harold	McDougal	7115 Elizabeth Lane	Phoenix	AZ	85009	247823	$775.75

PhoenixClientClaimsOver$500Query

Project 1h

Client	Sales2010	Sales2011	Total
Bering Company	$289,563.00	$327,541.00	$617,104.00
Fairhaven Developers	$101,210.00	$95,630.00	$196,840.00
Clearwater Service	$125,436.00	$144,328.00	$269,764.00
Landower Company	$97,653.00	$130,239.00	$227,892.00
Harford Systems	$215,420.00	$441,000.00	$656,420.00
Providence, Inc.	$85,628.00	$75,462.00	$161,090.00
Gallagher Systems	$199,346.00	$221,379.00	$420,725.00
Karris Supplies	$61,349.00	$105,000.00	$166,349.00
HE Systems	$554,120.00	$721,923.00	$1,276,043.00
Blue Ridge, Inc.	$17,542.00	$83,210.00	$100,752.00
Alderton Metals	$9,547.00	$45,230.00	$54,777.00
DV Corporation	$138,560.00	$200,540.00	$339,100.00
Franklin Services	$141,670.00	$65,411.00	$207,081.00
Milltown Contractors	$2,356.00	$31,230.00	$33,586.00
Wheeling Products	$115,423.00	$103,400.00	$218,823.00
Martin Manufacturing	$35,679.00	$61,539.00	$97,218.00
Valley Construction	$15,248.00	$22,478.00	$37,726.00
AeroTech	$156,439.00	$175,011.00	$331,450.00
Miles & Harrisburg	$201,430.00	$222,133.00	$423,563.00
Paragon Corporation	$51,237.00	$20,137.00	$71,374.00
Madison Electrics	$99,450.00	$103,435.00	$202,885.00
Haute Contractors	$174,319.00	$125,900.00	$300,219.00
Eagleton Industries	$300,137.00	$265,439.00	$565,576.00
Hoosier Corporation	$24,880.00	$31,935.00	$56,815.00
Dover Industries	$151,003.00	$120,890.00	$271,893.00
Northstar Services	$9,457.00	$15,094.00	$24,551.00
Zinn-Harris Electronics	$214,000.00	$176,420.00	$390,420.00

SalesTotalQuery

Client	Sales2010	Sales2011	Difference
Bering Company	$289,563.00	$327,541.00	$37,978.00
Fairhaven Developers	$101,210.00	$95,630.00	($5,580.00)
Clearwater Service	$125,436.00	$144,328.00	$18,892.00
Landower Company	$97,653.00	$130,239.00	$32,586.00
Harford Systems	$215,420.00	$441,000.00	$225,580.00
Providence, Inc.	$85,628.00	$75,462.00	($10,166.00)
Gallagher Systems	$199,346.00	$221,379.00	$22,033.00
Karris Supplies	$61,349.00	$105,000.00	$43,651.00
HE Systems	$554,120.00	$721,923.00	$167,803.00
Blue Ridge, Inc.	$17,542.00	$83,210.00	$65,668.00
Alderton Metals	$9,547.00	$45,230.00	$35,683.00
DV Corporation	$138,560.00	$200,540.00	$61,980.00
Franklin Services	$141,670.00	$65,411.00	($76,259.00)
Milltown Contractors	$2,356.00	$31,230.00	$28,874.00
Wheeling Products	$115,423.00	$103,400.00	($12,023.00)
Martin Manufacturing	$35,679.00	$61,539.00	$25,860.00
Valley Construction	$15,248.00	$22,478.00	$7,230.00
AeroTech	$156,439.00	$175,011.00	$18,572.00
Miles & Harrisburg	$201,430.00	$222,133.00	$20,703.00
Paragon Corporation	$51,237.00	$20,137.00	($31,100.00)
Madison Electrics	$99,450.00	$103,435.00	$3,985.00
Haute Contractors	$174,319.00	$125,900.00	($48,419.00)
Eagleton Industries	$300,137.00	$265,439.00	($34,698.00)
Hoosier Corporation	$24,880.00	$31,935.00	$7,055.00
Dover Industries	$151,003.00	$120,890.00	($30,113.00)
Northstar Services	$9,457.00	$15,094.00	$5,637.00
Zinn-Harris Electronics	$214,000.00	$176,420.00	($37,580.00)

SalesDifferencesQuery

SupplierName	Order#	UnitsOrdered	Amount	Total
Hopewell, Inc.	1010	10	$199.50	$1,995.00
Hopewell, Inc.	1011	15	$44.85	$672.75
Hopewell, Inc.	1018	15	$104.25	$1,563.75
Bayside Supplies	1021	5	$124.25	$621.25
Bayside Supplies	1022	5	$99.75	$498.75
Langley Corporation	1033	5	$196.25	$981.25
Langley Corporation	1036	20	$397.00	$7,940.00
Sound Supplies	1002	10	$887.90	$8,879.00
Sound Supplies	1003	10	$887.90	$8,879.00
Sound Supplies	1005	10	$887.90	$8,879.00
Sound Supplies	1030	10	$752.90	$7,529.00
Sound Supplies	1031	10	$752.90	$7,529.00
Sound Supplies	1034	10	$752.90	$7,529.00
Sound Supplies	1035	8	$602.32	$4,818.56
Emerald City Products	1032	5	$2,145.00	$10,725.00
Fraser Valley Product	1004	15	$2,397.75	$35,966.25
Fraser Valley Product	1007	10	$1,495.00	$14,950.00
Manning, Inc.	1024	10	$1,199.50	$11,995.00
Manning, Inc.	1025	10	$1,137.50	$11,375.00
Manning, Inc.	1027	15	$1,945.25	$29,178.75
Cascade Gear	1019	10	$1,285.00	$12,850.00
Cascade Gear	1026	5	$599.50	$2,997.50
Cascade Gear	1028	10	$1,285.00	$12,850.00
Cascade Gear	1029	5	$599.50	$2,997.50
Freedom Corporation	1008	20	$145.80	$2,916.00
Freedom Corporation	1009	25	$180.00	$4,500.00
Freedom Corporation	1012	25	$162.25	$4,056.25
Freedom Corporation	1013	15	$97.35	$1,460.25
Freedom Corporation	1014	20	$199.00	$3,980.00
Freedom Corporation	1015	20	$199.00	$3,980.00
Freedom Corporation	1016	10	$129.50	$1,295.00
Freedom Corporation	1017	25	$173.75	$4,343.75
Macadam, Inc.	1020	10	$45.95	$459.50
Macadam, Inc.	1023	5	$129.75	$648.75
KL Distributions	1001	10	$1,288.50	$12,885.00
KL Distributions	1006	15	$2,999.85	$44,997.75

UnitsOrderedTotalQuery

Project 2 Create Aggregate Functions, Crosstab, Find Duplicates, and Fund Unmatched Queries

Project 2a

SumOfAmount	AvgOfAmount	MaxOfAmount	MinOfAmount	CountOfAmount
$26,530.27	$736.95	$2,999.85	$44.85	36

AmountsQuery

SumOfAmountOfClaim	AvgOfAmountOfClaim	MaxOfAmountOfClaim	MinOfAmountOfClaim
$38,711.95	$2,037.47	$5,230.00	$535.00

ClaimAmountsQuery

Project 2b

Client#	SumOfAmountO	AvgOfAmountO
1331	$1,797.00	$1,797.00
1574	$2,696.25	$1,348.13
4300	$10,088.30	$5,044.15
4567	$1,840.00	$1,840.00
4868	$2,675.00	$2,675.00
4875	$875.00	$875.00
5982	$3,250.50	$3,250.50
6478	$925.75	$925.75
7335	$834.95	$834.95
8223	$2,830.50	$2,830.50
8854	$3,100.50	$1,550.25
9383	$1,770.00	$885.00
9775	$4,500.00	$4,500.00
9879	$1,528.20	$764.10

SumAvgClaimAmountsQuery

SumOfAmount	AvgOfAmount	Supplier#	SupplierName
$348.60	$116.20	10	Hopewell, Inc.
$224.00	$112.00	15	Bayside Supplies
$593.25	$296.63	25	Langley Corporation
$5,524.72	$789.25	31	Sound Supplies
$2,145.00	$2,145.00	35	Emerald City Products
$3,892.75	$1,946.38	42	Fraser Valley Products
$4,282.25	$1,427.42	54	Manning, Inc.
$3,769.00	$942.25	60	Cascade Gear
$1,286.65	$160.83	68	Freedom Corporation
$175.70	$87.85	84	Macadam, Inc.
$4,288.35	$2,144.18	99	KL Distributions

SupplierAmountsQuery

Project 2c

SL 20-degrees s	SL 20-degrees s	Tech-lite ski hat	Tech-lite ski hat	Ten-piece hiker	Thermaline roll-	Thermaline slee	Two-person dor	Two-person ten
				$124.25				
		$162.25	$97.35					
$1,137.50	$1,							

Lantern hanger	Lite-tech ski glo	Lite-tech ski glo	Lite-tech ski glo	Multi-function c	Polar backpack,	Polar backpack,	Shursite angle-h	Shursite portabl	SL 15-degrees s
					$1,495.00	$2,397.75			
	$129.50	$199.00	$199.00						
$44.85									

Gordon wool sk	Gordon wool sk	Gordon wool sk	HT waterproof I	HT waterproof I	HT waterproof I	HT waterproof I	HT waterproof I	HT waterproof I	HT waterproof I
$173.75	$180.00	$145.80							

SupplierName	Total Of Amoun	Binoculars, 8 x 4	Cascade R4 jack	Cascade R4 jack	Cascade R4 jack	Cascade R4 jack	Deluxe map con	Eight-piece stair
Bayside Supplies	$224.00							$99.75
Cascade Gear	$3,769.00		$1,285.00	$1,285.00	$599.50	$599.50		
Emerald City Products	$2,145.00	$2,145.00						
Fraser Valley Products	$3,892.75							
Freedom Corporation	$1,286.65							
Hopewell, Inc.	$348.60							
KL Distributions	$4,288.35							
Langley Corporation	$593.25							
Macadam, Inc.	$175.70						$129.75	
Manning, Inc.	$4,282.25							
Sound Supplies	$5,524.72							

OrdersBySupplierByProductQuery

Claim#	Total Of Amoun	1331	1574	4300	4567	4868	4875	5982	6478	7335	8223	8854	9383	9775	9879
102394	$1,235.00												$1,235.00		
104366	$834.95									$834.95					
121039	$5,230.00			$5,230.00											
136695	$1,840.00				$1,840.00										
147851	$3,250.50							$3,250							
147858	$875.00						$875.00								
153001	$535.00												$535.00		
158954	$1,050.75		$1,050.75												
158962	$2,830.50										$2,830.50				
174223	$950.50											$950.50			
174589	$752.45														$752.45
178545	$4,858.30			$4,858.30											
198745	$1,797.00	$1,797.00													
200147	$925.75								$925.75						
210369	$2,675.00					$2,675.00									
211458	$1,645.50		$1,645.50												
241485	$4,500.00													$4,500.00	
247823	$775.75														$775.75
248210	$2,150.00											$2,150.00			

ClaimsByClaim#ByClient#Query

Project 2d

SupplierName	Supplier#	StreetAddress	City	Prov/State	PostalCode	EmailAddress	Telephone
Langley Corporation	25	805 First Avenue	Burnaby	BC	V3J 1C9	langley@emcp.net	(604) 555-1200
Langley Corporation	29	1248 Larson Avenue	Burnaby	BC	V5V 9K2	lc@emcp.net	(604) 555-1200

DuplicateSuppliersQuery

Project 2e

Supplier#	Order#	SupplierName	Product#	UnitsOrdered	Amount	OrderDate
10	1018	Hopewell, Inc.	155-20	15	$104.25	1/16/201:
10	1011	Hopewell, Inc.	152-H	15	$44.85	1/16/201:
10	1010	Hopewell, Inc.	155-35	10	$199.50	1/16/201:
15	1022	Bayside Supplies	201-CW	5	$99.75	2/1/201:
15	1021	Bayside Supplies	202-CW	5	$124.25	2/1/201:
25	1033	Langley Corporation	590-TL	5	$196.25	2/15/201:
25	1036	Langley Corporation	560-TL	20	$397.00	2/15/201:
31	1031	Sound Supplies	299-W5	10	$752.90	2/15/201:
31	1030	Sound Supplies	299-W4	10	$752.90	2/15/201:
31	1002	Sound Supplies	299-M5	10	$887.90	1/2/201:
31	1034	Sound Supplies	299-W3	10	$752.90	2/15/201:
31	1035	Sound Supplies	299-W1	8	$602.32	2/15/201:
31	1005	Sound Supplies	299-M2	10	$887.90	1/2/201:
31	1003	Sound Supplies	299-M3	10	$887.90	1/2/201:
42	1004	Fraser Valley Product	443-1B	15	$2,397.75	1/2/201:
42	1007	Fraser Valley Product	442-1B	10	$1,495.00	1/2/201:
54	1024	Manning, Inc.	101-S3R	10	$1,199.50	2/1/201:
54	1027	Manning, Inc.	101-S2R	15	$1,945.25	2/1/201:
54	1025	Manning, Inc.	101-S3B	10	$1,137.50	2/1/201:
60	1029	Cascade Gear	255-XL	5	$599.50	2/1/201:
60	1028	Cascade Gear	250-L	10	$1,285.00	2/1/201:
60	1026	Cascade Gear	255-M	5	$599.50	2/1/201:
60	1019	Cascade Gear	250-XL	10	$1,285.00	2/1/201:
68	1009	Freedom Corporation	209-XL	25	$180.00	1/16/201:
68	1017	Freedom Corporation	209-L	25	$173.75	1/16/201:
68	1008	Freedom Corporation	209-XXL	20	$145.80	1/16/201:
68	1016	Freedom Corporation	371-L	10	$129.50	1/16/201:
68	1012	Freedom Corporation	210-L	25	$162.25	1/16/201:
68	1013	Freedom Corporation	210-M	15	$97.35	1/16/201:
68	1014	Freedom Corporation	375-S	20	$199.00	1/16/201:
68	1015	Freedom Corporation	375-M	20	$199.00	1/16/201:
84	1023	Macadam, Inc.	100-05	5	$129.75	2/1/201:
84	1020	Macadam, Inc.	100-02	10	$45.95	2/1/201:
99	1001	KL Distributions	780-2	10	$1,288.50	1/2/201:
99	1006	KL Distributions	647-1	15	$2,999.85	1/2/201:

Page 1

DuplicateSuppliersOrdersQuery

Project 2f

Product#	Product	Supplier#	UnitsInStock	UnitsOnOrder	ReorderLevel
558-C	ICE snow goggles, clear	68	18	0	15
559-B	ICE snow goggles, bronze	68	22	0	20
570-TL	Thermaline light-weight cot	25	8	0	5
580-TL	Thermaline camp seat	25	12	0	10
602-XT	Binoculars, 10.5 x 45	35	5	0	4
602-XX	Binoculars, 10 x 50	35	7	0	5
648-2	Three-person dome tent	99	5	0	10
651-1	K-2 one-person tent	99	8	0	10
652-2	K-2 two-person tent	99	12	0	10
804-50	AG freestyle snowboard, X50	70	7	0	10
804-60	AG freestyle snowboard, X60	70	8	0	5
897-L	Lang blunt snowboard	70	8	0	7
897-W	Lang blunt snowboard, wide	70	4	0	3
901-S	Solar battery pack	38	16	0	15
917-S	Silo portable power pack	38	8	0	10
100-01	Wrist compass	84	12	0	10
100-03	Lenspro plastic compass	84	6	0	5
100-04	Lenspro metal compass	84	8	0	5
101-S1B	SL 0-degrees down sleeping bag, black	54	16	0	15
101-S1R	SL 0-degrees down sleeping bag, red	54	17	0	15
101-S2B	SL 15-degrees synthetic sleeping bag, blac	54	21	0	15
155-30	Shursite aluminum flashlight	10	8	0	5
155-45	Shursite propane lantern	10	12	0	10
155-55	Shursite waterproof headlamp	10	7	0	5
200-CW	Four-piece titanium cookware	15	6	0	5
210-XL	Tech-lite ski hat, XL	68	22	0	20
250-M	Cascade R4 jacket, MM	60	6	0	5
250-XXL	Cascade R4 jacket, MXXL	60	5	0	0
255-L	Cascade R4 jacket, WL	60	6	0	5
299-M1	HT waterproof hiking boots, MS13	31	8	0	10
299-M4	HT waterproof hiking boots, MS10	31	7	0	10
299-W2	HT waterproof hiking boots, WS10	31	9	0	8
299-W6	HT waterproof hiking boots, WS6	31	11	0	10
371-M	Lite-tech ski gloves, MM	68	5	0	15
371-XL	Lite-tech ski gloves, MXL	68	13	0	10
371-XXL	Lite-tech ski gloves, MXXL	68	12	0	10
375-L	Lite-tech ski gloves, WL	68	22	0	20
442-1A	Polar backpack, 150BR	42	12	0	10
443-1A	Polar backpack, 250BR	42	14	0	15

Products Without Matching Orders

Project 1 Design Queries — 8 Parts

You will design and run a number of queries including queries with fields from one table and queries with fields from more than one table. You will also use the Simple Query Wizard to design queries.

Performing Queries

Being able to extract (pull out) specific data from a table is one of the most important functions of a database. Extracting data in Access is referred to as performing a query. The word ***query*** means to ask a question. Access provides several methods for performing a query. You can design your own query, use a simple query wizard, or use complex query wizards. In this chapter, you will learn to design your own query; use the Simple Query Wizard; use aggregate functions in a query; and use the Crosstab, Find Duplicates, and Unmatched Query wizards.

HINT

The first step in building a query is to choose the fields that you wish to display in the query results datasheet.

Query Design

Designing a Query

Designing a query consists of identifying the table from which you are gathering data, the field or fields from which the data will be drawn, and the criteria for selecting the data. To design a query and perform the query, open a database, click the Create tab, and then click the Query Design button in the Queries group. This displays a query window in the work area and also displays the Show Table dialog box as shown in Figure 3.1.

Figure 3.1 Query Window with Show Table Dialog Box

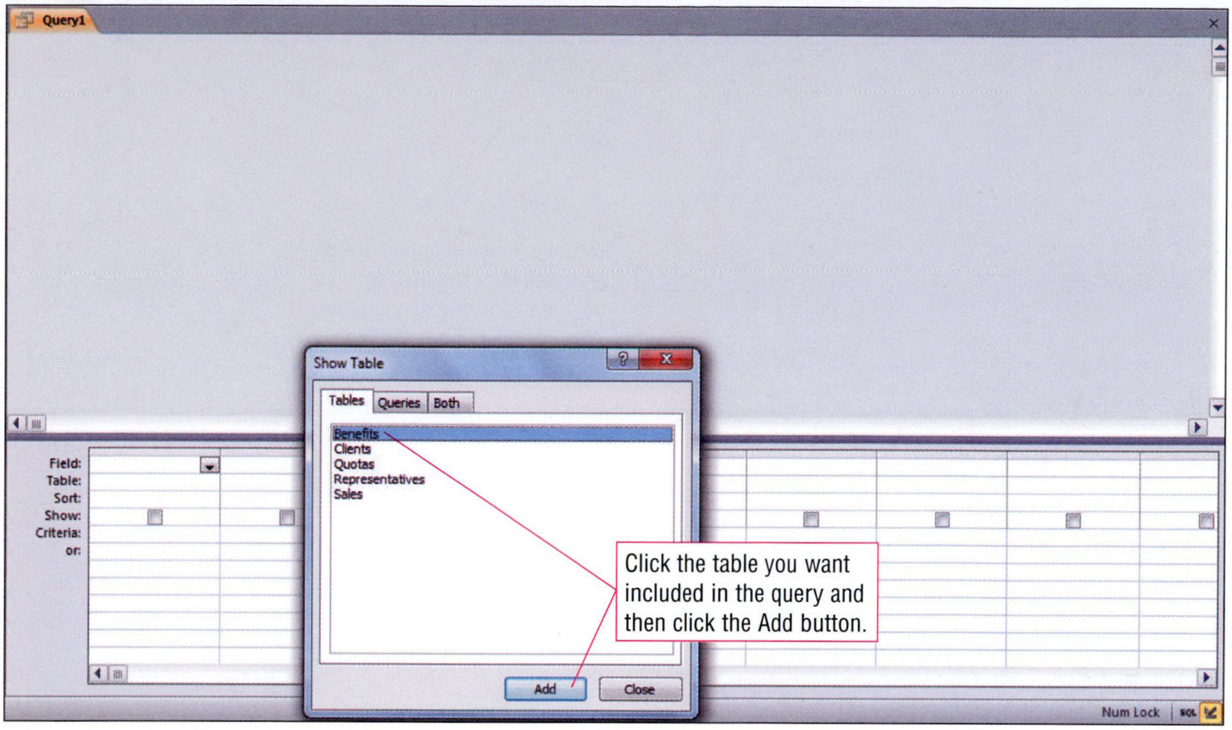

Click the table in the Show Table list box that you want included in the query and then click the Add button or double-click the desired table. Add any other tables required for the query. When all tables have been added, click the Close button. In the query window, click the down-pointing arrow at the right of the first *Field* row field in the query design grid and then click the desired field from the drop-down list. Figure 3.2 displays a sample query window.

To establish a criterion, click inside the *Criteria* row field in the column containing the desired field name in the query design grid and then type the criterion. With the fields and criteria established, click the Run button in the Results group in the Query Tools Design tab. Access searches the specified tables for records that match the criteria and then displays those records in the query results datasheet. If you plan to use the query in the future, save the query and name it. If you do not need the query again, close the query results datasheet without saving it.

You can click the down-pointing arrow at the right side of a *Field* row field and then click the desired field at the drop-down list. You can also double-click a field in a table and it is inserted in the first available *Field* row field in the query design grid. As an example, suppose you wanted to find out how many purchase orders were issued on a specific date. To do this, you would double-click *PurchaseOrderID* in the table (this inserts *PurchaseOrderID* in the first *Field* row field in the query design grid) and then double-click *OrderDate* in the table (this inserts *OrderDate* in the second *Field* row field in the query design grid). In this example, both fields are needed so the purchase order ID is displayed along with the specific order date. After inserting fields, you would then insert the criterion. The criterion for this example would be something like *#1/15/2012#*. After you insert the criterion, click the Run button in the Results group and the results of the query display in the query results datasheet.

Quick Steps

Design a Query

1. Click Create tab.
2. Click Query Design button.
3. At Show Table dialog box, click desired table, click Add button.
4. Add any additional tables.
5. In query design grid, click down-pointing arrow in *Field* row field and click desired field from drop-down list.
6. Insert criterion.
7. Click Run button.
8. Save query.

Run

Figure 3.2 Query Window

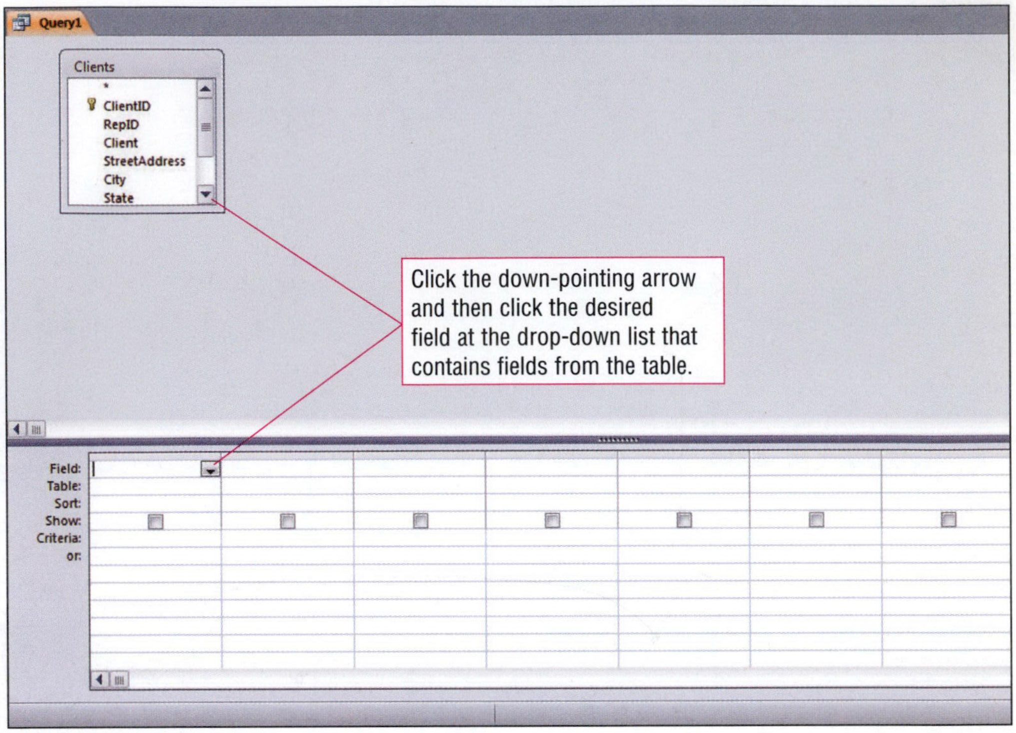

A third method for inserting a field in the query design grid is to drag a field from the table to the desired field in the query design grid. To do this, position the mouse pointer on the desired field in the table, hold down the left mouse button, drag to the desired *Field* row field in the query design grid, and then release the mouse button.

HINT

Insert fields in the *Field* row fields in the query design grid in the order in which you want the fields to display in the query results datasheet.

Establishing Query Criteria

Quick Steps

Establish Query Criterion

1. At query window, click in desired *Criteria* row field in query design grid.
2. Type criterion and then press Enter.
3. Click Run button.

A query does not require that specific criteria are established. In the example described on the previous page, if the criterion for the date was not included, the query would "return" (*return* is the term used for the results of the query) all Purchase Order numbers with the dates. While this information may be helpful, you could easily find this information in the table. The value of performing a query is to extract specific information from a table. To do this, you must insert a criterion like the one described in the example.

Access makes writing a criterion fairly simple because it inserts the necessary symbols in the criterion. If you type a city such as *Indianapolis* in the *Criteria* row field and then press Enter, Access changes the criterion to *"Indianapolis"*. The quotation marks are inserted by Access and are necessary for the query to run properly. You can either let Access put the proper symbols in the *Criteria* row field, or you can type the criterion with the symbols. Table 3.1 shows some criteria examples including what is typed and what is returned.

In Table 3.1, notice the quotation marks surrounding field values (such as "Smith"). If you do not type the quotation marks when typing the criterion, Access will automatically insert them. The same is true for the pound symbol (#). If you do not type the pound symbol around a date, Access will automatically

Table 3.1 Criteria Examples

Typing this Criteria	*Returns this*
"Smith"	Field value matching *Smith*
"Smith" or "Larson"	Field value matching either *Smith* or *Larson*
Not "Smith"	Field value that is not *Smith* (the opposite of "Smith")
"S*"	Field value that begins with *S* and ends in anything
"*s"	Field value that begins with anything and ends in *s*
"[A-D]*"	Field value that begins with *A* through *D* and ends in anything
#01/01/2012#	Field value matching the date 01/01/2012
<#04/01/2012#	Field value less than (before) 04/01/2012
>#04/01/2012#	Field value greater than (after) 04/01/2012
Between #01/01/2012# And #03/31/2012#	Any date between 01/01/2012 and 03/31/2012

insert the symbols. Access automatically inserts the correct symbol when you press the Enter key after typing the query criteria.

In the criteria examples, the asterisk is used as a wild card indicating any character. This is consistent with many other software applications where the asterisk is used as a wildcard character. Two of the criteria examples in Table 3.1 use the less than and greater than symbols. You can use these symbols for fields containing numbers, values, dates, amounts, and so forth. In the next several projects, you will be designing queries to extract specific information from different tables in databases.

HINT

Access inserts quotation marks around text criteria and the pound symbol around date criteria.

Project 1a **Performing Queries on Tables** Part 1 of 8

1. Display the Open dialog box with Access2010L1C3 on your storage medium the active folder.
2. Open the **AL1-C3-Dearborn.accdb** database and enable the contents.
3. Create the following relationships and enforce referential integrity (and cascade fields and records) for each relationship:
   a. Create a one-to-one relationship where the *ClientID* field in the Clients table is the "one" and the *ClientID* field in the Sales table is the "one."
   b. Create a one-to-one relationship where the *RepID* field in the Representatives table is the "one" and the *RepID* field in the Benefits table is the "one."
   c. Create a one-to-many relationship where the *RepID* field in the Representatives table is the "one" and the *RepID* field in the Clients table is the "many."
   d. Create a one-to-many relationship where the *QuotaID* field in the Quotas table is the "one" and the *QuotaID* field in the Representatives table is the "many."
4. Click the Save button on the Quick Access toolbar.
5. Print the relationships by completing the following steps:
   a. Click the Relationship Report button in the Tools group in the Relationship Tools Design tab.

b. At the relationship report window, click the Landscape button in the Page Layout group in the Print Preview tab.

c. Click the Print button that displays at the left side of the Print Preview tab.

d. At the Print dialog box, click OK.

6. Close the relationships report window without saving the report.

7. Close the Relationships window.

8. Extract records of those clients located in Indianapolis by completing the following steps:

a. Click the Create tab.

b. Click the Query Design button in the Queries group.

c. At the Show Table dialog box with the Tables tab selected (see Figure 3.1), click *Clients* in the list box, click the Add button, and then click the Close button.

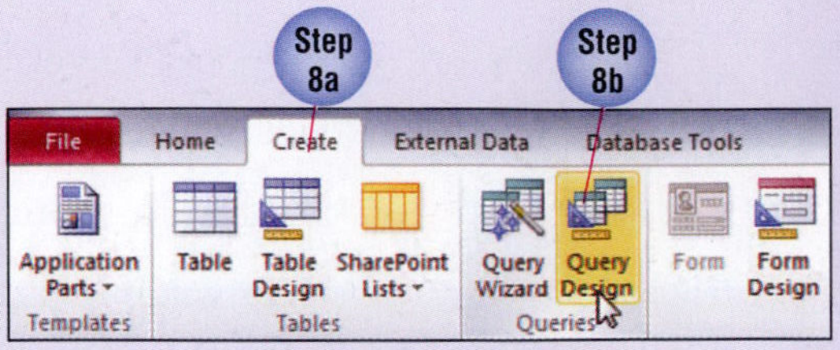

d. Insert fields from the table to *Field* row fields in the query design grid by completing the following steps:

1) Click the down-pointing arrow located at the right of the first *Field* row field in the query design grid and then click *Client* in the drop-down list.

2) Click inside the next *Field* row field (to the right of *Client*) in the query design grid, click the down-pointing arrow, and then click *StreetAddress* in the drop-down list.

3) Click inside the next *Field* row field (to the right of *StreetAddress*), click the down-pointing arrow, and then click *City* in the drop-down list.

4) Click inside the next *Field* row field (to the right of *City*), click the down-pointing arrow, and then click *State* in the drop-down list.

5) Click inside the next *Field* row field (to the right of *State*), click the down-pointing arrow, and then select *ZipCode* in the drop-down list.

Step 8d2		Step 8d3	Step 8d4	Step 8d5

Field:	Client	StreetAddress	City	State	ZipCode
Table:	Clients	Clients	Clients	Clients	Clients
Sort:					
Show:	✓	✓	✓	✓	✓
Criteria:					
or:

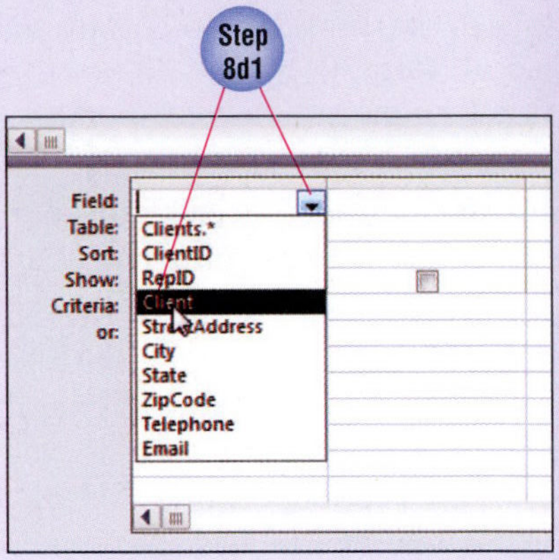

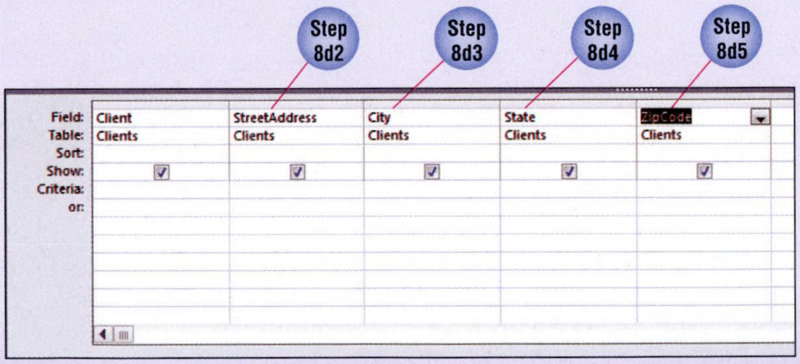

e. Insert the criterion text telling Access to display only those suppliers located in Indianapolis by completing the following steps:

Step 8e2

Field:	Client	StreetAddress	City	State
Table:	Clients	Clients	Clients	Clients
Sort:				
Show:	✓	✓	✓	
Criteria:			"Indianapolis"	
or:				

1) Click in the *Criteria* row field in the *City* column in the query design grid. (This positions the insertion point in the field.)

2) Type **Indianapolis** and then press Enter. (This changes the criterion to "Indianapolis".)

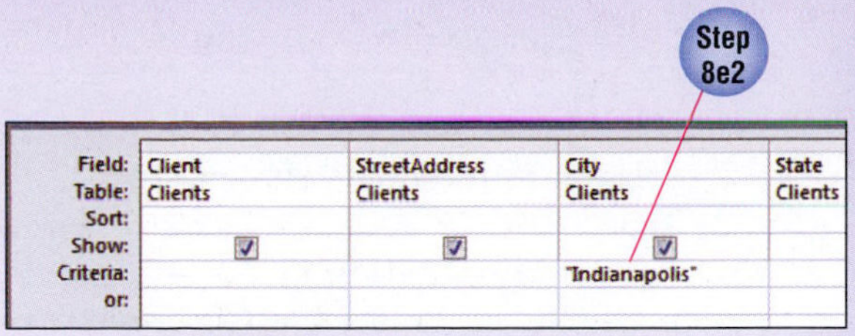

f. Return the results of the query by clicking the Run button in the Results group. (This displays the results in the query results datasheet.)

Step 8f

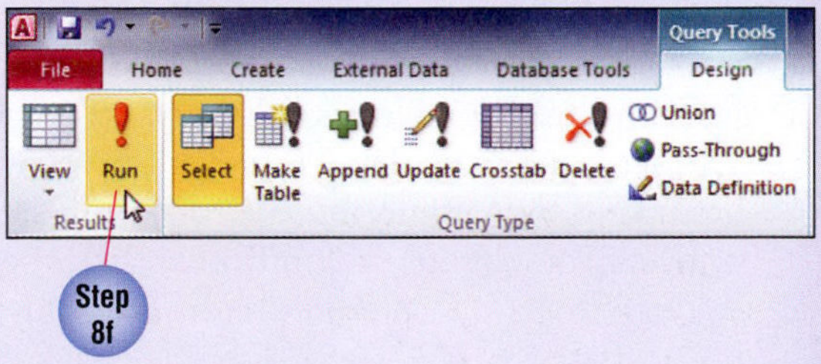

g. Save the results of the query by completing the following steps:

1) Click the Save button on the Quick Access toolbar.

2) At the Save As dialog box, type **ClientsIndianapolisQuery** and then press Enter or click OK. (See Project 1a query results on page 80.)

h. Print the query results datasheet by clicking the File tab, clicking the Print tab, and then clicking the *Quick Print* option.

i. Close ClientsIndianapolisQuery.

9. Extract those records with quota identification numbers higher than 2 by completing the following steps:

a. Click the Create tab and then click the Query Design button in the Queries group.

b. Double-click *Representatives* in the Show Table list box and then click the Close button.

c. In the query window, double-click *RepName*. (This inserts the field in the first *Field* row field in the query design grid.)

d. Double-click *QuotaID*. (This inserts the field in the second *Field* row field in the query design grid.)

e. Insert the query criterion by completing the following steps:

Field:	RepName	QuotaID
Table:	Representatives	Representatives
Sort:		
Show:	✓	✓
Criteria:		>"2"
or:		

Step 9e2

1) Click in the *Criteria* row field in the *QuotaID* column in the query design grid.

2) Type **>2** and then press Enter. (Access will automatically insert quotation marks around *2* since the data type for the field is set at *Text* [rather than *Number*].)

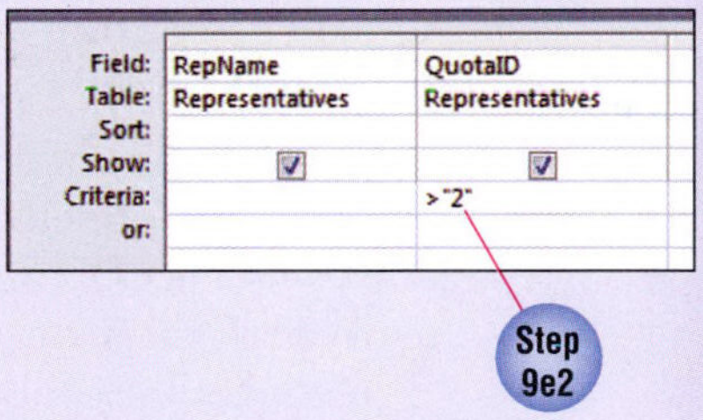

f. Return the results of the query by clicking the Run button in the Results group.

g. Save the query and name it *QuotaIDGreaterThanTwoQuery*. (See Project 1a query results on page 80.)

h. Print and then close the query.

10. Extract those 2011 sales greater than $99,999 by completing the following steps:

a. Click the Create tab and then click the Query Design button.

b. Double-click *Sales* in the Show Table dialog box and then click the Close button.

c. At the query window, double-click *ClientID*. (This inserts the field in the first *Field* row field in the query design grid.)

d. Insert the *Sales2011* field in the second *Field* row field.

e. Insert the query criterion by completing the following steps:
   1) Click in the *Criteria* row field in the *Sales2011* column in the query design grid.
   2) Type **>99999** and then press Enter. (Access will not insert quotation marks around *99999* since the field is identified as *Currency*.)

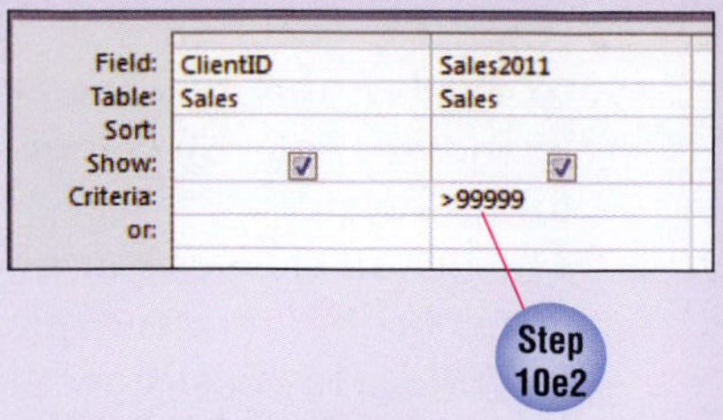

f. Return the results of the query by clicking the Run button in the Results group.
g. Save the query and name it *2011SalesOver$99999Query*. (See Project 1a query results on page 80.)
h. Print and then close the query.

11. Extract records of those representatives with a telephone number that begins with the 765 area code by completing the following steps:
   a. Click the Create tab and then click the Query Design button.
   b. Double-click *Representatives* in the Show Table dialog box and then click the Close button.
   c. Insert the *RepName* field in the first *Field* row field.
   d. Insert the *Telephone* field in the second *Field* row field.
   e. Insert the query criterion by completing the following steps:
      1) Click in the *Criteria* row field in the *Telephone* column.
      2) Type ***765*** and then press Enter.

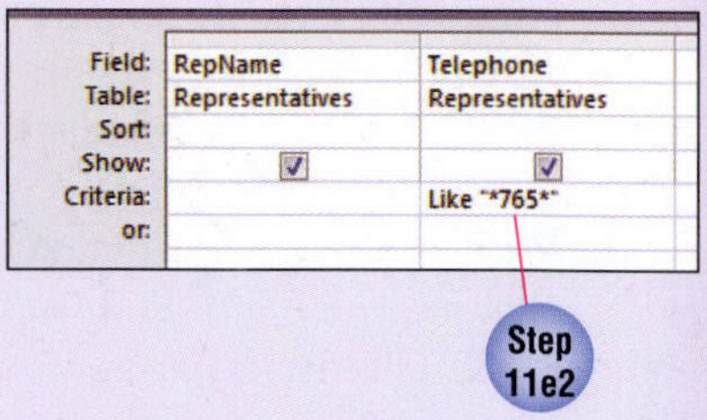

   f. Return the results of the query by clicking the Run button in the Results group.
   g. Save the query and name it *RepsWith765AreaCodeQuery*. (See Project 1a query results on page 80.)
   h. Print and then close the query.

In Project 1a, you performed several queries on specific tables. A query can also be performed on fields from more than one table. In Project 1b, you will perform queries on related tables.

When completing steps in Project 1b you will be instructed to open the AL1-C3-CopperState.accdb database. Two of the tables in the database contain yes/no check boxes. When designing a query, you can extract records containing a check mark or records that do not contain a check mark. If you want to extract records that contain a check mark, you would click in the *Criteria* row field in the desired column in the query design grid, type a *1*, and then press Enter. When you press the Enter key, Access changes the *1* to *True*. If you want to extract records that do not contain a check mark, you would type *0* in the *Criteria* row field and then press Enter. Access changes the 0 to *False*.

You can use the Zoom box when entering a criterion in a query to provide a larger area for typing. To display the Zoom box, press Shift + F2 or right-click in the desired Criteria row field and then click *Zoom* at the shortcut menu. Type the desired criterion in the Zoom box and then click OK.

Project 1b Performing a Query on Related Tables

Part 2 of 8

1. With the **AL1-C3-Dearborn.accdb** database open, extract information on representatives hired between March of 2008 and November of 2008 and include the representative's name by completing the following steps:
   a. Click the Create tab and then click the Query Design button.
   b. Double-click *Representatives* in the Show Table dialog box.
   c. Double-click *Benefits* in the Show Table dialog box list box and then click the Close button.
   d. At the query window, double-click *RepName* in the Representatives table.
   e. Double-click *HireDate* in the Benefits table.
   f. Insert the query criterion in the Zoom box by completing the following steps:
      1) Click in the *Criteria* row field in the *HireDate* column.
      2) Press Shift + F2 to display the Zoom box.
      3) Type **Between 3/1/2008 And 11/30/2008**. (Make sure you type zeros and not capital *O*s.)
      4) Click OK.
   g. Return the results of the query by clicking the Run button in the Results group.
   h. Save the query and name it *MarToNov2008HiresQuery*. (See Project 1b query results on page 80.)
   i. Print and then close the query.

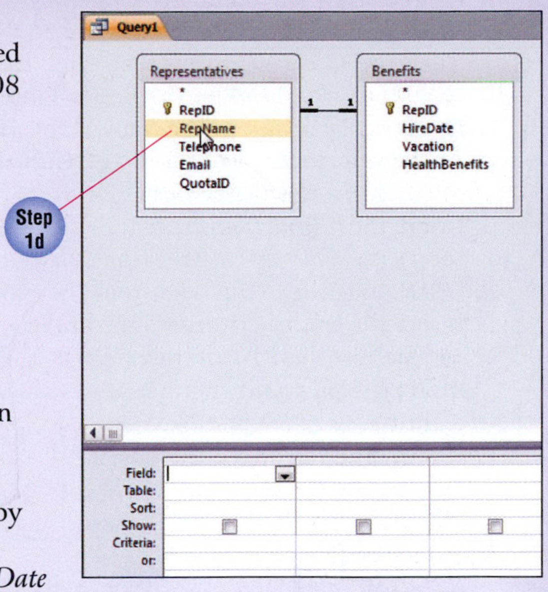

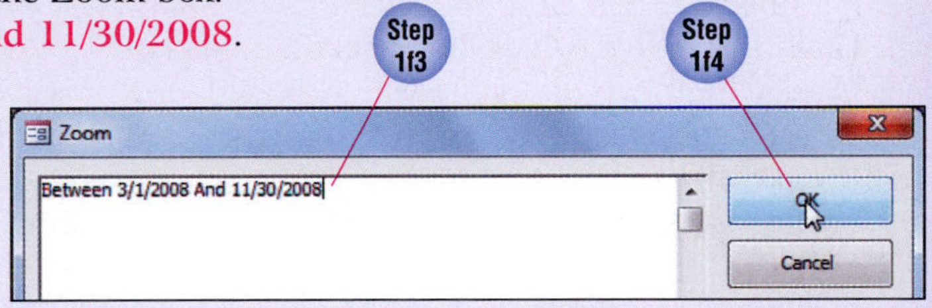

2. Extract records of those representatives who were hired in 2009 by completing the following steps:
   a. Click the Create tab and then click the Query Design button.
   b. Double-click *Representatives* in the Show Table dialog box.
   c. Double-click *Benefits* in the Show Table dialog box and then click the Close button.
   d. At the query window, double-click *RepID* field in the Representatives table.
   e. Double-click *RepName* in the Representatives table.
   f. Double-click *HireDate* in the Benefits table.
   g. Insert the query criterion by completing the following steps:
      1) Click in the *Criteria* row field in the *HireDate* column.
      2) Type ***2009** and then press Enter.
   h. Return the results of the query by clicking the Run button in the Results group.
   i. Save the query and name it *RepsHiredIn2009Query*. (See Project 1b query results on page 80.)
   j. Print and then close the query.

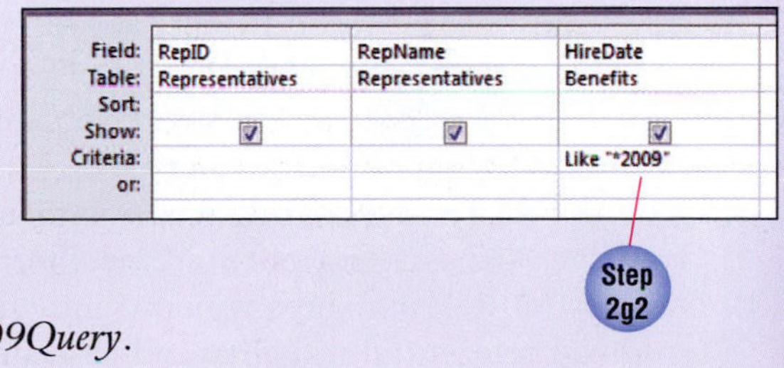

3. Suppose you need to determine 2010 and 2011 sales for a company but you can only remember that the company name begins with *Blue*. Create a query that finds the company and identifies the sales by completing the following steps:
 a. Click the Create tab and then click the Query Design button.
 b. Double-click *Clients* in the Show Table dialog box.
 c. Double-click *Sales* in the Show Table dialog box and then click the Close button.
 d. At the query window, insert the *ClientID* field from the Clients table in the first *Field* row field in the query design grid.
 e. Insert the *Client* field from the Clients table in the second *Field* row field.
 f. Insert the *Sales2010* field from the Sales table in the third *Field* row field.
 g. Insert the *Sales2011* field from the Sales table in the fourth *Field* row field.
 h. Insert the query criterion by completing the following steps:
 1) Click in the *Criteria* row field in the *Client* column.
 2) Type **Blue*** and then press Enter.
 i. Return the results of the query by clicking the Run button in the Results group.

Field:	ClientID	Client	Sales2010	Sales2011
Table:	Clients	Clients	Sales	Sales
Sort:				
Show:	☑	☑	☑	☑
Criteria:		Like "Blue*"		
or:				

Step 3h2

 j. Save the query and name it *BlueRidgeSalesQuery*. (See Project 1b query results on page 80.)
 k. Print and then close the query.
4. Close the **AL1-C3-Dearborn.accdb** database.
5. Display the Open dialog box with Access2010L1C3 on your storage medium the active folder.
6. Open the **AL1-C3-PacTrek.accdb** database and enable the contents.
7. Extract information on products ordered between February 1 and February 28, 2012, and include the supplier's name by completing the following steps:
 a. Click the Create tab and then click the Query Design button.
 b. Double-click *Products* in the Show Table dialog box.
 c. Double-click *Orders* in the Show Table dialog box and then click the Close button.
 d. At the query window, insert the *Product#* field from the Products table in the first *Field* row field.
 e. Insert the *Product* field from the Products table in the second *Field* row field.
 f. Insert the *OrderDate* field from the Orders table in the third *Field* row field.
 g. Insert the query criterion by completing the following steps:
 1) Click in the *Criteria* row field in the *OrderDate* column.
 2) Type **Between 2/1/2012 And 2/28/2012** and then press Enter. (Make sure you type zeros and not capital *O*s.)
 h. Return the results of the query by clicking the Run button in the Results group.

Field:	Product#	Product	OrderDate
Table:	Products	Products	Orders
Sort:			
Show:	☑	☑	☑
Criteria:			Between #2/1/2012#.
or:			

Step 7g2

 i. Save the query and name it *Feb1-28OrdersQuery*. (See Project 1b query results on page 80.)
 j. Print and then close the query.
8. Close the **AL1-C3-PacTrek.accdb** database.
9. Open the **AL1-C3-CopperState.accdb** database and enable the contents.
10. Display the Relationships window and create the following additional relationships (enforced referential integrity and cascade fields and records):
 a. Create a one-to-many relationships with the *AgentID* field in the Agents table the "one" and the *AgentID* field in the Assignments table the "many."

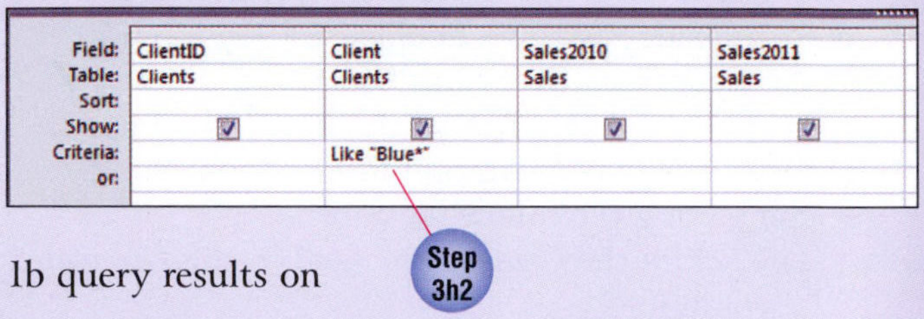

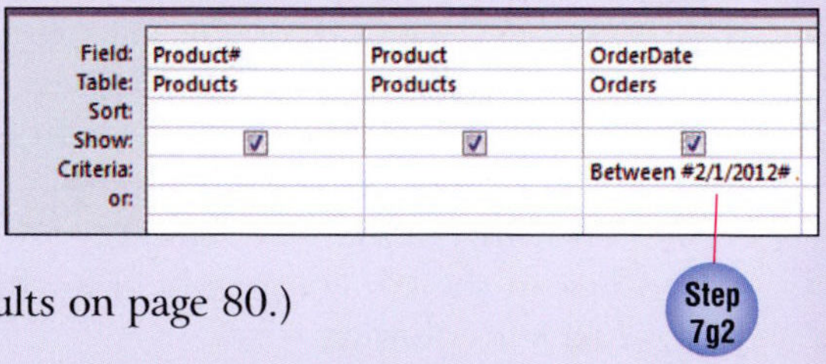

b. Create a one-to-many relationship with the *OfficeID* field in the Offices table the "one" and the *OfficeID* field in the Assignments table the "many."
c. Create a one-to-many relationship with the *OfficeID* field in the Offices table the "one" and the *OfficeID* field in the Agents table the "many."

11. Save and then print the relationships in landscape orientation.
12. Close the relationships report without saving it and then close the Relationships window.
13. Extract records of clients that have uninsured motorist coverage by completing the following steps:
    a. Click the Create tab and then click the Query Design button.
    b. Double-click *Clients* in the Show Table dialog box.
    c. Double-click *Coverage* in the Show Table dialog box and then click the Close button.
    d. At the query window, insert the *Client#* field from the Clients table in the first *Field* row field.
    e. Insert the *FirstName* field from the Clients table in the second *Field* row field.
    f. Insert the *LastName* field from the Clients table in the third *Field* row field.
    g. Insert the *UninsMotorist* field from the Coverage table in the fourth *Field* row field.
    h. Insert the query criterion by clicking in the *Criteria* row field in the *UninsMotorist* column, typing **1**, and then pressing the Enter. (Access changes the *1* to *True*.)

Field:	Client#	FirstName	LastName	UninsMotorist
Table:	Clients	Clients	Clients	Coverage
Sort:				
Show:	✓	✓	✓	✓
Criteria:				True
or:				

Step 13h

    i. Click the Run button in the Results group.
    j. Save the query and name it *UninsMotoristCoverageQuery*. (See Project 1b query results on page 80.)
    k. Print and then close the query.
14. Extract records of claims in January over $500 by completing the following steps:
    a. Click the Create tab and then click the Query Design button.
    b. Double-click *Clients* in the Show Table dialog box.
    c. Double-click *Claims* in the Show Table dialog box and then click the Close button.
    d. At the query window, insert the *Client#* field from the Clients table in the first *Field* row field.
    e. Insert the *FirstName* field from the Clients table in the second *Field* row field.
    f. Insert the *LastName* field from the Clients table in the third *Field* row field.
    g. Insert the *Claim#* field from the Claims table in the fourth *Field* row field.
    h. Insert the *DateOfClaim* field from the Claims table in the fifth *Field* row field.
    i. Insert the *AmountOfClaim* field from the Claims table in the sixth *Field* row field.
    j. Click in the *Criteria* row field in the *DateOfClaim* column, type **Between 1/1/2012 And 1/31/2012**, and then press Enter.
    k. With the insertion point positioned in the *Criteria* row field in the *AmountOfClaim* column, type **>500** and then press Enter.

Field:	Client#	FirstName	LastName	Claim#	DateOfClaim	AmountOfClaim
Table:	Clients	Clients	Clients	Claims	Claims	Claims
Sort:						
Show:	✓	✓	✓	✓	✓	✓
Criteria:					Between #1/1/2012#	>500
or:						

Step 14j

Step 14k

    l. Click the Run button in the Results group.
    m. Save the query and name it *JanClaimsOver$500Query*. (See Project 1b query results on page 80.)
    n. Print and then close the query.

Quick Steps

Sort Fields in Query

1. At query window, click in *Sort* row field in query design grid.
2. Click down arrow in *Sort* row field.
3. Click *Ascending* or *Descending.*

Sorting and Showing or Hiding Fields in a Query

When designing a query, you can specify the sort order of a field or fields. Click inside one of the columns in the *Sort* row field and a down-pointing arrow displays at the right of the field. Click this down-pointing arrow and a drop-down list displays with the choices *Ascending*, *Descending*, and *(not sorted)*. Click *Ascending* to sort from lowest to highest or click *Descending* to sort from highest to lowest. You can hide specific fields in the query result by removing the check mark from the check box in the *Show* row in the design grid for the field you do not want to show in the results.

Arranging Fields in a Query

With buttons in the Query Setup group in the Query Design Tools tab, you can insert a new field column in the query design grid and delete a field column from the query design grid. To insert a field column, click in a field in the column that you want to display immediately right of the new column and then click the Insert Columns button in the Query Setup group in the Query Design Tools tab. To remove a column, click in a field in the column you want to delete and then click the Delete Columns button in the Query Setup group. You would complete similar steps to insert or delete a row in the query design grid.

You can also rearrange columns in the query design grid by selecting the desired field column and then dragging the column to the desired position. To select a column in the query design grid, position the mouse pointer at the top of the column until the pointer turns into a small, black, down-pointing arrow and then click the left mouse button. Position the mouse pointer toward the top of the selected column until the mouse displays as a pointer, hold down the left mouse button, drag to the desired position in the design grid, and then release the mouse button. As you drag the column, a thick, black, vertical line displays identifying the location where the column will be inserted.

Project 1c **Performing a Query on Related Tables and Sorting in Field Values** **Part 3 of 8**

1. With the **AL1-C3-CopperState.accdb** database open, extract information on clients with agents from the West Bell Road Glendale office and sort the information alphabetically by client last name by completing the following steps:
   a. Click the Create tab and then click the Query Design button.
   b. Double-click *Assignments* in the Show Table dialog box.
   c. Double-click *Clients* in the Show Table dialog box and then click the Close button.
   d. At the query window, insert the *OfficeID* field from the Assignments table in the first *Field* row field.
   e. Insert the *AgentID* field from the Assignments table in the second *Field* row field.
   f. Insert the *FirstName* field from the Clients table in the third *Field* row field.
   g. Insert the *LastName* field from the Clients table in the fourth *Field* row field.

h. Click in the *Criteria* row field in the *OfficeID* column, type **GW**, and then press the Enter.

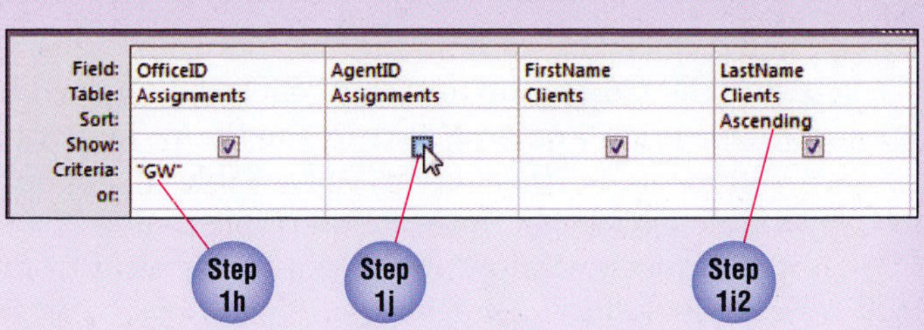

i. Sort the *LastName* field in ascending alphabetical order (A–Z) by completing the following steps:
   1) Click in the *Sort* row field in the *LastName* column. (This causes a down-pointing arrow to display at the right side of the field.)
   2) Click the down-pointing arrow at the right side of the *Sort* row field and then click *Ascending*.

j. Specify that you do not want the *AgentID* field to show in the query results by clicking in the check box in the *Show* row in the *AgentID* column to remove the check mark.

k. Click the Run button in the Results group.

l. Save the query and name it *GWClientsQuery*. (See Project 1c query results on page 81.)

m. Print and then close the query.

2. Close the **AL1-C3-CopperState.accdb** database.
3. Open the **AL1-C3-PacTrek.accdb** database.
4. Extract information on orders less than $1,500 by completing the following steps:
   a. Click the Create tab and then click the Query Design button.
   b. Double-click *Products* in the Show Table dialog box.
   c. Double-click *Orders* in the Show Table dialog box and then click the Close button.
   d. At the query window, insert the *Product#* field from the Products table in the first *Field* row field.
   e. Insert the *Supplier#* field from the Products table in the second *Field* row field.
   f. Insert the *UnitsOrdered* field from the Orders table in the third *Field* row field.
   g. Insert the *Amount* field from the Orders table in the fourth *Field* row field.
   h. Insert the query criterion by completing the following steps:

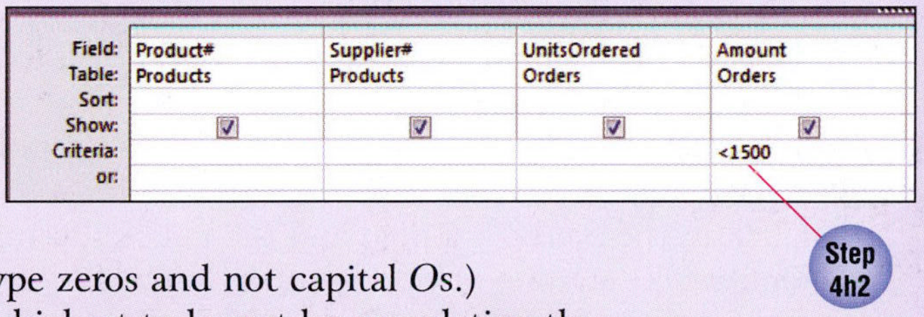

      1) Click in the *Criteria* row field in the *Amount* column.
      2) Type **<1500** and then press Enter. (Make sure you type zeros and not capital *O*s.)
   i. Sort the *Amount* field values from highest to lowest by completing the following steps:

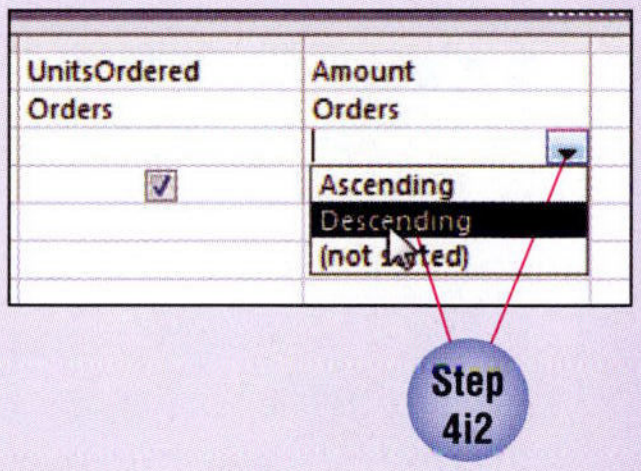

      1) Click in the *Sort* row field in the *Amount* column. (This causes a down-pointing arrow to display at the right side of the field.)
      2) Click the down-pointing arrow at the right side of the *Sort* field and then click *Descending*.
   j. Return the results of the query by clicking the Run button in the Results group.
   k. Save the query and name it *OrdersLessThan$1500Query*. (See Project 1c query results on page 81.)
   l. Print and then close the query.
5. Close the **AL1-C3-PacTrek.accdb** database.
6. Open the **AL1-C3-Dearborn.accdb** database.

7. Design a query by completing the following steps:
   a. Click the Create tab and then click the Query Design button.
   b. Double-click *Representatives* in the Show Table dialog box.
   c. Double-click *Clients* in the Show Table dialog box.
   d. Double-click *Sales* in the Show Table dialog box and then click the Close button.
   e. At the query window, insert the *RepID* field from the Representatives table in the first *Field* row field.
   f. Insert the *RepName* field from the Representatives table in the second *Field* row field.
   g. Insert the *ClientID* field from the Clients table in the third *Field* row field.
   h. Insert the *Sales2010* field from the Sales table in the fifth *Field* row field.
   i. Insert the *Sales2011* field from the Sales table in the sixth *Field* row field.
8. Move the *RepName* field by completing the following steps:
   a. Position the mouse pointer at the top of the *RepName* column until the pointer turns into a small, black, down-pointing arrow and then click the left mouse button. (This selects the entire column.)

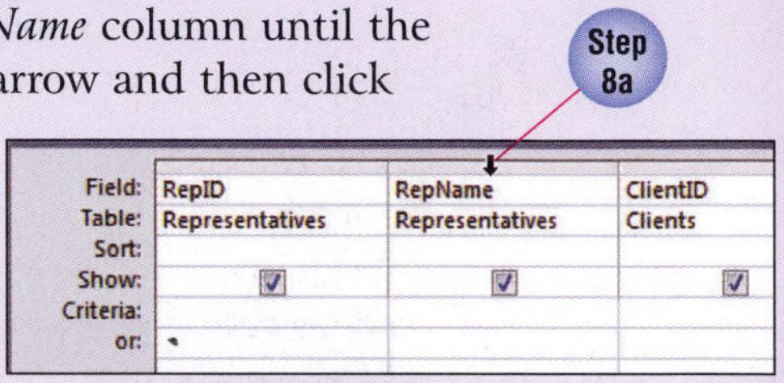

   b. Position the mouse pointer toward the top of the selected column until the pointer turns into a white arrow.
   c. Hold down the left mouse button, drag to the right until a thick, black, horizontal line displays between the *Sales2010* column and the *Sales2011* column, and then release the mouse button.

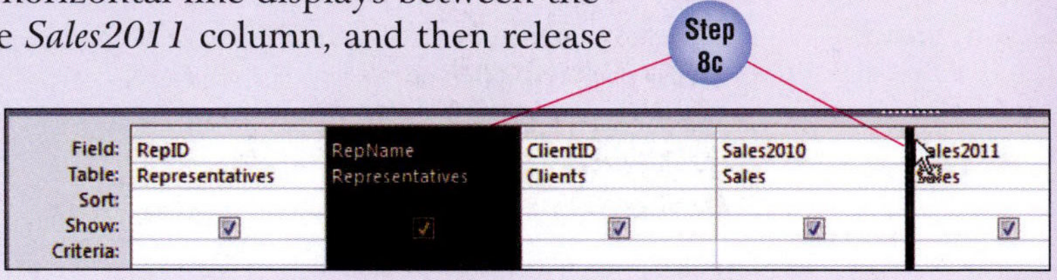

9. Delete the *Sales2011* column by clicking in a field in the column and then clicking the Delete Columns button in the Query Setup group in the Query Tools Design tab.
10. Delete the *RepID* field by clicking in a field in the column and then clicking the Delete Columns button in the Query Setup group.
11. Insert a new field column and insert a new field in the column by completing the following steps:
    a. Click in the *Sales2010* field and then click the Insert Columns button in the Query Setup group.
    b. Click the down-pointing arrow at the right side of the new field and then click *Clients.Client* at the drop-down list.

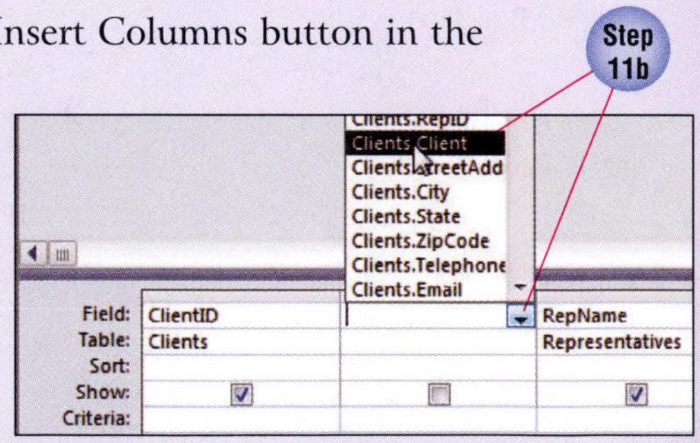

12. Hide the *ClientID* field so it does not display in the query results by clicking the *Show* check box in the *ClientID* column to remove the check mark.
13. Insert the query criterion that extracts information on sales over $100,000 for 2010 by completing the following steps:
    a. Click in the *Criteria* row field in the *Sales2010* column.
    b. Type **<100000** and then press Enter. (Make sure you type zeros and not capital *O*s.)
14. Sort the *Sales2010* field values from highest to lowest by completing the following steps:
    a. Click in the *Sort* row field in the *Sales2010* column.
    b. Click the down-pointing arrow at the right side of the *Sort* row field and then click *Descending*.

15. Return the results of the query by clicking the Run button in the Results group.
16. Save the query and name it *2010SalesLessThan$100000Query*. (See Project 1c query results on page 81.)
17. Print and then close the query.

Modifying a Query

You can modify a saved query. For example, suppose after designing the query that displays the 2010 sales that are less than $100,000, you decide that you want to find sales for 2011 that are less than $100,000. Rather than designing a new query, open the existing query, make any needed changes, and then run the query.

To modify an existing query, double-click the query in the Navigation pane. (This displays the query in Datasheet view.) Click the View button to display the query in Design view. You can also open a query in Design view by right-clicking the query in the Navigation pane and then clicking *Design View* at the shortcut menu. Make the desired changes and then click the Run button in the Results group. Click the Save button on the Quick Access toolbar to save the query with the same name. If you want to save the query with a new name, click the File tab, and then click Save Object As. At the Save As dialog box, type a name for the query and then press Enter.

If your database contains a number of queries, you can group and display them in the Navigation pane. To do this, click the down-pointing arrow in the Navigation pane Menu bar and then click *Object Type* at the drop-down list. This displays objects grouped in categories such as *Tables* and *Queries*.

Quick Steps

Modify a Query
1. Double-click query in Navigation pane.
2. Click View button.
3. Make desired changes to query.
4. Click Run button.
5. Click Save button.

HINT

Save time designing a query by modifying an existing query.

Project 1d **Modifying Queries** **Part 4 of 8**

1. With the **AL1-C3-Dearborn.accdb** database open, find the sales less than $100,000 for 20011 by completing the following steps:
   a. Change the display of objects in the Navigation pane by clicking the down-pointing arrow in the Navigation pane Menu bar and then clicking *Object Type* at the drop-down list.
   b. Double-click the *2010SalesLessThan$100000Query* in the *Queries* section of the Navigation pane.
   c. Click the View button in the Views group to switch to Design view.
   d. Click in the *Field* row field containing the text *Sales2010*.

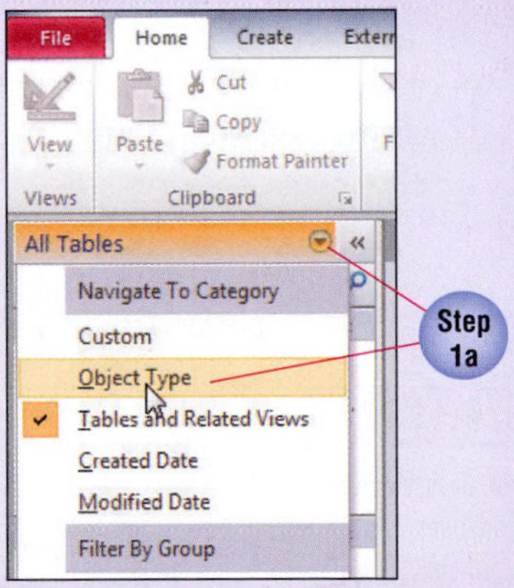

e. Click the down-pointing arrow that displays at the right side of the *Field* row field and then click *Sales2011* at the drop-down list.

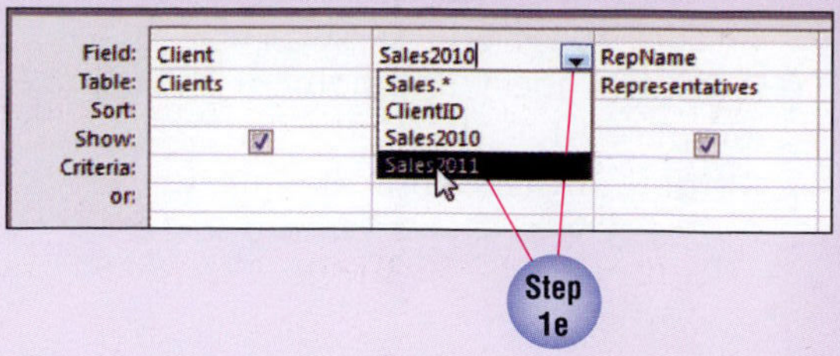

f. Click the Run button in the Results group.

2. Save the query with a new name by completing the following steps:
   a. Click the File tab and then click Save Object As.
   b. At the Save As dialog box, type **2011SalesLessThan$100000Query** and then press Enter. (See Project 1d query results on page 81.)

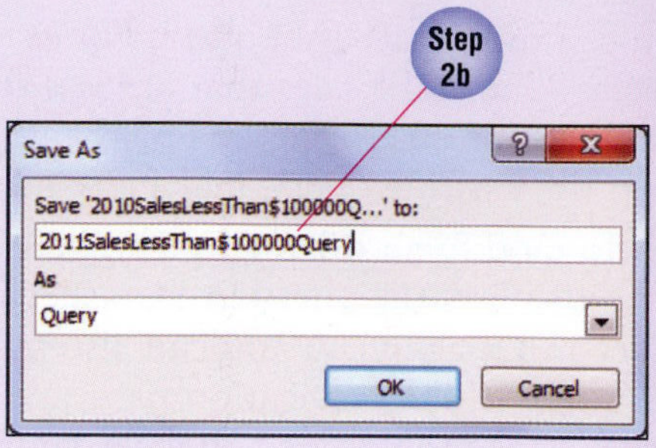

   c. Click the File tab to return to the query.
   d. Print and then close the query.
3. Modify an existing query and find employees with three weeks of vacation by completing the following steps:
   a. Right-click *MarToNov2008HiresQuery* in the Navigation pane and then click *Design View* at the shortcut menu.
   b. Click in the *Field* row field containing the text *HireDate*.
   c. Click the down-pointing arrow that displays at the right side of the field and then click *Vacation* at the drop-down list.
   d. Select the current text in the *Criteria* row field in the *Vacation* column, type **3 weeks**, and then press Enter.

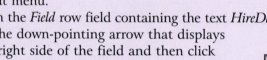

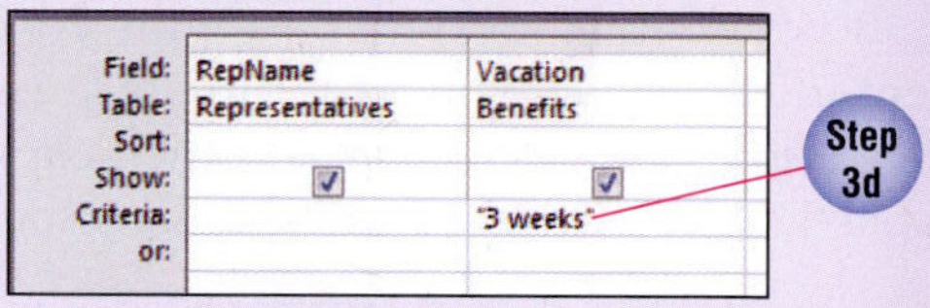

   e. Click the Run button in the Results group.
4. Save the query with a new name by completing the following steps:
   a. Click the File tab and then click Save Object As.
   b. At the Save As dialog box, type **RepsWith3WeekVacationsQuery** and then press Enter. (See Project 1d query results on page 81.)
   c. Click the File tab to return to the query.
   d. Print and then close the query.

Designing Queries with *Or* and *And* Criteria

HINT

You can design a query that combines *And* and *Or* statements.

The query design grid contains an *Or* row you can use to design a query that instructs Access to display records that match either of the two criteria. For example, to display a list of employees with three weeks of vacation *or* four weeks of vacation, you would type *3 weeks* in the *Criteria* row field for the *Vacation* column and then type *4 weeks* in the field immediately below *3 weeks* in the *Or* row. Other examples include finding clients that live in *Muncie* or *Lafayette* or finding representatives with a quota of *1* or *2*.

You can also select records by entering criteria statements into more than one *Criteria* field. Multiple criteria all entered in the same row become an *And* statement where each criterion must be met for Access to select the record. For example, you could search for clients in the Indianapolis area with sales greater than $100,000.

Project 1e Designing Queries with *Or* and *And* Criteria

Part 5 of 8

1. With the **AL1-C3-Dearborn.accdb** database open, modify an existing query and find employees with three weeks or four weeks of vacation by completing the following steps:
   a. Double-click the *RepsWith3WeekVacationsQuery*.
   b. Click the View button in the Views group to switch to Design view.
   c. Click in the empty field below *"3 weeks"* in the *Or* row, type **4 weeks**, and then press Enter.
   d. Click the Run button in the Results group.

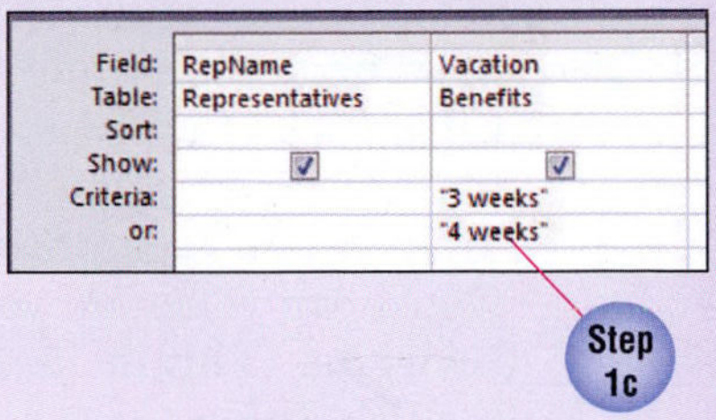

2. Save the query with a new name by completing the following steps:
   a. Click the File tab and then click Save Object As.
   b. At the Save As dialog box, type **RepsWith3Or4WeekVacationsQuery** and then press Enter. (See Project 1e query results on page 81.)
   c. Click the File tab to return to the query.
   d. Print and then close the query.
3. Design a query that finds records of clients in the Indianapolis area with sales over $100,000 for 2010 and 2011 by completing the following steps:
   a. Click the Create tab and then click the Query Design button.
   b. Double-click *Clients* in the Show Table dialog box.
   c. Double-click *Sales* in the Show Table dialog box and then click the Close button.
   d. At the query window, insert the *Client* field from the Clients table in the first *Field* row field.
   e. Insert the *City* field from the Clients table in the second *Field* row field.
   f. Insert the *Sales2010* field from the Sales table in the third *Field* row field.
   g. Insert the *Sales2011* field from the Sales table in the fourth *Field* row field.
   h. Insert the query criteria by completing the following steps:
      1) Click in the *Criteria* row field in the *City* column.
      2) Type **Indianapolis** and then press Enter.
      3) With the insertion point positioned in the *Criteria* row field in the *Sales2010* column, type **>100000** and then press Enter.
      4) With the insertion point positioned in the *Criteria* row field in the *Sales2011* column, type **>100000** and then press Enter.

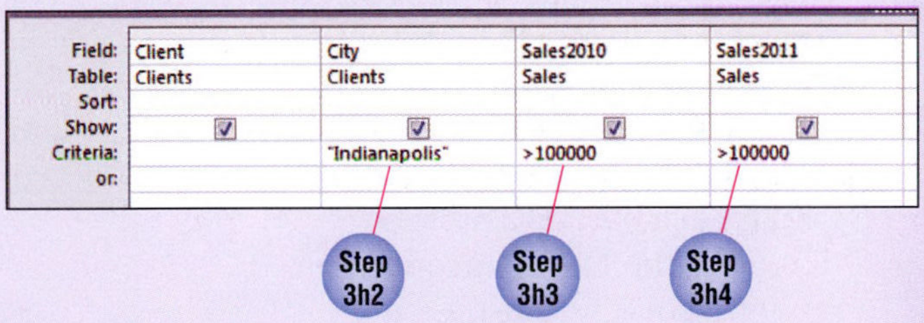

   i. Click the Run button in the Results group.
   j. Save the query and name it *SalesOver$100000IndianapolisQuery*. (See Project 1e query results on page 81.)
   k. Print and then close the query.
4. Close the **AL1-C3-Dearborn.accdb** database.
5. Open the **AL1-C3-PacTrek.accdb** database.
6. Design a query that finds products available from supplier numbers 25, 31, and 42 by completing the following steps:
   a. Click the Create tab and then click the Query Design button.
   b. Double-click *Suppliers* in the Show Table dialog box.
   c. Double-click *Products* in the Show Table dialog box and then click the Close button.

d. At the query window, insert the *Supplier#* field from the Suppliers table in the first *Field* row field.

e. Insert the *SupplierName* field from the Suppliers table in the second *Field* row field.

f. Insert the *Product* field from the Products table in the third *Field* row field.

g. Insert the query criteria by completing the following steps:

 1) Click in the *Criteria* row field in the *Supplier#* column.

 2) Type **25** and then press the Down Arrow key on your keyboard. (This makes active the field below *25*.)

 3) Type **31** and then press the Down Arrow key on your keyboard. (This makes active the field below *31*.)

 4) Type **42** and then press Enter.

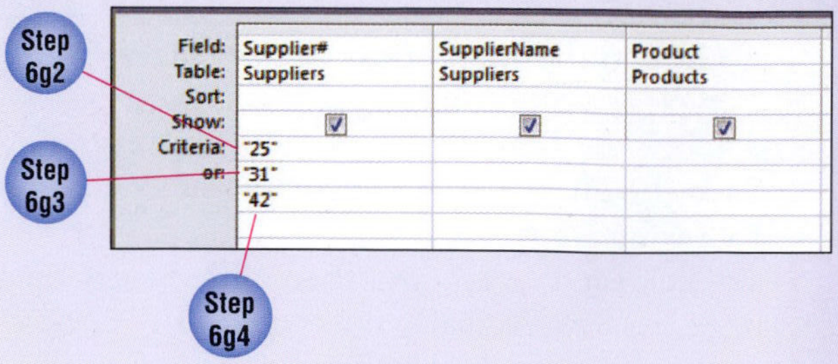

h. Click the Run button in the Results group.

i. Save the query and name it *Suppliers25-31-42Query*. (See Project 1e query results on page 81.)

j. Print and then close the query.

7. Design a query that finds ski hats and gloves on order and the number ordered by completing the following steps:

a. Click the Create tab and then click the Query Design button.

b. Double-click *Orders* in the Show Table dialog box.

c. Double-click *Suppliers* in the Show Table dialog box.

d. Double-click *Products* in the Show Table dialog box and then click the Close button.

e. At the query window, insert the *Order#* field from the Orders table in the first *Field* row field.

f. Insert the *SupplierName* field from the Suppliers table in the second *Field* row field.

g. Insert the *Product* field from the Products table in the third *Field* row field.

h. Insert the *UnitsOrdered* field from the Orders table in the fourth *Field* row field.

i. Insert the query criteria by completing the following steps:

 1) Click in the *Criteria* row field in the *Product* column.

 2) Type ***ski hat*** and then press the Down Arrow key on your keyboard. (You need to type the asterisk before and after *ski hat* so the query will find any product that includes the words *ski hat* in the description no matter what text comes before or after the words.)

Step 7i2

Step 7i3

Field:	Order#	SupplierName	Product	UnitsOrdered
Table:	Orders	Suppliers	Products	Orders
Sort:				
Show:	✓	✓	✓	✓
Criteria:			Like "*ski hat*"	
or:			Like "*gloves*"	

 3) Type ***gloves*** and then press Enter.

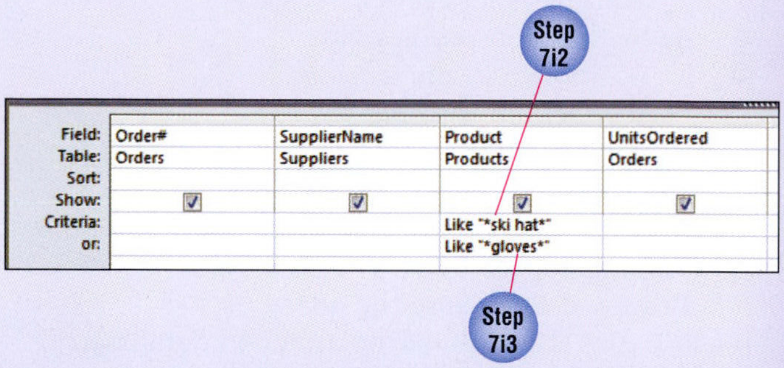

j. Click the Run button in the Results group.

k. Save the query and name it *SkiHatsGlovesOnOrderQuery*. (See Project 1e query results on page 81.)

l. Print and then close the query.

8. Design a query that finds boots, sleeping bags, and backpacks and the suppliers that produce them by completing the following steps:
   a. Click the Create tab and then click the Query Design button.
   b. Double-click *Products* in the Show Table dialog box.
   c. Double-click *Suppliers* in the Show Table dialog box and then click the Close button.
   d. At the query window, insert the *Product#* field from the Products table in the first *Field* row field.
   e. Insert the *Product* field from the Products table in the second *Field* row field.
   f. Insert the *SupplierName* field from the Suppliers table in the third *Field* row field.
   g. Insert the query criteria by completing the following steps:
      1) Click in the *Criteria* row field in the *Product* column.
      2) Type ***boots*** and then press the Down Arrow key on your keyboard.
      3) Type ***sleeping bag*** and then press the Down Arrow key on your keyboard.
      4) Type ***backpack*** and then press Enter.

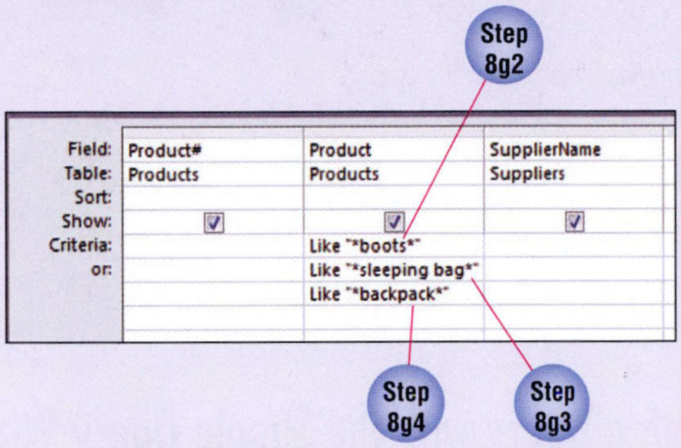

   h. Click the Run button in the Results group.
   i. Save the query and name it *BootsSleepingBagsBackpacksQuery*. (See Project 1e query results on page 81.)
   j. Print and then close the query.
9. Close the **AL1-C3-PacTrek.accdb** database.
10. Open the **AL1-C3-CopperState.accdb** database.
11. Design a query that finds clients that have only liability coverage by completing the following steps:
   a. Click the Create tab and then click the Query Design button.
   b. Double-click *Clients* in the Show Table dialog box.
   c. Double-click *Coverage* in the Show Table dialog box and then click the Close button.
   d. At the query window, insert the *Client#* field from the Clients table in the first *Field* row field.
   e. Insert the *FirstName* field from the Clients table in the second *Field* row field.
   f. Insert the *LastName* field from the Clients table in the third *Field* row field.
   g. Insert the *Medical* field from the Coverage table in the fourth *Field* row field.
   h. Insert the *Liability* field from the Coverage table in the fifth *Field* row field.
   i. Insert the *Comprehensive* field from the Coverage table in the sixth *Field* row field.
   j. Insert the *UninsMotorist* field from the Coverage table in the seventh *Field* row field.
   k. Insert the *Collision* field from the Coverage table in the eighth *Field* row field. (You will need to scroll down the Coverage table to display the *Collision* field.)

1. Insert the query criteria by completing the following steps:
 1) Click in the *Criteria* row field in the *Medical* column, type **0**, and then press Enter. (Access changes the *0* to *False*.)
 2) With the insertion point in the *Liability* column, type **1**, and then press Enter. (Access changes the *1* to *True*.)
 3) With the insertion point in the *Comprehensive* column, type **0**, and then press Enter.
 4) With the insertion point in the *UninsMotorist* column, type **0**, and then press Enter.
 5) With the insertion point in the *Collision* column, type **0**, and then press Enter.

Field:	Client#	FirstName	LastName	Medical	Liability	Comprehensive	UninsMotorist	Collision
Table:	Clients	Clients	Clients	Coverage	Coverage	Coverage	Coverage	Coverage
Sort:								
Show:	☑	☑	☑	☑	☑	☑	☑	☑
Criteria:				False	True	False	False	False
or:								

Step 11l1 Step 11l2 Step 11l3 Step 11l4 Step 11l5

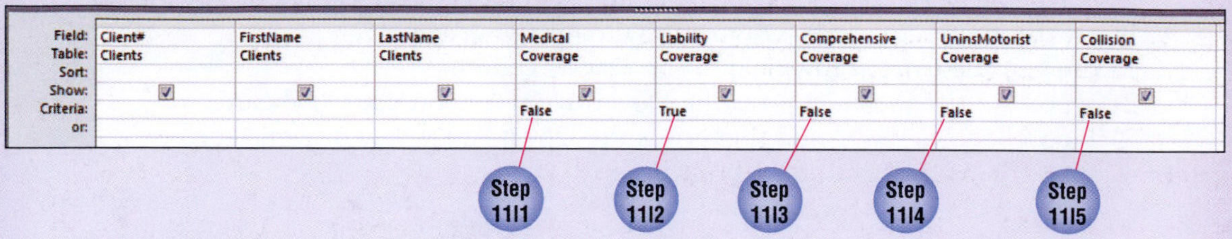

 m. Click the Run button in the Results group.
 n. Save the query and name it *ClientsWithOnlyLiabilityQuery*. (See Project 1e query results on page 81.)
 o. Print the query in landscape orientation.
 p. Close the query.
12. Close the **AL1-C3-CopperState.accdb** database.

Performing a Query with the Simple Query Wizard

Query Wizard

The Simple Query Wizard provided by Access guides you through the steps for preparing a query. To use this wizard, open the database, click the Create tab, and then click the Query Wizard button in the Queries group. At the New Query dialog box, make sure *Simple Query Wizard* is selected in the list box and then click the OK button. At the first Simple Query Wizard dialog box, shown in Figure 3.3, specify the table(s) in the *Tables/Queries* option box. After specifying the table, insert the fields you want included in the query in the *Selected Fields* list box, and then click the Next button.

Figure 3.3 First Simple Query Wizard Dialog Box

Specify the table in the *Tables/Queries* option box.

Click the One Field button to insert the selected field in the *Available Fields* list box into the *Selected Fields* list box.

Click the All Fields button to insert all of the fields in the *Available Fields* list box into the *Selected Fields* list box.

Insert in the *Selected Fields* list box the fields you want included in the query.

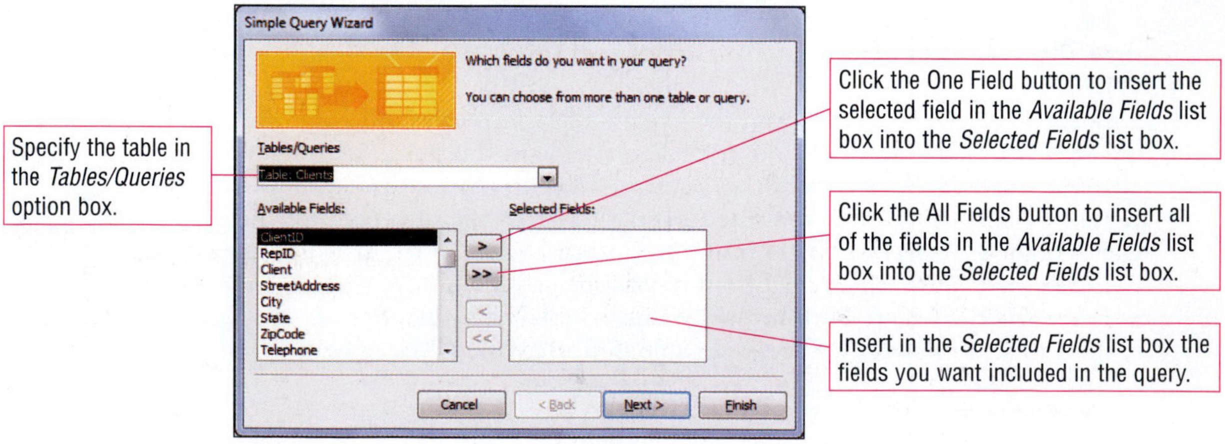

At the second Simple Query Wizard dialog box, specify whether you want a detail or summary query, and then click the Next button. At the third (and last) Simple Query Wizard dialog box, shown in Figure 3.4, type a name for the completed query or accept the name provided by the wizard. At this dialog box, you can also specify that you want to open the query to view the information or modify the query design. If you want to extract specific information, be sure to choose the *Modify the query design* option. After making any necessary changes, click the Finish button.

If you do not modify the query design in the last Simple Query Wizard dialog box, the query displays all records for the fields identified in the first Simple Query Wizard dialog box. In Project 1f you will perform a query without modifying the design, and in Project 1g you will modify the query design.

Quick Steps

Create a Query with Simple Query Wizard

1. Click Create tab.
2. Click Query Wizard button.
3. Make sure *Simple Query Wizard* is selected in list box and then click OK.
4. Follow query steps.

Figure 3.4 Last Simple Query Wizard Dialog Box

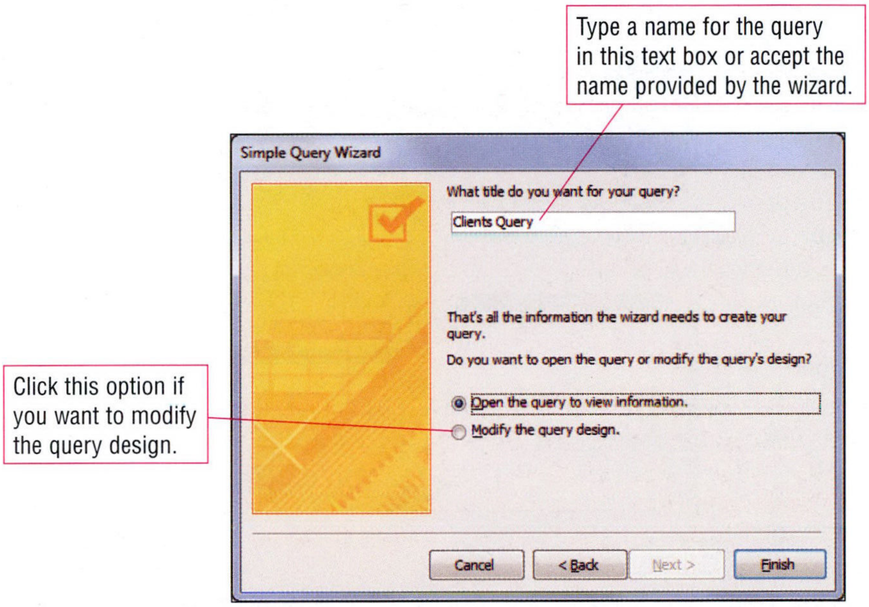

Project 1f Performing Queries with the Simple Query Wizard — Part 6 of 8

1. Open the **AL1-C3-Dearborn.accdb** database and then use the Simple Query Wizard to create a query that displays client names along with 2010 and 2011 sales by completing the following steps:
   a. Click the Create tab and then click the Query Wizard button in the Queries group.
   b. At the New Query dialog box, make sure *Simple Query Wizard* is selected in the list box and then click OK.
   c. At the first Simple Query Wizard dialog box, click the down-pointing arrow at the right of the *Tables/Queries* option box and then click *Table: Clients*. (You will need to scroll up the list to display this table.)

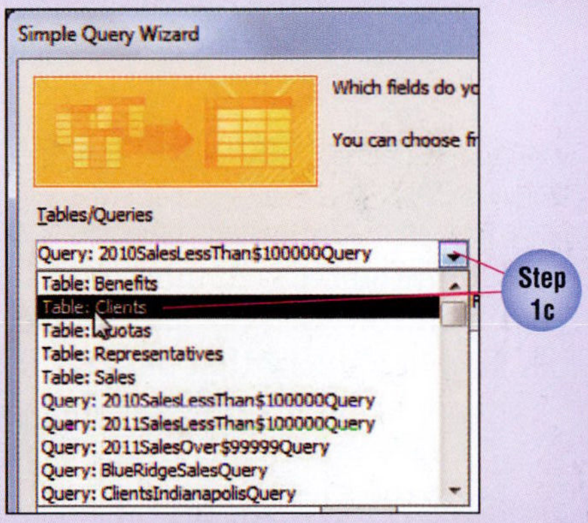

d. With *ClientID* selected in the *Available Fields* list box, click the One Field button (button containing the greater than symbol.) This inserts the *ClientID* field in the *Selected Fields* list box.
e. Click *Client* in the *Available Fields* list box and then click the One Field button.
f. Click the down-pointing arrow at the right of the *Tables/Queries* option box and then click *Table: Sales*.
g. Click *Sales2010* in the *Available Fields* list box and then click the One Field button.
h. With *Sales2011* selected in the *Available Fields* list box, click the One Field button.
i. Click the Next button.
j. At the second Simple Query Wizard dialog box, click the Next button.
k. At the last Simple Query Wizard dialog box, select the name in the *What title do you want for your query?* text box, type **Client2010-2011SalesQuery**, and then press Enter.

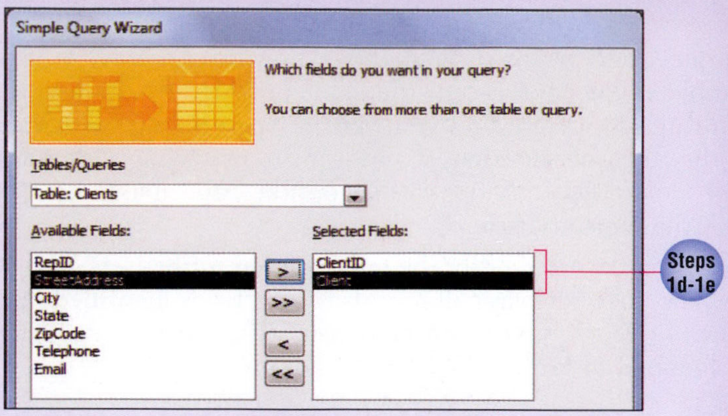

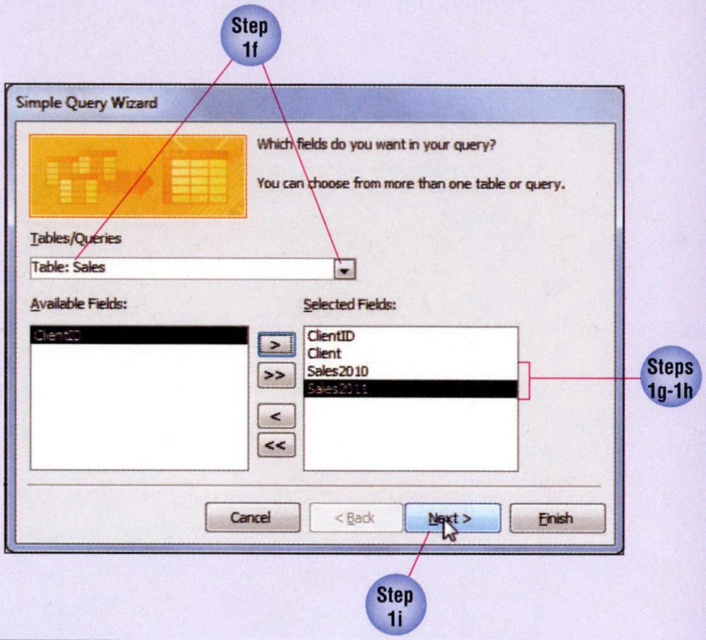

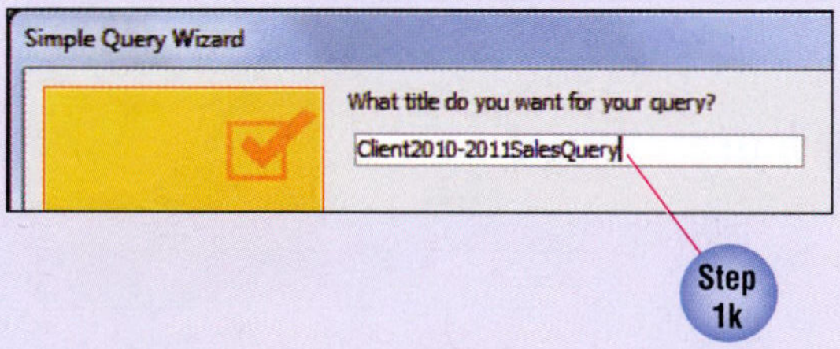

l. When the results of the query display, print the results. (See Project 1f query results on page 82.)
m. Close the query window.
2. Close the **AL1-C3-Dearborn.accdb** database.
3. Open the **AL1-C3-PacTrek.accdb** database.
4. Create a query that displays the products on order, the order amount, and the supplier name by completing the following steps:
a. Click the Create tab and then click the Query Wizard button.
b. At the New Query dialog box, make sure *Simple Query Wizard* is selected in the list box and then click OK.

c. At the first Simple Query Wizard dialog box, click the down-pointing arrow at the right side of the *Tables/Queries* option box and then click *Table: Suppliers*.

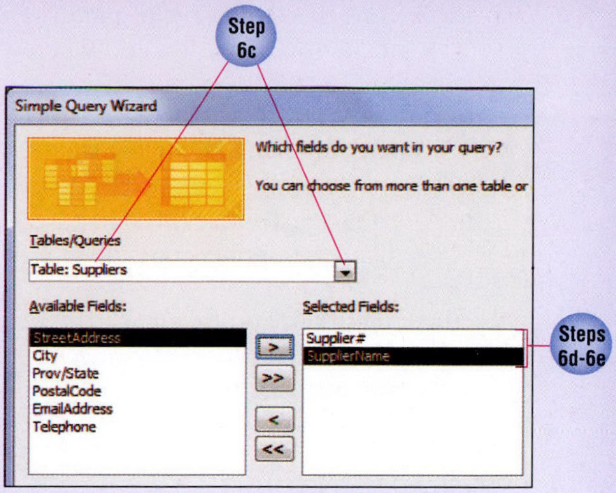

d. With *Supplier#* selected in the *Available Fields* list box, click the One Field button. (This inserts the *Supplier#* field in the *Selected Fields* list box.)

e. With *SupplierName* selected in the *Available Fields* list box, click the One Field button.

f. Click the down-pointing arrow at the right of the *Tables/Queries* option box and then click *Table: Orders*.

g. Click *Product#* in the *Available Fields* list box and then click the One Field button.

h. Click *Amount* in the *Available Fields* list box and then click the One Field button.

i. Click the Next button.

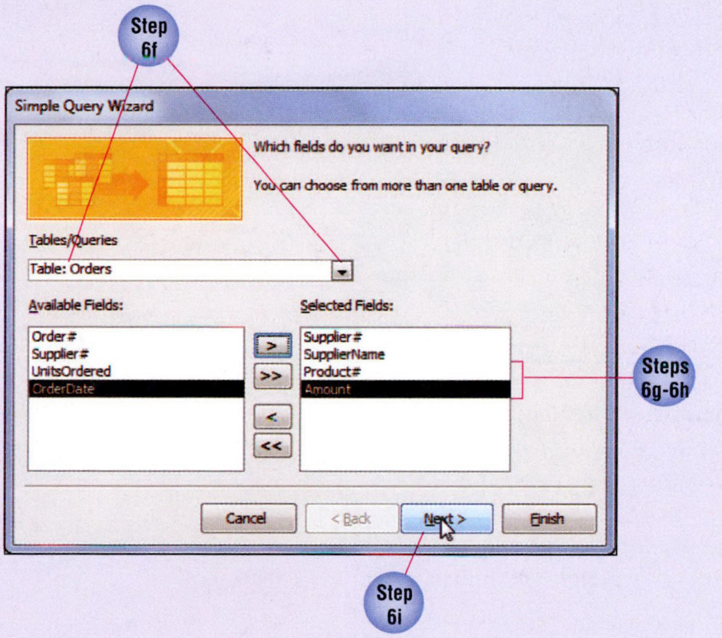

j. At the second Simple Query Wizard dialog box, click the Next button.

k. At the last Simple Query Wizard dialog box, select the text in the *What title do you want for your query?* text box, type **ProductOrderAmountsQuery**, and then press Enter.

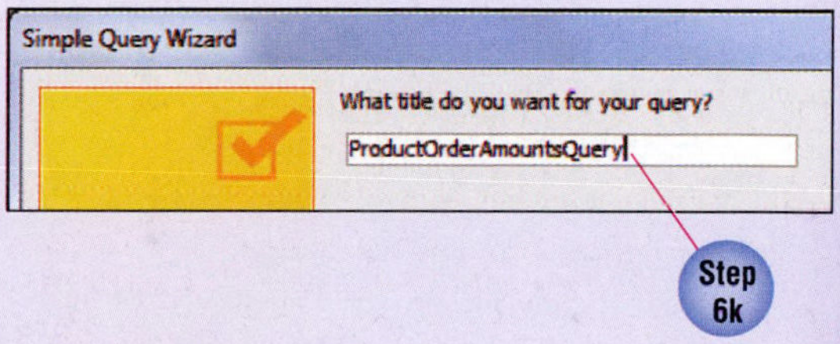

l. When the results of the query display, print the results. (See Project 1f query results on page 82.)

m. Close the query window.

To extract specific information when using the Simple Query Wizard, tell the wizard that you want to modify the query design. This displays the query window with the query design grid where you can insert query criteria.

Project 1g Performing and Modifying Queries with the Simple Query Wizard — Part 7 of 8

1. With the **AL1-C3-PacTrek.accdb** database open, use the Simple Query Wizard to create a query that displays suppliers outside of British Columbia by completing the following steps:
   a. Click the Create tab and then click the Query Wizard button.
   b. At the New Query dialog box, make sure *Simply Query Wizard* is selected and then click OK.
   c. At the first Simple Query Wizard dialog box, click the down-pointing arrow at the right side of the *Tables/Queries* option box and then click *Table: Suppliers*.
   d. Insert the following fields in the *Selected Fields* list box:
      SupplierName
      StreetAddress
      City
      Prov/State
      PostalCode

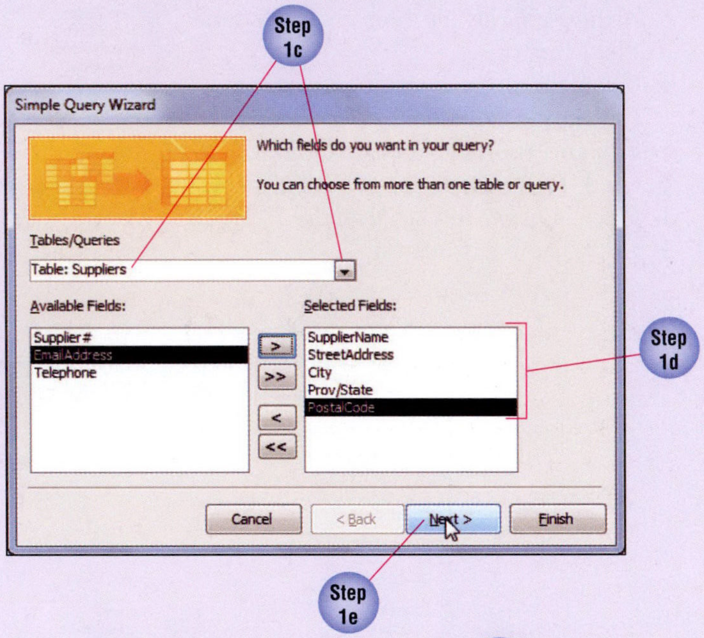

   e. Click the Next button.
   f. At the last Simple Query Wizard dialog box, select the current text in the *What title do you want for your query?* text box and then type **SuppliersNotBCQuery**.
   g. Click the *Modify the query design* option and then click the Finish button.
   h. At the query window, complete the following steps:
      1) Click in the *Criteria* row field in the *Prov/State* column in the query design grid.
      2) Type **Not BC** and then press Enter.
   i. Specify that the fields are to be sorted in descending order by postal code by completing the following steps:

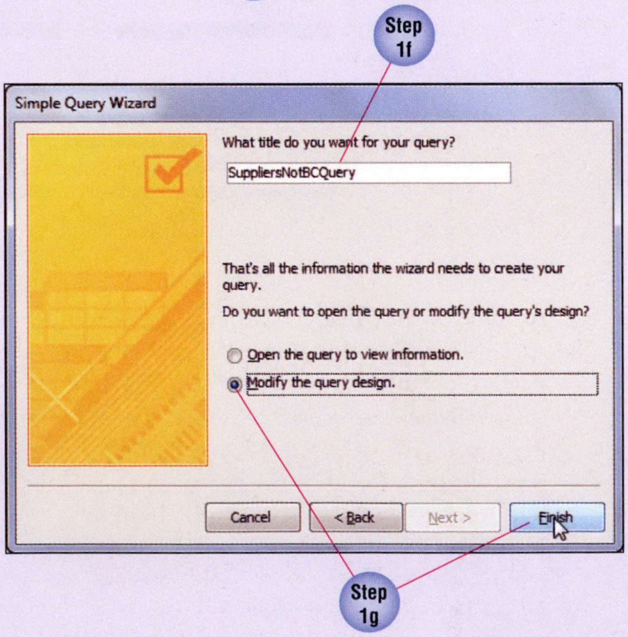

1) Click in the *Sort* row field in the *PostalCode* column.
2) Click the down-pointing arrow that displays at the right side of the field and then click *Descending*.

Field:	[SupplierName]	[StreetAddress]	[City]	[Prov/State]	[PostalCode]
Table:	Suppliers	Suppliers	Suppliers	Suppliers	Suppliers
Sort:					
Show:	✓	✓	✓	✓	Ascending
Criteria:				Not "BC"	Descending
or:					(not sorted)

Step 1i2

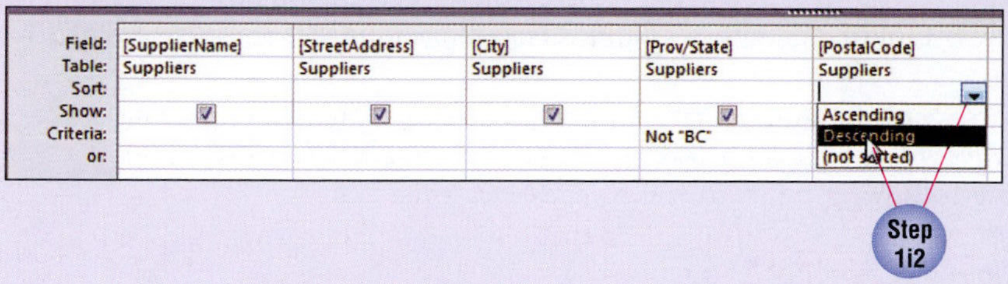

 j. Click the Run button in the Results group. (This displays suppliers that are not located in British Columbia and displays the records sorted by PostalCode in decending order. See Project 1g query results on page 82.)

 k. Save, print, and then close the query.

2. Close the **AL1-C3-PacTrek.accdb** database.
3. Open the **AL1-C3-Dearborn.accdb** database.
4. Use the Simple Query Wizard to create a query that displays clients in Muncie by completing the following steps:

 a. Click the Create tab and then click the Query Wizard button.

 b. At the New Query dialog box, make sure *Simple Query Wizard* is selected and then click OK.

 c. At the first Simple Query Wizard dialog box, click the down-pointing arrow at the right of the *Tables/Queries* option box and then click *Table: Clients*. (You will need to scroll up the list to display this table.)

 d. Insert the following fields in the *Selected Fields* list box:

 Client
 StreetAddress
 City
 State
 ZipCode

 e. Click the Next button.

 f. At the last Simple Query Wizard dialog box, select the current text in the *What title do you want for your query?* text box and then type **ClientsMuncieQuery**.

 g. Click the *Modify the query design* option and then click the Finish button.

 h. At the query window, complete the following steps:

 1) Click in the *Criteria* row field in the *City* column.

 2) Type **Muncie** and then press Enter.

Field:	[Client]	[StreetAddress]	[City]	[State]	[ZipCode]
Table:	Clients	Clients	Clients	Clients	Clients
Sort:					
Show:	✓	✓	✓	✓	✓
Criteria:			"Muncie"		
or:					

Step 4h2

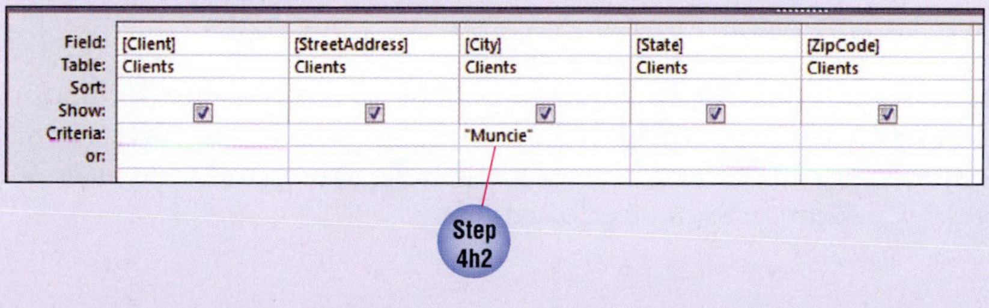

 i. Click the Run button in the Results group. (This displays clients located in Muncie. See Project 1g query results on page 82.)

 j. Save, print, and then close the query.

5. Close the **AL1-C3-Dearborn.accdb** database.

6. Open the **AL1-C3-CopperState.accdb** database.
7. Use the Simple Query Wizard to display clients that live in Phoenix with claims over $500 by completing the following steps:
   a. Click the Create tab and then click the Query Wizard button in the Queries group.
   b. At the New Query dialog box, make sure *Simple Query Wizard* is selected in the list box and then click OK.
   c. At the first Simple Query Wizard dialog box, click the down-pointing arrow at the right of the *Tables/Queries* option box and then click *Table: Clients*.
   d. Insert the following fields in the *Selected Fields* list box:
      Client#
      FirstName
      LastName
      StreetAddress
      City
      State
      ZIP
   e. Click the down-pointing arrow at the right of the *Tables/Queries* option box and then click *Table: Claims*.
   f. With *Claim#* selected in the *Available Fields* list box, click the One Field button.
   g. Click *AmountOfClaim* in the *Available Fields* list box and then click the One Field button.
   h. Click the Next button.
   i. At the second Simple Query Wizard dialog box, click the Next button.
   j. At the last Simple Query Wizard dialog box, select the current text in the *What title do you want for your query?* text box and then type **PhoenixClientClaimsOver$500Query**.
   k. Click the *Modify the query design* option and then click the Finish button.
   l. At the query window, complete the following steps:
      1) Click in the *Criteria* row field in the *City* column.
      2) Type **"Phoenix"** and then press Enter. (Type the quotation marks to tell Access that this is a criterion rather than an Access built-in function.)
      3) Click in the *Criteria* row field in the *AmountOfClaim* column. (You will need to scroll to the right to display this field.)
      4) Type **>500** and then press Enter.

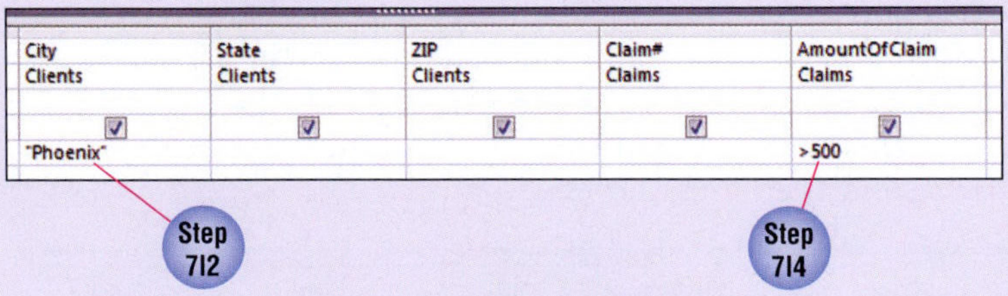

   m. Click the Run button in the Results group. (This displays clients located in Phoenix with a claim amount greater than $500. See Project 1g query results on page 82.)
   n. Save the query, print the query in landscape orientation, and then close the query.
8. Close the **AL1-C3-CopperState.accdb** database.

Creating a Calculated Field

In a query, you can calculate values from fields by inserting a *calculated field* in a *Field* row field in the query design grid. To insert a calculated field, click in the *Field* row field, type the desired field name followed by a colon, and then type the equation. For example, to add 2010 sales amounts with 2011 sales amounts, you would type *Total:[Sales2010]+[Sales2011]* in the *Field* row field. Use brackets to specify field names and use mathematical operators to perform the equation. Some basic operators include the plus symbol (+) for addition, the hyphen symbol (-) for subtraction, the asterisk (*) for multiplication, and the forward slash (/) for division.

You can type a calculated field in the field or in the Expression Builder dialog box. To display the Expression building dialog box, display the query in Design view, click in the field where you want the calculated field expression inserted, and then click the Builder button in the Query Setup group in the Query Tools Design tab. You can type field names in the Expression Builder and when you click OK the equation is inserted in the field with the correct symbols. For example, you can type *Sales2010+Sales2011* in the Expression Builder and, when you click OK, *Expr1: [Sales2010]+[Sales2011]* is inserted in the *Criteria* row field. If you do not type a name for the field, Access creates the alias *Expr1* for the field name. If you want a specific name for the field, such as *Total*, first type that in the Expression Builder followed by a colon and then type the expression.

Project 1h Creating a Calculated Field in a Query **Part 8 of 8**

1. Open the **AL1-C3-Dearborn.accdb** database.
2. Create a query that displays 2010 and 2011 sales and totals the sales by completing the following steps:
 a. Click the Create tab and then click the Query Design button.
 b. Double-click *Clients* in the Show Table dialog box.
 c. Double-click *Sales* in the Show Table dialog box and then click the Close button.
 d. At the query window, insert the *Client* field from the Clients table in the first *Field* row field.
 e. Insert the *Sales2010* field from the Sales table in the second *Field* row field.
 f. Insert the *Sales2011* field from the Sales table in the third *Field* row field.
 g. Click in the fourth *Field* row field.
 h. Type **Total:[Sales2010]+[Sales2011]** and then press Enter.

Step 2h

Field:	Client	Sales2010	Sales2011	Total: [Sales2010]+[Sa	▼
Table:	Clients	Sales	Sales		
Sort:					
Show:	☑	☑	☑	☑	☐
Criteria:					
or:					

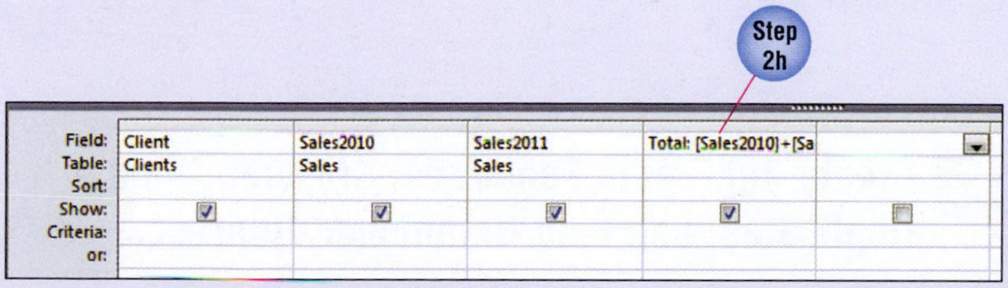

 i. Click the Run button in the Results group.
 j. Save the query and name it *SalesTotalQuery*. (See Project 1h query results on page 82.)
 k. Print and then close the query.

3. Modify the *SalesTotalQuery* and use the Expression Builder to write an equation finding the differences between sales by completing the following steps:
   a. Right-click *SalesTotalQuery* in the Navigation pane and then click *Design View* at the shortcut menu.
   b. Click in the field containing *Total:[Sales2010]+[Sales2011]*.
   c. Click the Builder button in the Query Setup group in the Query Tools Design tab.
   d. In the Expression Builder, select the existing expression *Total: :[Sales2010]+[Sales2011]*.
   e. Type **Difference:Sales2011-Sales2010** and then click OK.

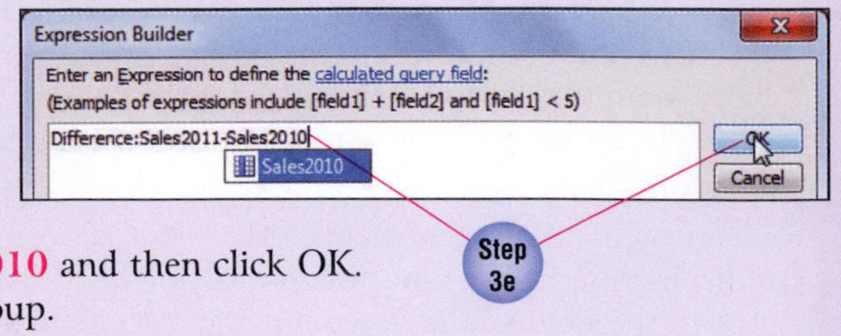

4. Click the Run button in the Results group.
5. Save the query by completing the following steps:
   a. Click the File tab and then click Save Object As.
   b. At the Save As dialog box, type **SalesDifferencesQuery** and then click OK.
6. Print and then close the query.
7. Close the **AL1-C3-Dearborn.accdb** database.
8. Open the **AL1-C3-PacTrek.accdb** database.
9. Create a query that displays order and total order amounts by completing the following steps:
   a. Click the Create tab and then click the Query Design button.
   b. Double-click *Suppliers* in the Show Table dialog box.
   c. Double-click *Orders* in the Show Table dialog box and then click the Close button.
   d. At the query window, insert the *SupplierName* field from the Suppliers table in the first *Field* row field.
   e. Insert the *Order#* field from the Orders table in the second *Field* row field.
   f. Insert the *UnitsOrdered* field from the Orders table in the third *Field* row field.
   g. Insert the *Amount* field from the Orders table in the fourth *Field* row field.
   h. Click in the fifth *Field* row field.
   i. Click the Builder button in the Query Setup group in the Query Tools Design tab.
   j. Type **Total:Amount*UnitsOrdered** in the Expression Builder and then click OK.
   k. Click the Run button in the Results group.
   l. Save the query and name it *UnitsOrderedTotalQuery*. (See Project 1h query results on page 82.)
   m. Print and then close the query.

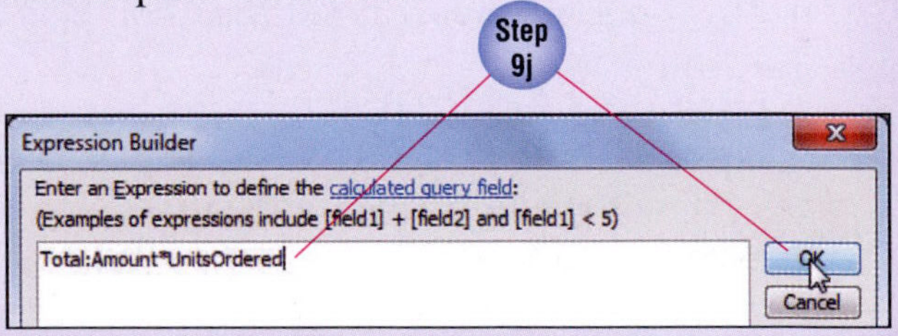

Project 2 Create Aggregate Functions, Crosstab, Find Duplicates, and Find Unmatched Queries

6 Parts

You will create an aggregate functions query that determines the total, average, minimum, and maximum order amounts and determine total and average order amounts grouped by supplier. You will also use the Crosstab, Find Duplicates, and Find Unmatched query wizards to design queries.

Figure 3.5 Query Results for Project 2a, Step 1

Access automatically determined the column heading names.

The aggregate functions calculated the order amounts in the *Amount* column in the Orders table.

AmountsQuery				
SumOfAmount	AvgOfAmount	MaxOfAmount	MinOfAmount	CountOfAmount
$26,530.27	$736.95	$2,999.85	$44.85	36

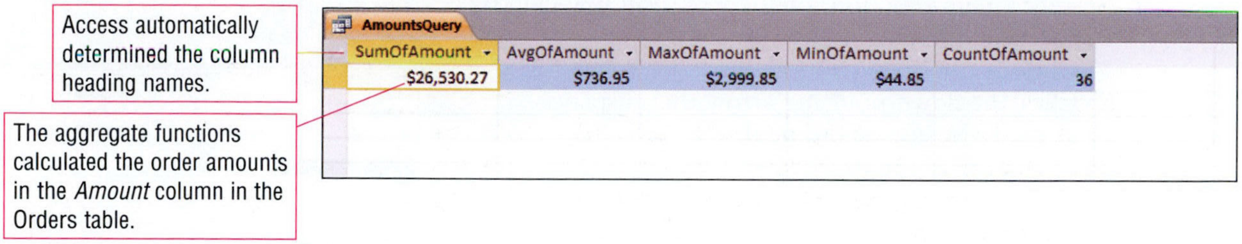

Designing Queries with Aggregate Functions ■■■■■■■

You can include an *aggregate function* such as Sum, Avg, Min, Max, or Count in a query to calculate statistics from numeric field values of all the records in the table. When an aggregate function is used, Access displays one row in the query results datasheet with the formula result for the function used. For example, in a table with a numeric field containing the annual salary amounts, you could use the Sum function to calculate the total of all salary amount values.

To display the aggregate function list, click the Totals button in the Show/Hide group in the Query Tools Design tab. Access adds a Total row to the design grid with a drop-down list from which you select the desired function. Access also inserts the words *Group By* in the *Total* row field. Click the down-pointing arrow and then click the desired aggregate function from the drop-down list. In Project 2a, Step 1, you will create a query in Design view and use aggregate functions to find the total of all sales, the average sales amount, the maximum and the minimum sales, and the total number of sales. The completed query will display as shown in Figure 3.5. Access automatically chooses the column heading names.

▼ **Quick Steps**

Design Query with Aggregate Function
1. At query window, click the Totals button.
2. Click the down-pointing arrow in *Total* row field.
3. Click desired aggregate function.

Σ

Totals

Project 2a **Using Aggregate Functions in Queries** **Part 1 of 6**

1. With the **AL1-C3-PacTrek.accdb** database open, create a query with aggregate functions that determines total, average, minimum, and maximum order amounts as well as the total number of orders by completing the following steps:
 a. Click the Create tab and then click the Query Design button.
 b. At the Show Table dialog box, make sure *Orders* is selected in the list box, click the Add button, and then click the Close button.
 c. Insert the *Amount* field in the first, second, third, fourth, and fifth *Field* row fields.
 d. Click the Totals button in the Show/Hide group in the Query Tools Design tab. (This adds a *Total* row to the design grid between *Table* and *Sort* with the default option of *Group By*.)

Step 1c

Field:	Amount	Amount	Amount	Amount	Amount
Table:	Orders	Orders	Orders	Orders	Orders
Sort:					
Show:	☑	☑	☑	☑	☑
Criteria:					
or:					

Step 1d

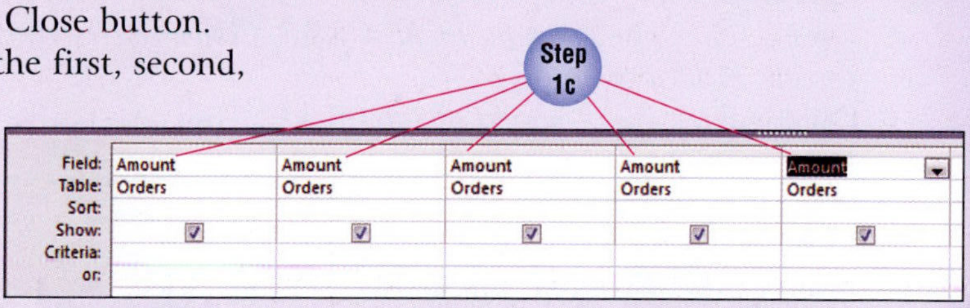

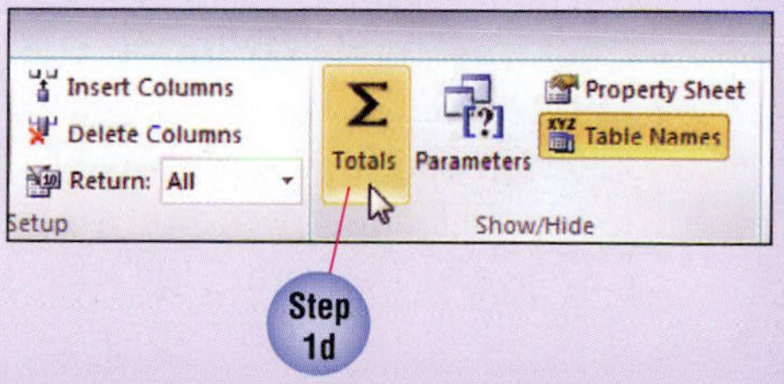

e. Specify a Sum function for the first *Total* row field by completing the following steps:
   1) Click in the first *Total* row field.
   2) Click the down-pointing arrow that displays at the right side of the field.
   3) Click *Sum* at the drop-down list.

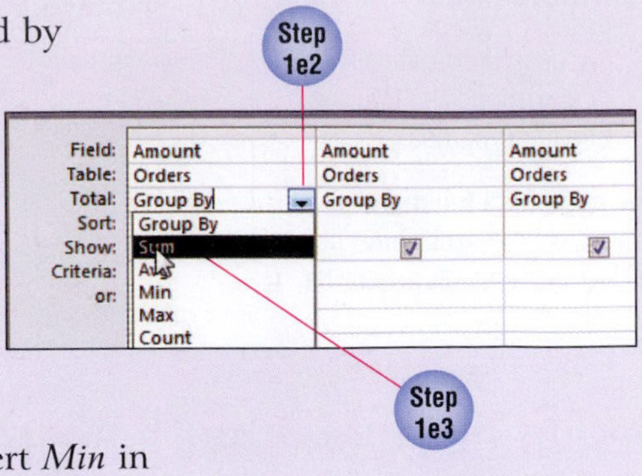

f. Complete steps similar to those in Step 1e to insert *Avg* in the second *Total* row field.
g. Complete steps similar to those in Step 1e to insert *Max* in the third *Total* row field.
h. Complete steps similar to those in Step 1e to insert *Min* in the fourth *Total* row field.
i. Complete steps similar to those in Step 1e to insert *Count* in the fifth *Total* row field.

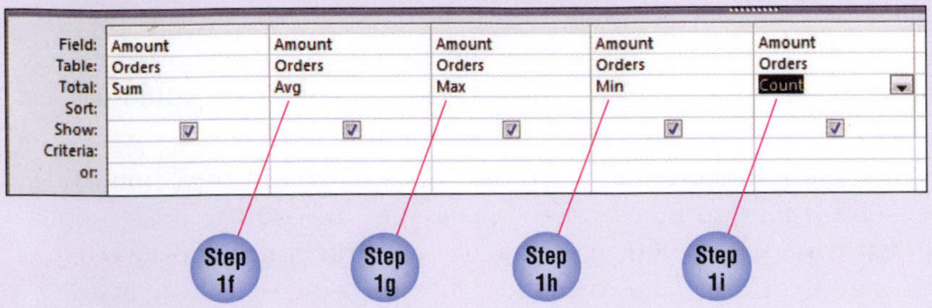

j. Click the Run button in the Results group. (Notice the headings that Access chooses for the columns.)
k. Automatically adjust the widths of the columns.
l. Save the query and name it *AmountsQuery*. (See Project 2a query results on page 82.)
m. Print and then close the query.

2. Close the **AL1-C3-PacTrek.accdb** database.
3. Open the **AL1-C3-CopperState.accdb** database.
4. Create a query with aggregate functions that determines total, average, minimum, and maximum claim amounts by completing the following steps:
   a. Click the Create tab and then click the Query Design button.
   b. At the Show Table dialog box, double-click *Claims*.
   c. Click the Close button to close the Show Table dialog box.
   d. Double-click the *AmountOfClaim* field. (This inserts the *AmountOfClaim* field in the first *Field* row field.)
   e. Double-click the *AmountOfClaim* field. (This inserts the *AmountOfClaim* field in the second *Field* row field.)
   f. Double-click the *AmountOfClaim* field. (This inserts the *AmountOfClaim* field in the third *Field* row field.)
   g. Double-click the *AmountOfClaim* field. (This inserts the *AmountOfClaim* field in the fourth *Field* row field.)
   h. Click the Totals button in the Show/Hide group.
   i. Click in the first *Total* row field, click the down-pointing arrow that displays at the right side of the field, and then click *Sum* at the drop-down list.

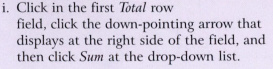

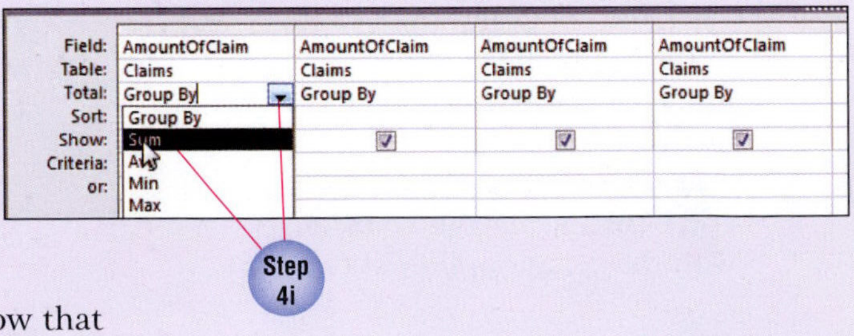

j. Click in the second *Total* row field, click the down-pointing arrow, and then click *Avg* at the drop-down list.

k. Click in the third *Total* row field, click the down-pointing arrow, and then click *Max* at the drop-down list.

l. Click in the fourth *Total* row field, click the down-pointing arrow, and then click *Min* at the drop-down list.

m. Click the Run button in the Results group. (Notice the headings that Access chooses for the columns.)

n. Automatically adjust the widths of the columns.

o. Save the query and name it *ClaimAmountsQuery*. (See Project 2a query results on page 82.)

p. Print the query in landscape orientation and then close the query.

Using the *Group By* option in the *Total* field you can add a field to the query upon which you want Access to group records for statistical calculations. For example, to calculate the total of all orders for a specific supplier, add the *Supplier#* field to the design grid with the *Total* field set to *Group By*. In Project 2b, Step 1, you will create a query in Design view and use aggregate functions to find the total of all order amounts and the average order amounts grouped by the supplier number.

Project 2b **Using Aggregate Functions and Grouping Records** Part 2 of 6

1. With the **AL1-C3-CopperState.accdb** database open, determine the sum and average of client claims by completing the following steps:

 a. Click the Create tab and then click the Query Design button.

 b. At the Show Table dialog box, double-click *Clients* in the list box.

 c. Double-click *Claims* in the list box and then click the Close button.

 d. Insert the *Client#* field from the Clients table list box to the first *Field* row field.

 e. Insert the *AmountOfClaim* field from the Claims table list box to the second *Field* row field.

 f. Insert the *AmountOfClaim* field from the Claims table list box to the third *Field* row field.

 g. Click the Totals button in the Show/Hide group.

 h. Click in the second *Total* row field, click the down-pointing arrow, and then click *Sum* at the drop-down list.

 i. Click in the third *Total* row field, click the down-pointing arrow, and then click *Avg* at the drop-down list.

 j. Make sure *Group By* displays in the first *Total* row field.

 k. Click the Run button in the Results group.

 l. Automatically adjust column widths.

 m. Save the query and name it *SumAvgClaimAmountsQuery*. (See Project 2b query results on page 83.)

 n. Print and then close the query.

2. Close the **AL1-C3-CopperState.accdb** database.

Field:	Client#	AmountOfClaim	AmountOfClaim
Table:	Clients	Claims	Claims
Total:	Group By	Sum	Avg
Sort:			
Show:	✓	✓	✓
Criteria:			
or:			

Step 1j Step 1h Step 1i

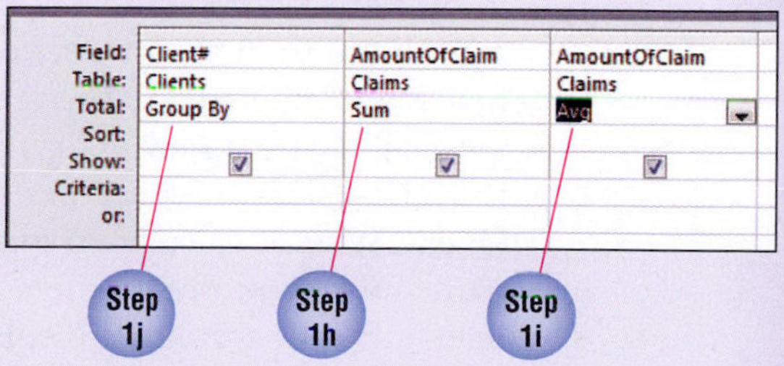

3. Open the **AL1-C3-PacTrek.accdb** database.
4. Determine the total and average order amounts for each supplier by completing the following steps:
   a. Click the Create tab and then click the Query Design button.
   b. At the Show Table dialog box, make sure *Orders* is selected in the list box and then click the Add button.
   c. Click *Suppliers* in the list box, click the Add button, and then click the Close button.
   d. Insert the *Amount* field from the Orders table list box to the first *Field* row field.
   e. Insert the *Amount* field from the Orders table list box to the second *Field* row field.
   f. Insert the *Supplier#* field from the Orders table list box to the third *Field* row field.
   g. Insert the *SupplierName* field from the Suppliers table to the fourth *Field* row field.
   h. Click the Totals button in the Show/Hide group.
   i. Click in the first *Total* row field, click the down-pointing arrow, and then click *Sum* at the drop-down list.
   j. Click in the second *Total* row field, click the down-pointing arrow, and then click *Avg* at the drop-down list.
   k. Make sure *Group By* displays in the third and fourth *Total* row fields.
   l. Click the Run button in the Results group.
   m. Save the query and name it *SupplierAmountsQuery*. (See Project 2b query results on page 83.)
   n. Print and then close the query.

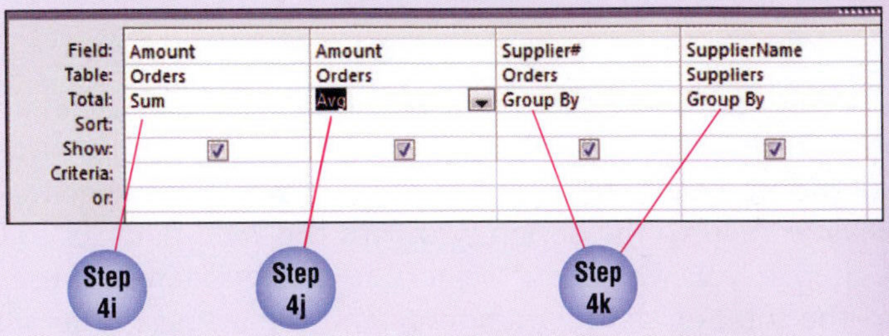

Creating a Crosstab Query

Quick Steps

Create a Crosstab Query
1. Click Create tab.
2. Click Query Wizard button.
3. Double-click *Crosstab Query Wizard*.
4. Complete wizard steps.

A ***crosstab query*** calculates aggregate functions such as Sum and Avg in which field values are grouped by two fields. A wizard is included that guides you through the steps to create the query. The first field selected causes one row to display in the query results datasheet for each group. The second field selected displays one column in the query results datasheet for each group. A third field is specified that is the numeric field to be summarized. The intersection of each row and column holds a value that is the result of the specified aggregate function for the designated row and column group.

Create a crosstab query from fields in one table. If you want to include fields from more than one table, you must first create a query containing the desired fields, and then create the crosstab query. For example, in Project 2c, Step 2, you will create a new query that contains fields from each of the three tables in the AL1-C3-PacTrek.accdb database. Using this query, you will use the Crosstab Query Wizard to create a query that summarizes the order amounts by supplier name and by product ordered. Figure 3.6 displays the results of that crosstab query. The first column displays the supplier names, the second column displays the total of amounts for each supplier, and the remaining columns display the amounts by suppliers for specific items.

Figure 3.6 Crosstab Query Results for Project 2c, Step 2

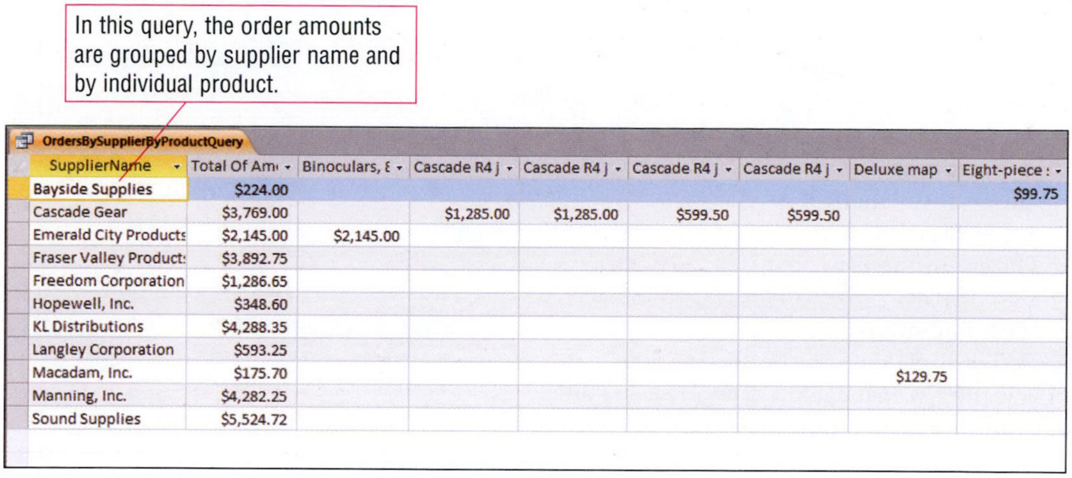

In this query, the order amounts are grouped by supplier name and by individual product.
OrdersBySupplierByProductQuery

SupplierName	Total Of Am	Binoculars, 8	Cascade R4 j	Cascade R4 j	Cascade R4 j	Cascade R4 j	Deluxe map	Eight-piece :
Bayside Supplies	$224.00							$99.75
Cascade Gear	$3,769.00		$1,285.00	$1,285.00	$599.50	$599.50		
Emerald City Products	$2,145.00	$2,145.00						
Fraser Valley Product:	$3,892.75							
Freedom Corporation	$1,286.65							
Hopewell, Inc.	$348.60							
KL Distributions	$4,288.35							
Langley Corporation	$593.25							
Macadam, Inc.	$175.70						$129.75	
Manning, Inc.	$4,282.25							
Sound Supplies	$5,524.72							

Project 2c Creating a Crosstab Query

Part 3 of 6

1. With the **AL1-C3-PacTrek.accdb** database open, create a query containing fields from the three tables by completing the following steps:
   a. Click the Create tab and then click the Query Design button.
   b. At the Show Table dialog box with *Orders* selected in the list box, click the Add button.
   c. Double-click *Products* in the Show Table dialog box.
   d. Double-click *Suppliers* in the list box and then click the Close button.
   e. Insert the following fields to the specified *Field* row fields:
      1) From the Orders table, insert the *Product#* field in the first *Field* row field.
      2) From the Products table, insert the *Product* field in the second *Field* row field.
      3) From the Orders table, insert the *UnitsOrdered* field in the third *Field* row field.
      4) From the Orders table, insert the *Amount* field in the fourth *Field* row field.
      5) From the Suppliers table, insert the *SupplierName* field in the fifth *Field* row field.
      6) From the Orders table, insert the *OrderDate* field in the sixth *Field* row field.

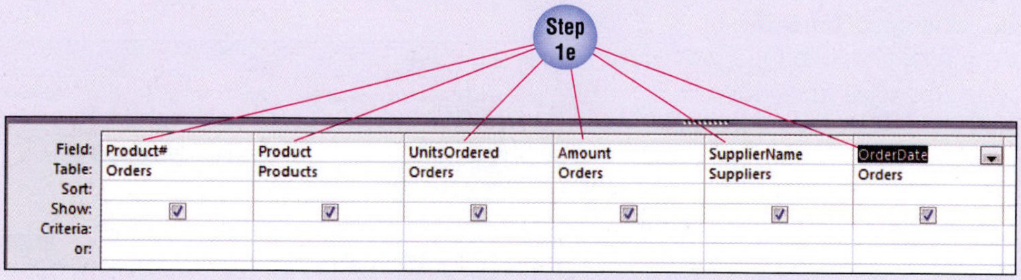

Field:	Product#	Product	UnitsOrdered	Amount	SupplierName	OrderDate
Table:	Orders	Products	Orders	Orders	Suppliers	Orders
Sort:						
Show:	☑	☑	☑	☑	☑	☑
Criteria:						
or:						

   f. Click the Run button to run the query.
   g. Save the query and name it *ItemsOrderedQuery*.
   h. Close the query.

2. Create a crosstab query that summarizes the orders by supplier name and by product ordered by completing the following steps:
   a. Click the Create tab and then click the Query Wizard button.
   b. At the New Query dialog box, double-click *Crosstab Query Wizard* in the list box.

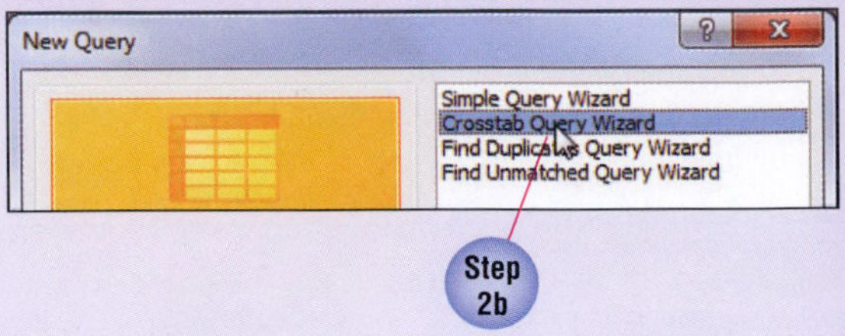

   c. At the first Crosstab Query Wizard dialog box, click the *Queries* option in the *View* section and then click *Query: ItemsOrderedQuery* in the list box.

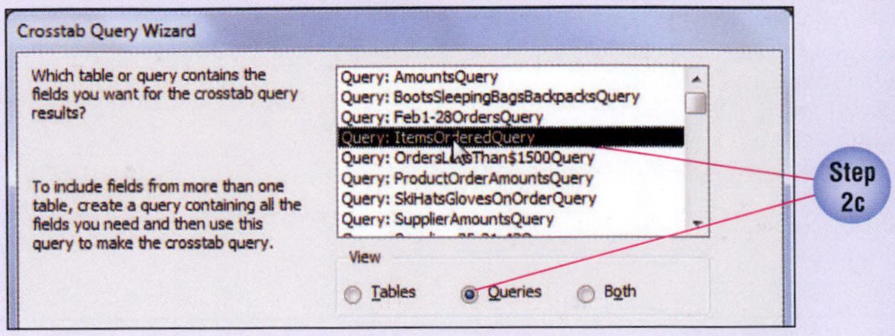

   d. Click the Next button.
   e. At the second Crosstab Query Wizard dialog box, click *SupplierName* in the *Available Fields* list box and then click the One Field button. (This inserts *SupplierName* in the *Selected Fields* list box and specifies that you want *SupplierName* for the row headings.)

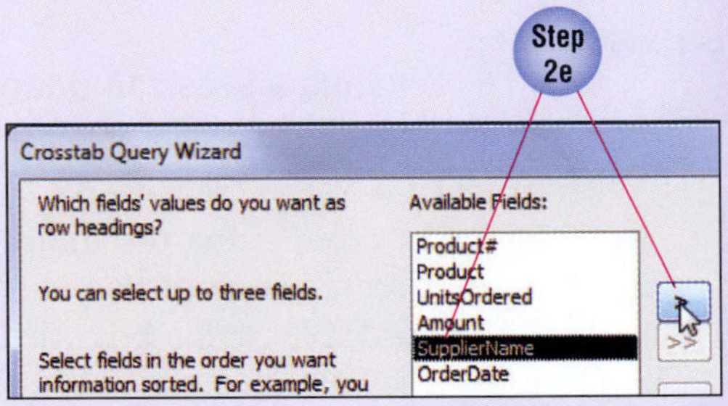

   f. Click the Next button.
   g. At the third Crosstab Query Wizard dialog box, click *Product* in the list box. (This specifies that you want *Product* for the column headings.)

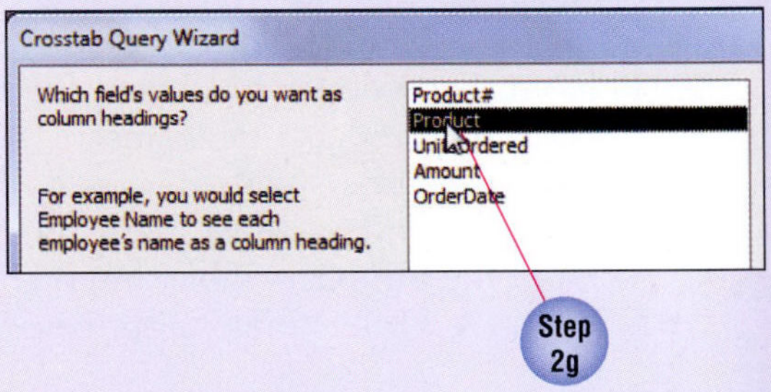

   h. Click the Next button.
   i. At the fourth Crosstab Query Wizard dialog box, click *Amount* in the *Fields* list box and click *Sum* in the *Functions* list box.
   j. Click the Next button.

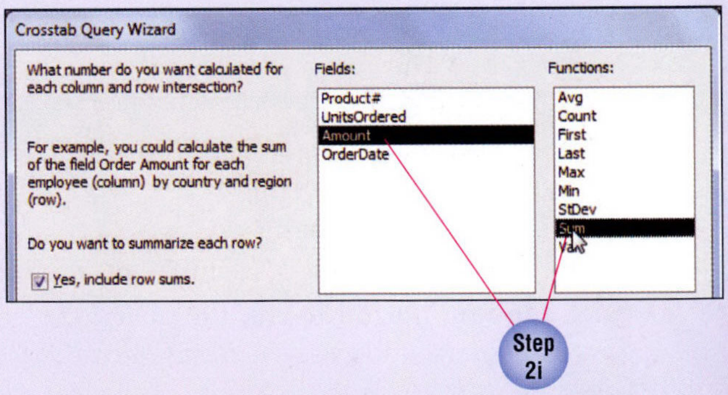

   k. At the fifth Crosstab Query Wizard dialog box, select the current text in the *What do you want to name your query?* text box and then type **OrdersBySupplierByProductQuery**.
   l. Click the Finish button. (See Project 2c query results on page 83.)
3. Display the query in Print Preview, change the orientation to landscape, change the left and right margins to 0.5 inch, and then print the query. (The query will print on four pages.)
4. Close the query.

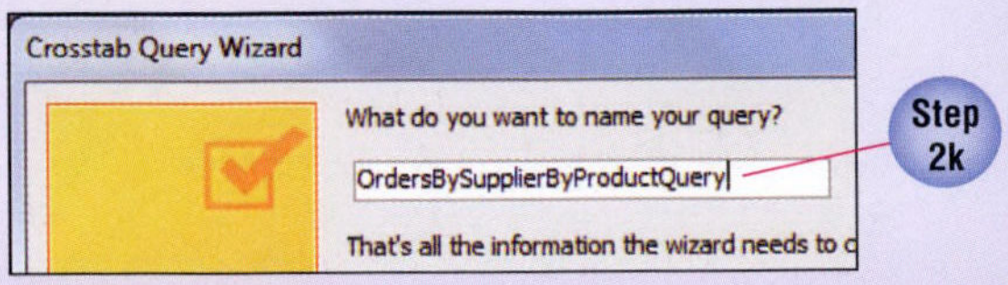

5. Close the **AL1-C3-PacTrek.accdb** database.
6. Open the **AL1-C3-CopperState.accdb** database.
7. Create a crosstab query from fields in one table that summarizes the claims by clients by completing the following steps:
   a. Click the Create tab and then click the Query Wizard button.
   b. At the New Query dialog box, double-click *Crosstab Query Wizard* in the list box.
   c. At the first Crosstab Query Wizard dialog box, click *Table: Claims* in the list box.
   d. Click the Next button.
   e. At the second Crosstab Query Wizard dialog box, click the One Field button. (This inserts the *Claim#* field in the *Selected Fields* list box.)
   f. Click the Next button.
   g. At the third Crosstab Query Wizard dialog, make sure *Client#* is selected in the list box and then click the Next button.
   h. At the fourth Crosstab Query Wizard dialog box, click *AmountOfClaim* in the *Fields* list box and click *Sum* in the *Functions* list box.
   i. Click the Next button.
   j. At the fifth Crosstab Query Wizard dialog box, select the current text in the *What do you want to name your query?* text box and then type **ClaimsByClaim#ByClient#Query**.
   k. Click the Finish button.
8. Change the orientation to landscape and then print the query. (The query will print on two pages. See Project 2c query results on page 83.)
9. Close the query.
10. Close the **AL1-C3-CopperState.accdb** database.

Creating a Find Duplicates Query

Use the ***find duplicates query*** to search a specified table or query for duplicate field values within a designated field or fields. Create this type of query, for example, if you suspect a record, such as a product record, has inadvertently been entered twice under two different product numbers. A find duplicates query has many applications. A few other examples of how you can use a find duplicates query include:

- Find the records in an Orders table with the same customer number so that you can identify your loyal customers.
- Find the records in a Customers table with the same last name and mailing address so that you send only one mailing to a household to save on printing and postage costs.
- Find the records in an EmployeeExpenses table with the same employee number so that you can see which employee is submitting the most claims.

Access provides the Find Duplicates Query Wizard that builds the query based on the selections made in a series of dialog boxes. To use this wizard, open the desired table, click the Create tab, and then click the Query Wizard button. At the New Query dialog box, double-click *Find Duplicates Query Wizard* in the list box, and then complete the steps provided by the wizard.

In Project 2d, you will assume that you have been asked to update the address for a supplier in the AL1-C3-PacTrek.accdb database. Instead of updating the address, you create a new record. You will then use the Find Duplicates Query Wizard to find duplicate field values in the Suppliers table.

Quick Steps

Create a Find Duplicates Query
1. Click Create tab.
2. Click Query Wizard button.
3. Double-click *Find Duplicates Query Wizard.*
4. Complete wizard steps.

Project 2d Creating a Find Duplicates Query

1. Open the **AL1-C3-PacTrek.accdb** database and then open the Suppliers table.
2. Add the following record to the table:

Supplier#	**29**
SupplierName	**Langley Corporation**
StreetAddress	**1248 Larson Avenue**
City	**Burnaby**
Prov/State	**BC**
PostalCode	**V5V 9K2**
EmailAddress	**lc@emcp.net**
Telephone	**(604) 555-1200**

3. Close the Suppliers table.
4. Use the Find Duplicates Query Wizard to find any duplicate supplier names by completing the following steps:
   a. Click the Create tab and then click the Query Wizard button.
   b. At the New Query dialog box, double-click *Find Duplicates Query Wizard*.
   c. At the first wizard dialog box, click *Table: Suppliers* in the list box.

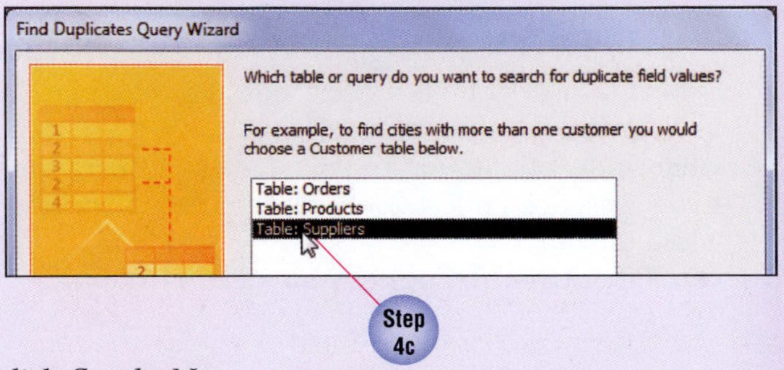

   d. Click the Next button.
   e. At the second wizard dialog box, click *SupplierName* in the *Available fields* list box and then click the One Field button. (This moves the *SupplierName* field to the *Duplicate-value fields* list box.)

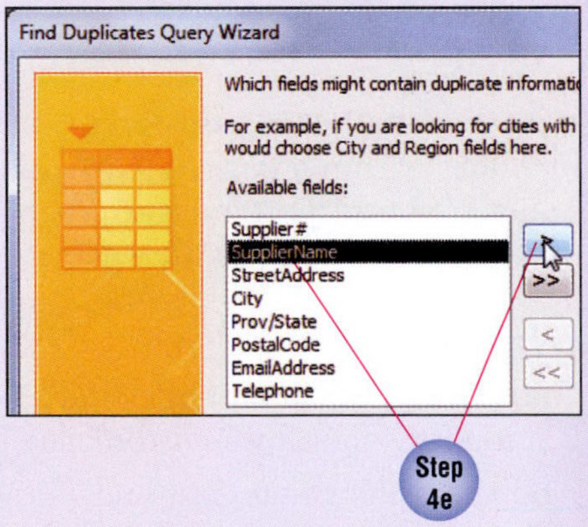

   f. Click the Next button.
   g. At the third wizard dialog box, click the All Fields button (button containing the two greater than (>>) symbols). This moves all the fields to the *Additional query fields* list box. You are doing this because if you find a duplicate supplier name, you want to view all the fields to determine which record is accurate.
   h. Click the Next button.
   i. At the fourth (and last) wizard dialog box, type **DuplicateSuppliersQuery** in the *What do you want to name your query?* text box.

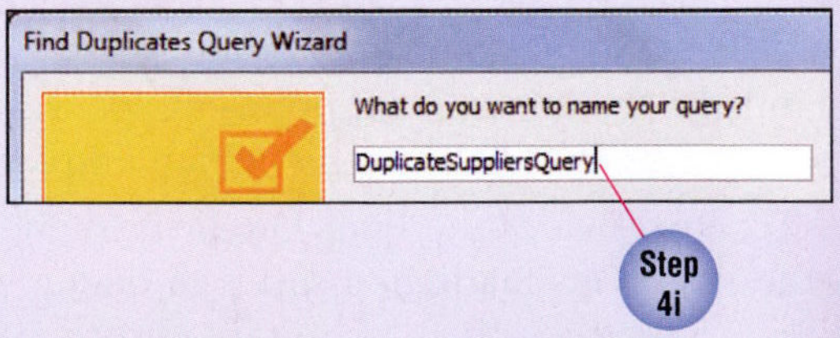

   j. Click the Finish button.
   k. Change the orientation to landscape and then print the query. (See Project 2d query results on page 83.)
5. As you look at the query results, you realize that an inaccurate record was entered for Langley so you decide to delete one of the records. To do this, complete the following steps:

a. With the query open, click in the record selector bar next to the second record (the one with a Supplier# of *29*). (This selects the entire row.)
b. Click the Home tab and then click the Delete button in the Records group.
c. At the message asking you to confirm, click the Yes button.
d. Close the query.

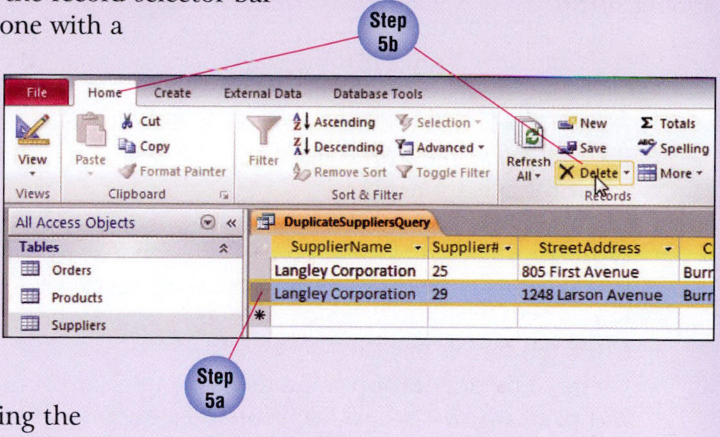

6. Change the street address for Langley Corporation by completing the following steps:
   a. Open the Suppliers table.
   b. With the Suppliers table open in Datasheet view, change the address for Langley Corporation from *805 First Avenue* to *1248 Larson Avenue*. Leave the other fields as displayed.
   c. Close the Suppliers table.

In Project 2d, you used the Find Duplicates Query Wizard to find records containing the same field. In Project 2e, you will use the Find Duplicates Query Wizard to find information on the suppliers you order from the most. You could use this information to negotiate for better prices or to ask for discounts.

Project 2e Finding Duplicate Orders

Part 5 of 6

1. With the **AL1-C3-PacTrek.accdb** database open, create a query with the following fields (in the order shown) from the specified tables:

Order#	Orders table
Supplier#	Orders table
SupplierName	Suppliers table
Product#	Orders table
UnitsOrdered	Orders table
Amount	Orders table
OrderDate	Orders table

2. Run the query.
3. Save the query with the name *SupplierOrdersQuery* and then close the query.
4. Use the Find Duplicates Query Wizard to find the suppliers you order from the most by completing the following steps:
   a. Click the Create tab and then click the Query Wizard button.
   b. At the New Query dialog box, double-click *Find Duplicates Query Wizard*.

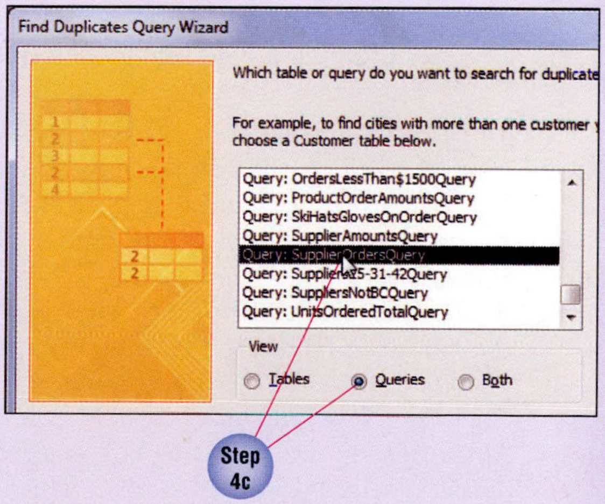

   c. At the first wizard dialog box, click *Queries* in the *View* section, and then click *Query: SupplierOrdersQuery*. (You may need to scroll down the list to display this query.)

d. Click the Next button.
e. At the second wizard dialog box, click *Supplier#* in the *Available fields* list box and then click the One Field button.
f. Click the Next button.
g. At the third wizard dialog box, click the All Fields button. (This moves all the fields to the *Additional query fields* list box.)
h. Click the Next button.
i. At the fourth (and last) wizard dialog box, type **DuplicateSupplierOrdersQuery** in the *What do you want to name your query?* text box.

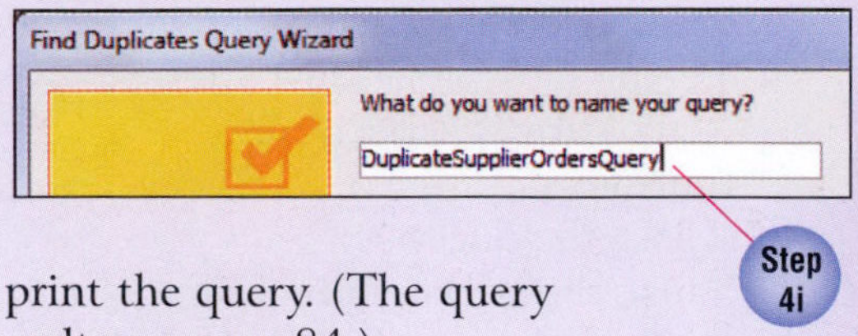

j. Click the Finish button.
k. Change the orientation to landscape and then print the query. (The query will print on two pages. See Project 2e query results on page 84.)

5. Close the query.

Creating a Find Unmatched Query

Quick Steps

Create a Find Unmatched Query
1. Click Create tab.
2. Click Query Wizard button.
3. Double-click *Find Unmatched Query Wizard.*
4. Complete wizard steps.

Create a ***find unmatched query*** to compare two tables and produce a list of the records in one table that have no matching record in the other related table. This type of query is useful to produce lists such as customers who have never placed an order or an invoice with no payment record. Access provides the Find Unmatched Query Wizard that builds the select query by guiding you through a series of dialog boxes.

In Project 2f, you will use the Find Unmatched Query Wizard to find all products that have no units on order. This information is helpful because it indicates which products are not selling and might need to be discontinued or returned. To use the Find Unmatched Query Wizard, click the Create tab and then click the Query Wizard button in the Queries group. At the New Query dialog box, double-click *Find Unmatched Query Wizard* in the list box and then follow the wizard steps.

Project 2f Creating a Find Unmatched Query — Part 6 of 6

1. With the **AL1-C3-PacTrek.accdb** database open, use the Find Unmatched Query Wizard to find all products that do not have any units on order by completing the following steps:
   a. Click the Create tab and then click the Query Wizard button.
   b. At the New Query dialog box, double-click *Find Unmatched Query Wizard.*
   c. At the first wizard dialog box, click *Table: Products* in the list box. (This is the table containing the fields you want to see in the query results.)

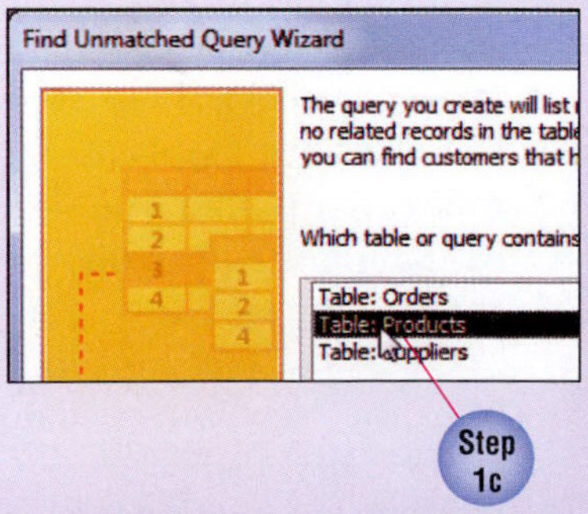

   d. Click the Next button.
   e. At the second wizard dialog box, make sure *Table: Orders* is selected in the list box. (This is the table containing the related records.)
   f. Click the Next button.

g. At the third wizard dialog box, make sure *Product#* is selected in the *Fields in 'Products'* list box and in the *Fields in 'Orders'* list box.
h. Click the Next button.
i. At the fourth wizard dialog box, click the All Fields button to move all fields from the *Available fields* list box to the *Selected fields* list box.
j. Click the Next button.
k. At the fifth wizard dialog box, click the Finish button. (Let the wizard determine the query name: *Products Without Matching Orders*. See Project 2f query results on page 84.)

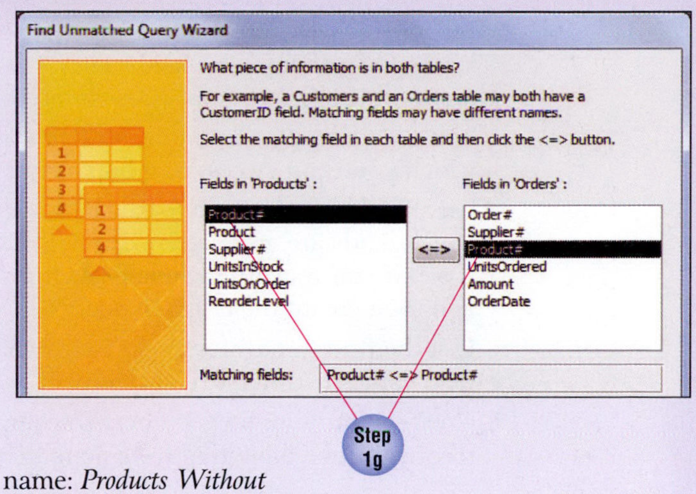

Find Unmatched Query Wizard
What piece of information is in both tables?
For example, a Customers and an Orders table may both have a CustomerID field. Matching fields may have different names.
Select the matching field in each table and then click the <=> button.
Fields in 'Products' :
Product#
Product
Supplier#
UnitsInStock
UnitsOnOrder
ReorderLevel
Fields in 'Orders' :
Order#
Supplier#
Product#
UnitsOrdered
Amount
OrderDate
<=>
Matching fields:
Product# <=> Product#
Step 1g

2. Print the query in landscape orientation and then close the query.
3. Close the **AL1-C3-PacTrek.accdb** database.

Chapter Summary

- Being able to extract specific information is one of the most important functions of a database. Data can be extracted from an Access database by performing a query, which can be accomplished by designing a query or using a query wizard.
- Designing a query consists of identifying the table, the field or fields from which the data will be drawn, and the criteria for selecting the data.
- During the designing of a query, write the criterion (or criteria) for extracting the specific data. Access inserts any necessary symbols in the criterion when the Enter key is pressed.
- In a criterion, quotation marks surround field values and pound symbols (#) surround dates. Use the asterisk (*) as a wildcard symbol.
- You can perform a query on fields within one table or on fields from related tables.
- When designing a query, you can specify the sort order of a field or fields.
- You can modify an existing query. To do this, double-click the query in the Navigation pane, click the View button to display the query in Design view, make the desired changes, and then click the Run button.
- Enter criterion in the *Or* row in the query design grid to instruct Access to display records that match either of the two criteria.
- Multiple criteria entered in the *Criteria* row in the query design grid become an *And* statement where each criterion must be met for Access to select the record.
- The Simple Query Wizard guides you through the steps for preparing a query. You can modify a query you create with the wizard.

- You can insert a calculated field in a *Field* row field when designing a query.
- Include an aggregate function such as Sum, Avg, Min, Max, or Count to calculate statistics from numeric field values. Click the Totals button in the Show/Hide group in the Query Tools Design tab to display the aggregate function list.
- Use the *Group By* option in the *Total* row field to add a field to a query upon which you want Access to group records for statistical calculations.
- Create a crosstab query to calculate aggregate functions such as Sum and Avg in which fields are grouped by two fields. Create a crosstab query from fields in one table. If you want to include fields from more than one table, create a query first, and then create the crosstab query.
- Use the find duplicates query to search a specified table or query for duplicate field values within a designated field or fields.
- Create a find unmatched query to compare two tables and produce a list of the records in one table that have no matching record in the other related table.

Commands Review

FEATURE	RIBBON TAB, GROUP	BUTTON, OPTION
Query design window	Create, Queries	
Run query	Query Tools Design, Results	
New Query dialog box	Create, Queries	
Simple Query Wizard	Create, Queries	, Simple Query Wizard
Add Total row to query design	Query Tools Design, Show/Hide	
Crosstab Query Wizard	Create, Queries	, Crosstab Query Wizard
Find Duplicates Query Wizard	Create, Queries	, Find Duplicates Query Wizard
Find Unmatched Query Wizard	Create, Queries	, Find Unmatched Query Wizard

Concepts Check Test Your Knowledge

Completion: In the space provided at the right, indicate the correct term, symbol, or command.

1. The Query Design button is located in the Queries group in this tab. ____________________
2. Click the Query Design button and the query window displays with this dialog box open. ____________________
3. To establish a criterion for the query, click in this row in the column containing the desired field name and then type the criterion. ____________________
4. This is the term used for the results of the query. ____________________
5. This is the symbol Access automatically inserts around a date when writing a criterion for the query. ____________________
6. Use this symbol to indicate a wildcard character when writing a query criterion. ____________________
7. This is the criterion you would type to return field values greater than $500. ____________________
8. This is the criterion you would type to return field values that begin with the letter *L*. ____________________
9. This is the criterion you would type to return field values that are not in Oregon. ____________________
10. You can sort a field in a query in ascending order or this order. ____________________
11. Enter a criterion in this row in the query design grid to instruct Access to display records that match either of the two criteria. ____________________
12. This wizard guides you through the steps for preparing a query. ____________________
13. This type of query calculates aggregate functions in which field values are grouped by two fields. ____________________
14. Use this type of query to compare two tables and produce a list of the records in one table that have no matching record in the other related table. ____________________

Skills Check Assess Your Performance

Assessment

1 DESIGN QUERIES IN A LEGAL SERVICES DATABASE

1. Display the Open dialog box with Access2010L1C3 on your storage medium the active folder.
2. Open the **AL1-C3-WarrenLegal.accdb** database and enable the contents.
3. Design a query that extracts information from the Billing table with the following specifications:
   a. Include the fields *Billing#*, *ClientID*, and *CategoryID* in the query.
   b. Extract those records with the *SE* category. (Type **"SE"** in the *Criteria* row field in the *CategoryID* column. You need to type the quotation marks to tell Access that SE is a criterion and not an Access built-in function.)
   c. Save the query and name it *SECategoryBillingQuery*.
   d. Print and then close the query.
4. Design a query that extracts information from the Billing table with the following specifications:
   a. Include the fields *Billing#*, *ClientID*, and *Date*.
   b. Extract those records in the *Date* field with dates between 6/11/2012 and 6/15/2012.
   c. Save the query and name it *June11-15BillingQuery*.
   d. Print and then close the query.
5. Design a query that extracts information from the Clients table with the following specifications:
   a. Include the fields *FirstName*, *LastName*, and *City*.
   b. Extract those records with any city other than Kent in the *City* field.
   c. Save the query and name it *ClientsNotInKentQuery*.
   d. Print and then close the query.
6. Design a query that extracts information from two tables with the following specifications:
   a. Include the fields *Billing#*, *ClientID*, *Date*, and *Rate#* from the Billing table.
   b. Include the field *Rate* from the Rates table.
   c. Extract those records with a rate number greater than 2.
   d. Save the query and name it *RateGreaterThan2Query*.
   e. Print and then close the query.
7. Design a query that extracts information from three tables with the following specifications:
   a. Include the fields *AttorneyID, FName,* and *LName* from the Attorneys table.
   b. Include the fields *FirstName* and *LastName* from the Clients table.
   c. Include the fields *Date* and *Hours* from the Billing table.
   d. Extract those records with an AttorneyID of *12*.
   e. Save the query and name it Attorney12Query.
   f. Print and then close the query.
8. Design a query that extracts information from four tables with the following specifications:
   a. Include the fields *AttorneyID*, *FName*, and *LName* from the Attorneys table.
   b. Include the field *Category* from the Categories table.
   c. Include the fields *Rate#* and *Rate* from the Rates table.

d. Include the fields *Date* and *Hours* from the Billing table.
e. Extract those records with an AttorneyID of *17* and a Rate# of *4*.
f. Save the query and name it *Attorney17Rate4Query*.
g. Print the query in landscape orientation and then close the query.

9. Open the Attorney17Rate4Query query, click the View button in the Home tab to display the query in Design view, and then modify the query so it displays records with a Rate# of *4* with an AttorneyID of *17* and also *19* by making the following changes:
   a. Click below the field value *"17"* in the *AttorneyID* column and then type **19**.
   b. Click below the field value *"4"* in the *Rate#* column, type **4**, and then press Enter.
   c. Run the query.
   d. Save the query with the new name *Attorney17&19Rate4Query*. ***Hint: Do this at the Save As dialog box. Display this dialog box by clicking the File tab and then clicking Save Object As.***
   e. Print the query in landscape orientation and then close the query.

Assessment 2

USE THE SIMPLE QUERY WIZARD AND DESIGN QUERIES

1. With **AL1-C3-WarrenLegal.accdb** database open, use the Simple Query Wizard to extract specific information from three tables with the following specifications:
   a. At the first Simple Query Wizard dialog box, include the following fields:
      From Attorneys table: *AttorneyID*, *FName,* and *LName*
      From Categories table: *Category*
      From Billing table: *Hours*
   b. At the second Simple Query Wizard dialog box, click Next.
   c. At the third Simple Query Wizard dialog box, click the *Modify the query design* option, and then click the Finish button.
   d. At the query window, insert *14* in the *Criteria* row field in the *AttorneyID* column.
   e. Run the query.
   f. Save the query with the default name.
   g. Print and then close the query.
2. Create a query in Design view with the Billing table with the following specifications:
   a. Insert the *Hours* field from the Billing table to the first, second, third, and fourth *Field* row fields.
   b. Click the Totals button in the Show/Hide group.
   c. Insert *Sum* in the first *Total* row field.
   d. Insert *Min* in the second *Total* row field.
   e. Insert *Max* in the third *Total* row field.
   f. Insert *Count* in the fourth *Total* row field.
   g. Run the query.
   h. Automatically adjust the widths of the columns.
   i. Save the query and name it *HoursAmountQuery*.
   j. Print and then close the query.
3. Create a query in Design view with the following specifications:
   a. Add the Attorneys table and the Billing table to the query window.
   b. Insert the *FName* field from the Attorneys table to the first *Field* row field.
   c. Insert the *LName* field from the Attorneys table to the second *Field* row field.

d. Insert the *AttorneyID* field from the Billing table to the third *Field* row field. (You will need to scroll down the Billing table list box to display the *AttorneyID* field.)
e. Insert the *Hours* field from the Billing table to the fourth *Field* row field.
f. Click the Totals button in the Show/Hide group.
g. Insert *Sum* in the fourth *Total* row field in the *Hours* column.
h. Run the query.
i. Save the query and name it *AttorneyHoursQuery*.
j. Print and then close the query.

4. Create a query in Design view with the following specifications:
   a. Add the Attorneys, Clients, Categories, and Billing tables to the query window.
   b. Insert the *AttorneyID* field from the Attorneys table to the first *Field* row field.
   c. Insert the *ClientID* field from the Billing table to the second *Field* row field.
   d. Insert the *Category* field from the Categories table to the third *Field* row field.
   e. Insert the *Hours* field from the Billing table to the fourth *Field* row field.
   f. Run the query.
   g. Save the query and name it *AttorneyClientHours*.
   h. Print and then close the query.

Assessment

3 CREATE A CROSSTAB QUERY AND USE THE FIND DUPLICATES AND FIND UNMATCHED QUERY WIZARDS

1. With the **AL1-C3-WarrenLegal.accdb** database open, create a crosstab query that summarizes the hours by attorney by category with the following specifications:
   a. At the first Crosstab Query Wizard dialog box, click the *Queries* option in the *View* section, and then click *Query: AttorneyClientHours* in the list box.
   b. At the second Crosstab Query Wizard dialog box with *AttorneyID* selected in the *Available Fields* list box, click the One Field button.
   c. At the third Crosstab Query Wizard dialog box, click *Category* in the list box.
   d. At the fourth Crosstab Query Wizard dialog box, click *Hours* in the *Fields* list box and click *Sum* in the *Functions* list box.
   e. At the fifth Crosstab Query Wizard dialog box, select the current name in the *What do you want to name your query?* text box and then type **HoursByAttorneyByCategory**.
   f. Display the query in Print Preview, change to landscape orientation, change the left and right margins to 0.5 inch, and then print the query.
   g. Close the query.
2. Use the Find Duplicates Query Wizard to find those clients with the same last name with the following specifications:
   a. At the first wizard dialog box, click *Table: Clients* in the list box.
   b. At the second wizard dialog box, click *LastName* in the *Available fields* list box and then click the One Field button.
   c. At the third wizard dialog box, click the All Fields button.
   d. At the fourth wizard dialog box, name the query *DuplicateLastNamesQuery*.
   e. Print the query in landscape orientation and then close the query.

3. Use the Find Unmatched Query Wizard to find all clients who do not have any billing hours with the following specifications:
   a. At the first wizard dialog box, click *Table: Clients* in the list box.
   b. At the second wizard dialog box, click *Table: Billing* in the list box.
   c. At the third wizard dialog box, make sure *ClientID* is selected in the *Fields in 'Clients'* list box and in the *Fields in 'Billing'* list box.
   d. At the fourth wizard dialog box, click the All Fields button to move all fields from the *Available fields* list box to the *Selected fields* list box.
   e. At the fifth wizard dialog box, click the Finish button. (Let the wizard determine the query name: *Clients Without Matching Billing*.)
4. Print the query in landscape orientation and then close the query.

Assessment 4

DESIGN AND HIDE FIELDS IN A QUERY

1. You can use the check boxes in the query design grid *Show* row to show or hide fields in the query. Experiment with these check boxes and then, with the **AL1-C3-WarrenLegal.accdb** database open, design the following query:
   a. At the Show Table dialog box, add the Clients table, the Billing table, and the Rates table.
   b. At the query window, insert the following fields in *Field* row fields:
      Clients table:
         FirstName
         LastName
      Billing table:
         Hours
      Rates table:
         Rate
   c. Insert in the fifth *Field* row field the calculated field *Total:[Hours]*[Rate]*.
   d. Hide the *Hours* and the *Rate* fields.
   e. Run the query.
   f. Save the query and name it *ClientBillingQuery*.
   g. Print and then close the query.
2. Close the **AL1-C3-WarrenLegal.accdb** database.

Visual Benchmark Demonstrate Your Proficiency

CREATING RELATIONSHIPS AND DESIGNING A QUERY

1. Open the **AL1-C3-MRInvestments.accdb** database from the Access2010L1C3 folder on your storage medium and enable the contents.
2. Display the Relationships window and then create the relationships shown in Figure 3.7. Enforce referential integrity and cascade fields and records. (The tables in Figure 3.7 have been rearranged in the Relationships window so you have a better view of the relationships.)
3. Save and then print the relationships.

4. Close the relationships report without saving it and then close the Relationships window.
5. Design the query shown in Figure 3.8.
6. Run the query.
7. Save the query with an appropriate name and then print the query.
8. Close the **AL1-C3-MRInvestments.accdb** database.

Figure 3.7 Visual Benchmark Relationships Window

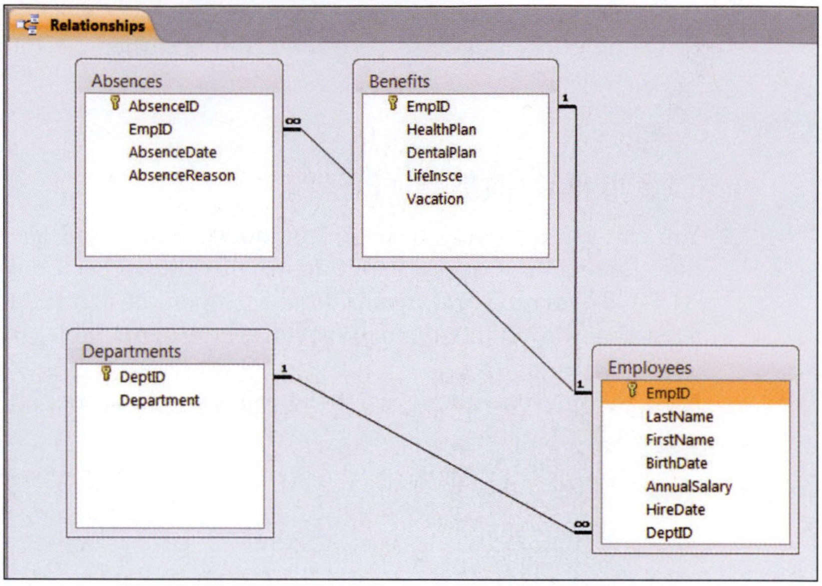

Figure 3.8 Visual Benchmark Query

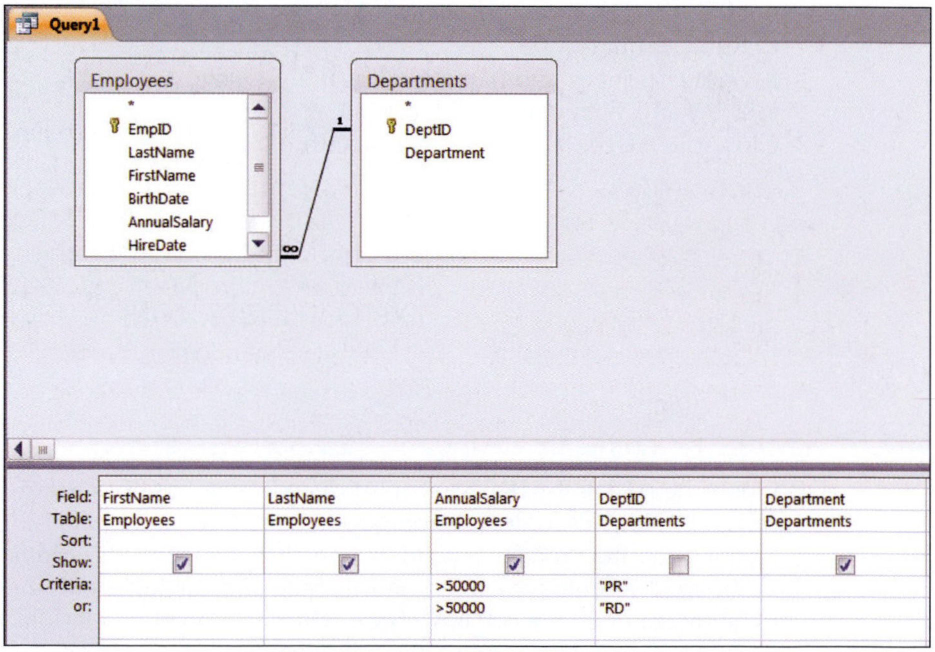

Case Study Apply Your Skills

Part 1

You work for the Skyline Restaurant in Fort Myers, Florida. Your supervisor is reviewing the restaurant operations and has asked for a number of query reports. Before running queries, you realize that the tables in the restaurant database, **AL1-C3-Skyline.accdb**, are not related. Open the **AL1-C3-Skyline.accdb** database, enable the contents, and then create the following relationships (enforce referential integrity and cascade fields and records):

Field Name	"One" Table	"Many" Table
EmployeeID	Employees	Banquets
Item#	Inventory	Orders
SupplierID	Suppliers	Orders
SupplierID	Suppliers	Inventory
EventID	Events	Banquets

Save and then print the relationships.

Part 2

As part of the review of the restaurant records, your supervisor has asked you for the following information. Create a separate query for each bulleted item listed below and save, name, and print the queries. (You determine the query names.)

- Suppliers in Fort Myers (from the Suppliers table include the supplier identification number, supplier name, city, and telephone number)
- Suppliers that are not located in Fort Myers (from the Suppliers table include the supplier identification number and supplier name, city, and telephone number)
- Employees hired in 2009 (from the Employees table include the employee identification number, first and last names, and hire date)
- Employees that are signed up for health insurance (from the Employees table include employee first and last names and the health insurance field)
- Wedding receptions (event identification "WR") booked in the banquet room (from the Banquets table include the reservation identification number; reservation date; event identification; and first name, last name, and telephone number of the person making the reservation)
- Banquet reservations between 6/14/2012 and 6/30/2012 and the employees making the reservations (from the Banquets table include reservation identification number; reservation date; and first name, last name, and telephone number of the person making the reservation; from the Employees table include the employee first and last names)
- Banquet reservations that have not been confirmed and the employees making the reservations (from the Banquets table include reservation identification number; reservation date; confirmed field; and first and last names of person making the reservation; from the Employees table include the employee first and last names)
- Banquet room reserved by someone whose last name begins with "Wie" (from the Employees table include the first and last names of the employee who booked the reservation and from the Banquets table include the first and last names and telephone number of the person making the reservation)

- A query that inserts a calculated field that multiplies the number of units ordered by the unit price for all orders for supplier number 2 (from the Orders table include the order number, the supplier identification number, the units ordered, and the unit price; from the Inventory table include the item field)

Part 3

Use the Find Duplicates Query Wizard to find duplicate items in the Orders table with the following specifications:

- At the first wizard dialog box, specify the Orders table.
- At the second wizard dialog box, specify *Item#* as the duplicate-value field.
- At the third wizard dialog, specify that you want all of the fields in the query.
- At the fourth wizard dialog box, you determine the query name.
- Print and then close the query.

Use the Find Unmatched Query Wizard to find all employees who have not made a banquet reservation with the following specifications:

- At the first wizard dialog box, specify the Employees table.
- At the second wizard dialog box, specify the Banquets table.
- At the third wizard dialog box, specify the *EmployeeID* field in both list boxes.
- At the fourth wizard dialog box, specify that you want all of the fields in the query.
- At the fifth wizard dialog box, you determine the query name.
- Print the query in landscape orientation and then close the query.

Use the Crosstab Query Wizard to create a query that summarizes order amounts by supplier with the following specifications:

- At the first wizard dialog box, specify the Orders table.
- At the second wizard dialog box, specify the *SupplierID* field for row headings.
- At the third wizard dialog box, specify the *Item#* field for column headings.
- At the fourth wizard dialog box, click *UnitPrice* in the *Fields* list box and click *Sum* in the *Functions* list box.
- At the fifth wizard dialog box, you determine the query name.
- Automatically adjust the columns in the query. (You will need to scroll to the right to view and adjust all of the columns containing data.)
- Display the query in Print Preview, change to landscape orientation, and then change the left and right margins to 0.3 inch.
- Print and then close the crosstab query.

Part 4

Design at least three additional queries that require fields from at least two tables. Run the queries and then save and print the queries. In Microsoft Word, write the query information and include specific information about each query and format the document to enhance the visual appeal. Save the document and name it **AL1-C3-CS-Queries**. Print and then close **AL1-C3-CS-Queries.docx**.

Microsoft®
Access®

CHAPTER 4

Creating and Modifying Tables in Design View

PERFORMANCE OBJECTIVES

Upon successful completion of Chapter 4, you will be able to:

- **Create a table in Design view**
- **Assign a default value**
- **Use the Input Mask Wizard and the Lookup Wizard**
- **Validate field entries**
- **Insert a total row**
- **Sort records and print specific records in a table**
- **Complete a spelling check**
- **Find specific records in a table and find data and replace with other data**
- **Apply text formatting**
- **Use the Help feature**

SNAP Training and Assessment. Simplified.

Tutorials

4.1 Creating a Table and Setting a Primary Key
4.2 Modifying Field Properties
4.3 Using the Input Mask Wizard and the Lookup Wizard
4.4 Validating Data in a Table
4.5 Modifying Table Fields
4.6 Deleting and Sorting Records
4.7 Completing a Spelling Check and Printing Specific Records
4.8 Finding and Replacing Specific Data in Records
4.9 Formatting a Datasheet
4.10 Using Help

In Chapter 1 you learned how to create a table in Datasheet view. You can also create a table in Design view where you can establish the table's structure and properties before entering data. In this chapter, you will learn how to create a table in Design view and use the Input Mask Wizard and Lookup Wizards; insert, move, and delete fields in Design view; sort records; check spelling in a table; find and replace data; apply text formatting to a table; and use the Access Help feature. Model answers for this chapter's projects appear on the following pages.

Access
Access2010L1C4

Note: Before beginning the projects, copy the Access2010L1C4 subfolder from the Access2010L1 folder on the CD that accompanies this textbook to your storage medium and make Access2010L1C4 the active folder.

Project 1 Create and Modify Tables in a Property Management Database

Project 1c

EmpID	EmpCategory	FName	LName	Address	City	State	ZIP	Telephone	HealthIns	DentalIns	LifeIns
02-59	Hourly	Christina	Solomon	12241 East 51st	Citrus Heights	CA	95611	(916) 555-8844	✓	✓	$100,000.00
03-23	Salaried	Douglas	Ricci	903 Mission Road	Roseville	CA	95678	(916) 555-4125	✓		$25,000.00
03-55	Hourly	Tatiana	Kasadev	6558 Orchard Drive	Citrus Heights	CA	95610	(916) 555-8534	✓		$0.00
04-14	Salaried	Brian	West	12232 142nd Avenue East	Citrus Heights	CA	95611	(916) 555-0967	✓	✓	$50,000.00
04-32	Temporary	Kathleen	Addison	21229 19th Street	Citrus Heights	CA	95621	(916) 555-3408	✓	✓	$50,000.00
05-20	Hourly	Teresa	Villanueva	19453 North 42nd Street	Citrus Heights	CA	95611	(916) 555-2302	✓	✓	$0.00
05-31	Salaried	Marcia	Griswold	211 Haven Road	North Highlands	CA	95660	(916) 555-1449			$100,000.00
06-24	Temporary	Tiffany	Gentry	12312 North 20th	Roseville	CA	95661	(916) 555-0043	✓	✓	$50,000.00
06-33	Hourly	Joanna	Gallegos	6850 York Street	Roseville	CA	95747	(916) 555-7446			$25,000.00
07-20	Salaried	Jesse	Scholtz	3412 South 21st Street	Fair Oaks	CA	95628	(916) 555-4204	✓		$0.00
07-23	Salaried	Eugene	Bond	530 Laurel Road	Orangevale	CA	95662	(916) 555-9412	✓		$100,000.00

Step 11, Employees Table

EmpID	FName	LName	Address	City	State	ZIP	Telephone	EmpCategory	HealthIns	LifeIns
02-59	Christina	Solomon	12241 East 51st	Citrus Heights	CA	95611	(916) 555-8844	Hourly	✓	$100,000.00
03-23	Douglas	Ricci	903 Mission Road	Roseville	CA	95678	(916) 555-4125	Salaried	✓	$25,000.00
03-55	Tatiana	Kasadev	6558 Orchard Drive	Citrus Heights	CA	95610	(916) 555-8534	Hourly	✓	$0.00
04-14	Brian	West	12232 142nd Avenue East	Citrus Heights	CA	95611	(916) 555-0967	Salaried	✓	$50,000.00
04-32	Kathleen	Addison	21229 19th Street	Citrus Heights	CA	95621	(916) 555-3408	Temporary	✓	$50,000.00
05-20	Teresa	Villanueva	19453 North 42nd Street	Citrus Heights	CA	95611	(916) 555-2302	Hourly	✓	$0.00
05-31	Marcia	Griswold	211 Haven Road	North Highlands	CA	95660	(916) 555-1449	Salaried		$100,000.00
06-24	Tiffany	Gentry	12312 North 20th	Roseville	CA	95661	(916) 555-0043	Temporary	✓	$50,000.00
06-33	Joanna	Gallegos	6850 York Street	Roseville	CA	95747	(916) 555-7446	Hourly		$25,000.00
07-20	Jesse	Scholtz	3412 South 21st Street	Fair Oaks	CA	95628	(916) 555-4204	Salaried	✓	$0.00
07-23	Eugene	Bond	530 Laurel Road	Orangevale	CA	95662	(916) 555-9412	Salaried	✓	$100,000.00

Step 16, Employees Table

Pymnt#	RenterID	PymntDate	PymntAmount	LateFee
1	130	3/1/2012	$1,800.00	
2	111	3/1/2012	$1,900.00	
3	136	3/1/2012	$1,250.00	
4	110	3/1/2012	$1,300.00	
5	135	3/2/2012	$1,900.00	
6	123	3/2/2012	$1,000.00	
7	117	3/2/2012	$1,100.00	
8	134	3/3/2012	$1,400.00	
9	131	3/3/2012	$1,200.00	
10	118	3/3/2012	$900.00	
11	125	3/5/2012	$1,650.00	
12	119	3/5/2012	$1,500.00	
13	133	3/8/2012	$1,650.00	
14	129	3/9/2012	$1,650.00	
15	115	3/12/2012	$1,375.00	$25.00
16	121	3/12/2012	$950.00	$25.00
17	127	3/19/2012	$1,300.00	$50.00
Total			**$23,825.00**	**$100.00**

Payments Table

Project 1d

RenterID	FirstName	LastName	PropID	EmpID	CreditScore	LeaseBegDate	LeaseEndDate
118	Mason	Ahn	1004	07-23	538	3/1/2012	2/28/2013
119	Michelle	Bertram	1001	03-23	621	3/1/2012	2/28/2013
110	Greg	Hamilton	1029	04-14	624	1/1/2012	12/31/2012
121	Travis	Jorgenson	1010	04-14	590	3/1/2012	2/28/2013
135	Marty	Lobdell	1006	04-14	510	6/1/2012	5/31/2013
129	Susan	Lowrey	1002	04-14	634	4/1/2012	3/31/2013
130	Ross	Molaski	1027	03-23	688	5/1/2012	4/30/2013
136	Nadine	Paschal	1022	05-31	702	6/1/2012	5/31/2013
111	Julia	Perez	1013	07-20	711	1/1/2012	12/31/2012
115	Dana	Rozinski	1026	02-59	538	2/1/2012	1/31/2013
131	Danielle	Rubio	1020	07-20	722	5/1/2012	4/30/2013
133	Katie	Smith	1018	07-23	596	5/1/2012	4/30/2013
123	Richard	Terrell	1014	07-20	687	3/1/2012	2/28/2013
117	Miguel	Villegas	1007	07-20	695	2/1/2012	1/31/2013
125	Rose	Wagoner	1015	07-23	734	4/1/2012	3/31/2013
134	Carl	Weston	1009	03-23	655	6/1/2012	5/31/2013
127	William	Young	1023	05-31	478	4/1/2012	3/31/2013

Step 2c, Renters Table

RenterID	FirstName	LastName	PropID	EmpID	CreditScore	LeaseBegDate	LeaseEndDate
125	Rose	Wagoner	1015	07-23	734	4/1/2012	3/31/2013
131	Danielle	Rubio	1020	07-20	722	5/1/2012	4/30/2013
111	Julia	Perez	1013	07-20	711	1/1/2012	12/31/2012
136	Nadine	Paschal	1022	05-31	702	6/1/2012	5/31/2013
117	Miguel	Villegas	1007	07-20	695	2/1/2012	1/31/2013
130	Ross	Molaski	1027	03-23	688	5/1/2012	4/30/2013
123	Richard	Terrell	1014	07-20	687	3/1/2012	2/28/2013
134	Carl	Weston	1009	03-23	655	6/1/2012	5/31/2013
129	Susan	Lowrey	1002	04-14	634	4/1/2012	3/31/2013
110	Greg	Hamilton	1029	04-14	624	1/1/2012	12/31/2012
119	Michelle	Bertram	1001	03-23	621	3/1/2012	2/28/2013
133	Katie	Smith	1018	07-23	596	5/1/2012	4/30/2013
121	Travis	Jorgenson	1010	04-14	590	3/1/2012	2/28/2013
118	Mason	Ahn	1004	07-23	538	3/1/2012	2/28/2013
115	Dana	Rozinski	1026	02-59	538	2/1/2012	1/31/2013
135	Marty	Lobdell	1006	04-14	510	6/1/2012	5/31/2013
127	William	Young	1023	05-31	478	4/1/2012	3/31/2013

Step 3c, Renters Table

PropID	CatID	MoRent	Address	City	State	ZIP
1007	A	$1,100.00	904 Everson Road	Fair Oaks	CA	95628
1004	A	$900.00	1932 Oakville Drive	North Highlands	CA	95660
1010	A	$950.00	19334 140th East	Citrus Heights	CA	95621
1014	A	$1,000.00	9045 Valley Avenue	Citrus Heights	CA	95611

Step 6f, Properties Table

PropID	CatID	MoRent	Address	City	State	ZIP
1007	A	$1,100.00	904 Everson Road	Fair Oaks	CA	95628
1004	A	$900.00	1932 Oakville Drive	North Highlands	CA	95660
1010	A	$950.00	19334 140th East	Citrus Heights	CA	95621
1014	A	$1,000.00	9045 Valley Avenue	Citrus Heights	CA	95611
1029	C	$1,300.00	155 Aldrich Road	Roseville	CA	95678
1002	C	$1,650.00	2650 Crestline Drive	Citrus Heights	CA	95611
1001	C	$1,500.00	4102 Tenth Street	Citrus Heights	CA	95611
1026	C	$1,375.00	10057 128th Avenue	Citrus Heights	CA	95611
1023	C	$1,300.00	750 Birch Drive	Orangevale	CA	95662
1009	C	$1,400.00	159 Meridian Street	Orangevale	CA	95662
1019	C	$1,700.00	765 Chellis Street	Fair Oaks	CA	95628
1018	C	$1,650.00	9945 North 20th Road	North Highlands	CA	95660
1017	D	$1,300.00	4500 Maple Lane	Orangevale	CA	95662
1011	D	$1,350.00	348 Hampton Avenue	Citrus Heights	CA	95611
1008	D	$1,575.00	5009 North Garden	Roseville	CA	95661
1020	D	$1,200.00	23390 South 22nd Street	Citrus Heights	CA	95610
1006	S	$1,900.00	3412 Mango Street	Orangevale	CA	95662
1003	S	$1,800.00	10234 122nd Avenue	North Highlands	CA	95660
1012	S	$1,775.00	1212 Fairhaven Road	North Highlands	CA	95660
1013	S	$1,900.00	2606 30th Street	Citrus Heights	CA	95610
1016	S	$1,825.00	21388 South 42nd Street	Citrus Heights	CA	95621
1030	S	$1,950.00	5430 112th Southeast	Citrus Heights	CA	95611
1021	S	$1,875.00	652 Seventh Street	Fair Oaks	CA	95628
1024	S	$1,650.00	1195 24th Street	North Highlands	CA	95660
1027	S	$1,800.00	2203 Center Road	Orangevale	CA	95662
1028	S	$1,750.00	488 Franklin Drive	Fair Oaks	CA	95628
1022	T	$1,250.00	4572 152nd Avenue	Citrus Heights	CA	95621
1005	T	$1,350.00	12110 55th Southeast	Citrus Heights	CA	95611
1025	T	$1,200.00	3354 North 62nd Street	Citrus Heights	CA	95610
1015	T	$1,650.00	560 Tenth Street East	North Highlands	CA	95660

Step 7f, Properties Table

Project 1d–*continued*

Pymnt#	RenterID	PymntDate	PymntAmount	LateFee
1	130	3/1/2012	$1,800.00	
2	111	3/1/2012	$1,900.00	
3	136	3/1/2012	$1,250.00	
4	110	3/1/2012	$1,300.00	
5	135	3/2/2012	$1,900.00	
6	123	3/2/2012	$1,000.00	
7	117	3/2/2012	$1,100.00	
8	134	3/3/2012	$1,400.00	
9	131	3/3/2012	$1,200.00	
10	118	3/3/2012	$900.00	
11	125	3/5/2012	$1,650.00	
12	119	3/5/2012	$1,500.00	
13	133	3/8/2012	$1,650.00	
14	129	3/9/2012	$1,650.00	
15	115	3/12/2012	$1,375.00	$25.00
16	121	3/12/2012	$950.00	$25.00
17	127	3/19/2012	$1,300.00	$50.00
Total			**$23,825.00**	**$100.00**

Step 8g, Payments Table

RenterID	FirstName	LastName	PropID	EmpID	CreditScore	LeaseBegDate	LeaseEndDate
110	Greg	Hamilton	1029	04-14	624	1/1/2012	12/31/2012
111	Julia	Perez	1013	07-20	711	1/1/2012	12/31/2012
115	Dana	Rozinski	1026	02-59	538	2/1/2012	1/31/2013
117	Miguel	Villegas	1007	07-20	695	2/1/2012	1/31/2013
118	Mason	Ahn	1004	07-23	538	3/1/2012	2/28/2013
119	Michelle	Bertram	1001	03-23	621	3/1/2012	2/28/2013
121	Travis	Jorgenson	1010	04-14	590	3/1/2012	2/28/2013
123	Richard	Terrell	1014	07-20	687	3/1/2012	2/28/2013
125	Rose	Wagoner	1015	07-23	734	4/1/2012	3/31/2013
127	William	Young	1023	05-31	478	4/1/2012	3/31/2013
129	Susan	Lowrey	1002	04-14	634	4/1/2012	3/31/2013
130	Ross	Molaski	1027	03-23	688	5/1/2012	4/30/2013
131	Danielle	Rubio	1020	07-20	722	5/1/2012	4/30/2013
133	Katie	Smith	1018	07-23	596	5/1/2012	4/30/2013
134	Carl	Weston	1009	03-23	655	6/1/2012	5/31/2013
135	Marty	Lobdell	1006	04-14	510	6/1/2012	5/31/2013
136	Nadine	Paschal	1022	05-31	702	6/1/2012	5/31/2013

Step 10j, Renters Table

Project 1e

EmpID	FName	LName	Address	City	State	ZIP	Telephone	EmpCategory	HealthIns
02-59	Christina	Solomon	12241 East 51st	Citrus Heights	CA	95611	(916) 555-8844	Hourly	✓
03-23	Douglas	Ricci	903 Mission Road	Roseville	CA	95678	(916) 555-4125	Salaried	✓
03-55	Tatiana	Kasadev	6558 Orchard Drive	Citrus Heights	CA	95610	(916) 555-8534	Hourly	✓
04-14	Brian	West	12232 142nd Avenue East	Citrus Heights	CA	95611	(916) 555-0967	Salaried	✓
04-32	Kathleen	Addison	21229 19th Street	Citrus Heights	CA	95621	(916) 555-3408	Temporary	✓
05-20	Teresa	Villanueva	19453 North 42nd Street	Citrus Heights	CA	95611	(916) 555-2302	Hourly	✓
05-31	Marcia	Griswold	211 Haven Road	North Highlands	CA	95660	(916) 555-1449	Salaried	
06-24	Tiffany	Gentry	12312 North 20th	Roseville	CA	95661	(916) 555-0043	Temporary	✓
06-33	Joanna	Gallegos	6850 York Street	Roseville	CA	95747	(916) 555-7446	Hourly	
07-20	Jesse	Scholtz	3412 South 21st Street	Fair Oaks	CA	95628	(916) 555-4204	Salaried	✓
07-23	Eugene	Bond	530 Laurel Road	Orangevale	CA	95662	(916) 555-9412	Salaried	✓
02-72	Robin	Wilder	9945 Valley Avenue	Citrus Heights	CA	95610	(916) 555-6522	Salaried	

Employees Table

Project 1f

PropID	CatID	MoRent	Address	City	State	ZIP
1007	A	$1,100.00	904 Everson Road	Fair Oaks	CA	95628
1004	A	$900.00	1932 Oakville Drive	North Highlands	CA	95668
1010	A	$950.00	19334 140th East	Citrus Heights	CA	95621
1014	A	$1,000.00	9045 Valley Avenue	Citrus Heights	CA	95611
1029	C	$1,300.00	155 Aldrich Road	Roseville	CA	95678
1002	C	$1,650.00	2650 Crestline Drive	Citrus Heights	CA	95611
1001	C	$1,500.00	4102 Tenth Street	Citrus Heights	CA	95611
1026	C	$1,375.00	10057 128th Avenue	Citrus Heights	CA	95611
1023	C	$1,300.00	750 Birch Drive	Orangevale	CA	95662
1009	C	$1,400.00	159 Meridian Street	Orangevale	CA	95662
1019	C	$1,700.00	765 Chellis Street	Fair Oaks	CA	95628
1018	C	$1,650.00	9945 North 20th Road	North Highlands	CA	95660
1017	D	$1,300.00	4500 Maple Lane	Orangevale	CA	95662
1011	D	$1,350.00	348 Hampton Avenue	Citrus Heights	CA	95611
1008	D	$1,575.00	5009 North Garden	Roseville	CA	95661
1020	D	$1,200.00	23390 South 22nd Street	Citrus Heights	CA	95610
1006	S	$1,900.00	3412 Mango Street	Orangevale	CA	95662
1003	S	$1,800.00	10234 122nd Avenue	North Highlands	CA	95668
1012	S	$1,775.00	1212 Fairhaven Road	North Highlands	CA	95660
1013	S	$1,900.00	2606 30th Street	Citrus Heights	CA	95610
1016	S	$1,825.00	21388 South 42nd Street	Citrus Heights	CA	95621
1030	S	$1,950.00	5430 112th Southeast	Citrus Heights	CA	95611
1021	S	$1,875.00	652 Seventh Street	Fair Oaks	CA	95628
1024	S	$1,650.00	1195 24th Street	North Highlands	CA	95660
1027	S	$1,800.00	2203 Center Road	Orangevale	CA	95662
1028	S	$1,750.00	488 Franklin Drive	Fair Oaks	CA	95628
1022	T	$1,250.00	4572 152nd Avenue	Citrus Heights	CA	95621
1005	T	$1,350.00	12110 55th Southeast	Citrus Heights	CA	95611
1025	T	$1,200.00	3354 North 62nd Street	Citrus Heights	CA	95610
1015	T	$1,650.00	560 Tenth Street East	North Highlands	CA	95668

PropertiesTable

Relationships Table

FName	LName	HealthIns
Christina	Solomon	✓
Douglas	Ricci	✓
Tatiana	Kasadev	✓
Brian	West	✓
Kathleen	Addison	✓
Teresa	Villanueva	✓
Tiffany	Gentry	✓
Jesse	Scholtz	✓
Eugene	Bond	✓

EmpsWithHealthInsQuery

PropID	Category	Address	City	State	ZIP
1001	Condominium	4102 Tenth Street	Citrus Heights	CA	95611
1002	Condominium	2650 Crestline Drive	Citrus Heights	CA	95611
1005	Townhouse	12110 55th Southeast	Citrus Heights	CA	95611
1010	Apartment	19334 140th East	Citrus Heights	CA	95621
1011	Duplex	348 Hampton Avenue	Citrus Heights	CA	95611
1013	Single-family house	2606 30th Street	Citrus Heights	CA	95610
1014	Apartment	9045 Valley Avenue	Citrus Heights	CA	95611
1016	Single-family house	21388 South 42nd Street	Citrus Heights	CA	95621
1020	Duplex	23390 South 22nd Street	Citrus Heights	CA	95610
1022	Townhouse	4572 152nd Avenue	Citrus Heights	CA	95621
1025	Townhouse	3354 North 62nd Street	Citrus Heights	CA	95610
1026	Condominium	10057 128th Avenue	Citrus Heights	CA	95611
1030	Single-family house	5430 112th Southeast	Citrus Heights	CA	95611

CitrusHeightsPropsQuery

Project 1f–*continued*

Pymnt#	PymntDate	PymntAmount	FirstName	LastName
1	3/1/2012	$1,800.00	Ross	Molaski
2	3/1/2012	$1,900.00	Julia	Perez
3	3/1/2012	$1,250.00	Nadine	Paschal
4	3/1/2012	$1,300.00	Greg	Hamilton
5	3/2/2012	$1,900.00	Marty	Lobdell
6	3/2/2012	$1,000.00	Richard	Terrell
7	3/2/2012	$1,100.00	Miguel	Villegas
8	3/3/2012	$1,400.00	Carl	Weston
9	3/3/2012	$1,200.00	Danielle	Rubio
10	3/3/2012	$900.00	Mason	Ahn
11	3/5/2012	$1,650.00	Rose	Wagoner
12	3/5/2012	$1,500.00	Michelle	Bertram

Pymnts3/1To3/5Query

Category	PropID	MoRent	Address	City	State	ZIP
Condominium	1001	$1,500.00	4102 Tenth Street	Citrus Heights	CA	95611
Townhouse	1005	$1,350.00	12110 55th Southeast	Citrus Heights	CA	95611
Condominium	1009	$1,400.00	159 Meridian Street	Orangevale	CA	95662
Apartment	1010	$950.00	19334 140th East	Citrus Heights	CA	95621
Duplex	1011	$1,350.00	348 Hampton Avenue	Citrus Heights	CA	95611
Apartment	1014	$1,000.00	9045 Valley Avenue	Citrus Heights	CA	95611
Duplex	1017	$1,300.00	4500 Maple Lane	Orangevale	CA	95662
Duplex	1020	$1,200.00	23390 South 22nd Street	Citrus Heights	CA	95610
Townhouse	1022	$1,250.00	4572 152nd Avenue	Citrus Heights	CA	95621
Condominium	1023	$1,300.00	750 Birch Drive	Orangevale	CA	95662
Townhouse	1025	$1,200.00	3354 North 62nd Street	Citrus Heights	CA	95610
Condominium	1026	$1,375.00	10057 128th Avenue	Citrus Heights	CA	95611

RentLessThan$1501InCHAndOVQuery

EmpID	FName	LName	Address	City	State	ZIP
07-20	Jesse	Scholtz	4102 Tenth Street	Citrus Heights	CA	95611
07-20	Jesse	Scholtz	2650 Crestline Drive	Citrus Heights	CA	95611
07-20	Jesse	Scholtz	12110 55th Southeast	Citrus Heights	CA	95611
07-20	Jesse	Scholtz	19334 140th East	Citrus Heights	CA	95621
07-20	Jesse	Scholtz	348 Hampton Avenue	Citrus Heights	CA	95611
07-20	Jesse	Scholtz	2606 30th Street	Citrus Heights	CA	95610
07-20	Jesse	Scholtz	9045 Valley Avenue	Citrus Heights	CA	95611
07-20	Jesse	Scholtz	21388 South 42nd Street	Citrus Heights	CA	95621
07-20	Jesse	Scholtz	23390 South 22nd Street	Citrus Heights	CA	95610
07-20	Jesse	Scholtz	4572 152nd Avenue	Citrus Heights	CA	95621
07-20	Jesse	Scholtz	3354 North 62nd Street	Citrus Heights	CA	95610
07-20	Jesse	Scholtz	10057 128th Avenue	Citrus Heights	CA	95611
07-20	Jesse	Scholtz	5430 112th Southeast	Citrus Heights	CA	95611

Emp07-20CHPropsQuery

Project 1 Create and Modify Tables in a Property Management Database — 8 Parts

You will open the Sun Properties database, create two new tables in Design view, modify existing tables, and sort data in tables. You will also complete a spelling check on data in tables, find data in a table and replace with other data, create relationships and perform queries, and get help using the Access Help feature.

Creating a Table in Design View

In Datasheet view you can create a table by assigning each column a data type and typing the field name. Once the columns are defined, you enter the data into records. You can also create a table in Design view where you can set field properties before you begin entering data. To display a table in Design view, open the desired database, click the Create tab, and then click the Table button. This opens a new blank table in Datasheet view. Display the table in Design view by clicking the View button that displays at the left side of the Table Tools Design tab in the Views group. When you click the View button in a new table, Access displays the Save As dialog box where you type the table name and then press Enter or click OK. Figure 4.1 displays the Properties table in Design view in the AL1-C4-SunProperties.accdb database.

View

In Design view, each row in the top section represents one field in the table and is used to define the field name, the field's data type, and a description. The *Field Properties* section in the lower half of the work area displays the properties for the active field. The properties will vary depending on the active field. In the lower right corner of Design view, Help information displays about an option as you make an option active in the Design window. In Figure 4.1, the *PropID* field name is active in Design view, so Access displays information in the Help area on field names.

Figure 4.1 Properties Table in Design View

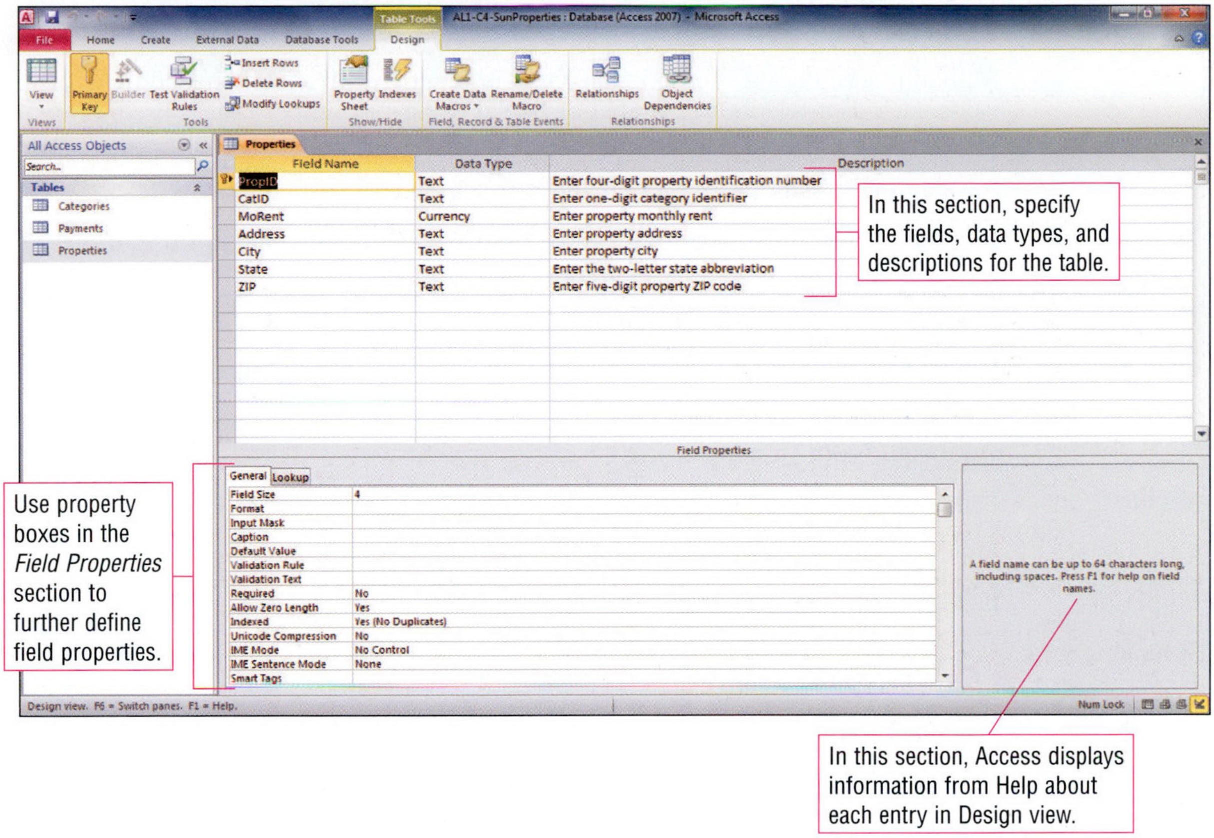
In this section, specify the fields, data types, and descriptions for the table.
Use property boxes in the *Field Properties* section to further define field properties.
In this section, Access displays information from Help about each entry in Design view.
Field Name
Data Type
Description
PropID
Text
Enter four-digit property identification number
CatID
Text
Enter one-digit category identifier
MoRent
Currency
Enter property monthly rent
Address
Text
Enter property address
City
Text
Enter property city
State
Text
Enter the two-letter state abbreviation
ZIP
Text
Enter five-digit property ZIP code
Field Properties
A field name can be up to 64 characters long, including spaces. Press F1 for help on field names.

Define each field in the table in the rows in the top section of Design view. When you create a new table in Design view, Access automatically assigns the first field the name *ID* and assigns the AutoNumber data type. You can leave this field name or type a new name and you can also change the data type. To create a new field in the table, click in the field in the *Field Name* column, type the field name, and then press the Tab key or the Enter key. This makes active the *Data Type* field. Click the down-pointing arrow in the *Data Type* field and then click the desired data type at the drop-down list. In Chapter 1, you created tables in Datasheet view and assigned data types of Text, Date/Time, Currency, or Yes/No. The *Data Type* field drop-down list includes these data types as well as additional types as described in Table 4.1.

When you click the desired data type at the drop-down list and then press the Tab key, the *Description* field becomes active. Type a description in the field that provides useful information to someone entering data in the table. When typing a description, consider the field's purpose or contents, or provide instructional information for data entry. The description you type displays in the Status bar when the field is active in the table in Datasheet view.

When creating the table, continue typing field names, assigning a data type to each field, and typing field descriptions. When the table design is complete, save the table by clicking the Save button on the Quick Access toolbar. Return to Datasheet view by clicking the View button in the Views group in the Table Tools Design tab. In Datasheet view, type the records for the table.

Quick Steps

Create Table in Design View

1. Open database.
2. Click Create tab.
3. Click Table button.
4. Click View button.
5. Type name for table.
6. Press Enter or click OK.
7. Type field names, specify data types, and include descriptions.
8. Click Save button.

Save

Table 4.1 Data Types

Data Type	*Description*
Text	Alphanumeric data up to 255 characters in length, such as a name, address, or value such as a telephone number or Social Security number that is used as an identifier and not for calculating.
Memo	Alphanumeric data up to 64,000 characters in length.
Number	Positive or negative values that can be used in calculations. Do not use for value that will calculate monetary amounts (see Currency).
Date/Time	Use this type to ensure dates and times are entered and sorted properly.
Currency	Values that involve money. Access will not round off during calculations.
AutoNumber	Access automatically numbers each record sequentially (incrementing by 1) when you begin typing a new record.
Yes/No	Data in the field will be either *Yes* or *No*, *True* or *False*, or *On* or *Off*.
OLE Object	Used to embed or link objects created in other Office applications.
Hyperlink	Field that will store a hyperlink such as a URL.
Attachment	Use this data type to add file attachments to a record such as a Word document or an Excel workbook.
Lookup Wizard	Use the Lookup Wizard to enter data in the field from another existing table or display a list of values in a drop-down list from which the user chooses.

Project 1a Creating a Table in Design View

Part 1 of 8

1. Open Access and then open the **AL1-C4-SunProperties.accdb** database located in the Access2010L1C4 folder on your storage medium.
2. Click the Enable Content button in the message bar. (The message bar will display immediately below the ribbon.)
3. View the Properties table in Design view by completing the following steps:
   a. Open the Properties table.
   b. Click the View button in the Views group in the Home tab. (This displays the table in Design view.)
   c. Click each of the field names and then look at the information that displays in the *Field Properties* section.
   d. Click in various options and then read the information that displays in the Help area located in the lower right corner of Design view.
   e. Click the View button to return the table to Datasheet view.
   f. Close the Properties table.

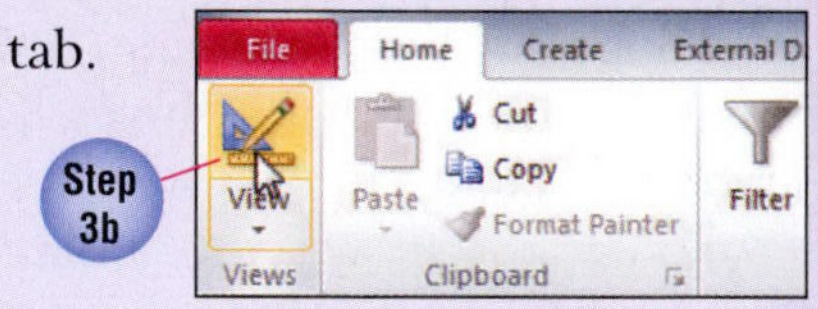

4. Create a new table in Design view as shown in Figure 4.2 by completing the following steps:
   a. Click the Create tab and then click the Table button in the Tables group.
   b. Click the View button in the Views group in the Table Tools Fields tab.
   c. At the Save As dialog box, type **Renters** and then press Enter.

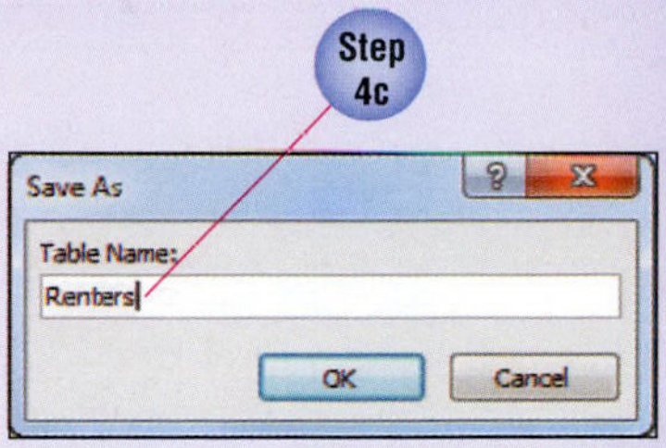

   d. Type **RenterID** in the *Field Name* column in the first row and then press the Tab key.
   e. Change the data type to Text by clicking the down-pointing arrow located in the *Data Type* column and then clicking *Text* at the drop-down list.

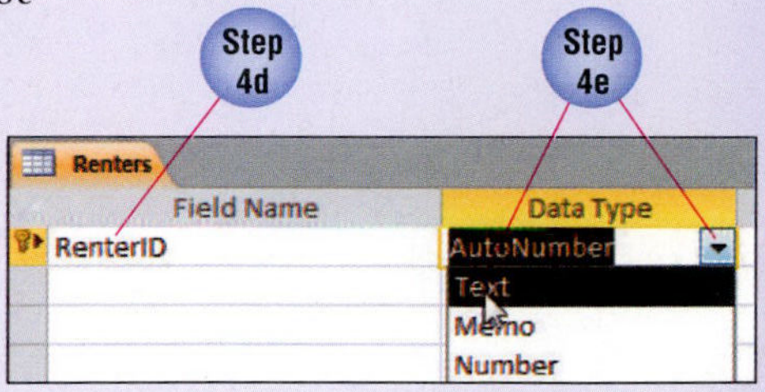

   f. Change the field size from the default of *255* to *3* by selecting *255* that displays in the *Field Size* property box in the *Field Properties* section and then typing **3**.

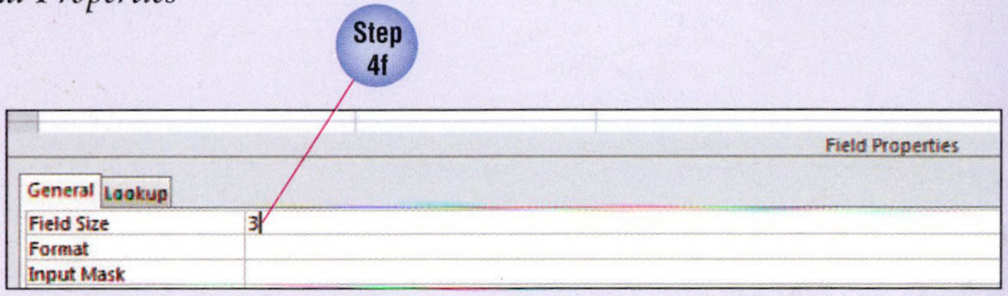

   g. Click in the *Description* column for the *RenterID* row, type **Enter three-digit renter identification number**, and then press the Tab key.

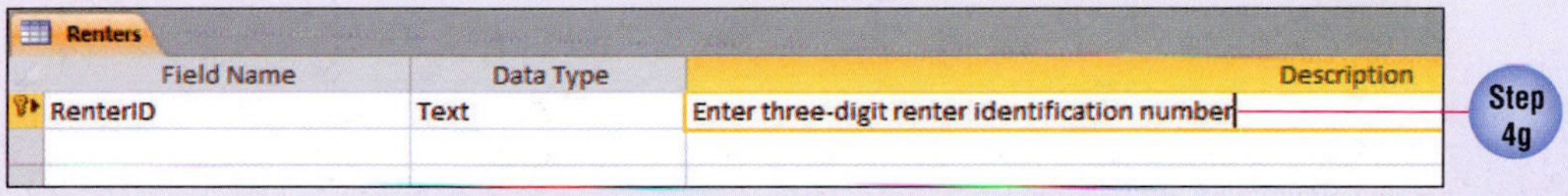

   h. Type **FirstName** in the *Field Name* column and then press the Tab key.
   i. Select *255* that displays in the *Field Size* property box in the *Field Properties* section and then type **20**.
   j. Click in the *Description* column for the *FirstName* row, type **Enter renter's first name**, and then press the Tab key.
   k. Type **LastName** in the *Field Name* column and then press the Tab key.
   l. Change the field size to *30* (at the *Field Size* property box).
   m. Click in the *Description* column for the *LastName* row, type **Enter renter's last name**, and then press the Tab key.
   n. Enter the remaining field names, data types, and descriptions as shown in Figure 4.2. (Change the field size to *4* for the *PropID* field, the field size to *5* for the *EmpID* field, and the field size to *3* for the *CreditScore* field.)
   o. When all fields are entered, click the Save button on the Quick Access toolbar.
   p. Make sure the *RenterID* field is identified as the primary key (a key icon displays in the *RenterID* field selector bar).
   q. Click the View button to return the table to Datasheet view.
5. Enter the records in the Renters table as shown in Figure 4.3.
6. After all records are entered, automatically adjust column widths.
7. Save and then close the Renters table.

Figure 4.2 Project 1a Renters Table in Design View

Renters

Field Name	Data Type	Description
RenterID	Text	Enter three-digit renter identification number
FirstName	Text	Enter renter's first name
LastName	Text	Enter renter's last name
PropID	Text	Enter four-digit property identification number
EmpID	Text	Enter five-digit employee identification number
CreditScore	Text	Enter renter's current credit score
LeaseBegDate	Date/Time	Enter beginning date of lease
LeaseEndDate	Date/Time	Enter ending date of lease

Field Properties

General | Lookup

Field Size	3
Format	
Input Mask	
Caption	
Default Value	
Validation Rule	
Validation Text	
Required	No
Allow Zero Length	Yes
Indexed	Yes (No Duplicates)
Unicode Compression	No
IME Mode	No Control
IME Sentence Mode	None
Smart Tags	

Figure 4.3 Project 1a Renters Table in Datasheet View

Renters

RenterID	FirstName	LastName	PropID	EmpID	CreditScore	LeaseBegDate	LeaseEndDate	Click
110	Greg	Hamilton	1029	04-14	624	1/1/2012	12/31/2012	
111	Julia	Perez	1013	07-20	711	1/1/2012	12/31/2012	
115	Dana	Rozinski	1026	02-59	538	2/1/2012	1/31/2013	
117	Miguel	Villegas	1007	07-20	695	2/1/2012	1/31/2013	
118	Mason	Ahn	1004	07-23	538	3/1/2012	2/28/2013	
119	Michelle	Bertram	1001	03-23	621	3/1/2012	2/28/2013	
121	Travis	Jorgenson	1010	04-14	590	3/1/2012	2/28/2013	
123	Richard	Terrell	1014	07-20	687	3/1/2012	2/28/2013	
125	Rose	Wagoner	1015	07-23	734	4/1/2012	3/31/2013	
127	William	Young	1023	05-31	478	4/1/2012	3/31/2013	
129	Susan	Lowrey	1002	04-14	634	4/1/2012	3/31/2013	
130	Ross	Molaski	1027	03-23	688	5/1/2012	4/30/2013	
131	Danielle	Rubio	1020	07-20	722	5/1/2012	4/30/2013	
133	Katie	Smith	1018	07-23	596	5/1/2012	4/30/2013	
134	Carl	Weston	1009	03-23	655	6/1/2012	5/31/2013	
135	Marty	Lobdell	1006	04-14	510	6/1/2012	5/31/2013	
136	Nadine	Paschal	1022	05-31	702	6/1/2012	5/31/2013	
*								

Assigning a Default Value

In Chapter 1, you learned how to specify a default value for a field in a table in Datasheet view using the Default Value button in the Properties group in the Table Tools Fields tab. In addition to this method, you can create a default value for a field in Design view with the *Default Value* property box in the *Field*

Properties section. Click in the *Default Value* property box and then type the desired field value. In Project 1b, you will create a health insurance field with a Yes/No data type. Since most of the agents of Sun Properties have signed up for health insurance benefits, you will set the default value for the field to *Yes*. If you add a new field that contains a default value to an existing table, the existing records will not reflect the default value, only new records entered in the table.

Using the Input Mask

For some fields, you may want to control the data entered in the field. For example, in a ZIP code field, you may want the nine-digit ZIP code entered (rather than the five-digit ZIP code); or you may want the three-digit area code included in a telephone number. Use the *Input Mask* field property to set a pattern for how data is entered in a field. An input mask ensures that data in records conforms to a standard format. Access includes an Input Mask Wizard that guides you through creating an input mask.

Use the Input Mask Wizard when assigning a data type to a field. In Design view, click in the Input Mask property box in the *Field Properties* section and then run the Input Mask Wizard by clicking the Build button (button containing three black dots) that appears at the right side of the Input Mask property box. This displays the first Input Mask Wizard dialog box as shown in Figure 4.4. In the *Input Mask* list box, choose which input mask you want your data to look like and then click the Next button. At the second Input Mask Wizard dialog box, as shown in Figure 4.5, specify the appearance of the input mask and the desired placeholder character and then click the Next button. At the third Input Mask Wizard dialog box, specify whether you want the data stored with or without the symbol in the mask and then click the Next button. At the fourth dialog box, click the Finish button.

Quick Steps

Use Input Mask Wizard

1. Open table in Design view.
2. Type text in *Field Name* column.
3. Press Tab key.
4. Change data type to *Text*.
5. Click Save button.
6. Click in *Input Mask* property box.
7. Click Build button.
8. Complete wizard steps.

HINT

An input mask is a set of characters that control what you can and cannot enter in a field.

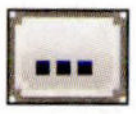

Build

Figure 4.4 First Input Mask Wizard Dialog Box

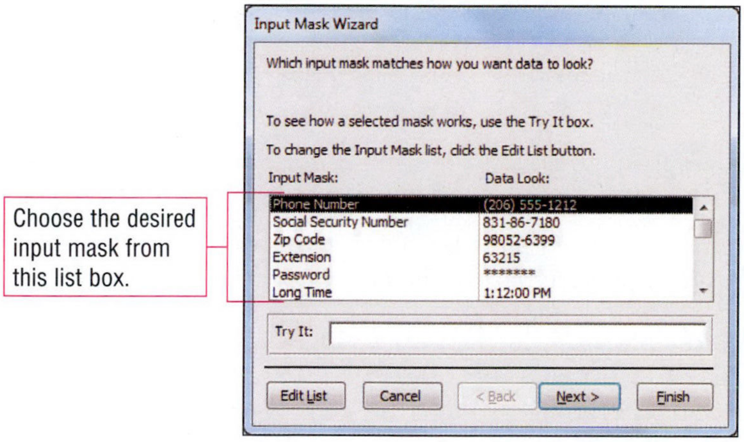

Figure 4.5 Second Input Mask Wizard Dialog Box

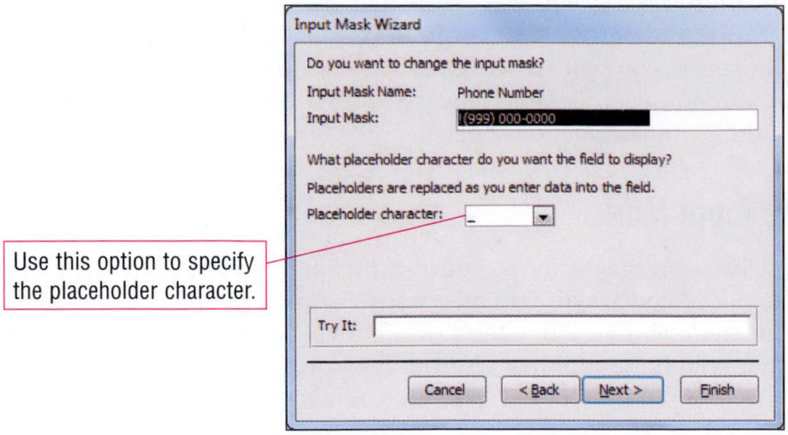

Project 1b Creating an Employees Table Part 2 of 8

1. With the **AL1-C4-SunProperties.accdb** database open, create the Employees table in Design view as shown in Figure 4.6 on page 142. Begin by clicking the Create tab and then clicking the Table button.
2. Click the View button.
3. At the Save As dialog box, type **Employees** and then press Enter.
4. Type **EmpID** in the *Field Name* column in the first row and then press the Tab key.
5. Change the data type to Text by clicking the down-pointing arrow located in the *Data Type* column and then clicking *Text* at the drop-down list.
6. Change the field size from the default of *255* to *5* by selecting *255* that displays in the *Field Size* property box in the *Field Properties* section and then typing **5**.
7. Click in the *Description* column for the *EmpID* row, type **Enter five-digit employee identification number**, and then press the Tab key.

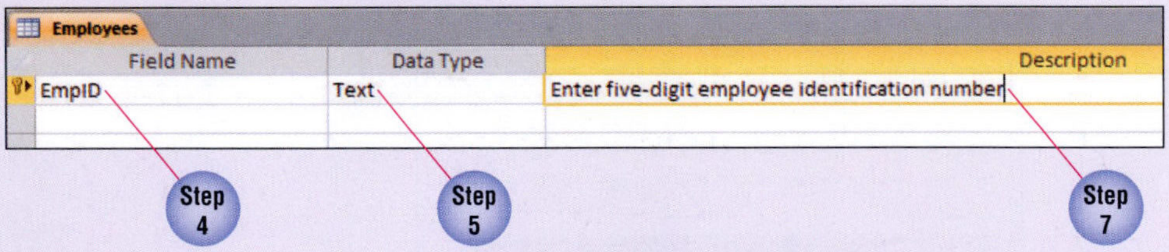

8. Type **FName** in the *Field Name* column and then press the Tab key.
9. Select *255* that displays in the *Field Size* property box in the *Field Properties* section and then type **20**.
10. Click in the *Description* column for the *FName* row, type **Enter employee's first name**, and then press the Tab key.
11. Complete steps similar to those in Steps 8 through 10 to create the *LName*, *Address*, and *City* fields as shown in Figure 4.6. Change the field size for the *LName* field and *Address* field to *30* and change the *City* field to *20*.
12. Create the *State* field with a default value of *CA*, since all employees live in California, by completing the following steps:
    a. Type **State** in the *Field Name* column in the row below the *City* row and then press the Tab key.

b. Click in the *Default Value* property box in the *Field Properties* section and then type **CA**.

c. Click in the *Description* column for the *State* row, type **CA automatically entered as state**, and then press the Tab key.

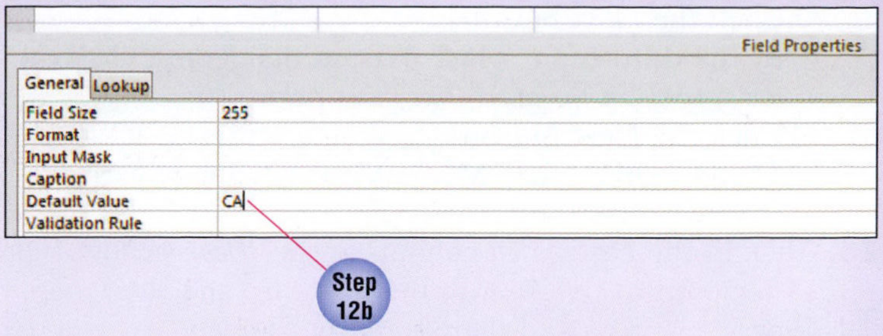

13. Type **ZIP** and then press the Tab key.
14. Select *255* that displays in the *Field Size* property box in the *Field Properties* section and then type **5**.
15. Click in the *Description* column for the *ZIP* row, type **Enter five-digit ZIP code**, and then press the Tab key.
16. Type **Telephone** and then press the Tab key.
17. Create an input mask for the telephone number by completing the following steps:
    a. Click the Save button to save the table. (You must save the table before using the Input Mask Wizard.)
    b. Click in the *Input Mask* property box in the *Field Properties* section.
    c. Click the Build button (button containing three black dots) that displays at the right side of the *Input Mask* property box.

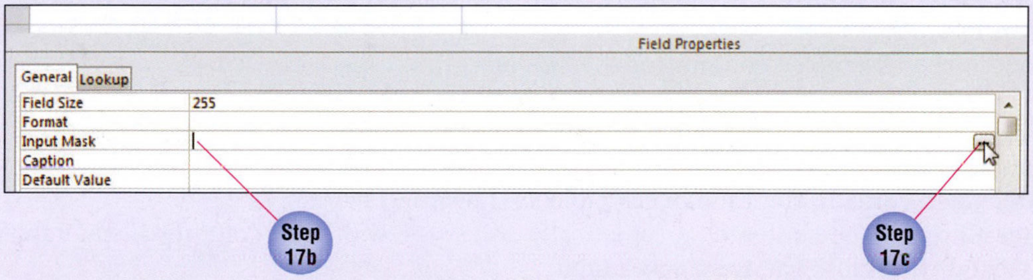

    d. At the first *Input Mask* Wizard dialog box, make sure *Phone Number* is selected in the *Input Mask* list box and then click the Next button.
    e. At the second Input Mask Wizard dialog box, click the down-pointing arrow at the right side of the *Placeholder character* box and then click # at the drop-down list.

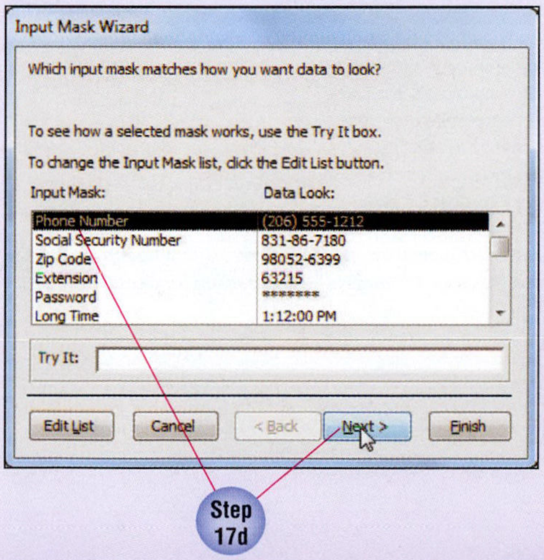

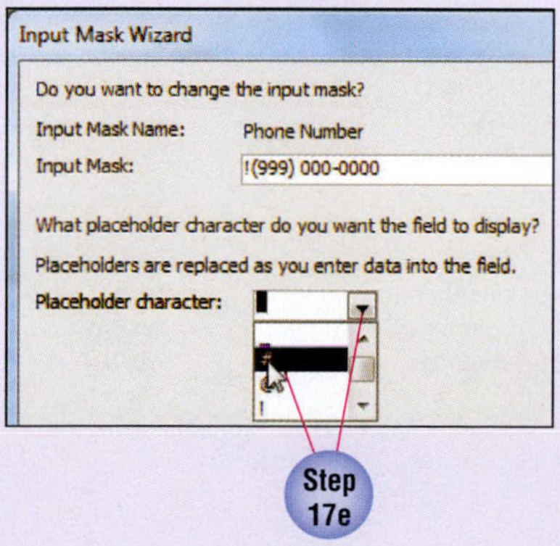

f. Click the Next button.

g. At the third Input Mask Wizard dialog box, click the *With the symbols in the mask, like this* option.

h. Click the Next button.

i. At the fourth Input Mask Wizard dialog box, click the Finish button.

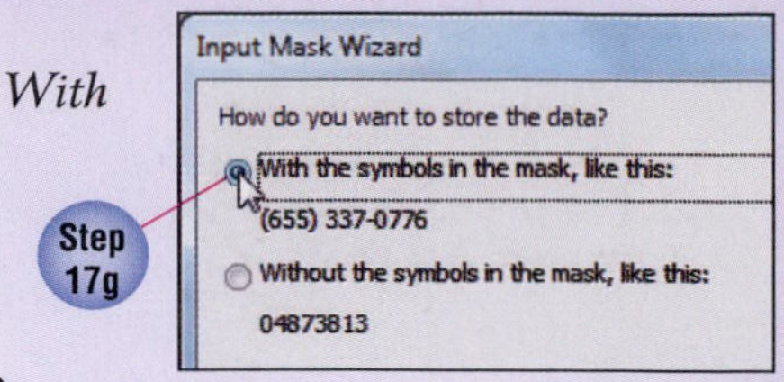

18. Click in the *Description* column in the *Telephone* row, type **Enter employee's telephone number**, and then press the Tab key.
19. Type **HealthIns** and then press the Tab key.
20. Click the down-pointing arrow in the *Data Type* column and then click *Yes/No* at the drop-down list.
21. Click in the *Default Value* property box in the *Field Properties* section and then type **Yes**.

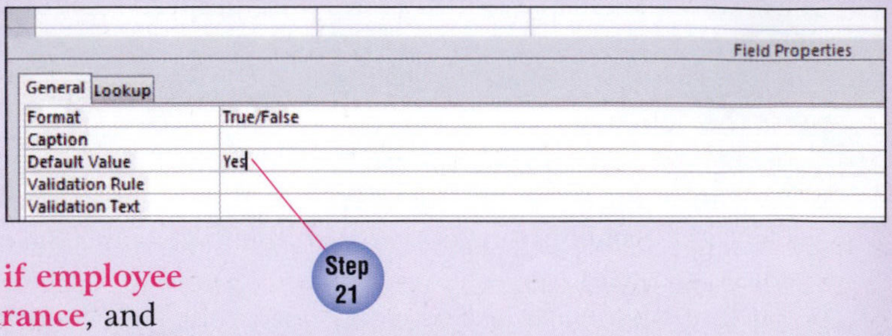

22. Click in the *Description* column for the *HealthIns* row, type **Leave check mark if employee is signed up for health insurance**, and then press the Tab key.
23. Type **DentalIns** and then press the Tab key.
24. Click the down-pointing arrow in the *Data Type* column and then click *Yes/No* at the drop-down list.
25. Click in the *Description* column for the *DentalIns* row, type **Insert check mark if employee is signed up for dental insurance**, and then press the Tab key.
26. When all fields are entered, click the Save button on the Quick Access toolbar.
27. Click the View button to return the table to Datasheet view.
28. Enter the records in the Employees table as shown in Figure 4.7.
29. After all records are entered, automatically adjust the widths of columns in the table.
30. Save and then close the Employees table.

Figure 4.6 Project 1b Employees Table in Design View

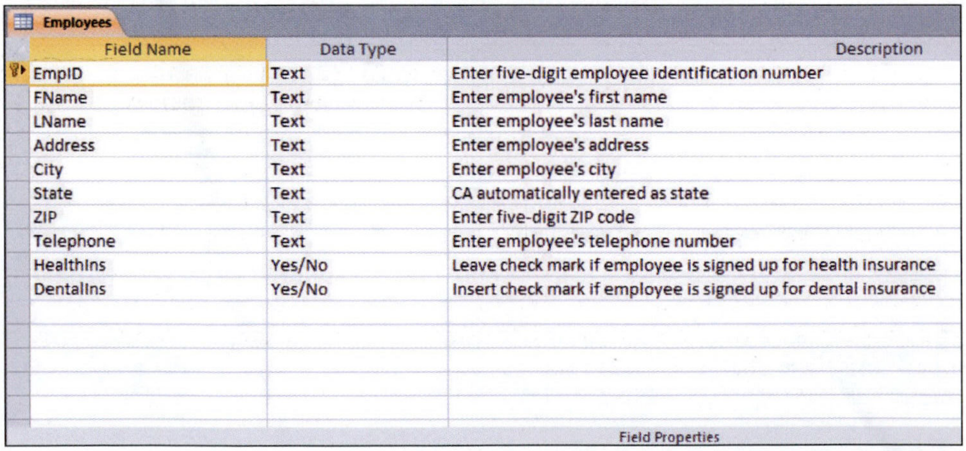
Employees

Field Name	Data Type	Description
EmpID	Text	Enter five-digit employee identification number
FName	Text	Enter employee's first name
LName	Text	Enter employee's last name
Address	Text	Enter employee's address
City	Text	Enter employee's city
State	Text	CA automatically entered as state
ZIP	Text	Enter five-digit ZIP code
Telephone	Text	Enter employee's telephone number
HealthIns	Yes/No	Leave check mark if employee is signed up for health insurance
DentalIns	Yes/No	Insert check mark if employee is signed up for dental insurance

Field Properties

Figure 4.7 Project 1b Employees Table in Datasheet View

Employees

	EmpID	FName	LName	Address	City	State	ZIP	Telephone	HealthIns	DentalIns	Click
	02-59	Christina	Solomon	12241 East 51st	Citrus Heights	CA	95611	(916) 555-8844	☑	☑	
	03-23	Douglas	Ricci	903 Mission Road	Roseville	CA	95678	(916) 555-4125	☑	☐	
	03-55	Tatiana	Kasadev	6558 Orchard Drive	Citrus Heights	CA	95610	(916) 555-8534	☑	☐	
	04-14	Brian	West	12232 142nd Avenue East	Citrus Heights	CA	95611	(916) 555-0967	☑	☑	
	04-32	Kathleen	Addison	21229 19th Street	Citrus Heights	CA	95621	(916) 555-3408	☑	☑	
	05-20	Teresa	Villanueva	19453 North 42nd Street	Citrus Heights	CA	95611	(916) 555-2302	☑	☑	
	05-31	Marcia	Griswold	211 Haven Road	North Highlands	CA	95660	(916) 555-1449	☐	☐	
	06-24	Tiffany	Gentry	12312 North 20th	Roseville	CA	95661	(916) 555-0043	☑	☑	
	06-33	Joanna	Gallegos	6850 York Street	Roseville	CA	95747	(916) 555-7446	☐	☐	
	07-20	Jesse	Scholtz	3412 South 21st Street	Fair Oaks	CA	95628	(916) 555-4204	☑	☐	
	07-23	Eugene	Bond	530 Laurel Road	Orangevale	CA	95662	(916) 555-9412	☑	☐	
*						CA			☑	☐	

Validating Field Entries

Use the *Validation Rule* property box in the *Field Properties* section in Design view to enter a statement containing a conditional test that is checked each time data is entered into a field. If you enter data that fails to satisfy the conditional test, Access does not accept the entry and displays an error message. By entering a conditional statement in the *Validation Rule* property box that checks each entry against the acceptable range, you can reduce errors. Enter in the *Validation Text* property box the content of the error message that you want to display.

HINT

Enter a validation rule in a field to control what is entered in the field and to reduce errors. Create validation text that displays when someone enters invalid data in the field.

Using the Lookup Wizard

Like the Input Mask Wizard, you can use the Lookup Wizard to control the data entered in a field. Use the Lookup Wizard to confine the data entered into a field to a specific list of items. For example, in Project 1c you will use the Lookup Wizard to restrict the new *EmpCategory* field to one of three choices—*Salaried*, *Hourly*, and *Temporary*. When the user clicks in the field in the datasheet, a down-pointing arrow displays. The user clicks this down-pointing arrow to display a drop-down list of available entries and then clicks the desired item.

Quick Steps

Use Lookup Wizard

1. Open table in Design view.
2. Type text in *Field Name* column.
3. Press Tab key.
4. Click down-pointing arrow.
5. Click *Lookup Wizard.*
6. Complete wizard steps.

Use the Lookup Wizard when assigning a data type to a field. Click in the desired field in the *Data Type* column and then click the down-pointing arrow that displays at the right side of the field. At the drop-down list that displays, click *Lookup Wizard*. This displays the first Lookup Wizard dialog box as shown in Figure 4.8. At this dialog box, indicate that you want to enter the field choices by clicking the *I will type in the values that I want* option and then click the Next button. At the second Lookup Wizard dialog box shown in Figure 4.9, click in the blank text box below *Col1* and then type the first choice. Press the Tab key and then type the second choice. Continue in this manner until all desired choices are entered and then click the Next button. At the third Lookup Wizard dialog box, make sure the proper name displays in the *What label would you like for your lookup column?* text box and then click the Finish button.

Figure 4.8 First Lookup Wizard Dialog Box

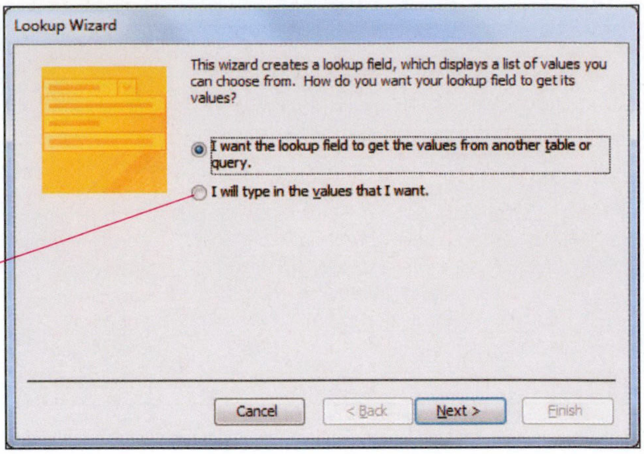
Lookup Wizard
This wizard creates a lookup field, which displays a list of values you can choose from. How do you want your lookup field to get its values?
I want the lookup field to get the values from another table or query.
I will type in the values that I want.
Cancel
< Back
Next >
Finish

Click this option if you want to type your own lookup values.

Figure 4.9 Second Lookup Wizard Dialog Box

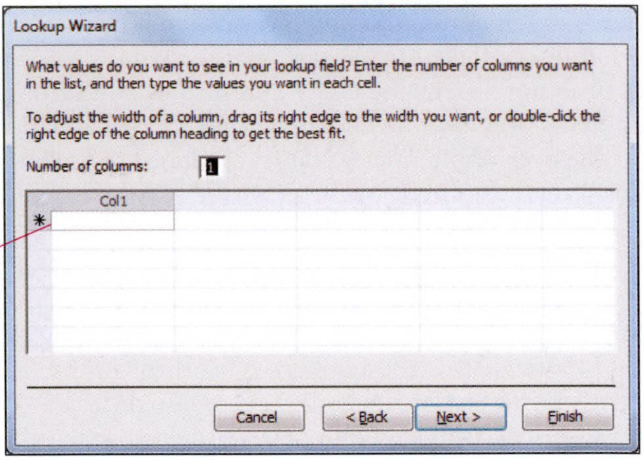
Lookup Wizard
What values do you want to see in your lookup field? Enter the number of columns you want in the list, and then type the values you want in each cell.
To adjust the width of a column, drag its right edge to the width you want, or double-click the right edge of the column heading to get the best fit.
Number of columns:
1
Col1
Cancel
< Back
Next >
Finish

Click this text box, type the first choice, and then press Tab. Continue typing and pressing Tab until all desired choices are entered.

Quick Steps

Insert Field in Design View
1. Open table in Design view.
2. Click in row that will follow new field.
3. Click Insert Rows button.

Delete Field in Design View
1. Open table in Design view.
2. Click in row to be deleted.
3. Click Delete Rows button.
4. Click Yes.

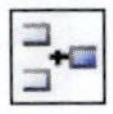

Insert Rows

Inserting, Moving, and Deleting Fields in Design View

In Chapter 1, you learned how to insert, move, and delete fields in a table in Datasheet view. You can also perform these tasks in Design view. To insert a new field in a table in Design view, position the insertion point in a field in the row that will be located immediately *below* the new field and then click the Insert Rows button in the Tools group in the Table Tools Design tab. Or, position the insertion point on any text in the row that will display immediately *below* the new field, click the right mouse button, and then click *Insert Rows* at the shortcut menu. If you insert a row for a new field and then change your mind, immediately click the Undo button on the Quick Access toolbar. Remember that a *row* in the Design view creates a *field* in the table.

You can move a field in a table to a different location in Datasheet view or Design view. To move a field in Design view, click in the field selector bar at the left side of the row you want to move. With the row selected, position the arrow pointer in the field selector bar at the left side of the selected row, hold down the left mouse button, drag the arrow pointer with a gray square attached until a thick black line displays in the desired position, and then release the mouse button.

Delete a field in a table and all data entered in that field is also deleted. When you delete a field, it cannot be undone with the Undo button. Delete a field only if you are sure you really want it and the data associated with it completely removed from the table. To delete a field in Design view, click in the field selector bar at the left side of the row you want to delete and then click the Delete Rows button in the Tools group. At the message asking if you want to permanently delete the field and all of the data in the field, click Yes. You can also delete a row by positioning the mouse pointer in the row you want to delete, clicking the right mouse button, and then clicking *Delete Rows* at the shortcut menu.

Delete Rows

Inserting a Total Row ■■■■■■■■■■■■■■■■■■■■■

You can add a total row in a table in Datasheet view and then choose from a list of functions to find the sum, average, maximum, minimum, count, standard deviations, or variance result in a numeric column. To insert a total row, click the Totals button in the Records group in the Home tab. Access adds a row to the bottom of the table with the label *Total* at the left. Click in the *Total* row, click the down-pointing arrow that appears, and then click the desired function at the drop-down list.

▼ **Quick Steps**

Insert a Total Row
1. Open table in Datasheet view.
2. Click Totals button.
3. Click in *Total* row.
4. Click down-pointing arrow.
5. Click desired function.

Totals

Project 1c **Validating Field Entries; Using the Lookup Wizard; and Inserting, Moving, and Deleting a Field** Part 3 of 8

1. With the **AL1-C4-SunProperties.accdb** database open, open the Employees table.
2. Insert in the Employees table a new field and apply a validation rule by completing the following steps:
 a. Click the View button to switch to Design view.
 b. Click in the empty field immediately below the *DentalIns* field in the *Field Name* column and then type **LifeIns**.
 c. Press the Tab key.
 d. Click the down-pointing arrow at the right side of the *Data Type* field and then click *Currency* at the drop-down list.
 e. Click in the *Validation Rule* property box, type **<=100000**, and then press Enter.
 f. With the insertion point positioned in the *Validation Text* property box, type **Enter a value that is equal to or less than $100,000**.
 g. Click in the field in the *Description* column for the *LifeIns* row and then type **Enter optional life insurance amount**.
 h. Click the Save button on the Quick Access toolbar. Since the validation rule was created *after* data was entered into the table, Access displays a warning message indicating that some data may not be valid. At this message, click No.
 i. Click the View button to switch to Datasheet view.
3. Click in the first empty field in the *LifeIns* column, type **200000**, and then press the Down Arrow key.

Step 2e

Field Properties

General	Lookup	
Format	Currency	
Decimal Places	Auto	
Input Mask		
Caption		
Default Value		
Validation Rule	<=100000	
Validation Text	Enter a value that is equal to or less than $100,000	
Required	No	

Step 2f

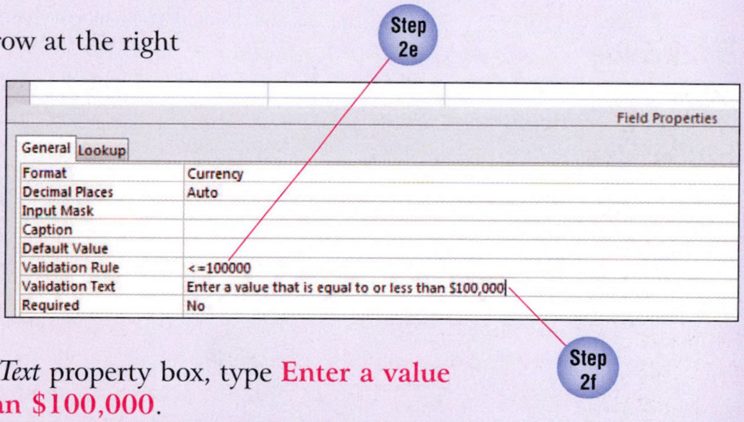

4. Access inserts the error message telling you to enter an amount that is equal to or less than $100,000. At this error message, click OK.
5. Edit the amount in the field so it displays as 100000 and then press the Down Arrow key.
6. Type the following entries in the remaining fields in the *LifeIns* column:
   25000
   0
   50000
   50000
   0
   100000
   50000
   25000
   0
   100000
7. Insert the field *EmpCategory* in the Employees table and use the Lookup Wizard to specify field choices by completing the following steps:

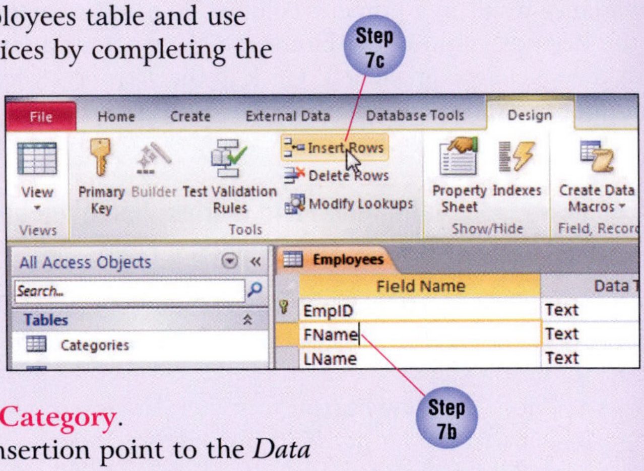

   a. Click the View button to change to Design view.
   b. Click on any character in the *FName* field entry in the *Field Name* column.
   c. Click the Insert Rows button in the Tools group.
   d. With the insertion point positioned in the new blank field in the *Field Name* column, type **EmpCategory**.
   e. Press the Tab key. (This moves the insertion point to the *Data Type* column.)
   f. Click the down-pointing arrow at the right side of the *Data Type* field and then click *Lookup Wizard* at the drop-down list.
   g. At the first Lookup Wizard dialog box, click the *I will type in the values that I want* option and then click the Next button.

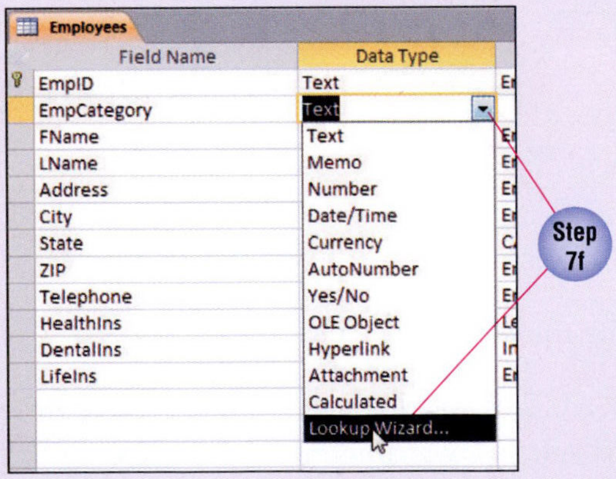

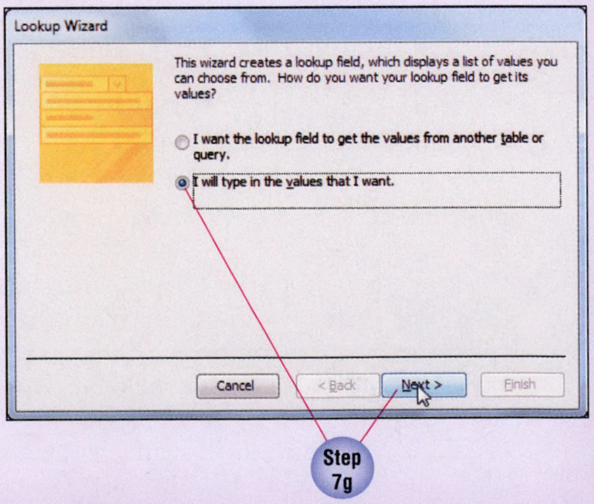

h. At the second Lookup Wizard dialog box, click in the blank text box below *Col1*, type **Salaried**, and then press the Tab key.

i. Type **Hourly** and then press the Tab key.

j. Type **Temporary**.

k. Click the Next button.

l. At the third Lookup Wizard dialog box, click the Finish button.

m. Press the Tab key and then type **Click down-pointing arrow and then click employee category** in the *Description* column.

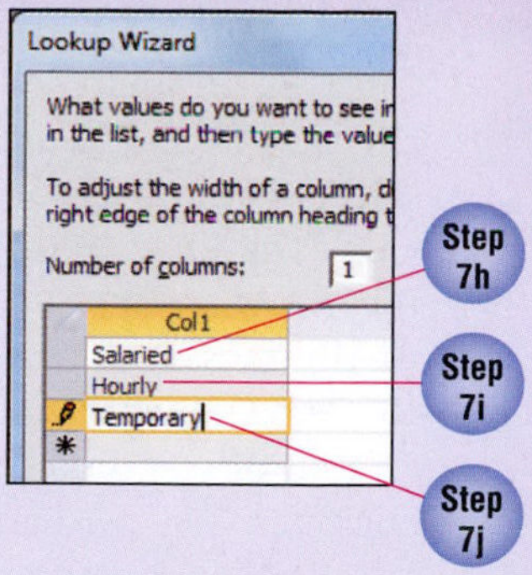

8. Click the Save button on the Quick Access toolbar.
9. Click the View button to switch to Datasheet view.
10. Insert information in the *EmpCategory* column by completing the following steps:

    a. Click in the first blank field in the new *EmpCategory* field.

    b. Click the down-pointing arrow at the right side of the field and then click *Hourly* at the drop-down list.

    c. Click in the next blank field in the *EmpCategory* column, click the down-pointing arrow, and then click *Salaried* at the drop-down list.

    d. Continue entering information in the *EmpCategory* column by completing similar steps. Choose the following in the specified record:

    Third record: *Hourly*
    Fourth record: *Salaried*
    Fifth record: *Temporary*
    Sixth record: *Hourly*
    Seventh record: *Salaried*
    Eighth record: *Temporary*
    Ninth record: *Hourly*
    Tenth record: *Salaried*
    Eleventh record: *Salaried*

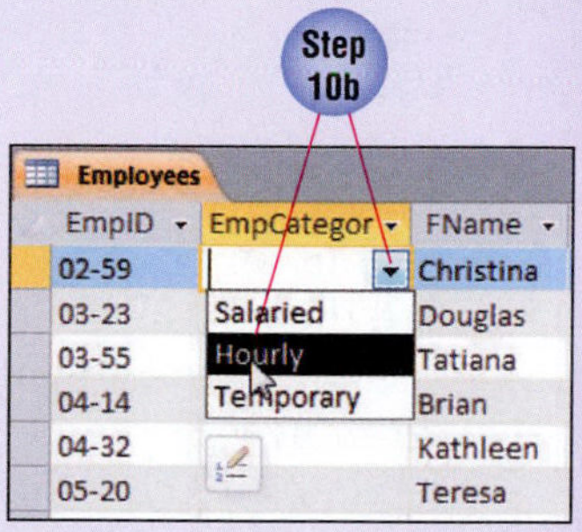

11. Print the Employees table. (The table will print on two pages.)
12. After looking at the printing of the table, you decide to move the *EmpCategory* field. You also need to delete the *DentalIns* field since Sun Properties no longer offers dental insurance benefits to employees. Move the *EmpCatgory* field and delete the *DentalIns* field in Design view by completing the following steps:

    a. With the Employees table open, click the View button to switch to Design view.

    b. Click in the field selector bar at the left side of the *EmpCategory* field to select the row.

    c. Position the arrow pointer in the *EmpCategory* field selector bar, hold down the left mouse button, drag down until a thick black line displays below the *Telephone* field, and then release the mouse button.

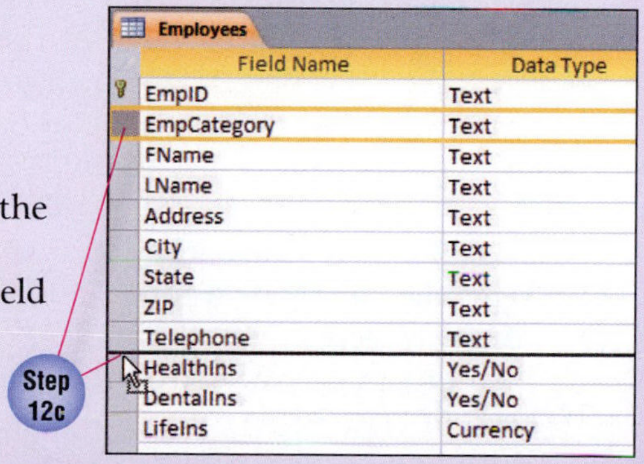

13. Delete the *DentalIns* field by completing the following steps:
    a. Click in the field selector bar at the left side of the *DentalIns* row. (This selects the row.)
    b. Click the Delete Rows button in the Tools group.
    c. At the message asking if you want to permanently delete the field and all of the data in the field, click Yes.

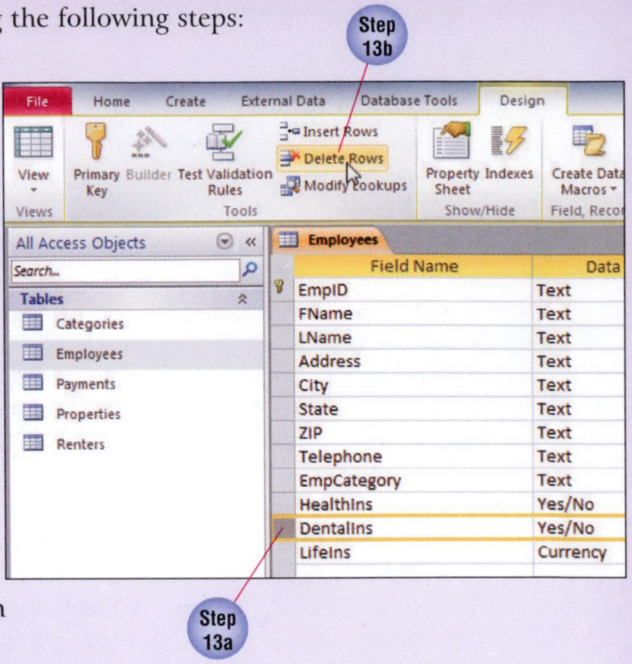

14. Click the Save button on the Quick Access toolbar.
15. Click the View button to switch to Datasheet view.
16. Print the Employees table. (The table will print on two pages.)
17. Close the Employees table.
18. Open the Payments table and then insert a new field and apply a validation rule by completing the following steps:
    a. Click the View button to switch to Design view.
    b. Click in the empty field immediately below the *PymntAmount* field in the *Field Name* column and then type **LateFee**.
    c. Press the Tab key.
    d. Click the down-pointing arrow at the right side of the *Text* box and then click *Currency* at the drop-down list.
    e. Click in the *Validation Rule* property box, type **<=50**, and then press Enter.
    f. With the insertion point positioned in the *Validation Text* property box, type **Late fee must be $50 or less**.
    g. Click in the box in the *Description* column for the *LateFee* field and then type **Enter a late fee amount if applicable**.
    h. Click the Save button on the Quick Access toolbar. Since the validation rule was created *after* data was entered into the table, Access displays a warning message indicating that some data may not be valid. At this message, click No.
    i. Click the View button to switch to Datasheet view.

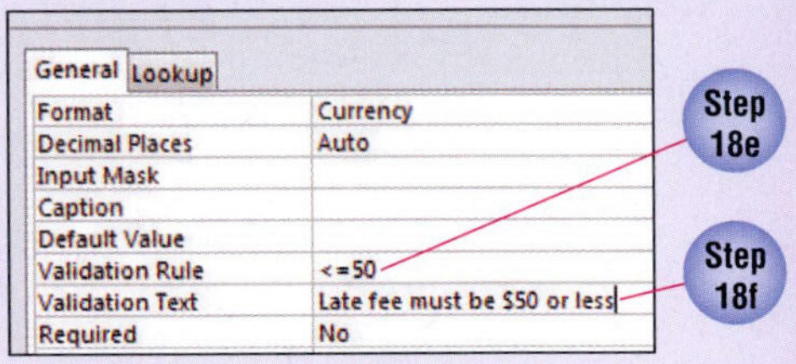

19. Insert late fees for the last three records by completing the following steps:
    a. Click in the *LateFee* field for record 15, type **25**, and then press the Down Arrow key.
    b. With the *LateFee* field for record 16 active, type **25** and then press the Down Arrow key.
    c. With the *LateFee* field for record 17 active, type **50** and then press the Up Arrow key.

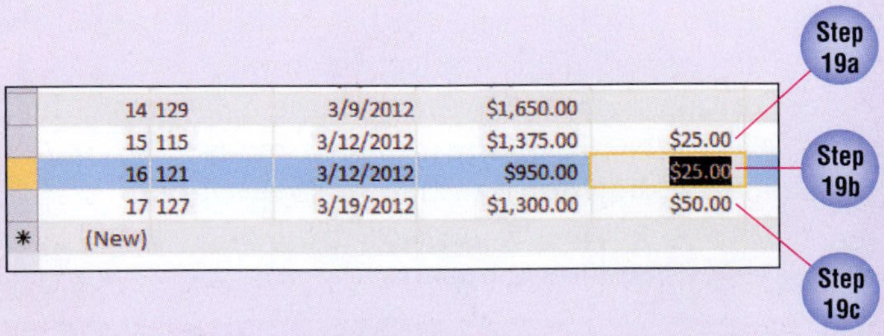

20. Insert a total row by completing the following steps:
 a. In Datasheet view, click the Totals button in the Records group in the Home tab.
 b. Click in the blank field in the *PymntAmount* column in the *Total* row.
 c. Click the down-pointing arrow at the left side of the field and then click *Sum* at the drop-down list.
 d. Click in the blank field in the *LateFee* column in the *Total* row.
 e. Click the down-pointing arrow at the left side of the field and then click *Sum* at the drop-down list.
 f. Click in any other field.
21. Save, print, and then close the Payments table.

Step 20a

Step 20c

Pymnt#	RenterID	PymntDate	PymntAmount	Late
1	130	3/1/2012	$1,800.00	
2	111	3/1/2012	$1,900.00	
3	136	3/1/2012	$1,250.00	
4	110	3/1/2012	$1,300.00	
5	135	3/2/2012	$1,900.00	
6	123	3/2/2012	$1,000.00	
7	117	3/2/2012	$1,100.00	
8	134	3/3/2012	$1,400.00	
9	131	3/3/2012	$1,200.00	
10	118	3/3/2012	$900.00	
11	125	3/5/2012	$1,650.00	
12	119	3/5/2012	$1,500.00	
13	133	3/8/2012	$1,650.00	
14	129	3/9/2012	$1,650.00	
15	115	3/12/2012	$1,375.00	
16	121	3/12/2012	$950.00	
17	127	3/19/2012	$1,300.00	
*	(New)			
	Total			

None
Sum
Average
Count

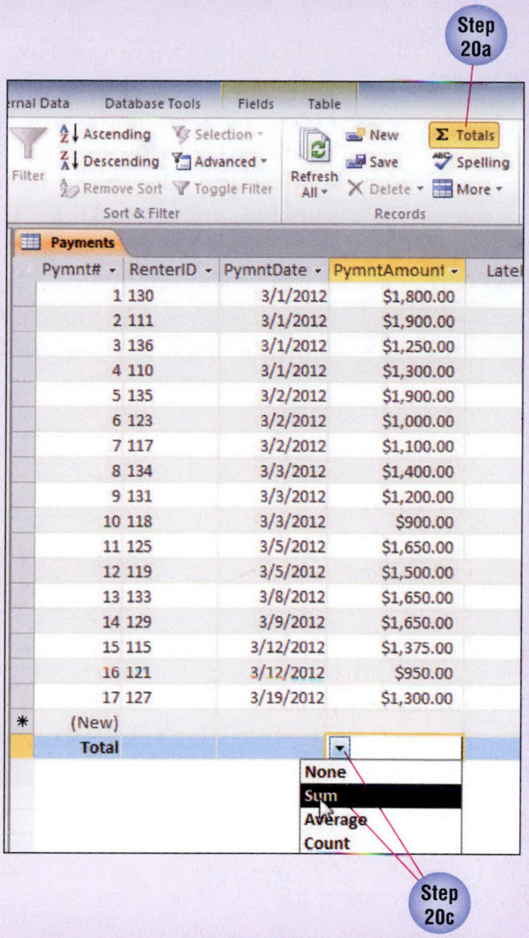

Sorting Records ■■■■■■■■■■■■■■■■■■■■■■■■■

The Sort & Filter group in the Home tab contains two buttons you can use to sort data in records. Click the Ascending button to sort data in the active field in alphabetic order from A to Z or numbers from lowest to highest, or click the Descending button to sort data in alphabetic order from Z to A or numbers from highest to lowest.

Printing Specific Records ■■■■■■■■■■■■■■■■■■■■■

If you want to print specific records in a table, select the records and then display the Print dialog box by clicking the File tab, clicking the Print tab, and then clicking the *Print* option. At the Print dialog box, click the *Selected Record(s)* option in the *Print Range* section and then click OK. To select specific records, display the table in Datasheet view, click the record selector of the first record and then drag to select the desired records. The record selector is the light blue square that displays at the left side of the record. When you position the mouse pointer on the record selector, the pointer turns into a right-pointing black arrow.

▼ **Quick Steps**

Sort Records
1. Open table in Datasheet view.
2. Click in field in desired column.
3. Click Ascending button or Descending button.

Ascending

Descending

Formatting Table Data

Quick Steps

Print Selected Records

1. Open table and select records.
2. Click File tab.
3. Click Print tab.
4. Click *Print* option.
5. Click *Selected Record(s)*.
6. Click OK.

In Datasheet view, you can apply formatting to data in a table. Formatting options are available in the Text Formatting group in the Home tab as shown in Figure 4.10. To apply formatting, open a table in Datasheet view and then click the desired button in the Text Formatting group. The button formatting is applied to all of the data in the table. (Some of the buttons in the Text Formatting are dimmed and unavailable. These buttons are available for fields formatted as rich text.) The buttons available for formatting a table are shown in Table 4.2.

Click the Align Text Left, Center, or Align Text Right button and formatting is applied to text in the currently active column. Click one of the other buttons shown in Table 4.2 and formatting is applied to all columns and rows of data in

Figure 4.10 Home Tab Text Formatting Group

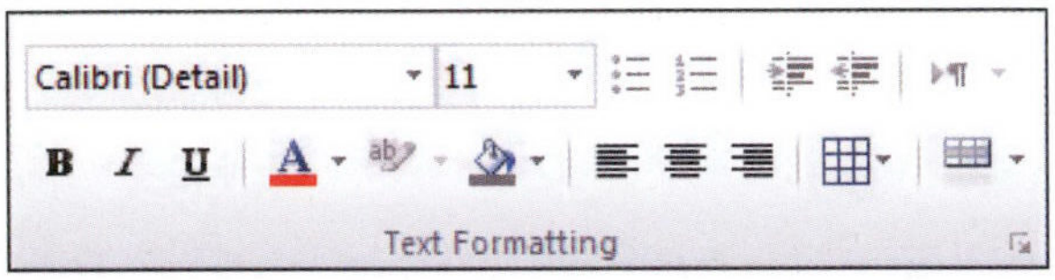

Table 4.2 Text Formatting Buttons

Button	*Name*	*Description*
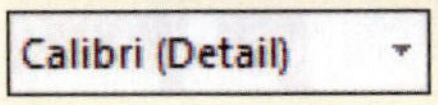	Font	Change text font.
	Font Size	Change text size.
	Bold	Bold text.
	Italic	Italicize text.
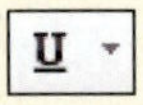	Underline	Underline text.
	Font Color	Change text color.
	Background Color	Apply a background color to all fields.
	Align Text Left	Align all text in the currently active column at the left side of the fields.
	Center	Center all text in the currently active column in the center of the fields.
	Align Text Right	Align all text in the currently active column at the right side of the fields.
	Gridlines	Specify whether or not you want vertical and/or horizontal gridlines displayed.
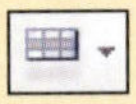	Alternate Row Color	Apply specified color to alternating rows in the table.

the table except the Background Color button that applies formatting to all fields in the table.

When creating a table, you specify a data type for a field such as the Text, Date, or Currency data type. If you want to format text in a field rather than all fields in a column or the entire table, you need to choose the Memo data type and then specify rich text formatting. For example, in Project 1d you will format specific credit scores in the *CreditScore* field column. To be able to format specific scores, you need to change the data type to Memo and then specify rich text formatting. Use the Memo data type only for fields containing text and not fields containing currency amounts, numbers, and dates.

To change the data type to Memo, open the table in Design view, click in the *Data Type* column for the desired field, click the down-pointing arrow, and then click *Memo* at the drop-down list. By default, the Memo data type uses plain text formatting. To change to rich text, click in the *Text Format* property box in the *Field Properties* section (displays with the text *Plain Text*), click the down-pointing arrow that displays at the right side of the property box, and then click *Rich Text* at the drop-down list.

Project 1d **Sorting, Printing, and Formatting Records and Fields in Tables** Part 4 of 8

1. With the **AL1-C4-SunProperties.accdb** database open, open the Renters table.
2. With the table in Datasheet view, sort records in ascending alphabetical order by last name by completing the following steps:
   a. Click any last name in the *LastName* field in the table.
   b. Click the Ascending button in the Sort & Filter group in the Home tab.
   c. Print the Renters table in landscape orientation.

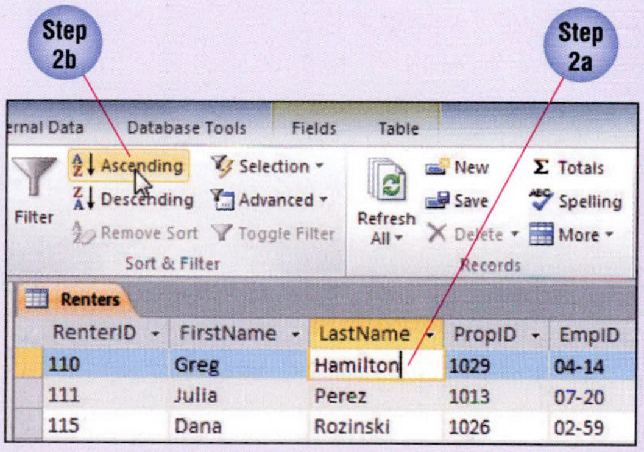

3. Sort records in descending order (highest to lowest) by credit score number by completing the following steps:
   a. Click any number in the *CreditScore* field.
   b. Click the Descending button in the Sort & Filter group.
   c. Print the Renters table in landscape orientation.
4. Close the Renters table without saving the changes.
5. Open the Properties table.
6. Sort and then print selected records with the apartment property type by completing the following steps:
   a. Click any entry in the *CatID* field.
   b. Click the Ascending button in the Sort & Filter group.
   c. Position the mouse pointer on the record selector of the first record with *A* for a category ID, hold down the mouse button, and then drag to select the four records with a category ID of *A*.

d. Click the File tab, click the Print tab, and then click the *Print* option.

e. At the Print dialog box, click the *Selected Record(s)* option in the *Print Range* section.

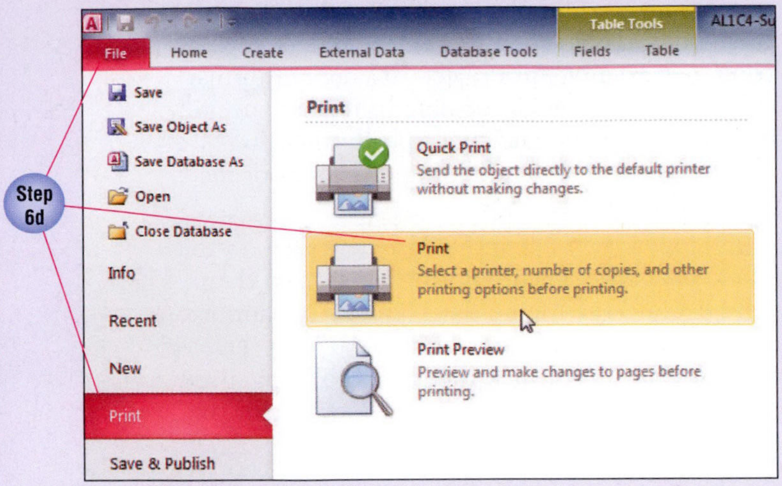

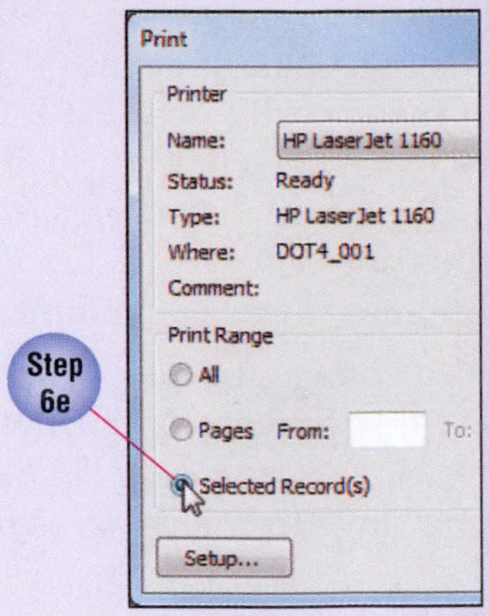

f. Click OK.

7. With the Properties table open, apply the following text formatting:

a. Click in any field in the *CatID* column and then click the Center button in the Text Formatting group in the Home tab.

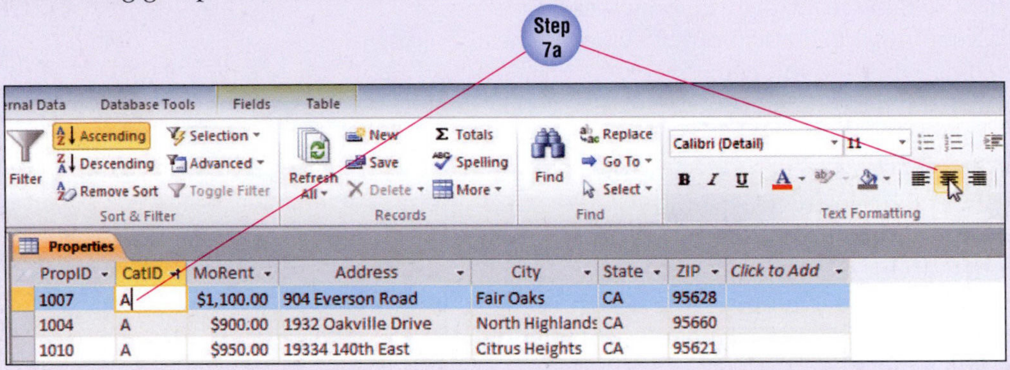

b. Click in any field in the *PropID* column and then click the Center button in the Text Formatting group.

c. Click the Bold button in the Text Formatting group. (This applies bold to all text in the table.)

d. Click the Font Color button arrow and then click the *Dark Blue* color (located in the top row in the fourth column from the left in the *Standard Colors* section).

e. Adjust the column widths.

f. Save, print, and then close the Properties table.

8. Open the Payments table and apply the following text formatting:

a. With the first field active in the *Pymnt#* column, click the Center button in the Text Formatting group in the Home tab.

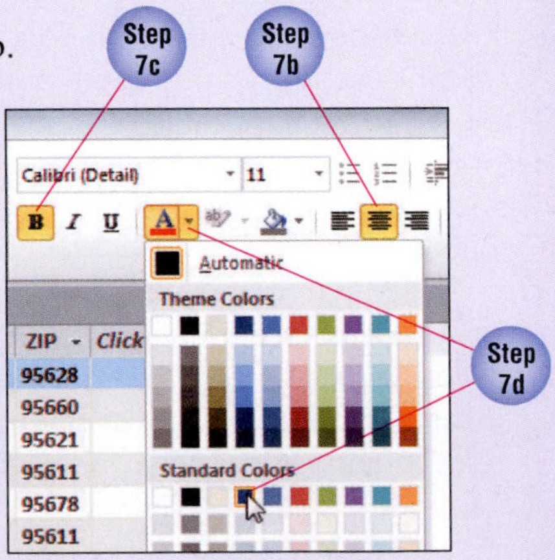

b. Click in any field in the *RenterID* column and then click the Center button in the Text Formatting group.

c. Click the Font button arrow, scroll down the drop-down list that displays, and then click *Candara*. (Fonts are listed in alphabetical order in the drop-down list.)
d. Click the Font Size button arrow and then click *12* at the drop-down list.
e. Click the Alternate Row Color button arrow and then click the *Green 2* color (located in the third row of the seventh column from the left in the *Standard Colors* section).

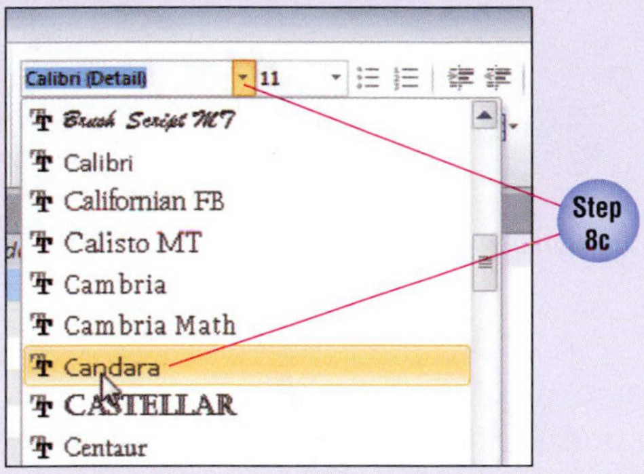

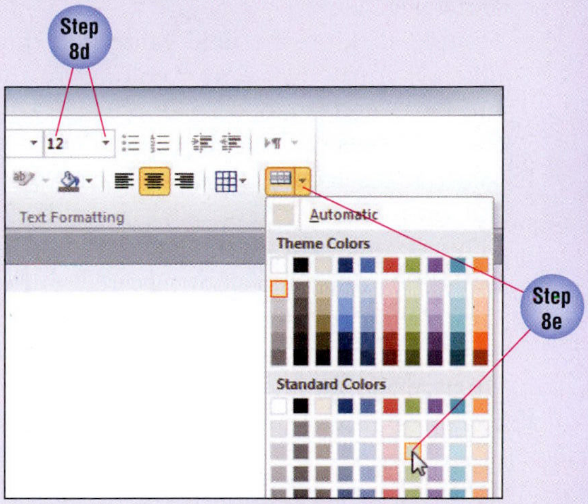

f. Adjust the column widths.
g. Save, print, and then close the Payments table.
9. Open the Renters table and then apply the following formatting to columns in the table:
a. With the first field active in the *RenterID* column, click the Center button in the Text Formatting group in the Home tab.
b. Click in any field in the *PropID* column and then click the Center button.
c. Click in any field in the *EmpID* column and then click the Center button
d. Click in any field in the *CreditScore* column and then click the Center button.
10. Change the data type for the *CreditScore* field to Memo with rich text formatting, and apply formatting by completing the following steps:
a. Click the View button to switch to Design view.
b. Click in the *Data Type* column in the *CreditScore* row, click the down-pointing arrow that displays in the field, and then click *Memo* at the drop-down list.
c. Click in the *Text Format* property box in the *Field Properties* section (displays with the words *Plain Text*), click the down-pointing arrow that displays at the right side of the property box, and then click *Rich Text* at the drop-down list.

d. At the message that displays telling you that the field will be converted to rich text, click the Yes button.
e. Click the Save button on the Quick Access toolbar.
f. Click the View button to switch to Datasheet view.
g. Double-click on the field value *538* that displays in the *CreditScore* column in the row for Dana Rozinski. (Double-clicking in the field selects the field value *538*.)
h. With *538* selected, click the Font Color button in the Text Formatting group. (This changes the number to red. If the font color does not change to red, click the Font Color button arrow and then click the *Red* color in the bottom row of the *Standard Colors* section.)
i. Change the font to red for any credit scores below 600.
j. Print the Renters table in landscape orientation and then close the table.

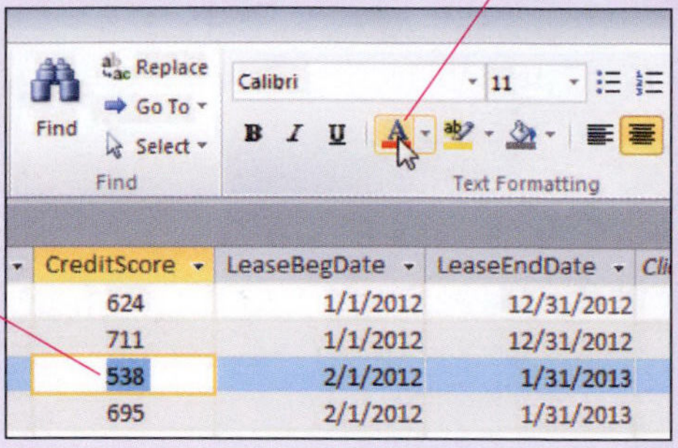

Quick Steps

Complete a Spelling Check
1. Open table in Datasheet view.
2. Click Spelling button.
3. Change or ignore spelling as needed.
4. Click OK.

HINT

You can also begin spell checking with the keyboard shortcut F7.

Spelling

Completing a Spelling Check

The spell checking feature in Access finds misspelled words and offers replacement words. It also finds duplicate words and irregular capitalizations. When you spell check an object in a database such as a table, the spelling checker compares the words in your table with the words in its dictionary. If a match is found, the word is passed over. If no match is found for the word, the spelling checker selects the word and offers replacement suggestions.

To complete a spelling check, open the desired table in Datasheet view and then click the Spelling button in the Records group in the Home tab. If the spelling checker does not find a match for a word in your table, the Spelling dialog box displays with replacement options. Figure 4.11 displays the Spelling dialog box with the word *Citruis* selected and possible replacements displayed in the *Suggestions* list box. At the Spelling dialog box, you can choose to ignore the word (for example, if the spelling checker has selected a proper name), change to one of the replacement options, or add the word to the dictionary or AutoCorrect feature. You can also complete a spelling check on other objects in a database such as a query, form, or report. (You will learn about forms and reports in future chapters.)

Figure 4.11 Spelling Dialog Box

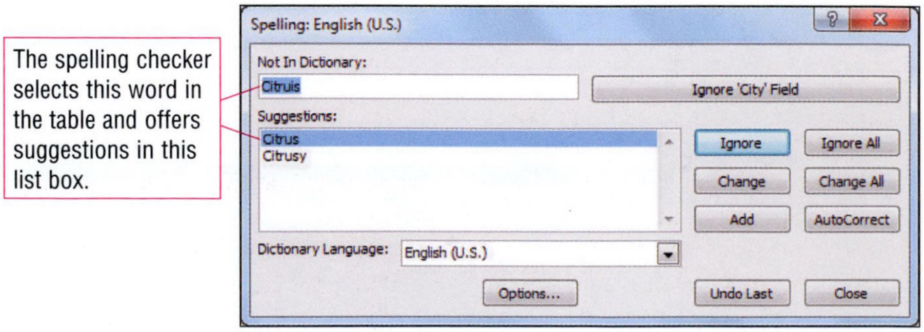

Project 1e Checking Spelling in a Table

Part 5 of 8

1. With the **AL1-C4-SunProperties.accdb** database open, open the Employees table.
2. Delete the *LifeIns* field by completing the following steps:
   a. Click the View button to switch to the Design view.
   b. Click in the field selector bar at the left side of the *LifeIns* row. (This selects the row.)
   c. Click the Delete Rows button in the Tools group.
   d. At the message asking if you want to permanently delete the field and all of the data in the field, click Yes.
   e. Click the Save button on the Quick Access toolbar.
   f. Click the View button to switch to Datasheet view.
3. Add the following record to the Employees table. (Type the misspelled words as shown below. You will correct the spelling in a later step.)

EmpID	=	**02-72**
FName	=	**Roben**
LName	=	**Wildre**
Address	=	**9945 Valley Avenue**
City	=	**Citruis Heights**
State	=	(CA automatically inserted)
ZIP	=	**95610**
Telephone	=	**9165556522**
EmpCategory	=	(choose *Salaried*)
HealthIns	=	No (Remove check mark)

4. Save the Employees table.
5. Click in the first entry in the *EmpID* column.
6. Click the Spelling button in the Records group in the Home tab.
7. The spelling checker selects the name *Kasadev*. This is a proper name, so click the Ignore button to tell the spelling checker to leave the name as written.

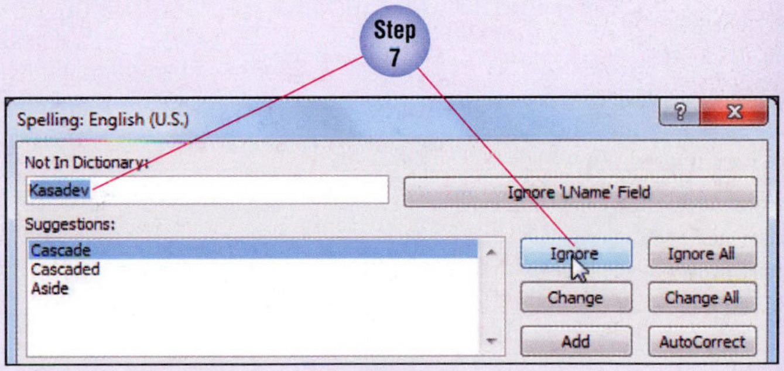

8. The spelling checker selects the name *Scholtz*. This is a proper name, so click the Ignore button to tell the spelling checker to leave the name as written.
9. The spelling checker selects *Roben*. The proper spelling *(Robin)* is selected in the *Suggestions* list box, so click the Change button.

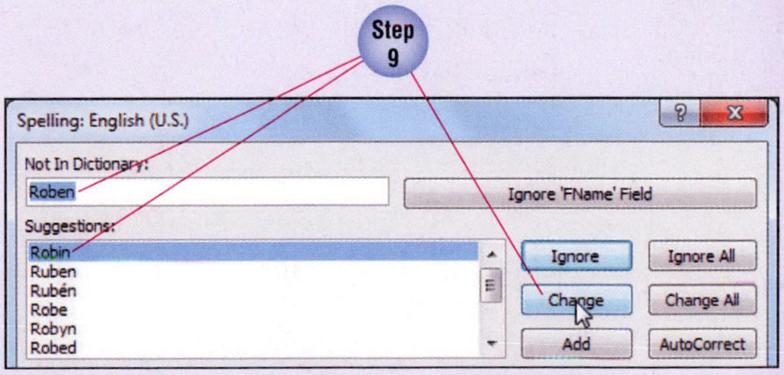

10. The spelling checker selects *Wildre*. The proper spelling *(Wilder)* is selected in the *Suggestions* list box, so click the Change button.
11. The spelling checker selects *Citruis*. The proper spelling *(Citrus)* is selected in the *Suggestions* list box, so click the Change button.
12. At the message telling you that the spelling check is complete, click the OK button.
13. Print the Employees table and then close the table.

Finding and Replacing Data ■■■■■■■■■■■■■■■■■■■■■■

▼ Quick Steps

Find Data
1. Open table in Datasheet view.
2. Click Find button.
3. Type data in *Find What* text box.
4. Click Find Next button.

Find and Replace Data
1. Open table in Datasheet view.
2. Click Replace button.
3. Type find data in *Find What* text box.
4. Type replace data in *Replace With* text box.
5. Click Find Next button.
6. Click Replace button or Find Next button.

If you need to find a specific entry in a field in a table, consider using options at the Find and Replace dialog box with the Find tab selected as shown in Figure 4.12. Display this dialog box by clicking the Find button in the Find group in the Home tab. At the Find and Replace dialog box, enter the data for which you are searching in the *Find What* text box. By default, Access will look in the specific column where the insertion point is positioned. Click the Find Next button to find the next occurrence of the data or click the Cancel button to remove the Find and Replace dialog box.

The *Look In* option defaults to the column where the insertion point is positioned. You can choose to look in the entire table by clicking the down-pointing arrow at the right side of the option and then clicking the table name at the drop-down list. The *Match* option has a default setting of *Whole Field*. You can change this to *Any Part of Field* or *Start of Field*. The *Search* option has a default setting of *All*, which means that Access will search all data in a specific column. This can be changed to *Up* or *Down*. If you want to find data that contains specific uppercase and lowercase letters, insert a check mark in the *Match Case* check box. By default, Access will search fields as they are formatted.

You can use the Find and Replace dialog box with the Replace tab selected to search for specific data and replace with other data. Display this dialog box by clicking the Replace button in the Find group in the Home tab.

HINT

Press Ctrl + F to display the Find and Replace dialog box with the Find tab selected.

HINT

Press Ctrl + H to display the Find and Replace dialog box with the Replace tab selected.

Find

Replace

Figure 4.12 Find and Replace Dialog Box with Find Tab Selected

Enter the data for which you are searching in this text box.

Find and Replace

Find | Replace

Find What: |

Find Next
Cancel

Look In: Current field
Match: Whole Field
Search: All
☐ Match Case ☑ Search Fields As Formatted

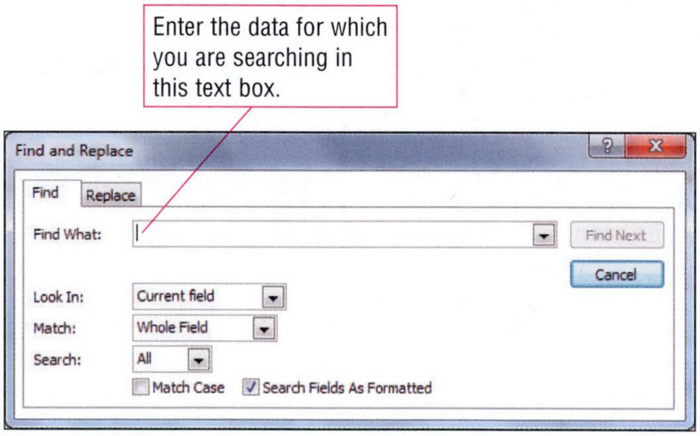

Project 1f Finding and Replacing Data, Creating Relationships, and Performing Queries

Part 6 of 8

1. With the **AL1-C4-SunProperties.accdb** database open, open the Properties table.
2. Find records containing the ZIP code *95610* by completing the following steps:
   a. Click in the first field in the *ZIP* column.
   b. Click the Find button in the Find group in the Home tab.
   c. At the Find and Replace dialog box with the Find tab selected, type **95610** in the *Find What* text box.
   d. Click the Find Next button. (Access finds and selects the first occurrence of *95610*. If the Find and Replace dialog box covers the data, drag the dialog box to a different location on the screen.)

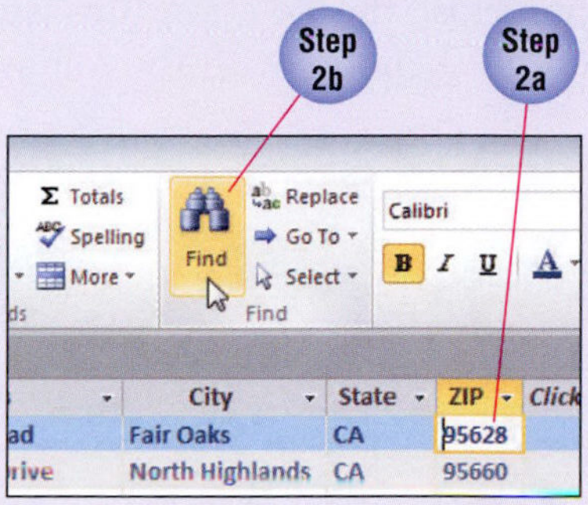

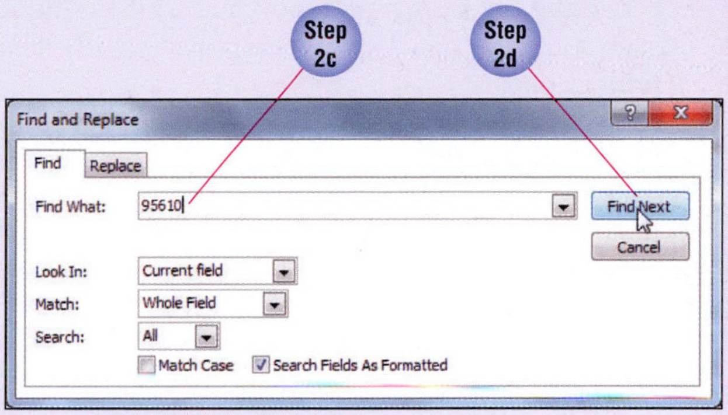

   e. Continue clicking the Find Next button until a message displays telling you that Access has finished searching the records. At this message, click OK.
   f. Click the Cancel button to close the Find and Replace dialog box.
3. Suppose a new ZIP code has been added to the city of North Highlands and you need to change to this new ZIP for some of the North Highlands properties. Complete the following steps to find *95660* and replace it with *95668*:
   a. Click in the first field in the *ZIP* column.
   b. Click the Replace button in the Find group.
   c. At the Find and Replace dialog box with the Replace tab selected, type **95660** in the *Find What* text box.
   d. Press the Tab key. (This moves the insertion point to the *Replace With* text box.)
   e. Type **95668** in the *Replace With* text box.
   f. Click the Find Next button.
   g. When Access selects the first occurrence of *95660*, click the Replace button.
   h. When Access selects the second occurrence of *95660*, click the Find Next button.

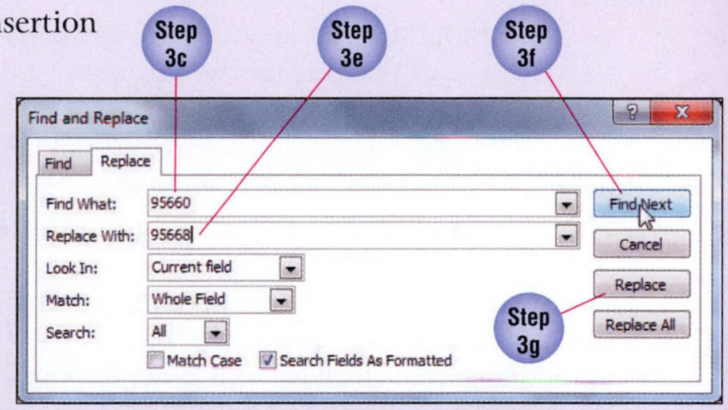

   i. When Access selects the third occurrence of *95660* click the Replace button.
   j. When Access selects the fourth occurrence of *95660*, click the Find Next button.
   k. When Access selects the fifth occurrence of *95660*, click the Find Next button.
   l. When Access selects the sixth occurrence of *95660*, click the Replace button.
   m. Access selects the first occurrence of *95660* (record 1018) in the table. Click the Cancel button to close the Find and Replace dialog box.
4. Print and then close the Properties table.

5. Display the Relationships window and then create the following relationships (enforce referential integrity and cascade fields and records):
   a. Create a one-to-many relationship with the *CatID* field in the Categories table the "one" and the *CatID* field in the Properties table the "many."
   b. Create a one-to-many relationship with the *EmpID* field in the Employees table the "one" and the *EmpID* field in the Renters table the "many."
   c. Create a one-to-many relationship with the *PropID* field in the Properties table the "one" and the *PropID* field in the Renters table the "many."
   d. Create a one-to-many relationship with the *RenterID* field in the Renters table the "one" and the *RenterID* field in the Payments table the "many."
   e. Save the relationships and then print the relationships in landscape orientation.
   f. Close the relationships report without saving it and then close the Relationships window.
6. Design a query that displays employees with health insurance benefits with the following specifications:
   a. Insert the Employees table in the query window.
   b. Insert the *EmpID* field in the first *Field* row field.
   c. Insert the *FName* field in the second *Field* row field.
   d. Insert the *LName* field in the third *Field* row field.
   e. Insert the *HealthIns* field in the fourth *Field* row field.
   f. Click in the check box in the *Show* row field in the *EmpID* column to remove the check mark. (This hides the EmpID numbers in the query results.)
   g. Extract those employees with health benefits. (Type a *1* for the criteria.)
   h. Run the query.
   i. Save the query and name it *EmpsWithHealthInsQuery*.
   j. Print and then close the query.

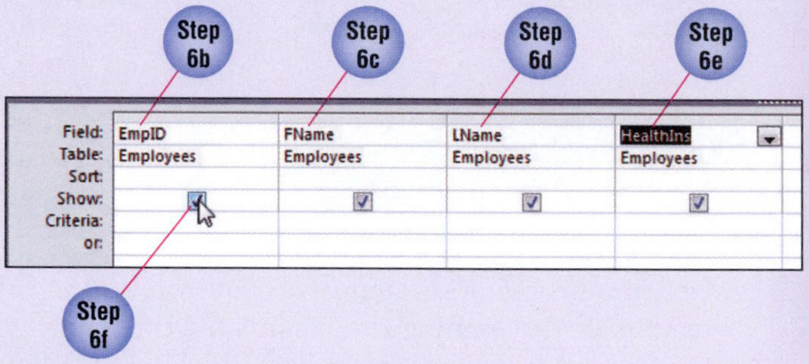

7. Design a query that displays all properties in the city of Citrus Heights with the following specifications:
   a. Insert the Properties table and the Categories table in the query window.
   b. Insert the *PropID* field from the Properties table in the first *Field* row field.
   c. Insert the *Category* field from the Categories table in the second *Field* row field.
   d. Insert the *Address*, *City*, *State*, and *ZIP* fields from the Properties table to the third, fourth, fifth, and sixth *Field* row fields.
   e. Extract those properties in the city of Citrus Heights.
   f. Run the query.
   g. Save the query and name it *CitrusHeightsPropsQuery*.
   h. Print and then close the query.
8. Design a query that displays rent payments made between 3/1/2012 and 3/5/2012 with the following specifications:
   a. Insert the Payments table and the Renters table in the query window.
   b. Insert the *Pymnt#*, *PymntDate*, and *PymntAmount* fields from the Payments table in the first, second, and third *Field* row fields.
   c. Insert the *FirstName* and *LastName* fields from the Renters table in the fourth and fifth *Field* row fields.
   d. Extract those payments made between 3/1/2012 and 3/5/2012.

e. Run the query.
f. Save the query and name it *Pymnts3/1To3/5Query*.
g. Print and then close the query.

9. Design a query that displays properties in Citrus Heights or Orangevale that rent for less than $1,501 a month as well as the type of property with the following specifications:
   a. Insert the Categories table and the Properties table in the query window.
   b. Insert the *Category* field from the Categories table.
   c. Insert the *PropID*, *MoRent*, *Address*, *City*, *State*, and *ZIP* fields from the Properties table.
   d. Extract those properties in Citrus Heights and Orangevale that rent for less than $1,501.
   e. Run the query.
   f. Save the query and name it *RentLessThan$1501InCHAndOVQuery*.
   g. Print the query in landscape orientation and then close the query.
10. Design a query that displays properties in Citrus Heights assigned to employee identification number *07-20* with the following specifications:
   a. Insert the Employees table and the Properties table in the query window.
   b. Insert the *EmpID*, *FName*, and *LName* fields from the Employees table.
   c. Insert the *Address*, *City*, *State*, and *ZIP* fields from the Properties table.
   d. Extract those properties in Citrus Heights assigned to EmpID 07-20.
   e. Run the query.
   f. Save the query and name it *Emp07-20CHPropsQuery*.
   g. Print and then close the query.

Using Help

Microsoft Access includes a Help feature that contains information about Access features and commands. This on-screen reference manual is similar to Windows Help and the Help features in Word, PowerPoint, and Excel. Click the Microsoft Access Help button (the circle with the question mark) located in the upper right corner of the screen or press the keyboard shortcut F1 to display the Access Help window. In this window, type a topic, feature, or question in the search text box and then press the Enter key. Topics related to the search text display in the Access Help window. Click a topic that interests you. If the topic window contains a Show All hyperlink in the upper right corner, click this hyperlink and the topic options expand to show additional help information related to the topic. When you click the Show All hyperlink, it becomes the Hide All hyperlink.

Quick Steps

Use the Help Feature
1. Click Microsoft Access Help button.
2. Type topic or feature.
3. Press Enter.
4. Click desired topic.

Display Help Tab Backstage View
1. Click File tab.
2. Click Help button.

HINT

Press F1 to display the Access Help window.

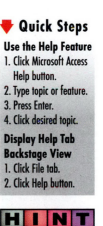

Help

Getting Help at the Help Tab Backstage View

The Help tab Backstage view, shown in Figure 4.13, contains an option for displaying the Access Help window as well as other options. Click the *Microsoft Office Help* option in the Support category to display the Access Help window and click the *Getting Started* option to access the Microsoft website that displays information about getting started with Access 2010. Click the *Contact Us* option in the Support category and the Microsoft Support website displays. Click *Options* in the Tools for Working With Office category and the Access Options dialog box displays. You will learn about this dialog box in a later chapter. Click the *Check for Updates* option and the Microsoft Update website displays with information on available updates. The right side of the Help tab Backstage view displays information about Office and Access.

Figure 4.13 Help Tab Backstage View

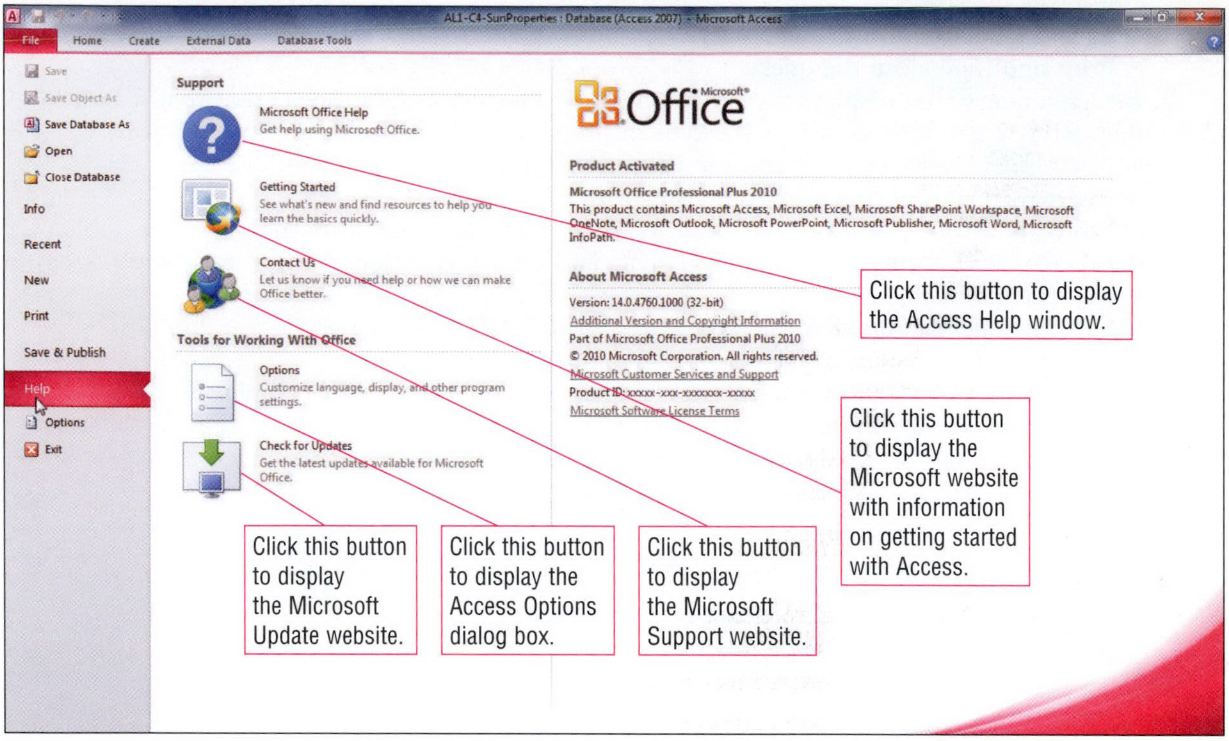

Project 1g Using the Help Feature

Part 7 of 8

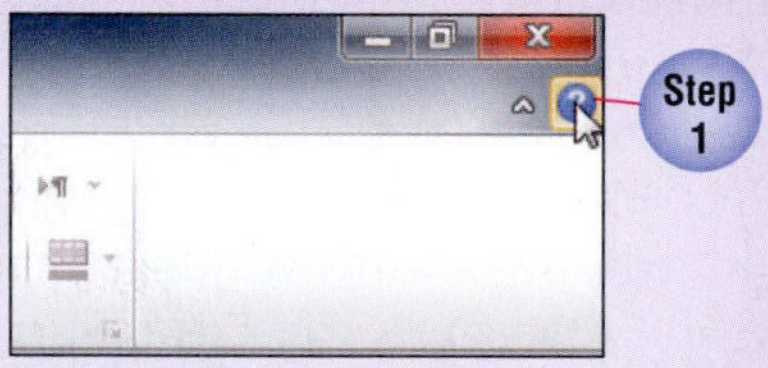

1. With the **AL1-C4-SunProperties.accdb** open, click the Microsoft Access Help button located in the upper right corner of the screen.
2. At the Access Help window, type **input mask** in the search text box and then press Enter. (Make sure that *Connected to Office.com* displays in the lower right corner of the window. If not, click the Search button arrow and then click *Content from Office.com* at the drop-down list.
3. When the list of topics displays, click the Control data entry formats with input masks hyperlink.
4. Read the information on creating an input mask. (If you want a printout of the information, you can click the Print button located toward the top of the Access Help window and then click the Print button at the Print dialog box.)
5. Close the Access Help window by clicking the Close button located in the upper right corner of the window.

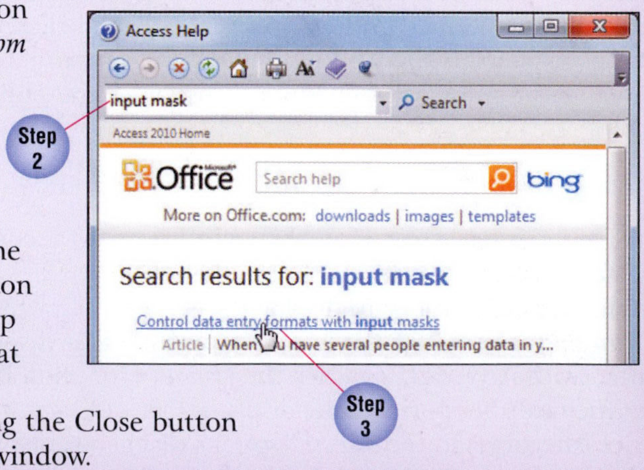

6. Click the File tab and then click the Help tab.
7. At the Help tab Backstage view, click the *Getting Started* option in the Support category. (You must be connected to the Internet to display the web page.)
8. Look at the information that displays at the website and then click the Close button located in the upper right corner of the web page.
9. Click the File tab and then click the Help tab.
10. Click the *Contact Us* option, look at the information that displays at the website, and then close the web page.

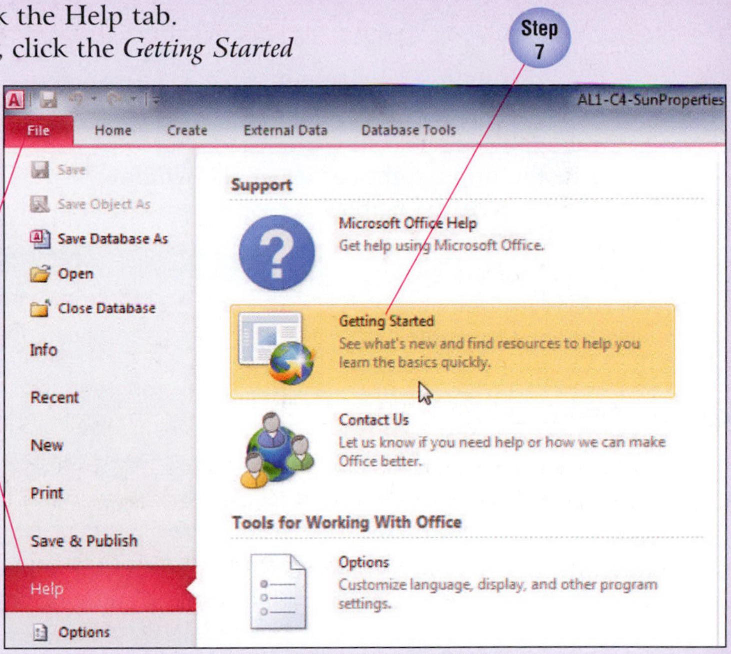

Getting Help on a Button

When you position the mouse pointer on a button, a ScreenTip displays with information about the button. Some button ScreenTips display with the message "Press F1 for more help" that is preceded by an image of the Help button. With the ScreenTip visible, press the F1 function key on your keyboard and the Access Help window opens and displays information about the specific button.

Getting Help in a Dialog Box or Backstage View

Some dialog boxes, as well as the Backstage view, contain a Help button you can click to display a help window with specific information about the dialog box or Backstage view. After reading and/or printing the information, close a dialog box by clicking the Close button located in the upper right corner of the dialog box or close the Backstage view by clicking the File tab or clicking any other tab in the ribbon.

Project 1h Getting Help in a Dialog Box and Backstage View — Part 8 of 8

1. With the **AL1-C4-SunProperties.accdb** database open, click the Create tab.
2. Hover the mouse pointer over the Table button in the Tables group until the ScreenTip displays and then press F1.
3. At the Access Help window, look over the information that displays and then close the window.
4. Click the File tab and then click the Save Database As button.

5. At the Save As dialog box, click the Help button located near the upper right corner of the dialog box.

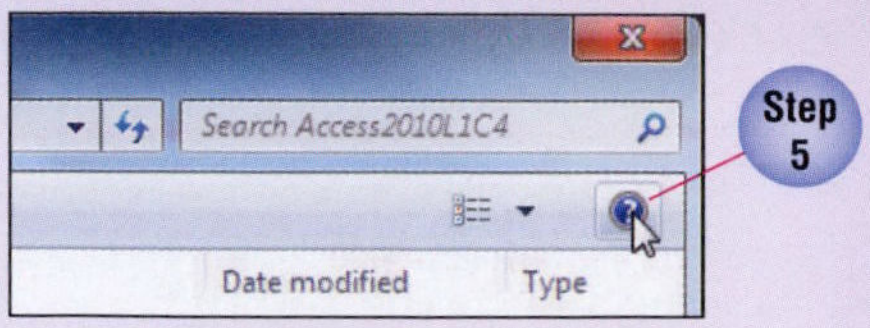

6. Read the information about saving files that displays in the Windows Help and Support window.
7. Close the window by clicking the Close button located in the upper right corner of the window.
8. Close the Save As dialog box.
9. Click the File tab.
10. At the Backstage view, click the Help button located near the upper right corner of the window.

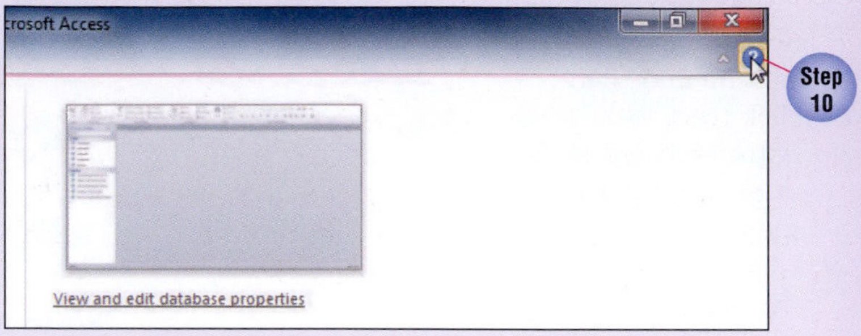

11. At the Access Help window, click a hyperlink that interests you.
12. Read the information and then close the Access Help window by clicking the Close button located in the upper right corner of the window.
13. Click the File tab to return to the database.
14. Close the **AL1-C4-SunProperties.accdb** database.

Chapter Summary

- You can create a table in Datasheet view or Design view. Click the View button in the Table Tools Design tab or the Home tab to switch between Datasheet view and Design view.
- Define each field in a table in the rows in the top section of Design view. Access automatically assigns the first field the name *ID* and assigns the AutoNumber data type.
- In Design view, specify a field name, data type, and description for each field.
- Assign a data type in Design view by clicking in the *Data Type* field in the desired row, clicking the down-pointing arrow at the right side of the field, and then clicking the desired data type at the drop-down list.
- Create a default value for a field in Design view with the *Default Value* property box in the *Field Properties* section.
- Use the Input Mask Wizard to set a pattern for how data is entered in a field.
- Use the *Validation Rule* property box in the *Field Properties* section in Design view to enter a statement containing a conditional test. Enter in the *Validation Text* property box the error message you want to display if the data entered violates the validation rule.
- Use the Lookup Wizard to confine data entered in a field to a specific list of items.
- Insert a field in Design view by clicking in the row immediately below where you want the new field inserted and then clicking the Insert Rows button.

- Move a field in Design view by clicking in the field selector bar of the field you want to move and then dragging with the mouse to the desired position.
- Delete a field in Design view by clicking in the field selector bar at the left side of the row you want deleted and then clicking the Delete Rows button.
- Insert a total row in a table in Datasheet view by clicking the Totals button in the Records group in the Home tab. Click the down-pointing arrow in the *Total* row field and then click the desired function at the drop-down list.
- Click the Ascending button in the Sort & Filter group in the Home tab to sort records in ascending order and click the Descending button to sort records in descending order.
- To print specific records in a table, select the records, display the Print dialog box, make sure *Selected Record(s)* is selected, and then click OK.
- Apply formatting to a table in Datasheet view with buttons in the Text Formatting group in the Home tab. Depending on the button you click in the Text Formatting group, formatting is applied to all data in a table or data in a specific column in the table.
- If you want to format text in a specific field, change the data type to Memo and then specify rich text formatting. Do this in Design view with the *Text Format* property box in the *Field Properties* section.
- Use the spelling checker to find misspelled words in a table and offer replacement words.
- Use options at the Find and Replace dialog box with the Find tab selected to search for specific field entries in a table. Use options at the Find and Replace dialog box with the Replace tab selected to search for specific data and replace with other data.
- Click the Microsoft Access Help button or press F1 to display the Access Help window. At this window, type a topic in the search text box and then press Enter.
- Some dialog boxes as well as the Backstage view contain a Help button you can click to display information specific to the dialog box or Backstage view.
- The ScreenTip for some buttons displays with a message telling you to press F1. Press F1 and the Access Help window opens with information about the button.

Commands Review

FEATURE	RIBBON TAB, GROUP	BUTTON, OPTION	KEYBOARD SHORTCUT
Design view	Home, Views OR Table Tools Fields, Views		
Insert field	Table Tools Design, Tools		
Delete field	Table Tools Design, Tools		
Totals row	Home, Records	Σ	
Sort records ascending	Home, Sort & Filter		

FEATURE	RIBBON TAB, GROUP	BUTTON, OPTION	KEYBOARD SHORTCUT
Sort records descending	Home, Sort & Filter		
Font	Home, Text Formatting	Calibri (Detail)	
Font size	Home, Text Formatting	11	
Bold	Home, Text Formatting		
Italic	Home, Text Formatting		
Underline	Home, Text Formatting	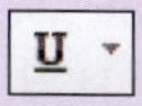	
Font color	Home, Text Formatting		
Background color	Home, Text Formatting		
Align text left	Home, Text Formatting		
Center	Home, Text Formatting		
Align text right	Home, Text Formatting		
Gridlines	Home, Text Formatting		
Alternate row color	Home, Text Formatting		
Spelling check	Home, Records		F7
Find and Replace dialog box with Find tab selected	Home, Find		Ctrl + F
Find and Replace dialog box with Replace tab selected	Home, Find		Ctrl + H
Access Help window			F1

Concepts Check Test Your Knowledge

Completion: In the space provided at the right, indicate the correct term, symbol, or command.

1. The lower half of the work area in Design view that displays the properties for the active field is referred to as this. ____________________

2. When you create a new table in Design view, Access automatically assigns the first field the name *ID* and assigns this data type. ____________________

3. The description you type in the *Description* field displays in this location when the field is active in the table in Datasheet view. ____________________

4. Use this field property to set a pattern for how data is entered in a field. ____________________

5. Use this property box in Design view to enter a statement containing a conditional test that is checked each time data is entered into a field. ____________________

6. Use this wizard to confine the data entered in a field to a specific list of items. ____________________

7. To insert a new field in a table in Design view, click this button. ____________________

8. To insert a total row in a table, click the Totals button in this group in the Home tab. ____________________

9. The Ascending and Descending sort buttons are located in this group in the Home tab. ____________________

10. Click this button to change the text size of data in a table. ____________________

11. Click this button to align all text in the active column in the center of the fields. ____________________

12. Click this button to specify a color for alternating rows in a table. ____________________

13. Use options at the Find and Replace dialog box with this tab selected to search for specific data and replace with other data. ____________________

14. The ScreenTip for some buttons displays with a message telling you to press this key to display the Access Help window with information about the button. ____________________

Skills Check Assess Your Performance

Assessment

1 CREATE AN EMPLOYEES TABLE WITH THE INPUT MASK AND LOOKUP WIZARDS

1. Open Access and then create a new database by completing the following steps:
   a. At the New tab Backstage view, click in the *File Name* text box located at the right side of the screen.
   b. Type **AL1-C4-Hudson**.
   c. Click the Browse button that displays at the right side of the *File Name* text box.
   d. At the File New Database dialog box, navigate to the Access2010L1C4 folder on your storage medium and then click OK.

e. At the New tab Backstage view, click the Create button located below the *File Name* text box.

2. Create the Employees table in Design view as shown in Figure 4.14 with the following specifications:
   a. Limit the *EmpID* field size to *4*, the *FirstName* and *LastName* fields to *20*, and the *Address* field to *30*.
   b. Create a default value of *Pueblo* for the *City* field since most of the employees live in Pueblo.
   c. Create a default value of *CO* for the *State* field since all of the employees live in Colorado.
   d. Create an input mask for the telephone number.
   e. Use the Lookup Wizard to specify field choices for the *Status* field and include the following choices: *Full-time*, *Part-time*, *Temporary*, and *Contract*.
3. Save the table, switch to Datasheet view, and then enter the records as shown in Figure 4.15.
4. Adjust the column widths.
5. Save the table and then print the table in landscape orientation.
6. Switch to Design view and then add a row immediately above the *FirstName* row. Type **Title** in the *Field Name* field, limit the field size to *20*, and type the description **Enter employee job title**.
7. Delete the *HireDate* field.
8. Move the *Status* field so it is positioned between the *EmpID* row and the *Title* row.
9. Save the table and then switch to Datasheet view.
10. Enter the following information in the *Title* field:

Emp#	Title	Emp#	Title
1466	**Design Director**	2301	**Assistant**
1790	**Assistant**	2440	**Assistant**
1947	**Resources Director**	3035	**Clerk**
1955	**Accountant**	3129	**Clerk**
1994	**Assistant**	3239	**Assistant**
2013	**Production Director**	4002	**Contractor**
2120	**Assistant**	4884	**Contractor**

11. Apply the following text formatting to the table:
    a. Change the font to Arial and the font size to 10.
    b. Center the data in the *EmpID* field column and the *State* field column.
    c. Apply a light turquoise (you determine the specific color) alternating row color to the table.
12. Adjust the column widths.

Figure 4.14 Employees Table in Design View

Employee

Field Name	Data Type	Description
EmpID	Text	Enter four-digit employee identification number
FirstName	Text	Enter employee first name
LastName	Text	Enter employee last name
Address	Text	Enter employee street address
City	Text	Pueblo automatically inserted
State	Text	CO automatically inserted
ZIP	Text	Enter employee ZIP code
Telephone	Text	Enter employee telephone number
Status	Text	Click down-pointing arrow and then click employee status
HireDate	Date/Time	Enter employee hire date

Figure 4.15 Employees Table in Datasheet View

Employee

	EmpID	FirstName	LastName	Address	City	State	ZIP	Telephone	Status	HireDate	Click
	1466	Samantha	O'Connell	9105 Pike Avenue	Pueblo	CO	81011	(719) 555-7658	Full-time	8/15/2010	
	1790	Edward	Sorrell	9958 Franklin Avenue	Pueblo	CO	81006	(719) 555-3724	Full-time	11/15/2006	
	1947	Brandon	Byrne	102 Hudson Avenue	Pueblo	CO	81012	(719) 555-1202	Full-time	8/1/2008	
	1955	Leland	Hughes	4883 Caledonia Road	Pueblo	CO	81005	(719) 555-1211	Full-time	3/1/2010	
	1994	Rosa	Martinez	310 Graham Avenue	Pueblo	CO	81004	(719) 555-8394	Part-time	8/15/2007	
	2013	Jean	Perrault	123 Chinook Lake	Pueblo	CO	82012	(719) 555-4027	Full-time	11/15/2006	
	2120	Michael	Turek	5503 East 27th Street	Boone	CO	81025	(719) 555-5423	Full-time	3/15/2008	
	2301	Gregory	Nitsche	12055 East 18th Street	Pueblo	CO	81007	(719) 555-6657	Part-time	3/15/2007	
	2440	Bethany	Rosario	858 West 27th Street	Pueblo	CO	81012	(719) 555-9481	Part-time	2/15/2011	
	3035	Alia	Shandra	7740 Second Street	Avondale	CO	81022	(719) 555-0059	Temporary	2/1/2010	
	3129	Gloria	Cushman	6590 East 14th Street	Pueblo	CO	81006	(719) 555-0332	Temporary	5/1/2012	
	3239	Rudolph	Powell	8874 Hood Avenue	Pueblo	CO	81008	(719) 555-2223	Temporary	4/1/2012	
	4002	Alice	Murray	4300 North 16th Street	Pueblo	CO	81003	(719) 555-4230	Contract	9/12/2006	
	4884	Simon	Banister	1022 Division Avenue	Boone	CO	81025	(719) 555-2378	Contract	5/15/2012	
*					Pueblo	CO					

13. Save the table and then print the table in landscape orientation.
14. Find all occurrences of *Director* and replace with *Manager*. ***Hint: Position the insertion point in the first entry in the* Title *column and then display the Find and Replace dialog box. At the dialog box, change the* Match *option to* Any Part of Field.**
15. Find all occurrences of *Assistant* and replace with *Associate*.
16. Save the table, print the table in landscape orientation with left and right margins of 0.5 inch, and then close the table.

Assessment 2

CREATE A PROJECTS TABLE

1. With the **AL1-C4-Hudson.accdb** database open, create a Projects table in Design view and include the following fields (make sure the *Proj#* field is identified as the primary key) and create an appropriate description for each field:

Field Name	Data Type
Proj#	Text (field size = 4)
EmpID	Text (field size = 4)
BegDate	Date/Time
EndDate	Date/Time
EstCosts	Currency

2. Save the table, switch to Datasheet view, and then type the following data or choose a field entry in the specified fields:

Proj#	08-A	*Proj#*	08-B
EmpID	2013	*EmpID*	1466
BegDate	08/01/2012	*BegDate*	08/15/2012
EndDate	10/31/2012	*EndDate*	12/15/2012
EstCosts	$5,250.00	EstCosts	$2,000.00
Proj#	10-A	*Proj#*	10-B
EmpID	1947	*EmpID*	2013
BegDate	10/01/2012	*BegDate*	10/01/2012
EndDate	01/15/2013	*EndDate*	12/15/2012
EstCosts	$10,000.00	*EstCosts*	$3,500.00

Proj#	11-A	*Proj#*	11-B
EmpID	1466	*EmpID*	1947
BegDate	11/01/2012	*BegDate*	11/01/2012
EndDate	02/01/2013	*EndDate*	03/31/2013
EstCosts	$8,000.00	*EstCosts*	$12,000.00

3. Adjust the column widths.
4. Save, print, and then close the Projects table.

Assessment 3

CREATE AN EXPENSES TABLE WITH A VALIDATION RULE AND INPUT MASK

1. With the **AL1-C4-Hudson.accdb** database open, create an Expenses table in Design view and include the following fields (make sure the *Item#* field is identified as the primary key) and include an appropriate description for each field:

Field Name	Data Type
Item#	AutoNumber
EmpID	Text (field size = 4)
Proj#	Text (field size = 4)
Amount	Currency (Type a condition in the *Validation Rule* property box that states the entry must be $500 or less. Type an error message in the *Validation Text* property box.)
DateSubmitted	Date/Time (Use the Input Mask to control the date so it is entered as a short date.)

2. Save the table, switch to Datasheet view, and then type the following data or choose a field entry in the specified fields (Access automatically inserts a number in the *Item#* field):

EmpID	1466	*EmpID*	2013
Proj#	08-B	*Proj#*	08-A
Amount	$245.79	*Amount*	$500.00
DateSubmitted	09/04/2012	*DateSubmitted*	09/10/2012
EmpID	4002	*EmpID*	1947
Proj#	08-B	*Proj#*	10-A
Amount	$150.00	*Amount*	$500.00
DateSubmitted	09/18/2012	*DateSubmitted*	10/03/2012
EmpID	2013	*EmpID*	1947
Proj#	10-B	*Proj#*	10-A
Amount	$487.25	*Amount*	$85.75
DateSubmitted	10/22/2012	*DateSubmitted*	10/24/2012
EmpID	1466	*EmpID*	1790
Proj#	08-B	*Proj#*	08-A
Amount	$175.00	*Amount*	$110.50
DateSubmitted	10/29/2012	*DateSubmitted*	10/30/2012
EmpID	2120	*EmpID*	1466
Proj#	10-A	*Proj#*	08-B
Amount	$75.00	*Amount*	$300.00
DateSubmitted	11/05/2012	*DateSubmitted*	11/07/2012
EmpID	1466	*EmpID*	2013
Proj#	11-A	*Proj#*	10-B
Amount	$75.00	*Amount*	$300.00
DateSubmitted	11/14/2012	*DateSubmitted*	11/19/2012

3. Adjust the column widths.
4. Insert a total row with the following specifications:
   a. Click the Totals button in the Records group in the Home tab.
   b. Click in the blank field in the *Amount* column in the *Total* row.
   c. Click the down-pointing arrow at the left side of the field and then click *Sum* at the drop-down list.
   d. Click in any other field.
5. Save, print, and then close the Expenses table.
6. Create a one-to-many relationship where *EmpID* in the Employees table is the "one" and *EmpID* in the Expenses table is the "many." (Enforce referential integrity and cascade fields and records.)
7. Create a one-to-many relationship where *EmpID* in the Employees table is the "one" and *EmpID* in the Projects table is the "many." (Enforce referential integrity and cascade fields and records.)
8. Create a one-to-many relationship where *Proj#* in the Projects table is the "one" and *Proj#* in the Expenses table is the "many." (Enforce referential integrity and cascade fields and records.)
9. Save the relationships, print the relationships, and then close the relationships report window and the relationships window.
10. Design and run a query that displays all full-time employees with the following specifications:
    a. Insert the Employees table in the query window.
    b. Insert the *EmpID*, *FirstName*, *LastName*, and *Status* fields.
    c. Click in the check box in the *Show* row field in the *EmpID* column to remove the check mark. (This hides the EmpID numbers in the query results.)
    d. Extract full-time employees.
    e. Save the query and name it *FTEmpsQuery*.
    f. Print and then close the query.
11. Design and run a query that displays projects managed by employee number 1947 with the following specifications:
    a. Insert the Employees table and the Projects table in the query window.
    b. Insert the *EmpID*, *FirstName*, and *LastName* fields from the Employees table.
    c. Insert the *Proj#* field from the Projects table.
    d. Extract those projects managed by employee number 1947.
    e. Save the query and name it *ProjsManagedByEmp1947Query*.
    f. Print and then close the query.
12. Design and run a query that displays expense amounts over $250.00 and the employee submitting the expense with the following specifications:
    a. Insert the Expenses table and the Employees table in the query window.
    b. Insert the *Item#*, *Amount*, and *DateSubmitted* fields from the Expenses table.
    c. Insert the *FirstName* and *LastName* fields from the Employees table.
    d. Hide the *Item#* field in the query results by clicking in the check box in the *Show* row field in the *Item#* column to remove the check mark.
    e. Extract those expense amounts over $250.
    f. Save the query and name it *ExpensesOver$250Query*.
    g. Print and then close the query.
13. Design and run a query that displays expenses submitted by employee number 1947 with the following specifications:
    a. Insert the Employees table and the Expenses table in the query window.
    b. Insert the *EmpID*, *FirstName*, and *LastName* fields from the Employees table.
    c. Insert the *Proj#*, *Amount*, and *DateSubmitted* from the Expenses table.

d. Click in the check box in the *Show* row field in the *EmpID* column to remove the check mark. (This hides the EmpID numbers in the query results.)
e. Extract those expenses submitted by employee number 1947.
f. Save the query and name it *ExpSubmittedBy1947Query*.
g. Print and then close the query.

Assessment 4

EDIT THE EMPLOYEES TABLE

1. With the **AL1-C4-Hudson.accdb** database open, open the Employees table.
2. Display the table in Design view, click in the *ZIP* field row *Data Type* column and then click in the *Input Mask* property box in the *Field Properties* section.
3. Use the Input Mask Wizard to create a nine-digit ZIP code input mask.
4. Save the table and then switch to Datasheet view.
5. Delete the record for employee number 3035 (Alia Shandra), employee number 3129 (Gloria Cushman), and employee number 4884 (Simon Banister).
6. Insert the following new records:

EmpID	**2286**	EmpID	**2970**
Status	**Full-time**	Status	**Full-time**
Title	**Associate**	Title	**Associate**
FirstName	**Erica**	FirstName	**Daniel**
LastName	**Bonari**	LastName	**Ortiz**
Address	**4850 55th Street**	Address	**12021 Cedar Lane**
City	(Pueblo automatically inserted)	City	(Pueblo automatically inserted)
State	(CO automatically inserted)	State	(CO automatically inserted)
ZIP	**81005-5002**	ZIP	**81011-1255**
Telephone	**(719) 555-1293**	Telephone	**(719) 555-0790**

7. Adjust the width of the *ZIP* column. (Only the two new records will contain the nine-digit ZIP code.)
8. Save the Employees table.
9. Display the table in Print Preview, change to landscape orientation, and then change the left and right margins to 0.5 inch. Print and then close the table.

Visual Benchmark Demonstrate Your Proficiency

EDIT THE EXPENSES TABLE

Note: The starting file for this activity is the file created after completing the previous Skills Check assessments.

1. With the **AL1-C4-Hudson.accdb** database open, open the Expenses table.
2. Insert fields, rearrange fields, insert new data, and apply text formatting as shown in Figure 4.16. Change the font of data in the table to Cambria and the font size to 12. Center align text as shown, add alternating row color, and adjust column widths.
3. Save the table, print the table in landscape orientation, and then close the Expenses table.

Figure 4.16 Visual Benchmark

Expenses

Item#	Proj#	EmpID	Expense	Amount	DateSubmitted	Approved	Click
1	08-B	1466	Design	$245.79	9 /4 /2012	☑	
2	08-A	2013	Consultation	$500.00	9 /10/2012	☐	
3	08-B	4002	Supplies	$150.00	9 /18/2012	☑	
4	10-A	1947	Equipment	$500.00	10/3 /2012	☑	
5	10-B	2013	Printer	$487.25	10/22/2012	☑	
6	10-A	1947	Supplies	$85.75	10/24/2012	☑	
7	08-B	1466	Consultation	$175.00	10/29/2012	☐	
8	08-A	1790	Design	$110.50	10/30/2012	☑	
9	10-A	2120	Announcements	$75.00	11/5 /2012	☑	
10	08-B	1466	Brochures	$300.00	11/7 /2012	☐	
11	11-A	1466	Printing	$75.00	11/14/2012	☐	
12	10-B	2013	Consultation	$300.00	11/19/2012	☐	
* (New)						☐	
Total				$3,004.29			

Case Study Apply Your Skills

Part 1

You work for Blue Ridge Enterprises and your supervisor has asked you to create a database with information about representatives and clients. Create a new database named **AL1-C4-BlueRidge.accdb** and then create a Representatives table with the following fields:

- Create a field for the representative identification number, change the data type to Text, and limit the field size to 3. (This is the primary key field.)
- Create a field for the representative's first name and limit the field size to 20.
- Create a field for the representative's last name and limit the field size to 20.
- Create a field for the representative's telephone number and use the Input Mask Wizard.
- Create a field for the insurance plan and use the Lookup Wizard and include four options: *Platinum*, *Premium*, *Standard*, and *None*.
- Create a field for the yearly bonus amount and type a validation rule that states that the bonus must be less than $10,001 and include an error message (you determine the message).

In Datasheet view, enter six records in the table. When entering the data, make sure that at least two representatives will receive a yearly bonus over $5000 and that at least two representatives are signed up for the *Platinum* insurance plan. Insert a total row that sums the yearly bonus amounts. Change the font for the data in the table to Cambria, change the font size to 10, and apply a light green alternating row color. Center the data in the representative identification column. Adjust the column widths and then save the Representatives table. Print the table in landscape orientation and then close the table.

Part 2

With the **AL-C4-BlueRidge.accdb** database open, create a second table named Clients (table contains information on companies doing business with Blue Ridge Enterprises) with the following fields:

- Create a field for the client identification number and limit the field size to 2. (This is the primary key field.)
- Create a field for the representative identification number (use the same field name you used in Part 1 in the Representatives table) and limit the field size to 3.
- Create fields for the company name, address, city, state (or province), and ZIP (or postal code). Insert the city you live in as the default value for the city field and insert the two-letter state or province abbreviation where you live as the default value for the state or province field.
- Create a field for the client's telephone number and use the Input Mask.
- Create a field for the client's type of business and insert the word *Wholesaler* as the default value.

In Datasheet view, enter at least eight companies. Make sure you use the representative identification numbers in the Clients table that match numbers in the Representatives table. Identify at least one company as a *Retailer* rather than a *Wholesaler* and make at least one representative represent two or more companies. Change the font for the data in the table to Cambria, change the font size to 10, and apply a light green alternating row color (the same color you chose in Part 1). Center the data in the client identification column, the representative identification column, and the state (or province) column. Adjust the column widths and then save the Clients table. Print the table in landscape orientation and then close the table.

Part 3

Create a one-to-many relationship with the representative identification number in the Representatives table as the "one" and the representative identification number in the Clients table as the "many." Save the relationship, print the relationships report, and then close the report without saving it.

Part 4

Your supervisor has asked you for specific information about representatives and clients. To provide answers to your supervisor, create and print the following queries:

- Create a query that extracts records of representatives earning a yearly bonus over $5000. (You determine the fields to insert in the query window.) Save, print, and then close the query.
- Create a query that extracts records of representatives signed up for the Platinum insurance plan. (You determine the fields to insert in the query window.) Save, print, and then close the query.
- Create a query that extracts records of wholesale clients. (You determine the fields to insert in the query window.) Save, print, and then close the query.
- Create a query that extracts records of companies represented by a specific representative. (Use the representative identification number you entered in Part 2 that represents two or more companies.) Save, print, and then close the query.

Microsoft® Access®

UNIT 1

Performance Assessment

Access2010L1U1

Note: The Student Resources CD does not include an Access Level 1, Unit 1 subfolder of files because no data files are required for the Unit 1 assessments. You will create all of the files yourself. Before beginning the assessments, create a folder for the new files called Access2010L1U1.

Assessing Proficiency

In this unit, you have learned to design, create, and modify tables and to create one-to-many relationships and one-to-one relationships between tables. You also learned how to perform queries on data in tables.

Assessment 1 Create Tables in a Cornerstone Catering Database

1. Use Access to create tables for Cornerstone Catering. Name the database **AL1-U1-Cornerstone**. Create a table named *Employees* that includes the following fields. If no data type is specified for a field, use the *Text* data type. You determine the field size and specify the same field size for a field that is contained in different tables. For example, if you specify a field size of *2* for the *Employee#* field in the Employees table, specify a field size of *2* for the *Employee#* field in the Events table. Provide a description for each field.

   Employee# (primary key)
   FirstName
   LastName
   CellPhone (Use the Input Mask Wizard for this field.)

2. After creating the table, switch to Datasheet view and then enter the following data in the appropriate fields:

   Employee#: **10**
   FirstName: **Erin**
   LastName: **Jergens**
   CellPhone: **(505) 555-3193**

   Employee#: **14**
   FirstName: **Mikio**
   LastName: **Ogami**
   CellPhone: **(505) 555-1087**

   Employee#: **19**
   FirstName: **Martin**
   LastName: **Vaughn**
   CellPhone: **(505) 555-4461**

   Employee#: **21**
   FirstName: **Isabelle**
   LastName: **Baptista**
   CellPhone: **(505) 555-4425**

Employee#: **24**
FirstName: **Shawn**
LastName: **Kettering**
CellPhone: **(505) 555-3885**

Employee#: **26**
FirstName: **Madison**
LastName: **Harris**
CellPhone: **(505) 555-2256**

Employee#: **28**
FirstName: **Victoria**
LastName: **Lamesa**
CellPhone: **(505) 555-6650**

Employee#: **30**
FirstName: **Isaac**
LastName: **Hobart**
CellPhone: **(505) 555-7430**

Employee#: **32**
FirstName: **Lester**
LastName: **Franklin**
CellPhone: **(505) 555-0440**

Employee#: **35**
FirstName: **Manuela**
LastName: **Harte**
CellPhone: **(505) 555-1221**

3. Change the font for data in the table to Cambria, the font size to 10, and apply a light blue alternating row color. Center-align the data in the *Employee#* column.
4. Adjust the column widths.
5. Save, print, and then close the Employees table.
6. Create a table named *Plans* that includes the following fields:

   PlanCode (primary key)
   Plan

7. After creating the table, switch to Datasheet view and then enter the following data in the appropriate fields:

   PlanCode: **A**
   Plan: **Sandwich Buffet**

   PlanCode: **B**
   Plan: **Cold Luncheon Buffet**

   PlanCode: **C**
   Plan: **Hot Luncheon Buffet**

   PlanCode: **D**
   Plan: **Combination Dinner**

   PlanCode: **E**
   Plan: **Vegetarian Luncheon Buffet**

   PlanCode: **F**
   Plan: **Vegetarian Dinner Buffet**

   PlanCode: **G**
   Plan: **Seafood Luncheon Buffet**

   PlanCode: **H**
   Plan: **Seafood Dinner Buffet**

8. Change the font for data in the table to Cambria, the font size to 10, and apply a light blue alternating row color. Center-align the data in the *PlanCode* column.
9. Adjust the column widths.
10. Save, print, and then close the Plans table.
11. Create a table named *Prices* that includes the following fields:

    PriceCode (primary key)
    PricePerPerson (identify this data type as Currency)

12. After creating the table, switch to Datasheet view and then enter the following data in the appropriate fields:

PriceCode: 1
PricePerPerson: $11.50

PriceCode: 2
PricePerPerson: $12.75

PriceCode: 3
PricePerPerson: $14.50

PriceCode: 4
PricePerPerson: $16.00

PriceCode: 5
PricePerPerson: $18.50

PriceCode: 6
PricePerPerson: $21.95

13. Change the font for data in the table to Cambria, the font size to 10, and apply a light blue alternating row color. Center-align the data in both columns.
14. Adjust the column widths.
15. Save, print, and then close the Prices table.
16. Create a table named *Clients* that includes the following fields:

Client# (primary key)
ClientName
StreetAddress
City
State (Insert *NM* as the default value.)
ZIP
Telephone (Use the Input Mask Wizard for this field.)

17. After creating the table, switch to Datasheet view and then enter the following data in the appropriate fields:

Client#: 104
ClientName: Sarco Corporation
StreetAddress: 340 Cordova Road
City: Santa Fe
State: NM
ZIP: 87510
Telephone: (505) 555-3880

Client#: 155
ClientName: Creative Concepts
StreetAddress: 1026 Market Street
City: Los Alamos
State: NM
ZIP: 87547
Telephone: (505) 555-1200

Client#: 218
ClientName: Allenmore Systems
StreetAddress: 7866 Second Street
City: Espanola
State: NM
ZIP: 87535
Telephone: (505) 555-3455

Client#: 286
ClientName: Sol Enterprises
StreetAddress: 120 Cerrillos Road
City: Santa Fe
State: NM
ZIP: 87560
Telephone: (505) 555-7700

Client#: 295
ClientName: Benson Productions
StreetAddress: 555 Junction Road
City: Santa Fe
State: NM
ZIP: 87558
Telephone: (505) 555-8866

Client#: 300
ClientName: Old Town Corporation
StreetAddress: 1035 East Adams Way
City: Santa Fe
State: NM
ZIP: 87561
Telephone: (505) 555-2125

Client#: 305
ClientName: Cromwell Company
StreetAddress: 752 Rialto Way
City: Santa Fe
State: NM
ZIP: 87512
Telephone: (505) 555-7500

Client#: 320
ClientName: GH Manufacturing
StreetAddress: 9550 Stone Road
City: Los Alamos
State: NM
ZIP: 87547
Telephone: (505) 555-3388

18. Change the font for data in the table to Cambria, the font size to 10, and apply a light blue alternating row color. Center-align the data in the *Client#* column.
19. Adjust the column widths.
20. Save the table and then print the table in landscape orientation.
21. Close the Clients table.
22. Create a table named *Events* that includes the following fields:

Event# (primary key; identify this data type as AutoNumber)
Client#
Employee#
DateOfEvent (identify this data type as Date/Time)
PlanCode
PriceCode
NumberOfPeople (identify this data type as Number)

23. After creating the table, switch to Datasheet view and then enter the following data in the appropriate fields:

Event#: (AutoNumber)
Client#: 218
Employee#: 14
DateOfEvent: 7/7/2012
PlanCode: B
PriceCode: 3
NumberOfPeople: 250

Event#: (AutoNumber)
Client#: 104
Employee#: 19
DateOfEvent: 7/8/2012
PlanCode: D
PriceCode: 5
NumberOfPeople: 120

Event#: (AutoNumber)
Client#: 155
Employee#: 24
DateOfEvent: 7/14/2012
PlanCode: A
PriceCode: 1
NumberOfPeople: 300

Event#: (AutoNumber)
Client#: 286
Employee#: 10
DateOfEvent: 7/15/2012
PlanCode: C
PriceCode: 4
NumberOfPeople: 75

Event#: (AutoNumber)
Client#: 218
Employee#: 14
DateOfEvent: 7/18/2012
PlanCode: C
PriceCode: 4
NumberOfPeople: 50

Event#: (AutoNumber)
Client#: 104
Employee#: 10
DateOfEvent: 7/20/2012
PlanCode: B
PriceCode: 3
NumberOfPeople: 30

Event#: (AutoNumber)
Client#: 305
Employee#: 30
DateOfEvent: 7/21/2012
PlanCode: H
PriceCode: 6
NumberOfPeople: 150

Event#: (AutoNumber)
Client#: 295
Employee#: 35
DateOfEvent: 7/22/2012
PlanCode: E
PriceCode: 4
NumberOfPeople: 75

Event#: (AutoNumber)
Client#: 300
Employee#: 32
DateOfEvent: 7/27/2012
PlanCode: B
PriceCode: 3
NumberOfPeople: 200

Event#: (AutoNumber)
Client#: 350
Employee#: 28
DateOfEvent: 7/28/2012
PlanCode: D
PriceCode: 6
NumberOfPeople: 100

24. Change the font for data in the table to Cambria, the font size to 10, and apply a light blue alternating row color. Center-align in all of the columns except the *DateOfEvent* column.
25. Adjust the column widths.
26. Save, print, and then close the Events table.

Assessment 2 Create Relationships between Tables

1. With the **AL1-U1-Cornerstone.accdb** database open, create the following one-to-many relationships and enforce referential integrity:
   a. *Client#* in the Clients table is the "one" and *Client#* in the Events table is the "many."
   b. *Employee#* in the Employees table is the "one" and *Employee#* in the Events table is the "many."
   c. *PlanCode* in the Plans table is the "one" and *PlanCode* in the Events table is the "many."
   d. *PriceCode* in the Prices table is the "one" and *PriceCode* in the Events table is the "many."
2. Save and then print the relationships in landscape orientation.

Assessment 3 Modify Tables

1. With the **AL1-U1-Cornerstone.accdb** database open, open the Plans table in Datasheet view and then add the following record at the end of the table:

   PlanCode: I
   Plan: Hawaiian Luau Dinner Buffet

2. Adjust the column widths.
3. Save, print, and then close the Plans table.
4. Open the Events table in Datasheet view and then add the following record at the end of the table:

   Event#: (AutoNumber)
   Client#: 104
   Employee#: 21
   Date: 7/29/2012
   PlanCode: I
   PriceCode: 5
   NumberOfPeople: 125

5. Save, print (in landscape orientation), and then close the Events table.

Assessment 4 Design Queries

1. With the **AL1-U1-Cornerstone.accdb** database open, create a query to extract records from the Events table with the following specifications:
   a. Include the fields *Client#*, *DateOfEvent*, and *PlanCode*.
   b. Extract those records with a PlanCode of C.
   c. Run the query.
   d. Save the query and name it *PlanCodeCQuery*.
   e. Print and then close the query.
2. Extract records from the Clients table with the following specifications:
   a. Include the fields *ClientName*, *City*, and *Telephone*.
   b. Extract those records with a city of Santa Fe.
   c. Run the query.
   d. Save the query and name it *SantaFeClientsQuery*.
   e. Print and then close the query.
3. Extract information from two tables with the following specifications:
   a. From the Clients table, include the fields *ClientName* and *Telephone*.
   b. From the Events table, include the fields *DateOfEvent*, *PlanCode*, and *NumberOfPeople*.
   c. Extract those records with a date between July 1 and July 15, 2012.
   d. Run the query.
   e. Save the query and name it *July1-15EventsQuery*.
   f. Print and then close the query.

Assessment 5 Design a Query with a Calculated Field Entry

1. With the **AL1-U1-Cornerstone.accdb** database open, create a query in Design view with the Events table and the Prices table and insert the following fields in the specified locations:
   a. Insert *Event#* from the Events table to the first *Field* row field.
   b. Insert *DateOfEvent* from the Events table to the second *Field* row field.
   c. Insert *NumberOfPeople* from the Events table to the third *Field* row field.
   d. Insert *PricePerPerson* from the Prices table to the fourth *Field* row field.
2. Insert the following calculated field entry in the fifth *Field* row field: *Amount: [NumberOfPeople]*[PricePerPerson]*.
3. Run the query.
4. Save the query and name it *EventAmountsQuery*.
5. Print and then close the query.

Assessment 6 Design a Query with Aggregate Functions

1. With the **AL1-U1-Cornerstone.accdb** database open, create a query in Design view using EventAmountsQuery with the following specifications:
   a. Click the Create tab and then click the Query Design button.
   b. At the Show Tables dialog box, click the Queries tab.
   c. Double-click *EventAmountsQuery* in the list box and then click the Close button.
   d. Insert the *Amount* field to the first, second, third, and fourth *Field* text boxes.
   e. Click the Totals button in the Show/Hide group.
   f. Insert *Sum* in the first *Total* row field.
   g. Insert *Avg* in the second *Total* row field.
   h. Insert *Min* in the third *Total* row field.
   i. Insert *Max* in the fourth *Total* row field.

2. Run the query.
3. Automatically adjust the column widths.
4. Save the query and name it *AmountTotalsQuery*.
5. Print and then close the query.

Assessment 7 Design a Query Using Fields from Tables and a Query

1. With the **AL1-U1-Cornerstone.accdb** database open, create a query in Design view using the Employees table, the Clients table, the Events table, and EventAmountsQuery with the following specifications:
   a. Click the Create tab and then click the Query Design button.
   b. At the Show Tables dialog box, double-click *Employees*.
   c. Double-click *Clients*.
   d. Double-click *Events*.
   e. Click the Queries tab, double-click *EventAmountsQuery* in the list box, and then click the Close button.
   f. Insert the *LastName* field from the Employees table to the first *Field* row field.
   g. Insert the *ClientName* field from the Clients table to the second *Field* row field.
   h. Insert the *Amount* field from EventAmountsQuery to the third *Field* row field.
   i. Insert the *DateOfEvent* field from the Events table to the fourth *Field* row field.
2. Run the query.
3. Save the query and name it *EmployeeEventsQuery*.
4. Close the query.
5. Using the Crosstab Query Wizard, create a query that summarizes the total amount of events by employee by client using the following specifications:
   a. At the first Crosstab Query Wizard dialog box, click the *Queries* option in the *View* section, and then click *Query: EmployeeEventsQuery* in the list box.
   b. At the second Crosstab Query Wizard dialog box, click *LastName* in the *Available Fields* list box and then click the One Field button.
   c. At the third Crosstab Query Wizard dialog box, make sure *ClientName* is selected in the list box.
   d. At the fourth Crosstab Query Wizard dialog box, make sure *Amount* is selected in the *Fields* list box, and then click *Sum* in the *Functions* list box.
   e. At the fifth Crosstab Query Wizard dialog box, type **AmountsByEmployeeByClientQuery** in the *What do you want to name your query?* text box.
6. Automatically adjust the column widths.
7. Print the query in landscape orientation and then close the query.

Assessment 8 Use the Find Duplicates Query Wizard

1. With the **AL1-U1-Cornerstone.accdb** database open, use the Find Duplicates Query Wizard to find employees who are responsible for at least two events with the following specifications:
   a. At the first wizard dialog box, double-click *Table: Events* in the list box.
   b. At the second wizard dialog box, click *Employee#* in the *Available fields* list box and then click the One Field button.
   c. At the third wizard dialog box, move the *DateOfEvent* field and the *NumberOfPeople* field from the *Available fields* list box to the *Additional query fields* list box.
   d. At the fourth wizard dialog box, name the query *DuplicateEventsQuery*.
2. Print and then close the query.

Assessment 9 Use the Find Unmatched Query Wizard

1. With the **AL1-U1-Cornerstone.accdb** database open, use the Find Unmatched Query Wizard to find any employees who do not have an upcoming event scheduled with the following specifications:
   a. At the first wizard dialog box, click *Table: Employees* in the list box.
   b. At the second wizard dialog box, click *Table: Events* in the list box.
   c. At the third wizard dialog box, make sure *Employee#* is selected in the *Fields in 'Employees'* list box and in the *Fields in 'Events'* list box.
   d. At the fourth wizard dialog box, click the All Fields button to move all fields from the *Available fields* list box to the *Selected fields* list box.
   e. At the fifth wizard dialog box, click the Finish button. (Let the wizard determine the query name: *Employees Without Matching Events*.)
2. Print and then close the *Employees Without Matching Events* query.

Writing Activities

The following activity gives you the opportunity to practice your writing skills along with demonstrating an understanding of some of the important Access features you have mastered in this unit. Use correct grammar, appropriate word choices, and clear sentence constructions.

Create a Payroll Table and Word Report

The manager of Cornerstone Catering has asked you to add information to the **AL1-U1-Cornerstone.accdb** database on employee payroll. You need to create another table that will contain information on payroll. The manager wants the table to include the following (you determine the appropriate field name, data type, field size, and description):

Employee Number: **10**
Status: **Full-time**
Monthly Salary: **$2,850**

Employee Number: **14**
Status: **Part-time**
Monthly Salary: **$1,500**

Employee Number: **19**
Status: **Part-time**
Monthly Salary: **$1,400**

Employee Number: **21**
Status: **Full-time**
Monthly Salary: **$2,500**

Employee Number: **24**
Status: **Part-time**
Monthly Salary: **$1,250**

Employee Number: **26**
Status: **Part-time**
Monthly Salary: **$1,000**

Employee number: **28**
Status: **Full-time**
Monthly salary: **$2,500**

Employee number: **30**
Status: **Part-time**
Monthly salary: **$3,000**

Employee number: **32**
Status: **Full-time**
Monthly salary: **$2,300**

Employee number: **35**
Status: **Full-time**
Monthly salary: **$2,750**

Print and then close the payroll table. Open Word and then write a report to the manager detailing how you created the table. Include a title for the report, steps on how the table was created, and any other pertinent information. Save the completed report and name it **AL1-U1-Act01-TableRpt**. Print and then close **AL1-U1-Act01-TableRpt.docx**.

Internet Research

Vehicle Search

In this activity you will search the Internet for information on different vehicles before doing actual test drives. Learning about a major product, such as a vehicle, can increase your chances of finding a good buy, can potentially guide you away from a poor purchase, and can help speed up the process of narrowing the search to the type of vehicle that will meet your needs. Before you begin, list the top five criteria you would look for in a vehicle. For example, it must be a four-door vehicle, needs to be four-wheel drive, etc.

Using key search words, find at least two websites that list vehicle reviews. Use the search engines provided within the different review sites to find vehicles that fulfill the criteria you listed to meet your particular needs. Create a database in Access and create a table in that database that will contain the results from your vehicle search. Design the table keeping in mind what type of data you need to record for each vehicle that meets your requirements. Include at least the make, model, year, price, description, and special problems in the table. Also, include the ability to rate the vehicle as poor, fair, good, or excellent. You will decide on the rating of each vehicle depending on your findings.

Microsoft®

Access® Level 1

Unit 2 ■ Creating Forms and Reports

Microsoft® Access®

CHAPTER 5

Creating Forms

PERFORMANCE OBJECTIVES

Upon successful completion of Chapter 5, you will be able to:

- **Create a form using the Form button**
- **Change views in a form**
- **Print and navigate in a form**
- **Add records to and delete records from a form**
- **Create a form with a related table**
- **Customize a form with options at the Form Layout Tools tab**
- **Create a split form and multiple items form**
- **Create a form using the Form Wizard**

SNAP Training and Assessment. Simplified.

Tutorials

5.1 Creating a Form Using the Form Button

5.2 Adding Records and Navigating in a Form

5.3 Adding and Modifying Objects

5.4 Modifying a Form

5.5 Modifying Forms Using Labels and Calculated Controls

5.6 Creating a Split Form and Multiple Items Form

5.7 Creating a Form

In this chapter, you will learn how to create forms from database tables, improving the data display and making data entry easier. Access offers several methods for presenting data on the screen for easier data entry. You will create a form using the Form button, create a split and multiple items form, and use the Form Wizard to create a form. You will also learn how to customize control objects in a form and insert control objects and fields in a form. Model answers for this chapter's projects appear on the following pages.

Access
Access2010L1C5

Note: Before beginning the projects, copy to your storage medium the Access2010L1C5 subfolder from the Access2010L1 folder on the CD that accompanies this textbook and make Access2010L1C5 the active folder.

Project 1 Create Forms with the Form Button

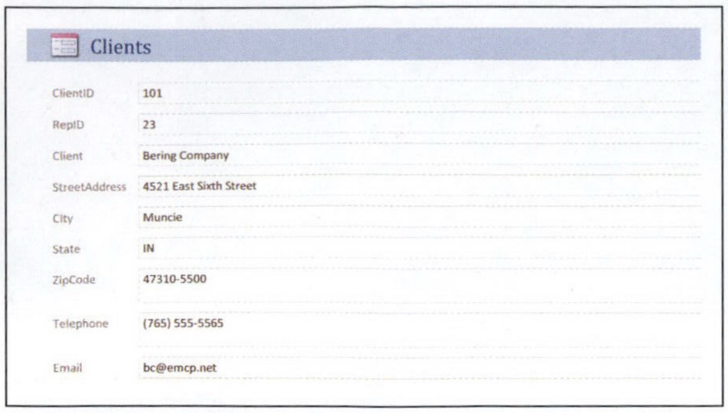
Clients

ClientID	101
RepID	23
Client	Bering Company
StreetAddress	4521 East Sixth Street
City	Muncie
State	IN
ZipCode	47310-5500
Telephone	(765) 555-5565
Email	bc@emcp.net

Project 1a, Dearborn Clients Form

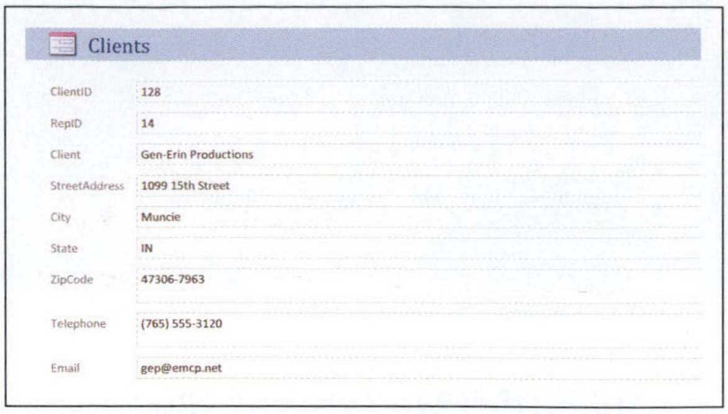
Clients

ClientID	128
RepID	14
Client	Gen-Erin Productions
StreetAddress	1099 15th Street
City	Muncie
State	IN
ZipCode	47306-7963
Telephone	(765) 555-3120
Email	gep@emcp.net

Project 1b, Dearborn Clients Form

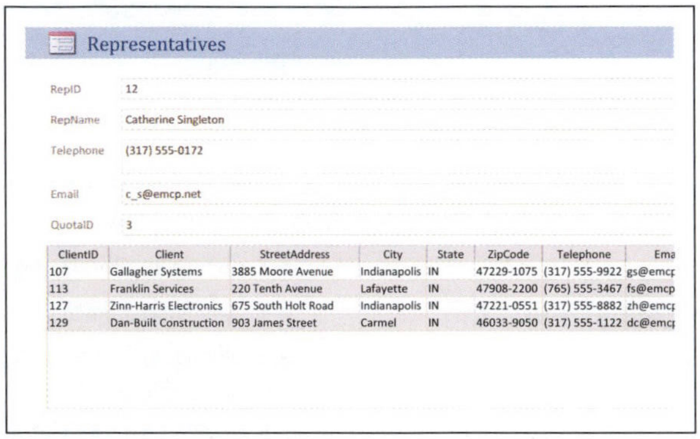
Representatives

RepID	12
RepName	Catherine Singleton
Telephone	(317) 555-0172
Email	c_s@emcp.net
QuotaID	3

ClientID	Client	StreetAddress	City	State	ZipCode	Telephone	Ema
107	Gallagher Systems	3885 Moore Avenue	Indianapolis	IN	47229-1075	(317) 555-9922	gs@emcp
113	Franklin Services	220 Tenth Avenue	Lafayette	IN	47908-2200	(765) 555-3467	fs@emcp
127	Zinn-Harris Electronics	675 South Holt Road	Indianapolis	IN	47221-0551	(317) 555-8882	zh@emcp
129	Dan-Built Construction	903 James Street	Carmel	IN	46033-9050	(317) 555-1122	dc@emcp

Project 1c, Dearborn Representatives Form

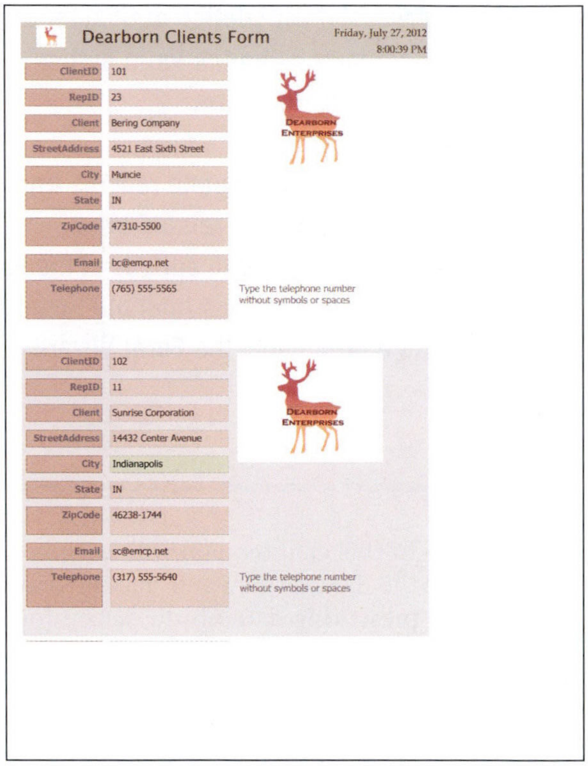
Dearborn Clients Form

Friday, July 27, 2012
8:00:39 PM

ClientID	101
RepID	23
Client	Bering Company
StreetAddress	4521 East Sixth Street
City	Muncie
State	IN
ZipCode	47310-5500
Email	bc@emcp.net
Telephone	(765) 555-5565

ClientID	102
RepID	11
Client	Sunrise Corporation
StreetAddress	14432 Center Avenue
City	Indianapolis
State	IN
ZipCode	46238-1744
Email	sc@emcp.net
Telephone	(317) 555-5640

Project 1g, Dearborn Clients Form

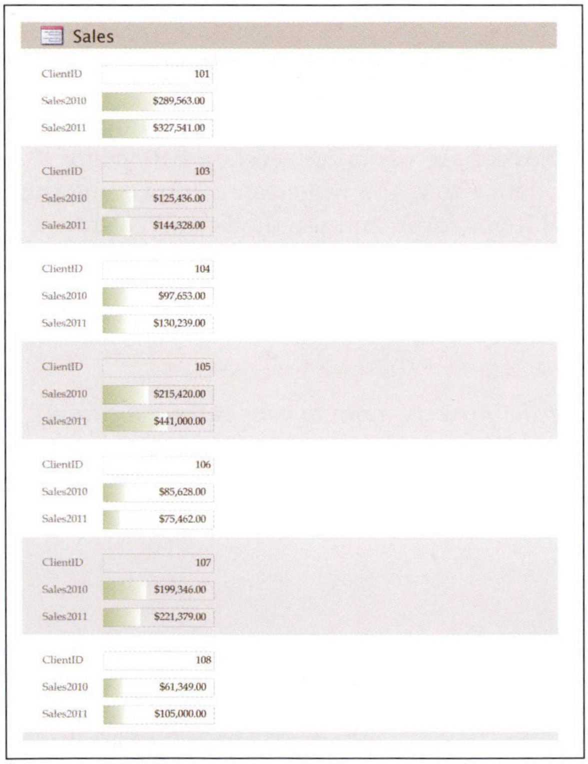
Sales

ClientID	Sales2010	Sales2011
101	$289,563.00	$327,541.00
103	$125,436.00	$144,328.00
104	$97,653.00	$130,239.00
105	$215,420.00	$441,000.00
106	$85,628.00	$75,462.00
107	$199,346.00	$221,379.00
108	$61,349.00	$105,000.00

Project 1g, Dearborn Sales Form

Project 2 Add Fields, Create a Split and Multiple Item Form, and Use the Form Wizard

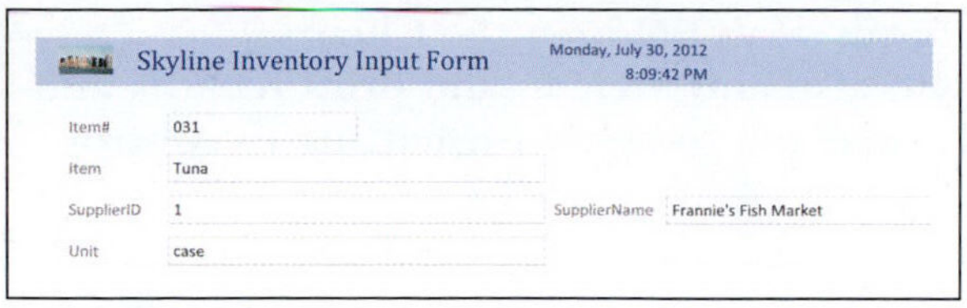

Skyline Inventory Input Form — Monday, July 30, 2012 8:09:42 PM

Item#	031
Item	Tuna
SupplierID	1
SupplierName	Frannie's Fish Market
Unit	case

Project 2a, Skyline Inventory Form

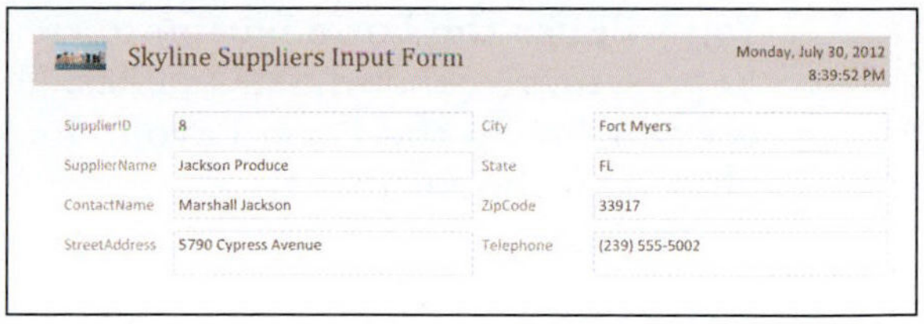

Skyline Suppliers Input Form — Monday, July 30, 2012 8:39:52 PM

SupplierID	8
SupplierName	Jackson Produce
ContactName	Marshall Jackson
StreetAddress	5790 Cypress Avenue
City	Fort Myers
State	FL
ZipCode	33917
Telephone	(239) 555-5002

Project 2b, Skyline Suppliers Form

Skyline Orders — Monday, July 30, 2012 9:15:30 PM

Order#	Item#	UnitsOrdered	UnitPrice	OrderDate	SupplierID
06-001	002	3	$10.50	6/1/2012	2
06-002	033	1	$73.50	6/1/2012	1
06-003	016	1	$24.00	6/4/2012	2
06-004	020	2	$18.75	6/4/2012	4
06-005	014	2	$15.75	6/4/2012	2
06-006	025	1	$28.50	6/5/2012	4
06-007	036	2	$17.00	6/6/2012	4
06-008	028	1	$315.00	6/7/2012	7
06-009	013	2	$14.00	6/7/2012	4
06-010	004	2	$10.95	6/11/2012	2
06-011	035	1	$17.00	6/11/2012	4
06-012	039	4	$3.50	6/11/2012	3
06-013	040	2	$4.95	6/12/2012	3
06-014	041	5	$6.50	6/12/2012	6
06-015	044	1	$50.25	6/13/2012	6
06-016	022	3	$16.50	6/15/2012	3
06-017	027	1	$22.00	6/15/2012	4
06-018	053	3	$52.00	6/18/2012	3
06-019	030	2	$175.00	6/18/2012	7
06-020	003	2	$7.25	6/18/2012	6
06-021	026	1	$29.25	6/20/2012	4
06-022	021	1	$31.00	6/20/2012	2
06-023	034	2	$13.75	6/20/2012	4
06-024	032	1	$101.50	6/22/2012	1
06-025	012	1	$30.25	6/22/2012	4
06-026	023	2	$12.95	6/25/2012	3
06-027	018	1	$45.00	6/25/2012	4
06-028	037	2	$11.25	6/25/2012	2
06-029	016	2	$39.40	6/26/2012	2
06-030	035	1	$17.00	6/26/2012	4
06-031	014	2	$15.75	6/28/2012	2
06-032	020	2	$18.75	6/28/2012	4

Project 2c, Skyline Orders Form

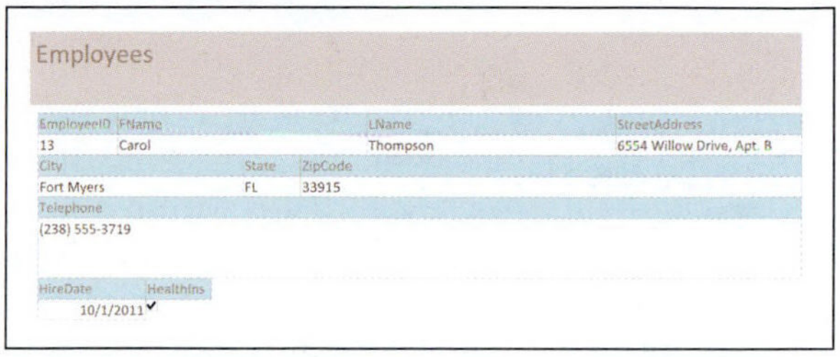

Employees

EmployeeID	FName	LName	StreetAddress
13	Carol	Thompson	6554 Willow Drive, Apt. B

City	State	ZipCode
Fort Myers	FL	33915

Telephone: (238) 555-3719

HireDate: 10/1/2011 HealthIns: ✓

Project 2d, Skyline Employees Form, Carol Thompson

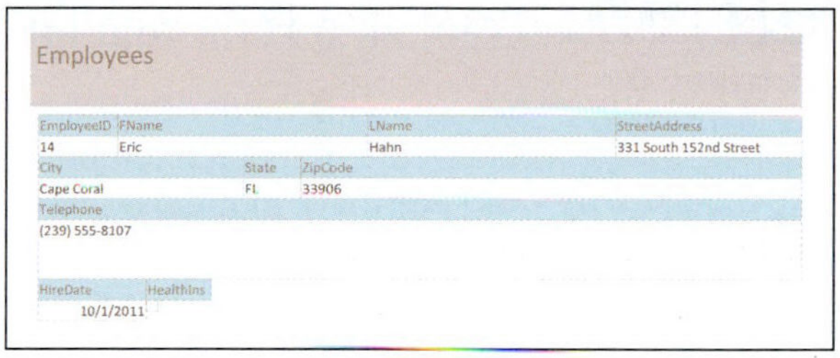

Employees

EmployeeID	FName	LName	StreetAddress
14	Eric	Hahn	331 South 152nd Street

City	State	ZipCode
Cape Coral	FL	33906

Telephone: (239) 555-8107

HireDate: 10/1/2011 HealthIns:

Project 2d, Skyline Employees Form, Eric Hahn

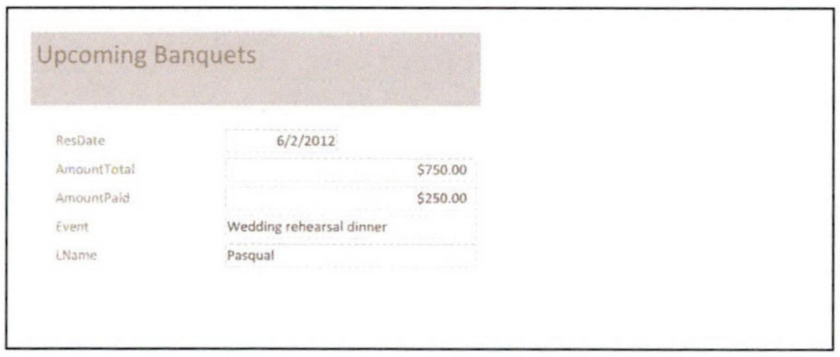

Upcoming Banquets

ResDate	6/2/2012
AmountTotal	$750.00
AmountPaid	$250.00
Event	Wedding rehearsal dinner
LName	Pasqual

Project 2e, Skyline Upcoming Banquets Form

Project 1 Create Forms with the Form Button — 7 Parts

You will use the Form button to create forms with fields in the Clients, Representatives, and Sales tables. You will also add, delete, and print records and use buttons in the Form Layout Tools Format tab to apply formatting to control objects in the forms.

Creating a Form

Access offers a variety of options for presenting data in a more easily read and attractive format. When entering data in a table in Datasheet view, multiple records display at the same time. If a record contains several fields, you may not be able to view all fields within a record at the same time. If you create a form, generally all fields for a record are visible on the screen. Several methods are available for creating a form. In this section, you will learn how to create a form using the Form, Split Form, and Multiple Items buttons as well as the Form Wizard.

Quick Steps

Create a Form with Form Button
1. Click desired table.
2. Click Create tab.
3. Click Form button.

HINT

A form allows you to focus on a single record at a time.

HINT

Save a form before making changes or applying formatting to the form.

Creating a Form with the Form Button

You can view, add, or edit data in a table in Datasheet view. You can also perform these functions on data inserted in a form. A ***form*** is an object you can use to enter and edit data in a table or query and is a user-friendly interface for viewing, adding, editing, and deleting records. A form is also useful in helping prevent incorrect data from being entered and it can be used to control access to specific data.

You can use a variety of methods to create a form. The simplest method to create a form is to click the Create tab and then click the Form button in the Forms groups. Figure 5.1 displays the form you will create in Project 1a with the Clients table in the AL1-C5-Dearborn.accdb database. Access creates the form using all fields in the table in a vertical layout and displays the form in Layout view with the Form Layout Tools Design tab active.

Form

View

Changing Views

When you click the Form button to create a form, the form displays in Layout view. This is one of three views you can use when working with forms. Use the Form view to enter and manage records. Use the Layout view to view the data as well as modify the appearance and contents of the form and use the Design view to view the structure of the form and modify the form. Change views with the View button in the Views group in the Form Layout Tools Design tab or with buttons in the view area located at the right side of the Status bar.

You can open an existing form in Layout view. To do this, right-click the form name in the Navigation pane and then click *Layout View* at the shortcut menu.

Quick Steps

Print Specific Record
1. Display form.
2. Click File tab, Print tab.
3. Click *Print* option.
4. Click *Selected Record(s)*.
5. Click OK.

Printing a Form

Print all records in the form by clicking the File tab, clicking the Print tab, and then clicking the *Quick Print* option. If you want to print a specific record in a form, click the File tab, click the Print tab, and then click the *Print* option. At the Print dialog box that displays, click the *Selected Record(s)* option and then click OK.

Figure 5.1 Form Created from Data in the Clients Table

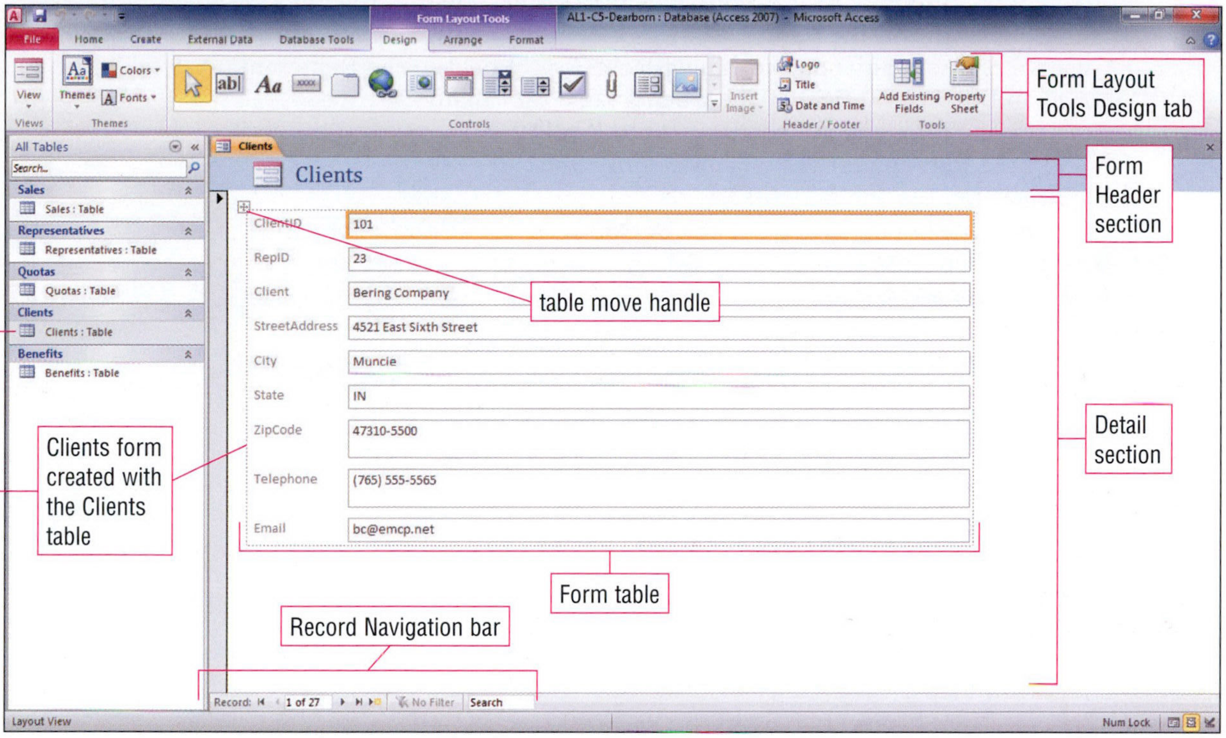

You can also print a range of records by clicking the *Pages* option in the *Print Range* section of the Print dialog box and then entering the beginning record number in the *From* text box and the ending record number in the *To* text box.

First Record

Previous Record

Next Record

Last Record

Navigating in a Form

When a form displays in either Form view or Layout view, navigation buttons display along the bottom of the form in the Record Navigation bar as identified in Figure 5.1. Using these navigation buttons, you can display the first record in the form, the previous record, the next record, the last record, and a new record.

Along with the Record Navigation bar, you can display records in a form using the keyboard. Press the Page Down key to move forward a single record or press the Page Up key to move back a single record. Press Ctrl + Home to display the first record or Press Ctrl + End to display the last record.

Project 1a Creating a Form with the Clients Table — Part 1 of 7

1. Display the Open dialog box with Access2010L1C5 on your storage medium the active folder.
2. Open the **AL1-C5-Dearborn.accdb** database and enable the contents.
3. Display the Relationships window, insert all of the tables in the window, and then create the following relationships and enforce referential integrity and cascade fields and records:
   a. Create a one-to-many relationship with the *RepID* field in the Benefits table the "one" and the *RepID* field in the Clients table the "many."
   b. Create a one-to-one relationship with the *ClientID* field in the Clients table the "one" and the *ClientID* field in the Sales table the "one."

c. Create a one-to-many relationship with the *QuotaID* field in the Quotas table the "one" and the *QuotaID* in the Representatives table the "many."

d. Create a one-to-many relationship with the *RepID* field in the Representatives table the "one" and the *RepID* field in the Clients table the "many."

e. Create a one-to-one relationship with the *RepID* field in the Representatives table the "one" and the *RepID* field in the Benefits table the "one."

f. Save and then close the Relationships window.

4. Create a form with the Clients table by completing the following steps:

   a. Click the Clients table in the Navigation pane.

   b. Click the Create tab.

   c. Click the Form button in the Forms group.

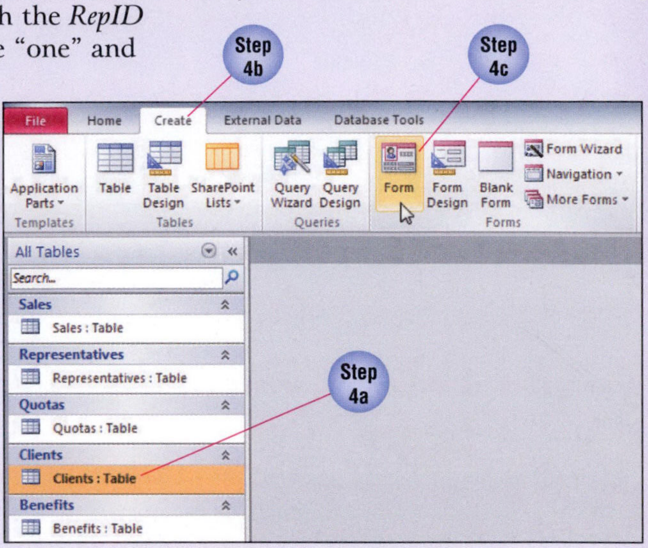

5. Switch to the Form view by clicking the View button in the Views group in the Form Layout Tools Design tab.

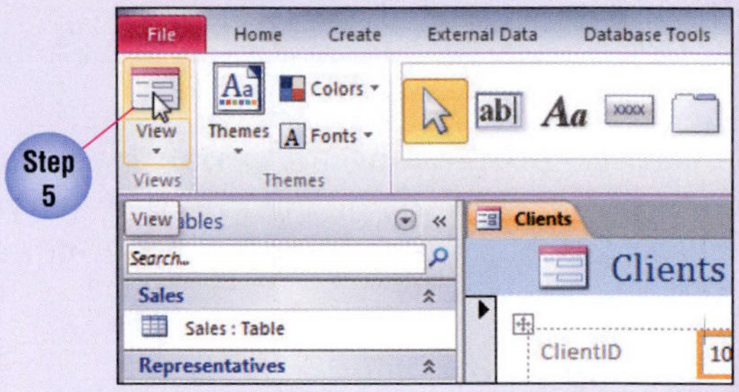

6. Navigate in the form by completing the following steps:

   a. Click the Next Record button in the Record Navigation bar to display the next record.

   b. Click the Last Record button in the Record Navigation bar to display the last record.

   c. Click the First Record button in the Record Navigation bar to display the first record.

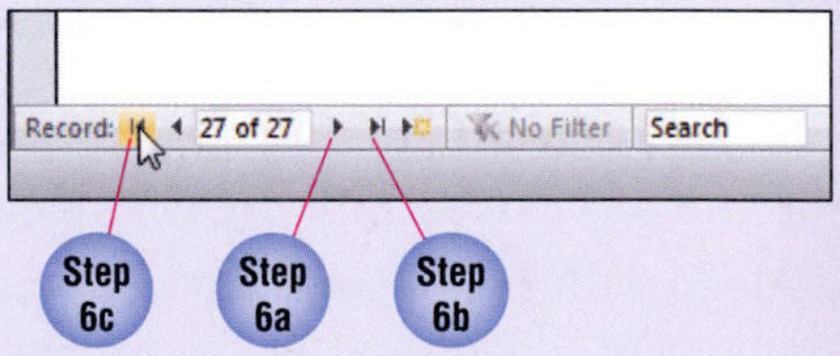

7. Save the form by completing the following steps:

   a. Click the Save button on the Quick Access toolbar.

   b. At the Save As dialog box, with *Clients* inserted in the *Form Name* text box, click OK.

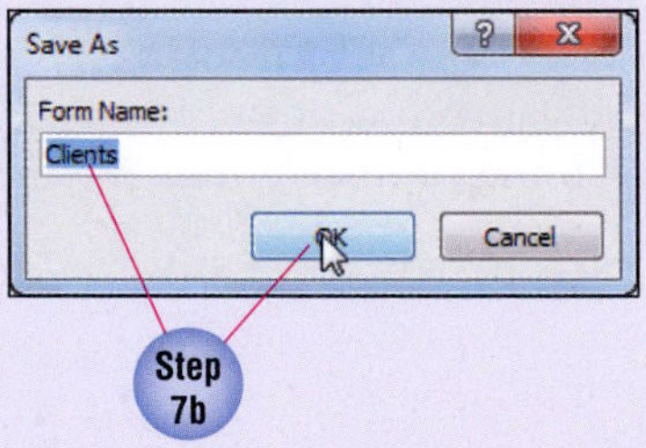

8. Print the current record in the form by completing the following steps:

   a. Click the File tab and then click the Print tab.

   b. Click the *Print* option.

   c. At the Print dialog box, click the *Selected Record(s)* option in the *Print Range* section, and then click OK.

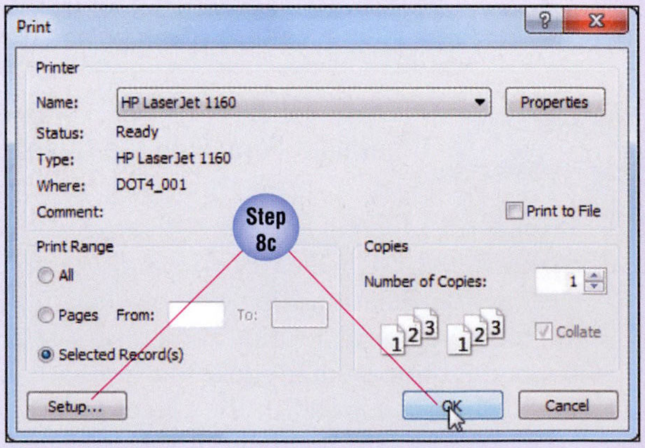

Adding and Deleting Records

Add a new record to the form by clicking the New (blank) Record button (contains a right arrow followed by a yellow asterisk) that displays in the Record Navigation bar along the bottom of the form. You can also add a new record to a form by clicking the Home tab and then clicking the New button in the Records group. To delete a record, display the record, click the Home tab, click the Delete button arrow in the Records group, and then click *Delete Record* at the drop-down list. At the message telling you that the record will be deleted permanently, click Yes.

Quick Steps

Add a Record
Click New (blank) Record button in Record Navigation bar.
OR
1. Click Home tab.
2. Click New button.

Delete a Record
1. Click Home tab.
2. Click Delete button arrow.
3. Click *Delete Record.*
4. Click Yes.

New Record

Delete

Sorting Records

You can sort data in a form by clicking in the field containing data on which you want to sort and then clicking the Ascending button or Descending button in the Sort & Filter group in the Home tab. Click the Ascending button to sort text in alphabetic order from A to Z or numbers from lowest to highest or click the Descending button to sort text in alphabetic order from Z to A or numbers from highest to lowest.

Project 1b **Adding and Deleting Records in a Form** Part 2 of 7

1. With the Clients form open and the first record displayed, add a new record by completing the following steps:
   a. Click the New (blank) Record button located in the Record Navigation bar.

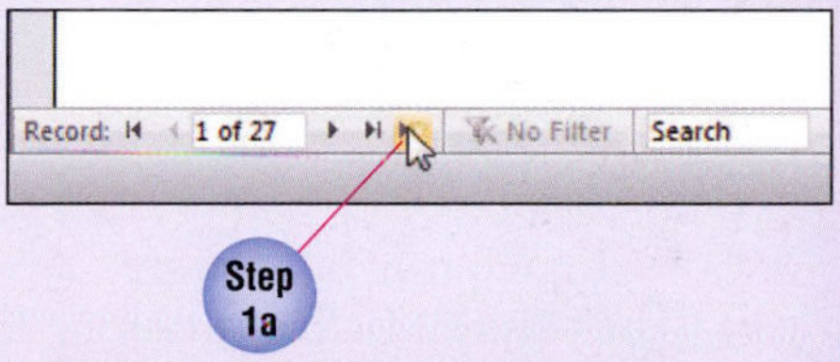

   b. At the new blank record, type the following information in the specified fields (move to the next field by pressing Tab or Enter; move to the previous field by pressing Shift + Tab):

ClientID	=	**128**
RepID	=	**14**
Client	=	**Gen-Erin Productions**
StreetAddress	=	**1099 15th Street**
City	=	**Muncie**
State	=	**IN**
ZipCode	=	**473067963**
Telephone	=	**7655553120**
Email	=	**gep@emcp.net**

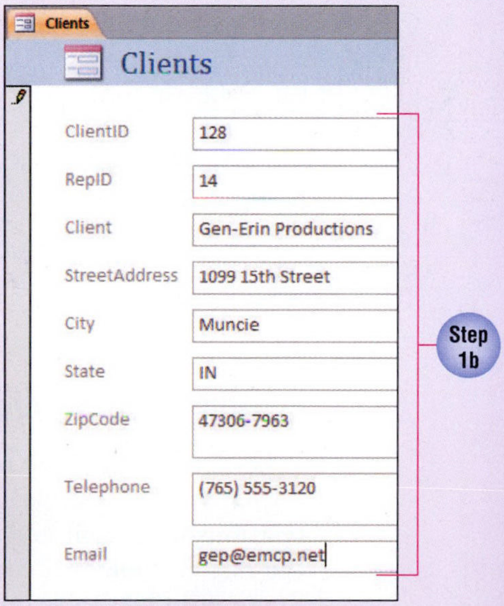

2. Print the current record in the form by completing the following steps:
   a. Click the File tab and then click the Print tab.
   b. Click the *Print* option.
   c. At the Print dialog box, click the *Selected Record(s)* option in the *Print Range* section, and then click OK.
3. Delete the second record (ClientID 102) by completing the following steps:
   a. Click the First Record button in the Record Navigation bar.
   b. Click the Next Record button in the Record Navigation bar.

c. With Record 2 active, click the Home tab.
d. Click the Delete button arrow and then click *Delete Record* at the drop-down list.

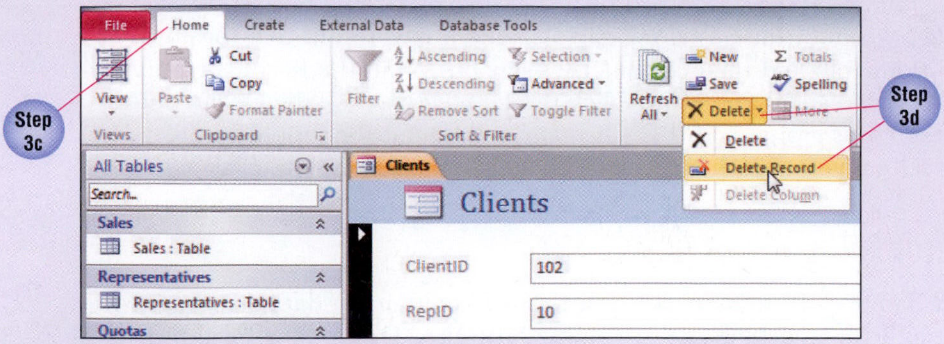

e. At the message that displays telling you that relationships that specify cascading deletes will cause records in the table to be deleted along with records in related tables, click the Yes button.

4. Click the New (blank) Record button in the Record Navigation bar and then type the following information in the specified fields.

ClientID	=	**102**
RepID	=	**11**
Client	=	**Sunrise Corporation**
StreetAddress	=	**14432 Center Avenue**
City	=	**Indianapolis**
State	=	**IN**
ZipCode	=	**462381744**
Telephone	=	**3175555640**
Email	=	**sc@emcp.net**

5. Sort the records in the form by completing the following steps:
   a. Click in the field containing the data *Sunrise Corporation* and then click the Ascending button in the Sort & Filter group in the Home tab.
   b. Click in the field containing the data *Indianapolis* and then click the Descending button in the Sort & Filter group.
   c. Click in the field containing the data *47310-5500* and then click the Ascending button in the Sort & Filter group.
   d. Click in the field containing the data *114* and then click the Ascending button in the Sort & Filter group.
6. Close the Clients form by clicking the Close button located in the upper right corner of the work area.

Creating a Form with a Related Table

When you created the form with the Clients table, only the Clients table fields displayed in the form. If you create a form with a table that has a one-to-many relationship established, Access adds a datasheet to the form that is based on the related table. For example, in Project 1c, you will create a form with the Representatives table and, since it is related to the Clients table by a one-to-many relationship, Access inserts a datasheet at the bottom of the form containing all of the records in the Clients table. Figure 5.2 displays the form you will create in Project 1c. Notice the datasheet that displays at the bottom of the form.

Figure 5.2 Representatives Form with Clients Datasheet

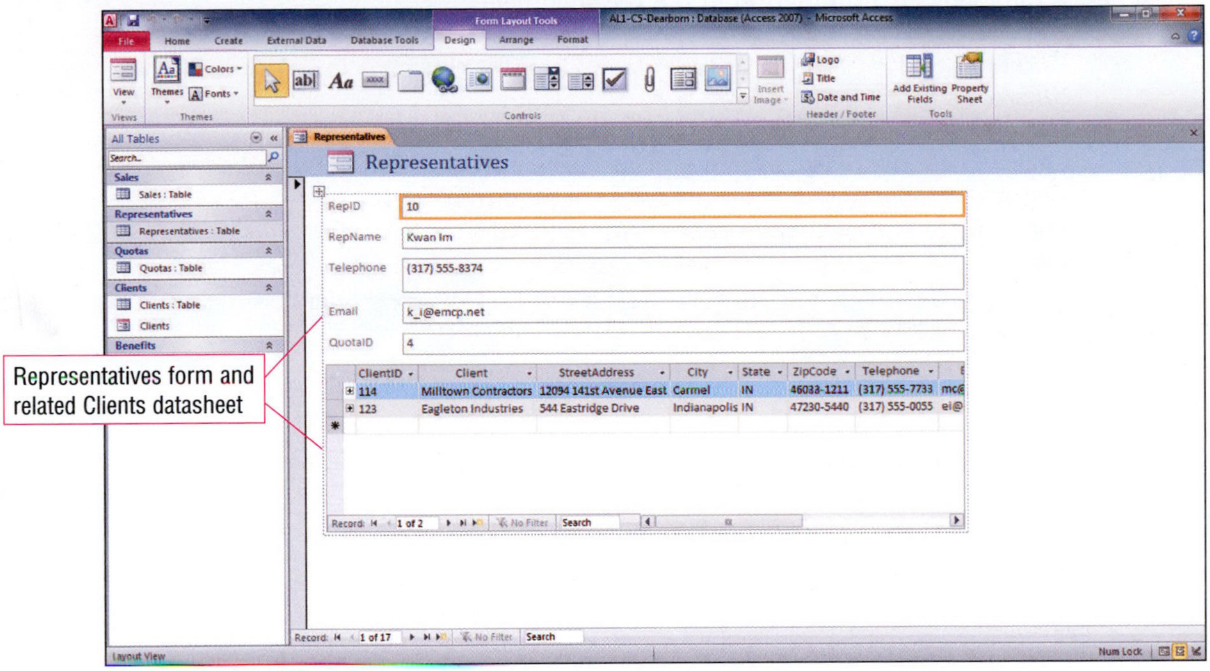

If you have created only a single one-to-many relationship, the datasheet for the related table displays in the form. If you have created more than a single one-to-many relationship in a table, Access will not display any datasheets when you create a form with the table.

Project 1c Creating a Form with a Related Table

Part 3 of 7

1. With the **AL1-C5-Dearborn.accdb** database open, create a form with the Representatives table by completing the following steps:
   a. Click the Representatives table in the Navigation pane.
   b. Click the Create tab.
   c. Click the Form button in the Forms group.
2. Insert a new record in the Clients table for representative 12 (Catherine Singleton) by completing the following steps:
   a. Click twice on the Next Record button in the Record Navigation bar at the bottom of the form window (not the Record Navigation bar in the Clients datasheet) to display the record for Catherine Singleton.
   b. Click in the cell immediately below *127* in the *ClientID* field in the Clients datasheet.

c. Type the following information in the specified fields:

ClientID	=	129
Client	=	Dan-Built Construction
StreetAddress	=	903 James Street
City	=	Carmel
State	=	IN
ZipCode	=	460339050
Telephone	=	3175551122
Email	=	dc@emcp.net

Representatives

RepID	12
RepName	Catherine Singleton
Telephone	(317) 555-0172
Email	c_s@emcp.net
QuotaID	3

	Client	StreetAddress	City	State	ZipCode	Telephone	Email
⊞	Gallagher Systems	3885 Moore Avenue	Indianapolis	IN	47229-1075	(317) 555-9922	gs@emcp.net
⊞	Franklin Services	220 Tenth Avenue	Lafayette	IN	47908-2200	(765) 555-3467	fs@emcp.net
⊞	Zinn-Harris Electronic:	675 South Holt Road	Indianapolis	IN	47221-0551	(317) 555-8882	zh@emcp.net
⊞	Dan-Built Constructio⌐	903 James Street	Carmel	IN	46033-9050	(317) 555-1122	dc@emcp.net

Step 2c

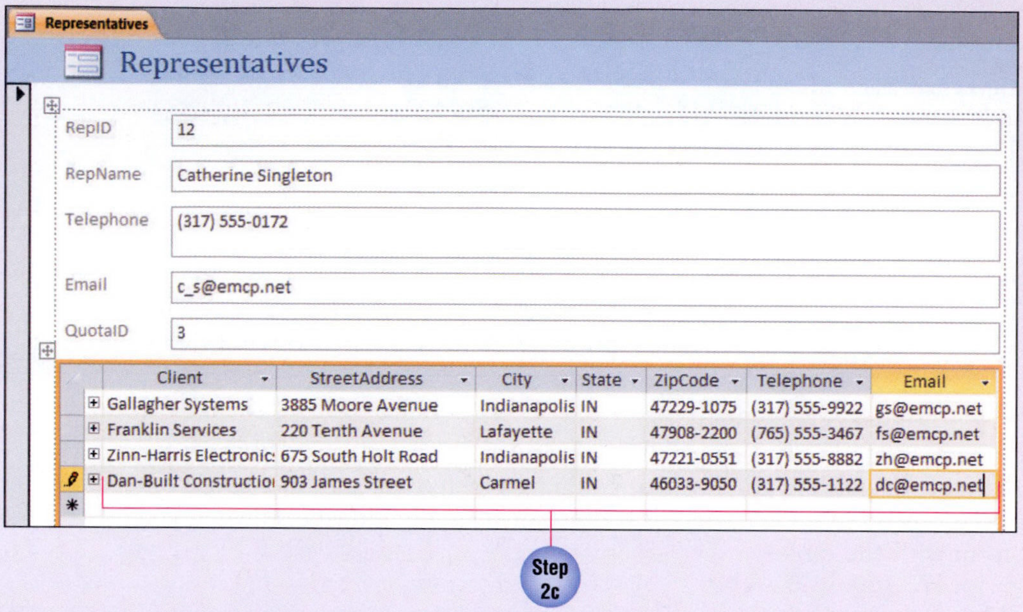

3. Click the Save button on the Quick Access toolbar and at the Save As dialog box with *Representatives* in the *Form Name* text box, click OK.
4. Print the current record in the form by completing the following steps:
 a. Click the File tab and then click the Print tab.
 b. Click the *Print* option.
 c. At the Print dialog box, click the *Select Record(s)* option in the *Print Range* section and then click OK.
5. Close the Representatives form.

Customizing a Form ■■■■■■■■■■ ■■■■■■■ ■■■■■ ■

You can make almost all changes to a form in Layout view.

A form is comprised of a series of *control objects*, which are objects that display titles or descriptions, accept data, or perform actions. Control objects are contained in the *Form Header* section and *Detail* section of the form. (Refer to Figure 5.1 on page 189.) The control objects in the *Detail* section are contained within a form table.

You can customize control objects in the *Detail* section and data in the *Form Header* section with buttons in the Form Layout Tools ribbon with the Design tab, Arrange tab, or Format tab selected. When you open a form in Layout view, the Form Layout Tools Design tab is active. This tab contains options for applying a theme, inserting controls, inserting header or footer data, and adding existing fields.

Applying Themes

Access provides a number of themes you can use to format objects in a database. A ***theme*** is a set of formatting choices that include a color theme (a set of colors) and a font theme (a set of heading and body text fonts). To apply a theme, click the Themes button in the Themes group in the Form Layout Tools Design tab. At the drop-down gallery that displays, click the desired theme. Position the mouse pointer over a theme and the ***live preview feature*** will display the form with the theme formatting applied. With the live preview feature you can see how the theme formatting affects your form before you make your final choice. When you apply a theme, any new objects you create in the database will be formatted with the theme.

You can further customize the formatting of a form with the Colors button and the Fonts button in the Themes group in the Form Layout Tools Design tab. If you want to customize the theme colors, click the Colors button in the Themes group, and then click the desired option at the drop-down list. Change the theme fonts by clicking the Themes button and then clicking the desired option at the drop-down list.

HINT

Themes available in Access are the same as the themes available in Word, Excel, and PowerPoint.

Themes

Colors

Font

Logo

Title

Date and Time

Inserting Data in the Form Header

Use buttons in the Header/Footer group in the Form Layout Tools Design tab to insert a logo, a form title, or the date and time. Click the Logo button and the Insert Picture dialog box displays. Browse to the folder containing the desired image and then double-click the image file. Click the Title button and the current title is selected. Type the new title and then press the Enter key. Click the Date and Time button in the Header/Footer group and the Date and Time dialog box displays. At this dialog box, choose the desired date and time format and then click OK. The date and time are inserted at the right side of the *Header* section.

You can resize and move control objects in the *Form Header* section. To resize an object, click the object to select it and then drag a left or right border to increase or decrease the width. Drag a top or bottom border to increase or decrease the height of the object as well as the *Form Header* section. To move a selected object in the *Form Header* section, position the mouse pointer over the selected object until the pointer displays with a four-headed arrow attached. Hold down the left mouse button, drag the object to the desired position, and then release the mouse button.

Modifying a Control Object

When Access creates a form from a table, the first column in the form contains the label control objects and displays the field names from the table. The second column contains the text box control objects that display the field values you entered in the table. You can resize the width of either column. To do this, click in any control object in the desired column, position the mouse pointer on the right or left border of the selected control object until the pointer displays as a black, two-headed arrow pointing left and right. Hold down the left mouse button, drag left or right to change the width of the column, and then release the mouse button. Complete similar steps to change the height of the row containing the selected control object.

To delete a control object from the form, click the desired object and then press the Delete key. You can also right-click the object and then click *Delete* at the shortcut menu. If you want to delete a form row, right-click an object in the row you want to delete and then click *Delete Row* at the shortcut menu. To delete a column, right-click in one of the objects in the column you want to delete and then click *Delete Column* at the shortcut menu. In addition to the label and text box control objects, you can modify the size and position of objects in the *Form Header* section such as the logo and title.

Inserting a Control

HINT
Each cell can contain only one control object.

Select

Text Box

Button

The Controls group in the Form Layout Tools Design tab contains a number of control objects you can insert in a form. By default, the Select button is active. With this button active, use the mouse pointer to select control objects. You can insert a new label control and text box control object in your form by clicking the Text Box button in the Controls group and then clicking in the desired position in the form. Click in the label control object, select the default text, and then type the label text. You can enter text in a label control object in Layout view but you cannot enter data in a text box control object. In Form view, you can enter data in a text box control object but you cannot edit text in a label control object. The Controls group contains a number of additional buttons for inserting control objects in a form such as a hyperlink, combo box, or image.

You can enter navigation control objects in a form by clicking the Button button in the Controls group and then clicking in the desired position in the form. This activates the Command Button Wizard. At the first Command Button Wizard dialog box, choose a category in the *Categories* list box and then choose the desired action in the *Actions* list box. The options in the *Actions* list box vary depending on the category you choose. Click the Next button and the second Command Button Wizard dialog box displays, choose whether you want text to display on the button or an image, and then click the Finish button.

Project 1d **Customizing the Design of a Form** **Part 4 of 7**

1. With the **AL1-C5-Dearborn.accdb** database open, open the Clients form you created in Project 1a by right-clicking the *Clients* form in the Navigation pane and then clicking *Layout View* at the shortcut menu.

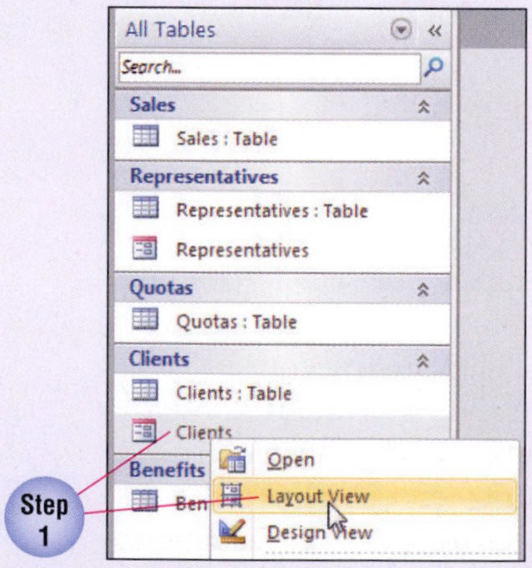

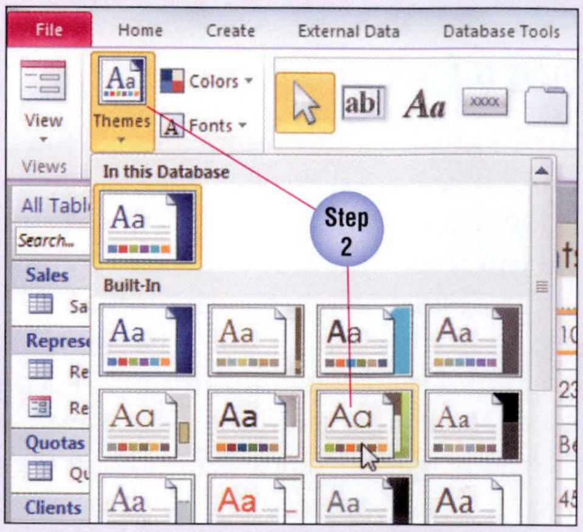

2. Apply a theme to the form by clicking the Themes button in the Themes group and then clicking *Austin* at the drop-down gallery.

3. Change the theme fonts by clicking the Fonts button in the Themes group and then clicking *Apex* at the drop-down gallery. (You may need to scroll down the list to display *Apex*.)

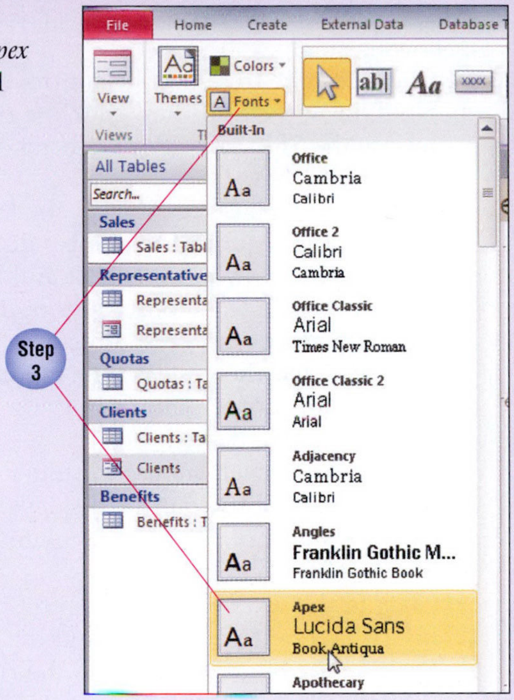

4. Insert a logo image in the *Form Header* section by completing the following steps:
   a. Right-click the logo object that displays in the *Form Header* section (located to the left of the title *Clients*) and then click *Delete* at the shortcut menu.

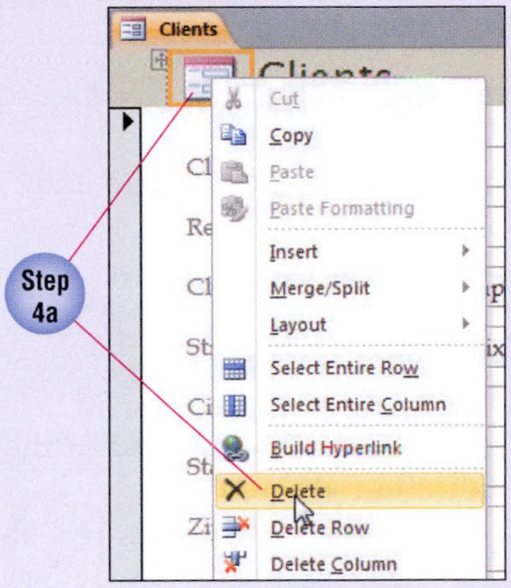

   b. Click the Logo button in the Header/Footer group.
   c. At the Insert Picture dialog box, navigate to the Access2010L1C5 folder on your storage medium and then double-click the file named ***DearbornLogo.jpg***.
5. Change the title by completing the following steps:
   a. Click the Title button in the Header/Footer group. (This selects *Clients* in the *Form Header* section.)
   b. Type **Dearborn Clients Form** and then press Enter.

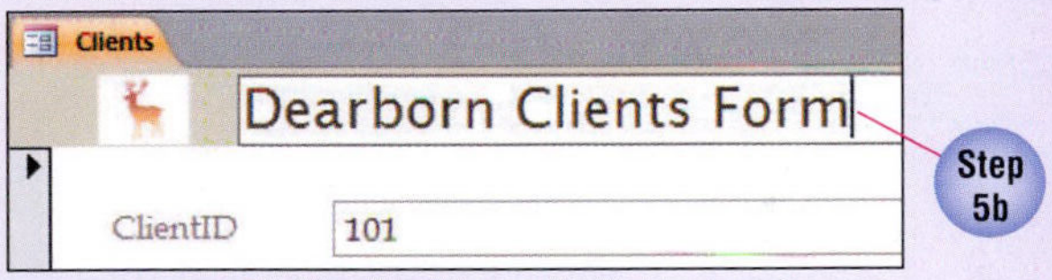

6. Insert the date and time in the *Form Header* section by completing the following steps:
   a. Click the Date and Time button in the Header/Footer group.
   b. At the Date and Time dialog box, click OK.
7. Size the control object containing the title by completing the following steps:
   a. Click in any field outside the title and then click the title to select the control object.
   b. Position the mouse pointer on the right border of the selected object until the pointer displays as a black, two-headed arrow pointing left and right.
   c. Hold down the left mouse button, drag to the left until the right border is immediately right of the title, and then release the mouse button.

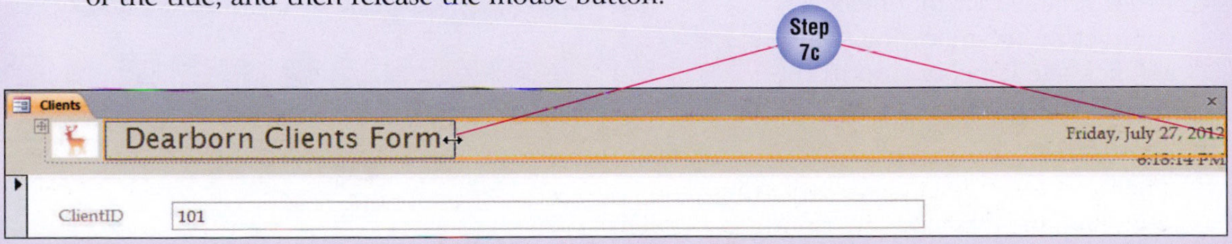

8. Size and move the control objects containing the date and time by completing the following steps:
   a. Click the date to select the control object.
   b. Hold down the Shift key, click the time, and then release the Shift key. (Both control objects should be selected.)
   c. Position the mouse pointer on the left border of the selected objects until the pointer displays as a black, two-headed arrow pointing left and right.
   d. Hold down the left mouse button, drag to the right until the border displays immediately left of the date and time, and then release the mouse button.

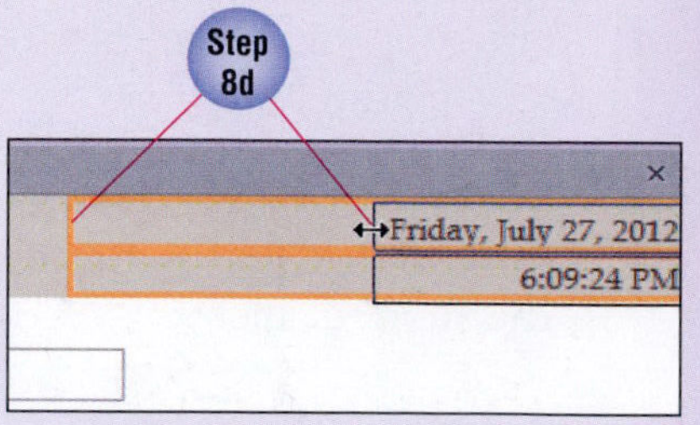

   e. Position the mouse pointer in the selected objects until the pointer displays with a four-headed arrow attached.
   f. Hold down the left mouse button and then drag the outline of the date and time objects to the left until the outline displays near the title.
9. Decrease the size of the second column of control objects in the *Detail* section by completing the following steps:
   a. Click in the text box control object containing the client number *101*. (This selects and inserts an orange border around the object.)
   b. Position the mouse pointer on the right border of the selected object until the pointer displays as a black, two-headed arrow pointing left and right.
   c. Hold down the left mouse button, drag to the left until the text box control objects are just slightly wider than the text, and then release the mouse button. (See image below.)

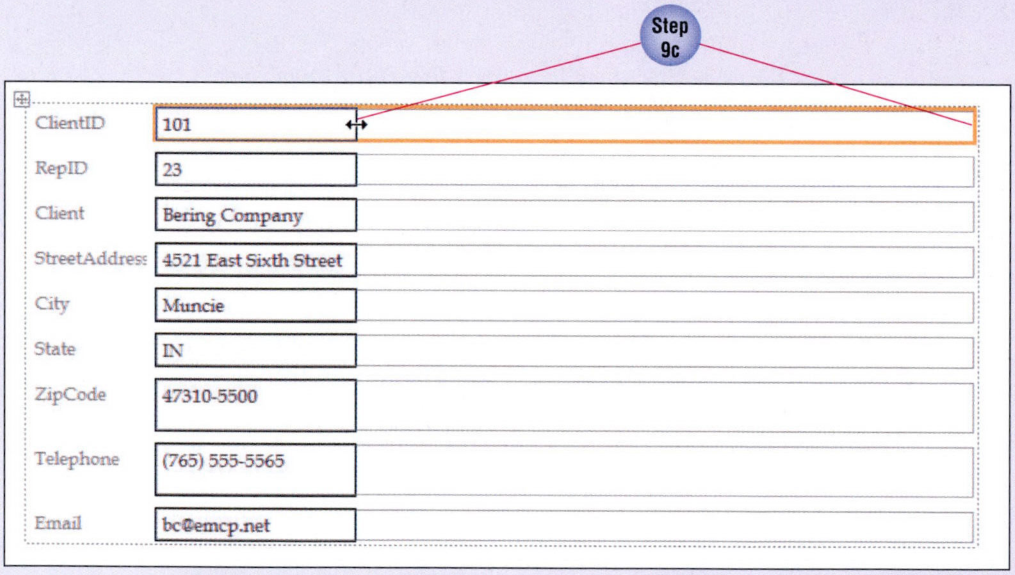

10. Insert a label control object by completing the following steps:
    a. Click the Label button in the Controls group.

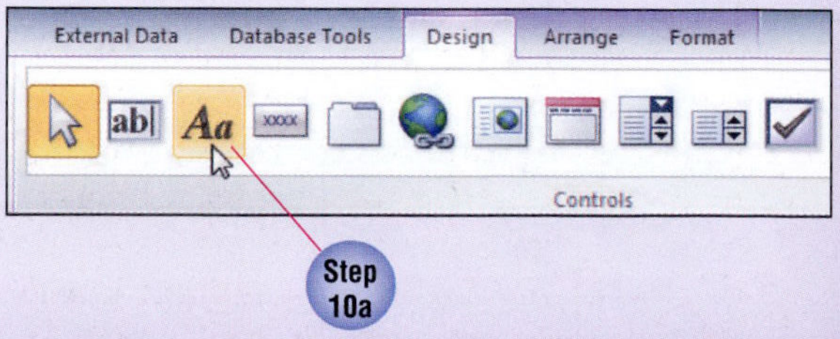

b. Click immediately right of the text box containing the telephone number *(765) 555-5565*. (This inserts the label to the right of the *telephone number* text box.)

c. With the insertion point positioned inside the label, type **Type the telephone number without symbols or spaces** and then press the Enter key.

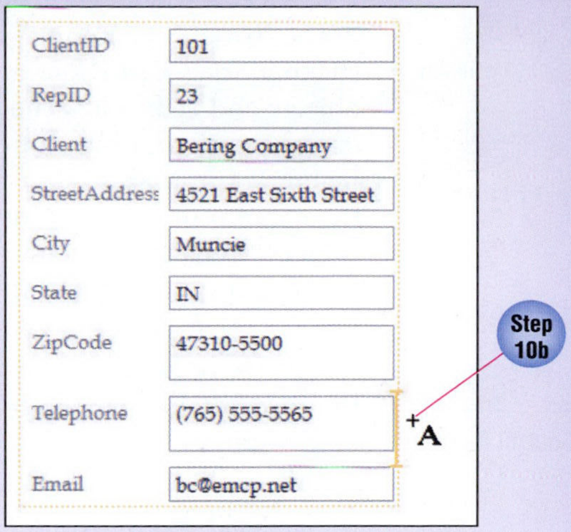

11. Change the size of the new label control object by completing the following steps:
    a. Position the arrow pointer on the right border of the new label control object until the pointer displays as a black, two-headed arrow pointing left and right.
    b. Hold down the left mouse button, drag the border to the right approximately an inch, and then release the mouse button. The text line in the label should break after the word *number*.
    c. Decrease the height of the new label control object by dragging the bottom border up so it is positioned just below the second line of text. (See image at right.)

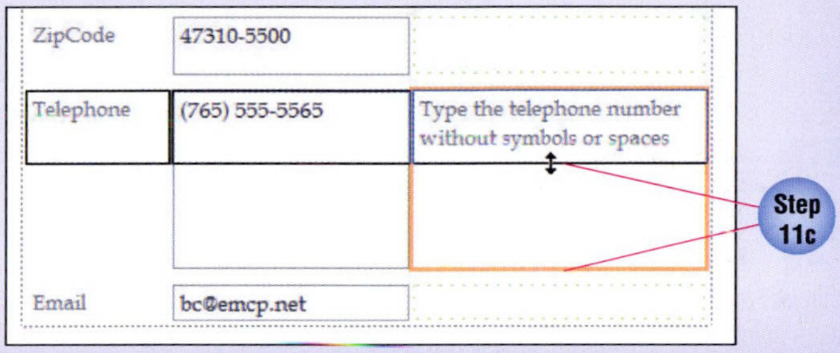

12. Click the Save button on the Quick Access toolbar to save the changes you made to the form.

Moving a Form Table

The control objects in the *Detail* section in a form in Layout view are contained within the form table. Click in a control object and the table is selected and the table move handle is visible. The table move handle is a small square with a four-headed arrow inside that displays in the upper left corner of the table. (Refer to Figure 5.1 on page 189.) You can move the table and all of the control objects within the table by dragging the table move handle using the mouse. When you position the mouse pointer on the table move handle and then hold down the left mouse button, all of the control objects are selected. You can also click the table move handle to select the control objects.

Select Row

Select Column

Insert Above

Insert Below

Merge

Arranging Objects

With options in the Form Layout Tools Arrange tab, you can select, insert, delete, arrange, merge, and split cells. When you inserted a label control object to the right of the *Telephone* text box control in Project 1d, empty cells were inserted in the form above and below the new label control object. You can select a control object or cell by clicking in the desired object or cell. You can select adjacent objects or cells by holding down the Shift key while clicking in the desired objects or cells. To select nonadjacent objects or cells, hold down the Ctrl key while clicking in the desired objects or cells.

Split Vertically

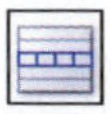
Split Horizontally

Control Margins

Control Padding

Select a row of control objects and cells by clicking the Select Row button in the Rows & Columns group or by right-clicking in an object or cell and then clicking *Select Entire Row* at the shortcut menu. To select a column of control objects and cells, click the Select Column button in the Rows & Columns group, or right-click an object or cell and then click *Select Entire Column* at the shortcut menu. You can also select a column by positioning the mouse pointer at the top of the column until the pointer displays as a small, down-pointing black arrow and then clicking the left mouse button.

The Rows & Columns group contains buttons for inserting a row or column of blank cells. To insert a new row, select a cell or object in a row and then click the Insert Above button to insert a row of blank cells above the current row or click the Insert Below button to insert a row below. Complete similar steps to insert a new column of blank cells either left or right of the current column.

You can merge adjacent selected cells by clicking the Merge button in the Merge/Split group in the Form Layout Tools Arrange tab. You can split a control object or a cell by clicking the object or cell to make it active and then clicking the Split Vertically button or Split Horizontally button in the Merge/Split group. When you split a control object, an empty cell is created to the right of the control object.

HINT

You can move a control object by dragging it to the desired location.

You can move up or down a row of control objects. To do this, select the desired row and then click the Move Up button in the Move group to move the row above the current row or click the Move Down button to move the row below the current row. Use the Control Margins button in the Position group to increase or decrease margins within control objects. The Position group also contains a Control Padding button you can use to increase or decrease spacing between control objects.

The Table group is located at the left side of the Form Layout Tools Arrange tab and contains buttons for applying gridlines to control objects and changing the layout of the objects to a stacked layout or columnar layout.

Project 1e **Arranging Objects in a Form** — Part 5 of 7

1. With the Clients form open in Layout view in the **AL1-C5-Dearborn.accdb** database, select and merge cells by completing the following steps:
   a. Click to the right of the text box control object containing the text *101*. (This selects the empty cell.)
   b. Hold down the Shift key and then click to the right of the text box control containing the text *Muncie*. (This selects five adjacent cells.)
   c. Click the Form Layout Tools Arrange tab.
   d. Click the Merge button in the Merge/Split group.

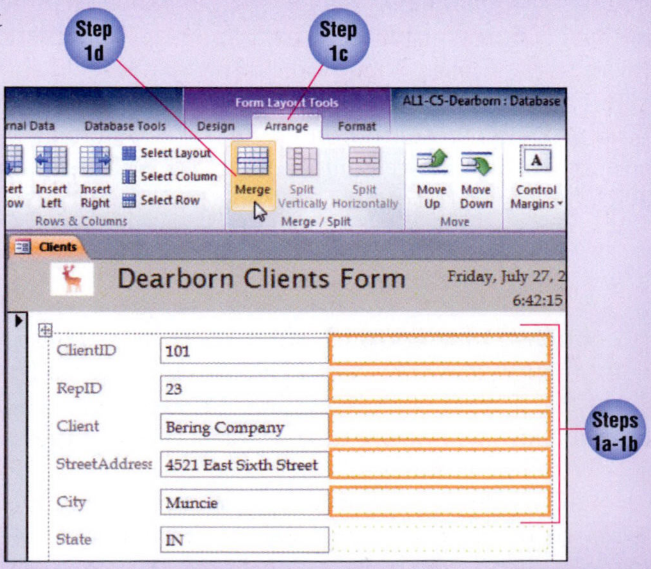

2. With the cells merged, insert an image control object and then insert an image by completing the following steps:
   a. Click the Form Layout Tools Design tab.
   b. Click the Image button in the Controls group.
   c. Move the mouse pointer (pointer displays as a plus symbol next to an image icon) to the location of the merged cell until the cell displays with yellow fill color and then click the left mouse button.
   d. At the Insert Picture dialog box, navigate to the Access2010L1C5 folder on your storage medium and then double-click ***Dearborn.jpg***.

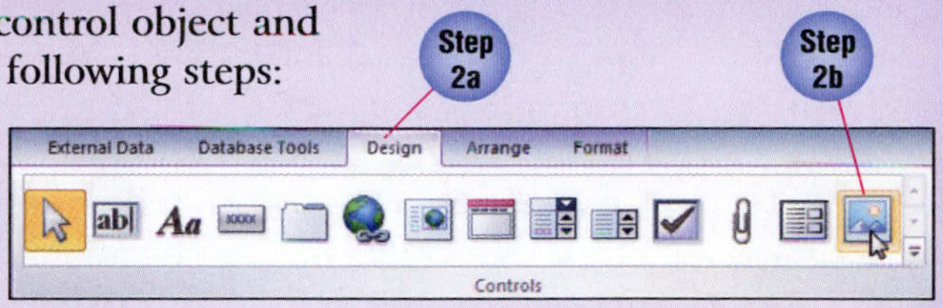

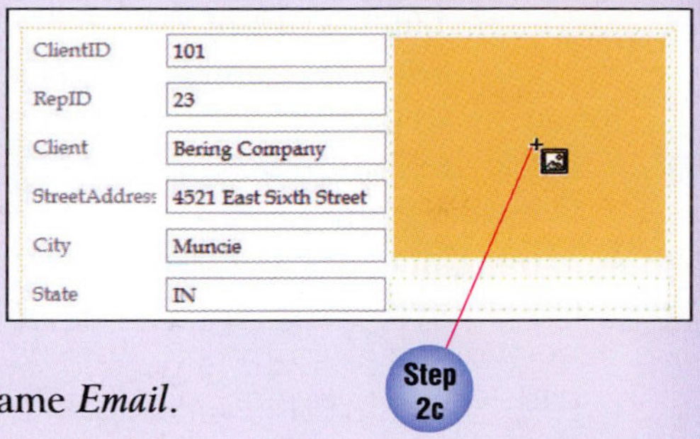

3. Insert a row by completing the following steps:
   a. Click in the control object containing the field name *Email*.
   b. Click the Form Layout Tools Arrange tab.
   c. Click the Insert Below button in the Rows & Columns group. (This inserts a row of blank cells at the bottom of the form.)

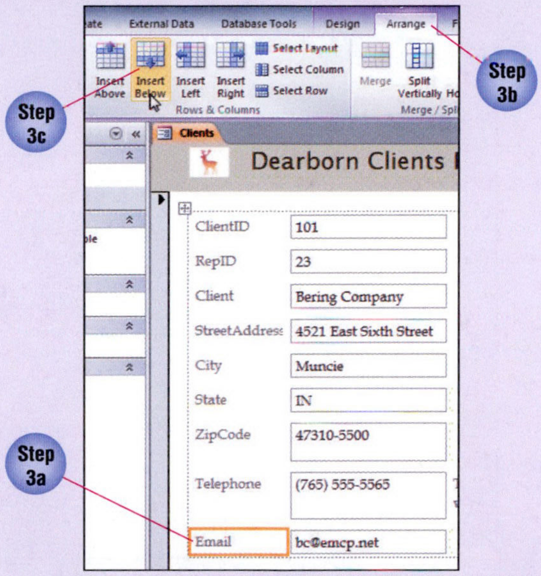

4. Split cells horizontally by completing the following steps:
   a. Click below the text box control object containing the text *bc@emcp.net*. (This selects the empty cell.)
   b. Click the Split Horizontally button in the Merge/Split group.
5. Insert a Previous button in the selected cell (the left empty cell below the text *bc@emcp.net*) by completing the following steps:
   a. Click the Form Layout Tools Design tab.
   b. Click the Button button in the Controls group.
   c. Move the mouse pointer to the left empty cell below the text *bc@emcp.net* until the cell displays with yellow fill color and then click the left mouse button.

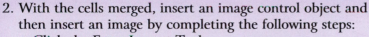

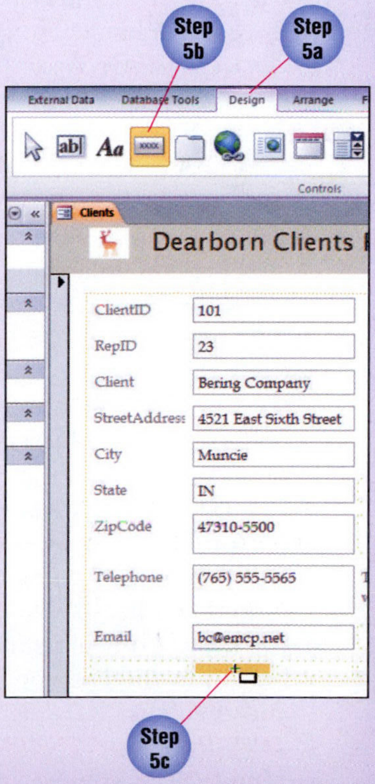

d. At the Command Button Wizard dialog box that displays, click the *Go To Previous Record* option in the *Actions* list box and then click the Finish button.

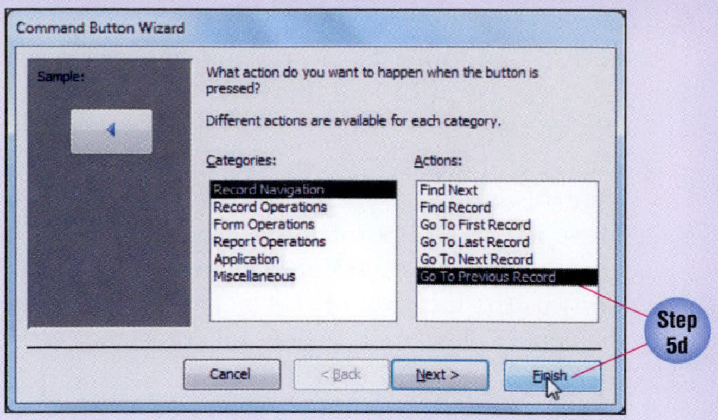

6. Insert a Next button in the cell immediately right of the Previous button by completing the following steps:
   a. Click the Button button in the Controls group.
   b. Move the mouse pointer to the cell to the right of the Previous button in the bottom row until the cell displays with yellow fill color and then click the left mouse button.
   c. At the Command Button Wizard dialog box, click the *Go To Next Record* option in the *Actions* list box and then click the Finish button.

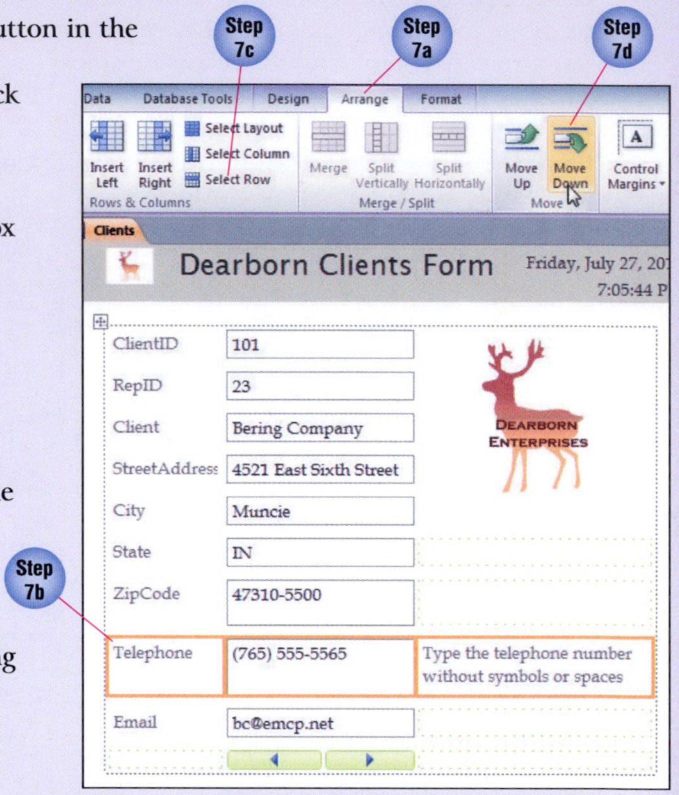

7. Move down the telephone row by completing the following steps:
   a. Click the Form Layout Tools Arrange tab.
   b. Click in the control object containing the text *Telephone*.
   c. Click the Select Row button in the Rows & Columns group.
   d. Click the Move Down button in the Move group.
8. Decrease the margins within objects and cells, increase the spacing (padding) between objects and cells in the form, and apply gridlines by completing the following steps:
   a. Click the Form Layout Tools Arrange tab.
   b. Click the Select Layout button in the Rows & Columns group. (This selects all objects and cells in the form.)
   c. Click the Control Margins button in the Position group and then click *Narrow* at the drop-down list.
   d. Click the Control Padding button in the Position group and then click *Medium* at the drop-down list.

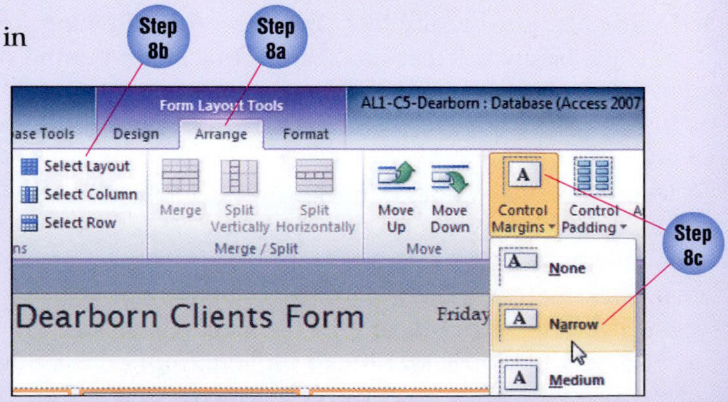

e. Click the Gridlines button in the Table group and then click *Top* at the drop-down list.
f. Click the Gridlines button in the Table group, point to *Color*, and then click the *Orange, Accent 6, Darker 50%* option (the last color option in the last column in the *Theme Colors* section).

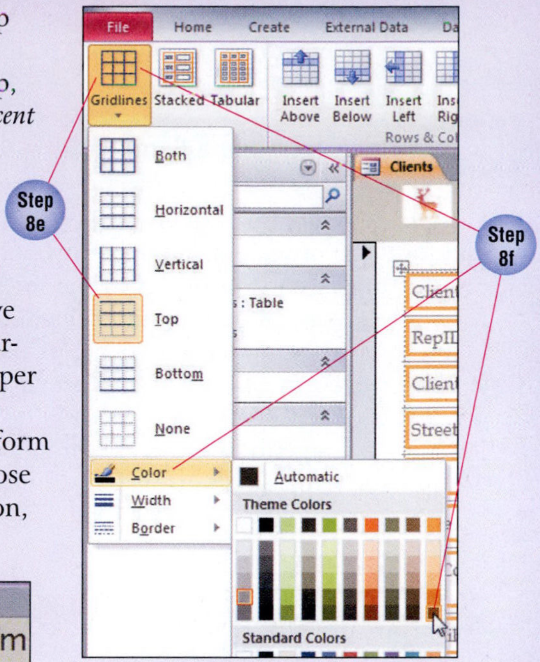

9. Move the form table by completing the following steps:
a. Position the mouse pointer on the table move handle (displays as a small square with a four-headed arrow inside and is located in the upper left corner of the table).
b. Hold down the left mouse button, drag the form table up and to the left so it is positioned close to the top and left border of the *Detail* section, and then release the mouse button.

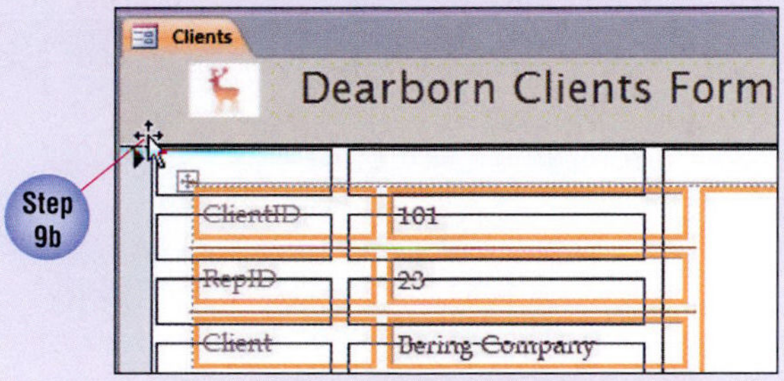

10. Click in the control object containing the field name *ClientID*.
11. Save the Clients form.

Formatting a Form

Object

Select All

Click the Form Layout Tools Format tab and buttons and options display for applying formatting to a form or specific objects in a form. If you want to apply formatting to a specific object, click the object in the form, or click the Object button arrow in the Selection group and then click the desired object at the drop-down list. To format all objects in the form, click the Select All button in the Selection group. This selects all objects in the form including objects in the *Form Header* section. If you want to select all of the objects in the *Detail* section (and not the *Form Header* section), click the selector button that displays in the upper left corner of form objects in the *Detail* section. Click an object in the *Detail* section to display the selector button, which displays as a small square with a four-headed arrow inside. You can also click the selector button and then drag the button to move the objects in the form.

With buttons in the Font, Number, Background, and Control Formatting groups, you can apply formatting to a control object or cell and to selected objects cells in a form. Use buttons in the Font group to change the font, apply a different font size, apply text effects such as bold and underline, and change the alignment of data in objects. If the form contains data with a data type of Number or Currency, use buttons in the Number group to apply specific formatting to numbers. Insert a background image in the form using the Background button and apply formatting to objects or cells with buttons in the Control Formatting group. Depending on what is selected in the form, some of the buttons may not be active.

Project 1f Formatting a Form

Part 6 of 7

1. With the Clients form open in the **AL1-C5-Dearborn.accdb** database, change the font and font size of text in the form by completing the following steps:
   a. Click in any control object in the form.
   b. Select all control objects and cells in the form by clicking the selector button that displays in the upper left corner of the *Detail* section. (See the image below.)
   c. Click the Form Layout Tools Format tab.
   d. Click the Font button arrow, scroll down the drop-down list, and then click *Tahoma*. (Fonts are alphabetized in the drop-down list.)
   e. Click the Font Size button arrow and then click *10* at the drop-down list.

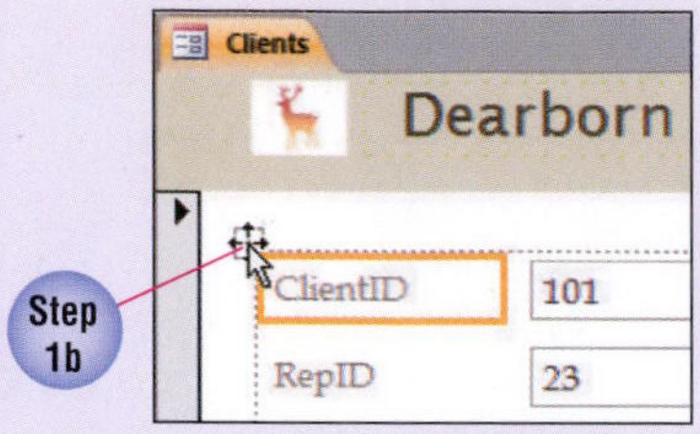

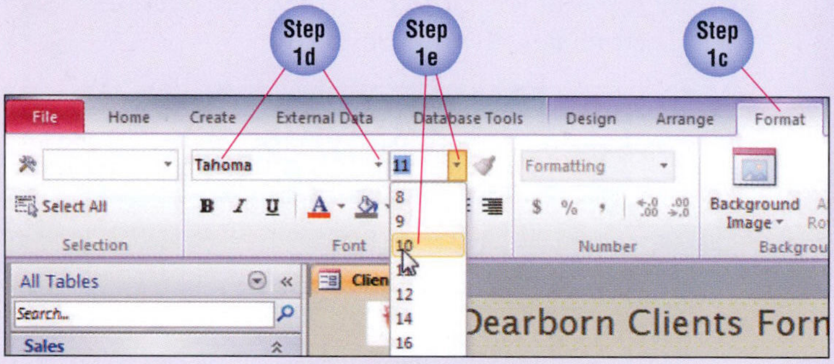

2. Apply formatting and change the alignment of the first column by completing the following steps:
   a. Click the control object containing the field name *ClientID*, hold down the Shift key, click the bottom control object containing field name *Telephone*, and then release the Shift key.
   b. Click the Bold button in the Font group.
   c. Click the Shape Fill button in the Control Formatting group and then click the *Brown, Accent 5, Lighter 60%* color option (located in the ninth column from the left in the *Theme Colors* section).
   d. Click the Shape Outline button in the Control Formatting group and then click the *Brown, Accent 5, Darker 50%* option (last option in the ninth column in the *Theme Colors* section).
   e. Click the Align Text Right button in the Font group.

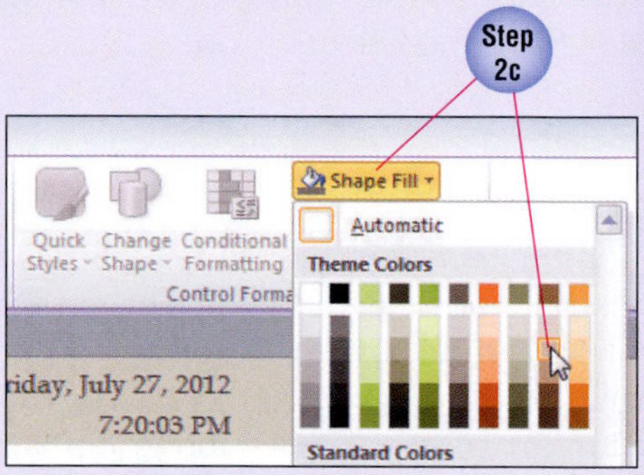

3. Apply shape fill to the second column by completing the following steps:
   a. Click the text box control object containing the text *101*.
   b. Position the mouse pointer at the top border of the selected object until the pointer displays as a small, black, down-pointing arrow and then click the left mouse button. (Make sure all of the objects in the second column are selected.)

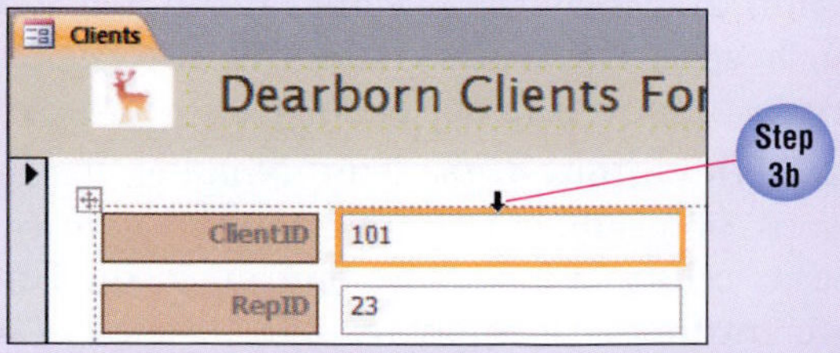

c. Click the Shape Fill button in the Control Formatting group and then click the *Brown, Accent 5, Lighter 80%* color option (located in the ninth column in the *Theme Colors* section).

4. Apply quick styles and change the shape of the Previous Record button by completing the following steps:
   a. Click the Previous Record button (the button on the left).
   b. Click the Quick Styles button in the Control Formatting group and then click the *Subtle Effect - Orange, Accent 6* option (last option in the fourth row).
   c. With the Previous Record button still selected, click the Change Shape button in the Control Formatting group and then click the *Rounded Rectangle* option (last option in the first row).

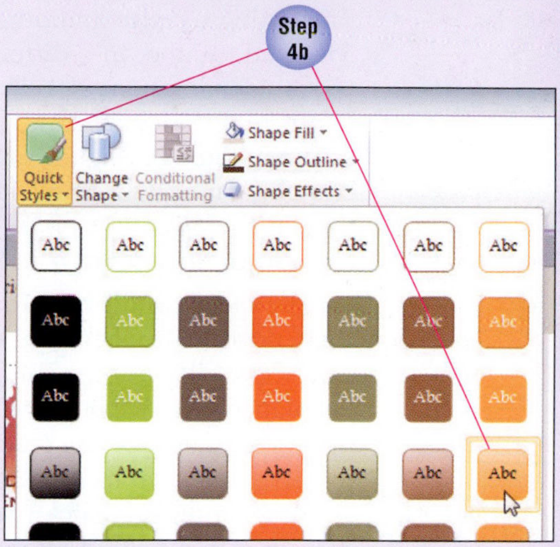

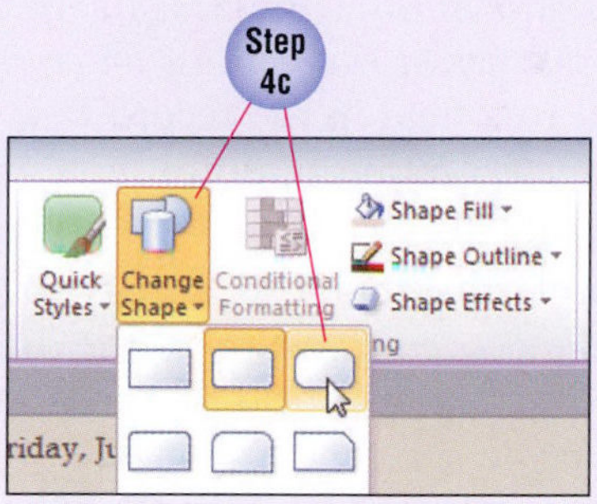

5. Select the Next Record button and then apply the same quick style and shape that you applied to the Previous Record button.
6. Remove the gridlines by completing the following steps:
   a. Click the Form Layout Tools Arrange tab.
   b. Click the Select Layout button in the Rows & Columns group.
   c. Click the Gridlines button in the Table group and then click *None* at the drop-down list.
7. Click the Save button on the Quick Access toolbar to save the Clients form.
8. Insert a background image by completing the following steps:
   a. Click the Form Layout Tools Format tab.
   b. Click the Background Image button in the Background group and then click *Browse* at the drop-down list.
   c. Navigate to the Access2010L1C5 folder on your storage medium and then double-click ***Mountain.jpg***.
   d. View the form and background image in Print Preview. (To display Print Preview, click the File tab, click the Print tab, and then click the Print Preview button.)
   e. After viewing the form in Print Preview, return to the form by clicking the Close Print Preview button.
9. Click the Undo button on the Quick Access toolbar to remove the background image. (If this does not remove the image, close the form without saving it and then reopen the form.)
10. Save the Clients form.

Applying Conditional Formatting

With the Conditional Formatting button in the Control Formatting group, you can apply formatting to data that meets a specific criterion or apply conditional formatting to data in all records in a form. For example, you can apply conditional formatting to sales amounts in a form that displays amounts higher than a specified number in a different color or you can apply conditional formatting to states' names and specify a specific color for companies in a particular state. You can also include conditional formatting that inserts data bars that visually compare data among records. The data bars provide a visual representation of the comparison of data in records. For example, in Project 1g, you will insert data bars in the *Sales 2010* field that provide a visual representation of how the sales amount in one record compares to the sales amount in other records.

To apply conditional formatting, click the Conditional Formatting button in the Control Formatting group and the Conditional Formatting Rules Manager dialog box displays. At this dialog box, click the New Rule button and the New Formatting Rule dialog box displays as shown in Figure 5.3. In the *Select a rule type* option box, choose the *Check values in the current record or use an expression* option if the conditional formatting is applied to a field in the record that matches a specific condition. Click the *Compare to other records* option if you want to insert data bars in a field in all records that compare the data among the records.

If you want to apply conditional formatting to a field, specify the field and field condition with options in the *Edit the rule description* section of the dialog box. Specify the type of formatting you want applied to data in a field that meets the specific criterion. For example, in Project 1g, you will specify that you want to change the shape fill to light green for all *City* fields containing *Indianapolis*. When you have made all the desired changes to the dialog box, click OK to close the dialog box and then click OK to close the Conditional Formatting Rules Manager dialog box.

To insert data bars in a field, click the Conditional Formatting button, click the New Rule button at the Conditional Formatting Rules Manager dialog box, and then click the *Compare to other records* option in the *Select a rule type* section. This changes the options in the dialog box as shown in Figure 5.4. Make the desired changes in the *Edit the rule description* section.

Figure 5.3 New Formatting Rule Dialog Box

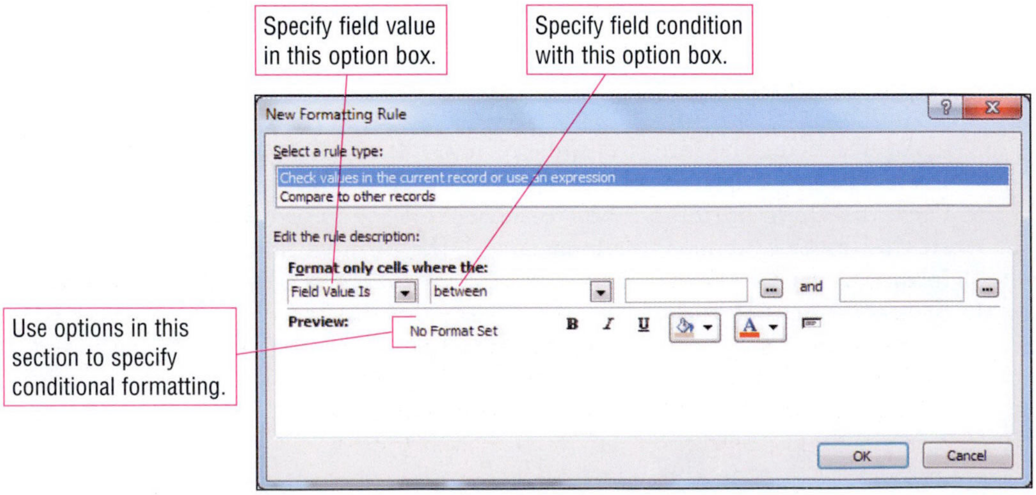

Figure 5.4 New Formatting Rule Dialog Box with Compare to Other Records Option Selected

Click this option to insert data bars that visually compare data among records.

Use options in this section to specify formatting of data bars.

New Formatting Rule

Select a rule type:

Check values in the current record or use an expression
Compare to other records

Edit the rule description:

Data Bar format settings:
☐ Show Bar only

	Shortest Bar	Longest bar
Type:	Lowest value	Highest value
Value:	(Lowest value)	(Highest value)

Bar color [] Preview: []

OK Cancel

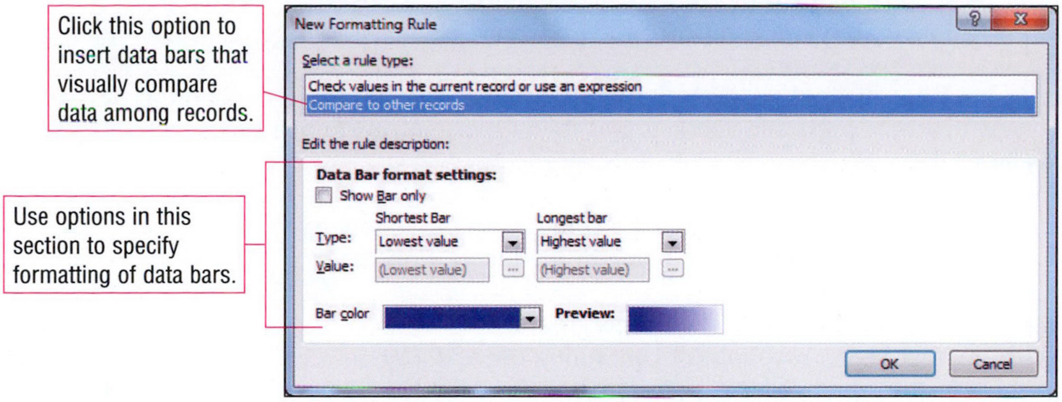

Project 1g **Applying Conditional Formatting to Fields in Forms** **Part 7 of 7**

1. With the Clients form open in the **AL1-C5-Dearborn.accdb** database, apply conditional formatting so that the *City* field displays any Indianapolis entries with a light green shape fill by completing the following steps:

 a. Click in the text box control object containing the text *Muncie*.

 b. Click the Form Layout Tools Format tab.

 c. Click the Conditional Formatting button in the Control Formatting group.

 d. At the Conditional Formatting Rules Manager dialog box, click the New Rule button.

 e. At the New Formatting Rule dialog box, click the down-pointing arrow at the right side of the option box containing the word *between* and then click *equal to* at the drop-down list.

 f. Click in the text box to the right of the *equal to* option box and then type **Indianapolis**.

 g. Click the Background color button arrow and then click the *Green 2* color option (located in the seventh column).

 h. Click OK to close the New Formatting Rule dialog box.

 i. Click OK to close the Conditional Formatting Rules Manager dialog box.

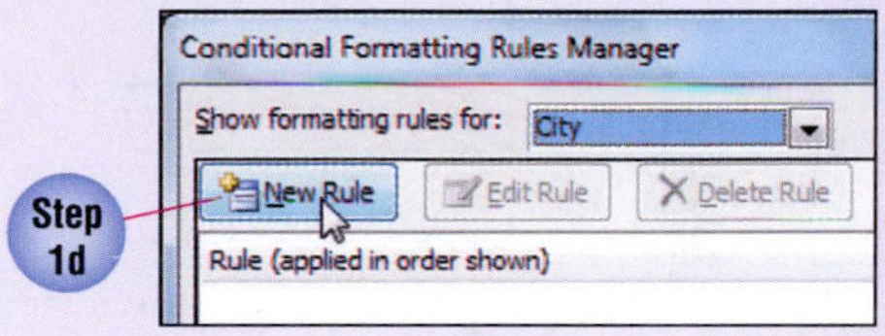

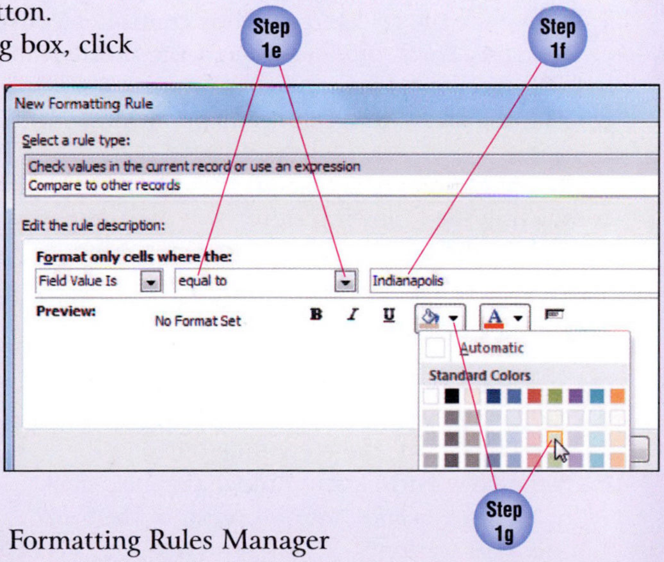

2. Click the Home tab and then click the View button to switch to Form view.

3. Click the Next Record button (one of the buttons you inserted) to display the next record in the form. Continue clicking the Next Record button to view records and notice that *Indianapolis* displays with light green shading fill.

4. Click the First Record button in the Navigation bar.

5. Click the Save button on the Quick Access toolbar.

Conditional Formatting Rules Manager

Show formatting rules for: City

🔧 New Rule ✏ Edit Rule ✖ Delete Rule

Rule (applied in order shown)

Step 1d

Step 1e *Step 1f*

New Formatting Rule

Select a rule type:

Check values in the current record or use an expression
Compare to other records

Edit the rule description:

Format only cells where the:

Field Value Is ▼ | equal to ▼ | Indianapolis

Preview: No Format Set **B** *I* <u>U</u> 🎨 ▼ **A** ▼ ▦

Automatic

Standard Colors

Step 1g

6. Print page 1 of the form by completing the following steps:
   a. Click the File tab and then click the Print tab.
   b. Click the *Print* option.
   c. At the Print dialog box, click the *Pages* option in the *Print Range* section, type 1 in the *From* text box, press the Tab key, and then type 1 in the *To* text box.
   d. Click OK.
7. Close the Clients form.
8. Create a form with the Sales table by completing the following steps:
   a. Click once on the Sales table name in the Navigation pane.
   b. Click the Create tab.
   c. Click the Form button in the Forms group.
9. With the text box control object containing the text *101* selected, drag the right border to the left until the border is positioned as shown in the image below. (The right border should be positioned approximately one inch to the right of the sales amounts.)

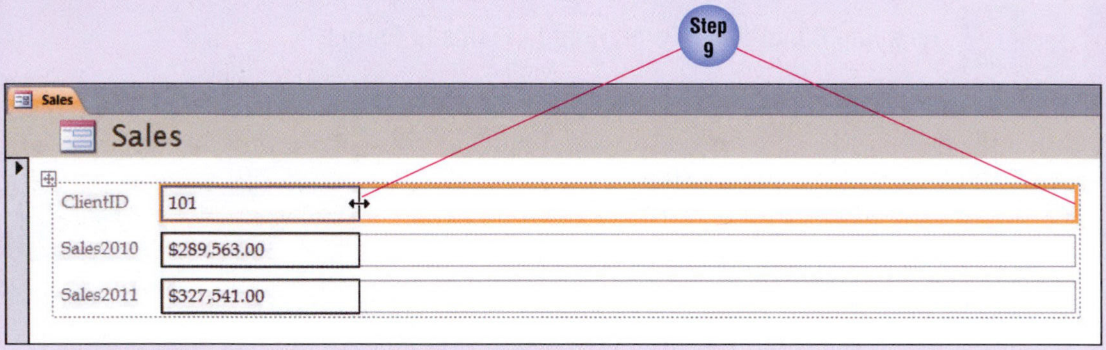

10. Change the alignment of text by completing the following steps:
    a. Right-click the selected text box control object (the object containing the text *101*) and then click *Select Entire Column* at the shortcut menu.
    b. Click the Form Layout Tools Format tab.
    c. Click the Align Text Right button in the Font group.
11. Apply data bars to the *Sales2010* field by completing the following steps:
    a. Click in the text box control object containing the text *$289,563.00*.
    b. Make sure the Form Layout Tools Format tab is active.
    c. Click the Conditional Formatting button.
    d. At the Conditional Formatting Rules Manager dialog box, click the New Rule button.
    e. At the New Formatting Rule dialog box, click the *Compare to other records* option in the *Select a rule type* section.
    f. Click the down-pointing arrow at the right side of the *Bar color* option box and then click the *Green 3* color option (located in the seventh column).
    g. Click OK to close the New Formatting Rule dialog box and then click OK to close the Conditional Formatting Rules Manager dialog box.

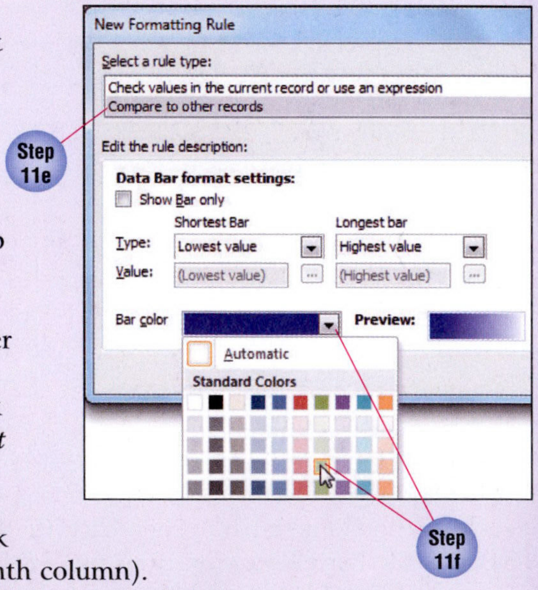

12. Click in the text box control object containing the text *$327,541.00* and then apply the same data bars that you applied to the *Sales2010* field.

13. Click the Next Record button in the Navigation bar to display the next record. Continue clicking the Next Record button and notice the data bars that display in the *Sales2010* and *Sales2011* fields.
14. Click the First Record button in the Navigation bar.
15. Click the Save button on the Quick Access toolbar. At the Save As dialog box with *Sales* inserted in the *Form Name* text box, click OK.
16. Print page 1 of the form by completing the following steps:
    a. Click the File tab and then click the Print tab.
    b. Click the *Print* option.
    c. At the Print dialog box, click the *Pages* option in the *Print Range* section, type 1 in the *From* text box, press the Tab key, type 1 in the *To* text box, and then click OK.
17. Close the Sales form.
18. Close the **AL1-C5-Dearborn.accdb** database.

Project 2 Add Fields, Create a Split and Multiple Items Form, and Use the Form Wizard — 5 Parts

You will open the Skyline database, create a form and add related fields to the form, create a split and multiple items form, and create a form using the Form Wizard.

Adding Existing Fields

If you create a form and then realize that you forgot a field or want to insert an existing field in the form, display the form in Layout view and then click the Add Existing Fields button located in the Tools group in the Form Layout Tools Design tab. When you click the Add Existing Fields button, the Field List pane opens and displays at the right side of the screen. This pane displays the fields available in the current view, fields available in related tables, and fields available in other tables. Figure 5.5 displays the Field List pane you will open in Project 2a.

HINT
Alt + F8 is the keyboard shortcut to display the Field List pane.

HINT
Use the Field List pane to add fields from a table or query to your form.

Add Existing Fields

In the *Fields available for this view* section, Access displays all fields in any tables used to create the form. So far, you have been creating a form with all fields in one table. In the *Fields available in related tables*, Access displays tables that are related to the table(s) used to create the form. To display the fields in the related table, click the plus symbol that displays before the table name in the Field List pane and the list expands to display all field names.

To add a field to the form, double-click the desired field in the Field List pane. This inserts the field below the existing fields in the form. You can also drag a field from the Field List pane into the form. To do this, position the mouse pointer on the desired field in the Field List window, hold down the left mouse button, drag into the form window, and then release the mouse button. A yellow insert indicator bar displays as you drag the field in the existing fields in the form. When you drag over a cell, the cell displays with yellow fill. When the insert indicator bar is in the desired position or the desired cell is selected, release the mouse button.

You can insert multiple fields in a form from the Field List pane. To do this, hold down the Ctrl key while clicking the desired fields and then drag the fields into the form. If you try to drag a field from a table in the *Fields available in other*

Figure 5.5 Field List Pane

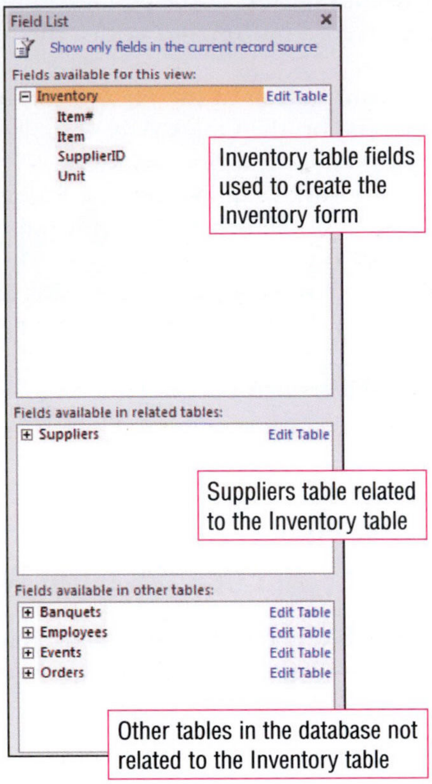

tables section, the Specify Relationship dialog box will display. To move a field from the Field List pane to the form, the field must be located in a table that is related to the table(s) used to create the form.

Project 2a Adding Existing Fields to a Form

Part 1 of 5

1. Display the Open dialog box with Access2010L1C5 on your storage medium the active folder, open the **AL1-C5-Skyline.accdb** database, and enable the contents.
2. Create a form with the Inventory table by clicking the Inventory table name in the Navigation pane, clicking the Create tab, and then clicking the Form button in the Forms group.
3. With the text box control object containing the text *001* selected, drag the right border to the left until the selected object is approximately one-half of the original width. (See the image below.)

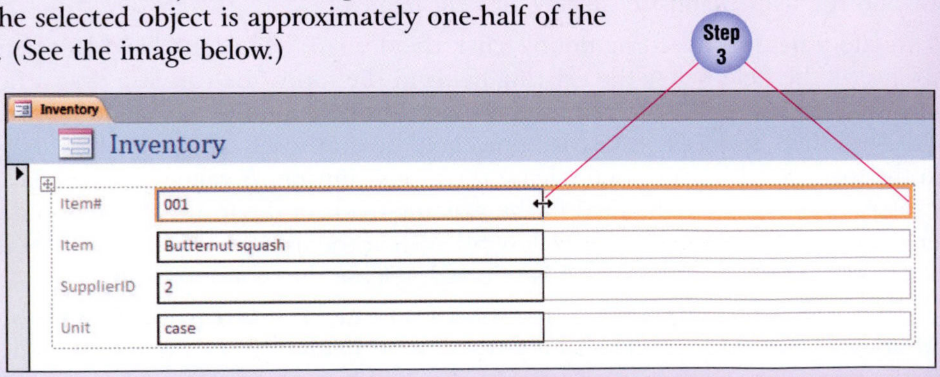

4. With the text box control object still selected, click the Form Layout Tools Arrange tab and then click the Split Horizontally button in the Merge/Split group. (This splits the text box control object into one object and one empty cell.)
5. You decide that you want to add the supplier name to the form so the name displays when entering a form. Add the supplier name field by completing the following steps:
   a. Click the Form Layout Tools Design tab.
   b. Click the Add Existing Fields button in the Tools group in the Form Layout Tools Design tab.
   c. Click the Show all tables hyperlink that displays toward the top of the Field List pane.

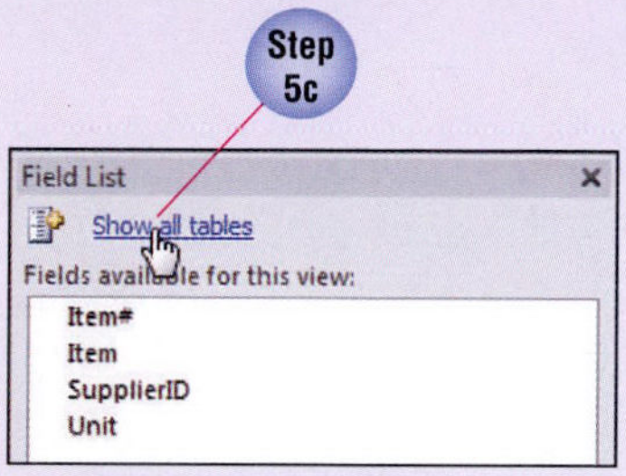

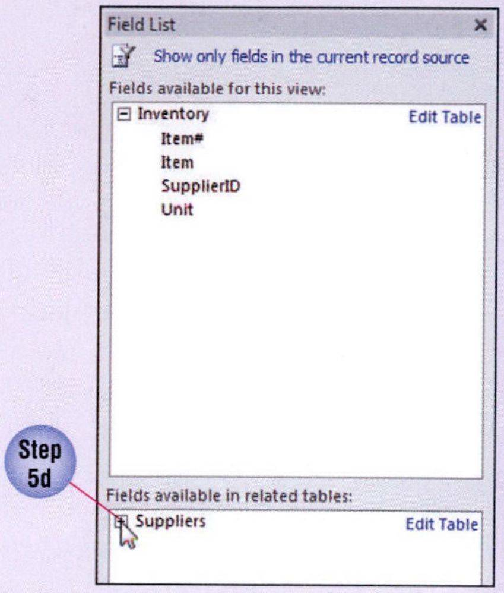

   d. Click the plus symbol that displays immediately left of the Suppliers table name located in the *Fields available in related tables* section of the Field List window.
   e. Position the mouse pointer on the *SupplierName* field, hold down the left mouse button, drag into the form until the yellow insert indicator bar displays immediately right of the text box control containing *2* (the text box control that displays at the right side of the *SupplierID* label control), and then release the mouse button. Access inserts the field as a Lookup field (down-pointing arrow displays at right side of field).

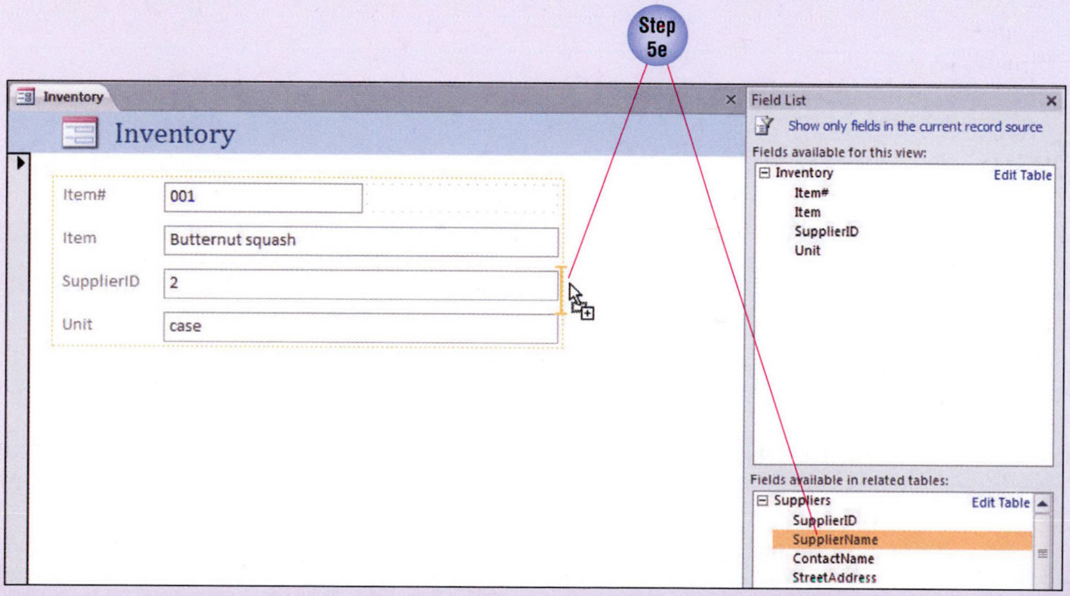

f. Change the *SupplierName* field from a Lookup field to a text box by clicking the Options button that displays below the field and then clicking *Change to Text Box* at the drop-down list. (This removes the down-pointing arrow at the right side of the field.)

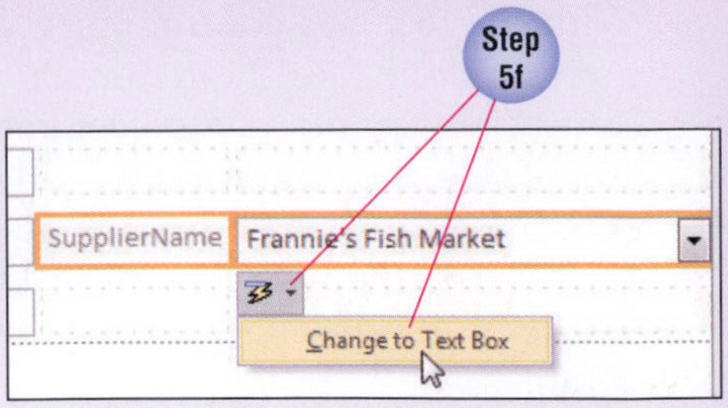

g. Close the Field List pane by clicking the Close button located in the upper right corner of the window.

6. Insert a logo image in the *Form Header* section by completing the following steps:
   a. Right-click the logo object that displays in the *Form Header* section (located to the left of the title *Inventory*) and then click *Delete* at the shortcut menu.
   b. Click the Logo button in the Header/Footer group.
   c. At the Insert Picture dialog box, navigate to the Access2010L1C5 folder on your storage medium and then double-click the file named ***Cityscape.jpg***.
7. Change the title by completing the following steps:
   a. Click the Title button in the Header/Footer group. (This selects *Inventory* in the *Form Header* section.)
   b. Type **Skyline Inventory Input Form** and then press Enter.
8. Insert the date and time in the *Form Header* section by clicking the Date and Time button in the Header/Footer group and then clicking OK at the Date and Time dialog box.
9. Click in any field outside the title, click the title to select the control object, and then drag the right border of the title control object to the left until the border displays near the title.
10. Select the date and time control objects, drag in the left border until the border displays near the date and time, and then drag the objects so they are positioned near the title.
11. Scroll through the records in the form.
12. Click the First Record button in the Record Navigation bar.
13. Click the Save button on the Quick Access toolbar and save the form with the name *Inventory*.
14. Print the current record.
15. Close the Inventory form.

Creating a Split Form

Quick Steps

Create a Split Form
1. Click desired table.
2. Click Create tab.
3. Click More Forms button.
4. Click *Split Form*.

More Forms

You can create a form by choosing the *Split Form* option at the More Forms button drop-down list in the Forms group in the Create tab. When you use this option to create a form, Access splits the screen in the work area and provides two views for the form. The top half of the work area displays the form in Layout view and the bottom half of the work area displays the form in Datasheet view. The two views are connected and are ***synchronous***, which means that displaying or modifying a specific field in the Form view portion will cause the same action to occur in the field in the Datasheet view portion. Figure 5.6 displays the split form you will create for Project 2b.

Figure 5.6 Split Form

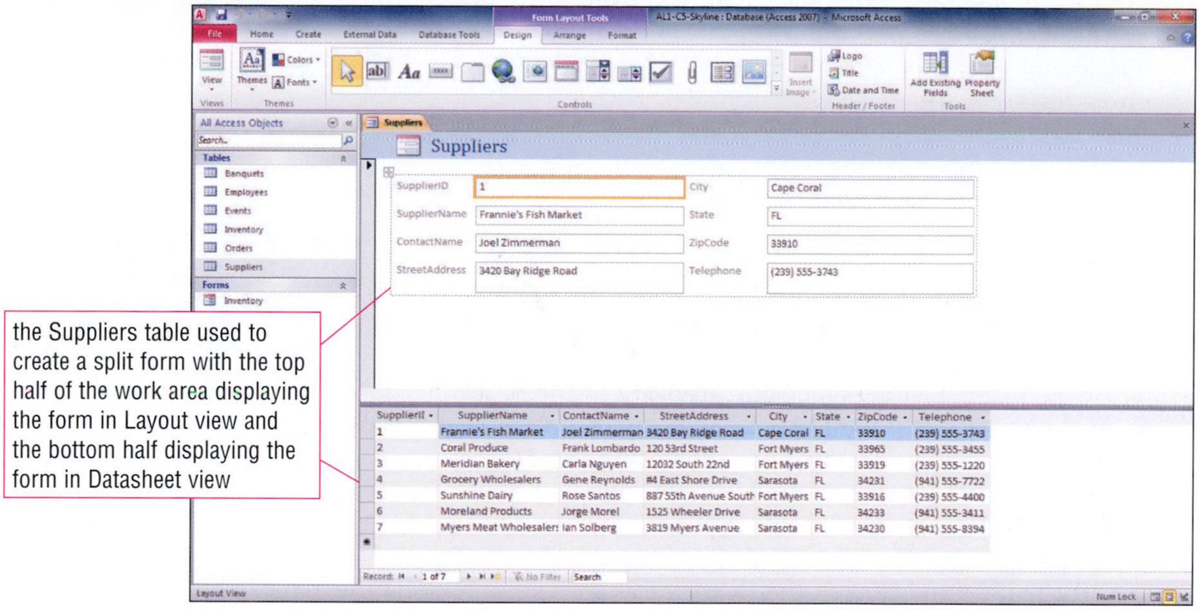

the Suppliers table used to create a split form with the top half of the work area displaying the form in Layout view and the bottom half displaying the form in Datasheet view

Project 2b Creating a Split Form

Part 2 of 5

1. With the **AL1-C5-Skyline.accdb** database open, create a split form with the Suppliers table by completing the following steps:
   a. Click the Suppliers table in the Navigation pane.
   b. Click the Create tab.
   c. Click the More Forms button in the Forms group and then click *Split Form* at the drop-down list.

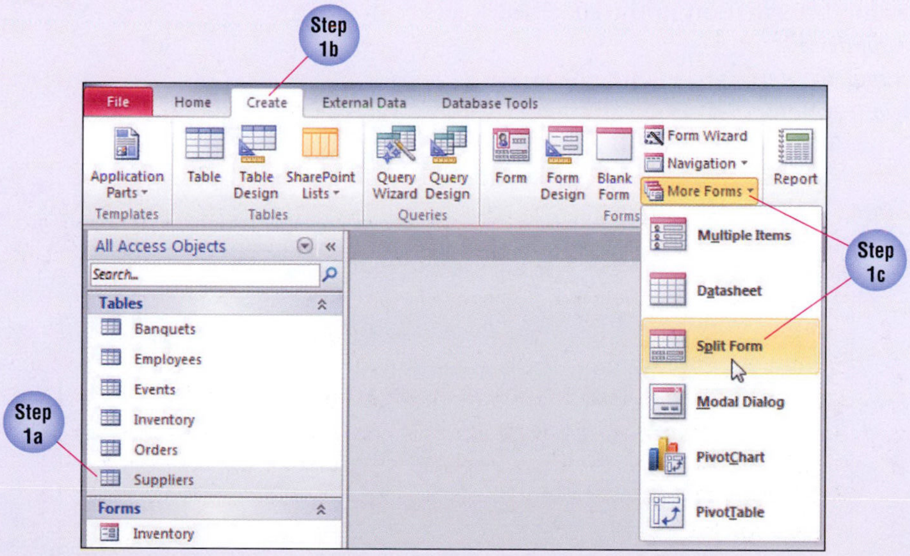

   d. Click several times on the Next Record button in the Navigation bar. (As you display records, notice that the current record in the Form view in the top portion of the window is the same record selected in Datasheet view in the lower portion of the window.)

2. Apply a theme by clicking the Themes button in the Themes group in the Form Layout Tools Design tab and then clicking *Adjacency* at the drop-down gallery.

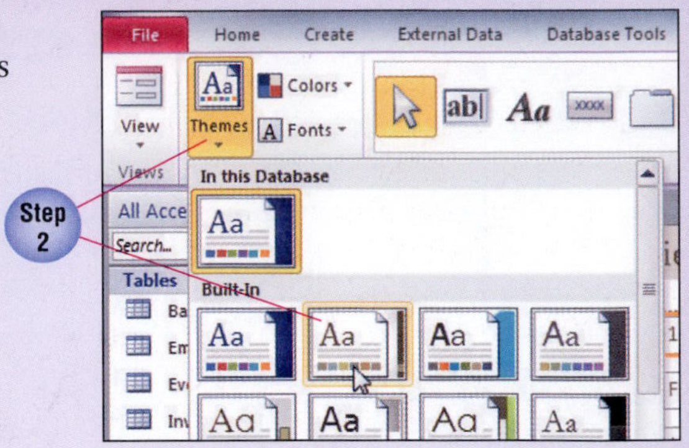

3. Insert a logo image in the *Form Header* section by completing the following steps:
   a. Right-click the logo object that displays in the *Form Header* section (located to the left of the title *Clients*) and then click *Delete* at the shortcut menu.
   b. Click the Logo button in the Header/Footer group.
   c. At the Insert Picture dialog box, navigate to the Access2010L1C5 folder on your storage medium and then double-click the file named ***Cityscape.jpg***.
4. Change the title by completing the following steps:
   a. Click the Title button in the Header/Footer group. (This selects *Suppliers* in the *Form Header* section.)
   b. Type **Skyline Suppliers Input Form** and then press Enter.
5. Insert the date and time in the *Form Header* section by clicking the Date and Time button in the Header/Footer group and then clicking OK at the Date and Time dialog box.
6. Click in any field outside the title, click the title to select the control object, and then drag the right border of the title control object to the left until the border displays near the title.
7. Select the date and time control objects, drag in the left border until the border displays near the date and time, and then drag the objects so they are positioned so the right border is aligned with the right side of the field value *Cape Coral*.
8. Insert a new record in the Suppliers form by completing the following steps:
   a. Click the View button to switch to Form view.
   b. Click the New (blank) Record button in the Record Navigation bar.
   c. Click in the *SupplierID* field in the Form view portion of the window and then type the following information in the specified fields:

      SupplierID = **8**
      SupplierName = **Jackson Produce**
      ContactName = **Marshall Jackson**
      StreetAddress = **5790 Cypress Avenue**
      City = **Fort Myers**
      State = **FL**
      ZipCode = **33917**
      Telephone = **2395555002**

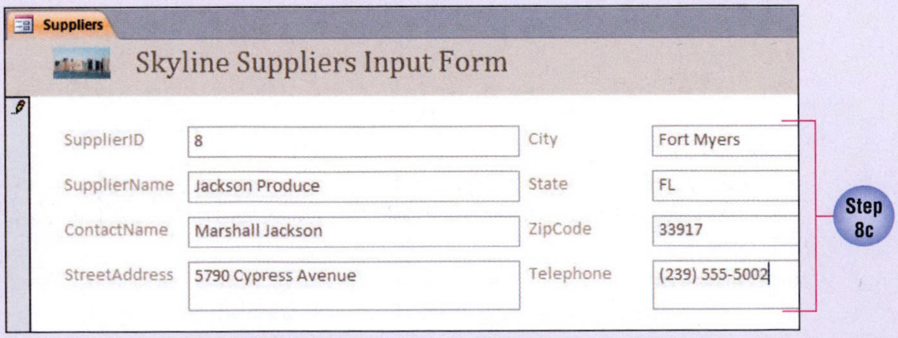

9. Click the Save button on the Quick Access toolbar and save the form with the name *Suppliers*.

10. Print the current form by completing the following steps:
    a. Click the File tab and then click the Print tab.
    b. Click the *Print* option.
    c. At the Print dialog box, click the Setup button.
    d. At the Page Setup dialog box, click the *Print Form Only* option in the *Split Form* section of the dialog box and then click OK.
    e. At the Print dialog box, click the *Selected Record(s)* option and then click OK.
11. Close the Suppliers form.

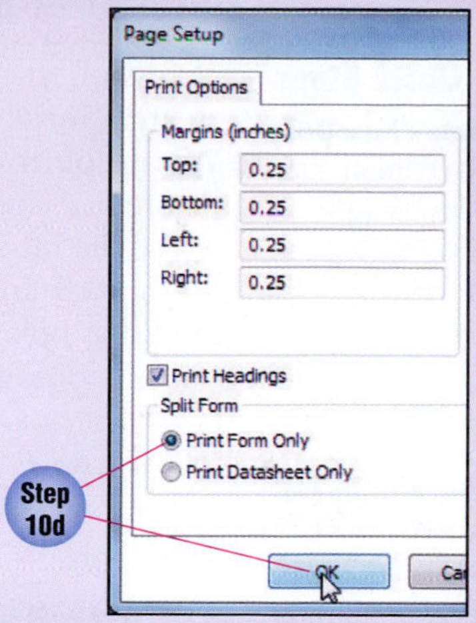

Creating a Multiple Items Form

When you create a form with the Form button, a single record displays. You can use the *Multiple Items* option at the More Forms button drop-down list to create a form that displays multiple records. The advantage to creating a multiple items form over displaying the table in Datasheet view is that you can customize the form using buttons in the Form Layout Tools ribbon with the Design, Arrange, or Format tab selected.

Quick Steps

Create a Multiple Items Form
1. Click desired table.
2. Click Create tab.
3. Click More Forms button.
4. Click *Multiple Items*.

Project 2c **Creating a Multiple Items Form** Part 3 of 5

1. With the **AL1-C5-Skyline.accdb** database open, create a multiple items form by completing the following steps:
    a. Click the Orders table in the Navigation pane.
    b. Click the Create tab.
    c. Click the More Forms button in the Forms group and then click *Multiple Items* at the drop-down list.
2. Insert the **Cityscape.jpg** image as the logo.
3. Insert the title *Skyline Orders*.
4. Insert the date and time in the *Form Header* section.
5. Decrease the border of the title control object and then size and move the date and time control objects so they display near the title.
6. Save the form with the name *Orders*.
7. Print the first record in the form by completing the following steps:
    a. Click the File tab and then click the Print tab.
    b. Click the *Print* option.
    c. At the Print dialog box, click the *Pages* option in the *Print Range* section.
    d. Type 1 in the *From* text box, press the Tab key, and then type 1 in the *To* text box.
    e. Click OK.
8. Close the Orders form.

Creating a Form Using the Form Wizard

Quick Steps

Create a Form Using Form Wizard

1. Click Create tab.
2. Click Form Wizard button.
3. Choose desired options at each Form Wizard dialog box.

HINT

With the Form Wizard, you can be more selective about what fields you insert in a form.

Form Wizard

Access offers a Form Wizard that guides you through the creation of a form. To create a form using the Form Wizard, click the Create tab and then click the Form Wizard button in the Forms group. At the first Form Wizard dialog box, shown in Figure 5.7, specify the table and then the fields you want included in the form. To select the table, click the down-pointing arrow at the right side of the *Table/Queries* option box and then click the desired table. Select the desired field in the *Available Fields* list box and then click the button containing the One Field button (the button containing the greater than symbol). This inserts the field in the *Selected Fields* list box. Continue in this manner until you have inserted all desired fields in the *Selected Fields* list box. If you want to insert all fields into the *Selected Fields* list box at one time, click the All Fields button (button containing two greater than symbols). After specifying fields, click the Next button.

At the second Form Wizard dialog box, specify the layout for the records. You can choose from *Columnar*, *Tabular*, *Datasheet*, and *Justified*. Click the Next button and the third and final Form Wizard dialog box displays and offers a title for the form and also provides the option *Open the form to view or enter information*. Make any necessary changes in this dialog box and then click the Finish button.

Figure 5.7 First Form Wizard Dialog Box

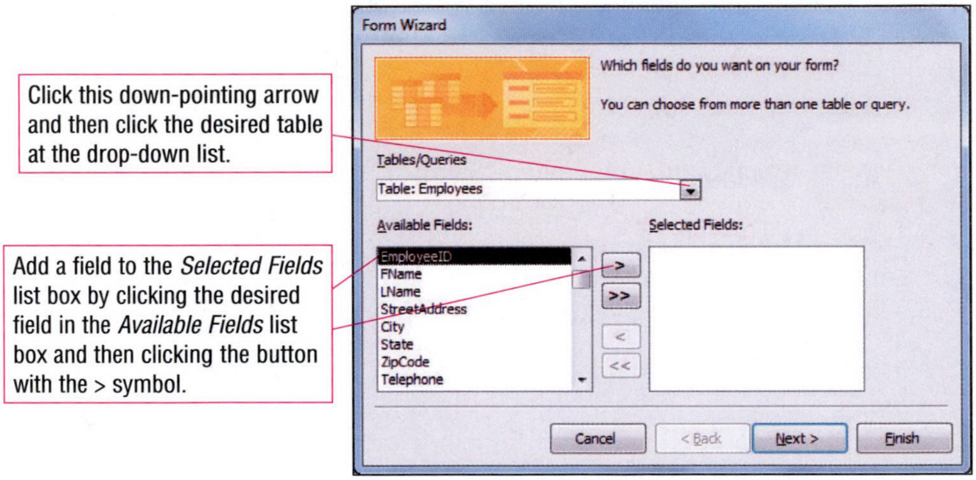
Click this down-pointing arrow and then click the desired table at the drop-down list.
Add a field to the Selected Fields list box by clicking the desired field in the Available Fields list box and then clicking the button with the > symbol.
Form Wizard
Which fields do you want on your form?
You can choose from more than one table or query.
Tables/Queries
Table: Employees
Available Fields:
Selected Fields:
EmployeeID
FName
LName
StreetAddress
City
State
ZipCode
Telephone
Cancel
< Back
Next >
Finish

Project 2d Creating a Form Using the Form Wizard — Part 4 of 5

1. With the **AL1-C5-Skyline.accdb** database open, create a form with the Form Wizard by completing the following steps:
   a. Click the Create tab.
   b. Click the Form Wizard button in the Forms group.

c. At the first Form Wizard dialog box, click the down-pointing arrow at the right side of the *Tables/Queries* option box and then click *Table: Employees* at the drop-down list.
d. Specify that you want all fields included in the form by clicking the All Fields button (button containing the two greater than symbols).
e. Click the Next button.
f. At the second Form Wizard dialog box, click the *Justified* option and then click the Next button.

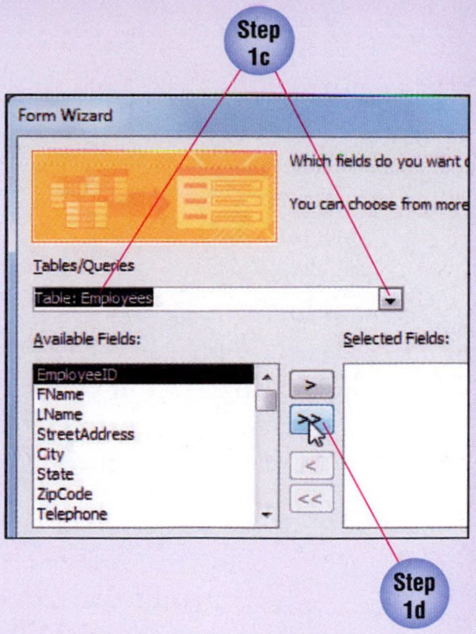

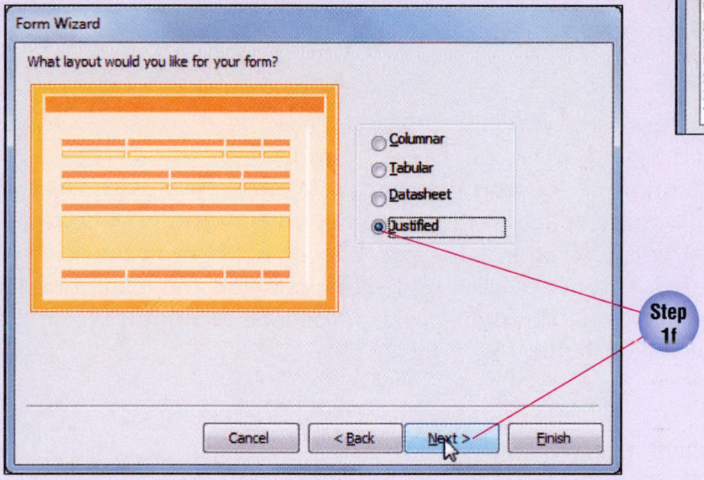

g. At the third and final Form Wizard dialog box, click the Finish button.
2. Format the field headings by completing the following steps:
a. Click the View button to switch to Layout view.
b. Click the *EmployeeID* label control object. (This selects the object.)
c. Hold down the Ctrl key and then click on each of the following label control objects: *FName*, *LName*, *StreetAddress*, *City*, *State*, *ZipCode*, *Telephone*, *HireDate*, and *HealthIns*.
d. With all of the label control objects selected, release the Ctrl key.
e. Click the Form Layout Tools Format tab.
f. Click the Shape Fill button and then click the *Aqua Blue 2* color option (located in the ninth column in the *Standard Colors* section).
g. Click the Form Layout Tools Design tab and then click the View button to switch to Form view.
3. In Form view, click the New (blank) Record button and then add the following records:

EmployeeID = 13
FirstName = Carol
LastName = Thompson
StreetAddress = 6554 Willow Drive, Apt. B
City = Fort Myers
State = FL
ZipCode = 33915
Telephone = 2395553719
HireDate = 10/1/2011
HealthIns = *(Click in the check box to insert a check mark.)*

EmployeeID	=	14
FirstName	=	Eric
LastName	=	Hahn
StreetAddress	=	331 South 152nd Street
City	=	Cape Coral
State	=	FL
ZipCode	=	33906
Telephone	=	2395558107
HireDate	=	10/1/2011
HealthIns	=	*(Leave blank.)*

4. Click the Save button on the Quick Access toolbar.
5. Print the record for Eric Hahn and then print the record for Carol Thompson.
6. Close the Employees form.

In Project 2d you used the Form Wizard to create a form with all of the fields in one table. If tables are related, you can create a form using fields from related tables. At the first Form Wizard dialog box, choose fields from the selected table and then choose fields from a related table. To change to the related table, click the down-pointing arrow at the right of the *Tables/Queries* option box and then click the name of the desired table.

Project 2e Creating a Form with Related Tables

Part 5 of 5

1. With the **AL1-C5-Skyline.accdb** database open, create a form with related tables by completing the following steps:
   a. Click the Create tab.
   b. Click the Form Wizard button in the Forms group.
   c. At the first Form Wizard dialog box, click the down-pointing arrow at the right of the *Tables/Queries* option box and then click *Table: Banquets*.
   d. Click *ResDate* in the *Available Fields* list box and then click the One Field button (button containing one greater than symbol). (This inserts *ResDate* in the *Selected Fields* list box.)
   e. Click *AmountTotal* in the *Available Fields* list box and then click the One Field button.
   f. Click *AmountPaid* in the *Available Fields* list box and then click the One Field button.
   g. Click the down-pointing arrow at the right side of the *Tables/Queries* option box and then click *Table: Events* at the drop-down list.
   h. Click *Event* in the *Available Fields* list box and then click the One Field button.
   i. Click the down-pointing arrow at the right side of the *Tables/Queries* option box and then click *Table: Employees* at the drop-down list.

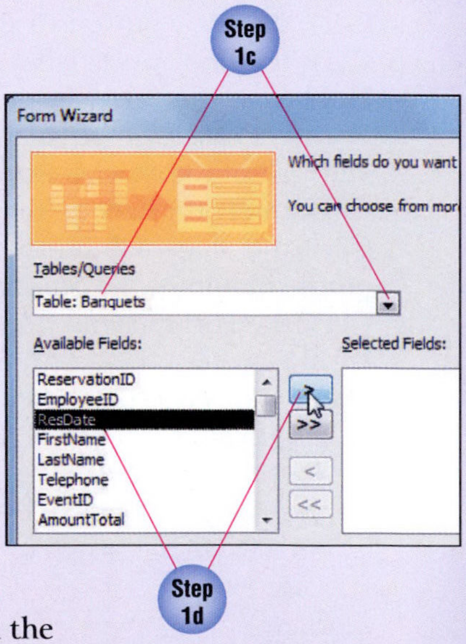

j. Click *LName* in the *Available Fields* list box and then click the One Field button.
k. Click the Next button.
l. At the second Form Wizard dialog box, click the Next button.
m. At the third Form Wizard dialog box, click the Next button.
n. At the fourth Form Wizard dialog box, select the text in the *What title do you want for your form?* text box, type **Upcoming Banquets**, and then click the Finish button.

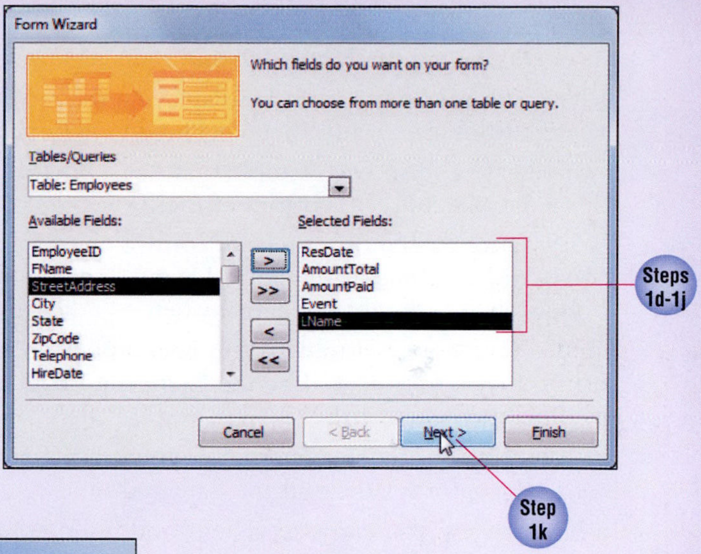

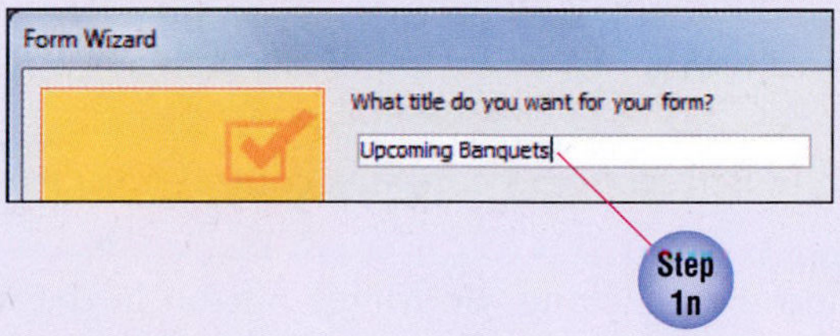

2. When the first record displays, print the record.
3. Save and then close the form.
4. Close the **AL1-C5-Skyline.accdb** database.

Chapter Summary

- A form generally improves the ease with which data is entered into a table. Some methods for creating a form include using the Form, Split Form, or Multiple Items buttons or the Form Wizard.
- A form is an object you can use to enter and edit data in a table or query and to help prevent incorrect data from being entered in a database.
- The simplest method for creating a form is to click a table in the Navigation pane, click the Create button, and then click the Form button in the Forms group.
- When you create a form, it displays in Layout view. Use this view to display data as well as modify the appearance and contents of the form. Other form views include Form view and Design view. Use Form view to enter and manage records and use Design view to view the structure of the form and modify the form.
- Open an existing form in Layout View by right-clicking the form in the Navigation pane and then clicking *Layout View* at the shortcut menu.
- Print a form with options at the Print dialog box. To print an individual record, display the Print dialog box, click the *Selected Record(s)* option, and then click OK.

- Navigate in a form with buttons in the Record Navigation bar.
- Add a new record to a form by clicking the New Record button in the Record Navigation bar or by clicking the Home tab and then clicking the New button in the Records group.
- Delete a record from a form by displaying the record, clicking the Home tab, clicking the Delete button arrow, and then clicking *Delete Record* at the drop-down list.
- If you create a form with a table that has a one-to-many relationship established, Access adds a datasheet at the bottom of the form.
- A form is comprised of a series of control objects and you can customize these control objects with buttons in the Form Layout Tools ribbon with the Design tab, Arrange tab, or Format tab. These tabs are active when you display a form in Layout view.
- Apply a theme to a form with the Themes button in the Themes group in the Form Layout Tools Design tab. Use the Colors and Fonts buttons in the Themes group to further customize a theme.
- With buttons in the Header/Footer group in the Form Layout Tools Design tab, you can insert a logo, form title, and the date and time.
- In Layout view, you can size, delete, and insert control objects.
- In the Rows & Columns group in the Form Layout Tools Arrange tab, you can use buttons to select or insert rows or columns.
- The Controls group in the Form Layout Tools Design tab contains control objects you can insert in a form.
- Merge cells in a form by selecting cells and then clicking the Merge button in the Merge/Split group in the Form Layout Tools Arrange tab. Split selected cells by clicking the Split Vertically or Split Horizontally button.
- Format control objects and cells in a form with buttons in the Form Layout Tools Format tab.
- Use the Conditional Formatting button in the Control Formatting group in the Form Layout Tools Format tab to apply specific formatting to data that matches a specific criterion.
- Click the Add Existing Fields button in the Tools group in the Form Layout Tools Design tab to display the Field List pane. Add fields to the form by double-clicking on or dragging the field from the pane.
- Create a split form by clicking the More Forms button and then clicking *Split Form* in the drop-down list. Access displays the form in Form view in the top portion of the work area and the form in Datasheet view in the bottom of the work area. The two views are connected and are synchronous.
- Create a Multiple Items form by clicking the More Forms button and then clicking *Multiple Items* in the drop-down list.
- The Form Wizard walks you through the steps for creating a form and lets you specify the fields you want included in the form, a layout for the records, and a name for the form.
- You can create a form with the Form Wizard that contains fields from tables connected by a one-to-many relationship.

Commands Review

FEATURE	RIBBON TAB, GROUP	BUTTON, OPTION
Form	Create, Forms	
Conditional Formatting Rules Manager dialog box	Form Layout Tools Format, Control Formatting	
Field List pane	Form Layout Tools Design, Tools	
Split Form	Create, Forms	, Split Form
Multiple Items form	Create, Forms	, Multiple Items
Form Wizard	Create, Forms	

Concepts Check Test Your Knowledge

Completion: In the space provided at the right, indicate the correct term, symbol, or command.

1. The simplest method to create a form is to click this tab and then click the Form button. ____________
2. When you click the Form button to create a form, the form displays in this view. ____________
3. To print the current record in a form, click this option at the Print dialog box and then click OK. ____________
4. Navigate in a form using buttons in this bar. ____________
5. Click this button to add a new record to a form. ____________
6. The Form Layout Tools Design tab is active when a form displays in this view. ____________
7. The Themes group in the Form Layout Tools Design tab contains three buttons—the Themes button, the Colors button, and this button. ____________
8. Click the Logo button in the Form Layout Tools Design tab and this dialog box displays. ____________
9. To select nonadjacent objects or cells, hold down this key on the keyboard while clicking the desired objects or cells. ____________

10. This group in the Form Layout Tools Arrange tab contains buttons for selecting and inserting rows and columns in a form. ____________

11. With this button in the Control Formatting group in the Form Layout Tools Format tab, you can apply formatting to data that meets a specific criterion. ____________

12. Click the Add Existing Fields button in the Tools group in the Form Layout Tools Design tab and this pane displays. ____________

13. When you create a form with the *Split Form* option, the form displays in this view in the top half of the work area. ____________

14. Create a split form or a multiple items form with options in this button drop-down list. ____________

Skills Check Assess Your Performance

Assessment 1

CREATE AND CUSTOMIZE A SALES FORM

1. Display the Open dialog box with Access2010L1C5 on your storage medium the active folder.
2. Open the **AL1-C5-PacTrek.accdb** database and enable the contents.
3. Use the Form button in the Forms group in the Create tab to create a form with the Suppliers table.
4. Switch to Form view and then add the following records to the Suppliers form:

Supplier#	=	**12**
SupplierName	=	**Seaside Suppliers**
StreetAddress	=	**4120 Shoreline Drive**
City	=	**Vancouver**
Prov/State	=	**BC**
PostalCode	=	**V2V 8K4**
EmailAddress	=	**seaside@emcp.net**
Telephone	=	**6045557945**

Supplier#	=	**34**
SupplierName	=	**Carson Company**
StreetAddress	=	**120 Plaza Center**
City	=	**Vancouver**
Prov/State	=	**BC**
PostalCode	=	**V2V 1K6**
EmailAddress	=	**carson@emcp.net**
Telephone	=	**6045551955**

5. Delete the record containing information on Manning, Inc.
6. Switch to Layout view and then apply the Civic theme to the form.

7. Select and delete the logo object in the *Form Header* section and then click the Logo button in the Header/Footer group. At the Insert Picture dialog box, navigate to the Access2010L1C5 folder on your storage medium and then double-click ***River.jpg***.
8. Create the title *Pacific Trek Suppliers* for the form. Click in any field outside the title and then click in the title (selects the title). Drag the right border of the title control object to the left until the border displays near the title.
9. Insert the date and time in the *Form Header* section.
10. Select the date and time control objects, drag in the left border until the border displays near the date and time, and then drag the objects so they are positioned near the title.
11. Click the text box control object containing the supplier number and then drag the right border to the left until the border displays approximately one inch to the right of the longest entry in the record.
12. Select the bottom row (the row containing the *Telephone* label control object) and the text box control object containing the telephone number and then insert a new row below the current row.
13. Click in the empty cell below the telephone number and then split the cell horizontally.
14. Click in the empty cell at the left side of the bottom row and then insert a Button control that, when clicked, displays the previous record.
15. Click in the empty cell at the right side of the bottom row and then insert a Button control that, when clicked, displays the next record.
16. Select the fields in the first column (*Supplier#* through *Telephone*) and then apply the following formatting:
    a. Apply bold formatting.
    b. Change the font color to *Dark Blue* (last option in the ninth column in the *Standard Colors* section).
    c. Change the alignment to Align Text Right.
    d. Apply the *Light Blue 2* shape fill (located in the fifth column in the *Standard Colors* section).
    e. Change the shape outline color to *Dark Blue* (last option in the ninth column in the *Standard Colors* section).
17. Select the second column and then apply the following formatting:
    a. Apply the *Light Blue 1* shape fill (located in the fifth column in the *Standard Colors* section).
    b. Change the shape outline color to *Dark Blue* (last option in the ninth column in the *Standard Colors* section).
18. Select both navigation buttons you inserted in the form. ***Hint: To select both buttons, click the first button, hold down the Ctrl key, and then click the second button.***
19. With both buttons selected, apply the *Subtle Effect - Teal, Accent 3* Quick Style.
20. Switch to Form view and then navigate in the form using the navigation buttons you inserted.
21. Save the form with the name *Suppliers*.
22. Make active the record for supplier number 12 (one of the new records you entered) and then print the record. (Make sure you only print the record for supplier number 12. The buttons do not print.)
23. Make active the record for supplier number 34 and then print the record.

24. Create a screen capture of the record, paste it in a Word file, and then print the file by completing the following steps:
    a. With the supplier number 34 record active, press the Print Screen button on your keyboard.
    b. Open Microsoft Word. (If necessary, check with your instructor to determine how to open Word.)
    c. Click the Paste button located in the Clipboard group in the Home tab. (This pastes the screen capture image in the Word document.)
    d. Click the File tab, click the Print tab, and then click the *Print* option at the Print tab Backstage view.
    e. Exit Word by clicking the Close button located in the upper right corner of the screen. At the message asking if you want to save the document, click the Don't Save button.
25. Close the Suppliers table.

Assessment 2

CREATE AND CUSTOMIZE AN ORDERS FORM AND A PRODUCTS FORM

1. With the **AL1-C5-PacTrek.accdb** database open, create a form with the Orders table using the Form button in the Create tab.
2. Insert a field from a related table by completing the following steps:
    a. Display the Field List pane and then, if necessary, click the Show all tables hyperlink.
    b. Expand the Suppliers table in the *Fields available in related tables* section.
    c. Drag the field named *SupplierName* into the form and position it between *Supplier#* and *Product#*.
    d. Change the *SupplierName* field from a Lookup field to a text box by clicking the Options button that displays below the field and then clicking *Change to Text Box* at the drop-down list.
    e. Close the Field List pane.
3. Click the text box control object containing the text *1010* and then drag the right border to the left until the border displays approximately one inch to the right of the longest entry in the record.
4. Select all of the objects in the *Detail* section by clicking an object in the *Detail* section and then clicking the selector button (small square button with a four-headed arrow inside). With the objects selected, apply the following formatting:
    a. Change the font to Cambria and the font size to 12.
    b. Change the alignment to Align Text Right.
5. Select the first column and then apply the following formatting:
    a. Apply the *Green 2* shape fill (located in the seventh column in the *Standard Colors* section).
    b. Apply bold formatting.
6. Apply conditional formatting that changes the font color to blue for any *Amount* field entry that contains an amount greater than $999. ***Hint: Click the Conditional Formatting button, click the New Rule button, change the second option in the*** **Edit the rule description** ***section to*** **greater than,** ***and then enter 999 in the third option box [without the dollar sign].***
7. Save the form with the name *Orders*.
8. Print the fifteenth record in the form and then close the form.

Assessment

3 CREATE A SPLIT FORM WITH THE PRODUCTS TABLE

1. With the **AL1-C5-PacTrek.accdb** database open, create a form with the Products table using the *Split Form* option from the More Forms button drop-down list.
2. Decrease the width of the second column so the second column is approximately twice the width of the first column.
3. Select the first column and then apply the following formatting:
   a. Apply bold formatting.
   b. Apply the *Aqua Blue 1* shape fill (located in the ninth column in the *Standard Colors* section).
   c. Change the shape outline color to *Blue* (located in the bottom row in the *Standard Colors* section).
4. Click in the text box control object containing the number *0* (the UnitsOnOrder number) and then apply conditional formatting that displays the number in red in any field value equal to 0 (zero).
5. Change to Form view, create a new record, and then enter the following information in the specified fields:

   Product# = **205-CS**
   Product = **Timberline solo cook set**
   Supplier# = **15**
   UnitsInStock = **8**
   UnitsOnOrder = **0**
   ReorderLevel = **5**

6. Save the form with the name *Products*.
7. Print the current record (the record you just typed). ***Hint: At the Print dialog box, click the Setup button. At the Page Setup dialog box, click the*** **Print Form Only** ***option.***
8. Close the Products form.
9. Close the **AL1-C5-PacTrek.accdb** database.

Assessment

4 CREATE AND CUSTOMIZE AN EMPLOYEES FORM

1. Open the **AL1-C5-Griffin.accdb** database from the Access2010L1C5 folder on your storage medium and enable the contents.
2. Suppose you want to create a form for entering employee information but you do not want to include the employee's salary since that is confidential information that only the account manager has access to. Use the Form Wizard to create an Employees form that includes all fields *except* the *AnnualSalary* field and name the form *Employees*.
3. Switch to Layout view and then apply the Slipstream theme to the form.
4. Switch to Form view and then type a new record with the following information in the specified fields:

   Emp# = **1099**
   LastName = **Williamson**
   FirstName = **Carrie**
   BirthDate = **6/24/1983**
   HireDate = **8/1/2011**
   DeptID = **RD**

5. Print the record you just typed.
6. Close the Employees form.

Assessment

5 CREATE AND CUSTOMIZE A BENEFITS FORM

1. With the **AL1-C5-Griffin.accdb** database open, create a form with the Benefits table using the Form button.
2. With the Benefits form in Layout view, decrease the width of the second column so it is approximately twice as wide as the first column.
3. Select the bottom row of control objects and then insert a row below. With the row still selected, insert another row below. (You should have two rows of empty cells at the bottom of the form.)
4. Click in the empty cell immediately below the text box control containing the text *4 weeks* and then split the cell horizontally.
5. Click in the empty cell immediately below the cell you just split and then split that cell horizontally.
6. Insert a button control by completing the following steps:
   a. Click the Form Layout Tools Design tab and then click the Button button.
   b. Click in the empty cell immediately below the label object control containing the label *Vacation*.
   c. At the first Command Button Wizard dialog box, click the *Go To Previous Record* in the *Actions* list box and then click the Next button.
   d. At the second Command Button Wizard dialog box, click the *Text* option and then click the Finish button.
7. Complete steps similar to those in Step 6 to insert in the cell at the right side of the first empty row of cells a Go To Next Record button that contains text on the button.
8. Complete steps similar to those in Step 6 to insert a button in the cell immediately below the Previous button that prints the current record. (To find this option, click the *Record Operations* option in the *Categories* list box. Specify that you want text on the button.)
9. Insert a button immediately below the Next Record button that closes the form. (To find this option, click the *Form Operations* option in the *Categories* list box. Specify that you want text on the button.)
10. Select each of the four new buttons and then change the font size to 10.
11. Save the form with the name *Benefits*.
12. Switch to Form view and then click the Print Record button you inserted. At the Print dialog box, make sure the *Selected Record(s)* option is selected and then click OK.
13. Create a screen capture of the record, paste it in a Word file, and then print the file by completing the following steps:
    a. With the current record displayed, press the Print Screen button on your keyboard.
    b. Open Microsoft Word.
    c. Click the Paste button located in the Clipboard group in the Home tab. (This pastes the screen capture image in the Word document.)
    d. Click the File tab, click the Print tab, and then click the *Print* option at the Print tab Backstage view.
    e. Exit Word by clicking the Close button located in the upper right corner of the screen. At the message asking if you want to save the document, click the Don't Save button.
14. Close the Benefits form.
15. Close the **AL1-C5-Griffin.accdb** database.

Visual Benchmark Demonstrate Your Proficiency

CREATE AND FORMAT A PROPERTIES FORM

1. Open the **AL1-C5-SunProperties.accdb** database located in the Access2010L1C5 folder on your storage medium and enable the contents.
2. Create a form with the Properties table and format your form so it appears in a manner similar to the form in Figure 5.8 with the following specifications:
   a. Apply the Thatch theme.
   b. Insert the logo, title, date, and time in the *Form Header* section as shown in the figure. (Insert the file **SunPropLogo.jpg** for the logo. Adjust the size of the title control object and then move the date and time as shown in the figure.)
   c. Select all of the objects in the *Detail* section and then change the font color to *Maroon 5* (located in the *Standard Colors* section).
   d. Select the first column, apply bold formatting, apply *Yellow, Accent 2, Lighter 60%* shape fill (color is located in the *Theme Colors* section), change the shape outline color to *Yellow, Accent 2, Darker 50%,* and then change to align text right.
   e. Insert a new column to the right of the second column, merge cells in the new column to accommodate the sun image and then insert the image **SunProp.jpg** (as a control object). Adjust the width of the third column so the image displays as shown in Figure 5.8.

Figure 5.8 Visual Benchmark

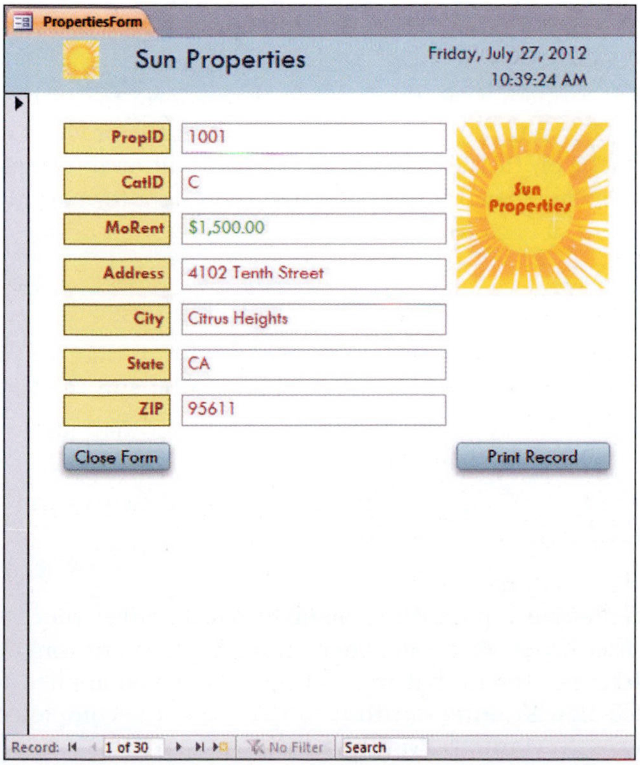

f. Apply conditional formatting to the *MoRent* field that displays in green any rent amount greater than $999.
g. Insert a new row at the bottom of the form and then insert the buttons as shown in the figure. Apply the *Subtle Effect - Blue-Gray, Accent 1* Quick Style to each button. Slightly increase the height of the bottom row containing the buttons until the text on the buttons displays as shown in the figure.

3. Save the form with the name *PropertiesForm* and then print the current record.
4. Use the Print Screen button to make a screen capture image of the current record, insert the image in a Word document, print the document, and then exit Word without saving the document.
5. Close the form and then close the **AL1-C5-SunProperties.accdb** database.

Case Study Apply Your Skills

Part 1

You are the office manager at the Lewis Vision Care Center and your center is switching over to Access to manage files. You have already created four basic tables and now need to create relationships and enter data. Open the **AL1-C5-LewisCenter.accdb** database and then create the following relationships between tables:

Field Name	**"One" Table**	**"Many" Table**
Patient#	Patients	Billing
ServiceID	Services	Billing
Doctor#	Doctors	Billing

Save and then print the relationships.

Part 2

Before entering data in the tables, create a form for each table and apply a theme of your choosing. Enter data in the forms in the order in which data appears in Figure 5.10 on the next page. Apply any additional formatting to enhance the visual appeal of each form. After entering the information in the forms, print the first record of each form.

Part 3

Apply the following conditions to fields in forms:

- In the Patients form, apply the condition that the city *Tulsa* displays in red and the city *Broken Arrow* displays in blue in the *City* field.
- In the Billing form, apply the condition that amounts in the *Fee* field over $99 display in green.

Print the first record of the form. Close the Patients form and then close the **AL1-C5-LewisCenter.accdb** database.

Part 4

Your center has a procedures manual that describes processes and procedures in the center. Open Word and then create a document for the procedures manual that describes the formatting and conditions you applied to the forms in the **AL1-C5-LewisCenter.accdb** database. Save the completed document and name it **AL1-C5-CS-Manual**. Print and then close **AL1-C5-CS-Manual.docx**.

Figure 5.10 Case Study Part 2

Patients form		
Patient number-030 Rhonda J. Mahler 130 East 41st Street Tulsa, OK 74155 (918) 555-3107	Patient number-076 Patrick S. Robbins 3281 Aspen Avenue Tulsa, OK 74108 (918) 555-9672	Patient number-092 Oren L. Vargas 21320 Tenth Street Broken Arrow, OK 74012 (918) 555-1188
Patient number-085 Michael A. Dempsey 506 Houston Street Tulsa, OK 74142 (918) 555-5541	Patient number-074 Wendy L. Holloway 23849 22nd Street Broken Arrow, OK 74009 (918) 555-8842	Patient number-023 Maggie M. Winters 4422 South 121st Tulsa, OK 74142 (918) 555-8833

Doctors form		
Doctor number-1 Carolyn Joswick (918) 555-4772	Doctor number-2 Gerald Ingram (918) 555-9890	Doctor number-3 Kay Feather (918) 555-7762
Doctor number-4 Sean Granger (918) 555-1039	Doctor number-5 Jerome Deltoro (918) 555-8021	

Services form		
Co = Consultation	V = Vision Screening	G = Glaucoma Testing
C = Cataract Testing	S = Surgery	E = Emergency

Billing form		
Patient number-076 Doctor number-2 Date of visit = 4/2/2012 Service ID = C Fee = $85	Patient number-076 Doctor number-3 Date of visit = 4/2/2012 Service ID = V Fee = $150	Patient number-085 Doctor number-1 Date of visit = 4/2/2012 Service ID = Co Fee = $0
Patient number-074 Doctor number-3 Date of visit = 4/2/2012 Service ID = V Fee = $150	Patient number-023 Doctor number-5 Date of visit = 4/2/2012 Service ID = S Fee = $750	Patient number-092 Doctor number-1 Date of visit = 4/2/2012 Service ID = G Fee = $85

Microsoft® Access®

CHAPTER 6

Creating Reports and Mailing Labels

PERFORMANCE OBJECTIVES

Upon successful completion of Chapter 6, you will be able to:

- **Create a report using the Report button**
- **Display a report in Print Preview**
- **Create a report with a query**
- **Format and customize a report**
- **Group and sort records in a report**
- **Create a report using the Report Wizard**
- **Create mailing labels using the Label Wizard**

SNAP Training and Assessment. Simplified.

Tutorials

6.1 Creating a Report

6.2 Modifying a Report

6.3 Modifying Reports Using Calculated Columns and Conditional Formatting

6.4 Creating a Report Using the Report Wizard

6.5 Creating Mailing Labels

In this chapter, you will learn how to prepare reports from data in a table using the Report button in the Reports group in the Create tab and with the Report Wizard. You will also learn how to format and customize a report and create mailing labels using the Label Wizard. Model answers for this chapter's projects appear on the following pages.

Access

Access2010L1C6

Note: Before beginning the projects, copy to your storage medium the Access2010L1C6 subfolder from the Access2010L1 folder on the CD that accompanies this textbook and make Access2010L1C6 the active folder.

Sales

Monday, July 30, 2012
8:46:28 PM

ClientID	Sales2010	Sales2011
101	$289,563.00	$327,541.00
102	$101,210.00	$95,630.00
103	$125,436.00	$144,328.00
104	$97,653.00	$130,239.00
105	$215,420.00	$441,000.00
106	$85,628.00	$75,462.00
107	$199,346.00	$221,379.00
108	$61,349.00	$105,000.00
109	$554,120.00	$721,923.00
110	$17,542.00	$83,210.00
111	$9,547.00	$45,230.00
112	$138,560.00	$200,540.00
113	$141,670.00	$65,411.00
114	$2,356.00	$31,230.00
115	$115,423.00	$103,400.00
116	$35,679.00	$61,539.00
117	$15,248.00	$22,478.00
118	$156,439.00	$175,011.00
119	$201,430.00	$222,133.00
120	$51,237.00	$20,137.00
121	$99,450.00	$103,435.00
122	$174,319.00	$125,900.00
123	$300,137.00	$265,439.00
124	$24,880.00	$31,935.00
125	$151,003.00	$120,890.00
126	$9,457.00	$15,094.00
127	$214,000.00	$176,420.00

Page 1 of 1

Project 1 Create and Customize Reports Using Tables and Queries

Project 1a, Dearborn Sales Report

Sales

Monday, July 30, 2012
11:05:46 AM

Client ID	Sales 2011	Sales 2010
109	$721,923.00	$554,120.00
105	$441,000.00	$215,420.00
101	$327,541.00	$289,563.00
123	$265,439.00	$300,137.00
119	$222,133.00	$201,430.00
107	$221,379.00	$199,346.00
112	$200,540.00	$138,560.00
127	$176,420.00	$214,000.00
118	$175,011.00	$156,439.00
103	$144,328.00	$125,436.00
104	$130,239.00	$97,653.00
122	$125,900.00	$174,319.00
125	$120,890.00	$151,003.00
108	$105,000.00	$61,349.00
121	$103,435.00	$99,450.00
115	$103,400.00	$115,423.00
102	$95,630.00	$101,210.00
110	$83,210.00	$17,542.00
106	$75,462.00	$85,628.00
113	$65,411.00	$141,670.00
116	$61,539.00	$35,679.00
111	$45,230.00	$9,547.00
124	$31,935.00	$24,880.00
114	$31,230.00	$2,356.00
117	$22,478.00	$15,248.00
120	$20,137.00	$51,237.00
126	$15,094.00	$9,457.00

Page 1 of 1

Project 1b, Dearborn Sales Report

Representatives

Monday, July 30, 2012
6:30:36 PM

RepID	RepName	Telephone	Email	QuotaID
10	Kwan Im	(317) 555-8374	k_i@emcp.net	4
11	William Ludlow	(317) 555-0991	w_l@emcp.net	4
12	Catherine Singleton	(317) 555-0172	c_s@emcp.net	3
13	Alfred Silva	(317) 555-3211	a_s@emcp.net	5
14	Jaren Newman	(317) 555-6790	j_n@emcp.net	2
15	Lee Hutchinson	(765) 555-4277	l_h@emcp.net	2
16	Cecilia Ortega	(317) 555-4810	c_o@emcp.net	1
17	Robin Rehberg	(317) 555-9812	r_r@emcp.net	1
18	Andre Kulisek	(317) 555-2264	a_k@emcp.net	1
19	Isabelle Marshall	(765) 555-8822	i_m@emcp.net	3
20	Craig Johnson	(317) 555-4391	c_j@emcp.net	2
21	Maureen Pascual	(317) 555-5513	m_p@emcp.net	3
22	Gina Tapparo	(317) 555-0044	g_t@emcp.net	5
23	Linda Foster	(317) 555-2101	l_f@empc.net	3
24	David DeBruler	(317) 555-8779	d_d@emcp.net	2
25	Lydia Alvarado	(765) 555-4996	l_a@emcp.net	4
26	Edward Harris	(317) 555-3894	e_h@emcp.net	1

Project 1b, Dearborn Representatives Report

InMunSalesOver$75000

Monday, July 30, 2012
9:10:42 PM

Client	StreetAddress	City	State	ZipCode	Sales2010
Bering Company	4521 East Sixth Street	Muncie	IN	47310-5500	$289,563.00
Fairhaven Developers	574 East Raymond Street	Indianapolis	IN	46219-3005	$101,210.00
Clearwater Service	10385 North Gavin Street	Muncie	IN	47308-1236	$125,436.00
Landower Company	1299 Arlington Avenue	Indianapolis	IN	46236-1299	$97,653.00
Harford Systems	9654 Jackson Street	Indianapolis	IN	46247-9654	$215,420.00
Providence, Inc.	12490 141st Street	Muncie	IN	47306-3410	$85,628.00
Gallagher Systems	3885 Moore Avenue	Indianapolis	IN	47229-1075	$199,346.00
DV Corporation	210 West Michigan Street	Indianapolis	IN	46251-4503	$138,560.00
Wheeling Products	5567 Washburn Avenue	Indianapolis	IN	46247-5567	$115,423.00
AeroTech	9905 West 16th Street	Indianapolis	IN	46241-9905	$156,439.00
Miles & Harrisburg	11029 47th Street East	Indianapolis	IN	46238-1120	$201,430.00
Paragon Corporation	4500 Meridian Street	Muncie	IN	47302-4338	$51,237.00
Haute Contractors	422 Kessler Boulevard	Indianapolis	IN	46218-4220	$174,319.00
Eagleton Industries	544 Eastridge Drive	Indianapolis	IN	47230-5440	$300,137.00
Dover Industries	4839 Huchins Road	Muncie	IN	47306-4839	$151,003.00
Northstar Services	5135 West Second Street	Muncie	IN	47301-7774	$9,457.00
Zinn-Harris Electronics	675 South Holt Road	Indianapolis	IN	47221-0551	$214,000.00
					$2,626,261.00

Project 1c, Dearborn InMun2010Sales Report

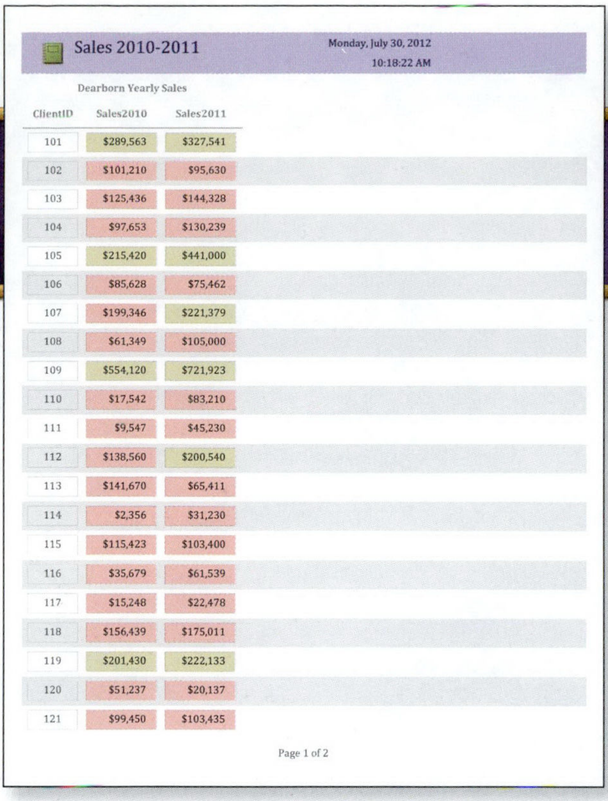

Sales 2010-2011

Monday, July 30, 2012
10:18:22 AM

Dearborn Yearly Sales

ClientID	Sales2010	Sales2011
101	$289,563	$327,541
102	$101,210	$95,630
103	$125,436	$144,328
104	$97,653	$130,239
105	$215,420	$441,000
106	$85,628	$75,462
107	$199,346	$221,379
108	$61,349	$105,000
109	$554,120	$721,923
110	$17,542	$83,210
111	$9,547	$45,230
112	$138,560	$200,540
113	$141,670	$65,411
114	$2,356	$31,230
115	$115,423	$103,400
116	$35,679	$61,539
117	$15,248	$22,478
118	$156,439	$175,011
119	$201,430	$222,133
120	$51,237	$20,137
121	$99,450	$103,435

Page 1 of 2

Dearborn Yearly Sales

ClientID	Sales2010	Sales2011
122	$174,319	$125,900
123	$300,137	$265,439
124	$24,880	$31,935
125	$151,003	$120,890
126	$9,457	$15,094
127	$214,000	$176,420
	$3,588,102	$4,131,934

Page 2 of 2

Project 1d, Dearborn Sales Report

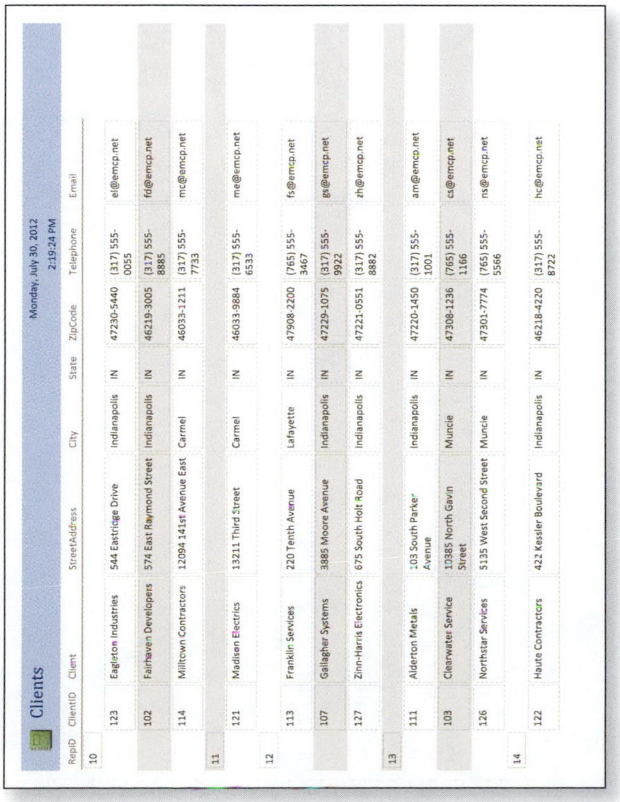

Clients

Monday, July 30, 2012
2:19:24 PM

RepID	ClientID	Client	StreetAddress	City	State	ZipCode	Telephone	Email
10								
	123	Eagleton Industries	544 Eastridge Drive	Indianapolis	IN	47230-5440	(317) 555-0055	el@emcp.net
	102	Fairhaven Developers	574 East Raymond Street	Indianapolis	IN	46219-3005	(317) 555-8885	fd@emcp.net
	114	Milltown Contractors	12094 141st Avenue East	Carmel	IN	46033-1211	(317) 555-7733	mc@emcp.net
11								
	121	Madison Electrics	13211 Third Street	Carmel	IN	46033-9884	(317) 555-6533	me@emcp.net
12								
	113	Franklin Services	220 Tenth Avenue	Lafayette	IN	47908-2200	(765) 555-3467	fs@emcp.net
	107	Gallagher Systems	3885 Moore Avenue	Indianapolis	IN	47229-1075	(317) 555-9922	gs@emcp.net
	127	Zinn-Harris Electronics	675 South Holt Road	Indianapolis	IN	47221-0551	(317) 555-8882	zh@emcp.net
13								
	111	Alderton Metals	103 South Parker Avenue	Indianapolis	IN	47220-1450	(317) 555-1001	am@emcp.net
	103	Clearwater Service	10385 North Gavin Street	Muncie	IN	47308-1236	(765) 555-1166	cs@emcp.net
	126	Northstar Services	5135 West Second Street	Muncie	IN	47301-7774	(765) 555-5566	ns@emcp.net
14								
	122	Haute Contractors	422 Kessler Boulevard	Indianapolis	IN	46218-4220	(317) 555-8722	hc@emcp.net

Project 1e, Dearborn ClientsGroupedRpt Report

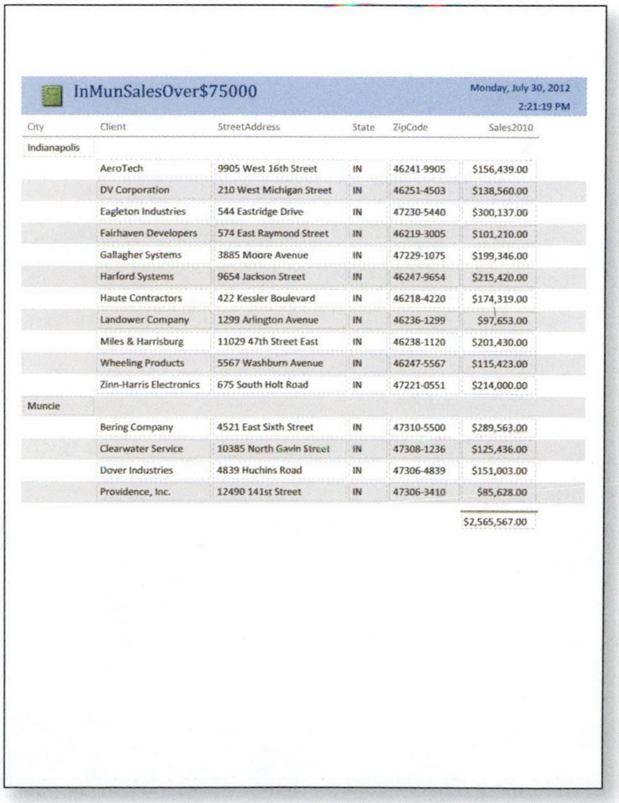

InMunSalesOver$75000

Monday, July 30, 2012
2:21:19 PM

City	Client	StreetAddress	State	ZipCode	Sales2010
Indianapolis					
	AeroTech	9905 West 16th Street	IN	46241-9905	$156,439.00
	DV Corporation	210 West Michigan Street	IN	46251-4503	$138,560.00
	Eagleton Industries	544 Eastridge Drive	IN	47230-5440	$300,137.00
	Fairhaven Developers	574 East Raymond Street	IN	46219-3005	$101,210.00
	Gallagher Systems	3885 Moore Avenue	IN	47229-1075	$199,346.00
	Harford Systems	9654 Jackson Street	IN	46247-9654	$215,420.00
	Haute Contractors	422 Kessler Boulevard	IN	46218-4220	$174,319.00
	Landower Company	1299 Arlington Avenue	IN	46236-1299	$97,653.00
	Miles & Harrisburg	11029 47th Street East	IN	46238-1120	$201,430.00
	Wheeling Products	5567 Washburn Avenue	IN	46247-5567	$115,423.00
	Zinn-Harris Electronics	675 South Holt Road	IN	47221-0551	$214,000.00
Muncie					
	Bering Company	4521 East Sixth Street	IN	47310-5500	$289,563.00
	Clearwater Service	10385 North Gavin Street	IN	47308-1236	$125,436.00
	Dover Industries	4839 Huchins Road	IN	47306-4839	$151,003.00
	Providence, Inc.	12490 141st Street	IN	47306-3410	$85,628.00
					$2,565,567.00

Project 1e, Dearborn InMun2010Sales Report

ClientBilling

Monday, July 30, 2012
6:57:21 PM

LastName	Date	Hours	Rate	Total
Aragato				
	6/6/2012	1.00	$250.00	$250.00
	6/12/2012	0.25	$250.00	$62.50
	6/15/2012	0.25	$250.00	$62.50
Briggs				
	6/1/2012	1.00	$300.00	$300.00
	6/4/2012	1.50	$325.00	$487.50
	6/4/2012	1.75	$300.00	$525.00
	6/5/2012	1.50	$300.00	$450.00
	6/7/2012	1.25	$325.00	$406.25
	6/13/2012	1.00	$325.00	$325.00
Cervantez				
	6/1/2012	2.00	$250.00	$500.00
	6/4/2012	0.75	$325.00	$243.75
	6/8/2012	2.00	$250.00	$500.00
Cordes				
	6/4/2012	1.00	$300.00	$300.00
	6/11/2012	1.00	$300.00	$300.00
Czubek				
	6/1/2012	1.75	$200.00	$350.00
	6/6/2012	1.50	$200.00	$300.00
	6/8/2012	0.50	$200.00	$100.00
	6/13/2012	0.25	$200.00	$50.00
Day				
	6/1/2012	1.50	$325.00	$487.50
	6/5/2012	0.75	$200.00	$150.00
	6/7/2012	1.00	$325.00	$325.00
	6/11/2012	1.50	$325.00	$487.50
	6/14/2012	1.00	$250.00	$250.00
	6/14/2012	1.25	$200.00	$250.00
Garvison				

Page 1 of 3

LastName	Date	Hours	Rate	Total
	6/14/2012	1.00	$300.00	$300.00
Hobart				
	6/4/2012	0.75	$300.00	$225.00
	6/11/2012	1.00	$300.00	$300.00
	6/14/2012	0.25	$300.00	$75.00
Jefferson				
	6/5/2012	1.00	$300.00	$300.00
	6/8/2012	1.00	$250.00	$250.00
	6/12/2012	0.50	$300.00	$150.00
	6/15/2012	1.50	$300.00	$450.00
Kasper				
	6/5/2012	2.00	$200.00	$400.00
	6/6/2012	1.00	$200.00	$200.00
	6/7/2012	1.50	$200.00	$300.00
Kendall				
	6/13/2012	1.00	$200.00	$200.00
McFadden				
	6/7/2012	0.25	$200.00	$50.00
Norheim				
	6/15/2012	1.00	$250.00	$250.00
O'Connor				
	6/11/2012	2.25	$200.00	$450.00
	6/13/2012	0.50	$200.00	$100.00
Reyes				
	6/12/2012	1.00	$200.00	$200.00
Rosenthal				
	6/13/2012	1.50	$250.00	$375.00
Saunders				
	6/8/2012	1.50	$250.00	$375.00
	6/14/2012	0.25	$250.00	$62.50
Singh				
	6/6/2012	1.50	$325.00	$487.50
Stein				

Page 2 of 3

Project 1e, Dearborn ClientBillingRpt Report

LastName	Date	Hours	Rate	Total
	6/13/2012	1.50	$325.00	$487.50
Valencia				
	6/1/2012	0.50	$200.00	$100.00
	6/4/2012	0.75	$250.00	$187.50
	6/5/2012	2.00	$200.00	$400.00
Waide				
	6/11/2012	1.00	$250.00	$250.00
Weyland				
	6/12/2012	1.50	$250.00	$375.00
	6/15/2012	0.50	$250.00	$125.00
	6/15/2012	0.50	$250.00	$125.00
				3,725.00

Page 3 of 3

Inventory

SupplierID	Item#	Item	Unit
1	033	Perch	case
	032	Swordfish	case
	031	Tuna	case
2	021	Cantaloupes	case
	017	Romaine lettuce	case
	008	Yellow peppers	case
	007	Red peppers	case
	016	Iceberg lettuce	case
	001	Butternut squash	case
	014	Green beans	case
	006	Green peppers	case
	004	Onions	25 lb bag
	002	Potatoes	50 lb bag
	051	Watermelon	case
	052	Kiwi	case
3	024	Kaiser rolls	flat
	023	Wheat bread	flat
	054	Ginger	case
	022	White bread	flat
	039	White flour	25 lb bag
	040	Wheat flour	25 lb bag
	044	Cinnamon	case
	045	Nutmeg	case
	046	Cloves	case
	047	Allspice	case
	053	Parsley	case
4	015	Brussel sprouts	flat
	027	Tortilla wraps	flat
	012	Cauliflower	case
	018	Bananas	case
	019	Pineapple	case
	020	Oranges	case
	013	Tomatoes	case
	026	Pita wraps	flat
	050	Pepper	case
	034	Ketchup	gallon
	035	Mustard	gallon
	036	Mayonnaise	gallon
	037	Relish	gallon

Monday, July 30, 2012 Page 1 of 2

Project 2 Use Wizards to Create Reports and Labels

Project 2a, Skyline Inventory Report

SupplierID	Item#	Item	Unit
4	038	Barbecue sauce	gallon
	025	English muffins	flat
	049	Salt	case
	048	Seasoned salt	case
6	041	White sugar	25 lb bag
	003	Carrots	25 lb bag
	005	Garlic	10 lb bag
	043	Baking soda	case
	042	Baking powder	case
	009	Radishes	case
	011	Broccoli	case
	010	Celery	case
7	028	Beef	side
	030	Chicken	case
	029	Pork	side

Monday, July 30, 2012 Page 2 of 2

BanquetEvents

Event	ResDate	FirstName	LastName	AmountTotal	AmountPaid
Birthday	6/9/2012	Joanne	Blair	$650.00	$200.00
	6/17/2012	Jason	Haley	$1,500.00	$400.00
	6/23/2012	Heidi	Thompson	$1,750.00	$750.00
	6/30/2012	Kirsten	Simpson	$750.00	$150.00
Bar mitzvah	6/25/2012	Robin	Gehring	$2,000.00	$700.00
	6/16/2012	Aaron	Williams	$2,000.00	$500.00
Bat mitzvah	6/9/2012	Tim	Drysdale	$1,000.00	$250.00
Other	6/15/2012	Tristan	Strauss	$1,400.00	$300.00
	6/10/2012	Gabrielle	Johnson	$300.00	$100.00
	6/8/2012	Bridget	Kohn	$500.00	$100.00
	6/29/2012	David	Fitzgerald	$800.00	$200.00
	6/19/2012	Lillian	Krakosky	$500.00	$100.00
Wedding rehearsal dinner	6/2/2012	Terrance	Schaefer	$750.00	$250.00
	6/13/2012	Cliff	Osborne	$800.00	$250.00
Wedding anniversary	6/30/2012	Shane	Rozier	$2,000.00	$500.00
	6/23/2012	Anthony	Wiegand	$900.00	$300.00
	6/7/2012	David	Hooper	$800.00	$300.00
Wedding reception	6/3/2012	Andrea	Wyatt	$1,250.00	$500.00
	6/24/2012	Julio	Rivas	$3,000.00	$1,000.00
	6/22/2012	Mallory	Satter	$2,500.00	$750.00
	6/15/2012	Janis	Semala	$2,000.00	$500.00
Wedding shower	6/16/2012	Willow	Earhart	$750.00	$200.00
	6/3/2012	Luis	Castillo	$575.00	$175.00

Monday, July 30, 2012 Page 1 of 1

Project 2b, Skyline BanquetEvents Report

Haley Brown
3219 North 33rd Street
Auburn, WA 98001

Margaret Kasper
40210 42nd Avenue
Auburn, WA 98001

Abigail Jefferson
1204 Meridian Road
Auburn, WA 98001

Doris Sturtevant
3713 Nelton Road
Auburn, WA 98001

Carlina McFadden
7809 52nd Street East
Auburn, WA 98001

Ewan Aragato
904 Marine View Drive
Auburn, WA 98002

Tricia O'Connor
3824 Sanders Court
Auburn, WA 98002

Carol Kendall
24 Ferris Parkway
Kent, WA 98003

James Weyland
2533 145th Street East
Kent, WA 98031

Janice Saunders
2757 179th Avenue East
Kent, WA 98032

Jeffrey Day
317 Meridian Street
Kent, WA 98033

Mindy Garvison
68 Queens Avenue
Kent, WA 98033

Kevin Stein
12034 South 22nd Avenue
Kent, WA 98035

Jean Briggs
2110 West Valley Avenue
Kent, WA 98036

Arthur Norheim
10533 Ashton Boulevard
Kent, WA 98036

Consuelo Day
13321 North Lake Drive
Kent, WA 98036

Christina Miles
13043 South 25th Avenue
Kent, WA 98036

Matthew Waide
18391 North 45th Street
Renton, WA 98055

Page 1

Karl Cordes
240 Mill Avenue
Renton, WA 98055

Mira Valencia
114 Springfield Avenue
Renton, WA 98056

Charles Hobart
11038 132nd Street
Renton, WA 98056

Taylor Reyes
201 Northwest Boulevard
Renton, WA 98056

Eric Rosenthal
1230 Maplewood Road
Auburn, WA 98071

Jennifer Czubek
8790 34th Avenue
Renton, WA 98228

Maddie Singh
450 Mill Avenue
Renton, WA 98228

Chris Cervantez
8722 Riverside Road
Renton, WA 98228

Arthur Jefferson
23110 North 33rd Street
Renton, WA 98230

Page 2

Project 2c, Warren Legal Mailing Labels

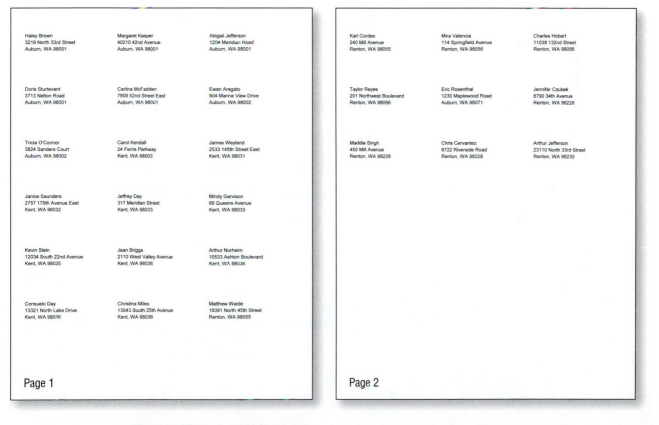

Project 1 Create and Customize Reports Using Tables and Queries — 5 Parts

You will create reports with the Report button using tables and queries. You will change the report views; select, move, and resize control objects; sort records; customize reports; apply conditional formatting; and group and sort fields in a report.

Creating a Report

Quick Steps

Create a Report
1. Click desired table or query in Navigation pane.
2. Click Create tab.
3. Click Report button.

HINT

Create a report to control what data appears on the page when printed.

The primary purpose for inserting data in a form is to improve the display of the data and to make data entry easier. You can also insert data in a report. The purpose for this is to control what data appears on the page when printed. Reports generally answer specific questions (queries). For example, a report could answer the question *What customers have submitted claims?* or *What products do we currently have on order?* You can use the Report button in the Reports group in the Create tab to create a report based on a table or query. You can also use the Report Wizard that walks you through the process of creating a report.

Creating a Report with the Report Button

To create a report with the Report button, click the desired table or query in the Navigation pane, click the Create tab, and then click the Report button in the Reports group. This displays the report in columnar style in Layout view with the Report Layout Tools Design tab active as shown in Figure 6.1. Access creates the report using all of the fields in the table.

Figure 6.1 Report Created with Sales Table

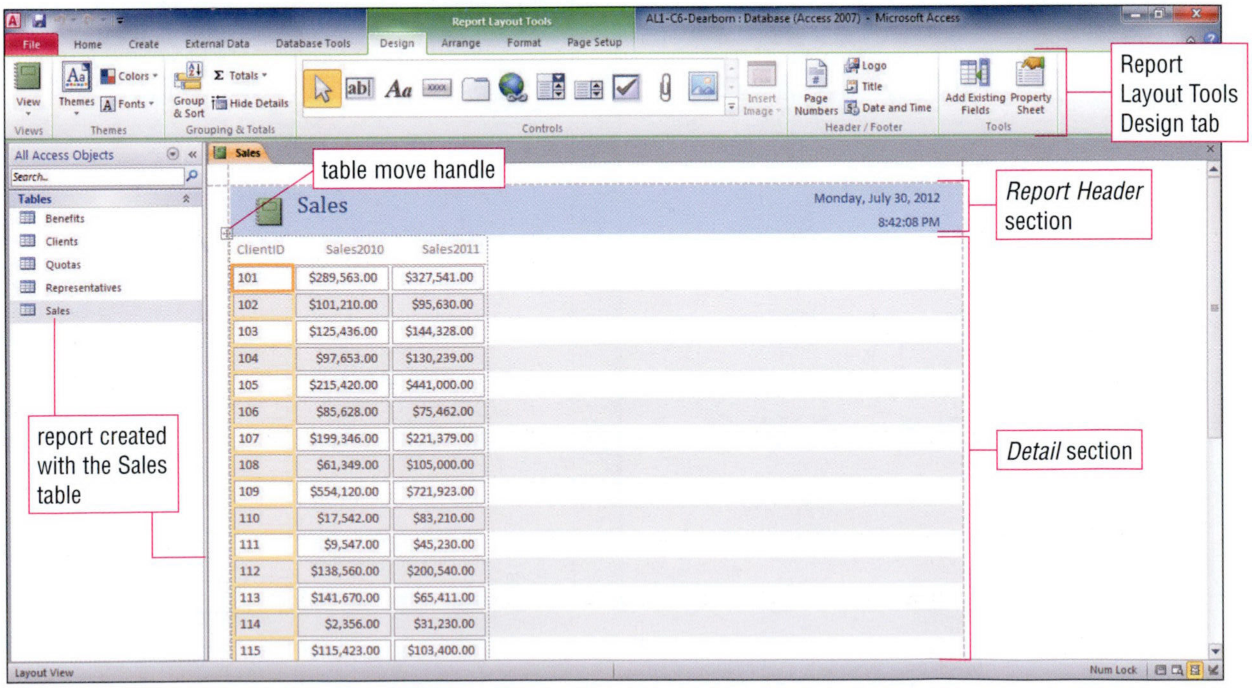

Project 1a Creating a Report with the Report Button

Part 1 of 5

1. Display the Open dialog box with Access2010L1C6 on your storage medium the active folder.
2. Open the **AL1-C6-Dearborn.accdb** database and enable the contents.
3. Create a report by completing the following steps:
   a. Click the Sales table in the Navigation pane.
   b. Click the Create tab.
   c. Click the Report button in the Reports group.

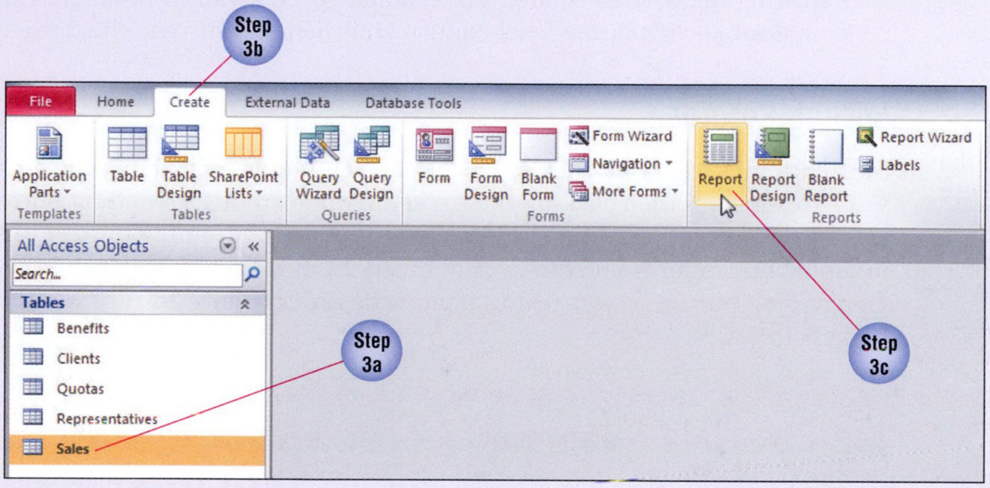

4. Access automatically inserted a total amount for the *Sales2011* column. Delete this amount by scrolling down to the bottom of the report, clicking the total amount at the bottom of the *Sales2011* column, and then pressing the Delete key. (This deletes the total amount but not the underline above the amount.)
5. Print the report by clicking the File tab, clicking the Print tab, and then clicking the *Quick Print* option.
6. Save the report by clicking the Save button on the Quick Access toolbar, making sure *Sales* displays in the *Report Name* text box in the Save As dialog box, and then clicking OK.

Modifying Control Objects

A report, like a form, is comprised of control objects such as a logo, title, labels, and text boxes. You can select an object in a report by clicking the object. A selected object displays with an orange border. If you click a data field in the report, Access selects all objects in the column except the column heading.

Like a form, a report contains a *Header* section and a *Detail* section. You can select all control objects in the report in both the *Header* and *Detail* sections by pressing Ctrl + A. Control objects in the *Detail* section are contained in a report table. To select the control objects in the report table, click in any cell in the report and then click the table move handle that displays in the upper left corner. The table move handle is a small square with a four-headed arrow inside that displays in the upper left corner of the table (see Figure 6.1). You can move the table and all of the control objects within the table by dragging the table move handle using the mouse.

You can adjust column widths in a report by dragging the column border left or right. In addition to adjusting column width, you can change the order of a selected column. To do this, select the desired column, position the mouse pointer in the column heading until the pointer displays with a four-headed arrow attached, and then drag the column left or right to the desired position. As you drag the column, a vertical orange bar displays indicating the location where the column will be placed when you release the mouse button.

Some control objects in a report, such as a column heading or title, are label control objects. You can edit a label control by double-clicking in the object and then making the desired change. For example, if you want to rename a label control, double-click in the label control and then edit or type the desired text.

Sorting Records

Quick Steps

Sort Records

1. Click in field containing data.
2. Click Ascending button or click Descending button.

Sort data in a report by clicking in the field containing the data on which you want to sort and then clicking the Ascending button or Descending button in the Sort & Filter group in the Home tab. Click the Ascending button to sort text in alphabetic order from A to Z or numbers from lowest to highest, or click the Descending button to sort text in alphabetic order from Z to A or numbers from highest to lowest.

Finding Data

Ascending

Descending

You can find specific data in a report with options at the Find dialog box. Display this dialog box by clicking the Find button in the Find group in the Home tab. At the Find dialog box, enter the data for which you are searching in the *Find What* text box. The *Match* option at the Find dialog box is set at *Whole Field* by default. At this setting, the data you enter must match the entire entry in a field. If you are searching for partial data in a field, change the *Match* option to *Any Part of Field* or *Start of Field*. If you want the text you enter in the *Find What* text box to match the case in a field entry, click the *Match Case* option check box to insert a check mark. Access will search the entire report by default. You can change this to *Up* if you want to search from the currently active field to the beginning of the report or *Down* if you want to search from the currently active field to the end of the report. Click the Find Next button to find data that matches the data in the *Find What* text box.

Displaying and Customizing a Report in Print Preview

Print Preview

View

When you create a report, the report displays in the work area in Layout view. This is one of four views available including Report view, Print Preview, and Design view. Use Print Preview to display the report as it will appear when printed. To change to Print Preview, click the Print Preview button in the view area located at the right side of the Status bar. You can also click the View button arrow in the Views group in either the Home tab or the Report Layout Tools Design tab and then click *Print Preview* at the drop-down list.

At the Print Preview tab, send the report to the printer by clicking the Print button. Use options in the Page Size group to change the page size and change margins. If you want to print only the report data and not the column headings, report title, shading, and gridlines, insert a check mark in the *Print Data Only* check box. Use options in the Page Layout group to specify the page orientation, specify columns, and display the Page Setup dialog box. Click the Page Setup button and the Page Setup dialog box displays with options for customizing margins, orientation, size, and columns.

Project 1b **Adjusting Control Objects, Renaming Labels, Finding and Sorting Data, and Displaying a Report in Print Preview** — Part 2 of 5

1. With the Sales report open, reverse the order of the *Sales2010* and *Sales2011* columns by completing the following steps:
   a. Make sure the report displays in Layout view.
   b. Click the *Sales2011* column heading.
   c. Hold down the Shift key and then click in the last control object containing text (*$176,420.00*).
   d. Position the mouse pointer inside the *Sales2011* column heading until the pointer displays with a four-headed arrow attached.
   e. Hold down the left mouse button, drag to the left until the vertical orange bar displays between *ClientID* and *Sales2010*, and then release the mouse button.

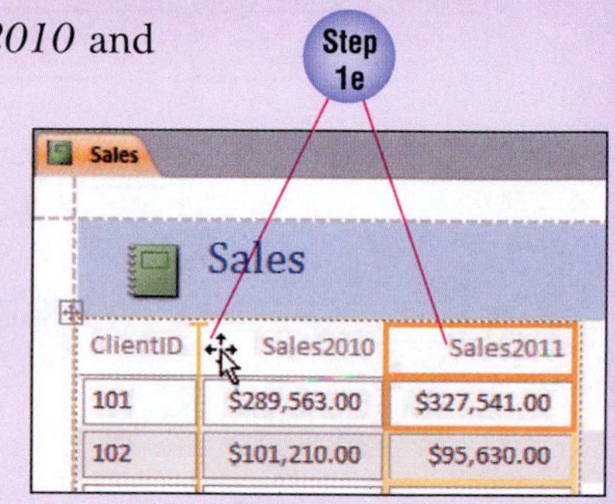

2. Sort the data in the *Sales2011* column in descending order by completing the following steps:
   a. Click the Home tab.
   b. Click in any field in the *Sales2011* column.
   c. Click the Descending button in the Sort & Filter group.

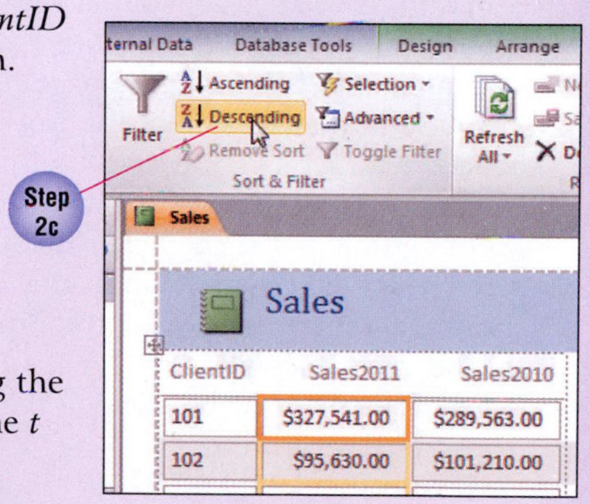

3. Rename the *ClientID* label control to *Client ID* by double-clicking in the label control object containing the text *ClientID*, moving the insertion point between the *t* and the *I*, and then pressing the spacebar.
4. Double-click in the *Sales2011* label control and then rename it *Sales 2011*.
5. Double-click in the *Sales2010* label control and then rename it *Sales 2010*.
6. Move the report table by completing the following steps:
   a. Click in a cell in the report.
   b. Position the mouse pointer on the table move handle (displays as a small square with a four-headed arrow inside and is located in the upper left corner of the table).

c. Hold down the left mouse button, drag the report table to the right until it is centered between the left and right sides of the *Detail* section, and then release the mouse button. (When you drag with the mouse, you will see only an outline of some of the control objects.)

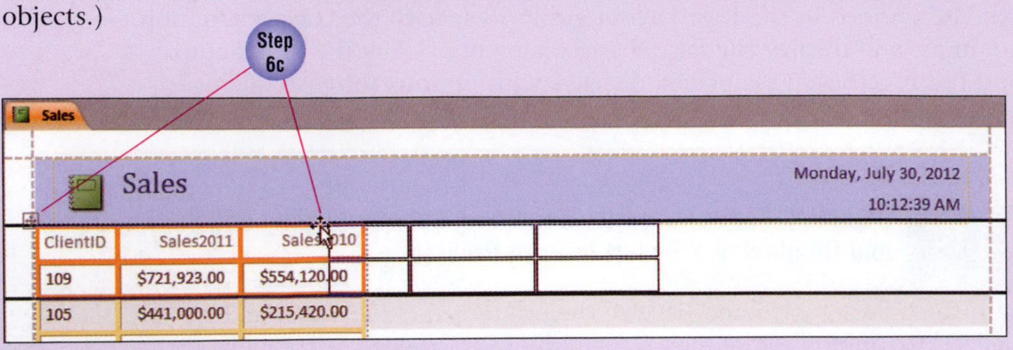

7. Display the report in Print Preview by clicking the Print Preview button in the view area at the right side of the Status bar.

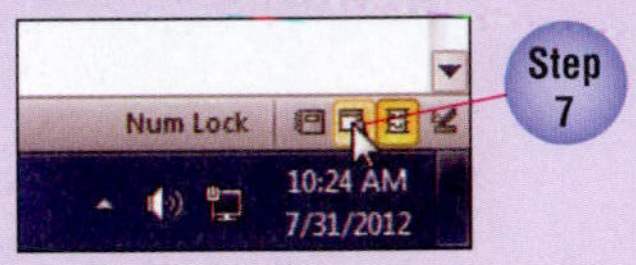

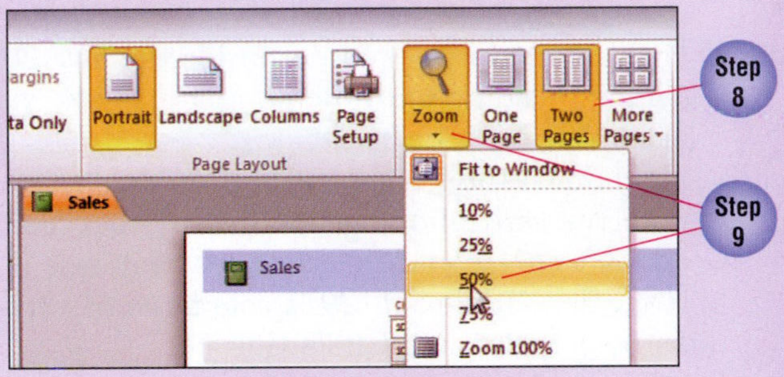

8. Click the Two Pages button in the Zoom group. (Since this report contains only one page, the page displays at the left side of the work area.)
9. Click the Zoom button arrow in the Zoom group and then click *50%* at the drop-down list.
10. Click the One Page button in the Zoom group.
11. Print the report by clicking the Print button in the Print Preview tab and then clicking OK at the Print dialog box.
12. Close Print Preview by clicking the Close Print Preview button located at the right side of the Print Preview tab.
13. Save and then close the Sales report.
14. Create a report with the Representatives table by completing the following steps:
    a. Click the Representatives table in the Navigation pane.
    b. Click the Create tab.
    c. Click the Report button in the Reports group.
15. Adjust the width of the second column by completing the following steps:
    a. Click in the *RepName* column heading.
    b. Drag the right border of the selected column heading to the left until the border displays near the longest entry in the column.
16. Complete steps similar to those in Step 15 to decrease the width of the third column (*Telephone*) and the fourth column (*Email*).
17. Search for fields containing a quote of *2* by completing the following steps:
    a. Click in the *RepID* column heading.
    b. Click the Home tab and then click the Find button in the Find group.

c. At the Find dialog box, type **2** in the *Find What* text box.
d. Make sure the *Match* option is set at *Whole Field*. (If not, click the down-pointing arrow at the right side of the *Match* option and then click *Whole Field* at the drop-down list.)

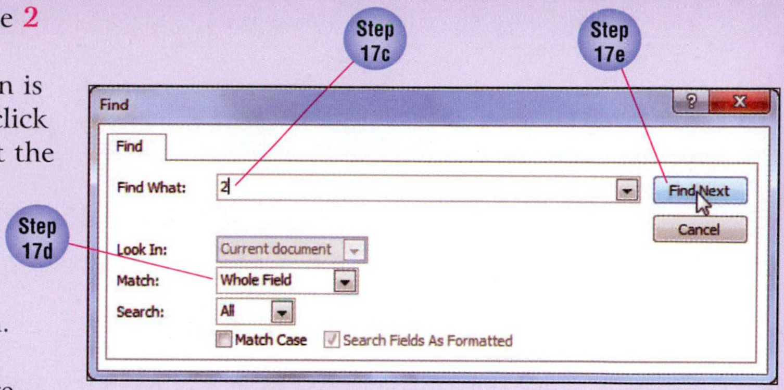

e. Click the Find Next button.
f. Continue clicking the Find Next button until a message displays telling you that Access has finished searching the records. At this message, click OK.
g. Click the Cancel button to close the Find dialog box.

18. Suppose you want to find information on a representative and you remember the first name but not the last name. Search for a field containing the first name of *Lydia* by completing the following steps:
    a. Click in the *RepID* column heading.
    b. Click the Find button in the Find group.
    c. At the Find dialog box, type **Lydia** in the *Find What* text box.
    d. Click the down-pointing arrow at the right side of the *Match* option and then click *Any Part of Field* at the drop-down list.
    e. Click the Find Next button. (Access will find and select the representative name *Lydia Alvarado*.)
    f. Click the Cancel button to close the Find dialog box.

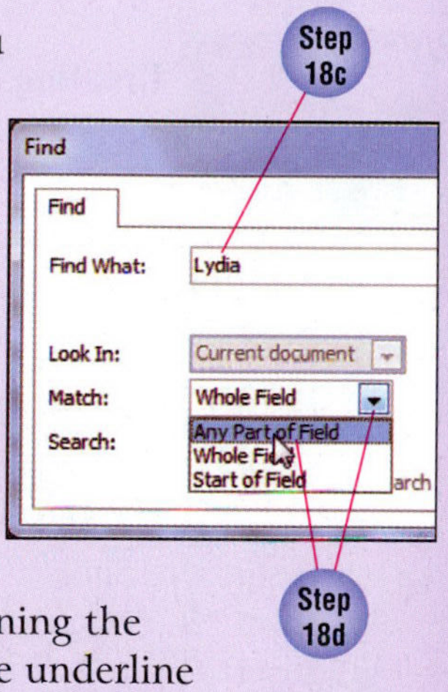

19. Click the control object at the bottom of the *RepID* column containing the number *17* and then press the Delete key. (This does not delete the underline above the amount.)
20. Switch to Print Preview by clicking the View button arrow in the Views group in the Report Layout Tools Design tab and then clicking *Print Preview* at the drop-down list.
21. Click the Margins button in the Page Size group and then click *Normal* at the drop-down list.

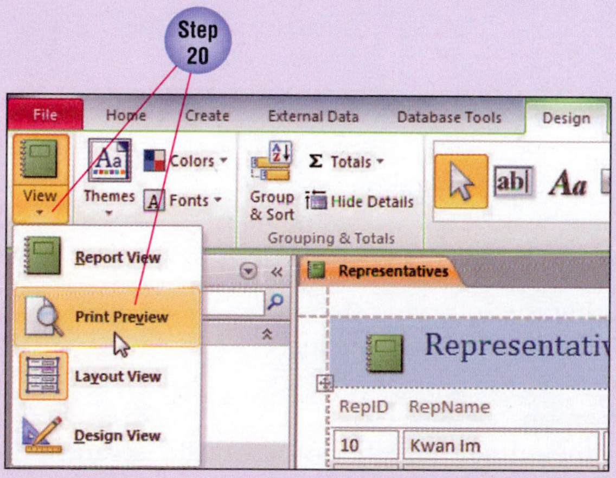

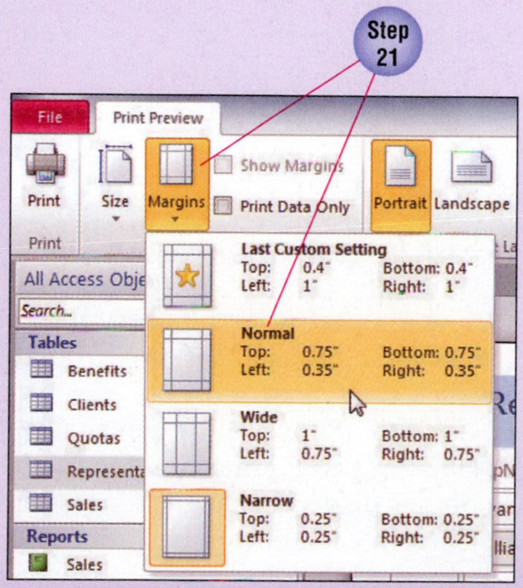

22. Print the report by clicking the Print button at the left side of the Print Preview tab and then clicking OK at the Print dialog box. (The report will print on three pages. The second and third pages contain only shading.)
23. Close Print Preview by clicking the Close Print Preview button.
24. Save the report with the name *Representatives*.
25. Close the Representatives report.

Creating a Report with a Query

Since one of the purposes of a report is to answer specific questions, design and run a query and then create a report based on that query. Create a report from a query in the same manner as creating a report from a table.

Project 1c **Creating a Report with a Query** **Part 3 of 5**

1. With the **AL1-C6-Dearborn.accdb** database open, design a query that extracts records from two tables with the following specifications:
   a. Add the Clients and Sales tables to the query window.
   b. Insert the *Client* field from the Clients table to the first *Field* row field.
   c. Insert the *StreetAddress* field from the Clients table to the second *Field* row field.
   d. Insert the *City* field from the Clients table to the third *Field* row field.
   e. Insert the *State* field from the Clients table to the fourth *Field* row field.
   f. Insert the *ZipCode* field from the Clients table to the fifth *Field* row field.
   g. Insert the *Sales2010* field from the Sales table to the sixth *Field* row field.
   h. Insert the criterion *Indianapolis Or Muncie* in the *Criteria* row field in the *City* column.
   i. Insert the criterion *>75000* in the *Criteria* row field in the *Sales2010* column.

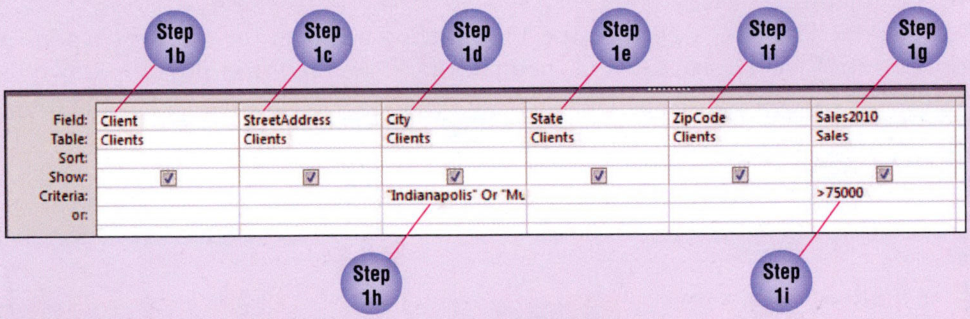

   j. Run the query.
   k. Save the query and name it *InMunSalesOver$75000*.
   l. Close the query.
2. Create a report with the query by completing the following steps:
   a. Click the *InMunSalesOver$75000* query in the Navigation pane.
   b. Click the Create tab.
   c. Click the Report button in the Reports group.
   d. Click in the column heading *Client* and then drag the right border to the left until the border displays near the longest entry in the column.
   e. Click in each of the remaining column headings and reduce the column widths. (Make sure the longest entry in each column is visible.)

f. Access automatically inserted a total amount for the *Sales2010* column. Scroll down the report to display the total amount, click the amount, and then increase the height and width of the object so the entire amount is visible.

3. Display the report in Print Preview by clicking the View button arrow in the Views group in the Report Layout Tools Design tab and then clicking *Print Preview* at the drop-down list.
4. Make sure that all columns of data display on the first page.
5. Change the top margin by completing the following steps:
   a. Click the Page Setup button in the Page Layout group.
   b. At the Page Setup dialog box, select the current measurement in the *Top* measurement box and then type 1.
   c. Click OK.

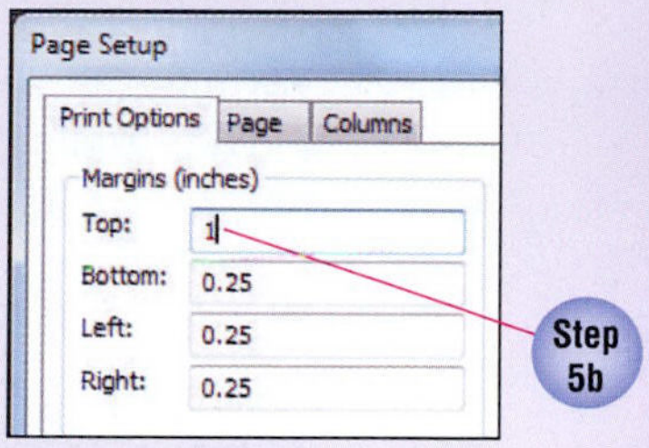

6. Print the first page of the report (the second page contains only shading) by completing the following steps:
   a. Click the Print button that displays at the left side of the Print Preview tab.
   b. At the Print dialog box, click the *Pages* option in the *Print Range* section.
   c. Type 1 in the *From* text box, press the Tab key, and then type 1 in the *To* text box.
   d. Click OK.
7. Close Print Preview.
8. Save the report and name it *InMun2010Sales*.
9. Close the report.

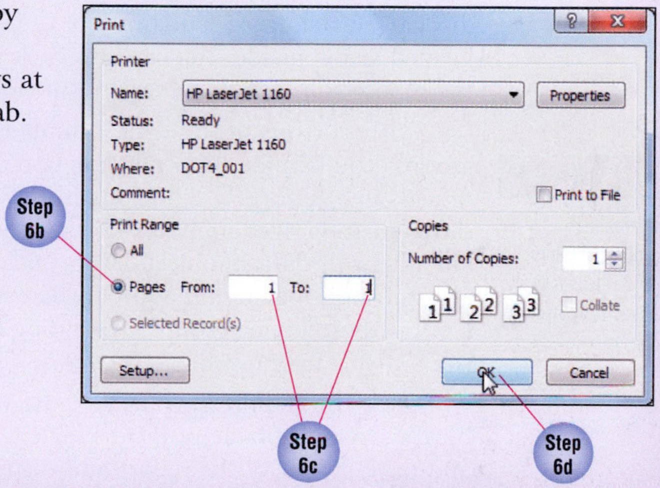

Customizing a Report

You can customize a report in much the same manner as customizing a form. When you first create a report, the report displays in Layout view and the Report Layout Tools Design tab is active. You can customize control objects in the *Detail* section and the *Header* section with buttons in the Report Layout Tools ribbon with the Design tab, the Arrange tab, the Format tab, or the Page Setup tab selected.

The Report Layout Tools Design tab contains many of the same options at the Form Layout Tools Design tab. With options in this tab, you can apply a theme, insert controls, insert header or footer data, and add existing fields. The tab also contains the Grouping & Totals group, which you will learn about in the next section. Use the Totals button in the Grouping & Totals group to perform functions such as finding the sum, average, maximum, or minimum of the numbers in a column. To use the Totals button, click the column heading of the column containing data you want to total, click the Totals button, and then click the desired function at the drop-down list. Use the Page Number button in the Report Layout Tools Design tab to insert and format page numbers.

HINT

The themes available in Access are the same as the themes available in Word, Excel, and PowerPoint.

Totals

Click the Report Layout Tools Arrange tab and options display for inserting and selecting rows, splitting cells horizontally and vertically, moving data up or down, controlling margins, and changing the padding between objects and cells. The options in the Report Layout Tools Arrange tab are the same as the options in the Form Layout Tools Arrange tab.

Select and format data in a report with options at the Report Layout Tools Format tab. The options in this tab are the same as the options in the Form Layout Tools Format tab. You can apply formatting to a report or specific objects in a report. If you want to apply formatting to a specific object, click the object in the report or click the Object button arrow in the Selection group in the Report Layout Tools Format tab and then click the desired object at the drop-down list. To format all objects in the report, click the Select All button in the Selection group. This selects all objects in the report including objects in the *Header* section. If you want to select all of the objects in the report form, click the table move handle that displays in the upper left corner of the report table as a small square with a four-headed arrow inside. You can also click the table move handle and then drag with the mouse to move the objects in the form.

HINT

Customize the formatting of control objects with options at the Report Layout Tools Format tab.

With buttons in the Font, Number, Background, and Control Formatting groups, you can apply formatting to a control object or cell and to selected objects or cells in a report. Use buttons in the Font group to change the font, apply a different font size, apply text effects such as bold and underline, and change the alignment of data in objects. Insert a background image in the report using the Background button and apply formatting to objects or cells with buttons in the Control Formatting group. Depending on what is selected in the report, some of the buttons may not be active.

Click the Report Layout Tools Page Setup tab and the buttons that display are buttons also available in Print Preview. For example, you can change the page size and page layout of the report and display the Page Setup dialog box.

Project 1d Applying Formatting to a Report

Part 4 of 5

1. With **AL1-C6-Dearborn.accdb** database open, delete the Sales report by right-clicking *Sales* in the *Reports* section of the Navigation pane and then clicking the *Delete* option at the shortcut menu. At the message asking if you want to permanently delete the report, click Yes.
2. Create a new report with the Sales table by clicking *Sales* in the *Tables* section of the Navigation pane, clicking the Create tab, and then clicking the Report button in the Reports group.
3. Click the Themes button in the Themes group in the Report Layout Tools Design tab and then click *Elemental* at the drop-down gallery. (You may need to scroll down the gallery to display this option.)

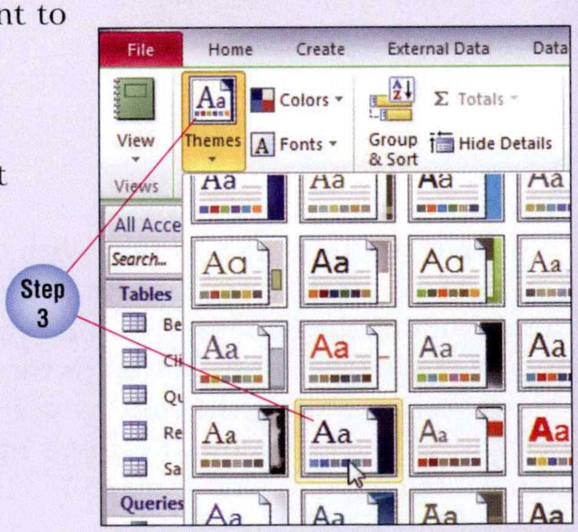

4. Insert new control objects by completing the following steps:
   a. Click in the *ClientID* cell.
   b. Click the Report Layout Tools Arrange tab.
   c. Click the Insert Above button in the Rows & Columns group.

5. Merge the cells in the new row by completing the following steps:
   a. Click in the blank cell immediately above the *ClientID* cell.
   b. Hold down the Shift key and then click immediately above the *Sales2011* cell. (This selects three cells.)
   c. Click the Merge button in the Merge/Split group.
   d. Type **Dearborn Yearly Sales** in the new cell.

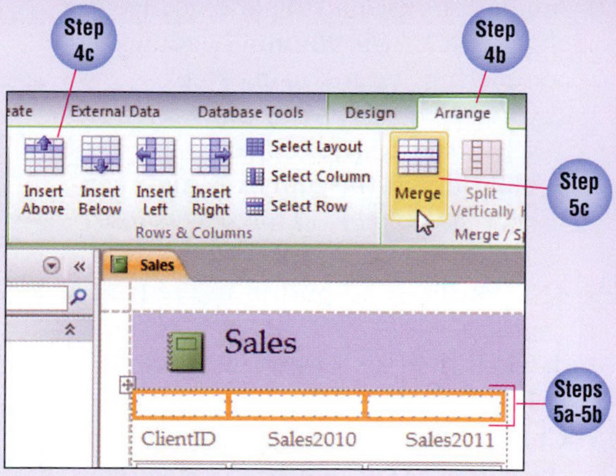

6. Split a cell by completing the following steps:
   a. Click in the *Sales* title in the *Header* section.
   b. Split the cell containing the title by clicking the Split Horizontally button in the Merge/Split group.
   c. Click in the empty cell immediately right of the cell containing the title *Sales* and then press the Delete key. (Deleting the empty cell causes the date and time to move to the left in the *Header* section.)
7. Click in the *Dearborn Yearly Sales* cell and then drag down the bottom border so all of the text in the cell is visible.
8. Change the report table margins and padding by completing the following steps:
   a. Click the table move handle that displays in the upper left corner of the *Dearborn Yearly Sales* cell. (This selects the control objects in the report table in the *Detail* section.)
   b. Click the Control Margins button in the Position group and then click *Narrow* at the drop-down list.
   c. Click the Control Padding button in the Position group and then click *Medium* at the drop-down list.

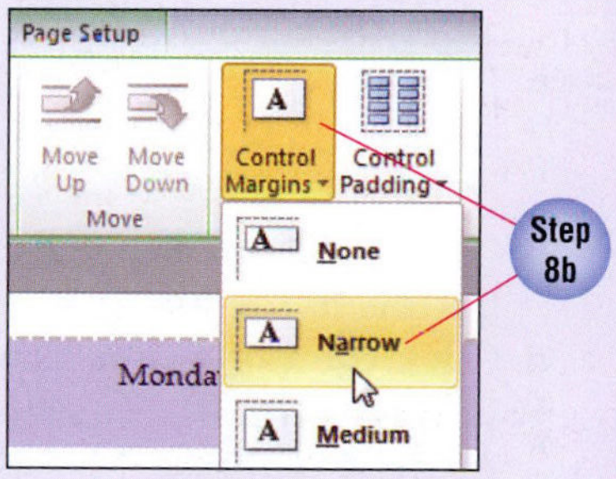

9. Change the font for all control objects in the report by completing the following steps:
   a. Press Ctrl + A to select all control objects in the report. (An orange border displays around selected objects.)
   b. Click the Report Layout Tools Format tab.
   c. Click the Font button arrow in the Font group and then click *Cambria* at the drop-down list. (You may need to scroll down the list to display *Cambria*.)

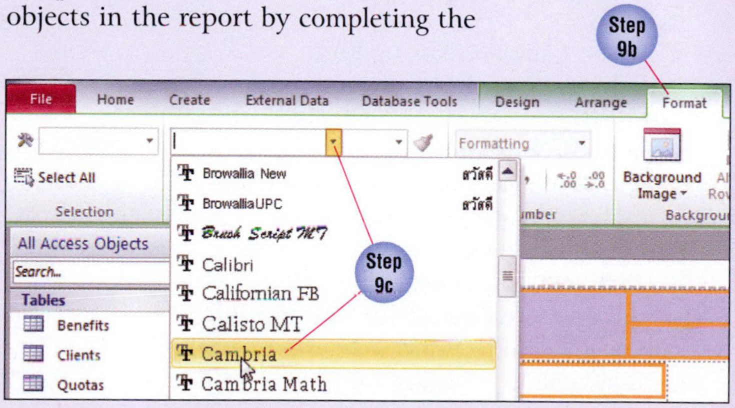

10. Apply bold formatting and change the alignment of the column headings by completing the following steps:
    a. Click *Dearborn Yearly Sales* to select the control object.
    b. Hold down the Shift key and then click *Sales2011*. (This selects four cells.)
    c. Click the Bold button in the Font group.
    d. Click the Center button in the Font group.

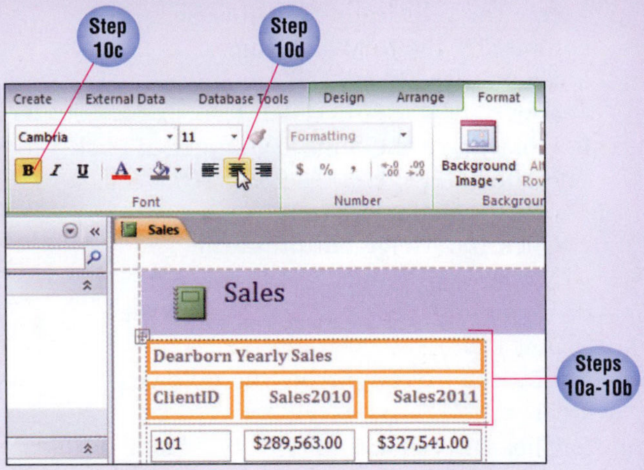

11. Change the alignment of data in the *ClientID* column by clicking the field value *101* (located below the *ClientID* column heading) and then clicking the Center button in the Font group.
12. Format amounts and apply conditional formatting to the amounts by completing the following steps:
    a. Click the first field value below the *Sales2010* column heading. (This selects all of the amounts in the column.)
    b. Hold down the Shift key and then click the first field value below the *Sales2011* column heading.
    c. Click twice on the Decrease Decimals button in the Number group.
    d. Click the Conditional Formatting button in the Control Formatting group.
    e. At the Conditional Formatting Rules Manager dialog box, click the New Rule button.
    f. At the New Formatting Rule dialog box, click the down-pointing arrow at the right side of the second option box in the *Edit the rule description* section and then click *greater than* at the drop-down list.
    g. Click in the text box immediately right of the option box containing *greater than* and then type **199999**.
    h. Click the Background color button arrow and then click the *Green 2* color option (located in the seventh column).
    i. Click the OK button.
    j. At the Conditional Formatting Rules Manager dialog box, click the New Rule button.

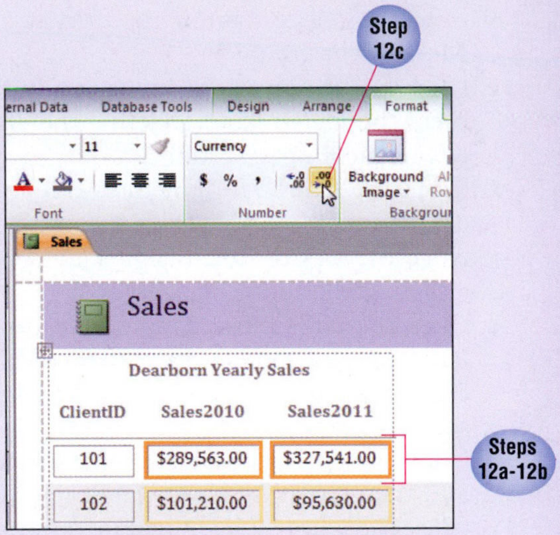

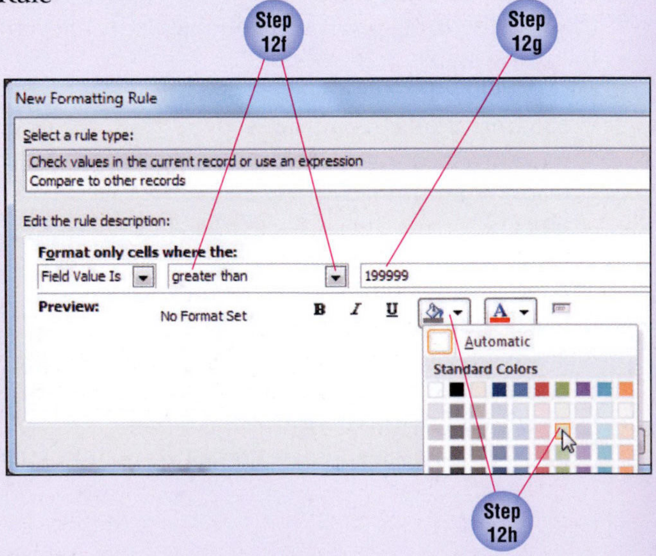

k. At the New Formatting Rule dialog box, click the down-pointing arrow at the right side of the second option box in the *Edit the rule description* section and then click *less than* at the drop-down list.

l. Click in the text box immediately right of the option containing *less than* and then type 200000.

m. Click the Background color button arrow and then click the *Maroon 2* color option (located in the sixth column).

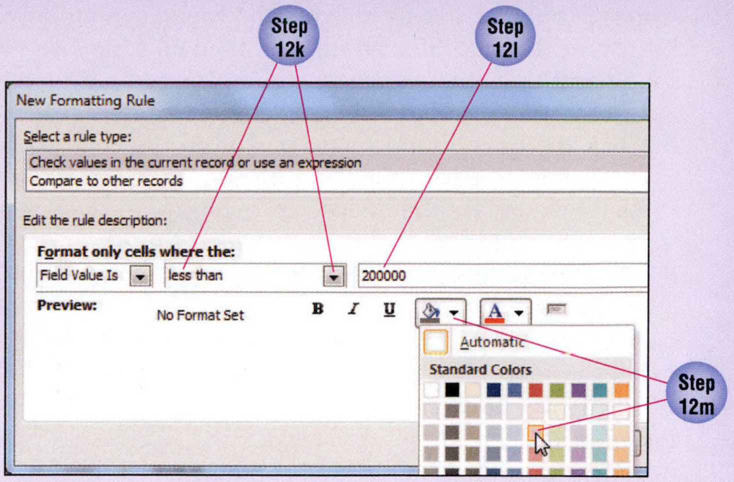

n. Click OK to close the New Formatting Rule dialog box.

o. Click OK to close the Conditional Formatting Rules Manager dialog box.

13. Sum the totals in the *Sales2010* column by completing the following steps:

a. Click in the *Sales2010* column heading.

b. Click the Report Layout Tools Design tab.

c. Click the Totals button in the Grouping & Totals group and then click *Sum* at the drop-down list.

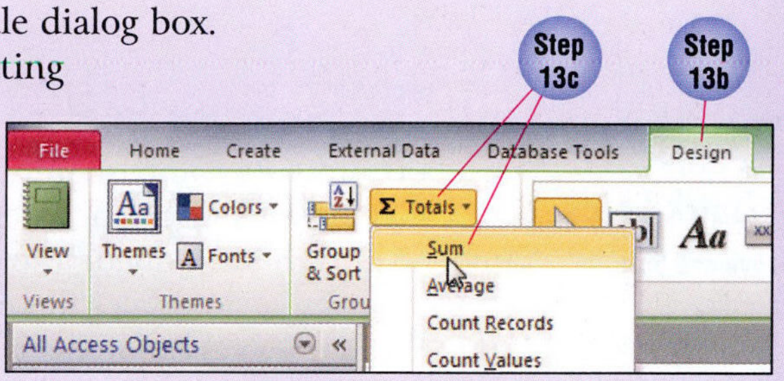

14. Click in the *Sales2011* sum amount (located at the bottom of the *Sales2011* column), click the Report Layout Tools Format tab, and then click the Decrease Decimals button two times.

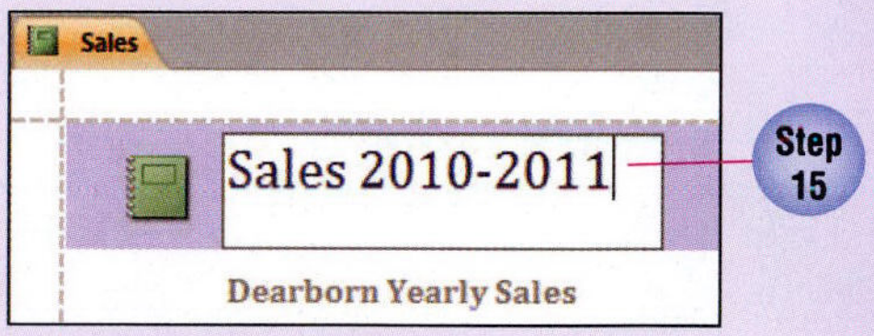

15. Edit the title by double-clicking in the *Sales* title in the *Header* section of the report and then editing the title so it reads *Sales 2010-2011*.

16. Change the top margin by completing the following steps:

a. Click in the *ClientID* column heading and then click the Report Layout Tools Page Setup tab.

b. Click the Page Setup button in the Page Layout group.

c. At the Page Setup dialog box with the Print Options tab selected, select the current measurement in the *Top* measurement box and then type 0.5.

d. Click OK to close the Page Setup dialog box.

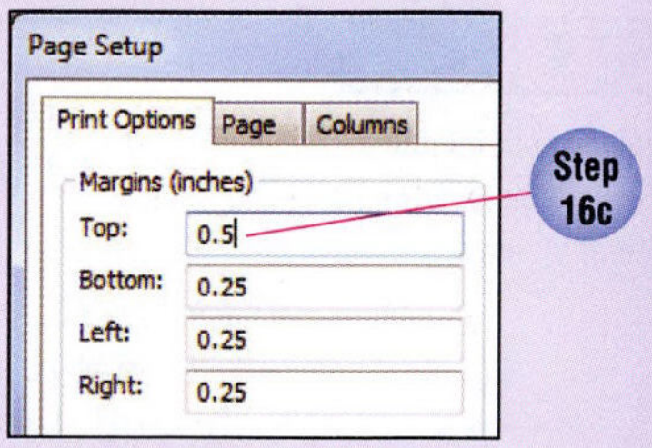

17. Change the page size by clicking the Size button in the Page Size group in the Report Layout Tools Page Setup tab and then clicking *Legal* at the drop-down list.

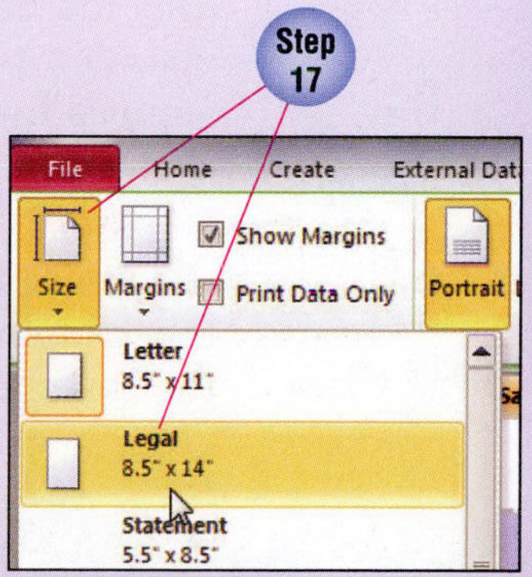

18. Display the report in Print Preview by clicking the File tab, clicking the Print tab, and then clicking the *Print Preview* option. Click the Two Pages button in the Zoom group and notice that the entire report will print on one legal-sized page.

19. Click the Close Print Preview button to return to the report.

20. Change the page size by clicking the Page Layout Tools Page Setup tab, clicking the Size button in the Page Size group, and then clicking *Letter* at the drop-down list.
21. Insert and then remove a background image by completing the following steps:
    a. Click the Report Layout Tools Format tab.
    b. Click the Background Image button in the Background group and then click *Browse* at the drop-down list.
    c. At the Insert Picture dialog box, navigate to the Access2010L1C6 folder on your storage medium and then double-click ***Mountain.jpg***.
    d. Display the report in Print Preview, notice the mountain image, and then close Print Preview.
    e. At the report, click the Undo button on the Quick Access toolbar to remove the background image. (You may need to click the Undo button more than once.)
22. Print the report by clicking the File tab, clicking the Print tab, and then clicking the *Quick Print* option.
23. Save the report and name it *Sales* and then close the report.

Grouping and Sorting Records

Quick Steps

Group and Sort Records
1. Open desired report in Layout view.
2. Click Group & Sort button.
3. Click Add a group button.
4. Click desired group field.

HINT

Grouping allows you to separate groups of records visually.

Group & Sort

Add a group

Add a sort

A report presents database information in a printed form and generally displays data that answers a specific question. To make the data in a report easy to understand, you can divide the data into groups. For example, you can divide data in a report by region, sales, dates, or any other division that helps identify the data to the reader. Access contains a powerful group and sort feature you can use in a report. In this section you will complete basic group and sort functions. For more detailed information on grouping and sorting, please refer to the Access help files.

Click the Group & Sort button in the Grouping & Totals group in the Report Layout Tools Design tab and the Group, Sort, and Total pane displays at the bottom of the work area as shown in Figure 6.2. Click the Add a group button in the Group, Sort, and Total pane and Access adds a new grouping level row to the pane along with a list of available fields. Click the field on which you want to group data in the report and Access adds the grouping level in the report. With options in the grouping level row, you can change the group, specify the sort order, and expand the row to display additional options.

When you specify a grouping level, Access automatically sorts that level in ascending order (from A to Z or from lowest to highest). You can then sort additional data within the report by clicking the Add a sort button in the Group, Sort, and Total pane. This inserts a sorting row in the pane below the grouping level row along with a list of available fields. At this list, click the field on which you want to sort. For example, in Project 1e you will specify that a report is grouped by city (which will display in ascending order) and then specify that the client names display in alphabetical order within the city.

To delete a grouping or sorting level in the Group, Sort, and Total pane, click the Delete button that displays at the right side of the level row. After specifying the grouping and sorting levels, close the Group, Sort, and Total pane by clicking the close button located in the upper right corner of the pane.

Figure 6.2 Group, Sort, and Total Pane

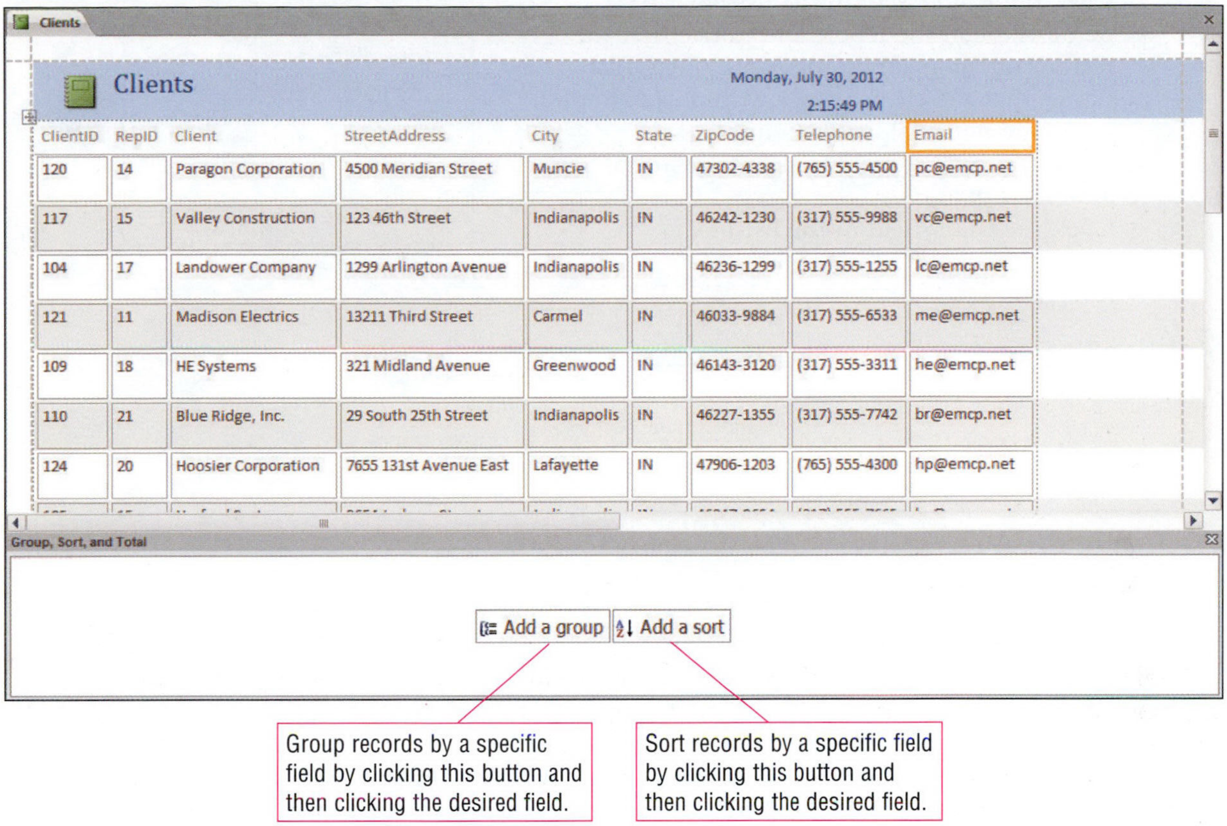

Clients
Clients
Monday, July 30, 2012
2:15:49 PM
ClientID RepID Client StreetAddress City State ZipCode Telephone Email
120 14 Paragon Corporation 4500 Meridian Street Muncie IN 47302-4338 (765) 555-4500 pc@emcp.net
117 15 Valley Construction 123 46th Street Indianapolis IN 46242-1230 (317) 555-9988 vc@emcp.net
104 17 Landower Company 1299 Arlington Avenue Indianapolis IN 46236-1299 (317) 555-1255 lc@emcp.net
121 11 Madison Electrics 13211 Third Street Carmel IN 46033-9884 (317) 555-6533 me@emcp.net
109 18 HE Systems 321 Midland Avenue Greenwood IN 46143-3120 (317) 555-3311 he@emcp.net
110 21 Blue Ridge, Inc. 29 South 25th Street Indianapolis IN 46227-1355 (317) 555-7742 br@emcp.net
124 20 Hoosier Corporation 7655 131st Avenue East Lafayette IN 47906-1203 (765) 555-4300 hp@emcp.net
Group, Sort, and Total
Add a group
Add a sort
Group records by a specific field by clicking this button and then clicking the desired field.
Sort records by a specific field by clicking this button and then clicking the desired field.

Project 1e Grouping and Sorting Data

Part 5 of 5

1. With the **AL1-C6-Dearborn.accdb** database open, create a report with the Clients table using the Report button in the Create tab.
2. Click each of the column headings individually and then decrease the size of each column so the right border of the column is just right of the longest entry in each column.
3. Change the orientation to landscape by completing the following steps:
   a. Click the Report Layout Tools Page Setup tab.
   b. Click the Landscape button in the Page Layout group.
4. Group the report by RepID and then sort by clients by completing the following steps:
   a. Click the Report Layout Tools Design tab.
   b. Click the Group & Sort button in the Grouping & Totals group.
   c. Click the Add a group button in the Group, Sort, and Total pane.

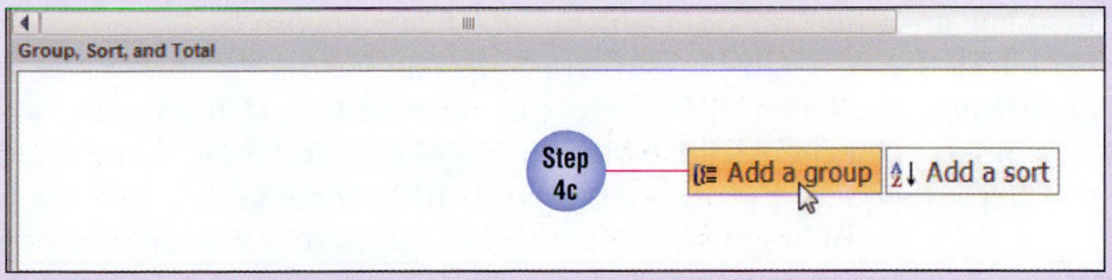

d. Click the *RepID* field in the list box.
e. Scroll through the report and notice that the records are grouped by the *RepID* field. Also, notice that the client names within each RepID group are not in alphabetic order.
f. Click the Add a sort button in the Group, Sort, and Total pane.
g. Click the *Client* field in the list box.

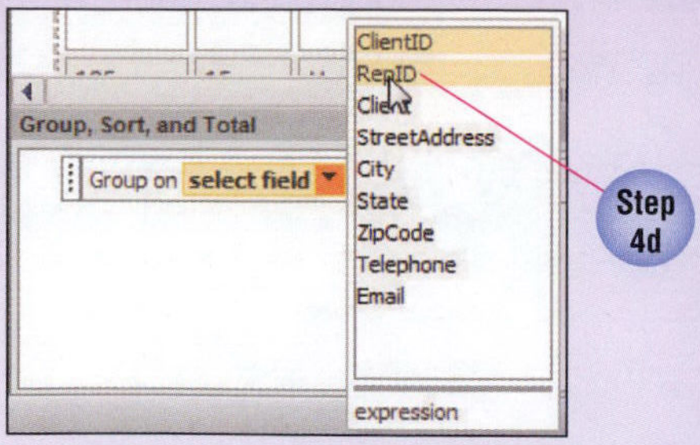

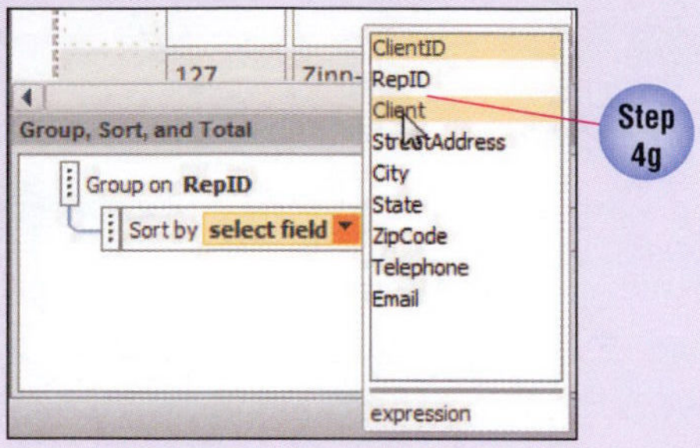

h. Scroll through the report and notice that client names are now alphabetized within RepID groups.
i. Close the Group, Sort, and Total pane by clicking the Close button located in the upper right corner of the pane.

5. Save the report and name it *ClientsGroupedRpt*.
6. Print the first page of the report by completing the following steps:
   a. Click the File tab, click the Print tab, and then click the *Print* option.
   b. At the Print dialog box, click *Pages* option in the *Print Range* section.
   c. Type 1 in the *From* text box, press the Tab key, and then type 1 in the *To* text box.
   d. Click OK.
7. Close the *ClientsGroupedRpt* report.
8. Open the InMun2010Sales report in Layout view.
9. Group the report by city and then sort by clients by completing the following steps:
   a. Click the Group & Sort button in the Grouping & Totals group in the Report Layout Tools Design tab.
   b. Click the Add a group button in the Group, Sort, and Total pane.
   c. Click the *City* field in the list box.
   d. Click the Add a sort button in the Group, Sort, and Total pane and then click the *Client* field in the list box.
   e. Close the Group, Sort, and Total pane by clicking the Close button located in the upper right corner of the pane.
10. Print the first page of the report (refer to Step 6).
11. Save and then close the InMun2010Sales report.
12. Close the **AL1-C6-Dearborn.accdb** database.
13. Display the Open dialog box with Access2010L1C6 on your storage medium the active folder, open the **AL1-C6-WarrenLegal.accdb** database and enable the contents.
14. Design a query that extracts records from three tables with the following specifications:
    a. Add the Billing, Clients, and Rates tables to the query window.

b. Insert the *LastName* field from the Clients table to the first *Field* row field.
c. Insert the *Date* field from the Billings table to the second *Field* row field.
d. Insert the *Hours* field from the Billings table to the third *Field* row field.
e. Insert the *Rate* field from the Rates table to the fourth *Field* row field.
f. Click in the fifth *Field* row field, type **Total: [Hours]*[Rate]**, and then press Enter.

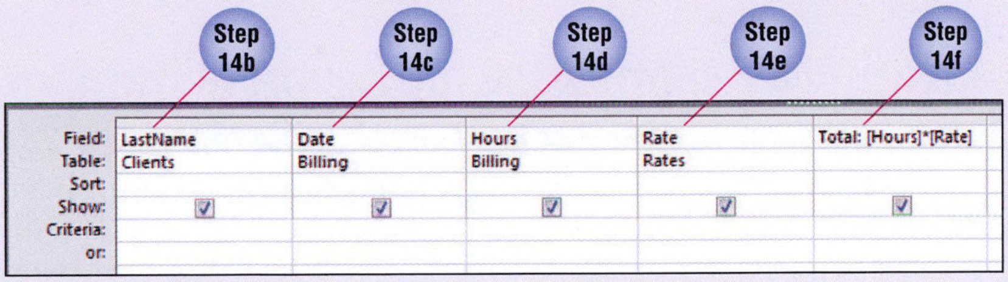

g. Run the query.
h. Save the query and name it *ClientBilling*.
i. Close the query.

15. Create a report with the ClientBilling query using the Report button in the Create tab.
16. Click each of the column headings individually and then decrease the size of each column so the right border of the column is near the longest entry.
17. Apply Currency formatting to the numbers in the *Total* column by completing the following steps:
    a. Click the Report Layout Tools Format tab.
    b. Click in the first field below the *Total* column (the field containing the number *350*).
    c. Click the Apply Currency Format button in the Number group.

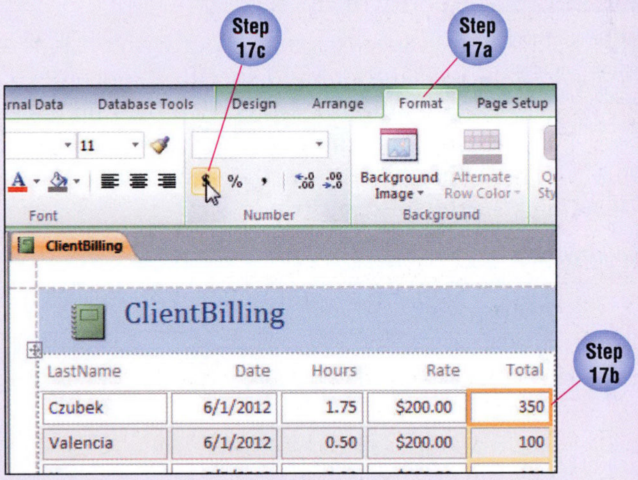

18. Group the report by last name by completing the following steps:
    a. Click the Report Layout Tools Design tab.
    b. Click the Group & Sort button in the Grouping & Totals group.
    c. Click the Add a group button in the Group, Sort, and Total pane.
    d. Click the *LastName* field in the list box.
    e. Click the Add a sort button in the Group, Sort, and Total pane.
    f. Click the *Date* field in the list box.
    g. Close the Group, Sort, and Total pane by clicking the Close button located in the upper right corner of the pane.
19. Save the report and name it *ClientBillingRpt*.
20. Print and then close the report. (The report will print on three pages.)
21. Close the **AL1-C6-WarrenLegal.accdb** database.

Project 2 Use Wizards to Create Reports and Labels 3 Parts

You will create reports using the Report Wizard and prepare mailing labels using the Label Wizard.

Creating a Report Using the Report Wizard

Quick Steps

Create a Report Using Report Wizard

1. Click Create tab.
2. Click Report Wizard button.
3. Choose desired options at each of the Report Wizard dialog boxes.

HINT

Use the Report Wizard to select specific fields and specify how data is grouped and sorted.

Report Wizard

Access offers a Report Wizard that will guide you through the steps for creating a report. To create a report using the wizard, click the Create tab and then click the Report Wizard button in the Reports group. At the first wizard dialog box, shown in Figure 6.3, choose the desired table or query with options from the *Tables/Queries* option box. Specify the fields you want included in the report by inserting them in the *Selected Fields* list box and then clicking the Next button.

At the second Report Wizard dialog box, shown in Figure 6.4, you can specify the grouping level of data in the report. To group data by a specific field, click the field in the list box at the left side of the dialog box and then click the One Field button. Use the button containing the left-pointing arrow to remove an option as a grouping level. Use the up-pointing and down-pointing arrows to change the priority of the field.

Specify a sort order with options at the third Report Wizard dialog box shown in Figure 6.5. To specify a sort order, click the down-pointing arrow at the right of the option box preceded by a number 1 and then click the field name. The default sort order is ascending. You can change this to descending by clicking the button that displays at the right side of the text box. After identifying the sort order, click the Next button.

Figure 6.3 First Report Wizard Dialog Box

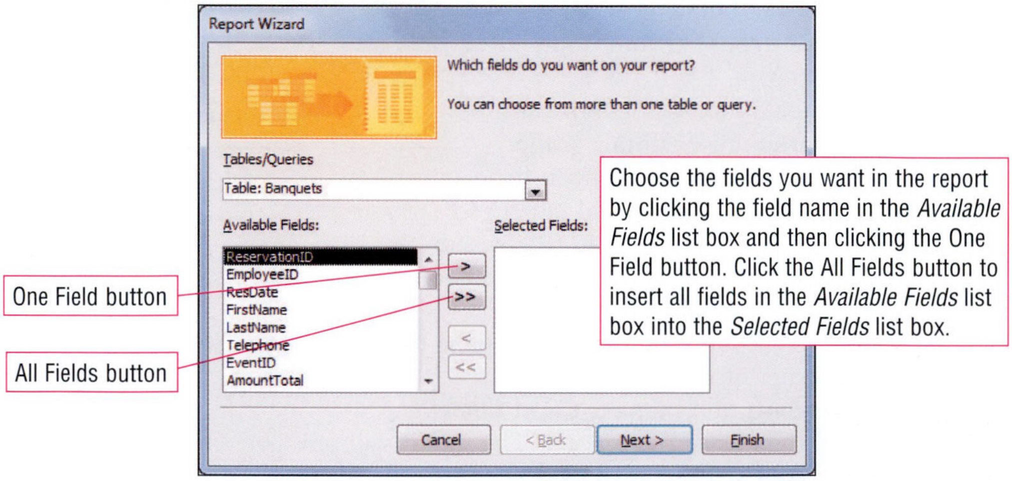
Report Wizard
Which fields do you want on your report?
You can choose from more than one table or query.
Tables/Queries
Table: Banquets
Available Fields:
Selected Fields:
ReservationID
EmployeeID
ResDate
FirstName
LastName
Telephone
EventID
AmountTotal
>
>>
<
<<
Cancel
< Back
Next >
Finish
One Field button
All Fields button
Choose the fields you want in the report by clicking the field name in the Available Fields list box and then clicking the One Field button. Click the All Fields button to insert all fields in the Available Fields list box into the Selected Fields list box.

Figure 6.4 Second Report Wizard Dialog Box

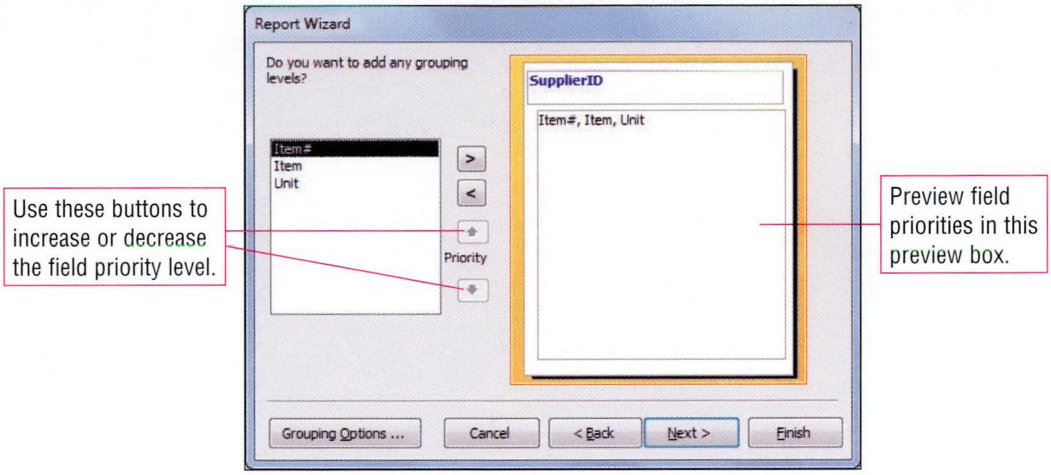

Figure 6.5 Third Report Wizard Dialog Box

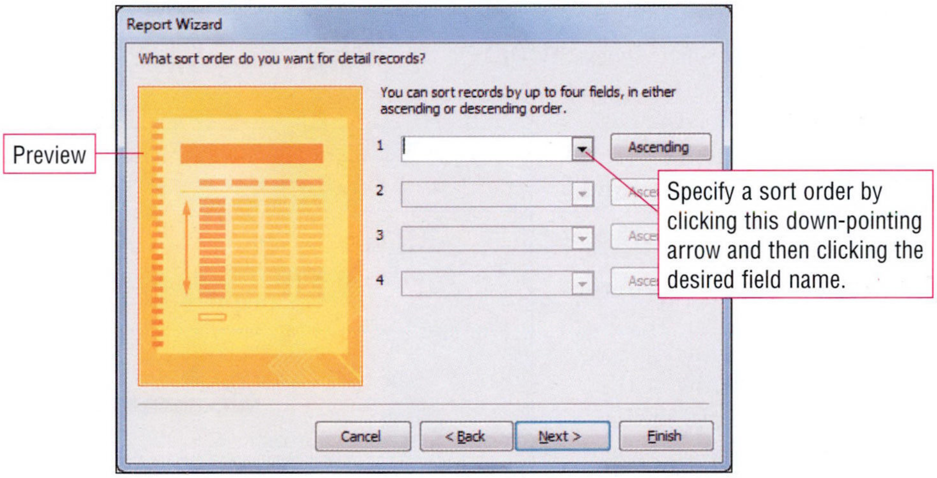

Use options at the fourth Report Wizard dialog box as shown in Figure 6.6 to specify the layout and orientation of the report. The *Layout* option has a default setting of *Stepped*. You can change this to *Block* or *Outline*. By default the report will print in *Portrait* orientation. You can change this to *Landscape* in the *Orientation* section of the dialog box. Access will adjust field widths in the report so all fields fit on one page. If you do not want Access to make the adjustment, remove the check mark from the *Adjust the field width so all fields fit on a page* option.

At the fifth and final Report Wizard dialog box, type a name for the report and then click the Finish button.

Figure 6.6 Fourth Report Wizard Dialog Box

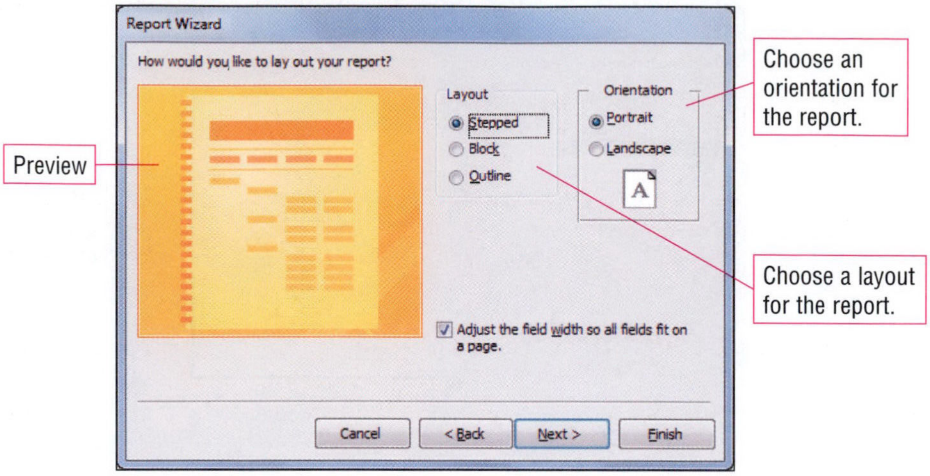

Project 2a Using the Report Wizard to Prepare a Report

Part 1 of 3

1. Display the Open dialog box with Access2010L1C6 on your storage medium the active folder.
2. Open the **AL1-C6-Skyline.accdb** database and enable the contents.
3. Create a report using the Report Wizard by completing the following steps:
   a. Click the Create tab.
   b. Click the Report Wizard button in the Reports group.
   c. At the first Report Wizard dialog box, click the down-pointing arrow at the right side of the *Tables/Queries* option box and then click *Table: Inventory* at the drop-down list.
   d. Click the All Fields button to insert all Inventory fields in the *Selected Fields* list box.
   e. Click the Next button.
   f. At the second Report Wizard dialog box, make sure *Supplier ID* displays in blue at the top of the preview page at the right side of the dialog box and then click the Next button.
   g. At the third Report Wizard dialog box, click the Next button. (You want to use the sorting defaults.)
   h. At the fourth Report Wizard dialog box, click the *Block* option in the *Layout* section and then click the Next button.

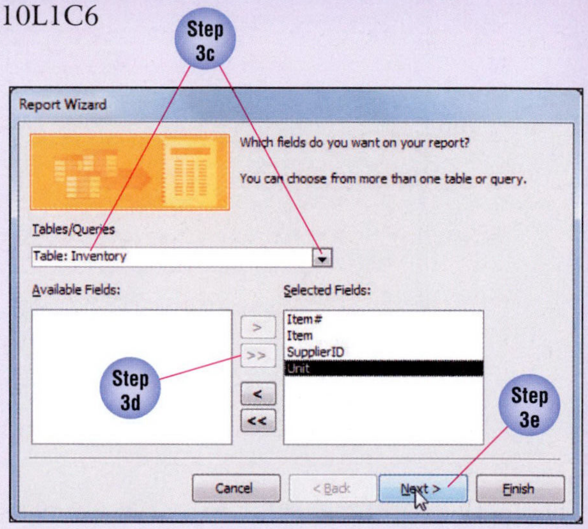

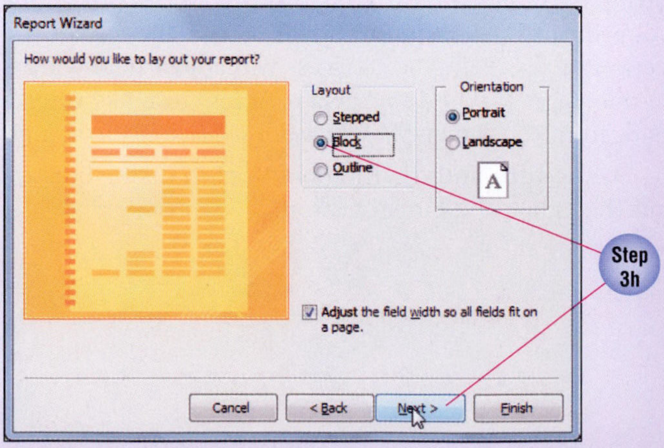

i. At the fifth Report Wizard dialog box, make sure *Inventory* displays in the *What title do you want for your report?* text box and then click the Finish button. (The report displays in Print Preview.)

4. With the report in Print Preview, click the Print button at the left side of the Print Preview tab and then click OK at the Print dialog box. (The report will print on two pages.)
5. Close Print Preview.
6. Switch to Report view by clicking the View button in the Report Design Tools Design tab.
7. Close the Inventory report.

If you create a report with fields from only one table, you will choose options from five Report Wizard dialog boxes. If you create a report with fields from more than one table, you will choose options from six Report Wizard dialog boxes. After choosing the tables and fields at the first dialog box, the second dialog box that displays asks how you want to view the data. For example, if you specify fields from a Suppliers table and fields from an Orders table, the second Report Wizard dialog box will ask you if you want to view data "by Suppliers" or "by Orders."

Project 2b Creating a Report with Fields from Multiple Tables Part 2 of 3

1. With the **AL1-C6-Skyline.accdb** database open, create a report with the Report Wizard by completing the following steps:
   a. Click the Create tab.
   b. Click the Report Wizard button in the Reports group.
   c. At the first Report Wizard dialog box, click the down-pointing arrow at the right side of the *Tables/Queries* option box and then click *Table: Events* at the drop-down list.
   d. Click the *Event* field in the *Available Fields* list box and then click the One Field button.
   e. Click the down-pointing arrow at the right side of the *Tables/Queries* option box and then click *Table: Banquets* at the drop-down list.
   f. Insert the following fields in the *Selected Fields* list box:
      ResDate
      FirstName
      LastName
      AmountTotal
      AmountPaid
   g. After inserting the fields, click the Next button.
   h. At the second Report Wizard dialog box, make sure *by Events* is selected and then click the Next button.

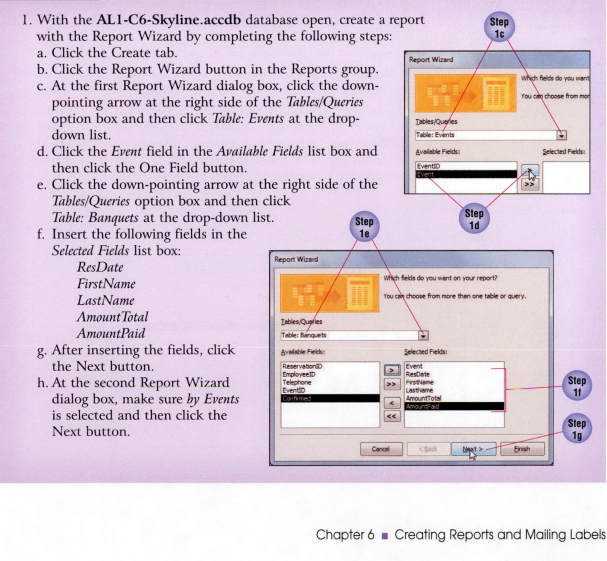

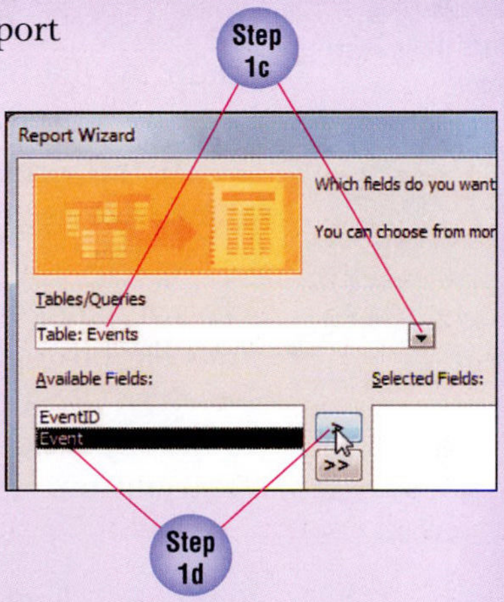

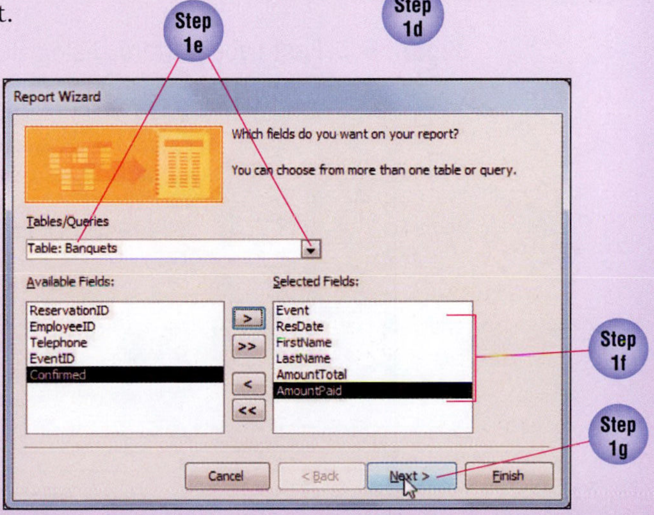

i. At the third Report Wizard dialog box, click the Next button. (The report preview shows that the report will be grouped by event.)
j. At the fourth Report Wizard dialog box, click the Next button. (You want to use the sorting defaults.)
k. At the fifth Report Wizard dialog box, click the *Block* option in the *Layout* section, click *Landscape* in the *Orientation* section, and then click the Next button.
l. At the sixth Report Wizard dialog box, select the current name in the *What title do you want for your report?* text box, type **BanquetEvents**, and then click the Finish button.

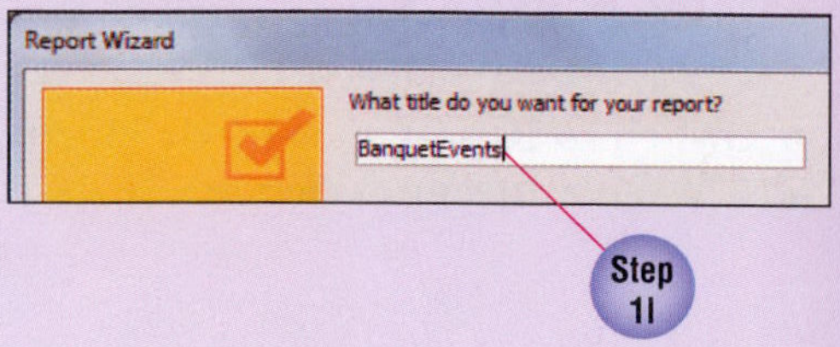

2. Close Print Preview and then change to Layout view.
3. Print and then close the BanquetEvents report.
4. Close the **AL1-C6-Skyline.accdb** database.

Preparing Mailing Labels

Quick Steps

Create Mailing Labels Using Label Wizard
1. Click the desired table.
2. Click Create tab.
3. Click Labels button.
4. Choose desired options at each of the Label Wizard dialog boxes.

Labels

Access includes a mailing label wizard that walks you through the steps for creating mailing labels with fields in a table. To create mailing labels, click the desired table, click the Create tab, and then click the Labels button in the Reports group. At the first Label Wizard dialog box shown in Figure 6.7, specify the label size, units of measure, and the label type, and then click the Next button.

At the second Label Wizard dialog box shown in Figure 6.8, specify the font name, size, weight, and color, and then click the Next button.

Specify the fields you want included in the mailing labels at the third Label Wizard dialog box shown in Figure 6.9. To do this, click the field in the *Available fields* list box, and then click the One Field button. This moves the field to the *Prototype label* box. Insert the fields in the *Prototype label* box as you want the text to display on the label. After inserting the fields in the *Prototype label* box, click the Next button.

Figure 6.7 First Label Wizard Dialog Box

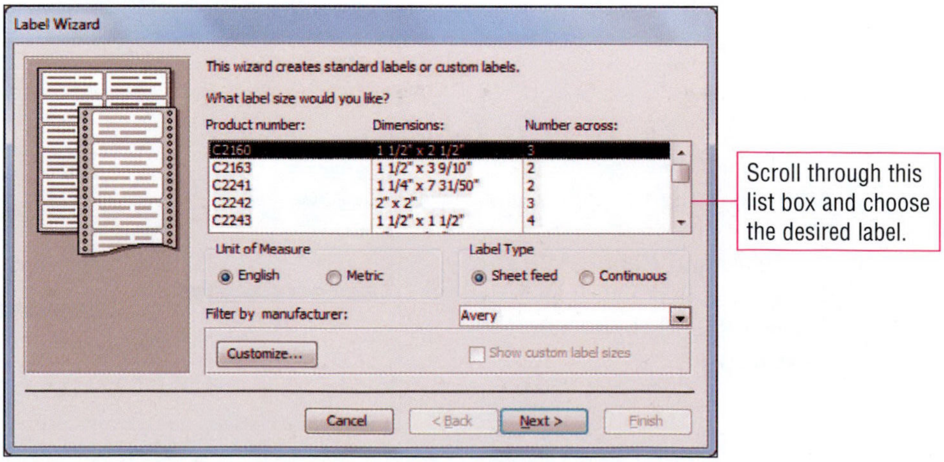

Figure 6.8 Second Label Wizard Dialog Box

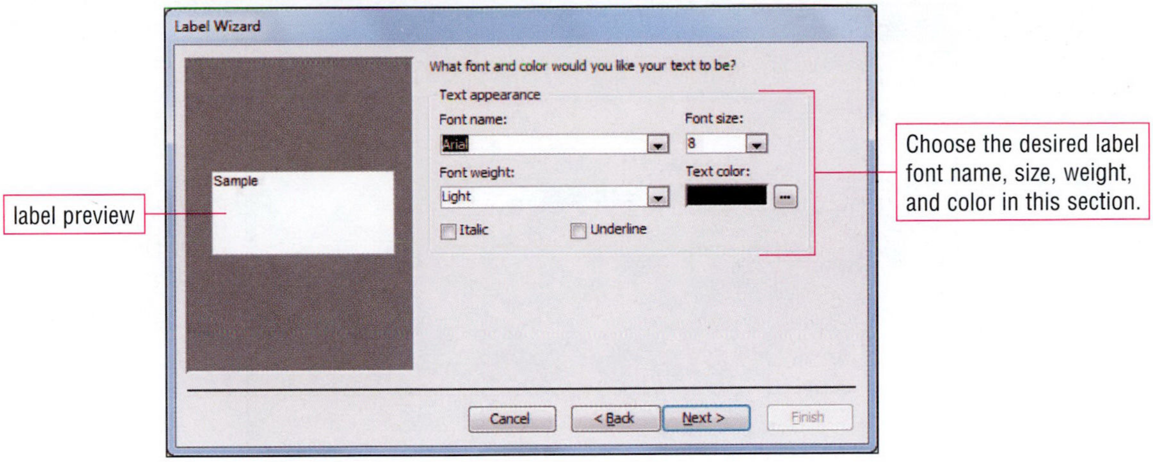

Figure 6.9 Third Label Wizard Dialog Box

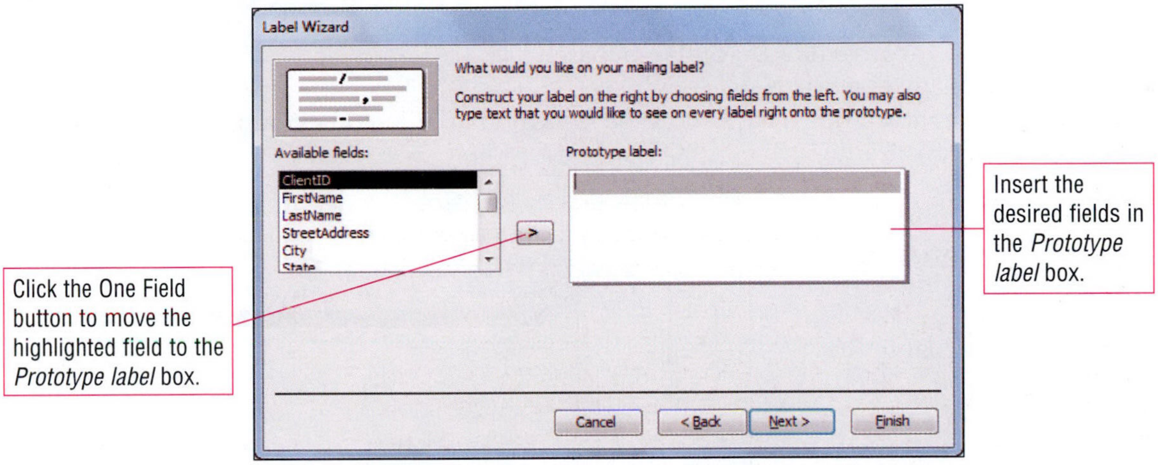

At the fourth Label Wizard dialog box, shown in Figure 6.10, you can specify a field from the database by which the labels are sorted. If you want the labels sorted (for example, by last name, postal code, etc.), insert the field by which you want the fields sorted in the *Sort by* list box and then click the Next button.

At the last Label Wizard dialog box, type a name for the label file, and then click the Finish button. After a few moments, the labels display on the screen in Print Preview. Print the labels and/or close Print Preview.

Figure 6.10 Fourth Label Wizard Dialog Box

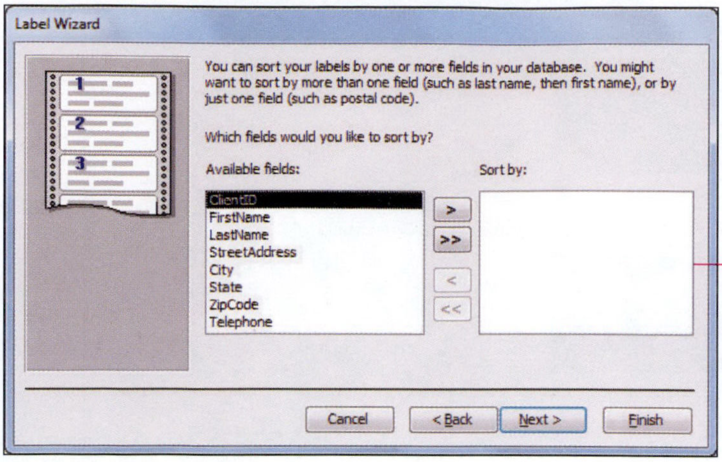

If you want labels sorted by a particular field, insert that field in the *Sort by* box.

Project 2c Preparing Mailing Labels

Part 3 of 3

1. Open the **AL1-C6-WarrenLegal.accdb** database.
2. Click the Clients table in the Navigation pane.
3. Click the Create tab and then click the Labels button in the Reports group.
4. At the first Label Wizard dialog box, make sure *English* is selected in the *Unit of Measure* section, *Avery* is selected in the *Filter by manufacturer* list box, *Sheet feed* is selected in the *Label Type* section, *C2160* is selected in the *Product number* list box, and then click the Next button.

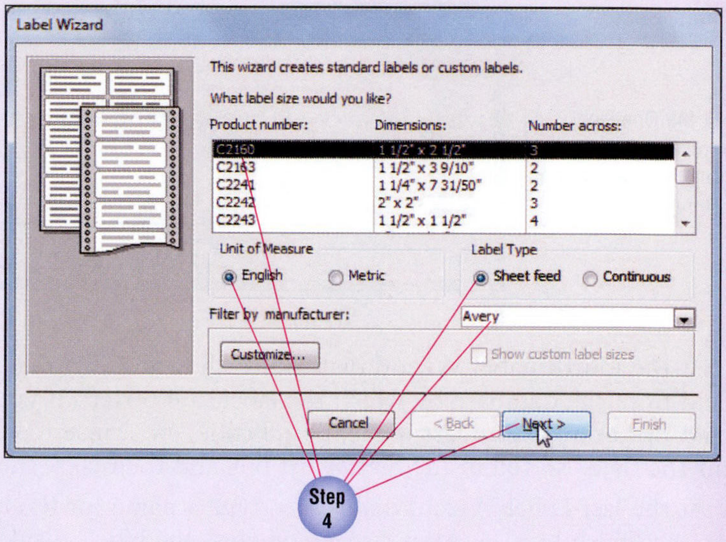

5. At the second Label Wizard dialog box, change the font size to 10, and then click the Next button.
6. At the third Label Wizard dialog box, complete the following steps to insert the fields in the *Prototype label* box:
   a. Click *FirstName* in the *Available fields* list box and then click the One Field button.
   b. Press the spacebar, make sure *LastName* is selected in the *Available fields* list box, and then click the One Field button.
   c. Press the Enter key. (This moves the insertion point down to the next line in the *Prototype label* box.)
   d. With *StreetAddress* selected in the *Available fields* list box, click the One Field button.
   e. Press the Enter key.
   f. With *City* selected in the *Available fields* list box, click the One Field button.
   g. Type a comma (,) and then press the spacebar.

h. With *State* selected in the *Available fields* list box, click the One Field button.
i. Press the spacebar.
j. With *ZipCode* selected in the *Available fields* list box, click the One Field button.
k. Click the Next button.

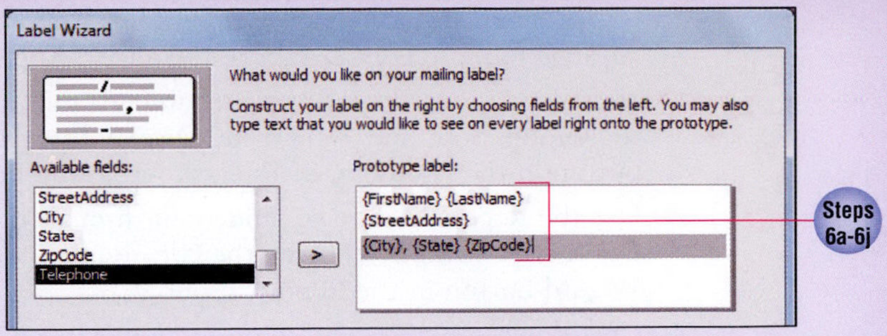

7. At the fourth Label Wizard dialog box, sort by ZIP code. To do this, click *ZipCode* in the *Available fields* list box and then click the One Field button.
8. Click the Next button.
9. At the last Label Wizard dialog box, click the Finish button. (The Label Wizard automatically names the label report *Labels Clients*.)
10. Print the labels by clicking the Print button that displays at the left side of the Print Preview tab and then click OK at the Print dialog box.
11. Close Print Preview.
12. Switch to Report view by clicking the View button in the Report Design Tools Design tab.
13. Close the labels report and then close the **AL1-C6-WarrenLegal.accdb** database.

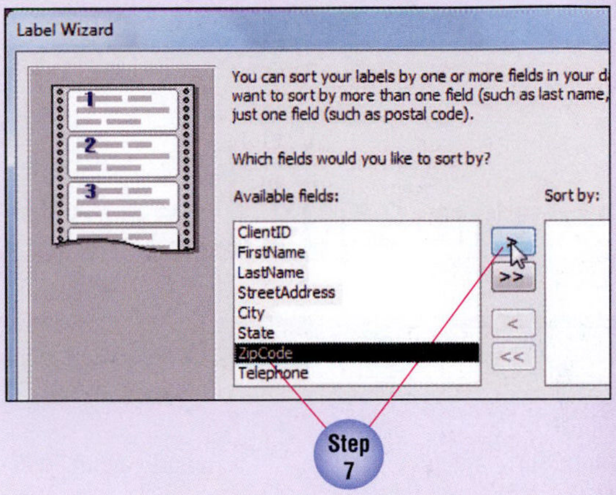

Chapter Summary

- You can create a report with data in a table or query to control how data appears on the page when printed.
- Create a report with the Report button in the Reports group in the Create tab.
- Four views are available for viewing a report — Report view, Print Preview, Layout view, and Design view.
- Use options in the Print Preview tab to specify how a report prints.
- In Layout view, you can select a report control object and then size or move the object. You can also change column width by clicking a column heading and then dragging the border to the desired width.
- Sort data in a record using the Ascending or Descending buttons in the Sort & Filter group in the Home tab.
- Customize a report with options in the Report Layout Tools ribbon with the Design tab, Arrange tab, Format tab, or Page Setup tab selected.

- You can customize control objects in the *Detail* section and the *Header* section with buttons in the Report Layout Tools ribbon with the Design tab, the Arrange tab, the Format tab, or the Page Setup tab selected.
- To make data in a report easier to understand, divide the data into groups using the Group, Sort, and Total pane. Display this pane by clicking the Group & Sort button in the Grouping & Totals group in the Report Layout Tools Design tab.
- Use the Report Wizard to guide you through the steps for creating a report. Begin the wizard by clicking the Create tab and then clicking the Report Wizard button in the Reports group.
- Create mailing labels with data in a table using the Label Wizard. Begin the wizard by clicking the desired table, clicking the Create tab, and then clicking the Labels button in the Reports group.

Commands Review

FEATURE	RIBBON TAB, GROUP	BUTTON
Report	Create, Reports	
Group, Sort, and Total pane	Report Layout Tools Design, Grouping & Totals	
Report Wizard	Create, Reports	
Labels Wizard	Create, Reports	

Concepts Check Test Your Knowledge

Completion: In the space provided at the right, indicate the correct term, symbol, or command.

1. The Report button is located in the Reports group in this tab. ____________
2. Layout view is one of four views available in a report including Report view, Design view, and this. ____________
3. Press these keys to select all control objects in a report in Layout view. ____________
4. The Ascending button is located in this group in the Home tab. ____________
5. Click this button in the Grouping & Totals group in the Report Layout Tools Design tab to perform functions such as finding the sum, average, maximum, or minimum of the numbers in a column. ____________

6. With options in this tab, you can insert controls, insert headers or footers data, and add existing fields. ____________________

7. The Group & Sort button is located in this group in the Report Layout Tools Design tab. ____________________

8. Click the Group & Sort button and this pane displays. ____________________

9. Use this to guide you through the steps for creating a report. ____________________

10. To create mailing labels, click the desired table, click the Create tab, and then click the Labels button in this group. ____________________

Skills Check Assess Your Performance

Assessment 1

CREATE AND FORMAT REPORTS IN THE HILLTOP DATABASE

1. Open the **AL1-C6-Hilltop.accdb** database and enable the contents.
2. Create a report with the Inventory table using the Report button.
3. With the report in Layout view, apply the following formatting:
   a. Center the data below each of the following column headings: *Equipment#*, *AvailableHours*, *ServiceHours*, and *RepairHours*.
   b. Select all of the control objects and then change the font to Constantia.
   c. Select the money amounts below the *PurchasePrice* column heading and then decrease the decimal so the money amounts display without a decimal point.
   d. Click in the *$473,260.00* amount and then decrease the decimal so the amount displays without a decimal.
   e. Change the title of the report to *Inventory Report*.
4. Save the report and name it *InventoryReport*.
5. Print and then close InventoryReport.
6. Create a query in Design view with the following specifications:
   a. Add the Customers, Equipment, Invoices, and Rates tables to the query window.
   b. Insert the *Customer* field from the Customers table in the first *Field* row field.
   c. Insert the *Equipment* field from the Equipment table in the second *Field* row field.
   d. Insert the *Hours* field from the Invoices table in the third *Field* row field.
   e. Insert the *Rate* field from the Rates table in the fourth *Field* row field.
   f. Click in the fifth *Field* row field, type **Total: [Hours]*[Rate]**, and then press Enter.
   g. Run the query.
   h. Save the query and name it *CustomerRentals* and then close the query.

7. Create a report with the CustomerRentals query using the Report button.
8. With the report in Layout view, apply the following formatting:
   a. Decrease the width of columns so the right border of each column displays near the right side of the longest entry.
   b. Select the money amounts and then decrease the decimal so the amounts display with no decimal point.
   c. Click in the *Total* column and then total the amounts by clicking the Report Layout Tools Design tab, clicking the Totals button in the Grouping & Totals group, and then clicking *Sum* at the drop-down list.
   d. Click the total amount (located at the bottom of the *Total* column), click the Report Layout Tools Format tab, and then click the Apply Currency Format button.
   e. Increase the height of the total amount until the entire amount is visible.
   f. Select and then delete the amount that displays at the bottom of the *Rate* column.
   g. Display the Group, Sort, and Total pane, group the records by *Customer*, sort by *Equipment*, and then close the pane.
   h. Apply the Grid theme. (Do this with the Themes button in the Themes group in the Report Layout Tools Design tab.)
   i. Select the five column headings and change the font color to black.
   j. Change the title to *Rentals*.
9. Save the report and name it *RentalReport*.
10. Print and then close RentalReport.

Assessment 2

CREATE REPORTS USING THE REPORT WIZARD

1. With the **AL1-C6-Hilltop.accdb** database open, create a report using the Report Wizard with the following specifications:
   a. At the first Report Wizard dialog box, insert the following fields in the *Selected Fields* list box:
      From the Equipment table:
         Equipment
      From the Inventory table:
         PurchaseDate
         PurchasePrice
         AvailableHours
   b. Do not make any changes at the second Report Wizard dialog box.
   c. Do not make any changes at the third Report Wizard dialog box.
   d. At the fourth Report Wizard dialog box, choose the *Columnar* option.
   e. At the fifth and last Report Wizard dialog box, click the Finish button. (This accepts the default report name of *Equipment*.)
2. Print and then close the report.

3. Create a report using the Report Wizard with the following specifications:
   a. At the first Report Wizard dialog box, insert the following fields in the *Selected Fields* list box:
      From the Customers table:
         Customer
      From the Invoices table:
         BillingDate
         Hours
      From the Equipment table:
         Equipment
      From the Rates table:
         Rate
   b. Do not make any changes at the second Report Wizard dialog box.
   c. Do not make any changes at the third Report Wizard dialog box.
   d. Do not make any changes at the fourth Report Wizard dialog box.
   e. At the fifth Report Wizard dialog box, choose the *Block* option.
   f. At the sixth and last Report Wizard dialog box, name the report *Rentals*.
4. Print and then close the report.

Assessment 3

CREATE MAILING LABELS

1. With the **AL1-C6-Hilltop.accdb** database open, click the Customers table in the Navigation pane.
2. Use the Label Wizard to create mailing labels (you determine the label type) with the customer names and addresses and sorted by customer names. Name the mailing label report *CustomerMailingLabels*.
3. Print the mailing labels.
4. Close the mailing labels.

Assessment 4

ADD A FIELD TO A REPORT

1. In Chapter 5, you added a field list to an existing form using the Field List pane. Experiment with adding a field to an existing report and then complete the following:
   a. Open the report named RentalReport (created in Assessment 1) in Layout view.
   b. Display the Field List pane and display all tables.
   c. Drag the *BillingDate* field from the Invoices table so the field is positioned between the *Equipment* column and the *Hours* column.
   d. At the message indicating that Access will modify the RecordSource property and asking if you want to continue, click Yes.
   e. Close the Field List pane.
3. Save, print, and then close the report.
4. Close the **AL1-C6-Hilltop.accdb** database.

Visual Benchmark Demonstrate Your Proficiency

DESIGN A QUERY AND CREATE A REPORT WITH THE QUERY

1. Open the **AL1-C6-Skyline.accdb** database and then create and run the query shown in Figure 6.11.
2. Save the query and name it *Suppliers2&4Orders* and then close the query.
3. Use the Report button to create the report shown in Figure 6.12 using the *Suppliers2&4Orders* query with the following specifications:
   a. Apply the *Concourse* theme.
   b. Adjust column widths and change the alignment of data as shown in Figure 6.12.
   c. Change the title as shown in the figure.
   d. Select the column headings and then change the font color to black.
   e. Insert the sum total of the amounts in the *Total* column. Format the total amount as shown in the figure.
   f. Delete the sum amount at the bottom of the *UnitPrice* column.
4. Save the report and name it *Suppliers2&4OrdersRpt*.
5. Print the report, close the report, and then close the **AL1-C6-Skyline.accdb** database.

Figure 6.11 Visual Benchmark Query

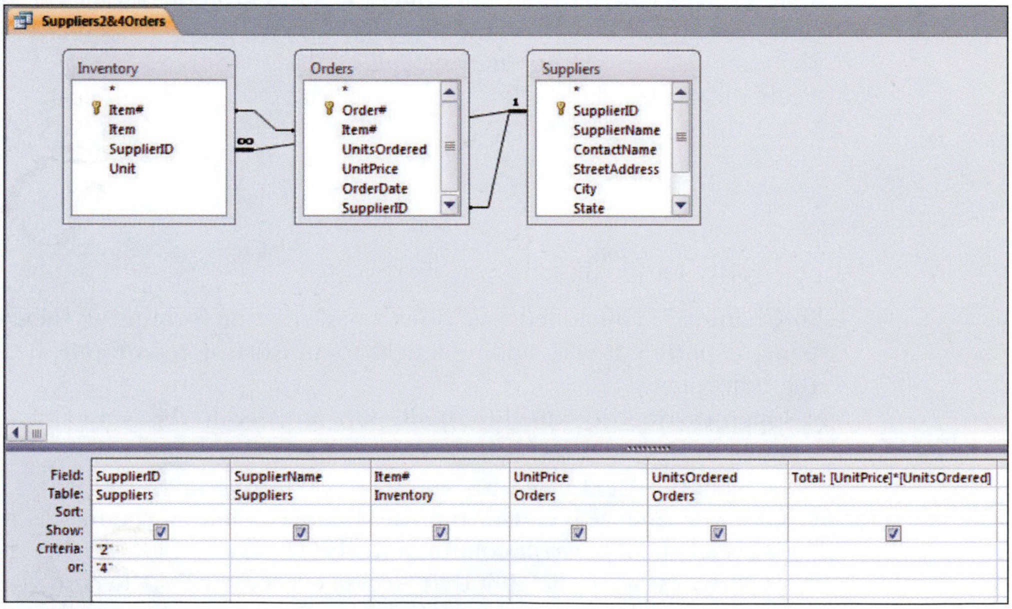

Figure 6.12 Visual Benchmark Report

Suppliers 2 and 4 Orders

Monday, July 30, 2012
9:00:15 PM

SupplierID	SupplierName	Item#	UnitPrice	UnitsOrdered	Total
2	Coral Produce	002	$10.50	3	$31.50
2	Coral Produce	016	$24.00	1	$24.00
4	Grocery Wholesalers	020	$18.75	2	$37.50
2	Coral Produce	021	$31.00	1	$31.00
4	Grocery Wholesalers	026	$29.25	1	$29.25
4	Grocery Wholesalers	034	$13.75	2	$27.50
4	Grocery Wholesalers	035	$17.00	1	$17.00
4	Grocery Wholesalers	025	$28.50	1	$28.50
4	Grocery Wholesalers	013	$14.00	2	$28.00
4	Grocery Wholesalers	036	$17.00	2	$34.00
2	Coral Produce	014	$15.75	2	$31.50
4	Grocery Wholesalers	027	$22.00	1	$22.00
2	Coral Produce	004	$10.95	2	$21.90
4	Grocery Wholesalers	012	$30.25	1	$30.25
4	Grocery Wholesalers	018	$45.00	1	$45.00
2	Coral Produce	016	$39.40	2	$78.80
4	Grocery Wholesalers	035	$17.00	1	$17.00
2	Coral Produce	014	$15.75	2	$31.50
4	Grocery Wholesalers	020	$18.75	2	$37.50
					$603.70

Case Study Apply Your Skills

Part 1

As the office manager at Millstone Legal Services, you need to enter records for three new clients in the **AL1-C6-Millstone.accdb** database. Using the following information, enter the data in the appropriate tables:

Client number 42 Martin Costanzo 1002 Thomas Drive Casper, WY 82602 (307) 555-5001 Mr. Costanzo saw Douglas Sheehan regarding divorce proceedings with a billing date of 3/15/2012 and a fee of $150.	Client number 43 Susan Nordyke 23193 Ridge Circle East Mills, WY 82644 (307) 555-2719 Ms. Nordyke saw Loretta Ryder regarding support enforcement with a billing date of 3/15/2012 and a fee of $175.	Client number 44 Monica Sommers 1105 Riddell Avenue Casper, WY 82609 (307) 555-1188 Ms. Sommers saw Anita Leland regarding a guardianship with a billing date of 3/15/2012 and a fee of $250.

Part 2

Create and print the following queries, reports, and labels:

- Create a report with the Clients table. Apply formatting to enhance the visual appeal of the report.
- Create a query that displays the client ID, first name, and last name; attorney last name; billing date; and fee. Name the query *ClientBilling*.
- Create a report with the ClientBilling query. Group the records in the report by attorney last name (the *LName* field in the drop-down list) and sort alphabetically in ascending order by client last name (the *LastName* field in the drop-down list). Apply formatting to enhance the visual appeal of the report.
- Create a telephone directory by creating a report that includes client last names, first names, and telephone numbers. Sort the records in the report alphabetically by last name and in ascending order.
- Edit the ClientBilling query so it includes a criterion that displays only billing dates between 3/12/2012 and 3/15/2012. Save the query with Save Object As and name it *ClientBilling12-15*.
- Create a report with the ClientBilling12-15 query. Apply formatting to enhance the visual appeal of the report.
- Create mailing labels for the clients.

Part 3

Apply the following conditions to fields in reports and then print the reports:

- In the Clients report, apply the condition that the city *Casper* displays in red and the city *Mills* displays in blue in the *City* field.
- In the ClientBilling report, apply the condition that fees over $199 display in green and fees less than $200 display in blue.

Part 4

Your center has a procedures manual that describes processes and procedures in the center. Open Word and then create a document for the procedures manual that describes the process for creating a report using the Report button, the Report Wizard, and the process for preparing mailing labels using the Label Wizard. Save the completed document and name it **A4-C6-CS-Manual**. Print and then close **A4-C6-CS-Manual.docx**.

Microsoft® Access®

CHAPTER 7

Modifying, Filtering, and Viewing Data

PERFORMANCE OBJECTIVES

Upon successful completion of Chapter 7, you will be able to:

- **Filter data by selection and by form**
- **Remove a filter**
- **View object dependencies**
- **Compact and repair a database**
- **Encrypt a database with a password**
- **View and customize document properties**
- **Customize the Recent tab Backstage view**
- **Save a database in an earlier version of Access**
- **Save a database object in PDF format**

SNAP Training and Assessment. Simplified.

Tutorials

7.1 Filtering Records

7.2 Compacting, Repairing, and Backing Up a Database

7.3 Encrypting a Database with a Password and Modifying Document Properties

7.4 Customizing the Recent Tab in Backstage View

7.5 Saving Databases and Database Objects in Different Formats

You can filter data in a database object to view specific records without having to change the design of the object. In this chapter, you will learn how to filter data, filter by selection, and filter by form. You will also learn how to view object dependencies, manage a database with options at the Info tab and Recent tab Backstage views, save a database in an earlier version, and save a database object in PDF format. Model answers for this chapter's projects appear on the following pages.

Access

Access2010L1C7

Note: Before beginning the projects, copy to your storage medium the Access2010L1C7 subfolder from the Access2010L1 folder on the CD that accompanies this textbook and make Access2010L1C7 the active folder.

Project 1 Filter Records

Project 1a

EmployeeID	FName	LName	StreetAddress	City	State	ZipCode
02	Wayne	Weber	17362 North Tenth	Fort Myers	FL	33994
03	Owen	Pasqual	4010 Shannon Drive	Fort Myers	FL	33910
04	Vadim	Sayenko	1328 St. Paul Avenue	Fort Myers	FL	33907
07	Donald	Sellars	23103 Summer Highway	Fort Myers	FL	33919
09	Elizabeth	Mohr	1818 Brookdale Road	Fort Myers	FL	33902
11	Nicole	Bateman	5001 150th Street	Fort Myers	FL	33908

Skyline Employees Filtered Records, Page 1

Telephone	HireDate	HealthIns
(239) 555-6041	4/1/2007	☐
(239) 555-3492	4/15/2006	☐
(239) 555-9487	6/15/2006	✓
(239) 555-4348	6/6/2008	✓
(239) 555-0430	5/1/2008	✓
(239) 555-2631	2/1/2010	☐

Skyline Employees Filtered Records, Page 2

Project 1b

ResDate	FirstName	LastName	Telephone	Event	EmployeeID
6/2/2012	Terrance	Schaefer	(239) 555-6239	Wedding rehearsal dinner	03
6/3/2012	Andrea	Wyatt	(239) 555-4282	Wedding reception	01
6/3/2012	Luis	Castillo	(239) 555-4001	Wedding shower	11
6/7/2012	David	Hooper	(941) 555-2338	Wedding anniversary	04
6/8/2012	Bridget	Kohn	(239) 551-1299	Other	02
6/9/2012	Joanne	Blair	(239) 555-7783	Birthday	03
6/9/2012	Tim	Drysdale	(941) 555-0098	Bat mitzvah	02
6/10/2012	Gabrielle	Johnson	(239) 555-1882	Other	05
6/13/2012	Cliff	Osborne	(239) 555-7823	Wedding rehearsal dinner	12
6/15/2012	Janis	Semala	(239) 555-0476	Wedding reception	06
6/15/2012	Tristan	Strauss	(941) 555-7746	Other	03

Skyline Banquet Reservations Query

BanquetReservations Monday, July 30, 2012 3:11:57 PM

ResDate	FirstName	LastName	Telephone	Event	EmployeeID
6/9/2012	Joanne	Blair	(239) 555-7783	Birthday	03
6/2/2012	Terrance	Schaefer	(239) 555-6239	Wedding rehearsal dinner	03

Skyline Banquet Report

Project 1c

Item#	Item	SupplierID	Unit
003	Carrots	6	25 lb bag
005	Garlic	6	10 lb bag
009	Radishes	6	case
010	Celery	6	case
011	Broccoli	6	case
041	White sugar	6	25 lb bag
042	Baking powder	6	case
043	Baking soda	6	case

Skyline Filtered Inventory Records, Step 2c

Item#	Item	SupplierID	Unit
006	Green peppers	2	case
007	Red peppers	2	case
008	Yellow peppers	2	case

Skyline Filtered Inventory Records, Step 3d

ResDate	FirstName	LastName	Telephone	Event	EmployeeID
6/3/2012	Luis	Castillo	(239) 555-4001	Wedding shower	11
6/16/2012	Willow	Earhart	(239) 555-0034	Wedding shower	04
6/9/2012	Joanne	Blair	(239) 555-7783	Birthday	03
6/17/2012	Jason	Haley	(239) 555-6641	Birthday	06
6/23/2012	Heidi	Thompson	(941) 555-3215	Birthday	01
6/30/2012	Kirsten	Simpson	(941) 555-4425	Birthday	02
6/16/2012	Aaron	Williams	(239) 555-3821	Bar mitzvah	04
6/25/2012	Robin	Gehring	(239) 555-0126	Bar mitzvah	06
6/9/2012	Tim	Drysdale	(941) 555-0098	Bat mitzvah	02
6/8/2012	Bridget	Kohn	(239) 551-1299	Other	02
6/10/2012	Gabrielle	Johnson	(239) 555-1882	Other	05
6/15/2012	Tristan	Strauss	(941) 555-7746	Other	03
6/19/2012	Lillian	Krakosky	(239) 555-8890	Other	03
6/29/2012	David	Fitzgerald	(941) 555-3792	Other	01
6/2/2012	Terrance	Schaefer	(239) 555-6239	Wedding rehearsal dinner	03
6/13/2012	Cliff	Osborne	(239) 555-7823	Wedding rehearsal dinner	12
6/7/2012	David	Hooper	(941) 555-2338	Wedding anniversary	04
6/23/2012	Anthony	Wiegand	(239) 555-7853	Wedding anniversary	11
6/30/2012	Shane	Rozier	(239) 555-1033	Wedding anniversary	12

Skyline Filtered Banquet Reservations Records, Step 6c

ResDate	FirstName	LastName	Telephone	Event	EmployeeID
6/16/2012	Aaron	Williams	(239) 555-3821	Bar mitzvah	04
6/25/2012	Robin	Gehring	(239) 555-0126	Bar mitzvah	06
6/9/2012	Tim	Drysdale	(941) 555-0098	Bat mitzvah	02

Skyline Filtered Banquet Reservations Records, Step 7d

Project 1d

ReservationID	EmployeeID	ResDate	FirstName	LastName	Telephone	EventID	AmountTotal	AmountPaid	Confirmed
1	03	6/2/2012	Terrance	Schaefer	(239) 555-6239	RD	$750.00	$250.00	✓
6	03	6/9/2012	Joanne	Blair	(239) 555-7783	BD	$650.00	$200.00	✓
11	03	6/15/2012	Tristan	Strauss	(941) 555-7746	OT	$1,400.00	$300.00	☐
15	03	6/19/2012	Lillian	Krakosky	(239) 555-8890	OT	$500.00	$100.00	☐

Skyline Filtered Banquet Records

Item#	Item	SupplierID	Unit
001	Butternut squash	2	case
002	Potatoes	2	50 lb bag
004	Onions	2	25 lb bag
006	Green peppers	2	case
007	Red peppers	2	case
008	Yellow peppers	2	case
014	Green beans	2	case
016	Iceberg lettuce	2	case
017	Romaine lettuce	2	case
021	Cantaloupes	2	case
028	Beef	7	side
029	Pork	7	side
030	Chicken	7	case
051	Watermelon	2	case
052	Kiwi	2	case

Skyline Filtered Inventory Records

Project 2 View Object Dependencies and Manage a Database with Options in the Info Tab and Recent Tab Backstage View

Orders 7/31/2012

Order#	Item#	UnitsOrdered	UnitPrice	OrderDate	SupplierID
06-001	002	3	$10.50	6/1/2012	2
06-002	033	1	$73.50	6/1/2012	1
06-003	016	1	$24.00	6/4/2012	2
06-004	020	2	$18.75	6/4/2012	4
06-005	014	2	$15.75	6/4/2012	2
06-006	025	1	$28.50	6/5/2012	4
06-007	036	2	$17.00	6/6/2012	4
06-008	028	1	$315.00	6/7/2012	7
06-009	013	2	$14.00	6/7/2012	4
06-010	004	2	$10.95	6/11/2012	2
06-011	035	1	$17.00	6/11/2012	4
06-012	039	4	$3.50	6/11/2012	3
06-013	040	2	$4.95	6/12/2012	3
06-014	041	5	$6.50	6/12/2012	6
06-015	044	1	$50.25	6/13/2012	6
06-016	022	3	$16.50	6/15/2012	3
06-017	027	1	$22.00	6/15/2012	4
06-018	053	3	$52.00	6/18/2012	3
06-019	030	2	$175.00	6/18/2012	7
06-020	003	2	$7.25	6/18/2012	6
06-021	026	1	$29.25	6/20/2012	4
06-022	021	1	$31.00	6/20/2012	2
06-023	034	2	$13.75	6/20/2012	4
06-024	032	1	$101.50	6/22/2012	1
06-025	012	1	$30.25	6/22/2012	4
06-026	023	2	$12.95	6/25/2012	3
06-027	018	1	$45.00	6/25/2012	4
06-028	037	2	$11.25	6/25/2012	2
06-029	016	2	$39.40	6/26/2012	2
06-030	035	1	$17.00	6/26/2012	4
06-031	014	2	$15.75	6/28/2012	2
06-032	020	2	$18.75	6/28/2012	4
06-033	033	1	$33.50	6/29/2012	1

Project 2e, Skyline Orders Table

Project 1 Filter Records — 4 Parts

You will filter records in a table, query, and report in the Skyline database using the Filter button, Selection button, Toggle Filter button, and shortcut menu. You will also remove filters and filter by form.

Filtering Data

You can place a set of restrictions, called a ***filter***, on records in a table, query, form, or report to isolate temporarily specific records. A filter, like a query, lets you view specific records without having to change the design of the table, query, form, or report. Access provides a number of buttons and options for filtering data. You can filter data using the Filter button in the Sort & Filter group in the Home tab, right-click specific data in a record and then specify a filter, and use the Selection and Advanced buttons in the Sort & Filter group.

Quick Steps

Filter Records

1. Open desired object.
2. Click in entry of desired field column to filter.
3. Click Filter button.
4. Select desired sorting option at drop-down list.

Filtering Using the Filter Button

You can use the Filter button in the Sort & Filter group in the Home tab to filter records in an object (table, query, form or report). To use this button, open the desired object, click in any entry in the field column on which you want to filter, and then click the Filter button. This displays a drop-down list with sorting options and a listing of all of the field entries. In a table, you can also display this drop-

HINT

Filters available depend on the type of data selected in a column.

Figure 7.1 *City* Field Drop-down List

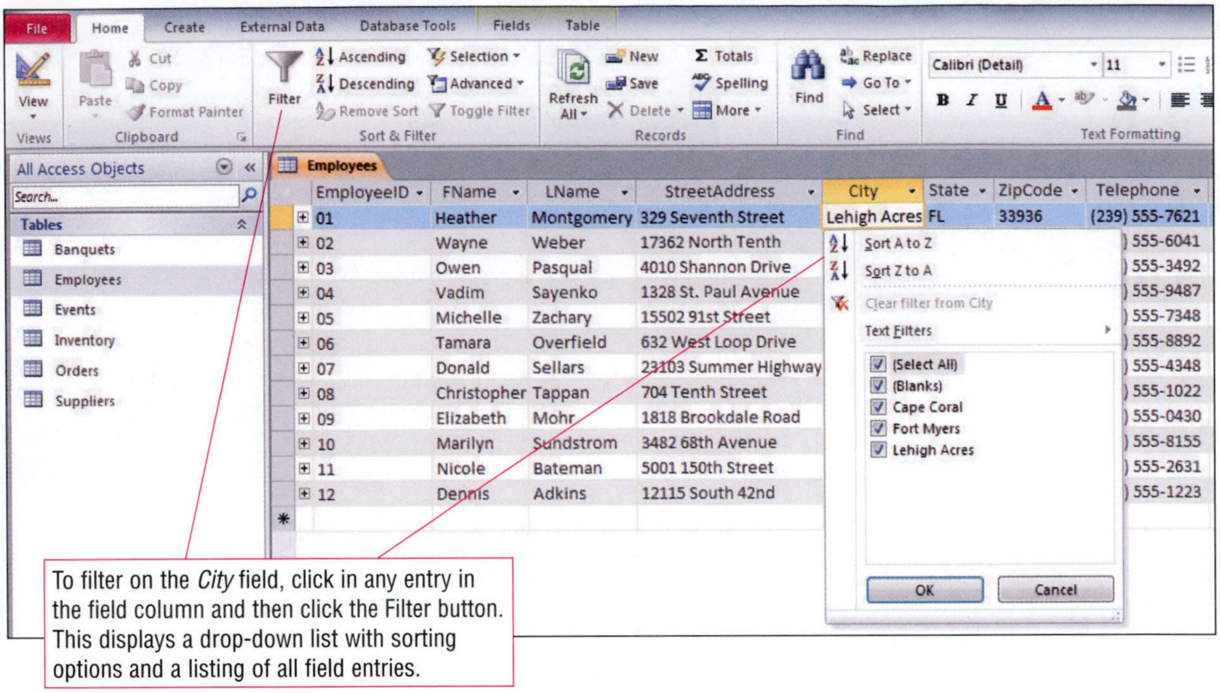

Filter

down list by clicking the filter arrow that displays at the right side of a column heading. Figure 7.1 displays the drop-down list that displays when you click in the *City* field and then click the Filter button. To sort on a specific criterion, click the *(Select All)* check box to move all check marks from the list of field entries. Click the item in the list box on which you want to sort and then click OK.

When you open a table, query, or form, the Record navigation bar contains the dimmed words *No Filter* preceded by a filter icon with a delete symbol (an X). If you filter records in one of these objects, *Filtered* displays in place of *No Filter*, the delete symbol is removed, and the text and filter icon display with an orange background. In a report, the word *Filtered* displays at the right side of the Status bar if you apply a filter to records.

Removing a Filter

Quick Steps

Remove a Filter

1. Click in field column containing filter.
2. Click Filter button.
3. Click *Clear filter from xxx.*

OR

1. Click Advanced button.
2. Click *Clear All Filters* at drop-down list.

When you filter data, the underlying data in the object is not deleted. You can switch back and forth between the data and the filtered data by clicking the Toggle Filter button in the Sort & Filter group in the Home tab. If you click the Toggle Filter button and turn off the filter, all of the data in a table, query, or form displays and the message *Filtered* in the Record navigation bar changes to *Unfiltered*.

Clicking the Toggle Filter button may redisplay all data in an object but it does not remove the filter. To remove the filter, click in the field column containing the filter and then click the Filter button in the Sort & Filter group in the Home tab. At the drop-down list that displays, click the *Clear filter from xxx* (where *xxx* is the name of the field). You can remove all filters from an object by clicking the Advanced button in the Sort & Filter group and then clicking the *Clear All Filters* option.

Project 1a Filtering Records in a Table, Form, and Report

Part 1 of 4

1. Display the Open dialog box with Access2010L1C7 on your storage medium the active folder.
2. Open the **AL1-C7-Skyline.accdb** database and enable the contents.
3. Filter records in the Employees table by completing the following steps:
   a. Open the Employees table.
   b. Click in any entry in the *City* field.
   c. Click the Filter button in the Sort & Filter group in the Home tab. (This displays a drop-down list in the *City* field.)

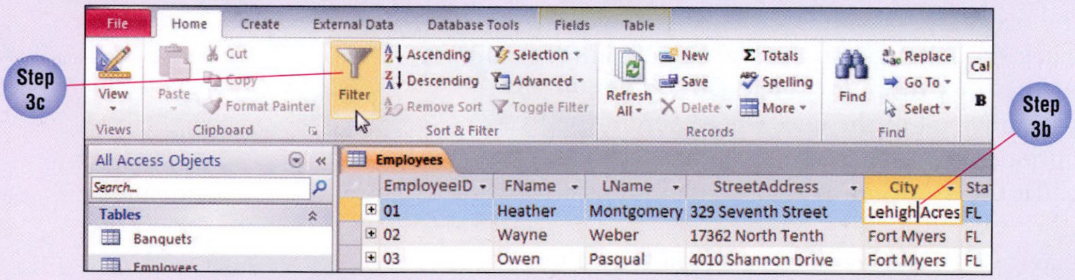

   d. Click the *(Select All)* check box in the filter drop-down list box. (This removes all check marks from the list options.)
   e. Click the *Fort Myers* check box in the list box. (This inserts a check mark in the check box.)
   f. Click OK. (Access displays only those records with a city field of *Fort Myers* and also displays *Filtered* and the filter icon with an orange background in the Record navigation bar.)
   g. Print the filtered records by pressing Ctrl + P (the keyboard shortcut to display the print dialog box) and then clicking OK at the Print dialog box.

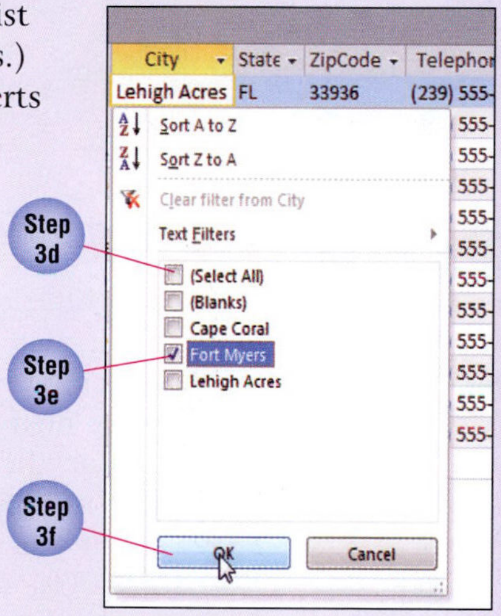

4. Toggle the display of filtered data by clicking the Toggle Filter button in the Sort & Filter group in the Home tab. (This redisplays all data in the table.)
5. Remove the filter by completing the following steps:
   a. Click in any entry in the *City* field.
   b. Click the Filter button in the Sort & Filter group.
   c. Click the *Clear filter from City* option at the drop-down list. (Notice that the message on the Record navigation bar changes to *No Filter* and dims the words.)

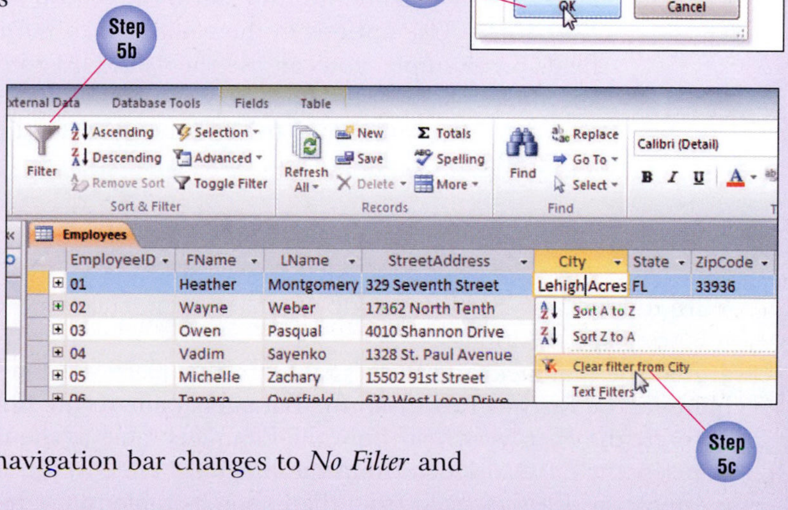

6. Save and then close the Employees table.
7. Create a form by completing the following steps:
   a. Click the Orders table in the Navigation pane.
   b. Click the Create tab and then click the Form button in the Forms group.
   c. Click the Form View button in the view area at the right side of the Status bar.
   d. Save the form with the name *Orders*.
8. Filter the records and display only those records with a supplier identification number of 2 by completing the following steps:
   a. Click in the *SupplierID* field containing the text *2*.
   b. Click the Filter button in the Sort & Filter group.
   c. At the filter drop-down list, click *(Select All)* to remove all of the check marks from the list options.
   d. Click the *2* option to insert a check mark.
   e. Click OK.
   f. Navigate through the records and notice that only the records with a supplier identification number of 2 display.
   g. Close the Orders form.

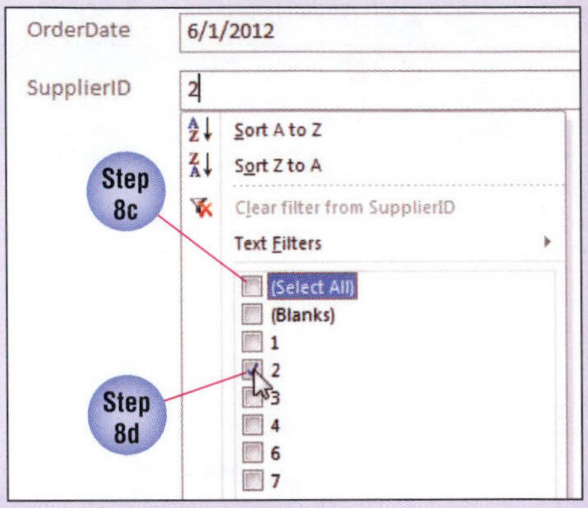

HINT

Hover the mouse over a column heading to display a tip showing the filter criteria.

Filtering on Specific Values

When you filter on a specific field, you can display a list of unique values for that field. If you click the Filter button for a field containing text, the drop-down list for the specific field will contain a *Text Filters* option. Click this option and a values list displays next to the drop-down list. The options in the values list will vary depending on the type of data in the field. If you click the Filter button for a field containing number values, the option in the drop-down list displays as *Number Filters* and if you are filtering dates, the option at the drop-down list displays as *Date Filters*. Use options in the values list to refine further a filter for a specific field. For example, you can use the values list to display money amounts within a specific range or order dates between certain dates. You can use the values list to find fields that are "equal to" or "not equal to" text in the current field.

Project 1b **Filtering Records in a Query and a Report** **Part 2 of 4**

1. With the **AL1-C7-Skyline.accdb** database open, create a query in Design view with the following specifications:
   a. Add the Banquets and Events tables to the query window.
   b. Insert the *ResDate* field from the Banquets table to the first *Field* row field.
   c. Insert the *FirstName* field from the Banquets table to the third *Field* row field.
   d. Insert the *LastName* field from the Banquets table to the second *Field* row field.
   e. Insert the *Telephone* field from the Banquets table to the fourth *Field* row field.
   f. Insert the *Event* field from the Events table to the fifth *Field* row field.
   g. Insert the *EmployeeID* field from the Banquets table to the sixth *Field* row field.
   h. Run the query.
   i. Save the query and name it *BanquetReservations*.

2. Filter records of reservations on or before June 15, 2012 in the query by completing the following steps:
   a. With the BanquetReservations query open, make sure the first entry is selected in the *ResDate* field.
   b. Click the Filter button in the Sort & Filter group in the Home tab.
   c. Point to the *Date Filters* option in the drop-down list box.
   d. Click *Before* in the values list.
   e. At the Custom Filter dialog box, type **6/15/2012** and then click OK.

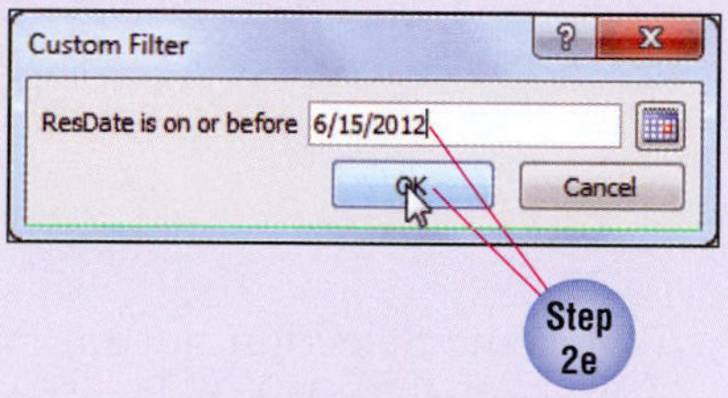

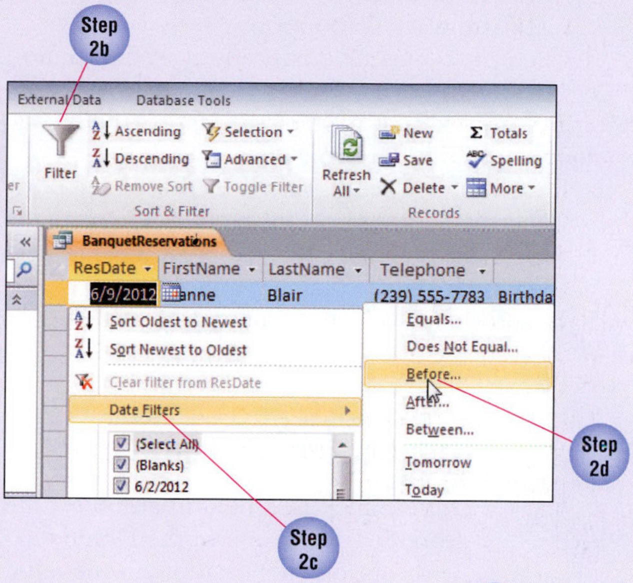

   f. Print the filtered query by pressing Ctrl + P and then clicking OK at the Print dialog box.
3. Remove the filter by clicking the filter icon that displays at the right side of the *ResDate* column heading and then clicking *Clear filter from ResDate* at the drop-down list.

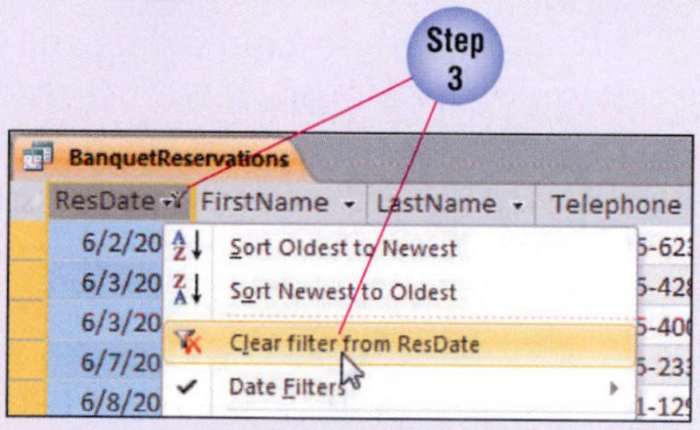

4. Save and then close the BanquetReservations query.
5. Create a report by completing the following steps:
   a. Click the BanquetReservations query in the Navigation pane.
   b. Click the Create tab and then click the Report button in the Reports group.
   c. Delete the total amount at the bottom of the *ResDate* column.
   d. With the report in Layout view, decrease the column widths so the right column border displays near the longest entry in each column.
   e. Click the Report View button in the view area at the right side of the Status bar.
   f. Save the report and name it *BanquetReport*.
6. Filter the records and display all records of events except *Other* events by completing the following steps:
   a. Click in the first entry in the *Event* field.
   b. Click the Filter button in the Sort & Filter group.
   c. Point to the *Text Filters* option in the drop-down list box and then click *Does Not Equal* at the values list.
   d. At the Custom Filter dialog box, type **Other** and then click OK.

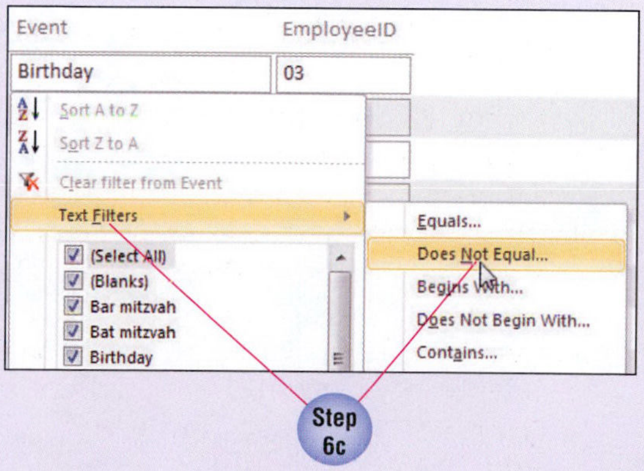

7. Further refine the filter by completing the following steps:
   a. Click in the first entry in the *EmployeeID* field.
   b. Click the Filter button.
   c. At the filter drop-down list, click the *(Select All)* check box to remove all of the check marks from the list options.
   d. Click the *03* check box to insert a check mark.
   e. Click OK.
8. Print only the first page of the report (the second page only contains shading) by completing the following steps:
   a. Press Ctrl + P to display the Print dialog box.
   b. Click the *Pages* option in the *Print Range* section.
   c. Type **1** in the *From* text box, press the Tab key, and then type **1** in the *To* text box.
   d. Click OK.
9. Save and then close the BanquetReport report.

Filtering by Selection

Selection

If you click in a field in an object and then click the Selection button in the Sort & Filter group in the Home tab, a drop-down list displays below the button with options for filtering on the data in the field. For example, if you click in a field containing the city name *Fort Myers*, clicking the Selection button will cause a drop-down list to display as shown in Figure 7.2. Click one of the options at the drop-down list to filter records. You can select specific text in a field entry and then filter based on the specific text. For example, in Project 1c you will select the word *peppers* in the entry *Green peppers* and then filter records containing the word *peppers*.

Figure 7.2 Selection Button Drop-down List

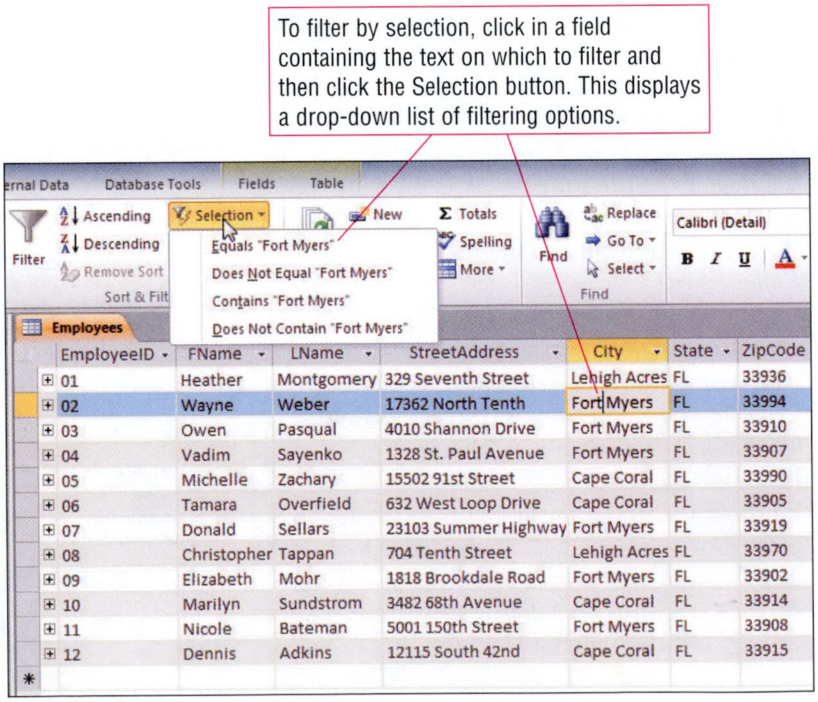

Filtering by Shortcut Menu

If you right-click on a field entry, a shortcut menu displays with options to sort the text, display a values list, or filter on a specific value. For example, if you right-click the field entry *Birthday* in the *Event* field, a shortcut menu displays as shown in Figure 7.3. Click a sort option to sort text in the field in ascending or descending order, point to the *Text Filters* option to display a values list, or click one of the values filters located toward the bottom of the menu. You can also select specific text within a field entry and then right-click the selection to display the shortcut menu.

Figure 7.3 Filtering Shortcut Menu

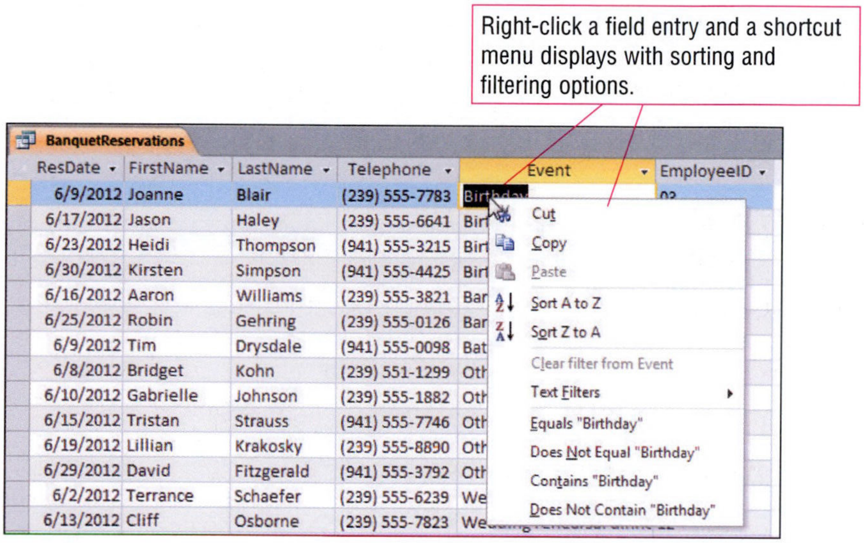

Project 1c **Filtering Records by Selection** Part 3 of 4

1. Open the Inventory table.
2. Filter only those records with a supplier number of 6 by completing the following steps:
   a. Click in the first entry containing *6* in the *SupplierID* field.
   b. Click the Selection button and then click *Equals "6"* at the drop-down list.
   c. Print the filtered table by pressing Ctrl + P and then clicking OK at the Print dialog box.
   d. Click the Toggle Filter button in the Sort & Filter group.

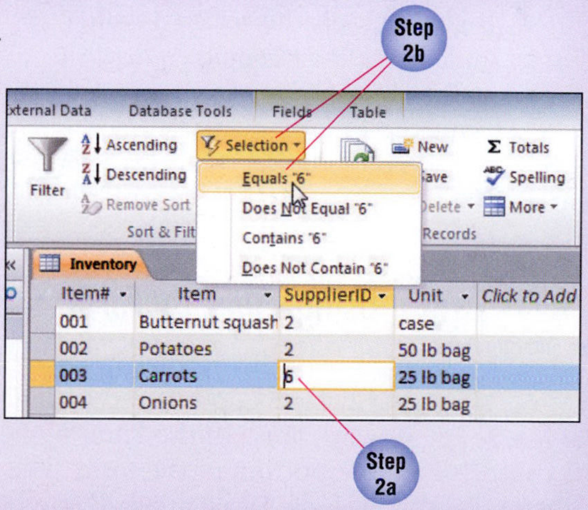

3. Filter any records in the *Item* field containing the word "pepper" by completing the following steps:
   a. Click in an entry in the *Item* field containing the entry *Green peppers*.
   b. Using the mouse, select the word *peppers*.
   c. Click the Selection button and then click *Contains "peppers"* at the drop-down list.
   d. Print the filtered table by pressing Ctrl + P and then clicking OK at the Print dialog box.
4. Close the Inventory table without saving the changes.
5. Open the BanquetReservations query.
6. Filter records in the *Event* field except *Wedding reception* by completing the following steps:
   a. Right-click in the first *Wedding reception* entry in the *Event* field.
   b. Click *Does Not Equal "Wedding reception"* at the shortcut menu.
   c. Print the filtered query.
   d. Click the Toggle Filter button in the Sort & Filter group.
7. Filter any records in the *Event* field containing the word *mitzvah* by completing the following steps:
   a. Click in an entry in the *Event* field containing the entry *Bar mitzvah*.
   b. Using the mouse, select the word *mitzvah*.
   c. Right-click on the selected word and then click *Contains "mitzvah"* at the shortcut menu.
   d. Print the filtered query.
8. Close the BanquetReservations query without saving the changes.

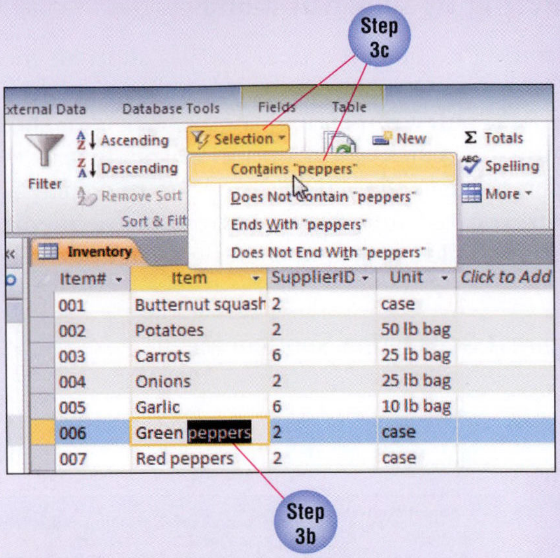

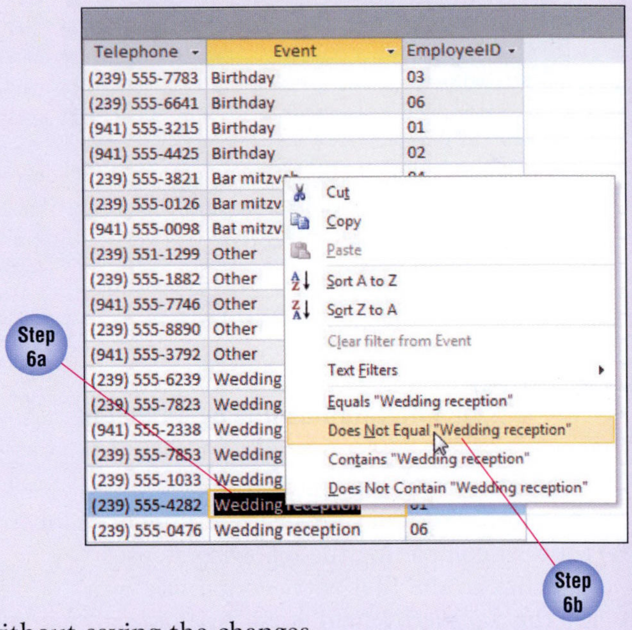

Quick Steps

Use *Filter By Form*
1. Click Advanced button.
2. Click *Filter By Form* at drop-down list.
3. Click in empty field below desired column to filter.
4. Click down-pointing arrow.
5. Click on item to filter.

Using *Filter By Form*

One of the options from the Advanced button drop-down list is *Filter By Form*. Click this option and a blank record displays in a Filter by Form window in the work area. In the Filter by Form window, the *Look for* and *Or* tabs display toward the bottom of the form. The Look for tab is active by default and tells Access to look for whatever data you insert in a field. Click in the empty field below the desired column and a down-pointing arrow displays at the right side of the field. Click the down-pointing arrow and then click the item on which you want to filter. Click the Toggle Filter button to display the desired records. Add an additional value to a filter by clicking the Or tab at the bottom of the form.

Project 1d Using *Filter By Form* to Display Specific Records Part 4 of 4

1. With the **AL1-C7-Skyline.accdb** database open, open the Banquets table.
2. Filter records for a specific employee identification number by completing the following steps:
   a. Click the Advanced button in the Sort & Filter group in the Home tab and then click *Filter By Form* at the drop-down list.

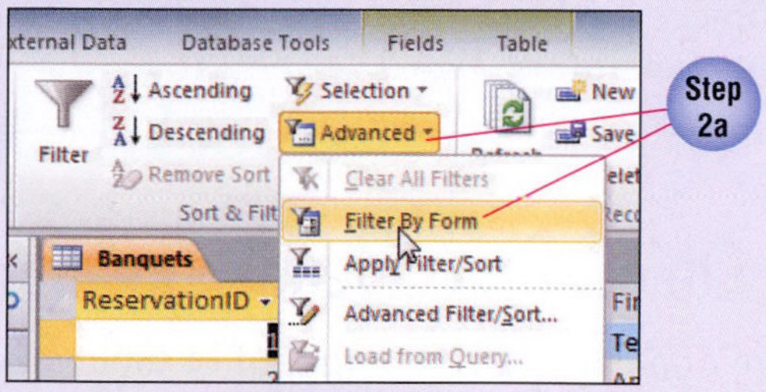

   b. At the Filter by Form window, click in the blank record below the *EmployeeID* field.
   c. Click the down-pointing arrow at the right side of the field and then click *03* at the drop-down list.
   d. Click the Toggle Filter button in the Sort & Filter group.

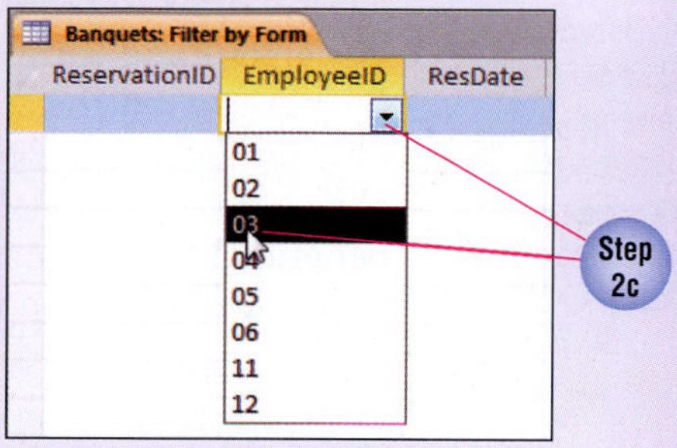

3. Print the filtered table by completing the following steps:
   a. Click the File tab, click the Print tab, and then click the *Print Preview* option.
   b. Click the Landscape button in the Page Layout group.
   c. Click the Print button and then click OK at the Print dialog box.
   d. Click the Close Print Preview button.
4. Close the Banquets table without saving the changes.
5. Open the Inventory table.
6. Filter records for supplier numbers 2 or 7 by completing the following steps:
   a. Click the Advanced button in the Sort & Filter group in the Home tab and then click *Filter By Form* at the drop-down list.
   b. At the Filter by Form window, click in the blank record below the *SupplierID* field.
   c. Click the down-pointing arrow at the right side of the field and then click *2* at the drop-down list.
   d. Click the Or tab located toward the bottom of the form.
   e. If necessary, click in the blank record below the *SupplierID* field.
   f. Click the down-pointing arrow at the right side of the field and then click *7* at the drop-down list.
   g. Click the Toggle Filter button in the Sort & Filter group.
   h. Print the filtered table.
   i. Click the Toggle Filter button to redisplay all records in the table.
   j. Click the Advanced button and then click *Clear All Filters* from the drop-down list.

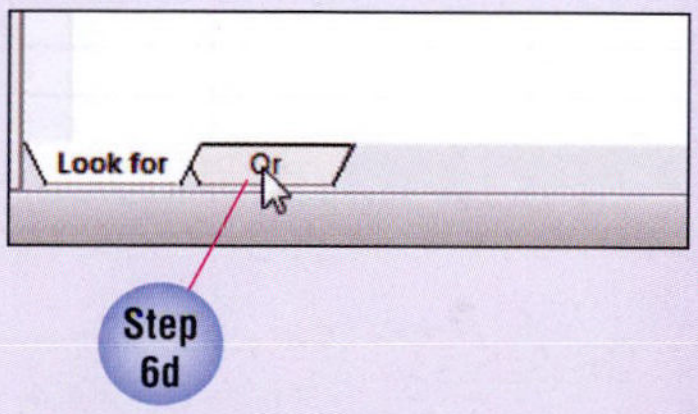

7. Close the Inventory table without saving the changes.

Project 2 **View Object Dependencies and Manage a Database with Options in the Info Tab and Recent Tab Backstage View** **4 Parts**

You will display object dependencies in the Skyline database, compact and repair the database, encrypt it with a password, view and customize document properties, save an object in the database in the PDF file format, and save the database in a previous version of Word.

Viewing Object Dependencies

Quick Steps

View Object Dependencies
1. Open desired database.
2. Click object in Navigation pane.
3. Click Database Tools tab.
4. Click Object Dependencies button.

Object Dependencies

The structure of a database is comprised of table, query, form, and report objects. Tables are related to other tables by creating relationships. Queries, forms, and reports draw the source data from records in the tables to which they have been associated and forms and reports can include subforms and subreports which further expand the associations between objects. A database with a large number of interdependent objects is more complex to work with. Viewing a list of the objects within a database and viewing the dependencies between objects can be beneficial to ensure an object is not deleted or otherwise modified causing an unforeseen effect on another object.

Display the structure of a database, including tables, queries, forms, and reports as well as relationships, at the Object Dependencies task pane. Display this task pane by opening the database, clicking the desired object in the Navigation pane, clicking the Database Tools tab, and then clicking the Object Dependencies button in the Relationships group. The Object Dependencies task pane in Figure 7.4 displays the objects in the AL1-C7-Skyline.accdb database that depend on the Banquets table.

Figure 7.4 Object Dependencies Task Pane

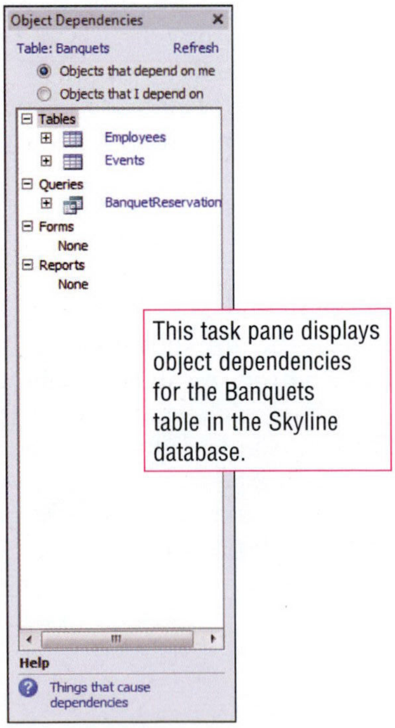

By default, *Objects that depend on me* is selected in the Object Dependencies task pane and the list box displays the names of objects for which the selected object is the source. Next to each object in the task pane list is an expand button (plus symbol). Clicking the expand button will show objects dependent at the next level. For example, if a query is based upon the Banquets and Events tables and the query is used to generate a report, clicking the expand button next to the query name would show the report name. Clicking an object name in the Object Dependencies task pane opens the object in Design view.

Project 2a Viewing Object Dependencies — Part 1 of 5

1. With the **AL1-C7-Skyline.accdb** database open, display the structure of the database by completing the following steps:
   a. Click the Banquets table in the Navigation pane.
   b. Click the Database Tools tab and then click the Object Dependencies button in the Relationships group. (This displays the Object Dependencies task pane. By default, *Objects that depend on me* is selected and the task pane lists the names of objects for which the Banquets table is the source.)

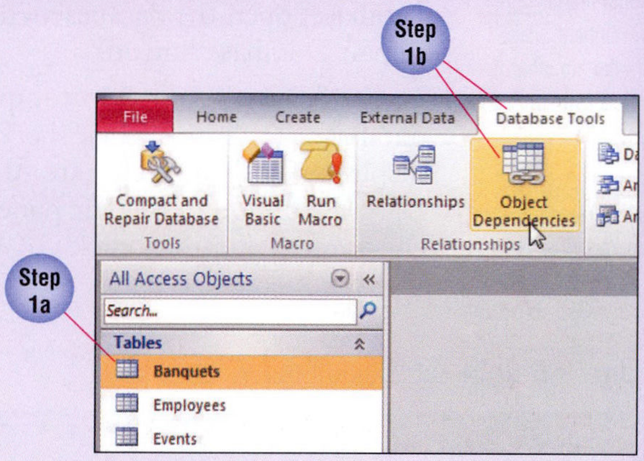

   c. Click the expand button (plus symbol) to the left of *Employees* in the *Tables* section. (This displays all objects that are dependent on the Employees table.)

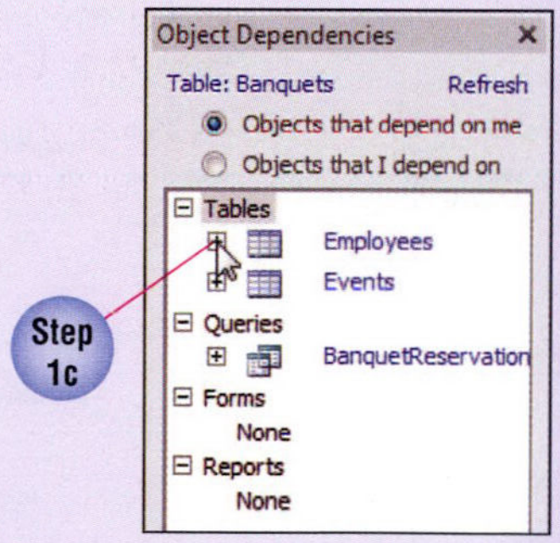

   d. Click the *Objects that I depend on* option located toward the top of the Object Dependencies task pane.

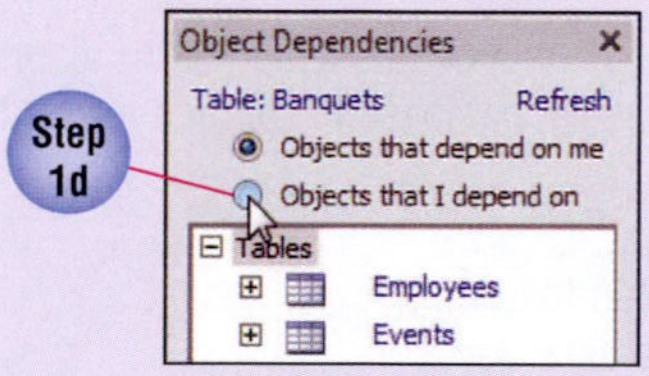

   e. Click the Events table in the Navigation pane. (Click the Events table in the Navigation pane and not the Object Dependencies task pane.)
   f. Click the Refresh hyperlink located in the upper right corner of the Object Dependencies task pane.
   g. Click the *Objects that depend on me* option located toward the top of the Object Dependencies task pane.

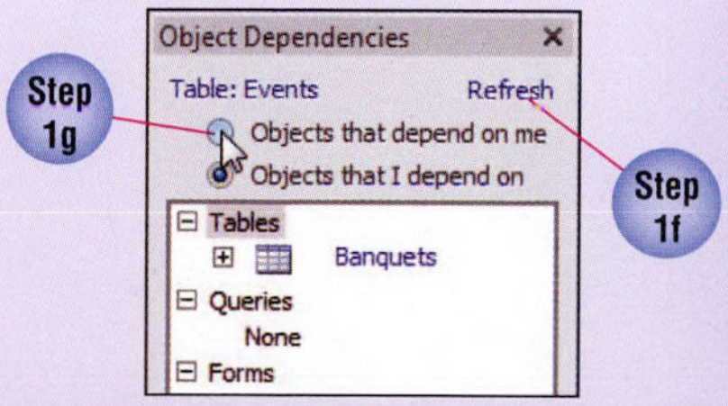

2. Close the Object Dependencies task pane.

Using Options at the Info Tab Backstage View

Quick Steps

Compact and Repair Database
1. Open database.
2. Click File tab.
3. Click Compact & Repair Database button.

HINT

Before compacting and repairing a database in a multi-user environment, make sure that no other user has the database open.

Compact & Repair Database

The Info tab Backstage view contains options for compacting and repairing a database, encrypting a database with a password, and displaying and customizing database properties. Display the Info tab Backstage view as shown in Figure 7.5 by opening a database and then clicking the File tab.

Compacting and Repairing a Database

To optimize the performance of your database, compact and repair the database on a regular basis. As you work with a database, data in the database can become fragmented causing the amount of space the database takes on the storage medium or in the folder to be larger than necessary. To compact and repair a database, open the database, click the File tab and then click the Compact & Repair Database button.

You can tell Access to compact and repair a database each time you close the database. To do this, click the File tab and then click the Options button that displays below the Help tab. At the Access Options dialog box, click the *Current Database* option in the left panel. Click the *Compact on Close* option to insert a check mark and then click OK to close the dialog box.

Figure 7.5 Info Tab Backstage View

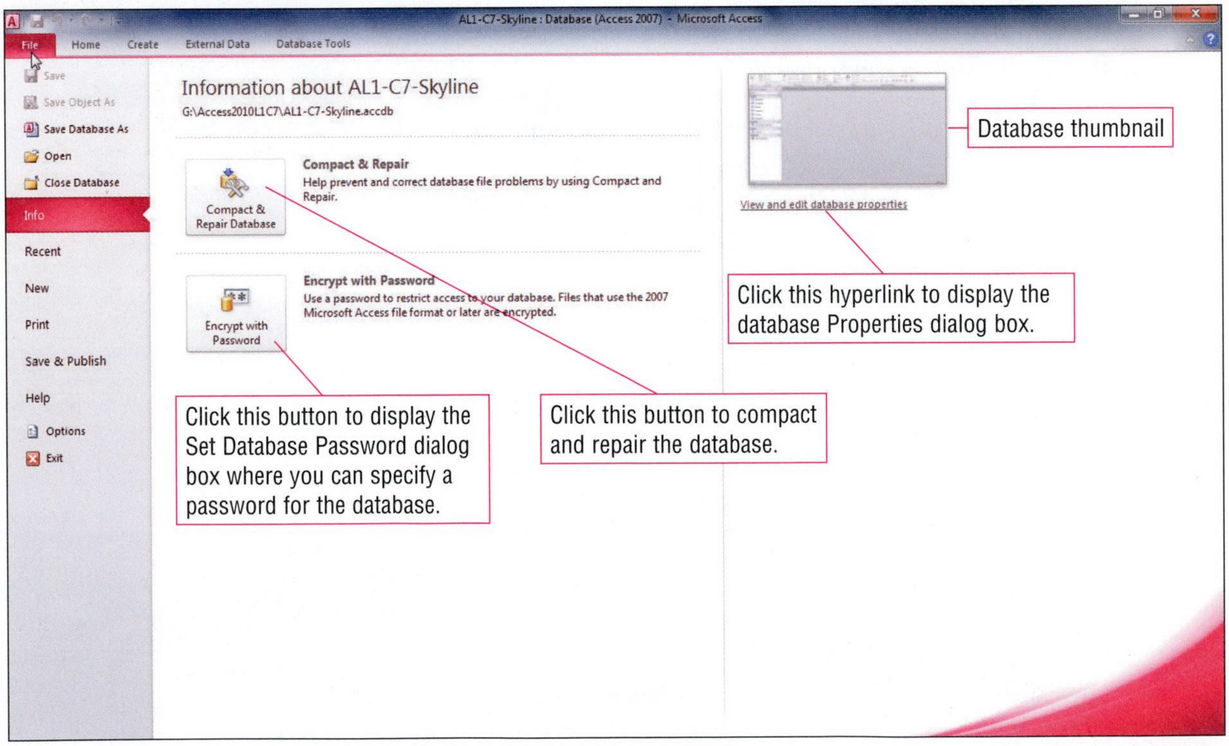

Encrypting a Database with a Password

If you want to prevent unauthorized access to a database, encrypt the database with a password to ensure that the database is opened only by someone who knows the password. Be careful when encrypting a database with a password because if you lose the password, you will be unable to use the database. You will not be able to remove a password from a database if you do not remember the password.

To encrypt a database with a password, you must open the database in Exclusive mode. To do this, display the Open dialog box, navigate to the desired folder, and then click the database to select it. Click the down-pointing arrow at the right side of the Open button located in the lower right corner of the dialog box, and then click *Open Exclusive* at the drop-down list. When the database opens, click the File tab and then click the Encrypt with Password button in the Info tab Backstage view. This displays the Set Database Password dialog box shown in Figure 7.6. At this dialog box, type a password in the *Password* text box, press the Tab key, and then type the password again. The text you type will display as asterisks. Click OK to close the Set Database Password dialog box. To remove a password from a database, open the database in Exclusive mode, click the File tab, and then click the Decrypt Database button. At the Unset Database Password dialog box, type the password and then click OK.

Quick Steps

Open Database in Exclusive Mode
1. Display Open dialog box.
2. Click desired database.
3. Click down-pointing arrow at right of Open button.
4. Click *Open Exclusive*.

Encrypt Database with Password
1. Open database in Exclusive mode.
2. Click File tab.
3. Click Encrypt with Password button.
4. Type password, press Tab, type password again.
5. Click OK.

HINT

When encrypting a database with a password, use passwords that combine uppercase and lowercase letters, numbers, and symbols.

Encrypt

Decrypt

Figure 7.6 Set Database Password Dialog Box

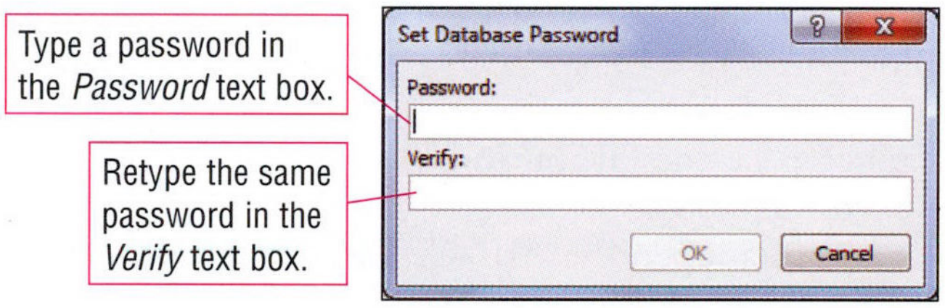

Project 2b **Compact and Repair and Encrypt a Database** Part 2 of 5

1. With the **AL1-C7-Skyline.accdb** database open, compact and repair the database by completing the following steps:
   a. Click the File tab. (This displays the Info tab Backstage view.)
   b. Click the Compact & Repair Database button.
2. Close the **AL1-C7-Skyline.accdb** database.

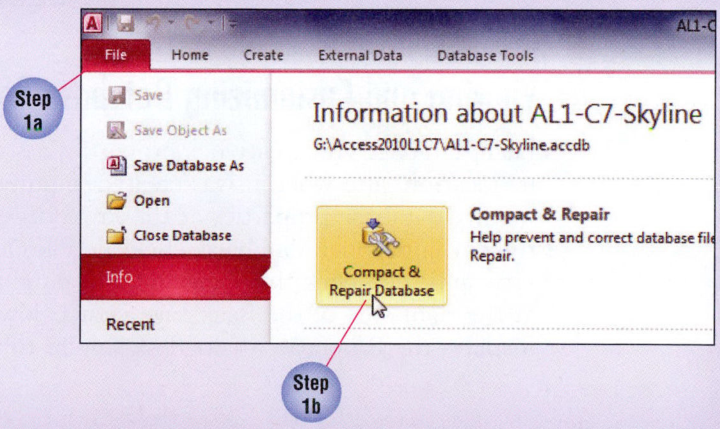

3. Open the database in Exclusive mode by completing the following steps:
   a. Display the Open dialog box.
   b. Click the **AL1-C7-Skyline.accdb** database in the Content pane to select it.
   c. Click the down-pointing arrow at the right side of the Open button that displays in the lower right corner of the dialog box and then click *Open Exclusive* at the drop-down list.

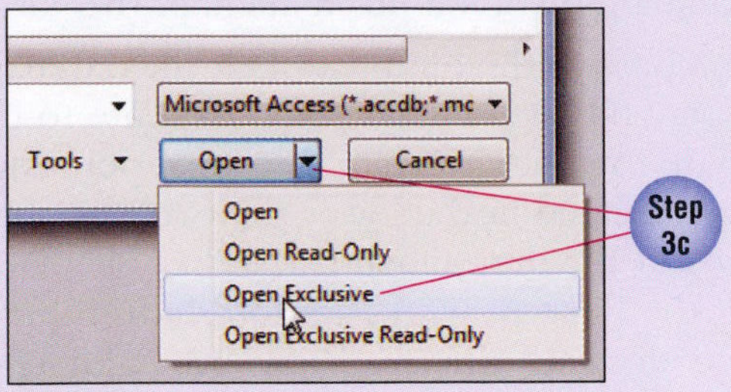

4. Encrypt the database with a password by completing the following steps:
   a. Click the File tab.
   b. At the Info tab Backstage view, click the Encrypt with Password button.
   c. At the Set Database Password dialog box, type your first and last names in all lowercase letters with no space, press the Tab key, and then type your first and last names again in lowercase letters.
   d. Click OK to close the dialog box.
   e. If a message displays with information about encrypting with a block cipher, click the OK button.

5. Close the **AL1-C7-Skyline.accdb** database.
6. Display the Open dialog box and then open the **AL1-C7-Skyline.accdb** database in Exclusive mode.
7. At the Password Required dialog box, type your password (first and last names) and then click OK.
8. Remove the password by completing the following steps:
   a. Click the File tab.
   b. Click the Decrypt Database button.
   c. At the Unset Database Password dialog box, type your first and last names in lowercase letters and then press the Enter key.

Viewing and Customizing Database Properties

Each database you create has properties associated with it such as the type of file, its location, and when it was created, modified, and accessed. You can view and modify database properties at the Properties dialog box. To view properties for the currently open database, click the File tab to display the Info tab Backstage view and then click the View and edit database properties hyperlink that displays at the right side of the Backstage view below the thumbnail of the database. This displays the Properties dialog box similar to what you see in Figure 7.7.

Figure 7.7 Properties Dialog Box

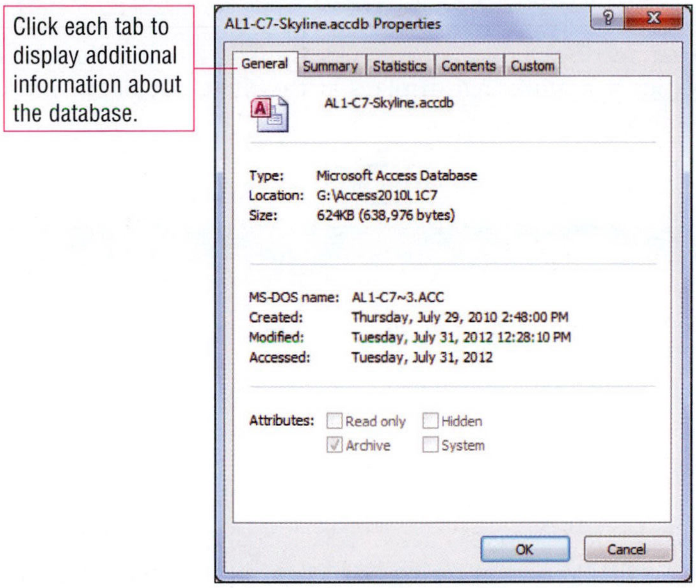

The Properties dialog box for an open database contains tabs with information about the database. With the General tab selected, the dialog box displays information about the database type, size, and location. Click the Summary tab and fields display such as title, subject, author, category, keywords, and comments. Some fields may contain data and others may be blank. You can insert, edit, or delete text in the fields. Move the insertion point to a field by clicking in the field or by pressing the Tab key until the insertion point is positioned in the desired field.

Click the Statistics tab and information displays such as dates for when the database was created, modified, accessed, and printed. You can view the objects in the database by clicking the Contents tab. The *Document contents* section displays the objects in the database including tables, queries, forms, reports, macros, and modules.

Use options at the Properties dialog box with the Custom tab selected to add custom properties to the database. For example, you can add a property that displays the date the database was completed, information on the department in which the database was created, and much more. The list box below the *Name* option box displays the predesigned properties provided by Access. You can choose a predesigned property or create your own.

To choose a predesigned property, select the desired property in the list box, specify what type of property it is (value, date, number, yes/no), and then type a value. For example, to specify the department in which the database was created, you would click *Department* in the list box, make sure the *Type* displays as *Text*, click in the *Value* text box, and then type the name of the department.

Project 2c Viewing and Customizing Database Properties Part 3 of 5

1. With the **AL1-C7-Skyline.accdb** database open, click the File tab and then click the View and edit database properties hyperlink that displays at the right side of the Backstage view below the database thumbnail.

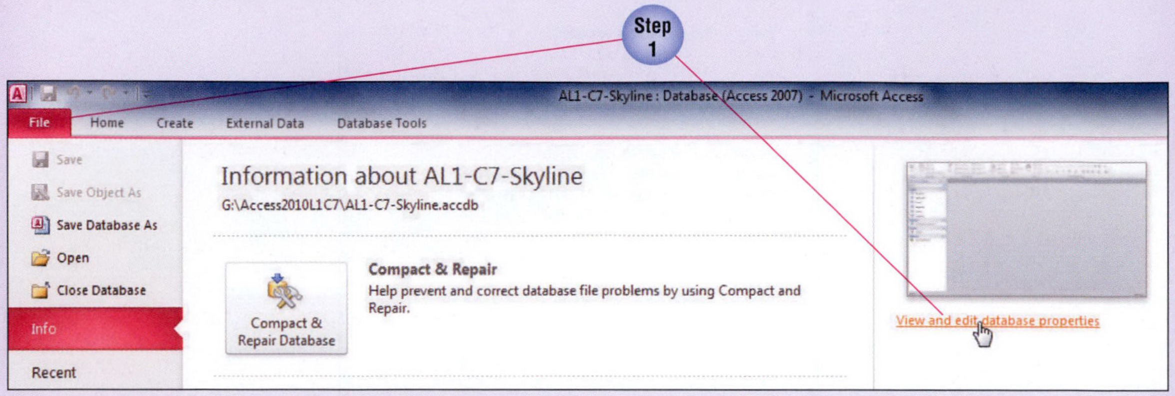

2. At the **AL1-C7-Skyline.accdb** Properties dialog box, click the General tab and then read the information that displays in the dialog box.
3. Click the Summary tab and then type the following text in the specified text boxes:

Title	=	**AL1-C7-Skyline database**
Subject	=	**Restaurant and banquet facilities**
Author	=	*(type your first and last names)*
Category	=	**restaurant**
Keywords	=	**restaurant, banquet, event, Fort Myers**
Comments	=	**This database contains information on Skyline Restaurant employees, banquets, inventory, and orders.**

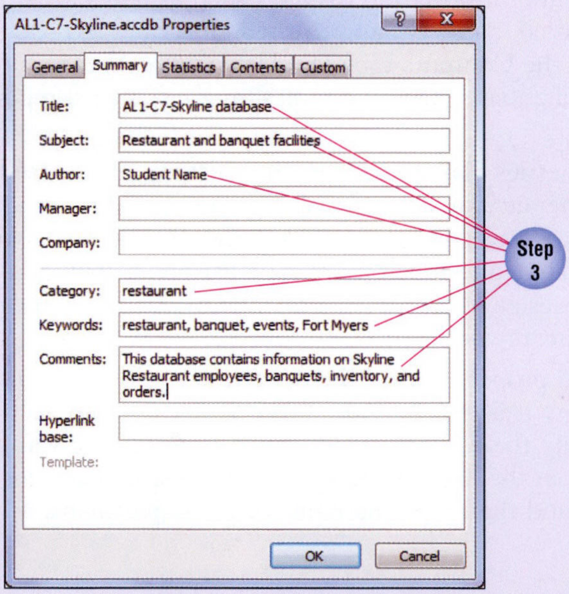

4. Click the Statistics tab and read the information that displays in the dialog box.
5. Click the Contents tab and notice that the *Document contents* section of the dialog box displays the objects in the database.

6. Click the Custom tab and then create custom properties by completing the following steps:
   a. Click the *Date completed* option in the *Name* list box.
   b. Click the down-pointing arrow at the right of the *Type* option box and then click *Date* at the drop-down list.

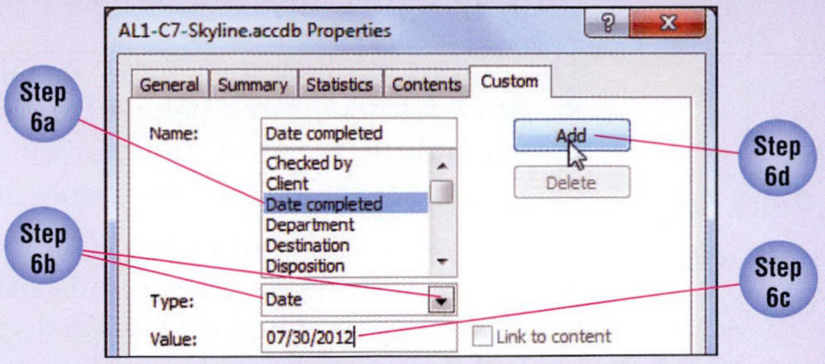

   c. Click in the *Value* text box and then type the current date in this format: *dd/mm/yyyy*.
   d. Click the Add button.
   e. With the insertion point positioned in the *Name* text box, type **Course**.
   f. Click the down-pointing arrow at the right of the *Type* option box and then click *Text* at the drop-down list.
   g. Click in the *Value* text box, type your current course number, and then press Enter.
   h. Click OK to close the dialog box.
7. Click the File tab to return to the database.

Customizing the Recent Tab Backstage View

When you open and close databases, Access keeps a list of the most recently opened databases. To view this list, click the File tab and then click the Recent tab. This displays the Recent tab Backstage view similar to what you see in Figure 7.8. (Your database file names may vary from what you see in the figure.) The most recently opened database names display in the *Recent Databases* list. Generally, the 20 most recently opened database names display in the list. To open a database, scroll down the list and then click the desired database name.

Figure 7.8 Recent Tab Backstage View

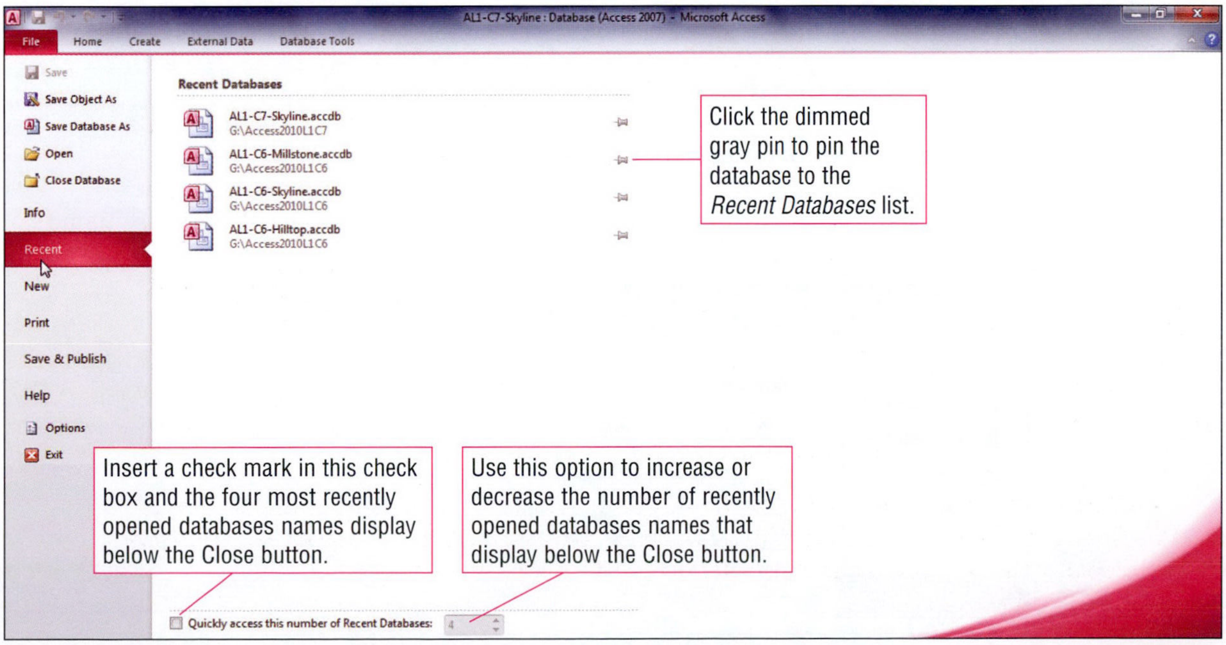

Displaying a Quick List

The Recent tab Backstage view contains the option *Quickly access this number of Recent Databases* located below the *Recent Databases* list. Insert a check mark in this option and the names of the four most recently opened databases display in the Backstage navigation bar (the panel at the left) below the Close Database button.

You can increase or decrease the number of displayed database names by increasing or decreasing the number that displays at the right side of the *Quickly access this number of Recent Databases* option. To remove the list of most recently opened databases from the navigation bar, click the *Quickly access this number of Recent Databases* option to remove the check mark.

Quick Steps

Display Recent Documents in Backstage Navigation Bar
1. Click File tab.
2. Click Recent tab.
3. Click *Quickly access this number of Recent Databases* check box.

Pin Database File Name
1. Click File tab.
2. Click Recent tab.
3. Click dimmed gray pin at right of desired database file name.

Pinning a Database

If you want a database name to remain at the top of the *Recent Databases* list, pin the database name. To do this, click the dimmed gray pin that displays at the right side of the database name. This changes the dimmed gray pin to a blue pin. The next time you display the Recent tab Backstage view, the database name you pinned displays at the top of the list. To unpin a database name, click the blue pin to change it to a dimmed gray pin. You can also pin a database name to the *Recent Databases* list by right-clicking the database name and then clicking *Pin to list* at the shortcut menu. To unpin the database name, right-click the database name and then click *Unpin from list* at the shortcut menu.

Clearing the *Recent Databases* List

You can clear the contents (except pinned databases) of the *Recent Databases* list by right-clicking a database name in the list and then clicking *Clear unpinned items* at the shortcut menu. At the message asking if you are sure you want to remove the items, click the Yes button.

Project 2d **Managing Databases at the Recent Tab Backstage View** Part 4 of 5

1. Close the **AL1-C7-Skyline.accdb** database.
2. Click the Recent tab.
3. Notice the database names that display in the *Recent Databases* list.
4. Pin the **AL1-C7-Skyline.accdb** database to the *Recent Databases* list by clicking the dimmed gray pin that displays at the right side of the *AL1-C7-Skyline.accdb* database name in the *Recent Databases* list. (This changes the gray pin to a blue pin.)

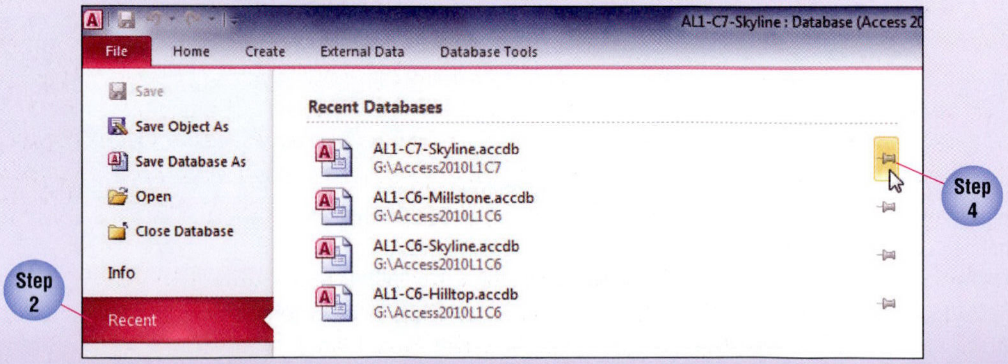

5. Click the *Quickly access this number of Recent Databases* check box located toward the bottom of the screen to insert a check mark. (With this option active, the four most recently opened database file names display in the Backstage navigation bar located below the Close Database button.)

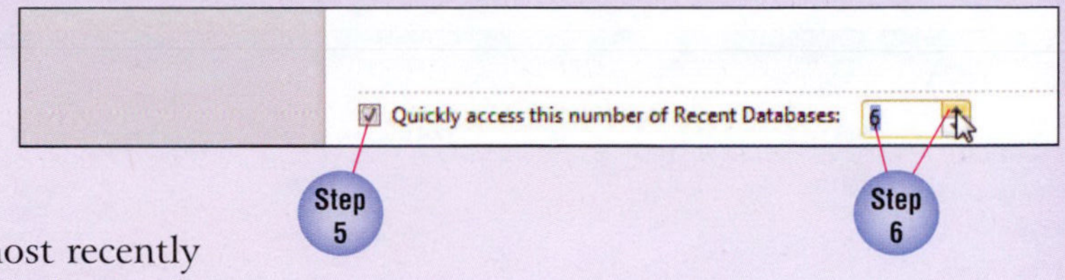

6. Increase the number of database file names in the navigation bar by clicking twice on the up-pointing arrow in the option box located to the right of the *Quickly access this number of Recent Databases*. (This changes the number from *4* to *6*.)
7. Open the **AL1-C7-Skyline.accdb** database by clicking ***AL1-C7-Skyline.accdb*** that displays at the top of the *Recent Databases* list.
8. Click the File tab, click the Recent tab, and then make the following changes at the Recent tab Backstage view:
   a. Click the twice on the down-pointing arrow in the option box located to the right of the *Quickly access this number of Recent Databases*. (This changes the number from *6* to *4*.)
   b. Click the *Quickly access this number of Recent Databases* check box to remove the check mark.
   c. Unpin the **AL1-C7-Skyline.accdb** database by clicking the blue pin that displays at the right side of the database name. (This changes the blue pin to a gray pin.)
   d. Click the File tab to return to the database.

Saving a Database and Database Object

An Access 2010 or Access 2007 database is saved with the .accdb file extension. Earlier versions of Access such as 2003, 2002, or 2000 save a database with the .mdb file extension. To open an Access 2010 or 2007 database in an earlier version, you need to save the database in the .mdb file format.

To save an Access database in the 2002-2003 file format, open the database, click the File tab, and then click the Save & Publish tab. This displays the Save & Publish tab Backstage view as shown in Figure 7.9. Click the *Access 2002-2003 Database (*.mdb)* option in the *Save Database As* section and then click the Save As button that displays at the bottom of the *Save Database As* section. This displays the Save As dialog box with the *Save as type* option set to *Microsoft Access Database (2002-2003) (*.mdb)* and the current database file name with the *.mdb* file extension inserted in the *File name* text box. At this dialog box, click the Save button.

Click the *Save Object As* option in the File Types category of the Save & Publish tab Backstage view and options display for saving the currently selected object. Click the *Save Object As* option to save the selected object in the database or click the *PDF or XPS* option if you want to save the object in the PDF or XPS file format. The letters *PDF* stand for *portable document format*, which is a file format developed by Adobe Systems® that captures all of the elements of a file as an electronic image. An XPS file is a Microsoft file format for publishing content in an easily viewable format. The letters *XPS* stand for *XML paper specification* and the letters *XML* stand for *Extensible Markup Language*, which is a set of rules for encoding files electronically.

To save an object in the PDF or XPS file format, click the desired object in the database Navigation pane, click the File tab, and then click the Save & Publish tab. At the Save & Publish tab Backstage view, click the *Save Object As* option

Quick Steps

Save Object in PDF Format
1. Click desired object in Navigation pane.
2. Click File tab.
3. Click Save & Publish tab.
4. Click *Save Object As* option.
5. Click *PDF or XPS* option.
6. Click Save As button.

Save a Database in an Earlier Version
1. Open database.
2. Click File tab.
3. Click Save & Publish tab.
4. Click desired version in Save Database As category.
5. Click Save As button.

Figure 7.9 Save & Publish Tab Backstage View

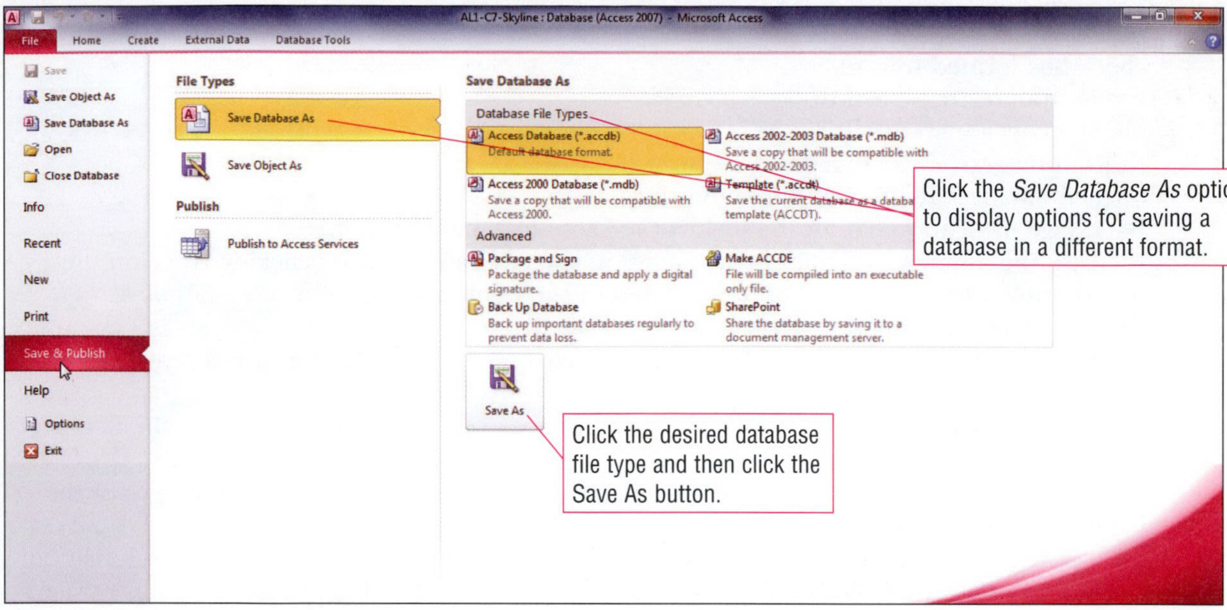

Click the *Save Database As* option to display options for saving a database in a different format.
Click the desired database file type and then click the Save As button.

HINT

An Access 2007 or 2010 database cannot be opened with an earlier version of Access.

in the File Types category, click the *PDF or XPS* option in the Save the current database object category, and then click the Save As button. This displays the Publish as PDF or XPS dialog box with the name of the object inserted in the *File name* text box followed by the file extension *.pdf*, and the *Save as type* option set at *PDF (*.pdf)*. Click the Publish button and the object is saved in PDF format and opens in Adobe Reader. Close Adobe Reader by clicking the Close button that displays in the upper right corner of the screen.

You can open a PDF file in Adobe Reader or in your web browser, and you can open an XPS file in your web browser. To open a PDF file or XPS file in your web browser, click the *File* option on the browser Menu bar and then click *Open* at the drop-down list. At the Open dialog box, click the Browse button. At the browser window Open dialog box, change the *Files of type* to *All Files (*.*)*, navigate to the desired folder, and then double-click the document.

Project 2e Saving a Database in a Previous Version and Saving an Object in PDF Format

Part 5 of 5

1. With the **AL1-C7-Skyline.accdb** database open, save the Orders table in PDF file format by completing the following steps:
   a. Click the Orders table in the Navigation pane.
   b. Click the File tab and then click the Save & Publish tab.
   c. At the Save & Publish tab Backstage view, click the *Save Object As* option in the File Types category.
   d. Click the *PDF or XPS* option in the Save the current database object category.
   e. Click the Save As button.

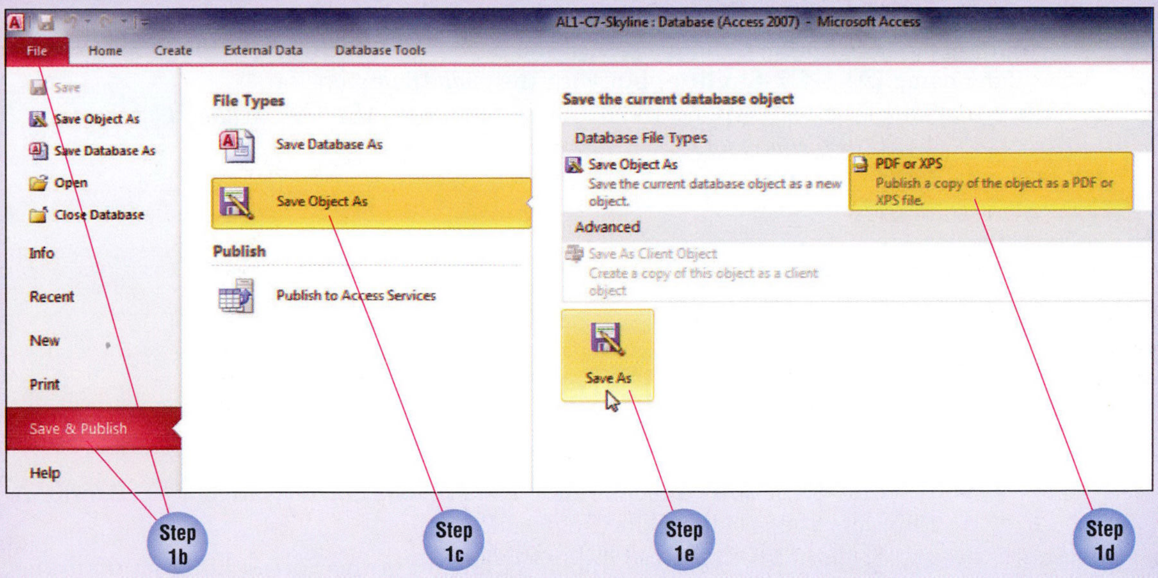

f. At the Publish as PDF or XPS dialog box, make sure the Access2010L1C7 folder on your storage medium is the active folder and then click the Publish button.

g. When the Orders table opens in Adobe Reader, scroll through the file, and then close the file by clicking the Close button located in the upper right corner of the screen.

2. Save the database in a previous version of Access by completing the following steps:

a. Click the File tab and then click the Save & Publish tab.

b. At the Save & Publish tab Backstage view, click the *Access 2002-2003 Database (*.mdb)* option in the Save Database As category.

c. Click the Save As button.

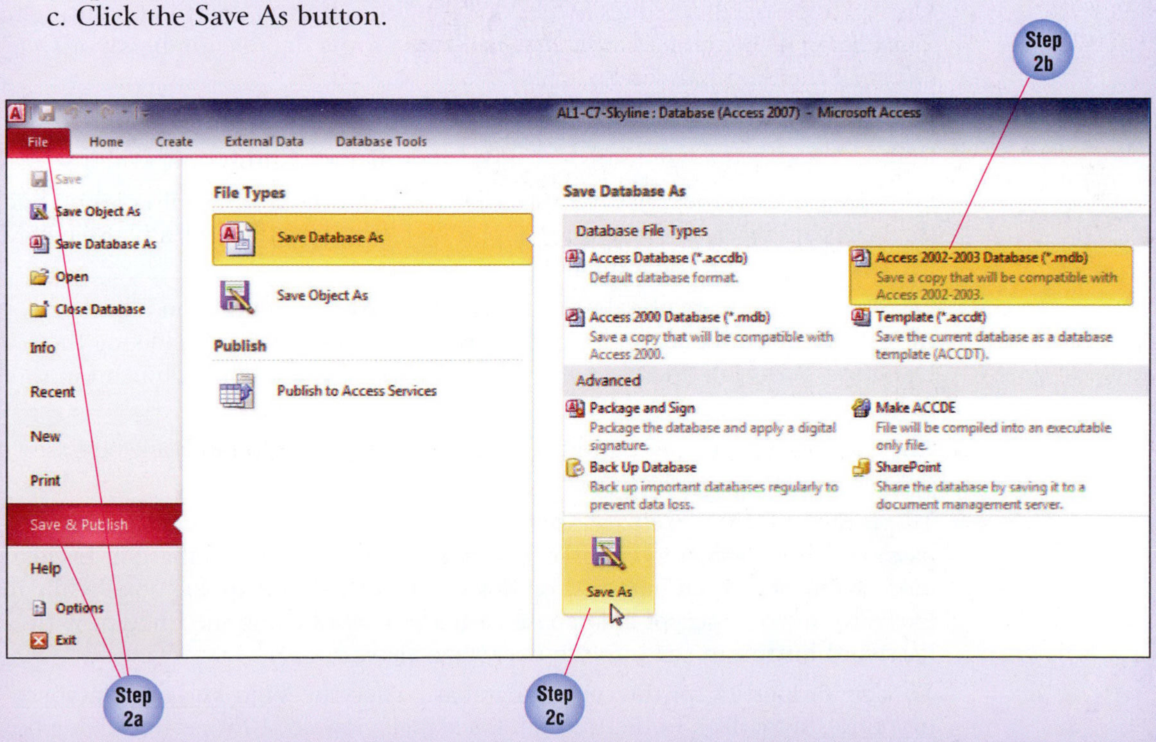

d. At the Save As dialog box, make sure the Access2010L1C7 folder on your storage medium is the active folder and then click the Save button. This saves the database with the same name (**AL1-C7-Skyline**) but with the *.mdb* file extension.
e. Notice that the Title bar displays the database file name *AL1-C7-Skyline : Database (Access 2002 - 2003 file format)*.

3. Close the database.

Chapter Summary

- A set of restrictions, called a filter, can be set on records in a table or form. A filter lets you select specific field values.
- You can filter records with the Filter button in the Sort & Filter group in the Home tab.
- Click the Toggle Filter button in the Sort & Filter group to switch back and forth between data and filtered data.
- Remove a filter by clicking the Filter button in the Sort & Filter group and then clicking the *Clear filter from xxx* (where *xxx* is the name of the field).
- Another method for removing a filter is to click the Advanced button in the Sort & Filter group and then click *Clear All Filters*.
- Display a list of filter values by clicking the Filter button and then pointing to *Text Filters* (if the data is text), *Number Filters* (if the data is numbers), or *Date Filters* (if the data is a date).
- Filter by selection by clicking the Selection button in the Sort & Filter group.
- Right-click a field entry to display a shortcut menu with filtering options.
- Filter by form by clicking the Advanced button in the Sort & Filter group and then clicking *Filter By Form* at the drop-down list. This displays a blank record with two tabs Look for and Or.
- Display the structure of a database and the relationship between objects at the Object Dependencies task pane. Display this task pane by clicking the Database Tools tab and then clicking the Object Dependencies button in the Relationships group.
- Click the Compact & Repair Database button in the Info tab Backstage view to optimize database performance.
- To prevent unauthorized access to a database, encrypt the database with a password. To encrypt a database, you must first open the database in Exclusive mode using the Open button drop-down list in the Open dialog box. While in Exclusive mode, encrypt a database with a password using the Encrypt with Password button in the Info tab Backstage view.
- To view properties for the current database, click the View and edit database properties hyperlink in the Info tab Backstage view. The Properties dialog box contains a number of tabs containing information about the database.

- The Recent tab Backstage view displays a list of the most recently opened databases. Insert a check mark in the *Quickly access this number of Recent Databases* check box to display the four most recently opened databases in the Backstage navigation bar.

- At the Recent tab Backstage view, click the gray pin to the right of the desired database in order to pin the database to the top of the *Recent Databases* list.

- Save a database in a previous version of Access using options in the Save Database As category of the Save & Publish tab Backstage view.

- To save a database object in PDF or XPS format, display the Save & Publish tab Backstage view, click the *Save Object As* option, and then click the *PDF or XPS* option.

Commands Review

FEATURE	RIBBON TAB, GROUP	BUTTON, OPTION
Filter	Home, Sort & Filter	▽
Toggle filter	Home, Sort & Filter	▼
Remove filter	Home, Sort & Filter	▽ , *Clear filter from xxx* OR ▦ , Clear All Filters
Filter by selection	Home, Sort & Filter	⚡
Filter by form	Home, Sort & Filter	▦ , Filter By Form
Object Dependencies task pane	Database Tools, Relationships	▦
Info tab Backstage view	File, Info	
Recent tab Backstage view	File, Recent

Concepts Check Test Your Knowledge

Completion: In the space provided at the right, indicate the correct term, symbol, or command.

1. The Filter button is located in this group in the Home tab. ____________
2. If you filter data, you can switch between the data and the filtered data by clicking this button. ____________
3. Remove all filtering from an object with the Filter button or by clicking this button and then clicking *Clear All Filters*. ____________
4. In the Filter by Form window, these two tabs display toward the bottom of the form. ____________
5. Display the structure of a database at this task pane. ____________
6. Do this to a database to optimize database performance. ____________
7. Before encrypting a database with a password, you have to open the database in this mode. ____________
8. Display the Set Database Password dialog box by clicking this button in the Info tab Backstage view. ____________
9. Data in this dialog box describes details about a database such as title, author name, and subject. ____________
10. Insert a check mark in this option and the names of the four most recently opened databases display in the Backstage navigation bar. ____________
11. Do this to a database file name if you want it to remain at the top of the *Recent Databases* list at the Recent tab Backstage view. ____________
12. Save a database object in PDF file format with the *PDF or XPS* option in this Backstage view tab. ____________

Skills Check Assess Your Performance

Assessment 1

FILTER RECORDS IN TABLES

1. Display the Open dialog box with Access2010L1C7 on your storage medium the active folder.
2. Open the **AL1-C7-WarrenLegal.accdb** database and enable the contents.
3. Open the Clients table and then filter the records to display the following records:
   a. Display only those records of clients who live in Renton. When the records of clients in Renton display, print the results in landscape orientation and then remove the filter. ***Hint: Change to landscape orientation in Print Preview.***
   b. Display only those records of clients with the ZIP code of 98033. When the records of clients with the ZIP code 98033 display, print the results in landscape orientation and then remove the filter.
4. Close the Clients table without saving the changes.
5. Open the Billing table and then filter records by selection to display the following records:
   a. Display only those records with a Category of CC. Print the CC records and then remove the filter.
   b. Display only those records with an Attorney ID of 12. Print the records and then remove the filter.
   c. Display only those records between the dates 6/1/2012 and 6/10/2012. Print the records and then remove the filter.
6. Close the Billing table without saving the changes.
7. Open the Clients table and then use Filter By Form to display clients in Auburn or Renton. (Be sure to use the Or tab at the very bottom of the table.) Print the table in landscape orientation and then remove the filter.
8. Close the Clients table without saving the changes.
9. Open the Billing table and then use Filter By Form to display categories G or P. Print the table and then remove the filter.
10. Close the Billing table without saving the changes.
11. Close the **AL1-C7-WarrenLegal.accdb** database.

Assessment 2

SAVE A TABLE AND DATABASE IN DIFFERENT FILE FORMATS

1. Open the **AL1-C7-Hilltop.accdb** database in Exclusive mode and enable the contents.
2. Create a password for the database and, with the Set Database Password dialog box open, create a screen capture of the screen with the dialog box by completing the following steps:
   a. Press the Print Screen button on your keyboard.
   b. Open Microsoft Word.
   c. Click the Paste button located in the Clipboard group in the Home tab. (This pastes the screen capture image in the Word document.)
   d. Click the File tab, click the Print tab, and then click the *Print* option at the Print tab Backstage view.

e. Exit Word by clicking the Close button located in the upper right corner of the screen. At the message asking if you want to save the document, click the Don't Save button.

3. Click OK to close the Set Database Password dialog box.
4. At the message telling you that block cipher is incompatible with row level locking, click OK.
5. Close the database.
6. Open the **AL1-C7-Hilltop.accdb** database in Exclusive mode and enter the password when prompted.
7. Remove the password. ***Hint: Do this with the Decrypt Database button in the Info tab Backstage view.***
8. Customize the Recent tab Backstage view by completing the following steps:
   a. Insert a check mark in the *Quickly access this number of Recent Databases* check box.
   b. Change the number of database files names that display to *6*.
   c. Pin the **AL1-C7-Hilltop.accdb** database to the *Recent Databases* list.
9. Use the Print Screen button on the keyboard to make a screen capture of the Recent tab Backstage view. Open Word and then paste the screen capture image in the Word document. Print the document containing the screen capture image and then exit Word without saving the changes to the document.
10. Change the Recent tab Backstage view options back by changing the number of database file names to display to *4*, removing the check mark from the *Quickly access this number of Recent Databases* check box, and unpinning the **AL1-C7-Hilltop.accdb** database.
11. Save the Invoices table in PDF format. When the table displays in Adobe Reader, print the table by clicking the Print button located toward the upper left side of the screen and then clicking OK at the Print dialog box. (If the Print button is not visible, click the File option, click *Print* at the drop-down list, and then click OK at the Print dialog box.)
12. Close Adobe Reader.
13. Save the **AL1-C7-Hilltop.accdb** database in the *Access 2002-2003 Database (*.mdb)* file format.
14. With the database open, make a screen capture using the Print Screen button on the keyboard. Open Word, paste the screen capture image in the Word document, print the document, and then exit Word without saving the changes.
15. Close the database.

Assessment 3

DELETE AND RENAME OBJECTS

1. Open the **AL1-C7-Hilltop.accdb** database.
2. Right-click an object in the Navigation pane, experiment with options in the shortcut menu, and then complete these steps using the shortcut menu:
   a. Delete the Inventory form.
   b. Rename the form Equipment to *EquipForm*.
   c. Rename the report InvReport to *InventoryReport*.
   d. Export (using the shortcut menu) the *EquipmentQuery* to a Word RTF file. ***Hint: Click the Browse button at the Export - RTF File dialog box and make Access2010L1C7 the active folder.***
   e. Open the *EquipmentQuery.rtf* file in Word, print the file, and then exit Word.
3. Close the **AL1-C7-Hilltop.accdb** database.

Visual Benchmark Demonstrate Your Proficiency

DESIGN A QUERY AND FILTER THE QUERY

1. Open the **AL1-C7-PacTrek.accdb** database and enable the contents.
2. Create and run the query shown in Figure 7.10.
3. Save the query and name it *ProductsOnOrderQuery.*
4. Print the query.
5. Filter the query so the records display as shown in Figure 7.11. ***Hint: Filter the supplier names as shown in Figure 7.11 and then filter the UnitsOnOrder field to show records that do not equal 0.***
6. Print the filtered query.
7. Remove the filters and then close the query without saving the changes.
8. Close the **AL1-C7-PacTrek.accdb** database.

Figure 7.10 Visual Benchmark Query

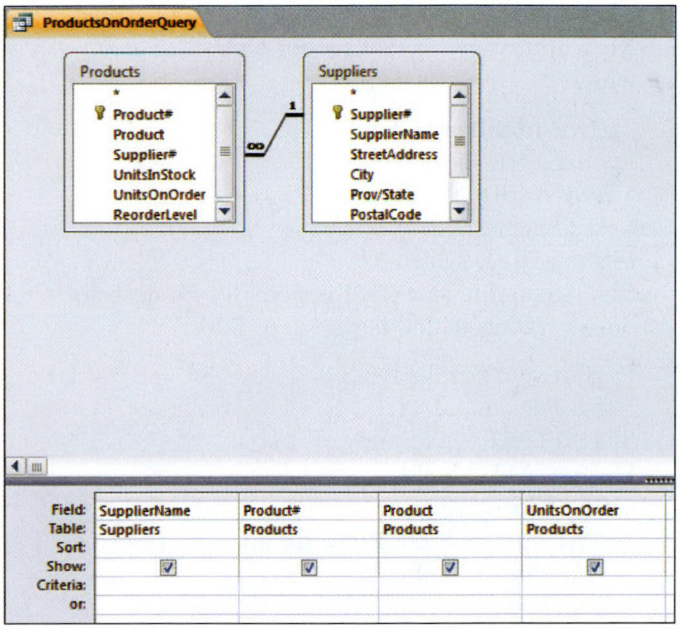

Figure 7.11 Visual Benchmark Filtered Query

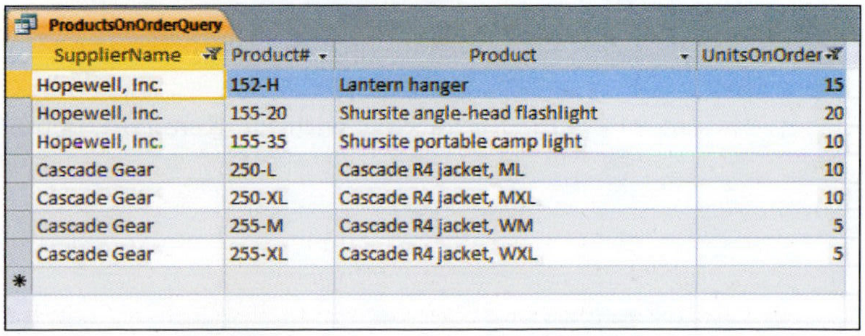

ProductsOnOrderQuery

SupplierName	Product#	Product	UnitsOnOrder
Hopewell, Inc.	152-H	Lantern hanger	15
Hopewell, Inc.	155-20	Shursite angle-head flashlight	20
Hopewell, Inc.	155-35	Shursite portable camp light	10
Cascade Gear	250-L	Cascade R4 jacket, ML	10
Cascade Gear	250-XL	Cascade R4 jacket, MXL	10
Cascade Gear	255-M	Cascade R4 jacket, WM	5
Cascade Gear	255-XL	Cascade R4 jacket, WXL	5

Case Study Apply Your Skills

Part 1

As the office manager at Summit View Medical Services, you are responsible for maintaining clinic records. Open the **AL1-C7-SummitView.accdb** database, enable the contents, and then insert the following additional services into the appropriate table:

- Edit the *Doctor visit* entry in the Services table so it displays as *Clinic visit*.
- Add the entry *X-ray* with a service identification of *X*.
- Add the entry *Cholesterol screening* with a service identification of *CS*.

Add the following new patient information in the database in the appropriate tables:

Patient number 121
Brian M. Gould
2887 Nelson Street
Helena, MT 59604
(406) 555-3121
Mr. Gould saw Dr.Wallace for a clinic visit on 4/6/2012, which has a fee of $75.

Patient number 122
Ellen L. Augustine
12990 148th Street
East Helena, MT 59635
(406) 555-0722
Ms. Augustine saw Dr. Kennedy for cholesterol screening on 4/6/2012, which has a fee of $90.

Patient number 123
Jeff J. Masura
3218 Eldridge Avenue
Helena, MT 59624
(406) 555-6212
Mr. Masura saw Dr. Rowe for an x-ray on 4/6/2012, which has a fee of $75.

Add the following information to the Billing table:

- Patient 109 came for cholesterol screening with Dr. Kennedy on 4/6/2012 with a $90 fee.
- Patient 106 came for immunizations with Dr. Pena on 4/6/2012 with a $100 fee.
- Patient 114 came for an x-ray with Dr. Kennedy on 4/6/2012 with a $75 fee.

Part 2

Create the following filters and queries:

- Open the Billing table and then filter and print the records for the date 04/2/2012. Clear the filter and then filter and print the records with a doctor number of 18. Save and then close the table.
- Create a report that displays the patient's first name, last name, street address, city, state, and ZIP code. Apply formatting to enhance the visual appeal of the report. Filter and print the records of those patients living in Helena, remove the filter, and then filter and print the records of those patients living in East Helena. Close the report.
- Design a query that includes the doctor number, doctor last name, patient number, date of visit, and fee. Save the query with the name *DoctorBillingFees* and then print the query. Filter and print the records for Dr. Kennedy and Dr. Pena, remove the filter, and then filter and print the records for the dates 4/5/2012 and 4/6/2012. Save and then close the query.

Part 3

You want to make the Billing table available for viewing on computers without Access so you decide to save the table in PDF format. Save the Billing table in PDF format, print the table in Adobe Reader, and then close Adobe Reader. Close the **AL1-C7-SummitView.accdb** database.

Part 4

Your clinic has a procedures manual that describes processes and procedures in the center. Open Word and then create a document for the procedures manual that describes the steps you followed to create the *DoctorBillingFees* query and the steps you followed to create and print the two filters. Save the completed document and name it **AL1-C7-CS-Manual**. Print and then close **AL1-C7-CS-Manual.docx**.

Microsoft® Access®

CHAPTER 8

Importing and Exporting Data

PERFORMANCE OBJECTIVES

Upon successful completion of Chapter 8, you will be able to:

- **Export Access data to Excel**
- **Export Access data to Word**
- **Merge Access data with a Word document**
- **Import data to a new table**
- **Link data to a new table**
- **Use the Office Clipboard**

SNAP Training and Assessment Simplified

Tutorials

8.1 Exporting Access Data to Excel and Word

8.2 Merging Access Data with a Word Document

8.3 Importing and Linking Data to a New Table

8.4 Using the Office Clipboard

Microsoft Office 2010 is a suite of programs that allows easy data exchange between programs. In this chapter you will learn how to export data from Access to Excel and Word, merge Access data with a Word document, import and link data to a new table, and copy and paste data between programs. You will also learn how to copy and paste data between applications. Model answers for this chapter's projects appear on the following pages.

Access
Access2012L1C8

Note: Before beginning the projects, copy to your storage medium the Access2010L1C8 subfolder from the Access2010L1 folder on the CD that accompanies this textbook and make Access2010L1C8 the active folder.

Project 1 Export Data to Excel and Export and Merge Data to Word

Project 1a

Equipment#	PurchaseDate	PurchasePrice	AvailableHours	ServiceHours	RepairHours
10	05-Feb-08	$65,540.00	120	15	10
11	01-Sep-09	$105,500.00	125	20	15
12	01-Jun-07	$55,345.00	140	10	10
13	05-May-10	$86,750.00	120	20	20
14	15-Jul-09	$4,500.00	160	5	5
15	01-Oct-07	$95,900.00	125	25	20
16	01-Dec-10	$3,450.00	150	10	5
17	10-Apr-09	$5,600.00	160	5	10
18	15-Jun-10	$8,000.00	150	5	5
19	30-Sep-11	$42,675.00	120	20	25

Hilltop Inventory

BillingDate	Customer	Hours	Rate	Total
01-May-12	Lakeside Trucking	8	$75.00	$600.00
01-May-12	Lakeside Trucking	8	$100.00	$800.00
01-May-12	Martin Plumbing	4	$50.00	$200.00
02-May-12	Country Electrical	16	$75.00	$1,200.00
02-May-12	Able Construction	5	$100.00	$500.00
03-May-12	Able Construction	5	$25.00	$125.00
03-May-12	Miles Contracting	10	$50.00	$500.00
04-May-12	Miles Contracting	10	$35.00	$350.00
04-May-12	Evergreen Painting	8	$25.00	$200.00
07-May-12	Barrier Concrete	8	$25.00	$200.00
07-May-12	Barrier Concrete	8	$25.00	$200.00
07-May-12	Cascade Enterprises	10	$100.00	$1,000.00
08-May-12	Cascade Enterprises	10	$75.00	$750.00
08-May-12	Allied Builders	6	$50.00	$300.00
08-May-12	Martin Plumbing	8	$35.00	$280.00
09-May-12	Evergreen Painting	8	$25.00	$200.00
09-May-12	Evergreen Painting	8	$25.00	$200.00
09-May-12	Able Construction	4	$75.00	$300.00
10-May-12	Able Construction	4	$100.00	$400.00
10-May-12	Miles Contracting	4	$50.00	$200.00
10-May-12	Country Electrical	6	$50.00	$300.00
11-May-12	Martin Plumbing	5	$75.00	$375.00
11-May-12	Lakeside Trucking	6	$100.00	$600.00
11-May-12	Cascade Enterprises	8	$25.00	$200.00
14-May-12	Miles Contracting	6	$25.00	$150.00
14-May-12	Evergreen Painting	6	$35.00	$210.00
14-May-12	Barrier Concrete	4	$100.00	$400.00
15-May-12	Allied Builders	4	$100.00	$400.00
15-May-12	Martin Plumbing	4	$50.00	$200.00
15-May-12	Miles Contracting	8	$25.00	$200.00

Hilltop Customer Invoices Query in Excel

CustomerReport

Customer	Equipment	BillingDate	Hours
Miles Contracting	Hydraulic pump	5/4/2012	10
	Trencher	5/10/2012	4
	Scaffolding	5/14/2012	6
	Sandblaster	5/15/2012	8
	Forklift	5/3/2012	10
Barrier Concrete	Sandblaster	5/7/2012	8
	Pressure sprayer	5/7/2012	8
	Tractor	5/14/2012	4
Country Electrical	Backhoe	5/2/2012	16
	Forklift	5/10/2012	6
Cascade Enterprises	Front loader	5/7/2012	10
	Flatbed truck	5/8/2012	10
	Pressure sprayer	5/11/2012	8
Martin Plumbing	Flatbed truck	5/11/2012	5
	Hydraulic pump	5/8/2012	8
	Forklift	5/15/2012	4
	Trencher	5/1/2012	4
Evergreen Painting	Pressure sprayer	5/4/2012	8
	Sandblaster	5/9/2012	8
	Pressure sprayer	5/9/2012	8
	Hydraulic pump	5/14/2012	6
Able Construction	Tractor	5/2/2012	5
	Scaffolding	5/3/2012	5
	Backhoe	5/9/2012	4
	Tractor	5/10/2012	4
Lakeside Trucking	Backhoe	5/1/2012	8
	Front loader	5/1/2012	8
	Front loader	5/11/2012	6
Allied Builders	Front loader	5/15/2012	4
	Forklift	5/8/2012	6

Tuesday, July 31, 2012 Page 1 of 1

Project 1b, Hilltop Customer Report in Access

Project 1b

Invoice#	BillingDate	Customer#	Equipment#	Hours	RateID
1	5/1/2012	310	10	8	D
2	5/1/2012	310	11	8	E
3	5/1/2012	267	12	4	C
4	5/2/2012	196	10	16	D
5	5/2/2012	305	13	5	E
6	5/3/2012	305	14	5	A
7	5/3/2012	106	15	10	C
8	5/4/2012	106	16	10	B
9	5/4/2012	275	17	8	A
10	5/7/2012	154	18	8	A
11	5/7/2012	154	17	8	A
12	5/7/2012	209	11	10	E
13	5/8/2012	209	19	10	D
14	5/8/2012	316	15	6	C
15	5/8/2012	267	16	8	B
16	5/9/2012	275	18	8	A
17	5/9/2012	275	17	8	A
18	5/9/2012	305	10	4	D
19	5/10/2012	305	13	4	E
20	5/10/2012	106	12	4	C
21	5/10/2012	196	15	6	C
22	5/11/2012	267	19	5	D
23	5/11/2012	310	11	6	E
24	5/11/2012	209	17	8	A
25	5/14/2012	106	14	6	A
26	5/14/2012	275	16	6	B
27	5/14/2012	154	13	4	E
28	5/15/2012	316	11	4	E
29	5/15/2012	267	15	4	C
30	5/15/2012	106	18	8	A

Hilltop Customer Invoices in Word

CustomerReport

Customer	Equipment	BillingDate	Hours
Miles Contracting	Hydraulic pump	5/4/2012	10
	Trencher	5/10/2012	4
	Scaffolding	5/14/2012	6
	Sandblaster	5/15/2012	8
	Forklift	5/3/2012	10
Barrier Concrete	Sandblaster	5/7/2012	8
	Pressure sprayer	5/7/2012	8
	Tractor	5/14/2012	4
Country Electrical	Backhoe	5/2/2012	16
	Forklift	5/10/2012	6
Cascade Enterprises	Front loader	5/7/2012	10
	Flatbed truck	5/8/2012	10
	Pressure sprayer	5/11/2012	8
Martin Plumbing	Flatbed truck	5/11/2012	5
	Hydraulic pump	5/8/2012	8
	Forklift	5/15/2012	4
	Trencher	5/1/2012	4
Evergreen Painting	Pressure sprayer	5/4/2012	8
	Sandblaster	5/9/2012	8
	Pressure sprayer	5/9/2012	8
	Hydraulic pump	5/14/2012	6
Able Construction	Tractor	5/2/2012	5
	Scaffolding	5/3/2012	5
	Backhoe	5/9/2012	4
	Tractor	5/10/2012	4
Lakeside Trucking	Backhoe	5/1/2012	8
	Front loader	5/1/2012	8
	Front loader	5/11/2012	6
Allied Builders	Front loader	5/15/2012	4
	Forklift	5/8/2012	6

Tuesday, July 31, 2012 Page 1 of 1

Project 1b, Hilltop Customer Report in Word

July 31, 2012

Miles Contracting
640 Smith Road
Aurora, CO 80041-6400

Ladies and Gentlemen:

Please join us June 1 for our annual equipment sales auction. Some of the choice items up for auction include three forklifts, two flatbed trucks, a front loader, and a bulldozer. We will also be auctioning painting equipment including pressure sprayers, ladders, and scaffolding.

The auction begins at 7:30 a.m. in the parking lot of our warehouse at 2605 Evans Avenue in Denver. For a listing of all equipment available for auction, stop by our store or call us at (303) 555-9066 and we will mail you the list.

Sincerely,

Lou Galloway
Manager

XX
HilltopLetter.docx

July 31, 2012

Barrier Concrete
220 Colorado Boulevard
Denver, CO 80125-2204

Ladies and Gentlemen:

Please join us June 1 for our annual equipment sales auction. Some of the choice items up for auction include three forklifts, two flatbed trucks, a front loader, and a bulldozer. We will also be auctioning painting equipment including pressure sprayers, ladders, and scaffolding.

The auction begins at 7:30 a.m. in the parking lot of our warehouse at 2605 Evans Avenue in Denver. For a listing of all equipment available for auction, stop by our store or call us at (303) 555-9066 and we will mail you the list.

Sincerely,

Lou Galloway
Manager

XX
HilltopLetter.docx

Project 1c, Hilltop Letters

July 31, 2012

Vernon Cook
1230 South Mesa
Phoenix, AZ 85018

Ladies and Gentlemen:

At the Grant Street West office of Copper State Insurance, we have hired two additional insurance representatives as well as one support staff member to ensure that we meet all your insurance needs. To accommodate the new staff, we have moved to a larger office just a few blocks away. Our new address is 3450 Grant Street West, Suite 110, Phoenix, AZ 85003. Our telephone number, (602) 555-6200, has remained the same.

If you have any questions or concerns about your insurance policies or want to discuss adding or changing current coverage, please stop by or give us a call. We are committed to providing our clients with the most comprehensive automobile insurance coverage in the country.

Sincerely,

Lou Galloway
Manager

XX
AL1-C8-CSLtrs.docx

July 31, 2012

Helena Myerson
9032 45th Street East
Phoenix, AZ 85009

Ladies and Gentlemen:

At the Grant Street West office of Copper State Insurance, we have hired two additional insurance representatives as well as one support staff member to ensure that we meet all your insurance needs. To accommodate the new staff, we have moved to a larger office just a few blocks away. Our new address is 3450 Grant Street West, Suite 110, Phoenix, AZ 85003. Our telephone number, (602) 555-6200, has remained the same.

If you have any questions or concerns about your insurance policies or want to discuss adding or changing current coverage, please stop by or give us a call. We are committed to providing our clients with the most comprehensive automobile insurance coverage in the country.

Sincerely,

Lou Galloway
Manager

XX
AL1-C8-CSLtrs.docx

Project 1d, Copper State Main Document

Model Answers

Coverage 7/31/2010

License#	Client#	Medical	Liability	Comprehensive	UninsMotorist	Collision
014 BZW	1574	☑	☐	☑	☑	☑
019 TMW	8223	☐	☑	☐	☑	☑
027 BWP	7139	☑	☑	☐	☑	☑
106 WRT	4786	☑	☐	☑	☑	☐
154 EDC	4868	☑	☐	☑	☑	☐
207 ZAR	9872	☑	☐	☑	☑	☑
273 BNE	9746	☐	☑	☐	☐	☐
297 QES	7521	☐	☑	☐	☑	☑
310 YTV	3120	☑	☐	☑	☑	☑
328 BZS	3156	☐	☑	☐	☐	☐
341 BNV	8223	☐	☑	☑	☐	☐
341 VIT	3120	☑	☐	☐	☑	☐
349 IPN	4852	☑	☐	☑	☑	☑
353 GWA	9879	☑	☐	☐	☑	☐
362 PAZ	9775	☑	☑	☑	☑	☑
387 GOE	2768	☑	☐	☐	☑	☐
439 PQC	1379	☐	☑	☑	☐	☑
452 XOS	0214	☑	☐	☐	☑	☐
458 IRD	5231	☑	☐	☐	☑	☐
473 GHM	3156	☐	☑	☐	☐	☐
489 WIF	9897	☑	☑	☑	☑	☑
587 ERI	3976	☑	☐	☐	☐	☐
717 TUQ	6478	☑	☐	☐	☑	☑
734 APL	4875	☐	☑	☑	☑	☑
758 BQI	5645	☑	☐	☐	☑	☑
763 ARM	4852	☑	☑	☑	☑	☑
776 ERU	9383	☑	☐	☐	☐	☐
823 IUN	5982	☑	☐	☐	☑	☑
852 YRN	1331	☑	☑	☑	☐	☐
877 BNN	4300	☐	☑	☑	☑	☑
923 HSC	5665	☑	☐	☐	☑	☐
937 PQX	4567	☑	☑	☑	☑	☑
948 NLQ	3164	☐	☑	☐	☐	☐
958 HGN	8854	☐	☑	☐	☐	☐
958 RMD	5645	☑	☐	☑	☑	☑
984 CWS	7335	☐	☑	☑	☑	☑

Page 1

Project 1e, Copper State Coverage Table

Project 2 Import and Link Excel Worksheets with an Access Table

Project 2a

Policy#	Client#	Premium
110-C-39	0214	$1,450
115-C-41	3120	$935
120-B-33	3156	$424
122-E-30	1331	$745
127-E-67	3164	$893
129-D-55	3976	$770
131-C-90	4300	$1,255
135-E-31	4567	$1,510
136-E-77	4786	$635
139-B-59	4852	$338
141-E-84	4875	$951
143-D-20	1379	$920
145-D-12	5231	$1,175
147-C-10	5645	$1,005
150-C-36	5665	$805
152-B-01	5982	$411
155-E-88	6478	$988
168-B-65	7139	$1,050
170-C-20	7335	$875
173-D-77	7521	$556
180-E-05	8223	$721
185-E-19	2768	$734
188-D-63	8854	$1,384
192-C-29	1574	$1,390

Project 2b

Policy#	Client#	Premium
110-C-39	0214	$ 1,450
122-E-30	1331	$ 850
143-D-20	1379	$ 920
192-C-29	1574	$ 1,390
185-E-19	2768	$ 734
115-C-41	3120	$ 935
120-B-33	3156	$ 424
127-E-67	3164	$ 893
129-D-55	3976	$ 770
131-C-90	4300	$ 1,255
135-E-31	4567	$ 1,510
136-E-77	4786	$ 635
139-B-59	4852	$ 338
141-E-84	4875	$ 951
145-D-12	5231	$ 1,175
147-C-10	5645	$ 1,005
150-C-36	5665	$ 805
152-B-01	5982	$ 411
155-E-88	6478	$ 988
168-B-65	7139	$ 1,050
170-C-20	7335	$ 875
173-D-77	7521	$ 556
180-E-05	8223	$ 721
188-D-63	8854	$ 1,384
190-C-28	3120	$ 685

Project 3 Collect Data in Word and Paste in an Access Table

Project 3

Customer#	Customer	StreetAddress	City	State	ZipCode
106	Miles Contracting	640 Smith Road	Aurora	CO	80041-6400
154	Barrier Concrete	220 Colorado Boulevard	Denver	CO	80125-2204
196	Country Electrical	12032 Sixth Avenue	Aurora	CO	80023-5473
209	Cascade Enterprises	24300 Quincy Avenue	Englewood	CO	80118-3800
267	Martin Plumbing	1010 Santa Fe Drive	Littleton	CO	80135-4886
275	Evergreen Painting	1045 Calfax Avenue	Denver	CO	80130-4337
305	Able Construction	8800 Evans Avenue	Denver	CO	80128-3488
310	Lakeside Trucking	566 Jewell Avenue	Denver	CO	80125-1298
316	Allied Builders	550 Alameda Avenue	Denver	CO	80135-7643
178	Stone Construction	9905 Broadway	Englewood	CO	80118-9008
225	Laughlin Products	997 Speer Boulevard	Denver	CO	80129-7446

Export Data to Excel and Export and Merge Data to Word **5 Parts**

You will export a table and query to Excel and export a table and report to Word. You will also merge data in an Access table and query with a Word document.

Exporting Data ▪▪▪▪▪▪▪▪▪▪▪▪▪▪▪▪▪▪▪▪▪▪▪▪

One of the advantages of a suite like Microsoft Office is the ability to exchange data between programs. Access, like other programs in the suite, offers a feature to export data from Access into Excel and/or Word. The Export group in the External Data tab contains buttons for exporting a table, query, form, or report to other programs such as Excel and Word.

Exporting Data to Excel

Use the Excel button in the Export group in the External Data tab to export data in a table, query, or form to an Excel worksheet. Click the object containing data you want to export to Excel, click the External Data tab, click the Excel button in the Export group and the first Export - Excel Spreadsheet wizard dialog box displays as shown in Figure 8.1.

▼ **Quick Steps**
Export Data to Excel
1. Click the desired table, query, or form.
2. Click the External Data tab.
3. Click Excel button in Export group.
4. Make desired changes at Export - Excel Spreadsheet dialog box.
5. Click OK.

Excel

Figure 8.1 Export - Excel Spreadsheet Dialog Box

Export - Excel Spreadsheet

Select the destination for the data you want to export

Specify the destination file name and format.

File name: G:\Access2010L1C8\Inventory.xlsx Browse...

File format: Excel Workbook (*.xlsx)

> Click the Browse button and then navigate to the desired folder and files.

Specify export options.

☑ **Export data with formatting and layout.**
Select this option to preserve most formatting and layout information when exporting a table, query, form, or report.

> Insert a check mark in this check box to export all object formatting and layout.

☐ **Open the destination file after the export operation is complete.**
Select this option to view the results of the export operation. This option is available only when you export formatted data.

> Insert a check mark in this check box to open the file in the destination program.

☐ **Export only the selected records.**
Select this option to export only the selected records. This option is only available when you export formatted data and have records selected.

OK Cancel

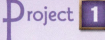

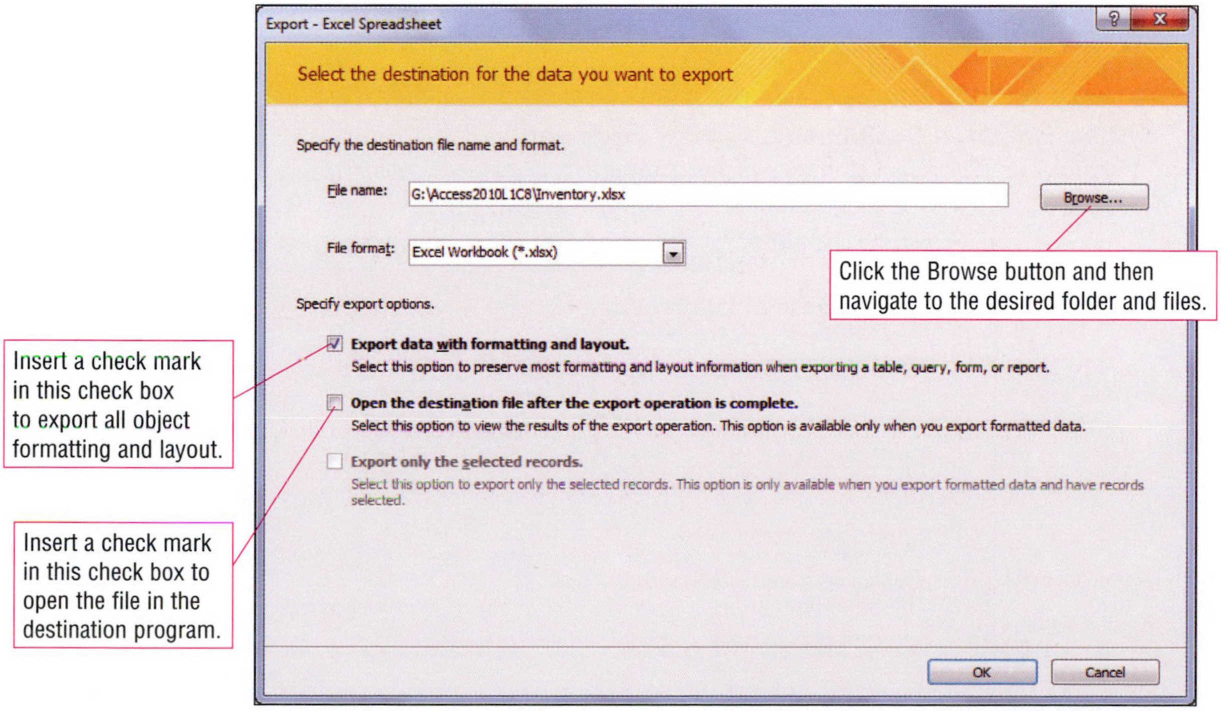

HINT

Data exported from Access to Excel is saved as an Excel workbook with the .xlsx file extension.

HINT

You can export only one database object at a time, and you cannot export reports to Excel.

At the first wizard dialog box, Access uses the name of the object as the Excel workbook name. You can change this by selecting the current name and then typing a new name and you can specify the file format with the *File format* option. Click the *Export data with formatting and layout* check box to insert a check mark. This exports all data formatting to the Excel workbook. If you want Excel to open with the exported data, click the *Open the destination file after the export operation is complete* option to insert a check mark. When you have made all desired changes, click the OK button. This opens Excel with the data in a workbook. Make any desired changes to the workbook and then save, print, and close the workbook. Exit Excel and Access displays with a second wizard dialog box asking if you want to save the export steps. At this dialog box, insert a check mark in the *Save export steps* if you want to save the export steps, or leave the option blank and then click the Close button.

Project 1a Exporting a Table and Query to Excel

Part 1 of 5

1. Display the Open dialog box with Access2010L1C8 on your storage medium the active folder.
2. Open the **AL1-C8-Hilltop.accdb** database and enable the contents.
3. Save the Inventory table as an Excel worksheet by completing the following steps:
   a. Click the Inventory table in the Navigation pane.
   b. Click the External Data tab and then click the Excel button in the Export group.
   c. At the Export - Excel Spreadsheet dialog box, click the Browse button.
   d. At the File Save dialog box, navigate to the Access2010L1C8 folder on your storage medium and then click the Save button.
   e. Click the *Export data with formatting and layout* option to insert a check mark in the check box.
   f. Click the *Open the destination file after the export operation is complete* option to insert a check mark in the check box.

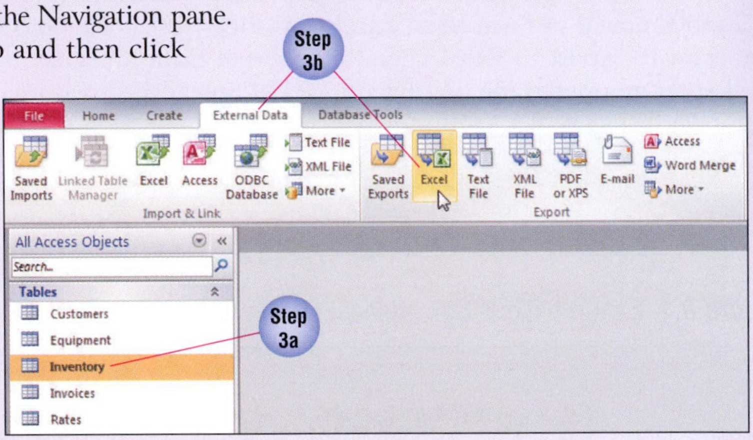
Step 3b
File
Home
Create
External Data
Database Tools
Saved Imports
Linked Table Manager
Excel
Access
ODBC Database
Text File
XML File
More
Import & Link
Saved Exports
Excel
Text File
XML File
PDF or XPS
E-mail
Access
Word Merge
More
Export
All Access Objects
Search...
Tables
Customers
Equipment
Inventory
Invoices
Rates
Step 3a

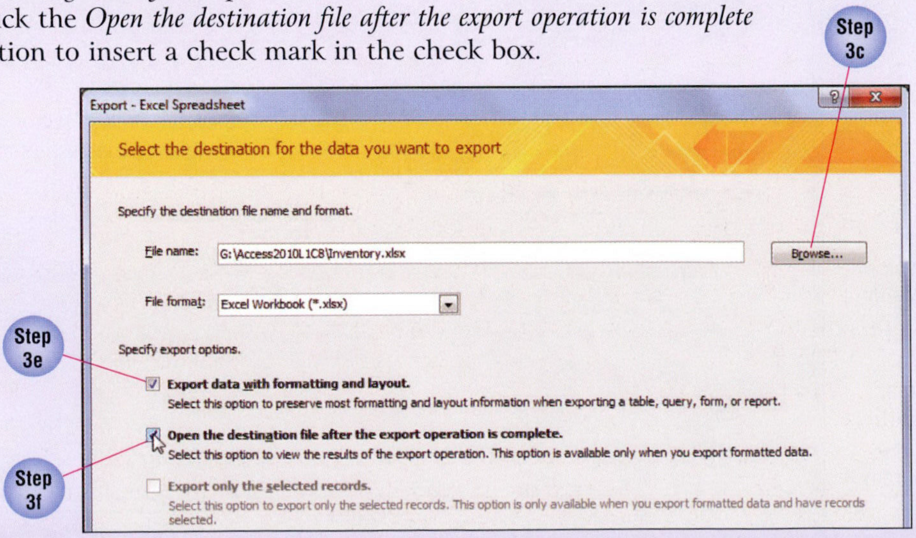
Step 3c
Export - Excel Spreadsheet
Select the destination for the data you want to export
Specify the destination file name and format.
File name:
G:\Access2010L1C8\Inventory.xlsx
Browse...
File format:
Excel Workbook (*.xlsx)
Specify export options.
Step 3e
Export data with formatting and layout.
Select this option to preserve most formatting and layout information when exporting a table, query, form, or report.
Step 3f
Open the destination file after the export operation is complete.
Select this option to view the results of the export operation. This option is available only when you export formatted data.
Export only the selected records.
Select this option to export only the selected records. This option is only available when you export formatted data and have records selected.

g. Click OK.

h. When the data displays on the screen in Excel as a worksheet, select cells A2 through A11 and then click the Center button in the Alignment group in the Home tab.

i. Select cells D2 through F11 and then click the Center button.

j. Click the Save button on the Quick Access toolbar.

k. Print the worksheet by pressing Ctrl + P and then clicking the *Print* option at the Print tab Backstage view.

Step 3h

	A	B	C	D	E	F
1	Equipment#	PurchaseDate	PurchasePrice	AvailableHours	ServiceHours	RepairHours
2	10	05-Feb-08	$65,540.00	120	15	10
3	11	01-Sep-09	$105,500.00	125	20	15
4	12	01-Jun-07	$55,345.00	140	10	10
5	13	05-May-10	$86,750.00	120	20	20
6	14	15-Jul-09	$4,500.00	160	5	5
7	15	01-Oct-07	$95,900.00	125	25	20
8	16	01-Dec-10	$3,450.00	150	10	5
9	17	10-Apr-09	$5,600.00	160	5	10
10	18	15-Jun-10	$8,000.00	150	5	5
11	19	30-Sep-11	$42,675.00	120	20	25
12						

l. Close the worksheet and then exit Excel.

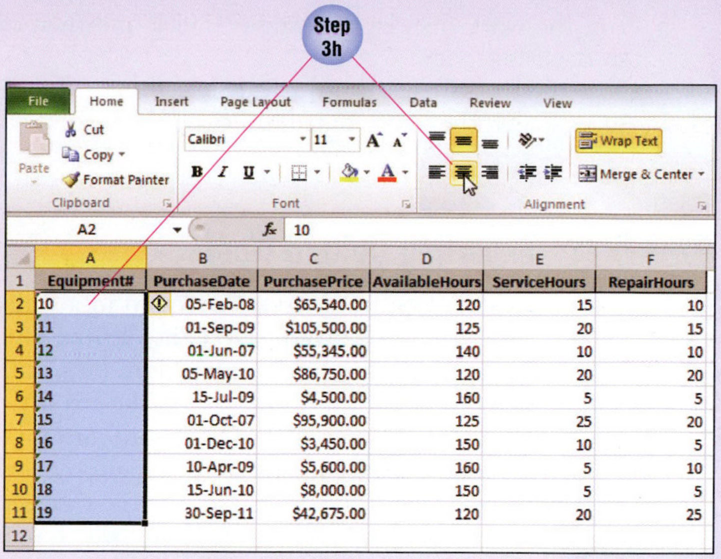

4. In Access, click the Close button to close the second wizard dialog box.

5. Design a query that extracts records from three tables with the following specifications:

a. Add the Invoices, Customers, and Rates tables to the query window.

b. Insert the *BillingDate* field from the Invoices table to the first *Field* row field.

c. Insert the *Customer* field from the Customers table to the second *Field* row field.

d. Insert the *Hours* field from the Invoices table to the third *Field* row field.

e. Insert the *Rate* field from the Rates table to the fourth *Field* row field.

f. Click in the fifth *Field* row field, type **Total: [Hours]*[Rate]**, and then press Enter.

Step 5b **Step 5c** **Step 5d** **Step 5e** **Step 5f**

Field:	BillingDate	Customer	Hours	Rate	Total: [Hours]*[Rate]
Table:	Invoices	Customers	Invoices	Rates	
Sort:					
Show:	✓	✓	✓	✓	✓
Criteria:					
or:					

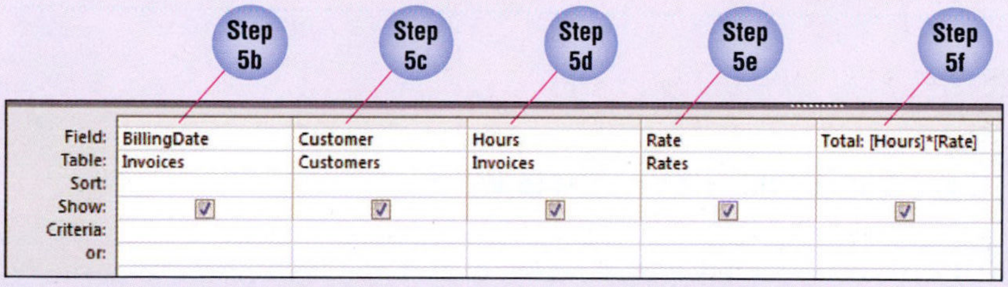

g. Run the query.

h. Automatically adjust the column width of the *Customer* field.

i. Save the query and name it *CustomerInvoices*.

j. Close the query.

6. Export the CustomerInvoices query to Excel by completing the following steps:

a. Click the CustomerInvoices query in the Navigation pane.

b. Click the External Data tab and then click the Excel button in the Export group.

c. At the Export - Excel Spreadsheet dialog box, click the *Export data with formatting and layout* option to insert a check mark in the check box.

d. Click the *Open the destination file after the export operation is complete* option to insert a check mark in the check box.

e. Click OK.

f. When the data displays on the screen in Excel as a worksheet, select cells C2 through C31 and then click the Center button in the Alignment group in the Home tab.

g. Click the Save button on the Quick Access toolbar.

h. Print the worksheet by pressing Ctrl + P and then clicking the *Print* option at the Print tab Backstage view.

i. Close the worksheet and then exit Excel.

7. In Access, click the Close button to close the second wizard dialog box.

Quick Steps

Export Data to Word

1. Click the desired table, query, form, or report.
2. Click External Data tab.
3. Click More button in Export group.
4. Click Word.
5. Make desired changes at Export - RTF File dialog box.
6. Click OK.

HINT

Data exported from Access to Word is saved with the .rtf file extension.

More

Exporting Data to Word

Export data from Access to Word in a similar manner as exporting to Excel. To export data to Word, select the desired object in the Navigation pane, click the External Data tab, click the More button in the Export group, and then click *Word* at the drop-down list. At the Export - RTF File dialog box, make desired changes and then click OK. Word automatically opens and the data displays in a Word document that is saved automatically with the same name as the database object. The difference is that the file extension .rtf is added to the name. An RTF file is saved in "rich-text format," which preserves formatting such as fonts and styles. You can export a document saved with the .rtf extension in Word and other Windows word processing or desktop publishing programs.

Project 1b **Exporting a Table and Report to Word** **Part 2 of 5**

1. With the **AL1-C8-Hilltop.accdb** database open, click the Invoices table in the Navigation pane.
2. Click the External Data tab, click the More button in the Export group, and then click *Word* at the drop-down list.

Step 2

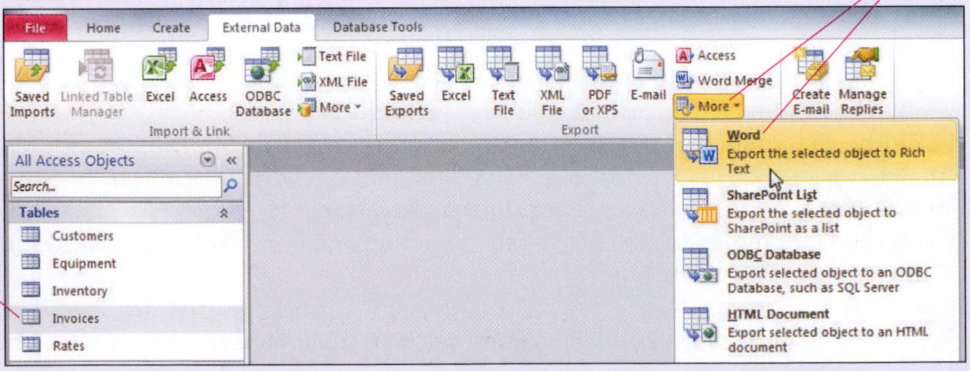

Step 1

3. At the Export - RTF File wizard dialog box, click the Browse button.

4. At the File Save dialog box, navigate to the Access2010L1C8 folder on your storage medium and then click the Save button.
5. At the Export - RTF File wizard dialog box, click the *Open the destination file after the export operation is complete* check box to insert a check mark.

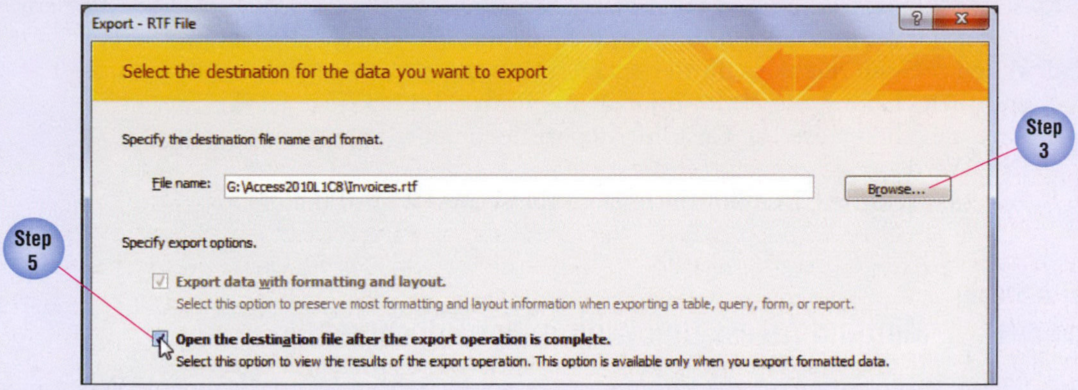

Export - RTF File
Select the destination for the data you want to export
Specify the destination file name and format.
File name:
G:\Access2010L1C8\Invoices.rtf
Browse...
Specify export options.
Export data with formatting and layout.
Select this option to preserve most formatting and layout information when exporting a table, query, form, or report.
Open the destination file after the export operation is complete.
Select this option to view the results of the export operation. This option is available only when you export formatted data.
Step 3
Step 5

6. Click OK.
7. With the **Invoices.rtf** file open in Word, print the document by pressing Ctrl + P and then clicking the *Print* option at the Print tab Backstage view.
8. Close the **Invoices.rtf** file and then exit Word.
9. In Access click the Close button to close the wizard dialog box.
10. Create a report with the Report Wizard by completing the following steps:
    a. Click the Create tab and then click the Report Wizard button in the Reports group.
    b. At the first Report Wizard dialog box, insert the following fields in the *Selected Fields* list box:
        From the Customers table:
            Customer
        From the Equipment table:
            Equipment
        From the Invoices table:
            BillingDate
            Hours
    c. After inserting the fields, click the Next button.
    d. At the second Report Wizard dialog box, make sure *by Customers* is selected in the list box in the upper left corner and then click the Next button.

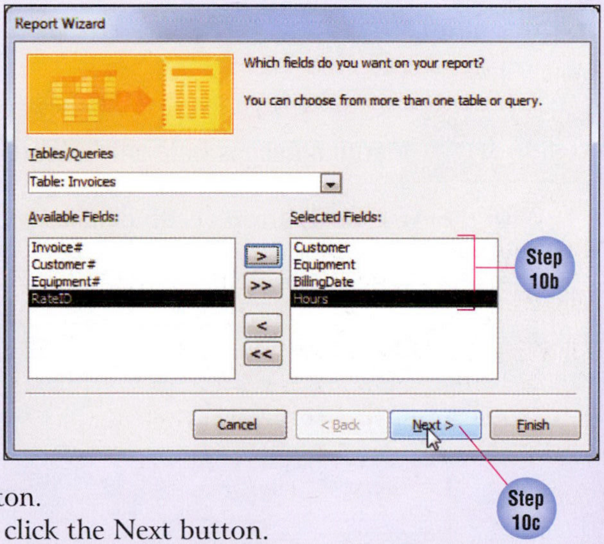

Report Wizard
Which fields do you want on your report?
You can choose from more than one table or query.
Tables/Queries
Table: Invoices
Available Fields:
Invoice#
Customer#
Equipment#
RateID
Selected Fields:
Customer
Equipment
BillingDate
Hours
Cancel
< Back
Next >
Finish
Step 10b
Step 10c

    e. At the third Report Wizard dialog box, click the Next button.
    f. At the fourth Report Wizard dialog box, click the Next button.
    g. At the fifth Report Wizard dialog box, click *Block* in the *Layout* section and then click the Next button.
    h. At the sixth and final Report Wizard dialog box, select the current name in the *What title do you want for your report?* text box, type **CustomerReport**, and then click the Finish button.
    i. When the report displays in Print Preview, click the Print button at the left side of the Print Preview tab and then click OK at the Print dialog box.
    j. Save and then close the CustomerReport report.

11. Export the CustomerReport report to Word by completing the following steps:
    a. Click the CustomerReport report in the Navigation pane.
    b. Click the External Data tab, click the More button in the Export group, and then click *Word* at the drop-down list.
    c. At the Export - RTF File wizard dialog box, click the *Open the destination file after export operation is complete* option to insert a check mark in the check box and then click OK.
    d. When the data displays on the screen in Word, print the document by pressing Ctrl + P and then clicking the *Print* option at the Print tab Backstage view.
    e. Save and then close the CustomerReport document.
    f. Exit Word.
12. In Access, click the Close button to close the second wizard dialog box.

Quick Steps

Merge Data with Word
1. Click the desired table or query.
2. Click External Data tab.
3. Click Word Merge button.
4. Make desired choices at each wizard dialog box.

Word Merge

Merging Access Data with a Word Document

You can merge data from an Access table with a Word document. When merging data, the data in the Access table is considered the data source and the Word document is considered the main document. When the merge is completed, the merged documents display in Word. To merge data, click the desired table in the Navigation pane, click the External Data tab, and then click the Word Merge button. When merging Access data, you can either type the text in the main document or merge Access data with an existing Word document.

Project 1c **Merging Access Data with a Word Document** **Part 3 of 5**

1. With the **AL1-C8-Hilltop.accdb** database open, click the Customers table in the Navigation pane.
2. Click the External Data tab.

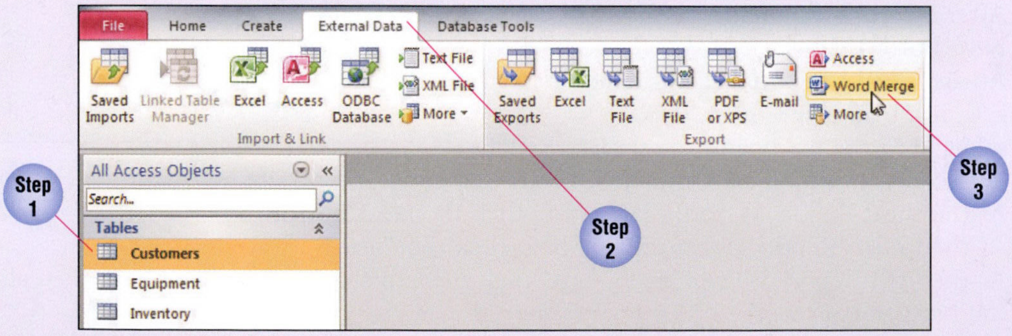

3. Click the Word Merge button in the Export group.
4. At the Microsoft Word Mail Merge Wizard dialog box, make sure *Link your data to an existing Microsoft Word document* is selected and then click OK.
5. At the Select Microsoft Word Document dialog box, make the Access2010L1C8 folder on your storage medium the active folder and then double-click the document named ***HilltopLetter.docx***.

6. Click the Word button on the Taskbar.
7. Click the Maximize button located at the right side of the HilltopLetter.docx title bar and then close the Mail Merge task pane.
8. Press the down arrow key six times (not the Enter key) and then type the current date.
9. Press the down arrow key four times and then insert fields for merging from the Customers table by completing the following steps:
   a. Click the Insert Merge Field button arrow located in the Write & Insert Fields group and then click *Customer1* in the drop-down list. (This inserts the *«Customer1»* field in the document. The drop-down list contains a *Customer* and a *Customer1* option. The first *Customer* option is actually the *Customer#* field. Word dropped the # symbol from the field name and added the *1* to the second *Customer* field to differentiate the two fields.)

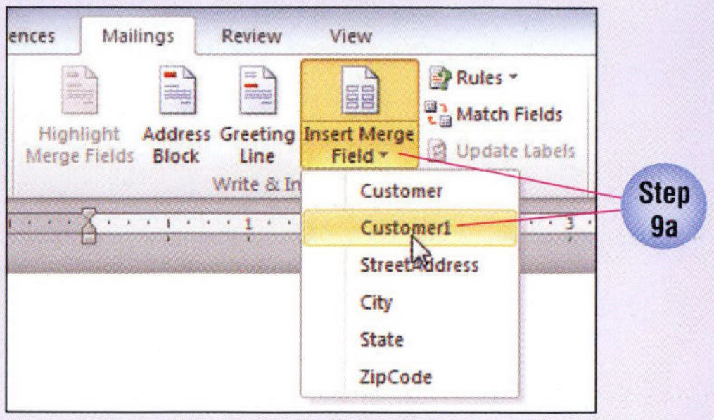

   b. Press Enter, click the Insert Merge Field button arrow, and then click *StreetAddress* in the drop-down list.
   c. Press Enter, click the Insert Merge Field button arrow, and then click *City* in the drop-down list.
   d. Type a comma (,) and then press the spacebar.
   e. Click the Insert Merge Field button arrow and then click *State* in the drop-down list.
   f. Press the spacebar, click the Insert Merge Field button arrow, and then click *ZipCode* in the drop-down list.

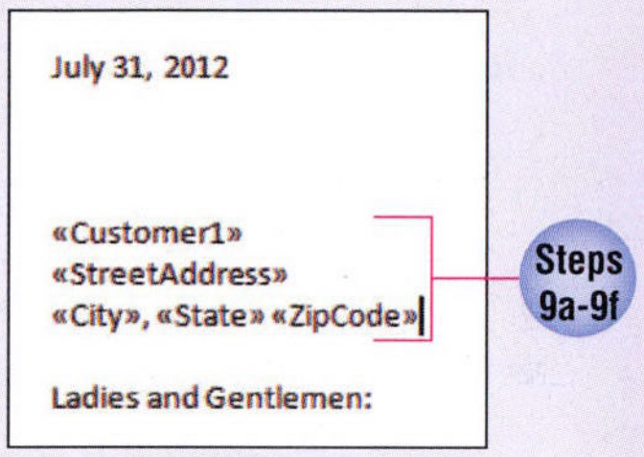

   g. Replace the letters *XX* that display toward the bottom of the letter with your initials.
   h. Click the Finish & Merge button in the Finish group and then click *Edit Individual Documents* in the drop-down list.
   i. At the Merge to New Document dialog box, make sure *All* is selected and then click OK.
   j. When the merge is completed, save the new document and name it **AL1-C8-HilltopLtrs** in the Access2010L1C8 folder on your storage medium.

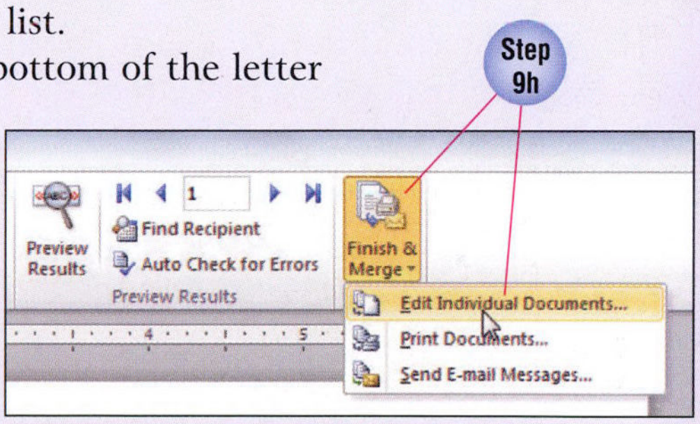

10. Print just the first two pages (two letters) of **AL1-C8-HilltopLtrs.docx**.
11. Close **AL1-C8-HilltopLtrs.docx** and then close **HilltopLetter.docx** without saving the changes.
12. Exit Word.
13. Close the **AL1-C8-Hilltop.accdb** database.

Merging Query Data with a Word Document

You can perform a query in a database and then use the query to merge with a Word document. In Project 1c you merged a table with an existing Word document. You can also merge a table or query and then type the Word document. You will create a query in Project 1d and then merge data in the query with a new document in Word.

In Project 1c, you inserted a number of merge fields for the inside address of a letter. You can also insert a field that will insert all of the fields required for the inside address of a letter with the Address Block button in the Write & Insert

Fields group in the Mailings tab. When you click the Insert the Address Block button, the Insert Address Block dialog box displays with a preview of how the fields will be inserted in the document to create the inside address; the dialog box also contains buttons and options for customizing the fields. Click OK and the *«AddressBlock»* field is inserted in the document. The *«AddressBlock»* field is an example of a composite field that groups a number of fields together.

In Project 1c you could not use the *«AddressBlock»* composite field because the *Customer1* field was not recognized by Word as a field for the inside address. In Project 1d you will create a query that contains the *FirstName* and *LastName* fields, which Word recognizes and uses for the *«AddressBlock»* composite field.

Project 1d Performing a Query and Then Merging with a Word Document

Part 4 of 5

1. Display the Open dialog box with Access2010L1C8 on your storage medium the active folder.
2. Open the **AL1-C8-CopperState.accdb** database and enable the contents.
3. Perform a query with the Query Wizard and modify the query by completing the following steps:
   a. Click the Create tab and then click the Query Wizard button in the Queries group.
   b. At the New Query dialog box, make sure Simple Query Wizard is selected and then click OK.
   c. At the first Simple Query Wizard dialog box, click the down-pointing arrow at the right of the *Tables/Queries* option box and then click *Table: Clients*.
   d. Click the All Fields button to insert all of the fields in the *Selected Fields* list box.
   e. Click the Next button.
   f. At the second Simple Query Wizard dialog box, make the following changes:
      1) Select the current name in the *What title do you want for your query?* text box and then type **ClientsPhoenixQuery**.
      2) Click the *Modify the query design* option.
      3) Click the Finish button.
   g. At the query window, click in the *Criteria* field in the *City* column, type **Phoenix**, and then press Enter.
   h. Click the Run button in the Results group. (Only clients living in Phoenix will display.)
   i. Save and then close the query.

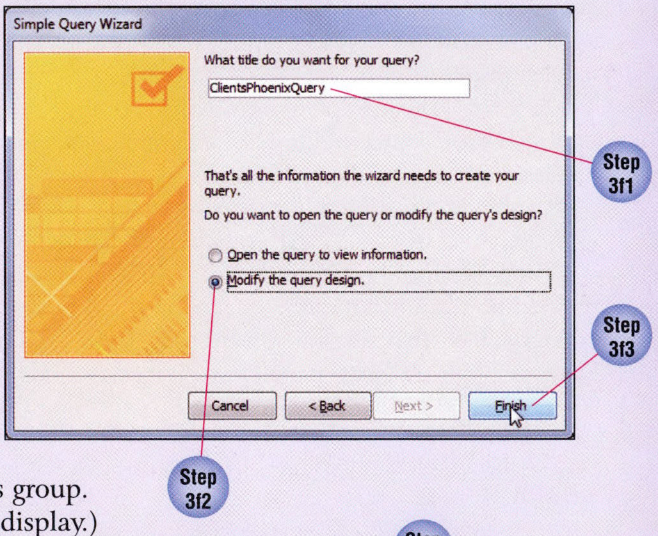

4. Click the ClientsPhoenixQuery query in the Navigation pane.
5. Click the External Data tab and then click the Word Merge button in the Export group.
6. At the Microsoft Word Mail Merge Wizard dialog box, click the *Create a new document and then link the data to it* option and then click OK.

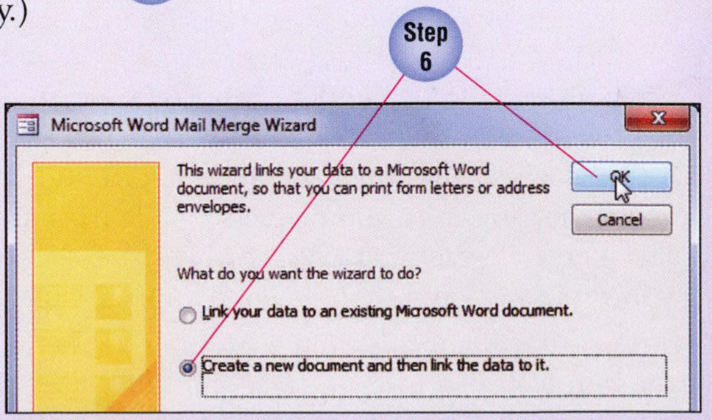

7. Click the Word button on the Taskbar.
8. Click the Maximize button located at the right side of the Document1 title bar and then close the Mail Merge task pane.
9. Complete the following steps to type text and insert the «AddressBlock» in the blank Word document:
   a. Click the Home tab and then click the No Spacing style in the Styles group.
   b. Press Enter six times.
   c. Type the current date.
   d. Press Enter four times.
   e. Click the Mailings tab.
   f. Insert the «AddressBlock» field by clicking the Address Block button in the Write & Insert Fields group in the Mailings tab and then clicking OK at the Insert Address Block dialog box. (This inserts the composite field «AddressBlock» in the document.)
   g. Press Enter twice and then type the salutation **Ladies and Gentlemen:**.
   h. Press Enter twice and then type the following paragraphs of text:

      At the Grant Street West office of Copper State Insurance, we have hired two additional insurance representatives as well as one support staff member to ensure that we meet all your insurance needs. To accommodate the new staff, we have moved to a larger office just a few blocks away. Our new address is 3450 Grant Street West, Suite 110, Phoenix AZ 85003. Our telephone number, (602) 555-6200, has remained the same.

      If you have any questions or concerns about your insurance policies or want to discuss adding or changing current coverage, please stop by or give us a call. We are committed to providing our clients with the most comprehensive automobile insurance coverage in the county.

   i. Press Enter twice and then type the following complimentary close (at the left margin):

      Sincerely,

      Lou Galloway
      Manager

      XX (Type your initials instead of XX.)
      AL1-C8-CSLtrs.docx

   j. Click the Finish & Merge button in the Finish group on the Mailings tab and then click *Edit Individual Documents* in the drop-down menu.
   k. At the Merge to New Document dialog box, make sure *All* is selected, and then click OK.
   l. When the merge is complete, save the new document and name it **AL1-C8-CSLtrs** in the Access2010L1C8 folder on your storage medium.
10. Print the first two pages (two letters) of **AL1-C8-CSLtrs.docx**.
11. Close **AL1-C8-CSLtrs.docx**.
12. Save the main document as **AL1-C8-CSMainDoc** in the Access2010L1C8 folder on your storage medium and then close the document.
13. Exit Word.

Exporting an Access Object to a PDF or XPS File

Quick Steps

Export Access Object to PDF File

1. Click object in the Navigation pane.
2. Click External Data tab.
3. Click PDF or XPS button.
4. Navigate to desired folder.
5. Click Publish button.

PDF or XPS

With the PDF or XPS button in the Export group in the External Data tab, you can export an Access object to a PDF or XPS file. As you learned in Chapter 7, the letters *PDF* stand for *portable document format*, which is a file format that captures all of the elements of a file as an electronic image. The letters *XPS* stand for *XML paper specification* and the letters *XML* stand for *Extensible Markup Language*, which is a set of rules for encoding files electronically.

To export an Access object to the PDF or XPS file format, click the desired object, click the External Data tab, and then click the PDF or XPS button in the Export group. This displays the Publish as PDF or XPS dialog box with the *PDF (*.pdf)* option selected in the *Save as type* option box. If you want to save the Access object in XPS format, click in the *Save as type* option box and then click *XPS Document (*.xps)* at the drop-down list. At the Save As dialog box, type a name in the *File name* text box and then click the Publish button. If you save the Access object in PDF format, the Access object opens in Adobe Reader, and if you save the Access object in XPS format, the object opens in your browser window.

You can open a PDF file in Adobe Reader or in your web browser, and you can open an XPS file in your web browser. To open a PDF file or XPS file in your web browser, click File in the browser Menu bar and then click *Open* at the drop-down list. At the Open dialog box, click the Browse button. At the browser window Open dialog box, change the *Files of type* to *All Files (*.*)*, navigate to the desired folder, and then double-click the document.

Project 1e **Exporting an Access Object to a PDF File** Part 5 of 5

1. With the **AL1-C8-CopperState.accdb** database open, export the Coverage table to a PDF format by completing the following steps:
   a. Click the Coverage table in the Navigation pane.
   b. Click the External Data tab.
   c. Click the PDF or XPS button in the Export group.
   d. At the Publish as PDF or XPS dialog box, navigate to the Access2010L1C8 folder on your storage medium and then click the Publish button.
   e. When the Coverage table data displays in Adobe Reader, scroll through the file and notice how it displays.
   f. Print the PDF file by clicking the Print button that displays at the left side of the toolbar and then clicking OK at the Print dialog box.
   g. Close Adobe Reader by clicking the Close button located in the upper right corner of the screen.
2. In Access, click the Close button to close the wizard dialog box.

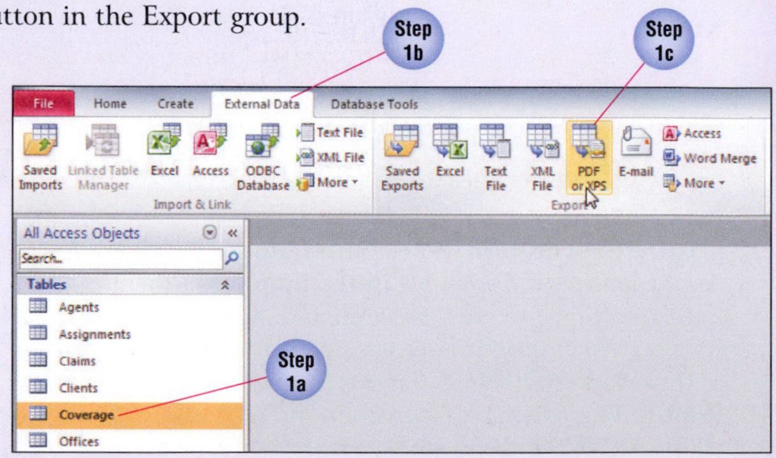

Project 2 Import and Link Excel Worksheets with an Access Table — 2 Parts

You will import an Excel worksheet into an Access table. You will also link an Excel worksheet into an Access table and then add a new record to the Access table.

Importing and Linking Data to a New Table

In this chapter, you learned how to export Access data to Excel and Word. You can also import data from other programs into an Access table. For example, you can import data from an Excel worksheet and create a new table in a database using data from the worksheet. Data in the original program is not connected to the data imported into an Access table. If you make changes to the data in the original program, those changes are not reflected in the Access table. If you want the imported data connected to the original program, link the data.

Quick Steps

Import Data to a New Table

1. Click External Data tab.
2. Click desired application in Import & Link group.
3. Click Browse button.
4. Double-click desired file name.
5. Make desired choices at each wizard dialog box.

Importing Data to a New Table

To import data, click the External Data tab and then determine where you would like to retrieve data with options in the Import & Link group. At the Import dialog box that displays, click Browse and then double-click the desired file name. This activates the Import Wizard and displays the first wizard dialog box. The appearance of the dialog box varies depending on the file selected. Complete the steps of the Import Wizard specifying information such as the range of data, whether or not the first row contains column headings, whether you want to store the data in a new table or store it in an existing table, the primary key, and the name of the table.

HINT

Store data in Access and use Excel to analyze data.

HINT

You can import and link data between Access databases.

Project 2a Importing an Excel Worksheet into an Access Table — Part 1 of 2

1. With the **AL1-C8-CopperState.accdb** database open, import an Excel worksheet into a new table in the database by completing the following steps:
   a. Click the External Data tab and then click the Excel button in the Import & Link group.
   b. At the Get External Data - Excel Spreadsheet dialog box, click Browse and then make the Access2010L1C8 folder on your storage medium the active folder.

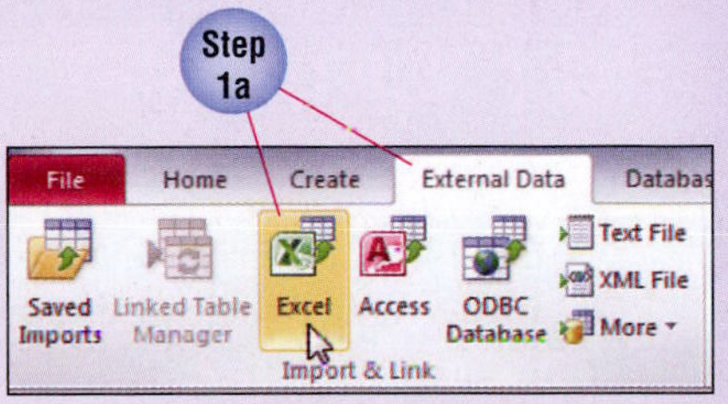

   c. Double-click ***AL1-C8-Policies.xlsx*** in the list box.
   d. Click OK at the Get External Data - Excel Spreadsheet dialog box.
   e. At the first Import Spreadsheet Wizard dialog box, click the Next button.

f. At the second Import Spreadsheet Wizard dialog box, make sure the *First Row Contains Column Headings* option contains a check mark and then click the Next button.
g. At the third Import Spreadsheet Wizard dialog box, click the Next button.
h. At the fourth Import Spreadsheet Wizard dialog box, click the *Choose my own primary key* option (this inserts *Policy#* in the text box located to the right of the option) and then click the Next button.

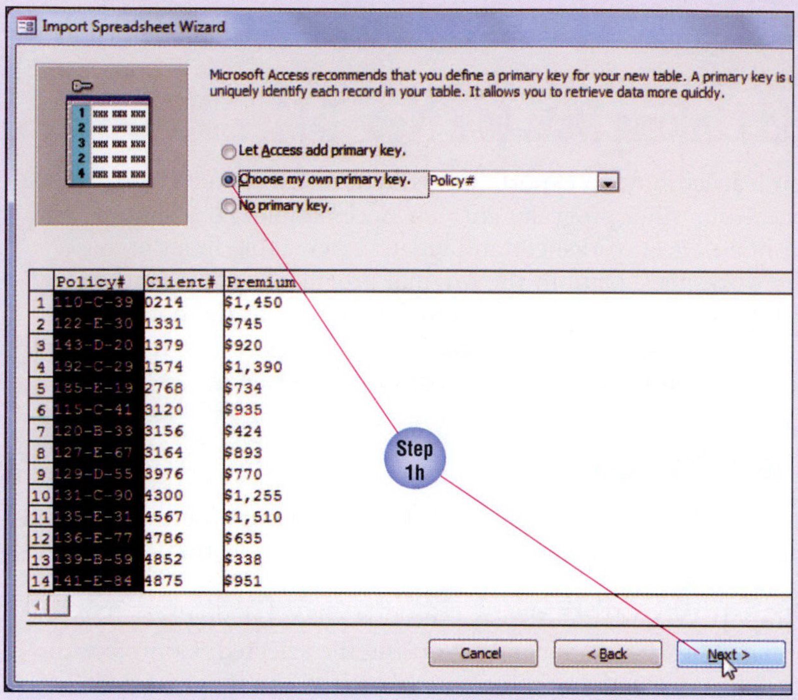

i. At the fifth Import Spreadsheet Wizard dialog box, type **Policies** in the *Import to Table* text box and then click the Finish button.

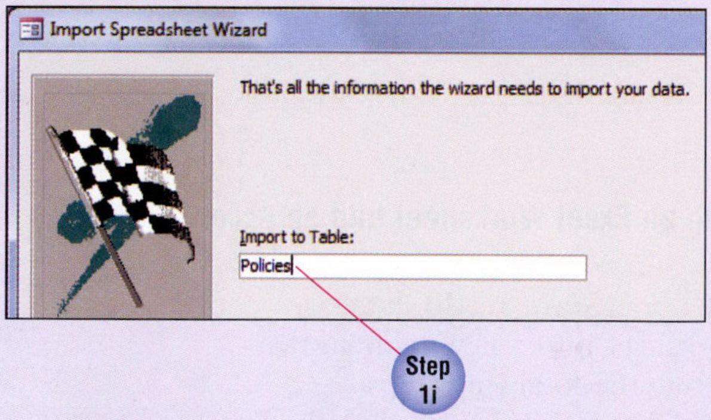

j. At the Get External Data - Excel Spreadsheet dialog box, click the Close button.
2. Open the new Policies table in Datasheet view.
3. Print and then close the Policies table.

Linking Data to an Excel Worksheet

Imported data is not connected to the source program. If you know that you will use your data only in Access, import it. However, if you want to update data in a program other than Access, link the data. Changes made to linked data in the source program file are reflected in the destination program file. For example, you can link an Excel worksheet with an Access table and when you make changes in the Excel worksheet, the changes are reflected in the Access table.

To link data to a new table, click the External Data tab and then click the Excel button in the Import group. At the Get External Data - Excel Spreadsheet dialog box, click the Browse button, double-click the desired file name, click the *Link to a data source by creating a linked table* option, and then click OK. This activates the Link Wizard and displays the first wizard dialog box. Complete the steps of the Link Wizard, specifying the same basic information as the Import Wizard.

Quick Steps

Link Data to Excel Worksheet

1. Click External Data tab.
2. Click Excel button in Import & Link group.
3. Click Browse button.
4. Double-click desired file name.
5. Click *Link to a data source by creating a linked table.*
6. Make desired choices at each wizard dialog box.

Import Excel

Project 2b **Linking an Excel Worksheet with an Access Table** Part 2 of 2

1. With the **AL1-C8-CopperState.accdb** database open, click the External Data tab and then click the Excel button in the Import & Link group.
2. At the Get External Data - Excel Spreadsheet dialog box, click the Browse button, navigate to the Access2010L1C8 folder on your storage medium, and then double-click ***AL1-C8-Policies.xlsx***.
3. At the Get External Data - Excel Spreadsheet dialog box, click the *Link to the data source by creating a linked table* option and then click OK.

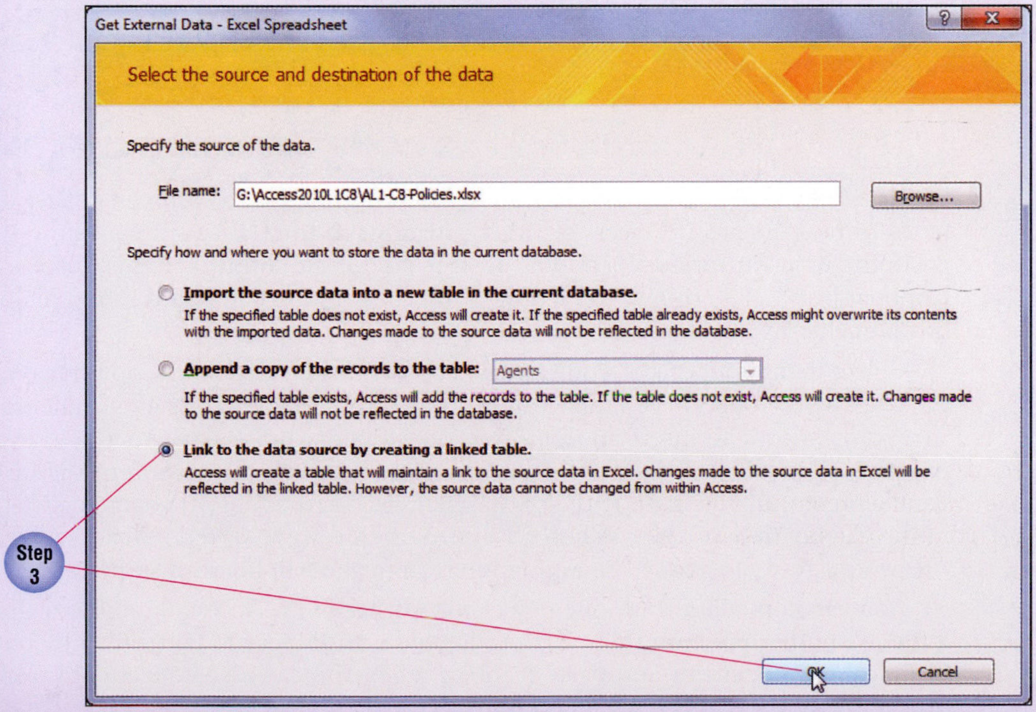

4. At the first Link Spreadsheet Wizard dialog box, make sure *Show Worksheets* and *Sheet 1* are selected in the list box and then click the Next button.
5. At the second Link Spreadsheet Wizard dialog box, make sure the *First Row Contains Column Headings* option contains a check mark and then click the Next button.
6. At the third Link Spreadsheet Wizard dialog box, type **LinkedPolicies** in the *Linked Table Name* text box and then click the Finish button.
7. At the message stating the linking is finished, click OK.
8. Open the new LinkedPolicies table in Datasheet view.
9. Close the LinkedPolicies table.
10. Open Excel, open the **AL1-C8-Policies.xlsx** workbook, and then make the following changes:
    a. Change the amount *$745* in cell C3 to *$850*.
    b. Add the following information in the specified cells:
        A26 = **190-C-28**
        B26 = **3120**
        C26 = **$685**

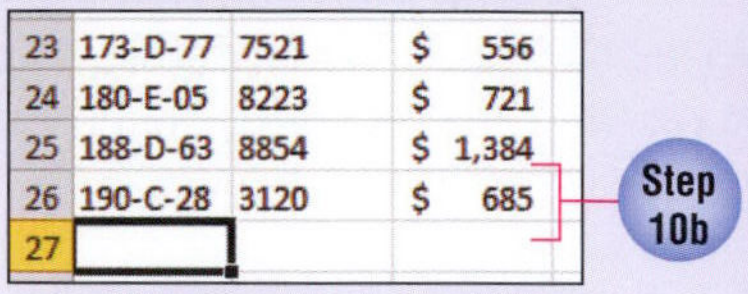

23 173-D-77 7521 $ 556
24 180-E-05 8223 $ 721
25 188-D-63 8854 $ 1,384
26 190-C-28 3120 $ 685
27
Step 10b

11. Save, print, and then close **AL1-C8-Policies.xlsx**.
12. Exit Excel.
13. With Access the active program and the **AL1-C8-CopperState.accdb** database open, open the LinkedPolicies table. Notice the changes you made in Excel are reflected in the table.
14. Close the LinkedPolicies table.
15. Close the **AL1-C8-CopperState.accdb** database.

Project 3 Collect Data in Word and Paste in an Access Table — 1 Part

You will open a Word document containing Hilltop customer names and addresses and then copy the data and paste it into an Access table.

Using the Office Clipboard

Quick Steps
Display Clipboard Task Pane
Click Clipboard group dialog box launcher.

Use the Office Clipboard to collect and paste multiple items. You can collect up to 24 different items in Access or other programs in the Office suite and then paste the items in various locations. To copy and paste multiple items, display the Clipboard task pane shown in Figure 8.2 by clicking the Clipboard group dialog box launcher in the Home tab.

Select data or an object you want to copy and then click the Copy button in the Clipboard group in the Home tab. Continue selecting text or items and clicking the Copy button. To insert an item from the Clipboard task pane to a field in an Access table, make the desired field active and then click the button in the task pane representing the item. If the copied item is text, the first 50 characters display in the Clipboard task pane. When all desired items are inserted, click the Clear All button to remove any remaining items from the Clipboard task pane.

You can copy data from one object to another in an Access database or from a file in another program to an Access database. In Project 3, you will copy data from a Word document and paste it into a table. You can also collect data from other programs such as PowerPoint and Excel.

Figure 8.2 Office Clipboard Task Pane

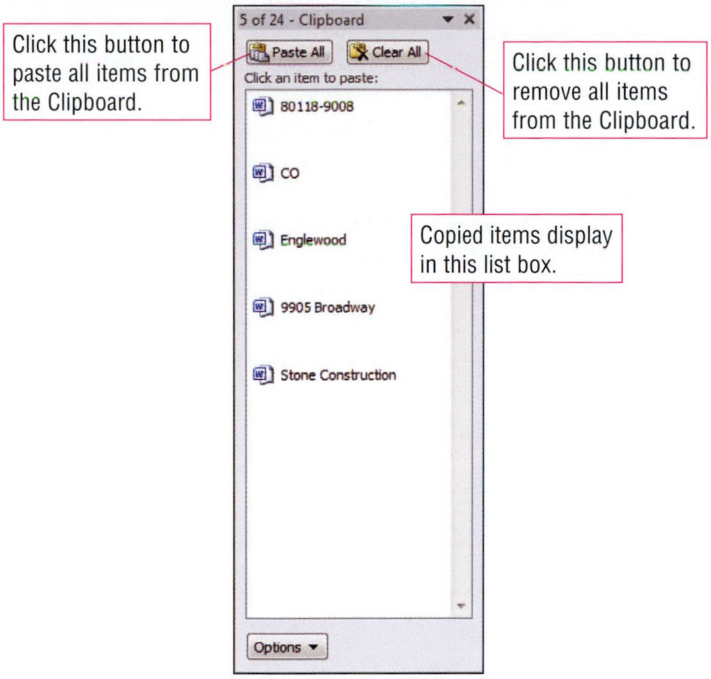

Project 3 Collecting Data in Word and Pasting It in an Access Table

Part 1 of 1

1. Open the **AL1-C8-Hilltop.accdb** database.
2. Open the Customers table.
3. Copy data from Word and paste it into the Customers table by completing the following steps:
   a. Open Word, make the Access2010L1C8 folder active, and then open **HilltopCustomers.docx**.
   b. Make sure the Home tab is active.
   c. Click the Clipboard group dialog box launcher to display the Clipboard task pane.
   d. Select the first company name, *Stone Construction*, and then click the Copy button in the Clipboard group.

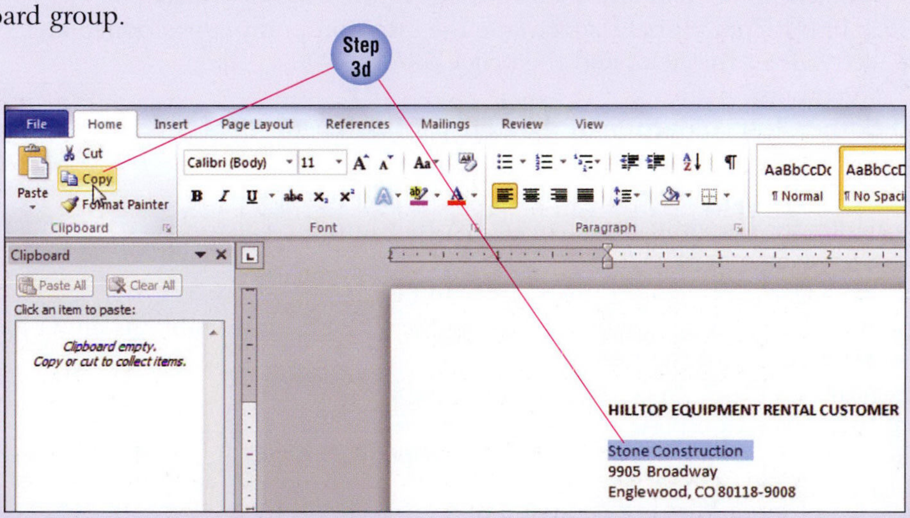

e. Select the street address, *9905 Broadway*, and then click the Copy button.
f. Select the city, *Englewood*, and then click the Copy button.
g. Select the state, *CO* (select only the two letters and not the space after the letters), and then click the Copy button.
h. Select the ZIP code, *80118-9008*, and then click the Copy button.
i. Click the button on the Taskbar representing Access. (Make sure the Customer table is open and displays in Datasheet view.)
j. Click in the first empty cell in the *Customer#* field and then type 178.
k. Display the Clipboard task pane by clicking the Home tab and then clicking the Clipboard group dialog box launcher.
l. Close the Navigation pane by clicking the Shutter Bar Open/Close Button.
m. Click in the first empty cell in the *Customer* field and then click *Stone Construction* in the Clipboard task pane.

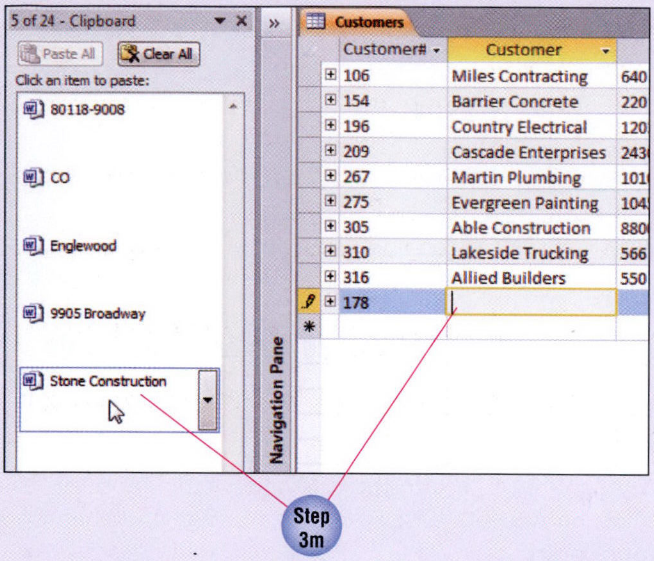

n. Click in the *StreetAddress* field and then click *9905 Broadway* in the Clipboard task pane.
o. Click in the *City* field and then click *Englewood* in the Clipboard task pane.
p. Click in the *State* field and then click *CO* in the Clipboard task pane.
q. Click in the *ZipCode* field, make sure the insertion point is positioned at the left side of the field, and then click *80118-9008* in the Clipboard task pane.
r. Click the Clear All button in the Clipboard task pane. (This removes all entries from the Clipboard.)

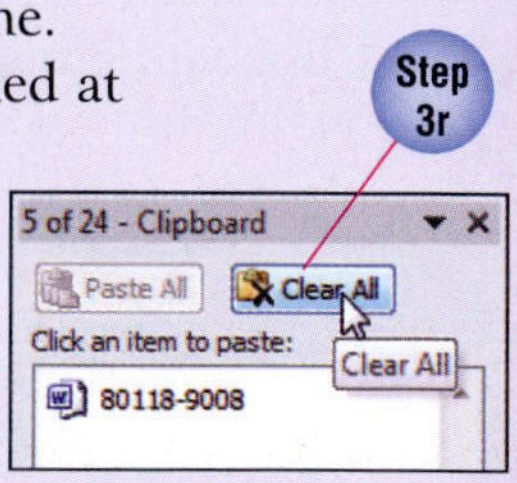

4. Complete steps similar to those in 3d through 3q to copy the information for Laughlin Products and paste it into the Customers table. (The Customer# is 225.)
5. Click the Clear All button in the Clipboard task pane.
6. Close the Clipboard task pane by clicking the Close button (contains an *X*) located in the upper right corner of the task pane.
7. Save, print, and then close the Customers table.
8. Open the Navigation pane by clicking the Shutter Bar Open/Close Button.
9. Make Word the active program, close **HilltopCustomers.docx** without saving changes, and then exit Word.
10. Close the **AL1-C8-Hilltop.accdb** database.

Chapter Summary

- Use the Excel button in the Export group in the External Data tab to export data in a table, query, or form to an Excel worksheet.
- Export data in a table, query, form, or report to a Word document by clicking the More button and then clicking *Word* at the drop-down list. Access exports the data to an RTF (rich-text format) file.
- Export an Access object to a PDF or XPS file with the PDF or XPS button in the Export group in the External Data tab.
- You can merge Access data with a Word document. The Access data is the data source and the Word document is the main document. To merge data, click the desired table or query, click the External Data tab, and then click the Word Merge button in the Export group.
- Use the Excel button in the Import group in the External Data tab to import Excel data to an Access table.
- You can link imported data. Changes made to the data in the source program file are reflected in the destination source file.
- If you want to link imported data, click the *Link to the data source by creating a linked table* option at the Get External Data dialog box.
- Use the Clipboard task pane to collect up to 24 different items in Access or other programs and paste them in various locations.
- Display the Clipboard task pane by clicking the Clipboard group dialog box launcher in the Home tab.

Commands Review

FEATURE	RIBBON TAB, GROUP	BUTTON
Export object to Excel	External Data, Export	
Export object to Word	External Data, Export	, Word
Merge Access data with Word	External Data, Export	
Export object to PDF or XPS	External Data, Export	
Import Excel data	External Data, Import & Link	
Clipboard task pane	Home, Clipboard	

Concepts Check Test Your Knowledge

Completion: In the space provided at the right, indicate the correct term, symbol, or command.

1. Click this tab to display the Export group. ____________
2. Click this button in the Export group to display the Export - Excel Spreadsheet wizard dialog box. ____________
3. At the first Export - Excel Spreadsheet wizard dialog box, click this option if you want Excel to open with the exported data. ____________
4. To export Access data to Word, click this button in the Export group in the External Data tab and then click *Word* at the drop-down list. ____________
5. When you export Access data to Word, the document is saved in this file format. ____________
6. When merging data, the data in the Access table is considered this. ____________
7. To merge data, click this button in the Export group in the External Data tab. ____________
8. You can export an Access object to the PDF file format and the letters PDF stand for this. ____________
9. Import an Excel worksheet into an Access database with the Excel button in this group in the External Data tab. ____________
10. If you want imported data connected to the original program, do this to the data. ____________
11. Use this task pane to collect and paste multiple items. ____________

Skills Check Assess Your Performance

Assessment

1 EXPORT A FORM TO EXCEL AND A REPORT TO WORD

1. Display the Open dialog box with Access2010L1C8 on your storage medium the active folder.
2. Open the **AL1-C8-WarrenLegal.accdb** database and enable the contents.
3. Create a form named *Billing* using the Form Wizard with the following fields:
   From the Billing table:
   Billing#
   ClientID
   BillingDate
   Hours
   From the Rates table:
   Rate
4. When the form displays, close it.
5. Create an Excel worksheet with the Billing form.
6. Make the following changes to the Excel Billing worksheet:
   a. Select columns A through E and then adjust the column widths.
   b. Select cells A2 through B42 and then click the Center button in the Alignment group in the Home tab.
   c. Save the Billing worksheet.
   d. Print and then close the Billing worksheet.
   e. Exit Excel.
7. In Access, close the Export Wizard.
8. Create a report named *ClientBilling* using the Report Wizard (at the fifth wizard dialog box, change the layout to *Block*) with the following fields:
   From the Clients table:
   FirstName
   LastName
   From the Billing table:
   BillingDate
   Hours
   From the Rates table:
   Rate
9. When the report displays, close Print Preview, change to Layout view, and then decrease the size of the columns so the right border of the column displays just right of the longest entry in the column.
10. Save and then close the report.
11. Create a Word document with the ClientBilling report and save it to the Access2010L1C8 folder on your storage medium with the default name. In the Word document, make the following changes:
    a. Press Ctrl + A to select the entire document, change the font color to black, and then deselect the text.
    b. Insert a space between *Client* and *Billing* in the title.
    c. Position the insertion point immediately right of the word *Billing*, press the spacebar, and then type **of Legal Services**.

12. Save and then print **ClientBilling.rtf**.
13. Close the document and then exit Word.
14. In Access, close the wizard dialog box.

Assessment 2

MERGE TABLE AND QUERY DATA WITH A WORD DOCUMENT

1. With the **AL1-C8-WarrenLegal.accdb** database open, merge data in the Clients table to a new Word document using the Word merge button.
2. Maximize the Word document, close the Mail Merge task pane, and then compose a letter with the following elements:
   a. Click the Home tab and then click the No Spacing style in the Styles group.
   b. Press Enter six times, type the current date, and then press Enter four times.
   c. Click the Mailings tab and then insert the «AddressBlock» composite field.
   d. Insert a proper salutation.
   e. Compose a letter to clients that includes the following information:

      The last time you visited our offices, you may have noticed how crowded we were. To alleviate the overcrowding, we are leasing new offices in the Meridian Building and will be moving in at the beginning of next month.

      Stop by and see our new offices at our open house planned for the second Friday of next month. Drop by any time between 2:00 and 5:30 p.m. We look forward to seeing you.

   f. Include an appropriate complimentary close for the letter. Use the name and title *Marjorie Shaw, Senior Partner* for the signature and add your reference initials and the document name (**AL1-C8-WLLtrs.docx**).
3. Merge to a new document and then save the document with the name **AL1-C8-WLLtrs**.
4. Print only the first two letters in the document and then close **AL1-C8-WLLtrs.docx**.
5. Save the main document and name it **AL1-C8-WLLtrMD1**, close the document, and then exit Word.
6. With the **AL1-C8-WarrenLegal.accdb** database open, extract the records from the Clients table of those clients located in Kent and then name the query *ClientsKentQuery*. (Include all of the fields from the table in the query.)
7. Merge the ClientsKentQuery to a new Word document using the Word Merge Button.
8. Maximize the Word document, close the Mail Merge task pane, and then compose a letter with the following elements:
   a. Click the Home tab and then click the No Spacing style in the Styles group.
   b. Press Enter six times, type the current date, and then press Enter four times.
   c. Click the Mailings tab and then insert the «AddressBlock» composite field.
   d. Insert a proper salutation.
   e. Compose a letter to clients that includes the following information:

      The City of Kent Municipal Court has moved from 1024 Meeker Street to a new building located at 3201 James Avenue. All court hearings after the end of this month will be held at the new address. If you need directions to the new building, please call our office.

f. Include an appropriate complimentary close for the letter. Use the name *Thomas Zeiger* and the title *Attorney* in the complimentary close and add your reference initials and the document name (**AL1-C8-WLKentLtrs.docx**).

9. Merge the letter to a new document and then save the document with the name **AL1-C8-WLKentLtrs**.
10. Print only the first two letters in the document and then close **AL1-C8-WLKentLtrs.docx**.
11. Save the main document and name it **AL1-C8-WLLtrMD2**, close the document, and then exit Word.

Assessment 3

LINK AN EXCEL WORKBOOK

1. With the **AL1-C8-WarrenLegal.accdb** database open, link **AL1-C8-Cases.xlsx** into a new table named *Cases*.
2. Open the Cases table in Datasheet view.
3. Print and then close the Cases table.
4. Open Excel, open the **AL1-C8-Cases.xlsx** workbook and then add the following data in the specified cell:

   A8 = 57-D
   B8 = 130
   C8 = $1,100

   A9 = 42-A
   B9 = 144
   C9 = $3,250

   A10 = 29-C
   B10 = 125
   C10 = $900

5. Save, print, and then close **AL1-C8-Cases.xlsx**.
6. Exit Excel.
7. In Access, open the Cases table in Datasheet view. (Notice the changes you made in Excel are reflected in the table.)
8. Print and then close the Cases table.
9. Close the **AL1-C8-WarrenLegal.accdb** database.

Visual Benchmark Demonstrate Your Proficiency

CREATE A REPORT AND EXPORT THE REPORT TO WORD

1. Open the **AL1-C8-Dearborn.accdb** database and enable the contents.
2. Use the Report Wizard to create the report shown in Figure 8.3. (Use the Quotas table and the Representatives table when creating the report.) Save the report and name it *RepQuotas* and then print the report.
3. Use the RepQuotas report and export it to Word. Format the report in Word as shown in Figure 8.4. Print the Word document and then exit Word.
4. In Access, close the **AL1-C8-Dearborn.accdb** database.

Figure 8.3 Visual Benchmark Report

RepQuotas

RepQuotas

Quota	RepName	Telephone
$100,000.00		
	Robin Rehberg	(317) 555-9812
	Andre Kulisek	(317) 555-2264
	Edward Harris	(317) 555-3894
	Cecilia Ortega	(317) 555-4810
$150,000.00		
	David DeBruler	(317) 555-8779
	Jaren Newman	(317) 555-6790
	Lee Hutchinson	(317) 555-4277
	Craig Johnson	(317) 555-4391
$200,000.00		
	Isabelle Marshall	(765) 555-8822
	Maureen Pascual	(317) 555-5513
	Linda Foster	(317) 555-2101
	Catherine Singleton	(317) 555-0172
$250,000.00		

Figure 8.4 Visual Benchmark Word Document

Representatives Quotas

Quota	RepName	Telephone
$100,000.00		
	Robin Rehberg	(317) 555-9812
	Andre Kulisek	(317) 555-2264
	Edward Harris	(317) 555-3894
	Cecilia Ortega	(317) 555-4810
$150,000.00		
	David DeBruler	(317) 555-8779
	Jaren Newman	(317) 555-6790
	Lee Hutchinson	(317) 555-4277
	Craig Johnson	(317) 555-4391
$200,000.00		
	Isabelle Marshall	(765) 555-8822
	Maureen Pascual	(317) 555-5513
	Linda Foster	(317) 555-2101
	Catherine Singleton	(317) 555-0172
$250,000.00		
	Kwan Im	(317) 555-8374
	William Ludlow	(317) 555-0991
	Lydia Alvarado	(317) 555-4996

Case Study Apply Your Skills

Part 1

As the office manager at Woodland Dermatology Center, you are responsible for managing the center database. In preparation for an upcoming meeting, open the **AL1-C8-Woodland.accdb** database and prepare the following with data in the database:

- Create a query that displays the patient number, first name, and last name; doctor last name; date of visit; and fee. Name the query *PatientBilling*.
- Export the PatientBilling query to an Excel worksheet. Apply formatting to enhance the appearance of the worksheet and then print the worksheet.
- Create mailing labels for the patients.
- Export the patient labels to a Word (.rtf) document and then print the document.
- Import and link the **AL1-C8-Payroll.xlsx** Excel worksheet to a new table named *WeeklyPayroll*. Print the WeeklyPayroll table.

You have been given some updated information about the weekly payroll and need to make the following changes to the **AL1-C8-Payroll.xlsx** worksheet: Change the hours for Irene Vaughn to *30*, change the wage for Monica Saunders to *$10.50*, and change the hours for Dale Jorgensen to *20*. After making the changes, open, print, and then close the WeeklyPayroll table.

Part 2

The center is expanding and will be offering cosmetic dermatology services at the beginning of next month to residents in the Altoona area. Design a query that extracts records of patients living in the city of Altoona and then merge the query with Word. At the Word document, write a letter describing the new services which include microdermabrasion, chemical peels, laser resurfacing, sclerotherapy, and photorejuvenation as well as an offer for a free facial and consultation. Insert the appropriate fields in the document and then complete the merge. Save the merged document and name it **AL1-C8-WLDLtr**. Print the first two letters of the document and then close the document. Close the main document without saving it and then exit Word.

Part 3

You need to save objects in the Woodland database in a format that can be read by employees that do not have Access available. You have researched the various file formats available and have determined that the PDF format is the most universal. Use the Access Help feature to learn how to save a database object in PDF format. Save the Patients table in PDF format and then print the PDF file. Save the Doctors table in PDF format and then print the PDF file.

Part 4

Since you are responsible for updating the clinic procedures manual, you decide to create a Word document that describes the steps for saving an object in PDF format. Save the completed document and name it **AL1-C8-CS-Manual**. Print and then close **AL1-C8-CS-Manual.docx**.

Microsoft® Access®

UNIT 2

Performance Assessment

Access

Access2010L1U2

Note: Before beginning unit assessments, copy to your storage medium the Access2010L1U2 subfolder from the Access2010L1 folder on the CD that accompanies this textbook and then make Access2010L1U2 the active folder.

Assessing Proficiency

In this unit, you have learned to create forms, reports, and mailing labels; and to filter data. You also learned how to modify document properties; view object dependencies; and export, import, and link data between programs.

Assessment 1 Create Tables in a Clinic Database

1. Use Access to create a database for clients of a mental health clinic. Name the database **AL1-U2-LancasterClinic**. Create a table named *Clients* that includes the following fields (you determine the field name, data type, field size, and description):

   ClientNumber (primary key)
   ClientName
   StreetAddress
   City
   State
   ZipCode
   Telephone
   DateOfBirth
   DiagnosisID

2. After creating the table, switch to Datasheet view and then enter the following data in the appropriate fields:

   ClientNumber: 1831
   George Charoni
   3980 Broad Street
   Philadelphia, PA 19149
   (215) 555-3482
   DateOfBirth: 4/12/1958
   DiagnosisID: SC

   ClientNumber: 3219
   Marian Wilke
   12032 South 39th
   Jenkintown, PA 19209
   (215) 555-9083
   DateOfBirth: 10/23/1981
   DiagnosisID: OCD

ClientNumber: **2874**
Arthur Shroeder
3618 Fourth Avenue
Philadelphia, PA 19176
(215) 555-8311
DateOfBirth: **3/23/1958**
DiagnosisID: **OCD**

ClientNumber: **5831**
Roshawn Collins
12110 52nd Court East
Cheltenham, PA 19210
(215) 555-4779
DateOfBirth: **11/3/1965**
DiagnosisID: **SC**

ClientNumber: **4419**
Lorena Hearron
3112 96th Street East
Philadelphia, PA 19132
(215) 555-3281
DateOfBirth: **7/2/1984**
DiagnosisID: **AD**

ClientNumber: **1103**
Raymond Mandato
631 Garden Boulevard
Jenkintown, PA 19209
(215) 555-0957
DateOfBirth: **9/20/1979**
DiagnosisID: **MDD**

3. Automatically adjust column widths.
4. Save, print, and then close the Clients table.
5. Create a table named *Diagnoses* that includes the following fields:

   DiagnosisID (primary key)
   Diagnosis

6. After creating the table, switch to Datasheet view and then enter the following data in the appropriate fields:

   DiagnosisID = **AD**
   Diagnosis = **Adjustment Disorder**

   DiagnosisID = **MDD**
   Diagnosis = **Manic-Depressive Disorder**

   DiagnosisID = **OCD**
   Diagnosis = **Obsessive-Compulsive Disorder**

   DiagnosisID = **SC**
   Diagnosis = **Schizophrenia**

7. Automatically adjust column widths.
8. Save, print, and then close the Diagnoses table.
9. Create a table named *Fees* that includes the following fields (you determine the field name, data type, field size, and description):

   FeeCode (primary key)
   HourlyFee

10. After creating the table, switch to Datasheet view and then enter the following data in the appropriate fields:

FeeCode	=	A	*FeeCode*	=	E
HourlyFee	=	$75.00	*HourlyFee*	=	$95.00
FeeCode	=	B	*FeeCode*	=	F
HourlyFee	=	$80.00	*HourlyFee*	=	$100.00
FeeCode	=	C	*FeeCode*	=	G
HourlyFee	=	$85.00	*HourlyFee*	=	$105.00
FeeCode	=	D	*FeeCode*	=	H
HourlyFee	=	$90.00	*HourlyFee*	=	$110.00

11. Automatically adjust column widths.
12. Save, print, and then close the Fees table.
13. Create a table named *Employees* that includes the following fields (you determine the field name, data type, field size, and description):

    ProviderNumber (primary key)
    ProviderName
    Title
    Extension

14. After creating the table, switch to Datasheet view and then enter the following data in the appropriate fields:

    ProviderNumber: 29
    ProviderName: James Schouten
    Title: Psychologist
    Extension: 399

    ProviderNumber: 33
    ProviderName: Janice Grisham
    Title: Psychiatrist
    Extension: 11

    ProviderNumber: 15
    ProviderName: Lynn Yee
    Title: Child Psychologist
    Extension: 102

    ProviderNumber: 18
    ProviderName: Craig Chilton
    Title: Psychologist
    Extension: 20

15. Automatically adjust column widths.
16. Save, print, and then close the Employees table.
17. Create a table named *Billing* that includes the following fields (you determine the field name, data type, field size, and description):

BillingNumber	(primary key; identify the data type as AutoNumber)
ClientNumber	
DateOfService	(apply the Date/Time data type)
Insurer	
ProviderNumber	
Hours	(Change the data type to *Number*, the *Field Size* option in the *Field Properties* section to *Double*, and the *Decimal Places* option in the *Field Properties* section in Design view to *1*. Two of the records will contain a number requiring this format.)
FeeCode	

18. After creating the table, switch to Datasheet view and then enter the following data in the appropriate fields:

ClientNumber: **4419**
DateOfService: **3/1/2012**
Insurer: **Health Plus**
ProviderNumber: **15**
Hours: **2**
FeeCode: **B**

ClientNumber: **1831**
DateOfService: **3/1/2012**
Insurer: **Self**
ProviderNumber: **33**
Hours: **1**
FeeCode: **H**

ClientNumber: **3219**
DateOfService: **3/2/2012**
Insurer: **Health Plus**
ProviderNumber: **15**
Hours: **1**
FeeCode: **D**

ClientNumber: **5831**
DateOfService: **3/2/2012**
Insurer: **Penn-State Health**
ProviderNumber: **18**
Hours: **2**
FeeCode: **C**

ClientNumber: **4419**
DateOfService: **3/5/2012**
Insurer: **Health Plus**
ProviderNumber: **15**
Hours: **1**
FeeCode: **A**

ClientNumber: **1103**
DateOfService: **3/5/2012**
Insurer: **Penn-State Health**
ProviderNumber: **18**
Hours: **0.5**
FeeCode: **A**

ClientNumber: **1831**
DateOfService: **3/6/2012**
Insurer: **Self**
ProviderNumber: **33**
Hours: **1**
FeeCode: **H**

ClientNumber: **5831**
DateOfService: **3/6/2012**
Insurer: **Penn-State Health**
ProviderNumber: **18**
Hours: **0.5**
FeeCode: **C**

19. Automatically adjust column widths.
20. Save, print in landscape orientation, and then close the Billing table.

Assessment 2 Relate Tables and Create Forms in a Clinic Database

1. With the **AL1-U2-LancasterClinic.accdb** database open, create the following one-to-many relationships and enforce referential integrity and cascade fields and records:
   a. *ClientNumber* in the Clients table is the "one" and *ClientNumber* in the Billing table is the "many."
   b. *DiagnosisID* in the Diagnoses table is the "one" and *DiagnosisID* in the Clients table is the "many."
   c. *ProviderNumber* in the Employees table is the "one" and *ProviderNumber* in the Billing table is the "many."
   d. *FeeCode* in the Fees table is the "one" and *FeeCode* in the Billing table is the "many."
2. Create a form with the data in the Clients table.

3. After creating the form, add the following record to the Clients form:

   ClientNumber: 1179
   Timothy Fierro
   1133 Tenth Southwest
   Philadelphia, PA 19178
   (215) 555-5594
   DateOfBirth: 12/7/1987
   DiagnosisID: AD

4. Save the form, print the form in landscape orientation, and then close the form.
5. Add the following records to the Billing table:

ClientNumber: 1179	*ClientNumber:* 1831
DateOfService: 3/6/2012	*DateOfService:* 3/6/2012
Insurer: Health Plus	*Insurer:* Self
ProviderNumber: 15	*ProviderNumber:* 33
Hours: 0.5	*Hours:* 1
FeeCode: C	FeeCode: H

6. Save and then print the Billing table in landscape orientation.
7. Close the Billing table.

Assessment 3 Create Forms Using the Form Wizard

1. With the **AL1-U2-LancasterClinic.accdb** database open, create a form with fields from related tables using the Form Wizard with the following specifications:
   a. At the first Form Wizard dialog box, insert the following fields in the Selected Fields list box:

From the Clients table:	From the Billing table:
ClientNumber	*Insurer*
DateOfBirth	*ProviderNumber*
DiagnosisID	

   b. Do not make any changes at the second Form Wizard dialog box.
   c. Do not make any changes at the third Form Wizard dialog box.
   d. At the fourth Form Wizard dialog box, type the name ProviderInformation in the *Form* text box.
2. When the first record displays, print the first record.
3. Close the form.

Assessment 4 Create Labels with the Label Wizard

1. With the **AL1-U2-LancasterClinic.accdb** database open, use the Label Wizard to create mailing labels with the client names and addresses and sorted by ZIP code. Name the mailing label file **ClientMailingLabels**.
2. Print the mailing labels.
3. Close the mailing labels file.

Assessment 5 Filter Records in Tables

1. With the **AL1-U2-LancasterClinic.accdb** database open, open the Billing table and then filter the records to display the following records:
   a. Display only those records with the Health Plus insurer. Print the results and then remove the filter.
   b. Display only those records with the 4419 client number. Print the results and then remove the filter.
2. Filter records by selection to display the following records:
   a. Display only those records with a C fee code. Print the results and then remove the filter.
   b. Display only those records between the dates of 3/1/2012 and 3/5/2012. Print the results and then remove the filter.
3. Close the Billing table without saving the changes.
4. Open the Clients table and then use Filter By Form to display clients in Jenkintown or Cheltenham. Print the results and then remove the filter.
5. Close the Clients table without saving the changes.

Assessment 6 Export a Table to Excel

1. With the **AL1-U2-LancasterClinic.accdb** database open, export the Billing table to an Excel workbook.
2. Apply formatting to the cells in the Excel workbook to enhance the appearance of the data.
3. Change the page orientation to landscape.
4. Save, print, and then close the workbook.
5. Exit Excel.

Assessment 7 Merge Records to Create Letters in Word

1. With the **AL1-U2-LancasterClinic.accdb** database open, merge data in the Clients table to a blank Word document. ***Hint: Use the Word Merge button in the Export group in the External Data tab.*** You determine the fields to use in the inside address and an appropriate salutation. Type March 12, 2012 as the date of the letter and type the following text in the body of the document:

   The building of a new wing for the Lancaster Clinic will begin April 1, 2012. We are excited about this new addition to our clinic. With the new facilities, we will be able to offer additional community and group services along with enhanced child-play therapy treatment.

   During the construction, the main entrance will be moved to the north end of the building. Please use this entrance until the construction of the wing is completed. We apologize in advance for any inconvenience this causes you.

   Include an appropriate complimentary close for the letter. Use the name and title *Marianne Lambert, Clinic Director* for the signature and add your reference initials and the document name (**AL1-U2-A7-LCLtrs.docx**).
2. Merge to a new document and then save the document with the name **AL1-U2-A7-LCLtrs**.
3. Print the first two letters of the document and then close **AL1-U2-A7-LCLtrs.docx**.

4. Save the main document as **AL1-U2-A7-ConstLtrMD** and then close the document.
5. Exit Word.

Assessment 8 Import and Link Excel Data to an Access Table

1. With the **AL1-U2-LancasterClinic.accdb** database open, import and link **AL1-U2-StaffHours.xlsx** into a new table named *StaffHours*.
2. Open the StaffHours table in Datasheet view.
3. Print and then close the StaffHours table.
4. Open **AL1-U2-StaffHours.xlsx** in Excel.
5. Insert a formula in cell D2 that multiplies B2 with C2 and then copy the formula down to cells D3 through D7.
6. Save and then close **AL1-U2-StaffHours.xlsx**.
7. Exit Excel.
8. In Access with the **AL1-U2-LancasterClinic.accdb** database open, open the StaffHours table.
9. Print and then close the StaffHours table.

Writing Activities

The following activities give you the opportunity to practice your writing skills along with demonstrating an understanding of some of the important Access features you have mastered in this unit. Use correct grammar, appropriate word choices, and clear sentence constructions.

Activity 1 Add a Table to the Clinic Database

The director at Lancaster Clinic has asked you to add information to the **AL1-U2-LancasterClinic.accdb** database on insurance companies contracted by the clinic. You need to create a table that will contain information on insurance companies. The director wants the table to include the insurance company name, address, city, state, and ZIP code along with a telephone number and the name of a representative. You determine the field names, data types, field sizes, and description for the table and then include the following information (in the appropriate fields):

Health Plus
4102 22nd Street
Philadelphia, PA 19166
(212) 555-0990
Representative: Byron Tolleson

Penn-State Health
5933 Lehigh Avenue
Philadelphia, PA 19148
(212) 555-3477
Representative: Tracey Pavone

Quality Medical
51 Cecil B. Moore Avenue
Philadelphia, PA 19168
(212) 555-4600
Representative: Lee Stafford

Delaware Health
4418 Front Street
Philadelphia, PA 19132
(212) 555-6770
Representative: Melanie Chon

Save, print, and then close the insurance company table. Open Word and then write a report to the clinic director detailing how you created the table. Include a title for the report, steps on how you created the table, and any other pertinent information. Save the completed report and name it **AL1-U2-Act1-LCRpt**. Print and then close **AL1-U2-Act1-LCRpt.docx**.

Activity 2 Merge Records to Create Letters to Insurance Companies

Merge data in the insurance company database to a blank Word document. You determine the fields to use in the inside address and an appropriate salutation. Compose a letter to the insurance companies informing them that Lancaster Clinic is providing mental health counseling services to people with health insurance through their company. You are sending an informational brochure about Lancaster Clinic and are requesting information from the insurance companies on services and service limitations. Include an appropriate complimentary close for the letter. Use the name and title *Marianne Lambert, Clinic Director* for the signature and add your reference initials. When the merge is completed, name the document containing the merged letters **AL1-U2-Act2-LCIns**. Print the first two letters in the merged document and then close **AL1-U2-Act2-LCIns.docx**. Close the main document without saving it and then exit Word. Close the **AL1-U2-LancasterClinic.accdb** database.

Internet Research

Health Information Search

In this activity, you will search the Internet for information on a health concern or disease that interests you. You will be looking for specific organizations, interest groups, or individuals who are somehow connected to the topic you have chosen. Your topic may be an organization that raises money to support research, it may be a support group that posts information or answers questions, or you may find information about clinics or doctors who specialize in your topic. Try to find at least ten different groups that support the health concern you are researching.

Create a database in Access and create a table that includes information from your search. Design the table so that you can store the name, address, phone number, and web address of the organizations you find. You will also want to identify the connection the group has to your topic (supports research, interest group, treats patients, etc.). Create a report to summarize your findings. In Microsoft Word, create a letter that you can use to write for further information about the organization. Use the names and addresses in your database to merge with the letter. Select and then print the first two letters that result from the merge. Finally, write a paragraph describing information you learned about the health concern that you previously did not know.

Job Study

City Improvement Projects

In this activity, you are working with the city council in your area to keep the public informed of the progress being made on improvement projects throughout the city. These projects are paid for through tax dollars voted on by the public, and the city council feels that an informed public leads to good voter turnout when it is time to make more improvements.

Your job is to create a database and a table in the database that will store the following information for each project: a project ID number, a description of the project, the budgeted dollar amount to be spent, the amount spent so far, the amount of time allocated to the project, and the amount of time spent so far. Enter five city improvement projects into the table (sample data created by you). Create a query based on the table that calculates the percent of budgeted dollars spent so far and the percent of budgeted time spent so far. Print the table and the query.

E

F

S

T

U

V

W

X

Y

Z

Unit 1 ■ Advanced Tables, Relationships, Queries, and Forms

Microsoft® Access®

CHAPTER 1

Designing the Structure of Tables

PERFORMANCE OBJECTIVES

Upon successful completion of Chapter 1, you will be able to:

- **Design the structure of tables to optimize efficiency and accuracy of data**
- **Select the appropriate field data type based on analysis of source data**
- **Disallow blank field values**
- **Allow or disallow zero-length strings in a field**
- **Create a custom format for text, number, and date fields**
- **Create a custom input mask**
- **Define rich text formatting for a memo field**
- **Store history of changes to a memo field**
- **Define and use an attachment field with multiple attachments**

SNAP Training and Assessment. Simplified.

Tutorials

1.1 Diagramming a Database

1.2 Creating Tables in Design View

1.3 Restricting Data Entry and Data

1.4 Creating a Custom Format for a Text Field, a Numeric Field, and a Date/Time Field

1.5 Restricting Data Entry Using Input Masks

1.6 Working with Memo Fields

1.7 Creating an Attachment Field

1.8 Attaching Files to Records

Designing tables in Access is the most important task when creating a database since tables are the objects upon which all other objects are based. A query, form, or report relies on a table for the data source. Designing a new database involves planning the number of tables needed, the fields that will be included in each table, and the methods with which Access can be used to check and/or validate new data as the data is being entered. In this chapter you will learn the basic steps to plan a new database by analyzing existing data. In addition to organizing the data structure, you will also learn to select appropriate data types and use field properties to control, restrict, or otherwise validate data.

In this chapter, prior knowledge of the steps to create a new table, including changing the data type and field size and assigning the primary key, as well as the meaning of the terms *field*, *record*, *table*, and *database* is assumed.

Model answers for this chapter's projects appear on the following page.

Access

Access2010L2C1

Note: Before beginning the projects, copy to your storage medium the Access2010L2C1 subfolder from the Access2010L2 folder on the CD that accompanies this textbook. Steps on how to copy a folder are presented on the inside of the back cover of this textbook. Do this every time you start a chapter's projects.

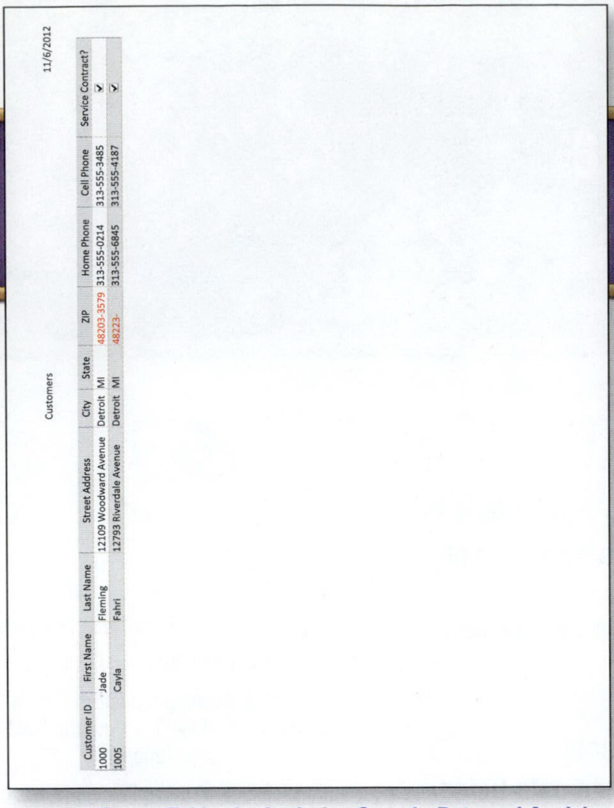

Customers

11/6/2012

Customer ID	First Name	Last Name	Street Address	City	State	ZIP	Home Phone	Cell Phone	Service Contract?
1000	Jade	Fleming	12109 Woodward Avenue	Detroit	MI	48203-3579	313-555-0214	313-555-3485	✓
1005	Cayla	Fahri	12793 Riverdale Avenue	Detroit	MI	48223-	313-555-6845	313-555-4187	✓

Project 1 Create Tables by Analyzing Sample Data and Applying Database Design Techniques

Project 1c, Customers Table

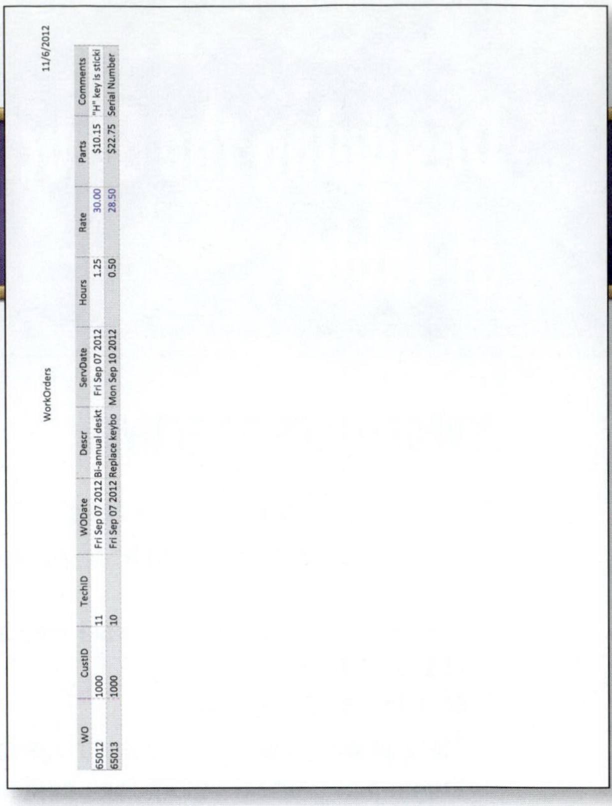

WorkOrders

11/6/2012

WO	CustID	TechID	WODate	Descr	ServDate	Hours	Rate	Parts	Comments
65012	1000	11	Fri Sep 07 2012	Bi-annual deskt	Fri Sep 07 2012	1.25	30.00	$10.15	"H" key is sticki
65013	1000	10	Fri Sep 07 2012	Replace keybo	Mon Sep 10 2012	0.50	28.50	$22.75	Serial Number

Project 1f, WorkOrders Table

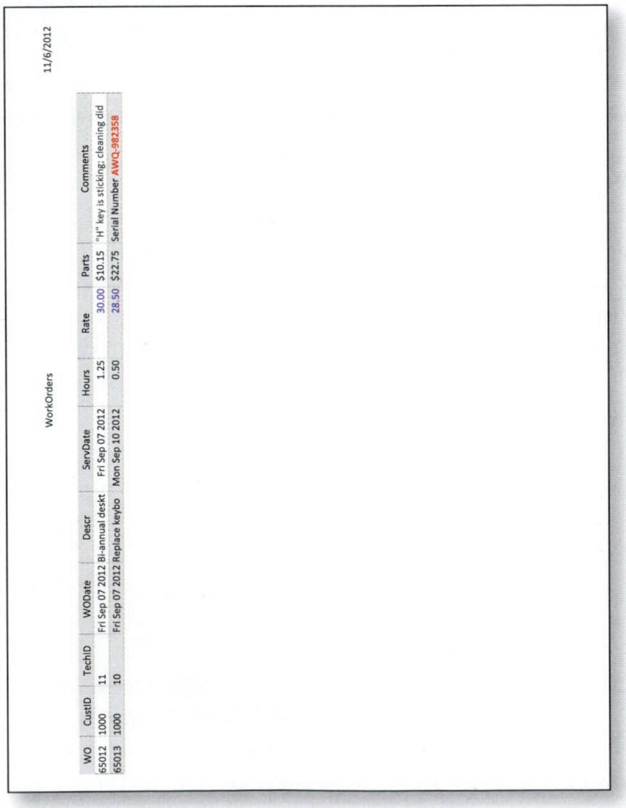

WorkOrders

11/6/2012

WO	CustID	TechID	WODate	Descr	ServDate	Hours	Rate	Parts	Comments
65012	1000	11	Fri Sep 07 2012	Bi-annual deskt	Fri Sep 07 2012	1.25	30.00	$10.15	"H" key is sticking; cleaning did
65013	1000	10	Fri Sep 07 2012	Replace keybo	Mon Sep 10 2012	0.50	28.50	$22.75	Serial Number AWQ-982358

Project 2 Work with Memo and Attachment Fields

Project 2a, WorkOrders Table

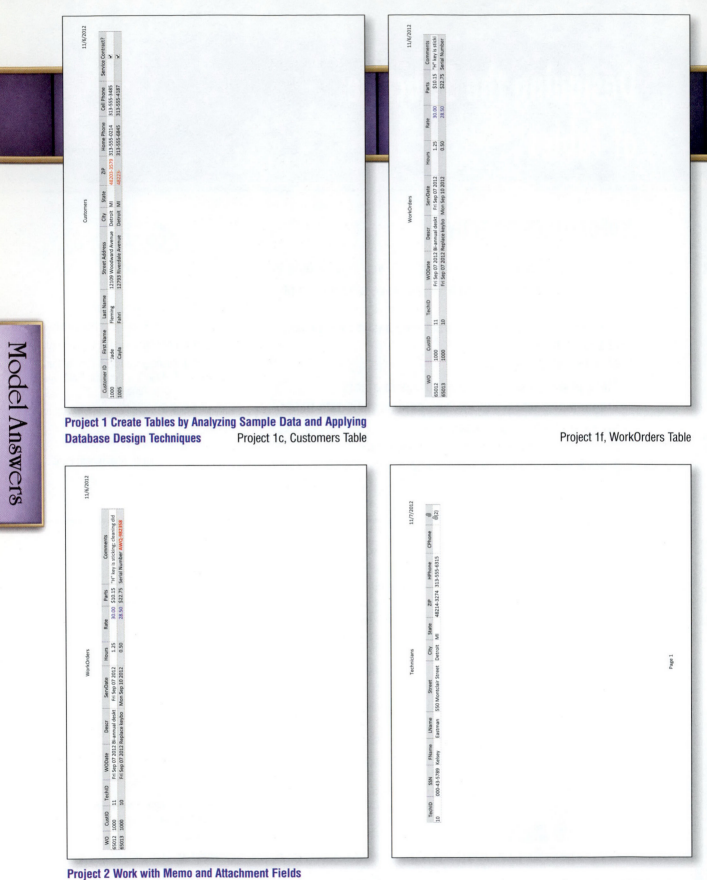

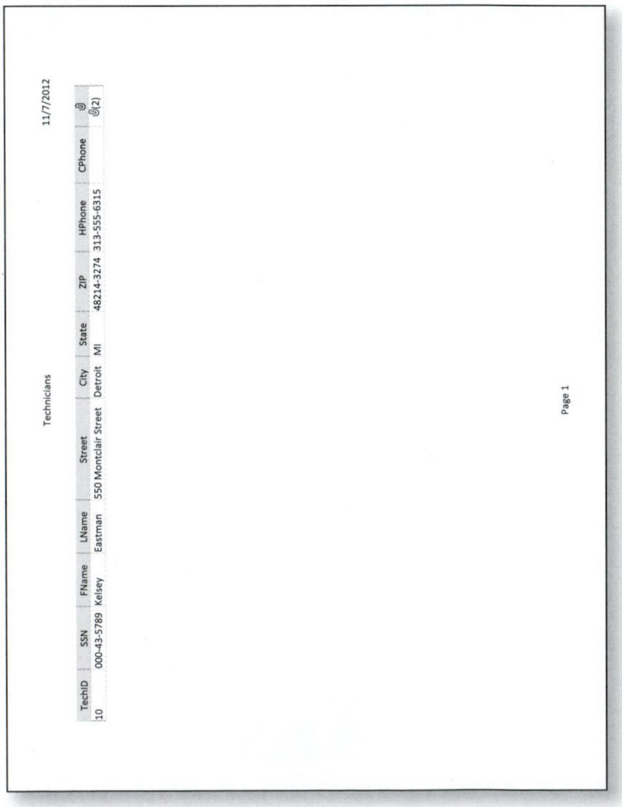

Technicians

11/7/2012

TechID	SSN	FName	LName	Street	City	State	ZIP	HPhone	CPhone	📎
10	000-43-5789	Kelsey	Eastman	550 Montclair Street	Detroit	MI	48214-3274	313-555-6315		📎(2)

Page 1

Project 2b, Technicians Table

Project 1 Create Tables by Analyzing Sample Data and Applying Database Design Techniques — 6 Parts

You will use sample data to decide how to structure a new database to track computer service work orders using best practices for table design and then create the tables.

Designing Tables and Fields for a New Database

Most of the databases you will work with in the workplace will have already been created by database designers. An introduction to the process involved in creating a new database will be of benefit to you so that you will better understand the reasons why objects are organized and related. Creating a new database from scratch involves careful advance planning. Database designers spend considerable time analyzing existing data and asking questions of users and managers. Designers will want to know how data will be used to help identify the required forms, queries, and reports to be generated from the data. Often, designers begin by modeling a report required from the database to see data that is required to populate the report. A ***data dictionary*** (a list of fields and attributes of each field) is then compiled from which the designer can next map out the number of required tables.

In Project 1, you will be analyzing a sample work order for RSR Computer Services. RSR started out as a small computer service company. The owners used Excel worksheets to enter information from service records and then produced revenue reports. The company's success has led to a need to move to a relational database to track customer information. The owners want to be able to generate queries and reports from the service records to assist with decision making. Examine the data in a typical work order shown in Figure 1.1. The work order form that the technicians have been filling out at the customer site will be used as the input source document for the database.

Figure 1.1 Sample Work Order for RSR Computer Services

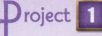

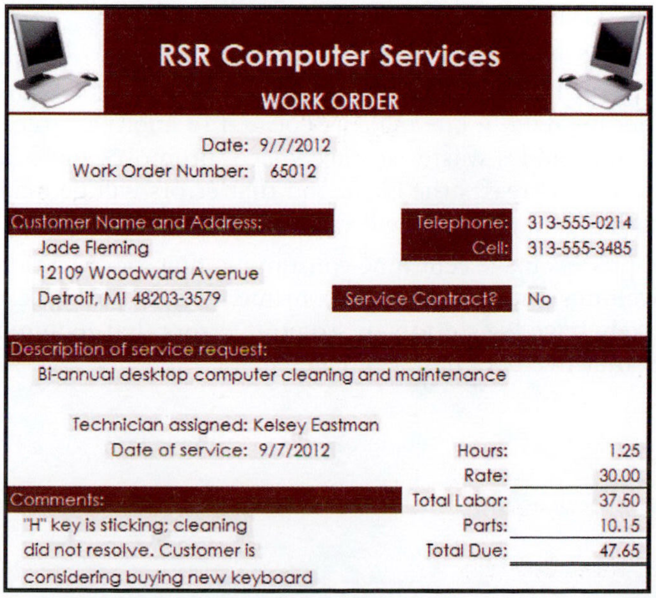

RSR Computer Services
WORK ORDER

Date: 9/7/2012
Work Order Number: 65012

Customer Name and Address:
Jade Fleming
12109 Woodward Avenue
Detroit, MI 48203-3579

Telephone: 313-555-0214
Cell: 313-555-3485

Service Contract? No

Description of service request:
Bi-annual desktop computer cleaning and maintenance

Technician assigned: Kelsey Eastman
Date of service: 9/7/2012

Hours: 1.25
Rate: 30.00
Total Labor: 37.50
Parts: 10.15
Total Due: 47.65

Comments:
"H" key is sticking; cleaning did not resolve. Customer is considering buying new keyboard

Designers analyze all input documents and output requirements to capture the entire set of data elements that need to be created. Once all data has been identified, the designer maps out the number of tables required to hold the data. During the process in which the designer is mapping the tables and fields to be associated with each table, the designer incorporates the following techniques:

- Each table is considered an ***entity*** and should describe a single person, place, object, event, or other subject. Each table should store facts that are related to the entity's subject only.
- Data should be segmented until it is in its smallest unit that you will want to manipulate. For example, in the work order shown in Figure 1.1, the customer's name and address would be split into separate fields for first name, last name, street address, city, state, and ZIP code. This approach provides maximum flexibility for generating other objects and allows the designer to sort or filter by any individual data element.
- Fields that can be calculated by using data in other fields are not included. For example, the total labor and total due amounts in the work order can be calculated using other numeric data elements.
- Identify fields that can be used to answer questions from the data. Queries and reports can be designed to extract information based on the results of a conditional expression (sometimes referred to as Boolean logic). For example, the technician enters on the work order whether the customer has a service contract or not. A field that stores a Yes or No (true or false) condition for the service contract data element allows the business to generate reports of customers that have subscribed to a service contract (true condition) and those that have not subscribed (false condition).
- Identify a field in each table that will hold data that uniquely identifies each record. This field becomes the primary key. If the source documents used for design do not reveal a unique identifier, Access provides an ID field automatically in new tables with the AutoNumber data type that can be used as a primary key.
- Determine each table that will relate to another table and the field you will use to join the two when you create relationships. Identifying relationships at this stage helps you determine if you need to add a field to a related table to allow you to join the table.
- Relational databases are built upon the concept that data redundancy should be avoided except for fields that will be used to join tables in a relationship. ***Data redundancy*** means data in one table is repeated in another table. Repeating fields in multiple tables wastes storage space, promotes inefficiency, inconsistency, and increases the likelihood that errors will be made when adding, updating, and deleting field values.

The design process may seem time-consuming; however, the time expended to produce a well-designed database saves time later. A database that is poorly designed will likely have logic errors or structure errors that require redefining of data or objects after live data has been entered.

Diagramming a Database

Recall from Level 1, Chapter 1 that designers often create a visual representation of the database's structure in a diagram similar to the one shown in Figure 1.2. Each table is represented in a box with the table name at the top of the box. Within each box, the fields that will be stored in the table are listed with the field names that will be used when the tables are created. The primary key field is denoted with an asterisk. Tables that will be joined have lines drawn connecting them together at the common field that exists in both tables. You will begin to build this database in the remainder of this chapter and create the relationships in Chapter 2.

Notice that many of the field names in the diagram are abbreviated. Although a field name can contain up to 64 characters, field names that are short enough to be understood are easier to manage and type into expressions. For abbreviated field names, the Caption property is used to display descriptive headings that contain spaces and/or longer words when viewing the data in a datasheet, form, or report. Also notice that none of the field names contain spaces. Spaces are allowed in field names; however, most database designers avoid using spaces and separate compound words by changing the case, by using an underscore character (_) or by using a hyphen (-) as a separator.

HINT

Words such as *Name* and *Date* are reserved words in Access and cannot be used as a field name. Access prompts you if the field name you used is a reserved word when you try to save the table.

Assigning Data Types

Each field is assigned a data type by the designer based on the type of entries that the designer wants to allow into the field and the operations that will need to be used to manipulate the data. Selecting the appropriate data type is important since restrictions will be placed on a field based upon the field's data type. For example, in a field designated with the Number data type, only numbers, a period to represent a decimal point, and a plus or minus sign can be entered into the field in a datasheet or form. Table 1.1 reviews the available data types.

Figure 1.2 Diagram of Table Structure for RSR Computer Services Database

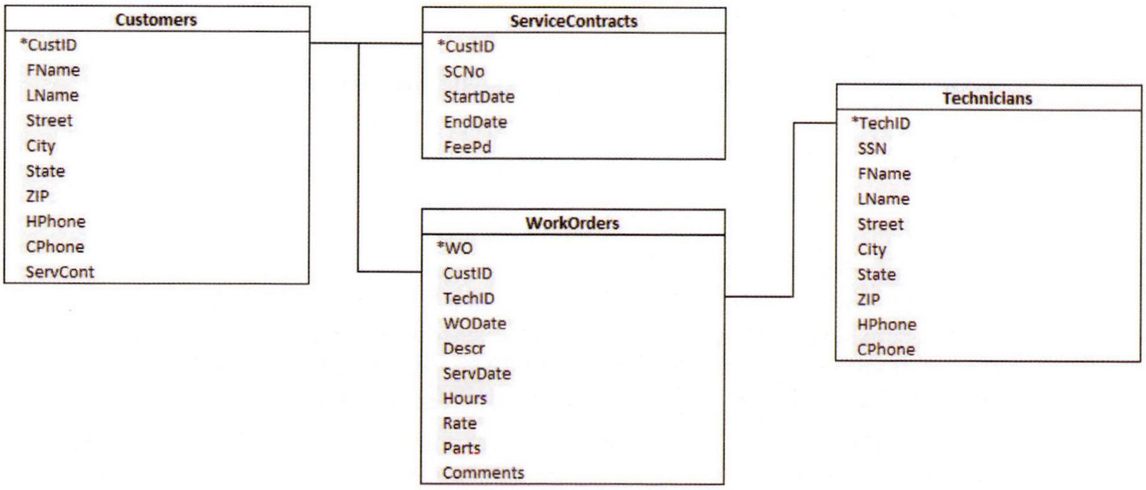

Table 1.1 Data Types

Data Type	*Description*
Text	Alphanumeric data up to 255 characters such as a name or address. Text fields can also store values such as a customer number, telephone number, or social security number that is used as an identifier and not for calculating.
Memo	Alphanumeric data longer than 255 characters with up to 65,535 characters displayed in the field. Use a Memo field to store longer passages of text in a record. You can add rich text formatting in a Memo field such as bold, italics, or font color.
Number	Positive or negative values that can be used in calculations. Do not use for monetary values (see *Currency*).
Date/Time	Accepts only valid dates and times into the field. Use to ensure dates and times are entered and sorted properly.
Currency	Holds monetary values. Access does not round off during calculations.
AutoNumber	Field value is automatically assigned by Access by sequentially incrementing the field value by 1 when a new record is added.
Yes/No	Entry in the field is restricted to conditional logic of Yes or No, True or False, On or Off.
OLE Object	Stores an embedded or linked object created in other Microsoft Office applications.
Hyperlink	Links to a URL.
Attachment	Attach a file to the record such as a picture, Word document, or Excel worksheet.
Calculated	The field's value is calculated using a mathematical expression that uses data from other fields within the same table.

Using the Field Size Property to Restrict Field Length

By default, text fields are set to a width of 255 in the Field Size property. Access uses only the amount of space needed for the data that is entered even when the field size allows for more characters, so you may wonder why one would change the property to a smaller value. One reason to consider is that changing the Field Size property becomes a means to restrict the length of data allowed into the field. For example, if RSR Computer Services has developed a 4-character numbering system for customer numbers, setting the field size for the *CustID* field to *4* will ensure that no one enters a customer number longer than 4 characters by accident since Access will disallow all characters typed after the fourth character.

Figure 1.3 shows the table structure diagram for the RSR Computer Services database expanded to include each field's data type and field size property. You will use this diagram in Project 1a to create the tables.

Figure 1.3 Expanded Table Structure Diagram with Data Types and Field Sizes for Project 1a

Customers		
*CustID	Text	4
FName	Text	20
LName	Text	30
Street	Text	35
City	Text	25
State	Text	2
ZIP	Text	10
HPhone	Text	14
CPhone	Text	14
ServCont	Yes/No	

ServiceContracts		
*CustID	Text	4
SCNo	Text	6
StartDate	Date/Time	
EndDate	Date/Time	
FeePd	Currency	

WorkOrders		
*WO	Text	5
CustID	Text	4
TechID	Text	2
WODate	Date/Time	
Descr	Text	255
ServDate	Date/Time	
Hours	Number	
Rate	Currency	
Parts	Currency	
Comments	Memo	

Technicians		
*TechID	Text	2
SSN	Text	11
FName	Text	20
LName	Text	30
Street	Text	35
City	Text	25
State	Text	2
ZIP	Text	10
HPhone	Text	14
CPhone	Text	14

Project 1a Creating Tables in Design View

Part 1 of 6

1. Start Access.
2. At the New tab Backstage view, complete the following steps to create a new database to store the work orders for RSR Computer Services:
   a. Click the Browse button located at the right of the *File Name* text box (currently displays *Database1.accdb*) in the *Blank database* section.
   b. At the File New Database dialog box, navigate to the Access2010L2C1 folder on your storage medium, select the current text in the *File Name* text box, type **AL2-C1-RSRCompServ**, and then click OK.
   c. Click the Create button located below the *File Name* text box.

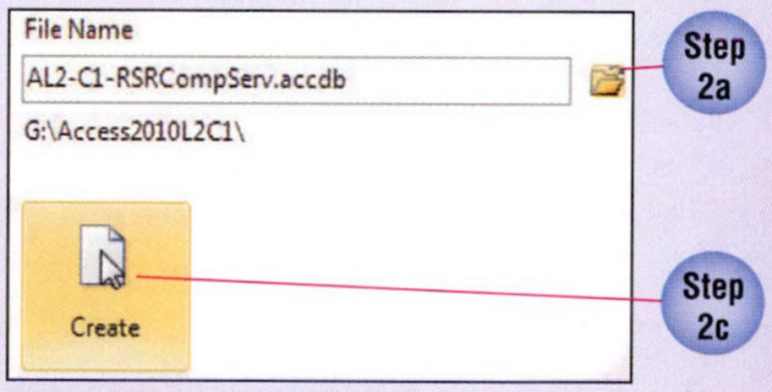

3. Close the Table1 blank table datasheet that displays. You will work with tables in Design view to access all of the field properties available for fields.
4. Click the Create tab and then click the Table Design button in the Tables group. Create the fields shown in the Customers table in Figure 1.3 including the data type and field size setting.
5. Assign the primary key to the *CustID* field.
6. Save the table and name it *Customers*.

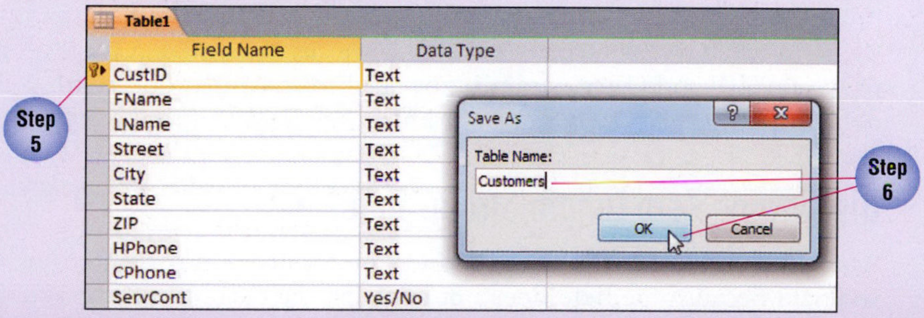

7. Close the table.
8. Create the ServiceContracts, WorkOrders, and Technicians tables shown in Figure 1.3 by completing steps similar to those in Steps 4–7. Assign the primary key in each table using the field denoted with an asterisk in Figure 1.3.
9. Make sure all tables are closed.

Restricting Data Entry and Data Display Using Field Properties

The properties that are available for a field depend on the field's data type. For example, a Yes/No field has 7 properties while a Text field has 14 and a Number field has 12. Use the options available in the *Field Properties* section in Design view to place restrictions on data accepted into the field and to ensure data is entered and displayed consistently. Field properties should be defined for the fields before other objects, such as forms or reports are created. The properties carry over to the other objects and taking the time to define the properties when the table is created reduces the number of times you have to make changes if you decide to modify properties later on.

You have already used the Field Size property in Project 1a to restrict the length of entries allowed in fields. In this section you will learn to apply other field properties to fields to further control data entry and display.

Quick Steps

Add a Caption to Existing Field
1. Open table in Design view.
2. Activate desired field.
3. Click in *Caption* property box.
4. Type descriptive text.
5. Save table.

Require Data in Field
1. Open table in Design view.
2. Activate desired field.
3. Click in *Required* property box.
4. Click down-pointing arrow.
5. Click Yes.
6. Save table.

Disallow Zero-Length String in Field
1. Open table in Design view.
2. Activate desired field.
3. Click in *Allow Zero Length* property box.
4. Click down-pointing arrow.
5. Click No.
6. Save table.

Adding Captions

In Level 1 you learned about the Caption property in the Name & Caption dialog box when creating a new table using a Table datasheet. The same property appears in Design view in the *Field Properties* section. Recall that the Caption property allows you to enter a more descriptive title for the field if the field name has been truncated or abbreviated. You can also use a caption to display spaces between words in a field name rather than underscore or hyphen characters. In the absence of an entry in the Caption property, Access displays the field name in datasheets, queries, forms, and reports.

Requiring Data in a Field

A field that you want to make sure is never left empty when a new record is added can be controlled using the Required field property. By default, the Required property is set to No. Change this value to Yes to make sure data is typed into the field when a new record is added. For example, you can force all new records to have a ZIP code entry. You do not need to set this property for a field that is defined as a primary key, since a primary key field cannot be left empty.

Disallowing Zero-Length Strings in a Field

A zero-length field can be used to indicate a value is not going to be entered into the field because the field does not apply to the current record. When you are entering a new record and leave a field blank, Access records a null value in the field. For example, if you are adding a new record for a customer and you do not know the customer's cell phone number, you can leave the field empty with the intention of updating the field at a later time. This is an example of leaving the field blank with a null value. Alternatively, if you know the customer does not own a cell phone, you can enter a zero-length string in the field to indicate no field value applies to this record.

To enter a zero-length string, type two double quotation symbols with no space between (""). When viewing the field in a datasheet, query, form, or report, you cannot distinguish between a field with a null value and a field with a zero-length string because both display as blanks; however, you can create a control in a form or report that returns a user-defined message in the blank fields that distinguishes one from the other. For example, you could display the word *Unknown* in a field with a null value and *Not applicable* in a field with a zero-length string. In some cases, you will want to see in a form or report which records will not have a value in the field as opposed to those records that are incomplete.

By default, Text, Memo, and Hyperlink data fields can have zero-length strings entered into the field. Change the Allow Zero Length property to *No* to disallow zero-length strings.

HINT

You can also press the spacebar to insert a zero-length string.

HINT

Set the *Required* field to *Yes* and *Allow Zero Length* to *No* to make sure a field value (and not a space) has to be entered at the time the record is added.

Project 1b Modifying Field Properties to Add Captions and Disallow Blank Values in a Field

Part 2 of 6

1. With the **AL2-C1-RSRCompServ.accdb** database open, add captions to the fields in the Customers table by completing the following steps:
   a. Right-click *Customers* in the Tables group of the Navigation pane and then click *Design View* at the shortcut menu.
   b. With *CustID* the active field, click in the *Caption* property box in the *Field Properties* section and then type **Customer ID**.
   c. Click in the *FName* field row to activate the field, click in the *Caption* property box in the *Field Properties* section, and then type **First Name**.
   d. Add captions to the following fields by completing a step similar to Step 1c.

LName	**Last Name**
Street	**Street Address**
HPhone	**Home Phone**
CPhone	**Cell Phone**
ServCont	**Service Contract?**

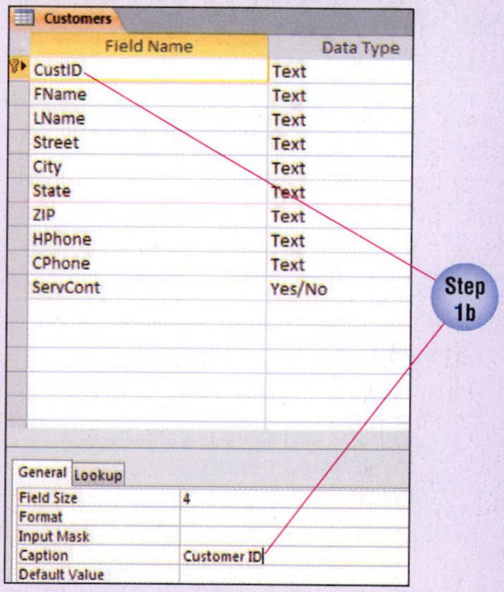

   e. Click the Save button on the Quick Access toolbar.
   f. Click the View button (do not click the down-pointing arrow on the button) to switch to Datasheet view and then select all columns in the datasheet. If necessary, click the Shutter Bar Open/Close button (two left-pointing chevrons located at the top of the Navigation pane) to minimize the Navigation pane.
   g. Click the More button in the Records group in the Home tab, click *Field Width* at the drop-down list, and then click the Best Fit button at the Column Width dialog box to adjust the widths to the length of the longest entry.
   h. Click in the *Customer ID* field in the first row of the datasheet to deselect the columns.

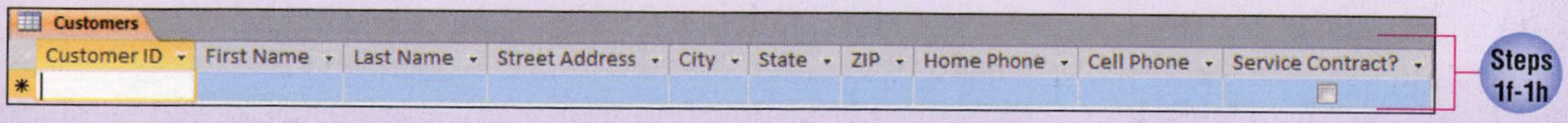

2. Switch to Design View and click the Shutter Bar Open/Close button (two right-pointing chevrons) to redisplay the Navigation pane if you minimized the pane in Step 1f.
3. You want to ensure that no record is entered without an entry in the *ZIP* field and you also want to disallow blank values in the field, including zero-length strings.
 a. Click in the *ZIP* field row to activate the field.
 b. Click in the *Required* property box in the *Field Properties* section (currently displays *No*), click the down-pointing arrow that appears, and then click *Yes* at the drop-down list.

Step
3b

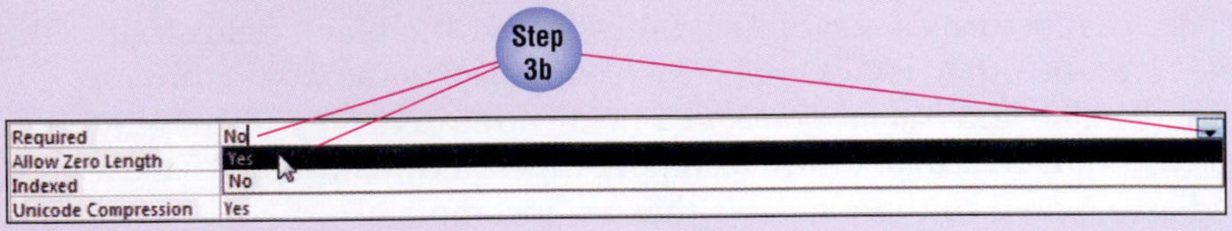

 c. Click in the *Allow Zero Length* property box (currently displays *Yes*), click the down-pointing arrow that appears, and then click *No* at the drop-down list.

Step
3c

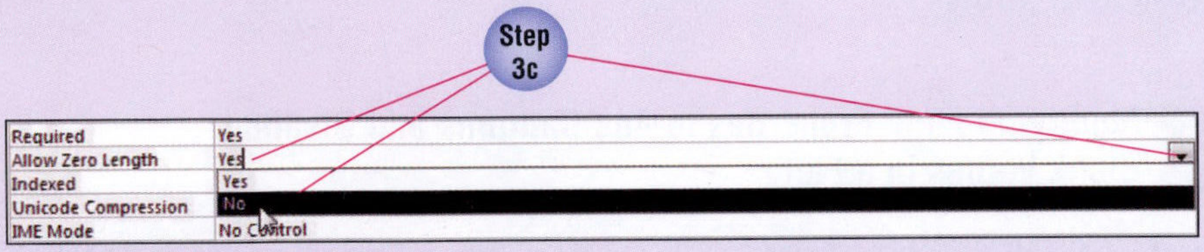

 d. Save the changes to the table design.
4. Test the restrictions on the *ZIP* field using a new record by completing the following steps:
 a. Switch to Datasheet view.
 b. Add the following data in the fields indicated.
Customer ID	1000
First Name	Jade
Last Name	Fleming
Street Address	12109 Woodward Avenue
City	Detroit
State	MI
 c. At the *ZIP* field, press Enter or Tab to move past the field, leaving the field blank.
 d. Type 313-555-0214 in the *Home Phone* field.
 e. Type 313-555-3485 in the *Cell Phone* field.
 f. Press the spacebar in the *Service Contract?* field to insert a check mark in the check box.
 g. Press Enter. Access displays an error message since the record cannot be saved without an entry in the *ZIP* field.
 h. Click OK at the Microsoft Access message box.
 i. Click in the *ZIP* field, type 48203-3579, and then press Enter four times to move to the *Customer ID* field in the second row of the datasheet.

Step
4h

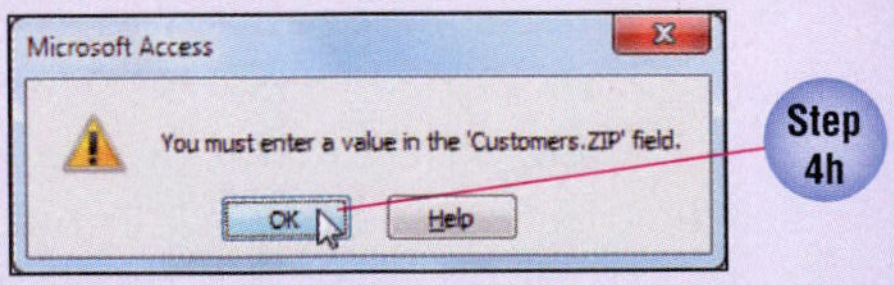

5. Double-click the right column boundary of the *Street Address* and *ZIP* columns to adjust the widths so that you can read the entire field value in the columns.

Step
5

Customer ID	First Name	Last Name	Street Address	City	State	ZIP	Home Phone	Cell Phone	Service Contract?
1000	Jade	Fleming	12109 Woodward Avenue	Detroit	MI	48203-3579	313-555-0214	313-555-3485	☑
*									☐

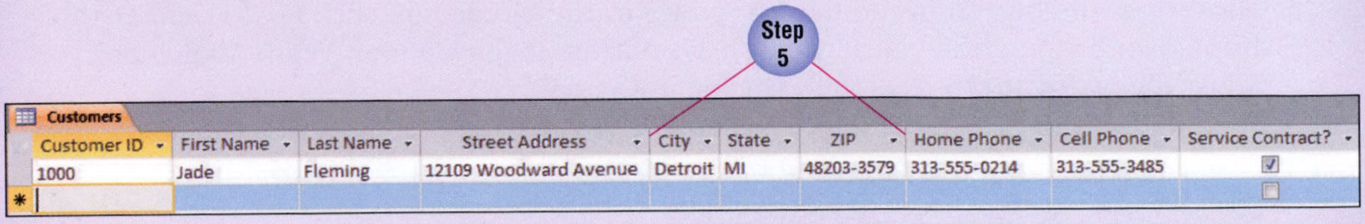

6. Close the Customers table. Click Yes when prompted to save changes to the layout of the table.

Creating a Custom Format for a Text Field

The Format property controls how data is displayed in the field in the datasheet, query, form, or report. The available formats that you can use are dependent on the field's data type. Some data types have predefined formats available which can be selected from a drop-down list in the *Format* property box. No predefined formats exist for Text or Memo fields. If no predefined format exists or if the predefined format options do not meet your needs, you can create your own custom format. Table 1.2 displays commonly used format codes for text or memo fields. The Format property does not control how data is entered into the field. Formatting a field controls the display of accepted field values. Refer to the section on input masks (starting on page 18) to learn how to control new data as the data is being entered.

Quick Steps

Format Text Field
1. Open table in Design view.
2. Activate desired field.
3. Click in *Format* property box.
4. Type desired format codes.
5. Save table.

Table 1.2 Format Codes for Text or Memo Fields

Code	Description	Format Property Example
@	Use as a placeholder, one symbol for each character position. Unused positions in a field value are replaced with blank spaces to the left of the text entered into the field.	@@@@ Field value is 123. Access displays one blank space followed by 123, left-aligned in the field.
!	Access fills the placeholder positions with characters from left to right instead of the default right to left sequence.	!@@@@ Field value entered is 123. Access displays 123 left-aligned in the field with one blank space after 3.
>	All text is converted to uppercase.	> Field value is mi. Access displays MI in the field.
<	All text is converted to lowercase.	< Field value is Jones@EMCP.NET. Access displays jones@emcp.net in the field.
[color]	Text is displayed in the font color specified. Available colors are: black, blue, cyan, green, magenta, red, yellow, and white.	[red]@@@@@-@@@@ Field value entered is 482033579. Access displays 48203-3579.

Project 1c Formatting Text Fields Using a Custom Format Part 3 of 6

1. With the **AL2-C1-RSRCompServ.accdb** database open, format the *State* field to ensure all text is displayed uppercase by completing the following steps:
   a. Right-click *Customers* in the Tables group of the Navigation pane and then click *Design View* at the shortcut menu.
   b. Click in the *State* field row to activate the field.
   c. Click in the *Format* property box and then type **>**.
   d. Save the table.

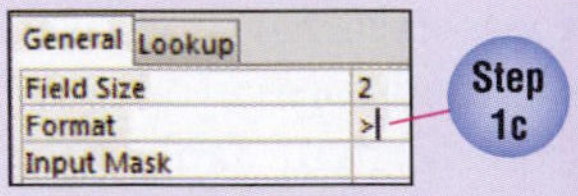

2. Format the *ZIP* field to fill the field with characters from left to right, display the text in red, and provide for the five-plus-four–character U.S. ZIP code separated by a hyphen by completing the following steps:
   a. Click in the *ZIP* field row to activate the field.
   b. Click in the *Format* property box and then type **![red]@@@@@-@@@@**.
   c. Save the table.

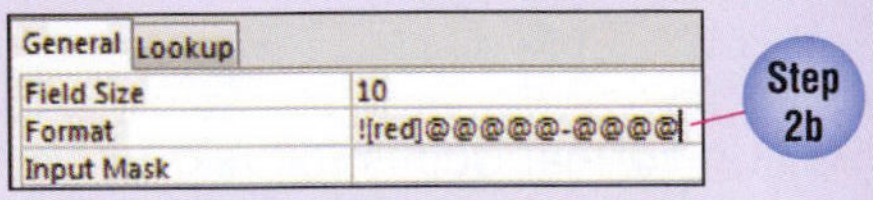

3. Test the custom formats in the *State* and *ZIP* fields using a new record by completing the following steps:
   a. Switch to Datasheet view.
   b. Add the following data in a new record. Type the text for the *State* field as indicated in lowercase text. Notice when you move to the next field, Access automatically converts the lowercase text to uppercase. As you type the ZIP text, notice the text is displayed in red. Since no field values are entered for the last four characters of the ZIP field, Access displays blank spaces in these positions.

Customer ID	**1005**
First Name	**Cayla**
Last Name	**Fahri**
Street Address	**12793 Riverdale Avenue**
City	**Detroit**
State	**mi**
ZIP	**48223**
Home Phone	**313-555-6845**
Cell Phone	**313-555-4187**
Service Contract?	Press spacebar for *Yes*

4. Look at the data in the *ZIP* field for the first record. This data was entered before you formatted the *ZIP* field. Since a hyphen was typed when the data was entered and the field is now formatted to automatically add the hyphen, two hyphen characters appear in the existing record. Edit the field value for record 1 in the *ZIP* field to remove the extra hyphen.

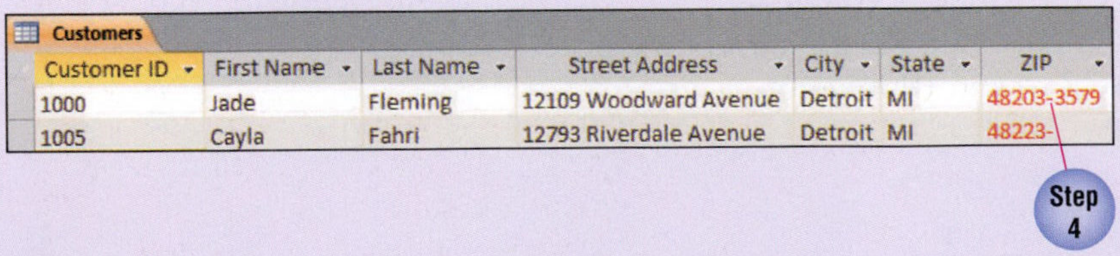

Customers
Customer ID
First Name
Last Name
Street Address
City
State
ZIP
1000
Jade
Fleming
12109 Woodward Avenue
Detroit
MI
48203-3579
1005
Cayla
Fahri
12793 Riverdale Avenue
Detroit
MI
48223-
Step 4

5. Display the datasheet in Print Preview. Change the orientation to landscape. Set the margins to a top margin of 1-inch and the bottom, left, and right margins of 0.25 inch. Print the datasheet and then close Print Preview.
6. Close the Customers table.

Creating a Custom Format for a Numeric Field

Access provides predefined formats for Number, AutoNumber, and Currency fields that include options for fixed decimal places, commas in the thousands, the currency symbol, percentages and exponential notation. Table 1.3 displays commonly used format codes that you can use to create a custom format. Use the placeholders shown in Table 1.3 in combination with other characters such as a dollar symbol, comma, and period to create the desired custom numeric format.

You can specify up to four different formats for a numeric field to include different options for displaying positive values, negative values, zero values, and null values. Examine the following custom format code:

#,###.00;-#,###.00[Red];0.00;"Unknown"

Each of the four sections is separated with a semicolon (;). The first section *#,###.00* defines the format for positive values that includes the comma in thousands and two decimal places with zeros used if no decimal value is entered. The second section *-#,###.00[Red]* defines negative values with the same placeholders as positive but starts the field with a minus symbol and displays the numbers in red. The third section *0.00* instructs Access to show 0.00 in the field if a zero is entered. Finally, a field value that is left blank would display the text *Unknown* [italics for emphasis only] in the field. Note that the example shown indicates the text that you want shown in the field includes a quotation symbol at the beginning and end of the desired text.

Quick Steps

Format Number Field

1. Open table in Design view.
2. Activate desired field.
3. Click in *Format* property box.
4. Type desired format codes or select from predefined list.
5. Save table.

Table 1.3 Format Codes for Numeric Fields

Code	*Description*	*Format Property Example*
#	Used as a placeholder to display a number.	#.## Field value entered is 123.45. Access displays 123.45 in the field. Note that the number of placeholder positions does not restrict the data entered into the field.
0	Used as a placeholder to display a number. Access displays a zero in place of a position for which no value is entered.	000.00 Field value entered is 55.4. Access displays 055.40 in the field.
%	Multiplies the value times 100 and adds a percent symbol.	#.0% Field value entered is .1242. Access displays 12.4% in the field. Notice that only one decimal position causes rounding up or down to occur.

Project 1d **Formatting Numeric Fields Using a Custom Format and a Predefined Format** Part 4 of 6

1. With the **AL2-C1-RSRCompServ.accdb** database open, format the *Rate* field in the WorkOrders table with a custom format by completing the following steps:
   a. Open the WorkOrders table in Design view.
   b. Make the *Rate* field active.
   c. Click in the *Format* property box, delete the current entry, and then type **#.00[blue];;;"Not Available"**. Notice that three semicolons are typed after the first custom format option *#.00[blue]*. When you do not need a custom format for negative or zero values in the property you include the semicolon to indicate no format setting for each option not specified. Since an hourly rate would never be a negative value or a zero value, you do not need to include custom formats for those situations since they would never occur.

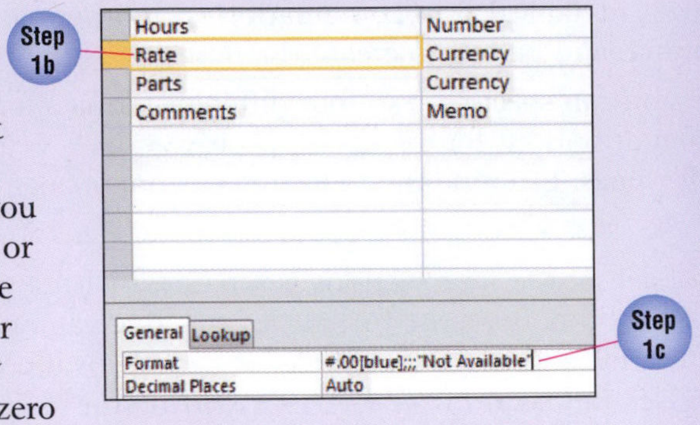

   d. Save the table.
2. Format the *Hours* field using a predefined format and change the field size by completing the following steps:
   a. Make the *Hours* field active.
   b. Click in the *Field Size* property box, click the down-pointing arrow that appears, and then click *Double*. The default setting for a Number field is *Long Integer*, which stores whole numbers only, meaning a decimal value entered into the field is rounded. Changing the field size property to *Double* allows you to store decimal values.
   c. Click in the *Format* property box, click the down-pointing arrow that appears, and then click *Standard* at the drop-down list.

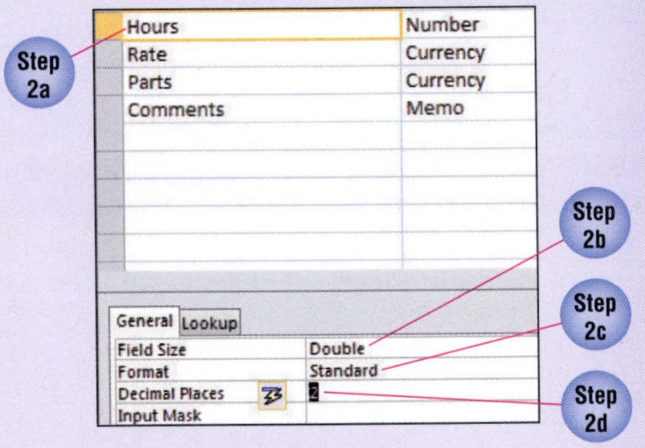

   d. Click in the *Decimal Places* property box, click the down-pointing arrow that appears and then click *2* at the pop-up list.
   e. Save the table.
3. Switch to Datasheet view.
4. Add the following data in a new record to test the custom format and the predefined format. Notice when you move past the Rate field, the value is displayed in blue.

WO	**65012**
CustID	**1000**
TechID	**11**
WODate	**09-07-2012**
Descr	**Bi-annual desktop computer cleaning and maintenance**
ServDate	**09-07-2012**
Hours	**1.25**
Rate	**30**
Parts	**10.15**
Comments	**"H" key is sticking; cleaning did not resolve. Customer is considering buying a new keyboard.**

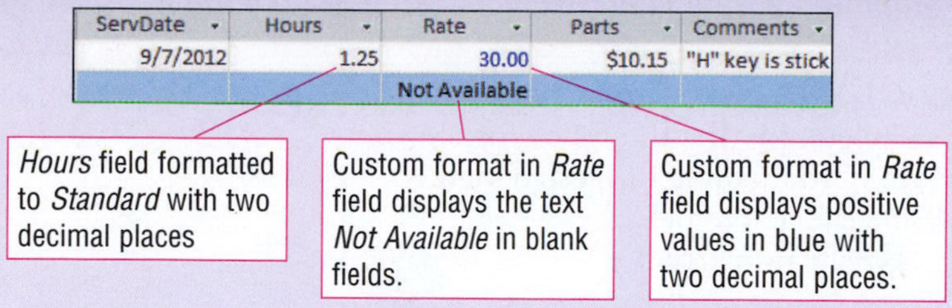
ServDate
Hours
Rate
Parts
Comments
9/7/2012
1.25
30.00
$10.15
"H" key is stick
Not Available
Hours field formatted to *Standard* with two decimal places
Custom format in *Rate* field displays the text *Not Available* in blank fields.
Custom format in *Rate* field displays positive values in blue with two decimal places.

5. Close the WorkOrders table.

Creating a Custom Format for a Date/Time Field

Access provides predefined formats for fields with a data type of Date/Time that provide for a variety of combinations of month, day, and year display options for dates, and hours and minutes display options for time. If the predefined formats do not meet your needs, you can create your own custom format using a combination of the codes described in Table 1.4 along with the desired symbols such as hyphens or slashes between parts of the date. If you do not specify a format option for a Date/Time field, Access displays the date in the format m/d/yyyy. For example, in Project 1d, the date entered into the *WODate* field displayed as 9/7/2012.

A custom format for a Date/Time field can contain two sections separated by a semicolon. The first section specifies the format for displaying dates. To add a format for displaying times, type a semicolon and then add the format codes to specify the time.

Quick Steps

Format Date Field/ Time Field

1. Open table in Design view.
2. Activate desired field.
3. Click in *Format* property box.
4. Type desired format codes or select from predefined list.
5. Save table.

Table 1.4 Format Codes for Date/Time Fields

Code	*Description*
d or dd	Displays the day of the month as one digit (d) or two digits (dd).
ddd or dddd	Spells out the day of the week abbreviated (ddd) or in full (dddd).
m or mm	Displays the month as one digit (m) or two digits (mm).
mmm or mmmm	Spells out the month abbreviated (mmm) or in full (mmmm).
yy or yyyy	Displays the year as the last two digits (yy) or all four digits (yyyy).
h or hh	Displays the hour as one digit (h) or two digits (hh).
n or nn	Displays the minutes as one digit (n) or two digits (nn).
s or ss	Displays the seconds as one digit (s) or two digits (ss).
AM/PM	Displays 12-hour clock values followed by AM or PM.

Project 1e Formatting a Date Field Using a Custom Date Format

1. With the **AL2-C1-RSRCompServ.accdb** database open, format the *WODate* field with a custom format by completing the following steps:
   a. Open the WorkOrders table in Design view.
   b. Make *WODate* the active field.
   c. Click in the *Format* property box and then type **ddd mmm dd yyyy**. This format will display dates beginning with the day of the week in abbreviated form, followed by the month in abbreviated form, the day of the month as two digits, and then the year as four digits. A space separates each section of the date.
   d. Save the table.

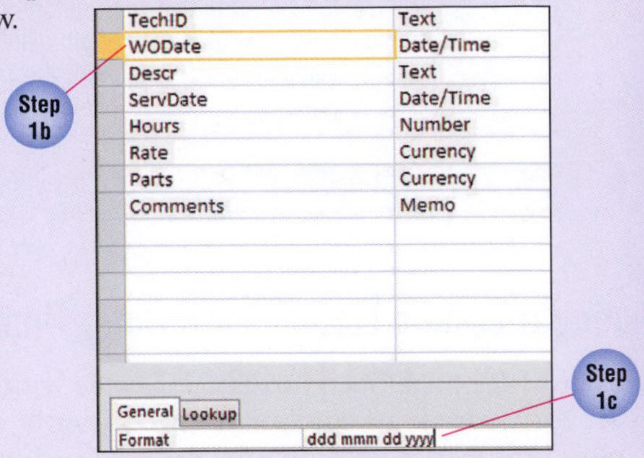

2. Switch to Datasheet view.
3. If necessary, adjust the column width of the *WODate* field to read the entire entry.

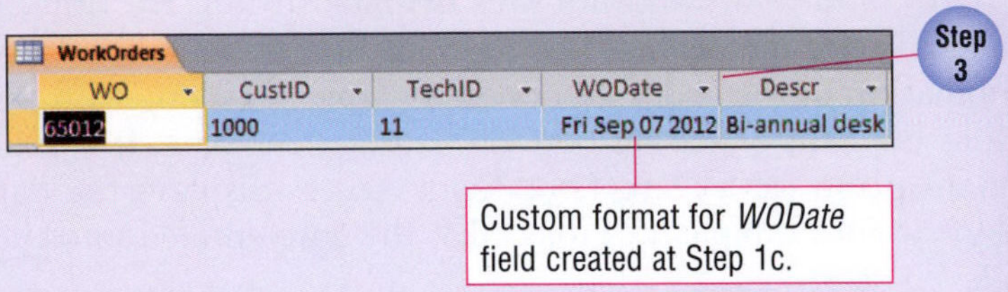

4. Switch to Design view.
5. Format the *ServDate* field using the same custom format as the one entered for *WODate* by completing steps similar to those in Steps 1b through 1c.
6. Save the table and then switch to Datasheet view.
7. Double-click the right column boundary of the *ServDate* field and view the custom date format.

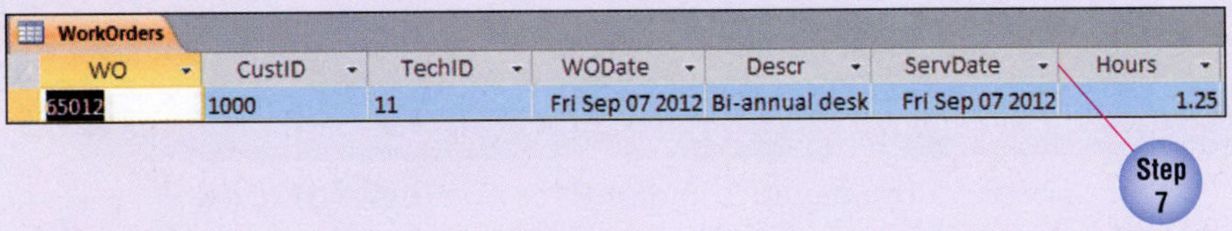

WorkOrders
WO CustID TechID WODate Descr ServDate Hours
65012 1000 11 Fri Sep 07 2012 Bi-annual desk Fri Sep 07 2012 1.25
Step 7

8. Close the WorkOrders table. Click Yes when prompted to save changes to the table layout.

Restricting Data Entry Using Input Masks

Quick Steps

Create Custom Input Mask
1. Open table in Design view.
2. Activate desired field.
3. Click in *Input Mask* property box.
4. Type input mask codes.
5. Save table.

An ***input mask*** is used when you want to control the type of data and the pattern in which the data is entered into a field. Using input masks ensures data is entered consistently in all records. For example, to force all telephone numbers to have the area code entered, you can create an input mask that requires ten numbers. As you learned in Level 1, Chapter 4, Access includes the Input Mask Wizard that can be used to create an input mask for a text or date field. Commonly used masks are predefined within the wizard for telephone numbers, social security numbers, ZIP codes, dates, and times. To create your own input mask without the wizard, use the codes described in Table 1.5.

Table 1.5 Commonly Used Input Mask Codes

Code	*Description*
0	Required digit.
9	Optional digit.
#	Digit, space, plus or minus symbol. If no data is typed at this position, Access leaves a blank space.
L	Required letter.
?	Optional letter.
A	Required letter or digit.
a	Optional letter or digit.
&	Required character or space.
C	Optional character or space.
!	The field is filled from left to right instead of right to left.
\	Access displays the character that immediately follows in the field.

An input mask can contain up to three sections separated by semicolons. The first section contains the input mask codes for the data entry in the field. The second section instructs Access to store the display characters used in the field (such as hyphens or brackets) or not store the characters. A zero indicates that Access should store the characters. Leaving the second section blank means the display characters will not be stored. The third section specifies the placeholder character to display in the field when the field becomes active for data entry.

An example of an input mask to store a four-digit customer identification number with a pound symbol (#) as the placeholder would be: 0000;;#. The first section *0000* is the four required digits for the customer identification. Since the mask contains no display characters (such as a hyphen), the second section is blank. The pound symbol after the second semicolon is the placeholder character.

In addition to the symbols in Table 1.5, you can include the format code > to force characters to be uppercase or < to force characters to be lowercase, as well as decimal points, hyphens, slashes, or other punctuation symbols between parts of the mask.

HINT

If you create a custom input mask for a date field that also contains a custom format, make sure the two properties do not conflict to avoid confusion. For example, a format code that displays dates with the year first followed by the month and then the day would be confusing if the input mask required the date to be entered as month first followed by day and then year.

Project 1f Creating Custom Input Masks

Part 6 of 6

1. With the **AL2-C1-RSRCompServ.accdb** database open, create a custom input mask for the work order numbers by completing the following steps:
   a. Open the WorkOrders table in Design view.
   b. With *WO* the active field, click in the *Input Mask* property box and then type **00000;;_**. This mask will require that a five-digit work order number is entered. The underscore character is used as the placeholder character that displays when the field becomes active.

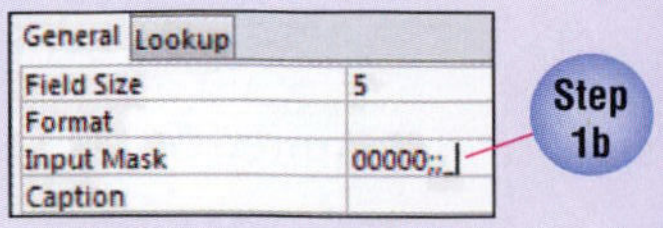

   c. Save the table.
2. Create an input mask to require the two date fields to be entered as three characters for the month with the first letter uppercase followed by two digits for the day and four digits for the year by completing the following steps:
   a. Make *WODate* the active field.

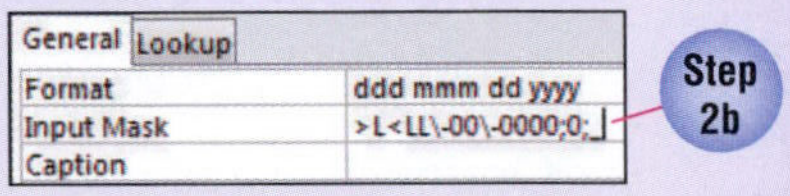

   b. Click in the *Input Mask* property box and then type **>L<LL\-00\-0000;0;_**. This mask requires three letters for the month with the first letter converted to uppercase and the remaining two letters converted to lowercase. The \- symbols instruct Access to display the hyphen character after the month as data is entered. Two digits are required for the day followed by another hyphen character and then four digits required for the year. The zero after the first semicolon instructs Access to store the display characters. Ending the mask, the underscore character is again used as the placeholder character.
   c. Make *ServDate* the active field, click in the *Input Mask* property box, and then type **>L<LL\-00\-0000;0;_**.
   d. Save the table.
3. Switch to Datasheet view.
4. Test the input masks using a new record by completing the following steps:
   a. Click the New button in the Records group of the Home tab.
   b. Type **6501**. Notice that as soon as you type the first character, the placeholders appear in the field.
   c. Press Tab or Enter to move to the next field in the datasheet. Since the mask contained five zeros indicating five required digits, Access displays a message box informing you the value entered is not appropriate for the input mask.
   d. Click OK at the Microsoft Access message box.

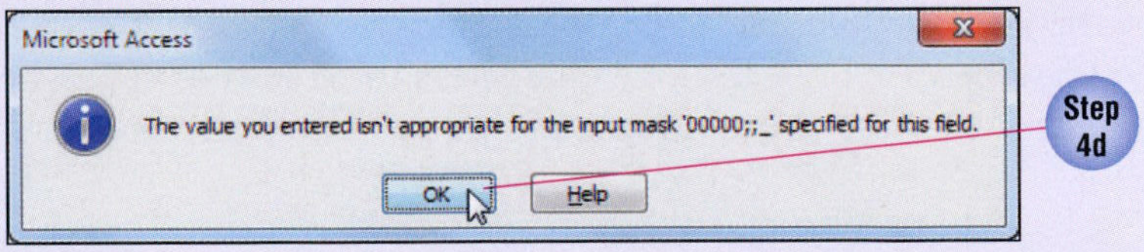

   e. Type **3** in the last position in the *WO* field and then press Tab or Enter to move to the next field.
   f. Type **1000** in the *CustID* field and then press Tab or Enter.
   g. Type **10** in the *TechID* field and then press Tab or Enter.
   h. Type **sep072012** in the *WODate* field and then press Tab or Enter. Notice that the placeholder characters and the hyphens appear as soon as you type the first letter. Notice also that the first character is converted to uppercase and you do not need to type the hyphen characters since Access moves automatically to the next position after the month and the day are typed.
   i. Type **Replace keyboard** in the *Descr* field and then press Tab or Enter.

j. Type **sep102012** in the *ServDate* field and then press Tab or Enter.

k. Complete the remainder of the record as follows.

Hours	**.5**
Rate	**28.50**
Parts	**22.75**
Comments	**Serial Number AWQ-982358**

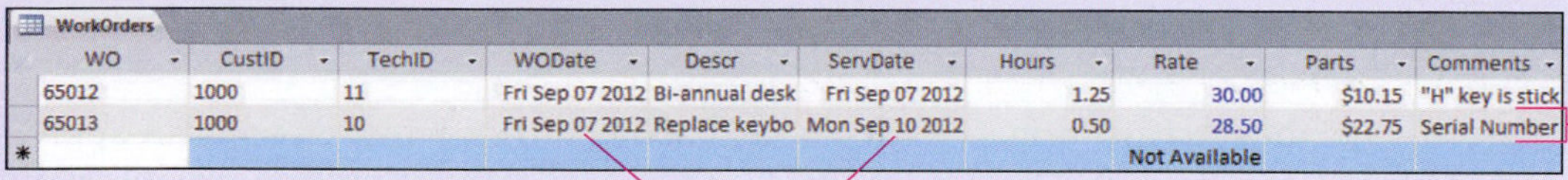

WorkOrders
WO | CustID | TechID | WODate | Descr | ServDate | Hours | Rate | Parts | Comments
65012 | 1000 | 11 | Fri Sep 07 2012 | Bi-annual desk | Fri Sep 07 2012 | 1.25 | 30.00 | $10.15 | "H" key is stick
65013 | 1000 | 10 | Fri Sep 07 2012 | Replace keybo | Mon Sep 10 2012 | 0.50 | 28.50 | $22.75 | Serial Number
Not Available

Steps 4e-4k

Notice that once the date is accepted into the field, the custom Format property controls how the date is presented in the datasheet with the abbreviated day of the week at the beginning of the field and spaces between month, day, and year instead of hyphens.

5. Display the datasheet in Print Preview. Change the orientation to landscape. Set the margins to a top margin of 1-inch and the bottom, left, and right margins of 0.25 inch. Print the datasheet and then close Print Preview.
6. Close the WorkOrders table.

Other field properties that should be considered for data accuracy when designing database tables include the Default Value, Validation Rule, and Validation Text properties. Use the Default Value property to populate the field in new records with a field value that is used most often. For example, in a table where most employees have an address within the same city and state, you could use a default value to ensure consistent spelling and capitalization. The text appears automatically in the fields when new records are added to the table. The user can choose to either accept the default value by pressing Tab or Enter to move past the field, or type new data in the field. In Level 1 you learned how to create a default value using the Default Value button in the Properties group of the Table Tools Fields tab. In Design view, the Default Value property is located below the Caption property.

Use the Validation Rule and Validation Text properties to enter conditional statements that are checked against new data entered into the field. Invalid entries that do not meet the conditional statement test are rejected. For example, a validation rule on a field used to store labor rates could check that a minimum labor rate value is entered in all records. In Level 1 you learned to add a validation rule using the Validation button in the Field Validation group of the Table Tools Fields tab. In Design view, the Validation Rule and Validation Text properties are located just above the Required property.

Project 2 Work with Memo and Attachment Fields

2 Parts

You will edit properties for a Memo field, apply rich text formatting to text, and attach files to records using an Attachment field.

Quick Steps

Enable Rich Text Formatting in Memo Field

1. Open table in Design view.
2. Select desired field defined as Memo.
3. Click in *Text Format* property box.
4. Click down-pointing arrow that appears.
5. Click *Rich Text*.
6. Click Yes.
7. Save table.

Track Changes in a Memo Field

1. Open table in Design view.
2. Select desired field defined as Memo.
3. If necessary, scroll down General tab.
4. Click in *Append Only* property box.
5. Click down-pointing arrow that appears.
6. Click Yes.
7. Save table.

Working with Memo Fields

By default, Access formats a Memo field as plain text; however, you can apply formatting attributes to text by enabling rich text formatting. For example, you can change the font, apply bold or italic formatting, or add font color to text in a Memo field. To add rich text formatting capability, change the Text Format property to *Rich Text*.

The Append Only property for a Memo field is set to *No* by default. Change the property to *Yes* to track changes made to the field value in the datasheet. You may need to scroll down the General tab in the *Field Properties* section to locate the Append Only property. When this property is set to *Yes*, Access maintains a history of additions to the field which can be viewed in the datasheet. Changing the Append Only property to *No* causes Access to delete any existing history.

Project 2a Enabling Rich Text Formatting and Maintaining a History of Changes in a Memo Field

Part 1 of 2

1. With the **AL2-C1-RSRCompServ.accdb** database open, enable rich text formatting and turn on tracking of history in a field defined as a Memo field by completing the following steps:
   a. Open the WorkOrders table in Design view.
   b. Make *Comments* the active field.
   c. Click in the *Text Format* property box (currently reads *Plain Text*), click the down-pointing arrow that appears, and then click *Rich Text* at the drop-down list.

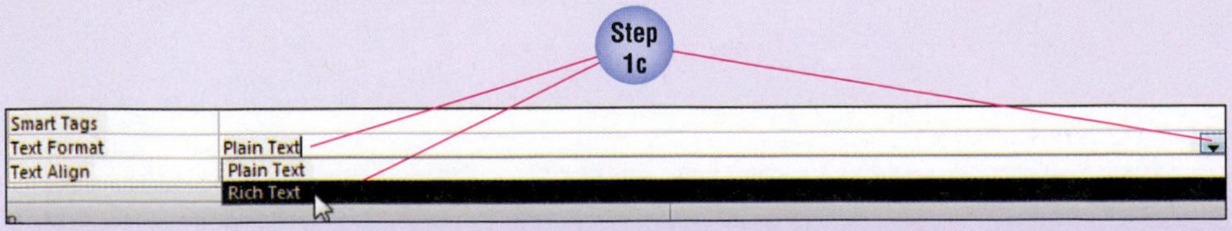

d. At the Microsoft Access message box indicating that the field will be converted to Rich Text, click Yes.

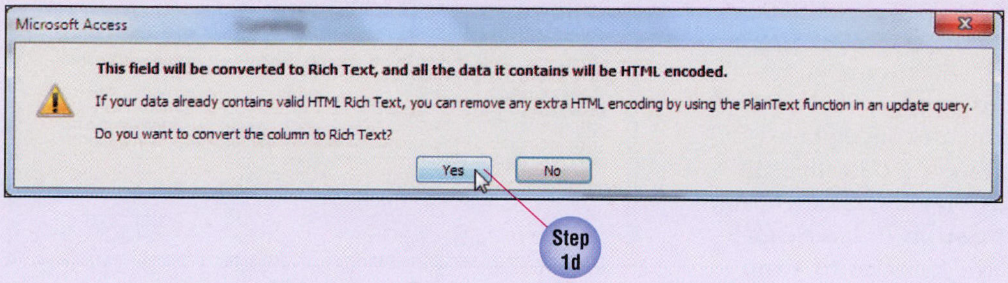

e. If necessary, scroll down the General tab in the *Field Properties* section until you can see the *Append Only* property box.

f. Click in the *Append Only* property box, click the down-pointing arrow that appears, and then click *Yes* at the drop-down list.

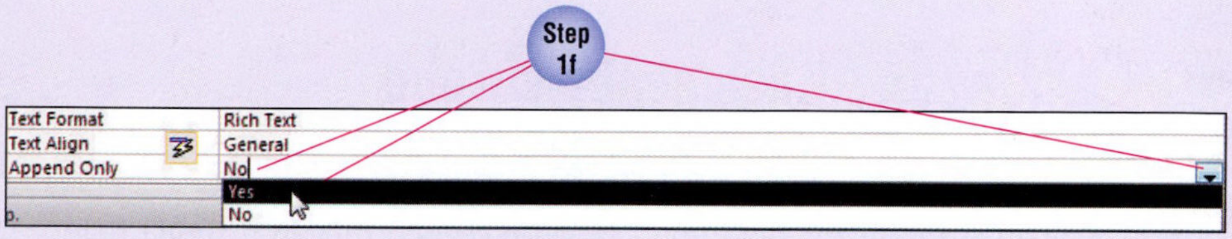

g. Save the table.

2. Switch to Datasheet view.
3. Minimize the Navigation pane and then adjust all column widths *except* the *Descr* and *Comments* fields to Best Fit.
4. Change the column width of the *Comments* field to 25.
5. Select the serial number text (AWQ-982358) in the second record in the *Comments* field and then apply bold and red font color using the buttons in the Text Formatting group of the Home tab. Click at the end of the serial number to deselect the text.

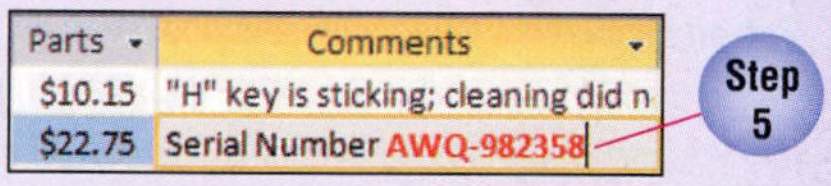

Parts
Comments
$10.15
"H" key is sticking; cleaning did n
$22.75
Serial Number AWQ-982358
Step 5

6. Click in the *Comments* field in the first record. Press the End key to move the insertion point to the end of the existing text. Press the spacebar once, type **Microsoft wireless keyboard was recommended.**, and then press Enter to save the changes and move to the next row.
7. Right-click the *Comments* field in the first record and then click *Show column history* at the shortcut menu.
8. Click OK after reading the text in the History for Comments dialog box.
9. Click in the *Comments* field in the first record. Press the End key to move the insertion point to the end of the current text. Press the spacebar once, type **See work order 65013 for replacement keyboard request.**, and then press Enter.

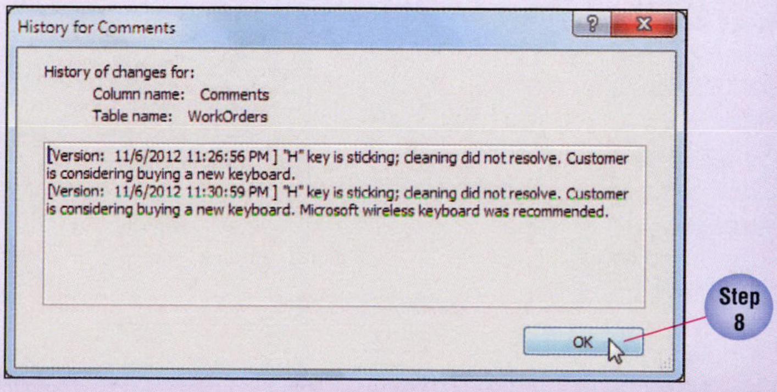

10. Right-click the *Comments* field in the first record and then click *Show column history* at the shortcut menu.
11. Click OK after reading the text in the History for Comments dialog box.
12. Display the datasheet in Print Preview. Change the orientation to landscape. Set the margins to a top margin of 1-inch and bottom, left, and right margins of 0.25-inch. Print the datasheet and then close Print Preview.
13. Close the WorkOrders table. Click Yes when prompted to save changes to the layout of the table and then redisplay the Navigation pane.

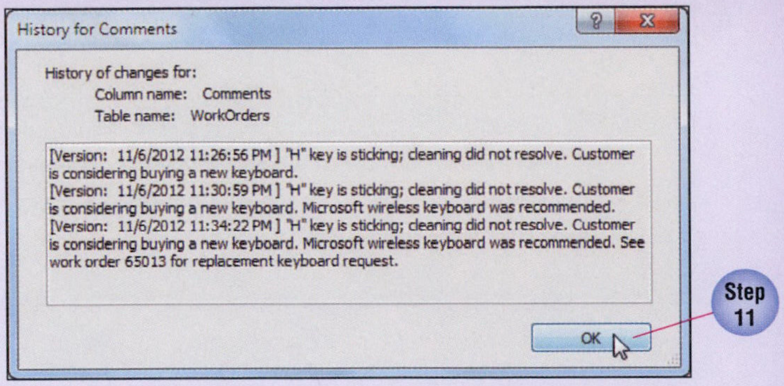
History for Comments
History of changes for:
Column name: Comments
Table name: WorkOrders
[Version: 11/6/2012 11:26:56 PM] "H" key is sticking; cleaning did not resolve. Customer is considering buying a new keyboard.
[Version: 11/6/2012 11:30:59 PM] "H" key is sticking; cleaning did not resolve. Customer is considering buying a new keyboard. Microsoft wireless keyboard was recommended.
[Version: 11/6/2012 11:34:22 PM] "H" key is sticking; cleaning did not resolve. Customer is considering buying a new keyboard. Microsoft wireless keyboard was recommended. See work order 65013 for replacement keyboard request.
OK
Step 11

Quick Steps

Create Attachment Field
1. Open table in Design view.
2. Click in first blank field row.
3. Type desired field name.
4. Click in *Data Type* column.
5. Click down-pointing arrow.
6. Click *Attachment.*
7. Save table.

Attach Files to Record
1. Open table in Datasheet view.
2. Double-click paper clip in desired record.
3. Click Add button.
4. Navigate to drive and/or folder location.
5. Double-click file name.
6. Click OK.

View Attached File
1. Open table in Datasheet view.
2. Double-click paper clip in desired record.
3. Double-click file name.
4. View file contents.
5. Exit source program.
6. Click OK.

Creating an Attachment Field and Attaching Files to Records

Using an Attachment field you can store several files in a single field attached to a record. The attachments can be opened within Access and are viewed and edited in the program from which the document originated. For example, you can attach a Word document to a field in a record. Opening the attached file in the Access table causes Microsoft Word to start with the document opened for editing. A file that is attached to a record cannot be larger than 256 megabytes.

An Attachment field displays with a paper clip in Datasheet view. Double-click the paper clip to open the Attachments dialog box shown in Figure 1.4 in which you manage attached files. A field that is created with a data type set to Attachment cannot be changed. You can attach multiple files to a record provided the total size of all files attached does not exceed two gigabytes.

Any file created within the Microsoft Office suite can be attached to a record as well as image files (.bmp, .jpg, .gif, .png), log files (.log), text files (.txt), and compressed files (.zip). Some files, such as files ending with .com and .exe are considered potential security risks and are blocked by Access.

Figure 1.4 Attachments Dialog Box

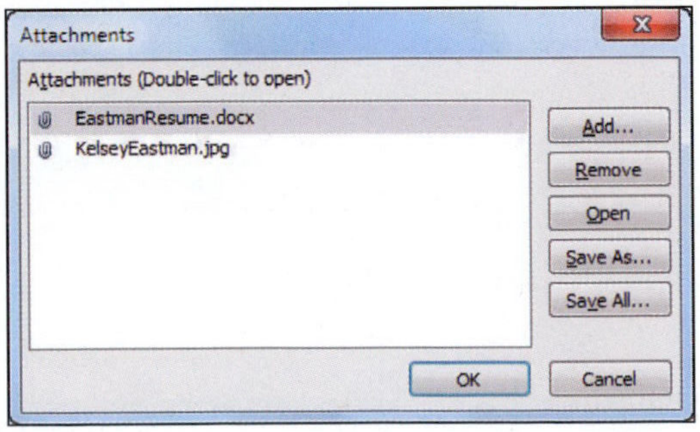
Attachments
Attachments (Double-click to open)
EastmanResume.docx
KelseyEastman.jpg
Add...
Remove
Open
Save As...
Save All...
OK
Cancel

Project 2b — Creating an Attachment Field, Attaching Files to a Record, and Viewing the Contents of Attached Files

Part 2 of 2

1. With the **AL2-C1-RSRCompServ.accdb** database open, create a new field in which you will store file attachments by completing the following steps:
   a. Open the Technicians table in Design view.
   b. Click in the blank row below *CPhone*, type **Attachments**, and then press Tab or Enter.
   c. Click the down-pointing arrow in the *Data Type* column and then click *Attachment* at the drop-down list.
   d. Save the table.

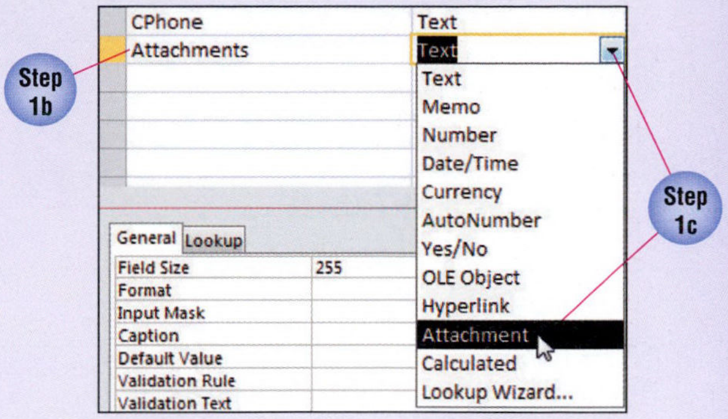

2. Switch to Datasheet view.
3. Add the following data in the first row of the datasheet.

TechID	**10**
SSN	**000-43-5789**
Fname	**Kelsey**
Lname	**Eastman**
StreetAdd	**550 Montclair Street**
City	**Detroit**
State	**MI**
ZIP	**48214-3274**
HPhone	**313-555-6315**
CPhone	"" (Recall that double quotation marks indicate a zero-length field.)

4. Attach two files to the record for Kelsey Eastman by completing the following steps:
   a. Double-click the paper clip in the first row of the datasheet. Attachment fields display a paper clip in each record in a column with a paper clip in the field name row. The number in brackets next to the paper clip indicates the number of files attached to the record.

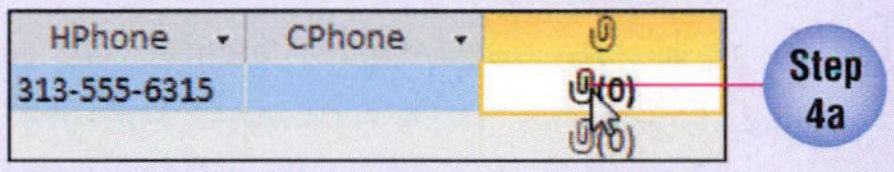

   b. At the Attachments dialog box, click the Add button.

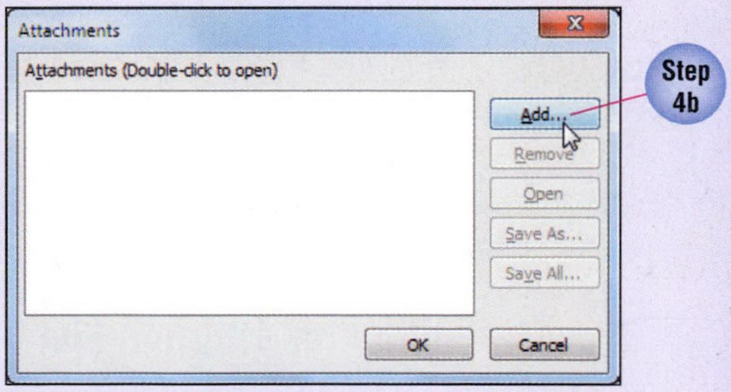

   c. At the Choose File dialog box, navigate to the Access2010L2C1 folder on your storage medium.
   d. Click the file named ***EastmanResume.docx***.
   e. Hold down the Ctrl key and click the file named ***KelseyEastman.jpg***.
   f. Click the Open button.
   g. Click OK. Access closes the Attachments dialog box and displays *(2)* next to the paper clip in the first record.

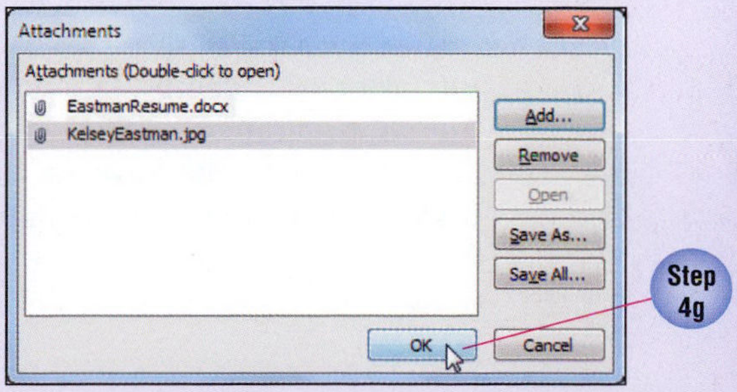

5. Open the attached files by completing the following steps:
   a. Double-click the paper clip in the first row of the datasheet to open the Attachments dialog box.
   b. Double-click ***EastmanResume.docx*** in the *Attachments* list box to open the Word document.

c. Read the resume in Microsoft Word and then exit Word.

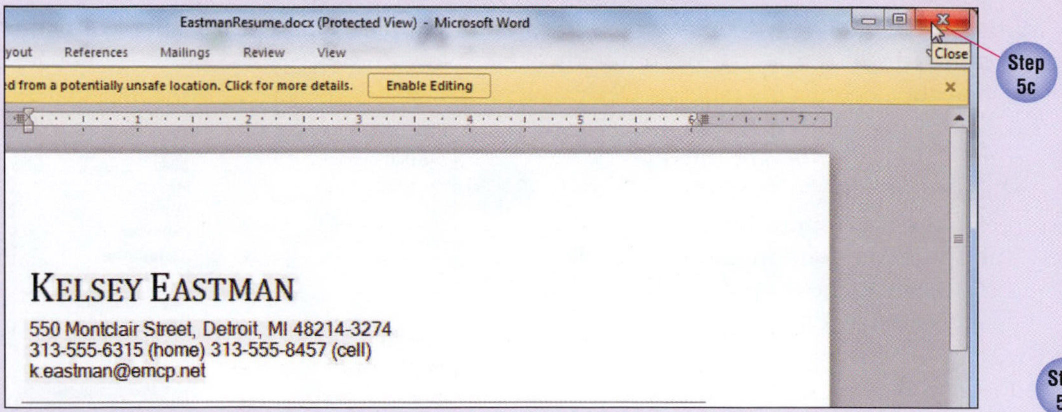

d. Double-click ***KelseyEastman.jpg*** in the *Attachments* list box to open the picture file.

e. View the picture and then exit the photo viewer program.

f. Click OK to close the Attachments dialog box.

6. Adjust all column widths to Best Fit.
7. Display the datasheet in Print Preview. Change the orientation to landscape, print the datasheet, and then close Print Preview.
8. Close the Technicians table. Click Yes when prompted to save changes to the table layout.
9. Close the **AL2-C1-RSRCompServ.accdb** database.

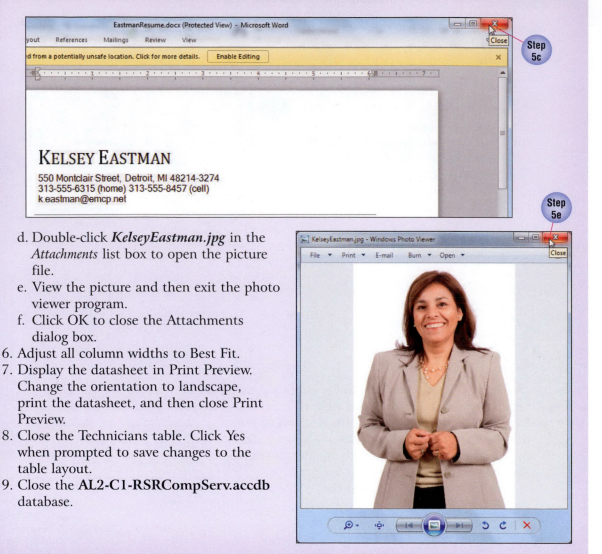

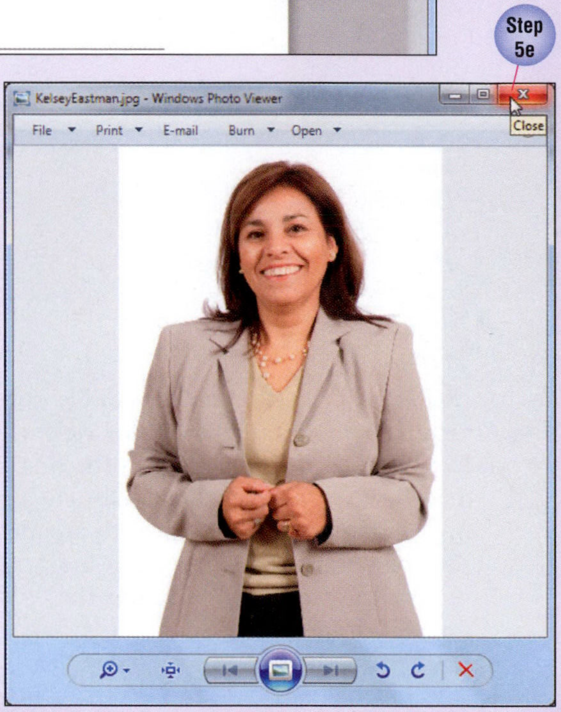

Editing an Attached File

If you open a file attachment and make changes to the file, click the Save button in the source program to save changes. The changes are saved to a temporary folder on your computer's hard drive. To save the changes permanently, exit the Source program and then click OK at the Attachments dialog box in Access. Access displays the Save Attachment dialog box shown in Figure 1.5. Click Yes to update the changes in the database.

Figure 1.5 Save Attachment Dialog Box

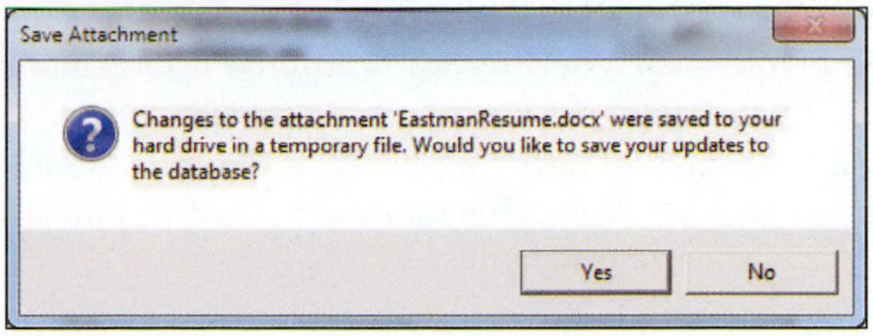

Saving an Attached File to Another Location

You can export a file that is attached to a record to make a copy of the document in another storage location by selecting the file and then clicking the Save As button in the Attachments dialog box. At the Save Attachment dialog box, navigate to the drive and/or folder in which you want to save the duplicate copy of the file, click the Save button, and then click OK to close the Attachments dialog box.

Removing an Attached File

If you no longer need to store a file attached to a record in the database, open the Attachments dialog box in the record containing the file attachment, click the file name for the file you want to delete, click the Remove button, and then click OK to close the Attachments dialog box.

Chapter Summary

- Database designers plan the tables needed for a new database by analyzing sample data, input documents, and output requirements to generate the entire set of data elements needed.
- Once all data has been identified, the designer maps out the number of tables required.
- Each table holds data for a single topic only with data split out into the smallest unit that will be manipulated.
- Designers also consider relationships that will be needed in case a field needs to be added to a table in order to join the tables.
- Data redundancy should be avoided, which means a field should not be repeated in another table except for those fields needed to join tables in a relationship.
- A diagram of a database portrays the database tables with field names, data types, field sizes, and notation of the primary key.
- Fields are assigned a data type by selecting a data type appropriate for the kind of data that will be accepted into the field.
- Changing the field size property can be used to restrict entries in the field to a maximum length as one way to prevent longer entries that might be added to the field by accident.

- Change the Required property to *Yes* to force an entry into the field when a new record is added to the table.
- Leaving a field blank when a new record is entered results in a null value stored in the field.
- A zero-length field is entered into a record by typing two double quotation symbols with no space between. This method is used to indicate a field value does not apply to the current record.
- You can disallow zero-length strings by changing the Allow Zero Length property to *No*.
- The Format property controls the display of data accepted into a field. A custom format can be created by typing the appropriate format codes in the *Format* property box.
- A custom numeric format can contain four sections; one section for positive values, one section for negative values, one section for zero values, and the last section for null values.
- Use an input mask to control the type and pattern of data entered into the field.
- Create a custom input mask for a Text or Date/Time field by typing the appropriate input mask codes in the *Input Mask* property box.
- A Memo field can be formatted using rich text formatting options in the Text Formatting group of the Home tab by changing the Text Format property to Rich Text.
- Change the Append Only property of a Memo field to *Yes* to track changes made to field values.
- A field with the data type set to *Attachment* can be used to store files associated with a record.
- Double-click the paper clip in the Attachment field for a record to add, view, save, or remove a file attachment.

Commands Review

FEATURE	RIBBON TAB, GROUP	BUTTON	KEYBOARD SHORTCUT
Create table in Design view	Create, Tables		
Minimize Navigation pane		«	F11
Redisplay Navigation pane		»	F11
Switch to Datasheet view from Design view	Table Tools Design, Views		
Switch to Design view from Datasheet view	Home, Views		

Concepts Check Test Your Knowledge

Completion: In the space provided at the right, indicate the correct term, command, or number.

1. Use this data type for a field that will hold numeric data that is not a monetary value. ____________
2. Use this data type to store alphanumeric text longer than 255 characters. ____________
3. This data type is restricted to a field value used to test conditional logic that can be one of only two conditions. ____________
4. The available properties that display for a field in the *Field Properties* section in Design view are dependent on this option. ____________
5. This property is used to display a more descriptive title for the field in the datasheet. ____________
6. To ensure a field is never left empty, set this property to *Yes*. ____________
7. Typing two double quotation symbols with no space between assigns this field value. ____________
8. This is the format code to convert all text in the field to uppercase. ____________
9. This placeholder in a custom numeric format instructs Access to display a zero if the position is not used. ____________
10. Type this entry in the *Format* property box of a Date/Time field to display dates beginning with the day of the week abbreviated, followed by the month as two digits, the day of the month as two digits, and the year as two digits with all sections separated with a hyphen character. ____________
11. Type this entry in the *Input Mask* property box to require a three-digit identification number to be entered with the pound symbol (#) used as the placeholder. ____________
12. Rich text formatting is enabled for a Memo field by changing this property option to *Rich Text*. ____________
13. For a Memo field with the Append Only property active, right-click in a record and click this option at the shortcut menu to display a dialog box with the history of the text changes made to the field. ____________
14. Create a field with this data type to store a file with the record. ____________
15. Add a file to the record by double-clicking this object in the record in Datasheet view. ____________

Skills Check Assess Your Performance

Assessment 1

CREATE A NEW DATABASE

1. Create a new blank database named **AL2-C1-BenchmarkGolf.accdb**.
2. Create the tables shown in Figure 1.6 to store membership records for the Benchmark Golf and Country Club including setting the primary key and assigning data types and field sizes.
3. Close any tables that have been left open.

Figure 1.6 Assessment 1

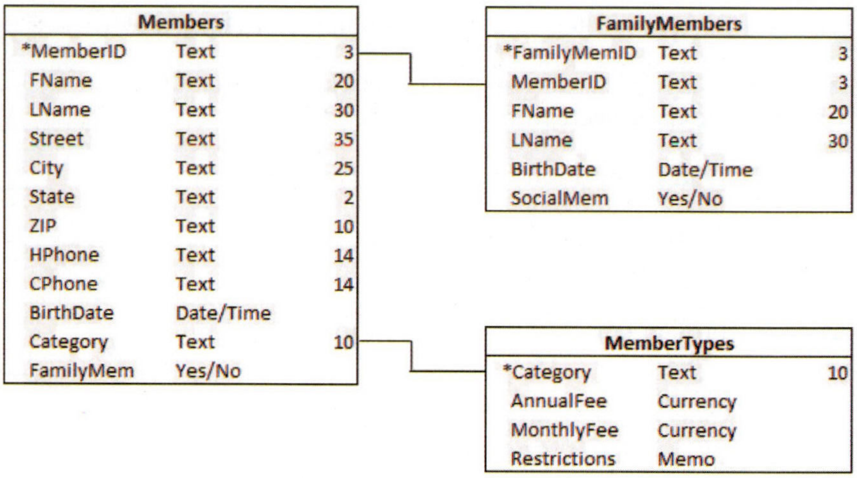

Assessment 2

ADD CAPTIONS AND DISALLOW BLANK VALUES

1. With the **AL2-C1-BenchmarkGolf.accdb** database open, create captions for the fields as follows:

Members Table

Field Name	**Caption**
MemberID	ID Number
FName	First Name
LName	Last Name
Street	Street Address
ZIP	ZIP Code
HPhone	Home Phone
CPhone	Cell Phone
BirthDate	Birth Date
FamilyMem	Family Member?

FamilyMembers Table

Field Name	Caption
FamilyMemID	Family ID Number
MemberID	Member ID Number
FName	First Name
LName	Last Name
BirthDate	Birth Date
SocialMem	Social Member?

MemberTypes Table

Field Name	Caption
AnnualFee	Annual Fee
MonthlyFee	Monthly Fee

2. Make the *ZIP* field a required field and disallow zero-length strings.
3. Save and then close all tables.

Assessment 3

CREATE CUSTOM FORMATS AND INPUT MASKS

1. With the **AL2-C1-BenchmarkGolf.accdb** database open, create the following custom formats:
   a. Display the state text in uppercase characters.
   b. Display all birth dates with the month spelled out in abbreviated form followed by the day of the month as two digits and the year as four digits with one space separating each section.
   c. Display the monthly fee in blue with two decimal values that will show zeros if no value is entered.
2. Create the following custom input masks:
   a. In the *MemberID* field in the Members table and the *FamilyMemID* field in the FamilyMembers table, require all three digits and display the underscore character as the placeholder.
   b. Require the *ZIP* field in the Members table to be entered in the pattern five required digits followed by a hyphen and then four required digits. Display the pound symbol (#) as the placeholder.
   c. Use the input mask wizard to create the standard input mask for the two telephone fields in the Members table. When the mask is finished, edit the codes in the property to make the three characters in the area code required digits as opposed to the optional digits that the wizard created.
   d. Create an input mask for both birth date fields that will match the custom format pattern created in Step 1b except include hyphens between each section. Store the display characters in the field and display the underscore character as the placeholder. For example, the custom format should display the date as *May 03 1964* in the datasheet. ***Hints: You do not need to worry about the first letter of the month being uppercase since the Format property will automatically use proper capitalization. Once you have the input mask created correctly, you can copy and paste the entry to the other birth date field.***
3. Save and then close all tables.

Assessment

4 ADD RECORDS

1. With the **AL2-C1-BenchmarkGolf.accdb** database open, add the following records. Type the text in the *State* field as shown to test your format code. Type ZIP codes, telephone numbers, and dates, being careful to watch the placeholders and enter in the required pattern.

Members Table

Field	**Record 1**	**Record 2**
ID Number	100	110
First Name	Hilary	Jesse
Last Name	Sampson	Reynolds
Street Address	300 South Saguaro Drive	7229 E University Drive
City	Apache Junction	Mesa
State	Az	Az
ZIP Code	85220 4956	85207 6501
Home Phone	602 555 1587	480 555 1385
Cell Phone	602 555 3496	480 555 1699
Birth Date	May 03 1964	Oct 15 1977
Category	Gold	Silver
Family Member?	Yes	No

FamilyMembers Table

Field	**Record 1**	**Record 2**
Family ID Number	610	611
Member ID Number	100	100
First Name	Kayla	Roy
Last Name	Sampson	Sampson
Birth Date	Jul 18 1992	Mar 16 1994
Social Member?	No	No

MemberTypes Table

Field	**Record 1**	**Record 2**	**Record 3**
Category	Gold	Silver	Bronze
Annual Fee	2500	1775	1550
Monthly Fee	60	52	35
Restrictions	Unlimited weekdays and weekends; weekend ballot first	Unlimited weekdays; weekend ballot second	Unlimited weekdays; weekends after 3 P.M.

2. Adjust all column widths to Best Fit and print each table in landscape orientation.
3. Close any tables that have been left open saving layout changes.
4. Close the **AL2-C1-BenchmarkGolf.accdb** database.

Visual Benchmark Demonstrate Your Proficiency

CREATE A NEW DATABASE

1. Create a new blank database named **AL2-C1-PawsParadise.accdb**.
2. Create the tables shown in the database diagram in Figure 1.7 for Paws Paradise Boarding Inc. to store the records of dog owners, dogs, and kennel categories including setting the primary key and assigning data types and field sizes.
3. Analyze the datasheets shown in Figure 1.8 and make the necessary changes to field properties. The datasheets show captions, default values, custom formats, and rich text formatting in the records. Use the following information to set other field properties not visible in the datasheet:
   a. Make *ZIP* a required field and then use the input mask wizard to create the default input mask for a zip code.
   b. Use the input mask wizard to create the default input mask for both telephone fields and then edit the masks to change the area code to three required digits.
4. Add the records shown in the datasheets to the tables.
5. Adjust all column widths to Best Fit and print each table in landscape orientation.
6. Save and then close all tables.
7. Close the **AL2-C1-PawsParadise.accdb** database.

Figure 1.7 Visual Benchmark Database Diagram

DogOwners		
*CustNum	Text	3
FName	Text	20
LName	Text	30
Street	Text	35
City	Text	25
State	Text	2
ZIP	Text	10
HPhone	Text	14
EPhone	Text	14
MultipleDogs	Yes/No	

Dogs		
*DogID	AutoNumber	
CustNum	Text	3
DogName	Text	20
Breed	Text	50
Color	Text	20
Bordetella	Yes/No	
Rabies	Yes/No	
Play	Yes/No	
KennelCat	Text	7

KennelCategories		
*KennelCat	Text	7
Type	Text	25
Descr	Memo	
DailyRate	Currency	

Figure 1.8 Visual Benchmark Datasheets

DogOwners

Customer Number	First Name	Last Name	Street Address	City	State	ZIP Code	Home Telephone	Emergency Telephone	Multiple Dogs?
100	Shawn	Jenkins	101 Davis Street	Bradford	PA	16701-	(814) 555-8446	(814) 555-7469	☑
110	Valerie	McTague	12 Bishop Street	Bradford	PA	16701-	(814) 555-3456	(814) 555-1495	☐
115	Glen	Waters	35 Vista Avenue	Bradford	PA	16701-2760	(814) 555-7496	(814) 555-6124	☐

Dogs

	Dog ID	Customer Number	Dog's Name	Breed	Color	Bordetella Vaccine Checked?	Rabies Vaccine Checked?	Play with other dogs?	Kennel Category
	1	100	Abby	Labrador Retriever	Black	☑	☑	☑	VIP
	2	100	Winnie	Cocker Spaniel	Buff	☑	☑	☑	VIP
	3	110	Chloe	Poodle	White	☑	☑	☐	Deluxe
	4	115	Barney	Pug	Black	☐	☐	☐	InOut
*	(New)					☑	☑	☑	

KennelCategories

Kennel Category	Kennel Type	Description	Daily Rate
DayCare	Day Care Boarding	Grassy play area where dogs can play with staff and other dogs throughout the day.	$16.50
Deluxe	Deluxe Suite	Designed for ***geriatric or special needs dogs***. Raised beds and quiet location.	$29.50
InOut	Indoor/Outdoor Suite	Indoor kennel attached to covered outdoor patio.	$25.50
VIP	V.I.P. Suite	***Indoor upgraded kennel*** attached to covered outdoor patio and grass play area.	$38.50

Case Study Apply Your Skills

Part 1

You started an internship today at Bestar Plumbing Service. Examine the customer invoice shown in Figure 1.9. This is a typical invoice for which the owner would like to start using an Access database. Design tables for the data using the invoice and the following additional information from the owner:

- Customer numbers are assigned using the first three letters of the customer's last name all uppercase and are followed by three digits after a hyphen character.
- Some invoices include parts with a labor charge. Individual parts are not itemized on the customer invoice. The service technician shows a single line on the invoice for all parts used.
- Bestar has two labor rates: $41.75 for a senior service technician and $28.00 for an apprentice technician.

Using Microsoft Word, create a document that diagrams the tables including table names, field names, data types, and field sizes. Use the asterisk to denote the primary key field in each table. Ask your instructor for the required format of the diagram in text boxes or tables in Word, or if a handwritten diagram is acceptable. Save the Word document and name it **AL2-C1-CS-P1-BestarPlumbing**. Save, print, and close **AL2-C1-CS-P1-BestarPlumbing.docx**.

Part 2

Using the table diagram created in Part 1, create a new database named **AL2-C1-BestarPlumbing.accdb** and then create the tables including setting the primary key in each table.

Part 3

Consider the field properties learned in this chapter that can be used to ensure data integrity and consistency. Modify field properties in your tables that can be used to restrict data accepted into the field and display the data after it has been accepted. Use the data in Figure 1.9 to enter a sample record in each table to test your field properties. Print each table with all column widths set to Best Fit.

Figure 1.9 Invoice for Case Study, Part 1

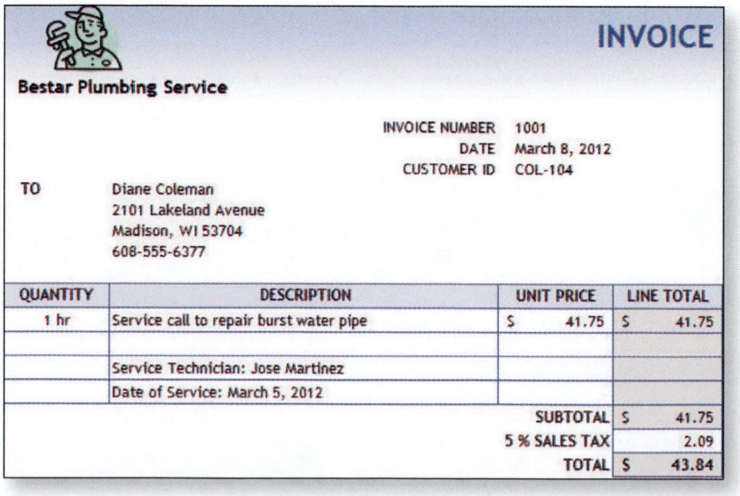

INVOICE

Bestar Plumbing Service

INVOICE NUMBER 1001
DATE March 8, 2012
CUSTOMER ID COL-104

TO Diane Coleman
2101 Lakeland Avenue
Madison, WI 53704
608-555-6377

QUANTITY	DESCRIPTION	UNIT PRICE	LINE TOTAL
1 hr	Service call to repair burst water pipe	$ 41.75	$ 41.75
	Service Technician: Jose Martinez		
	Date of Service: March 5, 2012		
		SUBTOTAL	$ 41.75
		5 % SALES TAX	2.09
		TOTAL	$ 43.84

Microsoft® Access®

CHAPTER 2

Building Relationships and Lookup Fields

PERFORMANCE OBJECTIVES

Upon successful completion of Chapter 2, you will be able to:

- **Create and edit relationships between tables including one-to-many, one-to-one, and many-to-many relationships**
- **Define a table with a multiple-field primary key**
- **Create and modify a lookup field to populate records with data from another table**
- **Create a lookup field that allows multiple values in records**
- **Create single-field and multiple-field indexes**
- **Define what is meant by normalization**
- **Determine if a table is in first, second, and third normal form**

SNAP Training and Assessment. Simplified.

Tutorials

2.1 Creating a One-to-Many Relationship

2.2 Creating a Second One-to-Many Relationship

2.3 Editing Relationship Options

2.4 Establishing a Many-to-Many Relationship

2.5 Defining a Multiple-Field Primary Key

2.6 Creating a Field to Look Up Values in Another Table

2.7 Creating a Field that Allows Multiple Values

2.8 Creating Indexes

2.9 Normalizing a Database

Once table design is completed, establishing relationships and relationship options between tables involves analyzing the type of relationship that exists between two tables. Some database designers will draw a relationship diagram to depict the primary table and the related table's matching record frequency. You will create and edit relationships and lookup fields, multiple-field primary keys, multiple-value fields, and indexes in this chapter. The concept of database normalization and three forms of normalization are introduced to complete the examination of database design fundamentals. Model answers for this chapter's projects appear on the following page.

Access
Access2010L2C2

Note: Before beginning the projects, copy to your storage medium the Access2010L2C2 subfolder from the Access2010L2 folder on the CD that accompanies this textbook and then make Access2010L2C2 the active folder.

Model Answers

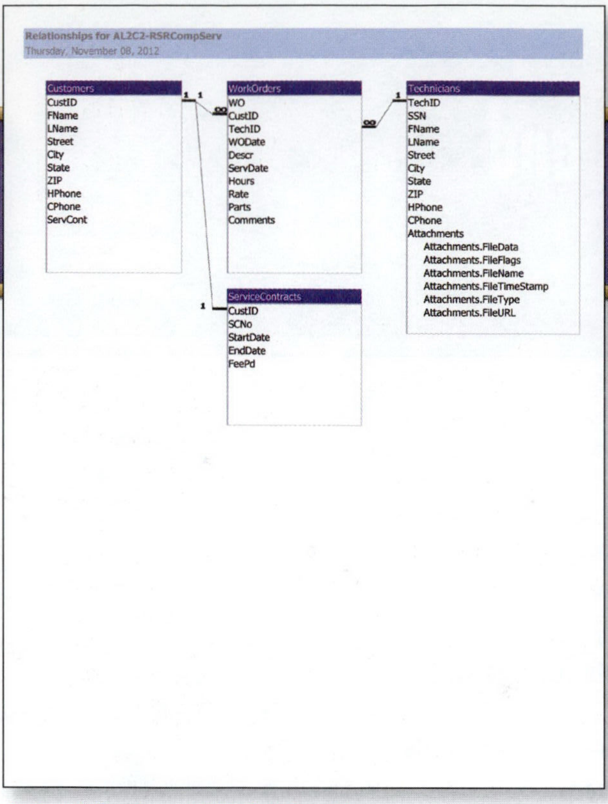

Project 1 Create and Edit Relationships

Project 1d, Relationships Report

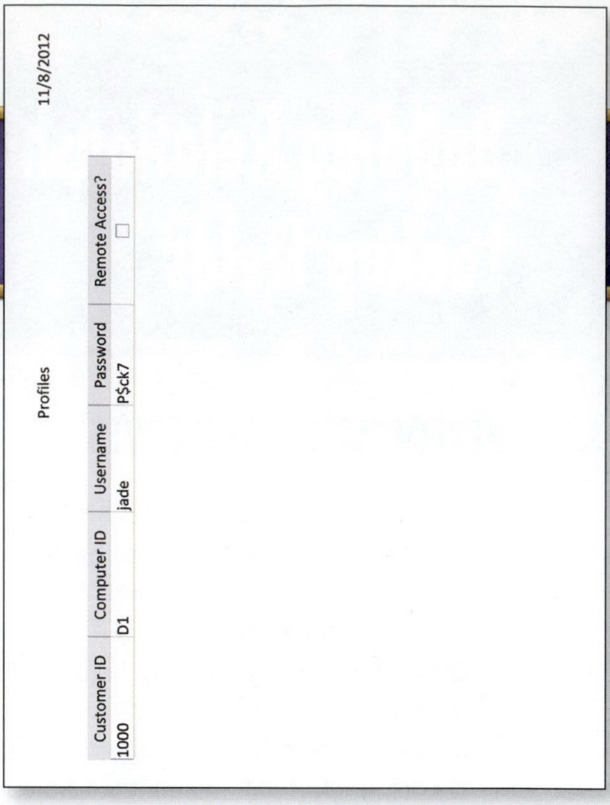

Profiles 11/8/2012

Customer ID	Computer ID	Username	Password	Remote Access?
1000	D1	jade	P$ck7	☐

Project 2 Create a Table with a Multiple-Field Primary Key and Lookup Fields

Project 2c, Profiles Datasheet

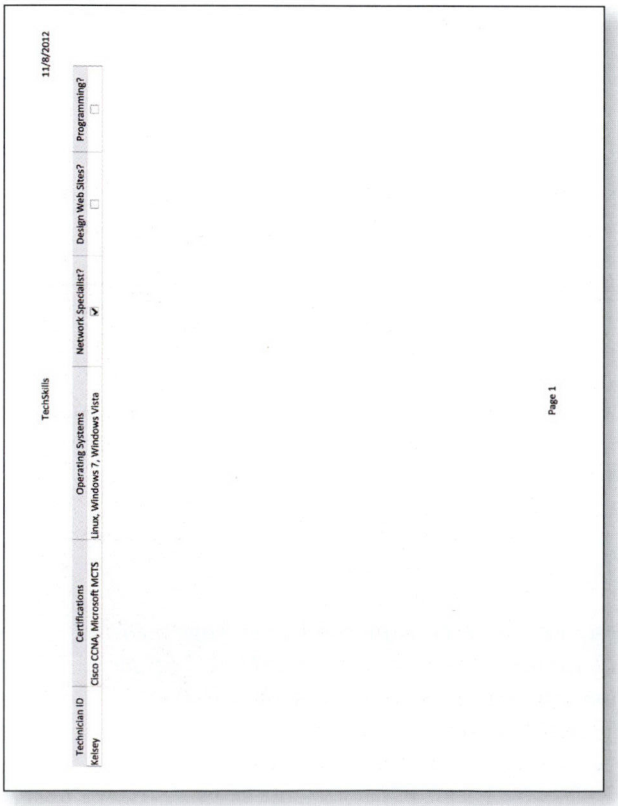

TechSkills 11/8/2012

Technician ID	Certifications	Operating Systems	Network Specialist?	Design Web Sites?	Programming?
Kelsey	Cisco CCNA, Microsoft MCTS	Linux, Windows 7, Windows Vista	☑	☐	☐

Page 1

Project 2e, TechSkills Table

Project 1 Create and Edit Relationships 4 Parts

You will create relationships and edit relationship options for the tables designed to track work orders for RSR Computer Services.

Building Relationships

Continuing the process of designing tables discussed in Chapter 1, which included determining which tables would be related to each other, the next step is to examine the types of relationships that exist. A relationship is based upon an association between two tables. For example, in the computer service database created in Chapter 1 for RSR Computer Services there is an association between the Customers table and the WorkOrders table. A customer is associated with all of his or her work orders involving computer maintenance requests, and a work order is associated with the individual customer for which the service was requested.

HINT

Not sure if two tables should be related? Consider if you would ever need to extract data from both tables in the same query, form, or report. If yes, then the tables should be joined in a relationship.

When building relationships, consider associations between tables and how the associations affect data that will be entered into the tables. In the database diagram presented in Chapter 1, relationships were shown by lines connecting the common field name between tables. In this chapter, you consider the type of relationship that should exist between the tables and the relationship options that you want to use to place restrictions on data entry. Access provides for three types of relationships: one-to-many, one-to-one, and many-to-many. In Access Level 1, Chapter 2, you learned about one-to-many and one-to-one relationships. You will begin by reviewing these two relationship types before you learn how to establish a many-to-many relationship.

Relationships

Establishing a One-to-Many Relationship

In the computer service database in Chapter 1, the Customers table is related to the WorkOrders table. This relationship exists because a work order involves computer maintenance for a specific customer. The customer is identified by the customer's number stored in the Customers table. In the Customers table only one record exists per customer. In the WorkOrders table, the same customer number can be associated with several work orders. This means the relationship between the Customers table and the WorkOrders table is a one-to-many relationship.

Quick Steps

Create One-to-Many Relationship

1. Click Database Tools tab.
2. Click Relationships button.
3. Add tables from Show Table dialog box.
4. Close Show Table dialog box.
5. Drag primary key field name from primary table to foreign key field name in related table.
6. Click Create button.

One-to-many relationships are the most common type of relationship created in Access. A common field is needed to join the Customers table and the WorkOrders table, so the *CustID* field was included in both tables. In the Customers table, *CustID* is the primary key field because each customer has only one record with a unique identification number. In the WorkOrders table, *CustID* cannot be the primary key because the same customer could be associated with several computer service work orders. In the WorkOrders table, *CustID* is the ***foreign key***. A foreign key is a field included in a table for the purpose of creating a relationship to a field that is a primary key in the other table. The Customers-to-WorkOrders one-to-many relationship can be illustrated using a diagram similar to the one shown in Figure 2.1.

Figure 2.1 One-to-Many Relationship between Customers Table and WorkOrders Table

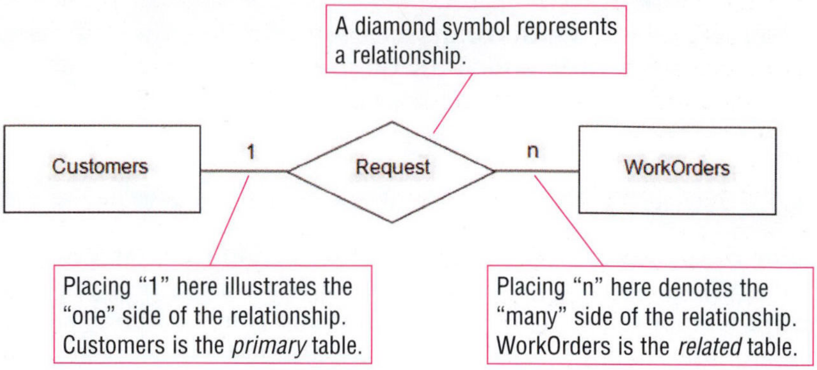

More than one method can be used to diagram a relationship if a database designer chooses to show relationships in a separate diagram from the database diagram shown in Chapter 1. In the version shown in Figure 2.1, table names are displayed in rectangles with lines drawn to a diamond symbol that represents a relationship. Inside the diamond, a word (usually a verb) describes the action that relates the two tables. For example, in the relationship shown in Figure 2.1, the word *Request* is used to show that "Customers *Request* WorkOrders." On the join line, a *1* is placed next to the table that represents the primary table, or the "one" side in the relationship, and *n* is placed next to the related table, or the "many" side of the relationship.

Project 1a Creating a One-to-Many Relationship

Part 1 of 4

1. Open **AL2-C2-RSRCompServ.accdb**. This database has the same structure as the database created in Chapter 1; however, additional field properties have been defined and several records have been added to each table to provide data with which to test relationships and lookup lists.
2. If the Security Warning message bar appears with the message indicating that some active content has been disabled, click the Enable Content button.
3. Create a one-to-many relationship between the Customers table and the WorkOrders table by completing the following steps:
   a. Click the Database Tools tab.
   b. Click the Relationships button in the Relationships group.
   c. At the Show Table dialog box with the Tables tab active and with *Customers* selected in the Tables list box, hold down the Ctrl key, click *WorkOrders*, and then click the Add button.
   d. Click the Close button to close the Show Table dialog box.
   e. Drag the bottom border of each table's field list box to resize the box until all field names are shown.

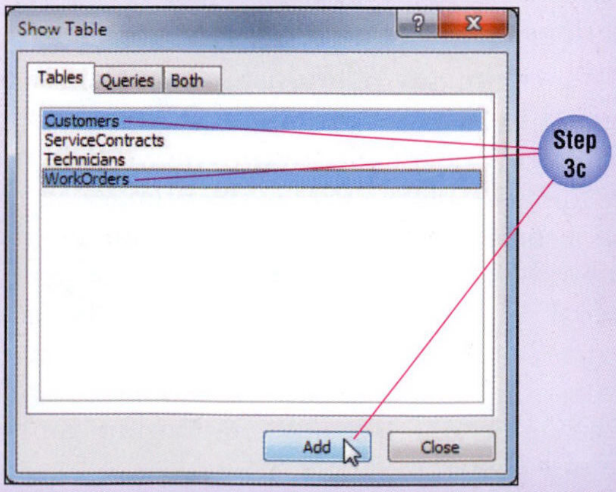

f. Drag the *CustID* field from the Customers table field list box to the *CustID* field in the WorkOrders table field list box. Be careful to drag the common field name starting from the primary table (Customers) in a relationship.

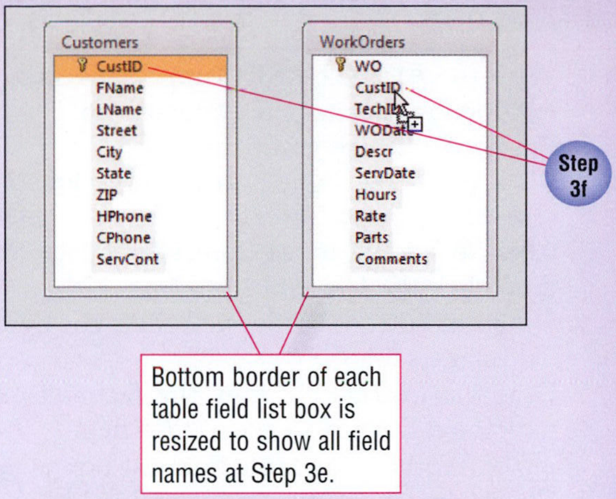

g. At the Edit Relationships dialog box, notice *One-To-Many* appears in the *Relationship Type* section. Access detected the correct type of relationship because the field used to join the tables is a primary key in only one of the tables. Always check that the correct table and field names are shown below the *Table/Query* and *Related Table/Query* list boxes. If the table name and/or the common field name is not shown correctly in the *Table/Query* list boxes and/or the *Related Table/Query* list boxes, click the Cancel button. This error occurs when you drag the mouse starting or ending at the wrong table or field. Return to Step 3f and try again.

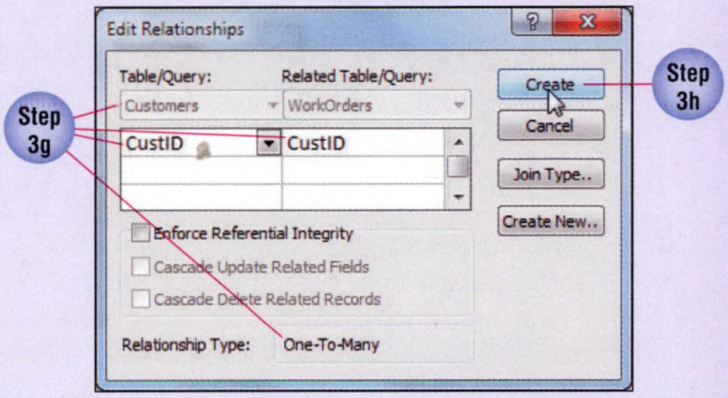

h. Click the Create button.

4. Click the Close button in the Relationships group of the Relationship Tools Design tab.
5. Click Yes at the Microsoft Access message box asking if you want to save changes to the layout of the 'Relationships' window.

Another one-to-many association exists between the Technicians table and the WorkOrders table. A technician is associated with all of the work orders that he or she has been assigned and a work order is associated with the technician that carried out the service request. The Technicians to WorkOrders relationship diagram is shown in Figure 2.2.

Figure 2.2 One-to-Many Relationship between Technicians Table and WorkOrders Table

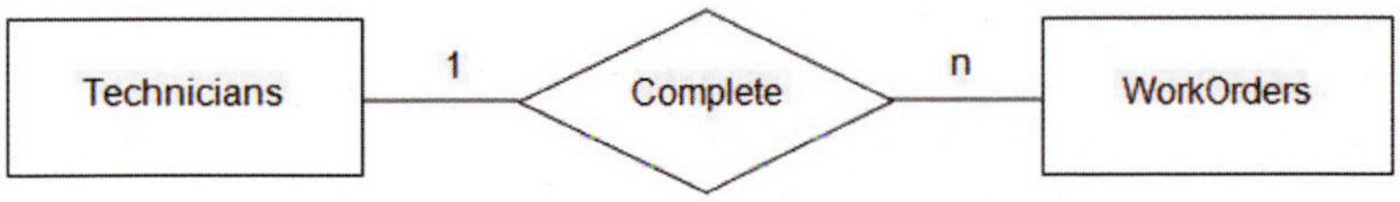

Project 1b Creating a Second One-to-Many Relationship

Part 2 of 4

1. With the **AL2-C2-RSRCompServ.accdb** database open, display the Relationships window by clicking the Database Tools tab and then clicking the Relationships button in the Relationships group.
2. Click the Show Table button in the Relationships group in the Relationships Tools Design tab.
3. Click *Technicians* in the Tables list at the Show Table dialog box, click the Add button, and then click the Close button.
4. Drag the bottom border and the right border of the Technicians table field list box until all field names are fully visible.
5. Drag the *TechID* field from the Technicians table field list box to the *TechID* field in the WorkOrders table field list box.
6. Check that the correct table and field names appear in the *Table/Query* and *Related Table/Query* list boxes. If necessary, click Cancel, and try Step 5 again.
7. Click the Create button at the Edit Relationships dialog box.

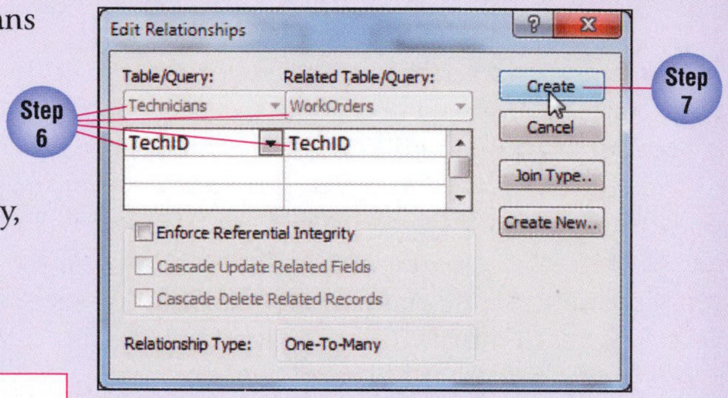

one-to-many relationship created between Technicians and WorkOrders at Steps 1 through 7

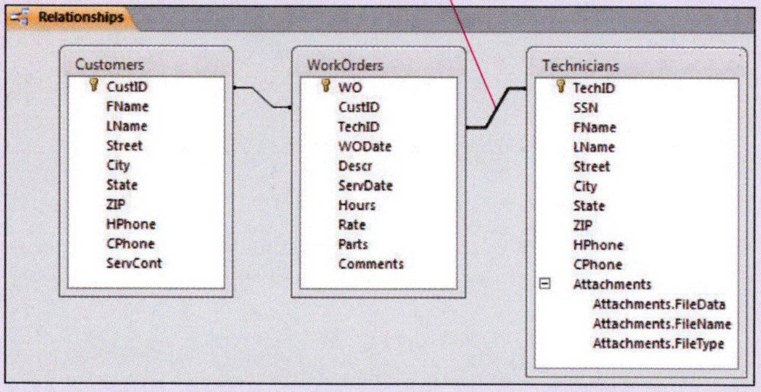

8. Click the Close button in the Relationships group of the Relationship Tools Design tab.
9. Click Yes at the Microsoft Access message box asking if you want to save changes to the layout of the 'Relationships' window.

Quick Steps

Edit Relationship

1. Click Database Tools tab.
2. Click Relationships button.
3. Click black join line between tables.
4. Click Edit Relationships button.
5. Select desired options.
6. Click OK.

Editing Relationship Options

At the Edit Relationships dialog box shown in Figure 2.3 you can elect to turn on relationship options and/or specify the type of join to create. The *Cascade Update Related Fields* and *Cascade Delete Related Records* options do not become active unless referential integrity is turned on.

Figure 2.3 Edit Relationships Dialog Box

Enforce Referential Integrity places restrictions on data entry. A record will not be allowed in the related table (WorkOrders) with a value in the foreign key field (*TechID*) for which no matching record is already in existence in the primary table (Technicians). In other words, you cannot assign a technician to a work order if the technician does not exist in the Technicians table.

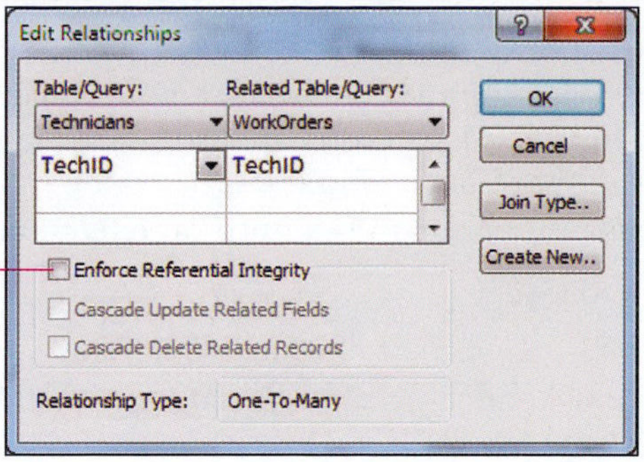

Edit Relationships

Turning on referential integrity in a one-to-many relationship is a good idea to ensure that orphan records do not occur. An ***orphan record*** is a record in a related table for which no "parent" record exists in the primary table. Assigning a technician to a work order in the WorkOrders table with no matching technician record in the Technicians table creates an orphan record in the WorkOrders table. Once referential integrity is turned on, Access checks for the existence of a matching record in the primary table as a new record is added to the related table. If no match is found, Access does not allow the record to be saved.

With referential integrity active, Access can automatically update all occurrences of the same data in the foreign key field in the related table when a change is made to the primary key field in the primary table (Cascade Update Related Fields). If a record is deleted from the primary table for which related records exist in the related table, Access can automatically delete the related records (Cascade Delete Related Records).

You will learn about join types and situations in which changing the join type is warranted in Chapter 3.

HINT

To enable referential integrity, the primary key and foreign key fields must be the same data type. If you receive an error message when attempting to activate referential integrity, open each table in Design view and compare the data type for each field used to join the tables.

Project 1c Editing Relationships

Part 3 of 4

1. With the **AL2-C2-RSRCompServ.accdb** database open, edit the one-to-many relationship between the Customers table and the WorkOrders table by completing the following steps:
   a. Open the Relationships window.
   b. Click to select the black join line between the Customers table and the WorkOrders table.
   c. Click the Edit Relationships button in the Tools group in the Relationship Tools Design tab.
   d. At the Edit Relationships dialog box, click the *Enforce Referential Integrity* check box, the *Cascade Update Related Fields* check box, and the *Cascade Delete Related Records* check box.
   e. Click OK at the Edit Relationships dialog box. The *1* at the primary table (one side) of the join line and the infinity symbol (∞) at the related table (many side) of the join line indicate referential integrity has been turned on.

Step 1d

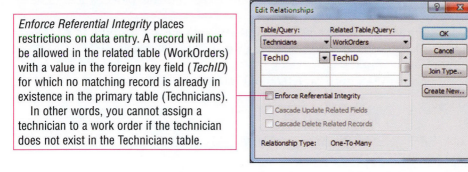

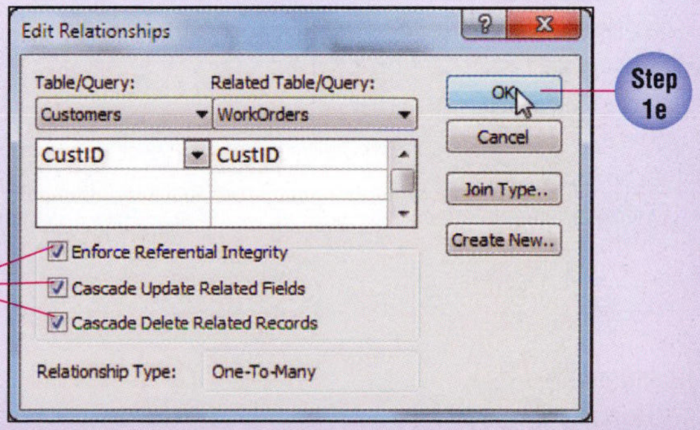

2. Edit the one-to-many relationship between the Technicians table and the WorkOrders table by completing the following steps:
   a. Double-click the black join line between the Technicians table and the WorkOrders table in the Relationships window. (You can also right-click the join line and click *Edit Relationship* at the shortcut menu.)
   b. At the Edit Relationships dialog box, turn on referential integrity and the two cascade options.
   c. Click OK.

Steps 2a-2c

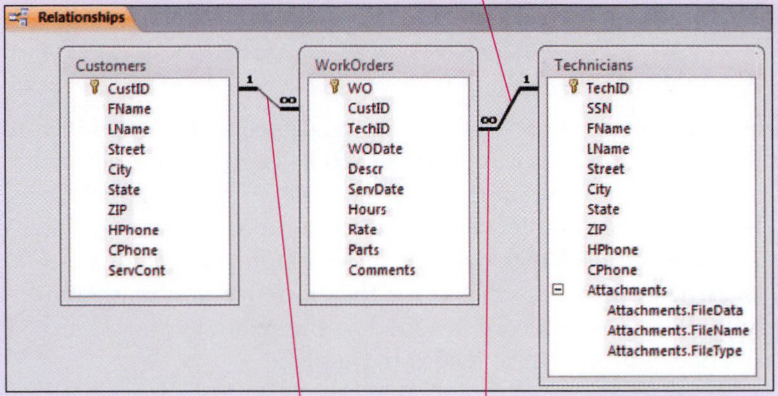

With referential integrity turned on, the 1 and infinity symbol (∞) display on the join lines.

3. Close the Relationships window.

Quick Steps

Create One-to-One Relationship

1. Click Database Tools tab.
2. Click Relationships button.
3. Add tables from Show Table dialog box.
4. Close Show Table dialog box.
5. Drag primary key field name from primary table to primary key field name in related table.
6. Select desired relationship options.
7. Click Create button.

Relationship Report

Establishing a One-to-One Relationship

In the database for RSR Computer Services, a table is used to store service contract information for each customer. This table, named ServiceContracts, is associated with the Customers table. Only one record exists for a customer in the Customers table and each customer subscribes to only one service contract in the ServiceContracts table. This means the two tables are related in a one-to-one relationship as shown in Figure 2.4.

Figure 2.4 One-to-One Relationship between Customers Table and ServiceContracts Table

Project 1d Creating a One-to-One Relationship — Part 4 of 4

1. With the **AL2-C2-RSRCompServ.accdb** database open, create a one-to-one relationship between the Customers table and the ServiceContracts table by completing the following steps:
   a. Open the Relationships window.
   b. Click the Show Table button in the Relationships group.
   c. Double-click *ServiceContracts* in the Tables list box and then click the Close button.
   d. Drag the *CustID* field from the Customers table field list box to the *CustID* field in the ServiceContracts table field list box.
   e. At the Edit Relationships dialog box, check that the correct table and field names appear in the *Table/Query* and *Related Table/Query* list boxes. If necessary, click Cancel, and try Step 1d again.
   f. Notice *One-To-One* appears in the *Relationship Type* section. Access detected the correct type of relationship because the field used to join the tables is a primary key in both tables.
   g. Click the *Enforce Referential Integrity* check box, the *Cascade Update Related Fields* check box, and the *Cascade Delete Related Records* check box.
   h. Click the Create button.

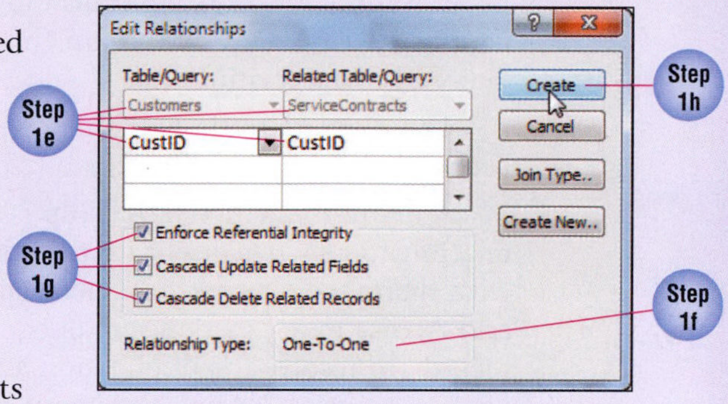

2. Drag the title bar of the ServiceContracts table field list box to the approximate location shown in the Relationships window. By moving the table field list box you are better able to view the join line and the *1* at each end of the line between Customers and ServiceContracts.

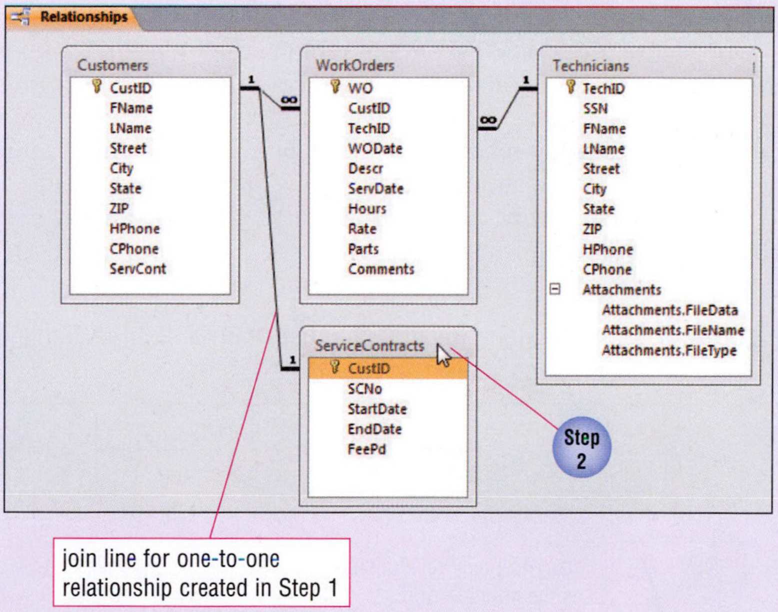

3. Create a relationships report by clicking the Relationship Report button in the Tools group of the Relationship Tools Design tab.
4. Access displays the report in Print Preview. Click the Print button in the Print group of the Print Preview tab and then click OK at the Print dialog box.

5. Close the Relationships for AL2-C2-RSRCompServ report. Click Yes to save the report and click OK to accept the default name at the Save As dialog box.
6. Close the Relationships window. Click Yes to save changes to the layout.

Establishing a Many-to-Many Relationship

Consider the association between the Customers table and the Technicians table in the RSR Computer Services database. Over time, any individual customer can have computer service work done by many different technicians and any individual technician can perform computer service work at any number of different customer locations. In other words, a record in the Customers table can be matched to many records in the Technicians table and a record in the Technicians table can be matched to many records in the Customers table. This is an example of a many-to-many relationship.

The diagram to show the many-to-many relationship between Customers and Technicians is depicted in Figure 2.5.

A many-to-many relationship is problematic because the nature of the relationship creates duplicate records. If the same customer number is associated with many technicians, and vice versa, many duplicates occur in the two tables and Access may experience data conflicts when trying to identify a unique record. To resolve the duplication and create unique entries, a third table is used to associate or link the many-to-many tables. The third table is called a junction table. A ***junction table*** is a table that contains at least two foreign keys—the primary key field from each table in the many-to-many relationship. Using the junction table, two one-to-many relationships are created. Examine the Relationships window shown in Figure 2.6.

In Figure 2.6, the WorkOrders table is the junction table. Notice the WorkOrders table contains two foreign keys—*CustID*, which is the primary key in the Customers table, and *TechID*, which is the primary key in the Technicians table. A one-to-many relationship exists between Customers and WorkOrders and a one-to-many relationship also exists between Technicians and WorkOrders. These two one-to-many relationships create a many-to-many relationship between Customers and Technicians.

Figure 2.5 Many-to-Many Relationship between Customers Table and Technicians Table

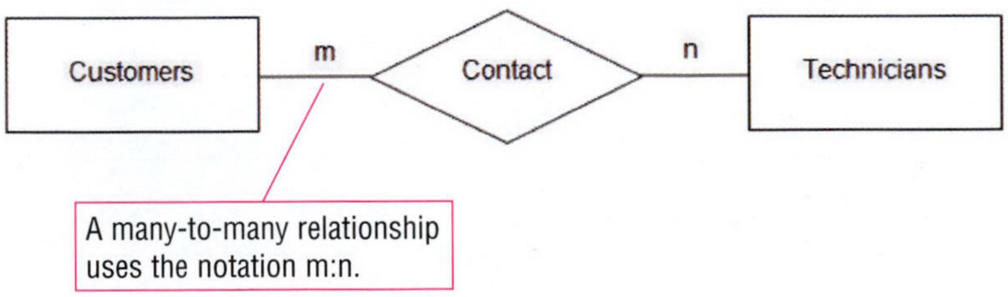

Figure 2.6 Relationships Window Showing Many-to-Many Relationship between Customers Table and Technicians Table

Customers and Technicians have many-to-many relationship via the WorkOrders junction table.

The WorkOrders junction table contains two foreign keys—the primary key from each table in the many-to-many relationship.

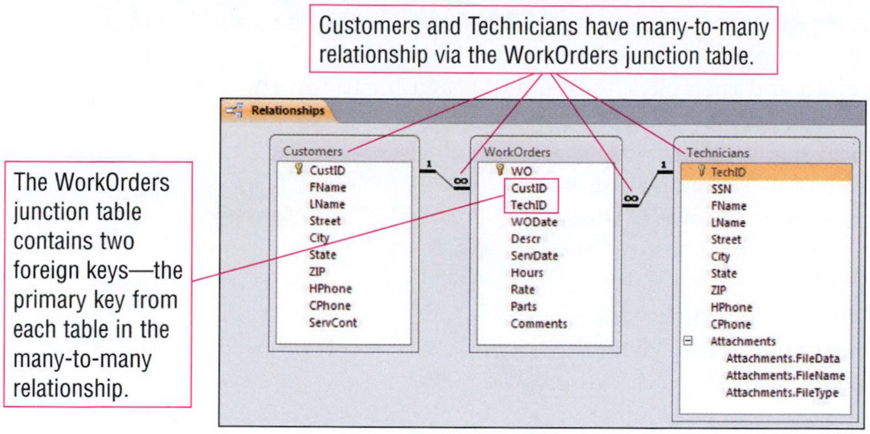

Project 2 Create a Table with a Multiple-Field Primary Key and Lookup Fields 5 Parts

You will create a new table that requires two fields to uniquely identify each record. To restrict data entry in the table, you will create fields that display a list from which the user selects the field value(s).

Defining a Multiple-Field Primary Key ■■■■■■■■■■

In most tables one field is designated as the primary key. However, in some situations, a single field may not always be guaranteed to hold unique data. Look at the fields in the table shown in Figure 2.7. This is a new table you will create in the RSR Computer Services database to store computer profiles for RSR customers. The company stores the profiles as a service to RSR clients in case the client forgets his or her logon credentials. Technicians can also access the credentials data when troubleshooting at the customer's site.

Some customers may have more than one computer in their home or office and each computer can have a different profile for each username. The *CustID* field will not serve as the primary key field if the customer has more than one record in the Profiles table. However, a combination of the three fields *CustID*, *CompID*, and *Username* will uniquely identify each record. In this table, you will define all three fields as a primary key. A primary key that is made up of two or more fields is called a ***composite key***.

Figure 2.7 Project 2a Profiles Table

Profiles		
*CustID	Text	4
*CompID	Text	2
*Username	Text	15
Password	Text	15
Remote	Yes/No	

▼ **Quick Steps**

Create Multiple-Field Primary Key
1. Open table in Design view.
2. Select first field.
3. Hold down Shift key (adjacent row) or Ctrl key (nonadjacent row) and select second field.
4. Click Primary Key button.
5. Save table.

HINT

Delete a primary key by opening the table in Design view, activating the primary key field, and then clicking the Primary Key button to remove the key.

Primary Key

Project 2a Creating a New Table with a Multiple-Field Primary Key — Part 1 of 5

1. With the **AL2-C2-RSRCompServ.accdb** database open, create a new table to store customer profiles by completing the following steps:
   a. Click the Create tab and then click the Table Design button in the Tables group.
   b. Type the field names, assign the data types, and change the field sizes as per the data structure shown in Figure 2.7.
2. Point in the field selector bar (blank column at left of field names) next to *CustID* until the pointer changes to a right-pointing black arrow and then click to select the field.
3. Hold down the Shift key and click in the field selector bar next to *Username*. The three adjacent fields *CustID*, *CompID*, and *Username* are now selected.

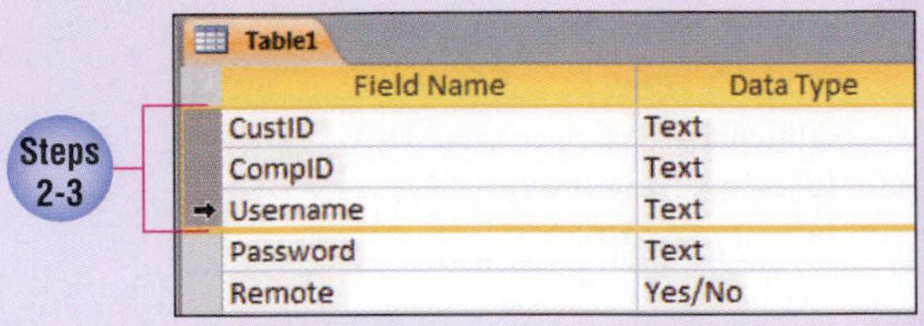

4. Click the Primary Key button in the Tools group in the Table Tools Design tab. Access displays the key icon next to each field.
5. Click in any field to deselect the first three rows.
6. Save the table and name it *Profiles*.
7. Close the table.

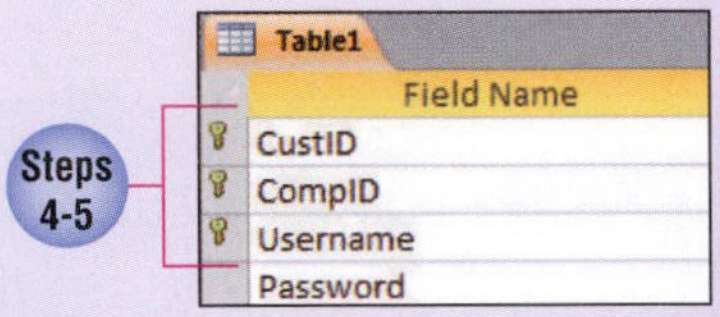

Quick Steps

Create Lookup Field to Another Table

1. Open table in Design view.
2. Click in *Data Type* column of lookup field.
3. Click down-pointing arrow.
4. Click *Lookup Wizard*.
5. Click Next.
6. Choose table and click Next.
7. Choose fields to display in column.
8. Click Next.
9. Choose field by which to sort.
10. Click Next.
11. If necessary, expand column widths.
12. Clear *Hide key column* if desired.
13. Click Next.
14. Choose field value to store in table.
15. Click Next.
16. Click Finish.
17. Click Yes.

Creating a Field to Look Up Values in Another Table

In Level 1, Chapter 4, you learned how to create a lookup list in which you typed the values that you wanted to appear in the list as you worked through the steps of the Lookup Wizard. A lookup field can also be created in which you display in the drop-down list the values found in records from another table. The user enters data by pointing and clicking rather than typing the field's entry. A lookup field that draws its data from a field in another table has many advantages. Data can be restricted to items within the list, which avoids orphan records, data entry errors, or inconsistencies in spelling. The lookup list can display more than one clue to the user so that the correct data is selected. For example, assume a lookup field requires the user to select a customer's identification number. Looking at a drop-down list of identification numbers is not very helpful; however, if the lookup field displayed the identification number as well as the customer's name, the correct entry is easily identifiable. By choosing the field entry based on the name, the correct identification number is automatically entered by Access. To assist with creating lookup fields, Access provides the Lookup Wizard. Create lookup list fields before you create relationships. If a relationship already exists between the table for the lookup field and the source data table, Access prompts you to delete the relationship before the Lookup Wizard can run.

Project 2b **Creating a Field to Look Up Data in Another Table** Part 2 of 5

1. With the **AL2-C2-RSRCompServ.accdb** database open, open the Profiles table in Design view.
2. Create a lookup field to enter a customer's identification number by selecting from a list of customers in the Customers table by completing the following steps:
   a. With *CustID* the active field, click in the *Data Type* column, click the down-pointing arrow that appears, and then click *Lookup Wizard* at the drop-down list.
   b. At the first Lookup Wizard dialog box with *I want the lookup field to get the values from another table or query* selected, click Next.

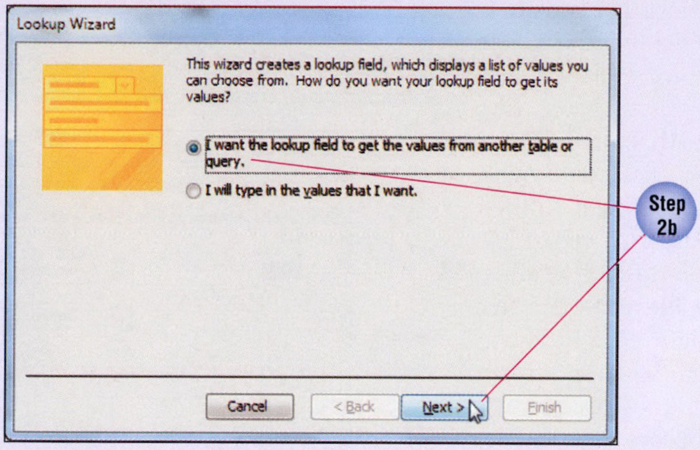

   c. At the second Lookup Wizard dialog box with *Table: Customers* already selected in the *Which table or query should provide the values for your lookup field?* list box, click Next.

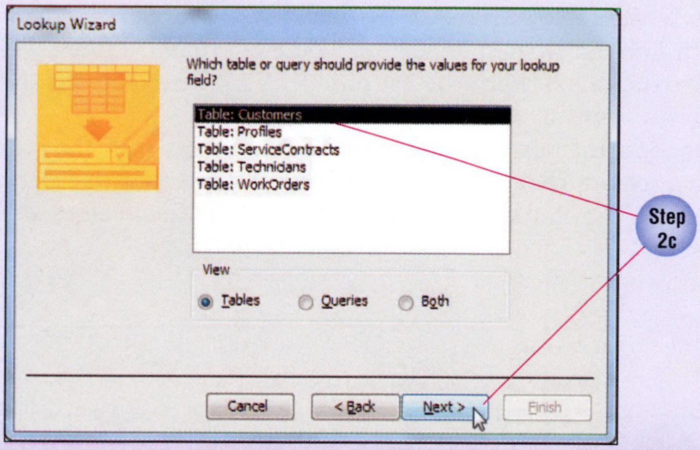

d. At the third Lookup Wizard dialog box you choose the fields you want to display in the drop-down list when the user clicks in the field. Double-click *FName* in the *Available Fields* list box to move the field to the *Selected Fields* list box.

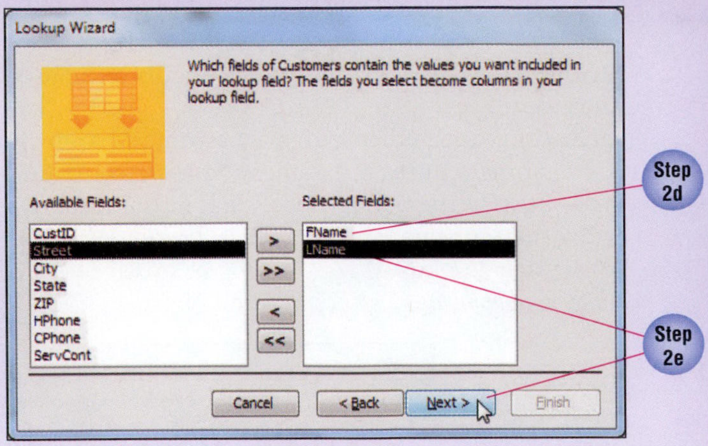

e. Double-click *LName* in the *Available Fields* list box to move the field to the *Selected Fields* list box and then click Next.

f. At the fourth Lookup Wizard dialog box, click the down-pointing arrow next to the first sort list box, click *LName* at the drop-down list, and then click Next. Notice that you can define up to four sort keys to sort the lookup list and that an Ascending button appears next to each *Sort* list box. You can change the sort order from Ascending to Descending by clicking the Ascending button.

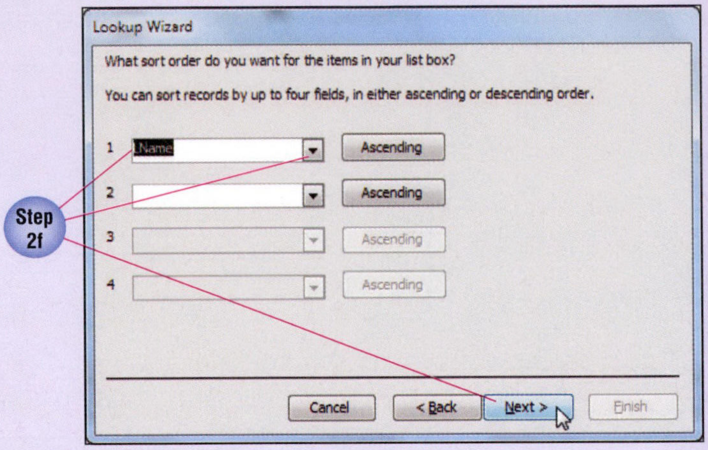

g. At the fifth Lookup Wizard dialog box you can expand column widths if necessary to display all data. Scroll down the list of entries in the dialog box. Notice the column widths are sufficient to show all of the text.

h. In order to view the customer identification numbers with the names while the list is opened in a record, click the *Hide key column (recommended)* check box to clear the check mark. Clearing the check mark displays the *CustID* field values as the first column in the lookup list.

i. Click Next.

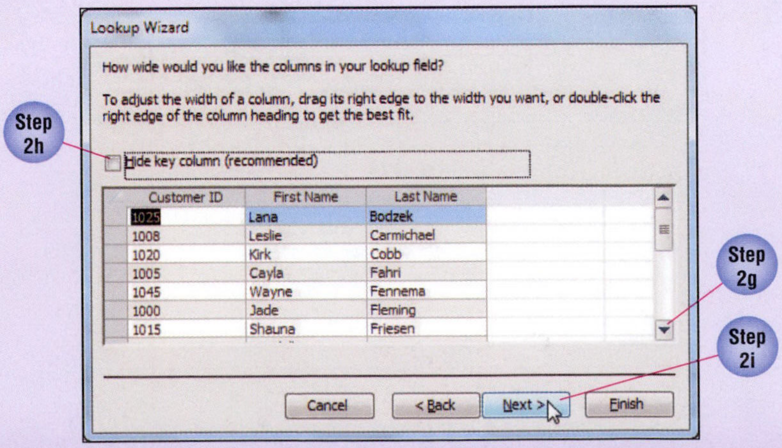

j. At the sixth Lookup Wizard dialog box with *CustID* already selected in the *Available Fields* list box, click Next. At this dialog box you choose the field value that you want to store in the table when an entry is selected in the drop-down list.

k. Click Finish at the last Lookup Wizard dialog box to accept the existing field name for the lookup field of *CustID*.

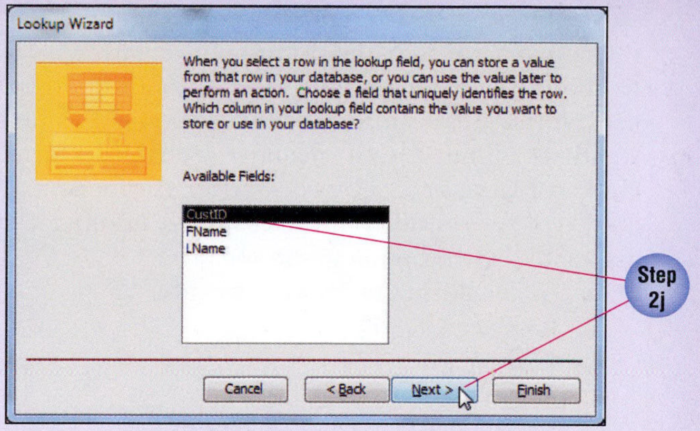

l. Click Yes to save the table at the Lookup Wizard message box that states the table must be saved before relationships can be created. Access automatically creates a relationship between the Customers table and the Profiles table based on the *CustID* field used to create the lookup field.

3. Close the Profiles table.

Project 2c Modifying Lookup List Properties and Using a Lookup List Field in a Record

Part 3 of 5

1. With the **AL2-C2-RSRCompServ.accdb** database open, open the Profiles table in Design view.
2. Add the following text to the Caption property of the fields noted.

   CustID Customer ID
   CompID Computer ID
   Remote Remote Access?

3. Modify the lookup list properties to restrict entries in new records to an item within the list by completing the following steps:
   a. Make *CustID* the active field.
   b. Click the Lookup tab in the *Field Properties* section.
   c. Look at the entries in each of the Lookup tab's property boxes. These entries were created by the Lookup Wizard.
   d. Click in the *Limit To List* property box, click the down-pointing arrow that appears, and then click *Yes* at the drop-down list. Changing *Limit To List* to *Yes* means that the field will accept data from existing customer records only. A user will not be able to type in an entry that is not in the list.

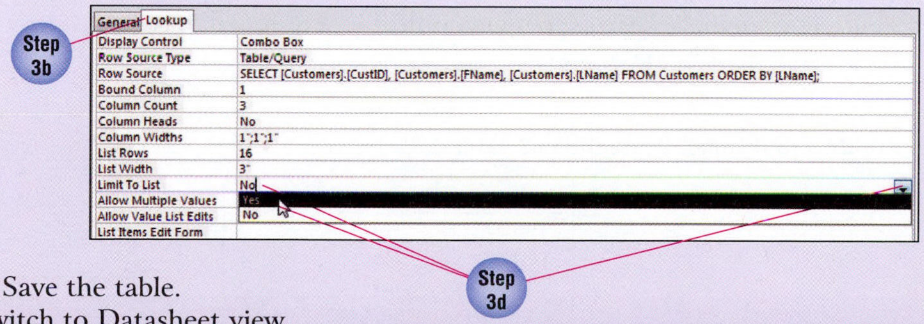

General
Lookup
Display Control
Combo Box
Row Source Type
Table/Query
Row Source
SELECT [Customers].[CustID], [Customers].[FName], [Customers].[LName] FROM Customers ORDER BY [LName];
Bound Column
1
Column Count
3
Column Heads
No
Column Widths
1";1";1"
List Rows
16
List Width
3"
Limit To List
No
Allow Multiple Values
Yes
Allow Value List Edits
No
List Items Edit Form
Step 3b
Step 3d

   e. Save the table.
4. Switch to Datasheet view.

5. With *Customer ID* in the first row of the datasheet the active field, click the down-pointing arrow in the field and then click *Jade Fleming* at the drop-down list. Notice Access inserts *1000* as the field value in the first column. You were able to select the correct entry for *Customer ID* by clicking a customer's name and then Access filled in the customer number associated with the name for you.
6. Type the remaining fields as indicated.

   Computer ID **D1**
   Username **jade**
   Password **P$ck7**
   Remote Access? No (leave blank)

7. Adjust all column widths to Best Fit.

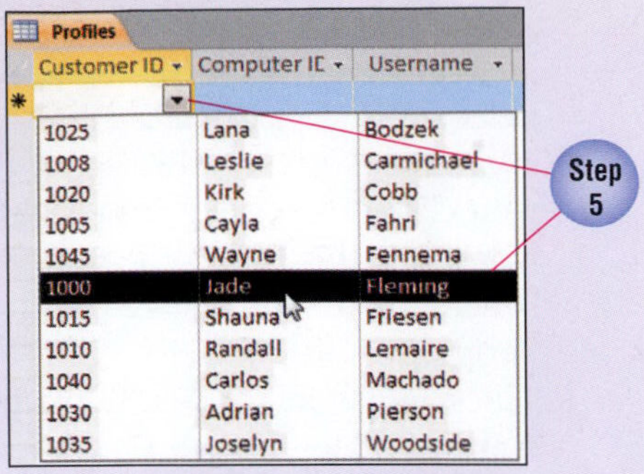

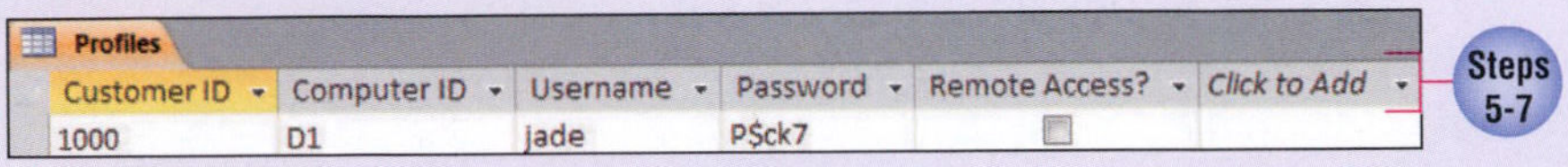

8. Print and then close the Profiles datasheet. Click Yes when prompted to save changes to the table layout.

Creating a Field That Allows Multiple Values

Quick Steps

Create Multiple-Value Lookup List
1. Open table in Design view.
2. Start Lookup Wizard for desired field.
3. Create list by typing values or binding data to field in another table.
4. At last Lookup Wizard dialog box, click *Allow Multiple Values.*
5. Click Finish.
6. Click Yes.

HINT

Multiple-value fields are suited to those occasions where you want to store more than one choice from a small list without having to create an advanced database design.

Assume you want to keep track of the industry certifications a technician has achieved. You could organize this data by creating a separate field for each certification. However, this approach might cause the table to require numerous fields in which only one or two technicians might have an entry. As an alternative, you can create a single field that displays a list of certifications with check boxes. Look at the fields in the table structure shown in Figure 2.8. In this table, for each technician, you would open a list in the *Certifications* field and click the check box next to the applicable certification title. In the field named *OperatingSys*, another list could be used to keep track of the operating systems for which the technician is considered an expert.

Create a field to store multiple values using the Lookup Wizard. You can choose to look up the values in a field in another table or create your own value list. At the last Lookup Wizard dialog box, click the *Allow Multiple Values* check box. Do not create a multiple-value field if the possibility exists the Access database could be moved to Microsoft SQL Server in the future. An Access multiple-value field upsizes to a memo field in a SQL database, causing additional conversion work to be required.

Figure 2.8 Project 2d TechSkills Table

TechSkills		
*TechID	Text	2
Certifications	Text	20
OperatingSys	Text	20
NetworkSpc	Yes/No	
WebDesign	Yes/No	
Programming	Yes/No	

Project 2d Creating a Table with Lookup Fields Including a Multiple-Value Field Part 4 of 5

1. With the **AL2-C2-RSRCompServ.accdb** database open, create a new table to store technician competencies by completing the following steps:
   a. Create a new table using Design view.
   b. Type the field names, assign the data types, and change the field sizes as per the data structure shown in Figure 2.8.
   c. Assign the primary key to the field denoted with the asterisk.
   d. Save the table and name it *TechSkills*.
2. Create a lookup field to select the technician from a list of technician names in the Technicians table by completing the following steps:
   a. Click in the *Data Type* column for the *TechID* field, click the down-pointing arrow that appears, and then click *Lookup Wizard*.
   b. Click Next at the first dialog box to look up the values in a table or query.
   c. Click *Table: Technicians* and then click Next.
   d. Double-click *FName* in the *Available Fields* list box to move the field to the *Selected Fields* list box.
   e. Double-click *LName* in the *Available Fields* list box and then click Next.
   f. Sort by *LName* and then click Next.
   g. With the *Hide key column* check box selected, click Next to accept the current column widths. In this lookup example, you are electing not to show the technician's ID field value. Although you will view and select by the names, Access stores the primary key value in the table. *TechID* is considered the bound field, while *FName* and *LName* are considered display fields.
   h. Click Finish and then click Yes to save the table.

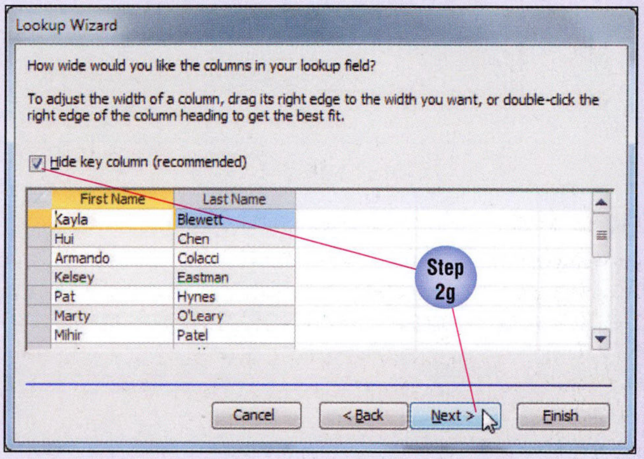
Lookup Wizard
How wide would you like the columns in your lookup field?
To adjust the width of a column, drag its right edge to the width you want, or double-click the right edge of the column heading to get the best fit.
Hide key column (recommended)
First Name
Last Name
Kayla
Blewett
Hui
Chen
Armando
Colacci
Kelsey
Eastman
Pat
Hynes
Marty
O'Leary
Mihir
Patel
Step 2g
Cancel
< Back
Next >
Finish

3. Create a lookup field that allows multiple values for certification information by completing the following steps:
   a. Click in the *Data Type* column for the *Certifications* field, click the down-pointing arrow that appears, and then click *Lookup Wizard*.
   b. Click *I will type in the values that I want* and then click Next.
   c. At the second Lookup Wizard dialog box, type the entries in *Col1* as shown at the right.
   d. Click Next.

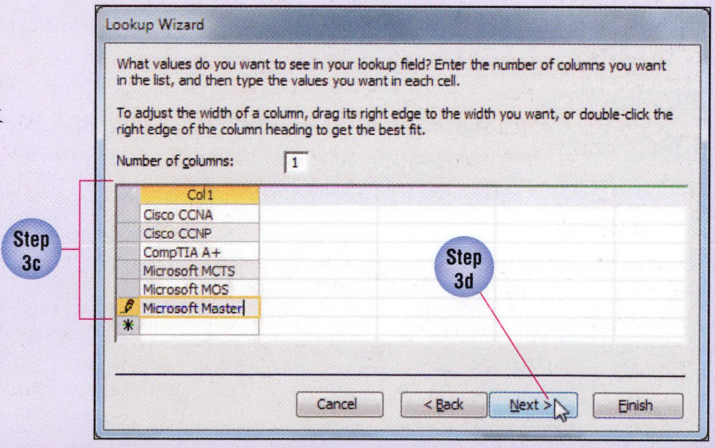
Step 3c
Lookup Wizard
What values do you want to see in your lookup field? Enter the number of columns you want in the list, and then type the values you want in each cell.
To adjust the width of a column, drag its right edge to the width you want, or double-click the right edge of the column heading to get the best fit.
Number of columns:
1
Col1
Cisco CCNA
Cisco CCNP
CompTIA A+
Microsoft MCTS
Microsoft MOS
Microsoft Master
Step 3d
Cancel
< Back
Next >
Finish

e. At the last Lookup Wizard dialog box, click the *Allow Multiple Values* check box and then click Finish.

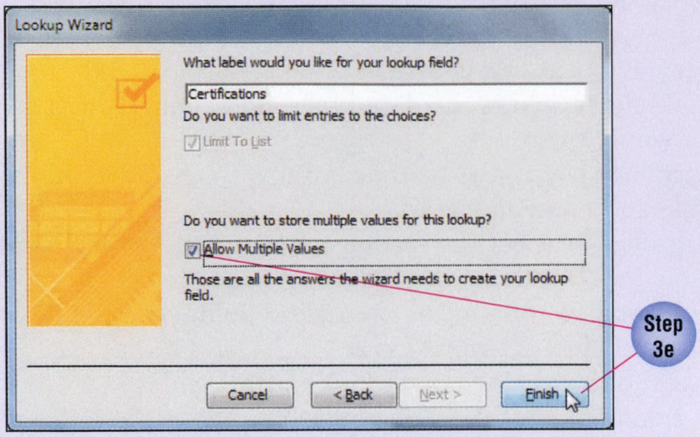

f. At the message box indicating that once the field is set to store multiple values, the action cannot be undone, click Yes to change the *Certifications* field to multiple values.

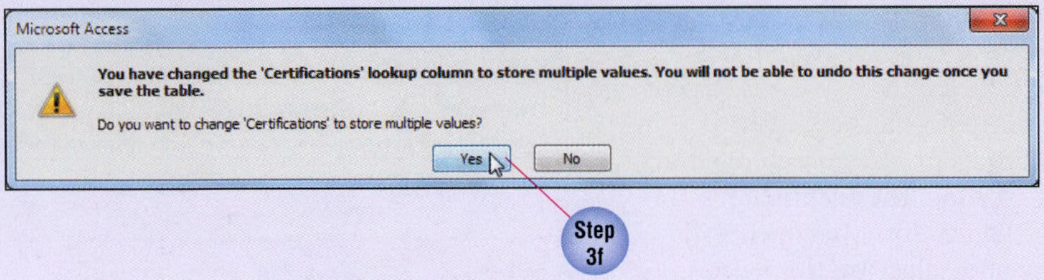

4. Create a lookup list to store multiple values in the *OperatingSys* field using the value list shown below by completing steps similar to those in Steps 3a through 3f.
   Windows 7
   Windows Vista
   Windows XP
   Linux
   Unix
   Mac OS X
5. Save and close the TechSkills table.

Project 2e Assigning Multiple Values in a Lookup List

Part 5 of 5

1. With the **AL2-C2-RSRCompServ.accdb** database open, open the TechSkills table in Design view.
2. Add the following text to the Caption property of the fields noted.

TechID	**Technician ID**
OperatingSys	**Operating Systems**
NetworkSpc	**Network Specialist?**
WebDesign	**Design Web Sites?**
Programming	**Programming?**

3. Save the table and then switch to Datasheet view.

4. Add a new record to the table by completing the following steps:
   a. With the insertion point positioned in the *Technician ID* column, click the down-pointing arrow and then click *Kelsey Eastman* at the drop-down list. Notice Access displays the technician's first name in the column. *FName* is considered a display field for this column; however, the identification number associated with Kelsey Eastman is stored in the table.
   b. Press Tab and then click the down-pointing arrow in the *Certifications* column.
   c. Since *Certifications* is a multiple-value field, the drop-down list displays with check boxes next to each item in the list. Click the *Cisco CCNA* check box and the *Microsoft MCTS* check box and then click OK.
   d. Press Tab and then click the down-pointing arrow in the *Operating System* column.
   e. Click the *Windows 7, Windows Vista*, and *Linux* check boxes and then click OK.
   f. Press Tab and then press the spacebar to insert a check mark in the *Network Specialist?* check box.
   g. Press Tab three times to finish the record, leaving the check boxes blank in the *Design Web Sites?* and *Programming?* columns.
5. Adjust the width of all columns to Best Fit.
6. Print the TechSkills table in landscape orientation with a left and right margin of 0.25-inch.
7. Close the TechSkills table. Click Yes when prompted to save changes to the layout.

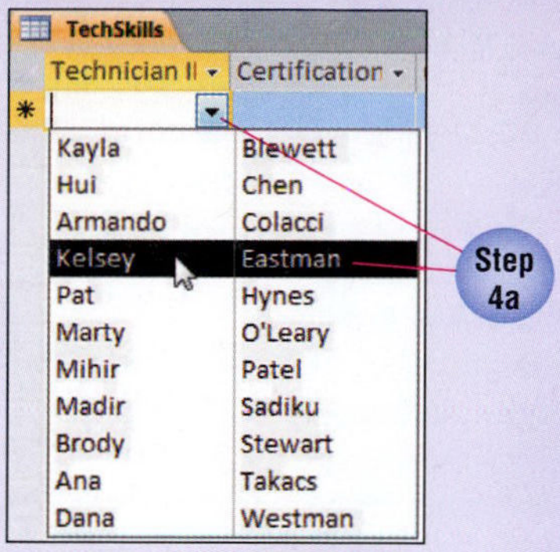

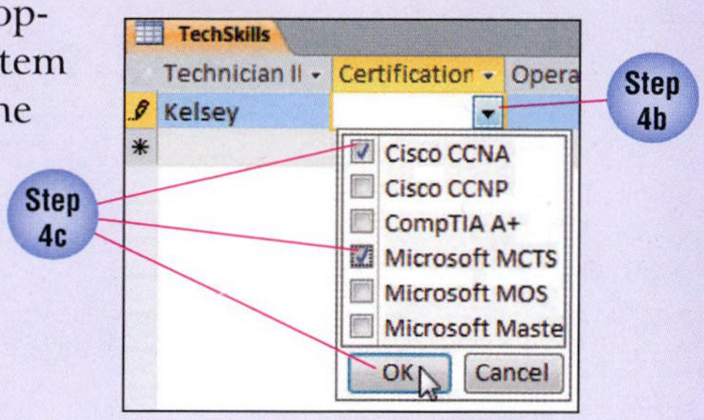

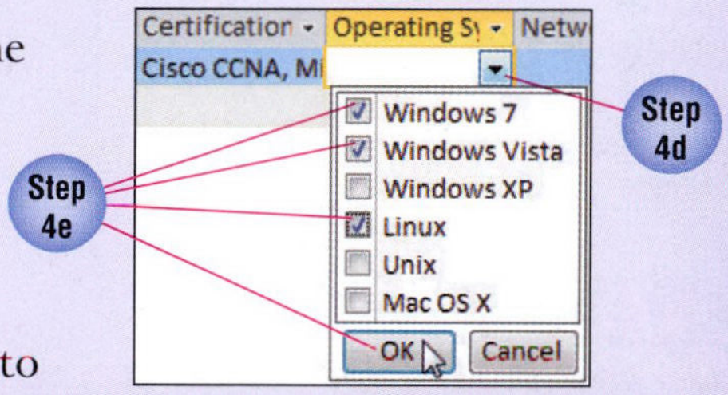

Project 3 Create an Index — 1 Part

You will create indexes to speed up database processing.

Creating Indexes

An ***index*** is a list created by Access containing pointers that direct Access to the location of a record in a table. A database index is very similar to an index you would find printed at the back of a textbook. You search an index for a keyword that is associated with the topic you want to find and are directed to the page number(s) in the book. You use a book's index because you want to find the information quickly and more directly. Access table indexes operate the same way. Access uses the index to locate a record in a table more quickly. A field that is specified as the primary key has an index generated by Access automatically. You can add additional indexed fields to the database to speed up sorting and searching. For example, in the Customers table in the RSR Computer Services database, creating an index for the *LName* field is a good idea since the table data will be frequently sorted by last names.

Quick Steps

Create Single-Field Index
1. Open table in Design view.
2. Make desired field active.
3. Click in *Indexed* property box.
4. Click down-pointing arrow.
5. Click *Yes (Duplicates OK)* or *Yes (No Duplicates)*.
6. Save table.

Quick Steps

Create Multiple-Field Index

1. Open table in Design view.
2. Click Indexes button.
3. Click in first blank row in *Index Name* column.
4. Type name for index.
5. Press Tab.
6. Click down-pointing arrow in *Field Name* column.
7. Click desired field.
8. If necessary, change sort order.
9. Click in *Field Name* column in next row.
10. Click down-pointing arrow.
11. Click desired field.
12. If necessary, change sort order.
13. Continue Steps 9–12 until finished.
14. Close Indexes window.

HINT

An index cannot be generated for fields with a data type of OLE Object or Attachment.

Indexes

An index can be created that restricts data in the field to unique values. This creates a field similar to a primary key in that Access will not allow two fields to hold the same data. For example, an e-mail field in a table that is frequently searched is a good candidate for an index. To avoid data entry errors in a field that should contain unique values (and is not the primary key), set up the index to not accept duplicates.

Create a multiple-field index if you frequently sort or search a large table by two or more fields at the same time. In Table Design view, click the Indexes button to open the Indexes window shown in Figure 2.9 and create an index for the combination of fields. Up to 10 fields can be included in a multiple-field index in the Indexes window.

Figure 2.9 Indexes Window

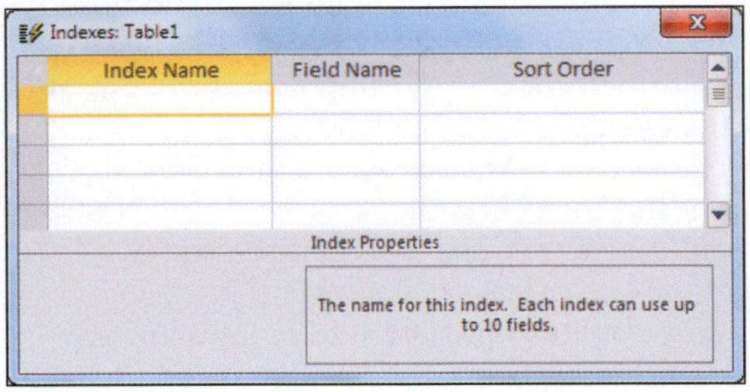

Project 3 Creating Indexes

Part 1 of 1

1. With the **AL2-C2-RSRCompServ.accdb** database open, open the Customers table in Design view.
2. Create a single-field index for the *ZIP* field by completing the following steps:
   a. Make *ZIP* the active field.
   b. Click in the *Indexed* property box, click the down-pointing arrow that appears, and then click *Yes (Duplicates OK)* at the drop-down list.

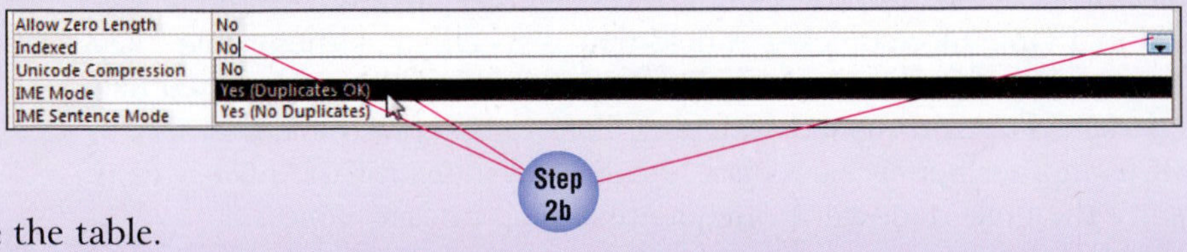

   c. Save the table.

3. Create a multiple-field index for the *LName* and *FName* fields by completing the following steps:
   a. Click the Indexes button in the Show/Hide group in the Table Tools Design tab.
   b. At the Indexes: Customers window, click in the first blank row in the *Index Name* column (below *ZIP*) and then type **Names**.
   c. Press Tab, click the down-pointing arrow that appears in the *Field Name* column, and then click *LName* at the drop-down list. The sort order for *LName* defaults to *Ascending*.

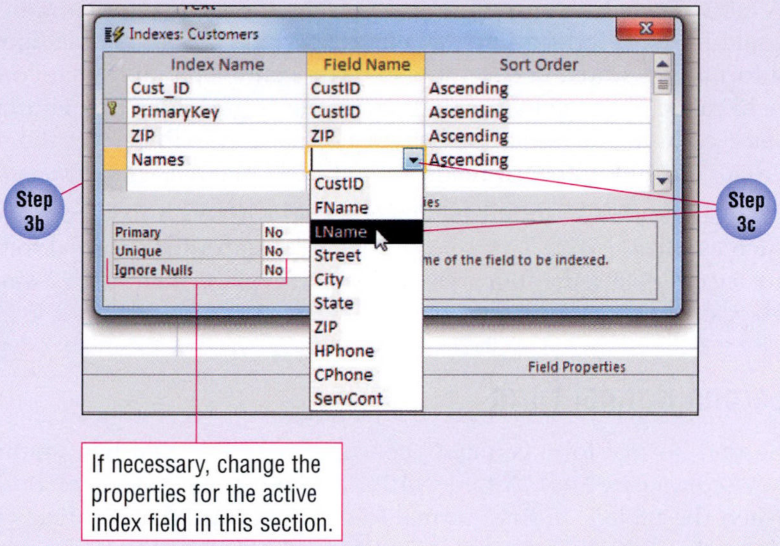

   d. Click in the row in the *Field Name* column below *LName*, click the down-pointing arrow that appears, and then click *FName*.
   e. Close the Indexes: Customers window.

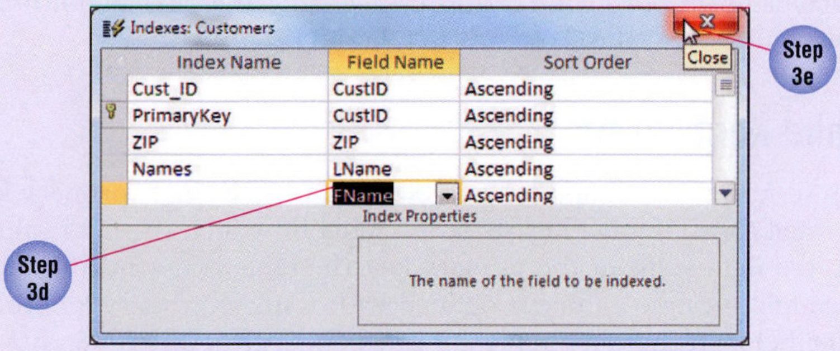

   f. Save the table.
4. Close the Customers table.
5. Close the **AL2-C2-RSRCompServ.accdb** database.

You cannot view an index. Access uses the index behind the scenes to work more efficiently. In a database with a large number of records, consider fields other than the primary key that are sorted or searched and create indexes for these fields.

Normalizing the Database

Normalizing a database involves reviewing the database structure and ensuring the tables are set up to eliminate redundancy. Three normalization states are tested: first normal form, second normal form, and third normal form.

First Normal Form

A table meets first normal form when the table does not contain any fields that could be broken down into smaller units and when the table does not have similar information stored in several fields. For example, a table that contains a single field called *TechnicianName* that stores the technician's first and last names in the same column is in violation of first normal form. To correct the structure, split *TechnicianName* into two fields such as *TechLastName* and *TechFirstName*.

A table that has multiple fields set up with each field containing similar data, such as *Week1*, *Week2*, *Week3*, and *Week4* violates first normal form. To correct this structure, delete the four week fields and replace them with a single field named *WeekNumber*.

Second Normal Form

Second normal form is only of concern for a table that has a multiple-field primary key (composite key). A table with a composite key meets second normal form when the table is in first normal form and when all of the fields in the table are dependent on all of the fields that form the primary key. For example, assume a table is defined with two fields that form the primary key: *CustID* and *ComputerID*. A field in the same table is titled *EmailAdd*. The contents of the *EmailAdd* field are dependent on the customer only (not the computer). Since *EmailAdd* is not dependent on **both** *CustID* **and** *ComputerID*, the table is not in second normal form. To correct the structure, delete the *EmailAdd* field.

Third Normal Form

Third normal form applies to a table that has a single primary key and is in first normal form. If a field exists in the table for which the field value is not dependent on the field value of the primary key, the table is not in third normal form. For example, assume a table is defined with a single primary key titled *TechnicianID*. Two fields in the same table are titled *PayCode* and *PayRate*. Assume also that a technician's pay rate is dependent on the pay code assigned to the technician. Since a pay rate is dependent on the field value in the pay code field and not on the technician's identification number, the table is not in third normal form. To convert the table to third normal form, delete the *PayRate* field from the table. (The *PayRate* field would belong in another table in the database.)

Normalizing a database often involves splitting fields into smaller units, and/or breaking larger tables down into smaller tables and creating relationships to remove repeating groups of data.

Chapter Summary

- When building relationships consider the frequency of matching data in the common field in both tables to determine if the relationship is one-to-many, one-to-one, or many-to-many.
- One-to-many relationships are the most common type of relationship that involves joining the tables by dragging the primary key from the "one" table to the foreign key in the "many" table.
- In a one-to-many relationship, only one record for a matching field value exists in the primary table while many records for the same value can exist in the related table.
- A relationship diagram depicts the tables joined in the relationship as well as the type of relationship between the two tables.
- At the Edit Relationships dialog box you can turn on referential integrity and the two cascade options.
- Referential integrity places restrictions on new data entered into the related table. A record is not allowed in the related table if a matching record does not already exist in the primary table.
- *Cascade Update Related Fields* automatically updates all occurrences of the same data in the foreign key field when a change is made to the primary key data.
- *Cascade Delete Related Records* automatically deletes related records when a record is deleted from the primary table.
- In a one-to-one relationship only one record exists with a matching value in the joined field in both tables.
- In a many-to-many relationship many records can exist with a matching value in the joined field in both tables.
- To create a many-to-many relationship, a junction table is used that contains a minimum of two fields which are the primary key fields from each table in the many-to-many relationship.
- Two one-to-many relationships using the junction table form a many-to-many relationship.
- In some tables, two or more fields are used to create the primary key if a single field is not guaranteed to hold unique data.
- A primary key that is made up of two or more fields is called a composite key.
- A lookup field displays a drop-down list in a field in which the user points and clicks to enter the field value. The list can be generated from records in a related table, or by typing in a value list.
- Once the lookup field is created, use the Lookup tab in the *Field Properties* section in Table Design view to modify individual properties.
- The Limit To List property allows you to restrict entries in the field to items within the lookup list.
- A field that allows multiple entries to be selected from a drop-down list can be created by clicking *Allow Multiple Values* at the last Lookup Wizard dialog box.

- A field that is defined as a multiple-value field cannot be changed back to a single-value field.
- Access displays check boxes next to items in the drop-down list if the field has been set to allow multiple values.
- An index is a list generated by Access that includes pointers that direct Access to the location of records in a table.
- Access creates an index for a primary key field automatically.
- Create a single-field table index by changing the Indexed property to *Yes (Duplicates OK)* or *Yes (No Duplicates)*.
- A multiple-field index is created using the Indexes window.
- Normalizing a database involves reviewing the database structure to eliminate redundancy. Three normalization states are checked: first normal form, second normal form, and third normal form.

Commands Review

FEATURE	RIBBON TAB, GROUP	BUTTON
Edit relationships	Relationship Tools Design, Tools	
Indexes	Table Tools Design, Show/Hide	
Primary key	Table Tools Design, Tools	
Print relationships report	Relationship Tools Design, Tools	
Relationships window	Database Tools, Show/Hide	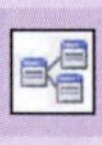
Show table	Relationship Tools Design, Relationships	

Concepts Check Test Your Knowledge

Completion: In the space provided at the right, indicate the correct term, command, or number.

1. This is the term for a field added to a related table for the purpose of creating a relationship that is the primary key in the other table. ____________
2. The Relationships button is found in this tab in the ribbon. ____________
3. Add a table to the Relationships window using this dialog box. ____________
4. At the Edit Relationships dialog box, the two cascade options do not become active until this option is turned on. ____________
5. This symbol appears on the join line next to the many side of a relationship when referential integrity is on. ____________
6. Open the Edit Relationships dialog box for an existing relationship by doing this action with the mouse while pointing at the black join line in the Relationships window. ____________
7. This type of relationship exists if only one matching record will be found in both tables in the relationship. ____________
8. A many-to-many relationship is created by establishing two one-to-many relationships using a third table referred to by this term. ____________
9. A primary key that is made up of two or more fields is referred to by this term. ____________
10. A lookup field can be restricted to items within the list by setting this property to *Yes*. ____________
11. Specify a field as a multiple-value field by clicking this check box at the last Lookup Wizard dialog box. ____________
12. Set the *Indexed* property to this option for an index field that is likely to contain more than one record with the same field value, such as a zip code. ____________
13. Open this window to create an index that uses two or more fields. ____________
14. These are the three normalization states that are tested. ____________
15. If a field exists in a table for which the field value is not dependent on the primary key, the table is not in this normalization state. ____________

Skills Check Assess Your Performance

Assessment 1

CREATE A LOOKUP LIST

1. Open the database named **AL2-C2-VantageVideos** and enable content.
2. Open each table in Datasheet view and review the table's fields and records to familiarize yourself with the database. Close all tables when finished.
3. Open the Relationships window and close the Show Table dialog box. Notice that no relationships have been created in the database. Close the Relationships window.
4. The *CustID* field in the WebOrders table can be made easier to use if the field is changed to a lookup list that presents customer names and numbers from the WebCustomers table. Open the WebOrders table in Design view, make *CustID* the active field, and create a lookup list to display values from another table using the following information.
   a. Display the *CustID*, *FirstName*, and *LastName* fields from the WebCustomers table.
   b. Sort the list in ascending order by the *LastName* field.
   c. Clear the *Hide key column* check box.
   d. Store the *CustID* value.
   e. Accept the default label for the column of *CustID*.
5. Modify the Lookup property for the *CustID* field that will ensure only items within the list are allowed to be entered into the field.
6. Save the table, switch to Datasheet view, and then enter the following record to test the lookup list.

Web Order ID	10007
Customer ID	Select *106 Gary Gallagher* in the lookup list.
Date Ordered	Feb 26 2012

7. Print the datasheet.
8. Close the WebOrders table.

Assessment 2

CREATE A TABLE WITH A MULTIPLE-FIELD PRIMARY KEY AND LOOKUP LISTS

1. With the **AL2-C2-VantageVideos** database open, create a new table using Design view to track the videos ordered by a customer using the following information.

Field Name	Data Type	Field Size	Caption
WebOrdID	Text	5	Web Order ID
WebProdID	Text	7	Product ID
Qty	Number		Quantity

2. A customer can choose to buy more than one video on the same order. When this occurs, the same order number can be associated with more than one record in the table; therefore, the primary key cannot be based on the *WebOrdID* field alone. Assign a multiple-field primary key using both the *WebOrdID* and *WebProdID* fields. The combination of the order identification number and product identification number will uniquely describe each record in the table.
3. Save the table and name it *WebOrderDetails*.

4. Create a lookup list for the *WebOrdID* field that connects to the *WebOrdID* field in the WebOrders table. Add all three fields in the WebOrders table to the lookup list, do not specify a sort field, clear the *Hide key column*, store *WebOrdID* in the field, and accept the default field name. Modify the Lookup property to ensure only items within the list are allowed to be entered into the field.
5. Create a lookup list for the *WebProdID* field that connects to the *WebProdID* field in the WebProducts table. Display the *Product* field sorted in ascending order, make sure the column width is wide enough to display the entire video title in the list, hide the key column, and accept the default field name. Modify the Lookup property to ensure only items within the list are allowed to be entered into the field.
6. Save the table and switch to Datasheet view. Add the following records to the WebOrderDetails datasheet to test the lookup lists.

Web Order ID	Product ID	Quantity
10001	To Kill a Mockingbird	1
10001	Blue Hawaii	1
10002	The Great Escape	2
10003	Cool Hand Luke	1
10003	Doctor Zhivago	1
10003	The Longest Day	2
10004	Dial M for Murder	1

7. Adjust all column widths to Best Fit and print the datasheet.
8. Close the WebOrderDetails table. Click Yes when prompted to save changes to the layout.

Assessment 3

EDIT RELATIONSHIPS

1. With the **AL2-C2-VantageVideos** database open, open the Relationships window to view the relationships created by Access when the lookup lists were created.
2. Resize and move the table field list boxes to the approximate size and location shown in Figure 2.10.
3. Edit the relationships as follows:
   a. Edit the one-to-many relationship between WebCustomers and WebOrders to turn on referential integrity and the two cascade options.
   b. Edit the one-to-many relationship between WebOrders and WebOrderDetails to turn on referential integrity and the two cascade options.
   c. Edit the one-to-many relationship between WebProducts and WebOrderDetails to turn on referential integrity and the two cascade options.

Figure 2.10 Assessment 3

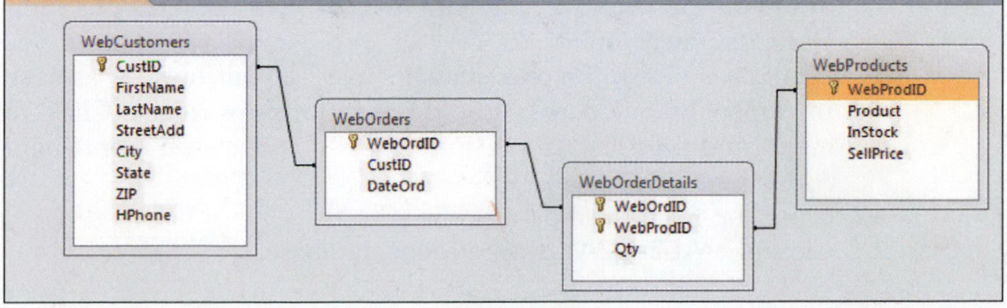

4. Create and print a relationship report.
5. On your relationship report printout write the type of relationship that exists between WebOrders and WebProducts.
6. Close the Relationships for **AL2-C2-VantageVideos** report. Click Yes to save the report and accept the default name in the Save As dialog box.
7. Close the Relationships window.

Assessment

4 CREATE A TABLE WITH A ONE-TO-ONE RELATIONSHIP

1. With the **AL2-C2-VantageVideos** database open, create a new table using Design view to store a customer's credit card information using the following information.

Field Name	Data Type	Field Size	Caption
CustID	Text	3	**Customer ID**
CCType	Text	20	**Credit Card Type**
CCNumber	Text	16	**Credit Card Number**
CCExpMonth	Number		**Expiry Month**
CCExpYear	Number		**Expiry Year**
EmailAdd	Text	30	**Email Address**

2. Assign the primary key to the *CustID* field.
3. Save the table and name it *WebCustPymnt*.
4. Create a lookup list for the *CustID* field that connects to the *CustID* field in the WebCustomers table by following steps similar to those in Assessment 1, Step 4. Modify the Lookup property to ensure only items within the list are allowed to be entered into the field.
5. Save the table, switch to Datasheet view, and enter the following record.

Customer ID	Select *106 Gary Gallagher* in the lookup list
Credit Card Type	**Visa**
Credit Card Number	**0009100876453152**
Expiry Month	**7**
Expiry Year	**2014**
Email Address	**garyg@emcp.net**

6. Adjust all column widths to Best Fit and print the datasheet in landscape orientation.
7. Close the WebCustPymnt table. Click Yes when prompted to save changes to the layout.
8. Open the Relationships window and open the Show Table dialog box.
9. Add the WebCustPymnt table to the window. Edit the one-to-one relationship between WebCustomers and WebCustPymnt to turn on referential integrity and the two cascade options.
10. If necessary, rearrange the table field list boxes in the Relationships window until you can better see the join line between the WebCustPymnt and WebCustomers tables.
11. Print a relationship report changing page layout options as necessary to fit the report on one page. Close the Relationships report. Click Yes to save the report and type **Relationships-Assessment4** as the report name in the Save As dialog box.
12. Close the Relationships window.
13. Close the **AL2-C2-VantageVideos** database.

Visual Benchmark Demonstrate Your Proficiency

CREATE LOOKUP LISTS AND EDIT RELATIONSHIPS

1. Open **AL2-C2-PawsParadise.accdb**.
2. This database is similar to the Visual Benchmark database created in Chapter 1; however, an additional table has been created and several records added to the database. Spend a few moments familiarizing yourself with the tables and records.
3. Create the following lookup lists, making sure the field value saved is always the primary key field:
   a. In the Dogs table, look up the Kennel Category in the KennelCategories table. Hide the key column in this list.
   b. In the Dogs table, look up the Customer Number in the DogOwners table. Clear the *Hide key column* in this list.
   c. In the Reservations table, look up the Customer Number in the DogOwners table. Clear the *Hide key column* in this list.
4. Open the Relationships window and edit relationships to enforce referential integrity and turn on both cascade options for each relationship.
5. Rearrange and move table field list boxes as necessary so that your Relationships window appears similar to the one shown in Figure 2.11.
6. Create and print a relationships report.
7. Save the relationships report using the default name and then close the report and the Relationships window.
8. Close the **AL2-C2-PawsParadise.accdb** database.

Figure 2.11 Visual Benchmark Relationships Window

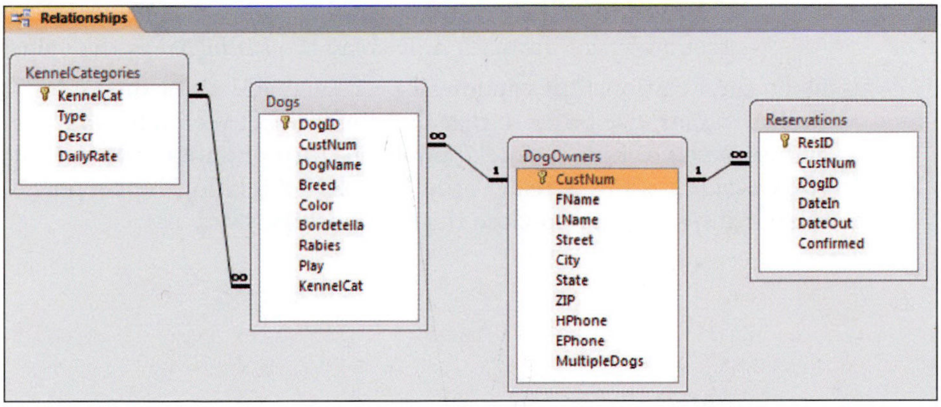

Case Study Apply Your Skills

Part 1

You are working as an intern at Hillsdale Realty. The intern that worked at the company before you started work on a database to be used for managing sales agents, listings, sales, and commission quotas. The previous intern did not have time to finish the database. Open **AL2-C2-HillsdaleRealty.accdb** and enable content. Open each table and review the fields and records to familiarize yourself with the database. The Agents table is not in first normal form. The field named *AgentName* contains both the first and last names of each sales agent. To improve the table design, modify the table so that two separate fields are used for representative names. Add captions to the name fields. Correct the data in the datasheet so that the names are correctly split into the two columns. Print the revised Agents table datasheet with all column widths adjusted to Best Fit. Close the table.

Part 2

You decide to improve the efficiency of data entry by creating lookup lists as follows:

- In the Listings table you want to be able to select the correct Agent ID by viewing the agent names in a sorted drop-down list. Display the *AgentID* as the value in the field.
- In the Agents table you want to be able to select the quota code by viewing all of the quota codes and amounts in a drop-down list. Display the Commission Quota in the datasheet but store *QuotaID* as the field value. Edit the caption for the field to read *Quota* (instead of *Quota Code*).
- In the SalesAndComm table you want to be able to select the correct Listing Number by viewing the listing numbers and addresses from the Listings table. Make sure the column width is wide enough to display all of the street address information. Display the *ListingNo* as the value in the field.

Open the Relationships window. If necessary, add all of the tables to the window. Resize and arrange boxes so that the join lines between tables are easy to follow and understand. Edit each relationship to turn on referential integrity and the two cascade options. Create, print, and save a relationships report. Close the relationships report and close the relationships window.

Part 3

You have decided to add another table named *Preferences* to the database. Create the table using the information below. You determine appropriate data types and other field properties.

Field Name	Lookup Lists
ClientID	
ListingNo	Create a lookup list to the Listings table.
AgentID	Create a lookup list to the Agents table.
Preferences	Create a multiple-value list with the following items: Exclusive listing MLS listing Pre-sale inspection Staging service

A client could have more than one listing at Hillsdale Realtors so you do not want to use *ClientID* as the primary key. Assign the primary key as a combination of two fields: *ClientID* and *ListingNo*. Add a sample record to the table to test your lookup lists and multiple-value field. Adjust all column widths to Best Fit, print the datasheet, and close the table saving the layout. Open the relationships window, add the new table, and arrange the layout so that join lines are not overlapping. Edit the relationships between Preferences and Listings and Agents to turn on referential integrity and the two cascade options. Create, print, and save a new relationships report named *Relationships-Part3*.

Microsoft® Access®

CHAPTER 3

Advanced Query Techniques

PERFORMANCE OBJECTIVES

Upon successful completion of Chapter 3, you will be able to:

- **Save a filter as a query**
- **Create and run a parameter query to prompt for criteria**
- **Add tables to and remove tables from a query**
- **Create an inner join, left join, and right join to modify query results**
- **Create a self-join to match two fields in the same table**
- **Create a query that includes a subquery**
- **Assign an alias to a table and a field name**
- **Select records using a multiple-value field in a query**
- **Create a new table using a make-table query**
- **Remove records from a table using a delete query**
- **Add records to the end of an existing table using an append query**
- **Modify records using an update query**

SNAP Training and Assessment. Simplified.

Tutorials

3.1 Saving a Filter as a Query

3.2 Prompting for Criteria Using a Parameter Query

3.3 Creating a Query with Right Outer Join

3.4 Creating a Self-Join Query

3.5 Creating and Using Subqueries

3.6 Assigning Aliases and Using a Multivalued Field in a Query

3.7 Performing Operations Using Action Queries

3.8 Creating a New Table Using a Query

3.9 Adding and Deleting Records to a Table Using a Query

3.10 Modifying Records Using an Update Query

In this chapter you create, save, and run queries that incorporate advanced query features such as saving a filter as a query, prompting for criteria on single and multiple fields, modifying join properties to view alternative query results, and using action queries to perform operations on groups of records. In addition to these topics, you will also create an alias for a table and a field and incorporate subqueries to manage multiple calculations. Model answers for this chapter's projects appear on the following pages.

Access
Access2010L2C3

Note: Before beginning the projects, copy to your storage medium the Access2010L2C3 subfolder from the Access2010L2 folder on the CD that accompanies this textbook and then make Access2010L2C3 the active folder.

Model Answers

WO2orMoreHrsRate30 — 11/12/2012

Work Order	Customer ID	Technician ID	WO Date	Descripton	Service Date	Hours	Rate	Parts
65015	1008	04	Mon Sep 10 2012	Restore operating system	Tue Sep 11 2012	2.25	30.00	$0.00
65019	1025	02	Sat Sep 15 2012	Upgrade to Windows 7	Mon Sep 17 2012	2.50	30.00	$0.00
65021	1035	06	Tue Sep 18 2012	Customer has blue screen upon boot	Tue Sep 18 2012	3.25	30.00	$0.00
65028	1030	04	Tue Oct 02 2012	Reinstall operating system	Tue Oct 02 2012	2.25	30.00	$0.00
65032	1008	02	Fri Oct 12 2012	Install second hard drive	Sat Oct 13 2012	2.00	30.00	$425.75
65033	1000	01	Fri Oct 12 2012	Install Windows 7	Sat Oct 13 2012	3.25	30.00	$335.75
65035	1020	02	Sun Oct 14 2012	Office 2010 training	Mon Oct 15 2012	2.50	30.00	$0.00
65038	1010	01	Fri Oct 19 2012	Install Windows 7	Fri Oct 19 2012	2.50	30.00	$0.00
65046	1010	10	Fri Oct 26 2012	Windows 7 training	Fri Oct 26 2012	2.00	30.00	$0.00

Page 1

Project 1 Select Records Using Filtered Criteria and Prompted Criteria Project 1a, WO2orMoreHrsRate30 Query

PromptedTechnicianLabor — 11/12/2012

Work Order	First Name	Last Name	Service Date	Hours	Rate
65020	Pat	Hynes	Mon Sep 17 2012	1.50	22.50
65033	Pat	Hynes	Sat Oct 13 2012	3.25	30.00
65038	Pat	Hynes	Fri Oct 19 2012	2.50	30.00

Page 1

Project 1b, PromptedTechnicianLabor Query

PromptedServiceDate — 11/12/2012

Work Order	Customer ID	Descripton	Service Date	Hours	Rate	Parts
65027	1010	Replace hard drive	Tue Oct 02 2012	1.50	30.00	$375.50
65028	1030	Reinstall operating system	Tue Oct 02 2012	2.25	30.00	$0.00
65029	1035	Set up automatic backup	Wed Oct 03 2012	0.50	22.50	$0.00
65030	1000	Clean malware from system	Sat Oct 06 2012	1.00	15.50	$0.00
65031	1045	Customer reports noisy hard drive	Sat Oct 06 2012	1.75	30.00	$0.00
65032	1008	Install second hard drive	Sat Oct 13 2012	2.00	30.00	$425.75
65033	1000	Install Windows 7	Sat Oct 13 2012	3.25	30.00	$335.75
65034	1035	File management training	Sun Oct 14 2012	1.50	30.00	$0.00
65035	1020	Office 2010 training	Mon Oct 15 2012	2.50	30.00	$0.00

Page 1

Project 1c, PromptedServiceDate Query

UnassignedWorkOrders — 11/13/2012

First Name	Last Name	Work Order	WO Date	Descripton
		65047	Sat Oct 27 2012	Set up automatic backup
		65048	Mon Oct 29 2012	Replace LCD monitor
		65049	Tue Oct 30 2012	Set up dual monitor system
		65050	Tue Oct 30 2012	Reinstall Windows 7
Pat	Hynes	65020	Mon Sep 17 2012	Troubleshoot noisy fan
Pat	Hynes	65033	Fri Oct 12 2012	Install Windows 7
Pat	Hynes	65038	Fri Oct 19 2012	Install Windows 7
Hui	Chen	65014	Mon Sep 10 2012	Replace power supply
Hui	Chen	65019	Sat Sep 15 2012	Upgrade to Windows 7
Hui	Chen	65026	Sat Sep 29 2012	Upgrade memory
Hui	Chen	65032	Fri Oct 12 2012	Install second hard drive
Hui	Chen	65035	Sun Oct 14 2012	Office 2010 training
Kayla	Blewett	65023	Sat Sep 22 2012	Upgrade RAM
Kayla	Blewett	65036	Mon Oct 15 2012	Set up home network
Kayla	Blewett	65041	Mon Oct 22 2012	Bi-annual computer maintenance
Mihir	Patel	65015	Mon Sep 10 2012	Restore operating system
Mihir	Patel	65022	Fri Sep 21 2012	Customer reports screen is fuzzy
Mihir	Patel	65024	Mon Sep 24 2012	Install malware protection
Mihir	Patel	65028	Tue Oct 02 2012	Reinstall operating system
Madir	Sadiku	65037	Fri Oct 19 2012	Semiannual computer maintenance
Brody	Stewart	65016	Tue Sep 11 2012	Install upgraded video card
Brody	Stewart	65021	Tue Sep 18 2012	Customer has blue screen upon boot
Brody	Stewart	65025	Fri Sep 28 2012	Troubleshoot hard drive noise
Brody	Stewart	65039	Fri Oct 19 2012	Set up automatic backup
Brody	Stewart	65042	Mon Oct 22 2012	File management training
Ana	Takacs	65029	Tue Oct 02 2012	Set up automatic backup
Ana	Takacs	65034	Fri Oct 12 2012	File management training
Ana	Takacs	65044	Tue Oct 23 2012	DVD drive is not working
Marty	O'Leary	65017	Fri Sep 14 2012	Replace DVD drive
Marty	O'Leary	65043	Mon Oct 22 2012	Troubleshoot video fuzziness
Armando	Colacci	65031	Sat Oct 06 2012	Customer reports noisy hard drive
Armando	Colacci	65040	Fri Oct 19 2012	Configure dual monitors
Kelsey	Eastman	65013	Fri Sep 07 2012	Replace keyboard
Kelsey	Eastman	65018	Fri Sep 14 2012	Upgrade Office suite
Kelsey	Eastman	65027	Sun Sep 30 2012	Replace hard drive
Kelsey	Eastman	65046	Fri Oct 26 2012	Windows 7 training
Dana	Westman	65012	Fri Sep 07 2012	Bi-annual computer maintenance
Dana	Westman	65030	Sat Oct 06 2012	Clean malware from system
Dana	Westman	65045	Tue Oct 23 2012	Set up automatic backup

Page 1

Project 2 Modify Query Results by Changing the Join Property

Project 2c, UnassignedWorkOrders Query

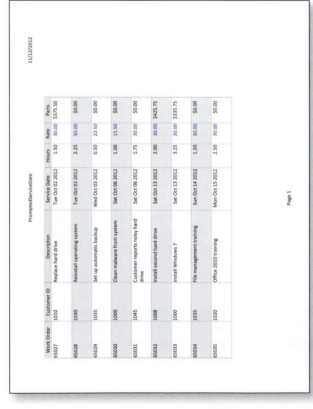

TotalWorkOrders 11/14/2012

Work Order	Service Date	Total Labor	Parts	Total Work Order
65012	Tue Sep 04 2012	$37.50	$10.15	$47.65
65013	Mon Sep 10 2012	$14.25	$42.75	$57.00
65014	Mon Sep 10 2012	$52.50	$62.77	$115.27
65015	Tue Sep 11 2012	$67.50	$0.00	$67.50
65016	Tue Sep 11 2012	$30.00	$48.75	$78.75
65017	Sat Sep 15 2012	$16.88	$55.87	$72.75
65018	Sat Sep 15 2012	$22.50	$0.00	$22.50
65019	Mon Sep 17 2012	$75.00	$0.00	$75.00
65020	Mon Sep 17 2012	$33.75	$62.77	$96.52
65021	Tue Sep 18 2012	$97.50	$0.00	$97.50
65022	Sat Sep 22 2012	$45.00	$55.47	$100.47
65023	Sun Sep 23 2012	$37.50	$62.50	$100.00
65024	Mon Sep 24 2012	$15.50	$75.50	$91.00
65025	Fri Sep 28 2012	$45.00	$0.00	$45.00
65026	Sat Sep 29 2012	$22.50	$75.75	$98.25
65027	Tue Oct 02 2012	$45.00	$375.50	$420.50
65028	Tue Oct 02 2012	$67.50	$0.00	$67.50
65029	Wed Oct 03 2012	$11.25	$0.00	$11.25
65030	Sat Oct 06 2012	$15.50	$0.00	$15.50
65031	Sat Oct 06 2012	$52.50	$0.00	$52.50
65032	Sat Oct 13 2012	$60.00	$425.75	$485.75
65033	Sat Oct 13 2012	$97.50	$335.75	$433.25
65034	Sun Oct 14 2012	$45.00	$0.00	$45.00
65035	Mon Oct 15 2012	$75.00	$0.00	$75.00
65036	Tue Oct 16 2012	$67.50	$85.22	$152.72
65037	Fri Oct 19 2012	$37.50	$8.75	$46.25
65038	Fri Oct 19 2012	$75.00	$0.00	$75.00
65039	Fri Oct 19 2012	$16.88	$0.00	$16.88
65040	Sat Oct 20 2012	$30.00	$0.00	$30.00
65041	Mon Oct 22 2012	$37.50	$10.15	$47.65
65042	Mon Oct 22 2012	$33.75	$0.00	$33.75
65043	Tue Oct 23 2012	$15.00	$0.00	$15.00
65044	Tue Oct 23 2012	$30.00	$55.40	$85.40
65045	Fri Oct 26 2012	$11.63	$0.00	$11.63
65046	Fri Oct 26 2012	$60.00	$0.00	$60.00

Page 1

Project 3 Calculate Work Order Totals

Project 3b, TotalWorkOrders Query

TechniciansOperatingSys 11/14/2012

First Name	Last Name	Operating System
Pat	Hynes	Windows 7
Hui	Chen	Windows 7
Madir	Sadiku	Windows 7
Armando	Colacci	Windows 7
Kelsey	Eastman	Windows 7

Page 1

Project 4 Query a Multiple-Value Field

TechnicianOperatingSys Query

Sept2012WorkOrders 11/14/2012

WO	CustID	TechID	WODate	Descr	ServDate	Hours	Rate	Parts
65012	1000	11	9/7/2012	Bi-annual com	9/4/2012	1.25	$30.00	$10.15
65013	1000	10	9/7/2012	Replace keybo	9/10/2012	0.5	$28.50	$42.75
65014	1005	02	9/10/2012	Replace power	9/10/2012	1.75	$30.00	$62.77
65015	1008	04	9/10/2012	Restore operati	9/11/2012	2.25	$30.00	$0.00
65016	1010	06	9/11/2012	Install upgrade	9/11/2012	1	$30.00	$48.75
65017	1015	08	9/14/2012	Replace DVD dr	9/15/2012	0.75	$22.50	$55.87
65018	1020	10	9/14/2012	Upgrade Office	9/15/2012	1	$22.50	$0.00
65019	1025	02	9/15/2012	Upgrade to Wi	9/17/2012	2.5	$30.00	$0.00
65020	1030	01	9/17/2012	Troubleshoot n	9/17/2012	1.5	$22.50	$62.77
65021	1035	06	9/18/2012	Customer has	9/18/2012	3.25	$30.00	$0.00
65022	1040	04	9/21/2012	Customer repo	9/22/2012	1.5	$30.00	$55.47
65023	1045	03	9/22/2012	Upgrade RAM	9/23/2012	1.25	$30.00	$62.50
65024	1005	04	9/24/2012	Install malware	9/24/2012	1	$15.50	$75.50
65025	1010	06	9/28/2012	Troubleshoot h	9/28/2012	1.5	$30.00	$0.00
65026	1025	02	9/29/2012	Upgrade mem	9/29/2012	0.75	$30.00	$75.75

Page 1

Project 5 Modify Records Using Action Queries

Project 5c, Sept2012WorkOrders Table

FeesSCPlans 11/14/2012

ID	Term	Plan	Max No. of Computers	Rate
1	6 months	A	1	$50.88
2	6 months	A	2	$63.07
3	6 months	B	3	$112.00
4	1 year	B	1	$82.50
5	1 year	B	2	$157.50
6	1 year	A	3	$169.07
7	1 year	C	3	$193.50
8	1 year	D	5	$242.00
9	2 years	A	4	$297.86
10	2 years	B	4	$297.50

Page 1

Project 5d, FeesSCPlans Table

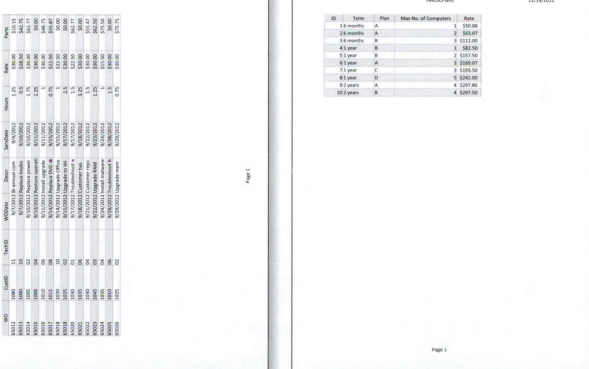

Project 1 Select Records Using Filtered Criteria and Prompted Criteria — 3 Parts

You will create queries to select records by saving a filter's criteria and by creating a query that prompts the user for the criteria when the query is run.

Quick Steps

Save Filter as Query

1. Open table.
2. Filter table as desired.
3. Click Advanced Filter Options button.
4. Click *Filter By Form.*
5. Click Advanced Filter Options button.
6. Click *Save As Query.*
7. Type desired query name.
8. Click OK.
9. Close Filter By Form datasheet.
10. Close table.

HINT

Consider filtering a datasheet and saving the filter as a query if you are more comfortable using filters to select records than typing criteria expressions in Query Design view.

Advanced Filter Options

Extracting Records Using Select Queries

A ***select query*** is the query type that is most often used in Access. Select queries extract records from a single table or from multiple tables that meet criteria that you specify. The subset of records that is displayed can be edited, viewed, and/or printed. In Query Design view, the criteria used to select records are entered by typing expressions in the *Criteria* row for the required field(s). Access provides other methods for which criteria can be specified for a query.

Saving a Filter as a Query

A ***filter*** is used in a datasheet or form to temporarily hide records that do not meet specified criteria. For example, you can filter a WorkOrders datasheet to display only those work orders completed on a specified date. The subset of records can be edited, viewed, or printed. Use the Filter by Form feature to filter a datasheet by multiple criteria using a blank datasheet. A filter is active until the filter is removed or the datasheet or form is closed. When the object is reopened, all records are redisplayed.

If you filter a datasheet and then decide that you may want to reuse the criteria, save the filter as a query. To do this, display the criteria in the Filter by Form datasheet, click the Advanced Filter Options button in the Sort & Filter group in the Home tab, and then click *Save as Query* at the drop-down list. Type a query name at the Save as Query dialog box and press Enter or click OK.

Saving a filter as a query means all columns in the table display in the query results datasheet. Use the Hide Fields feature to remove field(s) in the results.

Project 1a Saving a Filter as a Query — Part 1 of 3

1. Open the **AL2-C3-RSRCompServ.accdb** database and enable content.
2. Display only those service calls that required two or more hours of labor by technicians billed at $30.00 per hour using the Filter by Form feature by completing the following steps:
   a. Open the WorkOrders table in Datasheet view.
   b. Minimize the Navigation pane.
   c. Hide the *Comments* field by right-clicking the *Comments* column heading in the datasheet and then clicking *Hide Fields* at the shortcut menu.

d. Click the Advanced Filter Options button in the Sort & Filter group in the Home tab and then click *Filter By Form* at the drop-down list.

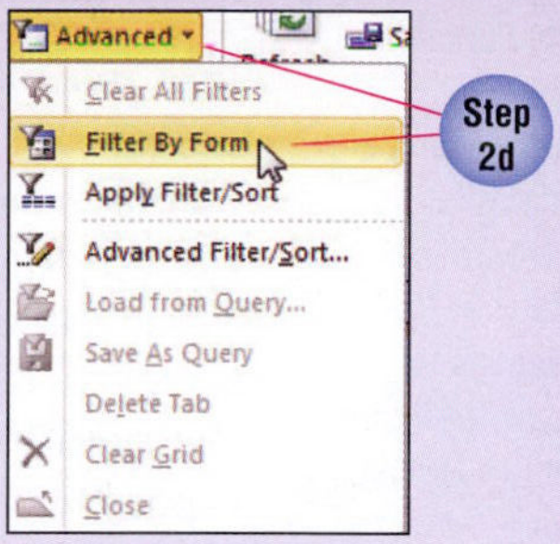

e. Click in the empty record in the *Hours* column. Use the down-pointing arrow if you want to filter the table by a specific value within the field. Type **>=2** and then press Tab.

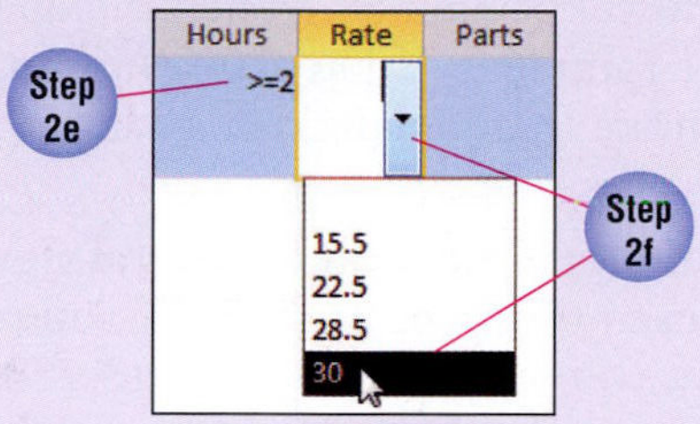

f. With the insertion point positioned in the *Rate* column, click the down-pointing arrow that appears and then click *30* at the drop-down list.

g. Click the Toggle Filter button (displays the ScreenTip *Apply Filter*) in the Sort & Filter group in the Home tab to apply the filter's criteria and display records that meet the filter conditions.

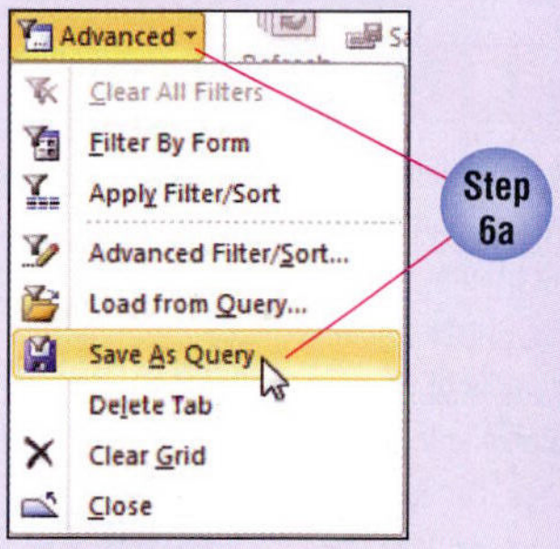

3. Review the nine filtered records in the datasheet.
4. Click the Toggle Filter button (displays the ScreenTip *Remove Filter*) to redisplay all records.
5. Click the Advanced Filter Options button and then click *Filter By Form* at the drop-down list. Notice the filter criteria in the *Hours* and *Rate* columns are intact.
6. Save the filter as a query so that you can reuse the criteria by completing the following steps:
   a. Click the Advanced Filter Options button and then click *Save As Query* at the drop-down list.
   b. At the Save As Query dialog box, type **WO2orMoreHrsRate30** in the *Query Name* text box and then press Enter or click OK.

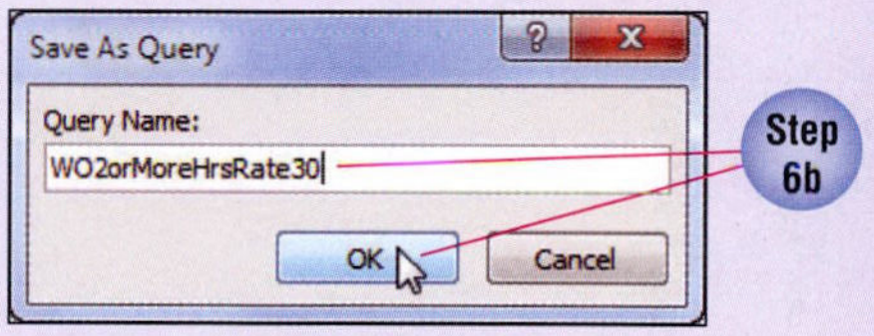

   c. Click the Advanced Filter Options button and then click *Close* at the drop-down list to close the Filter By Form datasheet.
   d. Close the WorkOrders table. Click No when prompted to save changes to the table design.

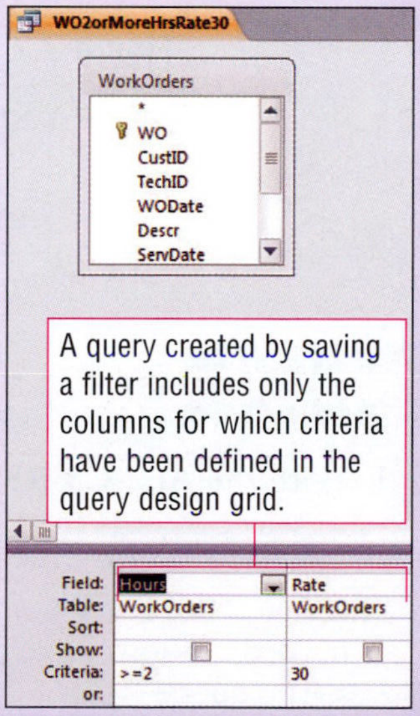

7. Expand the Navigation pane.
8. Double-click the query object named *WO2orMoreHrsRate30* to open the query and review the query results.
9. Hide the *Comments* column in the query results datasheet.
10. Print the datasheet in landscape orientation with the left and right margins set to 0.5 inch.
11. Switch to Design view. Notice a query created from a filter creates columns in the query design grid for only those columns upon which a criterion has been defined.
12. Close the query. Click Yes when prompted to save changes to the query layout.

Quick Steps

Create Parameter Query

1. Start new query in Design view.
2. Add desired table(s).
3. Close Show Table dialog box.
4. Add desired fields to query design grid.
5. Click in *Criteria* row in field to be prompted.
6. Type message text encased in square brackets.
7. Repeat Steps 5–6 for each additional criteria field.
8. Save query.
9. Close query.

H I N T

If you are creating a parameter query that will be used by other people, consider adding an example of an acceptable entry in the message. For example, the message *Type the service date in the format mmm-dd-yyyy (example Oct-31-2012)* is more informative than *Type the service date*.

Prompting for Criteria Using a Parameter Query

In a **parameter query**, specific criteria for a field are not stored with the query design. Instead, the field(s) used to select records have a prompt message that displays when the query is run. The prompt message instructs the user to type the criteria by which to select records. Figure 3.1 illustrates an Enter Parameter Value dialog box that is displayed when a parameter query is run to select by a technician's name. The message that is shown in the dialog box is created in the field for which the criterion will be applied. When the query is run, the user types the criterion at the Enter Parameter Value dialog box and Access selects the records based on the entry. If more than one field contains a parameter, Access prompts the user one field at a time.

A parameter query is useful if you run a query several times on the same field but use different criteria each time. For example, if you require a list of work orders by individual technician, you would have to create a separate query for each technician. This would create several query objects in the Navigation pane. Creating a parameter query that prompts you to enter the technician's name means you only have to create one query.

To create a parameter query, start a new query in Design view and add the desired tables and fields to the query design grid. Type a message encased in square brackets to prompt the user for the required criterion in the *Criteria* row of the field to be used to select records. The text inside the square brackets is displayed in the Enter Parameter Value dialog box when the query is run. Figure 3.2 displays the entry in the *Criteria* row of the *FName* field that generated the Enter Parameter Value message shown in Figure 3.1.

Figure 3.1 Enter Parameter Value Dialog Box

Figure 3.2 Criterion to Prompt for the Name in the *FName* Field

Field:	WO	FName
Table:	WorkOrders	Technicians
Sort:		
Show:	✓	✓
Criteria:		[Type the technician's first name]
or:		

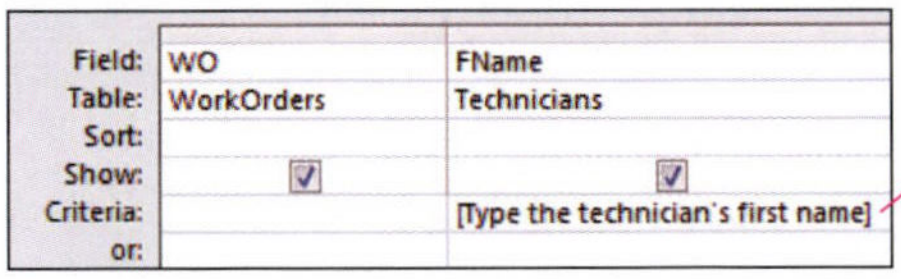

Type a message in square brackets to prompt the user for the criterion by which to select records.

Project 1b Creating a Query to Prompt for Technician Names **Part 2 of 3**

1. With the **AL2-C3-RSRCompServ.accdb** database open, create a query in Design view to select records from the Technicians table and the WorkOrders table by completing the following steps:
 a. Click the Create tab and then click the Query Design button in the Queries group.
 b. At the Show Table dialog box, add the Technicians table and the WorkOrders table to the query.

c. Close the Show Table dialog box.

d. Drag the bottom border of each table's field list box at the top of the query until all field names are visible in the box.

e. Add the following fields in order to the query design grid: *WO*, *FName*, *LName*, *ServDate*, *Hours*, *Rate*.

Step 1e

Field:	WO	FName	LName	ServDate	Hours	Rate
Table:	WorkOrders	Technicians	Technicians	WorkOrders	WorkOrders	WorkOrders
Sort:						
Show:	✓	✓	✓	✓	✓	✓

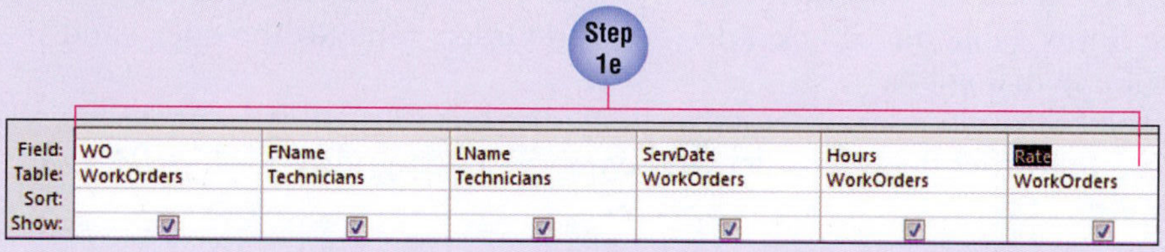

2. Click the Run button to run the query.

3. Add parameters to select records by a technician's first and last names by completing the following steps:

 a. Switch to Design view.

 b. Click in the *Criteria* row in the *FName* column in the query design grid, type **[Type the technician's first name]**, and then press Enter.

 c. Position the pointer on the vertical line between *FName* and *LName* in the gray field selector bar above the field names until the pointer changes to a vertical line with a left- and right-pointing arrow and then double-click to expand the width of the *FName* column so that you can see the entire criteria entry.

Step 3c

Step 3b

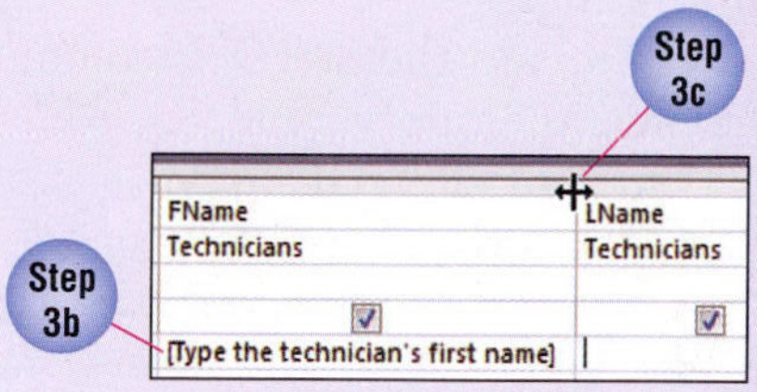

 d. With the insertion point positioned in the *Criteria* row in the *LName* column, type **[Type the technician's last name]** and then press Enter.

 e. Expand the width of the *LName* column so that you can see the entire criteria entry.

4. Click the Save button on the Quick Access toolbar, type **PromptedTechnicianLabor** in the *Query Name* text box at the Save As dialog box, and then press Enter or click OK.

5. Close the query.

6. Run the prompted query and extract a list of work orders for the technician named Pat Hynes by completing the following steps:

 a. Double-click the query named *PromptedTechnicianLabor* in the Navigation pane.

Step 6a

Step 6b

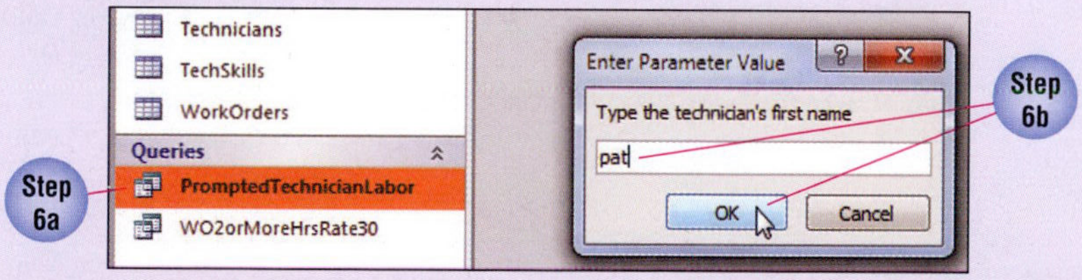

 b. Type **pat** at the Enter Parameter Value dialog box that displays the message *Type the technician's first name* and then press Enter or click OK. Note that Access is not case-sensitive when typing text strings.

 c. Type **hynes** at the second Enter Parameter Value dialog box that displays the message *Type the technician's last name* and then press Enter or click OK.

Step 6c

7. Review the records in the query results datasheet.

8. Print the query results datasheet.

9. Close the query.

Project 1c Creating a Query to Prompt for a Starting and Ending Date

Part 3 of 3

1. With the **AL2-C3-RSRCompServ.accdb** database open, create a query in Design view to prompt the user for a starting and ending date by which to select records using the WorkOrders table by completing the following steps:
   a. Click the Create tab and then click the Query Design button in the Queries group.
   b. At the Show Table dialog box, add the WorkOrders table to the query and then close the Show Table dialog box.
   c. Drag the bottom border of the table's field list box until all field names are visible.
   d. Add the following fields in order to the query design grid: *WO*, *CustID*, *Descr*, *ServDate*, *Hours*, *Rate*, *Parts*.
   e. Click in the *Criteria* row in the *ServDate* column, type the entry **Between [Type starting date] And [Type ending date]**, and then press Enter.

Descr	ServDate
WorkOrders	WorkOrders
☑	☑
	Between [Type starting date] And [Type ending date]

Step 1e

   f. Expand the *ServDate* column width until the entire criteria entry is visible.
2. Save the query, type **PromptedServiceDate** at the Save As dialog box, and then press Enter or click OK.
3. Close the query.
4. Double-click *PromptedServiceDate* in the Navigation pane. At the first Enter Parameter Value dialog box with *Type starting date* displayed, type **October 1, 2012** and press Enter or click OK. At the second Enter Parameter Value dialog box with *Type ending date* displayed, type **October 15, 2012** and press Enter or click OK.

PromptedServiceDate

Work Order	Customer ID	Descripton	Service Date	Hours	Rate	Parts
65027	1010	Replace hard drive	Tue Oct 02 2012	1.50	30.00	$375.50
65028	1030	Reinstall operating system	Tue Oct 02 2012	2.25	30.00	$0.00
65029	1035	Set up automatic backup	Wed Oct 03 2012	0.50	22.50	$0.00
65030	1000	Clean malware from system	Sat Oct 06 2012	1.00	15.50	$0.00
65031	1045	Customer reports noisy hard drive	Sat Oct 06 2012	1.75	30.00	$0.00
65032	1008	Install second hard drive	Sat Oct 13 2012	2.00	30.00	$425.75
65033	1000	Install Windows 7	Sat Oct 13 2012	3.25	30.00	$335.75
65034	1035	File management training	Sun Oct 14 2012	1.50	30.00	$0.00
65035	1020	Office 2010 training	Mon Oct 15 2012	2.50	30.00	$0.00

records selected within the date range October 1, 2012 to October 15, 2012 for the *Service Date* column at Step 4

5. Print the query results datasheet in landscape orientation.
6. Close the query.

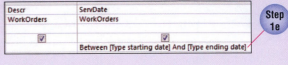

Project 2 Modify Query Results by Changing the Join Property

4 Parts

You will create and modify queries that obtain various results based on changing the join properties for related tables.

Modifying Join Properties in a Query

Join properties refers to the manner with which Access matches the field values in the common field between the two tables in a relationship. The method used determines how many records are selected for inclusion in the query results datasheet. Access provides for three join types in a relationship: an inner join, a left outer join, and a right outer join. By default, Access uses an inner join between the tables, which means that records are selected for display in a query only when a match on the joined field value exists in both tables. If a record exists in either table with no matching record in the other table, the record is not displayed in the query results datasheet. This means that in some cases you may not be viewing all records from both tables when you run a query.

HINT

You can edit a relationship if you always want the join type to be a left or right outer join. To do this, click the Join Type button in the Edit Relationships dialog box to open the Join Properties dialog box. Select the desired join type and click OK.

Specifying the Join Type

Double-click the black join line between tables in a query to open the Join Properties dialog box shown in Figure 3.3. By default, option 1 is selected, which is referred to as an ***inner join***. In an inner join, only those records where the primary key field value in the primary table matches a foreign key field value in the related table are displayed.

Options 2 and 3 are referred to as ***outer joins***. Option 2 is a ***left outer join.*** In this type of join, the primary table (referred to as the left table) displays all rows whereas the related table (referred to as the right table) shows only rows with a matching value in the foreign key field. For example, examine the query results datasheet shown in Figure 3.4. This query was created with the Technicians and TechSkills tables. All technician records are shown in the datasheet; however, notice that some technician records display with empty field values for the columns from the TechSkills table. These are the technicians who have not yet had a record created in the TechSkills table with their information. In a left outer join, all records from the primary table in the relationship are shown in the query results datasheet.

HINT

Changing the join type at a query window does not alter the join type for other objects based on the relationship—the revised join property applies to the query only.

Figure 3.3 Join Properties Dialog Box

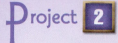

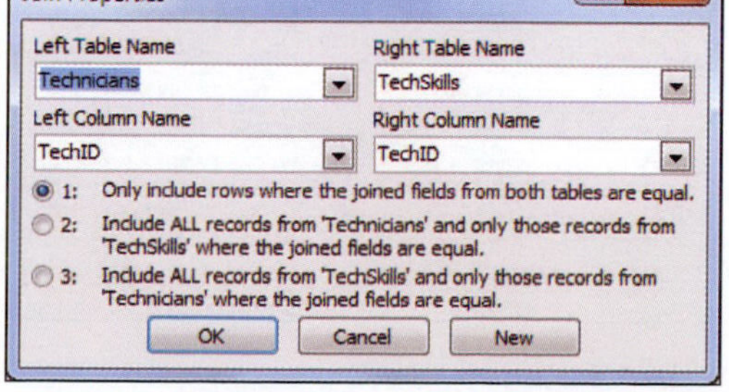

Join Properties
Left Table Name
Technicians
Right Table Name
TechSkills
Left Column Name
TechID
Right Column Name
TechID
1: Only include rows where the joined fields from both tables are equal.
2: Include ALL records from 'Technicians' and only those records from 'TechSkills' where the joined fields are equal.
3: Include ALL records from 'TechSkills' and only those records from 'Technicians' where the joined fields are equal.
OK
Cancel
New

Figure 3.4 Left Outer Join Example

First Name	Last Name	Certifications	Operating Systems	Network Specialist?	Design Websites?	Programming?
Pat	Hynes	Cisco CCNP, CompTIA A+, Microsoft MCTS	Linux, Unix, Windows 7, Windows XP	☑	☐	☑
Hui	Chen	Cisco CCNP, CompTIA A+	Linux, Unix, Windows 7	☑	☑	☐
Kayla	Blewett			■	■	■
Mihir	Patel	CompTIA A+, Microsoft MCTS	Unix, Windows Vista, Windows XP	☐	☐	☑
Madir	Sadiku	CompTIA A+, Microsoft MCTS	Mac OS X, Windows 7, Windows Vista	☐	☐	☐
Brody	Stewart			■	■	■
Ana	Takacs	Cisco CCNA	Mac OS X, Windows XP	☑	☐	☑
Marty	O'Leary	Cisco CCNP	Linux, Unix	☑	☑	☐
Armando	Colacci	Microsoft Master	Windows 7, Windows Vista, Windows XP	☐	☐	☑
Kelsey	Eastman	Cisco CCNA, Microsoft MCTS	Linux, Windows 7, Windows Vista	☑	☑	☐
Dana	Westman			■	■	■
*				■	■	■

Left outer join query results show related TechSkills fields blank for those technicians who do not yet have a record in the TechSkills table.

Option 3 is a ***right outer join.*** In this type of join, the related table (or right table) shows all rows whereas the primary table (or left table) shows only rows with a matching value in the common field. For example, examine the partial query results datasheet shown in Figure 3.5. This datasheet illustrates 15 of the 39 records in the query results datasheet from the Technicians and WorkOrders tables. Notice the first four records have no technician first or last name. These are the work orders that have not yet been assigned to a technician. In a right outer join, all records from the related table in the relationship are shown in the query results datasheet. In a left or right outer join, Access displays an arrow at the end of the join line pointing to the table that shows only matching rows.

To illustrate the difference in query results when no change is made to the join type, examine the query results datasheet shown in Figure 3.6. This is the datasheet you will create in Project 2a. In this project, you will create a list with the technician names and qualifications. Compare the number of records shown in Figure 3.6 with those shown in Figure 3.4. Notice that fewer records display in the datasheet. Since an inner join displays only those records where a matching entry exists in both tables, records from either table that do not have a matching

Figure 3.5 Right Outer Join Example

Right outer join query results show related technician fields blank for those work orders that have yet to be assigned to a technician.

First Name	Last Name	Work Order	Customer ID	WO Date	Descripton
		65047	1030	Sat Oct 27 2012	Set up automatic backup
		65048	1020	Mon Oct 29 2012	Replace LCD monitor
		65049	1040	Tue Oct 30 2012	Set up dual monitor system
		65050	1045	Tue Oct 30 2012	Reinstall Windows 7
Pat	Hynes	65020	1030	Mon Sep 17 2012	Troubleshoot noisy fan
Pat	Hynes	65033	1000	Fri Oct 12 2012	Install Windows 7
Pat	Hynes	65038	1010	Fri Oct 19 2012	Install Windows 7
Hui	Chen	65014	1005	Mon Sep 10 2012	Replace power supply
Hui	Chen	65019	1025	Sat Sep 15 2012	Upgrade to Windows 7
Hui	Chen	65026	1025	Sat Sep 29 2012	Upgrade memory
Hui	Chen	65032	1008	Fri Oct 12 2012	Install second hard drive
Hui	Chen	65035	1020	Sun Oct 14 2012	Office 2010 training
Kayla	Blewett	65023	1045	Sat Sep 22 2012	Upgrade RAM
Kayla	Blewett	65036	1008	Mon Oct 15 2012	Set up home network
Kayla	Blewett	65041	1020	Mon Oct 22 2012	Bi-annual computer maintenance

record in the other table are not displayed. Understanding that an inner join (the default join type) may not display all records that exist in the tables when you run a query is important.

Figure 3.6 Inner Join Example

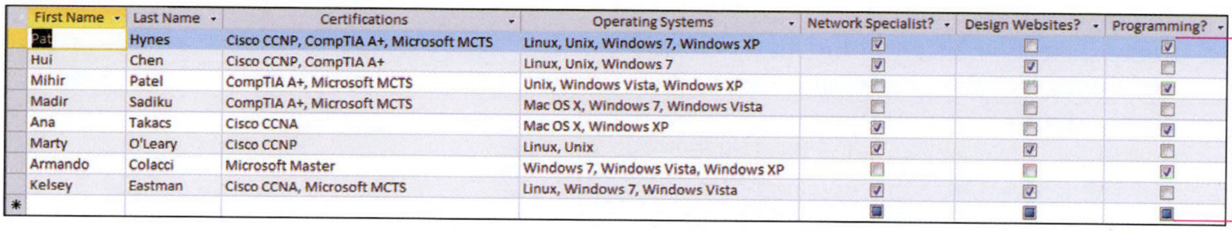

First Name	Last Name	Certifications	Operating Systems	Network Specialist?	Design Websites?	Programming?
Pat	Hynes	Cisco CCNP, CompTIA A+, Microsoft MCTS	Linux, Unix, Windows 7, Windows XP	✓	☐	✓
Hui	Chen	Cisco CCNP, CompTIA A+	Linux, Unix, Windows 7	✓	✓	☐
Mihir	Patel	CompTIA A+, Microsoft MCTS	Unix, Windows Vista, Windows XP	☐	☐	✓
Madir	Sadiku	CompTIA A+, Microsoft MCTS	Mac OS X, Windows 7, Windows Vista	☐	☐	☐
Ana	Takacs	Cisco CCNA	Mac OS X, Windows XP	✓	☐	✓
Marty	O'Leary	Cisco CCNP	Linux, Unix	✓	✓	☐
Armando	Colacci	Microsoft Master	Windows 7, Windows Vista, Windows XP	☐	☐	✓
Kelsey	Eastman	Cisco CCNA, Microsoft MCTS	Linux, Windows 7, Windows Vista	✓	✓	☐
*				☐	☐	☐

An inner join displays a record only when a matching value in the joined field exists in both tables—no blank records appear in the query results. However, notice that you are not viewing all records in the technicians table.

Project 2a Selecting Records in a Query Using an Inner Join Part 1 of 4

1. With the **AL2-C3-RSRCompServ.accdb** database open, create a query in Design view to display a list of technicians with each technician's skill specialties by completing the following steps:

 a. Create a new query in Design view. At the Show Table dialog box, add the Technicians and the TechSkills tables. Close the Show Table dialog box and then drag the bottom border of each table's field list box until all field names are visible in the box.

 b. Double-click the black join line between the two tables to open the Join Properties dialog box.

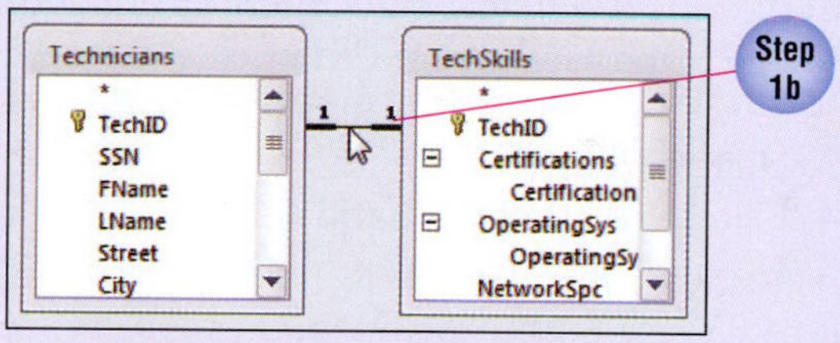

 c. At the Join Properties dialog box, notice that *1* is selected by default. Option 1 selects records only when the joined fields from both tables are equal. This represents an inner join. Click OK.

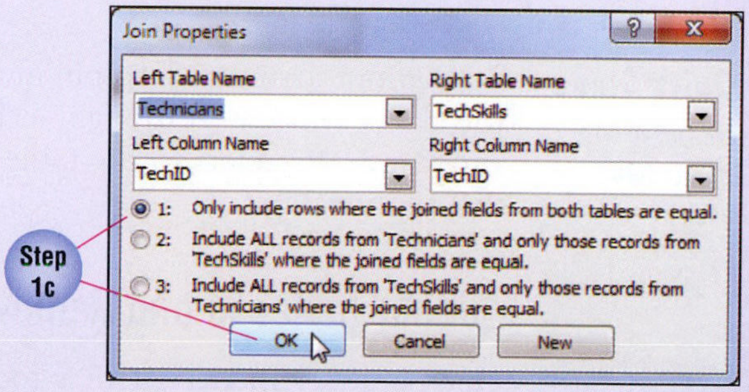

 d. Add the following fields in order to the query design grid: *FName, LName, Certifications, OperatingSys, NetworkSpc, WebDesign,* and *Programming*.

e. Run the query.

2. Minimize the Navigation pane and then compare your results with the query results datasheet displayed in Figure 3.6.

3. Save the query and name it **TechnicianSpecialties**.

4. Close the query.

5. Expand the Navigation pane.

Project 2b Selecting Records in a Query Using a Left Outer Join

Part 2 of 4

1. With the **AL2-C3-RSRCompServ.accdb** database open, modify the TechnicianSpecialties query to a left outer join to check if any technicians do not have a matching record in the TechSkills table by completing the following steps:
   a. Right-click the TechnicianSpecialties query and then click *Design view* at the shortcut menu.
   b. Right-click the black join line between the two tables and then click *Join Properties* at the shortcut menu.

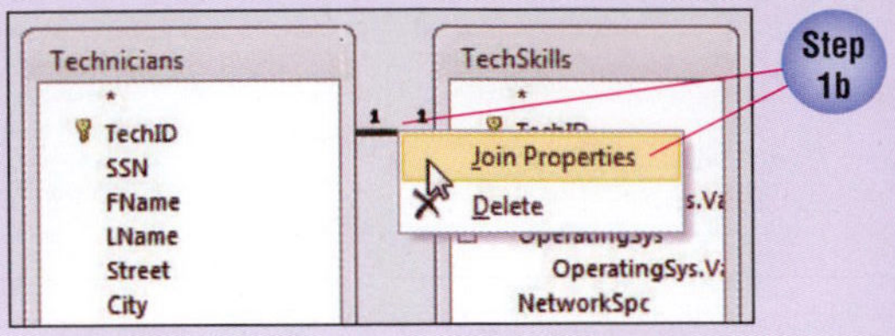

   c. At the Join Properties dialog box, click *2* and then click OK. Option 2 includes all records from the Technicians table and only those records from TechSkills where the joined fields are equal. The left table (Technicians) is the table that will show all records. If a technician does not have a matching record in the other table, the columns display empty fields next to the technician's name.

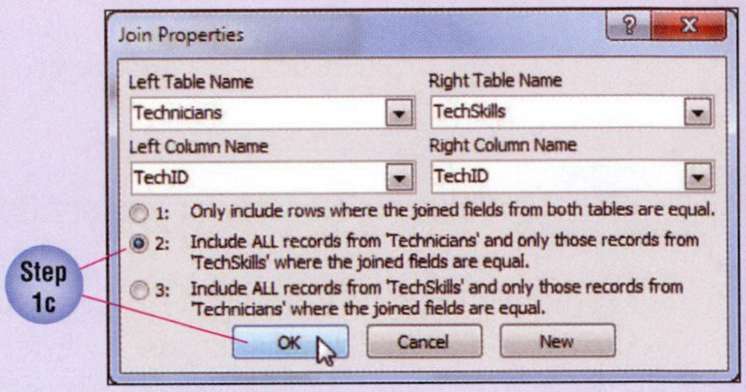

   d. Notice the join line between the two tables now displays with an arrow pointing to the joined field in the TechSkills table.
   e. Run the query.
2. Minimize the Navigation pane and then compare your results with the query results datasheet displayed in Figure 3.4 on page 76. Notice that 11 records display in this datasheet whereas only eight records displayed in the query results from Project 2a.
3. Click the File tab and then click Save Object As. At the Save As dialog box, type AllTechnicianSkills in the *Save 'TechnicianSpecialties' to* text box and then press Enter or click OK.
4. Click the Home tab and then close the query.
5. Expand the Navigation pane.

Quick Steps

Create Query with Left Outer Join

1. Create new query in Design view.
2. Add tables to query window.
3. Double-click join line between tables.
4. Select option *2*.
5. Click OK.
6. Add desired fields to query design grid.
7. Save and run query.

Do not assume a left join always occurs with the table that is the left table in the query window. Although Technicians was the left table in the Project 2b query window, "left" refers to the table that represents the one side (primary table) in the relationship.

Adding Tables to and Removing Tables from a Query

Open a query in Design view to add a table to a query. Click the Show Table button in the Query Setup group in the Query Tools Design tab and then add the desired table using the Show Table dialog box. Close the Show Table dialog box when finished.

To remove a table from a query, click any field within the table field list box to activate the table in the query window and then press the Delete key. The table is removed from the window and all fields associated with the table that were added to the query design grid are automatically removed. You can also right-click the table in the query window and click *Remove Table* at the shortcut menu.

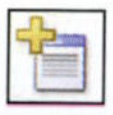

Show Table

Project 2c Selecting Records in a Query Using a Right Outer Join

Part 3 of 4

1. With the **AL2-C3-RSRCompServ.accdb** database open, create a new query to check for work orders that have not been assigned to a technician by modifying an existing query by completing the following steps:
   a. Open the TechnicianSpecialties query in Design view.
   b. Right-click the TechSkills table in the query window and then click *Remove Table* at the shortcut menu. Notice that the last five columns are removed from the query design grid along with the table.

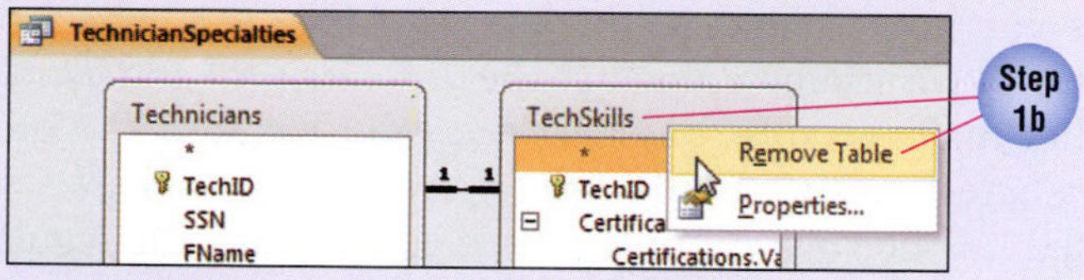

   c. Click the Show Table button in the Query Setup group in the Query Tools Design tab.
   d. At the Show Table dialog box, double-click *WorkOrders* in the Tables list, click the Close button, and then drag the bottom border of the WorkOrders table field list box until all fields are visible in the box.
   e. Double-click the black join line between the two tables.
   f. At the Join Properties dialog box, click *3* and then click OK. Option 3 includes all records from the WorkOrders table and only those records from the Technicians table where the joined fields are equal. The right table (WorkOrders) is the table that will show all records. If a work order does not have a matching record in the other table, the columns display empty fields for the technician names.

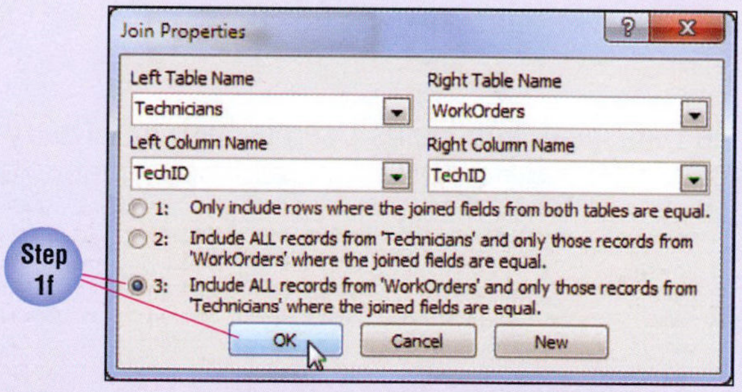

   g. Notice the join line between the two tables now displays with an arrow pointing to the joined field in the Technicians table.
   h. Add the following fields in order from the WorkOrders table to the query design grid: *WO*, *WODate*, and *Descr*.
2. Click the File tab and then click Save Object As. At the Save As dialog box, type **UnassignedWorkOrders** in the *Save 'TechnicianSpecialties' to* text box and then press Enter or click OK.
3. Click the Query Tools Design tab and then run the query.

4. Compare your results with the partial query results datasheet shown in Figure 3.5 on page 76. Notice the first four records in the query results datasheet have empty fields in the *First Name* and *Last Name* columns.
5. Double-click the right column boundary of the *Description* column to adjust the column width and then print the query results datasheet with the right margin set to 0.5-inch.
6. Close the query. Click Yes to save changes.

Quick Steps

Create Query with Right Outer Join

1. Create new query in Design view.
2. Add tables to query window.
3. Double-click join line between tables.
4. Select option *3*.
5. Click OK.
6. Add desired fields to query design grid.
7. Save and run query.

HINT

In a self-join query, the two fields joined together must have the same data type.

Do not assume a right join always occurs with the table that is the right table in the query window. Although WorkOrders was the right table in the Project 2c query window, "right" refers to the table that represents the *many* side (related table) in the relationship.

Creating a Self-Join Query

Assume you have a table in which two fields in the same table contain similar field values. For example, look at the *Technician ID* and *Tier 2 Supervisor* columns in the Technicians table datasheet shown in Figure 3.7. Notice that each column contains a technician's ID number. Tier 2 supervisors are senior technicians who are called in when a work order is too complex for the regular technician to solve. The ID number in the *Tier 2 Supervisor* column is the senior technician's ID who is assigned to the technician.

You may find it more informative to view the list of technicians with the Tier 2 supervisor's last name instead of ID number. If you have a table that has matching values in two separate fields, you can create a ***self-join query,*** which creates a relationship between fields in the same table. To create a self-join query, two copies of the same table are added to the query window. The second occurrence of the table is named using the original table name with *_1* added to the end. You can assign an alias to the second table to provide the table with a more descriptive name in the query. Next, join the two tables by dragging the field with matching values from one table field list to the other. Add the required fields to the query design grid and then run the query.

Figure 3.7 Technician's Table Datasheet with Fields Used in Self-Join Query

Technician ID	SSN	First Name	Last Name	Street Address	City	State	ZIP Code	Home Phone	Cell Phone	📎	Tier 2 Supervisor
01	000-45-5368	Pat	Hynes	206-31 Woodland Street	Detroit	MI	48202-1138	313-555-6874	313-555-6412	(1)	03
02	000-47-3258	Hui	Chen	12905 Hickory Street	Detroit	MI	48205-3462	313-555-7468	313-555-5234	(0)	06
03	000-62-7468	Kayla	Blewett	1310 Jarvis Street	Detroit	MI	48220-2011	313-555-3265	313-555-6486	(0)	
04	000-33-1485	Mihir	Patel	8213 Elgin Street	Detroit	MI	48234-4092	313-555-7458	313-555-6385	(1)	11
05	000-48-7850	Madir	Sadiku	8190 Kenwood Street	Detroit	MI	48220-1132	313-555-6327	313-555-8569	(0)	03
06	000-75-8412	Brody	Stewart	3522 Moore Place	Detroit	MI	48208-1032	313-555-7499	313-555-3625	(0)	
07	000-55-1248	Ana	Takacs	14902 Hampton Court	Detroit	MI	48215-3616	313-555-6142	313-555-4586	(0)	11
08	000-63-1247	Marty	O'Leary	14000 Vernon Drive	Detroit	MI	48237-1320	313-555-9856	313-555-4125	(0)	11
09	000-84-1254	Armando	Colacci	17302 Windsor Avenue	Detroit	MI	48224-2257	313-555-9641	313-555-8796	(0)	06
10	000-43-5789	Kelsey	Eastman	550 Montclair Street	Detroit	MI	48214-3274	313-555-6315	313-555-7411	(2)	06
11	000-65-4185	Dana	Westman	18101 Keeler Streeet	Detroit	MI	48223-1322	313-555-5488	313-555-4158	(0)	
*										(0)	

These two fields contain technician identification numbers. Tier 2 supervisors are senior-level technicians and are assigned to handle complex cases for other technicians.

Creating an Alias for a Table

An ***alias*** is another name that you want to use to reference a table in a query. The alias is temporary and applies to the query only. Generally, you create an alias if you want to assign a shorter name to a table or a more descriptive name in the case of a self-join query. For example, one of the tables that you will use in the query in Project 2d is named Technicians_1. You can assign the table a more descriptive name such as Supervisors to more accurately describe the second table's role in the query.

To assign an alias to a table, right-click the table name in the query window and click *Properties* at the shortcut menu to open the Property Sheet task pane. Click in the *Alias* property box, delete the existing table name, and type the name by which you want the table referenced. Access replaces all occurrences of the table name with the alias in the query design grid.

Quick Steps

Create Self-Join Query

1. Create query in Design view.
2. Add two copies of the table to the query.
3. Right-click second table name.
4. Click *Properties.*
5. Click in *Alias* property box and delete existing table name.
6. Type alias table name.
7. Close the Property Sheet.
8. Drag field name from left table to field name with matching values in right table.
9. Add fields as required to query design grid.
10. Run query.
11. Save query.

Project 2d **Creating a Self-Join Query** **Part 4 of 4**

1. With the **AL2-C3-RSRCompServ.accdb** database open, create a self-join query to display the last name of the Tier 2 supervisor instead of the identification number by completing the following steps:
   a. Create a new query in Design view.
   b. At the Show Table dialog box, double-click *Technicians* in the *Tables* list box twice to add two copies of the Technicians table to the query and then close the Show Table dialog box. Notice the second copy of the table is named *Technicians_1*.
   c. Drag the bottom border of both table field list boxes down until all field names are visible.
   d. Create an alias for the second table by completing the following steps:
      1) Right-click the *Technicians_1* table name.
      2) Click *Properties* at the shortcut menu.
      3) Select and delete the current name in the *Alias* property box in the Property Sheet task pane.

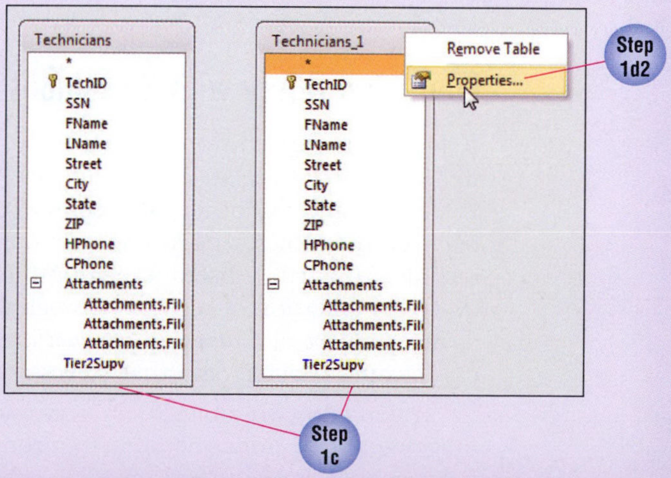

4) Type **Supervisors** and then close the Property Sheet task pane.

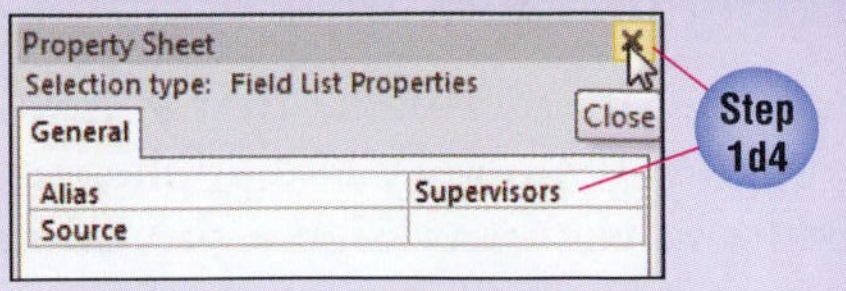

e. Drag the field named *Tier2Supv* from the Technicians table field list box at the left to the field named *TechID* in the Supervisors table field list box at the right. This creates a join line between the two tables.

f. Add the *FName* and *LName* fields from the Technicians table to the query design grid.

g. Add the *LName* field from the Supervisors table to the query design grid.

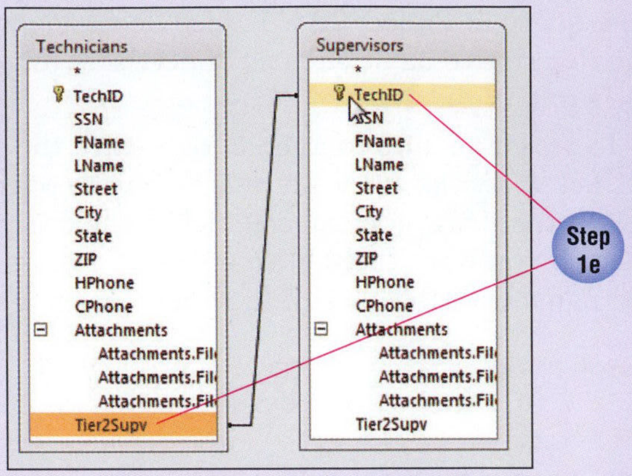

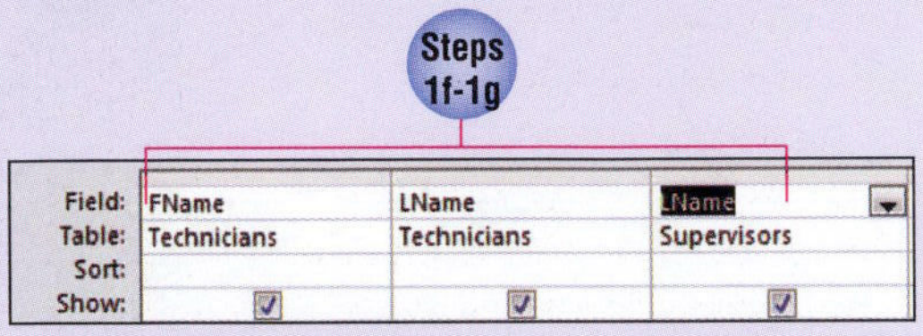

2. Run the query. The last names displayed in the second *Last Name* column represent the *Tier2Supv* name.
3. Switch to Design view.
4. Right-click the second *LName* column (from the Supervisors table) and click *Properties* at the shortcut menu. Click in the *Caption* property box in the Property Sheet task pane, type **Tier 2 Supervisor**, and then close the Property Sheet task pane.
5. Save the query. Type **Tier2Supervisors** at the Save As dialog box and then press Enter or click OK.
6. Run the query.
7. Double-click the right column boundary of the *Tier 2 Supervisor* column to adjust the width and then compare your results to the datasheet shown at the right.
8. Close the query. Click Yes to save changes.

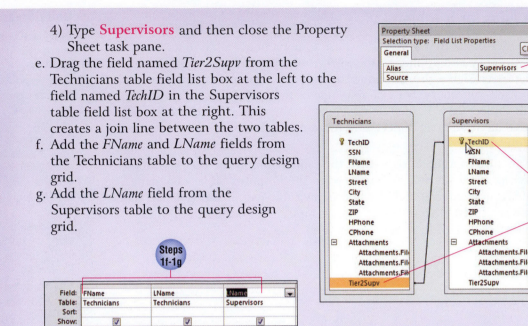

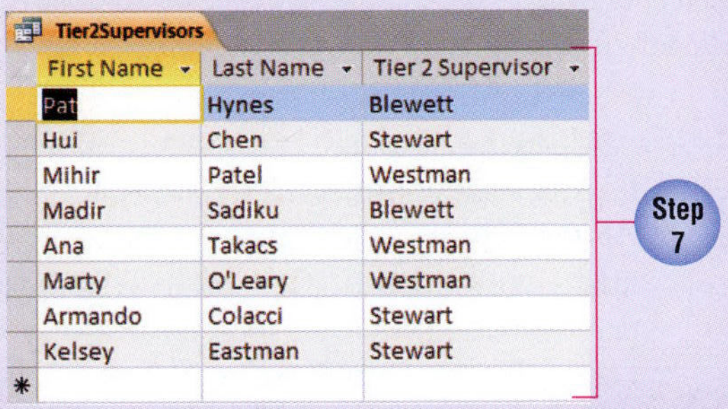

Running a Query with No Established Relationship

If a query is created from two tables for which no join is established, Access will not know how to relate records in each table. For example, if one table contains 20 records and the other table contains 10 records and no join is established between the tables, Access produces a query results datasheet containing 200 records (20 × 10). Absent a relationship, Access produces a datasheet representing every combination of records between the two tables. This type of query is called a ***cross product*** or ***Cartesian product*** query. The results of such a query in most cases would provide data that serves no purpose.

If you add two tables to a query and no join line appears, create a join by dragging a field from one table to a compatible field in the other table. The two fields should contain the same data type and be logically related in some way.

Project 3 Calculate Work Order Totals — 2 Parts

You will use a subquery nested within another query to calculate the total amount earned from each work order.

Creating and Using Subqueries

When performing multiple calculations based on numeric fields you may decide to create a separate query for each individual calculation and then use subqueries to generate the final total. A ***subquery*** is a query nested inside another query. Using subqueries to break the calculations into individual objects allows you to reuse a calculated field in multiple queries. For example, assume that you want to calculate the total amount for each work order. The WorkOrders table contains fields with the number of hours for each service call, the labor rate, and the total amount of the parts used. To find the total for each work order, you need to calculate the total labor by multiplying the hours times the rate and then add the parts value to the total labor value. However, you may want the total labor value to be in a separate query so that you can perform other calculations such as finding the average, maximum, or minimum labor on work orders. To be able to reuse the total labor value, you will need to create the calculated field in its own query.

Once the query is created to calculate the total labor, you can nest the query inside another query to add the labor to the parts to calculate the total for all work orders. Creating subqueries provides you with the flexibility to reuse calculations, thus avoiding duplication of effort and reducing the potential for calculation errors.

In Level 1, Chapter 3 you learned how to insert a calculated field in a query. Recall the format for an equation in a query is to type in a blank *Field* row the desired field name followed by a colon and then the equation with field names in square brackets. For example, Total:[Sales]+[SalesTax].

Quick Steps

Nest Query within a Query
1. Start new query in Design view.
2. At Show Table dialog box, click Queries tab.
3. Double-click query to be used as subquery.
4. Add other queries or tables as required.
5. Close Show Table dialog box.
6. Add fields as required.
7. Save and run query.

HINT

Subqueries are not restricted to nested calculations—use a subquery for any combination of fields that you want to be able to reuse in multiple queries.

Project 3a Creating a Query to Calculate Total Labor — Part 1 of 2

1. With the **AL2-C3-RSRCompServ.accdb** database open, create a query to calculate the total labor for each work order by completing the following steps:
   a. Create a new query in Design view. At the Show Table dialog box, add the WorkOrders table to the query window and then close the Show Table dialog box.
   b. Drag the bottom border of the WorkOrders table field list box down until all fields are visible.
   c. Add the following fields in order to the query design grid: *WO*, *ServDate*, *Hours*, and *Rate*.
   d. Click in the blank *Field* row next to *Rate* in the query design grid, type **Total Labor: [Hours]*[Rate]**, and then press Enter.
   e. Expand the width of the calculated column until you can see all of the formula in the *Field* row.

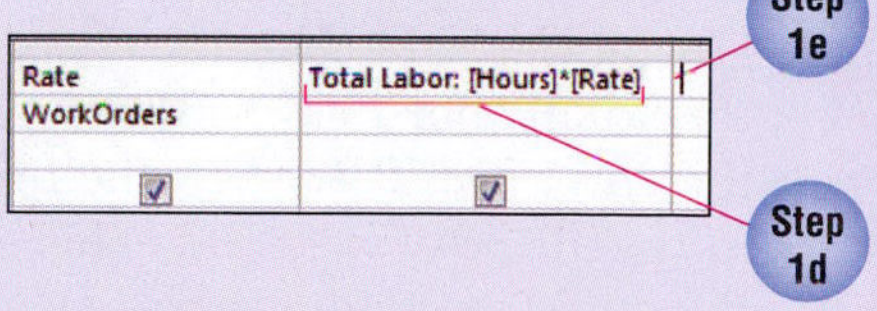

2. Run the query and view the query results. Notice the *Total Labor* column does not display a consistent number of decimal values.
3. Switch to Design view.
4. Format the *Total Labor* column by completing the following steps:
   a. Click the insertion point anywhere within the *Total Labor* field row to activate the field.
   b. Click the Property Sheet button in the Show/Hide group in the Query Tools Design tab.
   c. Click in the *Format* property box in the Property Sheet task pane, click the down-pointing arrow that appears, and then click *Standard* at the drop-down list.
   d. Close the Property Sheet task pane.

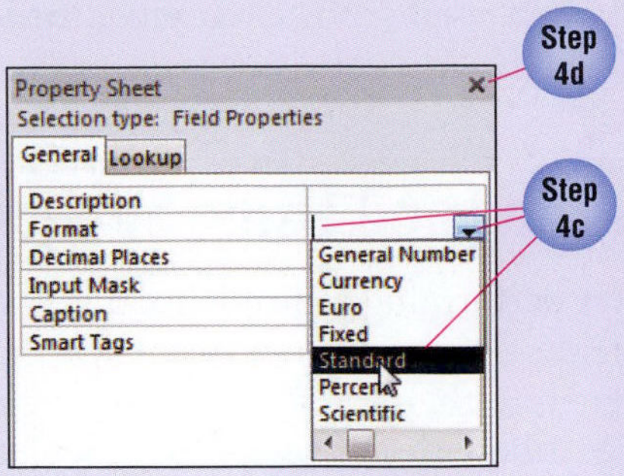

5. Save the query. Type **TotalLabor** at the Save As dialog box and then press Enter or click OK.
6. Run the query. Notice the last four rows contain no values since the service calls have not yet been completed.
7. Switch to Design view. Click in the *Criteria* row in the *Hours* column, type **>0**, and then press Enter.

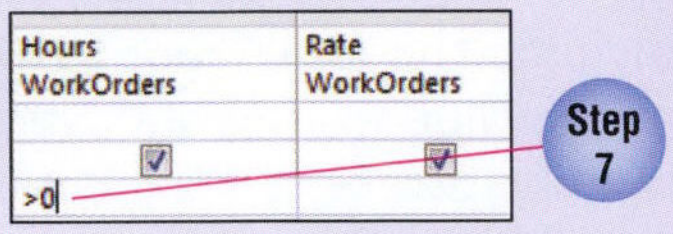

8. Save the revised query and then run the query.
9. Close the query.

Project 3b Nesting a Query within a Query

Part 2 of 2

1. With the **AL2-C3-RSRCompServ.accdb** database open, create a new query to calculate the total value of all work orders using the TotalLabor query as a subquery by completing the following steps:
   a. Create a new query in Design view.
   b. At the Show Table dialog box, click the Queries tab.
   c. Double-click *TotalLabor* in the Queries list.
   d. Click the Tables tab.
   e. Double-click *WorkOrders* in the Tables list and then close the Show Table dialog box. Notice that Access has automatically joined the two objects on the *WO* field.

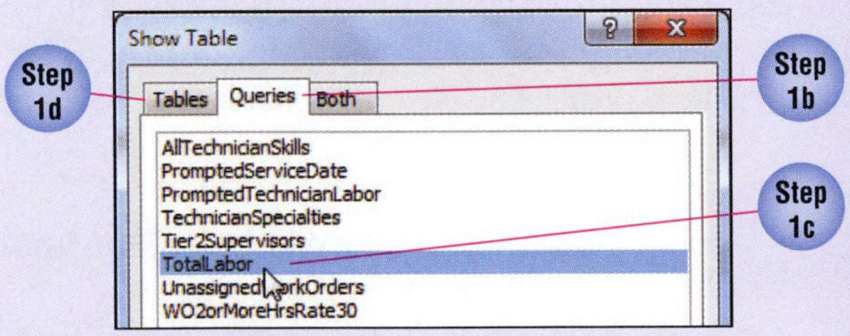

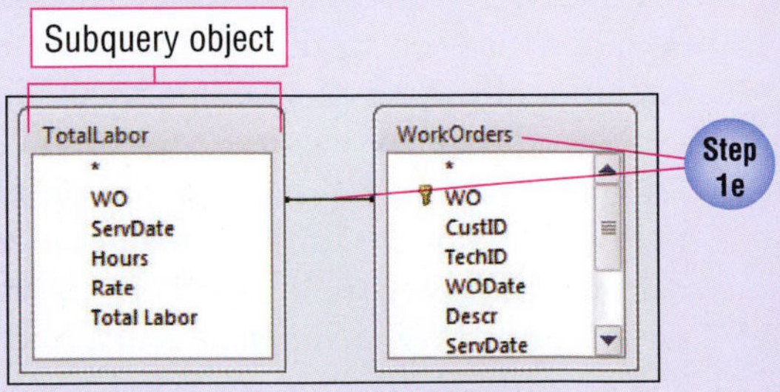

2. Add fields from the TotalLabor subquery and from the WorkOrders table by completing the following steps:
   a. Double-click the asterisk (*) at the top of the TotalLabor field list box. Access adds the entry *TotalLabor.** to the first column in the query design grid. This entry adds all of the fields from the query. Individual columns do not display in the grid; however, when you run the query, the datasheet will show all fields.

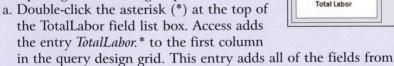

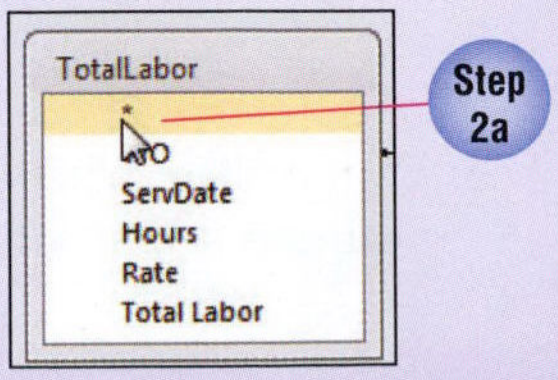

b. Run the query. Notice the query results datasheet shows all five columns from the TotalLabor query.
c. Switch to Design view. You decide to format the *Total Labor* column to *Currency* for this new query. In order to do this, you need to add the column to the query design grid.
d. Right-click in the field selector bar (gray bar above the *Field* row) for the *TotalLabor.** column and then click *Cut* at the shortcut menu to remove the column from the design grid.
e. Add the following fields from the TotalLabor query field list box in order to the query design grid: *WO*, *ServDate*, and *Total Labor*.
f. Format the *Total Labor* column to *Currency*.
g. Drag the bottom border of the WorkOrders table field list box down until all fields are visible and then double-click *Parts* to add the field to the query design grid.

3. Create the calculated field to add the total labor and parts by completing the following steps:
   a. Click in the blank *Field* row next to *Parts* in the query design grid, type **Total Work Order: [Total Labor]+[Parts]**, and then press Enter.
   b. Expand the width of the *Total Work Order* column until the entire formula is visible.
   c. Format the *Total Work Order* column to *Currency*.

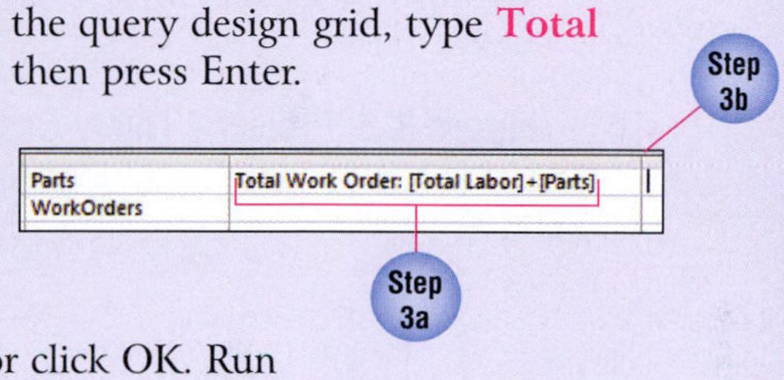

4. Save the query. Type **TotalWorkOrders** at the Save As dialog box and then press Enter or click OK. Run the query.
5. Double-click the column boundary for the *Total Work Order* column to adjust the column width and then print the query results datasheet.

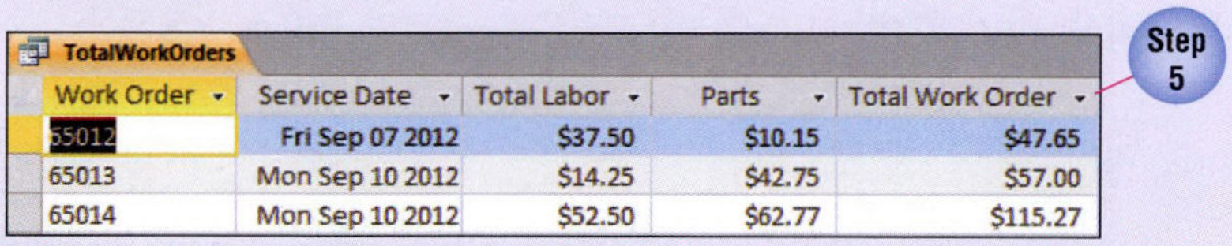

TotalWorkOrders
Work Order
Service Date
Total Labor
Parts
Total Work Order
65012
Fri Sep 07 2012
$37.50
$10.15
$47.65
65013
Mon Sep 10 2012
$14.25
$42.75
$57.00
65014
Mon Sep 10 2012
$52.50
$62.77
$115.27
Step
5

6. Close the query. Click Yes to save changes.

Smaller queries are easier to build and troubleshoot. Another reason to use subqueries is when you need to create a complex query. Create subqueries to build and test each section individually and then combine the subqueries into the final query.

Project 4 Query a Multiple-Value Field — 1 Part

You will select records using a multiple-value field in a query.

Quick Steps

Show Multiple-Value Field in Separate Rows in Query

1. Open query in Design view.
2. Click in *Field* box of multiple-value field in design grid.
3. Move insertion point to end of field name.
4. Type period (.).
5. Press Enter to accept *.Value*.
6. Save query.

Selecting Records Using a Multiple-Value Field

You learned to create and use multiple-value fields in Chapter 2. In a query, a multiple-value field can display as it does in a table datasheet with the multiple field values in the same column separated by commas, or you can elect to show each field value in a separate row. To show each value in a separate row, add the multiple-value field name with *.Value* at the end in the *Field* box in the query design grid. Figure 3.8 displays the query design grid for the query you will use in Project 4 that displays each entry in the *OperatingSys* field in a separate row in the datasheet.

To select records using criteria in a multiple-value field, type the criteria using the same procedures you would for a single-value field. For example, in the TechnicianSpecialties query, typing *Windows 7* in the *Criteria* row in the *OperatingSys* column causes Access to return the records of any technician with Windows 7 as one of the multiple field values.

Figure 3.8 Project 4 Query Design Grid

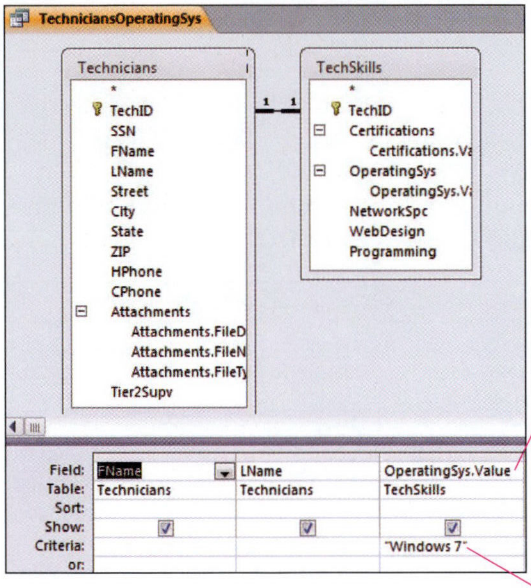

Adding *.Value* to the end of the multiple-value field *OperatingSys* causes Access to display each value in a separate row in the datasheet.

Only those records with *Windows 7* as one of the multiple-value field entries will be selected in the query results.

Project 4 **Using a Multiple-Value Field in a Query** **Part 1 of 1**

1. With the **AL2-C3-RSRCompServ.accdb** database open, open the TechnicianSpecialties query in Design view.
2. Right-click in the field selector bar above the *Certifications* field and click *Cut* at the shortcut menu to remove the field from the query design grid.
3. Delete the *NetworkSpc*, *WebDesign*, and *Programming* columns from the query design grid by completing a step similar to Step 2.

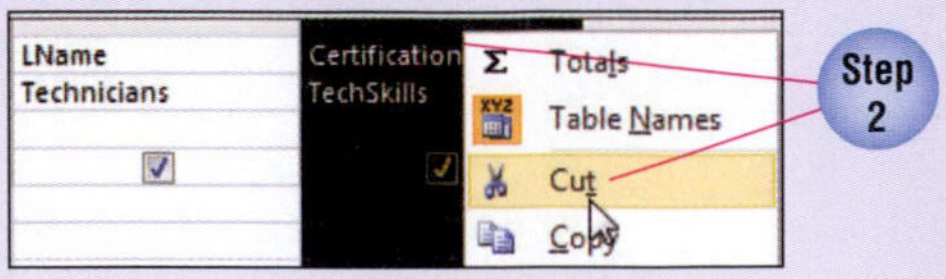

4. Run the query. Notice each record in the *Operating Systems* column displays the multiple values separated by commas.
5. Switch to Design view.
6. Click in the *OperatingSys* field box in the query design grid, move the insertion point to the end of the field name and then type a period (.). Access displays *.Value* in the *Field* box. Press Enter to accept the .Value property in the field name. ***Note: When creating a query from scratch, drag the multiple-value field name with the .Value property already attached from the table's field list box to the query design grid.***

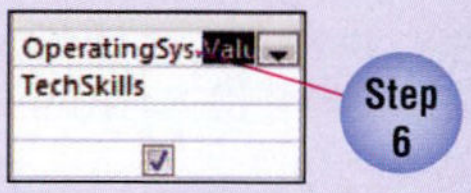

7. Click the File tab, click Save Object As, type **TechniciansOperatingSys** at the Save As dialog box, and then press Enter or click OK.
8. Click the Query Tools Design Tab and then run the query. Notice that each entry in the multiple-value field is now displayed in a separate row.
9. Switch to Design view.
10. Click in the *Criteria* row in the *OperatingSys.Value* column in the query design grid, type **Windows 7**, and then press Enter.

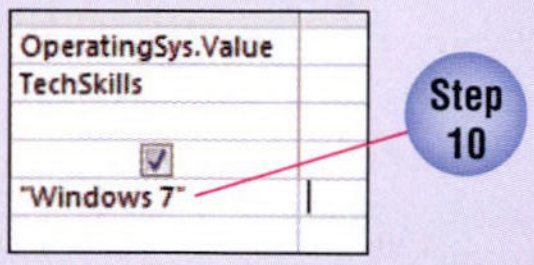

11. Run the query. Notice the column title for the multiple-value field in the query results datasheet is now *TechSkills. OperatingSys.Value*. Change the column heading for the field by completing the following steps:
    a. Switch to Design view.
    b. Click the insertion point anywhere within the *OperatingSys.Value* Field box in the query design grid.
    c. Click the Property Sheet button in the Show/Hide group of the Query Tools Design tab.
    d. Click in the *Caption* property box, type **Operating System**, and then press Enter.
    e. Close the Property Sheet task pane.

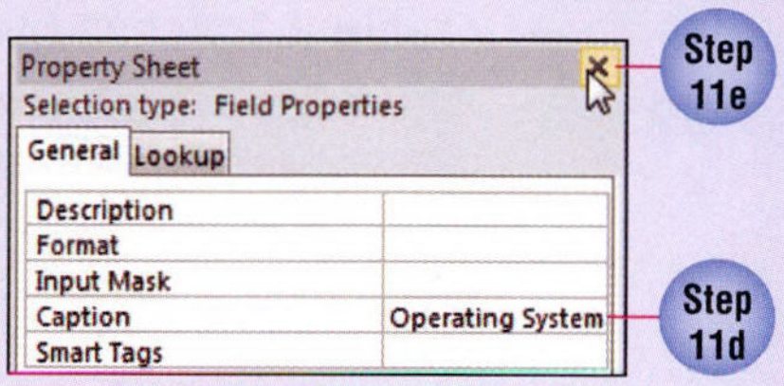

12. Run the query.

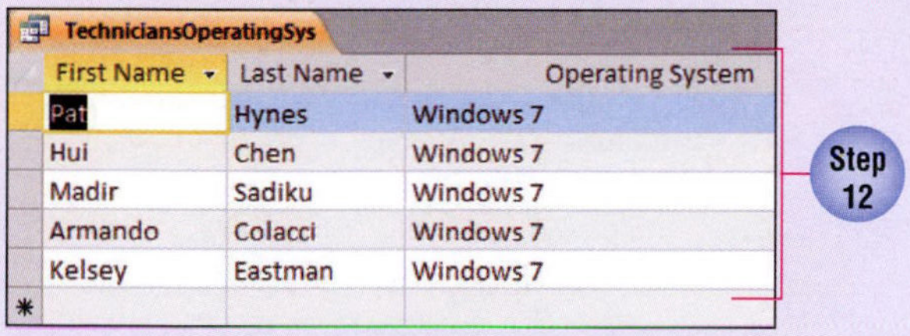

13. Print the query results datasheet and then close the query. Click Yes to save changes.

Project 5 Modify Records Using Action Queries **4 Parts**

You will create a new table, add and delete records, and update field values using action queries.

Quick Steps

Create Make-Table Query
1. Create query in Design view.
2. Add desired table(s) to query.
3. Add desired fields to query design grid.
4. If necessary, enter criteria to select records.
5. Run query.
6. Switch to Design view.
7. Click Make Table button.
8. Type table name.
9. If necessary, select destination database.
10. Click OK.
11. Run the query.
12. Click Yes.
13. Save query.

Performing Operations Using Action Queries

Action queries are used to perform an operation on a group of records. Building an action query is similar to building a select query with the extra step of specifying the action to perform on the group of selected records. Four types of action queries are available and are described in Table 3.1.

To create an action query, first build a select query by adding tables, fields, and criteria to the query design grid. Run the select query to make sure the desired group of records is being targeted for action. Once you are satisfied the correct records will be modified, change the query type using the Make Table, Append, Update, or Delete buttons in the Query Type group in the Query Tools Design tab shown in Figure 3.9.

Clicking the Run button once the query type has been changed to an action query causes Access to perform the make-table, append, update, or delete operation. Once an action query has been run, the results cannot be reversed.

Table 3.1 Action Query Types

Query Type	*Description*
Make Table	A new table is created from selected records in an existing table. For example, you could create a new table that combines fields from two other tables in the database.
Append	Selected records are added to the end of an existing table. This action is similar to performing a copy and paste.
Update	A global change is made to the selected group of records based on an update expression. For example, you could increase the labor rate by 10 percent in one step.
Delete	The selected group of records is deleted from a table.

Figure 3.9 Query Type Group in Query Tools Design Tab

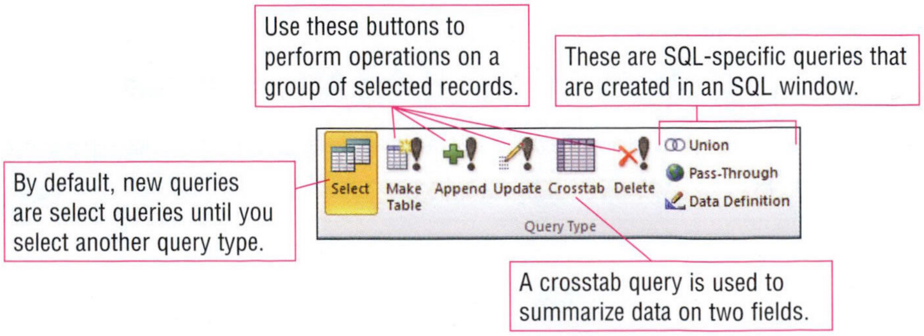
Use these buttons to perform operations on a group of selected records.
These are SQL-specific queries that are created in an SQL window.
By default, new queries are select queries until you select another query type.
Select
Make Table
Append
Update
Crosstab
Delete
Union
Pass-Through
Data Definition
Query Type
A crosstab query is used to summarize data on two fields.

Creating a New Table Using a Query

A ***make-table query*** creates a new table from selected records placed in the same database or in another database. This type of query is useful to create a history table prior to purging old records that are no longer required. The history table can be placed in the same database or in another database used as an archive copy. Once you have created a select query that will extract the records you want to copy to a new table, click the Make Table button in the Query Type group in the Query Tools Design tab to open the Make Table dialog box shown in Figure 3.10. Enter a table name, choose the destination database, and click OK.

HINT

Once you have run a make-table query, do not double-click the query name in the Navigation pane since doing so instructs Access to run the query again. Open the query in Design view to make changes to the criteria and/or query type if you need to use the query again.

Make Table

Figure 3.10 Make Table Dialog Box

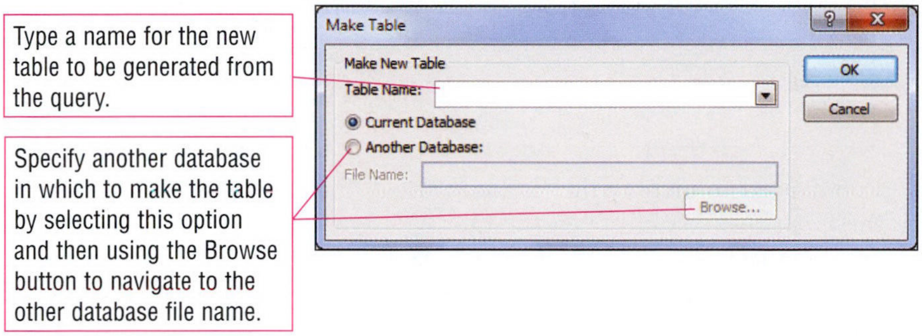

Project 5a Creating a New Table Using a Query

Part 1 of 4

1. With the **AL2-C3-RSRCompServ.accdb** database open, create a select query to select work order records for September 1, 2012 to September 15, 2012 inclusive by completing the following steps:
   a. Create a new query in Design view. Add the WorkOrders table to the query window and then close the Show Table dialog box. Drag the bottom border of the table field list box until you can see all of the field names.
   b. Double-click the WorkOrders table field list box title bar. This selects all records within the table.
   c. Position the arrow pointer anywhere within the selected field names in the field list box and drag the pointer to the first column in the query design grid. All fields in the table are added to the query design grid.
   d. Click in the *Criteria* row in the *ServDate* column, type **Between September 1, 2012 and September 15, 2012**, and then press Enter.

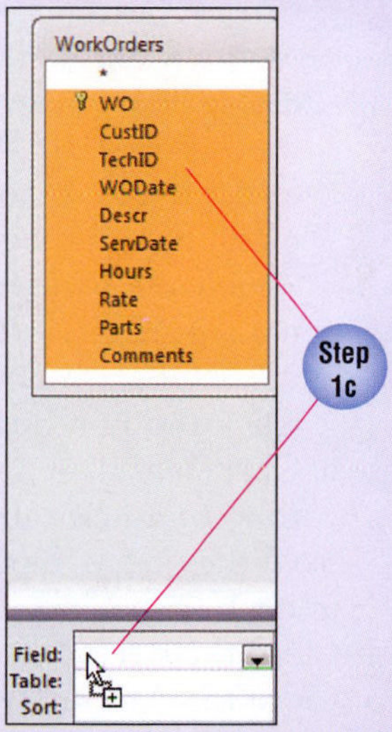

e. Run the query. The query results datasheet displays seven records.

records selected for make-table query at Step 1e

Work Order	Customer ID	Technician ID	WO Date	Descripton
65012	1000	11	Fri Sep 07 2012	Bi-annual computer maintenance
65013	1000	10	Fri Sep 07 2012	Replace keyboard
65014	1005	02	Mon Sep 10 2012	Replace power supply
65015	1008	04	Mon Sep 10 2012	Restore operating system
65016	1010	06	Tue Sep 11 2012	Install upgraded video card
65017	1015	08	Fri Sep 14 2012	Replace DVD drive
65018	1020	10	Fri Sep 14 2012	Upgrade Office suite

f. You decide you do not need to archive the *Comments* field data. Switch to Design view and then delete the *Comments* column from the query design grid.

2. Make a new table from the selected records and store the table in a history database used for archive purposes by completing the following steps:
   a. If necessary, switch to Design view.
   b. Click the Make Table button in the Query Type group in the Query Tools Design tab.
   c. With the insertion point positioned in the *Table Name* text box, type **Sept2012WorkOrders**.
   d. Click *Another Database* and then click the Browse button.
   e. At the Make Table dialog box, navigate to the Access2010L2C3 folder on your storage medium and then double-click the file named ***AL2-C3-RSRCompServHistory.accdb***.

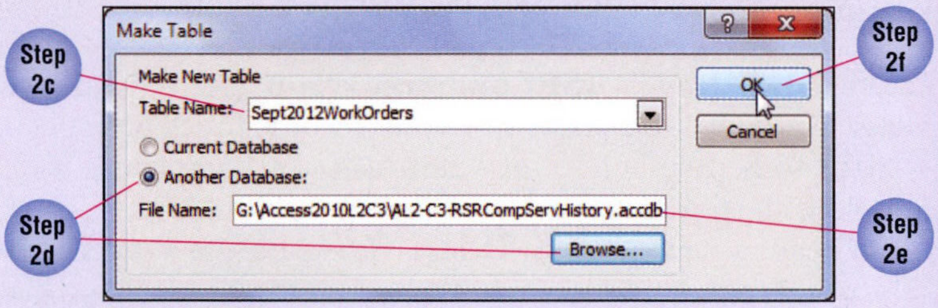

   f. Click OK.
   g. Click the Run button.
   h. Click Yes at the Microsoft Access message box indicating you are about to paste seven rows to a new table.
3. Save the query. Type **Sept2012MakeTable** at the Save As dialog box and then press Enter or click OK.
4. Close the query.
5. Close the **AL2-C3-RSRCompServ.accdb** database.
6. Open the **AL2-C3-RSRCompServHistory.accdb** database and enable content. Click OK to continue if a message appears stating that Access has to update object dependencies.
7. Open the Sept2012WorkOrders table.
8. Review the records that were copied to the new table from the make-table query.
9. Close the table.
10. Close the **AL2-C3-RSRCompServHistory.accdb** database.

Deleting a Group of Records Using a Query

A ***delete query*** is used to delete a group of records that meet specified criteria in one step. You can use this action query in any instance where the records to be deleted can be selected using a criteria statement. Using a query to remove the records is more efficient and reduces the chances of removing a record in error if deleting is done manually in the table.

The make-table query used in Project 5a created a duplicate copy of the records in the new table. The original records still exist in the WorkOrders table. The make-table query used to archive the records can be modified by changing the query type to a delete query and then using it to remove the records from the original table.

Action query names display with a black exclamation mark in the Navigation pane next to an icon that indicates the type of action that will be performed if the query is run.

Quick Steps

Create Delete Query

1. Create query in Design view.
2. Add desired table to query.
3. Add desired fields to query design grid.
4. Enter criteria to select records.
5. Run query.
6. Switch to Design view.
7. Click Delete button.
8. Run the query.
9. Click Yes.
10. Save query.

Delete

Project 5b **Deleting Records Using a Query** Part 2 of 4

1. Open the **AL2-C3-RSRCompServ.accdb** database and enable content.
2. Right-click the Sept2012MakeTable query and then click *Design View* at the shortcut menu.
3. Click the Delete button in the Query Type group in the Query Tools Design tab.
4. Click the File tab, click Save Object As, type Sept2012Delete at the Save As dialog box, and then press Enter or click OK.
5. Click the Query Tools Design tab and then run the query.
6. At the Microsoft Access message box indicating you are about to delete seven rows from the table and informing you the action cannot be reversed, click Yes to delete the selected records.

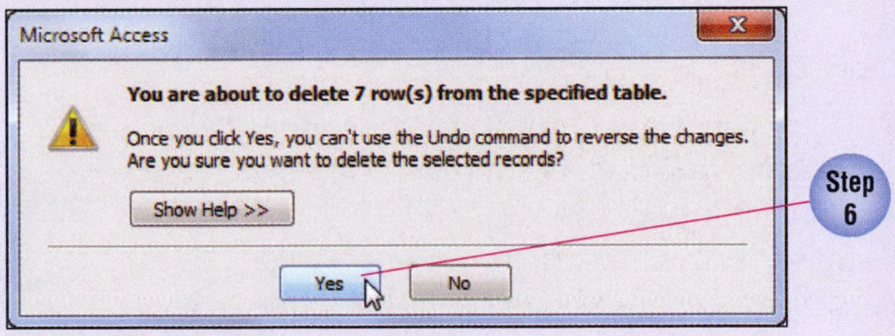

Microsoft Access
You are about to delete 7 row(s) from the specified table.
Once you click Yes, you can't use the Undo command to reverse the changes.
Are you sure you want to delete the selected records?
Show Help >>
Yes
No
Step 6

7. Close the query.
8. Open the WorkOrders table. Notice that no records exist with a *Service Date* before September 15, 2012.
9. Close the table.

Adding Records to a Table Using a Query

The ***append query*** is used to copy a group of records from one or more tables to the end of an existing table. Consider using an append query in any situation where you want to make a duplicate copy of records. For example, in Project 5a, the make table query was used to create a new table to store archive records. Once the table exists, you can use append queries to copy subsequent archive records to the end of the existing history table.

Append

Quick Steps

Create Append Query

1. Create query in Design view.
2. Add desired table to query.
3. Add desired fields to query design grid.
4. Enter criteria to select records.
5. Run query.
6. Switch to Design view.
7. Click Append button.
8. Type table name.
9. Select destination database.
10. Click OK.
11. Run the query.
12. Click Yes.
13. Save query.

Clicking the Append button in the Query Type group in the Query Tools Design tab causes the Append dialog box to open with the same options as the Make Table dialog box, as shown in Figure 3.11.

The receiving table should have the same structure as the query from which the records are selected.

Figure 3.11 Append Dialog Box

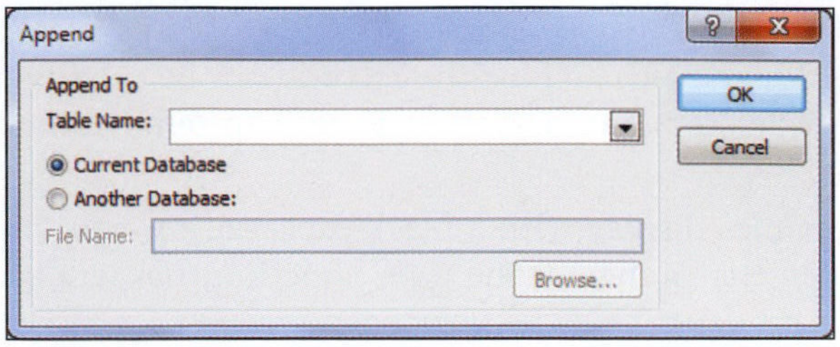

Project 5c Adding Records to a Table Using a Query

Part 3 of 4

1. With the **AL2-C3-RSRCompServ.accdb** database open, open the Sept2012MakeTable query in Design view.
2. Modify the criteria to select work order records for the last half of September 2012 by completing the following steps:
   a. Expand the width of the *ServDate* column until you can see the entire criteria statement.
   b. Click the insertion point in the *Criteria* row in the *ServDate* column, insert and delete text as necessary to modify the criteria statement to read **Between #9/16/2012# And #9/30/2012#**, and then press Enter.

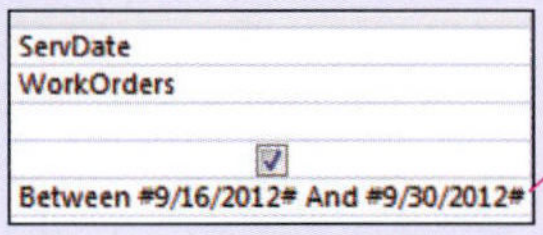

3. Click the Append button in the Query Type group in the Query Tools Design tab.
4. Since the query is being changed from a make-table query, Access inserts the same table name and database that was used to create the table in Project 5a. Click OK to accept the table name *Sept2012WorkOrders* and the *AL2-C3-RSRCompServHistory.accdb* database located in the Access2010L2C3 folder on your storage medium.

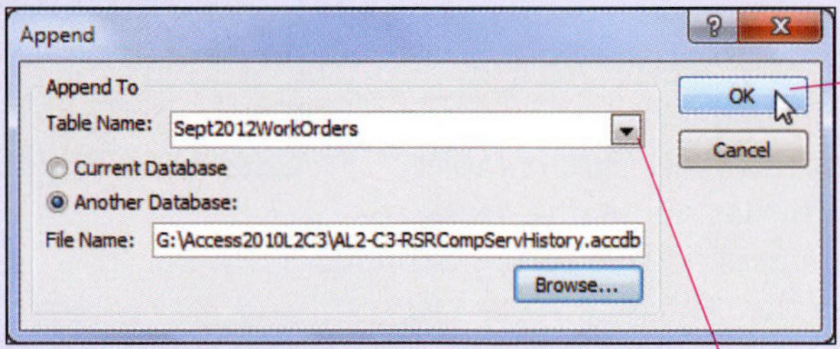

If you are appending to a table in the existing database, you can select the table name from the drop-down list.

5. Click the File tab, click Save Object As, type **Sept2012Append** at the Save As dialog box, and then press Enter or click OK.
6. Click the Query Tools Design tab and then run the query.
7. Click Yes at the Microsoft Access message box indicating you are about to append eight rows and the action cannot be undone.

8. Close the query.
9. Close the **AL2-C3-RSRCompServ.accdb** database.
10. Open the **AL2-C3-RSRCompServHistory.accdb** database.
11. Open the Sept2012WorkOrders table and print the datasheet in landscape orientation.
12. Close the table.
13. Close the **AL2-C3-RSRCompServHistory.accdb** database.

Modifying Records Using an Update Query

When you need to make a change to a group of records that can be selected in a query and the change to be incorporated is the same for all records, you can instruct Access to modify the data using an update query. Making a global change using an update query is efficient and reduces the potential for errors that could occur from manual editing of multiple records.

Clicking the Update button in the Query Type group in the Query Tools Design tab causes an *Update To* row to appear in the query design grid. Click in the *Update To* box in the column to be modified and type the expression that will change the field values as needed. Run the query to make the global change.

▼ **Quick Steps**

Create Update Query
1. Create query in Design view.
2. Add desired table to query.
3. Add desired fields to query design grid.
4. Enter criteria to select records.
5. Run query.
6. Switch to Design view.
7. Click Update button.
8. Click in *Update To* box in field to be changed.
9. Type update expression.
10. Run the query.
11. Click Yes.
12. Save query.

Update

Project 5d | **Changing Service Plan Rates Using an Update Query** | **Part 4 of 4**

1. Open the **AL2-C3-RSRCompServ.accdb** database and enable content.
2. Open the table named FeesSCPlans and review the current values in the *Rate* column. For example, take note that the current rate for Plan A's six month term for one computer is $48.00. Close the table when you are finished reviewing the current rates.
3. Create an update query to increase Plan A service contract rates by 6% by completing the following steps:
 a. Create a new query in Design view.
 b. Add the table named FeesSCPlans to the query and then close the Show Table dialog box.
 c. Add the *Plan* and *Rate* fields to the query design grid.
 d. Click in the *Criteria* row in the *Plan* column, type **A**, and then click in the Criteria row in the next column in the query design grid. *Note: The AutoComplete feature will show a list of functions as soon as you type **A**. You can ignore the AutoComplete drop-down list since you are not entering a mathematical expression for the criteria; however, pressing Enter causes Access to add Abs to the Criteria row. Clicking in another box in the query design grid will remove the AutoComplete drop-down list.*

Step 3d

Field:	Plan	Rate
Table:	FeesSCPlans	FeesSCPlans
Sort:		
Show:	☑	☑
Criteria:	"A"	
or:

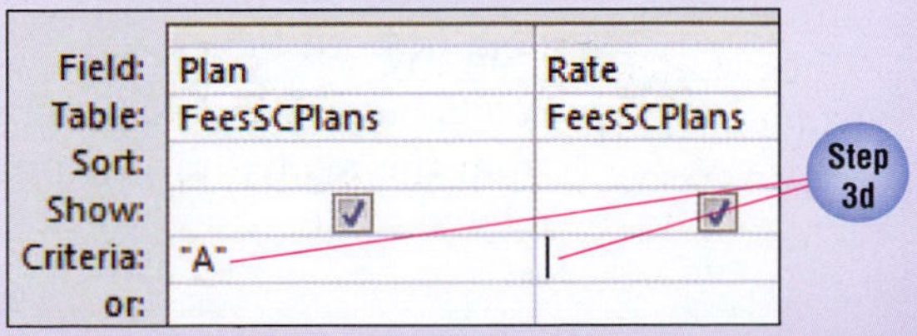

e. Run the query. Review the four records shown in the query results datasheet.

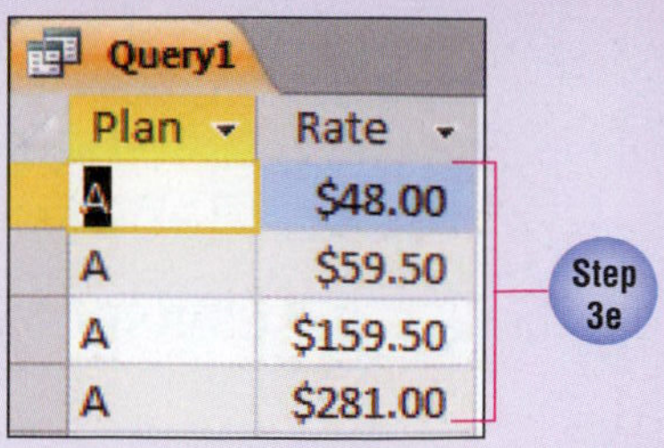

f. Switch to Design view.

g. Click the Update button in the Query Type group in the Query Tools Design tab. Access adds a row labeled *Update To* in the query design grid between the *Table* and *Criteria* rows.

h. Click in the *Update To* row in the *Rate* column, type **[Rate]*1.06**, and then press Enter.

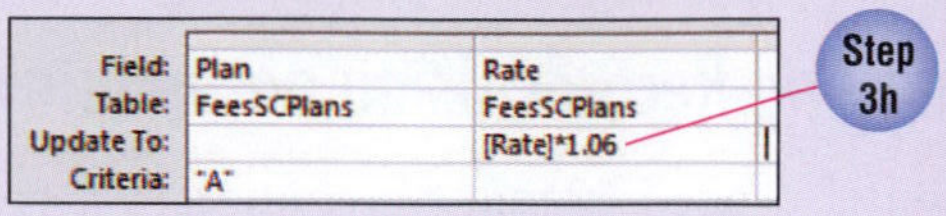

4. Save the query. Type **RateUpdate** at the Save As dialog box and then press Enter or click OK.
5. Run the query. Click Yes at the Microsoft Access message that says you are about to update four rows.
6. Close the query.
7. Open the FeesSCPlans table. Notice the *Rate* values for Plan A records have increased. For example, the value in the Rate column for Plan A's six month term for one computer is now $50.88. Print the datasheet.
8. Close the table and then close the **AL2-C3-RSRCompServ.accdb** database.

HINT

Create a backup copy of the database before running an action query.

Exercise caution when running any action query since the queries perform changes in database tables. For example, in Project 5d, if you ran the update query a second time, the rates for the Plan A service plans would increase another six percent. Once changed, the rates cannot be undone. To reverse the update, you would need to create a mathematical expression in a new update query to remove six percent from the prices if you ran the query twice by mistake.

Chapter Summary

- A filter can be saved as a query by displaying the filter criteria in a Filter By Form window, clicking the Advanced Filter Options button, and then clicking *Save as Query* at the drop-down list.
- Parameter queries prompt the user for the criteria by which to select records when the query is run.
- To create a parameter query, type a prompt message encased in square brackets in the *Criteria* row in the field you want to use to select records.
- Changing the join property can alter the number of records that are displayed in the query results datasheet.
- An inner join selects records only if a matching value is found in the joined field in both tables.
- A left outer join selects all records from the left table and matching records from the related table; empty fields display if no matching records exist in the related table.

- Click the Show Table button in the Query Setup group in the Query Tools Design tab to add a table or query to the query window.
- Remove a table from the query by clicking a field within the table's field list box and pressing the Delete key, or by right-clicking the table and clicking *Remove Table* at the shortcut menu.
- A right outer join selects all records from the right table and matching records from the primary table; empty fields display if no matching records exist in the primary table.
- A self-join query is created by adding two copies of the same table to the query window and joining the tables on a field containing matching field values.
- An alias is another name that you want to use to reference a table in a query.
- Right-click a table name in the query window, click *Properties* at the shortcut menu, and then enter the alias for the table in the *Alias* property box at the Property Sheet task pane.
- A query that contains two tables that are not joined creates a cross product or Cartesian product query, which means Access creates records for every possible combination from both tables, the results of which are generally not meaningful.
- A subquery is a query nested inside another query. Use subqueries to break down a complex query into manageable units. For example, a query with multiple calculations could be created by combining subqueries in which each calculation is built individually.
- Another reason for using subqueries is to have the ability to reuse a smaller query in many other queries, meaning you do not have to keep recreating the same structure.
- Create select queries on multiple-value fields using the same methods you would use for single-field criteria.
- Adding *.Value* to the end of a multiple-value field name in the *Field* box in the query design grid causes Access to place each field value in a separate row in the query results datasheet.
- A make-table query creates a new table in the active database or in another database with the structure defined in the query design grid and containing records selected by a criteria statement.
- Delete a group of records in one step by creating and running a delete query.
- Add a group of records to the bottom of an existing table in the active database or in another database using an append query.
- An update query allows you to make a global change to records by entering an expression such as a mathematical formula in the query design grid.

Commands Review

FEATURE	RIBBON TAB, GROUP	BUTTON
Advanced Filter Options	Home, Sort & Filter	
Append query	Query Tools Design, Query Type	
Create query in Design view	Create, Queries	
Delete query	Query Tools Design, Query Type	
Make table query	Query Tools Design, Query Type	
Run query	Query Tools Design, Results	
Show Table	Query Tools Design, Query Setup	
Update query	Query Tools Design, Query Type	

Concepts Check Test Your Knowledge

Completion: In the space provided at the right, indicate the correct term, command, or number.

1. Click this button at a Filter By Form datasheet to save the filter's criteria as a query. ____________________
2. This is the name for a query which prompts the user to type the criteria in a dialog box when the query is run. ____________________
3. Double-clicking the black join line between tables in a query window opens this dialog box. ____________________
4. This join type displays all records from the related table and empty fields if no matching record exists in the primary table. ____________________
5. Click this button in the Query Setup group in the Query Tools Design tab to add a table to an existing query. ____________________
6. This is the term for a query in which two copies of the same table are added to the query window and joined by two fields in the same table that contain matching field values. ____________________

7. This is the term used to describe another name with which you reference a table in a query. ________________

8. This is the term for a query in which two tables are used in the query window with no join established to connect one table to the other. ________________

9. This term describes a query nested inside another query. ________________

10. Add this entry to the end of a multiple-value field name in the *Field* box in the query design grid to display each field value in a separate row. ________________

11. Queries that perform operations on selected records are referred to by this term. ________________

12. Create this type of query to create a new table from existing records in the active database or in an archive database. ________________

13. This query removes a group of records that meet specified criteria. ________________

14. This query adds a group of records to the end of an existing table in the active database or in another database. ________________

15. Create this type of query to increase the prices in all records by 10%. ________________

Skills Check Assess Your Performance

Assessment

1 EXTRACT RECORDS USING A FILTER AND PROMPTED QUERIES

1. Open the database named **AL2-C3-VantageVideos.accdb** and enable content.
2. Open the table named WebCustomers.
3. Using the Filter By Form feature, display only those customers who reside in Burlington with a ZIP code that begins with 05401. ***Hint: Type* 05401* *in the ZIP field to specify only the first five characters in the ZIP code. The asterisk is a wildcard that allows you to filter by specifying only a portion of the field value.***
4. Save the filter as a query named *CustBurlington05401*.
5. Close the Filter By Form datasheet and close the table. Click No when prompted to save changes to the table design.
6. Open the CustBurlington05401 query.
7. Print the query results datasheet in landscape orientation and then close the query.

8. Create a new query in Design view using the following specifications:
   a. Add the tables WebOrderDetails, WebOrders, and WebProducts to the query.
   b. Add the fields *WebOrderID*, *DateOrd*, *Qty*, and *Product* to the query design grid. ***Note: Add* WebOrderID *from the WebOrders table*.**
   c. Create a parameter query to prompt the user to type the title of the video in the *Product* column. You determine the message that should display in the Enter Parameter Value dialog box.
   d. Save the query, name it *PromptedVideo*, and then close the query.
9. Run the PromptedVideo query. Type **The Longest Day** at the Enter Parameter Value dialog box. Print the query results datasheet and then close the query.
10. Open the PromptedVideo query in Design view. Delete the prompt message in the *Product* column. Create a parameter query to prompt the user to type a beginning and ending date to view Web orders in the *DateOrd* column. Use Save As to name the revised query *PromptedOrderDates* and then close the query.
11. Run the PromptedOrderDates query. Type **February 1, 2012** as the beginning date and **February 29, 2012** as the ending date. Print the query results datasheet and then close the query.

Assessment 2

MODIFY JOIN PROPERTIES

1. With the **AL2-C3-VantageVideos.accdb** database open, create a new query in Design view using the following specifications:
   a. Add the tables WebCustomers and WebOrders to the query.
   b. Add the fields *CustID*, *FirstName*, *LastName*, and *WebOrderID* to the query design grid.
   c. Modify the join type between the WebCustomers table and the WebOrders table to a left outer join.
   d. Save the query and name it *CustWebOrders*.
2. Run the query. Print the query results datasheet and then close the query.
3. Create a new query in Design view using the following specifications:
   a. Add the tables WebOrderDetails and WebProducts to the query.
   b. Add the fields *WebOrdID*, *WebProdID*, and *Product* to the query design grid. ***Note: Add* WebProdID *from the WebProducts table*.**
   c. Modify the join type between the WebProducts table and the WebOrderDetails table to a left outer join.
   d. Save the query and name it *WebProductOrders*.
4. Run the query. Print the query results datasheet and then close the query.

Assessment 3

ADD A TABLE TO A QUERY AND CREATE AND USE A SUBQUERY TO PERFORM CALCULATIONS

1. With the **AL2-C3-VantageVideos.accdb** database open, open the CustWebOrders query in Design view and modify the query as follows:
   a. Modify the join type between the WebCustomers table and the WebOrders table to an inner join.
   b. Add the WebOrderDetails table and the WebProducts table to the query.

c. Add the fields named *DateOrd*, *Qty*, *Product*, and *SellPrice* to the query design grid.
d. Delete the *CustID* field from the query.
e. Create a calculated field with the column label *Total Sale* that multiplies the quantity ordered times the selling price. Format the calculated column to *Currency*.
f. Use Save As to name the revised query *WebSalesWithTotal*.

2. Run the query. Print the query results datasheet in landscape orientation with a left and right margin set to 0.5 inch and then close the query.
3. Create a new query in Design view that calculates the total sale with tax as follows:
   a. Nest the WebSalesWithTotal query in the new query.
   b. Add the fields *WebOrdID*, *DateOrd*, and *Total Sale* to the query design grid.
   c. Create a calculated field with the column label *Tax* that multiples the value in the *Total Sale* column times .06 (decimal equivalent of 6%). Format the calculated column to *Standard*.
   d. Create a second calculated column with the column label *Total Sale with Tax* that adds the *Total Sale* column to the *Tax* column.
   e. Save the query and name it *WebSalesWithTotalAndTax*.
4. Run the query. Double-click the right column boundary for the last column in the query results datasheet to display the entire field heading and then print the query results datasheet. Close the query saving changes.

Assessment 4

USE ACTION QUERIES TO ARCHIVE RECORDS AND UPDATE SELLING PRICES

1. With the **AL2-C3-VantageVideos.accdb** database open, open the WebSalesWithTotal query in Design view and modify the query as follows:
   a. Delete the *SellPrice* and *Total Sale* columns from the query design grid.
   b. Add a criterion to select the records for sales during the month of February 2012.
   c. Run the query to make sure the correct records are being selected.
   d. Change the query to a make-table query, name the new table *Feb2012WebSales*, and store the table in the database named **AL2-C3-VantageVideosArchive.accdb** on your storage medium.
   e. Use Save As to name the revised query *Feb2012SalesMakeTable*.
   f. Run the query.
2. Close the query and then close the **AL2-C3-VantageVideos.accdb** database.
3. Open the **AL2-C3-VantageVideosArchive.accdb** and then open the Feb2012WebSales table.
4. Adjust column widths as necessary and then print the datasheet. Close the table saving changes to the layout and then close the **AL2-C3-VantageVideosArchive.accdb** database.
5. Open the **AL2-C3-VantageVideos.accdb** database and enable content if necessary.
6. Open the Feb2012SalesMakeTable query in Design view and modify the query as follows:
   a. Change the query to a delete query.
   b. Remove the WebCustomers, WebOrderDetails, and WebProducts tables from the query.
   c. Use Save As to name the revised query *Feb2012SalesDelete*.
   d. Run the query and then close the query window.

7. Open the WebSalesWithTotal query. Print the query results datasheet in landscape orientation with left and right margins of 0.5 inch and then close the query.
8. Create a new query in Design view to update the selling prices of all videos as follows:
   a. Add the WebProducts table to the query.
   b. Add the *SellPrice* field to the query design grid.
   c. Change the query to an update query and add a formula that will add $1.05 to the selling price of all videos.
   d. Save the query and name it *PriceUpdate*.
   e. Run the query and then close the query window.
9. Open the WebProducts table. Print the datasheet and then close the table.
10. Close the **AL2-C3-VantageVideos.accdb** database.

Visual Benchmark Demonstrate Your Proficiency

CALCULATE DAYS BOARDED AND AMOUNT DUE USING NESTED QUERIES

1. Open **AL2-C3-PawsParadise.accdb**.
2. Review the query results datasheet shown in Figure 3.12. This query is the result of nesting a query within a query. Create the calculations as follows:
   a. Create the first query to calculate the number of days a dog is boarded in the kennel. Show in the query results the reservation ID, the customer's name, the dog's name, and the two date fields. Calculate the days the dog was boarded. Save the query and name it *DaysBoarded*.
   b. Nest DaysBoarded in a new query. Add the Dogs and the KennelCategories tables to the query. Join the DaysBoarded query to the Dogs table on the common *DogName* field. Add the fields to the query design grid as shown in Figure 3.12 and then calculate the amount due for each reservation.
   c. Sort and format the query results as shown in Figure 3.12. The font used is Cambria 11-point. The alternate row color used is Maroon 1 in the *Standard Colors* section of the color palette. ***Note: The first row is not formatted differently from the remainder of the datasheet; the row displays with a different row color because the first row is selected.*** Save the query and name it ReservationTotals.
3. Print the ReservationTotals query results datasheet in landscape orientation with left and right margins set to 0.5 inch.
4. Close the query.
5. Close the **AL2-C3-PawsParadise.accdb** database.

Figure 3.12 Visual Benchmark

Reservation	First Name	Last Name	Dog's Name	Date Out	Days Boarded	Kennel Type	Daily Rate	Amount Due
1	Shawn	Jenkins	Abby	11/12/2012	3	V.I.P. Suite	$38.50	$115.50
2	Shawn	Jenkins	Winnie	11/12/2012	3	V.I.P. Suite	$38.50	$115.50
3	Sean	Gallagher	Tank	11/13/2012	3	V.I.P. Suite	$38.50	$115.50
4	Sofia	Ramos	Apollo	11/18/2012	7	Indoor/Outdoor Suite	$25.50	$178.50
5	Sofia	Ramos	Murphy	11/18/2012	7	Indoor/Outdoor Suite	$25.50	$178.50
6	Dina	Lombardi	Niko	11/16/2012	4	Indoor/Outdoor Suite	$25.50	$102.00
7	Natale	Rizzo	Dallas	11/14/2012	2	Indoor/Outdoor Suite	$25.50	$51.00
8	James	Chung	Lassie	11/13/2012	1	Deluxe Suite	$29.50	$29.50
9	Bernard	Jedicke	Kosmo	11/13/2012	1	Day Care Boarding	$16.50	$16.50
10	Bernard	Jedicke	Sierra	11/13/2012	1	Day Care Boarding	$16.50	$16.50
11	Bernard	Jedicke	Emma	11/13/2012	1	Day Care Boarding	$16.50	$16.50
12	Carlotta	Sanchez	Scrappy	11/19/2012	6	Deluxe Suite	$29.50	$177.00
13	Michael	Mancini	Harley	11/23/2012	10	Indoor/Outdoor Suite	$25.50	$255.00
14	Glen	Waters	Barney	11/29/2012	15	Indoor/Outdoor Suite	$25.50	$382.50
15	Lenora	Diaz	Zack	11/17/2012	3	Indoor/Outdoor Suite	$25.50	$76.50
16	Maeve	Murphy	King	11/19/2012	4	V.I.P. Suite	$38.50	$154.00
17	Valerie	McTague	Chloe	11/19/2012	3	Deluxe Suite	$29.50	$88.50
18	Nadia	Costa	Bailey	11/24/2012	7	Deluxe Suite	$29.50	$206.50
19	Juan	Torres	Taffy	11/21/2012	4	V.I.P. Suite	$38.50	$154.00
20	Liam	Doherty	Zeus	11/23/2012	5	V.I.P. Suite	$38.50	$192.50
21	Dillon	Farrell	Chico	11/22/2012	4	Indoor/Outdoor Suite	$25.50	$102.00
22	Diane	Ye	Elvis	11/25/2012	5	Indoor/Outdoor Suite	$25.50	$127.50
23	Lorenzo	Rivera	Fifi	11/27/2012	5	V.I.P. Suite	$38.50	$192.50
24	Lorenzo	Rivera	Lucky	11/27/2012	5	Indoor/Outdoor Suite	$25.50	$127.50
25	Bernard	Jedicke	Kosmo	11/27/2012	1	Day Care Boarding	$16.50	$16.50
26	Bernard	Jedicke	Sierra	11/27/2012	1	Day Care Boarding	$16.50	$16.50
27	Bernard	Jedicke	Emma	11/27/2012	1	Day Care Boarding	$16.50	$16.50

Case Study Apply Your Skills

Part 1

You are continuing your work as an intern at Hillsdale Realty. The office manager has requested a series of printouts with information from the database. Open the database named **AL2-C3-HillsdaleRealty.accdb** and enable content. Design, create, save, run, and print query results to provide the required information. You determine appropriate descriptive names for each query.

- A list of sales by agent that includes the date of sale, address, sale price, and commission rate. Sort the query results by the agent's last name and then by the date of sale with both fields sorted in ascending order.
- Modify the first query to allow the office manager to type the agent's name when she runs the query so that she can view individual sales reports by agent. To test your query, run the query using the agent name *Cecilia Ortega*. Save the revised query using a new name.
- A list that shows all of the agents and each agent's clients. Show the client ID, client first name, and client last name next to each agent's name. The manager wants to see which agents have not yet signed a client so you need to make sure the query results show all agents.

- A list of agents that shows his or her co-broker agent. The Agents table contains a field named *CoBroker*. This field is the agent ID for the person assigned to co-broker listings. The office manager has requested a list that shows the agent's last name instead of his or her ID number in the *CoBroker* field. Sort the list in ascending order by AgentLName. ***Hint: Create a self-join query and remember to use the alias and caption properties to rename the table and the column that will display the co-broker agent last name.***
- Modify the first query to add a column to calculate the amount of commission that will be owed on the sale by multiplying the sale price times the commission rate. Save the revised query using a new name.
- Use a query to update all commission quota values to add 15% to the existing quotas. After updating the values, create a new query to show each agent and his or her respective commission quota. Sort the list in ascending order by agent last name.

Part 2

Help

The office manager would like to see the five highest sale prices to date. Research in Help how to create a top values query. Using the information you learned in Help, modify the first query created in Part 1 to produce the top 5 list. Save the revised query using a new name and print the query results. ***Hint: Remove the sorting from the original query and then sort by the sale prices in descending order before converting the query to a top 5 values query.***

Part 3

The office manager would like to review the client preferences for each listing with each preference on a separate line. Include in the list the date of the listing, the street address, the client's name, and the client's telephone number. Add criteria to select only those records where the client has requested a pre-sale inspection or a staging service for his or her listing. Save and print the query.

Microsoft® Access®

CHAPTER 4

Creating and Using Custom Forms

PERFORMANCE OBJECTIVES

Upon successful completion of Chapter 4, you will be able to:

- **Create a custom form in Design view using all three form sections**
- **Add fields individually and as a group**
- **Move, size, and format control objects**
- **Change the tab order of fields**
- **Create tabbed pages in a form and insert a subform on each page**
- **Add and format a calculation to a custom form**
- **Group and ungroup multiple controls**
- **Adjust the alignment and spacing of controls**
- **Add graphics to a form**
- **Anchor a control to a position in the form**
- **Create a datasheet form**
- **Modify form properties to restrict actions allowed in records**
- **Create a blank form**
- **Add list boxes to a form**
- **Sort records in a form and locate a record using a wildcard character**

SNAP Training and Assessment. Simplified.

Tutorials

4.1 Creating Custom Forms Using Design View

4.2 Binding a Table to a Form and Adding Fields

4.3 Moving, Resizing, and Formatting Control Objects

4.4 Changing the Tab Order of Fields

4.5 Adding a Tab Control and a Subform

4.6 Adding Subforms and a New Page to the Tab Control

4.7 Adding Calculations to a Form in Design View

4.8 Grouping, Aligning, and Spacing Controls

4.9 Creating a Datasheet Form and Modifying Form Properties

4.10 Sorting and Finding Records in a Form

Forms provide an interface for data entry and maintenance that allows end users to work with data stored in the underlying tables more efficiently. For example, forms can be designed using a layout that uses the screen space more effectively than the tabular layout of a datasheet. Forms can include fields from multiple tables allowing data to be entered in one object that updates several tables. Generally, database designers provide forms for end users to use to perform data maintenance and restrict access to tables to protect the structure and integrity of the database. In this chapter you will learn how to build custom forms. Model answers for this chapter's projects appear on the following page.

Access

Access2010L2C4

Note: Before beginning the projects, copy to your storage medium the Access2010L2C4 subfolder from the Access2010L2 folder on the CD that accompanies this textbook and then make Access2010L2C4 the active folder.

Model Answers

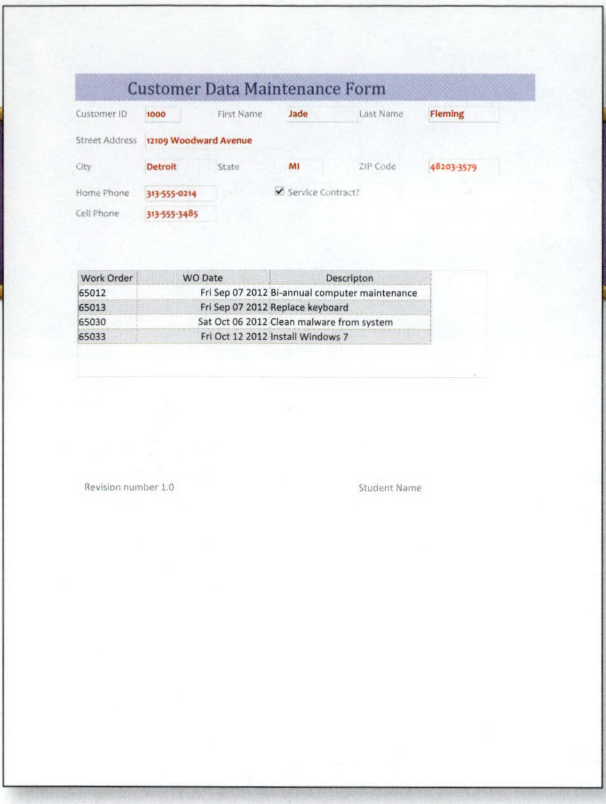

Customer Data Maintenance Form

Customer ID	1000	First Name	Jade	Last Name	Fleming
Street Address	12109 Woodward Avenue				
City	Detroit	State	MI	ZIP Code	48203-3579
Home Phone	313-555-0214	☑ Service Contract?			
Cell Phone	313-555-3485				

Work Order	WO Date	Descripton
65012	Fri Sep 07 2012	Bi-annual computer maintenance
65013	Fri Sep 07 2012	Replace keyboard
65030	Sat Oct 06 2012	Clean malware from system
65033	Fri Oct 12 2012	Install Windows 7

Revision number 1.0 Student Name

Project 1 Design and Create a Custom Form

Customer Data Maintenance Form

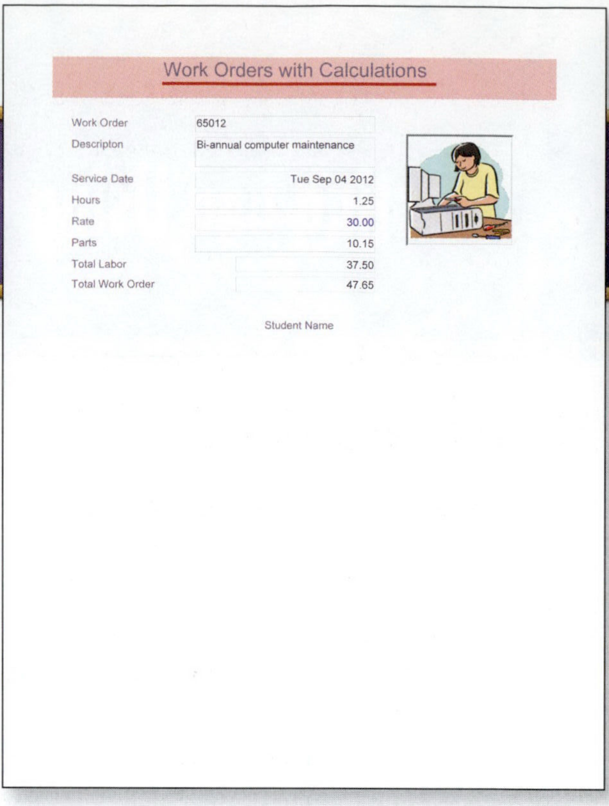

Work Orders with Calculations

Work Order	65012
Descripton	Bi-annual computer maintenance
Service Date	Tue Sep 04 2012
Hours	1.25
Rate	30.00
Parts	10.15
Total Labor	37.50
Total Work Order	47.65

Student Name

Project 2 Create a Form with Calculations and Graphics

Work Orders with Calculations Form

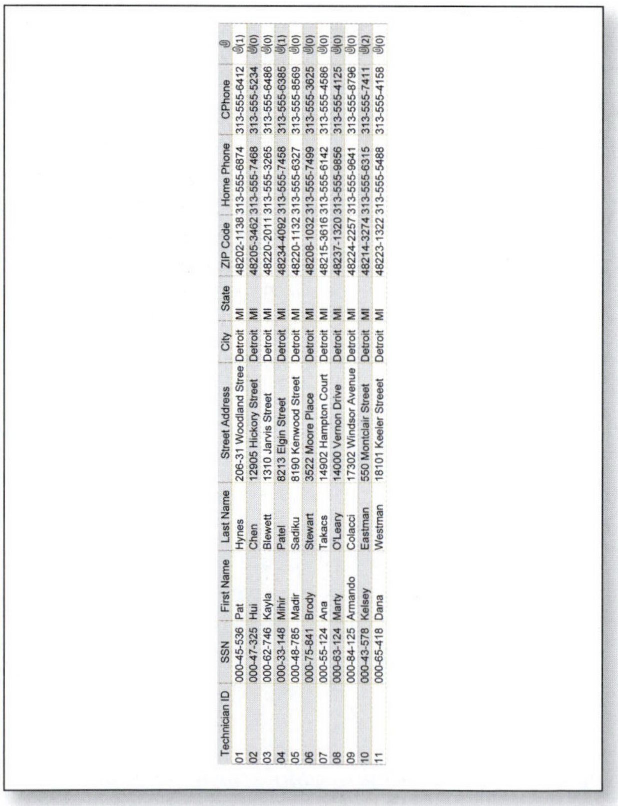

Technician ID	SSN	First Name	Last Name	Street Address	City	State	ZIP Code	Home Phone	CPhone	🖇
01	000-45-536	Pat	Hynes	206-31 Woodland Stree	Detroit	MI	48202-1138	313-555-6874	313-555-6412	🖇(1)
02	000-47-325	Hui	Chen	12905 Hickory Street	Detroit	MI	48205-3462	313-555-7468	313-555-5234	🖇(0)
03	000-62-746	Kayla	Blewett	1310 Jarvis Street	Detroit	MI	48220-2011	313-555-3265	313-555-6486	🖇(0)
04	000-33-148	Mihir	Patel	8213 Elgin Street	Detroit	MI	48234-4092	313-555-7458	313-555-6385	🖇(1)
05	000-48-785	Madir	Sadiku	8190 Kenwood Street	Detroit	MI	48220-1132	313-555-6327	313-555-8569	🖇(0)
06	000-75-841	Brody	Stewart	3522 Moore Place	Detroit	MI	48208-1032	313-555-7499	313-555-3625	🖇(0)
07	000-55-124	Ana	Takacs	14902 Hampton Court	Detroit	MI	48215-3616	313-555-6142	313-555-4586	🖇(0)
08	000-63-124	Marty	O'Leary	14000 Vernon Drive	Detroit	MI	48237-1320	313-555-9856	313-555-4125	🖇(0)
09	000-84-125	Armando	Colacci	17302 Windsor Avenue	Detroit	MI	48224-2257	313-555-9641	313-555-8796	🖇(0)
10	000-43-578	Kelsey	Eastman	550 Montclair Street	Detroit	MI	48214-3274	313-555-6315	313-555-7411	🖇(2)
11	000-65-418	Dana	Westman	18101 Keeler Streeet	Detroit	MI	48223-1322	313-555-5488	313-555-4158	🖇(0)

Project 3 Create a Restricted-Use Form

Technicians Form

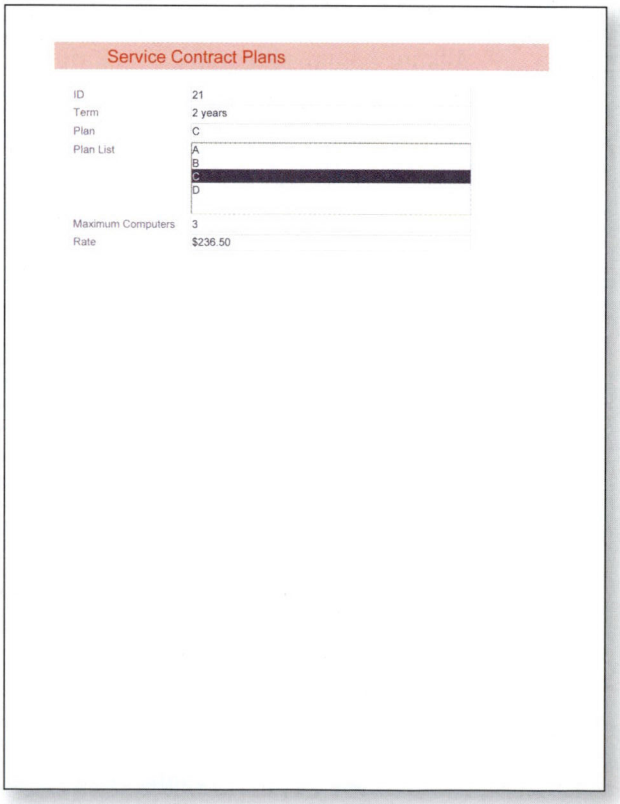

Service Contract Plans

ID	21
Term	2 years
Plan	C
Plan List	A B C D
Maximum Computers	3
Rate	$236.50

Project 4 Create a Blank Form with Lists

SCPlans Form

Project 1 **Design and Create a Custom Form** **7 Parts**

You will create a custom form in Design view that includes subforms in tabbed pages to provide a single object in which data stored in four tables can be entered, viewed, and printed.

Creating Custom Forms Using Design View

Access provides several tools with which you can create forms such as the Form tool, the Split Form tool, and the Form Wizard. These features allow you to build a form quickly. A form generated using one of these tools can be modified in Layout view or Design view to customize the content, format, or layout. If you require a form with several custom options, you can begin in Design view and build the form from scratch. Click the Create tab and click the Form Design button in the Forms group to begin a new form using the Design view window shown in Figure 4.1.

Quick Steps

Start New Form in Design View

1. Click Create tab.
2. Click Form Design button.

Form Design

Figure 4.1 Form Design View

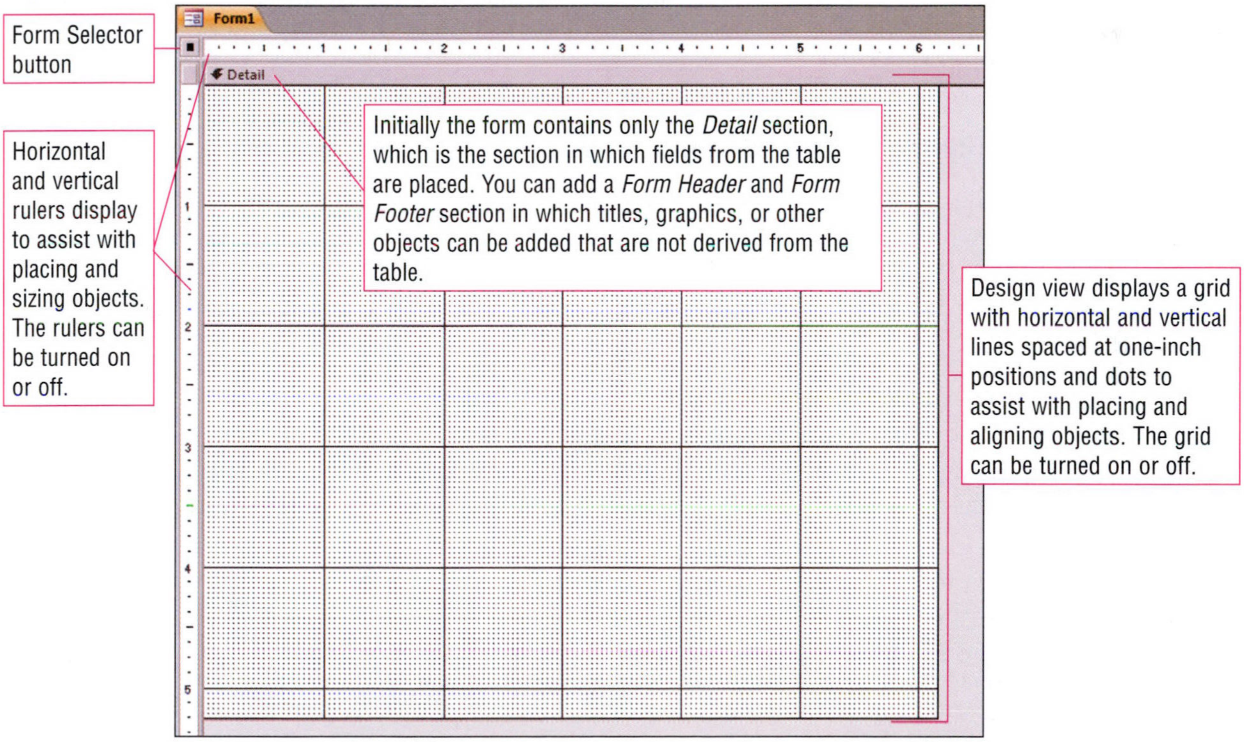

Form Selector button
Horizontal and vertical rulers display to assist with placing and sizing objects. The rulers can be turned on or off.
Form1
Detail
Initially the form contains only the *Detail* section, which is the section in which fields from the table are placed. You can add a *Form Header* and *Form Footer* section in which titles, graphics, or other objects can be added that are not derived from the table.
Design view displays a grid with horizontal and vertical lines spaced at one-inch positions and dots to assist with placing and aligning objects. The grid can be turned on or off.

Figure 4.2 Controls, Header/Footer, and Tools Groups in Form Design Tools Design Tab

The form displays the *Detail* section, which is used to display fields from the table associated with the form. Objects are added to the form using buttons in the Controls, Header/Footer, and Tools groups in the Form Design Tools Design tab shown in Figure 4.2.

Quick Steps

Add Form Title
1. Open form in Design view.
2. Click Title button.
3. Type title text.
4. Press Enter.

Add Label Object
1. Open form in Design view.
2. Click Label button.
3. Drag to create object the desired height and width.
4. Type label text.
5. Press Enter.

HINT

Before starting a new custom form in Design view it is a good idea to draw a sketch on a piece of paper that indicates the rough layout of the form. This will help you place the fields and determine other objects you need to create.

Label

Title

Bound, Unbound, and Calculated Control Objects

As you begin to build a custom form, understanding the three types of objects that can be created in a form is important. A form is comprised of a series of control objects. A ***control object*** in a form is bound, unbound, or calculated. ***Bound objects*** draw data displayed in the control from the field in the table to which the control is associated. In other words, the content that is displayed in the control object in Form view is drawn from a field in a record in a table. ***Unbound objects*** are used to display text or graphics and do not rely on the table for their content. For example, an object that contains a clip art image to enhance the visual appearance or an object that contains the hours of business for informational purposes are both unbound objects. A ***calculated object*** displays the result of a mathematical formula.

Creating Titles and Label Objects

Click the Title button in the Header/Footer group of the Form Design Tools Design tab to display the *Form Header* and *Form Footer* sections and automatically insert a label object with the name of the form inside the *Form Header* section. The text inside the title object is selected in order to type new text, delete, or otherwise modify the default title text. Click the Label button in the Controls group to draw a label control object within any section in the form and type descriptive or explanatory text inside the object.

Once a title or label control object has been created, the text can be formatted using buttons in the Font group in the Form Design Tools Format tab. You can also move and resize the control object to reposition it on the form.

The *Form Header* section is used to create objects that you want to display at the top of the form while scrolling records in Form view and is printed at the top of the page when a record or group of records is printed from Form view. Titles and company logos are generally placed in the *Form Header* section. The *Form Footer* section is used to create objects that you want to display at the bottom of the form while scrolling records in Form view and is printed at the end of a printout when a record or group of records is printed from Form view. Consider adding a creation date and/or revision number in the *Form Footer* section.

Project 1a — Starting a New Form Using Design View and Adding a Title and Label Object

Part 1 of 7

1. Open **AL2-C4-RSRCompServ.accdb** and enable content.
2. Click the Create tab and then click the Form Design button in the Forms group.

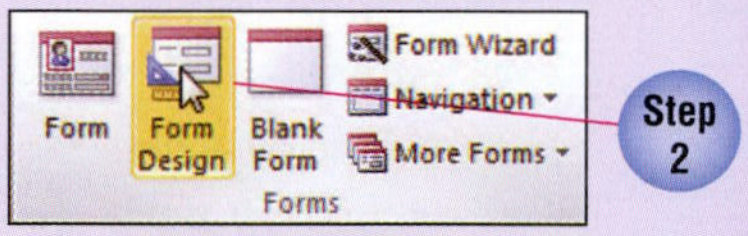

3. Add a title in the *Form Header* section of the form and center the text within the object by completing the following steps:
   a. With the Form Design Tools Design tab active, click the Title button in the Header/Footer group. Access displays the *Form Header* section above the *Detail* section and places a title object with the text *Form1* selected.

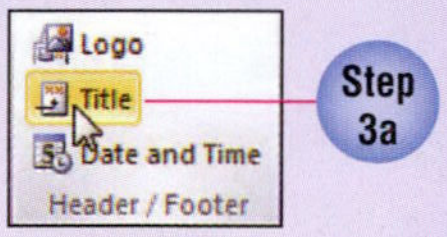

   b. Type **Customer Data Maintenance Form**. Notice the background behind the title object is shaded blue and the color of the text is blue. The colors and fonts that appear in controls are dependent on the current theme. The default theme for a database is *Office*.

   c. Press the Enter key.
   d. With the title object selected as indicated by the orange border around the title text, click the Form Design Tools Format tab and then click the Center button in the Font group.

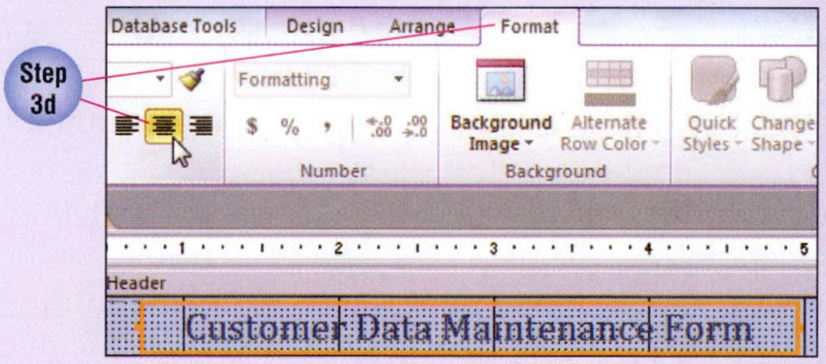

4. Scroll down the form until you can see the *Form Footer* section.
5. Position the mouse pointer at the bottom border of the form's grid until the pointer changes to a horizontal line with an up- and down-pointing arrow and then drag the bottom of the form down to the 0.5-inch position in the vertical ruler.

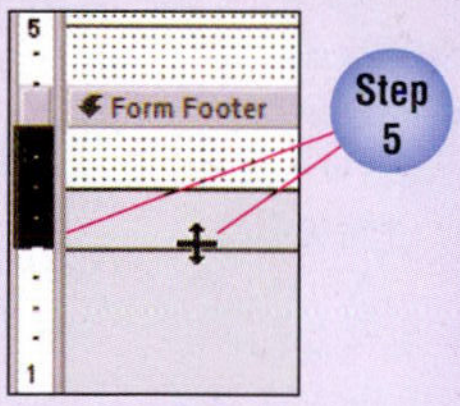

6. Add a label control object at the left edge of the form footer that contains a revision number and another label control object at the right edge of the form footer that contains your name by completing the following steps:
   a. Click the Form Design Tools Design tab and then click the Label button in the Controls group.
   b. Position the crosshairs with the label icon attached at the left side of the *Form Footer* section and drag to draw a label control object the approximate height and width shown. When you release the mouse, an insertion point appears inside the label control object.

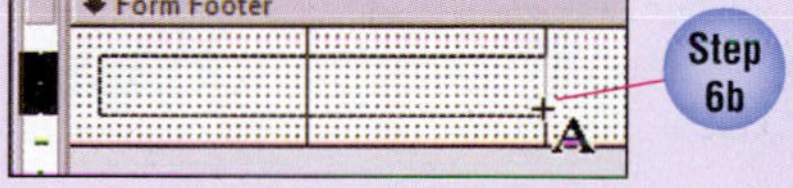

   c. Type **Revision number 1.0** and press Enter.

d. Create another label control object at the right side of the *Form Footer* section similar in height and width to the one shown, type your first and last names inside the label control object, and press Enter. If necessary, refer to Steps 6a through 6c if you need help with this step.

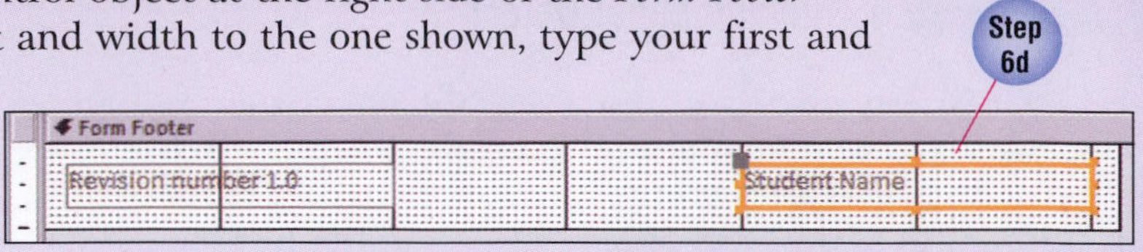

e. Click in any blank area of the form to deselect the label control object.

7. Click the Save button on the Quick Access toolbar, type **CustMaintenance** in the *Form Name* text box at the Save As dialog box, and then press Enter or click OK.

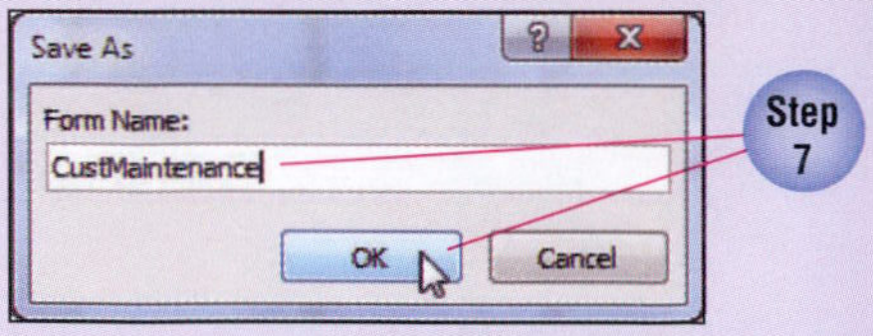

Quick Steps

Connect Table to Form
1. Open form in Design view.
2. Double-click Form Selector button.
3. Click Data tab in Property Sheet.
4. Click down-pointing arrow in *Record Source* property box.
5. Click desired table.
6. Close Property Sheet.

Add Fields to Form
1. Click Add Existing Fields button.
2. Drag field name from Field List pane to desired location in *Detail* section.

OR

1. Click first field name in Field List pane.
2. Hold down Shift key.
3. Click last field name in Field List pane.
4. Drag selected fields from Field List pane to desired location in *Detail* section.

Form Selector

Add Existing Fields

Adding Fields to a Form

Before you can add fields to the *Detail* section, you need to first connect a table to the form. The table to be connected with the form is specified in the Record Source property in the Data tab of the Form Property Sheet. Double-click the Form Selector button located above the vertical ruler and left of the horizontal ruler to open the form's Property Sheet at the right side of the work area. Click the Data tab, click the down-pointing arrow in the *Record Source* property box, click the desired table at the drop-down list, and then close the Property Sheet.

Click the Add Existing Fields button in the Tools group in the Form Design Tools Design tab to open the Field List pane. Select and drag a group of field names or an individual field name from the Field List pane to the *Detail* section of the form. Release the pointer in the *Detail* section near the location at which you want to display the data. For each field added to the form, two control objects are inserted. A label control object containing the field name or Caption property text is placed at the left of where you release the mouse pointer, and a text box control object that is bound to the field is placed at the right of where you release the mouse. The text box control object is the object that displays table data from the record in Form view. Figure 4.3 displays the fields from the Customers table that you will add to the CustMaintenance form in Project 1b.

Figure 4.3 Fields from Customer Table Added to Form in Project 1b

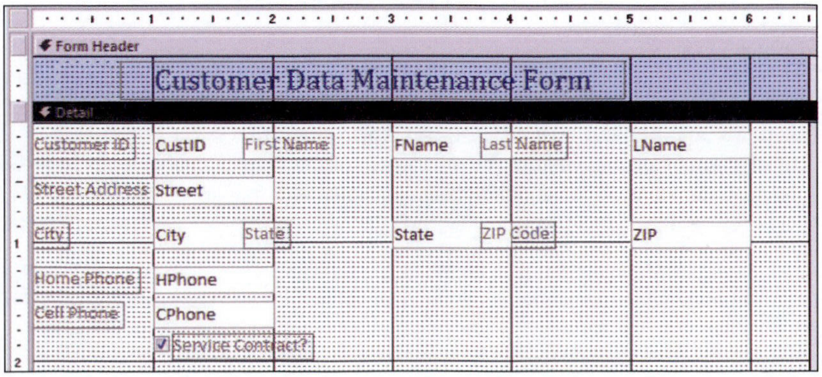

Project 1b Connecting a Table to a Form and Adding Fields

Part 2 of 7

1. With the **AL2-C4-RSRCompServ.accdb** database open and the CustMaintenance form open in Design view, scroll up to the top of the form in the work area.
2. Connect the Customers table to the form by completing the following steps:
   a. Double-click the Form Selector button (displays as a black or blue square) located at the top of the vertical ruler and left of the horizontal ruler to open the form's Property Sheet.

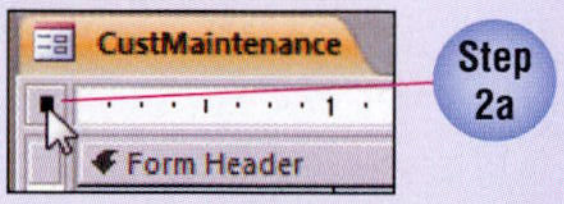

   b. Click the Data tab in the Property Sheet.
   c. Click the down-pointing arrow in the *Record Source* property box and then click *Customers* at the drop-down list.
   d. Close the Property Sheet.

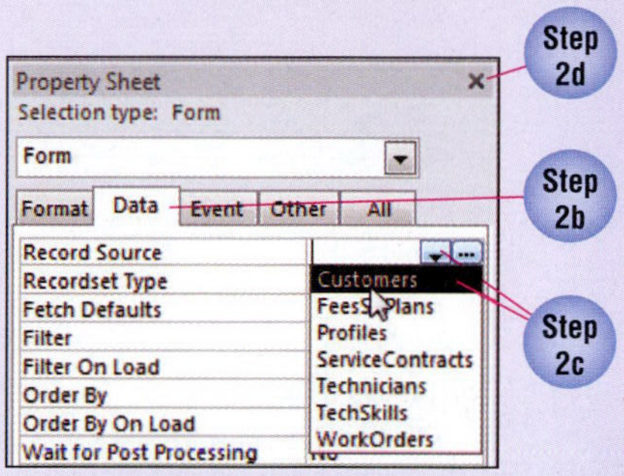

3. Add fields individually from the Customers table to the *Detail* section of the form by completing the following steps:
   a. Click the Add Existing Fields button in the Tools group in the Form Design Tools Design tab. The Field List pane opens at the right side of the work area.
   b. Position the mouse pointer at the right border of the form's grid until the pointer changes to a vertical line with a left- and right-pointing arrow and then drag the right edge of the form to the 6.5-inch position in the horizontal ruler.

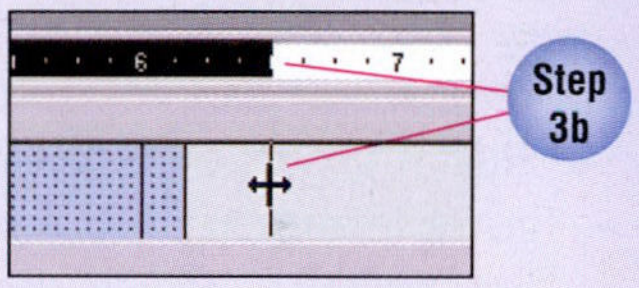

   c. If necessary, click *CustID* in the Field List pane to select the field and then drag the field name to the *Detail* section, releasing the mouse with the pointer near the top of the section at the 1-inch position in the horizontal ruler.

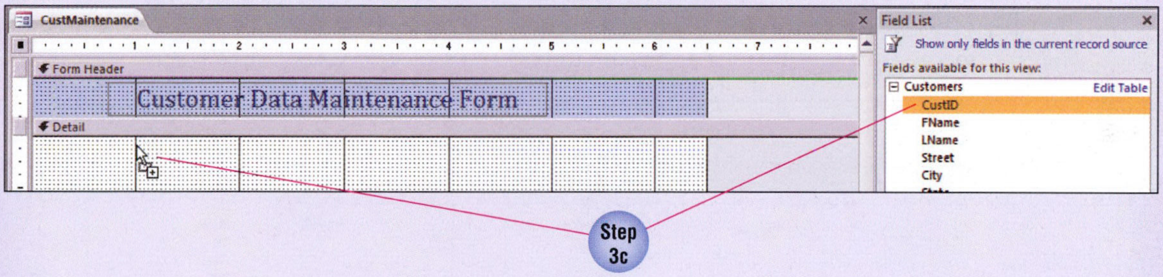

   d. Click to select *FName* in the Field List pane and then drag the field to the same vertical position as *CustID* in the *Detail* section, releasing the mouse with the pointer at the 3-inch position in the horizontal ruler.
   e. Click to select *LName* in the Field List pane and then drag the field to the same vertical position as *CustID* in the *Detail* section, releasing the mouse with the pointer at the 5-inch position in the horizontal ruler.

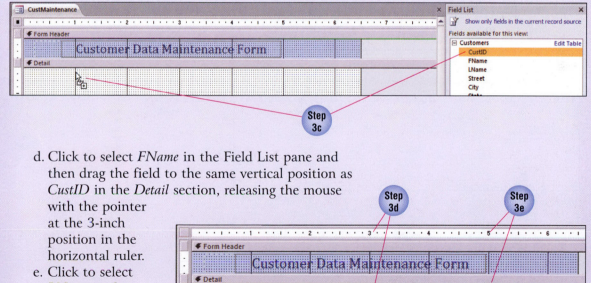

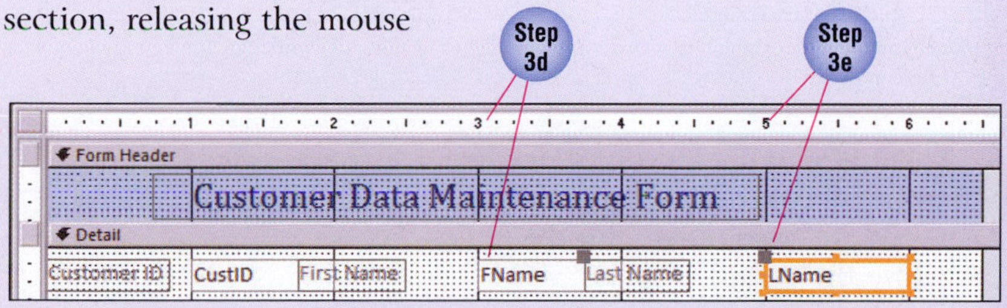

f. Drag the *Street* field from the Field List pane to the *Detail* section below *CustID*, releasing the mouse at the 1-inch position in the horizontal ruler and approximately 3 rows of grid dots below *CustID*.

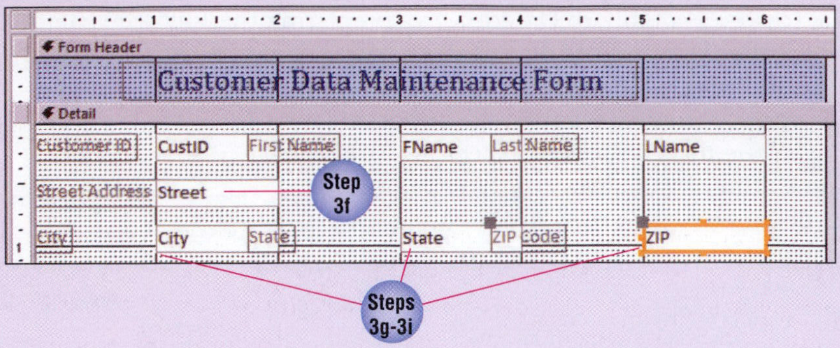

g. Drag the *City* field from the Field List pane to the *Detail* section below *Street*, releasing the mouse at approximately the 1-inch position in the horizontal ruler and approximately 3 rows of grid dots below *Street*.

h. Drag the *State* field from the Field List pane to the *Detail* section at the same horizontal position as *City*, releasing the mouse at the 3-inch position in the horizontal ruler.

i. Drag the *ZIP* field from the Field List pane to the *Detail* section at the same horizontal position as *City*, releasing the mouse at the 5-inch position in the horizontal ruler.

4. Add a group of fields from the Customers table to the *Detail* section of the form by completing the following steps:
   a. Click the *HPhone* field name in the Field List pane.
   b. Hold down the Shift key and click the *ServCont* field name in the Field List pane. Access selects all fields from the first field name clicked to the last field name clicked when the Shift key is used.
   c. Position the mouse pointer within the selected group of fields in the Field List pane and then drag the group to the *Detail* section below *City*, releasing the mouse at the 1-inch position in the horizontal ruler approximately 3 rows of grid dots below *City*.

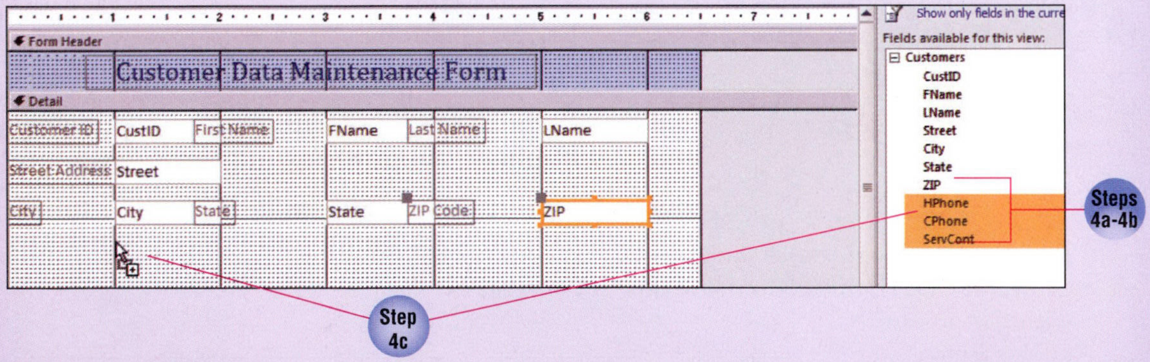

5. Click in any blank area to deselect the group of fields.
6. Compare your form with the one shown in Figure 4.3 on page 108.
7. Click the Save button on the Quick Access toolbar.
8. Close the Field List pane.

Moving and Resizing Control Objects

Once fields are placed on the form, move or resize objects to change the layout. In Project 1b, you saw that Access places two control objects for each field on the form. A label control object, which contains the caption or field name, is placed left of a text box control object, which displays the field value from the record or a blank entry box when adding a new record. Click the label control object or the text box control object for the field you want to move or resize to display an orange border with eight handles. Access displays a large dark gray square (called the move handle) at the top left of the selected field's label control object or text box control object.

Point to the orange border of the selected control object until the pointer displays with the four-headed arrow move icon and then drag the field to the new position on the form. Access moves the connected label control or text box control along with the object you drag to the new location. If you want to move a selected label control or text box control independently from its connected object, point to the large dark gray handle at the top left of the selected control and drag using the move handle to the new position as described in Figure 4.4.

To resize a selected control object, point to one of the sizing handles (small orange squares) in the border of the selected object until the pointer displays with an up- and down-pointing arrow, a left- and right-pointing arrow, or a two-headed diagonal arrow to resize the height and/or width.

By default, the Snap to Grid feature is turned on in Design view. This feature pulls a control to the nearest grid point when moving or resizing objects. If you want to move or resize an object very precisely in small increments, you may want to turn the feature off. To do this, click the Form Design Tools Arrange tab, click the Size/Space button in the Sizing & Ordering group, and then click *Snap to Grid* at the drop-down list. Snap to Grid is a toggle feature which is turned on or off by clicking the button.

Quick Steps

Move Objects in Design View
1. Select control object.
2. Drag using orange border or move handle to desired location.

Resize Objects in Design View
1. Select control object.
2. Drag middle top, bottom, left, or right sizing handle to resize the height or width.

OR
1. Select control object.
2. Drag corner sizing handle to resize the height and width at the same time.

HINT

Do not be overly concerned with exact placement and alignment as you initially add fields to the form. You will learn how to use alignment and spacing tools in the Form Design Tools Arrange tab to assist with layout.

Size/Space

Figure 4.4 Moving a Control Object in Design View

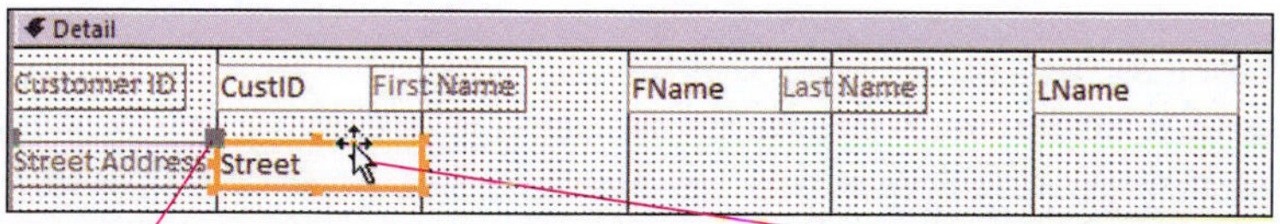

Point to the large dark gray square (called the move handle) at the top left of the selected control object to move the selected *Street* text box control object independently of the *Street Address* label control object.

Point to the orange border and drag the object to the desired location when you see this icon. The label control object containing the caption *Street Address* will move as well as the selected *Street* text box control object.

Quick Steps

Format Controls Using Selection Rectangle

1. In Design view, position pointer above top left control to be formatted.
2. Drag down and right to draw a rectangle around controls.
3. Release mouse.
4. Click desired formatting options.
5. Deselect controls.

Format Multiple Controls Using Shift

1. In Design view, click to select first control object.
2. Shift + click remaining control objects.
3. Click desired formatting options.
4. Deselect controls.

Formatting Controls

Use the buttons in the Font group in the Form Design Tools Format tab to change the font, font size, font color, background color, alignment, or apply bold, italic, or underline formatting to the selected control object. Use the Conditional Formatting button in the Control Formatting group to apply conditional formatting to the selected object.

Multiple control objects can be formatted at the same time by holding down the Shift key while clicking individual controls. You can also use the mouse pointer to draw a selection rectangle around a group of controls to select multiple objects inside the rectangle.

Apply a Theme to the form at the Form Design Tools Design tab. The Theme controls the default colors and fonts for objects on the form.

Themes

Form View

Design View

Project 1c Moving and Resizing Controls

Part 3 of 7

1. With the **AL2-C4-RSRCompServ.accdb** database open and the CustMaintenance form open in Design view, preview the form to determine the controls that need to be moved or resized by clicking the View button in the Views group of the Form Design Tools Design tab. (Do not click the down-pointing arrow on the button.)
2. The form is displayed in Form view with data from the first record displayed in the text box control objects. Notice that some label control objects are overlapping text box control objects and that the street address in the first record is not entirely displayed.
3. Click the Design View button located at the right end of the Status bar (last button in View buttons group).
4. Move the controls for those objects that are overlapping other objects by completing the following steps:
   a. Click the *First Name* label control object.
   b. Point to the large dark gray square (move handle) at the top left of the selected label control object until the pointer displays with the four-headed arrow attached and then drag right to the 2-inch position in the horizontal ruler. Notice the connected *FName* text box control object does not move because you are dragging using the move handle.

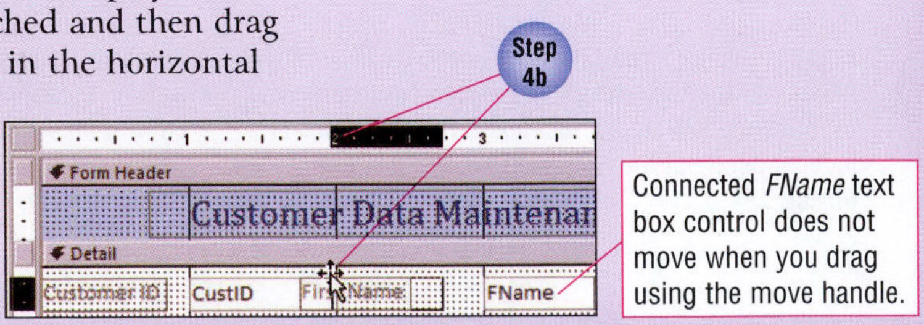

c. Click the *Last Name* label control object and then drag right using the move handle to the 4-inch position in the horizontal ruler.

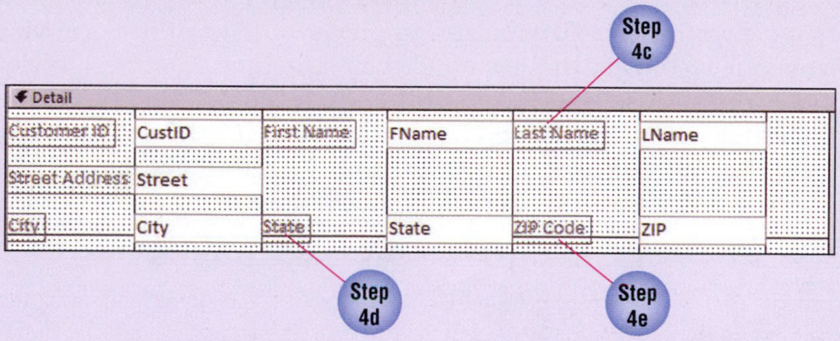

d. Move the *State* label control object right to the 2-inch position in the horizontal ruler.

e. Move the *ZIP Code* label control object right to the 4-inch position in the horizontal ruler.

f. Click in any blank area to deselect the *ZIP Code* label control.

5. Click the *Street* text box control object. Drag the right middle sizing handle to the right to the 3-inch position in the horizontal ruler.

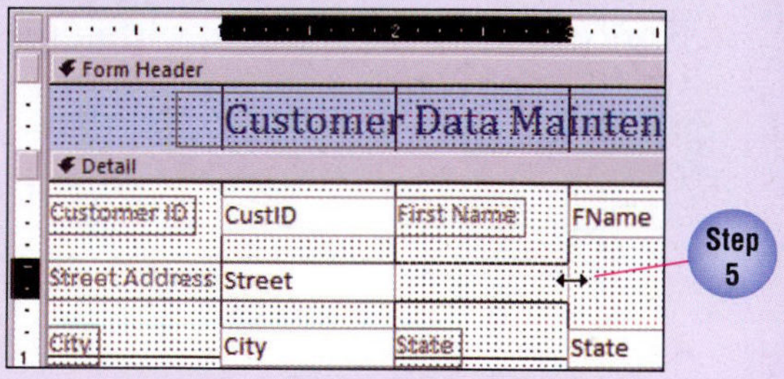

6. Click the *State* text box control object and then drag the right middle sizing handle to the left to the 3.5-inch position in the horizontal ruler. (Since the *State* field displays only two characters, this control object can be resized smaller.)
7. Resize the *CustID* text box control so that the right edge of the control is at the 1.5-inch position in the horizontal ruler.
8. Click the *Service Contract?* label control object. Point to any side of the selected object's orange border (not on a sizing handle) and then drag the object until the left edge is at the 3-inch position in the horizontal ruler adjacent to the *HPhone* field. Notice that both the label control object and the text box control object moved since you dragged the border (not the move handle).

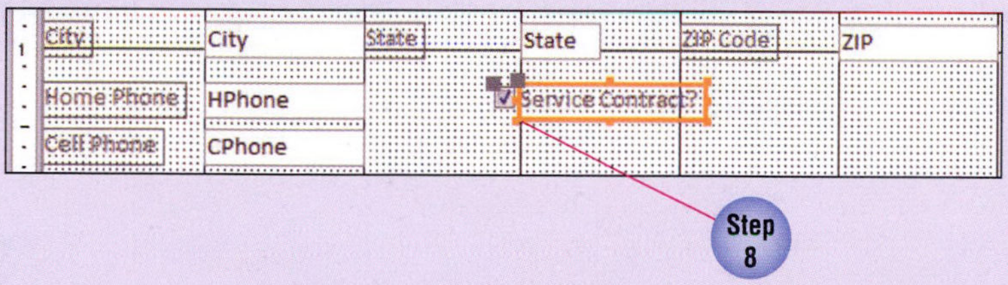

9. Deselect the *Service Contract?* control object.
10. Save the form.

Project 1d Formatting Multiple Controls

Part 4 of 7

1. With the **AL2-C4-RSRCompServ.accdb** database open and the CustMaintenance form open in Design view, click the View button to preview the form in Form view.
2. Scroll through a few records in the form and then switch back to Design view.
3. Format multiple controls using a selection rectangle by completing the following steps:
   a. Position the arrow pointer at the top left corner in the *Detail* section above the *Customer ID* label control object and then drag down and right until you have drawn a rectangle around all of the controls in the section as shown below and then release the mouse.

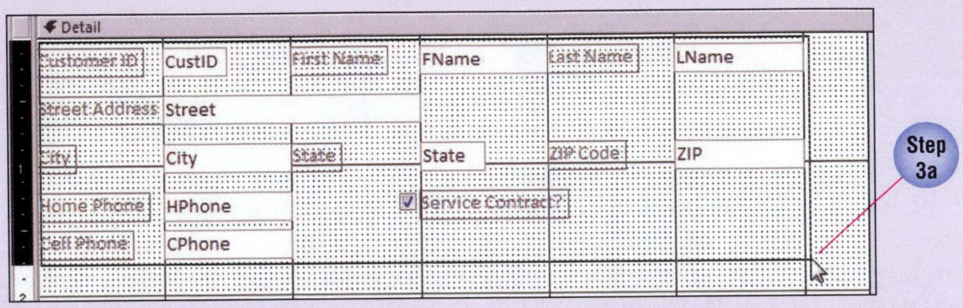

   b. Notice all objects contained within the rectangle are selected.
   c. Use the Font button in the Font group in the Form Design Tools Format tab to change the font to Candara.
   d. Use the Font Size button to change the font size to 10.

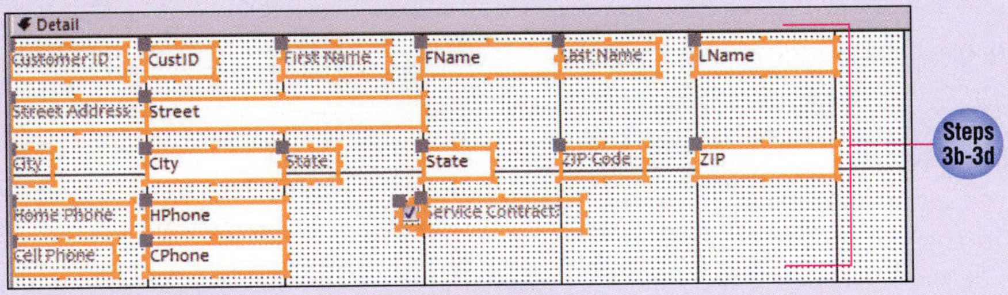

   e. Click in any blank area to deselect the controls.
4. Format by selecting multiple controls using the Shift key by completing the following steps:
   a. Click the *CustID* text box control object.
   b. Hold down the Shift key and click each of the other text box control objects in the *Detail* section.

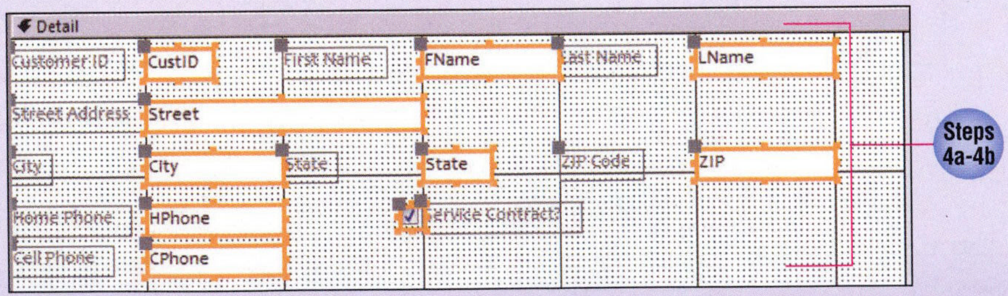

c. Click the down-pointing arrow on the Font Color button and then click *Dark Red* at the color palette (first option in last row).
d. Click the Bold button.
5. Click in any blank area to deselect the controls.
6. Click the Form Design Tools Design tab and then switch to Form view to view the formatting changes applied to the form.
7. Switch to Design view and then save the form.

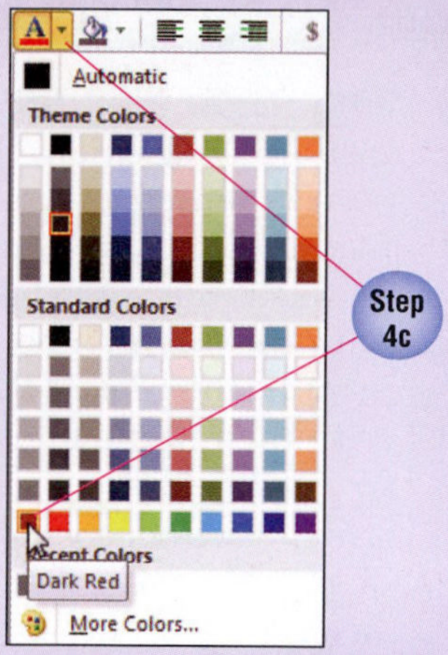
Automatic
Theme Colors
Standard Colors
Dark Red
More Colors...
Step 4c

Changing the Tab Order of Fields

Tab order refers to the order in which fields are selected when you press the Tab key while entering data in Form view. You do not have to enter data into a record in the order in which the fields are presented. Click the Tab Order button in the Tools group of the Form Design Tools Design tab to open the Tab Order dialog box shown in Figure 4.5.

Position the pointer in the gray field selector bar next to the field name that you want to move until the pointer displays as a right-pointing black arrow and click to select the field. Drag the selected field up or down to the desired position. The order of fields in the *Custom Order* list box in the Tab Order dialog box is the order in which the fields will be selected as the Tab key is pressed in a record in Form view. Click OK when you have finished relocating the fields.

Quick Steps

Change Tab Order of Fields
1. Open form in Design view.
2. Click Tab Order button.
3. Click in gray field selector bar next to field name.
4. Drag field to desired location.
5. Repeat Steps 3-4 as required.
6. Click OK.

Tab Order

Figure 4.5 Tab Order Dialog Box

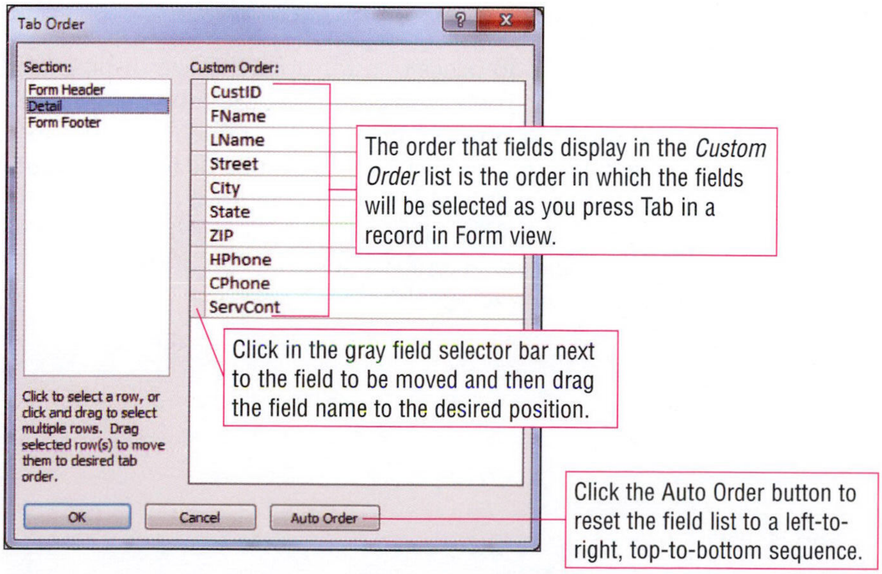
Tab Order
Section:
Form Header
Detail
Form Footer
Custom Order:
CustID
FName
LName
Street
City
State
ZIP
HPhone
CPhone
ServCont
Click to select a row, or click and drag to select multiple rows. Drag selected row(s) to move them to desired tab order.
OK
Cancel
Auto Order
The order that fields display in the *Custom Order* list is the order in which the fields will be selected as you press Tab in a record in Form view.
Click in the gray field selector bar next to the field to be moved and then drag the field name to the desired position.
Click the Auto Order button to reset the field list to a left-to-right, top-to-bottom sequence.

Project 1e Changing the Tab Order of Fields

Part 5 of 7

1. With the **AL2-C4-RSRCompServ.accdb** database open and the CustMaintenance form open in Design view, click the View button to display the form in Form view.
2. With the insertion point positioned in the *CustID* field in the first record in the table, press the Tab key seven times. As you press Tab, notice that the order in which the fields are selected is a left-to-right, top-to-bottom sequence.
3. With the insertion point in the *HPhone* field, press Tab. Notice the selected field moves down to the *CPhone* field instead of moving right to the *ServCont* field.
4. With the insertion point in the *CPhone* field, press Tab to move to the *ServCont* field.
5. Switch to Design view.
6. Change the tab order of the fields so that the *ServCont* field is selected after the *HPhone* field by completing the following steps:
   a. Click the Tab Order button in the Tools group of the Form Design Tools Design tab.
   b. At the Tab Order dialog box, move the pointer to the gray field selector bar next to *ServCont* until the pointer displays as a right-pointing black arrow.
   c. Click to select the field.
   d. With the pointer now displayed as a white arrow in the field selector bar, drag *ServCont* up until the horizontal black line indicating the location at which the field will be moved is positioned between *HPhone* and *CPhone* in the *Custom Order* list and then release the mouse.
   e. Click OK.
7. Switch to Form view.
8. Press the Tab key nine times to move through the fields in the first record. Notice when you reach the *HPhone* field and press Tab, the *ServCont* field is active next instead of the *CPhone* field.
9. Switch to Design view.
10. Save the form.

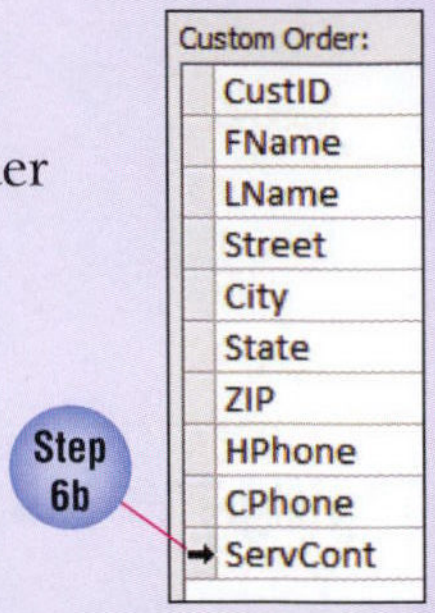

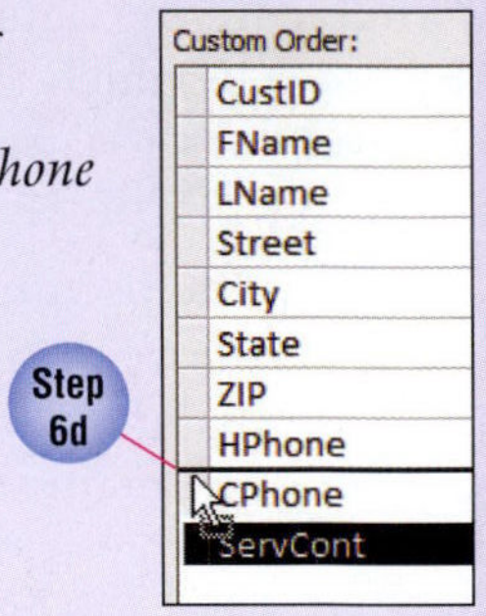

Quick Steps

Add Tab Control to Form
1. Open form in Design view.
2. Click Tab Control button.
3. Position crosshairs in *Detail* section at desired location for top left of object.
4. Drag down and right to draw object desired height and width.
5. Release mouse.

Adding a Tab Control to a Form

A tab control is an object used to add pages to a form. Each page displays with a tab at the top. When viewing the form, you click the page tab to display the contents of the page within the tab control object. Add a tab control to a form to organize fields in a large table into smaller related groups or to insert multiple subforms that display on separate pages within the tab control object. Examine the tab control shown in Figure 4.6. You will create this object in Projects 1f–1g. The tab control contains three pages. The tabs across the top of the control display the caption assigned to each page.

Figure 4.6 Tab Control with Three Pages Created in Projects 1f–1g

A tab displays at the top of each page added to a tab control object. Click the tab to change the contents in the tab control to the fields or subform added to the page.

Profiles	Service Contracts	Work Orders

Comp ▾	Username ▾	Password ▾	Remote Access? ▾
D1	jade	P$ck7	☐
*			☐

Record: ◄ ◄ 1 of 1 ► ►► ►⋇ No Filter Search

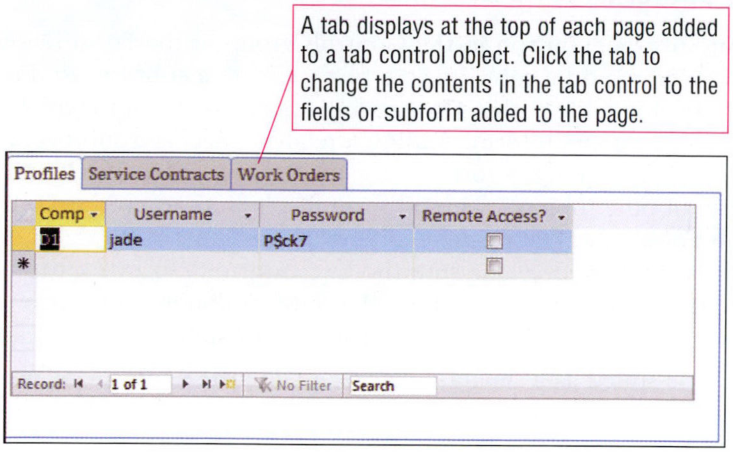

In Projects 1f–1g you will create a subform on each page within the tab control to display fields from a related table. When completed, the CustMaintenance form can be used to enter or view data related to customers that includes fields from four tables.

Tab Control

To add a tab control object to a form, click the Tab Control button in the Controls group in the Form Design Tools Design tab. Position the crosshairs with the tab control icon attached at the top left of the area in the *Detail* section where you want to begin the tab control and then drag down and right to draw the control the size that you want to make the tabbed pages. When you release the mouse, the tab control object initially displays with two pages as shown in Figure 4.7.

Change the text displayed in the tab at the top of the page by changing the Caption property in the page's Property Sheet. Add fields or create a subform on each page as needed. Add an additional page to the tab control by right-clicking an existing tab in the tab control object and then clicking *Insert Page* at the shortcut menu. To remove a page from the tab control, right-click the tab to be deleted and then click *Delete Page* at the shortcut menu.

▼ **Quick Steps**

Change Page Caption
1. Click desired tab in tab control.
2. Click Property Sheet button.
3. Click in *Caption* property box.
4. Type desired text.
5. Close Property Sheet.

Add New Page to Tab Control
1. Right-click existing tab in tab control.
2. Click *Insert Page* at shortcut menu.

Figure 4.7 New Tab Control Object with Two Pages

Your page numbers may vary.

Page16 Page17

A tab control object initially contains two pages. You can add and delete pages as needed.

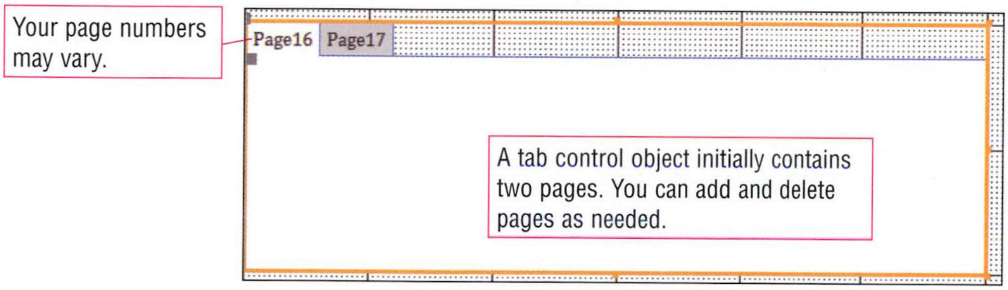

Creating a Subform

The Subform/Subreport button in the Controls group of the Form Design Tools Design tab is used to add a subform to a form. Create a subform to display fields from another related table within the existing form. The form in which a subform is created is called the main form. Adding a related table as a subform creates a control object within the main form that can be moved, formatted, and resized independently of other objects. The subform displays as a datasheet within the main form in Form view. Data can be entered or updated in the subform while the main form is being viewed. Make sure the Use Control Wizards button is toggled on in the Controls group before clicking the Subform/Subreport button so that you can add the subform using the Subform Wizard shown in Figure 4.8.

A subform is stored as a separate object outside the main form. You will notice an additional form name added in the Navigation pane with *subform* at the end of the name when you finish the steps in the Subform Wizard.

Figure 4.8 First Dialog Box in Subform Wizard

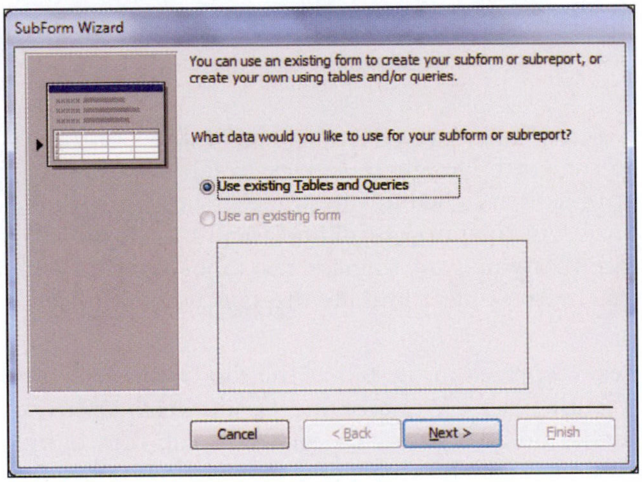

Quick Steps

Add Subform to Page

1. Click desired page tab in tab control.
2. Make sure Use Control Wizards is active.
3. Click More button in Controls scroll bar.
4. Click Subform/ Subreport button.
5. Click crosshairs inside selected page.
6. Click Next.
7. Choose table and fields.
8. Click Next.
9. Click Next.
10. Click Finish.
11. Delete subform label control object.
12. Move and resize subform object as required.

HINT

Do not delete a subform object in the Navigation pane. If the subform object is deleted, the main form will no longer display the fields from the related table in the tab control.

Subform/Subreport

Control Wizard

1. With the **AL2-C4-RSRCompServ.accdb** database open and the CustMaintenance form open in Design view, add a tab control object to the form by completing the following steps:
 a. Click the Tab Control button in the Controls group of the Form Design Tools Design tab.
 b. Position the crosshairs with the tab control icon attached at the left edge of the grid in the *Detail* section at the 2-inch position in the vertical ruler, drag down to the 4-inch position in the vertical ruler and right to the 6-inch position in the horizontal ruler, and then release the mouse.

Your page numbers may vary.

Step 1b

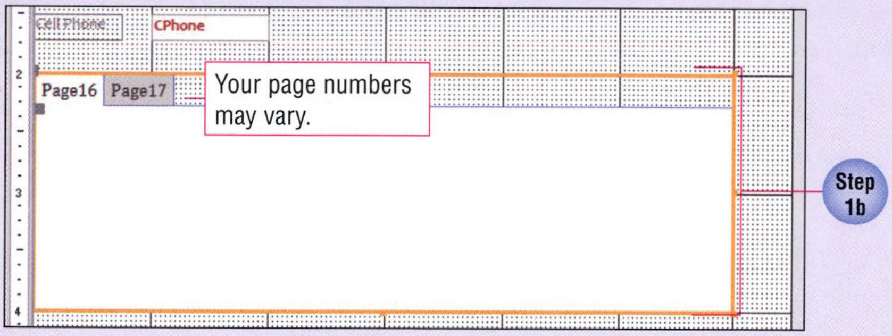

2. Change the page caption and add a subform to the first page within the tab control by completing the following steps:
 a. Click the first tab in the tab control that displays *Pagexx* where *xx* is the page number to select the page. (For example, click *Page16* in the image shown above.)
 b. Click the Property Sheet button in the Tools group.
 c. Click the Format tab in the Property Sheet, click in the *Caption* property box, type **Profiles**, and then close the Property Sheet. The tab displays the caption text in place of *Pagexx*.

Step 2c

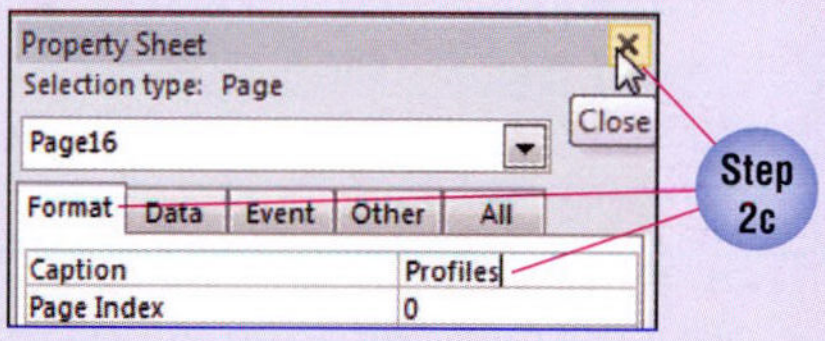

 d. By default, the Use Control Wizards feature is toggled on in the Controls group. Click the More button at the bottom of the Controls scroll bar to expand the Controls and view two rows of buttons and the Controls drop-down list. View the current status of the *Use Control Wizards* option. The button at the left of the option displays with an orange background when the feature is active. If the button is orange, click in a blank area to remove the expanded Controls list. If the feature is not active (displays with a white background), click the Use Control Wizards option to turn the feature on.

Step 2e

Check status of Use Control Wizards button at Step 2d. When the button displays as shown with an orange background, the feature is active. The control wizards allow you to add a subform more easily by responding to a series of dialog boxes.

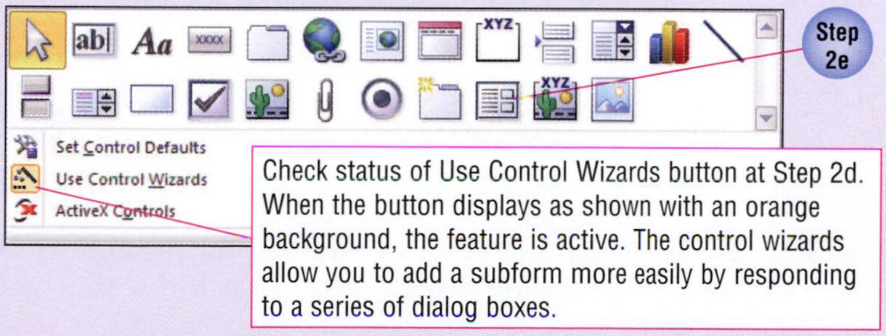

 e. Click the More button at the bottom of the Controls scroll bar and then click the Subform/Subreport button at the expanded Controls list.

f. Move the crosshairs with the subform icon attached to the Profiles page in the tab control. The background of the page turns black. Click the mouse to start the Subform Wizard.

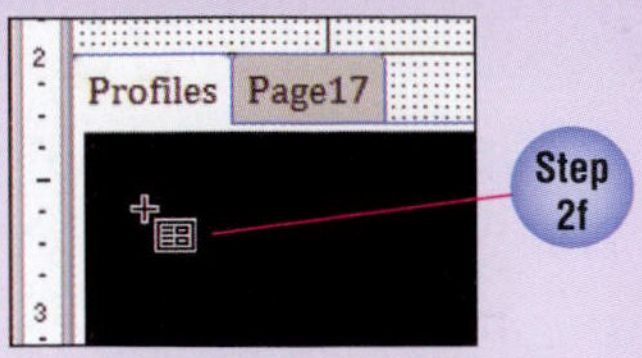

g. Click Next at the first Subform Wizard dialog box with *Use existing Tables and Queries* already selected.

h. At the second Subform Wizard dialog box, select the table and fields to be displayed in the subform by completing the following steps:

   1) Click the down-pointing arrow next to the *Tables/Queries* list box and then click *Table: Profiles* at the drop-down list.
   2) Move all of the fields except *CustID* from the *Available Fields* list box to the *Selected Fields* list box.
   3) Click Next.

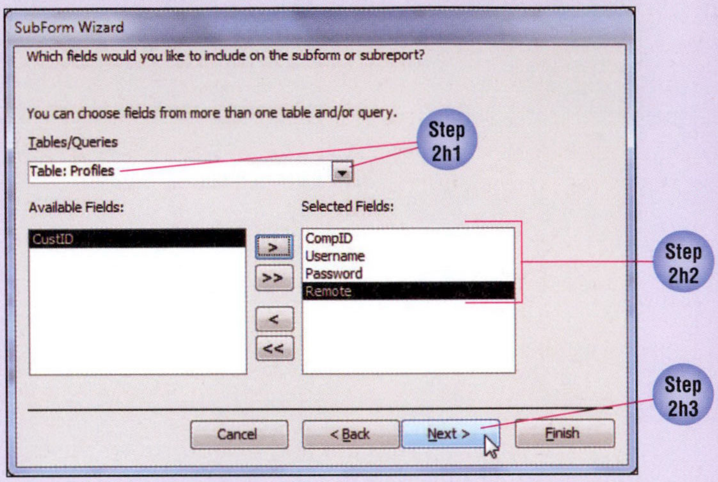

i. Click Next at the third Subform Wizard dialog box with *Show Profiles for each record in Customers using CustID* selected. Since the two tables have a relationship created with *CustID* as the joined field, Access knows the field that links records in the main form with the subform.

j. Click Finish at the last Subform Wizard dialog box to accept the default subform name *Profiles subform*.

3. Access creates the subform within the active page in the tab control with a label control object above the subform control. Click the label control object displaying the text *Profiles subform* to select the object and then press the Delete key.
4. Click the border of the subform control object to display the orange border and sizing handles and then move and resize the object as shown using the techniques you learned in Project 1c.

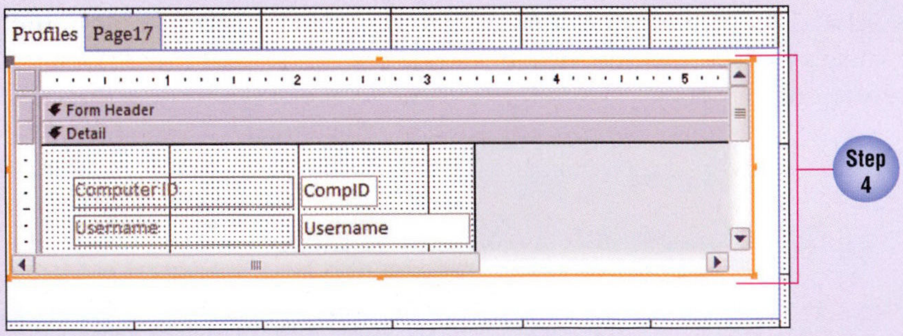

5. Click in a blank area outside the grid to deselect the subform control object and then switch to Form view. Notice the subform displays as a datasheet within the tab control object in the CustMaintenance form.

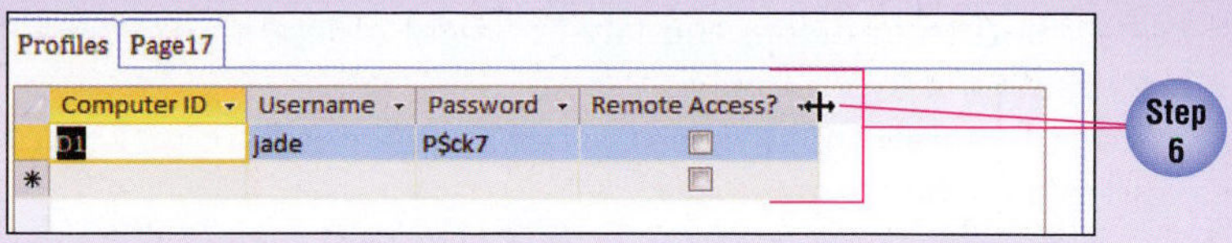

6. Position the pointer on the column boundary line in the field names row in the datasheet between each column and then double-click to adjust each column's width to Best Fit.
7. Notice that two sets of navigation buttons are displayed — one set at the bottom of the main form (just above the Status bar) and another set at the bottom of the datasheet in the subform. Use the navigation bar at the bottom of the main form to scroll a few records and watch the fields update in both the main form and the subform as you move to the next customer record.
8. Switch to Design view.
9. Save the form.
10. Notice in the Navigation pane a form object exists with the name *Profiles subform.* Subforms are separate objects within the database. If the main form is closed, you can open the subform individually to edit data.

In Design view the controls within the subform display one below another; however in Form view, the subform displays using a datasheet layout. If desired, you can change the Default View property in the subform's Property Sheet to *Single Form*. This view matches the layout of the controls in Design view to the layout of the fields in Form view. The fields display one below another in a single column in Form view. To do this, open the subform Property Sheet by double-clicking the Form Selector button at the top of the vertical ruler and left of the horizontal ruler in the subform control object in Design view. Click the down-pointing arrow in the Default View property in the Format tab and click *Single Form* at the drop-down list.

Project 1g Adding More Subforms and Adding a New Page to the Tab Control — Part 7 of 7

1. With the **AL2-C4-RSRCompServ.accdb** database open and the CustMaintenance form open in Design view, change the caption for the second page in the tab control to **Service Contracts** by completing steps similar to those in Steps 2a–2c of Project 1f.
2. With the Service Contracts page selected in the tab control, add a subform to display the fields from the ServiceContracts table on the page by completing the following steps:
   a. Click the More button at the bottom of the Controls scroll bar and then click the Subform/Subreport button at the expanded Controls list.
   b. Click inside the selected Service Contracts page in the tab control.
   c. Click Next at the first Subform Wizard dialog box.
   d. At the second Subform Wizard dialog box change the table displayed in the *Tables/ Queries* list box to *Table: ServiceContracts*.
   e. Move all fields from the table except the *CustID* field to the *Selected Fields* list box.
   f. Click Next.
   g. Click Next at the third Subform Wizard dialog box with *Show ServiceContracts for each record in Customers using CustID* selected.
   h. Click Finish at the last Subform Wizard dialog box to accept the default subform name *ServiceContracts subform*.

3. Select and then delete the label control object above the subform displaying the text *ServiceContracts subform*.
4. Click the subform control object to display the orange border and sizing handles and move and resize the form as shown.

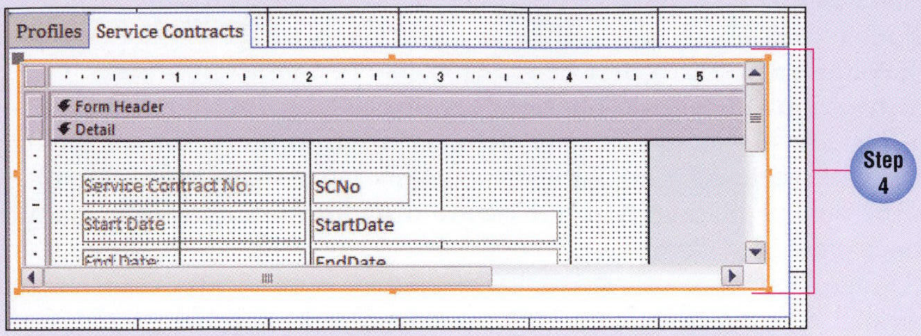

5. Deselect the subform control object and then switch to Form view.
6. Click the Service Contracts tab and adjust the column width for each column in the datasheet to Best Fit.

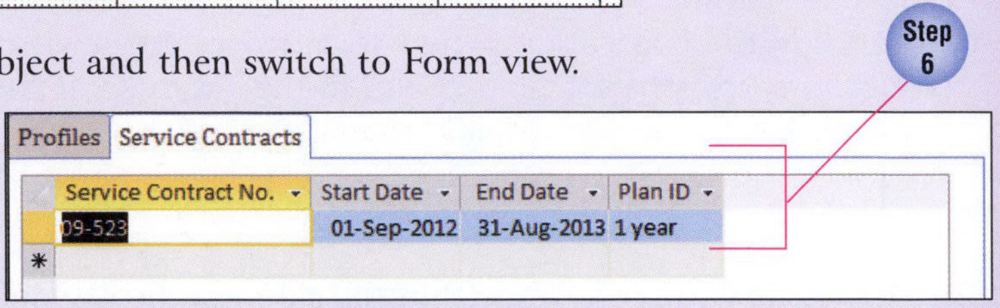

7. Switch to Design view and save the form.
8. Add a new page to the tab control and add a subform to display selected fields from the WorkOrders table in the new page by completing the following steps:
   a. Right-click the Service Contracts tab and then click *Insert Page* at the shortcut menu.
   b. With the new page already selected, display the Property Sheet, change the page caption to **Work Orders**, and then close the Property Sheet.
   c. Click the More button at the bottom of the Controls scroll bar and then click the Subform/Subreport button. Click inside the selected Work Orders page. Create a subform to display selected fields from the WorkOrders table by completing the following steps:
      1) Click Next at the first Subform Wizard dialog box.
      2) At the second Subform Wizard dialog box, change the table displayed in the *Tables/Queries* list box to *Table: WorkOrders*.
      3) Move the following fields from the *Available Fields* list box to the *Selected Fields* list box.
         WO
         WODate
         Descr
      4) Click Next.
      5) Click Next at the third Subform Wizard dialog box.
      6) Click Finish at the last Subform Wizard dialog box to accept the default subform name.
9. Select and then delete the label control object above the subform displaying the text *WorkOrders subform*.
10. Click the subform control object to display the orange border and sizing handles and move and resize the form as shown.

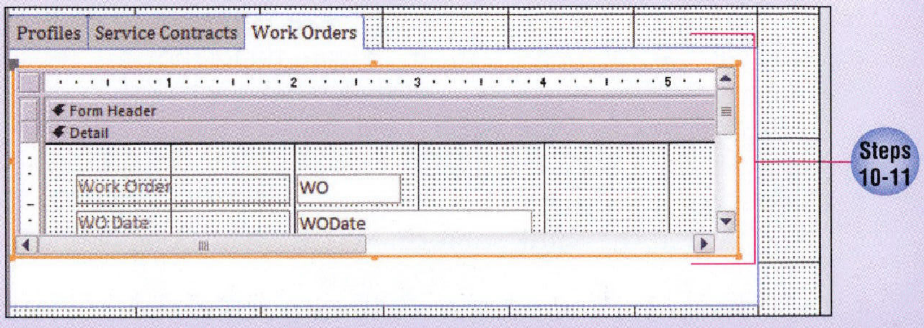

11. Access automatically extends a form's width and widens the tab control object if a table with many fields is added in a subform. If necessary, select the tab control object and decrease the width so that the right edge of the tab control is at the 6-inch position in the horizontal ruler. If necessary, decrease the width of the form so that the right edge of the grid is at the 6.5-inch position in the horizontal ruler. ***Hint: If Access resizes the tab control to the edge of the form, you may have to temporarily widen the grid in order to see the middle sizing handle at the right edge of the tab control object.***
12. Deselect the subform control object and then switch to Form view.
13. While viewing the form, you decide the title would look better if it was not centered. Switch to Design view, click the Title control object in the *Form Header* section, click the Form Design Tools Format tab, and then click the Align Text Left button in the Font group.
14. Click the Form Design Tools Design tab and then switch to Form view.
15. Click the Work Orders tab and adjust the column width for each column in the datasheet to Best Fit. Compare your CustMaintenance form with the one shown in Figure 4.9.
16. Print the selected record only. To do this, open the Print dialog box, click *Selected Record(s)* in the *Print Range* section and then click OK.
17. Save and then close the CustMaintenance form.

Figure 4.9 Completed CustMaintenance Form

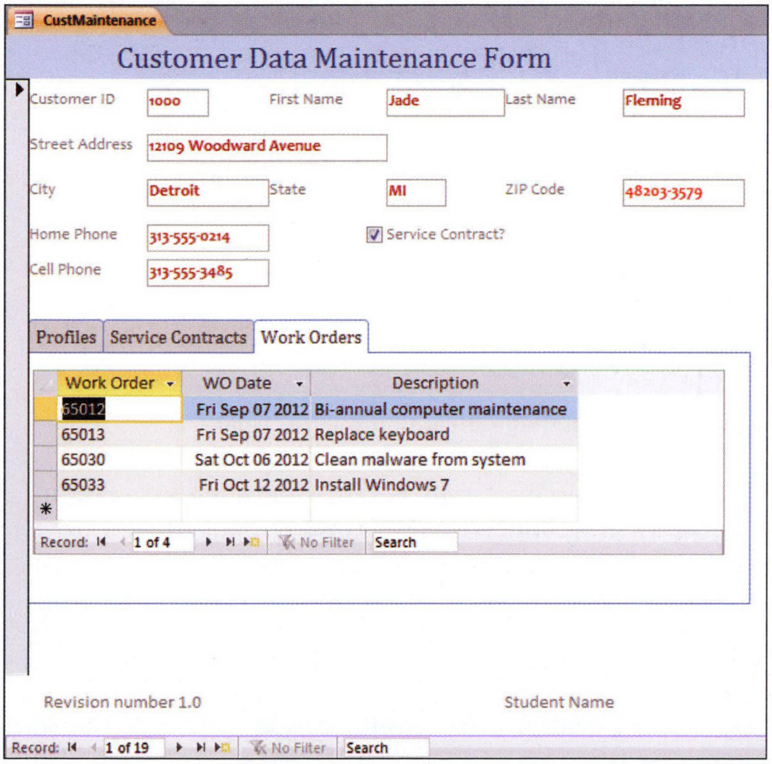

Adding the tab control with a separate page displaying a subform for each table related to the Customers table in the CustMaintenance form allowed you to create one object that can be used to view and update fields in multiple tables.

Project 2 Create a New Form with Calculations and Graphics 4 Parts

You will create a new form using the Form Wizard, add two calculations to the form, use features that assist with alignment and spacing of multiple control objects, and add graphics to the form.

Quick Steps

Add Calculated Control to Form

1. Open form in Design view.
2. Click Text Box button.
3. Position crosshairs in *Detail* section at desired location.
4. Drag to create control object the required height and width.
5. Release mouse.
6. Click in text box control.
7. Type formula.
8. Press Enter.
9. Delete text in label control object.
10. Type label text and press Enter.

Text Box

Adding Calculations to a Form in Design View

To display a calculated value in a form, you can create a query that includes a calculated column and then create a new form based on the query. Alternatively, you can create a calculated control object in an existing form using Design view. To do this, click the Text Box button in the Controls group in the Form Design Tools Design tab and then drag the crosshairs in the *Detail* section to create a control object the approximate height and width required to show the calculation. Access displays a text box control with *Unbound* displayed inside the object and a label control to the left displaying *Textxx* inside the object (where *xx* is the text box object number). A calculated control is considered an unbound object since the data displayed in the control is not drawn from a stored field value in a record. Click inside the text box control object (*Unbound* disappears when you click inside the control) and type the formula beginning with an equals sign. For example, the formula *=[Hours]*[Rate]* multiplies the value in the *Hours* field times the value in the *Rate* field. Field names in a formula are encased in square brackets.

Open the Property Sheet for the calculated control object to format the calculated values to *Fixed*, *Standard*, or *Currency* depending on the calculated value. Edit the label control object next to the calculated control to add a descriptive label that describes the calculated value.

Project 2a Adding and Formatting Calculated Control Objects — Part 1 of 4

1. With the **AL2-C4-RSRCompServ.accdb** database open, create a new form based on the WorkOrders table using the Form Wizard by completing the following steps:
   a. Click to select the WorkOrders table in the Navigation pane and then click the Create tab.
   b. Click the Form Wizard button in the Forms group.
   c. With *Table: WorkOrders* selected in the *Table/Queries* list box, complete the steps in the Form Wizard as follows:
      1) Move the following fields from the *Available Fields* list box to the *Selected Fields* list box and then click Next.
         WO, Descr, ServDate, Hours, Rate, Parts
      2) With *Columnar* layout selected, click Next.
      3) With *WorkOrders* the default text in the *What title do you want for your form?* text box, click *Modify the form's design* at the last dialog box and click Finish.

2. With the WorkOrders form displayed in Design view, change the theme and add a calculated control object to display the total labor for the work order by completing the following steps:
   a. Click the Themes button in the Themes group of the Form Design Tools Design tab and then click *Clarity* (second option in third row) at the drop-down gallery.
   b. Position the pointer on the top border of the gray *Form Footer* section bar until the pointer displays as a horizontal line with an up- and down-pointing arrow and then drag down just below the 3-inch position in the vertical ruler. This creates more grid space in the *Detail* section in which you can add controls.

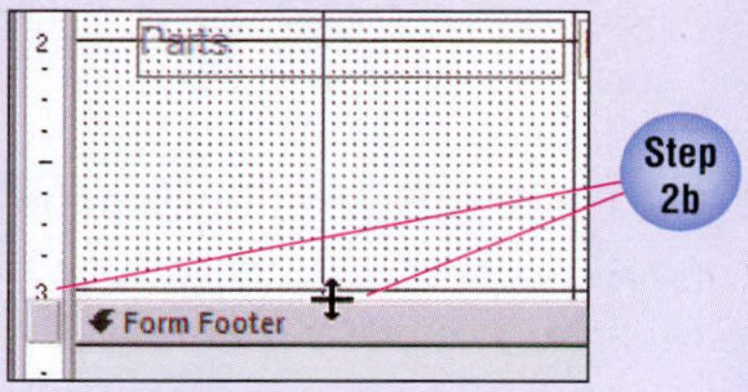

   c. Click the Text Box button in the Controls group.
   d. Position the crosshairs with the text box icon attached below the *Parts* text box control, drag to create an object the approximate height and width shown, and then release the mouse.

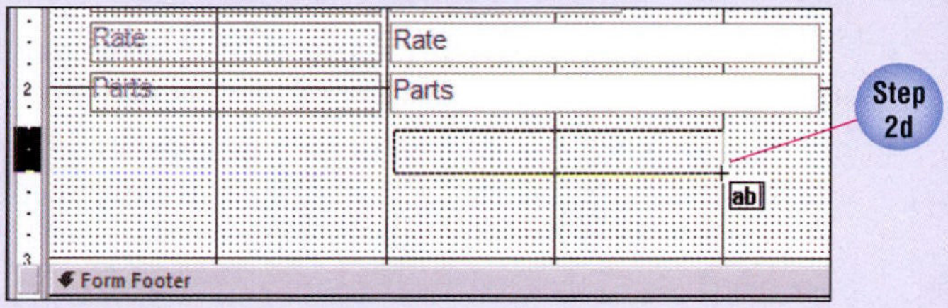

   e. Click in the text box control (displays *Unbound*) and type **=[Hours]*[Rate]**.
   f. Press the Enter key.

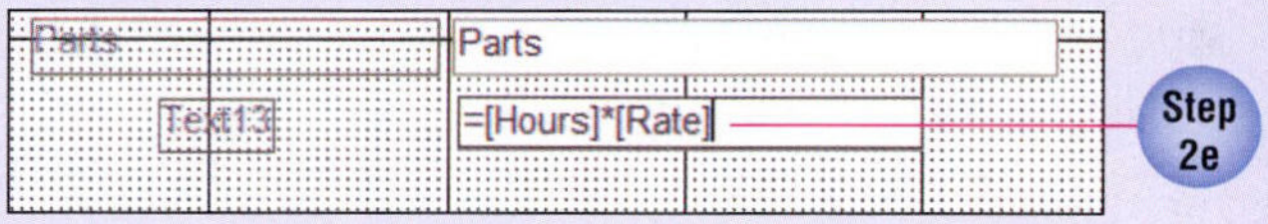

   g. With the calculated control object selected, click the Property Sheet button in the Tools group. With the Format tab in the Property Sheet active, click the down-pointing arrow in the *Format* property box, click *Standard* at the drop-down list, and then close the Property Sheet.

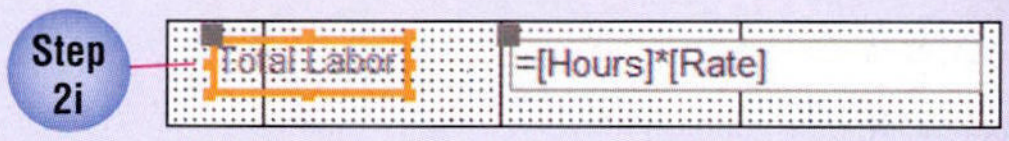

   h. With the calculated control object still selected, click the Form Design Tools Format tab and then click the Align Text Left button in the Font group. (By default, calculated values display right-aligned in Form view.)
   i. Click to select the label control object to the left of the calculated control object (displays *Textxx* [where *xx* is the text box label number]). Click inside the selected label control object a second time to display an insertion point. Delete *Textxx:*, type **Total Labor**, and press Enter. Notice the label control automatically expands to accommodate the width of the typed text.
3. Click the Form Design Tools Design tab. Click the View button to display the form in Form view and scroll a few records to view the calculated field. Do not be concerned with the size, position, alignment, and/or spacing of the controls since this will be fixed in a later project.
4. Switch to Design view and save the form.
5. A calculated control object can be used as a field in another formula. To do this, reference the calculated object in the formula by its *Name* property encased in square brackets. Change the name for the calculated object created in Step 2 to a more descriptive name by completing the following steps:
   a. Click the calculated control object (displays the formula *=[Hours]*[Rate]*).
   b. Click the Property Sheet button in the Tools group.

c. Click the Other tab in the Property Sheet.

d. Select and delete the existing text (displays *Textxx* [where *xx* is the text box number]) in the *Name* property box.

e. Type **LaborCalc** and then close the Property Sheet.

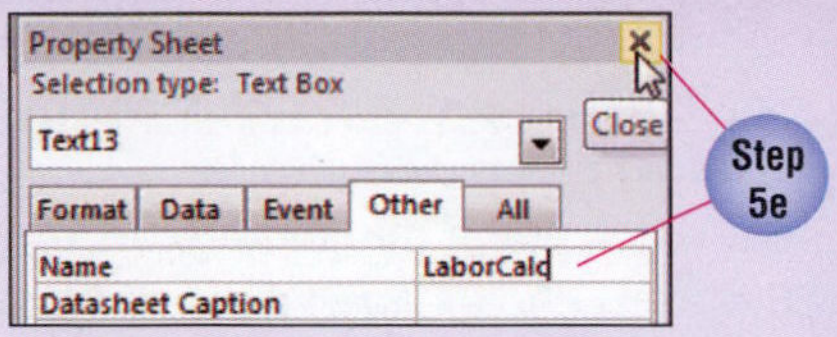

6. Add another calculated control object to the form to add the labor and parts to display the total value for the work order by completing the following steps:

a. Click the Text Box button.

b. Position the crosshairs with the text box icon attached below the calculated control created in Step 2, drag to create an object the approximate height and width as the first calculated control, and then release the mouse.

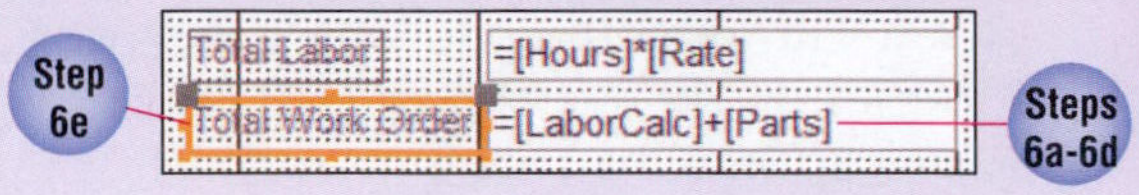

c. Click in the text box control (displays *Unbound*), type **=[LaborCalc]+[Parts]**, and press the Enter key.

d. Format the calculated control to *Currency* and align the text at the left side of the control. Refer to Steps 2g through 2h if you need assistance with this step.

e. Change the entry in the label control object to **Total Work Order**. Refer to Step 2i if you need assistance with this step.

7. Save the form. Display the form in Form view and scroll a few records to view the calculations.

8. Switch to Design view.

Quick Steps

Align Multiple Objects

1. In Design view, select desired control objects.
2. Click Form Design Tools Arrange tab.
3. Click Align button.
4. Click desired option at drop-down list.
5. Deselect controls.

Align

Adjusting Objects for Consistency in Appearance

When working in Design view, Access provides tools to assist with positioning, aligning, sizing, and spacing multiple controls to create a uniform and consistent appearance. Access these tools from the Size/Space and Align buttons in the Sizing & Ordering group of the Form Design Tools Arrange tab.

Aligning Multiple Controls at the Same Position

The Align button options in the Sizing & Ordering group of the Form Design Tools Arrange tab shown in Figure 4.10 can be used to align multiple selected controls at the same horizontal or vertical position. Using the Align button options saves the work of adjusting each control individually to the same position on the form.

Figure 4.10 Alignment Options in Align Button Drop-down List

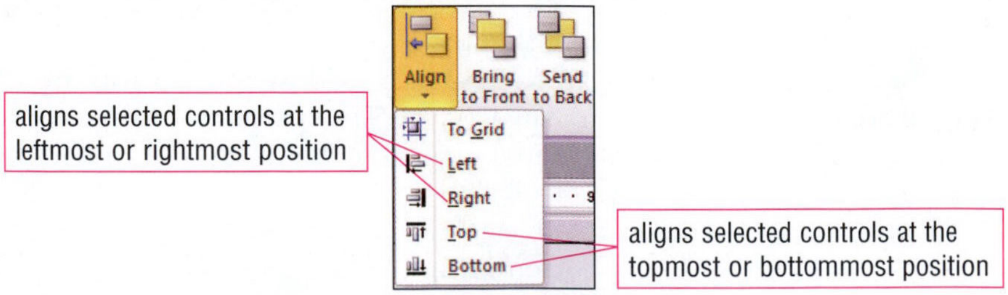

Adjusting the Sizing and Spacing between Controls

The Size/Space button drop-down list in the Sizing & Ordering group of the Form Design Tools Arrange tab shown in Figure 4.11 contains options to assist with consistent sizing of controls and spacing between controls. Use options in the *Size* section of the drop-down list to adjust the height or width to the tallest, shortest, widest, or narrowest of the selected control objects. Use options in the *Spacing* section to adjust the horizontal and vertical spacing between controls, to increase the space, decrease the space, or make all of the spaces between selected objects equal.

These tools are helpful when creating a new form by adding controls manually to the grid or after editing an existing form since the space between controls can easily change after adding or deleting objects. To precisely move individual control objects to adjust the spacing would be time-consuming.

Quick Steps

Adjust Spacing between Objects

1. In Design view, select desired control objects.
2. Click Form Design Tools Arrange tab.
3. Click Size/Space button.
4. Click desired option in *Spacing* section.
5. Deselect controls.

Size/Space

Figure 4.11 Size and Spacing Options in Size/Space Button Drop-Down List

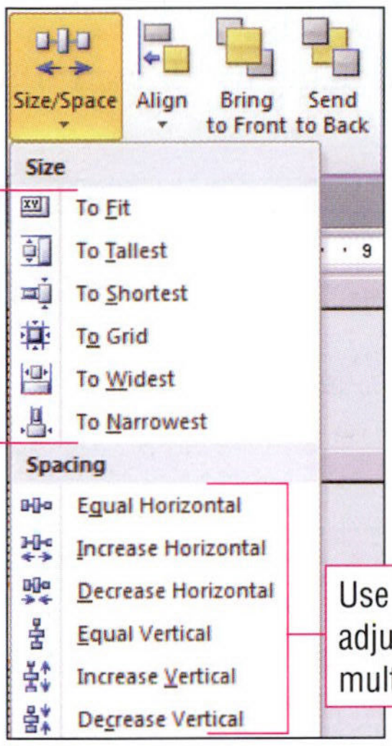

Project 2b **Sizing, Aligning, and Spacing Multiple Controls** Part 2 of 4

1. With the **AL2-C4-RSRCompServ.accdb** database open and the WorkOrders form open in Design view, edit the title in the *Form Header* section to **Work Orders with Calculations** and then widen the control object to fit the title text on one line.
2. With the title control object still selected, position the pointer on the orange border until the pointer changes to the four-headed arrow move icon and then drag the control to move it to the approximate center of the *Form Header* section.

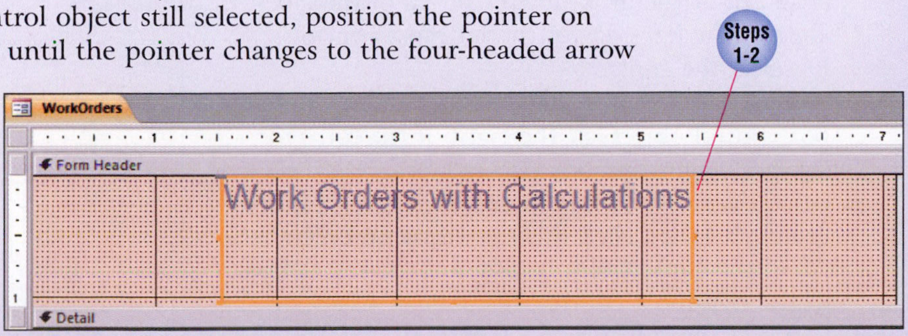

3. Point to the bottom gray border in the *Form Footer* section bar until the pointer displays as a horizontal line with an up- and down-pointing arrow and then drag down approximately 0.5 inch to create space in the *Form Footer* section. Create a label control object with your name in the center of the *Form Footer* section.

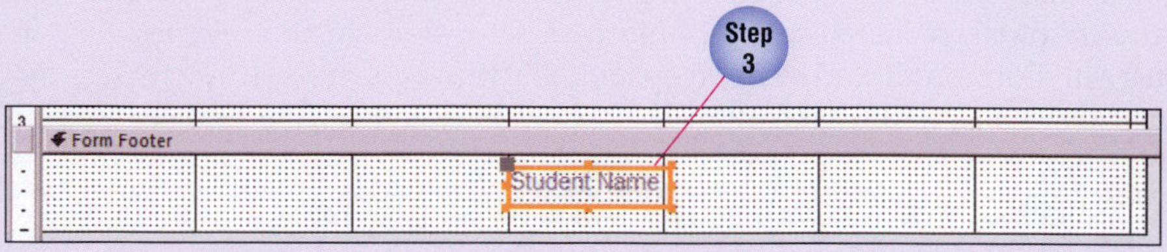

4. Click to select the *Descr* text box control object and then drag the right middle sizing handle left until the control is resized to approximately the 4.5-inch position in the horizontal ruler.
5. Shift + click to select the six text box control objects for the fields above the two calculated controls. Click the Form Design Tools Arrange tab, click the Size/Space button in the Sizing & Ordering group, and then click *To Widest* at the drop-down list. The six text box control objects are now all the same width, with the width set to the length of the widest selected object.

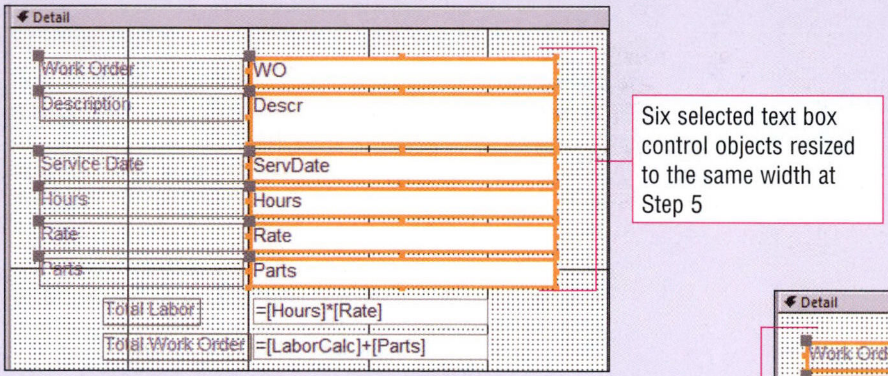

6. Click in any blank area to deselect the controls.
7. Use the Align button to align multiple controls by completing the following steps:
   a. Draw a selection rectangle around all of the label control objects at the left side of the form to select all eight label controls.
   b. Click the Align button in the Sizing & Ordering group and then click *Left* at the drop-down list. All of the label control objects align at the left edge of the leftmost control.
   c. Deselect the controls.
   d. Draw a selection rectangle around all of the text box control objects at the right of the form to select all eight text box controls.
   e. Click the Align button in the Sizing & Ordering group and then click *Right* at the drop-down list. All of the control objects align at the right edge of the rightmost control.
   f. Deselect the controls.

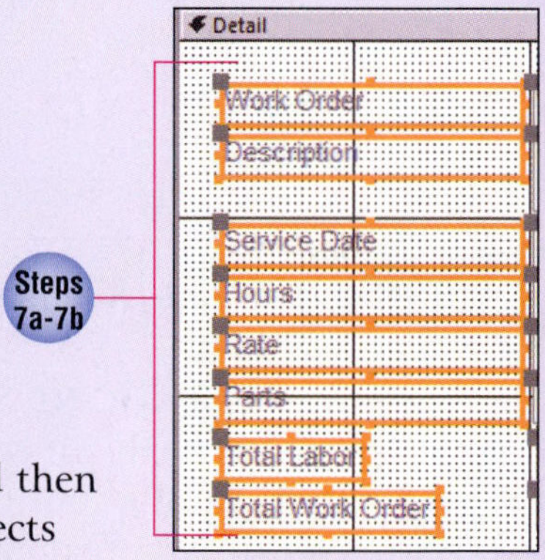

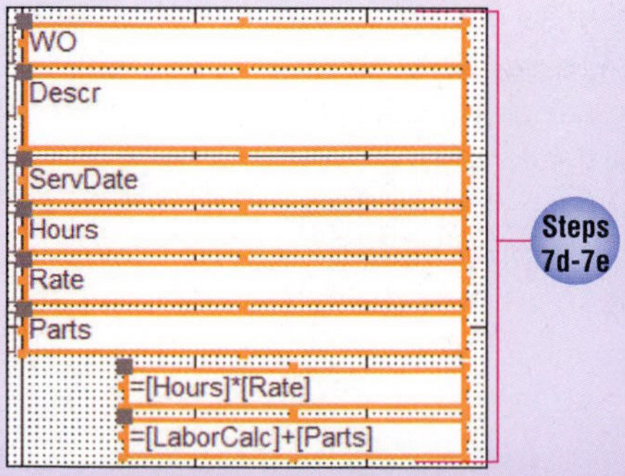

8. Adjust the vertical space between controls to make all of the control objects equally spaced in the *Detail* section by completing the following steps:

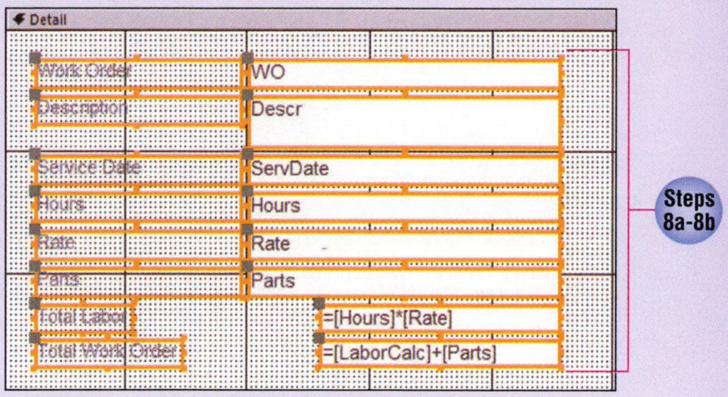

   a. Draw a selection rectangle around all of the control objects in the *Detail* section.
   b. Click the Size/Space button and then click *Equal Vertical* in the *Spacing* section of the drop-down list. All of the control objects now have the same amount of vertical space between each object.
   c. Deselect the controls.
9. Save the form.
10. Display the form in Form view and scroll a few records to view the revised alignment and spacing options.
11. Switch to Design view.

Adding Graphics to a Form in Design View

A picture that is saved in a graphic file format can be added to a form using the Logo button or the Insert Image button in the Controls group in the Form Design Tools Design tab. Click the Logo button and Access opens the Insert Picture dialog box. Navigate to the drive and/or folder in which the graphic file is stored and then double-click the image file name. Access automatically adds the image to the left side of the *Form Header* section. Move and/or resize the image as needed. Access supports these popular graphic file formats for a logo control object: *bmp*, *gif*, *jpeg*, *jpg*, and *png*.

Use the Insert Image button when you want to place the picture in another section or prefer to draw a larger control object to hold the picture at the start. Click the Insert Image button and then click *Browse* at the drop-down list to open the Insert Picture dialog box. Navigate to the drive and/or folder in which the graphic file is stored and then double-click the image file name. Next, position the crosshairs pointer with the image icon attached at the desired location in the form where you want to place the image, and then drag the crosshairs to draw a control object the approximate height and width desired. Access supports these popular graphic file formats for an image control object: *gif*, *jpeg*, *jpg*, and *png*.

Use the Line button in the Controls group to draw horizontal or vertical lines in the form. Hold down the Shift key while dragging to draw a straight line. Once the line is drawn, use the Shape Outline button in the Control Formatting group of the Form Design Tools Format tab to modify the line thickness, line type, and line color.

You can also add clip art images to a form. Access does not provide a clip art button in the Controls group; however, you can use Microsoft Word to insert a clip art image in a document and use standard Windows commands to copy the image to the clipboard and paste the clip art into a form. Access inserts the clip art in an unbound OLE control object.

Quick Steps

Add Clip Art to Form

1. Open form in Design view.
2. Start Microsoft Word.
3. Click Insert, Clip Art.
4. Locate and insert desired clip art into document.
5. Copy clip art image to clipboard.
6. Switch to Microsoft Access.
7. Paste image into desired form section.
8. Move and resize as required.
9. If necessary, display Property Sheet and change Size Mode property.
10. Switch to Microsoft Word.
11. Exit Word without saving.

Logo

Line

Insert Image

Project 2c Adding Graphics to a Form

Part 3 of 4

1. With the **AL2-C4-RSRCompServ.accdb** database open and the WorkOrders form open in Design view, start Microsoft Word.
2. Locate and insert a clip art image in a new document and copy and paste the image to the form in Microsoft Access by completing the following steps:

   a. At a blank Word document screen, click the Insert tab and then click the Clip Art button in the Illustrations group to open the Clip Art task pane.
   b. Select and delete existing text in the *Search for* text box, type **computer repairs**, and then press the Enter key.
   c. Scroll down the results list box and click the image shown to insert the clip art in the current document. If the image shown is not available, select a suitable alternative image.
   d. Right-click the clip art image in the Word document and click *Copy* at the shortcut menu.
   e. Click the button on the Taskbar representing Microsoft Access.

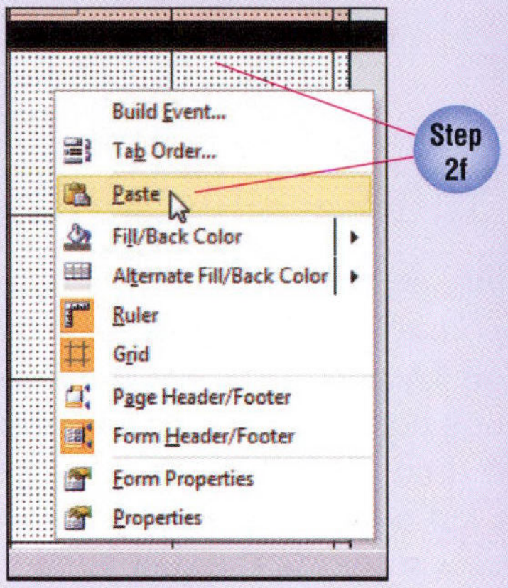

   f. Right-click in the *Detail* section of the form and click *Paste* at the shortcut menu. Access inserts the image overlapping existing controls and displays the orange border with selection handles.
   g. Move and resize the image to the approximate position and size shown below (your size and image may vary). You will notice when you resize the control object that Access cuts off parts of the image as you make the control object smaller. This action reflects the default *Clip* property for the object. You will correct this in Step 3.

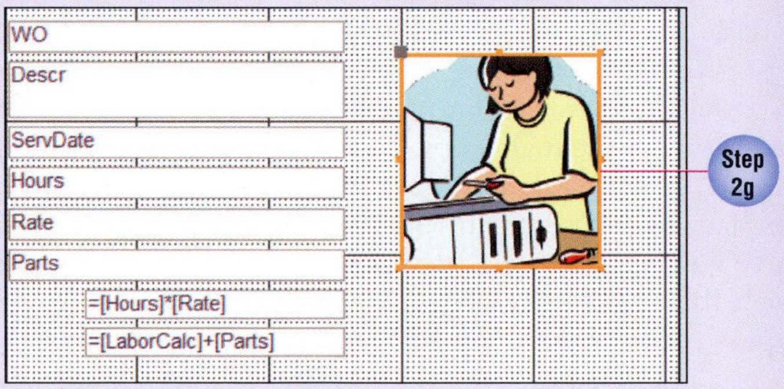

   h. Click the button on the Taskbar representing Microsoft Word and exit Word. Click Don't Save when prompted to save the document. Click No if prompted to make the Clipboard contents available for other applications.

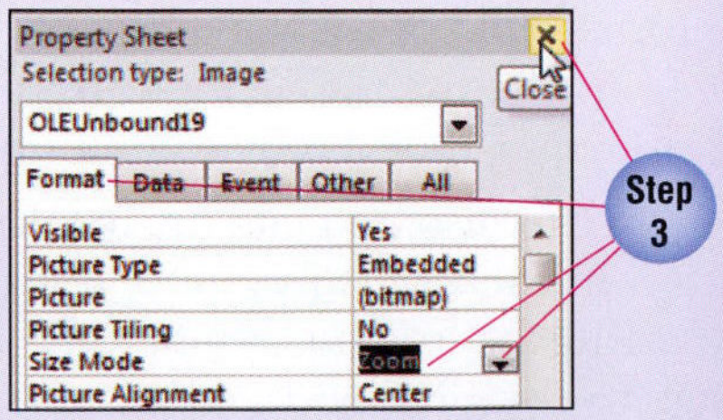

3. Right-click the clip art image pasted at the right side of the *Detail* section in the form and click *Properties* at the shortcut menu. With Format the active tab in the Property Sheet, click in the *Size Mode* property box, click the down-pointing arrow that appears, and then click *Zoom* at the drop-down list. Close the Property Sheet. Changing *Size Mode* to *Zoom* instructs Access to resize the image within the control object maintaining the original proportions to height and width. The *Size Mode* drop-down list also contains the *Stretch* option. Use this option to stretch the image to fit the height and width of the control object. Using *Stretch* may cause a skewed appearance to the image.

4. Deselect the control object containing the clip art image and display the form in Form view. You decide a line below the title would help improve the form's appearance. Draw and modify the line by completing the following steps:
   a. Switch to Design view and click the Line button in the Controls group.
   b. Position the crosshairs with the line icon attached below the title in the *Form Header* section beginning a few rows of grid dots below the first letter in the title, hold down the Shift key, drag right releasing the mouse below the last letter in the title, and then release the Shift key.

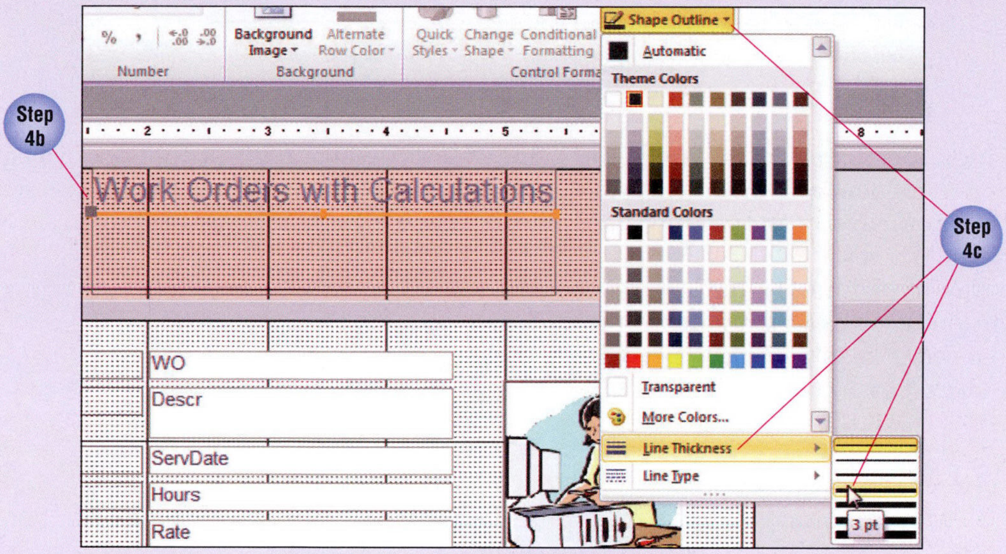

   c. Click the Form Design Tools Format tab, click the Shape Outline button in the Control Formatting group, point to *Line Thickness* at the drop-down list, and then click *3 pt* (fourth thickness option).
   d. With the line object still selected, click the Shape Outline button and then click the *Dark Red* color square (first option in last row of *Standard Colors*).
   e. Deselect the line object.
5. Display the form in Form view to view the line under the title.
6. Switch to Design view. If necessary, adjust the length and/or position of the line as desired.
7. Adjust alignment and formatting options of numeric fields by completing the following steps:
   a. Shift + click to select the *Hours*, *Rate*, *Parts*, and both calculated text box control objects.
   b. Click the Form Design Tools Format tab and then click the Align Text Right button in the Font group.
   c. Deselect the controls.
   d. Shift + click the *Parts* text box control and the bottom calculated control object that displays the formula *=[LaborCalc]+[Parts]*.
   e. Click the Form Design Tools Design tab and then click the Property Sheet button in the Tools group. Change the Format property to *Standard* and then close the Property Sheet.
   f. Deselect the controls.

8. Click to select the title text in the *Form Header* section and then drag the bottom middle sizing handle up to decrease the height of the control object to approximately 0.5 inch in the vertical ruler.

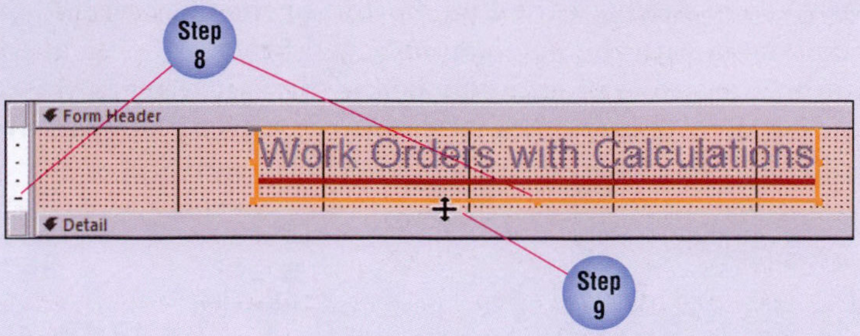

9. Position the pointer on the top of the gray *Detail* section bar until the pointer displays as a horizontal line with an up- and down-pointing arrow and then drag up to decrease the height of the *Form Header* section to approximately 0.6 inch in the vertical ruler.
10. Save the form.
11. Display the form in Form view and compare your form with the one shown in Figure 4.12.
12. Print the selected record only with the left and right margins set to 0.5 inch.
13. Close the form.

Figure 4.12 Completed WorkOrders Form

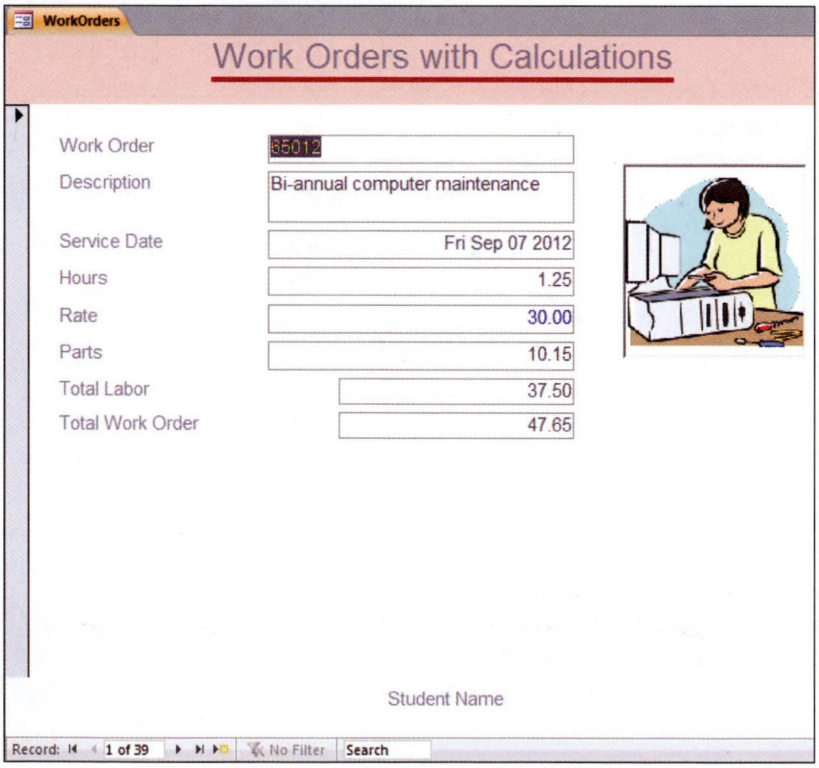

Anchoring Controls to a Form

A control object in a form can be anchored to a section or to another control object using the Anchoring button in the Position group in the Form Design Tools Arrange tab. When a control object is anchored, the object's position is maintained when the form is resized. For example, if a clip art image is anchored to the top right of the *Detail* section, when the form is resized in Form view, the image automatically moves in conjunction with the new form size so that the original distance between the image and the top right of the *Detail* section is maintained. If an image is not anchored and the form is resized, the position of the image relative to the edges of the form can change.

By default, *Top Left* is selected as the anchor position for each control object in a form. To change the anchor position, select the object(s), click the Form Design Tools Arrange tab, click the Anchoring button, and then click *Stretch Down*, *Bottom Left*, *Stretch Across Top*, *Stretch Down and Across*, *Stretch Across Bottom*, *Top Right*, *Stretch Down and Right*, or *Bottom Right*. Click the option that represents how you want the object to dynamically move as a form is resized. Some options will cause a control object to resize as well as move when the form is changed.

Quick Steps

Anchor Control in Form

1. Open form in Design view.
2. Select control object(s) to be anchored.
3. Click Form Design Tools Arrange tab.
4. Click Anchoring button.
5. Click desired anchor position.
6. Deselect object.
7. Save form.

Anchoring

Project 2d **Anchoring an Image to a Position within a Section** **Part 4 of 4**

1. With the **AL2-C4-RSRCompServ.accdb** database open, open the WorkOrders form in Form view.
2. Switch to Design view.
3. Anchor the clip art image to the top of the *Detail* section of the form by completing the following steps:
   a. Click to select the clip art image.
   b. Click the Form Design Tools Arrange tab.
   c. Click the Anchoring button in the Position group.

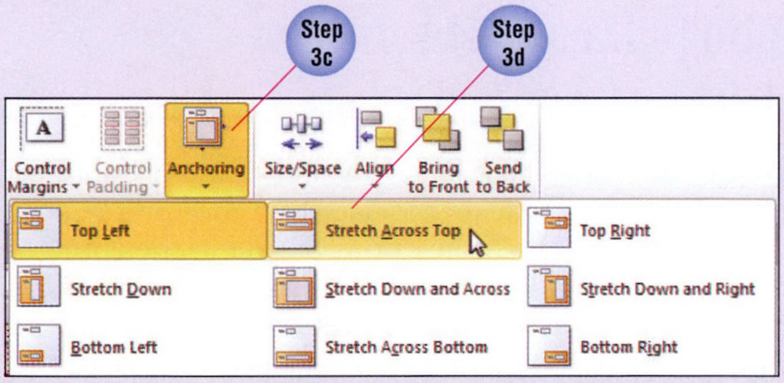

   d. Click *Stretch Across Top* at the drop-down list.
   e. Take note of the distance between the top border of the selected clip art image and the top of the *Detail* section.

4. Display the form in Form view. Notice the image has shifted up and become stretched across the top of the *Detail* section maintaining the distance between the top of the control object's boundary and the top of the *Detail* section.

Clip art image is shifted up and stretched across top of *Detail* section. The distance between the top of the image and the top of the *Detail* section is maintained when the form is resized.

WorkOrders

Work Orders with Calculations

Work Order	85012
Descripton	Bi-annual computer maintenance
Service Date	Fri Sep 07 2012
Hours	1.25
Rate	30.00
Parts	10.15

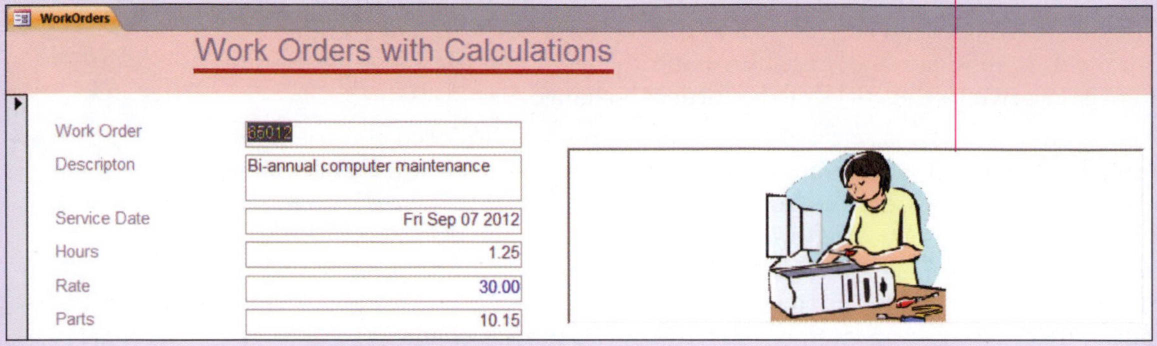

5. Click the File tab and then click Save Object As. Type **WorkOrdersAnchored** at the Save As dialog box and then press the Enter key or click OK.
6. Click the Home tab and then close the form.

Project 3 Create a Restricted-Use Form 1 Part

You will create a datasheet form to be used to enter information into a table and set the form's properties to prevent records from being deleted in the form.

▼ **Quick Steps**

Create Datasheet Form
1. Select table in Navigation pane.
2. Click Create tab.
3. Click More Forms button.
4. Click *Datasheet.*
5. Save form.

Restrict Record Actions for Form
1. Open form in Design view.
2. Double-click Form Selector button.
3. Click Data tab.
4. Change *Allow Additions, Allow Deletions, Allow Edits,* or *Allow Filters* to *No.*
5. Close Property Sheet.
6. Save form.

Creating a Datasheet Form and Restricting Form Actions ■■■■■■■■■■■■■■■■■■■■■

A form can be created that looks just like a table's datasheet. Click the table for which you want to create the datasheet form in the Navigation pane, click the Create tab, click the More Forms button in the Forms group, and then click *Datasheet* at the drop-down list. Access creates a form including all fields from the selected table presented in a datasheet layout.

Although the datasheet form has the look and feel of a table datasheet, the form object prevents end users from accessing and modifying the underlying table's structure.

Using options available in the Data tab of a form's Property Sheet shown in Figure 4.13, you can restrict actions that can be performed while a form is displayed in Form view. For example, you can prevent new records from being added and/or existing records from being deleted and/or edited and/or filtered. Setting the Data Entry property to *Yes* means the end user will see a blank form only when the form is opened. A data entry form is intended to be used to add new records only; the user is prevented from scrolling through existing records in the form.

Figure 4.13 Form Property Sheet with Data Tab Selected

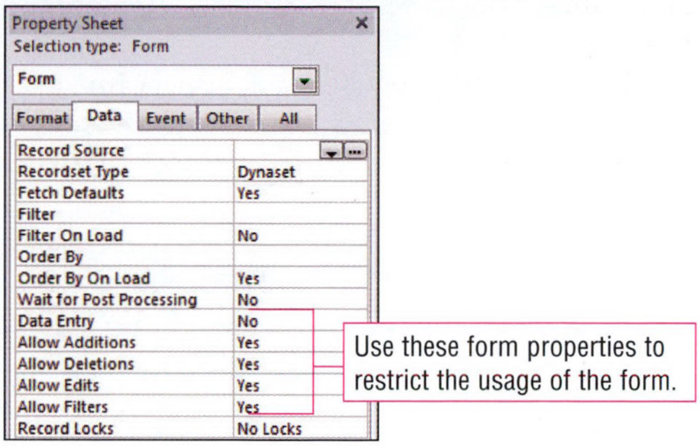

Project 3 Creating a Datasheet Form and Preventing Record Deletions

Part 1 of 1

1. With the **AL2-C4-RSRCompServ.accdb** database open, click the Technicians table in the Navigation pane, and then click the Create tab.
2. Click the More Forms button in the Forms group and then click *Datasheet* at the drop-down list.
3. Review the Technicians form in the work area. Notice the form resembles a table datasheet.
4. Switch to Design view.
5. Modify the Technician's form properties to prevent users from deleting records using the form by completing the following steps:
   a. Click in a blank area to deselect the controls.
   b. Double-click the Form Selector button (displays as a black square) located at the top of the vertical ruler and left of the horizontal ruler to open the form's Property Sheet.
   c. Click the Data tab.
   d. Click in the *Allow Deletions* property box, click the down-pointing arrow that appears, and then click *No* at the drop-down list.
   e. Close the Property Sheet.
6. Click the Save button and then click OK to accept *Technicians* as the *Form Name*.
7. Click the down-pointing arrow on the View button in the Views group in the Form Design Tools Design tab. Notice that *Datasheet View* and *Design View* are the only views available. The *Form View* option is not available in the drop-down list or in the View buttons at the right end of the Status bar.
8. Click in a blank area to remove the drop-down list and then close the form.

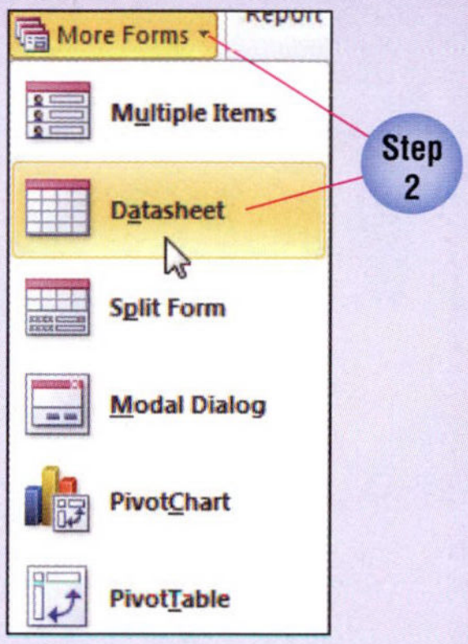

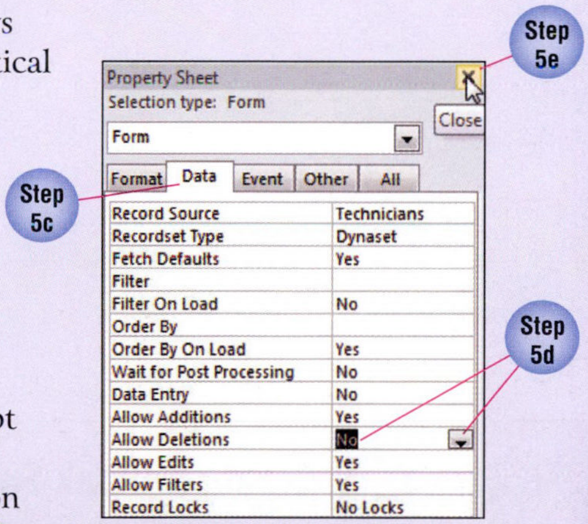

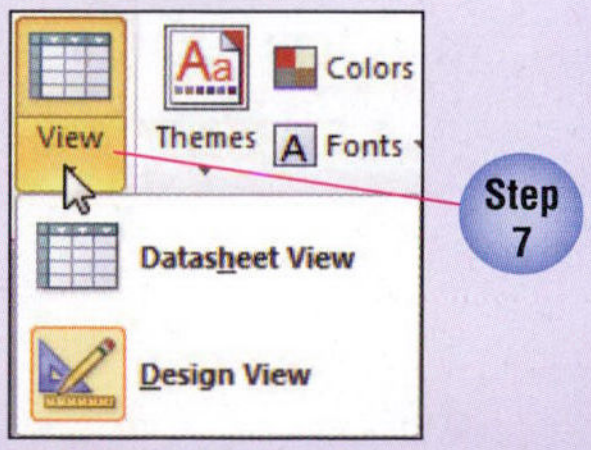

9. Double-click the Technicians form object in the Navigation pane. Be careful to open the form object and not the table object.
10. Click in the record selector bar next to the first row in the datasheet for Technician ID 01 to select the record.
11. Click the Home tab and then look at the Delete button in the Records group. Notice the Delete button is dimmed. The feature is unavailable since the *Allow Deletions* form property was set to *No*.

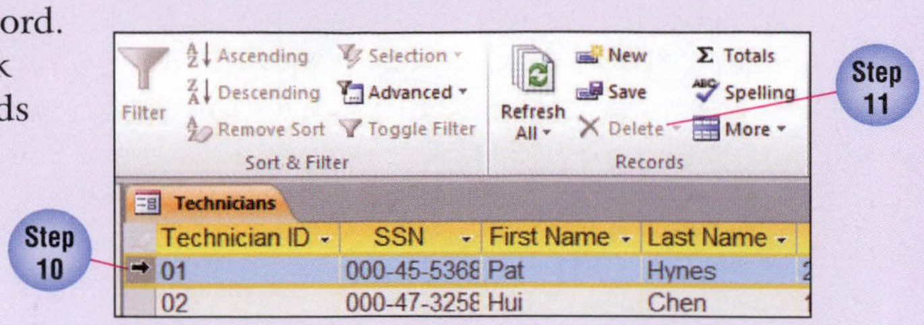

12. Print the first page only of the Technicians form in landscape orientation and then close the form.
13. Right-click the Technicians form object in the Navigation pane and then click *Layout View* at the shortcut menu. Notice the datasheet form displays in a columnar layout in Layout view. The Technicians table includes a field named *Attachments*. In this field in the first record a picture of the technician has been attached to the record. In Layout View, Access automatically opens the image file and displays the contents.

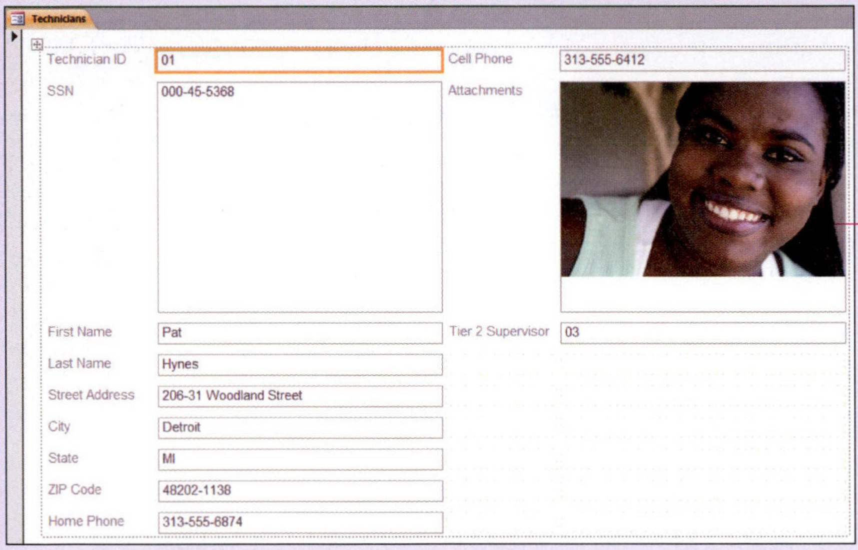

In Layout view the datasheet form displays in a columnar layout.

The *Attachments* field automatically displays an attached image file if one has been added to the *Attachments* field.

14. Close the form.

Project 4 Create a Blank Form with Lists — 1 Part

You will use the Blank Form tool to create a new form for maintaining the service plan fees table named FeesSCPlans. In the form, you will create list boxes to provide an easy way to enter data for new service contract plans.

Creating a Form Using the Blank Form Tool

When you need to create a form that contains a small number of fields you can use the Blank Form tool in Access to quickly build the form. A blank form begins with no controls or format and displays as a blank white page in Layout view. Click the Create tab and then click the Blank Form button in the Forms group to begin a new form. Access opens the Field List pane at the right side of the work area. Expand the list for the desired table and then add fields to the form as needed. If the Field List pane displays with no table names, click the hyperlink to Show all tables at the top of the pane.

Quick Steps

Create Blank Form
1. Click Create tab.
2. Click Blank Form button.
3. Expand field list for desired table.
4. Drag fields to form as needed.
5. Add a title, format, or make other design changes as needed.
6. Save form.

Create List Box
1. Open form in Layout or Design view.
2. Click List Box button in Controls group.
3. Click within form at desired location.
4. Create values within List Box Wizard.
5. Save form.

Create Combo Box
1. Open form in Layout or Design view.
2. Click Combo Box button in Controls group.
3. Click within form at desired location.
4. Create values within Combo Box Wizard.
5. Save form.

Blank Form

List Box

Combo Box

Adding a List Box to a Form

A list box displays a list of values for a field within the control object. In Form view, the user can easily see the entire list for the field. You can create the list of values when you create the control object or instruct Access to populate the list using values from a table or query. When you add a list box control to the form, the List Box Wizard begins as long as *Use Control Wizards* is active. Within the List Box Wizard you specify the values to be shown within the list box.

Adding a Combo Box to a Form

A combo box is similar to a list box; however, a combo box includes a text box within the control object so that the user can either type the value for the field or click the down-pointing arrow to display field values in a drop-down list and click the desired value. As with a list box, when you add a combo box control to the form, the Combo Box Wizard begins as long as *Use Control Wizards* is active. Within the Combo Box Wizard you specify the values to be shown within the drop-down list.

Project 4 **Creating a Blank Form with List Boxes** **Part 1 of 1**

1. With the **AL2-C4-RSRCompServ.accdb** database open, click the Create tab and then click the Blank Form button in the Forms group.
2. If the Field List pane at the right side of the work area does not display the table names, click the Show all tables hyperlink; otherwise, proceed to Step 3.
3. Add fields from the FeesSCPlans table to the form by completing the following steps:
   a. Click the plus symbol next to the table named *FeesSCPlans* to expand the field list.

b. Click the first field named *ID* in the Field List pane and then drag the field to the top left of the form.
c. Click the second field named *Term* in the Field List pane, hold down the Shift key, and then click the last field named *Rate* in the Field List pane to select the remaining fields in the FeesSCPlans table.
d. Position the mouse pointer within the selected field names and then drag the group of fields to the form below the *ID* field. Release the mouse when you see the gold bar displayed below *ID*.
e. With the four fields selected that were added to the table, hold down the Shift key and click the *ID* field.
f. Position the mouse pointer on the orange border at the right of any of the selected label control objects until the pointer changes to a left- and right-pointing arrow and then drag the right edge of the label control objects to the right until you can read all of the label text as shown below.

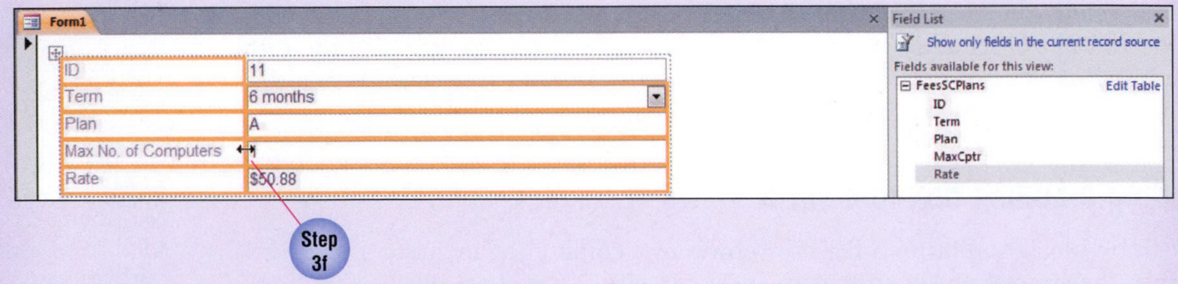

4. Add a List Box control object to show the plan letters in a list by completing the following steps:
a. Click the List Box control in the Controls group of the Form Layout Tools Design tab.
b. Position the pointer with the List Box icon attached below the *Plan* field text box control object in the form. Click the mouse when you see the gold bar displayed between *A* and *1* in the right column. The List Box Wizard starts when you release the mouse.
c. At the first List Box Wizard dialog box, click *I will type in the values that I want* and then click Next.

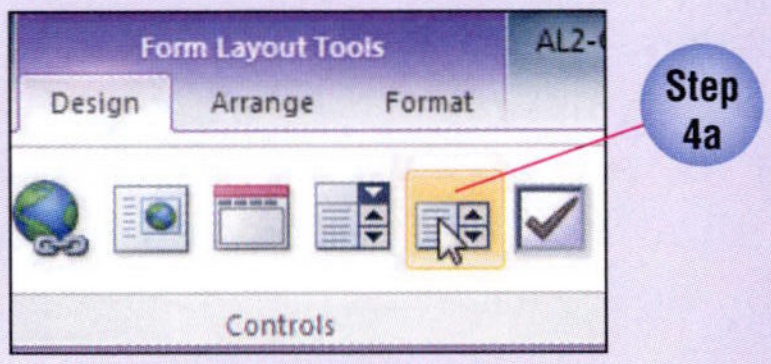

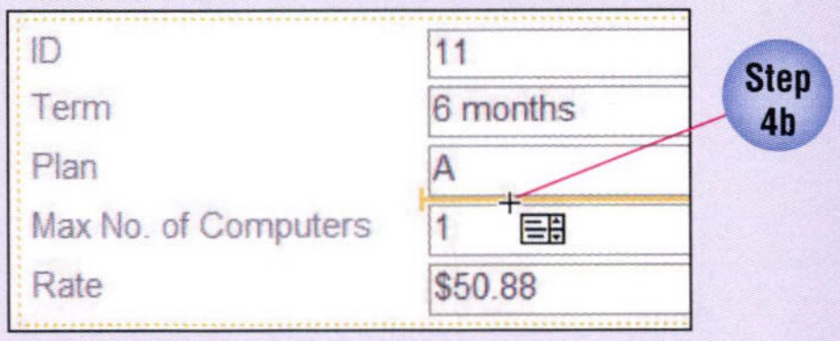

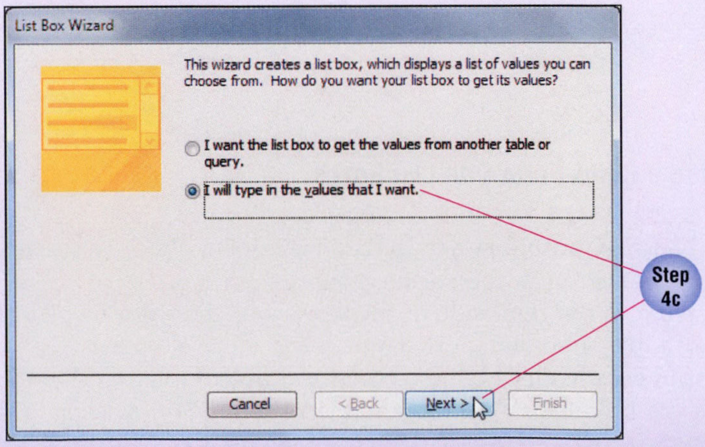

d. At the second List Box Wizard dialog box, click in the first cell below *Col1*, type **A**, and then press the Tab key.
e. Type **B**, press Tab, type **C**, press Tab, type **D**, and then click Next.
f. At the third List Box Wizard dialog box, click *Store that value in this field*, click the down-pointing arrow at the right of the list box, and then click *Plan* at the drop down list.
g. Click Next.

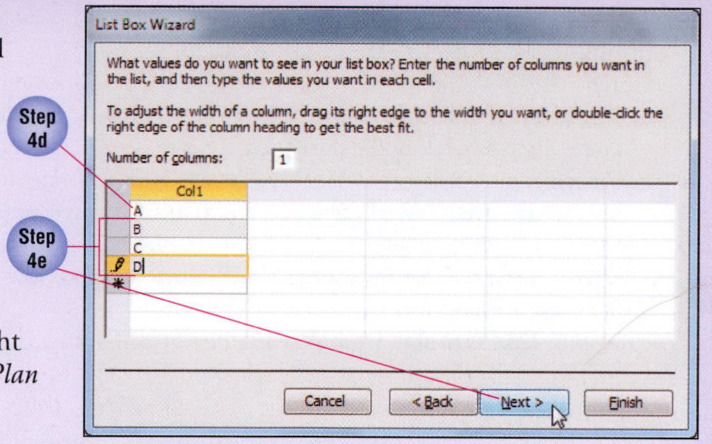
List Box Wizard
What values do you want to see in your list box? Enter the number of columns you want in the list, and then type the values you want in each cell.
To adjust the width of a column, drag its right edge to the width you want, or double-click the right edge of the column heading to get the best fit.
Number of columns:
1
Col1
A
B
C
D
Cancel
< Back
Next >
Finish
Step 4d
Step 4e

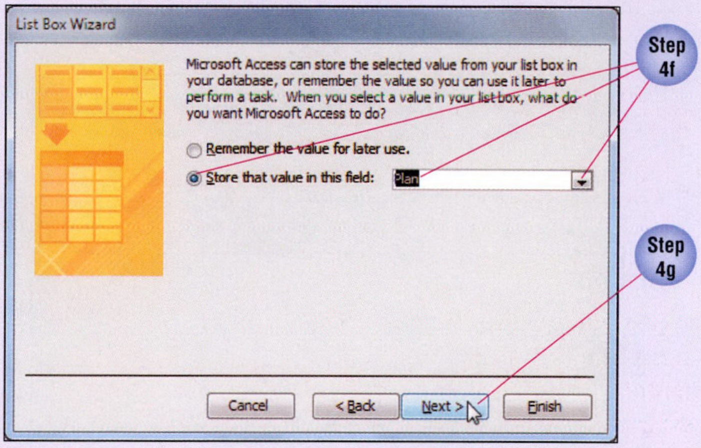
List Box Wizard
Microsoft Access can store the selected value from your list box in your database, or remember the value so you can use it later to perform a task. When you select a value in your list box, what do you want Microsoft Access to do?
Remember the value for later use.
Store that value in this field:
Plan
Cancel
< Back
Next >
Finish
Step 4f
Step 4g

h. At the last List Box Wizard dialog box, with the current text already selected in the *What label would you like for your list box?* text box, type **PlanList** and then click Finish. Access adds the list box to the form displaying all of the values you entered in the list.

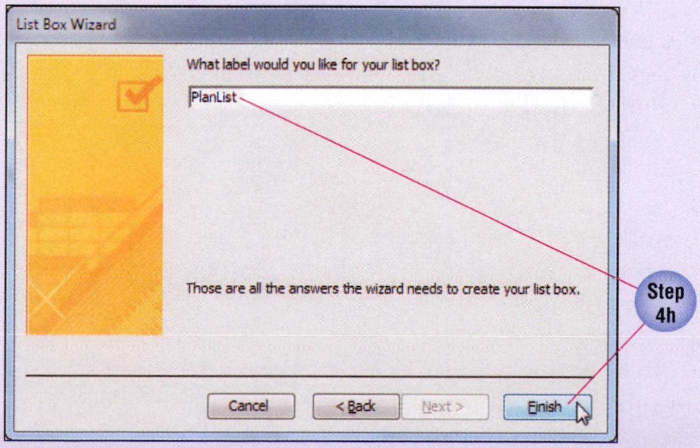
List Box Wizard
What label would you like for your list box?
PlanList
Those are all the answers the wizard needs to create your list box.
Cancel
< Back
Next >
Finish
Step 4h

5. Add a Combo Box control object to enter the maximum number of computers in a plan by completing the following steps:
   a. Click the Combo Box control in the Controls group of the Form Layout Tools Design tab.

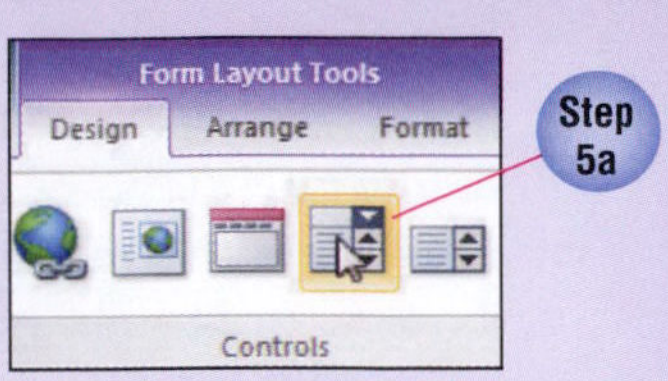

Form Layout Tools
Design
Arrange
Format
Controls
Step 5a

   b. Position the pointer with the Combo Box icon attached below the *Max No. of Computers* text box control object in the form. Click the mouse when you see the gold bar displayed between *1* and *$50.88* in the right column. The Combo Box Wizard starts when you release the mouse.

Step 5b
Max No. of Computers
1
Rate
$50.88

   c. At the first Combo Box Wizard dialog box, click *I will type in the values that I want* and then click Next.
   d. At the second Combo Box Wizard dialog box, click in the first cell below *Col1*, type **1**, and then press Tab.
   e. Type **2**, press Tab, type **3**, press Tab, type **4**, press Tab, type **5**, and then click Next.

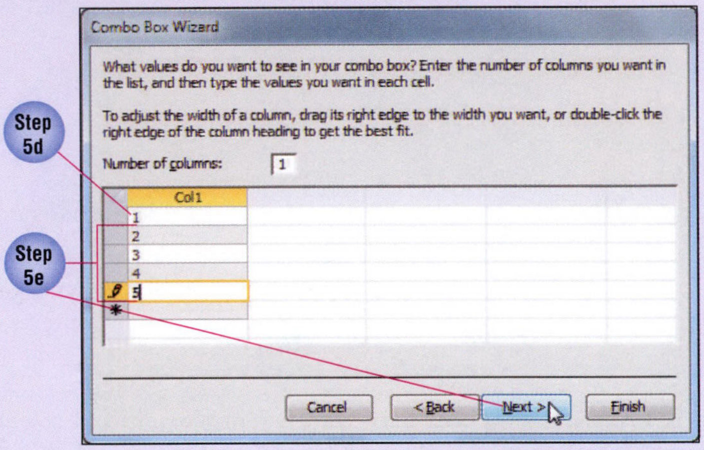

Combo Box Wizard
What values do you want to see in your combo box? Enter the number of columns you want in the list, and then type the values you want in each cell.
To adjust the width of a column, drag its right edge to the width you want, or double-click the right edge of the column heading to get the best fit.
Number of columns: 1
Col1
1
2
3
4
5
Cancel
< Back
Next >
Finish
Step 5d
Step 5e

   f. At the third Combo Box Wizard dialog box, click *Store that value in this field*, click the down-pointing arrow at the right of the list box, click *MaxCptr* at the drop down list, and then click Next.

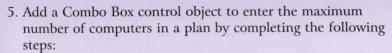

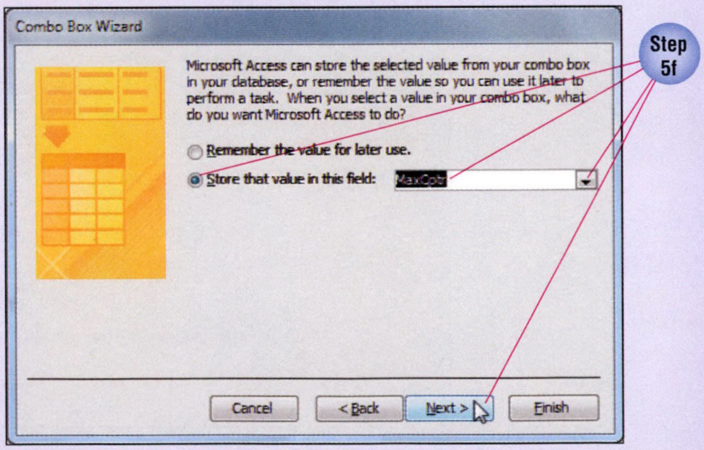

Combo Box Wizard
Microsoft Access can store the selected value from your combo box in your database, or remember the value so you can use it later to perform a task. When you select a value in your combo box, what do you want Microsoft Access to do?
Remember the value for later use.
Store that value in this field:
MaxCptr
Cancel
< Back
Next >
Finish
Step 5f

   g. At the last Combo Box Wizard dialog box, with the current text already selected in the *What label would you like for your list box?*, type **CptrList** and then click Finish. Access adds the combo box to the form displaying a value and a drop-down arrow at the right end of the text box.

6. Double-click the label for the combo box added in Step 5 (currently reads *CptrList*) and then type **Maximum Computers**. Edit the label for the list box added in Step 4 (currently reads *PlanList*) to add a space between *Plan* and *List*.
7. Right-click the label control object above the combo box that displays the text *Max No. of Computers* and then click *Select Entire Row* at the shortcut menu. Press Delete to remove the selected row from the form.
8. Click the Title button in the Header/Footer group of the Form Layout Tools Design tab and then type the title text **Service Contract Plans**.
9. Save the form and name it *SCPlans*.
10. Switch to Form view and scroll through the records in the form.
11. Add a new form to the table by completing the following steps:
    a. Click the New button in the Records group in the Home tab.
    b. Press Tab to move past the *ID* field since this field is an AutoNumber field.
    c. Click the down-pointing arrow at the *Term* field and then click *2 years* at the drop-down list.
    d. Click *C* in the *Plan List* list box that displays below *Plan*. Notice that *C* is entered into the *Plan* field text box control object when you click the letter *C* in the list box.
    e. Click the down-pointing arrow at the *Maximum Computers* field combo list box and then click *3* at the drop-down list.
    f. Click in the *Rate* text box and then type **236.50**.

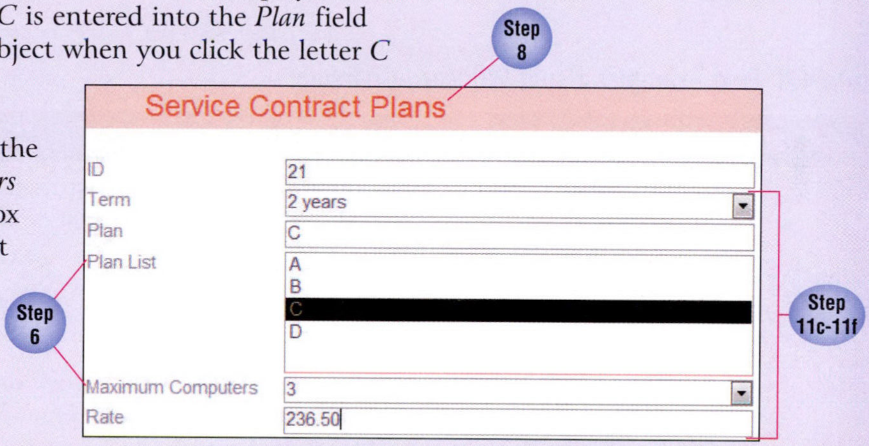

12. Print the selected record and then close the form.

Project 5 Sort and Find Records within a Form — 1 Part

You will open a custom-built form and use the form to sort and find records using a wildcard character and by searching backwards by date.

Sorting and Finding Records in Forms

One of the advantages to using a form for data entry and maintenance is that the form displays a single record at a time within the work area. This prevents distractions from viewing records other than the one on which you need to focus at the moment, reducing the likelihood of editing the wrong record. In a table with many records, quickly finding the specific record that you need to maintain or view is important. Use the Sort and Find features to move to the desired record quickly.

The Find feature allows you to search for records without specifying the entire field value. To do this, you substitute wildcard characters in the position(s) where you do not want to specify the exact text. Two commonly used wildcard characters are the asterisk (*) and the question mark (?). For example, you may want to search for a record by a person's last name but you are not sure of the correct spelling. The asterisk wildcard character is used in a position where there may be one or more characters that can vary. The question mark wildcard character is used in a fixed-width word where you want to view all records with the same number of characters in the field. In this case, substitute one question mark for each character not specified. Table 4.1 provides examples of the usage of the asterisk and question mark wildcard characters.

In Project 4, you will use the asterisk wildcard character to locate customer records for a specified street.

Quick Steps

Find Records Using Wildcard

1. Open form in Form view.
2. Click in field by which to search.
3. Click Find button.
4. Type search string including an asterisk for any variable text.
5. Click Find Next.
6. Continue clicking Find Next until search is finished.
7. Click OK.
8. Close Find and Replace dialog box.

Ascending

Find

Descending

Table 4.1 Find Examples Using Wildcard Characters

Find What Entry	*In This Field*	*Will Find*
104?	Customer ID	Customer records with a customer ID that begins with 104 and has one more character such as 1041, 1042, 1043 and so on up to 1049.
4820?	ZIP Code	Customer records with a zip code that begins with 4820 and has one more character such as 48201, 48202, and so on.
650??	Work Order	Work order records with a work order number that begins with 650 and has two more characters such as 65023, 65035, 65055 and so on.
313*	Home Phone	Customer records with a telephone number that begins with the 313 area code.
Peter*	Last Name	Customer records with a last name that begins with Peter and has any number of characters following such as Peters, Peterson, Petersen, Peterovski.
4820*	ZIP Code	Customer records with a zip code that begins with 4820 and has any number of characters after such as 48201 or 48203-4841.
oak	Street Address	Customer records with any street address that has oak in the middle such as 1755 Oak Drive, 12-234 Oak Street, or 9 Oak Boulevard.

Project 5 Sorting and Finding Records in a Form

Part 1 of 1

1. With the **AL2-C4-RSRCompServ.accdb** database open, open the CustMaintenance form in Form view.
2. Click in the *Last Name* field to place an insertion point in the field and then click the Ascending button in the Sort & Filter group in the Home tab. The records are now arranged in alphabetic order by the customer's last name in ascending order. Scroll through a few records in the form watching the last names to confirm the new sorted order.

3. Assume that you now need to locate the name of the customer that resides on Roselawn Street. You do not know the exact house number or the customer's name. Complete the following steps to find the record using a wildcard character in the criterion:
   a. Click the First Record button in the Record Navigation bar to return to record 1 and then click the insertion point in the *Street Address* field to activate the field by which you want to search records.
   b. Click the Find button in the Find group.
   c. With the insertion point positioned in the *Find What* text box, type ***roselawn*** and then click the Find Next button. Access displays the first record in the form in which a match was made. The entry **roselawn** means "Find any record in which any number of characters before roselawn and any number of characters after roselawn exist in the active field."

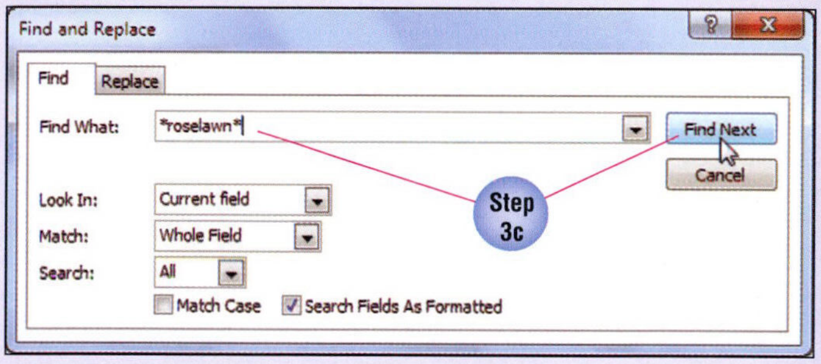

   d. Click the Find Next button a second time to see if any other records exist for customers on Roselawn Street.
   e. At the Microsoft Access message box indicating that Access has finished searching records, click OK.
   f. Close the Find and Replace dialog box.
4. Close the CustMaintenance form.
5. Open the WorkOrders form in Form view.
6. Click in the *Service Date* field and then click the Descending button in the Sort & Filter group to sort the records from the most recent service date to the oldest service date. Scroll through a few records in the form watching the service dates to confirm the new sorted order.
7. Find the records for work orders completed on October 19, 2012 by completing the following steps:
   a. Click the First Record button in the Record Navigation bar to return to record 1 and then click the Find button with the insertion point still active in the *Service Date* field.

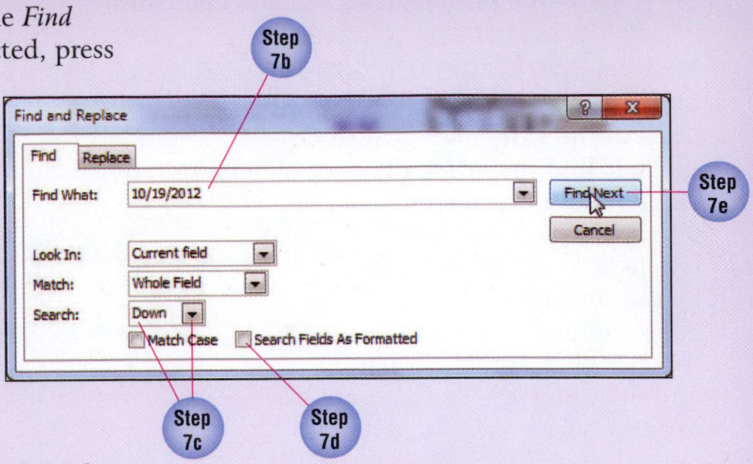

b. With the existing text in the *Find What* text box already selected, press Delete to remove the entry and then type **10/19/2012**.
c. Click the down-pointing arrow next to the *Search* list box and click *Down* at the drop-down list. Since the records are arranged in descending order, you need Access to search in a downward direction.
d. Click the *Search Fields As Formatted* check box to clear the check mark. Since the date entered in the *Find What* text box does not match the date format in the *Service Date* field, this check box must be cleared or Access will not match any records.
e. Click the Find Next button. Access moves to the first record for the specified date (Work Order 65039). If necessary, drag the Find and Replace dialog box down towards the bottom of the work area so that you can view the record details.
f. Click the Find Next button. Access moves to the next record (Work Order 65038).
g. Click the Find Next button. Access moves to the next record (Work Order 65037).
h. Click the Find Next button. At the Microsoft Access message box indicating Access has finished searching records, click OK.
i. Close the Find and Replace dialog box.

8. Close the WorkOrders form.
9. Close the **AL2-C4-RSRCompServ.accdb** database.

Remove Sort

Once a form has been sorted, Access displays the records in the sorted order whenever you open the form. To remove a sort and have the order revert to the order of the primary key, open the form in Form view and then click the Remove Sort (displays the ScreenTip *Clear All Sorts*) button in the Sort & Filter group in the Home tab. Access clears the sort order and the table's records are rearranged in ascending order by the primary key field value.

In this chapter you have learned techniques for building a custom form using Design view. As you learned in Project 2, you can create a form using one of the form tools such as the Form Wizard and then make changes to the form in Design view. As you become more experienced with Access, you will likely use a combination of three methods to build custom forms: a form tool to build the basic table and field structure of the form; Layout view to apply formatting options, add a title and logo, and make other appearance changes; and Design view to add advanced control objects such as tab controls, subforms, and calculations.

Chapter Summary

- A new form in Design view initially displays only the *Detail* section, which is the section in which fields are placed to display record data.
- A *Form Header* and *Form Footer* section can be added to the form. Objects placed in the Form Header display at the top of the form or print at the beginning of a printout of records from Form view. Objects placed in the *Form Footer* section display at the bottom of the form or print at the end of the printout of records from Form view.
- A form can contain three types of control objects: bound, unbound, and calculated.
- Click the Title button to display the *Form Header* and *Form Footer* sections and add a label control object in the Form Header that contains the form name.
- Click the Label button in the Controls group to add a label control object containing unbound text to any section within the form.
- Double-click the Form Selector button in Design view to open the form's Property Sheet and specify the table to be bound to the form in the Record Source property.
- Once a table has been associated with a form, click the Add Existing Fields button to open the Field List pane.
- Drag individual field names or a group of selected field names from the Field List pane to the *Detail* section in the form to add fields to the form.
- Use the move handle (large dark gray square at top left of selected control) to move a selected object independently of the control's associated label control or text box control.
- Use buttons in the Font group in the Form Design Tools Format tab to apply formatting options to selected controls.
- Multiple control objects can be selected in Design view by drawing a selection rectangle around a group of adjacent control objects or by holding down the Shift key while clicking controls.
- Open the Tab Order dialog box to change the order in which fields are selected as you press Tab to move from field to field in Form view.
- A tab control object in a form allows you to organize groups of related fields in pages.
- Click the Subform/Subreport button in the controls group to create a subform in a page within a tab control object.
- Create a calculated control object in a form using the Text Box button in the Controls group.
- Type a formula in the text box control object (displays *Unbound*) beginning with an equals sign (=). Field names within the formula are encased in square brackets.
- Use the Size/Space and Align buttons in the Sizing & Ordering group in the Form Design Tools Arrange tab to resize, align, or adjust spacing between multiple selected control objects.
- Images can be added to a form in Design view using the Logo button in the Header/Footer group or the Insert Image button in the Controls group.

- Draw a horizontal or vertical line in a form using the Line button in the Controls group. Hold down the Shift key while dragging to draw a straight line.
- Use the Shape Outline button in the Form Design Tools Format tab to adjust a line's thickness, type, or color.
- Clip art images can be copied to the clipboard from another Microsoft Office program such as Microsoft Word and then pasted to a form in Design view.
- Change a control object's Size Mode property if a clip art image has become truncated after resizing to *Zoom* or *Stretch*.
- A control object can be anchored to a position in a form so that the object's position relative to the edges of the form is maintained when the form is resized.
- A datasheet form is a form that looks like a table datasheet.
- Modify properties in the Data tab of a form's Property Sheet to restrict the actions a user can perform when viewing records in Form view.
- The Blank Form tool in the Forms group of the Create tab creates a new form with no controls or format applied. The form opens as a blank white page in Layout view with the Field List pane opened at the right of the work area.
- A list box control object displays all of the list values inside a rectangular-shaped control object in the form. Field values can be added to the list within the List Box Wizard by typing the values or by selecting a field from a table or query.
- A combo box control object displays a text box as well as a down-pointing arrow to a drop-down list of field values. The end user can type the field value into the text box or click the down-pointing arrow to pick the field value from a list. Field values are added within the Combo Box Wizard by typing the values or by selecting a field from a table or query.
- Sort a form in Form view by clicking in the field by which to sort records and then clicking the Ascending button or the Descending button.
- Click in a field by which to search records in Form view, click the Find button, and then enter the search criterion in the *Find What* text box. Typing an asterisk or question mark in the criterion allows you to search records using a wildcard character inserted for variable data.

Commands Review

FEATURE	RIBBON TAB, GROUP	BUTTON	KEYBOARD SHORTCUT
Add existing fields	Form Design Tools Design, Tools		
Adjust size of multiple controls	Form Design Tools Arrange, Sizing & Ordering		
Align multiple controls at same position	Form Design Tools Arrange, Sizing & Ordering		
Anchor controls to form	Form Design Tools Arrange, Position		
Blank Form	Create, Forms		
Change tab order of fields	Form Design Tools Design, Tools		
Combo Box control object	Form Layout Tools Design, Controls		
Create datasheet form	Create, Forms		
Design view	Home, Views		
Equal spacing between controls	Form Design Tools Arrange, Sizing & Ordering		
Find	Home, Find		Ctrl + F
Form view	Form Design Tools Design, Views		
Insert Image	Form Design Tools Design, Controls		
Label control object	Form Design Tools Design, Controls		
List Box control object	Form Layout Tools Design, Controls		
Line	Form Design Tools Design, Controls		
Property Sheet	Form Design Tools Design, Tools		
Sort ascending order	Home, Sort & Filter		
Sort descending order	Home, Sort & Filter		
Subform	Form Design Tools Design, Controls		
Tab control object	Form Design Tools Design, Controls		
Text box control object	Form Design Tools Design, Controls		
Title	Form Design Tools Design, Header/Footer		

Concepts Check Test Your Knowledge

Completion: In the space provided at the right, indicate the correct term, command, or number.

1. A new form in Design view initially displays only this section in the form. ________________
2. These are the three types of control objects found in a form. ________________
3. Use this button from the Controls group to create an object in the *Form Footer* section in which to display a form's version number. ________________
4. Before you can add fields to the table you must first connect a table to the form in this property box in the form's Property Sheet. ________________
5. The large dark gray handle at the top left of a selected control is referred to by this name. ________________
6. Hold down this key while clicking controls to select multiple control objects to be formatted. ________________
7. Open this dialog box to change the order in which fields are selected when the Tab key is pressed in Form view. ________________
8. Add this object to the bottom of a form to display subforms in individual pages. ________________
9. Make sure this feature is active in the Controls group before clicking the Subform/Subreport button so that the Subform Wizard is available. ________________
10. Click this button in the Controls group to add a calculation to a form. ________________
11. The *Equal Vertical* option is located on this button's drop-down list in the Form Design Tools Arrange tab. ________________
12. Change this property for a control object containing a clip art image to *Zoom* to proportionately adjust the image to the resized object's height and width. ________________
13. The *Datasheet* form is available from this button's drop-down list in the Forms group in the Create tab. ________________
14. Click this tab in a form's Property Sheet to locate the *Allow Deletions* property box. ________________
15. This form tool opens as a blank white page in Layout view. ________________
16. These two controls are used to add list boxes to a form. ________________

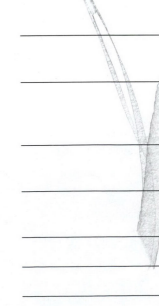

17. Type this entry in the *Find What* text box to search for all records in the active field that begin with the zip code 48221 and have any four-character extension. ____________________

Skills Check Assess Your Performance

Assessment

1 CREATE A CUSTOM FORM USING DESIGN VIEW

1. Open the database named **AL2-C4-VantageVideos.accdb** and enable content.
2. Create a query named **CustWebOrders** using the following specifications:
   a. Add the WebOrderDetails, WebOrders, and WebProducts tables to the query.
   b. Add the following fields in order:

WebOrders Table	WebOrderDetails Table	WebProducts Table
WebOrdID	*Qty*	*Product*
CustID		*SellPrice*
DateOrd		

   c. Run the query and then close the query results datasheet.
3. Create a new form using Design view and build the form using the following specifications:
   a. Expand the width of the form in the grid to the 6.5-inch position in the horizontal ruler.
   b. Add a title in the *Form Header* section with the text *Web Customer Orders*. Use the move handle that displays at the top and left of the selected title control to move the title until the first letter in the title text (W) is at approximately the 1.5-inch position in the horizontal ruler.
   c. Add your name in a label control object centered in the *Form Footer* section.
   d. Apply the Flow theme.
   e. Connect the WebCustomers table to the form and add all of the fields to the *Detail* section in the layout shown in Figure 4.14. Adjust the width of the control objects as shown. Remember to use the Size/Space and Align buttons to help you position multiple controls at the same horizontal or vertical position and adjust spacing between controls.

Figure 4.14 Assessment 1

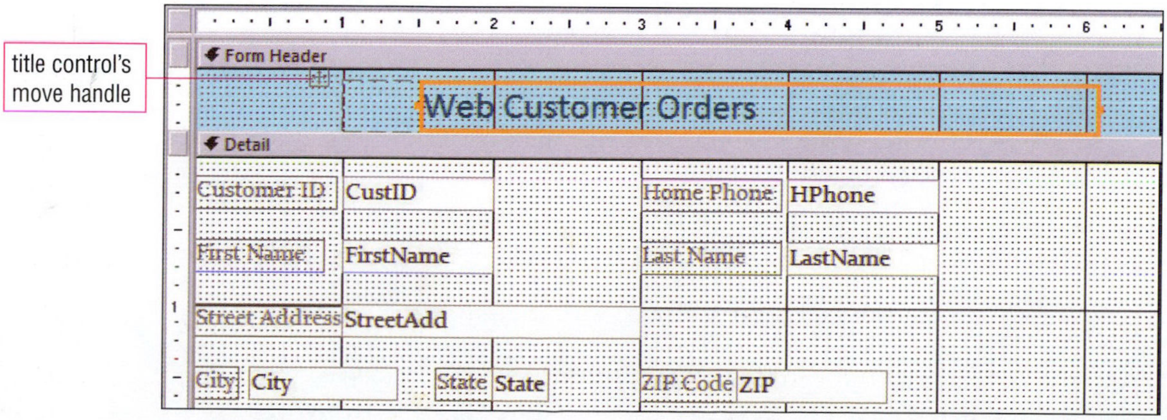

f. Change the tab order of the fields so that the *HPhone* field is selected after *CustID*.
g. Add a tab control object below the existing fields that is approximately two inches in height and with the width extended to the right edge of the form.
   1) On the first page, change the caption to *Web Orders* and add all fields from the CustWebOrders query in a subform. Delete the subform label control object. Delete the label control object and the text box control object for the CustID field in the subform and then move the remaining fields up to fill in the space. Move and resize the subform to fit the width of the page. Adjust column widths in Form view as needed to view all columns within the page.
   2) On the second page, change the caption to *Payment Information* and add all fields except *EmailAdd* from the WebCustPymnt table in a subform. Delete the subform label control object and move and resize the subform to fit the width of the page. Adjust column widths in Form view as needed.

4. Make any formatting changes you think would improve the appearance of the form.
5. Save the form and name it *WebCustOrders*.
6. Print the form in Form view with the first record displayed and the Web Orders page active.
7. Close the form.

Assessment 2

CREATE A FORM USING THE FORM WIZARD; ADD A CALCULATION AND GRAPHICS

1. With the **AL2-C4-VantageVideos.accdb** database open, create a new form using the Form Wizard as follows:
   a. Select all fields from the WebProducts table.
   b. Select the *Columnar* style.
   c. Accept the default form name *WebProducts*.
2. View the completed form in Form view.
3. Switch to Design view and edit the form to resemble the form shown in Figure 4.15 using the following additional information:
   a. Apply the Solstice theme.
   b. *Retail Value* is a calculated field that uses a formula to multiply the quantity of videos that are in stock times the selling price.
   c. The clip art image can be found by searching using the keyword *Movies*. Choose a suitable alternative image if the image shown is not available on the computer you are using.
   d. The font color for the title text and the lines is *Maroon 5* in the *Standard Colors* section of the color palette.
   e. Use your best judgment for other formatting options to match as closely as possible the form shown in Figure 4.15.
4. Print the form in Form view with the first record displayed.
5. Save and close the form.

Figure 4.15 Assessment 2

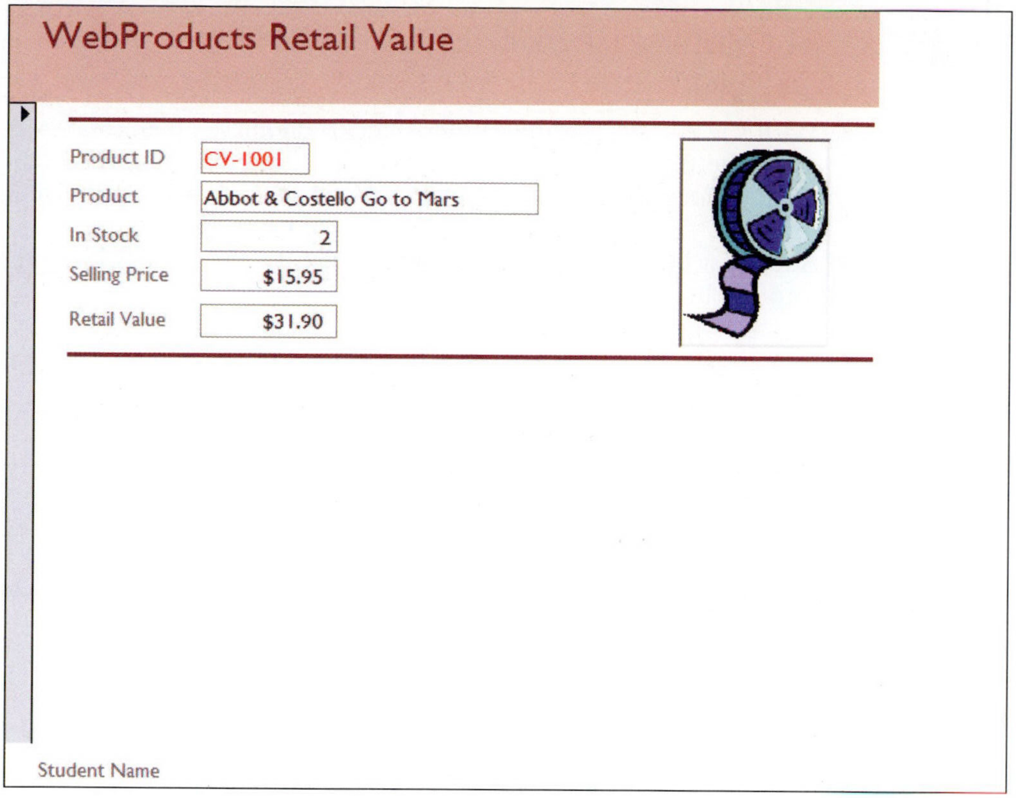

Assessment 3

CREATE A RESTRICTED-USE FORM

1. With the **AL2-C4-VantageVideos.accdb** database open, create a datasheet form using the WebCustPymnt table.
2. Modify the form so that records cannot be deleted when using the form.
3. Display the form in Datasheet view with the Home tab active and a record selected.
4. Use the PrintScreen key or the Windows Snipping tool to capture an image of the screen with the Delete button dimmed while the record is selected.
5. Paste the screen image into a blank Word document. Type your name, the chapter number and assessment number and any other identification information required by your instructor above or below the screen image.
6. Print the document.
7. Save the Word document and name it **AL2-C4-VantageVideosForm.**
8. Exit Word.
9. Save the form using the default form name *WebCustPymnt* and then close the form.

Assessment

4 CREATE A CUSTOM FORM USING THE BLANK FORM TOOL; ADD A LIST BOX

1. With the **AL2-C4-VantageVideos.accdb** database open, create a new form using the Blank Form tool that adds all of the fields from the WebCustomers table. Widen the labels column so that all of the label text is visible in the form.
2. Add a list box control object between the *City* and *State* fields. Type the values into the list as follows:

   Burlington
   Charlotte
   Colchester

   Store the values in the field named *City* and accept the default label for the control object at the last List Box Wizard dialog box.
3. Delete the label control object for the list box.
4. Add a title to the form with the text *Customer Maintenance Form*.
5. Save the form and name it *WebCustomerMaintenance*.
6. Switch to Form view and add the following new record to the WebCustomers table:

Customer ID	**121**
First Name	**Morgan**
Last Name	**Kalil**
Street Address	**29011 Greenbush Road**
City	Click *Charlotte* in the list box
State	Accept default value of *VT*
ZIP Code	**05445-9314**
Home Phone	**802-555-9185**

7. Print the selected record and then close the form.
8. Close the **AL2-C4-VantageVideos.accdb** database.

Visual Benchmark Demonstrate Your Proficiency

CREATE CUSTOM RESERVATIONS FORM

1. Open **AL2-C4-PawsParadise.accdb**.
2. Review the form shown in Figure 4.16 and Figure 4.17. This form was created from scratch in Design view. Create the form using your best judgment for alignment, spacing, sizing, and position of controls as well as the following information:
   a. Connect the Reservations table to the main form.
   b. Apply the Slipstream theme.
   c. The line color is *Dark Blue* and the thickness is *3 pt*.
   d. The Days Boarded value is calculated by subtracting the two date fields.
   e. Each subform's Default View property (Format tab) was changed from Datasheet to *Single Form*. This view displays the fields one below the other instead of in a tabular arrangement. ***Hint: Create the subform by including the linked common field in the wizard dialog box so that the correct relationship between the main form and the subform is established. You can then delete extra controls while editing the subform object.***
3. Save the form naming it *Reservations*.
4. Display the form in Form view and then print the first record only.
5. Close the form and then close the **AL2-C4-PawsParadise.accdb** database.

Figure 4.16 Visual Benchmark Custom Form with Dog Information Tab Displayed

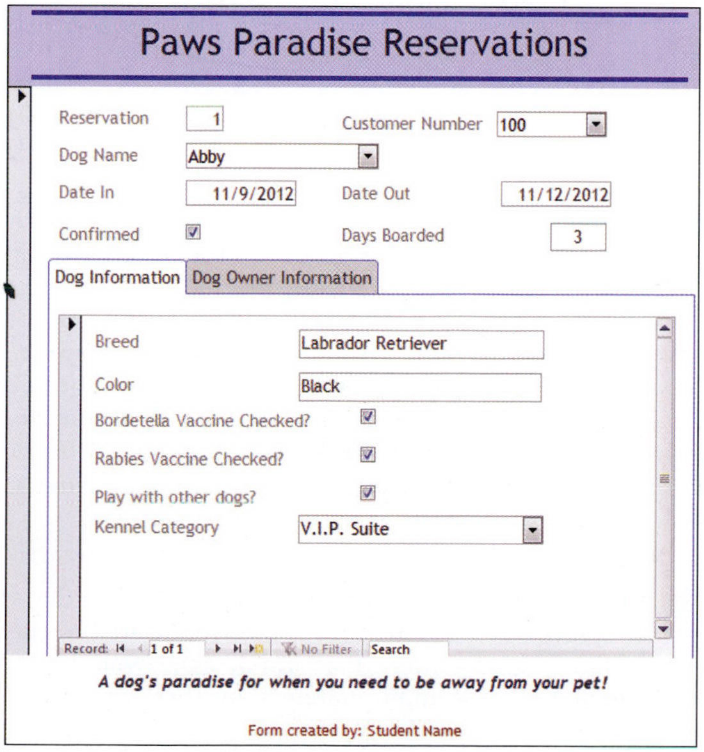

Figure 4.17 Visual Benchmark Custom Form with Dog Owner Information Tab Displayed

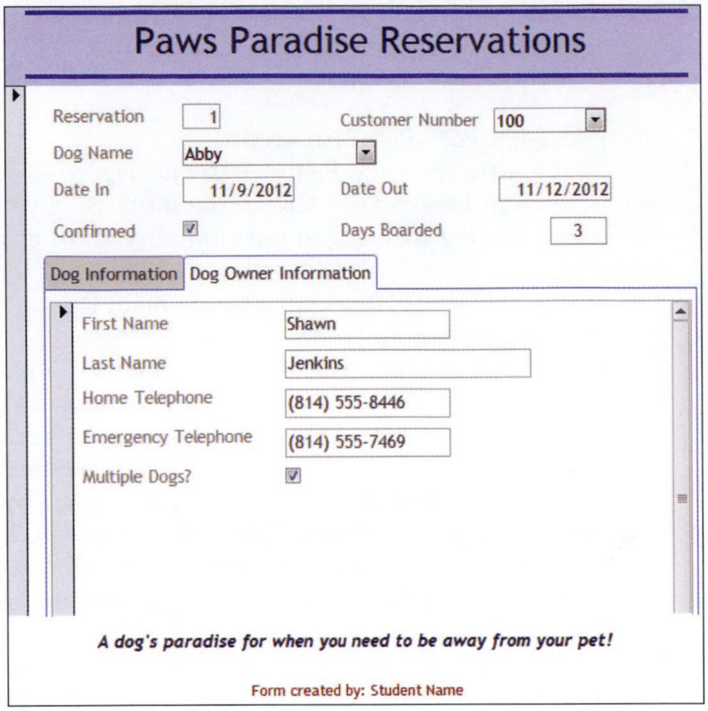

Case Study Apply Your Skills

Part 1

You are continuing your work as an intern with Hillsdale Realty. The office manager has requested that you create a form for easier data entry and maintenance of the listings and sales information. Open the database named **AL2-C4-HillsdaleRealty.accdb** and enable content. Design and create the form similar to the one shown in Figure 4.18 using the Listings and SalesAndComm tables. Apply the Hardcover theme. Include the calculated field at the bottom of the subform. Modify the tab order of the fields to match the arrangement of the fields in Figure 4.18. ***Hints: Change the default view for the subform to Single Form and add a calculated control in the subform control object that multiplies the sale price times the commission rate. Search for the clip art image using the keywords "for sale"; choose another suitable image if the one shown is not available on the computer you are using.*** Save the form and name it appropriately. Print the first record in the form.

Part 2

The office manager would like another form created that displays the information from the Agents table along with the clients related to each agent. Design and create a form. You determine the form design, layout, and formatting options. Save the form and name it appropriately. Print the form with the first record displayed in the main form.

Figure 4.18 Case Study Part 1 Form

Part 3

Open the main form created in Part 1. While viewing the form you realize that the Record Navigation bar at the bottom of the subform is not needed since a listing would only have one sale record. Remove the Record Navigation bar in the subform by opening the subform's Property sheet. At the Format tab, change the Navigation Buttons property to *No*. Close the Property sheet and then display the form in Form view. Notice the subform no longer displays a Record Navigation bar. Save the revised form. Capture a screen image of the revised form using the PrintScreen key or the Windows Snipping tool. Paste the screen image into a new Word document screen. Type your name, the chapter number, and any other identifying information required by your instructor above or below the screen image. Print the Word document. Save the Word document naming it **AL2-C4-CS-P3-HillsdaleRealty** and then exit Word.

UNIT 1

Microsoft® Access® Performance Assessment

Access

Access2010L2U1

Note: The Student Resources CD does not include an Access Level 2, Unit 1 subfolder of files because no data files are required for the Unit 1 assessments. You will create all of the files yourself. Before beginning the assessments, create a folder called Access2010L2U1 for the new files.

Assessing Proficiency

In this unit you have learned to design advanced tables that incorporate best practices in database design. You have created tables with multiple-field primary keys, multiple-value fields, attachment fields, and lookup fields to retrieve data from another table. You have learned to modify the join type in a relationship to achieve various query results and understand the concept of normalization as it applies to table design. You have created select queries, parameter queries, and action queries. Finally, you learned how to build a custom form using Design view that includes calculations, multiple pages, and subforms.

Assessment 1 Create Tables for a Property Management Database

1. Create a new database named **AL2-U1-BenchmarkPropMgt.accdb**.
2. Create the tables shown in Figure U1.1 to store residential building management and tenant information including setting the primary key and assigning data types and field sizes. Leave field sizes at the default setting for those fields that do not have a field size specified in Figure U1.1.
3. Close any tables that have been left open.

Figure U1.1 Assessment 1

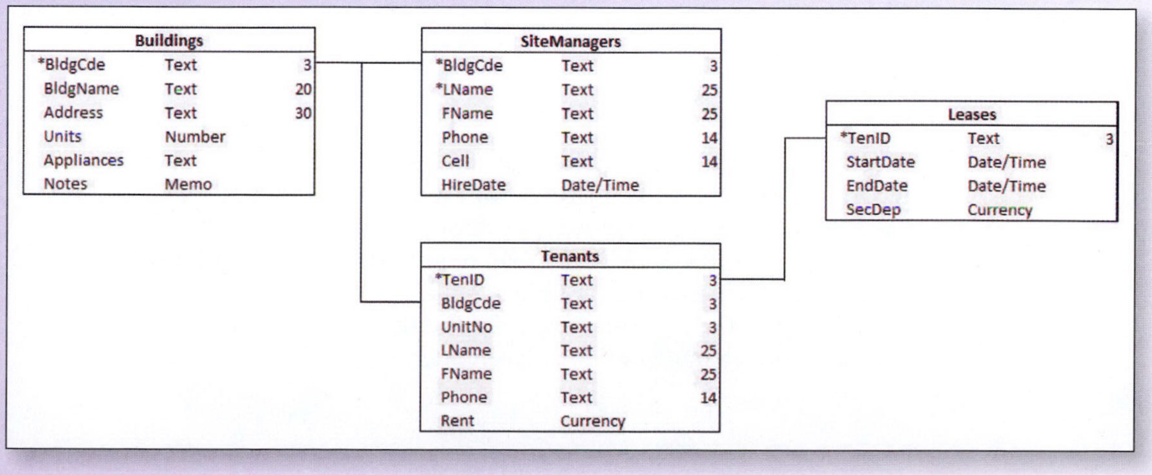

4. Open the Access Options dialog box and click the *Compact on Close* check box with the Current Database pane active to make sure the file size is optimized each time you close the database. Click OK at the message you must close and reopen the current database for the option to take effect.
5. Close **AL2-U1-BenchmarkPropMgt.accdb**.

Assessment 2 Add Captions and Modify Field Properties

1. Open the **AL2-U1-BenchmarkPropMgt.accdb** database and then create captions for the fields as follows:

Buildings Table

Field Name	Caption
BldgCde	Bldg Code
BldgName	Name

Leases Table

Field Name	Caption
TenID	Tenant ID
StartDate	Start Date
EndDate	End Date
SecDep	Security Deposit

SiteManagers Table

Field Name	Caption
BldgCde	Bldg Code
LName	Last Name
FName	First Name
Phone	Telephone
Cell	Cell Phone
HireDate	Hire Date

Tenants Table

Field Name	Caption
TenID	Tenant ID
BldgCde	Bldg Code
UnitNo	Unit No
LName	Last Name
FName	First Name
Phone	Telephone

2. Make *UnitNo* in the Tenants table a required field including disallowing zero-length strings.
3. Create a custom format for all date fields that displays dates in the short date format with leading zeroes for months and days. Use a slash to separate each section in the date, for example, *01/05/2012*.
4. Create the following custom input masks:
   a. In *BldgCde* in the Buildings table, require three digits and display the underscore character as the placeholder.
   b. In *TenID* in the Tenants table, require three digits and display the underscore character as the placeholder.

c. In all of the date fields, create an input mask that will require dates to be entered using the short date format created in Step 3 with all digits required. ***Hints: You can use the Input Mask Wizard to create the first input mask and then modify the code created by the wizard to change optional digits to required digits. Next, copy and paste the input mask codes to the other two date fields.***
d. Require all telephone numbers to include the area code with hyphens between each section of the number. Display the pound symbol (#) as the placeholder character. (Apply the same Hints for this step as provided for Step 4c.)

5. Enable rich text formatting in the *Notes* field in the Buildings table.
6. Make *995.00* the default value in the *Rent* field in the Tenants table.
7. Save and then close all tables.

Assessment 3 Add Records

1. With the **AL2-U1-BenchmarkPropMgt.accdb** database open, add the following records:

Buildings Table

Field	Record 1	Record 2	Record 3
Bldg Code	115	120	125
Name	Coventry Park	Mornington Place	Bayview Towers
Address	33 Westview Road	1100 Forrester Lane	12 Lakeview Circle
Units	38	60	110
Appliances	(leave blank)	(leave blank)	(leave blank)
Notes	New roof in 2010	Furnace and air conditioning units under warranty until 2015	Parking lot resurfaced in 2009

Leases Table

Field	Record 1	Record 2	Record 3
Tenant ID	101	102	103
Start Date	01 01 2012	02 01 2012	02 01 2012
End Date	12 31 2012	01 31 2013	01 31 2013
Security Deposit	995	995	1125

SiteManagers Table

Field	Record 1	Record 2	Record 3
Bldg Code	115	120	125
Last Name	Jenkins	Hernandez	Doxtator
First Name	Blair	Maria	Cody
Telephone	800 555 3485	800 555 8675	800 555 9677
Cell Phone	800 555 3748	800 555 3996	800 555 7795
Hire Date	02 08 2009	04 23 2010	09 15 2010

Tenants Table

Field	Record 1	Record 2	Record 3
Tenant ID	101	102	103
Bldg Code	115	115	115
Unit No	110	215	320
Last Name	Chen	Ayoub	Reiser
First Name	Wei	Mona	Helena
Telephone	519 555 8776	519 555 2286	519 555 7668
Rent	995	995	1125

2. Apply bold and red font color to the years entered in the *Notes* field in each record.
3. For each table, adjust column widths until all data is entirely visible and print the table, adjusting print options as necessary to fit the table on one page.
4. Save and then close all tables.

Assessment 4 Create Lookup Lists and Edit Relationships

1. With the **AL2-U1-BenchmarkPropMgt.accdb** database open, create the following lookup lists to display values from another table:
   a. In the SiteManagers table, create a lookup list for *BldgCde* that displays the building codes and names from the Buildings table. Sort the list by the building names and show the key column. Widen the column displaying the building names to accommodate longer names that may be added to the table in the future. Store the *BldgCde* value in the field.
   b. In the Tenants table, create a lookup list for *BldgCde* using the same specifications as Step 1a.
   c. In the Leases table, create a lookup list for *TenID* that displays the tenant IDs, first names, and last names from the Tenants table. Sort the list by the last names and show the key column. Store the *TenID* value in the field.
2. Create a multiple-value drop-down list for the *Appliances* field in the Buildings table with the following items.

   Refrigerator
   Stove
   Microwave
   Dishwasher
   Washer
   Dryer

3. Edit the three records to populate the *Appliances* field as follows:

Bldg Code	*Appliances*
115	Refrigerator, Stove, Microwave
120	Refrigerator, Stove, Microwave, Dishwasher
125	Refrigerator, Stove, Washer, Dryer

4. Adjust the field width of the *Appliances* column to Best Fit, change the field width of the *Notes* column to 35 and the row height to 30, and then print the Buildings table in landscape orientation with left and right margins set to 0.25 inch.
5. Close the Buildings table, saving changes to the table layout.
6. Open the Relationships window. Edit all relationships to turn on referential integrity and the two cascade options.
7. Arrange the table field list boxes in the window to show the relationships with the primary tables on the left and the related tables on the right. Make sure no join lines are overlapping each other so that each relationship is easily distinguished from others. Create, save, and print a relationships report using the default report name.
8. Close the relationship report window and the relationships window.

Assessment 5 Create Select Queries

1. With the **AL2-U1-BenchmarkPropMgt.accdb** database open, design and create the following select queries:
   a. A query named *PromptedTenant* that displays the *BldgCde* and *BldgName* fields from the Buildings table and the *UnitNo*, *FName*, *LName*, and *Phone* fields from the Tenants table. Include prompts to specify the building name and the unit number criteria when the query is run.
   b. A query named *PromptedLease* that displays the *TenID* from the Tenants table, the *BldgName* from the Buildings table, the *UnitNo*, *FName*, and *LName* fields from the Tenants table, and the *StartDate*, *EndDate*, and *SecDep* fields from the Leases table. Include prompts to specify the starting date and ending date criteria when the query is run.
   c. A query named *TenantsList* that displays the *BldgCde* and *BldgName* fields from the Buildings table and the *UnitNo*, *FName*, *LName* and *Rent* fields from the Tenants table. Sort in ascending order by the building names. Modify the join properties to show all records from the Buildings table in a left outer join.
   d. A query named *BuildingsList* that displays all of the fields in the Buildings table except the *Notes* field. Show each entry in the multiple-value *Appliances* field in a separate row in the query results datasheet and assign the field the caption *Supplied Appliances*.
2. Run the PromptedTenant query. Type **coventry park** when prompted for the building name and **110** when prompted for the unit number. Print the query results datasheet and then close the query.
3. Run the PromptedLease query. Type **02/01/2012** when prompted for the starting date and **01/31/2013** when prompted for the ending date. Print the query results datasheet in landscape orientation and then close the query.
4. Run the TenantsList query, print the query results datasheet, and then close the query.
5. Run the BuildingsList query, print the query results datasheet, and then close the query.

Assessment 6 Calculate in a Query and Use an Update Query to Increase Rents

1. With the **AL2-U1-BenchmarkPropMgt.accdb** database open, create a query to calculate the total rental income from each unit as follows:
   a. Open the TenantsList query in Design view and use Save Object As to name the query *RentalIncome*.
   b. Modify the join properties to show records only when the joined fields are equal in both tables using an inner join.
   c. Add a calculated field to the query with the column heading *Annual Rent* that calculates twelve months of rental income.
   d. Run the query and add a total row in the query results datasheet with a sum function in the *Rent* and *Annual Rent* columns.
   e. Print the query results datasheet in landscape orientation and then close the query saving changes.
2. Create an update query named *RentIncrease* to increase all rents by 4%. Run the query.
3. Close the RentIncrease query.
4. Open the RentalIncome query, print the query results datasheet in landscape orientation, and then close the query.

Assessment 7 Design and Create Forms

1. With the **AL2-U1-BenchmarkPropMgt.accdb** database open, design and create a form to enter data into the Buildings table as a main form with the SiteManagers table in a subform. Name the main form *BldgsAndMgrs*. You determine the form design, layout, and formatting options. Include an appropriate clip art image in the form. Add your name in the *Form Footer* section. Print the first record in the Buildings table displayed in Form view.
2. Design and create a form to enter data into the Tenants table as a main form with the Leases table in a subform similar to the one shown in Figure U1.2. Name the form *TenantsAndLeases*. Modify the tab order to move in the order *Tenant ID*, *Bldg Code*, *Unit No*, *Telephone*, *First Name*, *Last Name* and *Rent*. *Annual Rent* is a calculated control. Use your best judgment to match the color formatting as closely as possible within the theme colors. Add labels and graphics as shown. Note that the subform does not show a Record Navigation bar. Refer to Case Study Part 3 on page 149 in Chapter 4 if you need help turning off the bar.
3. Print all records using the TenantsAndLeases form and then close the form saving changes.
4. Close the **AL2-U1-BenchmarkPropMgt.accdb** database.

Figure U1.2 Assessment 7, Step 2

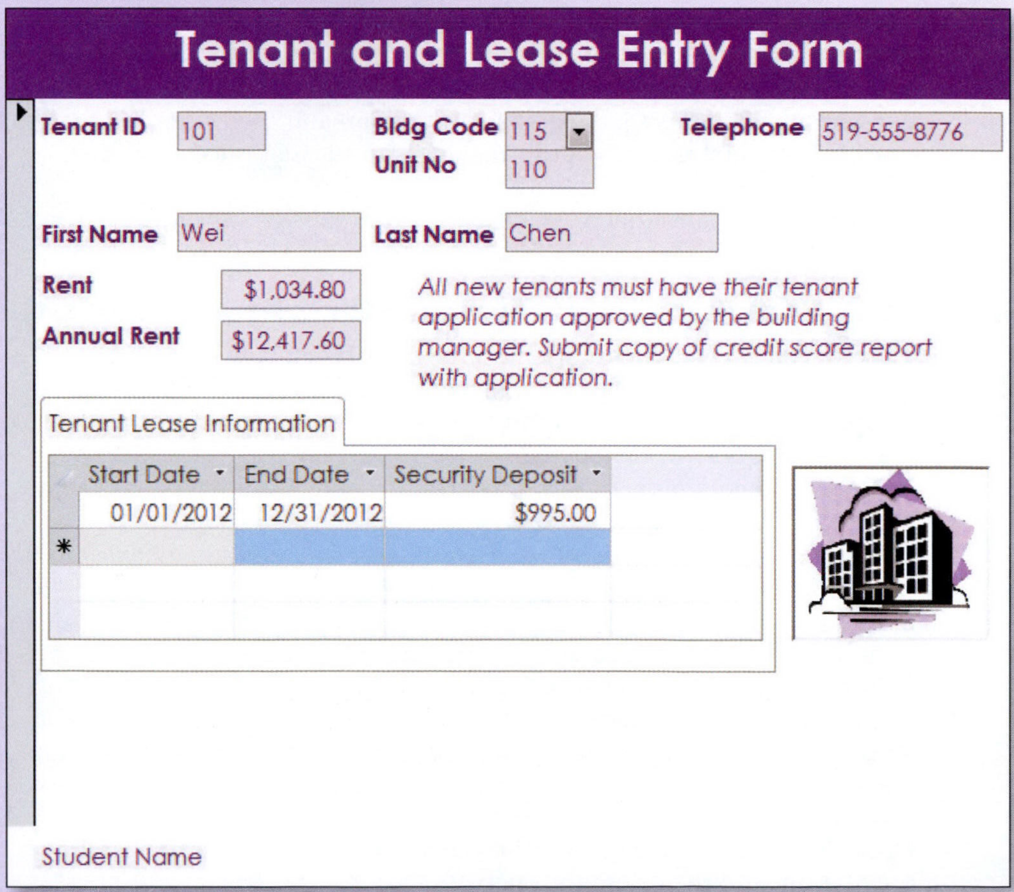

Writing Activities

The following activities give you the opportunity to practice your writing skills along with demonstrating an understanding of some of the important Access features you have mastered in this unit. Use correct grammar, appropriate word choices, and clear sentence constructions when required.

Activity 1 Design Tables for Parking Information in the Property Management Database

The office manager at Benchmark Property Management would like to add tables to the **AL2-U1-BenchmarkPropMgt.accdb** database to store information about assigned parking at each of the buildings. Design and create a table to store parking rates and another table to track rental information for each parking spot using the information provided below. Create two lookup lists in the assigned parking table, one to look up the correct parking rate in the rates table and another to look up the tenant's ID in the Tenants table. Add at least three records to test your tables.

Use the following information to assist you with the table design:

Parking Rates

- Coventry Park charges $30 per month for parking.
- Mornington Place charges $41 per month for parking.
- Bayview Towers charges $58 per month for parking.

Assigned Parking Table

- Include fields to store the vehicle make, model, color, and license plate number of the tenant's vehicle that will be parked in the spot.
- Include a field to store the date the tenant began renting the spot.

In Microsoft Word, document your table design by including each table's name and the fields created in each table including the data type and field properties that you set such as field size, caption, input mask, and so on. Indicate the primary key(s) in each table by typing an asterisk preceding the field name. Save the Word document and name it **AL2-U1-Act1-BenchmarkPropMgt**. Print the document and then exit Word.

Activity 2 Design Tables for a Soccer League Database

You are assisting the volunteer registration coordinator for a local soccer league. The registration coordinator would like to create an Access database in which to store information about this season's soccer players so that he can extract reports by age category to develop team lists and generate financial reports for the league treasurer. Design and create tables in a new database named **AL2-U1-SoccerRegn.accdb**. The registration coordinator has given you a sample registration form to help you design the tables. Refer to the sample form shown in Figure U1.3.

Figure U1.3 Activity 2

Minor League Soccer Registration

Date			
Youth name		**Circle gender**	
Birth Date		**Male**	**Female**
Parent or guardian name			
Address			
City/Town			
ZIP code			
Telephone			

Registering for:		**House league fee**
Under 6		**60.00**
Under 8		**95.00**
Under 10		**95.00**
Under 12		**95.00**
Under 14		**120.00**
Under 16		**120.00**
Under 18		**135.00**
Competitive surcharge		**75.00**
Late fee		**35.00**

Total Received			
Cash		**Check**	

Create one data entry form to enter information into the tables and add at least five records to test your table and form design. Print all of the records using the form. Design and create a prompted query that will print a list of soccer players selecting records by age category. Design and create another query to print the soccer players registered for the current season including the registration fee paid. Add a total row in the query results datasheet to show the total registration fees collected. Run each query to test your query design and print the query results datasheets.

In Microsoft Word, create a one-page quick reference guide for the registration coordinator and the treasurer that provides instructions on how to open the database and use the data entry form, the prompted query, and the registration fee query. Include in your instructions how to print objects in the database, including how to print a selected form. Save the Word document and name it **AL2-U1-Act2-SoccerRegistration**. Print the document and exit Word.

Internet Research

Plan Your Volunteer Work

You want to volunteer each week after school but are not sure which organization would be a good fit with your skills and interests. As you begin to consider where you would like to donate your time and expertise you decide to use your newly learned Access skills to develop a volunteer organization database that you can share with your friends and relatives. Research five to eight organizations in your area that need volunteers on a regular basis. Pick a variety of organizations so that your database will have at least one organization that will appeal to most people. Design tables in Access in a new database named **AL2-U1-VolunteerOrg.accdb** to store the organization name, address, telephone number, and volunteer coordinator (if applicable). Include a field with notes about the organization's mission. Look for annual fundraising events at which volunteers are needed and include an Events table related to the organization. Design and create a form for data entry and use the form to input records for the organizations that you researched. Print all of the records using the form. Using Microsoft Word, create a brief document with instructions for your friends and relatives on how to open the database, browse records using the form, and print information. Save and print the document naming it **AL2-U1-VolunteerInfo**.

Microsoft®

Access®

Level 2

Unit 2 ■ Advanced Reports, Access Tools, and Customizing Access

Chapter 5 ■ Creating and Using Custom Reports

Chapter 6 ■ Using Access Tools and Managing Objects

Chapter 7 ■ Automating, Customizing, and Securing Access

Chapter 8 ■ Integrating Access Data

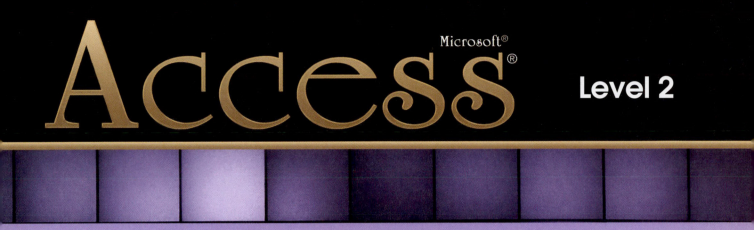

Microsoft® Access®

CHAPTER 5

Creating and Using Custom Reports

PERFORMANCE OBJECTIVES

Upon successful completion of Chapter 5, you will be able to:

- **Create a custom report in Design view using all five report sections**
- **Move, size, format, and align control objects**
- **Insert a subreport into a report**
- **Add page numbering, date and time controls**
- **Add graphics to a report**
- **Group records including adding functions and totals**
- **Modify section or group properties to control print options**
- **Create and modify charts in a report**
- **Create a blank report**
- **Add hyperlinks and list boxes to a report**
- **Change the shape of a tab control**
- **Change the tab order of fields**

SNAP Training and Assessment. Simplified.

Tutorials

5.1 Creating Custom Reports Using Design View

5.2 Connecting a Table or Query to a Report and Adding Fields

5.3 Moving Control Objects to Another Section

5.4 Inserting a Subreport

5.5 Formatting Controls in a Report

5.6 Grouping Records in a Report

5.7 Creating a Report with a Grouping Level Using the Report Wizard

5.8 Adding Functions to a Group; Keeping a Group Together

5.9 Modifying Section Properties; Inserting a Chart

5.10 Creating a Report Using the Blank Report Tool

Reports are used to generate printouts from the tables in a database. Although data can be printed from a table datasheet, query results datasheet, or form using the Print feature, these printouts do not allow you to customize the output and do not offer formatting options to present the data in a different manner. The Report feature provides tools and options that can be used to control the content and formatting in order to produce professional-quality reports that serve a particular purpose. In this chapter you will learn how to build custom reports. Model answers for this chapter's projects appear on the following pages.

Access

Access2010L2C5

Note: Before beginning the projects, copy to your storage medium the Access2010L2C5 subfolder from the Access2010L2 folder on the CD that accompanies this textbook and then make Access2010L2C5 the active folder.

RSR Computer Service Work Orders

Work Order	Customer ID	First Name	Last Name	WO Date	Descripton
65012	1000	Jade	Fleming	Fri Sep 07 2012	Bi-annual computer maintenance
Service Date	Total Labor	Parts	Total Work Order		
Tue Sep 04 2012	$37.50	$10.15	$47.65		
65013	1000	Jade	Fleming	Fri Sep 07 2012	Replace keyboard
Service Date	Total Labor	Parts	Total Work Order		
Mon Sep 10 2012	$14.25	$42.75	$57.00		
65030	1000	Jade	Fleming	Sat Oct 06 2012	Clean malware from system
Service Date	Total Labor	Parts	Total Work Order		
Sat Oct 06 2012	$15.50	$0.00	$15.50		
65033	1000	Jade	Fleming	Fri Oct 12 2012	Install Windows 7
Service Date	Total Labor	Parts	Total Work Order		
Sat Oct 13 2012	$97.50	$335.75	$433.25		
65014	1005	Cayla	Fahri	Mon Sep 10 2012	Replace power supply
Service Date	Total Labor	Parts	Total Work Order		
Mon Sep 10 2012	$52.50	$62.77	$115.27		
65024	1005	Cayla	Fahri	Mon Sep 24 2012	Install malware protection
Service Date	Total Labor	Parts	Total Work Order		
Mon Sep 24 2012	$15.50	$75.50	$91.00		
65015	1008	Leslie	Carmichael	Mon Sep 10 2012	Restore operating system
Service Date	Total Labor	Parts	Total Work Order		
Tue Sep 11 2012	$67.50	$0.00	$67.50		
65032	1008	Leslie	Carmichael	Fri Oct 12 2012	Install second hard drive
Service Date	Total Labor	Parts	Total Work Order		
Sat Oct 13 2012	$60.00	$425.75	$485.75		

Page 1 of 5

Work Order	Customer ID	First Name	Last Name	WO Date	Descripton
65036	1008	Leslie	Carmichael	Mon Oct 15 2012	Set up home network
Service Date	Total Labor	Parts	Total Work Order		
Tue Oct 16 2012	$67.50	$85.22	$152.72		
65044	1008	Leslie	Carmichael	Tue Oct 23 2012	DVD drive is not working
Service Date	Total Labor	Parts	Total Work Order		
Tue Oct 23 2012	$30.00	$55.40	$85.40		
65016	1010	Randall	Lemaire	Tue Sep 11 2012	Install upgraded video card
Service Date	Total Labor	Parts	Total Work Order		
Tue Sep 11 2012	$30.00	$48.75	$78.75		
65025	1010	Randall	Lemaire	Fri Sep 28 2012	Troubleshoot hard drive noise
Service Date	Total Labor	Parts	Total Work Order		
Fri Sep 28 2012	$45.00	$0.00	$45.00		
65027	1010	Randall	Lemaire	Sun Sep 30 2012	Replace hard drive
Service Date	Total Labor	Parts	Total Work Order		
Tue Oct 02 2012	$45.00	$375.50	$420.50		
65038	1010	Randall	Lemaire	Fri Oct 19 2012	Install Windows 7
Service Date	Total Labor	Parts	Total Work Order		
Fri Oct 19 2012	$75.00	$0.00	$75.00		
65046	1010	Randall	Lemaire	Fri Oct 26 2012	Windows 7 training
Service Date	Total Labor	Parts	Total Work Order		
Fri Oct 26 2012	$60.00	$0.00	$60.00		
65017	1015	Shauna	Friesen	Fri Sep 14 2012	Replace DVD drive
Service Date	Total Labor	Parts	Total Work Order		
Sat Sep 15 2012	$16.88	$55.87	$72.75		
65037	1015	Shauna	Friesen	Fri Oct 19 2012	Bi-annual computer maintenance
Service Date	Total Labor	Parts	Total Work Order		
Fri Oct 19 2012	$37.50	$8.75	$46.25		

Page 2 of 5

Projects 1 and 2 Design and Create a Custom Report, Add Features and Enhance a Report

Project 2b, WorkOrders Report

Work Order	Customer ID	First Name	Last Name	WO Date	Descripton
65018	1020	Kirk	Cobb	Fri Sep 14 2012	Upgrade Office suite
Service Date	Total Labor	Parts	Total Work Order		
Sat Sep 15 2012	$22.50	$0.00	$22.50		
65035	1020	Kirk	Cobb	Sun Oct 14 2012	Office 2010 training
Service Date	Total Labor	Parts	Total Work Order		
Mon Oct 15 2012	$75.00	$0.00	$75.00		
65041	1020	Kirk	Cobb	Mon Oct 22 2012	Bi-annual computer maintenance
Service Date	Total Labor	Parts	Total Work Order		
Mon Oct 22 2012	$37.50	$10.15	$47.65		
65043	1020	Kirk	Cobb	Mon Oct 22 2012	Troubleshoot video fuzziness
Service Date	Total Labor	Parts	Total Work Order		
Tue Oct 23 2012	$15.00	$0.00	$15.00		
65048	1020	Kirk	Cobb	Mon Oct 29 2012	Replace LCD monitor
Service Date	Total Labor	Parts	Total Work Order		
Mon Oct 29 2012	$15.00	$169.95	$184.95		
65019	1025	Lana	Bodzek	Sat Sep 15 2012	Upgrade to Windows 7
Service Date	Total Labor	Parts	Total Work Order		
Mon Sep 17 2012	$75.00	$0.00	$75.00		
65026	1025	Lana	Bodzek	Sat Sep 29 2012	Upgrade memory
Service Date	Total Labor	Parts	Total Work Order		
Sat Sep 29 2012	$22.50	$75.75	$98.25		
65040	1025	Lana	Bodzek	Fri Oct 19 2012	Configure dual monitors
Service Date	Total Labor	Parts	Total Work Order		
Sat Oct 20 2012	$30.00	$0.00	$30.00		
65045	1025	Lana	Bodzek	Tue Oct 23 2012	Set up automatic backup
Service Date	Total Labor	Parts	Total Work Order		
Fri Oct 26 2012	$11.63	$0.00	$11.63		

Page 3 of 5

WO Date	Descripton
Mon Sep 17 2012	Troubleshoot noisy fan
Parts	Total Work Order
$62.77	$96.52
Tue Oct 02 2012	Reinstall operating system
Parts	Total Work Order
$0.00	$67.50
Fri Oct 19 2012	Set up automatic backup
Parts	Total Work Order
$0.00	$16.88
Mon Oct 22 2012	File management training
Parts	Total Work Order
$0.00	$33.75
Sat Oct 27 2012	Set up automatic backup
Parts	Total Work Order
$0.00	$11.25
Tue Sep 18 2012	Customer has blue screen upon b
Parts	Total Work Order
$0.00	$97.50
Tue Oct 02 2012	Set up automatic backup
Parts	Total Work Order
$0.00	$11.25
Fri Oct 12 2012	File management training
Parts	Total Work Order
$0.00	$45.00
Fri Sep 21 2012	Customer reports screen is fuzzy
Parts	Total Work Order
$55.47	$100.47

Page 4 of 5

WO Date	Descripton
Tue Oct 30 2012	Set up dual monitor system
Parts	Total Work Order
$0.00	$22.50
Sat Sep 22 2012	Upgrade RAM
Parts	Total Work Order
$62.50	$100.00
Sat Oct 06 2012	Customer reports noisy hard drive
Parts	Total Work Order
$0.00	$52.50
Tue Oct 30 2012	Reinstall Windows 7
Parts	Total Work Order
$0.00	$45.00

Date Printed: 23-Nov-12
Time Printed: 2:46 PM

Page 5 of 5

Model Answers

Work Orders by Month
Student Name
Service Date by Month
Work Order
CustID
Description
Service Date
Total Labor
Parts
Total Work Order
September 2012
Work Order Count: 15
Month Total: $1,165.16
Monday, November 26, 2012
Page 1 of 2

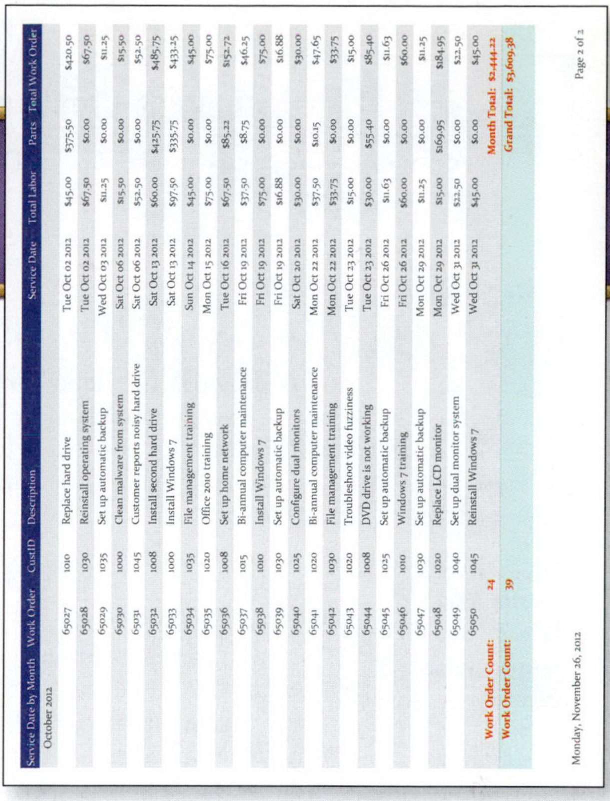
Service Date by Month
Work Order
CustID
Description
Service Date
Total Labor
Parts
Total Work Order
October 2012
Work Order Count: 24
Work Order Count: 39
Month Total: $2,444.22
Grand Total: $3,609.38
Monday, November 26, 2012
Page 2 of 2

Projects 3 and 4 Group Records and Add Functions to Count and Sum, Modify Section and Group Properties

Project 4, WorkOrdersbyMonth Report

Project 5 Create and Format a Chart

Project 5b, CustomersWOChart Report

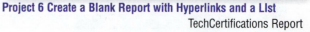

Project 6 Create a Blank Report with Hyperlinks and a LIst

TechCertifications Report

Project 1 Design and Create a Custom Report — 5 Parts

You will create a custom report in Design view with fields from two tables and insert a subreport.

Quick Steps

Start New Report in Design View
1. Click Create tab.
2. Click Report Design button.

Add Report Title
1. Open report in Design view.
2. Click Title button.
3. Type title text.
4. Press Enter.

Add Label Object
1. Open report in Design view.
2. Click Label button.
3. Drag to create object the desired height and width.
4. Type label text.
5. Press Enter.

Report Design

Creating Custom Reports Using Design View

Access provides the Report tool and the Report Wizard that can be used to create reports. These features allow you to build a report quickly that can be modified in Layout view or Design view to customize the content, format, or layout. In most cases, you will want to use one of the report tools to generate the report structure and then customize the report; however, if you require a report with several custom options, you can begin in Design view and build the report from scratch. Click the Create tab and click the Report Design button in the Reports group to begin a new report using the Design view window shown in Figure 5.1.

Creating a report in Design view involves using the same techniques that you learned in Chapter 4 for designing and building a custom form. You will add a title; connect a table or query to the report; add fields; and align, move, resize, and format controls the same way that you learned to do these tasks in a form.

A report can contain up to five sections, each of which is described in Table 5.1. You can also add a *Group Header* and a *Group Footer* section, which are used when you group records that contain repeating values in a field such as a department or city. You will learn how to use these additional sections in Project 3. A report that is grouped by more than one field can have multiple *Group Header* and *Group Footer* sections.

Figure 5.1 Report Design View

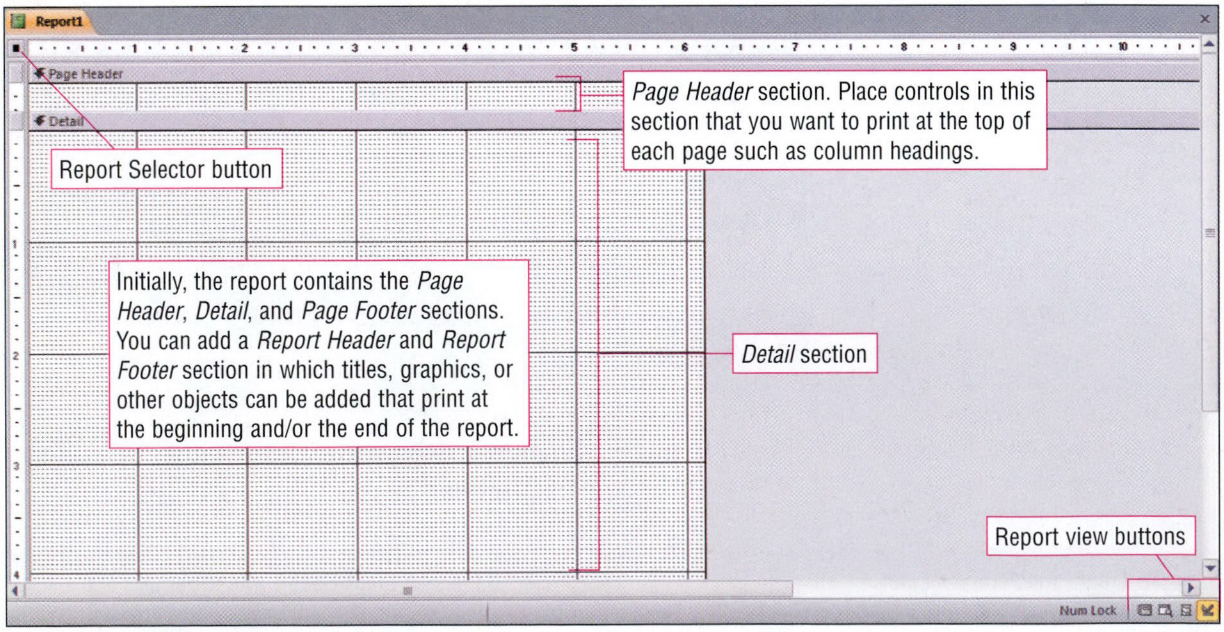

Report1
Page Header
Detail
Page Header section. Place controls in this section that you want to print at the top of each page such as column headings.
Report Selector button
Initially, the report contains the Page Header, Detail, and Page Footer sections. You can add a Report Header and Report Footer section in which titles, graphics, or other objects can be added that print at the beginning and/or the end of the report.
Detail section
Report view buttons
Num Lock

Table 5.1 Report Sections

Report Section	*Description*
Report Header	Content in the *Report Header* section prints at the beginning of the report and generally includes controls for the report title and company logo or other image.
Page Header	Content in the *Page Header* section prints at the top of each page in the report. Place controls for column headings in a tabular report format in the page header.
Detail	Similar to a form, controls for the fields from the table or query that make up the body of the report are placed in the *Detail* section.
Page Footer	Content in the *Page Footer* section prints at the bottom of each page in the report. Add a control to this section to print a page number at the bottom of each page.
Report Footer	Content in the *Report Footer* section prints at the end of the report. Add controls in this section to print grand totals or perform another function such as average, max, min, or count.

Project 1a Starting a New Report Using Design View and Adding a Title and Label Object

Part 1 of 5

1. Open **AL2-C5-RSRCompServ.accdb** and enable content.
2. Click the Create tab and then click the Report Design button in the Reports group.

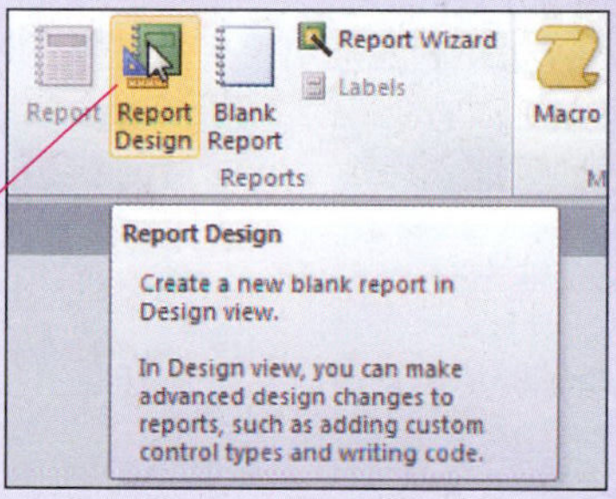

Step 2

3. Add a title in the *Report Header* section of the report by completing the following steps:
   a. With the Report Design Tools Design tab active, click the Title button in the Header/Footer group. Access adds the *Report Header* section above the *Page Header* section and places a title object with the text *Report1* selected.
   b. Type **RSR Computer Service Work Orders** and press Enter.

Steps 3a-3b

4. With the title control object still selected, click the Report Design Tools Format tab and then click the Center button in the Font group.
5. Drag the right edge of the report grid until the width is aligned at the 8-inch position in the horizontal ruler.
6. Scroll down the report until you can see the *Page Footer* and *Report Footer* sections. The *Report Footer* section was added to the design grid at the same time the *Report Header* section was added when the title was created in Step 3.

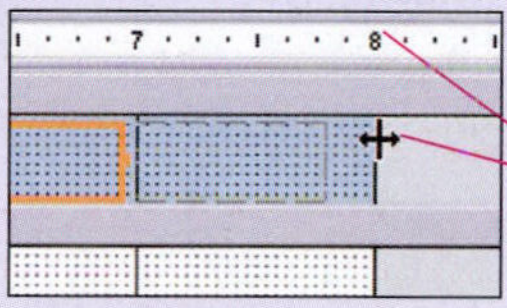

Step 5

7. Drag the bottom edge of the report grid down until the bottom of the report is at the 0.5-inch position in the vertical ruler.
8. Click the Report Design Tools Design tab and then click the Label button in the Controls group. Add a label control object at the left edge of the *Report Footer* section that contains your first and last names.
9. Click in any blank area of the report to deselect the label control object.
10. Save the report and name it *WorkOrders*.

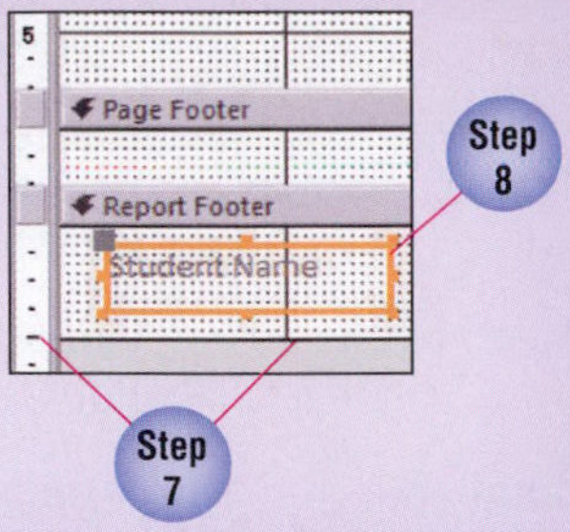

Connecting a Table or Query to the Report and Adding Fields

Quick Steps

Connect Table or Query to Report
1. Open report in Design view.
2. Double-click Report Selector button.
3. Click Data tab in Property Sheet.
4. Click down-pointing arrow in *Record Source* property box.
5. Click desired table or query.
6. Close Property Sheet.

Add Fields to Report
1. Click Add Existing Fields button.
2. Drag field name(s) from Field List pane to *Detail* section.

Add Fields from Related Table
1. Open Field List pane.
2. Click Show all tables hyperlink.
3. Click expand button next to desired table name in *Fields available in related tables* section.
4. Drag field name from related table list to *Detail* section.

Report Selector

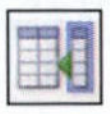
Add Existing Fields

A new report started in Design view does not have a table or query associated with it. In order to view data in the report, Access needs to know from which table the data should be gathered. Similar to a form, you connect a table or query to the report using the Record Source property in the report's Property Sheet. This step must be completed first before fields can be added to the *Detail* section. The steps to connect a table or query to the report are the same as the steps you learned to connect a table to a form. Double-click the Report Selector button located above the vertical ruler and left of the horizontal ruler to open the report's Property Sheet. Click the Data tab and then select the table or query name in the drop-down list in the *Record Source* property box.

Display the Field List pane and drag individual fields from the table or query or a group of fields to the *Detail* section. After fields have been added you can move and resize the control objects as needed.

The Field List pane displays in one of two states: with one section only with the fields from the table or query associated with the report, or with two additional sections with fields from other tables in the database. If the Field List pane contains only the fields from the associated table or query, you can add fields from other tables by displaying other table names from the database within the Field List pane. At the top of the pane, Access displays a hyperlink with the text Show all tables. Click the hyperlink to display two additional sections within the pane: *Fields available in related tables* and *Fields available in other tables*. Next to each table name is an expand button (displays as a plus symbol). Click the expand button next to a table name to display the fields stored within the table and then drag the field name to the *Detail* section of the report. You will perform these steps in Project1b.

Project 1b Connecting a Table to a Report and Adding Fields — Part 2 of 5

1. With the **AL2-C5-RSRCompServ.accdb** database open and the WorkOrders report open in Design view, scroll up to the top of the report in the work area.
2. Connect the WorkOrders table to the report so that Access knows which fields to display in the Field List pane by completing the following steps:
   a. Double-click the Report Selector button located at the top of the vertical ruler and left of the horizontal ruler to open the report's Property Sheet.
   b. Click the Data tab in the Property Sheet, click the down-pointing arrow in the *Record Source* property box, and then click *WorkOrders* at the drop-down list.
   c. Close the Property Sheet.

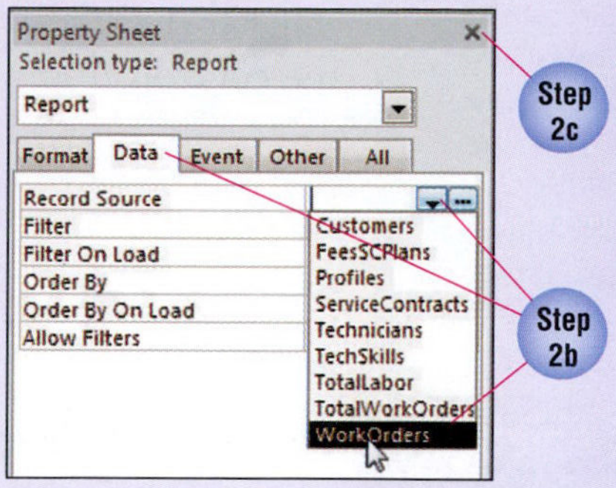

3. Click the Add Existing Fields button in the Tools group in the Report Design Tools Design tab to open the Field List pane.
4. Add fields from the WorkOrders table and related fields from the Customers table by completing the following steps:
   a. Click the Show all tables hyperlink at the top of the Field List pane. Access adds two sections to the pane. One section contains related tables and the other section contains other tables in the database which do not have an established relationship with the report's table. Next to each table name is an expand button (displays as a plus symbol) which is used to display field names for the table. ***Note: Skip this step if the hyperlink at the top of the Field List pane displays Show only fields in the current record source since the additional sections are already added to the pane.***

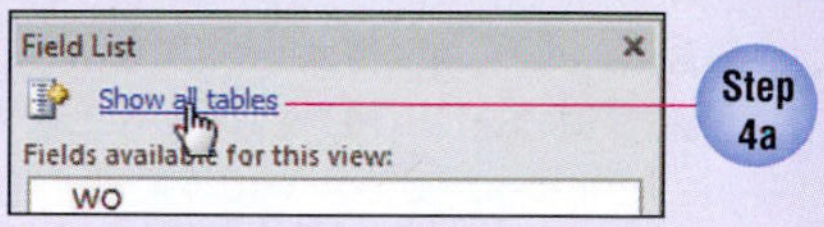

   b. Click the expand button next to *Customers* in the *Fields available in related tables* section of the Field List pane. Access expands the list to display the field names in the Customers table below the Customers table name.

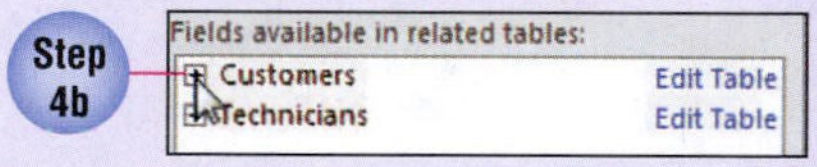

   c. Drag the *WO*, *CustID*, *WODate*, and *Descr* fields from the WorkOrders table to the design grid as shown.
   d. Drag the *FName* and *LName* fields from the Customers table to the design grid as shown. Notice the Customer table and field names move to the *Fields available for this view* section in the Field List pane once you add the first field from the Customers table to the *Detail* section.

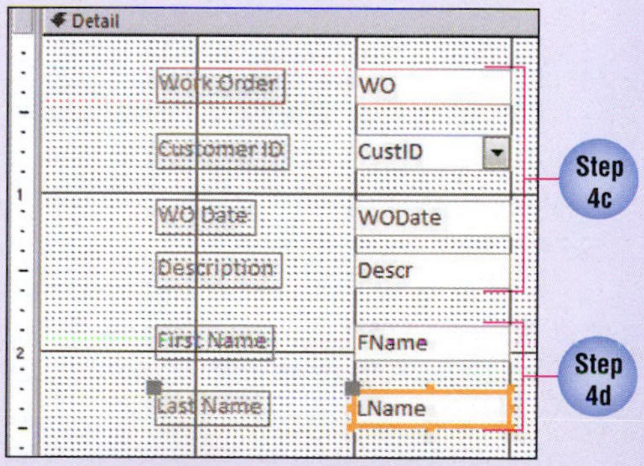

5. Close the Field List pane.
6. Save the report.

Quick Steps

Move Controls to Another Section

1. Open report in Design view.
2. Select controls to be moved.
3. Click Home tab.
4. Click Cut button.
5. Click section bar in which to move controls.
6. Click Paste button.
7. Deselect controls.

Moving Control Objects to Another Section

As with a form, when a field is added to the *Detail* section in a report, a label control object containing the caption or field name is placed left of a text box control object that displays the field value from the record when the report is viewed or printed. In the WorkOrders report, the label control object for each field needs to be moved to the *Page Header* section so that the field names or captions print at the top of each page as column headings. To do this, you will cut and paste the controls from the *Detail* section to the *Page Header* section in Project 1c.

Project 1c Moving Controls to Another Section

Part 3 of 5

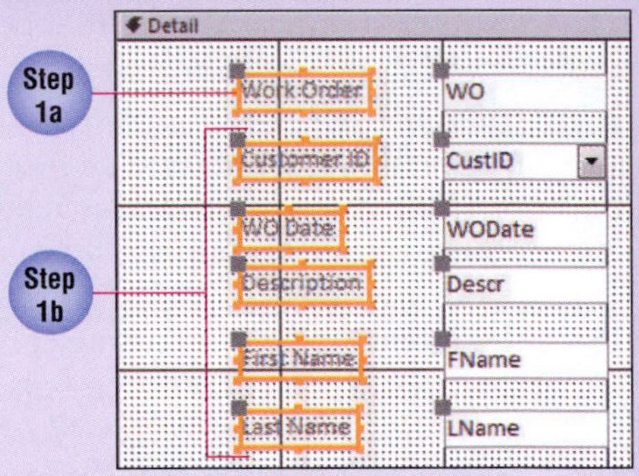

1. With the **AL2-C5-RSRCompServ.accdb** database open and the WorkOrders report open in Design view, move the label control objects from the *Detail* section to the *Page Header* section by completing the following steps:
   a. Click to select the *Work Order* label control object.
   b. Shift + click to select each of the other label control objects.
   c. Click the Home tab and then click the Cut button in the Clipboard group.
   d. Click the gray *Page Header* section bar.
   e. Click the Paste button in the Clipboard group. (Do not click the down-pointing arrow on the button.) Access pastes the label control objects and expands the *Page Header* section.
   f. Deselect the controls.

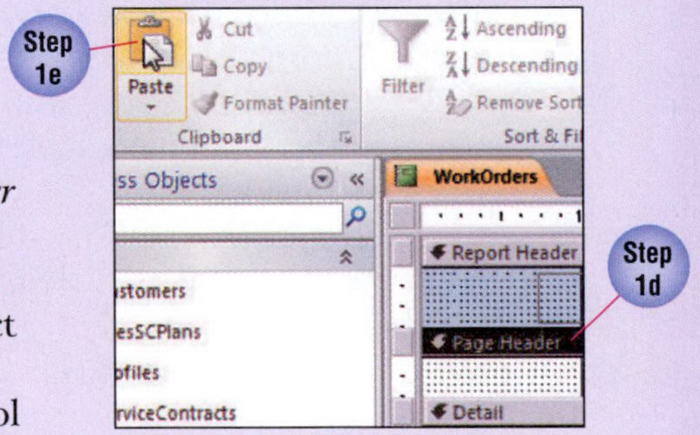

2. Click to select the *Customer ID* label control object and then move the control to the top of the *Page Header* section next to the *Work Order* label control as shown by dragging the object while pointing at the orange border with the four-headed arrow move icon displayed (not on a sizing handle).

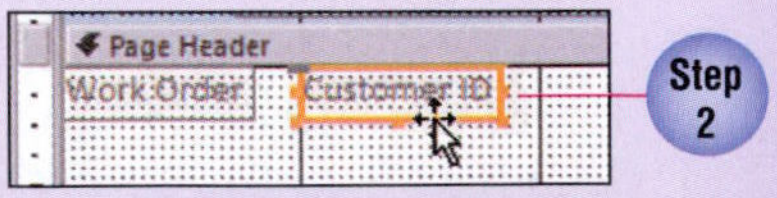

3. Move the remaining four label control objects to the top of the *Page Header* section in the order shown in the image at the top of the next page by completing a step similar to Step 2.

4. Drag the top of the gray *Detail* section bar up until the top of the bar is aligned at the bottom edge of the label control objects in the *Page Header* section as shown below.

5. Save the report.

Applying a Theme

Apply a theme to the report using the Themes button at the Report Design Tools Design tab. The theme controls the default colors and fonts for the report. The Themes options align with the themes available in Word, Excel, and PowerPoint so that you can maintain a consistent look for Access reports that you use for other documents, worksheets, or presentations. Note that changing a theme for one report automatically changes the theme for all reports in the database.

Quick Steps

Apply Theme
1. Open report in Design view.
2. Click Report Design Tools Design tab.
3. Click Themes button.
4. Click desired theme.

Themes

Project 1d **Moving Controls, Resizing Controls, and Applying a Theme** Part 4 of 5

1. With the **AL2-C5-RSRCompServ.accdb** database open and the WorkOrders report open in Design view, move each text box control object in the *Detail* section below the object's associated label control object in the *Page Header* section so that the field values will align below the correct column headings in the report as shown below.

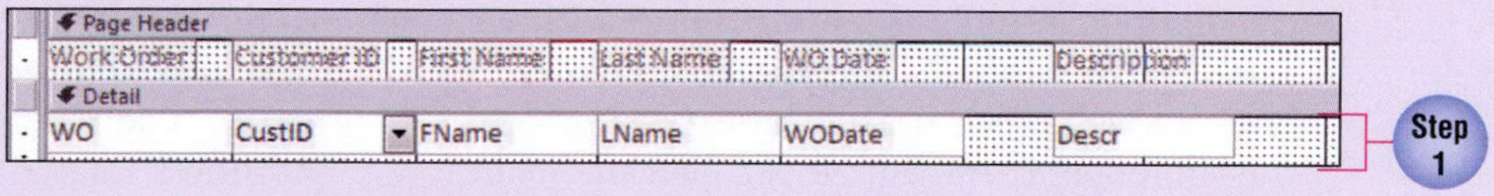

2. Click the Report Design Tools Design tab, click the View button arrow in the Views group, and then click *Print Preview* at the drop-down list. (Note that there is also a Print Preview button in the Views group at the right end of the Status bar.) Notice the field value in the *WO Date* column is displaying pound symbols indicating the field's text box control object needs to be widened.
3. Click the Design View button in the View group located at the right end of the Status bar next to the Zoom slider to return to Design view.

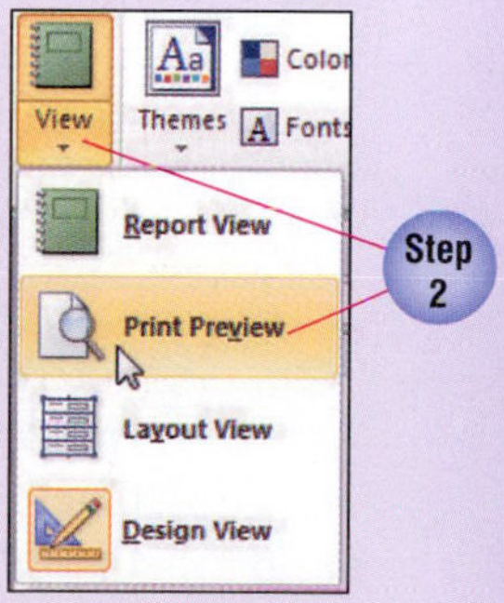

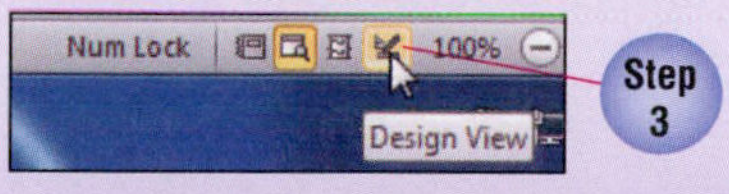

4. Resize the *WODate* text box control in the *Detail* section until the right edge of the control meets the left edge of the *Descr* text box control object.
5. Resize the *Descr* text box control in the *Detail* section until the right edge of the control is aligned approximately at the 7.75-inch position in the horizontal ruler.
6. Deselect the *Descr* control object.
7. Click the Themes button in the Themes group of the Report Design Tools Arrange tab and then click *Angles* at the drop-down gallery (third option in first row).

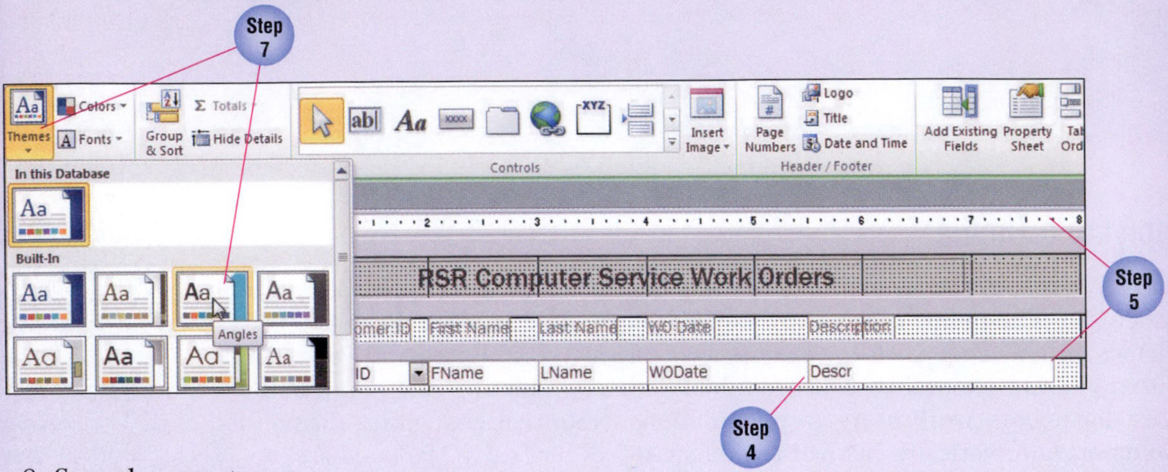

8. Save the report.
9. Display the report in Print Preview to review the changes made in this project. Switch back to Design view when finished previewing the report. ***Note: Do not be concerned if you only see one record in the report. Currently, the* Detail *section is sized such that only one record can fit on a page. This will be corrected in the next project.***

Inserting a Subreport

Subform/ Subreport

A ***subreport*** is a report that is inserted inside another report. Similar to a nested query, using a subreport allows you to reuse a group of fields, formatting, and calculations in more than one report without having to recreate the setup each time. The Subform/Subreport button in the Controls group of the Report Design Tools Design tab is used to insert a subreport into a report. The report into which the subreport is embedded is called the main report. Adding a related table or query as a subreport creates a control object within the main report that can be moved, formatted, and resized independently of the other control objects. Make sure the Use Control Wizards button is toggled on in the expanded Controls group before clicking the Subform/Subreport button so that you can add the subreport using the SubReport Wizard shown in Figure 5.2.

A subreport is stored as a separate object outside the main report. You will notice an additional report name added in the Navigation pane with *subreport* at the end of the name when you finish the steps in the SubReport Wizard. Do not delete a subreport object in the Navigation pane. If the subreport object is deleted, the main report will no longer be able to display the fields from the related table or query in the report.

Figure 5.2 First Dialog Box in SubReport Wizard

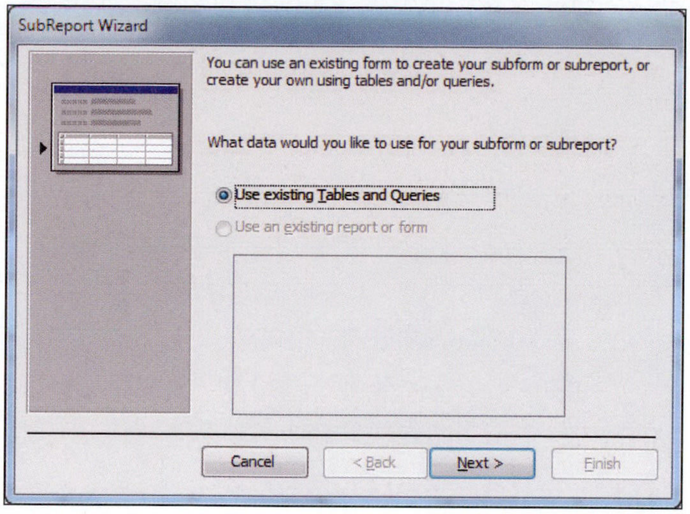

Quick Steps

Insert Subreport

1. Open report in Design view.
2. Make sure Use Control Wizards is active.
3. Click Subform/ Subreport button.
4. Drag crosshairs desired height and width in *Detail* section.
5. Click Next.
6. Choose table or query and fields.
7. Click Next.
8. Choose field by which to link main report with subreport.
9. Click Next.
10. Click Finish.
11. If desired, delete subreport label control object.
12. Move and/or resize subreport object as required.

Project 1e Inserting a Subreport

Part 5 of 5

1. With the **AL2-C5-RSRCompServ.accdb** database open and the WorkOrders report open in Design view, insert a subreport into the WorkOrders report with fields from a query for the service date, labor, and parts for each work order by completing the following steps:
   a. By default, the *Use Control Wizards* option is toggled on in the Controls group. Click the More button at the bottom of the Controls scroll bar to expand the Controls and view three rows of buttons and the Controls drop-down list. View the current status of the *Use Control Wizards* option. The button at the left of the option displays with an orange background when the feature is active. If the button is orange, click in a blank area to remove the expanded Controls list. If the feature is not active (displays with a white background), click *Use Control Wizards* to turn the feature on.
   b. Click the More button at the bottom of the Controls scroll bar and then click the Subform/Subreport button at the expanded Controls list.

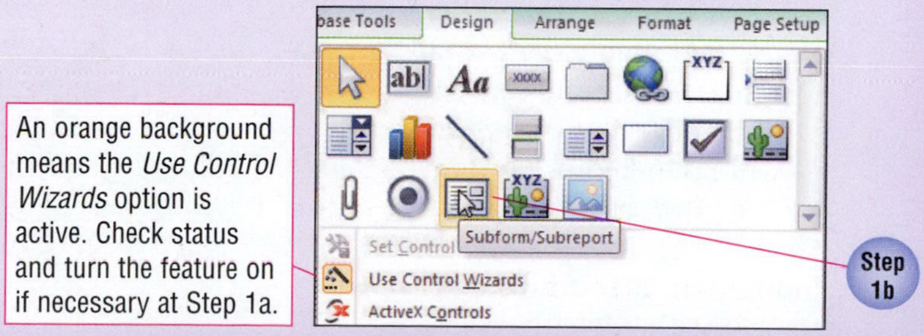

c. Move the crosshairs with the subreport icon attached to the *Detail* section below the *WO* text box control object and drag down and right to create a subreport object the approximate height and width shown below. When you release the mouse, the SubReport Wizard begins.

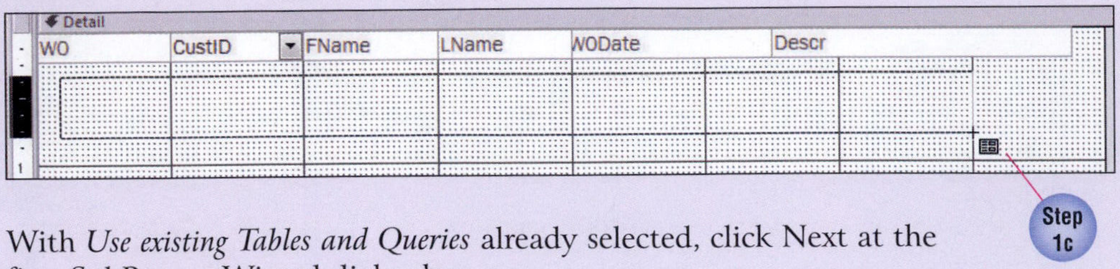

d. With *Use existing Tables and Queries* already selected, click Next at the first SubReport Wizard dialog box.

e. At the second SubReport Wizard dialog box, select the query fields to be displayed in the subreport by completing the following steps:
   1) Click the down-pointing arrow next to the *Tables/Queries* list box and then click *Query: TotalWorkOrders* at the drop-down list.
   2) Move all of the fields from the *Available Fields* list box to the *Selected Fields* list box.
   3) Click Next.

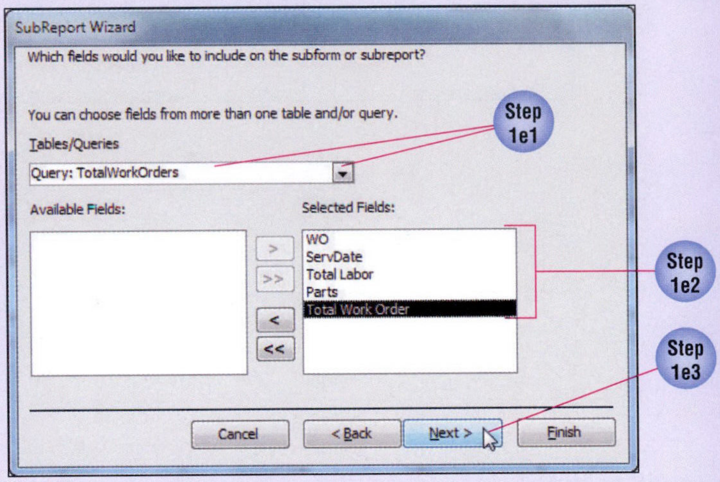

f. At the third SubReport Wizard dialog box, choose the field by which to link the main report with the subreport by completing the following steps:
   1) With *Choose from a list* and the first option in the list box selected, read the text that displays below the list box describing the linked field. The text indicates that the main report will be linked to the subreport using the *CustID* field. This is not the correct field since you want your report to show the service date, labor, and parts based on the work order number.
   2) Click the second option in the list box and then read the text below the list box.
   3) Since the second option indicates the two reports will be linked using the *WO field*, click Next.

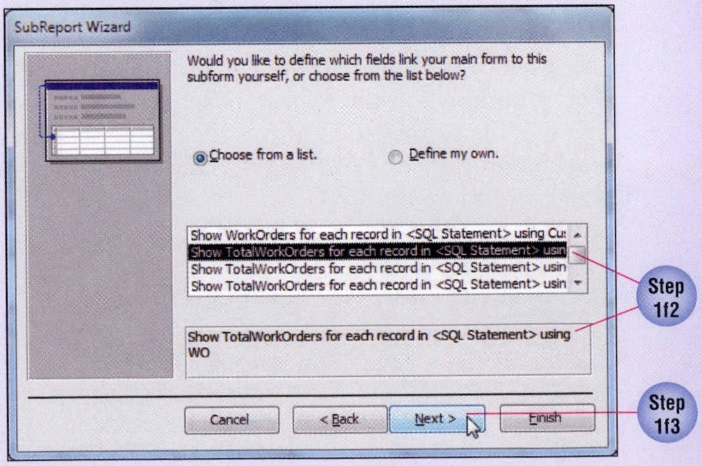

g. Click Finish at the last SubReport Wizard dialog box to accept the default subreport name *TotalWorkOrders subreport*.

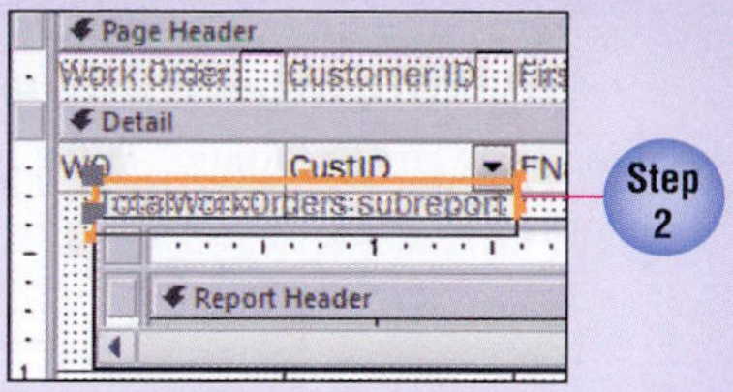

2. Access inserts the subreport with a label control object above the subreport control that contains the name of the subreport. Click the label control displaying the text *TotalWorkOrders subreport* to select the object and then press the Delete key.
3. Click the Report View button in the Views group of the Report Design Tools Design tab. Note that a Report View button is also located in the View group at the right end of the Status bar (first button). Report view is not the same as Print Preview. Report view will display the report with data in the fields and is useful for viewing reports within the database; however, this view does not show how the report will paginate when printed. For printing purposes, always use Print Preview to resize and adjust control objects.
4. Notice the work order number in the subreport is the same work order number that is displayed in the first record in the main report.

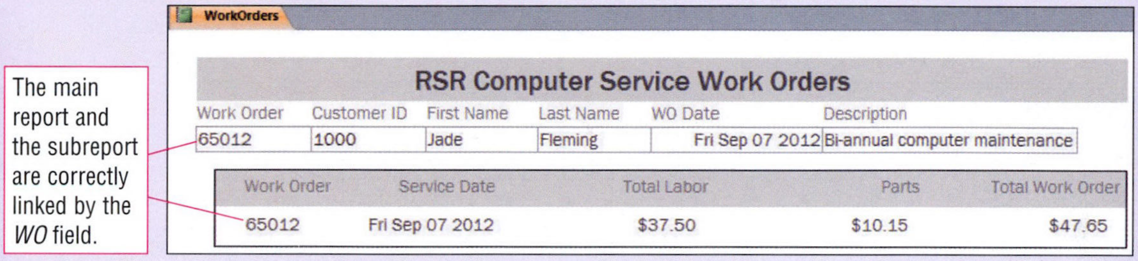

5. Switch back to Design view.
6. Now that you know the subreport is linked correctly to the main report, you do not need to display the work order number in the subreport. Delete the work order number control objects in the subreport by completing the following steps:
   a. Click to select the subreport control object and then drag the bottom middle sizing handle down to increase the height of the subreport until you can see all of the controls in the *Report Header* and *Detail* sections.
   b. Click to select the *Work Order* label control object in the *Report Header* section and then Shift + click the *WO* text box control object in the *Detail* section in the subreport.
   c. Press Delete.

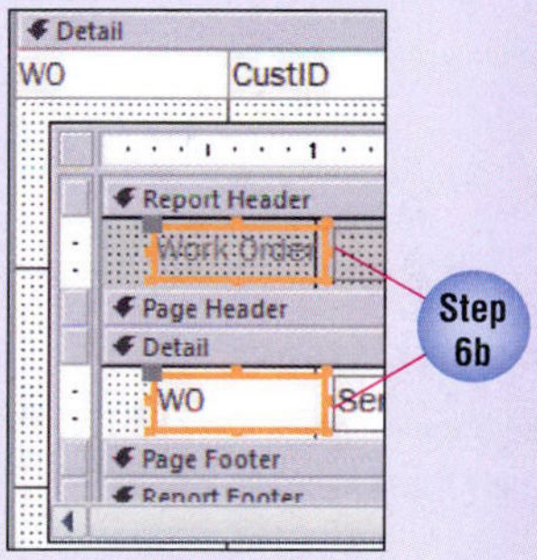

7. Click to select the subreport control object and then drag the bottom middle sizing handle of the control up until the height of the subreport is approximately 0.5 inch.
8. Scroll down the report until you can see the gray *Page Footer* section bar.
9. Drag the top of the *Page Footer* section bar up until the section bar is just below the subreport control object in the *Detail* section as shown below.

Height of subreport control object decreased at Step 7.

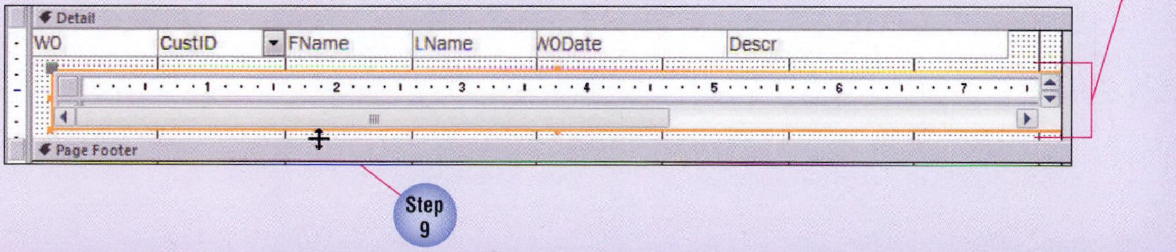

10. Save the report and then switch to Report view to view the revised report. Resizing the *Detail* section at Step 9 allowed the report to show more records and related subreport records on the page since the spacing between sections was reduced.

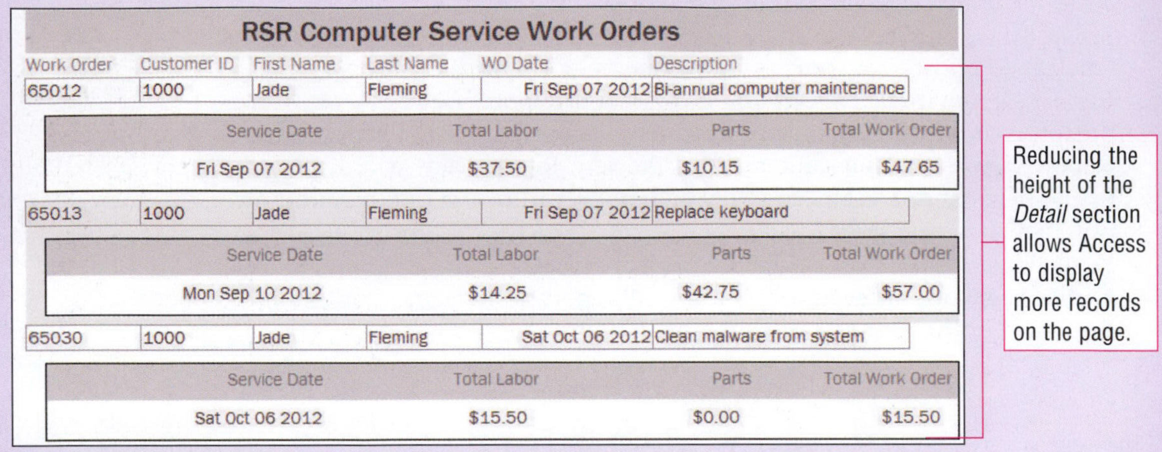

11. Close the report.

Project 2 Add Features and Enhance a Report — 2 Parts

You will modify the WorkOrders report to add page numbering, date and time controls, and graphics.

Adding Page Numbering and Date and Time Controls

Quick Steps

Add Page Numbers

1. Open Report in Design view.
2. Click Page Numbers button.
3. Select desired format, position, and alignment options.
4. Click OK.

Page Numbers

When you create a report using the Report tool, page numbering and the current date and time are automatically added to the top right of a report. The Report wizard automatically inserts the current date at the bottom left and page numbering at the bottom right of the report. In Design view, you can add page numbering to a report using the Page Numbers button in the Header/Footer group of the Report Design Tools Design tab. Clicking the button opens the Page Numbers dialog box

Figure 5.3 Page Numbers Dialog Box

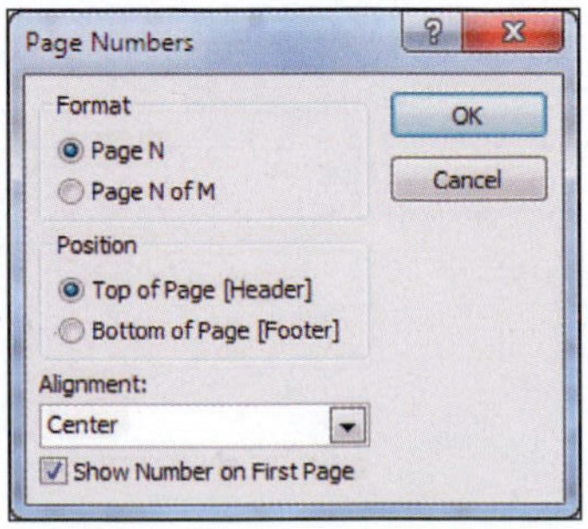

shown in Figure 5.3. Choose the desired format, position, and alignment for the page number and click OK. Access inserts a control object in either the Page Header or the *Page Footer* section depending on the *Position* option selected in the dialog box. Including the page number in a report is a good idea in case the pages become shuffled and need to be reorganized back into sequential order.

Add the current date and/or time in the *Report Header* section by clicking the Date and Time button in the Header/Footer group to open the Date and Time dialog box shown in Figure 5.4. By default both the *Include Date* and *Include Time* check boxes are selected. Access creates one control object for the desired date format and a separate control object for the desired time format. Access places the control objects with the date above the time aligned at the right edge of the *Report Header* section. Once inserted, you can move the controls to another section in the report. Adding a date and/or time control means that the current date and/or time the report is printed are included on the printout. This information is important for the reader of a report to know the currency of the data he or she is reading. Always include a date control as a minimum. Depending on the end user's needs, the time control may or may not be required.

Quick Steps

Add Date and/or Time

1. Open report in Design view.
2. Click Date and Time button.
3. Select desired date and/or time options.
4. Click OK.
5. If necessary, move and/or resize controls as required.

Date and Time

Figure 5.4 Date and Time Dialog Box

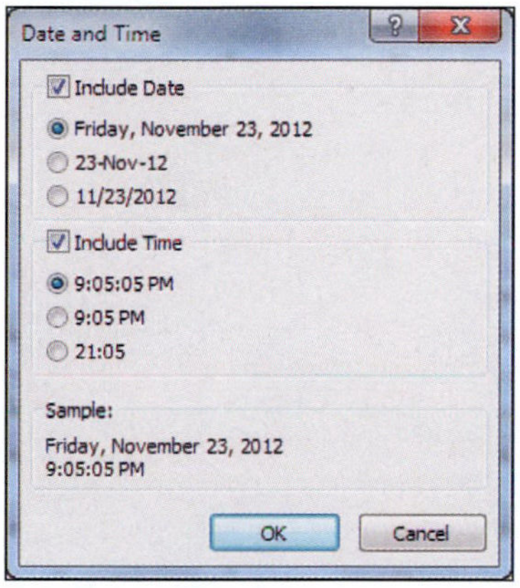

Project 2a **Adding Page Numbering and the Date and Time to a Report** Part 1 of 2

1. With the **AL2-C5-RSRCompServ.accdb** database open, right-click the WorkOrders report in the Navigation pane and click *Design View* at the shortcut menu.
2. When the subreport was inserted in Project 1e, the width of the report may have been automatically extended beyond the page width. Look at the Report Selector button. If a green diagonal triangle displays in the upper left corner of the button, correct the page width by completing the following steps; otherwise, skip this step if your Report Selector button does not display with a green diagonal triangle.
   a. Click the subreport control object to display the orange border and sizing handles. Point to the orange border and then drag the subreport control object left until the left edge of the control object is at the left edge of the *Detail* section. Next, drag the right middle sizing handle left to decrease the subreport width until the right edge of the subreport control object is aligned with the right edge of the *Descr* text box control object above it.

b. Click the green triangle to display the error checking options button and then click the error checking options button to display the drop-down list of options.

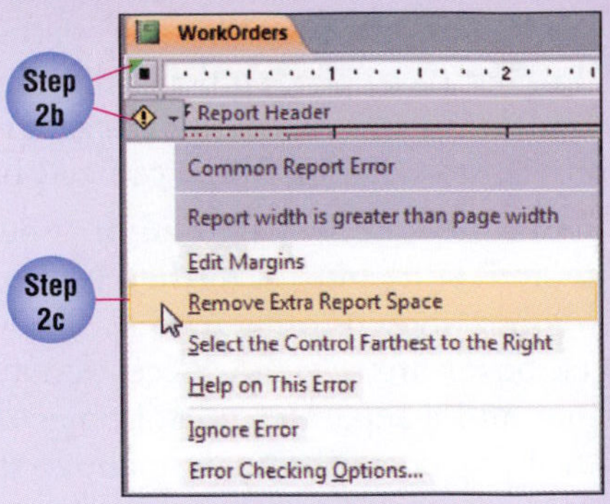

c. Click *Remove Extra Report Space* at the drop-down list to automatically decrease the width of the report. Notice the green diagonal triangle is removed from the Report Selector button once the report width has been corrected.

3. Add page numbering at the bottom center of each page by completing the following steps:
   a. Click the Page Numbers button in the Header/Footer group of the Report Design Tools Design tab.
   b. Click *Page N of M* in the *Format* section of the Page Numbers dialog box.
   c. Click *Bottom of Page [Footer]* in the *Position* section.
   d. With *Alignment* set to *Center* and a check mark in the *Show Number on First Page* check box, click OK. Access adds a control object in the center of the *Page Footer* section with the codes required to print the page numbers in the desired format.

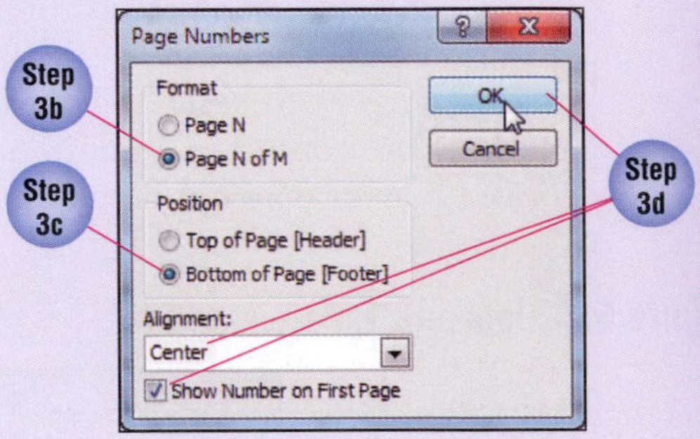

4. Add the current date and time to the end of the report along with a label control object containing the text *Date and Time Printed:* by completing the following steps:
   a. Click the Date and Time button in the Controls group.
   b. Click the second option in the *Include Date* section in the Date and Time dialog box that displays the date in the format *dd-mmm-yy*. For example, *23-Nov-12*.
   c. Click the second option in the *Include Time* section that displays the time in the format *hh:mm AM/PM*. For example, *11:08 AM*.
   d. Click OK. Access adds two control objects one above the other at the right end of the *Report Header* section with the date code *=Date()* and the time code *=Time()*.

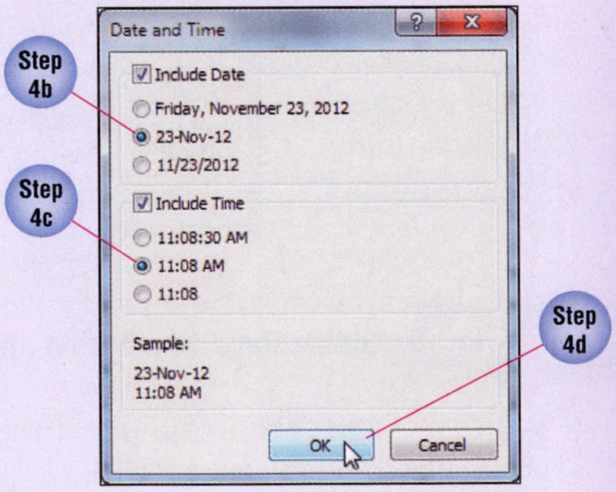

   e. Select both control objects added to the *Report Header* section containing the date and time codes. Click the Home tab and then click the Cut button in the Clipboard group.

f. Click the *Report Footer* section bar and then click the Paste button in the Clipboard group. Access pastes the two objects at the left side of the *Report Footer* section. With the date and time control objects still selected, position the mouse pointer on the orange border until the pointer displays with the four-headed arrow move icon and then drag the controls to the right side of the *Report Footer* section, aligning the right edge of the controls near the right edge of the report grid.

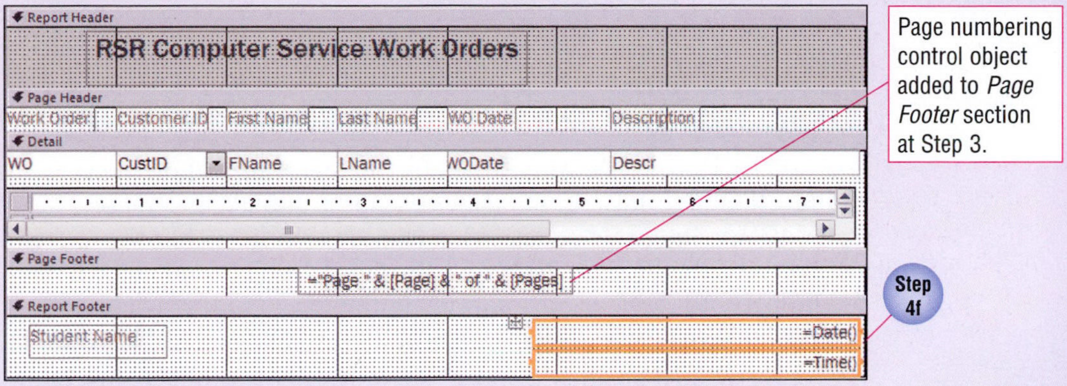

g. Resize and then move the date and time controls to arrange them as shown.

h. Create the two label control objects, type the text **Date Printed:** and **Time Printed:**, and position them left of the date control object and time control object as shown.

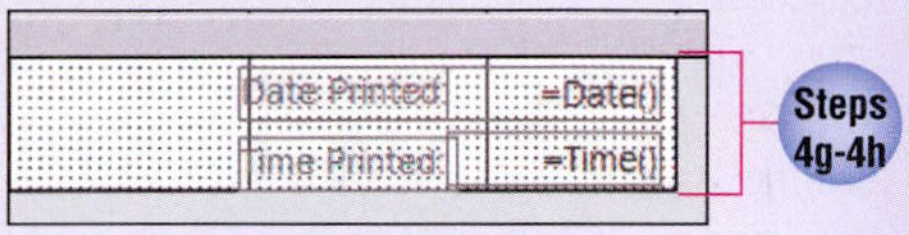

5. Save the report and then display Print Preview.
6. Scroll to the bottom of the first page to view the page numbering at the bottom center of the page.
7. Click the Last Page button in the Page Navigation bar to scroll to the last page in the report and view the date and time at the end of the report.
8. Notice in Print Preview the subreport data is being cut off at the right edge of the report, meaning that the total work order value is not visible. Exit Print Preview to switch back to Design view.
9. Adjust the size and placement of the subreport control objects by completing the following steps:
   a. Since the subreport's control objects are not visible within the WorkOrders report, making changes to the contents of the subreport is more easily completed by working within the separate TotalWorkOrders subreport. Close the WorkOrders report.
   b. Right-click the TotalWorkOrders subreport in the Navigation pane and then click Design View at the shortcut menu.
   c. Press Ctrl + A to select all objects (Ctrl + A is the shortcut for Select All).
   d. Position the mouse pointer on the edge of any selected control until the four-headed arrow move icon appears and then drag the controls to the left edge of the report grid.
   e. Click in any blank area to deselect the controls and then drag the right edge of the grid left to approximately the 7-inch position in the horizontal ruler.

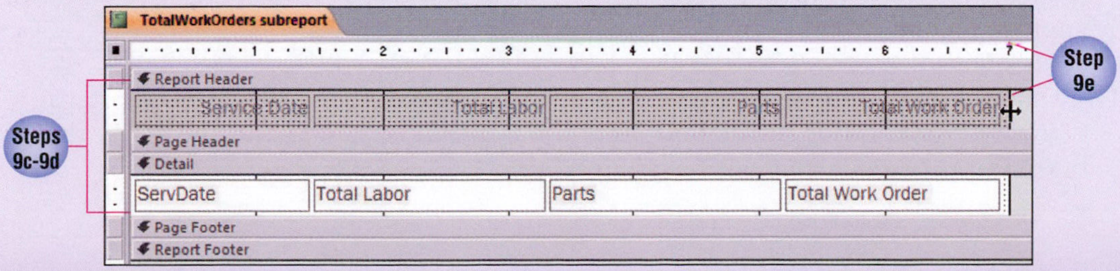

f. Click to select the *Parts* label control object in the *Page Header* section and then drag the right middle sizing handle left until the right edge of the control aligns at the 5-inch position in the horizontal ruler.

10. Save and close the TotalWorkOrders subreport.
11. Open the WorkOrders report. Notice the subreport data is no longer truncated at the right side of the report.
12. Display the report in Design view.

Adding Graphics to a Report

The same techniques that you learned in Chapter 4 to add pictures or clip art or to draw lines in a form in Design view can be applied to a report. Recall from Chapter 4 that clip art when resized is truncated to fit within the resized control object. Display the Property Sheet for the clip art object and change the Size Mode property to *Zoom* or *Stretch* to resize the image to the height and width of the control object.

Insert Image

A company logo or other company artwork that is available in a standard picture file format such as .gif, .jpg, or .png can be inserted in an image control object. Click the Insert Image button in the Controls group of the Report Design Tools Design tab, browse to the image file's drive and folder, double-click the image file name, and then drag to create the image control object the desired height and width within the report.

Project 2b Adding Graphics and Formatting Controls — Part 2 of 2

1. With the **AL2-C5-RSRCompServ.accdb** database open, insert a company logo in the report by completing the following steps:
   a. Position the mouse pointer on the top of the gray *Page Header* section bar until the pointer displays as a horizontal line with an up- and down-pointing arrow and then drag the section bar down approximately 0.5 inch to increase the height of the *Report Header* section.
   b. Click the Insert Image button in the Controls group of the Report Design Tools Design tab and then click *Browse* at the drop-down list.
   c. At the Insert Picture dialog box, navigate to the drive and or folder for the Access2010L2C5 data files on your storage medium and then double-click the file named ***RSRLogo.jpg***.
   d. Position the crosshairs with the image icon attached at the top of the *Report Header* section near the 6-inch position in the horizontal ruler and then drag to create an image control object the approximate height and width shown at the right.

2. Draw and format a horizontal line below the title by completing the following steps:
   a. Click the More button at the bottom of the Controls scroll bar and then click the Line button in the expanded Controls group.

b. Position the crosshairs with the line icon attached below the first letter in the title in the *Report Header* section, hold down the Shift key, drag right releasing the mouse below the last letter in the title, and then release the Shift key.
c. Click the Report Design Tools Format tab and then click the Shape Outline button.
d. Point to *Line Thickness* and then click *3 pt* (fourth option).
e. With the line still selected, click the Shape Outline button, click *Turquoise, Accent 3* (seventh option in first row in *Theme Colors* section of color palette) and then deselect the line.

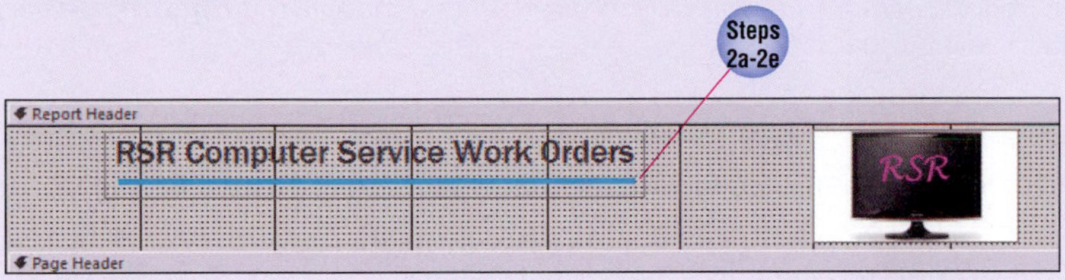

3. Draw and format a horizontal line below the report's column headings by completing the following steps:
   a. Drag the top of the *Detail* section bar down approximately 0.25 inch to add grid space in the *Page Header* section.
   b. Click the Report Design Tools Design tab, click the More button at the bottom of the Controls scroll bar, and then click the Line button in the expanded Controls group.
   c. Draw a straight horizontal line that extends the width of the report along the bottom of the label control objects in the *Page Header* section.
   d. Change the Line Thickness to *1 pt* and change the line color to the same turquoise applied to the line below the report title.
   e. Deselect the line.

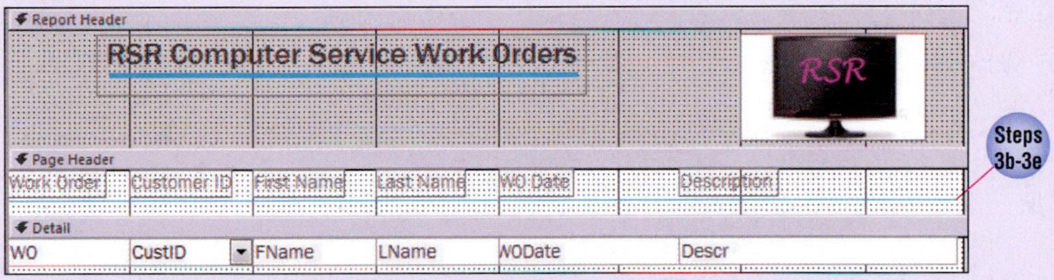

4. Format, move, and resize control objects as follows:
   a. Select all of the label control objects in the *Page Header* section, change the font size to *12* and the font color to *Turquoise, Accent 3, Darker 50%* (seventh option in last row of *Theme Colors* section).
   b. Resize the controls as needed to show all of the label text after increasing the font size.
   c. Move the report title and the line below the title until the first *R* in the title is aligned at the 1-inch position in the horizontal ruler.
   d. Move the *WO Date* label control object in the Page Header section until the left edge of the object is aligned at the 4.5-inch position in the horizontal ruler.
   e. Click the *Report Header* section bar, click the Shape Fill button in the Control Formatting group of the Report Design Tools Format tab, and then click *White, Background 1* (first option in first row in *Theme Colors* section).
   f. Select all of the text box control objects in the *Detail* section. Open the Property Sheet, click the Format tab, click in the *Border Style* property box, click the down-pointing arrow that appears, click *Transparent* at the drop-down list, and then close the Property Sheet. This removes the border around the data in the fields.

g. With all of the text box control objects still selected, change the font color to *Black, Text 1* (second option in first row of *Theme Colors* section).
5. Display the report in Report view.
6. Compare your report with the partial report shown in Figure 5.5. If necessary, return to Design view, make adjustments to formats, alignment, or position of control objects, and then redisplay the report in Report view.
7. Save the report.
8. Print the report. ***Note: This report is five pages long. Print only if required by your instructor.***
9. Close the WorkOrders report.

Figure 5.5 Partial View of Completed WorkOrders Report

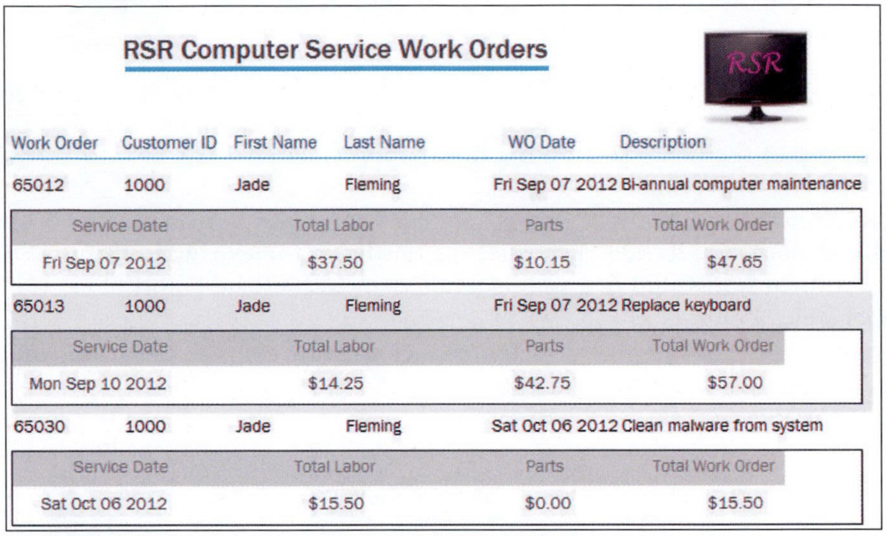
RSR Computer Service Work Orders
RSR
Work Order Customer ID First Name Last Name WO Date Description
65012 1000 Jade Fleming Fri Sep 07 2012 Bi-annual computer maintenance
Service Date Total Labor Parts Total Work Order
Fri Sep 07 2012 $37.50 $10.15 $47.65
65013 1000 Jade Fleming Fri Sep 07 2012 Replace keyboard
Service Date Total Labor Parts Total Work Order
Mon Sep 10 2012 $14.25 $42.75 $57.00
65030 1000 Jade Fleming Sat Oct 06 2012 Clean malware from system
Service Date Total Labor Parts Total Work Order
Sat Oct 06 2012 $15.50 $0.00 $15.50

Project 3 Group Records and Add Functions to Count and Sum — 2 Parts

You will create a new report using the Report Wizard and then modify the report in Design view to add sum and count functions.

Grouping Records and Adding Functions in a Report

A field included in a report that contains repeating field values such as a department, city, or name, is a suitable field by which to group records. For example, a report could be organized to show all records together for the same department or the same city. By summarizing the records by a common field value, you can add totals using functions to calculate the sum, average, max, min, or count for each group. For example, a report similar to the partial report shown in

Figure 5.6 Example Report with Work Order Records Grouped by Customer

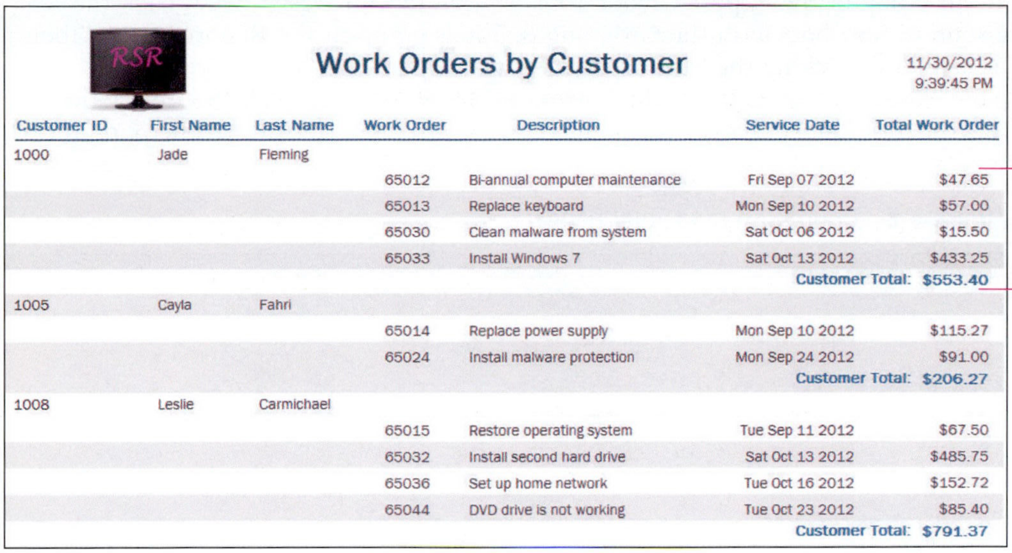

RSR

Work Orders by Customer

11/30/2012
9:39:45 PM

Customer ID	First Name	Last Name	Work Order	Description	Service Date	Total Work Order
1000	Jade	Fleming				
			65012	Bi-annual computer maintenance	Fri Sep 07 2012	$47.65
			65013	Replace keyboard	Mon Sep 10 2012	$57.00
			65030	Clean malware from system	Sat Oct 06 2012	$15.50
			65033	Install Windows 7	Sat Oct 13 2012	$433.25
					Customer Total:	$553.40
1005	Cayla	Fahri				
			65014	Replace power supply	Mon Sep 10 2012	$115.27
			65024	Install malware protection	Mon Sep 24 2012	$91.00
					Customer Total:	$206.27
1008	Leslie	Carmichael				
			65015	Restore operating system	Tue Sep 11 2012	$67.50
			65032	Install second hard drive	Sat Oct 13 2012	$485.75
			65036	Set up home network	Tue Oct 16 2012	$152.72
			65044	DVD drive is not working	Tue Oct 23 2012	$85.40
					Customer Total:	$791.37

Report is grouped on *CustID* field (displays with column heading *Customer ID*) allowing owners to easily see how many calls were made to each customer and how much revenue each customer generated.

Figure 5.6 that organizes the work orders by customer allows the owners of RSR Computer Service to easily see which customer has provided the most revenue to their service business. In this report, the *CustID* field (column heading *Customer ID*) is used to group the records and a sum function has been added to each group.

As you learned in Level 1, Chapter 6, you can group records in a report using the Report Wizard. At the Report Wizard dialog box shown in Figure 5.7, you can specify how you want to group the report. Double-click a field name in the field list box to add a grouping level. The preview window updates to display the grouped field in blue. More than one grouping level can be added to a report. If you change your mind after adding a grouping level, use the Remove Field button (button with left-pointing arrow) to remove the grouped level. Use the Priority buttons (buttons with up- and down-pointing arrows) to change the grouping order when you have multiple grouped fields.

If you created a report using the wizard and did not specify a grouping level, you can group records after the report has been generated using Layout view or

Quick Steps

Group Records Using Report Wizard

1. Click Create tab.
2. Click Report Wizard button.
3. Choose table or query and fields.
4. Click Next.
5. If necessary, remove default grouped field name.
6. Double-click field name by which to group records.
7. Click Next.
8. Choose field(s) by which to sort.
9. Click Next.
10. Choose layout options.
11. Click Next.
12. Enter title for report.
13. Click Finish.

Figure 5.7 Grouping by a Field Using the Report Wizard

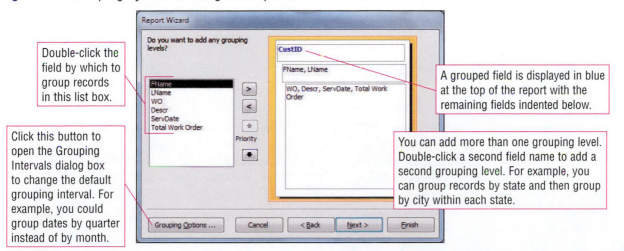

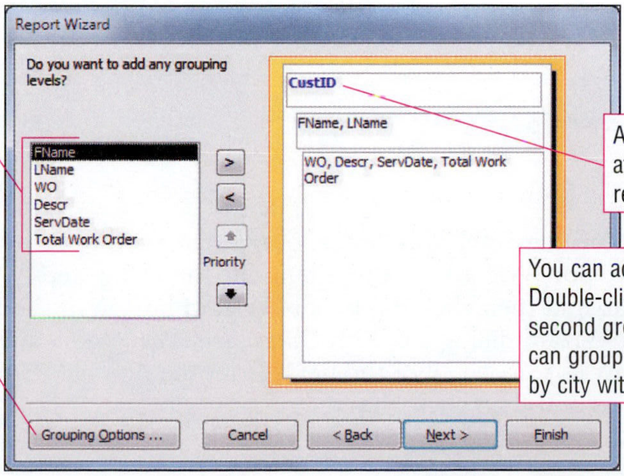

Double-click the field by which to group records in this list box.

Click this button to open the Grouping Intervals dialog box to change the default grouping interval. For example, you could group dates by quarter instead of by month.

A grouped field is displayed in blue at the top of the report with the remaining fields indented below.

You can add more than one grouping level. Double-click a second field name to add a second grouping level. For example, you can group records by state and then group by city within each state.

HINT

Use Layout view to group records using the Group, Sort, and Total pane since Access does all of the work for you after you select the group field. In Design view, Access creates the *Group Header* section but does not automatically place the field's text box control within the group section—you have to do this manually.

Group & Sort

Design view. In Layout view, click the Group & Sort button in the Grouping & Totals group of the Report Layout Tools Design tab. In Design view, click the Group & Sort button in the Grouping & Totals group in the Report Design Tools Design tab. Clicking the button in either view opens the Group, Sort, and Total pane shown in Figure 5.8 at the bottom of the work area. Click the Add a group button and then click the field name by which to group records in the pop-up list.

Figure 5.8 Group, Sort, and Total Pane

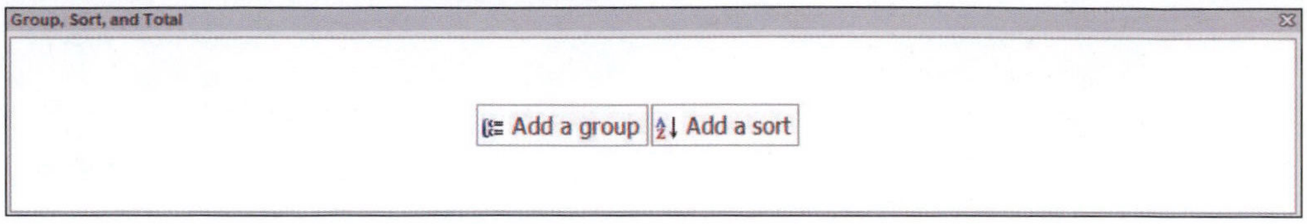

Project 3a Creating a Report with a Grouping Level Using the Report Wizard — Part 1 of 2

1. With the **AL2-C5-RSRCompServ.accdb** database open, modify the TotalWorkOrders query to add two fields you want to include in a report by completing the following steps:
   a. Open the TotalWorkOrders query in Design view.
   b. Drag the *CustID* field from the WorkOrders field list box to the *Field* box in the second column in the design grid. The existing *ServDate* and other fields will shift right to accommodate the new field.
   c. Drag the *Descr* field from the WorkOrders table to the *Field* box in the third column in the design grid.
   d. Save the revised query.
   e. Run the query.

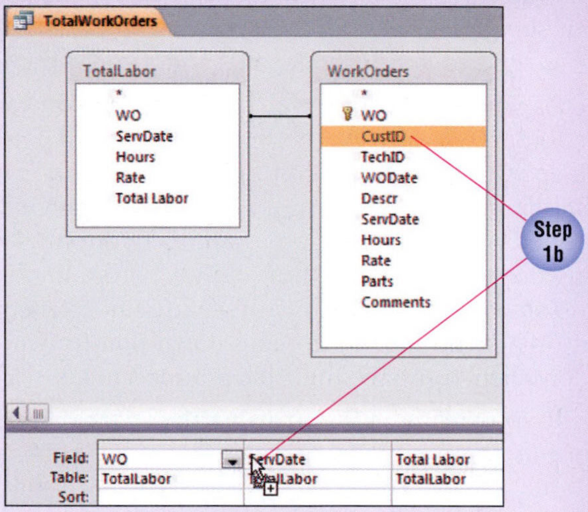

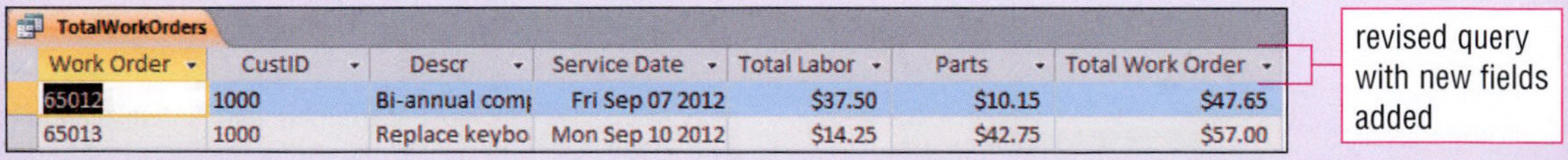

TotalWorkOrders
Work Order
CustID
Descr
Service Date
Total Labor
Parts
Total Work Order
65012
1000
Bi-annual com
Fri Sep 07 2012
$37.50
$10.15
$47.65
65013
1000
Replace keybo
Mon Sep 10 2012
$14.25
$42.75
$57.00
revised query with new fields added

   f. Close the query.
2. Create a report based on the TotalWorkOrders query that is grouped by the service dates by month using the Report Wizard by completing the following steps:
   a. Click the Create tab and then click the Report Wizard button in the Reports group.
   b. At the first Report Wizard dialog box with *Query: TotalWorkOrders* already selected in the *Tables/Queries* list box, move all of the fields from the *Available Fields* list box to the *Selected Fields* list box and then click Next.

c. At the second Report Wizard dialog box, specify the grouping level by the *ServDate* field by completing the following steps:

1) With *CustID* displayed in blue in the preview section indicating the report will be grouped by customer number, click the Remove field button (displays as a left-pointing arrow) to remove the grouping level.

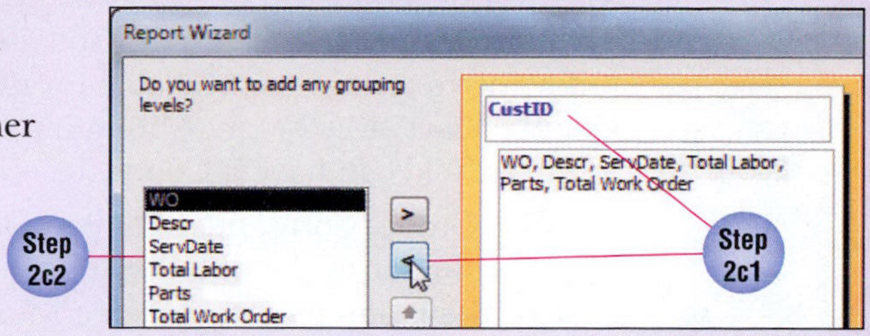

2) Double-click *ServDate* in the field list box to add a grouping level by the service date field. By default, Access groups the date field by month.

3) With the preview section now displaying that the report will be grouped by *ServDate by Month*, click Next.

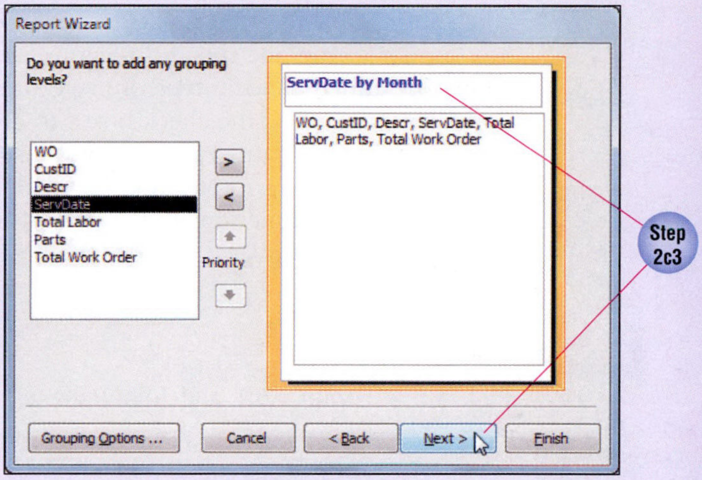

d. At the third Report Wizard dialog box, click the down-pointing arrow at the right of the first sort list box, click *WO* at the drop-down list to sort within each group by the work order numbers in ascending order, and then click Next.

e. At the fourth Report Wizard dialog box, click *Landscape* in the *Orientation* section and then click Next.

f. At the last Report Wizard dialog box, select the existing text in the *What title do you want for your report?* text box, type **WorkOrdersbyMonth**, and click Finish.

3. Minimize the Navigation pane.

4. Preview the report and then switch to Layout view or Design view. Edit text in the report title and column heading labels and adjust widths as necessary until the report looks similar to the one shown below. Change the theme to *Flow* and modify the colors for the *Report Header* and *Page Header* sections using your best judgment to match the theme colors as shown.

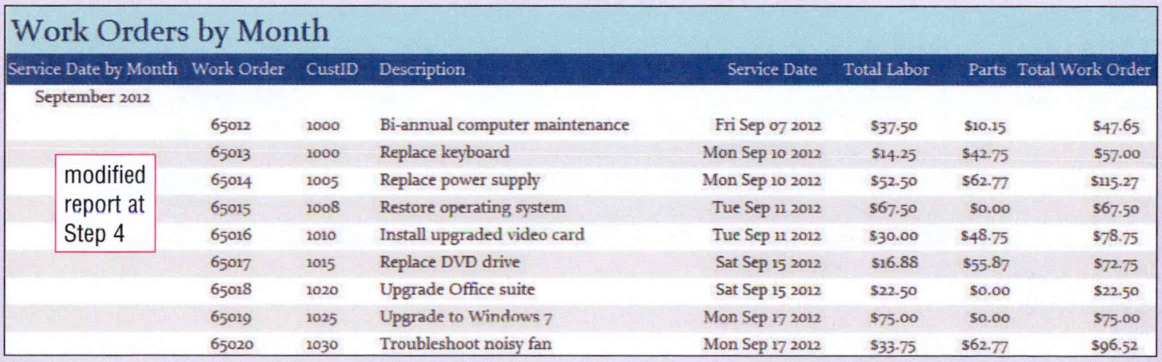

Work Orders by Month

Service Date by Month	Work Order	CustID	Description	Service Date	Total Labor	Parts	Total Work Order
September 2012							
	65012	1000	Bi-annual computer maintenance	Fri Sep 07 2012	$37.50	$10.15	$47.65
	65013	1000	Replace keyboard	Mon Sep 10 2012	$14.25	$42.75	$57.00
	65014	1005	Replace power supply	Mon Sep 10 2012	$52.50	$62.77	$115.27
	65015	1008	Restore operating system	Tue Sep 11 2012	$67.50	$0.00	$67.50
	65016	1010	Install upgraded video card	Tue Sep 11 2012	$30.00	$48.75	$78.75
	65017	1015	Replace DVD drive	Sat Sep 15 2012	$16.88	$55.87	$72.75
	65018	1020	Upgrade Office suite	Sat Sep 15 2012	$22.50	$0.00	$22.50
	65019	1025	Upgrade to Windows 7	Mon Sep 17 2012	$75.00	$0.00	$75.00
	65020	1030	Troubleshoot noisy fan	Mon Sep 17 2012	$33.75	$62.77	$96.52

5. Save the report.

Quick Steps

Add Functions to Group

1. Open report in Design view or Layout view.
2. Click Group & Sort button.
3. Click More Options button.
4. Click down-pointing arrow next to *with no totals*.
5. Choose field in *Total On* list box.
6. Choose function in *Type* list box.
7. If desired, click *Show Grand Total* check box.
8. If desired, click *Show group subtotal as % of Grand Total* check box.
9. Click *Show subtotal in group header* or *Show subtotal in group footer* check box.
10. Repeat Steps 5–9 as needed for other fields.
11. Click outside Totals option box.
12. Close Group, Sort, and Total pane.

HINT

Apply formatting options such as bold, color, or borders (in Property Sheet) to totals to make them stand out in the report. For totals without a border style, you can use the Line tool to draw lines below a total. For example, draw two lines below a grand total to double underline.

When a report is grouped, the Group, Sort, and Total pane can be used to add a calculation below a numeric field at the end of each group. You can add a function to more than one field within the group. For example you can calculate a Sum function on a sales field and a Count function on an invoice field. The following functions are available for numeric fields: Sum, Average, Count Records, Count Values, Maximum, Minimum, Standard Deviation, and Variance. A non-numeric field can have a Count Records or Count Values function added.

The Group, Sort, and Total pane for a report with an existing grouping level displays similar to the one shown in Figure 5.9. Click the More Options button next to the group level to which a total is to be added to expand the available group options.

Click the down-pointing arrow next to *with no totals* to open the *Totals* option box similar to the one shown in Figure 5.10. Select the field to which a function should be added and the type of aggregate function to calculate using the drop-down list boxes. Use the check boxes to choose to add a grand total to the end of the report, calculate group subtotals as a percentage of the grand total, and whether to add the subtotal function to the *Group Header* or *Group Footer* section. Continue adding functions to other fields as needed and click outside the *Totals* option box when finished to close the box.

Figure 5.9 Group, Sort, and Total Pane with a Grouping Level Added

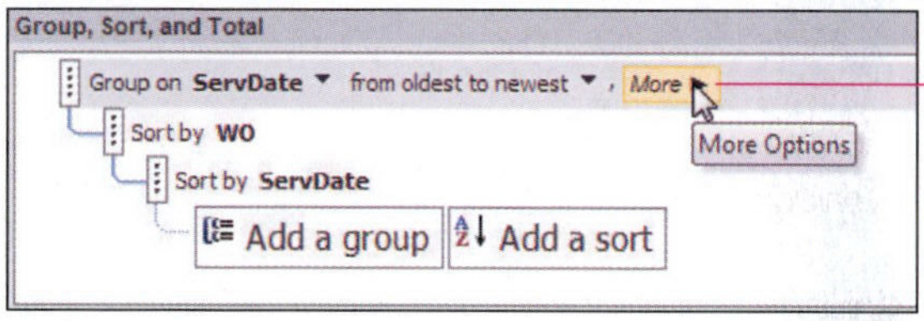

Click the More Options button to expand the pane to show group interval options, the *Totals* option, and other group options.

Figure 5.10 *Totals* Option Box in Group, Sort, and Total Pane

Click here in the expanded options list to open the *Totals* option box in which you specify the field(s) and function(s) to add to the report. You can also add functions to calculate a grand total at the end of the report and calculate group totals as a percentage of the grand total.

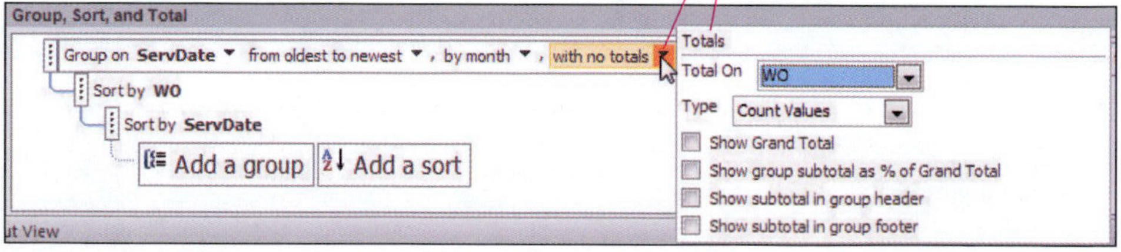

Project 3b Adding Functions to a Report

1. With the **AL2-C5-RSRCompServ.accdb** database open, display the WorkOrdersbyMonth report in Design view.
2. Add two functions at the end of each month to show the number of work orders and the total value of work orders by completing the following steps:

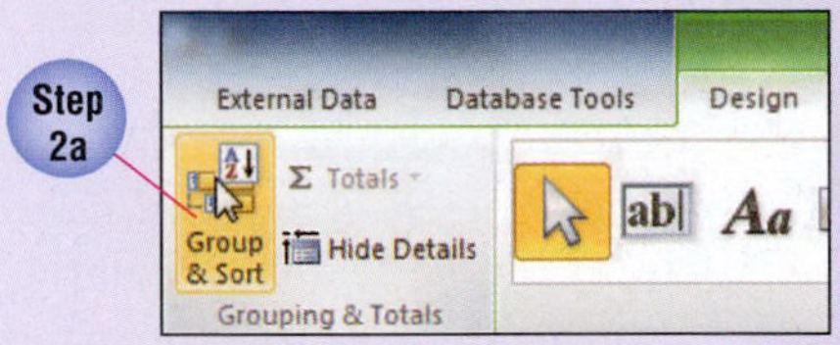

   a. In the Grouping & Totals group of the Report Design Tools Design tab, click the Group & Sort button.

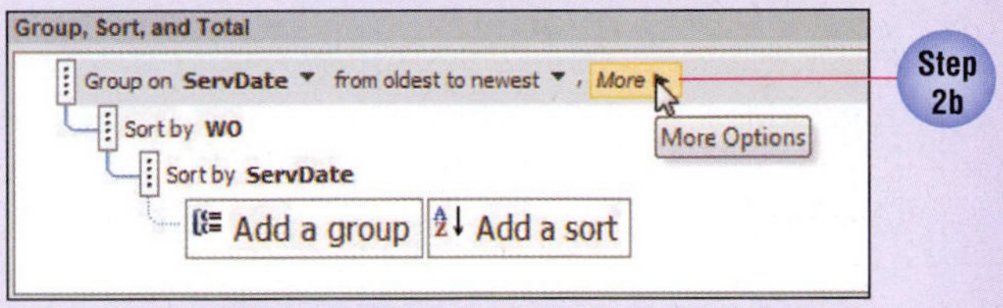

   b. At the Group, Sort, and Total pane located at the bottom of the work area, click the More Options button located next to *from oldest to newest* in the *Group on ServDate* group options.
   c. Click the down-pointing arrow next to *with no totals* in the expanded group options.
   d. At the *Totals* option box, with *WO* in the *Total On* list box, specify the type of function and the placement of the result by completing the following steps:
      1) Click the down-pointing arrow next to *Type* and then click *Count Records* at the drop-down list.
      2) Click the *Show Grand Total* check box to insert a check mark. Access adds a count function in a control object in the *Report Footer* section below the *WO* column.
      3) Click the *Show subtotal in group footer* check box to insert a check mark. Access displays a new section with the title *ServDate Footer* in the gray section bar below the *Detail* section and inserts a count function in a control object below the *WO* column.

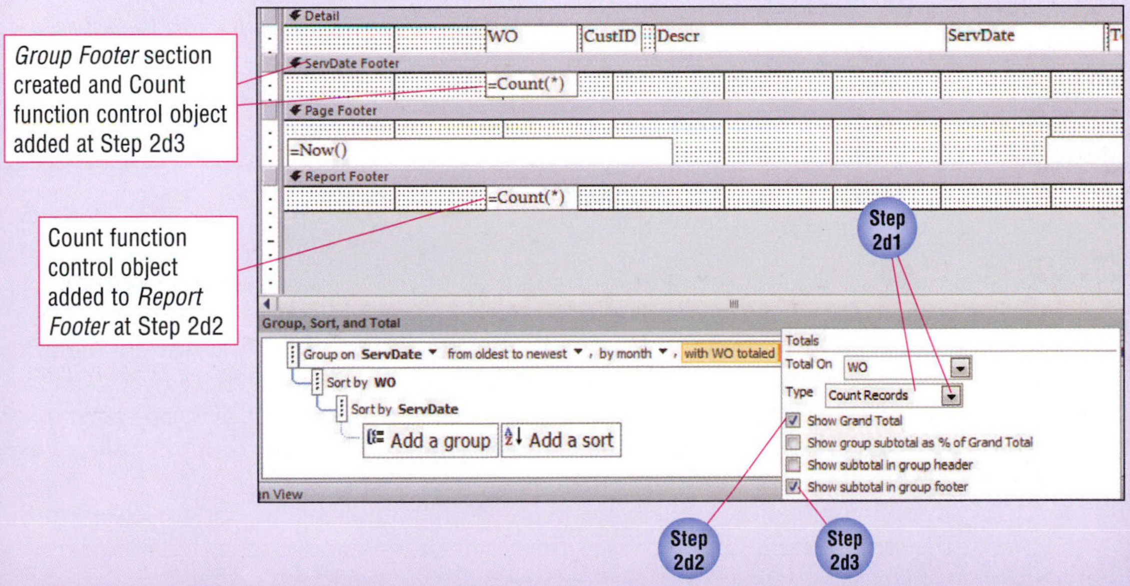

e. With the Totals option box still open, click the down-pointing arrow next to *Total On* and select *Total Work Order* at the drop-down list. The *Type* option defaults to *Sum* for a numeric field.

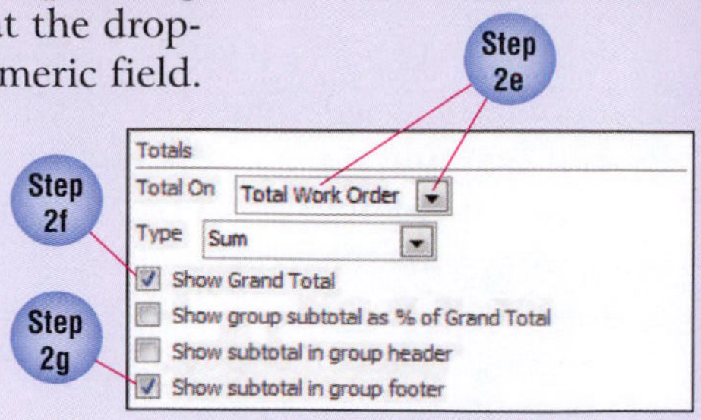

f. Click the *Show Grand Total* check box to insert a check mark. Access adds a Sum function in a control object in the *Report Footer* section.

g. Click the *Show subtotal in group footer* check box to insert a check mark. Access adds a Sum function in a control object in the *ServDate Footer* section.

h. Click outside the *Totals* option box to close the box.

3. Click the Group & Sort button to close the Group, Sort, and Total pane.
4. Review the two Count functions and the two Sum functions added to the report in Design view.
5. Display the report in Print Preview to view the calculated results. Notice the printout requires two pages with the report's grand totals printing on page 2. Also notice that Access added the Sum function below the Count function rather than at the bottom of the *Total Work Order* column.
6. Close Print preview to switch back to Design view.
7. Click to select the Sum function control object in the *ServDate Footer* section, Shift + click to select the Sum function control object in the *Report Footer* section. Position the mouse pointer on the orange border of either one of the selected control objects and then drag to move the two objects simultaneously to the right below the Total Work Order object in the *Detail* section.

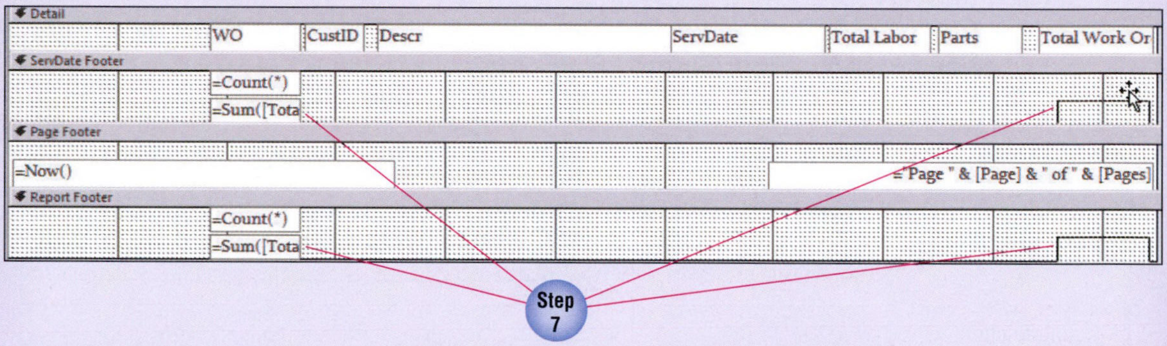

8. Add a label control object left of the Count function in the *ServDate Footer* section that displays the text *Work Order Count:* and another label control object left of the Sum function that displays the text *Month Total:*. Apply bold, red font color, and right-align the text in the two label control objects. Resize and align the two labels as necessary. ***Note: Access displays an error flag on the two label control objects indicating these objects are not associated with another control object. You can ignore these error flags since the labels have been added for descriptive text only.***
9. Move the Sum function control object and the Month Total label control object up until they are at the same horizontal position as the Count function and then decrease the height of the *ServDate Footer* section as shown below.

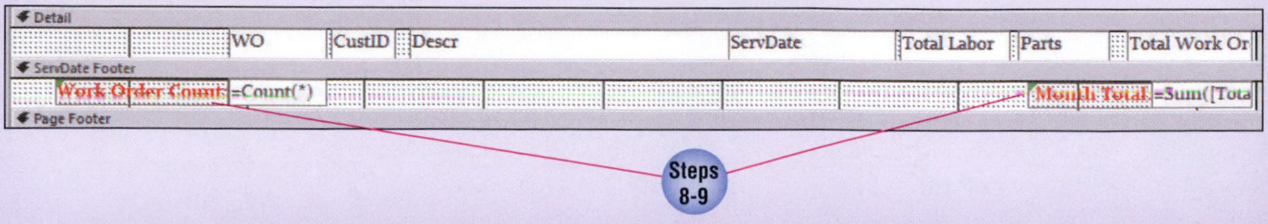

10. Display the report in Print Preview to view the labels. If necessary, return to Design view to make further size and alignment adjustments.

partial report displayed in Print Preview with labels and functions added

Service Date by Month	Work Order	CustID	Description	Service Date	Total Labor	Parts	Total Work Order
September 2012							
	65012	1000	Bi-annual computer maintenance	Fri Sep 07 2012	$37.50	$10.15	$47.65
	65013	1000	Replace keyboard	Mon Sep 10 2012	$14.25	$42.75	$57.00
	65014	1005	Replace power supply	Mon Sep 10 2012	$52.50	$62.77	$115.27
	65015	1008	Restore operating system	Tue Sep 11 2012	$67.50	$0.00	$67.50
	65016	1010	Install upgraded video card	Tue Sep 11 2012	$30.00	$48.75	$78.75
	65017	1015	Replace DVD drive	Sat Sep 15 2012	$16.88	$55.87	$72.75
	65018	1020	Upgrade Office suite	Sat Sep 15 2012	$22.50	$0.00	$22.50
	65019	1025	Upgrade to Windows 7	Mon Sep 17 2012	$75.00	$0.00	$75.00
	65020	1030	Troubleshoot noisy fan	Mon Sep 17 2012	$33.75	$62.77	$96.52
	65021	1035	Customer has blue screen upon boot	Tue Sep 18 2012	$97.50	$0.00	$97.50
	65022	1040	Customer reports screen is fuzzy	Sat Sep 22 2012	$45.00	$55.47	$100.47
	65023	1045	Upgrade RAM	Sun Sep 23 2012	$37.50	$62.50	$100.00
	65024	1005	Install malware protection	Mon Sep 24 2012	$15.50	$75.50	$91.00
	65025	1010	Troubleshoot hard drive noise	Fri Sep 28 2012	$45.00	$0.00	$45.00
	65026	1025	Upgrade memory	Sat Sep 29 2012	$22.50	$75.75	$98.25
Work Order Count:	15					Month Total:	$1,165.16

11. With the report displayed in Design view, select the Sum function control object in the *Report Footer* section and move the control up until it is positioned at the same horizontal position as the Count function below the *WO* column.
12. Click to select the *Work Order Count*: label control object, Shift + click to select the *Month Total*: label control object, click the Home tab, and then click the Copy button in the Clipboard group. Click the *Report Footer* section bar and then click the Paste button in the Clipboard group. Move and align the copied labels as shown below. Edit the *Month Total*: label control object to *Grand Total*: as shown.

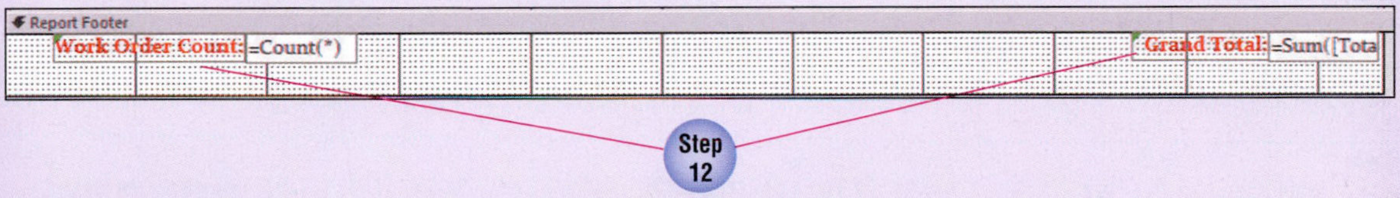

13. Display the report in Report view. Scroll to the bottom of the page to view the labels next to the grand totals. If necessary, return to Design view to make further size and alignment adjustments and then save and close the report.
14. Redisplay the Navigation pane.

Project 4 Modify Section and Group Properties — 1 Part

You will change a report's page setup and then modify section and group properties to control print options.

Modifying Section Properties

A report has a Property Sheet, each control object within the report has a Property Sheet, and each section within the report has a Property Sheet. Section properties control whether the section is visible when printed, the section's height, background color, special effects, and so on. Figure 5.11 displays the Format tab in the Property Sheet for the *Report Header* section. Some of the options can be

Figure 5.11 *Report Header* Section Property Sheet with Format Tab Selected

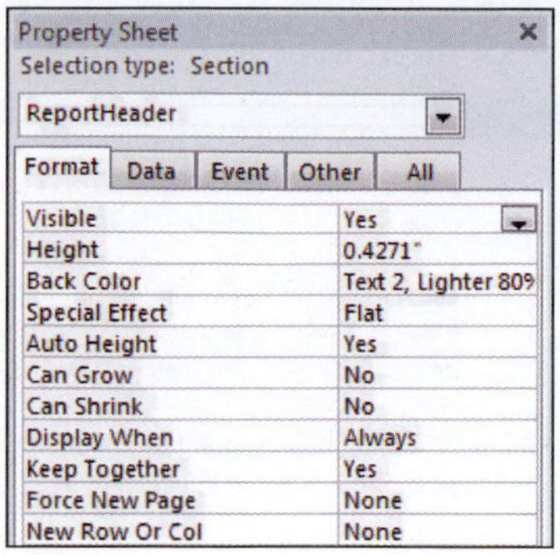

> **Quick Steps**
>
> **Modify Section Properties**
> 1. Open report in Design view.
> 2. Double-click gray section bar.
> 3. Change desired properties.
> 4. Close Property Sheet.
>
> **Keep Group Together on One Page**
> 1. Open report in Design view or Layout view.
> 2. Click Group & Sort button.
> 3. Click More Options button.
> 4. Click down-pointing arrow next to *do not keep group together on one page*.
> 5. Click desired print option.
> 6. Close Group, Sort, and Total pane.

changed without opening the Property Sheet. For example, you can increase or decrease the height of a section by dragging the top or bottom of a gray section bar in Design view. You can also set the background color using the Fill/Back Color button in the Font group of the Report Design Tools Format tab.

Use the Keep Together property to ensure that a section is not split over two pages by a page break. If necessary, Access starts printing the section at the top of the next page; however, if the section is longer than can fit on one page, Access continues printing the section on the following page. In that case, you can decrease margins and/or apply a smaller font size to fit the text for the section all on one page.

Use the Force New Page property to insert a page break before a section begins *(Before Section)*, after a section is finished *(After Section)*, or before and after a section *(Before & After)*.

Keeping a Group Together on the Same Page

Open the Group, Sort, and Total pane and click the More Options button for a group to specify whether you want to keep an entire group together on the same page. By default, Access does not keep a group together. Click the down-pointing arrow next to *do not keep group together on one page* and then click the desired option as shown in Figure 5.12.

Figure 5.12 Group, Sort, and Total Pane with Keep Group Together Print Options

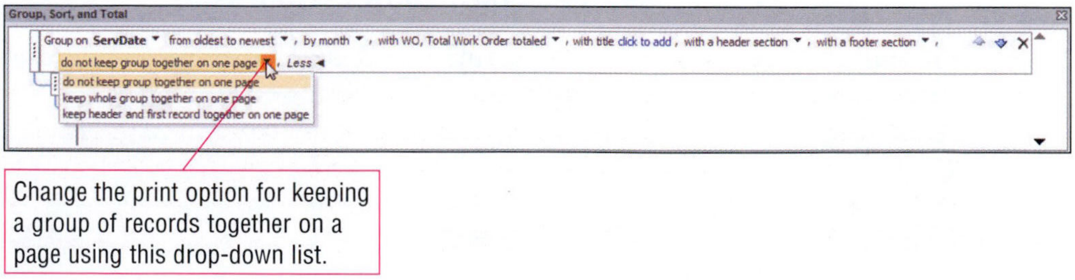

Change the print option for keeping a group of records together on a page using this drop-down list.

Project 4 Modifying Section Properties, and Keeping a Group Together

Part 1 of 1

1. With the **AL2-C5-RSRCompServ.accdb** database open, display the WorkOrdersbyMonth report in Print Preview, click the Zoom button (do not click the down-pointing arrow on the button) in the Zoom group to change the zoom to view an entire page within the window.
2. Click the Next Page button in the Page Navigation bar to view page 2 of the report with the grand totals.
3. Switch to Design view and minimize the Navigation pane.
4. Change the section properties for the *Group Footer* and the *Report Footer* sections displaying the Count and Sum functions by completing the following steps:
   a. Double-click the gray *ServDate Footer* section bar to open the section's Property Sheet.
   b. Click in the *Back Color* property box and click the Build button to open the color palette.
   c. Click *Light Turquoise, Background 2* (third option in first row of *Theme Colors* section).
   d. Close the Property Sheet.
   e. Select the Count function control object and the Sum function control object in the *ServDate Footer* section and change the font color to red and apply bold.
   f. With the Count and Sum function control objects still selected, right-click either one of the selected controls, point to *Fill/Back Color* at the shortcut menu, and then click *Transparent*. The controls by default displayed with a white fill color in the background. Changing to *Transparent* means the background color applied at Step 4c will now display behind the calculations.

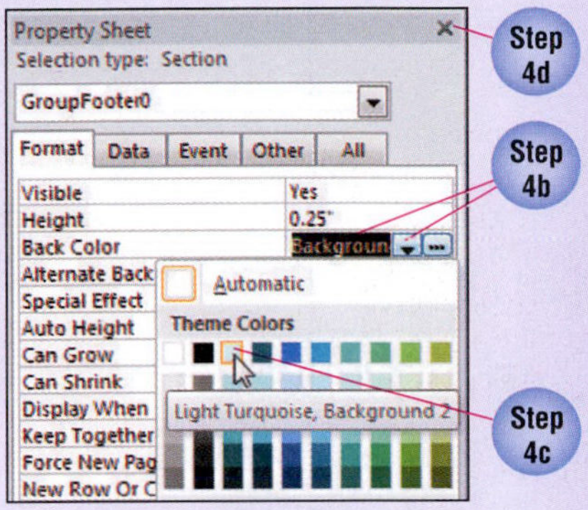

   g. Double-click the gray *Report Footer* section bar and then change the *Back Color* to the same color as the ServDate footer (see Steps 4b through 4c) and then close the Property Sheet.
   h. Apply the same formatting in Steps 4e through 4f to the Count and Sum function control objects in the *Report Footer* section.
5. Print each month's work orders on a separate page by completing the following steps:
   a. Click the Group & Sort button in the Report Design Tools Design tab.
   b. Click the More Options button in the Group, Sort, and Total pane.
   c. Click the down-pointing arrow next to *do not keep group together on one page* and then click *keep whole group together on one page* at the drop-down list.
   d. Close the Group, Sort, and Total pane.

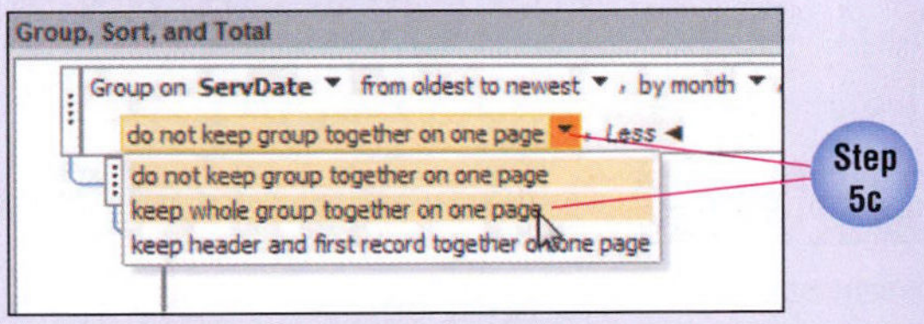

6. Create a label control object at the top right of the *Report Header* section with your first and last name. Bold the label control object and apply dark blue font color.
7. Display the report in Print Preview and zoom to One Page. Compare your report with the one shown in Figure 5.13. Scroll to page 2 to view all of October's work orders together on the same page.
8. Save, print, and then close the report.
9. Redisplay the Navigation pane.

Figure 5.13 Page 1 of Completed Report in Project 4

Work Orders by Month — Student Name

Service Date by Month	Work Order	CustID	Description	Service Date	Total Labor	Parts	Total Work Order
September 2012							
	65012	1000	Bi-annual computer maintenance	Fri Sep 07 2012	$37.50	$10.15	$47.65
	65013	1000	Replace keyboard	Mon Sep 10 2012	$14.25	$42.75	$57.00
	65014	1005	Replace power supply	Mon Sep 10 2012	$52.50	$62.77	$115.27
	65015	1008	Restore operating system	Tue Sep 11 2012	$67.50	$0.00	$67.50
	65016	1010	Install upgraded video card	Tue Sep 11 2012	$30.00	$48.75	$78.75
	65017	1015	Replace DVD drive	Sat Sep 15 2012	$16.88	$55.87	$72.75
	65018	1020	Upgrade Office suite	Sat Sep 15 2012	$22.50	$0.00	$22.50
	65019	1025	Upgrade to Windows 7	Mon Sep 17 2012	$75.00	$0.00	$75.00
	65020	1030	Troubleshoot noisy fan	Mon Sep 17 2012	$33.75	$62.77	$96.52
	65021	1035	Customer has blue screen upon boot	Tue Sep 18 2012	$97.50	$0.00	$97.50
	65022	1040	Customer reports screen is fuzzy	Sat Sep 22 2012	$45.00	$55.47	$100.47
	65023	1045	Upgrade RAM	Sun Sep 23 2012	$37.50	$62.50	$100.00
	65024	1005	Install malware protection	Mon Sep 24 2012	$15.50	$75.50	$91.00
	65025	1010	Troubleshoot hard drive noise	Fri Sep 28 2012	$45.00	$0.00	$45.00
	65026	1025	Upgrade memory	Sat Sep 29 2012	$22.50	$75.75	$98.25
Work Order Count:	15					Month Total:	$1,165.16

Friday, November 30, 2012 — Page 1 of 2

Project 5 Create and Format a Chart — 2 Parts

You will create and format a chart in a customers report to show the total parts and labor on work orders by month.

Inserting, Editing, and Formatting a Chart into a Report

HINT

The chart feature in Access is not the same Chart tool that is included with Word, Excel, and PowerPoint.

Insert Chart

A chart can be added to a report to graphically display numerical data from another table or query. The chart is linked to a field in the report that is common to both objects. Access summarizes and graphs the data from the charted table or query based on the fields you select for each record in the report.

With a report open in Design view, increase the height or width of the *Detail* section to make room for the chart, click the Insert Chart button in the Controls group of the Report Design Tools Design tab and drag the crosshairs with the chart icon attached the approximate height and width for the chart. When you release the mouse, Access launches the Chart Wizard with the first of six dialog boxes shown in Figure 5.14 that guide you through the steps of creating a chart.

Figure 5.14 First Dialog Box in Chart Wizard

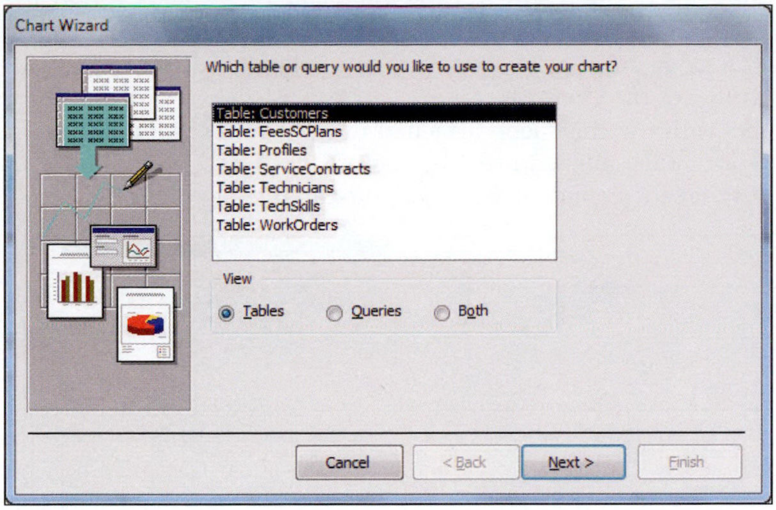

Quick Steps

Insert Chart in Report
1. Open report in Design view.
2. Click Insert Chart button.
3. Drag to create control object the height and width desired.
4. Select table or query for chart data.
5. Click Next.
6. Add fields to use in chart.
7. Click Next.
8. Click desired chart type.
9. Click Next.
10. Add fields as needed to chart layout.
11. Click Preview Chart.
12. Close Sample Preview window.
13. Click Next.
14. Select field to link report with chart.
15. Click Next.
16. Type chart name.
17. Click Finish.

In Project 5 you will use the Chart Wizard to insert a chart in a customer report that depicts the total value of work orders for each customer by month. The data for the chart will be drawn from a related query. A chart can also be inserted into a form and formatted by completing steps similar to those in Projects 5a and 5b.

Project 5a Creating a Report and Inserting a Chart

Part 1 of 2

1. With the **AL2-C5-RSRCompServ.accdb** database open, create a new report using the Report Wizard by completing the following steps:
   a. Select the Customers table in the Navigation pane, click the Create tab and then click the Report Wizard button.
   b. At the first Report Wizard dialog box with *Table: Customers* selected in the *Tables/Queries* list box, move *CustID*, *FName*, *LName*, and *ServCont* from the *Available Fields* list box to the *Selected Fields* list box and then click Next.
   c. Click Next at the second Report Wizard dialog box with no group field selected.
   d. Click Next at the third Report Wizard dialog to choose not to sort the report.
   e. Click *Columnar* at the fourth Report Wizard dialog box and then click Next.
   f. Click at the end of the current text in the *What title do you want for your report?* text box, type **WOChart** so that the report title is *CustomersWOChart*, and then click Finish.
2. Minimize the Navigation pane and display the report in Design view.
3. Edit the report title in the *Report Header* section to *Customers with Work Orders by Month*.
4. Drag the top of the *Page Footer* section bar down until the *Detail* section ends at the 2-inch position in the vertical ruler.

5. Insert a chart at the right side of the report to show the value of the work orders for each customer by month by completing the following steps:
   a. Click the More button at the bottom of the Controls scroll bar and then click the Chart button in the second row of the Controls.
   b. Position the crosshairs with the chart icon attached in the *Detail* section at the 5-inch position in the horizontal ruler aligned near the top of the *CustID* control object and drag down and right to create a chart object the approximate height and width shown.

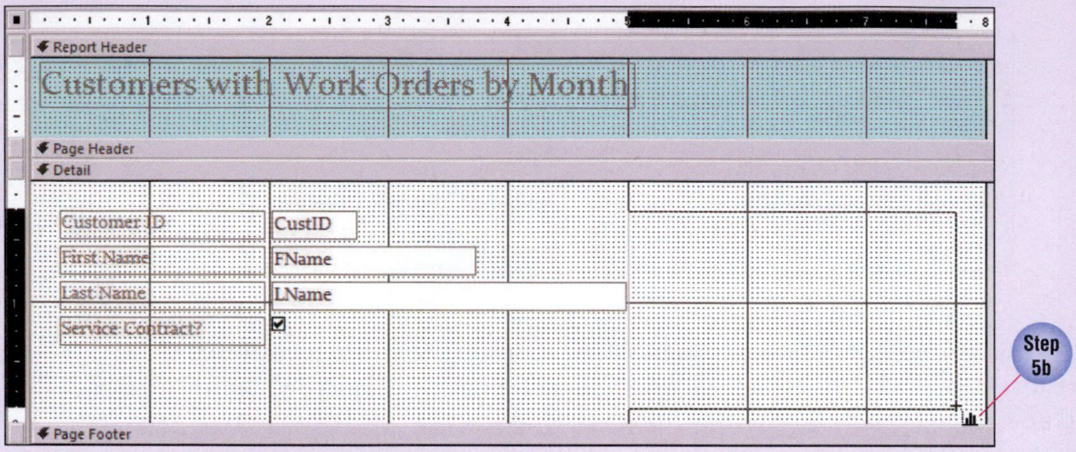

   c. At the first Chart Wizard dialog box, click *Queries* in the *View* section, click *Query: TotalWorkOrders* in the list box, and then click Next.

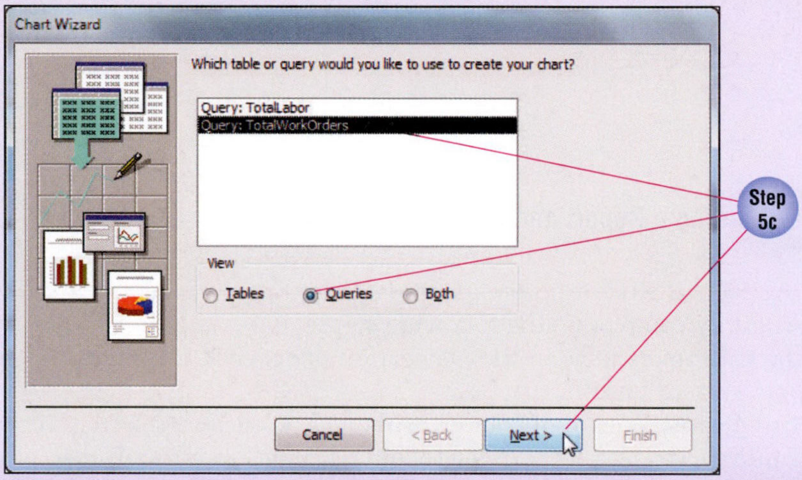

d. At the second Chart Wizard dialog box, double-click *ServDate* and *Total Work Order* in the *Available Fields* list box to move the fields to the *Fields for Chart* list box and then click Next.

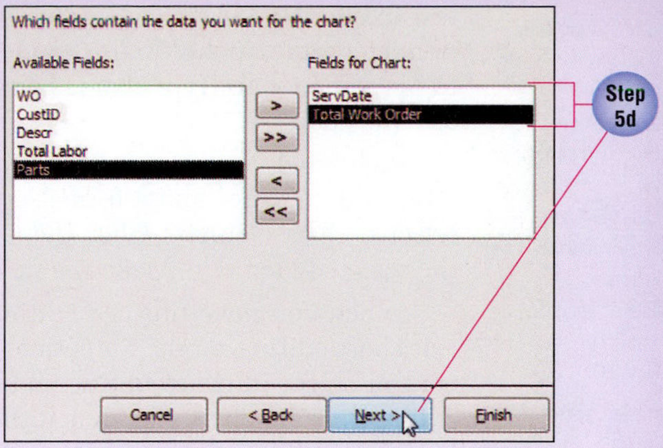

e. At the third Chart Wizard dialog box, click the second chart type in the first row (3-D Column Chart) and then click Next.

f. At the fourth Chart Wizard dialog box, look at the fields that Access has already placed to lay out the chart. Since only two fields were added, Access automatically used the numeric field with a Sum function as the data series for the chart and the date field as the *x*-axis category axis.

g. Click Next.

h. At the fifth Chart Wizard dialog box notice that Access has correctly detected the field to link records in the Customers report with the chart (based on the TotalWorkOrders query) as *CustID*. Click Next.

i. At the last Chart Wizard dialog box, click Finish. Access inserts a chart within the height and width of the chart control. The chart displayed in the control in Design view is not the actual chart based on the query data—it is only a sample to show the chart elements.

6. Display the report in Print Preview and scroll through the four pages in the report. Customers for which an empty chart displays have no work order data to be graphed.

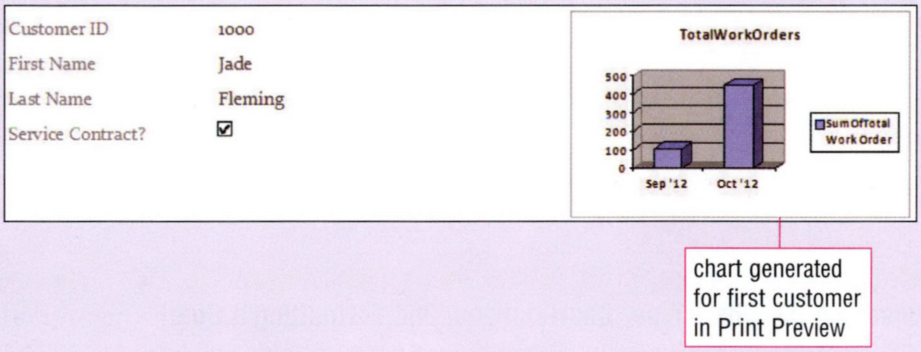

7. Save and close the report and then redisplay the Navigation pane.

The chart application within Access is not the same chart feature that is available in Microsoft Word, Microsoft Excel, and Microsoft PowerPoint. Access uses the Microsoft Graph application for charts. Open a report in Design view and double-click a chart object to edit the chart. In chart editing mode, a Menu bar and a toolbar display at the top of the Access window as well as a datasheet for the chart in the work area. You can change the chart type, add, remove, or change chart options, and format chart elements.

Quick Steps

Change Chart Type
1. Open report in Design view.
2. Double-click chart.
3. Click Chart on Menu bar.
4. Click *Chart Type*.
5. Click desired chart type in list box.
6. Click desired chart sub-type.
7. Click OK.

Change Chart Options
1. Open report in Design view.
2. Double-click chart.
3. Click Chart on Menu bar.
4. Click *Chart Options*.
5. Click tab for options to be changed.
6. Change options as required.
7. Click OK.

Format Chart Element
1. Open report in Design view.
2. Double-click chart.
3. Right-click chart element.
4. Click *Format* for selected chart element.
5. Change format options as required.
6. Click OK.

Click Chart on the Menu bar and click *Chart Options* to add, delete, or edit text in chart titles, to add or remove chart axes, gridlines, the legend, data labels, or a data table at the Chart Options dialog box. Click Chart and click *Chart Type* to open the Chart Type dialog box and choose a different chart such as a bar chart or a pie chart.

Right-click an object within the chart such as the chart title, legend, chart area, or data series and a format option displays in the shortcut menu for the selected chart element. Click the Format option to open a Format dialog box for the selected element. Make the desired changes and click OK.

When you have finished editing the chart, click outside the chart object to exit chart editing mode. Sometimes Access displays a sample chart within the control object in chart editing mode instead of the actual chart which can make editing specific chart elements difficult if your actual chart does not match the sample. If this occurs, exit chart editing mode, close and reopen the report in Design view, or switch views to cause Access to update the chart displayed in the control object.

Project 5b Changing the Chart Type, Chart Options, and Formatting a Chart — Part 2 of 2

1. With the **AL2-C5-RSRCompServ.accdb** database open, display the CustomersWOChart report in Design view.
2. Change the chart type, edit the chart title, and remove the legend in the chart by completing the following steps:
   a. Double-click within the chart to open the chart in chart editing mode. Access displays a datasheet with the chart and opens the Microsoft Graph application in which you edit charts.
   b. Click Chart on the Menu bar and then click *Chart Type*.

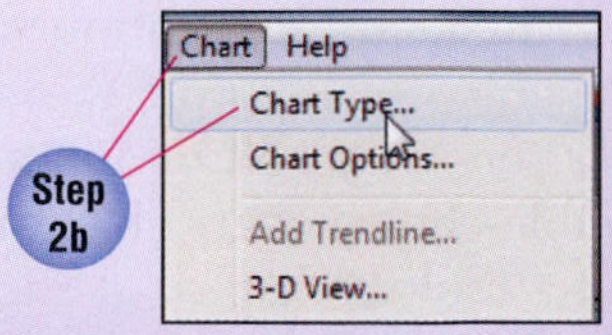

c. At the Chart Type dialog box with the Standard Types tab selected, click *Bar* in the *Chart type* list box and click the first chart in the second row in the *Chart sub-type* section.

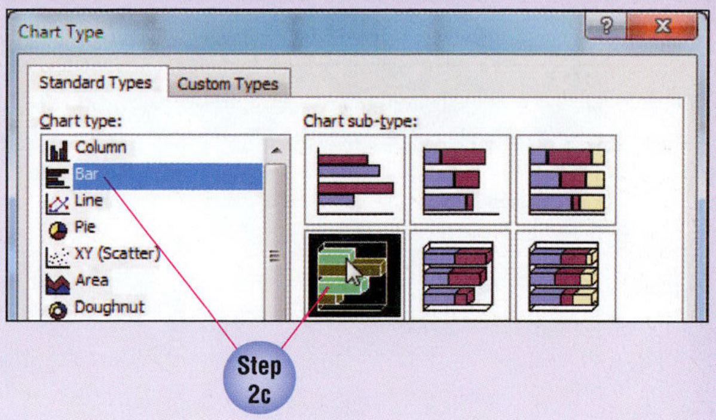

d. Click OK.

e. Click Chart on the Menu bar and then click *Chart Options*.

f. At the Chart Options dialog box with the Titles tab selected, edit the text in the *Chart title* text box by inserting a space between the words so that the title text reads *Total Work Orders*.

g. Click the Legend tab.

h. Click the *Show legend* check box to clear the check mark. Since there is only one data series, the chart title sufficiently describes the data and the legend can be removed from the chart.

i. Click OK.

3. Format the bars in the chart to change the shape and colors by completing the following steps. ***Note: If the chart shown is not the actual chart but the sample chart showing multiple data bars, click outside the chart object to exit chart editing mode, save, and then close the report. Reopen the report in Report view, switch to Design view, and then double-click the chart to open Microsoft Graph.***

a. Right-click the bar in the chart and click *Format Data Series* at the shortcut menu.

b. At the Format Data Series dialog box, click the Shape tab.

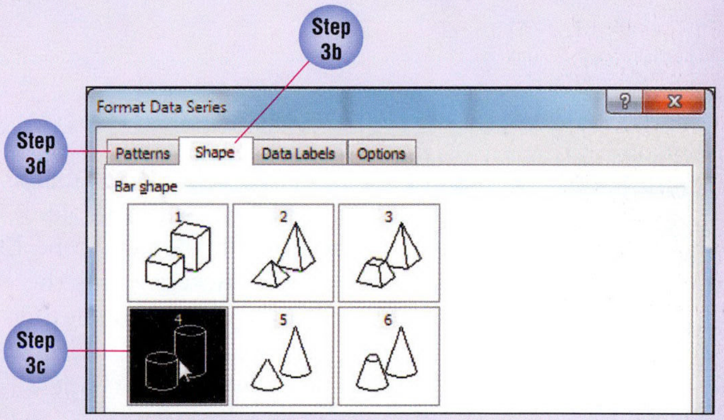

c. Click *4* in the *Bar shape* section (cylinder shape).

d. Click the Patterns tab.

e. Click the bright blue color square (last option in last row).

f. Click OK.

4. Right-click the chart title, click *Format Chart Title* at the shortcut menu, click the Font tab, change the *Color* to red (first option in third row at drop-down list), and then click OK.

5. Click outside the chart object to exit Microsoft Graph.

6. Create a label control object with your first and last names in the *Report Header* section with the right edge of the control aligned with the right edge of the chart.

7. Display the report in Print Preview.

Customers with Work Orders by Month Student Name

Customer ID 1000
First Name Jade
Last Name Fleming
Service Contract? ☑

Total Work Orders

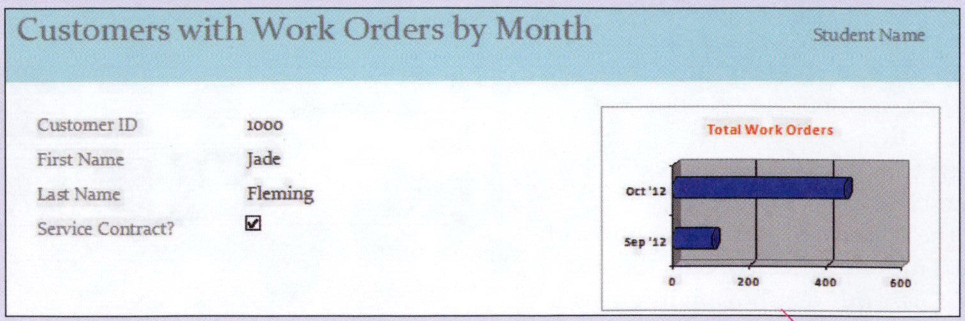

edited and formatted chart
for first customer record
displayed in Print Preview

8. Print the first page only of the report.
9. Save and close the report.

Project **6** **Create a Blank Report with Hyperlinks and a List** **1 Part**

You will use the Blank Report tool to create a new report for viewing technician certifications. In the report, you will reorder the tab fields, create a list box inside a tab control, change the shape of the tab control, and add hyperlinks.

Creating a Report Using the Blank Report Tool ■■■■■■

▼ **Quick Steps**

Create Blank Report
1. Click Create tab.
2. Click Blank Report button.
3. Expand field list for desired table.
4. Drag fields to report as needed.
5. Add a title, control objects, format, or make other design changes as needed.
6. Save report.

A blank report begins with no controls or format and displays as a blank white page in Layout view similar to the blank form tool you learned about in Chapter 4. Click the Create tab and then click the Blank Report button in the Reports group to begin a new report. Access opens the Field List pane at the right side of the work area. Expand the list for the desired table and then add fields to the report as needed. If the Field List pane displays with no table names, click the hyperlink to Show all tables at the top of the pane.

Adding a Tab Control to a Report

You learned how to add a tab control to a form in Chapter 4 in which you were able to display fields from different tables in pages. In Form view, you displayed a page by clicking the page tab. Similarly, a tab control can be used in a report to display fields from the same table or a different table in pages. To create a tab control in a report, follow the same steps you learned in Chapter 4 to add a tab control to a form.

Blank Report

Tab Control

List Box

Adding a List Box or a Combo Box to a Report

As with a form, a list box in a report displays a list of values for a field within the control object. In Report view, one can easily see the entire list for the field. If a list is too long for the size of the list box control, scroll bars display with which you can scroll up or down the list when viewing the report. Although you cannot edit data in a report, you can use a list box to view all of the field values and see which value has been selected for the current record.

A combo box added to a report does not display as a list; however, the field value that was entered into the field from the associated table, query, or form is shown in the combo box control object. Since you cannot edit data in a report, the combo box field is not shown as a drop-down list. A combo box can be changed to display as a list box within the report. In this case, the list box displays all of the field values with the value stored in the current record shown selected within the list.

Combo Box

A list box or a combo box can be added to a report by following the same steps as you learned in Chapter 4 to add a list box or a combo box to a form.

Adding Hyperlinks to a Report

With the Hyperlink button in the Controls group of the Report Layout Tools Design tab you can create a link in a report to a web page, a picture, an email address, or a program. Click the Hyperlink button and then click within the report at the desired location to open the Insert Hyperlink dialog box in which you provide the text to display in the control object and the address to which the object should be linked. Use the Places bar at the left of the Insert Hyperlink dialog box to choose to link to an existing file or web page, another object within the database, or an email address.

Changing the Shape of a Control Object

The Change Shape button in the Control Formatting group of the Report Layout Tools Format tab contains eight shape options in a drop-down list. You can use the shape options to modify the appearance of a command button, a toggle button, a navigation button, or a tab control. Select the control object you want to modify, click the Change Shape button and then click the desired shape at the drop-down list.

Quick Steps

Add Hyperlink to Report

1. Open report in Layout view or Design view.
2. Click Hyperlink button in Controls group.
3. Click in desired location with report.
4. Type text to display in control in *Text to display* text box.
5. Type URL in *Address* text box.
6. Click OK.

Change Shape of Control Object

1. Open report in Layout view.
2. Click to select control object.
3. Click Report Layout Tools Format tab.
4. Click Change Shape button.
5. Click desired shape.

Hyperlink

Change Shape

Changing the Tab Order of Fields

In Chapter 4 you learned how to open the Tab Order dialog box and change the order in which the tab key moves from field to field. In a report, you can also change the order in which the tab key moves from field to field in Report view. Although you do not add, delete, or edit data in Report view, you may want to use the tab key to move within a report. Display the report in Design view, click the Tab Order button in the Tools group of the Report Design Tools Design tab, and drag the fields up or down the *Custom Order* list as desired.

Tab Order

Project 6 **Creating a Blank Report with Hyperlinks and a List** **Part 1 of 1**

1. With the **AL2-C5-RSRCompServ.accdb** database open, click the Create tab and then click the Blank Report button in the Reports group.
2. If the Field List pane at the right side of the work area does not display the table names, click the Show all tables hyperlink; otherwise, proceed to Step 3.

3. Add fields from the Technicians table and a tab control object to the report by completing the following steps:
   a. Click the plus symbol next to the table named Technicians to expand the field list.
   b. Click the first field named *TechID* in the Field List pane and then drag the field to the top left of the report.
   c. Right-click the *Technician ID* column, point to *Layout* at the shortcut menu, and then click *Stacked*. A stacked layout is better suited to this report where you want to show each technician's certifications next to their name in a tab control object.
   d. Drag the *FName* field from the Field List pane below the first *Technician ID* text box control object. Release the mouse when you see the gold bar below the *01* text box control object next to *Technician ID*.
   e. Drag the *LName* field from the Field List pane below the first *First Name* text box control object. Release the mouse when the gold bar displays below *Pat*.
   f. Click the Tab Control button in the Controls group of the Report Layout Tools Design tab.
   g. Position the mouse pointer with the Tab Control icon attached at the right of the first *Technician ID* text box control in the report. Click the mouse when you see the gold bar displayed at the right of the *01* text box control object.
   h. Right-click the selected tab control object, point to *Layout*, and then click *Remove Layout* at the shortcut menu.
   i. Select the *HPhone* and *CPhone* fields in the Field List pane and then drag the two fields below the *Last Name* text box control object. Release the mouse when the gold bar displays below *Hynes*.
   j. Double-click over the first *Pagexx* tab (where *xx* is the page number) in the tab control object at the right of the report to select the tab control object. Point to the bottom orange border of the selected tab control object until the pointer displays as an up- and down-pointing arrow and then drag the bottom of the object down until the bottom aligns with the bottom of the *Cell Phone* control objects.

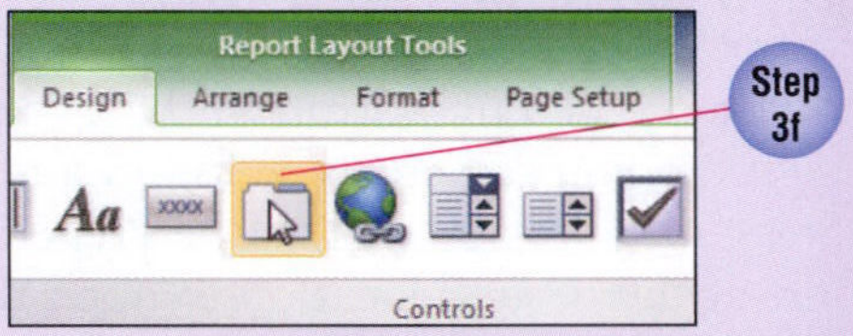

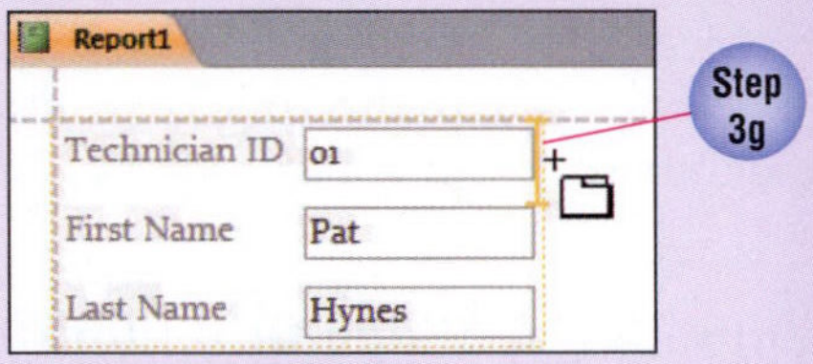

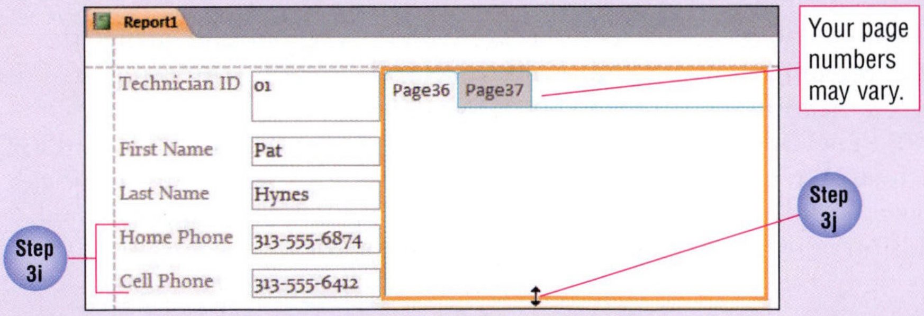

4. Add a field from the TechSkills table to the tab control object and change the control to a list box by completing the following steps:
   a. Click the plus symbol next to the TechSkills table name in the *Fields available in related tables* section of the Field List pane to expand the list.
   b. Click to select the *Certifications* field name and then drag the field to the first page in the tab control next to *Technician ID 01*.

c. Access inserts the field in the page with both the label control object and the text box control object selected. To change the field to display as a list box you need to select only the text box control object. Click to select the text box control object (displays *Cisco CCNP, CompTIA A+,* and *Microsoft MCTS* in the first record.

d. Right-click the selected text box control object, point to *Change To,* and then click *List Box* at the shortcut menu.

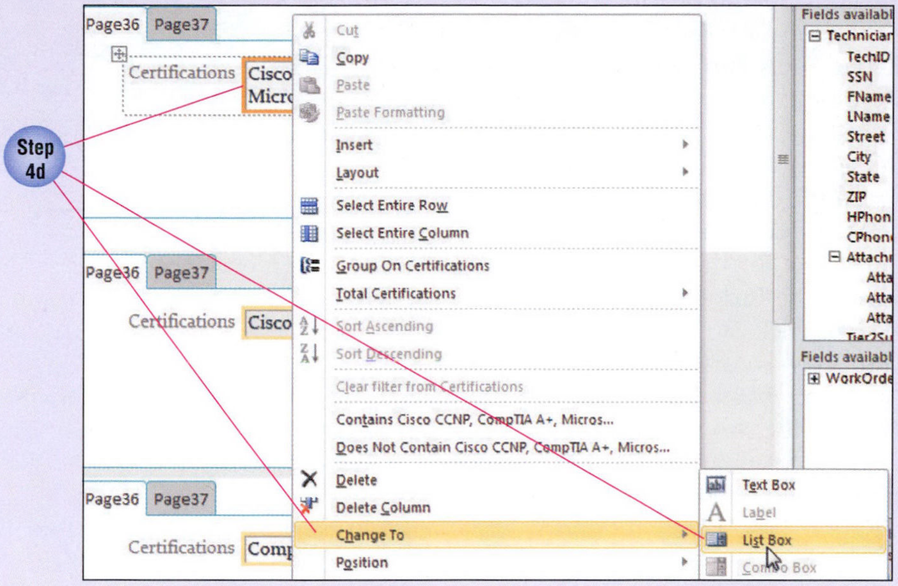

5. Add hyperlinks to the bottom of the tab control by completing the following steps:

a. Click the Hyperlink button in the Controls group of the Report Layout Tools Design tab.

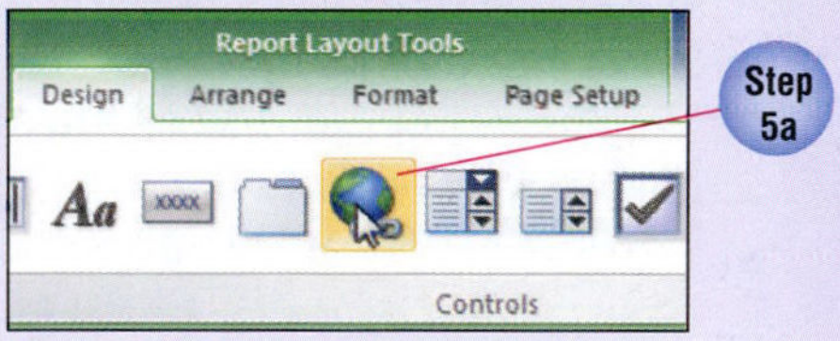

b. Position the mouse pointer with the Hyperlink icon attached below *Certifications* in the tab control object. Release the mouse when the gold bar displays.

c. At the Insert Hyperlink dialog box, click in the *Text to display* text box and then type **Cisco Certifications**.

d. Click in the *Address* text box, type **www.cisco.com/web/learning/netacad/course_catalog/index.html**, and then click OK.

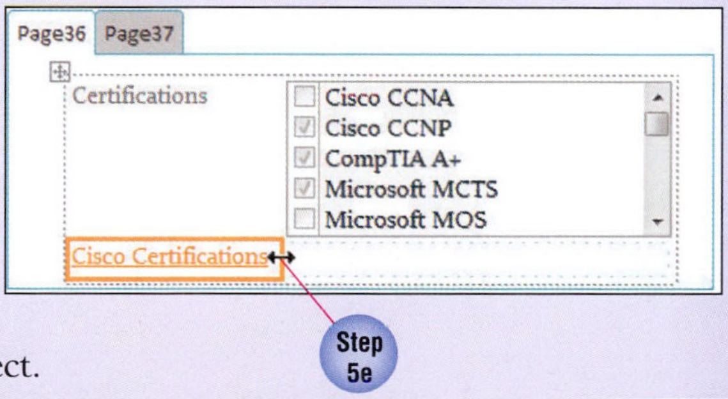

e. Drag the right orange border of the hyperlink control object right until the entire text displays within the control object.

f. Add a second hyperlink control object below the list box in the tab control object that displays the text *Microsoft Certifications* and links to the address *www.microsoft.com/learning/en/us/certification/cert-overview.aspx* by completing steps similar to those in Steps 5a to 5d.

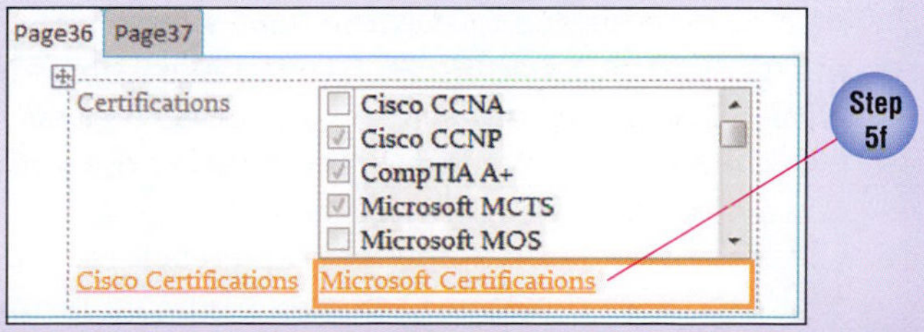

6. Right-click the second page in the tab control and then click *Delete Page* at the shortcut menu. Do not be concerned if Access displays the first page with an empty list box. The screen will refresh at the next step.

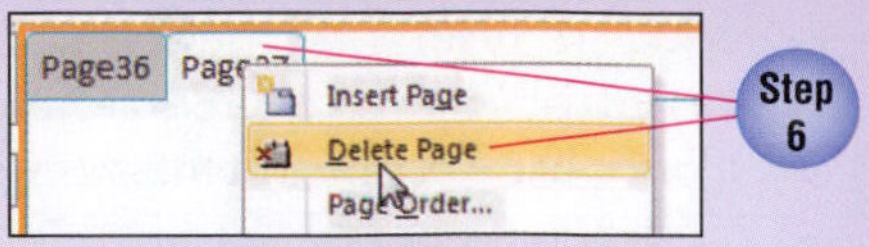

7. Double-click over *Pagexx* (where *xx* is the page number) in the tab control to select the entire tab control object. Click the Report Layout Tools Format tab, click the Change Shape button in the Control Formatting group, and then click *Snip Single Corner Rectangle* at the drop-down list (last option in second row of shapes).

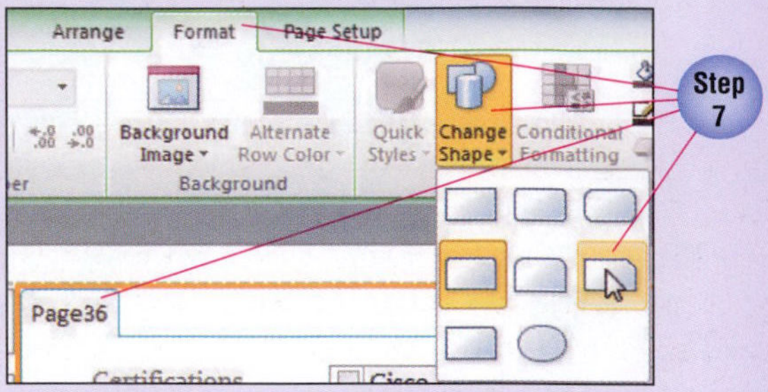

8. Click to select *Pagexx* (where *xx* is the page number), click the Report Layout Tools Design tab, and then click the Property Sheet button to open the Property Sheet. With *Selection Type: Page* displayed at the top of the Property Sheet, click in the *Caption* property, type **Technician's Certifications**, and then close the Property Sheet.
9. Right-click the *Technician ID* text box control object (displays *01*) and then click *Select Entire Column* at the shortcut menu. Click the Report Layout Tools Format tab, click the Shape Outline button, and then click *Transparent* at the drop-down list.
10. Save the report and name it *TechCertifications*.
11. Switch to Report view. Click in the first *Technician ID* text box and press Tab four times to see how the Tab key moves through the first fields in order at the left edge of the report.
12. Switch to Design view. Assume that you want the Tab key to move to the technician's last name first and then to the technician's first name. Change the tab order of the fields by completing the following steps:
    a. Click the Tab Order button in the Tools group of the Report Design Tools Design tab.
    b. At the Tab Order dialog box, click in the gray bar next to *LName* in the *Custom Order* section to select the field and then drag the field to the top of the list until the black line displays above *TechID*.
    c. Drag *TechID* to the bottom of the list.
    d. Click OK.

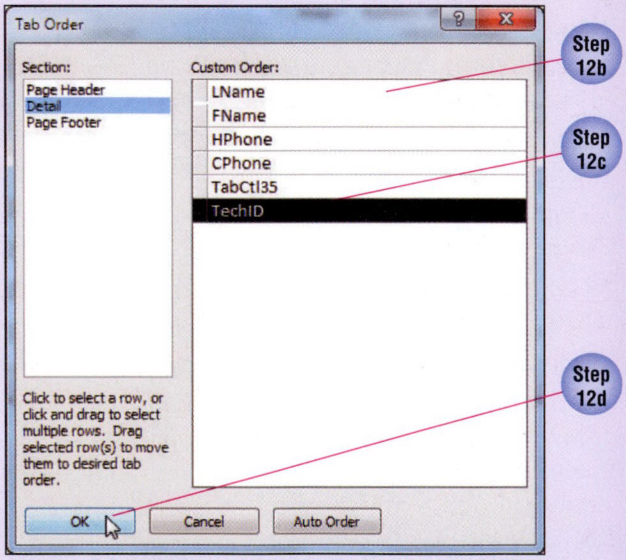

13. Save the revised form and then switch to Report view. Press the Tab key. Notice the first field selected is the *Last Name* field. Press Tab a second time. Notice the selected field moves to *First Name*. Press Tab two more times to watch the selected fields move to the *Home Phone* and *Cell Phone* fields below the *Last Name* field.
14. Click the *Cisco Certifications* hyperlink to open an Internet Explorer window and display the Cisco Courses & Certificatioins web page.
15. Close the browser window and then click the *Microsoft Certifications* hyperlink to display the Microsoft Certification Overview page in a browser window.

16. Close the browser window and then display the report in Print Preview.
17. Print the first page only of the report and then close Print Preview.
18. Close the TechCertifications report and then close the **AL2-C5-RSRCompServ.accdb** database.

In this chapter you have learned how to build a custom report from scratch using Design view. You have also created reports using the Report Wizard and the Blank Report tool and used options in Design view and Layout view to customize the reports. As you become more comfortable with reports, explore other tools available in Layout View and Design view using the Design, Arrange, Format, and Page Setup tabs. More features are available to assist you with creating professional-quality reports.

Chapter Summary

- A report generally contains five sections: *Report Header, Page Header, Detail, Page Footer,* and *Report Footer*.
- Drag a field or group of fields from the Field List pane to the *Detail* section of the report, which represents the body of the report.
- An additional *Group Header* and *Group Footer* section can be added if the report is grouped by a field containing repeating values such as a department or city.
- Click the Create tab and click the Report Design button to build a custom report from scratch.
- Connect a table or query to a report using the *Record Source* property box in the Data tab of the report's Property Sheet.
- Place label control objects to be used as column headings in a tabular report within the *Page Header* section in Design view.
- A related table or query can be inserted as a subreport within a main report. A subreport is stored as a separate object outside the main report.
- Click the Page Numbers button in the Header/Footer group to open the Page Numbers Dialog box in which you specify the format, position, and alignment options for page numbering in a report.
- The current date and/or time can be added as a control object within the *Report Header* section using the Date and Time button in the Header/Footer group.
- Add pictures, clip art images, or draw lines in a report using the same techniques that you learned for adding graphics to forms.
- A report can be grouped by a field at the Report Wizard or by opening the Group, Sort, and Total pane.
- Functions such as Sum, Average or Count can be added to each group within a report and grand totals added to the end of a report by expanding the group options in the Group, Sort, and Total pane.

- Each section within a report has a set of properties that can be viewed or changed by opening the section's Property Sheet.
- The Keep Together property for a section is used to prevent a section from being split by a page break.
- The Force New Page property in a section Property Sheet can be used to automatically insert a page break before a section begins, after the section ends, or before and after a section.
- At the Group, Sort, and Total pane, you can specify to keep an entire group together on the same page.
- A chart can be added to a report to graphically display numerical data from another table or query related to the report.
- Open a report in Design view, click the Chart button in the Controls group to create a chart control object in a report or form, and use the Chart Wizard to generate the chart.
- Double-click a chart control object in Design view to edit the chart using Microsoft Graph by changing the chart type; adding, removing, or changing chart options; and formatting chart elements.
- The Blank Report tool in the Reports group in the Create tab creates a new report with no controls or format applied. The report opens as a blank white page in Layout view with the Field List pane opened at the right of the work area.
- A tab control and a list box can be added to a blank report using the same techniques as you learned for adding these controls to a form.
- Use the Hyperlink button to create a link in a report to a web page, a picture, an email address, or a program.
- The shape of a command button, a toggle button, a navigation button, or a tab control can be modified using the Change Shape button in the Control Formatting group of the Report Layout Tools Format tab.
- You can alter the order of the fields in which the Tab key will move within a report at the Tab Order dialog box. Display a report in Design view to access the Tab Order button in the Tools group of the Report Design Tools Design tab.

Commands Review

FEATURE	RIBBON TAB, GROUP	BUTTON
Add existing fields	Report Design Tools Design, Tools	
Blank report	Create, Reports	
Change Shape of selected control	Report Layout Tools Format, Control Formatting	
Date and Time	Report Design Tools Design, Header/Footer	
Design view	Report Design Tools Design, Views	
Group & Sort	Report Design Tools Design, Grouping & Totals	
Insert a chart	Report Design Tools Design, Controls	
Insert a Hyperlink	Report Layout Tools Design, Controls	
Insert image	Report Design Tools Design, Controls	
Page numbering	Report Design Tools Design, Header/Footer	
Property Sheet	Report Design Tools Design, Tools	
Report Design	Create, Reports	
Report Wizard	Create, Reports	
Report view	Report Design Tools Design, Views	
Subreport	Report Design Tools Design, Controls	
Tab Control	Report Layout Tools Design, Controls	
Tab Order	Report Design Tools Design, Tools	
Theme	Report Design Tools Design, Themes	
Title	Report Design Tools Design, Header/Footer	

Concepts Check Test Your Knowledge

Completion: In the space provided at the right, indicate the correct term, command, or number.

1. Add controls in this section to print grand totals at the end of a report. ____________________
2. Double-click this button to open the Property Sheet for a report. ____________________
3. The Subform/Subreport button is found in this group within the Report Design Tools Design tab. ____________________
4. The Page Numbers button is located in this group in the Report Design Tools Design tab. ____________________
5. If the date and time are added to a report using the Date and Time dialog box, Access creates the control objects in this report section. ____________________
6. At the Report Wizard dialog box, Access displays a grouped field in this color in the preview section. ____________________
7. An existing report can have grouping added by opening this pane. ____________________
8. Click this button to expand the group options for a grouped field in order to add a Sum function to each group. ____________________
9. Modify this section property to instruct Access to insert a page break after the section is finished printing. ____________________
10. Double-click this element in report Design view to open the Property Sheet for a section. ____________________
11. Use this button in the expanded Controls group to insert a bar chart into a report. ____________________
12. Launch the Microsoft Graph application to edit a chart by doing this action with the mouse. ____________________
13. When finished editing a chart, exit Microsoft Graph by doing this action with the mouse. ____________________
14. This report tool opens as a blank white page in Layout view. ____________________
15. Click this button to create a control object within a report that will display a web page when clicked. ____________________
16. This button in the Control Formatting group of the Report Layout Tools Format tab can be used to change the shape of a selected control. ____________________

Skills Check Assess Your Performance

Assessment 1

CREATE A CUSTOM REPORT USING DESIGN VIEW

1. Open the database named **AL2-C5-VantageVideos.accdb** and enable content.
2. Create a new report using the Report Design button and build the report using the following specifications:
   a. Add a title in the *Report Header* section with the text **Web Products and Sales**.
   b. Add your name in a label control object in the center of the *Report Footer* section.
   c. Connect the WebProducts table to the report. Add all of the fields from the table to the report.
   d. Move the label control objects for each field from the *Detail* section to the *Page Header* section arranging the controls horizontally in the order the fields appeared in the table. You determine the amount of space to leave between controls. Resize the *Page Header* section when finished so that the extra space is removed.
   e. Align each text box control object in the *Detail* section below the object's associated label control object in the *Page Header* section.
   f. Use Report view to check alignment and width of controls to make sure data is not truncated in any of the control objects. Make adjustments as needed in Design view or Layout View.
   g. Apply the Opulent theme.
   h. Insert a subreport into the *Detail* section using the following specifications. ***Hint: You may need to first adjust the height of the* Detail *section to make room for the subreport if you have been using Layout view.***
      1) Use the WebSaleswithTotal query and add the fields in order *CustID, WebOrdID*, *DateOrd*, *WebProdID*, and *Qty* to the subreport.
      2) Accept the default link option to link the main report to the subreport on the *WebProdID* field.
      3) Accept the default subreport name.
      4) Edit the text in the subreport label control object to *Web Sales*.
      5) View the report to ensure the data is properly linked.
      6) Remove the *WebProdID* field (including the associated label control object) from the subreport since this data is duplicated in the main report and then move the *Qty* field (including the associated label control object) left to fill in the space.
      7) Move and/or resize the subreport control object as desired.
   i. Resize the *Detail* section so that the section ends just below the subreport.
   j. Format the *WebProdID, Product, InStock,* and *SellPrice* fields in the *Detail* section to 12-point bold.
   k. Make any additional adjustments to the position, height, width, alignment, or formatting of any control objects you think would improve the appearance of the report; however, do not add any further elements as you will continue work on this report in the next assessment.
3. Save the report and name it *WebProductsWithSales*.
4. Print and then close the report.

Assessment 2

ENHANCE THE REPORT

1. With the **AL2-C5-VantageVideos.accdb** database open, display the WebProductsWithSales report in Design view.
2. Add page numbering using the *Page N of M* format to the bottom left of each page.
3. Add the current date to the bottom right of each page aligning the right edge of the control in the *Page Footer* section at the 7-inch position in the horizontal ruler. You determine the date format.
4. Insert an appropriate clip art image to the top right of the report resized to a suitable height and width and with the right edge of the image aligned at the 7-inch position in the horizontal ruler. Adjust the position of the report title to center it vertically left of the clip art image and horizontally within the title control object.
5. Draw a horizontal line under the report title. You determine the line thickness, line type, and line color.
6. Change all four margins for the report to 0.5 inch.
7. The diagonal green triangle appears on the Report Selector button after changing the margins. Click the Error Checking button and then click *Select the Control Farthest to the Right*. This will remove the drop-down list and select the control object that is at the right edge of the report that would prevent you from resizing the grid to remove extra space. The control selected is part of the date and time controls that were added within the title placeholder at Step 3. Drag the right middle sizing handle of the selected control left to decrease the control's width aligning the control at the right edge of the clip art image. Click the Error Checking button again and then click *Remove Extra Report Space* at the drop-down list.
8. Save the report.
9. Print page 1 only of the revised report and then close the report.

Assessment 3

CREATE A NEW REPORT WITH GROUPING AND TOTALS

1. With the **AL2-C5-VantageVideos.accdb** database open, create a new report using the Report Wizard as follows:
   a. Use the WebSalesWithTotal query and add all fields to the report except *CustID* and *WebProdID*.
   b. Group by the *DateOrd* field by month.
   c. Click Next to leave the sort field blank.
   d. Use a *Stepped* layout in *Landscape* orientation.
   e. Edit the report title to *WebSalesByDate*.
2. Preview both pages of the report and then switch to Design view.
3. Add your name in a label control object at the left edge of the *Report Footer* section.
4. Open the Group, Sort, and Total pane and make the following changes:
   a. Add a Sum function to each month's *Total Sale* column. Show a grand total at the end of the report as well as the subtotal in the group footer.
   b. Add a sort by the *LastName* field.
5. Add an appropriate label next to the Sum function in the *DateOrd Footer* section and next to the Sum function in the *Report Footer* section.

6. Edit the report title to *Web Sales by Date* and edit the *DateOrd by Month* label to *Month*.
7. Display the report in Print Preview and note any column widths that need to be adjusted or labels that need to be edited in order to display the entire entry. Switch to Design view or Layout view and adjust column widths as necessary so that all data is entirely visible. If necessary, abbreviate long column labels. For example, *Quantity* could be abbreviated to *Qty*.
8. Change the top and bottom margin to 0.75 inch and then print the report.
9. Save and then close the report.

Assessment 4

CREATE AND FORMAT A NEW REPORT WITH A CHART

1. With the **AL2-C5-VantageVideos.accdb** database open, create a new report using the Report Wizard as follows:
   a. Use the WebCustomers table and add the customer number, customer name, and home telephone fields to the report.
   b. Do not group or sort the report.
   c. Use a *Columnar* layout in *Portrait* orientation.
   d. Edit the report title to *WebCustomersWithChart*.
2. Preview the report.
3. Switch to Design view.
4. Insert a chart at the right side of the page next to each customer record using the following information:
   a. Use the WebSalesWithTotal query.
   b. Add the *DateOrd* and *Total Sale* fields to the chart field list.
   c. Select a bar chart style. You determine which style to use.
   d. Accept the default chart layout that Access creates with *DateOrd by month* as the *x*-axis labels and *SumOfTotal Sale* as the value axis.
   e. Accept *CustID* as the linked field for the report and the chart.
   f. Edit the title for the chart to *Web Sales*.
5. Preview the report with the bar chart and then switch to Design view.
6. Edit the chart as follows:
   a. Change the chart type to a column chart. You determine the sub-type.
   b. Delete the legend.
   c. Change the color of the bar to dark purple.
7. Edit the report title to *Customers with Web Sales Chart*.
8. Add your name in a label control object at the bottom left of the report.
9. Make any other formatting changes you think would improve the appearance of the report.
10. Print page 1 only of the report.
11. Save and then close the report.

Assessment 5

CREATE A CUSTOM REPORT USING THE BLANK REPORT TOOL

1. With the **AL2-C5-VantageVideos.accdb** database open, create a new report using the Blank Report tool.
2. Add the first field named *CustID* from the WebCustomers table and then change the layout of the report to *Stacked*.

3. Add the remaining fields from the WebCustomers table below the *Customer ID* field. Make sure you release the mouse with the gold bar displayed below *101* for the first *Customer ID*.
4. Widen the labels column so that *Street Address* does not wrap to a second line in the label column.
5. Insert a tab control object at the right of the *Customer ID* field. Make sure you click the mouse when the gold bar displays at the right of *101*.
6. Remove the layout from the tab control column and then lengthen the tab control object to align with the bottom of the *Home Phone* field.
7. Expand the field list for the *WebCustPymnt* table and then add the following fields to the tab control object.
    CCType
    CCNumber
    CCExpMonth
    CCExpYear
8. Select all of the label control objects in the tab control and widen the objects so that all of the label text is visible.
9. Save the report and name it *CustomersWithCreditCards*.
10. Delete the second page in the tab control and then change the shape of the selected tab control object. You choose the shape.
11. Change the caption of the page in the tab control to *Credit Card Details*.
12. Insert a title at the top of the report with the text *Customers with Payment Information*.
13. Print the first page only of the report.
14. Save and close the report and then close the **AL2-C5-VantageVideos.accdb** database.

Visual Benchmark Demonstrate Your Proficiency

CREATE CUSTOM RESERVATIONS REPORT WITH TOTALS

1. Open **AL2-C5-PawsParadise.accdb** and enable content.
2. Review the partial report shown in Figure 5.15. This report was created based on the Dog Owners table with the Dogs table added as a subreport. Create the report with subreport with the following specifications and using your best judgment for formatting options as well as alignment, spacing, sizing, and position of controls:
   a. Apply the Austin theme.
   b. Substitute another suitable clip art image if the one shown is not available on the computer you are using.
   c. Add the current date and page numbering to the bottom of each page.
   d. Edit the labels in the subreport as shown in Figure 5.15.
   e. Add your name in the *Report Footer* section.
3. Save the report naming it *DogOwnersWithDogs*.
4. Preview the report. If necessary return to Layout view or Design view to make adjustments as needed. When finished, save and print the report.
5. Close the report and then close the **AL2-C5-PawsParadise.accdb** database.

Figure 5.15 Partial View of Completed Visual Benchmark Report

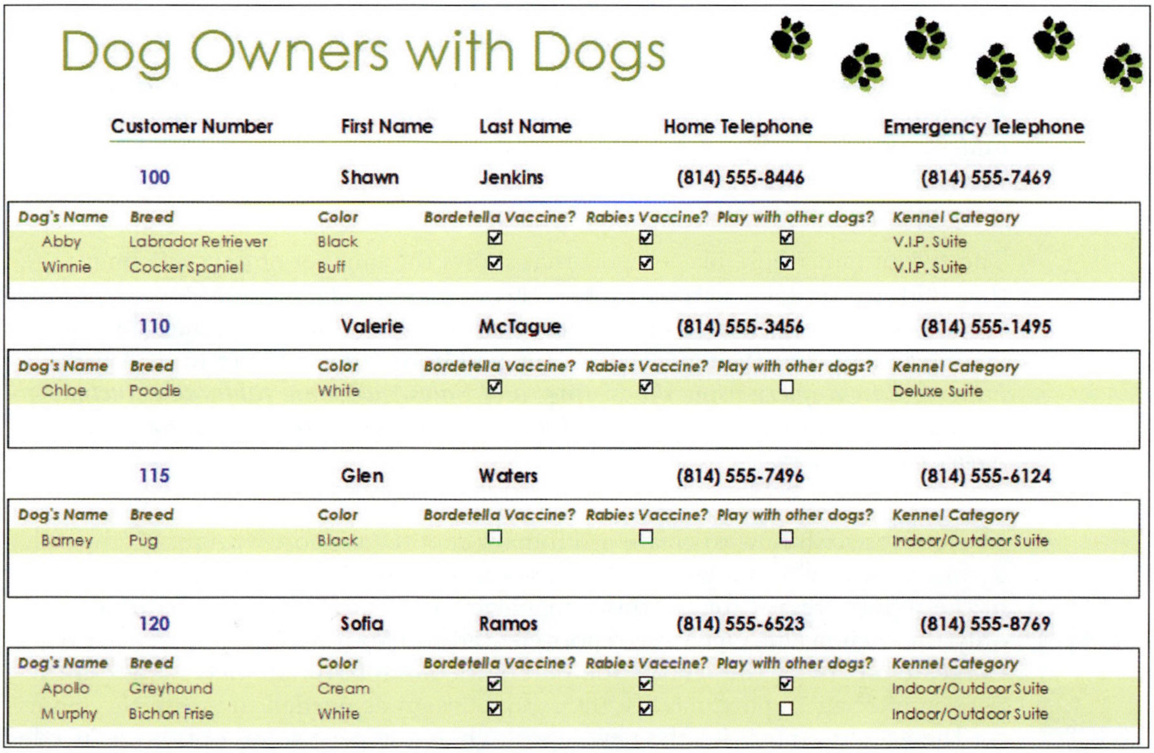
Dog Owners with Dogs

Customer Number	First Name	Last Name	Home Telephone	Emergency Telephone
100	Shawn	Jenkins	(814) 555-8446	(814) 555-7469

Dog's Name	Breed	Color	Bordetella Vaccine?	Rabies Vaccine?	Play with other dogs?	Kennel Category
Abby	Labrador Retriever	Black	☑	☑	☑	V.I.P. Suite
Winnie	Cocker Spaniel	Buff	☑	☑	☑	V.I.P. Suite

110	Valerie	McTague	(814) 555-3456	(814) 555-1495

Dog's Name	Breed	Color	Bordetella Vaccine?	Rabies Vaccine?	Play with other dogs?	Kennel Category
Chloe	Poodle	White	☑	☑	☐	Deluxe Suite

115	Glen	Waters	(814) 555-7496	(814) 555-6124

Dog's Name	Breed	Color	Bordetella Vaccine?	Rabies Vaccine?	Play with other dogs?	Kennel Category
Barney	Pug	Black	☐	☐	☐	Indoor/Outdoor Suite

120	Sofia	Ramos	(814) 555-6523	(814) 555-8769

Dog's Name	Breed	Color	Bordetella Vaccine?	Rabies Vaccine?	Play with other dogs?	Kennel Category
Apollo	Greyhound	Cream	☑	☑	☑	Indoor/Outdoor Suite
Murphy	Bichon Frise	White	☑	☑	☐	Indoor/Outdoor Suite

Case Study Apply Your Skills

Part 1

Continuing your work as an intern at Hillsdale Realty, your next task is to create reports for management. Open the database named **AL2-C5-HillsdaleRealty.accdb** and enable content. For each report created, add your name in a label control object in the Report Footer. The first report has been requested by the office manager. The office manager uses the SalesByAgentWithComm query frequently but has asked for a report that provides the information in a more useful format. Specifically, the office manager would like the report to be organized with each individual agent's sales together showing the total value of sales and commissions earned for that agent and sorted by the date the listing sold. The office manager would also like to see grand totals and the percentage of the grand total that each agent has achieved for the sale prices and commissions earned. Design and create the report including features such as page numbering, date and time controls, and graphics. Save the report and name it appropriately. Print the report with top and bottom margins set to 0.5 inch and making sure that an entire group is kept together on the same page.

Part 2

The office manager would like a printout of the listings with the client's preferences and the agent attached to the listing grouped by the city. (Note that not all listings have a preferences record but the office manager wants to see all listings on the report.) You determine an appropriate sort order within each city's group of records. Design and create the report. Save the report and name it appropriately. Print the report with a top margin of 0.75 inch and make sure that an entire group is kept together on the same page. ***Hint: Consider creating a query first with the relevant fields needed from the Listings, Preferences, and Agents tables and base the report on the query. For one of the relationships in the query you will need to modify the join properties.***

Part 3

The accountant would like a report that shows the number of days a listing that sold was on the market as well as the average number of days it took to sell a listing by city. Design and create the report. Save the report and name it appropriately. Print the report with a top and bottom margins set to 0.75 inch. ***Hint: Create a query using the Listings and SalesAndComm tables that includes a calculated field for the number of days a listing was on the market and base the report on the query.***

Part 4

Help

In Help research how to create a summary report (a report without the record details shown within a group). The accountant would like a compacted version of the report created for the office manager in Part 1 that shows the totals only for each agent. Open the report created in Part 1 and use *Save Object As* to create a copy of the report. You determine an appropriate new name. In the new copy of the report, modify the report design as needed to create the report for the accountant. Print the new report, changing page setup options as needed to fit the entire report on one page. Save and close the report. Close the **AL2-C5-HillsdaleRealty.accdb** database.

Microsoft® Access®

CHAPTER 6

Using Access Tools and Managing Objects

PERFORMANCE OBJECTIVES

Upon successful completion of Chapter 6, you will be able to:

- **Create a new database using a template**
- **Add a group of objects to a database using an Application Parts template**
- **Create a new form using an Application Parts Blank Form**
- **Create a form to be used as a template in a database**
- **Create a table by copying the structure of another table**
- **Evaluate a table using the Table Analyzer Wizard**
- **Evaluate a database using the Performance Analyzer**
- **Split a database**
- **Print documentation about a database using the Database Documenter**
- **Rename and delete objects**

SNAP Training and Assessment. Simplified.

Tutorials

6.1 Creating a Database Using a Template
6.2 Creating a Table Using a Table Template
6.3 Copying a Table Structure to a New Table
6.4 Modifying a Table Using the Table Analyzer Wizard
6.5 Optimizing Performance Using the Performance Analyzer
6.6 Splitting a Database
6.7 Documenting a Database
6.8 Renaming and Deleting Objects

Access provides tools to assist you with creating and managing databases and objects within databases. Templates are provided that can be used to create a new database or create a new table and/or related group of objects. Blank form templates provide you with a predefined layout and may include a form title and command buttons. If none of the predefined templates suit your needs, you can create your own template. Access provides wizards to assist with analyzing a table and a database in order to improve performance. A database can be split into two files to store the tables separate from the queries, forms, and reports. The Database Documenter can be used to print a report that provides details about objects and object properties. In this chapter you will learn how to use these Access tools and how to rename and delete objects in the Navigation pane. Model answers for this chapter's projects appear on the following pages.

Access
Access2010L2C6

Note: Before beginning the projects, copy to your storage medium the Access2010L2C6 subfolder from the Access2010L2 folder on the CD that accompanies this textbook and then make Access2010L2C6 the active folder.

Model Answers

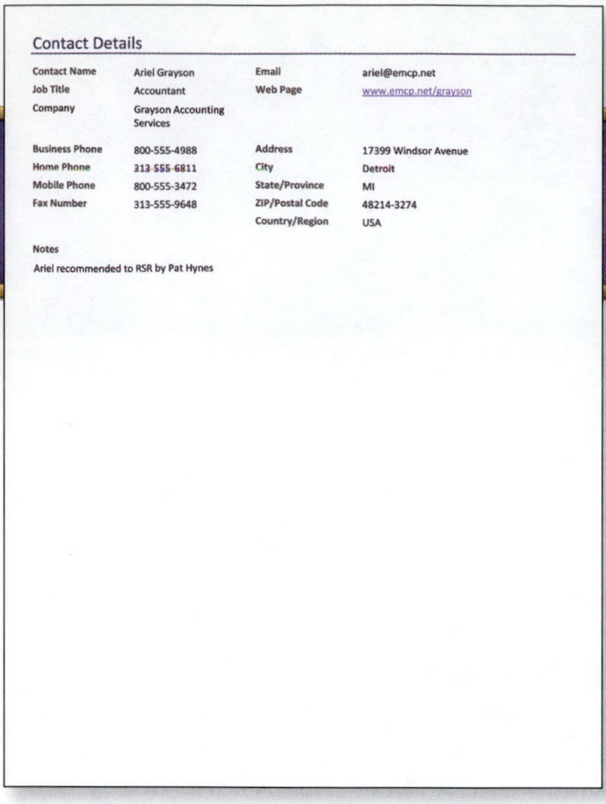
Contact Details

Contact Name	Ariel Grayson	Email	ariel@emcp.net
Job Title	Accountant	Web Page	www.emcp.net/grayson
Company	Grayson Accounting Services		
Business Phone	800-555-4988	Address	17399 Windsor Avenue
Home Phone	313-555-6811	City	Detroit
Mobile Phone	800-555-3472	State/Province	MI
Fax Number	313-555-9648	ZIP/Postal Code	48214-3274
		Country/Region	USA

Notes

Ariel recommended to RSR by Pat Hynes

Project 1 Create a New Database Using a Template

Project 1b, ContactDetails Report

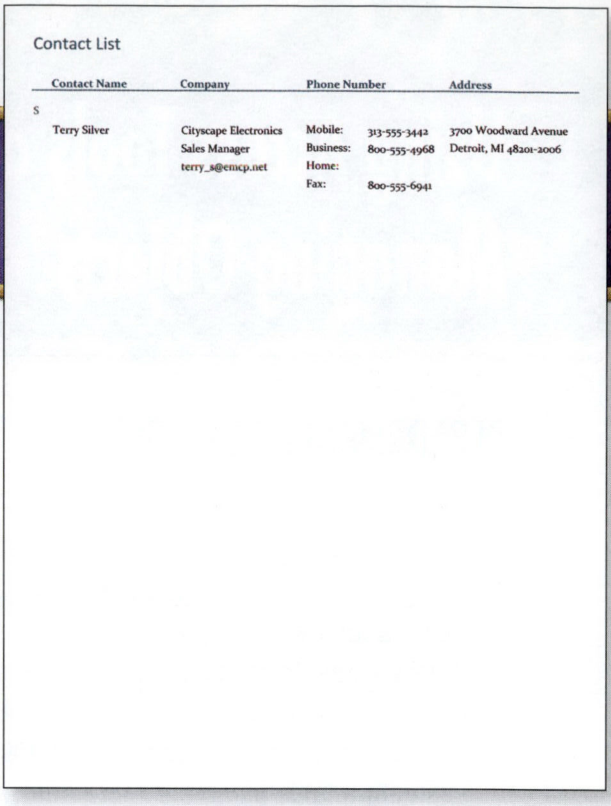
Contact List

Contact Name	Company	Phone Number		Address
S				
Terry Silver	Cityscape Electronics Sales Manager terry_s@emcp.net	Mobile: Business: Home: Fax:	313-555-3442 800-555-4968 800-555-6941	3700 Woodward Avenue Detroit, MI 48201-2006

Project 2 Create Objects Using a Template

Project 2a, ContactList Report

WorkOrders

Work Order	65012
Customer ID	1000
Technician ID	11
WO Date	Fri Sep 07 2012
Description	Bi-annual computer maintenance
Service Date	Fri Sep 07 2012
Hours	1.25
Rate	30.00
Parts	$10.15
Comments	"H" key is sticking; cleaning did not resolve. Customer is considering buying a new keyboard. Microsoft wireless keyboard. See work order 65013 for replacement keyboard request.

Project 2c, WorkOrders Form

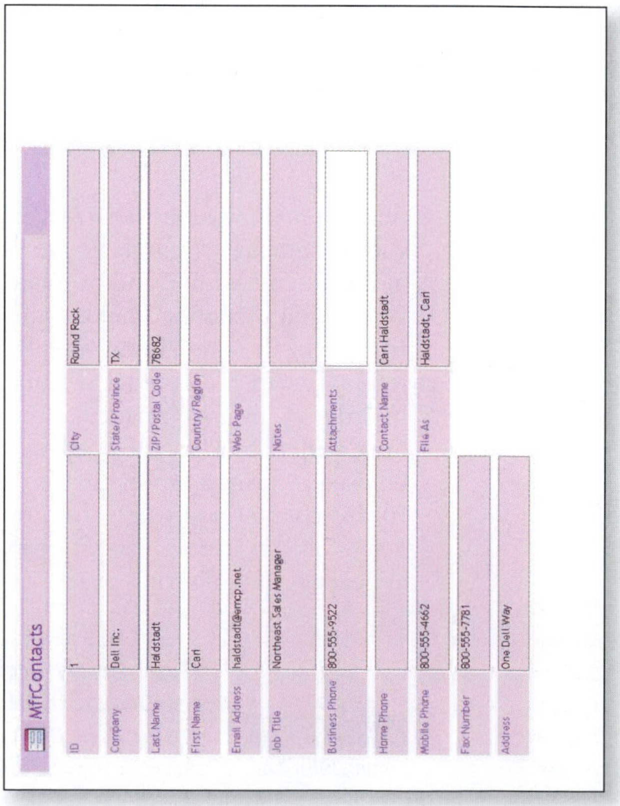
MfrContacts

ID	1	City	Round Rock
Company	Dell Inc.	State/Province	TX
Last Name	Haldstadt	ZIP/Postal Code	78682
First Name	Carl	Country/Region	
Email Address	haldstadt@emcp.net	Web Page	
Job Title	Northeast Sales Manager	Notes	
Business Phone	800-555-9522	Attachments	
Home Phone		Contact Name	Carl Haldstadt
Mobile Phone	800-555-4662	File As	Haldstadt, Carl
Fax Number	800-555-7781		
Address	One Dell Way		

Project 3 Copy Table Structure

MfrContacts Form

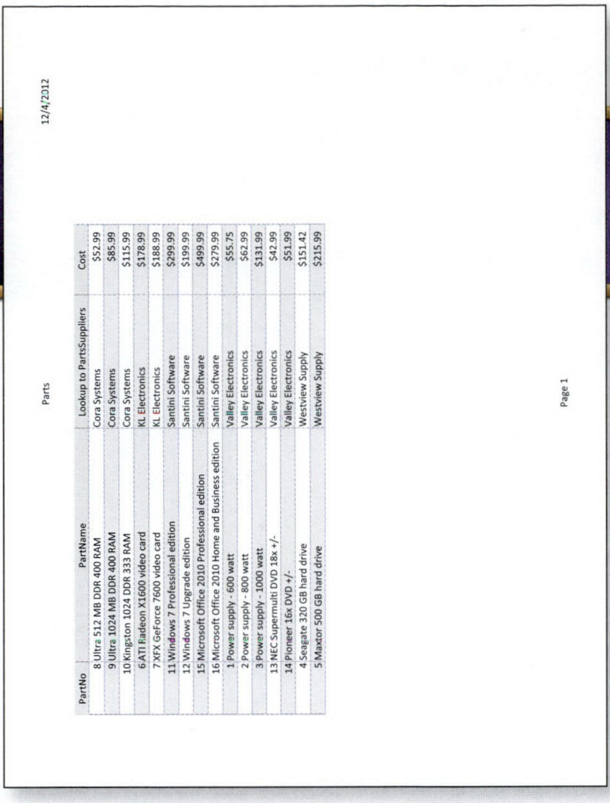

Parts 12/4/2012

PartNo	PartName	Lookup to PartsSuppliers	Cost
8	Ultra 512 MB DDR 400 RAM	Cora Systems	$52.99
9	Ultra 1024 MB DDR 400 RAM	Cora Systems	$85.99
10	Kingston 1024 DDR 333 RAM	Cora Systems	$115.99
6	ATI Radeon X1600 video card	KL Electronics	$178.99
7	XFX GeForce 7600 video card	KL Electronics	$188.99
11	Windows 7 Professional edition	Santini Software	$299.99
12	Windows 7 Upgrade edition	Santini Software	$199.99
15	Microsoft Office 2010 Professional edition	Santini Software	$499.99
16	Microsoft Office 2010 Home and Business edition	Santini Software	$279.99
1	Power supply - 600 watt	Valley Electronics	$55.75
2	Power supply - 800 watt	Valley Electronics	$62.99
3	Power supply - 1000 watt	Valley Electronics	$131.99
13	NEC Supermulti DVD 18x +/-	Valley Electronics	$42.99
14	Pioneer 16x DVD +/-	Valley Electronics	$51.99
4	Seagate 320 GB hard drive	Westview Supply	$151.42
5	Maxtor 500 GB hard drive	Westview Supply	$215.99

Page 1

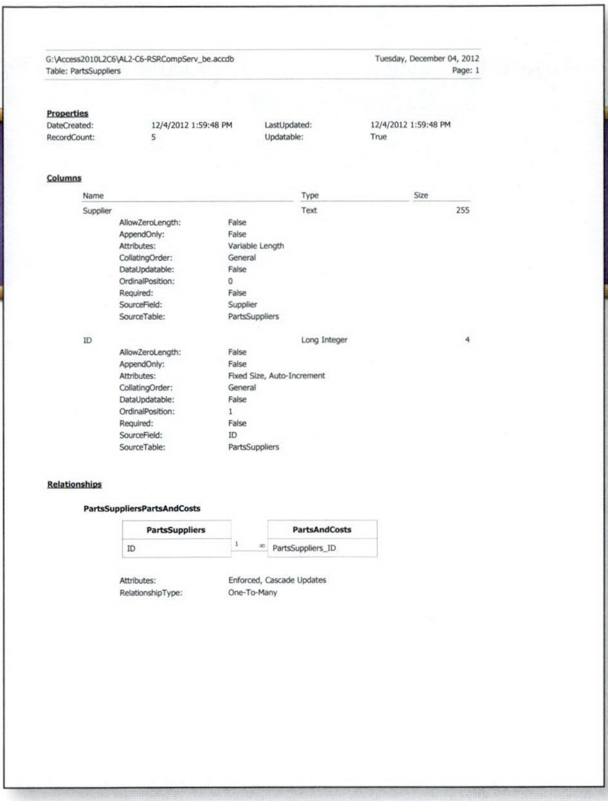

G:\Access2010L2C6\AL2-C6-RSRCompServ_be.accdb Tuesday, December 04, 2012
Table: PartsSuppliers Page: 1

Properties
DateCreated: 12/4/2012 1:59:48 PM LastUpdated: 12/4/2012 1:59:48 PM
RecordCount: 5 Updatable: True

Columns

Name	Type	Size
Supplier	Text	255
AllowZeroLength: False		
AppendOnly: False		
Attributes: Variable Length		
CollatingOrder: General		
DataUpdatable: False		
OrdinalPosition: 0		
Required: False		
SourceField: Supplier		
SourceTable: PartsSuppliers		
ID	Long Integer	4
AllowZeroLength: False		
AppendOnly: False		
Attributes: Fixed Size, Auto-Increment		
CollatingOrder: General		
DataUpdatable: False		
OrdinalPosition: 1		
Required: False		
SourceField: ID		
SourceTable: PartsSuppliers		

Relationships

PartsSuppliersPartsAndCosts

PartsSuppliers		PartsAndCosts
ID	1 ∞	PartsSuppliers_ID

Attributes: Enforced, Cascade Updates
RelationshipType: One-To-Many

Project 4 Use Access Tools to Optimize and Document a Database

Project 4a, Parts Query

Project 4d, PartsSuppliers Definition Report

Project 1 Create a New Database Using a Template — 2 Parts

You will create a new database using one of the database templates supplied with Access.

Creating a New Database Using a Template

At the New tab Backstage view, you can create a new database using one of the professionally designed templates provided by Microsoft. The database templates provide a complete series of objects including predefined tables, forms, reports, queries, and relationships. You can use a template as provided and immediately start entering data or you can base a new database on a template and modify the objects to suit your needs. If a template exists for a database application that you need, you can save time by creating the database based on one of the template designs.

To create a new database using a template, start Access and click *Sample Templates* in the Available Templates category in the center pane at the New tab Backstage view. The available template designs display in the center pane. Click a template name in the center pane, click the Browse button to navigate to the drive and/or folder in which you want to store the database, and then type a file name at the File New Database dialog box. This returns you to the previous screen with the new database file name entered below the *File Name* text box in the right pane of the New tab Backstage view. Click the Create button to create the database as shown in Figure 6.1.

Quick Steps

Create Database from Template
1. Start Access.
2. Click *Sample Templates.*
3. Click desired template.
4. Click Browse button.
5. Navigate to drive and/or folder.
6. Edit file name as required.
7. Click OK.
8. Click Create button.

Figure 6.1 AvailableTemplates in the *Sample Templates* Section of the New Tab Backstage View

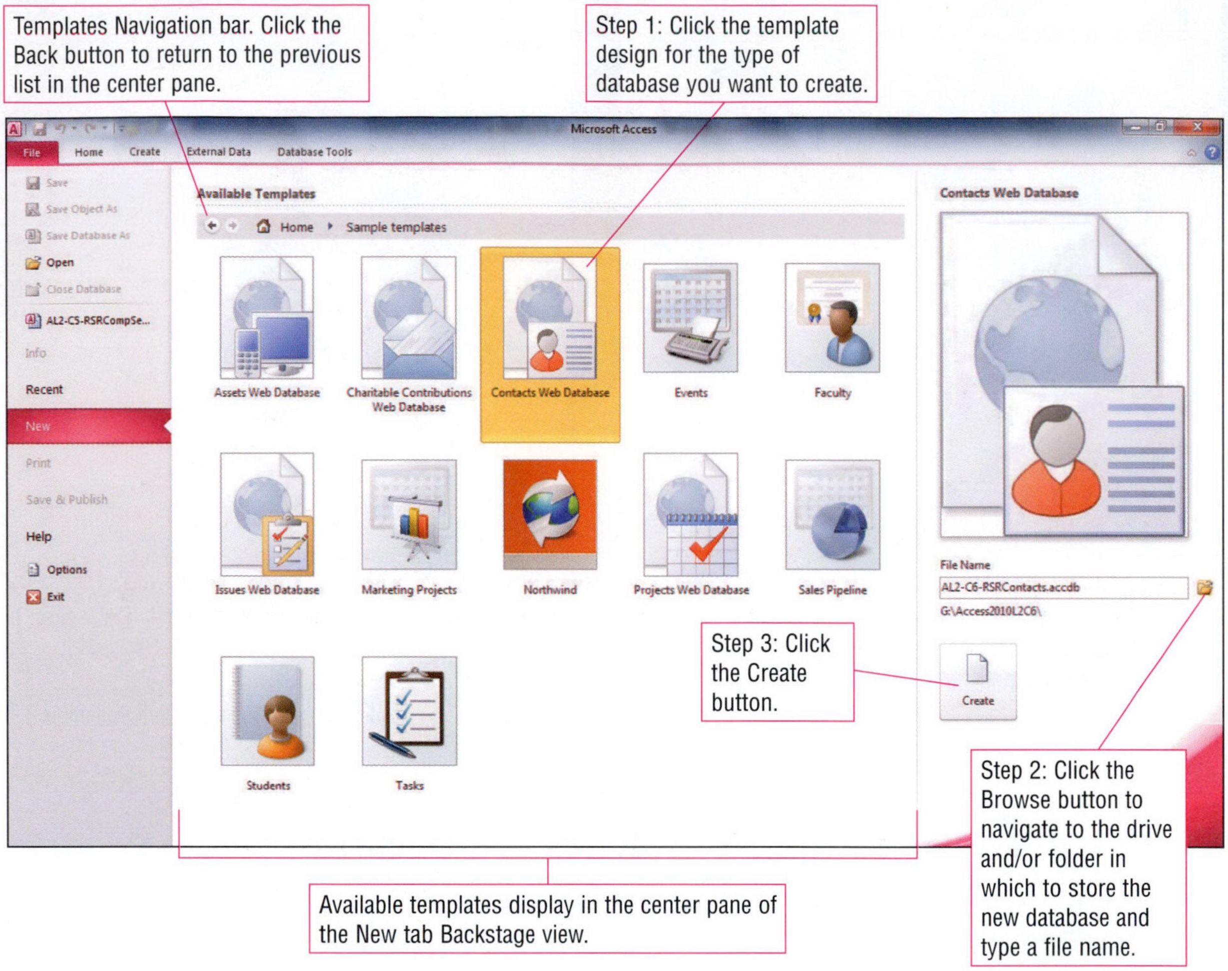

If one of the sample templates does not provide the type of application that you need, click the Back button in the Navigation bar below Available Templates and then click one of the categories below *Office.com Templates* to view a list of database templates that can be downloaded from the Microsoft Office Online website to your computer.

Project 1a Creating a New Contacts Database Using a Template — Part 1 of 2

1. Start Microsoft Access 2010.
2. At the New tab Backstage view, click *Sample Templates* in the center pane.

3. Click *Contacts Web Database* in the center pane and then click the Browse button (displays as a file folder icon) next to the *File Name* text box in the right pane.

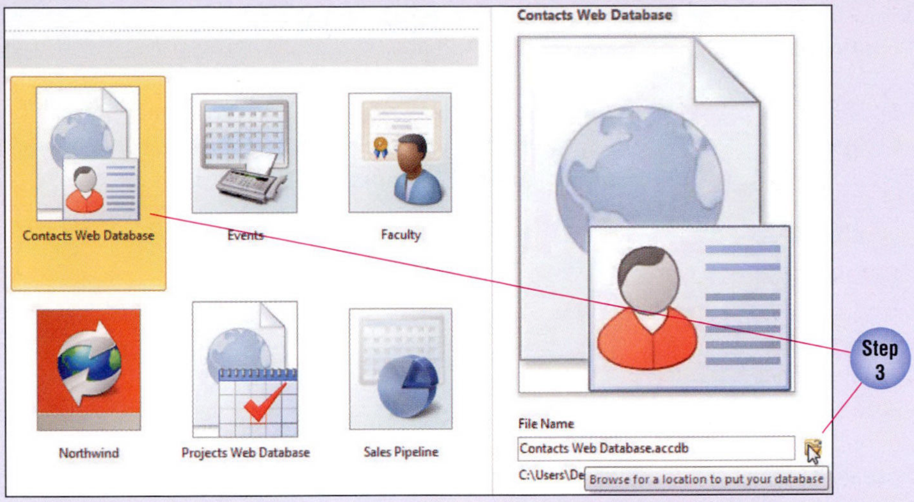

4. At the File New Database dialog box, navigate to the Access2010L2C6 folder on your storage medium, select and delete the current entry in the *File name* text box, and then type **AL2-C6-RSRContacts**.
5. Click OK.

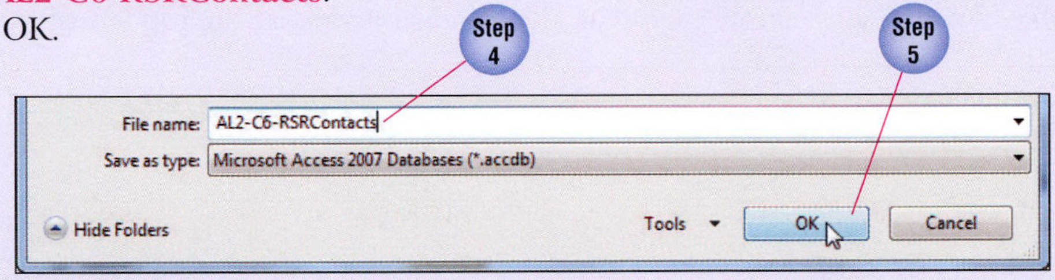

6. Click the Create button.
7. The database is created with all objects from the template loaded into the current window and the Main form opened with a *Welcome to the Contacts web database* page with links to Help information. Click the Enable Content button in the Security Warning message bar.
8. Click the Shutter Bar Open/Close button to display the Navigation pane.
9. Review the list of objects created for you by Access in the Navigation pane and then double-click to open the Contacts table.
10. Scroll right to view all of the fields in the Contacts table and then close the table.
11. Double-click *ContactDetails* in the *Forms* section of the Navigation pane and review the form in the work area.

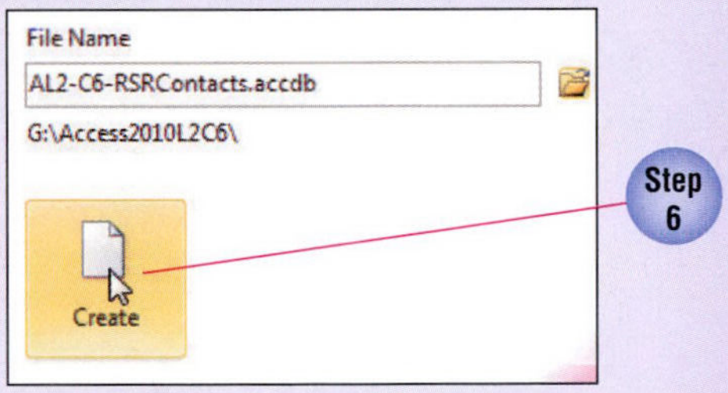

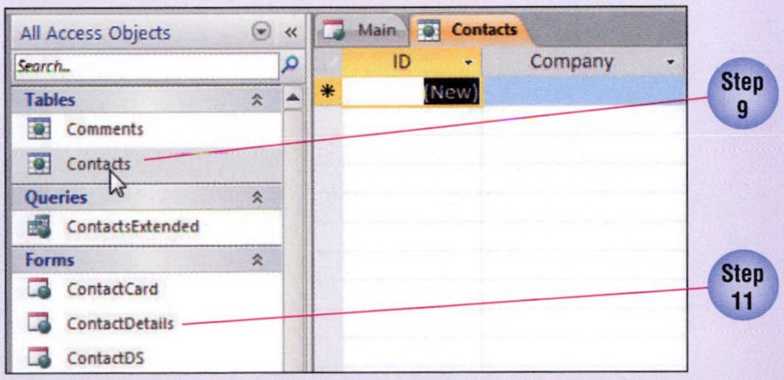

Project 1b — Entering and Viewing Data in the Contacts Database — Part 2 of 2

1. With the **AL2-C6-RSRContacts.accdb** database open and the ContactDetails form open in Form view, add the following record using the form:

First Name	**Ariel**
Last Name	**Grayson**
Job Title	**Accountant**
Company	**Grayson Accounting Services** ***Note: Press Tab or Enter twice after this field to move to the E-mail field.***
E-mail	**ariel@emcp.net**
Web Page	**www.emcp.net/grayson**
Business Phone	**800-555-4988**
Fax	**313-555-9648**
Home Phone	**313-555-6811**
Mobile Phone	**800-555-3472**
Address	**17399 Windsor Avenue**
City	**Detroit**
State/Province	**MI**
Zip/Postal Code	**48214-3274**
Country/Region	**USA**
Notes	**Ariel recommended to RSR by Pat Hynes**

2. Add a picture of the contact using the *Attachments* field by completing the following steps:
   a. Double-click the gray empty picture in the *Attachments* box at the top left of the form.

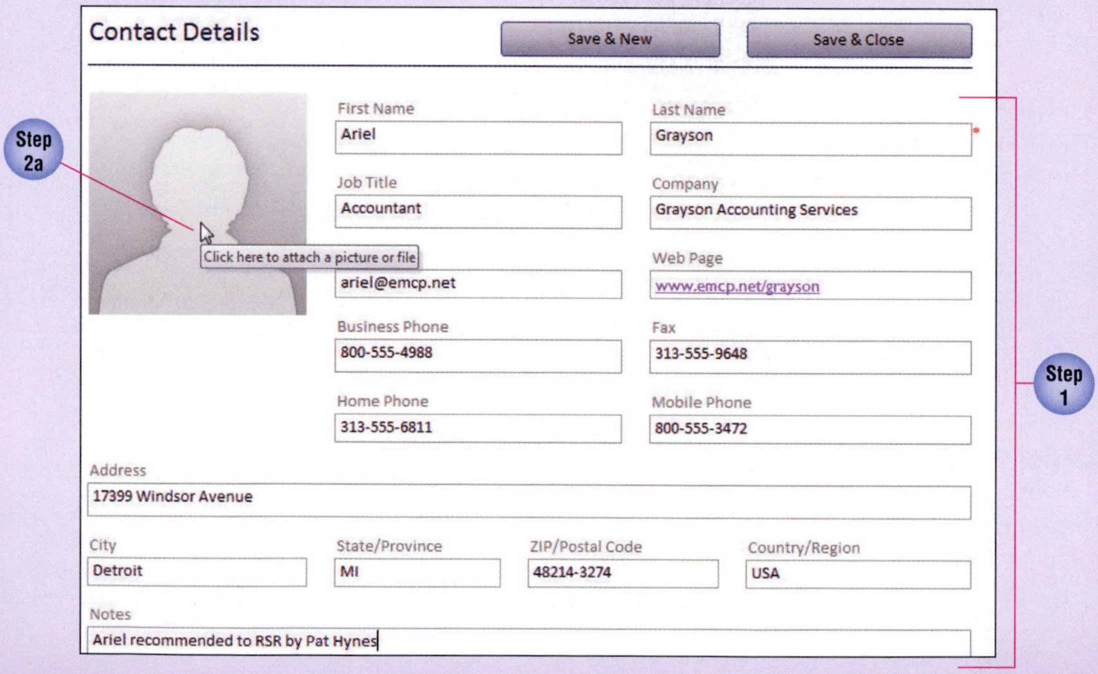

b. At the Attachments dialog box, click the Add button.

c. At the Choose File dialog box, navigate to the Access2010L2C6 folder on your storage medium.

d. Double-click ***ArielGrayson.jpg*** to add the file to the Attachments dialog box.

e. Click OK.

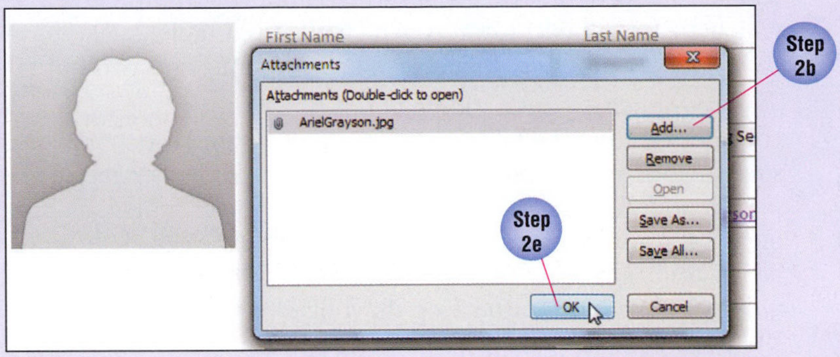

3. Click the Save & Close button located at the top right of the form.
4. Click the Address Book tab located at the top left of the Main form and review the contact information for Ariel Grayson in the Address Book.
5. Click the Report Center tab in the Main form and then click the Contact Details hyperlink in the Select a Report pane at the right side of the work area.
6. Click each of the other report hyperlinks in the Select a Report pane.
7. Close the Main form.
8. Double-click *ContactDetails* in the *Reports* section of the Navigation pane. Display the report in Print Preview and then print the report.
9. Close Print Preview, close the Contact Details report, and then close the **AL2-C6-RSRContacts.accdb** database.

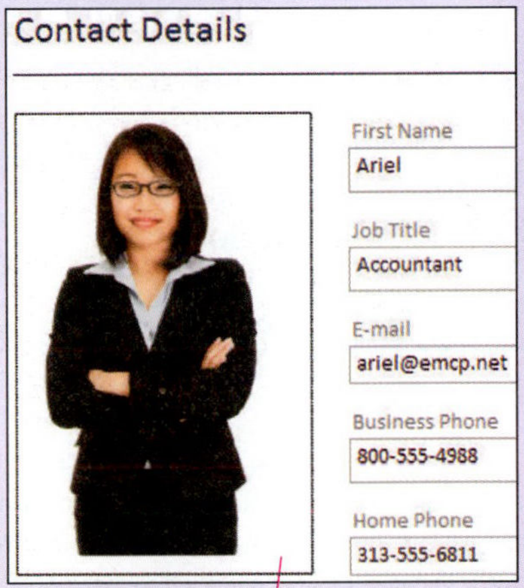

Picture displays in form after adding a .jpg file to Attachments dialog box. If you add a Word document in the *Attachments* box, a Word icon displays.

Project 2 Create Objects Using a Template — 3 Parts

You will create a series of objects in an existing database using Application Parts templates. You will also define a form as a template for all new forms in a database.

Quick Steps

Create Objects Using an Application Parts Template

1. Open database.
2. Click Create tab.
3. Click Application Parts button.
4. Click desired template.
5. Choose relationship options.
6. Add data or modify objects as required.

HINT

You can create your own Application Parts template by copying an object you will reuse in other databases to a new database and then save the database as a template at the Save & Publish tab Backstage view.

Application Parts

Creating Objects Using an Application Parts Template

Access 2010 provides templates that include prebuilt objects that can be inserted into an existing database using the Application Parts button in the Create tab. The *Quick Start* section of the Application Parts button drop-down list includes *Comments*, which creates a table; *Contacts*, which creates a table, query, forms and reports; and *Issues, Tasks,* and *Users*, which each create a table and two forms.

If you need to add a table about one of these topics to an existing database, consider creating the table using the Application Parts template since related objects such as forms and reports are also automatically generated. Once the application part is added, you can modify any of the object designs to suit your needs. To create a group of objects based on a template, click the Create tab and click the Application Parts button in the Templates group. Click the desired template in the *Quick Start* section of the drop-down list shown in Figure 6.2.

Access opens the Create Relationship Wizard to guide you through creating the relationship for the new table. Decide in advance of creating the new table what relationship, if any, will exist between the new table and an existing table in the database. At the first Create Relationship Wizard dialog box shown in Figure 6.3, click the first option if the new table will be the "many" table in a one-to-many relationship. Use the Tables drop-down list to choose the "one" table and click Next. Click the second option if the new table will be the "one" table in a one-to-many relationship, choose the "many" table from the Tables drop-down list, and choose Next. At the second Create Relationship Wizard dialog box you enter the settings for the lookup column between the two tables. Choose the field to be used to join the tables, choose a sort order if desired, assign the name for the lookup column, and then click the Create button. If the new table will not be related to any of the existing tables in the database, choose the *There is no relationship* option and click the Create button at the first Create Relationship Wizard dialog box.

Figure 6.2 Application Parts Button Drop-Down List

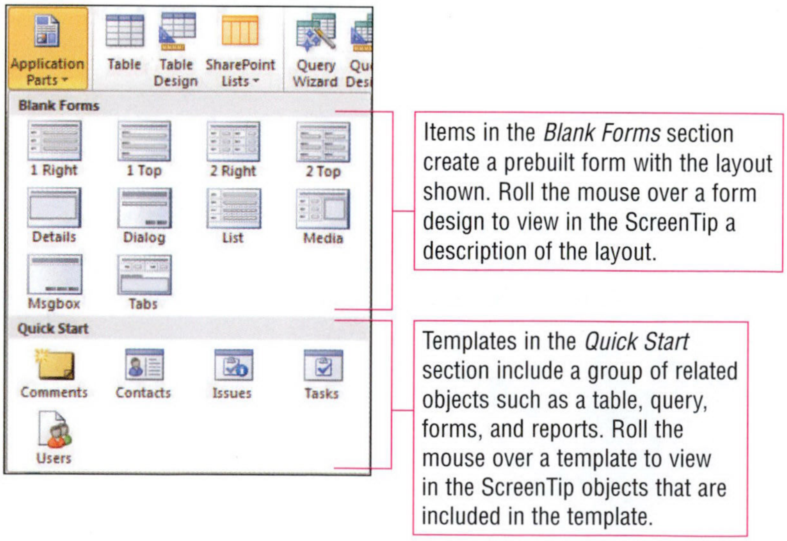
Application Parts
Table
Table Design
SharePoint Lists
Query Wizard
Blank Forms
1 Right
1 Top
2 Right
2 Top
Details
Dialog
List
Media
Msgbox
Tabs
Quick Start
Comments
Contacts
Issues
Tasks
Users
Items in the *Blank Forms* section create a prebuilt form with the layout shown. Roll the mouse over a form design to view in the ScreenTip a description of the layout.
Templates in the *Quick Start* section include a group of related objects such as a table, query, forms, and reports. Roll the mouse over a template to view in the ScreenTip objects that are included in the template.

Figure 6.3 Create Relationship Wizard Dialog Box

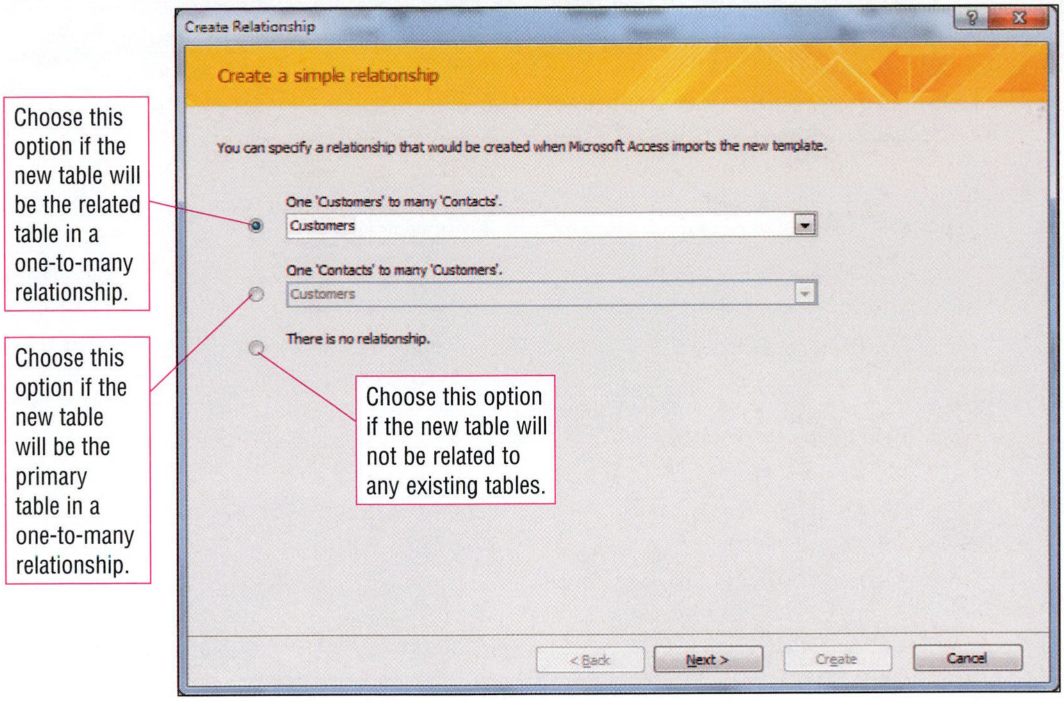

Project 2a Creating a Contacts Table, Query, Forms, and Reports Using a Template Part 1 of 3

1. Open **AL2-C6-RSRCompServ.accdb** and enable content.
2. Create a new table, query, forms, and reports related to contacts using a template by completing the following steps:
   a. Click the Create tab.
   b. Click the Application Parts button in the Templates group and click *Contacts* in the *Quick Start* section of the drop-down list.

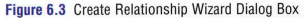

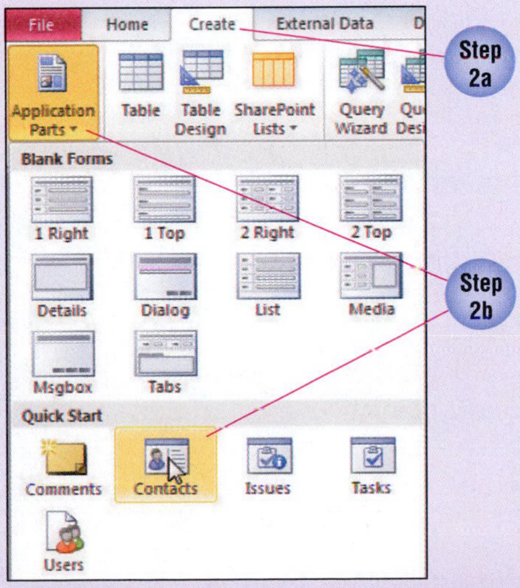

c. At the Create Relationship Wizard dialog box, click the *There is no relationship* option and then click Create. Access imports a Contacts table; a ContactsExtended query; a ContactDetails, ContactDS, and ContactList form; and a ContactAddressBook, ContactList, and ContactPhoneBook report into the database.

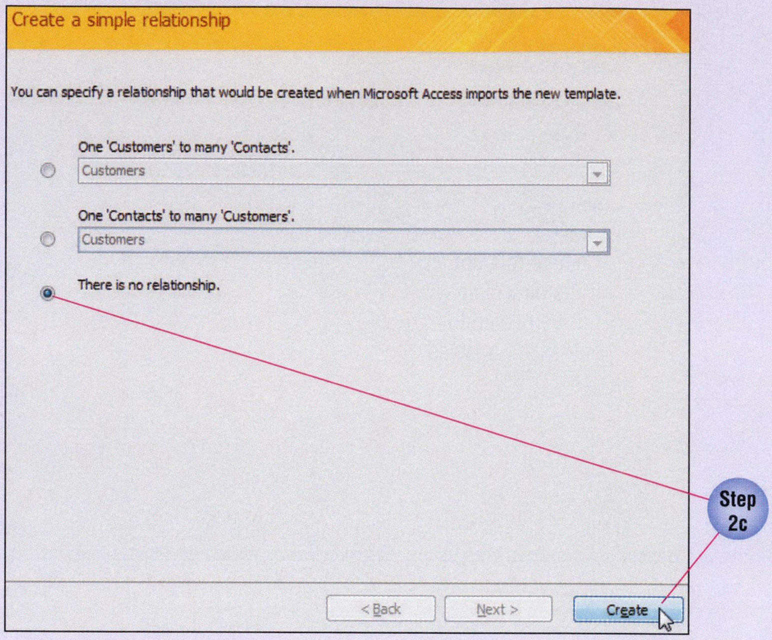

3. Double-click the Contacts table in the Navigation pane. Scroll right to view all of the fields in the new table and then close the table.
4. Double-click the ContactDetails form in the Navigation pane. Notice the form is the same ContactDetails form you used in Project 1b in the Contacts database.
5. Enter the following record using the ContactDetails form:

First Name	**Terry**
Last Name	**Silver**
Job Title	**Sales Manager**
Company	**Cityscape Electronics**
E-mail	**terry_s@emcp.net**
Web Page	**www.emcp.net/cityscape**
Business Phone	**800-555-4968**
Fax	**800-555-6941**
Home Phone	(leave blank)
Mobile Phone	**313-555-3442**
Address	**3700 Woodward Avenue**
City	**Detroit**
State/Province	**MI**
ZIP/Postal Code	**48201-2006**
Country/Region	(leave blank)
Notes	(leave blank)

6. Click the Save & Close button at the top right of the form.

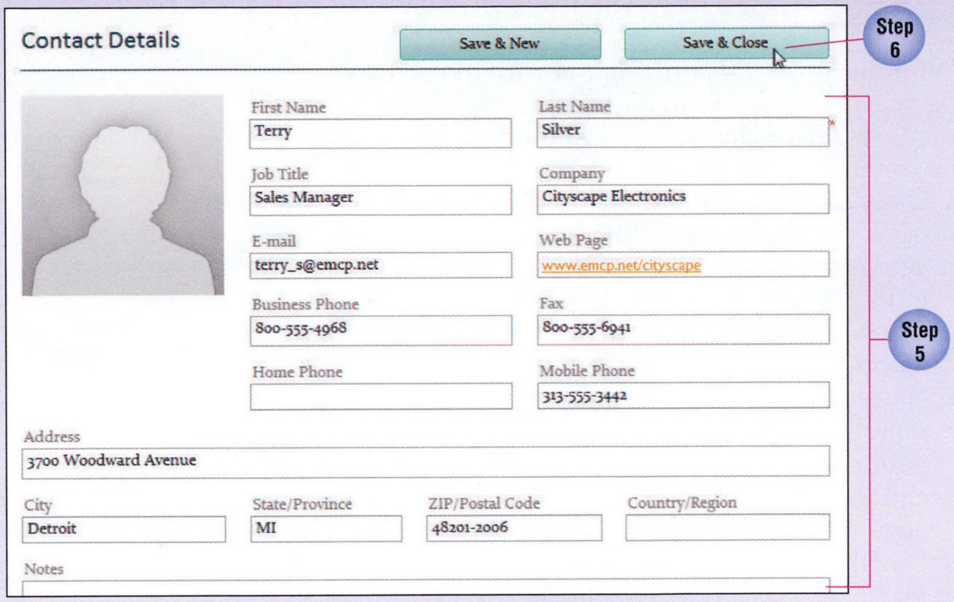

7. Open the ContactList report.
8. Display the report in Print Preview and then print the report.
9. Close Print Preview and then close the ContactList report.

Application Parts also includes various blank form layouts to make the task of creating a new form easier by allowing you to pick a layout that has already been defined. The *Blank Forms* section of the Application Parts button drop-down list contains 10 prebuilt blank forms. Most of the forms contain command buttons that perform actions such as saving changes or saving and closing the form. Resting the mouse pointer over a blank form option at the Application Parts button drop-down list displays a description of the form's layout in a ScreenTip. When you click a blank form option, Access creates the form object using a predefined form name. For example, if you click *1 Right*, Access creates a form named *SingleOneColumnRightLabels*. Locate the form name in the Navigation pane and open the form in Layout view or Design view to customize the form as needed.

Application Parts forms have a control layout applied so that all of the form's controls will move and resize together. Remove the control layout to make individual size adjustments. In Design view, select all of the controls and click the Remove Layout button in the Table group of the Arrange tab.

Quick Steps

Create Form Using Blank Form Application Parts

1. Click Create tab.
2. Click Application Parts button.
3. Click desired blank form layout.
4. Add fields to form.
5. Customize form as needed.
6. Save form.

Create a New Form Using an Application Parts Blank Form

1. With the **AL2-C6-RSRCompServ.accdb** database open, create a new form for maintaining records in the Parts table using an Application Parts blank form by completing the following steps:
   a. If necessary, click the Create tab.
   b. Click the Applications Parts button in the Templates group and then click *1 Right* in the *Blank Forms* section at the drop-down list. Access creates a form named *SingleOneColumnRightLabels*.
   c. If necessary, position the mouse pointer on the right border of the Navigation pane until the pointer changes to a left- and right-pointing arrow and then drag right to widen the Navigation pane until you can read all of the object names.
   d. Double-click the form named *SingleOneColumnRightLabels* in the Navigation pane.

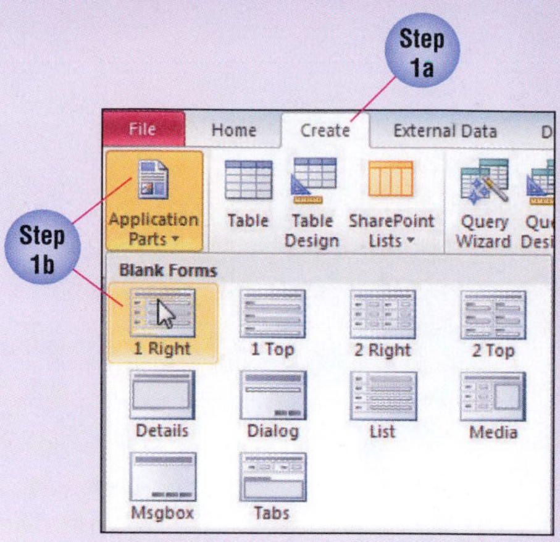

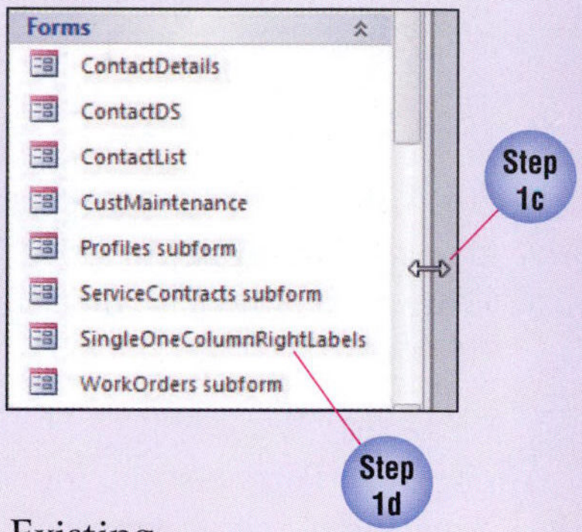

2. Switch to Layout view.
3. Click to select the *Field1* label control object. Shift + click to select the *Field2*, *Field3*, and *Field4* label control objects and then press Delete.
4. Associate the Parts table with the form and add fields from the Parts table by completing the following steps:
   a. If the Field List pane is not currently open, click the Add Existing Fields button in the Tools group of the Form Layout Tools Design tab.
   b. Click the Show all tables hyperlink at the top of the pane. Skip this step if your Field List pane already displays all of the table names in the database.
   c. Click the plus symbol next to *Parts* in the Field List pane to expand the list and show all of the fields in the Parts table.
   d. Drag the *PartNo* field to the second column in the row shown at the right.
   e. Drag the remaining fields *PartName*, *Supplier*, and *Cost* below *PartNo* as shown below.

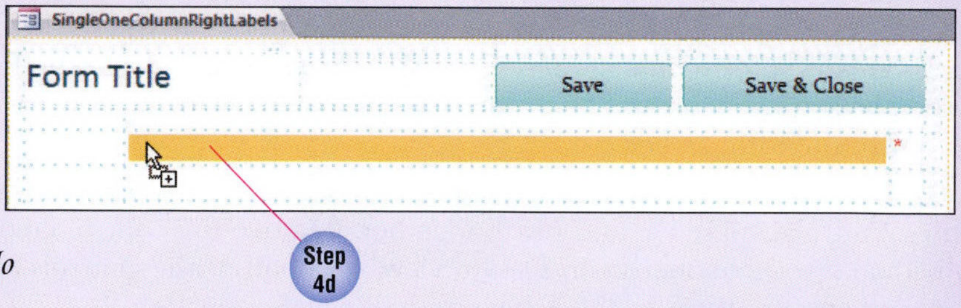

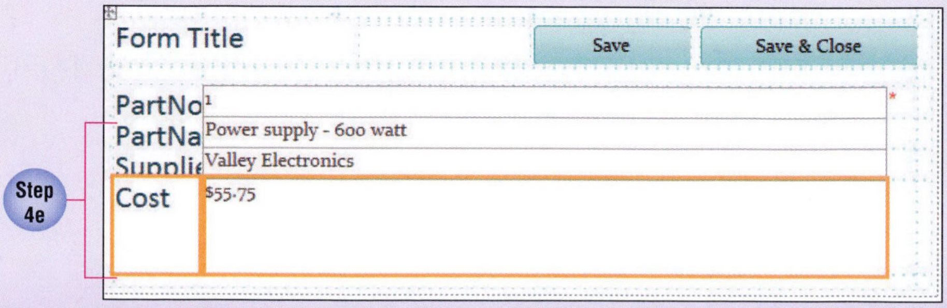

5. With the *Cost* field selected, drag the bottom orange border of the control up to decrease the height of the control object so that the bottom border is approximately 0.5 inch below the label text.
6. Select the four label control objects and drag the right orange border of the selected controls right to widen the labels until you can read all of the label text.
7. With the four label control objects still selected, click the Form Layout Tools Arrange tab, click the Control Padding button in the Position group, and then click *Wide* at the drop-down list.

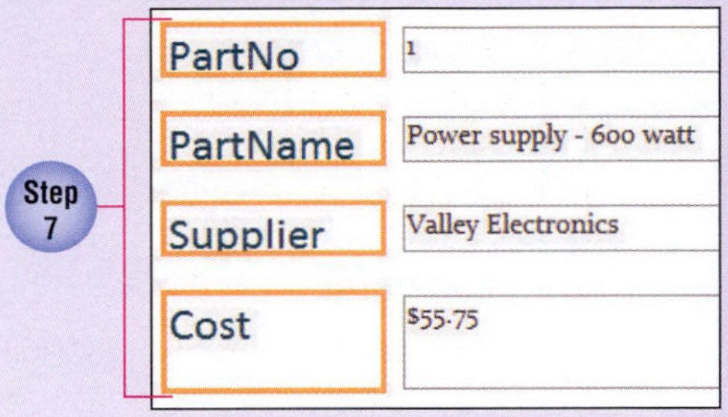

8. Double-click the form title to place an insertion point inside the title text, delete *Form Title*, type **Repair Parts**, and then press Enter.
9. Apply formatting changes to the form as follows:
   a. Select the two command buttons at the top right of the form (Save and Save & Close), click the Form Layout Tools Format tab, click the Quick Styles button, and then click *Intense Effect - Blue, Accent 1* at the drop-down list.
   b. Select the *Repair Parts* title control object and change the font color to *Blue, Accent 1* (fifth color option in first row of *Theme Colors* section).
   c. Apply *Blue, Accent 1* font color to the four label control objects.
   d. Apply *Light Turquoise, Background 2* (third color option in first row of *Theme Colors* section) background color to the four text box control objects adjacent to the labels.

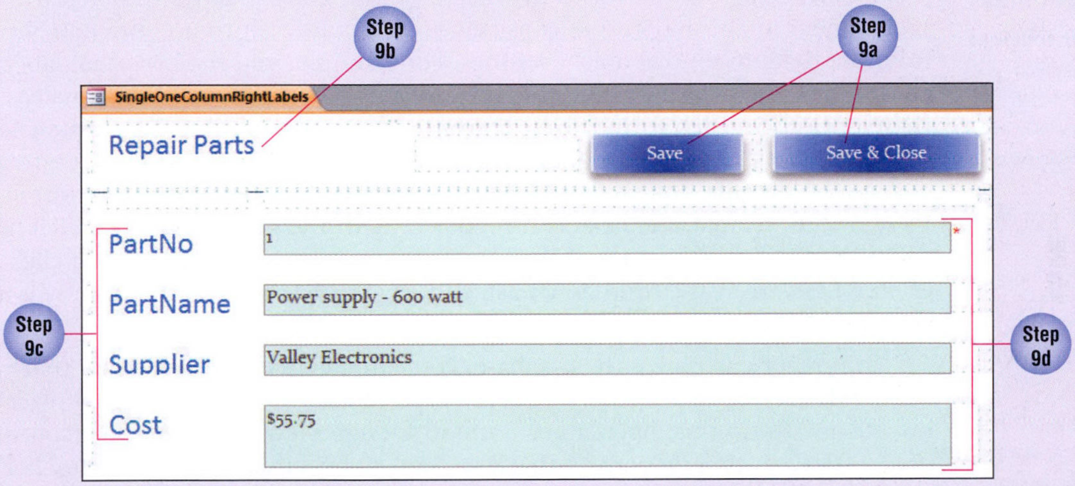

   e. Click in a blank area of the form to deselect the four text box control objects.
10. Click the File tab, click Save Object As, type **PartsForm** in the *Save 'SingleOneColumnRightLabels' to* text box at the Save As dialog box, and then click OK.
11. Click the Home tab and then switch to Form view.

12. Scroll through a few records in the PartsForm and then click the Save & Close button at the top right of the form to close the PartsForm.

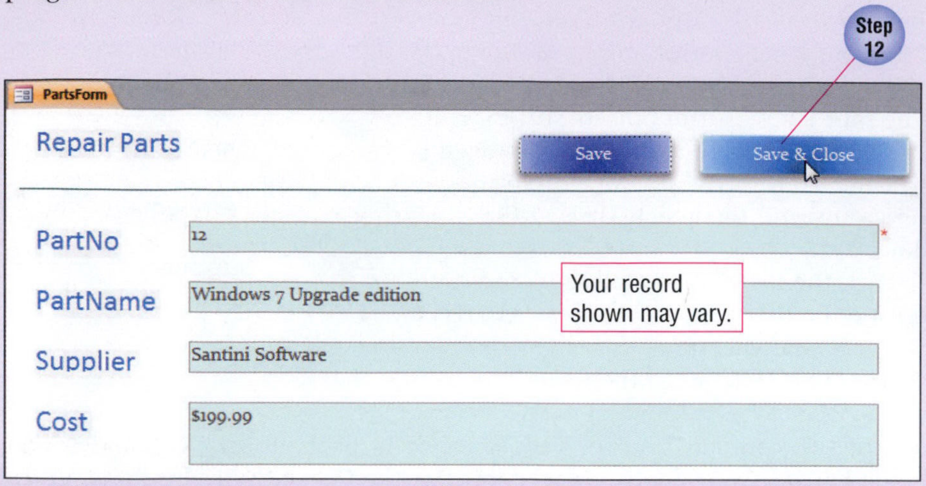

Setting Form Control Defaults and Creating a User-Defined Form Template

Quick Steps

Create User-Defined Form Template

1. Create new form in Design view.
2. Add control object to form.
3. Format control object as desired.
4. Click More button at bottom of Control group.
5. Click *Set Control Defaults.*
6. Repeat Steps 2 to 5 for each type of control to be used.
7. Save form naming it *Normal.*

HINT

Delete the Normal form if you want to go back to using the standard default options for control objects in forms.

A standard design for all forms in a database is a good practice to portray a professional image and ensure consistency. You may wish to use different settings from the default control object settings. For example, you may want all label control objects to be 14-point blue text on a gray background. To manually change these options in each form is time-consuming and may lead to inconsistencies. The *Set Control Defaults* option at the Controls drop-down list allows you to change the defaults for all new labels in a form. To do this, open the form in Design view, format one label control object with the desired settings, click the More button at the bottom of the Controls vertical scroll bar, and then click *Set Control Defaults* at the drop-down list. All new labels added to the form will have the format options already defined that you want to use.

To further customize the database, you can create a form template that will set the desired control defaults for each type of control object that you place on a form. To do this, open a new form in Design view and create one control object for each type of control that you want to specify a default setting. For example, add a label control object, a text box control object, a command button, a list box control object, and so on making sure you format each control object with the desired colors and backgrounds. As you finish each control, use the *Set Control Defaults* option to change the default settings or select all controls after you have finished the form and perform one *Set Control Defaults* command. When finished, save the form using the form name *Normal*. The Normal form becomes the template for all new forms in the database. Existing forms retain their initial format unless you manually change them.

Project 2c Creating and Using a User-Defined Form Template

Part 3 of 3

1. With the **AL2-C6-RSRCompServ.accdb** database open, create a form to be used as the form template for the database for all new forms by completing the following steps:
   a. Click the Create tab and then click the Form Design button in the Forms group.
   b. Click the Themes button in the Themes group and then click *Opulent* at the drop-down list.
   c. Click the Label button in the Controls group of the Form Design Tools Design tab, draw a label in the *Detail* section, type **Sample Label Text**, and then press Enter. The position and size of the label object is not of concern at this time since you are using this control object only to set new default formatting options.
   d. Click the Form Design Tools Format tab. Change the font color to *Purple, Accent 2* (sixth color option in first row of *Theme Colors* section) and the background color to *Lavender, Background 2* (third color option in first row of *Theme Colors* section).

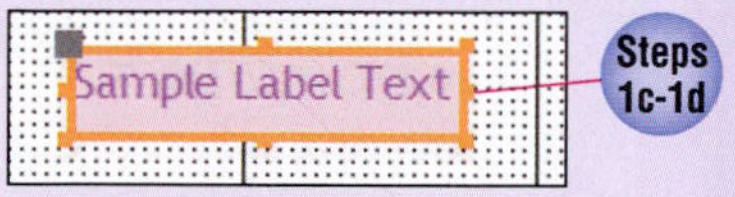

   f. Click the Form Design Tools Design tab, click the Text Box button in the Controls group, and then draw a text box control object in the *Detail* section. Format the text box control object and its associated label control object as follows:
      1) Apply the same font color and background color to the label control object attached to the text box as you applied to the label control object in Step 1d.
      2) Select the text box control object (displays *Unbound*) and apply the same background color as you applied to the label control object in Step 1d.

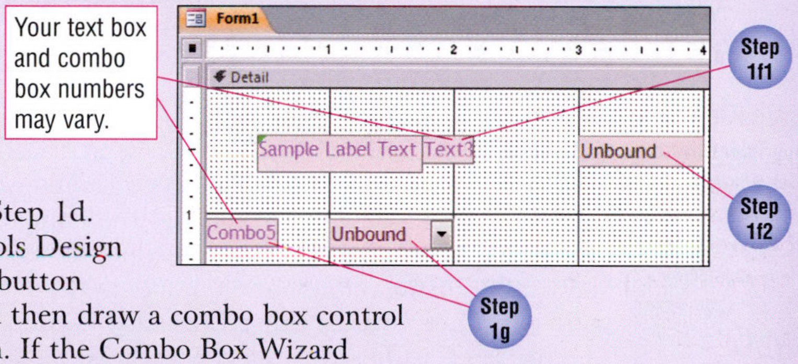

   g. Click the Form Design Tools Design tab, click the Combo Box button in the Controls group, and then draw a combo box control object in the *Detail* section. If the Combo Box Wizard begins, click the Cancel button. Format the combo box control object using the same format options as you applied to the text box control object in Steps 1f1 to 1f2.
   h. Press Ctrl + A to select all of the control objects in the form.
   i. Click the Form Design Tools Design tab, click the More button at the bottom of the Controls scroll bar, and then click *Set Control Defaults* at the drop-down list.

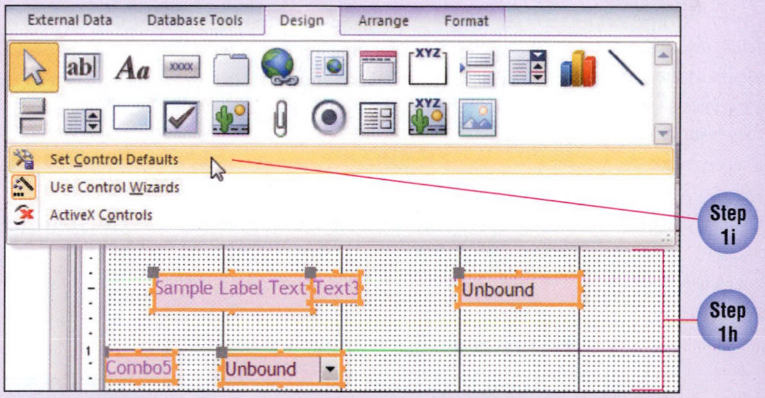

2. Save the form and name it *Normal*.

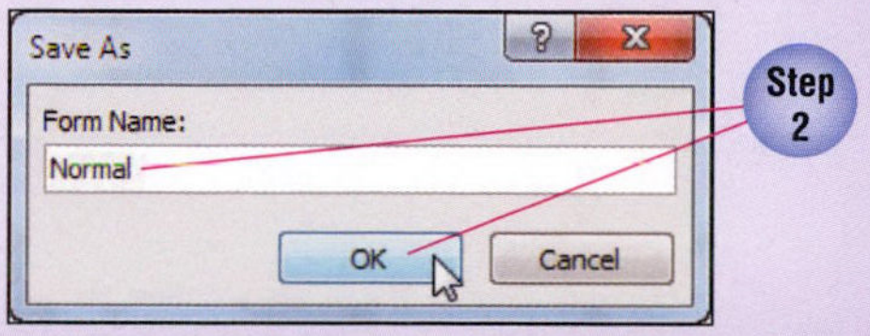

3. Close the Normal form. Normal becomes the form template for the *AL2-C6-RSRCompServ.accdb* database. Any new form created will have labels, text boxes, and combo boxes formatted as specified in Step 1.
4. Click the WorkOrders table name in the Navigation pane, click the Create tab, and then click the Form button in the Forms group. The new WorkOrders form uses the formatting applied to the labels, text boxes, and combo boxes in the Normal form template.
5. With the first record displayed in the WorkOrders form in Form view, open the Print dialog box. Click the Setup button and then click the Columns tab at the Page Setup dialog box. Select the current value in the *Width* text box in the *Column Size* section, type 8, and then click OK. Click *Selected Record(s)* in the *Print Range* section of the Print dialog box and then click OK.
6. Close the WorkOrders form. Click Yes when prompted to save changes to the design of the form and then click OK to accept the default form name *WorkOrders*.

Project 3 Copy Table Structure — 1 Part

You will create a new table to store contact information for manufacturer sales representatives by copying an existing table's field names and field properties.

Quick Steps

Copy Table Structure
1. Select table.
2. Click Copy button.
3. Click Paste button.
4. Type new table name.
5. Click *Structure Only*.
6. Click OK.

HINT

If a new table that is needed is similar to an existing table's fields and/or field properties, you can save time by copying the existing table's structure and then adding, deleting, and modifying fields in Design view.

Copying Table Structure to Create a New Table

Using copy and paste commands you can copy an existing table's structure if you need to create a new table that uses the same or similar fields as an existing table. For example, in Project 3 you will copy the Contacts table structure to create a new table for manufacturer contacts that you want to maintain separately from other contact records. Since the fields needed for manufacturer contact records are the same as those that already exist for the other contact records, you can base the new table on the existing table.

To copy a table's structure, click the existing table name in the Navigation pane and click the Copy button in the Clipboard group in the Home tab. Next, click the Paste button in the Clipboard group. When a table has been copied to the clipboard, clicking the Paste button causes the Paste Table As dialog box shown in Figure 6.4 to appear.

Type the desired name for the new table in the *Table Name* text box, click *Structure Only* in the *Paste Options* section, and then click OK. Once the table is created you can add, delete, or modify fields as needed.

Figure 6.4 Paste Table As Dialog Box

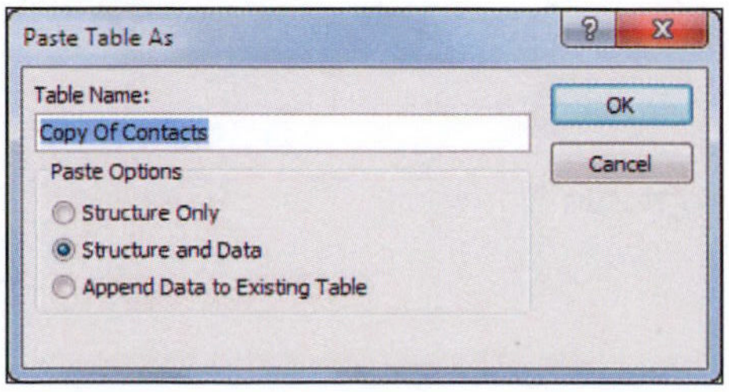

Project 3 Copying Table Structure to Create a New Table

Part 1 of 1

1. With the **AL2-C6-RSRCompServ.accdb** database open, click to select the Contacts table in the Navigation pane.
2. Click the Home tab and then click the Copy button in the Clipboard group.
3. Click the Paste button in the Clipboard group. (Do not click the down-pointing arrow on the button.)
4. At the Paste Table As dialog box, type MfrContacts in the *Table Name* text box, click *Structure Only* in the *Paste Options* section, and then press Enter or click OK.

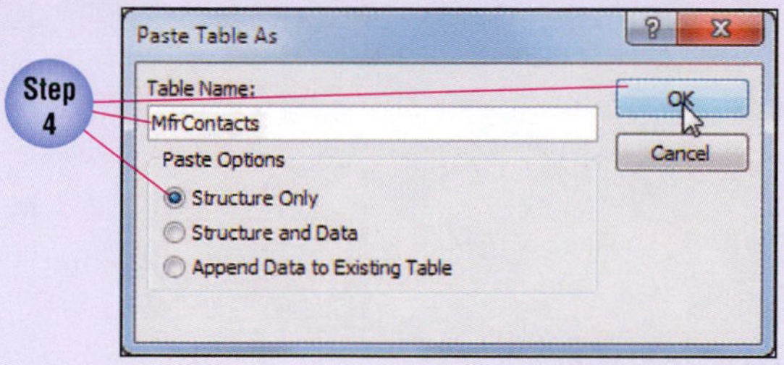

5. Open the MfrContacts table. The table structure contains the same fields as the Contacts table.
6. Enter the following data in a new record using Datasheet view. Press Tab or Enter past the remaining fields after *ZIP/Postal Code* to finish the record.

Company	Dell Inc.
Last Name	Haldstadt
First Name	Cari
Email Address	haldstadt@emcp.net
Job Title	Northeast Sales Manager
Business Phone	800-555-9522
Home Phone	(leave blank)
Mobile Phone	800-555-4662
Fax Number	800-555-7781
Address	One Dell Way
City	Round Rock
State/Province	TX
ZIP/Postal Code	78682

7. Close the table.

8. With MfrContacts selected in the Navigation pane, click the Create tab and then click the Form button in the Forms group to create a new form based on the table.

MfrContacts
ID
1
City
Round Rock
Company
Dell Inc.
State/Province
TX
Last Name
Haldstadt
ZIP/Postal Code
78682
First Name
Cari
Country/Region
Email Address
haldstadt@emcp.net
Web Page
Job Title
Northeast Sales Manager
Notes
Business Phone
800-555-9522
Attachments
Home Phone
Contact Name
Cari Haldstadt
Mobile Phone
800-555-4662
File As
Haldstadt, Cari
Fax Number
800-555-7781

MfrContacts form created at Step 8.

9. Click the File tab, click Print, and then click Print Preview to display the form in Print Preview. Change the page orientation to landscape and then close Print Preview.
10. Save the form using the default name *MfrContacts*.
11. Print the selected record and then close the form.

Project 4 Use Access Tools to Optimize and Document a Database — 5 Parts

You will use the Table Analyzer Wizard to improve a table's design, the Performance Analyzer to optimize database design, and split a database by separating tables from queries, forms, and reports. Finally, you will use the Database Documenter to print a report documenting table structure.

Modifying a Table Using the Table Analyzer Wizard

HINT

The Table Analyzer Wizard helps you normalize a table.

The Table Analyzer Wizard is used to examine a table and determine if duplicate information in the table can be split into smaller related tables to improve the table design. Repeated information in tables can result in inconsistencies and wasted storage space. The wizard presents a solution with fields that can be separated into a new table related to the original table with a lookup field. You can accept the proposed solution or modify the suggestion. In Project 4a you will use the Table Analyzer Wizard in a new Parts table. The table was created to store information about parts that are commonly used by the technicians at RSR Computer Service. Access will examine the table and propose that the *Supplier* field be moved to a separate table. The reason this solution is a better design is that several parts records can be associated with the same supplier. In the current table design, the supplier name is typed into a field in each record. With several parts associated with the same supplier name, the field contains many duplicated entries that use disk space. Furthermore, the potential exists for a typing mistake in a record, which could result in a query not producing the correct list.

To begin the Table Analyzer Wizard, click the Database Tools tab and then click the Analyze Table button in the Analyze group. This presents the first Table Analyzer Wizard dialog box shown in Figure 6.5. The first two dialog boxes in the wizard explain what the Table Analyzer does to improve the table design. At the third dialog box in the wizard, you select the table to be analyzed. At the fourth dialog box, you choose to let the wizard decide which fields to group together in the smaller tables or manually split the tables by dragging and dropping fields.

The wizard looks for fields with repetitive data and suggests a solution. You confirm the grouping of fields and the primary keys in the new tables and, at the final step in the wizard, you can elect to have Access create a query so that the fields in the split tables are presented together in a datasheet that resembles the original table.

Quick Steps

Evaluate Table with Table Analyzer Wizard

1. Click Database Tools tab.
2. Click Analyze Table button.
3. Click Next.
4. Click Next.
5. Click table name.
6. Click Next.
7. If necessary, click *Yes, let wizard decide.*
8. Click Next.
9. Confirm grouping of fields in proposed tables.
10. Rename each table.
11. Click Next.
12. Confirm and/or set primary key in each table.
13. Click Next.
14. If necessary, click *Yes, create the query.*
15. Click Finish.
16. Close Help window.
17. Close query.

Analyze Table

Figure 6.5 First Table Analyzer Wizard Dialog Box

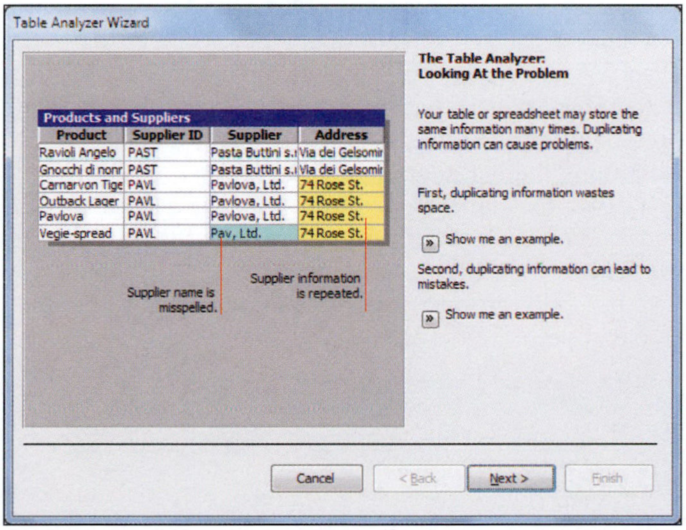

Project 4a Splitting a Table Using the Table Analyzer Wizard Part 1 of 5

1. With the **AL2-C6-RSRCompServ.accdb** database open, open the Parts table in Datasheet view and review the table structure and data. Notice the table includes four fields: *PartNo*, *PartName*, *Supplier*, and *Cost*. Also notice that supplier names are repeated in the *Supplier* field.
2. Close the Parts table.
3. Use the Table Analyzer Wizard to evaluate the Parts table design to determine if the table can be improved by completing the following steps:
   a. Click the Database Tools tab.

b. Click the Analyze Table button in the Analyze group.
c. Read the information at the first Table Analyzer Wizard dialog box and click Next.
d. Read the information at the second Table Analyzer Wizard dialog box and click Next.
e. With *Parts* selected in the *Tables* list box at the third Table Analyzer Wizard dialog box, click Next.

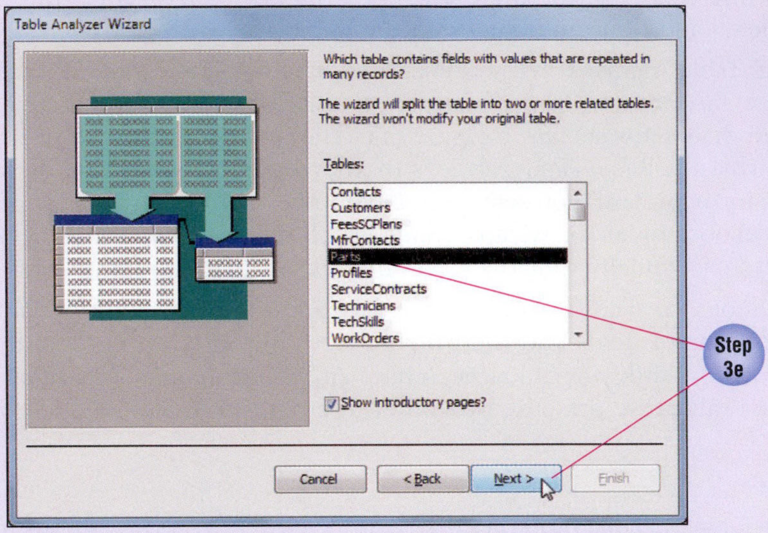

f. With *Yes, let the wizard decide* selected for *Do you want the wizard to decide what fields go in what tables?* at the fourth Table Analyzer Wizard dialog box, click Next.
g. At the fifth Table Analyzer Wizard dialog box, look at the two tables the wizard is proposing. Notice that the *Supplier* field has been moved to a new table with a one-to-many relationship created between the table with the supplier names ("one" table) and a new table with the remaining fields ("many" table). Access names the new tables *Table1* and *Table2* and asks two questions: *Is the wizard grouping information correctly?* and *What name do you want for each table?* ***Note: If necessary, resize the table list boxes in order to see the proposed fields.***
h. The proposed tables have the fields grouped correctly. Rename the first table by double-clicking the Table1 title bar.

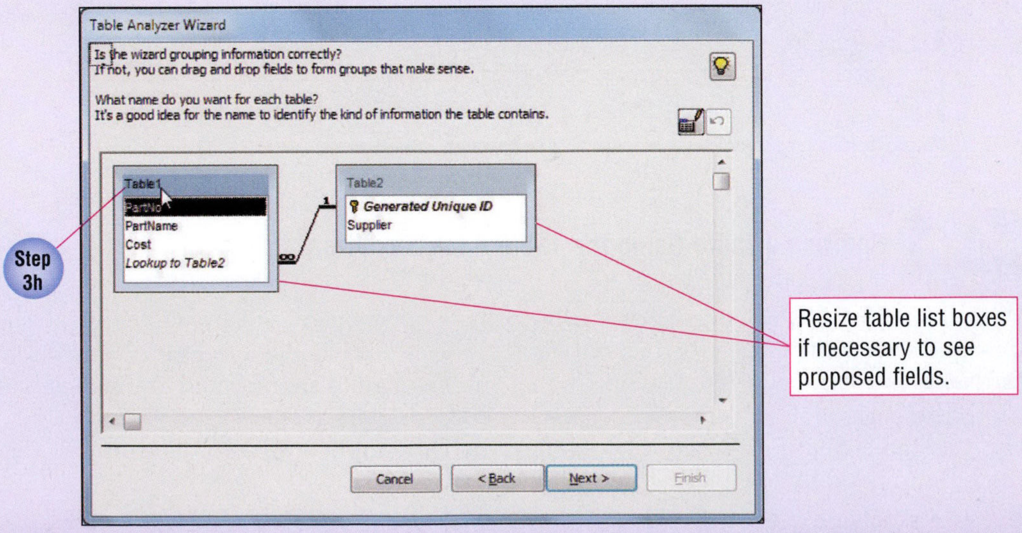

i. Type **PartsAndCosts** in the *Table Name* text box and press Enter or click OK.

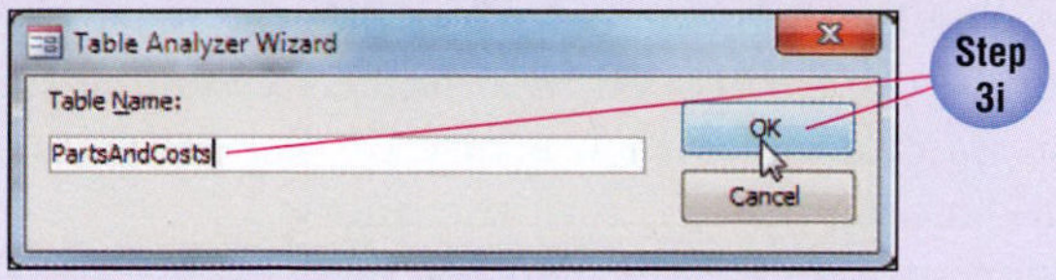

j. Click the Table2 title bar and click the Rename Table button located near the top right of the dialog box above the table list boxes. Type **PartsSuppliers** in the *Table Name* text box and press Enter or click OK.

k. Click Next.

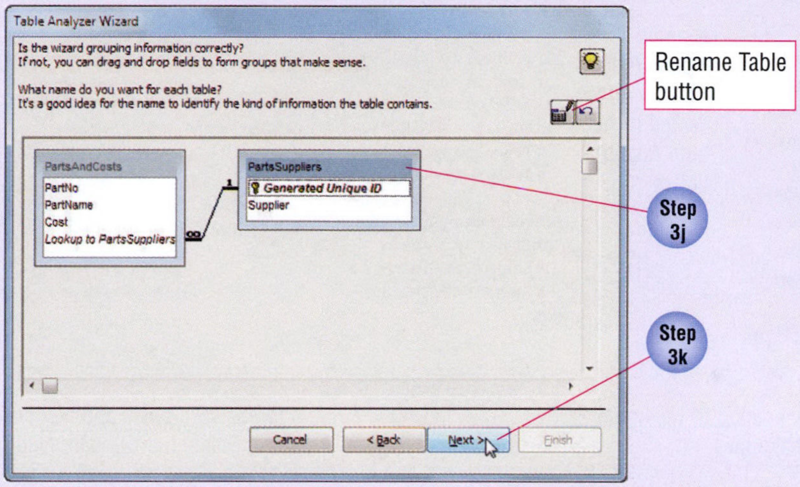

l. At the sixth Table Analyzer Wizard dialog box, the primary key fields for each table are set and/or confirmed. The primary key fields are displayed in bold in the table list boxes. Notice the PartsAndCosts table does not have a primary key defined. Click *PartNo* in the *PartsAndCosts table* list box and click the Primary Key button located near the top right of the dialog box. Access sets *PartNo* as the primary key field, displays a key icon, and applies bold to the field name.

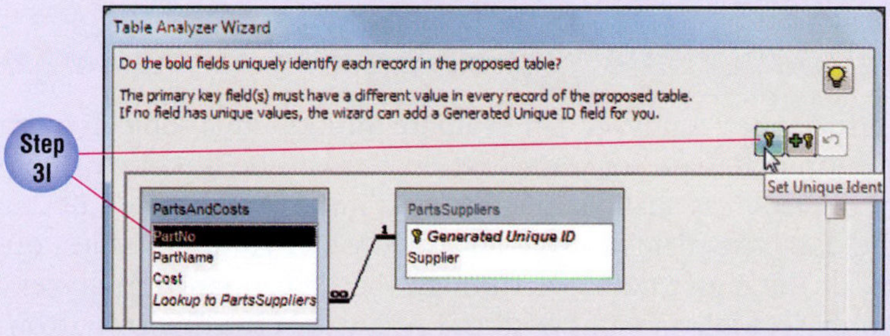

m. Click Next.

n. At the last Table Analyzer Wizard dialog box, you can choose to have Access create a query with the original table name that includes the fields from the new tables. Creating the query means existing forms or reports that were based on the original table will still operate. With *Yes, create the query* selected, click Finish. Access renames the original table *Parts_OLD*, creates the query with the name *Parts*, and opens the Parts query results datasheet with the Access Help window in the foreground.

o. Close the Help window.

4. Examine the Parts query datasheet and the object names added in the Navigation pane including the new tables PartsAndCosts and PartsSuppliers along with the original table named Parts_OLD. The Parts query looks just like the original table you opened at Step 1 with the exception of the additional field named *Lookup to PartsSupplier*. The lookup field displays the supplier name, which is also displayed in the original *Supplier* field. The second *Supplier* field can be deleted from the query.
5. Switch to Design view and delete the *Supplier* field.

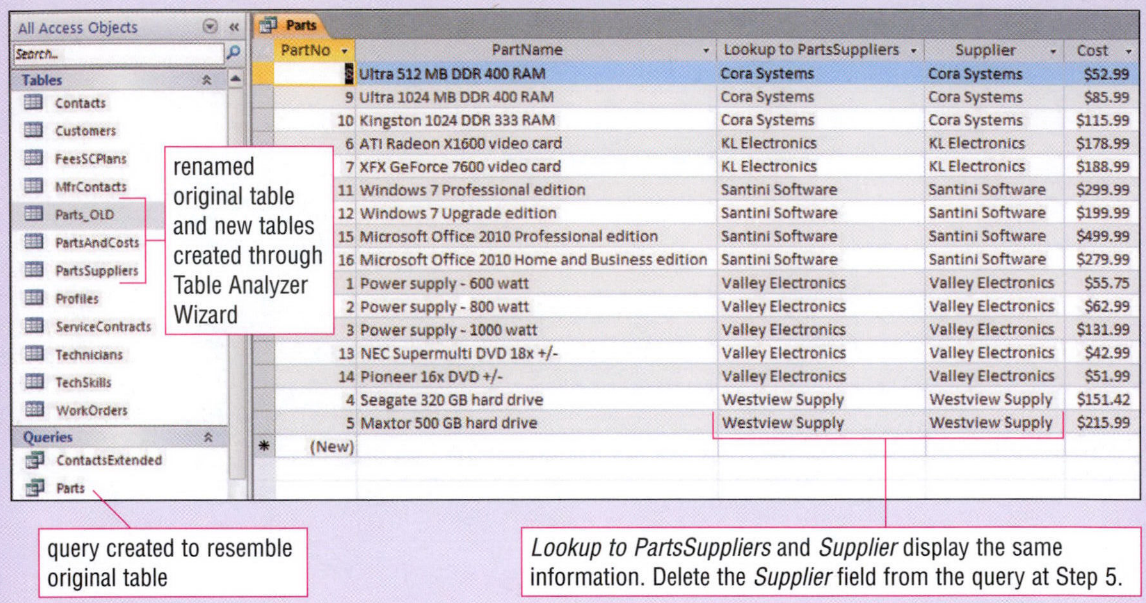

PartNo	PartName	Lookup to PartsSuppliers	Supplier	Cost
8	Ultra 512 MB DDR 400 RAM	Cora Systems	Cora Systems	$52.99
9	Ultra 1024 MB DDR 400 RAM	Cora Systems	Cora Systems	$85.99
10	Kingston 1024 DDR 333 RAM	Cora Systems	Cora Systems	$115.99
6	ATI Radeon X1600 video card	KL Electronics	KL Electronics	$178.99
7	XFX GeForce 7600 video card	KL Electronics	KL Electronics	$188.99
11	Windows 7 Professional edition	Santini Software	Santini Software	$299.99
12	Windows 7 Upgrade edition	Santini Software	Santini Software	$199.99
15	Microsoft Office 2010 Professional edition	Santini Software	Santini Software	$499.99
16	Microsoft Office 2010 Home and Business edition	Santini Software	Santini Software	$279.99
1	Power supply - 600 watt	Valley Electronics	Valley Electronics	$55.75
2	Power supply - 800 watt	Valley Electronics	Valley Electronics	$62.99
3	Power supply - 1000 watt	Valley Electronics	Valley Electronics	$131.99
13	NEC Supermulti DVD 18x +/-	Valley Electronics	Valley Electronics	$42.99
14	Pioneer 16x DVD +/-	Valley Electronics	Valley Electronics	$51.99
4	Seagate 320 GB hard drive	Westview Supply	Westview Supply	$151.42
5	Maxtor 500 GB hard drive	Westview Supply	Westview Supply	$215.99
(New)				

6. Save the revised query. Switch to Datasheet view, adjust all column widths to Best Fit, and print the query results datasheet in landscape orientation.
7. Close the query saving changes to the layout.

Quick Steps

Optimize Database Performance
1. Click the Database Tools tab.
2. Click Analyze Performance button.
3. Click All Object Types tab.
4. Click Select All button.
5. Click OK.
6. Review *Analysis Results* items.
7. Optimize desired *Recommendation* or *Suggestion* items.
8. Click Close button.

Analyze Performance

Optimizing Performance Using the Performance Analyzer

The Performance Analyzer can evaluate an individual object, a group of objects, or the entire database for ways that objects can be modified to optimize the use of system resources such as memory and improve the speed of data access. If you find the database seems to run slowly, consider running tables, queries, forms, reports, or the entire database through the Performance Analyzer. To do this, click the Database Tools tab and click the Analyze Performance button in the Analyze group to open the Performance Analyzer dialog box shown in Figure 6.6. Select a tab for the object type, click the check box next to an object to have the object analyzed, and click OK. You can select multiple objects or click the Select All button to select all objects in the current tab for analysis. To evaluate the entire database, click the All Object Types tab and then click the Select All button. Click OK to begin the analysis.

Figure 6.6 Performance Analyzer Dialog Box

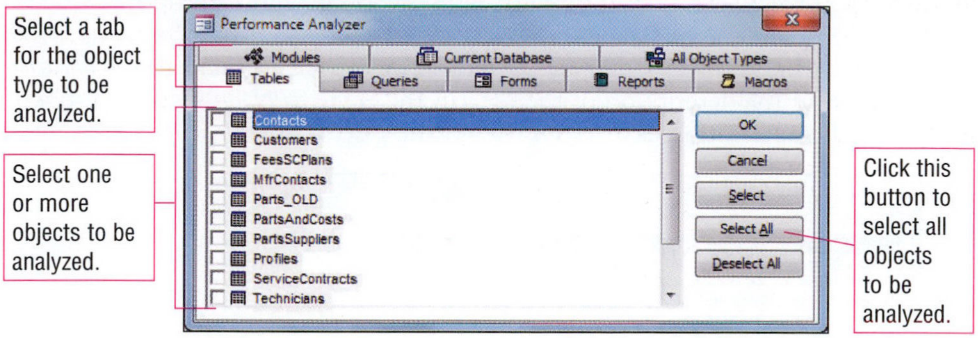

Three types of results are presented to optimize the selected objects: *Recommendation*, *Suggestion*, and *Idea*. Click an item in the *Analysis Results* list to read a description of the proposed optimization method in the *Analysis Notes* section. Click a recommendation or suggestion in the *Analysis Results* list box and then click the Optimize button to instruct Access to carry out the recommendation or suggestion. Access will modify the object and mark the item as *Fixed* when completed. The Performance Analyzer may provide items to improve the design such as assigning a different data type for a field based on the type of data that has been entered into records or creating relationships between tables that are not related.

HINT

Make sure objects are closed that will be evaluated using the Performance Analyzer–open objects are skipped when the evaluation is run.

Project 4b Analyzing a Database to Improve Performance

Part 2 of 5

1. With the **AL2-C6-RSRCompServ.accdb** database open, use the Performance Analyzer to evaluate the database for optimization techniques by completing the following steps:
   a. If necessary, click the Database Tools tab.
   b. Click the Analyze Performance button in the Analyze group.
   c. At the Performance Analyzer dialog box, click the All Object Types tab.
   d. Click the Select All button.

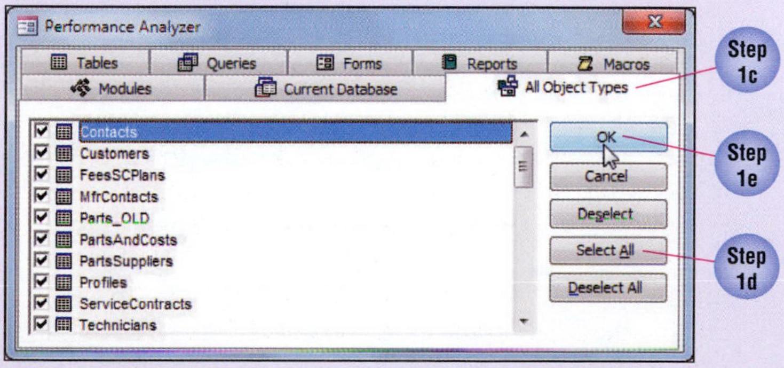

   e. Click OK. The Performance Analyzer displays the name of each object as the object is evaluated and presents the *Analysis Results* when completed.

2. Review the items in *Analysis Results* and optimize a relationship by completing the following steps:
   a. Click the first entry in the *Analysis Results* list with the text *Application: Save your application as an MDE file* and read the description of the idea in the *Analysis Notes* section. You will learn about saving the application as an MDE file in the next chapter.

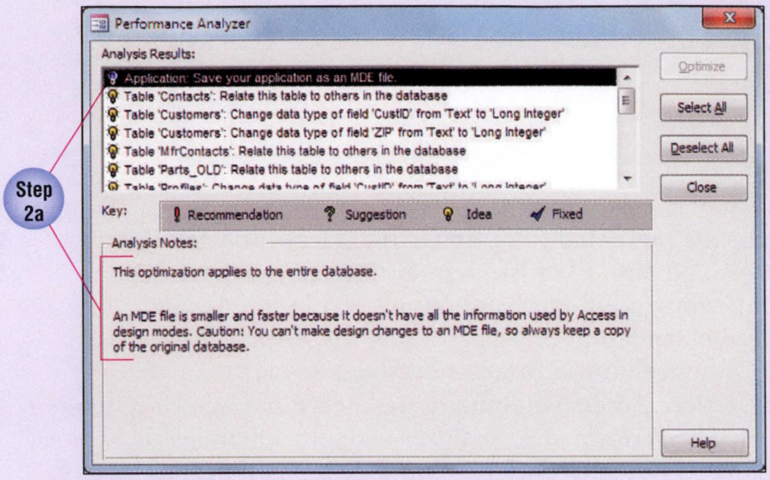

   b. Click the fifth entry in the *Analysis Results* with the text *Table MfrContacts: Relate this table to others in the database* and read the description of the idea in the *Analysis Notes* section. The contact information stored in this table is for manufacturer sales representatives and cannot be related to any other tables.
   c. Scroll down the *Analysis Results* list box and click the item with the green question mark representing a suggestion with the text *Table WorkOrders: Relate to table WorkOrders*. Read the description of the suggestion in the *Analysis Notes* section. Note that the optimization will benefit the TotalWorkOrders query. This optimization refers to a query that contains a subquery with two levels of calculations. The suggestion is referring to creating a relationship to speed up the query calculations.
   d. Click the Optimize button.

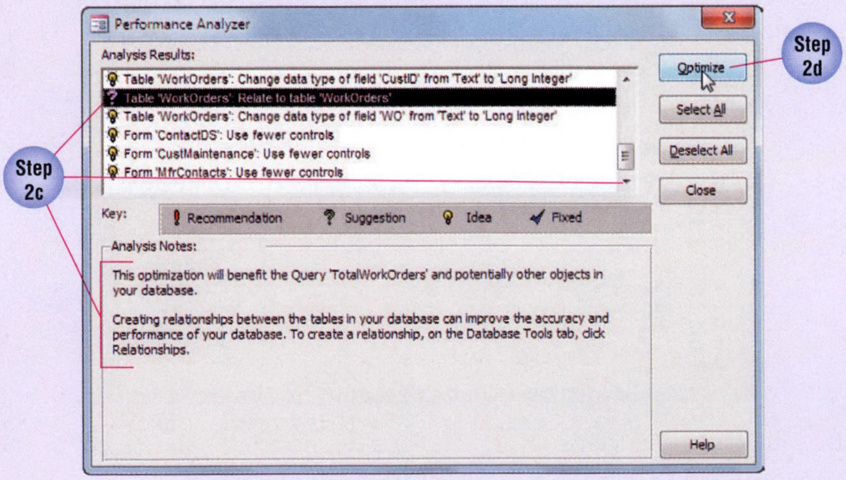

   e. Access creates the relationship and changes the question mark next to the item in the *Analysis Results* list box to a check mark. The check mark indicates the item has been fixed.

f. Click the second to the last item in the *Analysis Results* list box with the text *Form CustMaintenance: Use fewer controls* and read the description of the idea. Note that the idea is to break the form into multiple forms with information used often retained in the existing form. Information viewed less often should be split out into individual forms. To implement this optimization idea, you would need to redesign the form.

3. Click the Close button to close the Performance Analyzer dialog box.

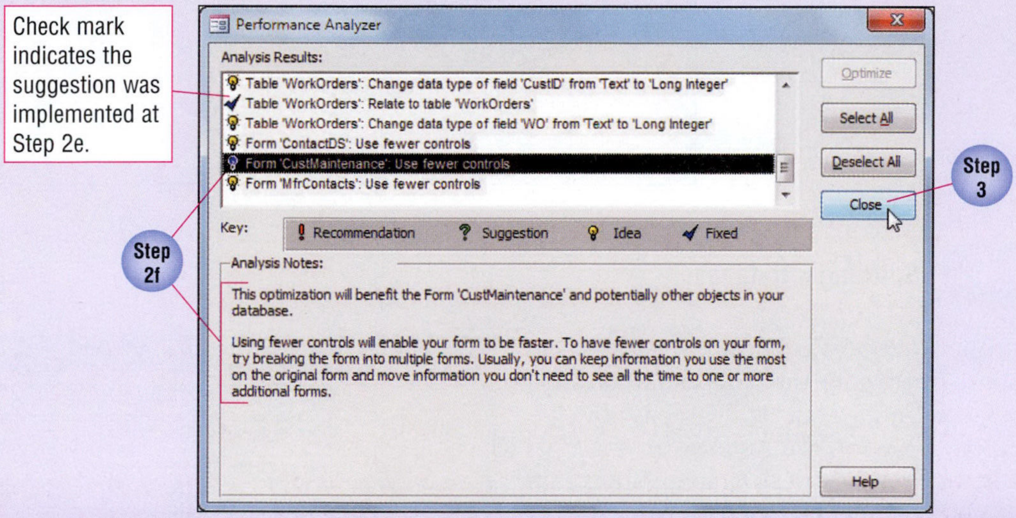

Splitting a Database

If a database is placed in a network where multiple users access the database simultaneously, the speed with which the data is accessed may decrease. One solution to improve the performance of the database is to split the database into two files: one file containing the tables (called the ***back-end***) is stored in the network share folder, and the other file containing the queries, forms, and reports (called the ***front-end***) is stored on the individual end-user computers. The individual end users can create and/or customize their own queries, forms, and reports to serve their individual purposes. The front-end database contains tables linked to the back-end data, so that each user is updating a single data source.

To split an existing database into a back-end and a front-end database, Access provides the Database Splitter Wizard. Click the Database Tools tab and click the Access Database button in the Move Data group to begin the Database Splitter Wizard shown in Figure 6.7.

Click the Split Database button to open the Create Back-end Database dialog box where you navigate to the drive and/or folder in which to store the database file containing the original tables. By default, Access uses the original database file name with *_be* appended to the end of the name before the file extension. Change the file name if desired and then click the Split button. Access moves the table objects to the back-end file, creates links to the back-end tables in the front-end file, and displays a message when the process is complete that the database was successfully split.

Quick Steps

Split a Database

1. Click Database Tools tab.
2. Click Access Database button.
3. Click Split Database button.
4. If necessary, navigate to desired drive and/or folder.
5. If necessary, edit the *File name.*
6. Click Split button.
7. Click OK.

HINT

Consider making a backup copy of the database before you split the file, in case you need to restore the database back to its original state.

Access Database

Figure 6.7 First Database Splitter Wizard Dialog Box

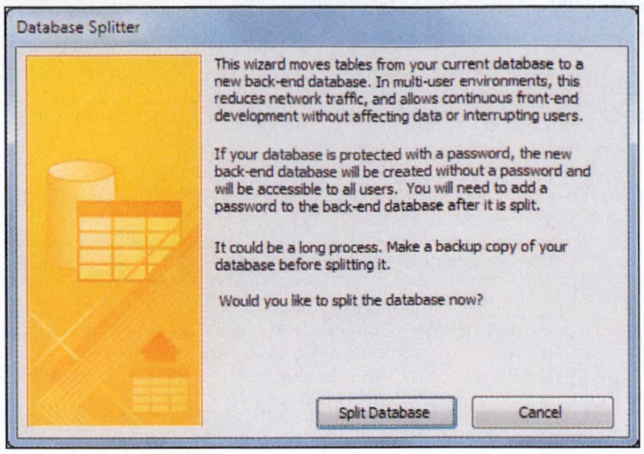

Project 4c Splitting a Database

Part 3 of 5

1. With the **AL2-C6-RSRCompServ.accdb** database open, split the database to create a back-end and a front-end database by completing the following steps:
   a. If necessary, click the Database Tools tab.
   b. Click the Access Database button in the Move Data group.
   c. Click the Split Database button at the first Database Splitter Wizard dialog box.
   d. At the Create Back-end Database dialog box with the default option to save the back-end database in the same folder from which the original database originated (Access2010L2C6) and the file name *AL2-C6-RSRCompServ_be.accdb* in the *File name* text box, click the Split button.

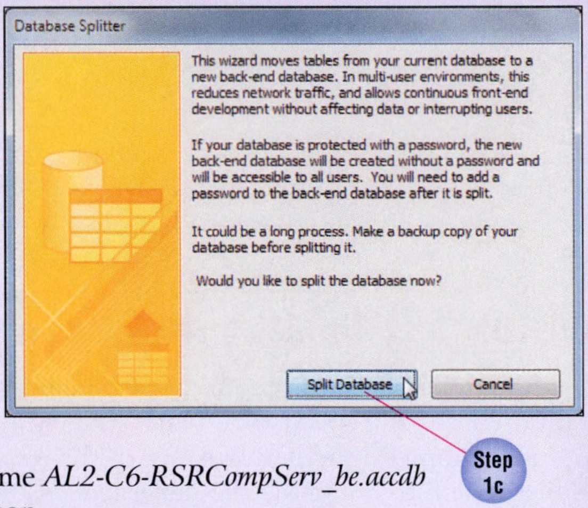

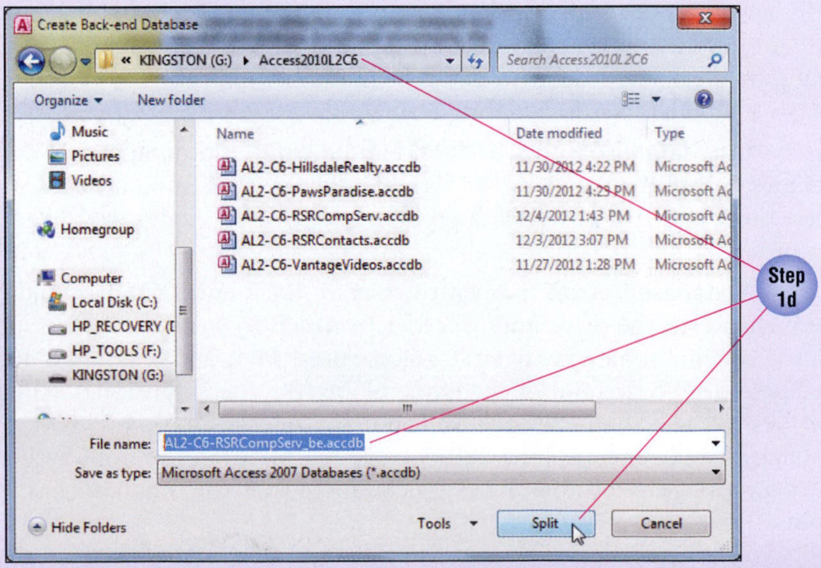

e. Click OK at the Database Splitter message box indicating the database was successfully split.

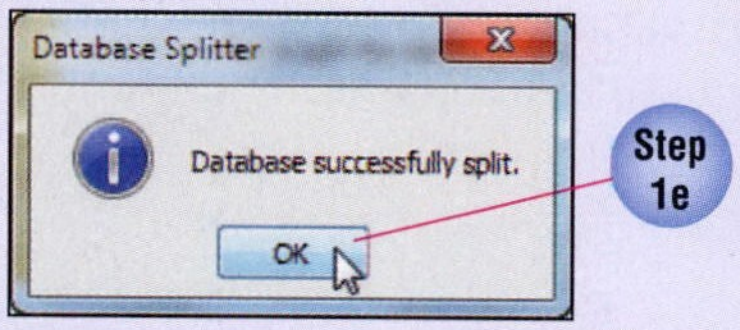

2. When the database was split, Access moved the tables to the back-end file and created links to the tables in the front-end file. Notice the table names in the Navigation pane are all preceded with a right-pointing arrow. The arrow indicates the table is a linked object. Opening a linked table causes Access to retrieve the records from the back-end database to display in the table datasheet. Open the linked Contacts table datasheet and review the data.

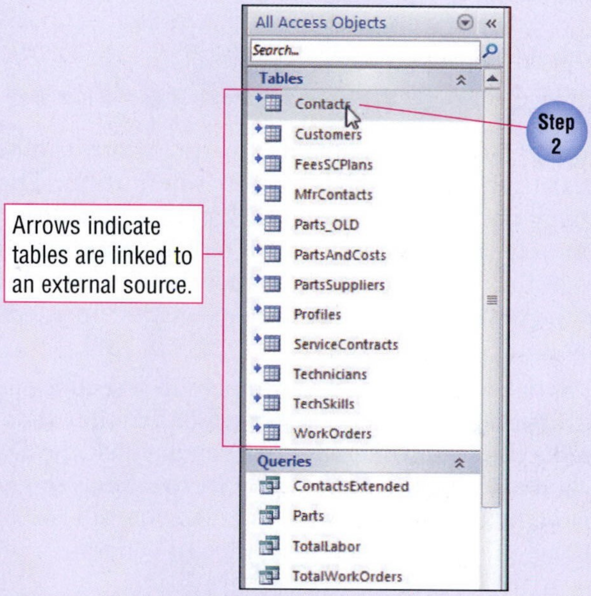

3. Switch to Design view. Since the table is linked to an external source, Access displays a message indicating the table design cannot be modified; changes to fields or field properties have to be made in the source database. Click No at the Microsoft Access message box asking if you want to open the table anyway.

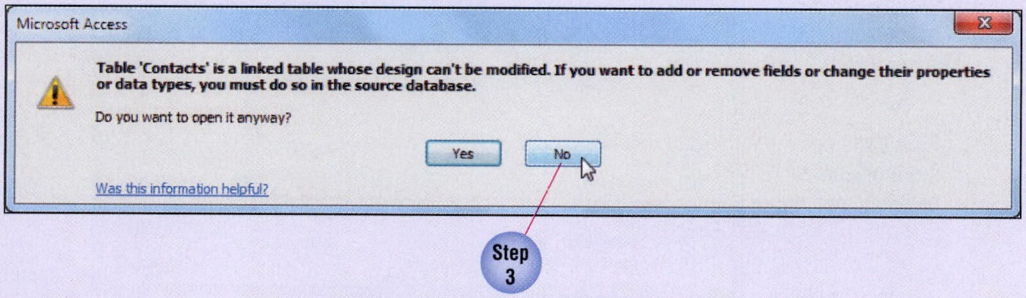

4. Close the table and then close the **AL2-C6-RSRCompServ.accdb** database.
5. Open the **AL2-C6-RSRCompServ_be.accdb** database and enable content.

6. Notice the back-end database file contains only the tables. Open the Customers table in Datasheet view and review the data.
7. Switch to Design view. Notice that in the back-end database you can switch to Design view to make changes without receiving the message box you saw at Step 3 since this database contains the original source table.
8. Close the table.

Another reason to split a database may be to overcome the file size restriction in Access 2010. Database specifications for Access 2010 place the maximum file size at 2 gigabytes. This size includes any space needed by Access to open system objects while working with the database; therefore, the actual maximum file size is less than 2 gigabytes. However, the size restriction does not include links to external data sources. By splitting a database you can extend the size beyond the 2-gigabyte limitation.

Quick Steps

Print Object Documentation

1. Click Database Tools tab.
2. Click Database Documenter button.
3. Click Options button.
4. Choose desired report options.
5. Click OK.
6. Click desired object name.
7. Click OK.
8. Print report.
9. Close report.

Database Documenter

Documenting a Database

Access provides the Database Documenter feature which can be used to print a report with details about a database object's definition. The report is used to obtain hard copy documentation of a table's structure with field properties or documentation regarding a query, form, or report definition. You can add the relationships to the report to include relationship diagrams for all defined relationships for the table. Relationship options are documented below each relationship diagram.

Storing the database documentation report in a secure place is a good idea in case of data corruption or other disaster which requires that the database be manually repaired, rebuilt, or otherwise recovered. Click the Database Tools tab and click the Database Documenter button in the Analyze group to open the Documenter dialog box shown in Figure 6.8. As you did for the Performance Analyzer, select the object for which you want to generate a report and then click OK.

Figure 6.8 Documenter Dialog Box

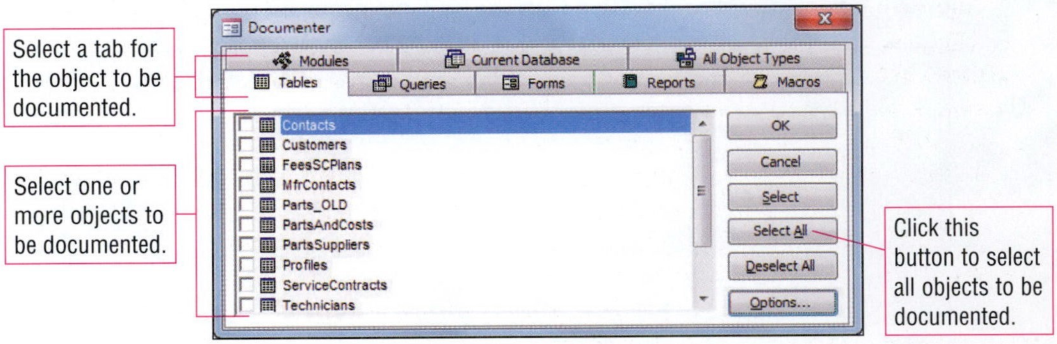

Project 4d Generating a Table Definition Documentation Report — Part 4 of 5

1. With the **AL2-C6-RSRCompServ_be.accdb** database open, generate a report providing details of the table structure, field properties, and relationships for an individual table by completing the following steps:
   a. Click the Database Tools tab.
   b. In the Analyze group, click the Database Documenter button.
   c. At the Documenter dialog box, click the Options button.
   d. At the Print Table Definition dialog box, click the *Permissions by User and Group* check box in the *Include for Table* section to clear the check mark.
   e. Make sure *Names, Data Types, Sizes, and Properties* is selected in the *Include for Fields* section.
   f. Click *Nothing* in the *Include for Indexes* section.
   g. Click OK.
   h. With Tables the active tab in the Documenter dialog box, click the *PartsSuppliers* check box to select the object.
   i. Click OK.

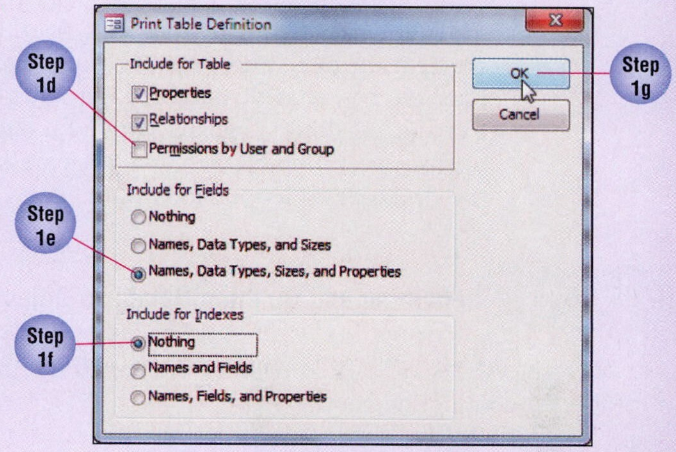

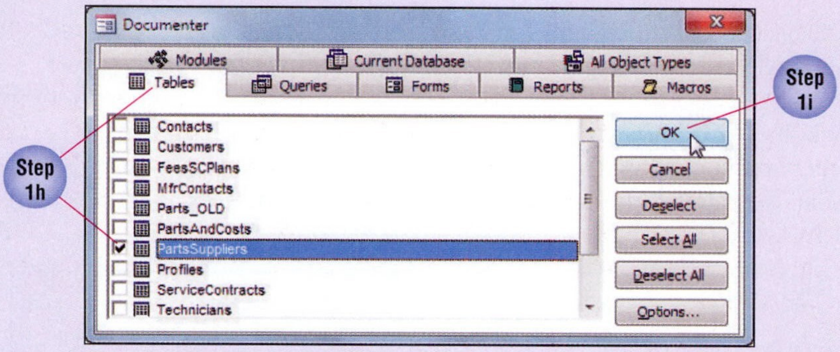

2. Access generates the table definition report and displays the report in Print Preview. Print the report.
3. Notice the Save option is dimmed. You cannot save a report generated by the Documenter.
4. Click the Close Print Preview button in the Close Preview group in the Print Preview tab.
5. Generate another report providing details of all of the tables and view the report by completing the following steps:
   a. Click the Database Documenter button.
   b. With Tables the active tab at the Documenter dialog box, click the Select All button to select all table objects and then click OK to generate the report.
   c. Change the Zoom to 100% and maximize the report window.
   d. Scroll down the first page of the report and review the data.
   e. Click the Last Page button in the Page navigation bar to navigate to the last page in the report. Review the relationship diagrams and relationship options documented on the last page of the report. Notice the page number is 55.
6. Close the report.

Renaming and Deleting Objects

Quick Steps

Rename Object
1. Right-click object in Navigation pane.
2. Click *Rename*.
3. Type new name.
4. Press Enter.

Delete Object
1. Right-click object in Navigation pane.
2. Click *Delete*.
3. Click Yes.

As part of managing a database you may decide to rename or delete objects within the database file. To do this, right-click the object name in the Navigation pane and click *Rename* or *Delete* at the shortcut menu. Be cautious with renaming or deleting objects which have dependencies to other objects. For example if you delete a table and a query exists which is dependent on fields within the table deleted, the query will no longer run. You will need to edit in Design view queries, forms, or reports that reference a table that was renamed for those objects that include fields from the renamed table.

You can also delete an object from the database by selecting the object in the Navigation pane and pressing the Delete key. Click Yes at the Microsoft Access message box that displays asking you to confirm you want to delete the object. Consider making a backup copy of a database before renaming or deleting objects in case several object dependencies are broken afterwards and you want to restore the database to its previous state.

Project 4e Renaming and Deleting Database Objects — Part 5 of 5

1. With the **AL2-C6-RSRCompServ_be.accdb** database open, rename the MfrContacts table by completing the following steps:
   a. Right-click *MfrContacts* in the Navigation pane.
   b. Click *Rename* at the shortcut menu.
   c. Type **ManufacturerContacts** and press Enter.

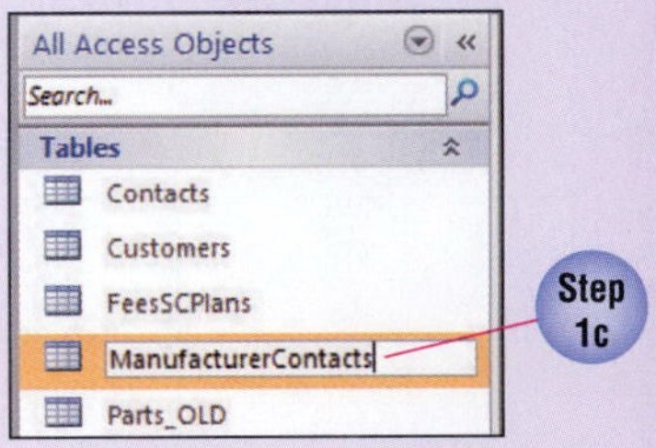
All Access Objects
Search...
Tables
Contacts
Customers
FeesSCPlans
ManufacturerContacts
Parts_OLD
Step 1c

2. Delete the original table that was split using the Table Analyzer Wizard in Project 4a by completing the following steps:
   a. Right-click *Parts_OLD* in the Navigation pane.
   b. Click *Delete* at the shortcut menu.
   c. Click Yes at the Microsoft Access message box asking if you want to delete the table Parts_OLD.

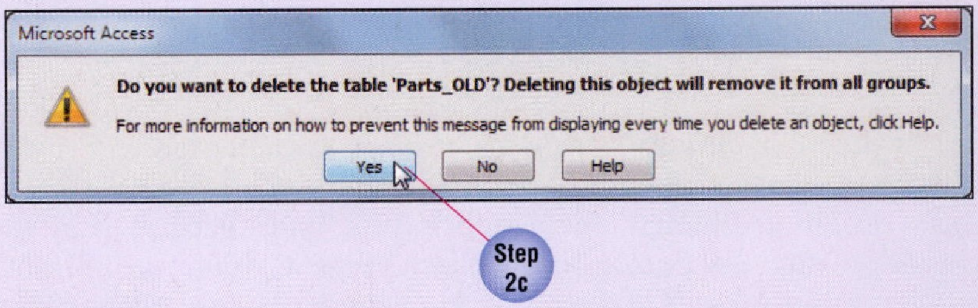
Microsoft Access
Do you want to delete the table 'Parts_OLD'? Deleting this object will remove it from all groups.
For more information on how to prevent this message from displaying every time you delete an object, click Help.
Yes
No
Help
Step 2c

3. Close the **AL2-C6-RSRCompServ_be.accdb** database.
4. Open the **AL2-C6-RSRCompServ.accdb** front-end database and enable content.
5. When the database was split in Project 4c, Access created links to the existing table objects at the time the database was split. Since you have now renamed and deleted a table object in the back-end database, the linked objects will no longer work.

6. Double-click the link to MfrContacts in the Navigation pane. Since the table was renamed at Step 1, Access can no longer find the source data. At the Microsoft Access message box informing you that the database engine cannot find the input table, click OK. The link would have to be recreated to establish a new connection to the renamed table. You will learn how to link to external tables in Chapter 8.

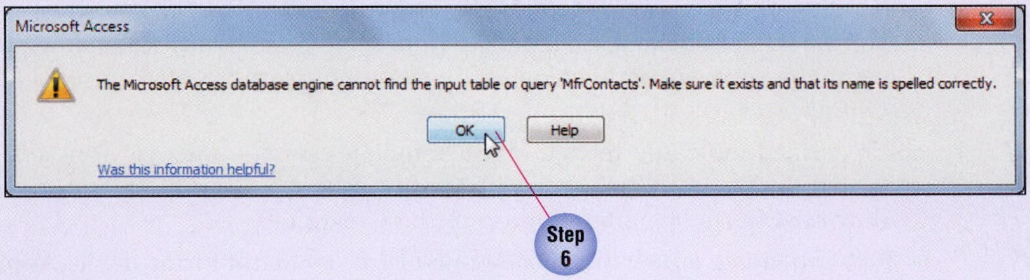

7. Double-click the link to Parts_OLD. Since this table was deleted, the same message appears. Click OK to close the message box.
8. Right-click *Parts_OLD* in the Navigation pane and click *Delete* at the shortcut menu. Click Yes at the Microsoft Access message asking if you want to remove the link.

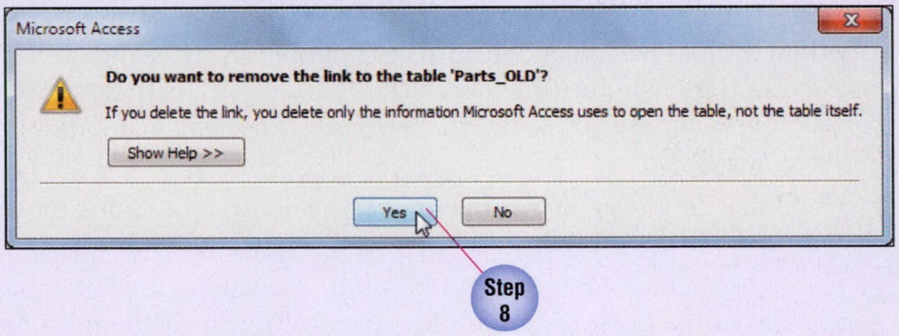

9. Close the **AL2-C6-RSRCompServ.accdb** database.

In this chapter you have learned to use some of the tools that Access provides to create a new database, create new tables and related objects, improve database or individual object design and performance, and document the database. You have also learned how to rename and delete objects.

Chapter Summary

- Access includes predefined database templates that include tables, queries, forms, and reports which can be used to create a new database.
- You can choose a database template from sample templates stored on your computer or you can download a database template from Microsoft Office Online.
- Predefined table and related object templates for Comments; Contacts; and Issues, Tasks, and Users are available from the Application Parts button drop-down list in the Templates group in the Create tab.
- You can create a new form using one of the 10 blank forms in the Application Parts button drop-down list. Most of the blank forms include command buttons that perform actions such as saving changes or saving and closing the form.
- Define your own form template by creating a form named *Normal* which includes a sample of each control object with the formatting options applied that you want to use for future forms. Select all of the controls and use the *Set Control Defaults* option to save the new settings.
- When a table has been copied to the clipboard from the Navigation pane, clicking the Paste button causes the Paste Table As dialog box to open in which you choose to paste *Structure Only*, *Structure and Data*, or *Append Data to Existing Table*.
- The Table Analyzer Wizard is used to evaluate a table for repeated data and determine if the table can be split into smaller related tables.
- The Performance Analyzer can be used to evaluate a single object, a group of objects, or the entire database for ways to optimize the use of system resources or disk space.
- The Performance Analyzer provides three types of results in the *Analysis Results* list: *Recommendation*, *Suggestion*, or *Idea*.
- Click an item in the *Analysis Results* list box that is a recommendation or suggestion and click the Optimize button to instruct Access to carry out the modification.
- A database can be split into two individual files, a back-end database and a front-end database, to improve performance for a multi-user database or to overcome the maximum database file size restriction.
- Split a database using the Database Splitter Wizard, which is started from the Access Database button in the Move Data group of the Database Tools tab.
- Access provides the Database Documenter feature, which is used to obtain hard copy reports providing object definition and field or control properties.
- Rename an object by right-clicking the object name in the Navigation pane, clicking *Rename* at the shortcut menu, typing a new name, and then pressing Enter.
- Delete an object by right-clicking the object name in the Navigation pane, clicking *Delete* at the shortcut menu, and then clicking Yes at the message box asking if you want to delete the object.

Commands Review

FEATURE	RIBBON TAB, GROUP	BUTTON	KEYBOARD SHORTCUT
Application Parts	Create, Templates		
Documenter	Database Tools, Analyze		
Paste Table As	Home, Clipboard		Ctrl + V
Performance Analyzer	Database Tools, Analyze		
Split database	Database Tools, Move Data		
Table Analyzer Wizard	Database Tools, Analyze		

Concepts Check Test Your Knowledge

Completion: In the space provided at the right, indicate the correct term, command, or number.

1. Click this option in the Available Templates category to view the database templates stored on the computer you are using. ____________________
2. A predefined table with related objects to store information about Contacts can be imported into the current database using this button in the Templates group in the Create tab. ____________________
3. Access provides 10 prebuilt forms with a defined layout and with most including titles and command buttons in this section of the Application Parts button drop-down list. ____________________
4. Name a form with this name to use the form as a template for all new forms. ____________________
5. Clicking the Paste button after copying a table in the Navigation pane causes this dialog box to open. ____________________
6. This wizard analyzes a table for repeated information and proposes a solution where the table can be split into smaller related tables. ____________________
7. Optimize a database using this button in the Analyze group in the Database Tools tab. ____________________

8. List the three types of solutions the Performance Analyzer provides to optimize the selected objects. ________________

9. Click an item in the *Analysis Results* list and read a description of the optimization method in this section of the Performance Analyzer dialog box. ________________

10. A database can be split into a front-end database file and a back-end database file using this button in the Move Data group in the Database Tools tab. ________________

11. When a database has been split, the back-end database file contains these objects. ________________

12. When a database has been split, the front-end database file contains links to these objects. ________________

13. Open this dialog box to print a report with a table's definition and field properties. ________________

14. Rename a database object in the Navigation pane by performing this action. ________________

15. Remove a selected object from the database by pressing this key. ________________

Skills Check Assess Your Performance

Assessment

1 CREATE A NEW DATABASE USING A TEMPLATE

1. Create a new database named **AL2-C6-VantageAssets.accdb** using the Assets Web Database template. At the Login dialog box that appears, click *New User* located at the bottom left of the dialog box. Type your name in the *Full Name* text box, your email address in the *E-mail* text box, and then click the Save & Close button. At the Login dialog box with your name added to the *Users* list, click the Close button in the dialog box title bar to close the dialog box and finish importing the database elements.
2. Click Enable Content in the Security Warning message bar. If necessary, at the Login dialog box, click your name in the *Users* list box and then click the Login button.
3. Display the Navigation pane and then spend a few moments opening and viewing various objects within the database. Close all objects when you are finished including the Main form.

4. Open the AssetDetails form, add the following records using the form and then close the form.

Asset	**Web Server**
Owner	(click your name in the drop-down list)
Location	**Head office**
Model	**TrueEdge 6500**
Attachments	(attach the data file named **WebServer.jpg**)
Manufacturer	**Edge Industries**
Condition	**New**
Acquired Date	(enter the current date)
Category	**Servers**
Current Value	**1850.00**
Retired Date	(leave blank)
Comments	(leave blank)

Asset	**Workstation**
Owner	(click your name in the drop-down list)
Location	**Head office**
Model	**EdgeConnect 100**
Attachments	(attach the data file named **Workstation1.jpg**)
Manufacturer	**Edge Industries**
Condition	**New**
Acquired Date	(enter the current date)
Category	**Desktop Computers**
Current Value	**985.00**
Retired Date	(leave blank)
Comments	(leave blank)

5. Print the two records as displayed in the AssetDetails form.
6. Close the form and then close the **AL2-C6-VantageAssets.accdb** database.

Assessment 2

CREATE TABLE USING AN APPLICATIONS PARTS TEMPLATE

1. Open **AL2-C6-VantageVideos.accdb** and enable content.
2. Create a new group of objects related to Tasks using the Tasks Application Part. Specify no relationship at the Create Relationship Wizard.
3. Using the TaskDetails form, add a record using the following information. Substitute your name for *Student Name* in the *Description* field.

Task	**Set up backup Web server**
Status	**Not started**
Priority	**(1) High**
Start Date	Enter the current date
Due Date	Enter a due date that is one week from the current date
Attachments	(leave blank)
% Complete	(leave at default value of 0%)
Description	**Configure hot server to be on standby in event of failover. Assigned to *Student Name*.**

4. Open the Tasks table to view the record added to the table using the form at Step 3. Close the table.
5. Print the selected record using the TaskDetails form.
6. Close the form.

Assessment 3

USE ACCESS TOOLS TO IMPROVE DESIGN AND PERFORMANCE

1. With the **AL2-C6-VantageVideos.accdb** database open, use the Table Analyzer Wizard to analyze the WebCustPymnt table using the following information.
   a. Rename the new table with all of the fields except the *CCType* field to *WebCustCreditCards*.
   b. Rename the new table with the *CCType* field to *CreditCardTypes*.
   c. Choose an appropriate field for the primary key in the WebCustCreditCards table.
   d. If the wizard determines that the Discover card is a typographical error, choose (*Leave as is*) at the *Correction* drop-down list and click Next.
   e. Create the query.
2. Close the Help window.
3. Delete the *CCType* field in the WebCustPymnt query. Adjust all column widths to Best Fit and print the query results datasheet using left and right margins of 0.25 inch.
4. Close the query saving the layout changes.
5. Delete the WebCustPymnt_OLD table.
6. Split the database to create a front-end database and a back-end database file. Accept the default file name for the back-end database.
7. Close the **AL2-C6-VantageVideos.accdb** database.
8. Open the **AL2-C6-VantageVideos_be.accdb** database and enable content.
9. Generate and print a report that provides the table and field property definitions for the CreditCardTypes table. Include the relationships in the report.
10. Close the **AL2-C6-VantageVideos_be.accdb** database.

Visual Benchmark Demonstrate Your Proficiency

1 CREATE TABLE TO STORE GROOMERS INFORMATION

1. Open **AL2-C6-PawsParadise.accdb** and enable content.
2. Review the table shown in Figure 6.9 and create the new table in the database by copying the structure of the DogOwners table.
3. Modify the table design as needed, add the records shown in the figure, and rename the table as shown.
4. Adjust all column widths and print the table.
5. Close the table.

Figure 6.9 Visual Benchmark 1

Groomers

	Groomer ID	First Name	Last Name	Street Address	City	State	ZIP Code	Home Telephone	Hourly Rate
	01	Max	Lahey	715 Irish Hollow	Smethport	PA	16749-	(814) 555-6253	$28.50
	02	Juan	Modesta	117 Spring Drive	Bradford	PA	16701-	(814) 555-3845	$28.50
	03	Pat	O'Connor	147 Lamont Drive	Bradford	PA	16701-	(814) 555-2118	$31.50
	04	Greg	Walczak	22 Foster Square	Allegheny	PA	15212-	(814) 555-7448	$35.50
	05	Melissa	Cochrane	140 Congress Street	Bradford	PA	16701-	(814) 555-6489	$28.50
*					Bradford	PA			

2 CREATE FORM TEMPLATE

1. With the **AL2-C6-PawsParadise.accdb** database open, examine the control objects shown in the form named *Normal* in Figure 6.10. Create a Normal form to be used as a template with the three control objects shown. Use font color *Green, Accent 1, Darker 50%* and background color *Green, Accent 1, Lighter 80%* for the formatting.
2. Create a new form for the Groomers table using the Form button in the Forms group of the Create tab. Decrease the width of the form title and text box control objects in the form so that one form will fit on one page and then print the first form only.
3. Save the Groomers form accepting the default name *Groomers*.
4. Close the form and then close the **AL2-C6-PawsParadise.accdb** database.

Figure 6.10 Visual Benchmark 2

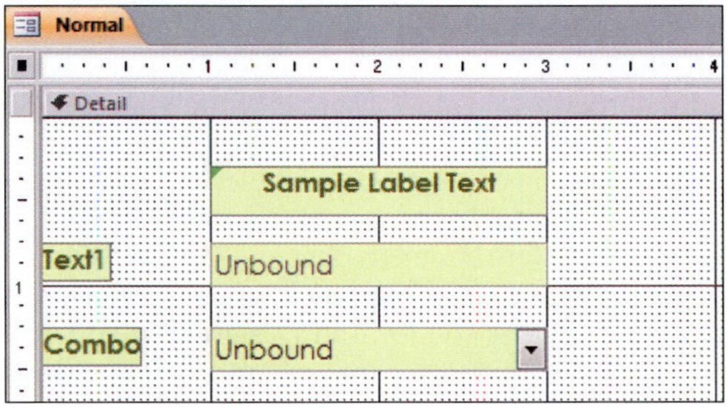

Case Study Apply Your Skills

Part 1

As an intern at Hillsdale Realty, you have been building a listings, sales, and commission database over the past weeks. You decide to create a new database to store information about home shows and conferences that Hillsdale Realty attends as an exhibitor. To save time developing new objects, use the Events sample template to create a new database in the Access2010L2C6 folder on your storage medium named **AL2-C6-HillsdaleShows.accdb**. Enable content and then add the following two trade show events to the database using the Event List form.

- The three-day Homebuilders Association Trade Show begins April 15, 2012 at the Phoenix Convention Center.
- The four-day Green Home Design Conference begins October 11, 2012 at the University of Phoenix Hohokam Campus.

The office manager likes the idea of tracking the trade shows in the database and would like you to create a similar table to keep track of conferences that agents attend as visitors. Close the Event List form and display the Navigation pane. Change the Navigation pane view to display objects by *Object Type*. Next, copy the structure of the Events table to create a new table named *AgentConferences*. Modify the AgentConferences table to delete the *Attachments* field and add a new field to store the number of people the company will send to the show. Create a form for the AgentConferences table using the Form button and add the following record.

- Five employees will attend the three-day Window and Door Manufacturers Association Annual Conference beginning November 7, 2012 at the Georgia International Convention Center.

Preview the AgentConferences form in Print Preview. If necessary, make adjustments to fit the form on one page. Print the AgentConferences form with the first record displayed. Save and close the form. Open the Event Details report. Print and then close the report. Close the **AL2-C6-HillsdaleShows.accdb** database.

Part 2

You want to see if Access tools can help you improve the database design of the database you have been building over the past weeks. Open the database named **AL2-C6-HillsdaleRealty.accdb** and enable content. Use the Table Analyzer Wizard to analyze the Listings table. Accept the proposed table split, create appropriate table names, assign primary key fields, and create the query. Modify the query as needed to remove duplicate columns. Sort the query in ascending order by the *ListDate* field. Print the query results datasheet with all column widths adjusted to Best Fit. Delete the original table with *_OLD* in the name. When changes are made to tables after other objects are created that are dependent on the table, errors can occur. Open the ListingsAndSales form. Notice the error in the control object named *City*. Since the Table Analyzer Wizard split the original Listings table on the *City* field, the original field added to the form no longer exists. Display the form in Design view and delete the *City* control object. Display the Field List task pane and add the appropriate field to the form. Size and align the controls as needed and then save and close the form.

Part 3

Help

Use the Performance Analyzer to analyze the entire database. When the Listings table was split in Part 2, the relationships between the original Listings table and other objects were removed, leaving the new split table not related to other tables. Select and optimize entries in the *Analysis Results* list that will create the relationships for you between the new Listings table and other objects. Next, notice that all of the fields that store identification numbers such as *AgentID*, *ClientID*, *ListingNo*, and *QuotaID* have the idea proposed that the data type should be changed from Text to Long Integer. Long Integer is not actually a data type but a field size setting for a numeric field. Research data types in Help. Specifically find out the difference between assigning a field the Text data type and the Number data type. Using Microsoft Word, compose a memo to your instructor with the following information:

- An explanation of the use of the Text data type
- An explanation of the use of the Number data type
- Your recommendation of which data type should be used for the four *ID* fields in the database and why

Save the memo and name it **AL2-C6-HillsdaleDBAnalysisMemo.docx**. Print the memo and exit Word. In the database, open the Relationships window. Delete the original Listings table from the window and display the new Listings table name to show the relationships created when the database was optimized. Rearrange the table field list boxes so that the join lines are easy to follow and generate a relationship report. Print the relationships report. Save and close the relationships report and then close the **AL2-C6-HillsdaleRealty.accdb** database.

Microsoft® Access®

CHAPTER 7

Automating, Customizing, and Securing Access

PERFORMANCE OBJECTIVES

Upon successful completion of Chapter 7, you will be able to:

- **Create, run, edit, and delete a macro**
- **Assign a macro to a command button on a form**
- **View macro code created in a form's Property Sheet for a command button**
- **Convert macros to Visual Basic**
- **Create and edit a Navigation form**
- **Change database startup options**
- **Show and hide the Navigation pane**
- **Customize the Navigation pane by hiding objects**
- **Define error checking options**
- **Customize the ribbon**
- **Create an ACCDE database file**
- **View trust center settings**

SNAP Training and Assessment. Simplified.

Tutorials

7.1 Creating and Editing a Macro

7.2 Creating a Command Button to Run a Macro

7.3 Creating a Navigation Form

7.4 Adding a Command Button to a Navigation Form

7.5 Limiting Ribbon Tabs and Menus in a Database

7.6 Customizing the Navigation Pane

7.7 Configuring Error Checking Options

7.8 Customizing the Ribbon

7.9 Creating an ACCDE Database File

7.10 Viewing Trust Center Settings

Macros are used to automate repetitive tasks or to store actions that can be executed by clicking a button in a form. A Navigaton form is a form used as a menu that provides an interface between the end user and the objects within the database file. In this chapter you will learn how to automate a database using macros and a Navigation form. You will also learn methods to secure and customize the Access environment to prevent changes to the design of objects. Model answers for this chapter's projects appear on the following page.

Access
Access2010L2C7

Note: Before beginning the projects, copy to your storage medium the Access2010L2C7 subfolder from the Access2010L2 folder on the CD that accompanies this textbook and then make Access2010L2C7 the active folder.

Model Answers

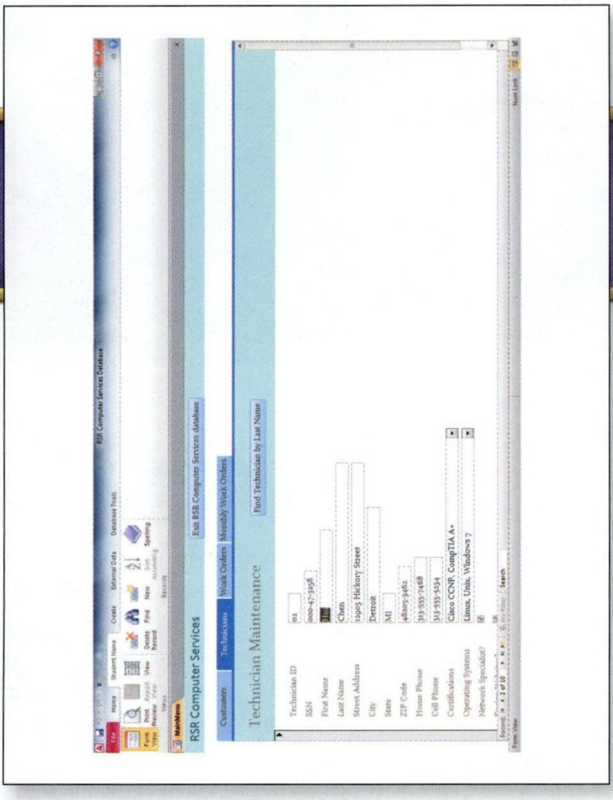

Project 3 Configure Database Options

Project 3d, Customized Database Startup Options, Navigation Pane, and Custom Ribbon Tab

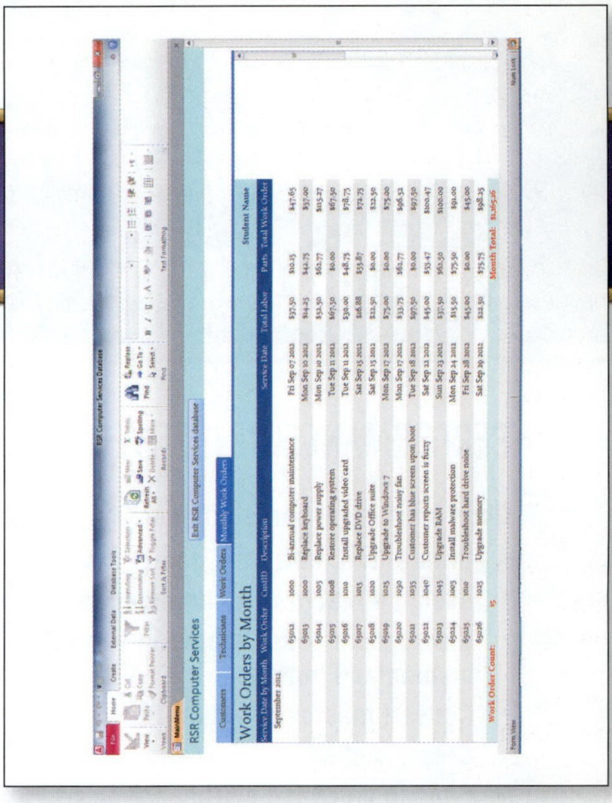

Project 4 Secure a Database

Project 4a, ACCDE Database Window

Project 1 Create Macros and Assign Macros to Command Buttons — 8 Parts

You will create macros to automate routine tasks and add macros to command buttons in forms that run the macros.

Creating a Macro

HINT

For a complex macro, consider working through the steps you want to save, writing down all of the parameters as you go before attempting to create the macro.

A ***macro*** is a series of instructions stored in sequence that can be recalled and carried out whenever the need arises. Macros are generally created when a task that is never varied is repeated frequently. For example, a macro could be created to open a query, form, or report. The macro object stores a series of instructions (called ***actions***) in the sequence in which the actions are to be performed. Macros appear as objects within the Navigation pane. Double-clicking the macro name causes Access to perform the instructions. A macro can also be assigned to a command button to enable the macro to be run using a single mouse click. For example, you could create a macro in a form that automates the process of finding a record by the last name field and assign the macro to a button. The macro would contain two instructions, the first instruction to move to the field in which the last name is stored, and the second instruction to open the Find dialog box.

To create a macro, click the Create tab and then click the Macro button in the Macros & Code group. This opens the Macro Builder Window shown in Figure 7.1. Click the down-pointing arrow at the right end of the *Add New Action* list box and click the desired instruction at the drop-down list. As an alternative, you can add an action using the Action Catalog pane as described in Figure 7.1.

Each new action entered into the Macro Builder window is associated with a set of ***arguments*** that displays once the action has been added. Similar to field properties in Table Design view, the arguments displayed in the *Action Arguments* section vary depending on the active action that has been expanded in the Macro Builder window. For example, Figure 7.2 displays the action arguments for the OpenForm action.

The OpenForm action is used to open a form similar to double-clicking a form name in the Navigation pane. Within the *Action Arguments* section you specify the name of the form to open and the view in which the form is to be presented. You can choose to open the form in Form view, Design view, Print Preview, Datasheet view, PivotTable view, PivotChart view, or Layout view. Use the *Filter Name* or *Where Condition* arguments to restrict the records displayed in the report. The Data Mode argument is used to place editing restrictions on records while the form is open. You can open the form in *Add* mode to allow adding new records only (users cannot view existing records), *Edit* mode to allow records to be added, edited, or deleted, or *Read Only* mode to allow records to be viewed only. The *Window Mode* argument is used to instruct Access to open the form in *Normal* mode (as you normally view forms in the work area), *Hidden* mode (form is hidden), *Icon* mode (form opens minimized), or *Dialog* mode (form opens in a separate window similar to a dialog box).

Quick Steps

Create Macro
1. Click Create tab.
2. Click Macro button.
3. Click *Add New Action* list arrow.
4. Click desired action.
5. Enter arguments as required in *Action Arguments* section.
6. Click Save button.
7. Type name for macro.
8. Press Enter or click OK.
9. Repeat Steps 3–6 as needed.

Run Macro
Double-click macro name in Navigation pane.
OR
1. Right-click macro name.
2. Click *Run*.

Macro

Figure 7.1 Macro Builder Window

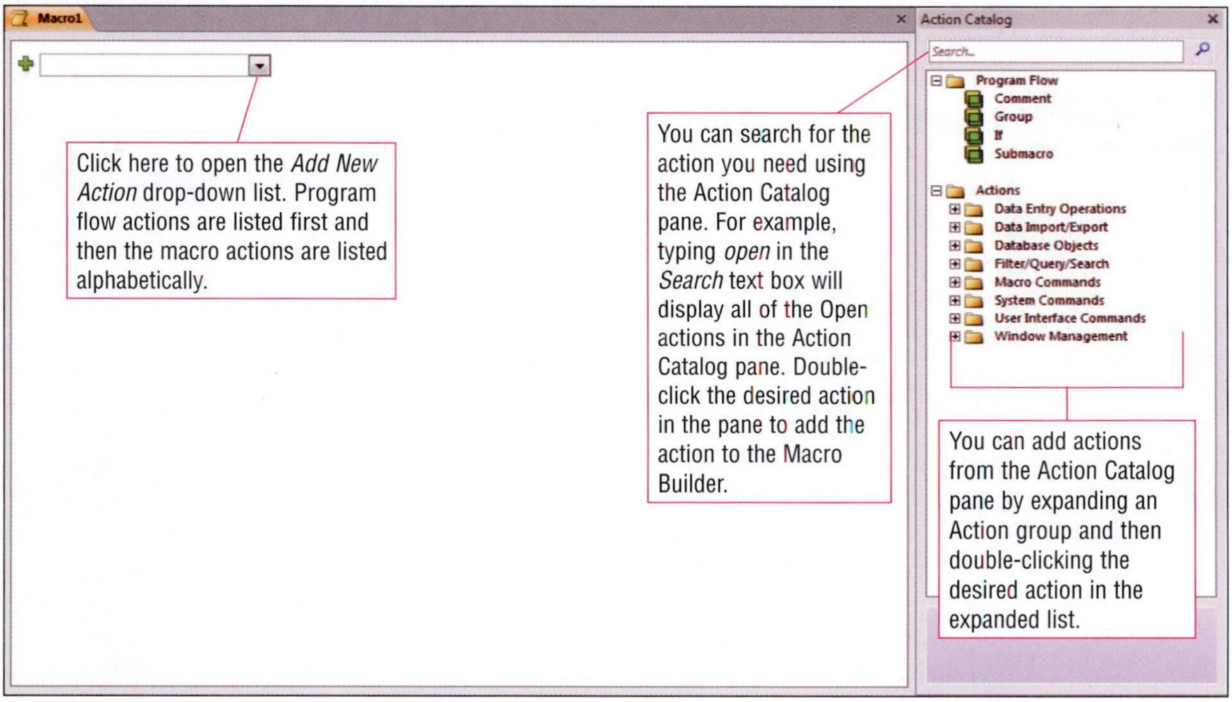

HINT

Hovering the mouse over an argument's entry box allows you to read a description of the argument and the available parameters in a ScreenTip.

To create a macro with multiple actions, add the second instruction in the *Add New Action* list box that appears below the first action. Access executes each action in the order they appear in the Macro Builder window. In Project 1a you will create a macro with multiple actions that will instruct Access to open a form, make active a control within the form, and then open the Find dialog box in order to search for a record. The *GoToControl* action is used to make active a control within a form or report and the *RunMenuCommand* action is used to execute an Access command. For each of these actions, a single argument specifies the name of the control to move to and the name of the command you want to run. As you add actions to the Macro Builder window, you can expand and collapse the *Action Arguments* section for actions as needed. When several actions are added to the Macro Builder window, collapsing arguments allows you to focus on only the current action you are editing.

Figure 7.2 Macro Builder Window with Action Arguments for *OpenForm* Action

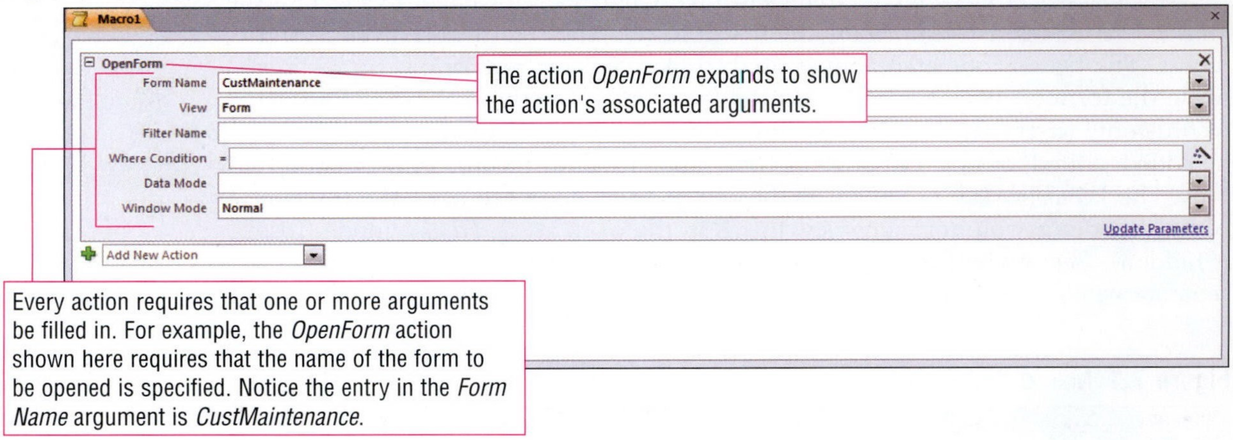

Project 1a Creating a Macro to Open a Form and Find a Record

Part 1 of 8

1. Open the **AL2-C7-RSRCompServ.accdb** database and enable content. Create a macro to open the TechMaintenance form by completing the following steps:
   a. Click the Create tab.
   b. Click the Macro button in the Macros & Code group.
   c. At the Macro Builder window, click the down-pointing arrow at the right of the *Add New Action* list box, scroll down the list, and then click *OpenForm*. Access adds the action and opens the *Action Arguments* section. Most actions require at least one action argument as a minimum.

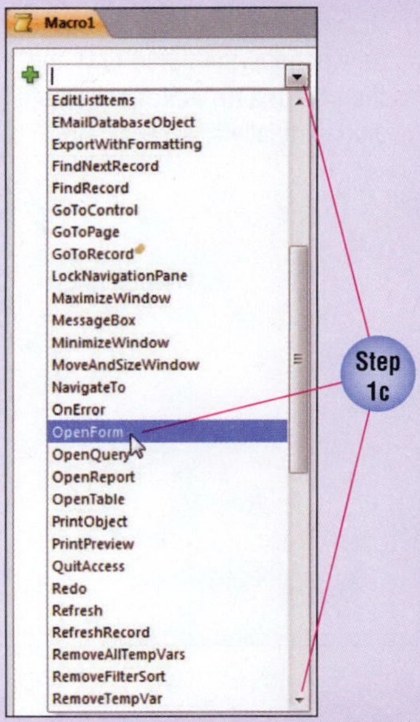

d. Click the down-pointing arrow at the right of the *Form Name* argument box in the *Action Arguments* section and then click *TechMaintenance* at the drop-down list.

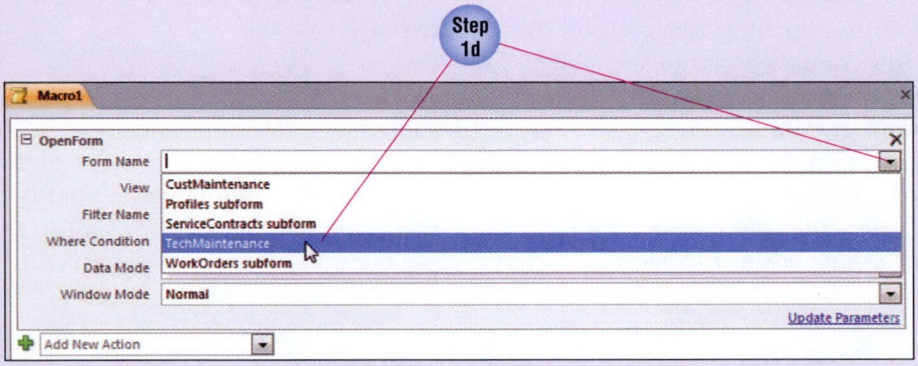

2. Add additional instructions to move to the technician's last name field and then open the Find dialog box by completing the following steps:
   a. Click the down-pointing arrow at the right of the *Add New Action* list box, scroll down the list, and then click *GoToControl*. Notice that only one action argument is required for the *GoToControl* action.
   b. Click in the *Control Name* argument box in the *Action Arguments* section and then type **LName**. (At the *Control Name* argument box, the name of the field that you want to make active in the form is required.)

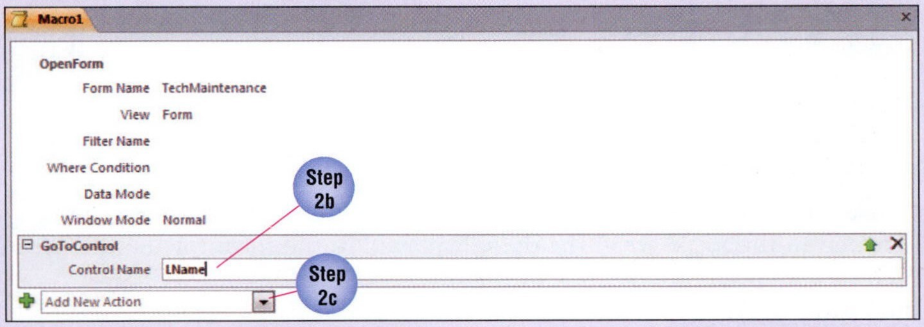

   c. Click the down-pointing arrow at the right of the *Add New Action* list box, scroll down the list box, and then click *RunMenuCommand* at the drop-down list.
   d. Click the down-pointing arrow at the right of the *Command* argument box, scroll down the list box, and then click *Find*.

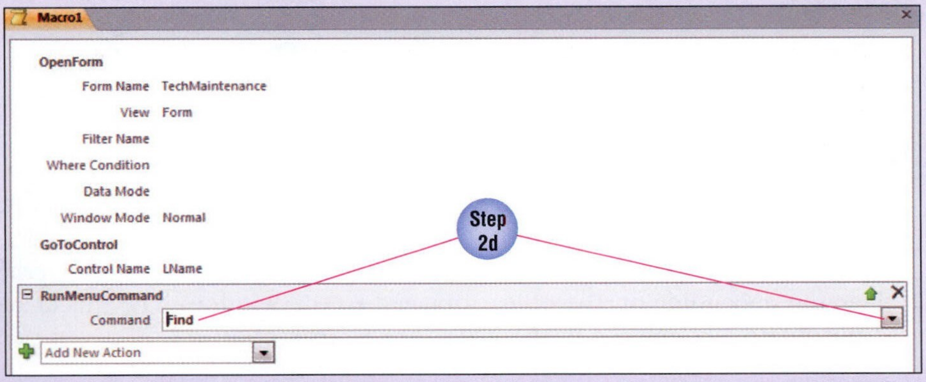

3. Click the Save button, type **FormFindTech** in the *Macro Name* text box at the Save As dialog box, and press Enter or click OK.

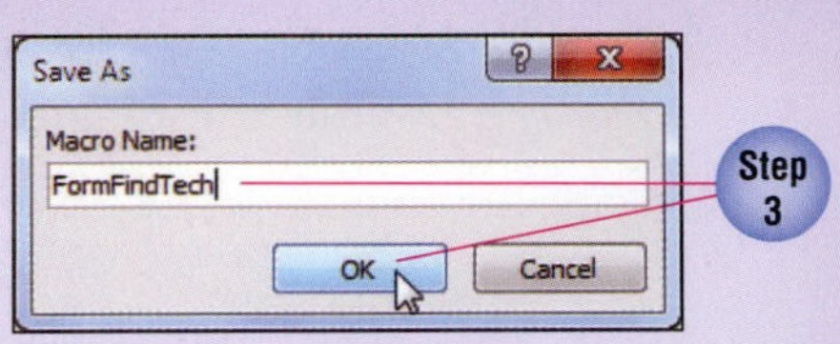

4. Click the Run button (displays as a red exclamation mark) in the Tools group of the Macro Tools Design tab. The Run button instructs Access to carry out the instructions in the macro. The TechMaintenance form opens, the active field is *Last Name,* and the Find and Replace dialog box appears with the last name of the first technician entered in the *Find What* text box. Type **Sadiku** and click the Find Next button. ***Note: If the Find and Replace dialog box is overlapping the*** **Last Name** ***field in the form, drag the dialog box to the bottom or right edge of the work area.***

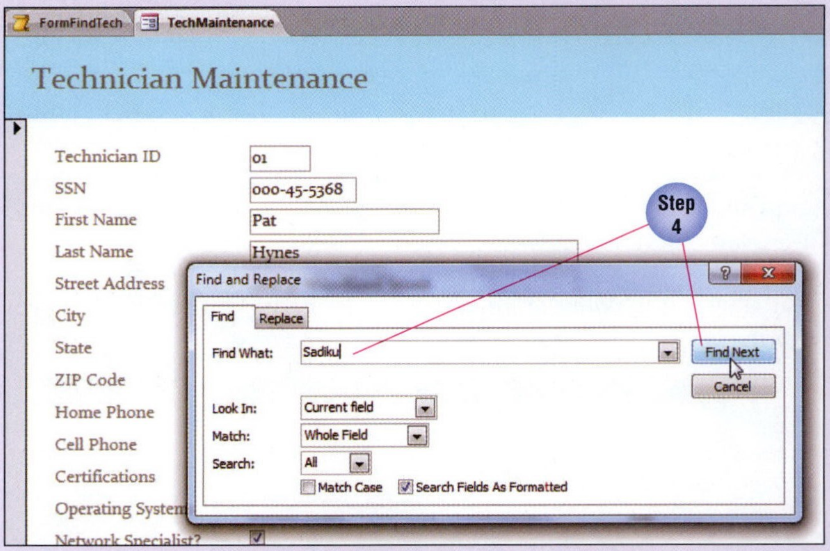

5. Access moves to record 5. Close the Find and Replace dialog box. Notice the last name text is selected in the form. Read the data displayed in the form for the technician named *Madir Sadiku.*
6. Close the form.
7. At the Macro Builder window, click the Close button located at the top right of the work area and left of the Action Catalog pane. This closes the FormTechFind macro. Notice a new category named Macros has been added to the Navigation pane and the FormTechFind macro name appears as an object below Macros.

A macro can also be created by dragging and dropping an object name from the Navigation pane to the *Add New Action* list box in a Macro Builder window. By default, Access creates an *OpenTable*, *OpenQuery*, *OpenForm*, or *OpenReport* action depending on the object dragged to the window. The object name is also automatically entered in the *Action Arguments* section.

Project 1b Creating a Macro by Dragging and Dropping an Object

Part 2 of 8

1. With the **AL2-C7-RSRCompServ.accdb** database open, create a macro to open the CustMaintenance form using the drag and drop method by completing the following steps:
   a. Click the Create tab.
   b. Click the Macro button in the Macros & Code group.
   c. Position the mouse pointer on the CustMaintenance form name in the Navigation pane, hold down the left mouse button, drag the object name to the *Add New Action* list box in the Macro Builder window, and then release the mouse. Access inserts an OpenForm action with *CustMaintenance* entered in the *Form Name* argument box.

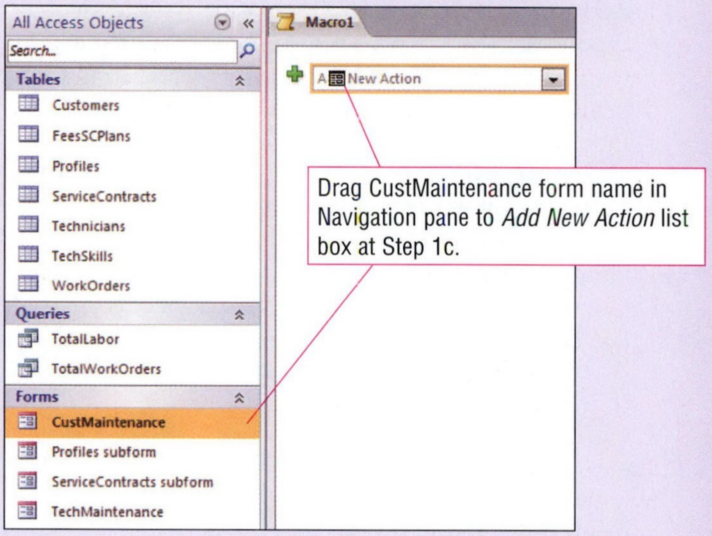

2. Click the Save button, type **FormCustMaint**, and then press the Enter key or click OK.
3. Click the Run button in the Tools group of the Macro Tools Design tab.
4. Close the form.
5. Click the Close button located at the top right of the work area and left of the Action Catalog pane to close the macro.

Project 1c Creating a Macro Using the Action Catalog Pane

Part 3 of 8

1. With the **AL2-C7-RSRCompServ.accdb** database open, create a macro using the Action Catalog pane to find a record in a form by making active the home telephone field, opening the Find dialog box, and then completing the following steps:
   a. Click the Create tab.
   b. Click the Macro button in the Macros & Code group.
   c. Click the Expand button (displays as a plus symbol) next to *Database Objects* in the *Actions* list in the Action Catalog pane to expand the category and display the actions available for changing controls or objects in the database. ***Note: If you accidentally closed the Action Catalog pane in a previous Macro Builder window and the pane does not redisplay in the new Macro Builder window, click the Action Catalog button in the Show/Hide group of the Macro Tools Design tab to restore the pane.***

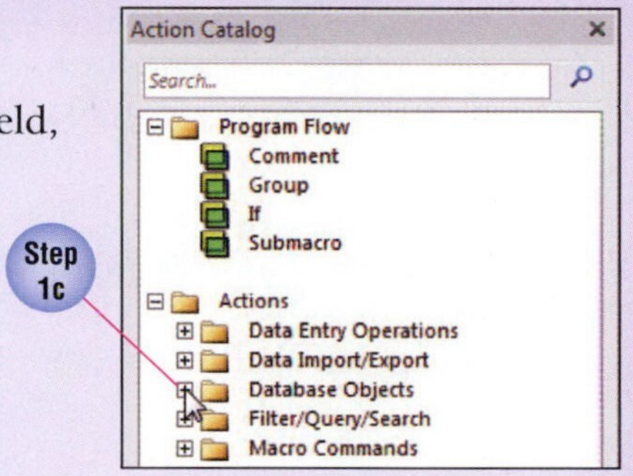

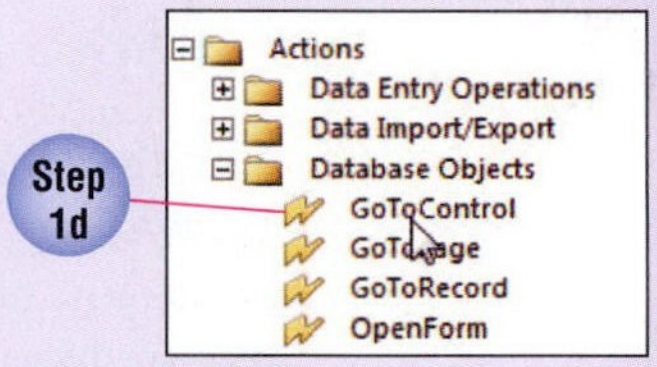

   d. Double-click *GoToControl* at the expanded *Database Objects* actions list in the Action Catalog pane to add the action to the Macro Builder window.

e. With the insertion point positioned in the *Control Name* argument box in the Macro Builder window, type **HPhone**.

Step 1e

Step 1f

Step 1g

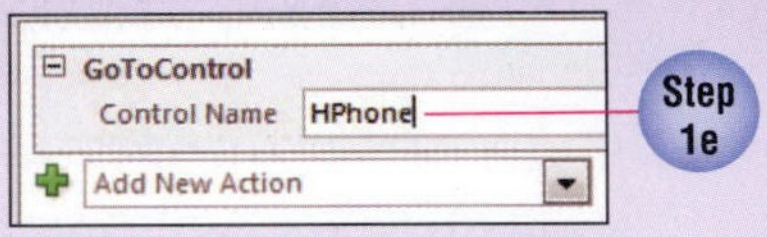

f. Click in the Search text box at the top of the Action Catalog pane and then type **Run**. As you type text in the Search text box, Access displays in the Action Catalog pane the available actions that begin with the same text as the text you typed.

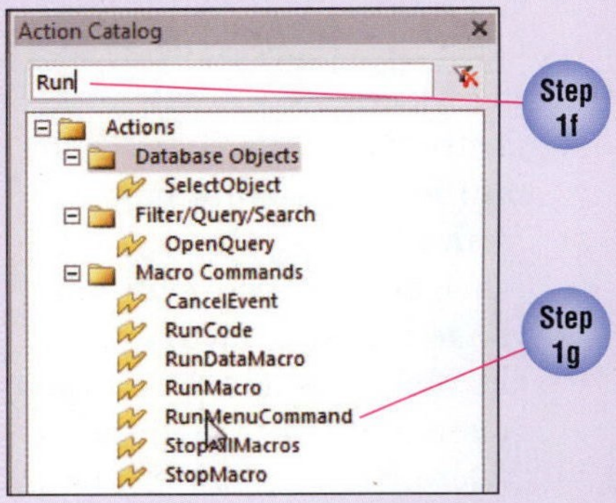

g. Double-click *RunMenuCommand* in the *Macro Commands* list in the Action Catalog pane.

h. With the insertion point positioned in the *Command* argument box in the Macro Builder window, type **Find**.

i. Click the Save button on the Quick Access toolbar.

j. At the Save As dialog box, type **HPhoneFind** and then press Enter or click OK.

k. Close the HPhoneFind macro.

2. Create a macro to close the current database and exit Access using the Action Catalog pane by completing the following steps:

a. Click the Create tab and then click the Macro button.

b. Click the Clear Filter button (displays as a red x over a funnel) at the right of the Search text box in the Action Catalog pane to clear *Run* from the Search text box and redisplay all action catalog categories.

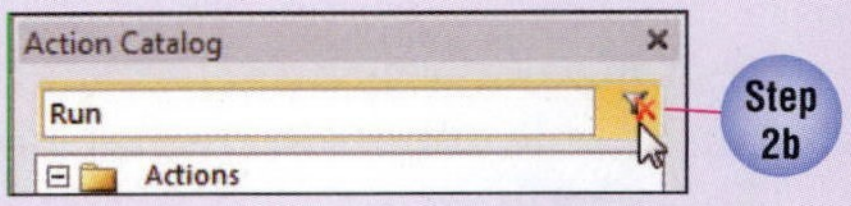

c. Click the Expand button (displays as a plus symbol) next to *System Commands* in the *Actions* list in the Action Catalog pane.

d. Double-click *QuitAccess* in the expanded *System Commands* actions list.

e. With *Save All* the default argument in the *Options* argument box, click the Save button on the Quick Access toolbar.

f. Type **ExitRSRdb** at the Save As dialog box and then press Enter or click OK.

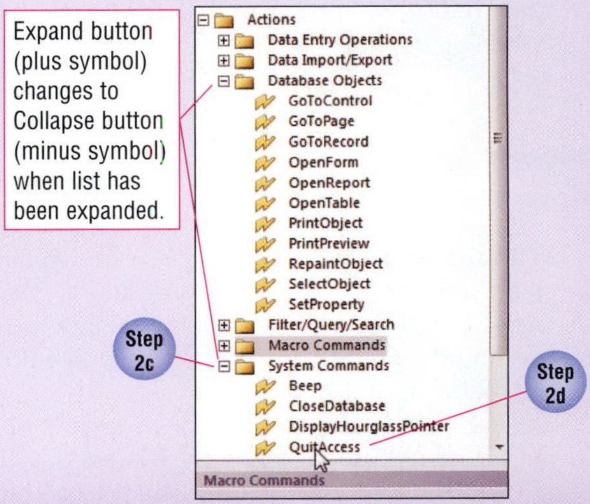

3. Close the ExitRSRdb macro.

Step 2b

Expand button (plus symbol) changes to Collapse button (minus symbol) when list has been expanded.

Step 2c

Step 2d

Editing and Deleting a Macro ■ ■ ■ ■ ■ ■ ■ ■ ■ ■ ■ ■

To edit a macro, right-click the macro name in the Navigation pane and click *Design View* at the shortcut menu. The macro opens in the Macro Builder window. Edit an action and/or the action's arguments, insert new actions, or delete actions as required. Save the revised macro and close the Macro Builder window when finished.

To delete a macro, right-click the macro name in the Navigation pane and then click *Delete* at the shortcut menu. At the Microsoft Access dialog box asking if you want to delete the macro, click Yes.

Project 1d **Editing and Deleting a Macro** Part 4 of 8

1. With the **AL2-C7-RSRCompServ.accdb** database open, assume you decide that the macro to find a technician record will begin with the TechMaintenance form already opened. This means you have to delete the first macro instruction to open the TechMaintenance form in the FormFindTech macro. To do this, complete the following steps:
   a. If necessary, scroll down the Navigation pane to view the macro object names.
   b. Right-click the macro named FormFindTech and then click *Design View* at the shortcut menu. The macro opens in the Macro Builder window.
   c. Position the mouse pointer over the *OpenForm* action in the Macro Builder window. As you point to an action in the Macro Builder window Access displays a collapse button at the left of the action to allow you to collapse the *Arguments* section, a down-pointing green arrow at the right side of the Macro Builder window to allow you to move the action, and a black x to delete the action.

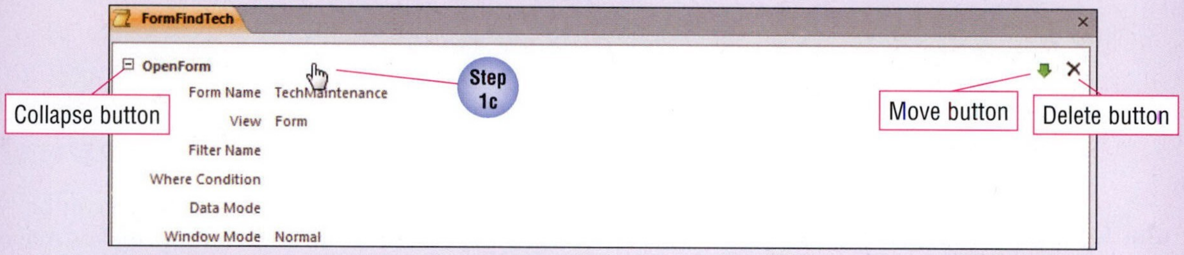

   d. Click the Delete button located at the right side of the Macro Builder window next to *OpenForm*. The action is removed from the Macro Builder window. ***Note: If the buttons at the right side of the Macro Builder window disappear as you move the mouse right, move the pointer up so that the pointer is on the same line as OpenForm to redisplay the buttons.***

2. Save the revised macro.
3. Close the macro.
4. The revised macro contains two instructions that activate the *LName* control and then open the Find dialog box. This macro could be used in any form that contains a field named *LName*; therefore, you decide to rename the macro. To begin, right-click FormFindTech in the Navigation pane, click *Rename* at the shortcut menu, type **LNameFind**, and then press Enter.

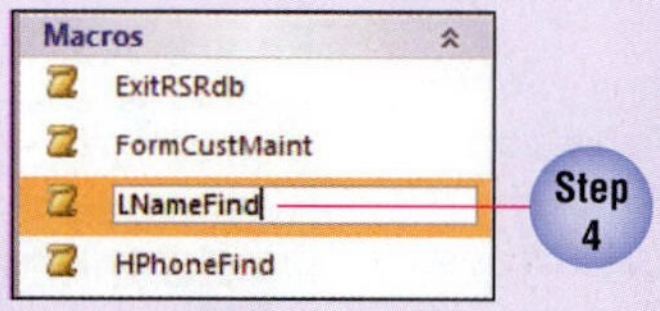

5. Delete the FormCustMaint macro by completing the following steps:
 a. Right-click *FormCustMaint* in the Navigation pane and then click *Delete* at the shortcut menu.
 b. At the Microsoft Access dialog box asking if you want to delete the macro, click Yes.

Reports
- TotalWorkOrders
- WorkOrders
- WorkOrdersbyMo

Macros
- ExitRSRdb
- FormCustMaint
- HPhoneFind
- LNameFind

Delete
Cut
Copy
Paste
Object Properties
Check Web Compatibility

Step 5a

Microsoft Access

⚠ Do you want to delete the macro 'FormCustMaint'? Deleting this object will remove it from all groups.

For more information on how to prevent this message from displaying every time you delete an object, click Help.

Yes No Help

Step 5b

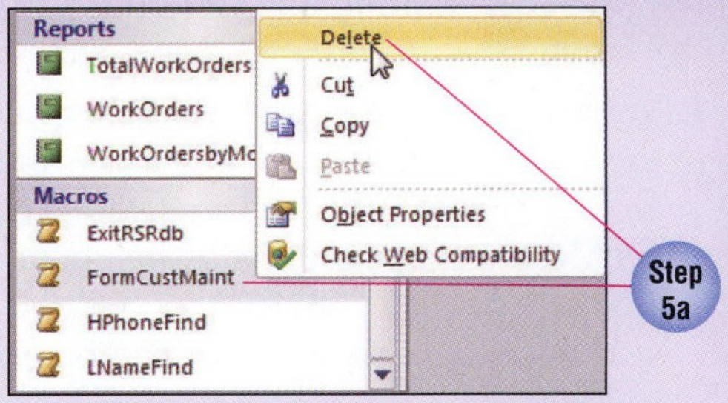

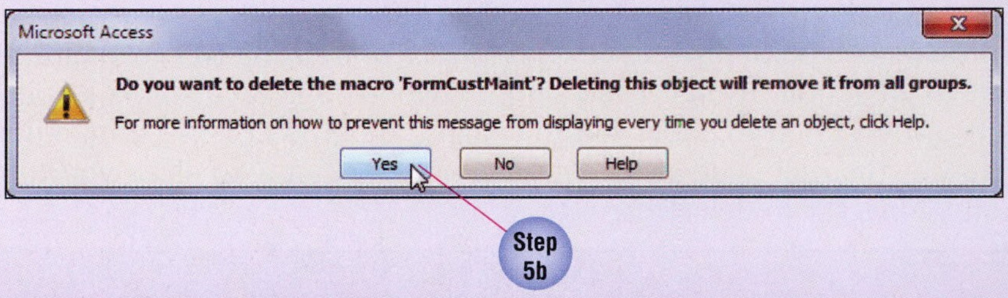

Creating a Command Button to Run a Macro ■■■■■■■■■

▼ **Quick Steps**

Create Command Button in Form
1. Open form in Design view.
2. Click Button button.
3. Drag to create button desired height and width.
4. Click *Miscellaneous*.
5. Click *Run Macro*.
6. Click Next.
7. Click desired macro name.
8. Click Next.
9. Click *Text*.
10. Select current text in *Text* text box.
11. Type desired text to appear on button.
12. Click Next.
13. Type name for command button.
14. Click Finish.

A macro can be assigned to a button added to a form so that the macro can be executed with a single mouse click. This method of running a macro makes macros more accessible and efficient. Open a form in Design view to add a button to the form to be used to run a macro. Click the Button button in the Controls group in the Form Design Tools Design tab and drag to create the button the approximate height and width in the desired form section. When you release the mouse, the Command Button Wizard launches if the Use Control Wizards feature is active. At the first Command Button Wizard dialog box shown in Figure 7.3, you begin by choosing the type of command to assign to the button.

Click *Miscellaneous* in the *Categories* list box and *Run Macro* in the *Actions* list box and click Next. At the second Command Button Wizard dialog box you choose the name of the macro to assign to the button. At the third dialog box, shown in Figure 7.4, specify text to display on the face of the button or choose to

Figure 7.3 First Command Button Wizard Dialog Box

Command Button Wizard

Sample:

What action do you want to happen when the button is pressed?

Different actions are available for each category.

Categories:
- Record Navigation
- Record Operations
- Form Operations
- Report Operations
- Application
- Miscellaneous

Actions:
- Auto Dialer
- Print Table
- Run Macro
- Run Query

Cancel < Back Next > Finish

Select the *Miscellaneous* category and the *Run Macro* action to assign a macro to the button at the first Command Button Wizard dialog box.

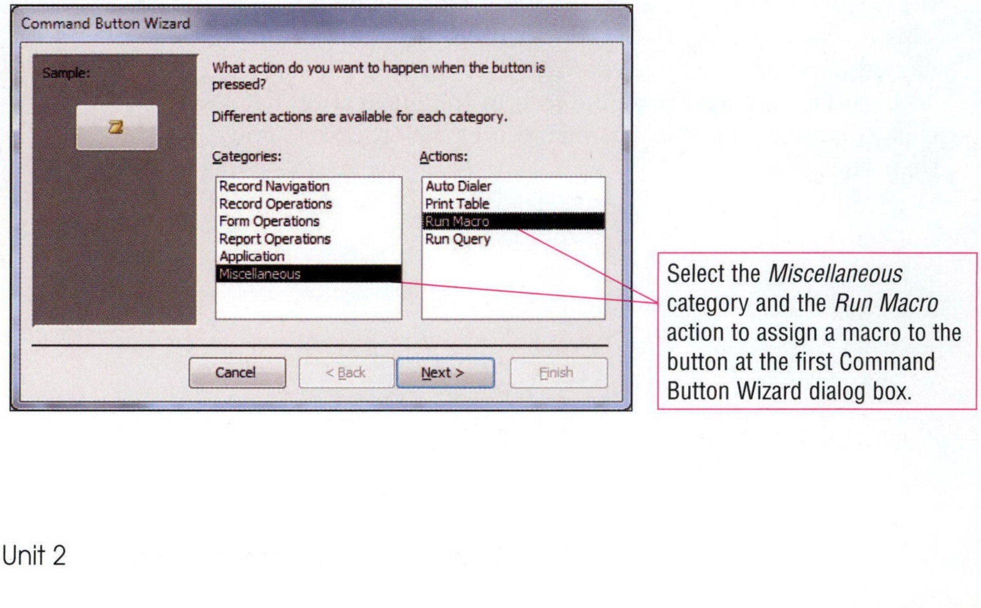

Figure 7.4 Third Command Button Wizard Dialog Box

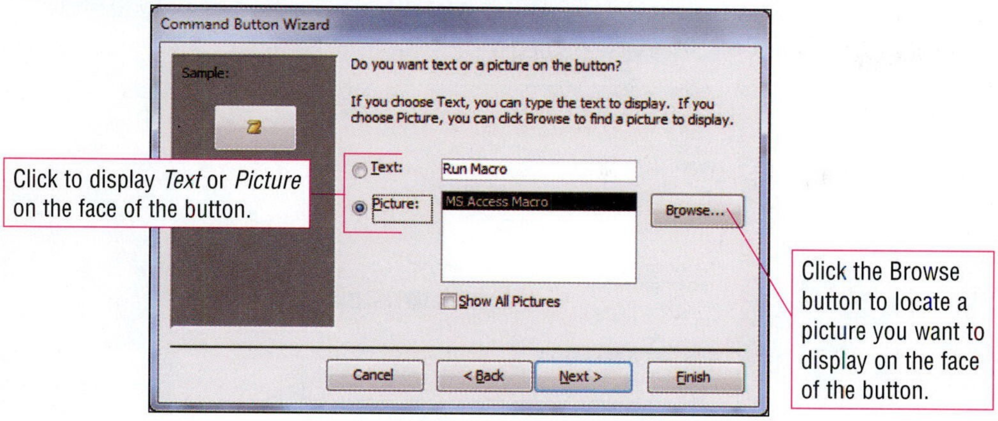

display a picture as an icon. The button in the *Sample* section of the dialog box updates to show how the button will appear as you enter text or select a picture file. At the last Command Button Wizard dialog box, assign a name to associate with the command button and click Finish.

HINT

Actions can be assigned to a command button without using a macro. Explore the categories and actions for each category at the first Command Button Wizard dialog box.

Button

Control Wizard

Project 1e **Creating a Button and Assigning a Macro to the Button in a Form** Part 5 of 8

1. With the **AL2-C7-RSRCompServ.accdb** database open, create a command button to run the macro to locate a technician record by last name in the TechMaintenance form by completing the following steps:
   a. Open the TechMaintenance form in Design view. To make room for the new button in the *Form Header* section, click to select the control object with the title text and then drag the right middle sizing handle left until the right edge is at approximately 3.5 inches in the horizontal ruler.
   b. By default, the Use Control Wizards feature is toggled on in the Controls group. Click the More button at the bottom of the Controls scroll bar to expand the Controls and display the *Controls* drop-down list. View the current status of the *Use Control Wizards* option. The button at the left of the option displays with an orange background when the feature is active. If the button is orange, click in a blank area to remove the expanded Controls list. If the feature is not active (displays with a white background), click *Use Control Wizards* to turn the feature on.
   c. Click the Button button in the Controls group in the Form Design Tools Design tab.
   d. Position the crosshairs with the button icon attached in the *Form Header* section, drag to create a button the approximate height and width shown, and then release the mouse.

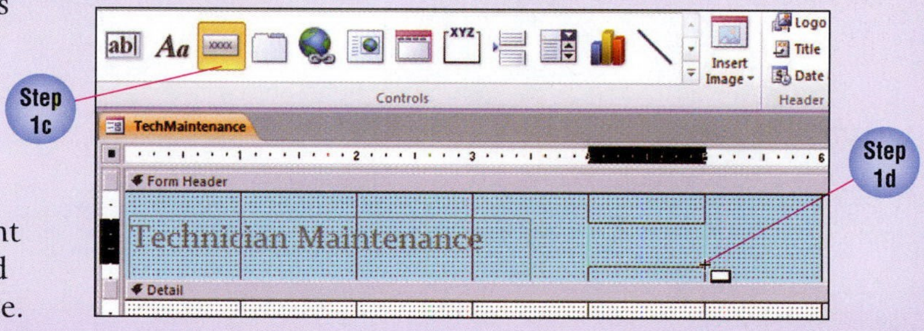

e. At the first Command Button Wizard dialog box, click *Miscellaneous* in the *Categories* list box.
f. Click *Run Macro* in the *Actions* list box and then click Next.

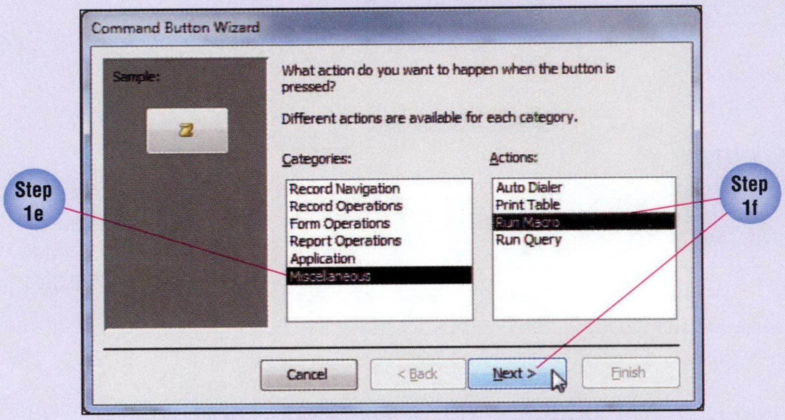

g. Click *LNameFind* in the *What macro would you like the command button to run?* list box at the second Command Button Wizard dialog box and then click Next.

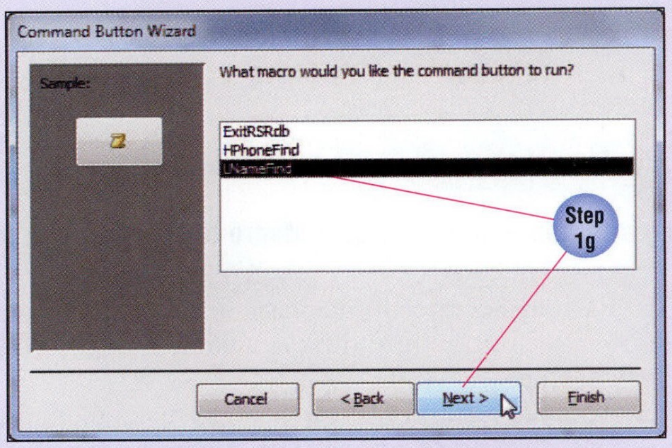

h. At the third Command Button Wizard dialog box, click *Text*.
i. Select the current text in the *Text* text box, type **Find Technician by Last Name**, and click Next.

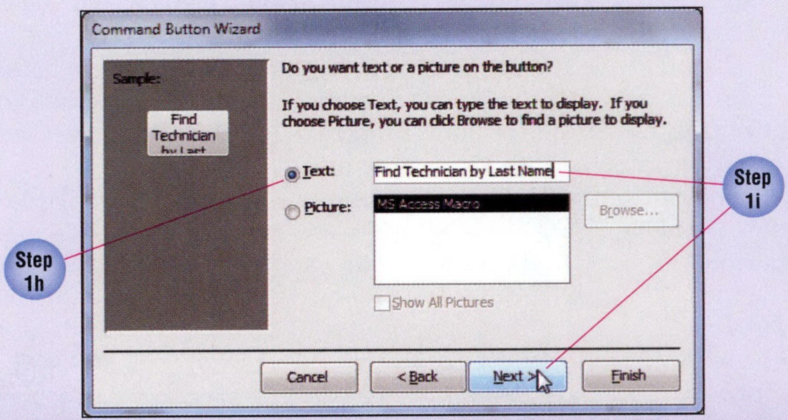

j. With *Command##* (where ## is the number of the command button) already selected in the *What do you want to name the button?* text box, type **FindTechRec** and then click Finish. Access automatically resizes the width of the button to accommodate the text to be displayed on the face of the button.

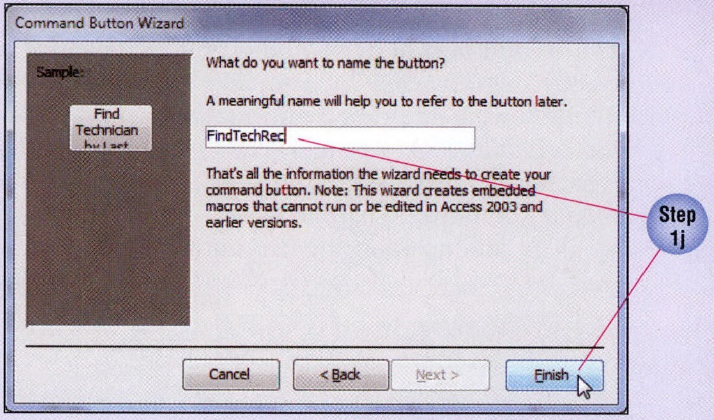

2. Save the revised form.
3. Switch to Form view.
4. Click the Find Technician by Last Name button to run the macro.

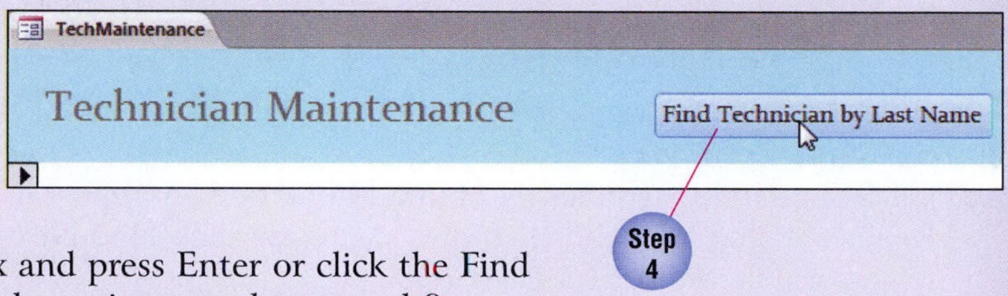

5. Type **Colacci** in the *Find What* text box at the Find and Replace dialog box and press Enter or click the Find Next button. Access moves the active record to record 9.
6. Close the Find and Replace dialog box.
7. Close the form.

Project 1f Creating Two Command Buttons and Assigning Macros to the Buttons Part 6 of 8

1. With the **AL2-C7-RSRCompServ.accdb** database open, create a command button to run the macro to find a record by the home telephone number field in the CustMaintenance form by completing the following steps:
   a. Open the CustMaintenance form in Design view.
   b. Click the Button button in the Controls group in the Form Design Tools Design tab.
   c. Position the crosshairs with the button icon attached in the *Detail* section below the *Service Contract?* label control object, drag to create a button the approximate height and width shown, and then release the mouse.

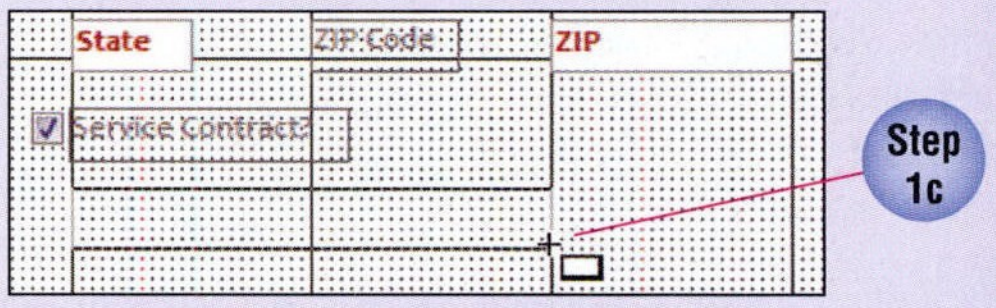

   d. Click *Miscellaneous* in the *Categories* list box, click *Run Macro* in the *Actions* list box, and then click Next.
   e. Click *HPhoneFind* and click Next.

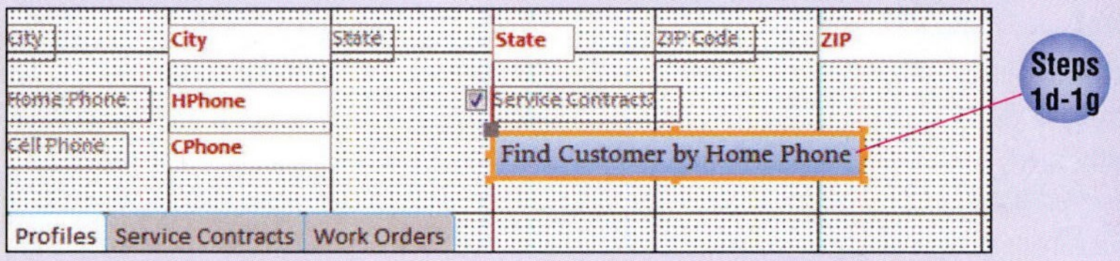

   f. Click *Text*, select the current text in the *Text* text box, type **Find Customer by Home Phone**, and click Next.
   g. Type **FindByPhone** and then click Finish.

2. Save the revised form.
3. Create a second button below the button you created in Step 1 to run the macro to find a record by the last name by completing steps similar to those in Steps 1b through 1g and with the following additional information:
    - Select *LNameFind* as the macro to assign to the button.
    - Display the text *Find Customer by Last Name* on the button.
    - Name the button *FindByLName.*
4. Resize, align, and position the two buttons as shown.

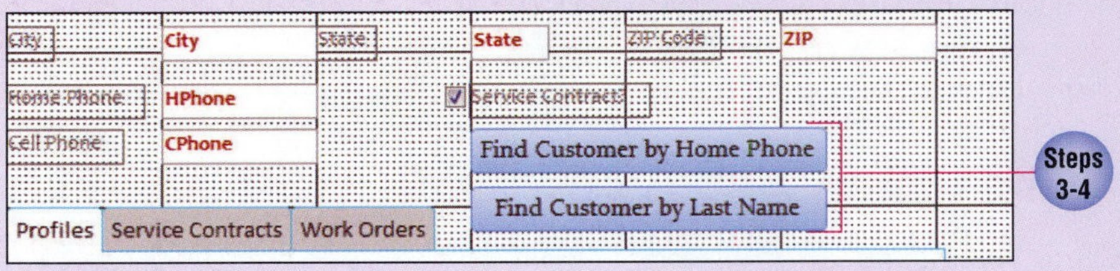

5. Save the revised form.
6. Switch to Form view.
7. Click the Find Customer by Home Phone button, type **313-555-7486** at the Find and Replace dialog box, and then press Enter or click Find Next. Close the dialog box and review the record for *Customer ID* 1025.
8. Click the Find Customer by Last Name button, type **Antone** at the Find and Replace dialog box, and then press Enter or click Find Next. Close the dialog box and review the record for *Customer ID* 1075.
9. Close the CustMaintenance form.

Quick Steps

View Macro Code for Command Button
1. Open form in Design view.
2. Click to select command button.
3. Display the Property Sheet.
4. Click the Event tab.
5. Click the Build button in the *On Click* property box.

HINT

To delete an embedded macro, open the Property Sheet, select *[Embedded Macro]* in the *On Click* property box and then press Delete. Close the Property Sheet and then save the form.

The Command Button Wizard used in Project 1e and 1f created an embedded macro in the Property Sheet of the button. An ***embedded macro*** is a macro that is stored within a form, report, or control that is run when a specific event occurs. For example, when the user clicks the button the macro is run. Clicking the button is the *event* that causes the macro action to be performed. You can view the embedded macro by opening the command button's Property Sheet and clicking the Event tab. In the *On Click* property box, you will see *[Embedded Macro]*. Click the Build button (button with three dots) at the right end of the *On Click* property box to open the Macro Builder window with the macro actions displayed. The macro and the macro actions were created for you by the Command Button Wizard. Embedded macros are not objects that you can see in the Navigation pane. To view or edit an embedded macro you need to open the form, report, or control Property Sheet.

Project 1g Viewing Macro Actions Created by Command Button Wizard

Part 7 of 8

1. With the **AL2-C7-RSRCompServ.accdb** database open, view the macro actions embedded in a command button when you used the Command Button Wizard by completing the following steps:
   a. Open the CustMaintenance form in Design view.
   b. Click to select the Find Customer by Home Phone command button.
   c. Click the Property Sheet button in the Tools group of the Form Design Tools Design tab or press function key F4.
   d. Click the Event tab in the Command Button Property Sheet.
   e. Notice the text in the *On Click* property box reads *[Embedded Macro]*.

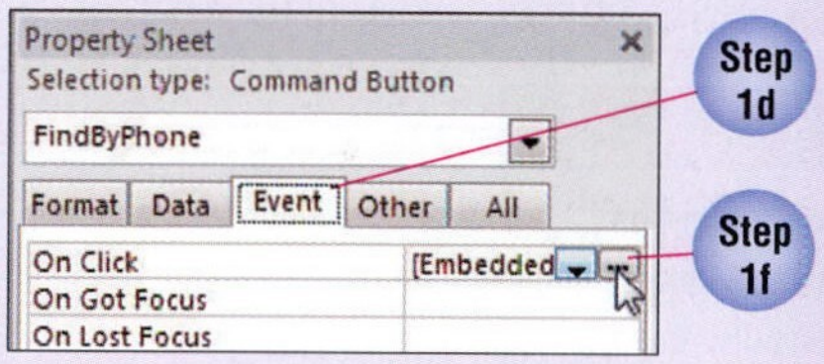

   f. Click the Build button (button with three dots) in the *On Click* property box. When you click the Build button, Access opens the Macro Builder window for the macro that was embedded in the command button.
   g. Notice the name of the macro created for you by the Command Button Wizard is *CustMaintenance: FindByPhone: On Click*. The form name, followed by the button name to which the macro is associated and then the event that causes the macro to run (*On Click*), comprise the embedded macro's name.
   h. Review the macro actions in the Macro Builder window. Notice the macro action is *RunMacro* with the name of the macro you selected at the second Command Button Wizard dialog box, *HPhoneFind*, entered in the *Macro Name* argument.
   i. Click the Close button in the Close group of the Macro Tools Design tab.

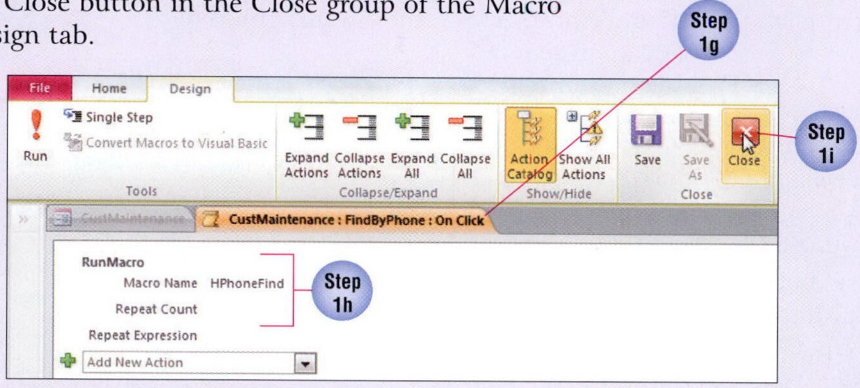

2. With the Property Sheet still open, click to select the Find Customer by Last Name command button and then click the Build button in the *On Click* property box of the Event tab in the Property Sheet. Review the embedded macro name and macro actions in the Macro Builder window and then click the Close button in the Close group of the Macro Tools Design tab.

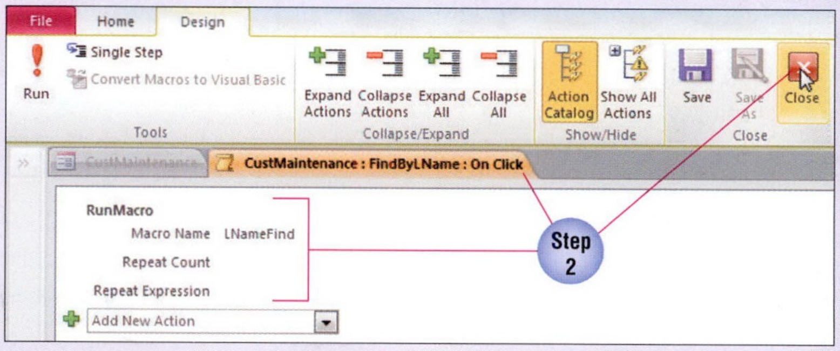

3. Close the CustMaintenance form.

Quick Steps

Convert Macro to Visual Basic
1. Open macro in Design view.
2. Click Convert Macros to Visual Basic button.
3. Click Convert button.
4. Click OK.

HINT

If you convert an embedded macro, Access also changes the property box in the form, report, or control Property Sheet to run the VBA procedure instead of the macro.

Macros enable you to add automation or functionality within Access without having to learn how to write programming code. In the Microsoft Office suite, Visual Basic for Applications (VBA) is the programming language used to build custom applications that operate within Word, Excel, PowerPoint, or Access. The macros used in this chapter have been simple and did not need VBA programming; however, when automation requires more complex tasks, a developer may prefer to write a program using VBA. A quick method to use to start a VBA program is to create a macro and then convert the macro to VBA code. To do this, open the macro in the Macro Builder window and then click the Convert Macros to Visual Basic button in the Tools group of the Macro Tools Design tab. Access opens a Microsoft Visual Basic window with the VBA code for the macro.

Convert Macros to Visual Basic

Project 1h Converting a Macro to Visual Basic for Applications

Part 8 of 8

1. With the **AL2-C7-RSRCompServ.accdb** database open, convert a macro to Visual Basic by completing the following steps:
   a. Right-click the HPhoneFind macro in the Macros group of the Navigation pane and then click *Design View* at the shortcut menu. The Macro Builder window opens with the macro actions and arguments for the HPhoneFind macro.
   b. Click the Convert Macros to Visual Basic button in the Tools group of the Macro Tools Design tab.
   c. At the Convert macro: HPhoneFind dialog box with the *Add error handling to generated functions* and *Include macro comments* check boxes selected, click the Convert button.
   d. At the *Convert macros to Visual Basic* message box with the message *Conversion Finished!*, click OK.

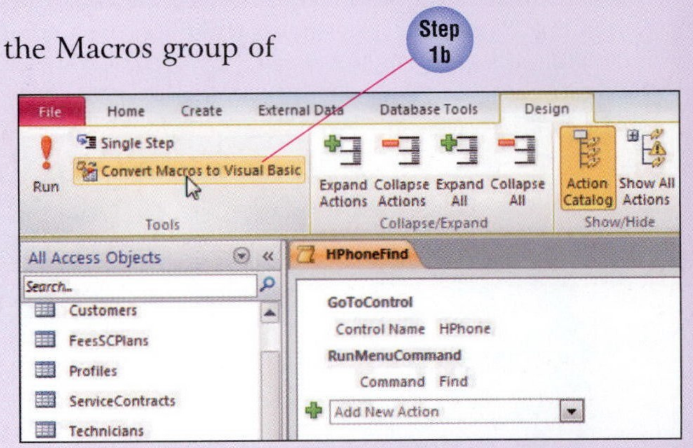

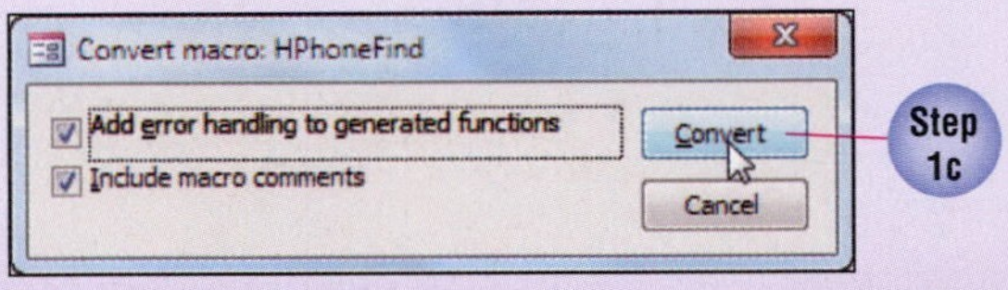

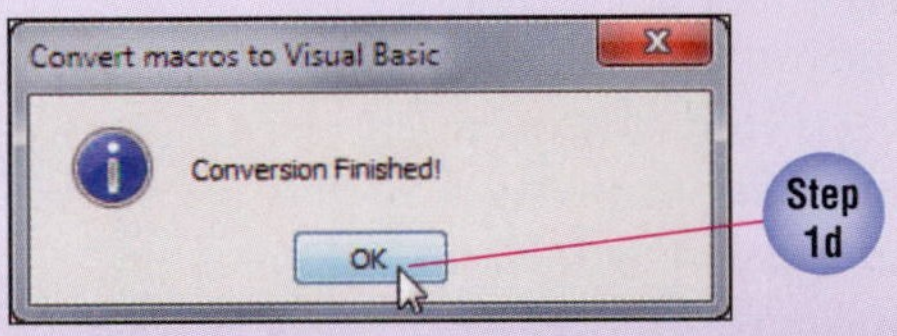

2. Access opens a Microsoft Visual Basic for Applications window when the macro is converted and displays the converted event procedure below an expanded Modules list in a Project window. If necessary, drag the right border of the Project window to expand the width in order to read the entire converted macro name and then double-click the macro name to open the event procedure in its class module window.

3. Read the VBA code in the Converted Macro-HPhoneFind (Code) window and then close the window.

Step 2

Step 3

```
Option Compare Database

'----------------------------------------
' HPhoneFind
'
'----------------------------------------
Function HPhoneFind()
On Error GoTo HPhoneFind_Err

    DoCmd.GoToControl "HPhone"
    DoCmd.RunCommand acCmdFind

HPhoneFind_Exit:
    Exit Function

HPhoneFind_Err:
    MsgBox Error$
    Resume HPhoneFind_Exit

End Function
```

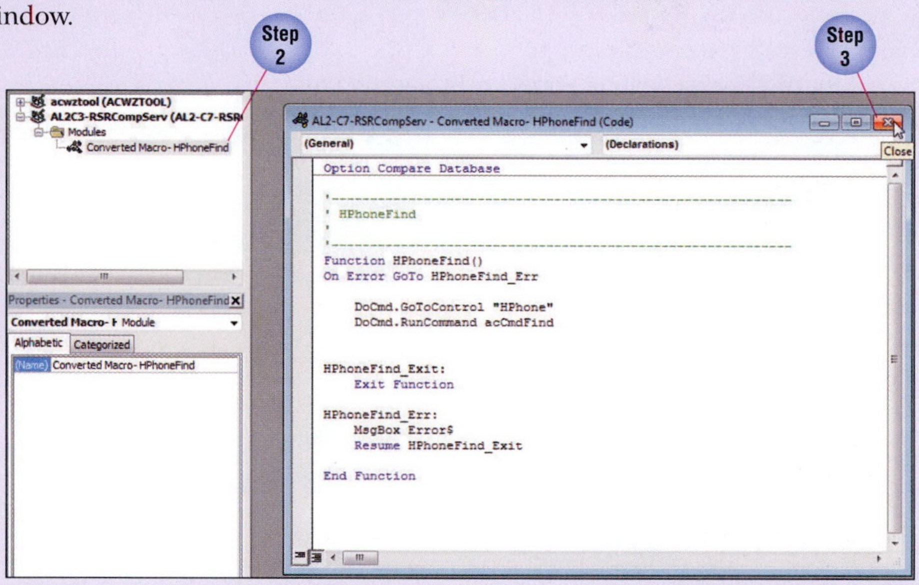

4. Click File on the Menu bar and then click *Close and Return to Microsoft Access* at the drop-down list.
5. Close the HPhoneFind Macro Builder window.

P**roject** **2** **Create a Navigation Form** **2 Parts**

You will create a Navigation form to be used as a main menu for the RSR Computer Services database.

Creating a Navigation Form ■■■■■■■■■■■■■■■■■■■■■■■

Database files are often accessed by multiple users who need to enter the file for a specific purpose such as updating a customer record or entering details related to a completed work order. These individuals may not be well versed in database applications and simply want an easy method with which to accomplish the data entry or maintenance task. A Navigation form with tabs along the top, left, or right is used as a menu with which end users can open the forms and reports needed to update, view, or print data. The Navigation form can be set to display automatically when the database file is opened so that end users do not need to know which objects are needed from the Navigation pane.

To create a Navigation form, click the Create tab and then click the Navigation button in the Forms group. At the Navigation button drop-down list, choose the type of menu form you want to create by selecting the option in the drop-down list

▼ **Quick Steps**

Create Navigation Form
1. Click Create tab.
2. Click Navigation button.
3. Click desired form style.
4. Drag form or report name to *[Add New]* in Navigation Form.
5. Repeat Step 4 as needed.
6. Click Save.
7. Type form name.
8. Press Enter or click OK.

Navigation Form

that positions the tabs where you want them to appear horizontally or vertically. A Navigation Form window opens with a title and tab bar created. Access displays *[Add New]* indicating the first tab in the form. Drag a form or report from the Navigation pane to *[Add New]* in the Navigation Form window to add a form or report to the form. Continue dragging form and/or report names from the Navigation pane to *[Add New]* in the Navigation Form window in the order you want them to appear. Figure 7.5 illustrates the navigation form you will create in Projects 2a and 2b.

Figure 7.5 Navigation Form for Projects 2a and 2b

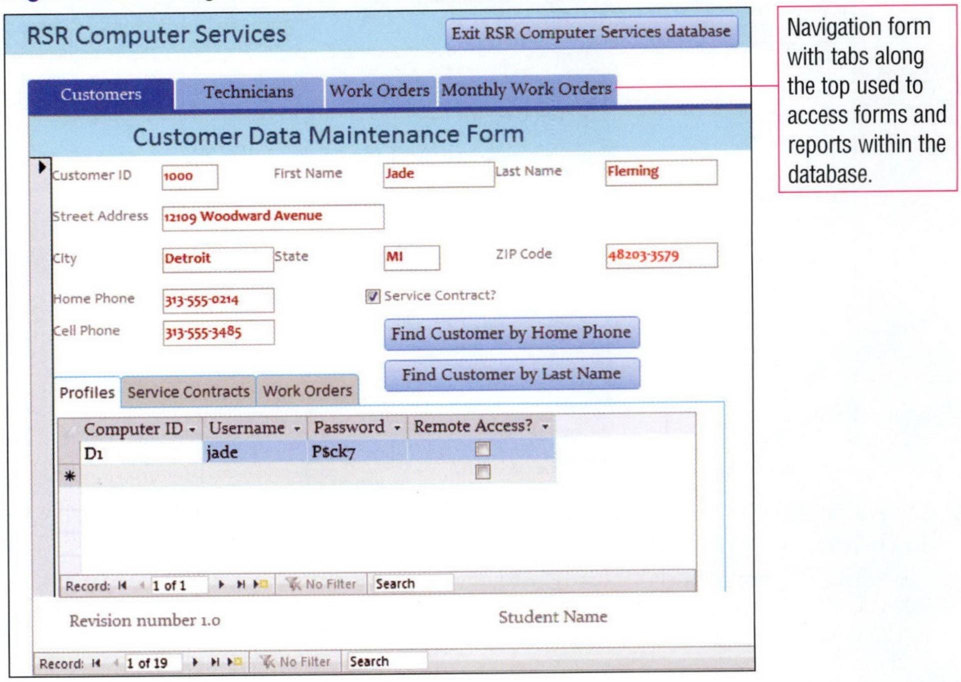

Project 2a Creating a Navigation Form

Part 1 of 2

1. With the **AL2-C7-RSRCompServ.accdb** database open, create a Navigation form with tabs along the top for accessing forms and reports by completing the following steps:
   a. Click the Create tab.
   b. Click the Navigation button in the Forms group.
   c. Click *Horizontal Tabs* at the drop-down list. Access opens a Navigation Form window with a Field List pane open at the right side of the work area. The horizontal tab across the top of the form is selected with *[Add New]* displayed in the first tab.

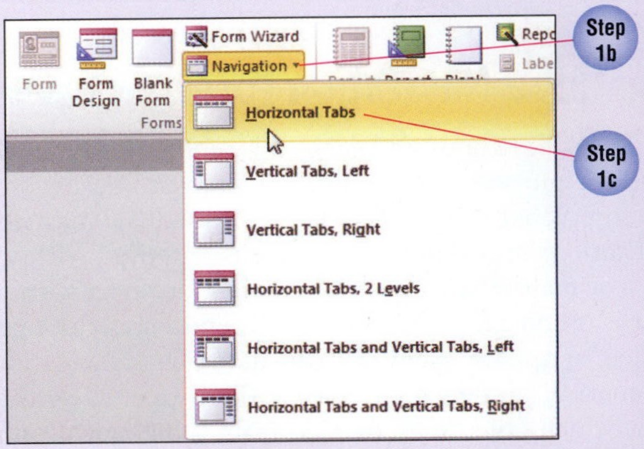

d. Position the mouse pointer on the CustMaintenance form name in the Navigation pane, hold down the left mouse button, drag the form name to *[Add New]* in the Navigation Form, and then release the mouse. Access adds the CustMaintenance form to the first tab in the form and displays a new tab with *[Add New]* to the right of the CustMaintenance tab.

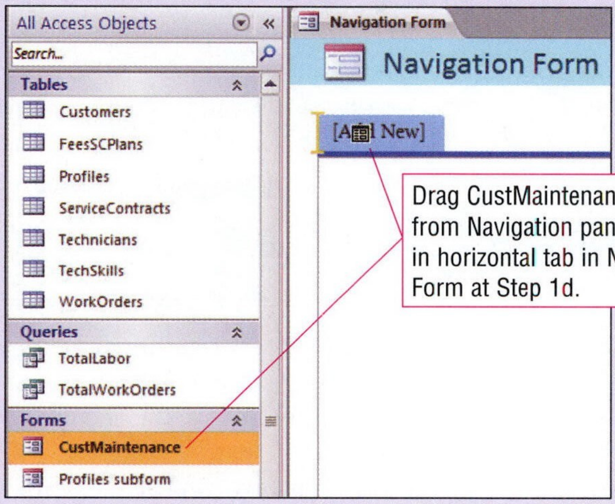

e. Drag the TechMaintenance form name from the Navigation pane to the second tab with *[Add New]* displayed as the tab name.

f. Drag the WorkOrders report name from the Navigation pane to the third tab with *[Add New]* in the Navigation Form.

g. Drag the WorkOrdersbyMonth report name from the Navigation pane to the fourth tab with *[Add New]* in the Navigaton Form.

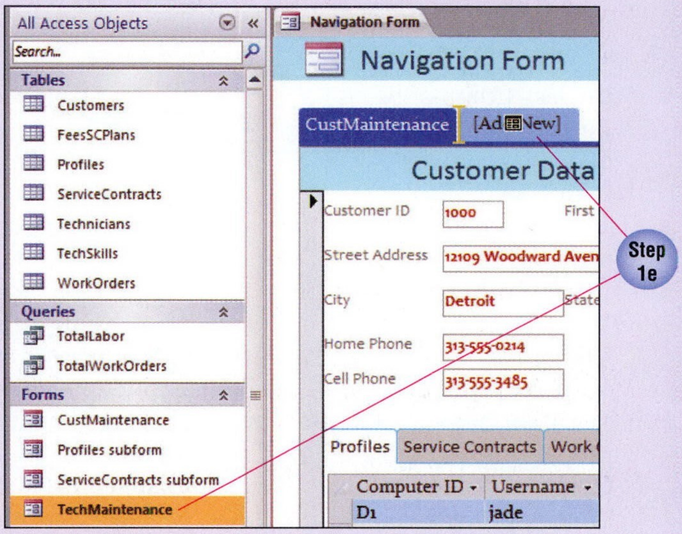

2. Close the Field List pane at the right side of the work area.
3. Click the Save button on the Quick Access toolbar. At the Save As dialog box, type **MainMenu** in the *Form Name* text box and then press Enter or click OK.

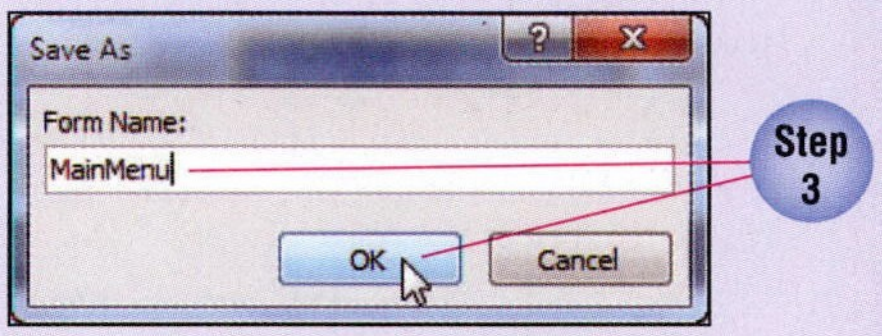

4. Switch to Form view.
5. Click each tab along the top of the Navigation form to view each form or report in the work area. When finished, leave the form open for the next project.

A Navigation form can be edited in Layout view or Form view using all of the tools and techniques you learned in Chapter 4 for working with forms. Consider changing the title, adding a logo, and renaming tabs to customize the Navigation form.

Project 2b Adding a Command Button to a Navigation Form and Editing the Form Part 2 of 2

1. With the **AL2-C7-RSRCompServ.accdb** database open and with the MainMenu form displayed in the work area, add a command button to the Navigation form by completing the following steps:
   a. Switch to Design view.
   b. Resize the title control object in the *Form Header* section to align the right edge of the object at approximately the 3-inch position in the horizontal ruler.
   c. Click the Button button in the Controls group and drag to create a button the approximate height and width shown in the *Form Header* section.

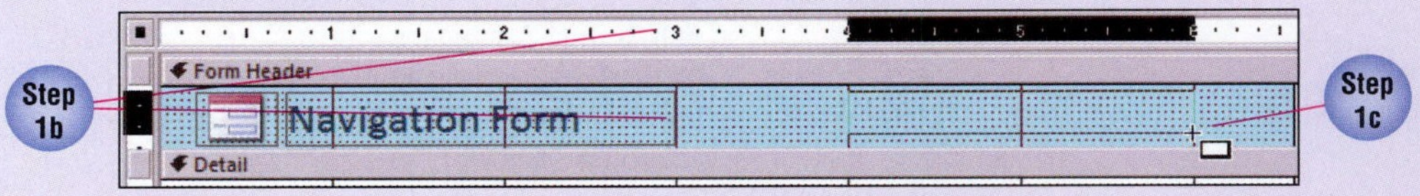

   d. Select *Miscellaneous* in the *Categories* list box and *Run Macro* in the *Actions* list box at the first Command Button Wizard dialog box and click Next.
   e. With *ExitRSRdb* already selected in the macros list box at the second Command Button Wizard dialog box, click Next.
   f. Click *Text*, select the current entry in the *Text* text box, type **Exit RSR Computer Services database**, and click Next at the third Command Button Wizard dialog box.
   g. Type **Exitdb** at the last Command Button Wizard dialog box and then click Finish.

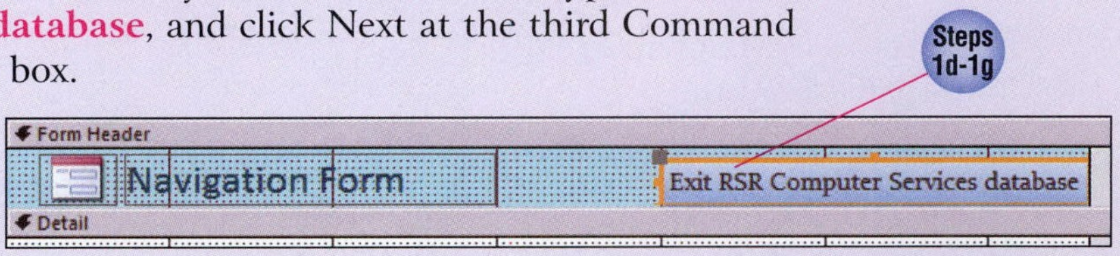

2. Click to select the logo container object at the left of the title in the *Form Header* section and then press Delete.
3. Edit the text in the Title control object in the *Form Header* section to *RSR Computer Services*.
4. Relabel the tabs along the top of the Navigation form by completing the following steps:
   a. Click to select the first tab with *CustMaintenance* as the tab name and then click the Property Sheet button in the Tools group of the Form Design Tools Design tab.
   b. With Format the active tab in the Property Sheet, select the current text in the *Caption* property box and then type **Customers**.
   c. Click the second tab with *TechMaintenance* as the tab name, select the current text in the *Caption* property box in the Property Sheet, and then type **Technicians**.
   d. Click the third tab with *WorkOrders* as the tab name, click in the *Caption* property box, and then insert a space between *Work* and *Orders* so that the tab name displays *Work Orders*.
   e. Click the fourth tab with *WorkOrdersbyMonth* as the tab name, select the current text in the *Caption* property box, and then type **Monthly Work Orders**.

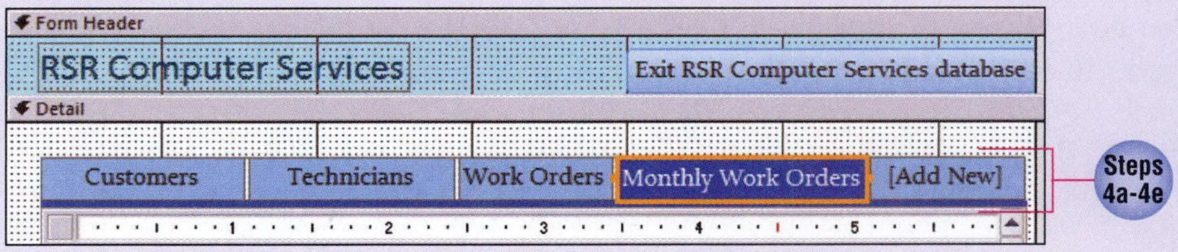

   f. Close the Property Sheet task pane.
5. Save the revised form and then switch to Form view.
6. Compare your form with the one shown in Figure 7.5 on page 274.

Project 3 Configure Database Options

5 Parts

You will configure database options for the active database and error checking options for all databases, and customize the ribbon.

Customizing the Access Environment

Click the File tab and then click the Options button located near the bottom of the left pane in the Info tab Backstage view to open the Access Options dialog box in which you can customize the Access environment. You can specify database options for all databases or for the current database. You can also define behavior for certain keys and set the default margins for printing. A form can be set to display automatically whenever the database file is opened. You can also choose to show or hide the Navigation pane in the current database. For example, if you have created a Navigation form that you want to use to provide limited access to only those objects that you want to make available, you may choose to hide the Navigation pane to prevent users from being able to open other objects within the database. Databases can be set to open by default in shared use or exclusive use. Exclusive use means the file is restricted to one individual user.

Figure 7.6 displays the Access Options dialog box with *Current Database* selected in the left pane. In the Current Database pane, you can define a startup form to open automatically when the database is opened. In Project 3a you will configure the current database to display the MainMenu form when the database is opened and in Project 3b you will customize the Navigation pane.

Quick Steps

Set Startup Form

1. Click File tab.
2. Click Options.
3. Click *Current Database* in left pane.
4. Click down-pointing arrow next to *Display Form.*
5. Click desired form.
6. Click OK.

Specify Application Title

1. Click File tab.
2. Click Options.
3. Click *Current Database* in left pane.
4. Click in *Application Title* text box.
5. Type desired title.
6. Click OK.

Options

Figure 7.6 Access Options Dialog Box with Current Database Pane Selected

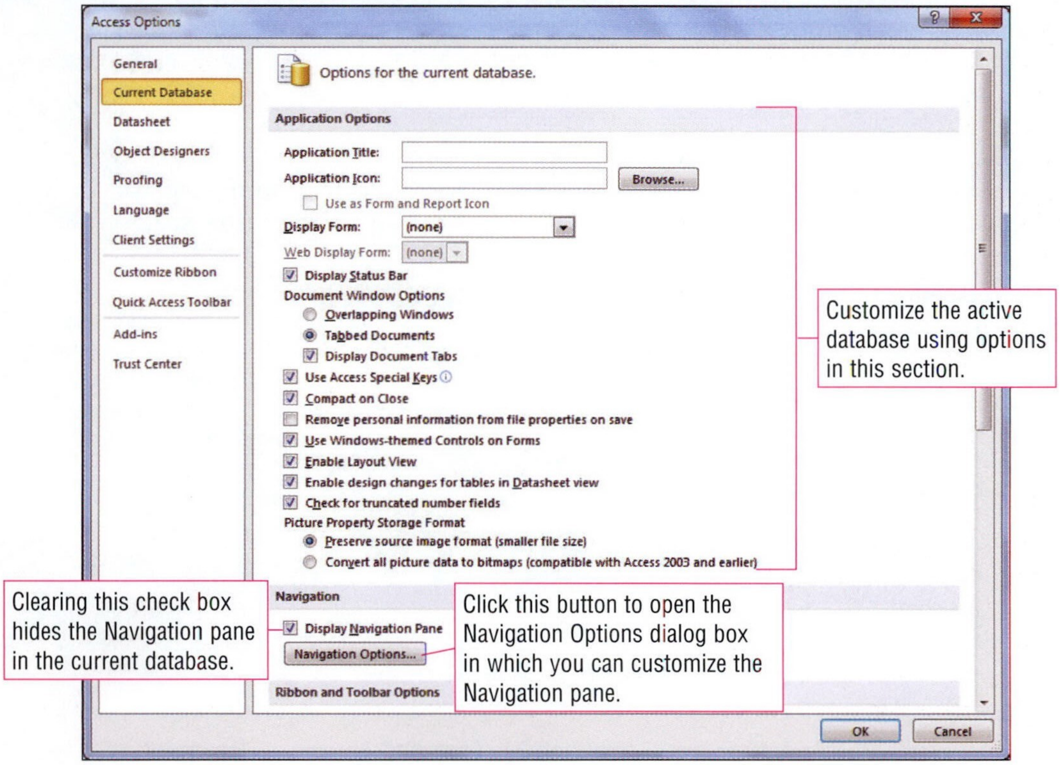

Project 3a Specifying a Startup Form and Application Title

Part 1 of 5

1. With the **AL2-C7-RSRCompServ.accdb** database open, specify a form to be opened automatically when the database file is opened and a title to appear in the Title bar by completing the following steps:
   a. Click the File tab.
   b. Click the Options button located near the bottom of the left pane at the Info tab Backstage view.
   c. Click *Current Database* in the left pane.
   d. Click the down-pointing arrow next to the *Display Form* list box (currently displays *[none]* in the *Application Options* section) and then click *MainMenu* at the drop-down list.

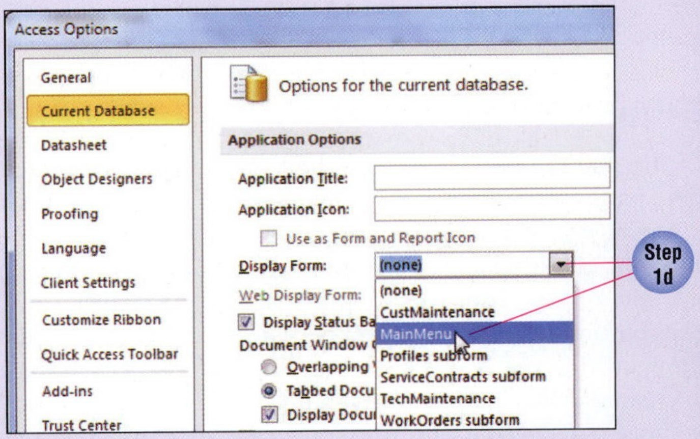

2. Click in the *Application Title* text box and type **RSR Computer Services Database**.
3. Click OK.
4. Click OK at the Microsoft Access message box indicating you have to close and reopen the database for the options to take effect.

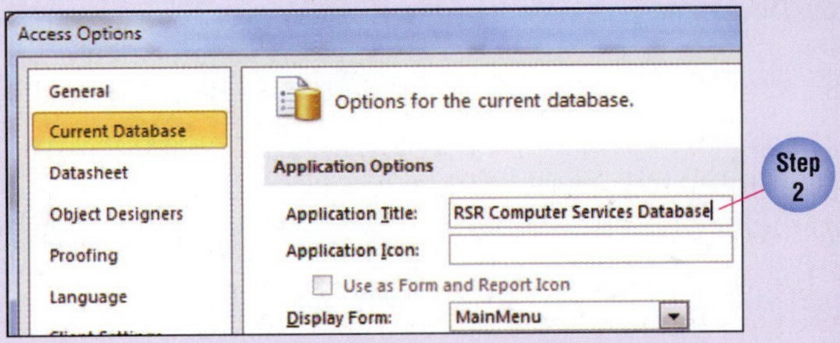

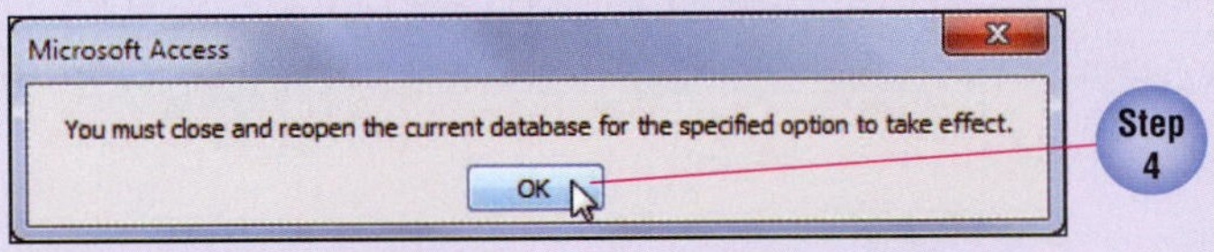

5. Close the **AL2-C7-RSRCompServ.accdb** database.
6. Reopen the **AL2-C7-RSRCompServ.accdb** database. The MainMenu form displays automatically in the work area and the Title bar displays the application title *RSR Computer Services Database*.

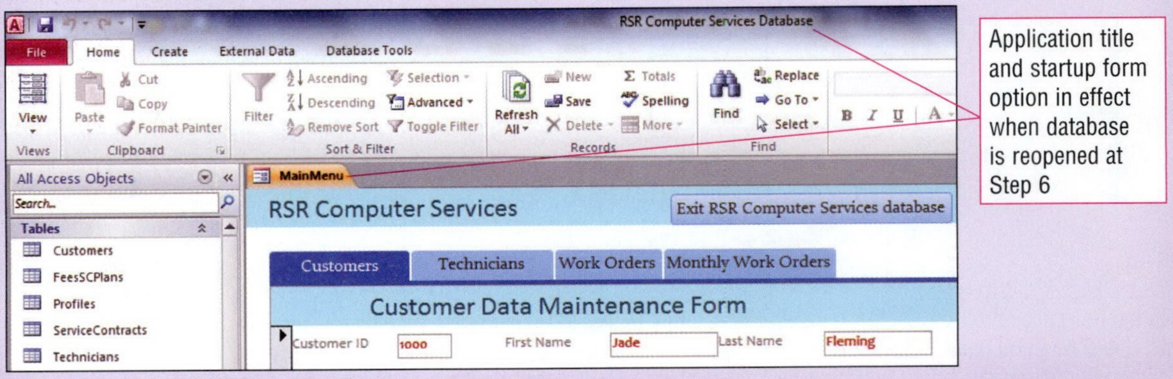

Limiting Ribbon Tabs and Menus in a Database

Often, when you are interested in securing the database by showing a startup form with limited access to objects, you also want to limit access to options in the ribbon and menus. Preventing an end user from seeing the full ribbon and shortcut menus allows you to avoid accidental changes made by someone switching views and editing or deleting objects without knowing the full impact of these changes. To do this, display the Access Options dialog box with the Current Database pane active. Scroll down the dialog box to the section titled *Ribbon and Toolbar Options*. Clear the check boxes for *Allow Full Menus* and *Allow Default Shortcut Menus* and then click OK. When the database is closed and reopened, only the Home tab will be available in the ribbon. The File tab Backstage view will only display Print options. You will not be able to switch views as the View buttons are removed and right-clicking will not show a shortcut menu.

If you need to work within the database and have access to the full ribbon and menus, you can bypass the startup options by holding the Shift key while double-clicking the file name to open the database.

Customizing the Navigation Pane

Often, when a startup form is used in a database, the Navigation pane is hidden to prevent users from accidentally making changes to other objects by opening an object from the Navigation pane. To hide the Navigation pane, open the Access Options dialog box, click *Current Database* in the left pane, and then clear the *Display Navigation Pane* check box in the *Navigation* section.

Click the Navigation Options button in the *Navigation* section to open the Navigation Options dialog box shown in Figure 7.7. At this dialog box you can elect to hide individual objects or groups of objects, set display options for the pane, and define whether objects are opened using a single mouse click or a double mouse click. For example, to prevent changes from being made to table design, you can hide the Tables group.

Quick Steps

Customize Navigation Pane

1. Click File tab.
2. Click Options.
3. Click *Current Database* in left pane.
4. Click Navigation Options button.
5. Select desired options.
6. Click OK.
7. Click OK.

Hide Navigation Pane

1. Click File tab.
2. Click Options.
3. Click *Current Database* in left pane.
4. Clear *Display Navigation Pane* check box.
5. Click OK.
6. Click OK.

HINT

Press F11 to display a hidden Navigation pane.

Figure 7.7 Navigation Options Dialog Box

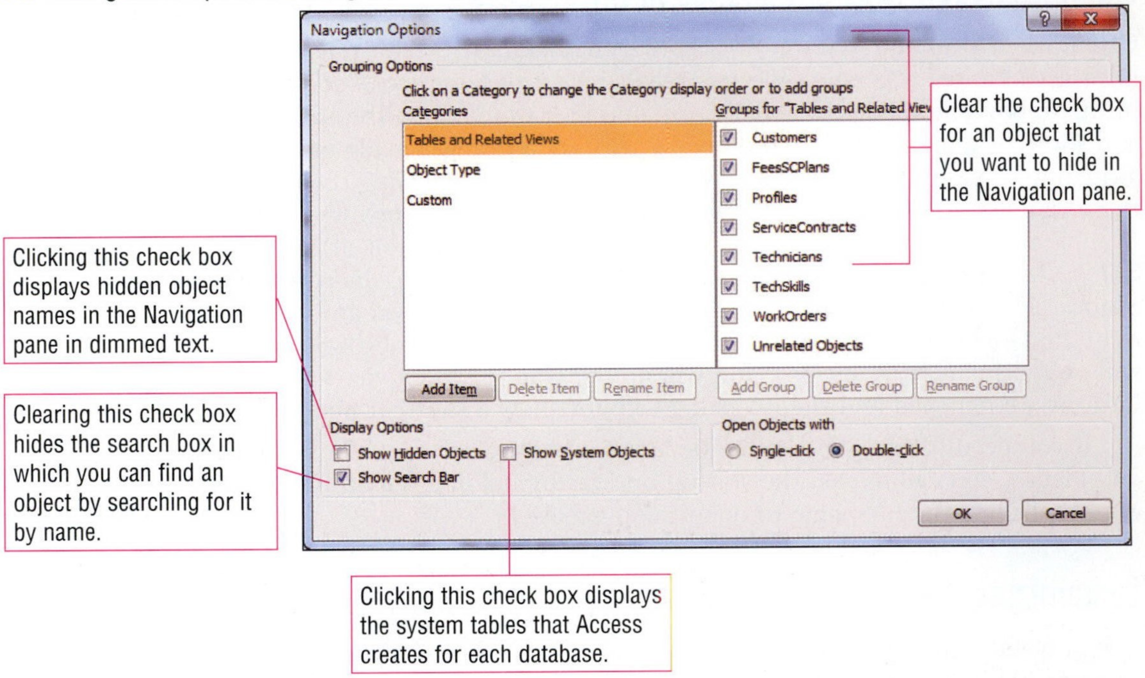

Project 3b Customizing the Navigation Pane

Part 2 of 5

1. With the **AL2-C7-RSRCompServ.accdb** database open, customize the Navigation pane to hide all of the table and macro objects by completing the following steps:
   a. Click the File tab and then click the Options button.
   b. If necessary, click *Current Database* in the left pane. Click the Navigation Options button in the *Navigation* section.
   c. Click *Object Type* in the *Categories* list box.
   d. Click the *Tables* check box in the *Groups for "Object Type"* list box to clear the check mark.
   e. Clear the check mark in the *Macros* check box.
   f. Click OK to close the Navigation Options dialog box.

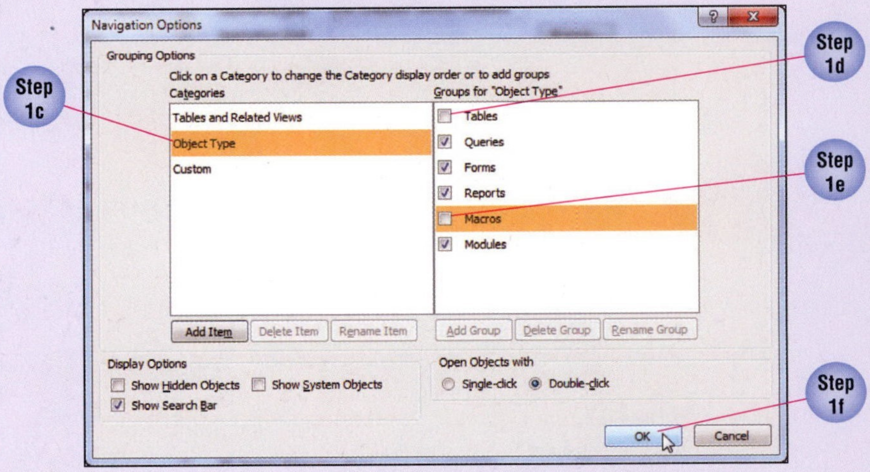

   g. Click OK to close the Access Options dialog box.

h. Click OK at the message box that says you must close and reopen the current database for the specified option to take effect.

2. Notice the Tables and Macros groups are hidden in the Navigation pane.

Tables and Macros groups are hidden in the Navigation pane.

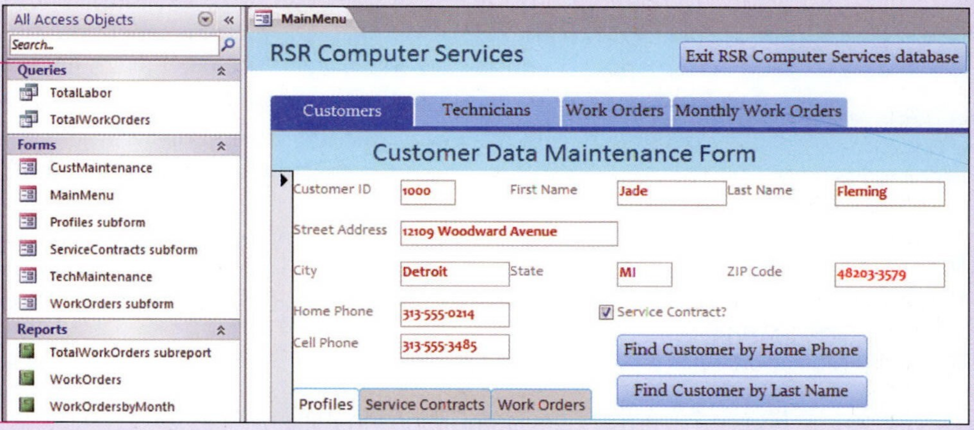

3. After reviewing the customized Navigation pane, you decide the database would be more secure if the pane were hidden when the database is opened. To do this, complete the following steps:
   a. Click the File tab and then click the Options button.
   b. With *Current Database* already selected in the left pane, click the *Display Navigation Pane* check box in the *Navigation* section to clear the check mark.
   c. Click OK.
   d. Click OK at the message box indicating you have to close and reopen the database for the option to take effect.

Step 3b

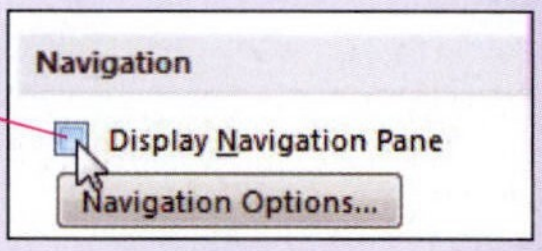

4. Close the **AL2-C7-RSRCompServ.accdb** database.
5. Reopen the **AL2-C7-RSRCompServ.accdb** database. The Navigation pane is hidden with the MainMenu form open in the work area.

Database opens with Navigation pane hidden.

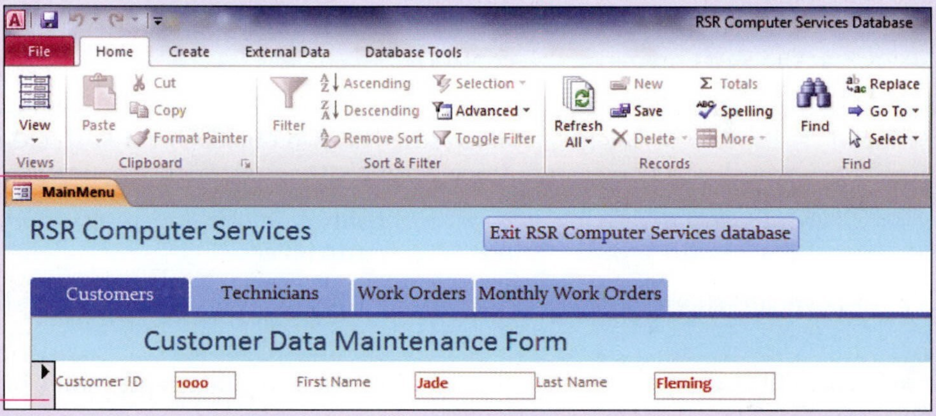

Configuring Error Checking Options

Quick Steps

Customize Error Checking Options

1. Click File tab.
2. Click Options.
3. Click *Object Designers* in left pane.
4. Scroll down to *Error checking in form and report design view* section.
5. Clear check boxes as required.
6. Click OK.

Recall from Chapter 5 that a green triangle displayed in the Report Selector button when the report width was wider than the page would allow. Clicking the error checking options button allowed you to access tools to automatically fix the report. A green triangle also appeared in a new label you added to a report to describe another control. Access flagged the label as an error because the label control object was not associated with another object.

By default, Access has error checking turned on with all error checking options active. Figure 7.8 displays the error checking option parameters that you can configure in Access. Open the Access Options dialog box and select *Object Designers* in the left pane. Scroll down the right pane to locate the *Error checking in form and report design view* section. Clear check boxes for those options for which you want to disable error checking and click OK. Table 7.1 provides a description of each option.

Figure 7.8 Error Checking Options in Access

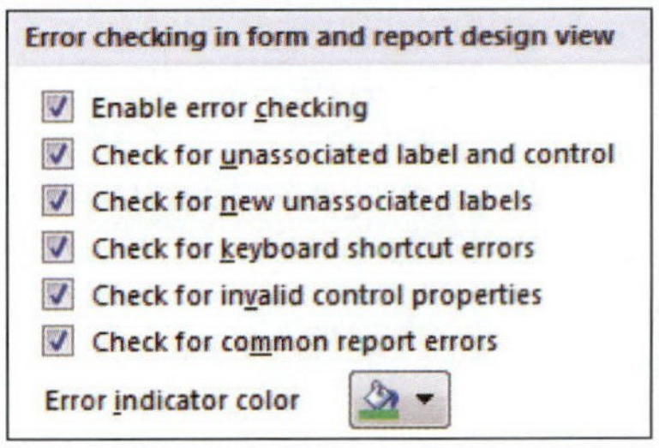

Table 7.1 Error Checking Options

Error Checking Option	*Description*
Enable error checking	Turn on or off error checking in forms and reports. An error is indicated by a green triangle in the upper left corner of a control.
Check for unassociated label and control	Access checks a selected label and text box control object to make sure the two objects are associated with each other. A Trace Error button appears if Access detects an error.
Check for new unassociated labels	New label control objects are checked for association with a text box control object.
Check for keyboard shortcut errors	Duplicate keyboard shortcuts or invalid shortcuts are flagged.
Check for invalid control properties	Invalid properties, formula expressions, or field names are flagged.
Check for common report errors	Reports are checked for errors such as invalid sort orders or reports that are wider than the selected paper size.
Error indicator color	A green triangle indicates an error in a control. Click the Color Picker button to change to a different color.

Project 3c **Customizing Error Checking Options** **Part 3 of 5**

1. With the **AL2-C7-RSRCompServ.accdb** database open, assume you frequently add label control objects to forms and reports to add explanatory text to users. You decide to customize the error checking options to prevent Access from flagging these independent label controls as errors. To do this, complete the following steps:
   a. Click the File tab and then click the Options button.
   b. Click *Object Designers* in the left pane.
   c. Scroll down the right pane to the *Error checking in form and report design view* section.
   d. Click the *Check for new unassociated labels* check box to clear the check mark.
   e. Click OK.
   f. Click OK.

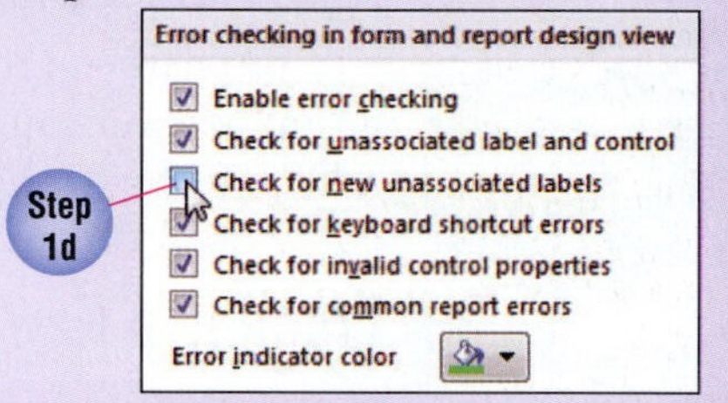

Customizing the Ribbon

You can customize the ribbon by creating a new tab. Within the new tab you can add groups and then add buttons within the groups. To customize the ribbon, click the File tab and then click the Options button. At the Access Options dialog box, click *Customize Ribbon* in the left pane to open the dialog box shown in Figure 7.9.

HINT

Consider creating a custom tab with the buttons you use on a regular basis to save mouse clicks from frequently switching tabs.

Figure 7.9 Access Options Dialog Box with *Customize Ribbon* Selected

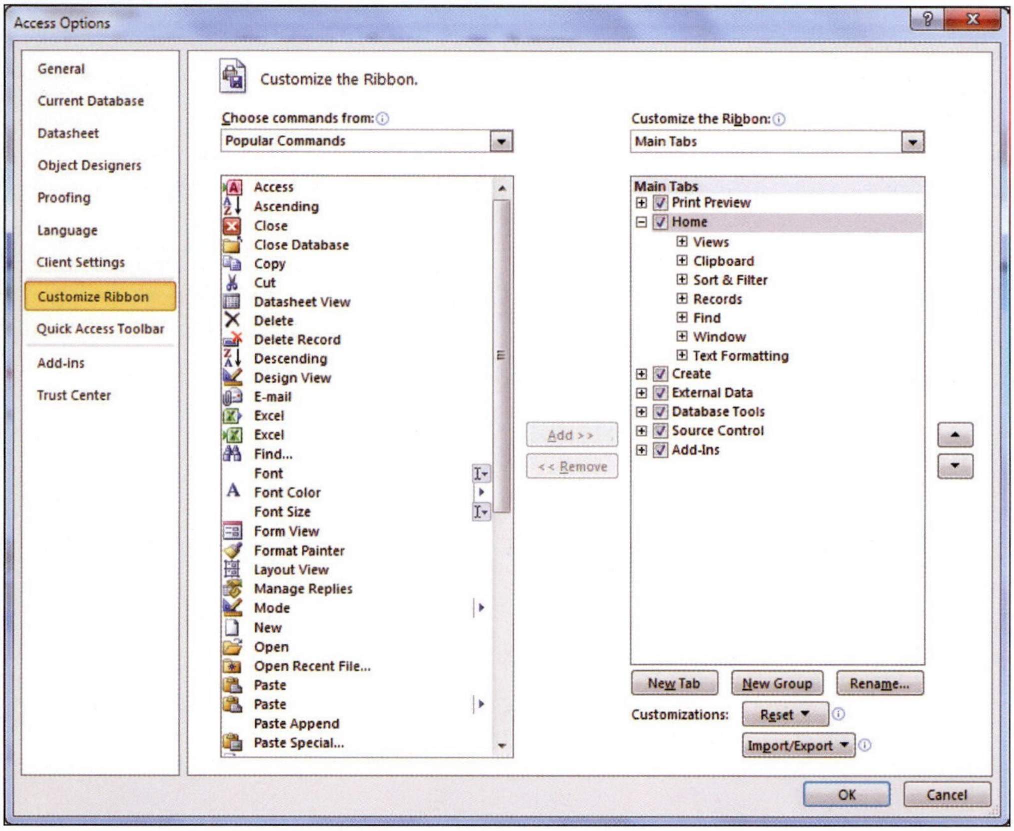

Quick Steps

Create a New Tab and Group
1. Click File tab.
2. Click Options.
3. Click *Customize Ribbon* in left pane.
4. Click tab name to precede new tab.
5. Click New Tab button.

Add New Group to Existing Tab
1. Click File tab.
2. Click Options.
3. Click *Customize Ribbon* in left pane.
4. Click tab name for which the new group is associated.
5. Click New Group button.

The commands shown in the left list box are dependent on the current option for *Choose commands from*. Click the down-pointing arrow at the right of the current option (displays *Popular Commands*) to select from a variety of command lists such as *Commands Not in the Ribbon* or *All Commands*. The tabs shown in the right list box are dependent on the current option for *Customize the Ribbon*. Click the down-pointing arrow at the right of the current option (displays *Main Tabs*) to select *All Tabs*, *Main Tabs*, or *Tool Tabs*.

You can create a new group in an existing tab and add buttons within the new group, or you can create a new tab, create a new group within the tab, and then add buttons to the new group.

Creating a New Tab

To create a new tab, click the tab name in the *Main Tabs* list box that you want the new tab positioned after and then click the New Tab button located below the *Main Tabs* list box. This inserts a new tab in the list box along with a new group below the new tab as shown in Figure 7.10. If you had selected the wrong tab name before clicking the New Tab button, you can move the new tab up or down the list box by clicking *New Tab (Custom)* and then clicking the Move Up or the Move Down buttons that display at the right side of the dialog box.

Figure 7.10 New Tab and Group Created in the Customize Ribbon Pane at the Access Options Dialog Box

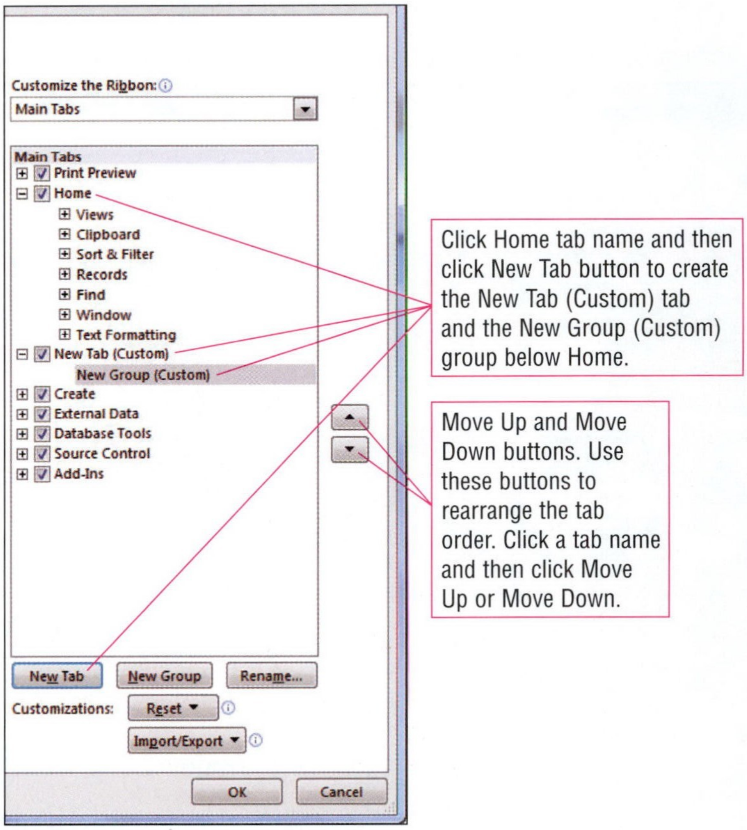

Renaming a Tab or Group

Rename a tab by clicking the tab name in the *Main Tabs* list box and then clicking the Rename button located below the *Main Tabs* list box. At the Rename dialog box, type the desired name for the tab and then press Enter or click OK. You can also display the Rename dialog box by right-clicking the tab name and then clicking *Rename* at the shortcut menu.

Complete similar steps to rename a group. The Rename dialog box for a group name or a command name contains a *Symbol* list as well as the *Display name* text box. Type the new name for the group in the *Display name* text box and press Enter or click OK. The symbols are useful to identify new buttons rather than the group name.

Adding Buttons to a Tab Group

Add commands to a tab by clicking the group name within the tab, clicking the desired command in the list box at the left, and then clicking the Add button that displays between the two list boxes. Remove commands in a similar manner. Click the command you want to remove from the tab group and then click the Remove button that displays between the two list boxes.

Quick Steps

Rename a Tab or Group
1. Click File tab.
2. Click Options.
3. Click *Customize Ribbon* in left pane.
4. Click tab or group to be renamed.
5. Click Rename button.
6. Type new name.
7. Press Enter or click OK.

Add Buttons to Group
1. Click File tab.
2. Click Options.
3. Click *Customize Ribbon* in left pane.
4. Click group name in which to insert new button.
5. Change *Choose commands from* to desired command list.
6. Scroll down and click desired command.
7. Click Add button.

Project 3d **Customizing the Ribbon** **Part 4 of 5**

1. With the **AL2-C7-RSRCompServ.accdb** database open, customize the ribbon by adding a new tab and two new groups within the tab by completing the following steps:
   a. Click the File tab and then click the Options button.
   b. Click *Customize Ribbon* in the left pane of the Access Options dialog box.
   c. Click the Home tab name in the *Main Tabs* list box located at the right of the dialog box.
   d. Click the New Tab button located below the list box. (This inserts a new tab below the Home tab and a new group below the new tab.)
   e. With *New Group (Custom)* selected below *New Tab (Custom)*, click the New Group button that displays below the list box. (This inserts another new group below the new tab.)

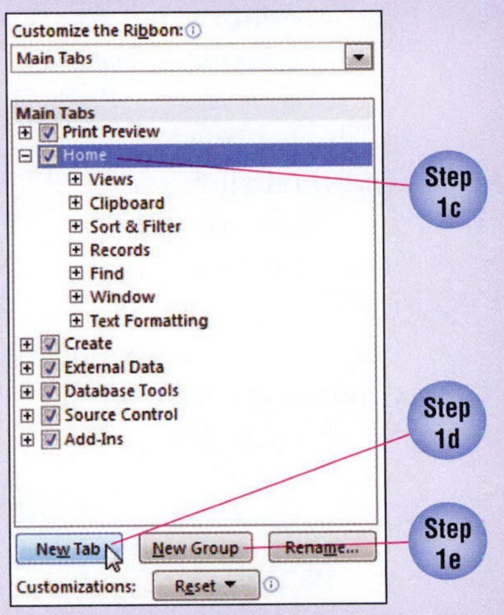

2. Rename the tab and the groups by completing the following steps:
   a. Click to select *New Tab (Custom)* in the *Main Tabs* list box.
   b. Click the Rename button that displays below the list box.
   c. At the Rename dialog box, type your first and last names and then press Enter or click OK.
   d. Click to select the first *New Group (Custom)* group name that displays below the new tab.
   e. Click the Rename button.
   f. At the Rename dialog box, type **Views** in the *Display name* text box and then press Enter or click OK. The Rename dialog box for a group or button displays symbols in addition to the *Display name* text box. You will apply a symbol to a button in a later step.
   g. Right-click the *New Group (Custom)* group name below *Views (Custom)* and then click *Rename* at the shortcut menu.
   h. Type **Records** in the *Display name* text box at the Rename dialog box and then press Enter or click OK.

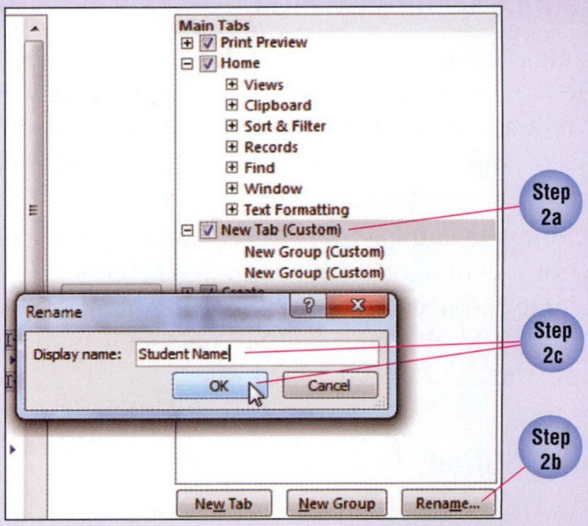

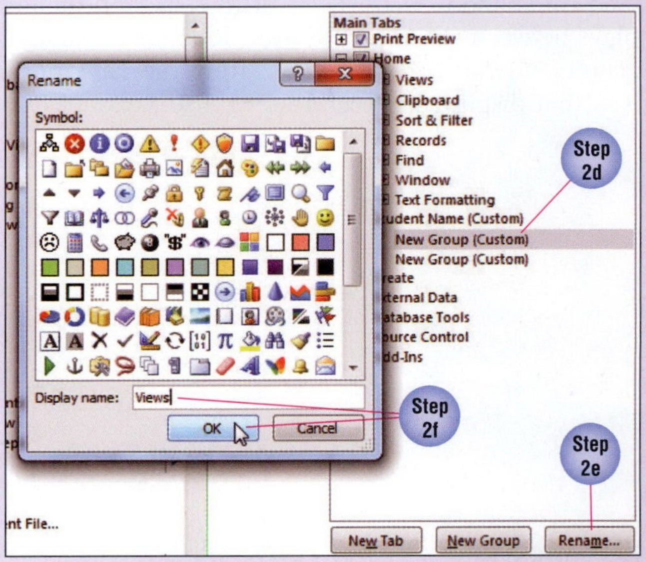

3. Add buttons to the Views (Custom) group by completing the following steps:
   a. Click to select *Views (Custom)* in the *Main Tabs* list box.
   b. With *Popular Commands* the current option for *Choose commands from*, click *Form View* in the list box and then click the Add button located between the two list boxes. This inserts the command below the Views (Custom) group name.

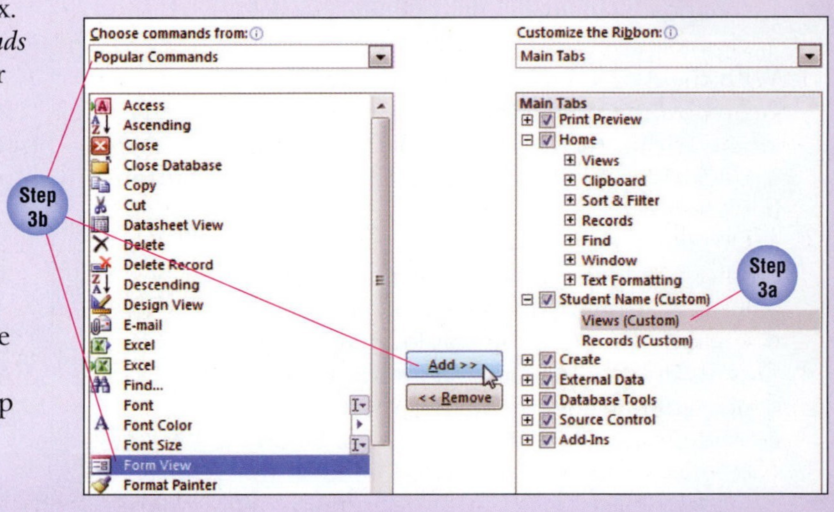

c. Scroll down the *Popular Commands* list box, click Print Preview, and then click the Add button.
d. Click *Report View* in the *Popular Commands* list box and then click the Add button.
e. If necessary, scroll to the bottom of the *Popular Commands* list box, click *View*, and then click the Add button.

4. Add buttons to the Records (Custom) group by completing the following steps:
   a. Click to select *Records (Custom)* in the *Main Tabs* list box.
   b. Click the down-pointing arrow at the right of the *Choose commands from* list box (currently displays *Popular Commands*) and then click *All Commands* at the drop-down list.
   c. Scroll down the *All Commands* list box (the list displays alphabetically), click *Delete Record*, and then click the Add button.
   d. Scroll down the *All Commands* list box, click *Find*, and then click the Add button.
   e. Scroll down the *All Commands* list box, click *New* (choose the *New* option that displays with the ScreenTip *Home Tab | Records | New (GoToNewRecord))*, and then click the Add button.
   f. Scroll down the *All Commands* list box, click *Sort Ascending*, and then click the Add button.
   g. If necessary, scroll down the *All Commands* list box, click *Spelling*, and then click the Add button.

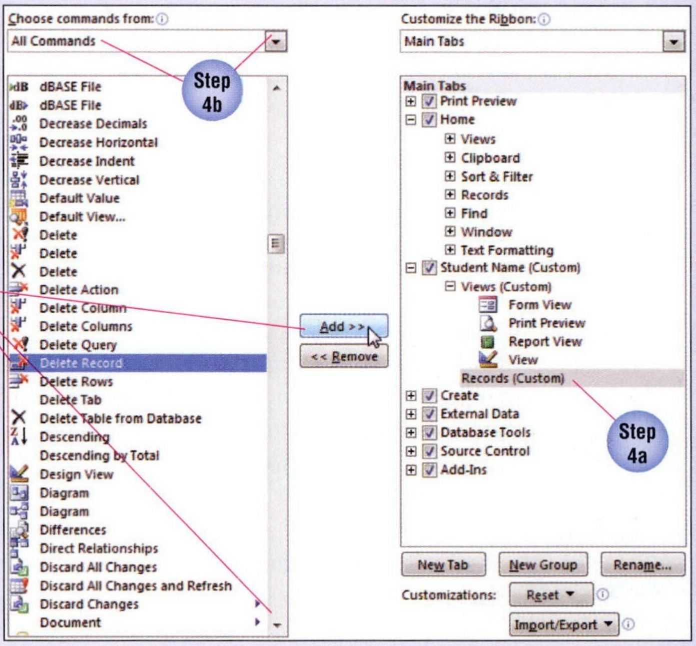

5. Change the symbol for the Spelling button by completing the following steps:
   a. Right-click *Spelling* below *Records (Custom)* in the *Main Tabs* list box.
   b. Click *Rename* at the shortcut menu.
   c. At the Rename dialog box, click the blue book icon in the *Symbol* list box (fourth icon in eighth row) and then click OK.

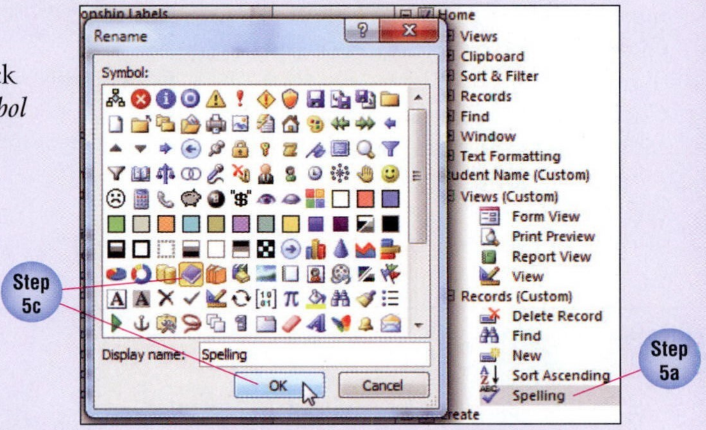

6. Click OK to close the Access Options dialog box.
7. Click OK at the message that displays saying that you have to close and reopen the database for the option to take effect.
8. Use buttons in the custom tab to change views and start a spelling check in a form by completing the following steps:
   a. Click the Technicians tab along the top of the MainMenu form.

b. Click the custom tab with your name and then click the Print Preview button in the Views group.
c. Click the Form View button in the Views group to switch back to the form.
d. Click in the *Last Name* field and then click the Spelling button.
e. Click the Cancel button at the Spelling dialog box.

9. Insert a screen image of the database window showing the custom tab in a new Microsoft Word document using either Print Screen with Paste or the Windows Snipping tool (Start button, *All Programs*, *Accessories*). Type your name a few lines below the screen image and add any other identifying information as instructed (for example, the chapter number and project number).
10. Save the Microsoft Word document and name it **AL2-C7-P3-CustomRibbon.docx**.
11. Print **AL2-C7-P3-CustomRibbon.docx** and then exit Word.

Resetting the Ribbon

Restore the original ribbon by clicking the Reset button that displays below the *Main Tabs* list box in the Access Options dialog box with the Customize Ribbon pane selected. Clicking the Reset button displays two options—*Reset only selected Ribbon tab* and *Reset all customizations*. Click *Reset all customizations* to restore the ribbon to its original settings and then click Yes at the Microsoft Office message box that displays the message *Delete all Ribbon and Quick Access Toolbar customizations for this program?*

Project 3e Restoring the Ribbon — Part 5 of 5

1. Open the Access Options dialog box.
2. If necessary, click *Customize Ribbon* in the left pane.
3. Click the Reset button located below the Main Tabs list box.
4. Click *Reset all customizations* at the drop-down list.
5. Click Yes at the Microsoft Office message box that appears.
6. Click OK to close the Access Options dialog box.
7. Click OK at the message that displays saying that you have to close and reopen the database for the option to take effect.

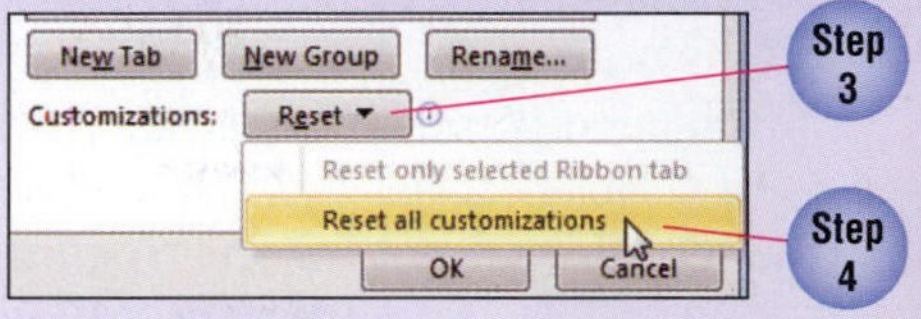

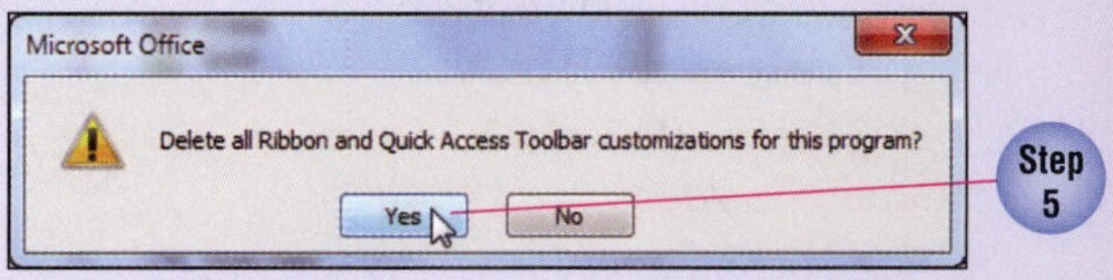

Project 4 Secure a Database — 2 Parts

You will secure a database by making an ACCDE file. You will also explore the default settings in the Trust Center.

Creating an ACCDE Database File

In Chapter 6 you learned how to split a database into two files to create a front-end and a back-end database. This method allowed you to improve performance and protect the table objects from changes by separating the tables from the queries, forms, and reports. Another method with which you can protect an Access database is to create an ACCDE file. In an ACCDE file, end users are prevented from making changes to the design of objects. An Access database stored as an ACCDE file is a locked-down version of the database that does not provide access to Design view or Layout view. In addition, if the database contains any Visual Basic for Application (VBA) code, the code cannot be modified or changed.

To save an Access database as an ACCDE file, click the File tab and then click the Save & Publish tab. Click *Make ACCDE* in the *Advanced* section of the Save Database As pane located at the right side of the Save & Publish tab Backstage view. Next, click the Save As button located at the bottom of the Save Database As pane to open the Save As dialog box. Navigate to the drive and/or folder in which to save the database, type the desired file name in the *File Name* text box, and click the Save button. Once the file is created, move the original database in .accdb format to a secure location and provide end users with the path to the .accde file for daily use.

Quick Steps

Make ACCDE File

1. Open database.
2. Click File tab.
3. Click Save & Publish tab.
4. Click *Make ACCDE*.
5. Click Save As button.
6. Navigate to required drive and/or folder.
7. Type name in *File name* text box.
8. Click Save button.

Project 4a **Making an ACCDE Database File** **Part 1 of 2**

1. With the **AL2-C7-RSRCompServ.accdb** database open, create an ACCDE file by completing the following steps:
   a. Click the File tab and then click the Save & Publish tab.
   b. Click *Make ACCDE* in the *Advanced* section of the Save Database As pane located at the right of the Save & Publish tab Backstage view.
   c. Click the Save As button located at the bottom of the Save Database As pane.

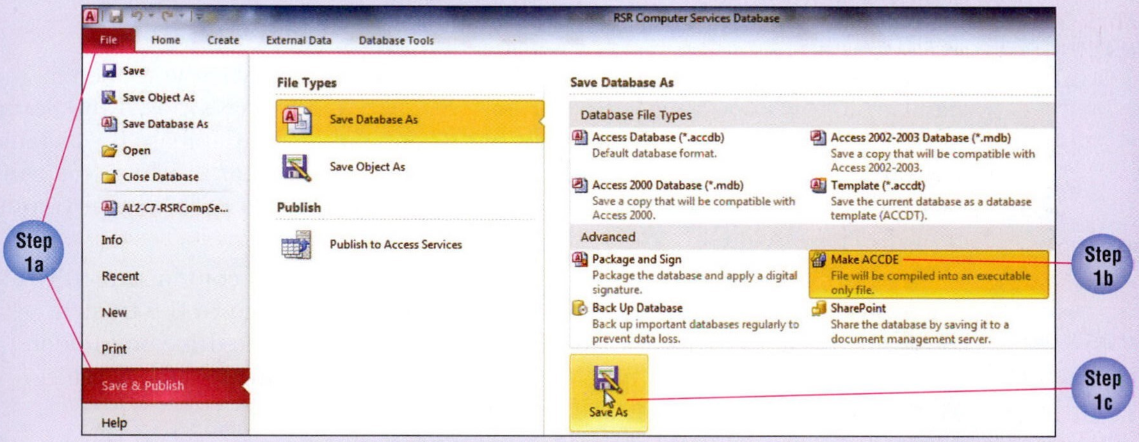

   d. At the Save As dialog box with the default location the Access2010L2C7 folder on your storage medium and ***AL2-C7-RSRCompServ.accde*** the default name in the *File name* text box, click the Save button.

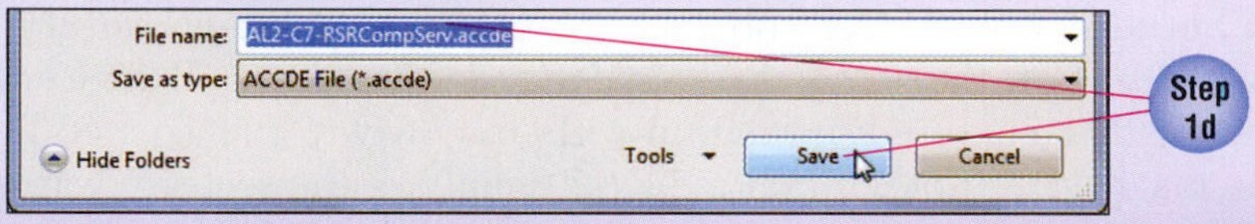

2. Close the **AL2-C7-RSRCompServ.accdb** database.
3. Open the **AL2-C7-RSRCompServ.accde** database.
4. At the Microsoft Access Security Notice dialog box informing you the file might contain unsafe content, click the Open button.

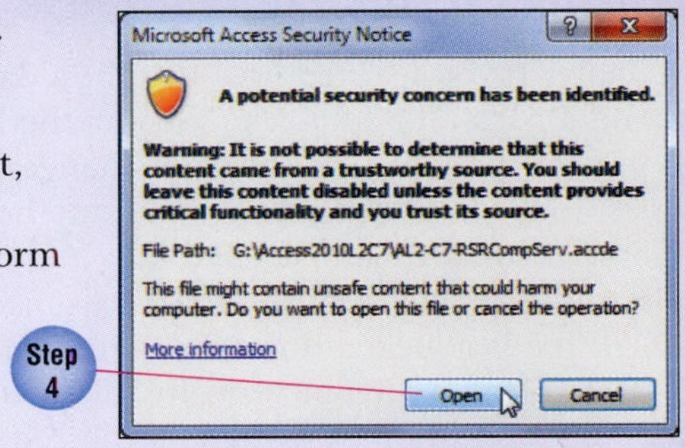

5. With Customers the active tab in the MainMenu form and the Customer Data Maintenance Form open in Form view, click the Home tab if necessary. Notice the View button in the Views group is dimmed.
6. Click the Monthly Work Orders tab in the MainMenu form to view the Work Orders by Month report. Notice the View button in the Home tab is still dimmed. Also notice only one view button is available in the View group located at the right end of the Status bar.

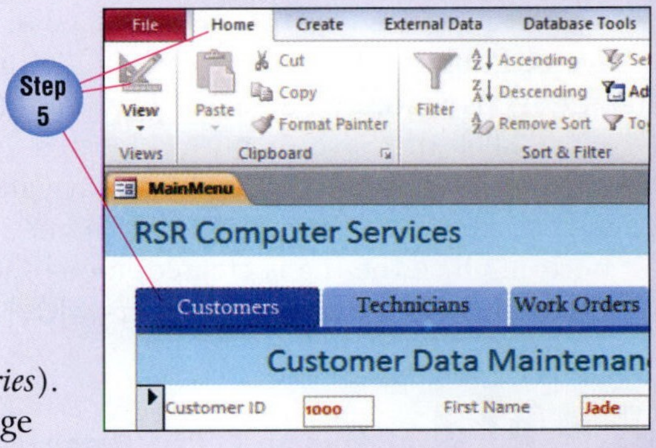

7. Insert a screen image of the database window in a new Microsoft Word document using either Print Screen with Paste or the Windows Snipping tool (Start button, *All Programs*, *Accessories*). Type your name a few lines below the screen image and add any other identifying information as instructed.
8. Save the Microsoft Word document and name it **AL2-C7-P4-ACCDEWindow.docx**.
9. Print **AL2-C7-P4-ACCDEWindow.docx** and then exit Word.
10. Close the **AL2-C7-RSRCompServ.accde** database.

Quick Steps

View Trust Center Options
1. Click File tab.
2. Click Options.
3. Click *Trust Center* in left pane.
4. Click Trust Center Settings button.
5. Click desired trust center category in left pane.
6. View and/or modify required options.
7. Click OK twice.

HINT

Changing the macro security setting in Access does not affect the macro security setting in other Microsoft programs such as Word or Excel.

Viewing Trust Center Settings for Access

In Access, the Trust Center is set to block unsafe content when you open a database file. As you have been working with Access, you have closed the Security Warning that appears in the message bar when you open a database by clicking the Enable Content button. Access provides the Trust Center in which you can view and/or modify the security options that are in place to protect your computer from malicious content.

The Trust Center maintains a *Trusted Locations* list with content stored within the location considered a trusted source. You can add a path to the trusted locations list and Access will treat any files opened from the drive and folder as safe. Databases opened from trusted locations do not display the Security Warning in the message bar and do not have content blocked.

Before a database can have macros enabled, the Trust Center checks for a valid and current digital signature signed by an entity that is stored in the *Trusted Publishers* list. The *Trusted Publishers* list is maintained by you on the computer you are using. A trusted publisher is added to the list when you enable content from an authenticated source and click the option to *Trust all content from this publisher*. Depending on the active macro security setting, if the Trust Center cannot match the digital signature information with an entity in the Trusted Publishers list or the macro does not contain a digital signature, the security warning displays in the message bar.

The default Macro Security option is *Disable all macros with notification*. Table 7.2 describes the four options for macro security. In some cases, you may decide to change the default macro security setting by opening the Trust Center dialog box. You will explore the Trust Center in Project 4b.

Table 7.2 Macro Security Settings for Databases Not Opened from a Trusted Location

Macro Setting	*Description*
Disable all macros without notification	All macros are disabled; security alerts will not appear.
Disable all macros with notification	All macros are disabled; security alert appears with the option to enable content if you trust the source of the file. This is the default setting.
Disable all macros except digitally signed macros	A macro that does not contain a digital signature is disabled; security alerts do not appear. If the macro is digitally signed by a publisher in your Trusted Publishers list, the macro is allowed to run. If the macro is digitally signed by a publisher not in your Trusted Publishers list, you receive a security alert.
Enable all macros (not recommended, potentially dangerous code can run)	All macros are allowed; security alerts do not appear.

Project 4b Exploring Trust Center Settings Part 2 of 2

1. At the New tab Backstage view, explore the current settings in the Trust Center by completing the following steps:
   a. Click the Options button.
   b. Click *Trust Center* in the left pane of the Access Options dialog box.

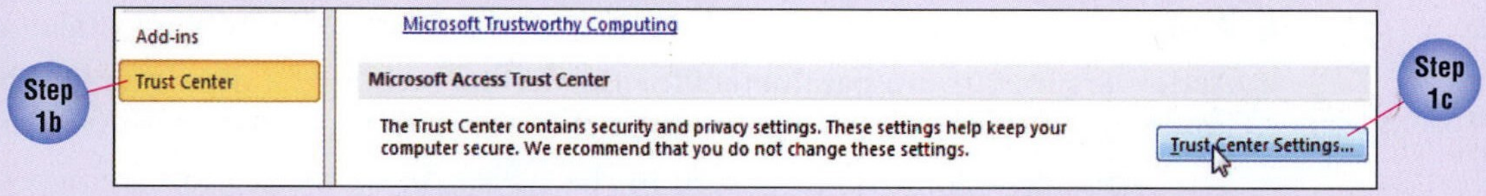

   c. Click the Trust Center Settings button in the *Microsoft Access Trust Center* section.
   d. At the Trust Center dialog box, click *Macro Settings* in the left pane.
   e. Review the options in the *Macro Settings* section. Note which option is active on the computer you are using. The default option is *Disable all macros with notification*. ***Note: The security setting on the computer you are using may be different than the default option. Do not change the security setting without the permission of your instructor.***

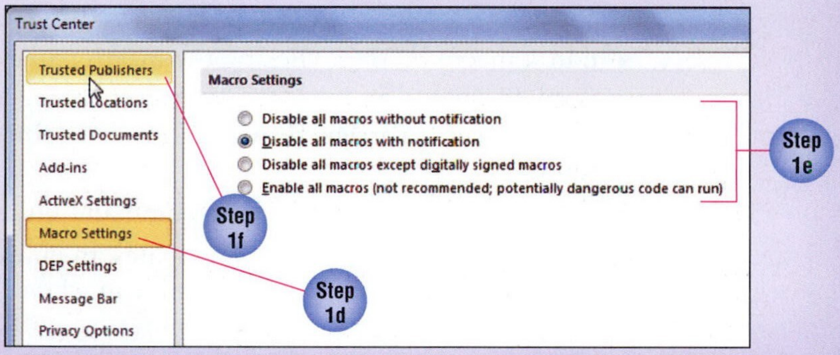

f. Click *Trusted Publishers* in the left pane. If any publishers have been added to the list on the computer you are using, the names of the entities will be shown in the list box. If the list box is empty, no trusted publishers have been added.
g. Click *Trusted Locations* in the left pane. Review the path and description of any folders added to the trusted locations list. By default, Access adds the folder created upon installation of Microsoft Access that contains the wizard database templates provided by Microsoft. Additional folders may also appear that have been added by a system administrator or network administrator.
h. Click OK to close the Trust Center dialog box.

2. Click OK to close the Access Options dialog box.

In this chapter you have learned some techniques to automate, customize, and secure an Access database. As you gain more experience with Access, explore further Access options to customize the environment that allow you to change behavior of actions and keys while editing. Also consider experimenting with other macro actions such as the OpenQuery action to automate queries.

Chapter Summary

- A macro is used to automate actions within a database such as opening a form or report.
- Click the Create tab and click the Macro button in the Macros & Code group to open a Macro Builder window in which you create the actions you want to store.
- Add a macro action using the *Add New Action* list box or the Action Catalog pane.
- Action arguments are parameters for the action such as the object name, the mode in which the object opens, and other restrictions placed on the action.
- The available arguments displayed in the *Action Arguments* section are dependent on the active action.
- Run a macro by clicking the Run button in the Macro Builder window or by double-clicking the macro name in the Navigation pane.
- A macro can also be created by dragging and dropping an object name from the Navigation pane to the *Add New Action* list box in the Macro Builder window.
- Edit a macro by right-clicking the macro name and clicking *Design View* at the shortcut menu.
- A macro can be assigned to a button in a form to provide single-click access to run the macro.
- Use the Button tool to create a command button in a form.
- The Command Button Wizard creates an embedded macro for you that instructs Access on which macro to run when the button is clicked. You can view the macro by opening the command button's Property Sheet, clicking the Event tab, and then clicking the Build button in the *On Click* property box.

- A macro can be converted to Visual Basic for Applications code by opening the macro in the Macro Builder window and then clicking the Convert Macros to Visual Basic button in the Tools group of the Macro Tools Design tab.
- A Navigation form with tabs along the top, left, or right is used as a menu. Users can open the forms and reports in the database by clicking a tab rather than using the Navigation pane.
- Click the Create tab and then click the Navigation button to create a Navigation form. Choose the desired form style at the drop-down list and then drag and drop form and/or report names from the Navigation pane to *[Add New]* in the tab bar.
- A form can be set to display automatically whenever the database is opened at the *Display Form* list box in the Access Options dialog box with *Current Database* selected in the left pane.
- Change the title that appears in the Title bar for the active database by typing an entry in the *Application Title* text box at the Access Options dialog box with *Current Database* selected in the left pane.
- You can set options for the Navigation pane such as hiding individual objects or groups of objects at the Navigation Options dialog box.
- Hide the Navigation pane by clearing the *Display Navigation Pane* check box at the Access Options dialog box with *Current Database* selected in the left pane.
- Change default error checking options in the Access Options dialog box with *Object Designers* selected in the left pane.
- You can customize the ribbon by creating a new tab, creating a new group within the new tab, and then adding buttons within the new group.
- To customize the ribbon, open the Access Options dialog box and click *Customize Ribbon* in the left pane.
- Create a new ribbon tab by clicking the tab name that will precede the new tab and then clicking the New Tab button. A new group is automatically added with the new tab.
- Rename a custom tab by clicking to select the tab name, clicking the Rename button, typing a new name, and then pressing Enter or clicking OK. Rename a group using a similar process.
- Add buttons within a group by clicking the group name, selecting the desired command in the commands list box and then clicking the Add button located between the two list boxes.
- Restore the ribbon to the default by clicking the Reset button located near the bottom right of the Access Options dialog box with *Customize Ribbon* selected and then clicking *Reset all customizations* at the drop-down list.
- Create an ACCDE database file at the Save & Publish tab Backstage view to create a locked-down version of the database in which objects are prevented from being opened in Design view or Layout view.
- Open the Access Options dialog box, click *Trust Center* in the left pane, and then click the Trust Center Settings button to view and/or modify trust center options.

Commands Review

FEATURE	RIBBON TAB, GROUP	BUTTON
Convert Macros to Visual Basic	Macro Tools Design, Tools	
Create ACCDE file	File, Save & Publish	
Create command button	Form Design Tools Design, Controls	
Create macro	Create, Macros & Code	
Customize Access options	File, Options	
Customize Navigation pane	File, Options	
Navigation Form	Create, Forms	
Run macro	Macro Tools Design, Tools	

Concepts Check Test Your Knowledge

Completion: In the space provided at the right, indicate the correct term, command, or number.

1. This is the name of the window in which you create actions with associated action arguments for a macro. ____________________
2. Add a macro action at the *Add New Action* list box or in this pane. ____________________
3. To cause Access to display the Find dialog box in a macro, choose this action in the *Add New Action* list box. ____________________
4. Drag a form name from the Navigation pane to the *Add New Action* list box to insert this macro action. ____________________
5. Edit a macro by right-clicking the macro name in the Navigation pane and selecting this option at the shortcut menu. ____________________
6. At the first Command Button Wizard dialog box, click this option in the *Categories* list box to locate the *Run Macro* action. ____________________
7. This type of macro is not shown as a macro object within the Navigation pane. ____________________

8. When a macro has been converted to Visual Basic, Access opens this window. ____________________

9. This type of form is used to create a menu to allow end users to select forms and reports by clicking tabs. ____________________

10. Open this dialog box to specify a display form to open whenever the database is opened. ____________________

11. Hide the Tables group in the Navigation pane by opening this dialog box. ____________________

12. Click this option in the left pane at the Access Options dialog box to change an error checking option. ____________________

13. Click this option in the left pane at the Access Options dialog box to create a custom ribbon tab. ____________________

14. Save a database as this type of file to disallow Design view and Layout view for the database objects. ____________________

15. View and/or change the macro security setting at this dialog box. ____________________

Skills Check Assess Your Performance

Assessment

1 CREATE AND RUN MACROS

1. Open the database named **AL2-C7-VantageVideos.accdb** and enable content.
2. Create the following macros. Run each macro to make sure the macro works properly and then close the macro.
   a. A macro named RPTWebOrders that opens the report named WebOrdersByProd. Use the macro action *OpenReport*. In the *Action Arguments* section, change the *View* argument to *Print Preview*.
   b. A macro named RPTWebSales to open the WebSalesByDate report in Report view.
   c. A macro named FORMCustOrd that opens the WebCustOrders form in Form view, activates the control named *LastName*, and then opens the Find dialog box. Test the macro using the customer last name *Gallagher*.
3. Open the RPTWebOrders macro in Design view. Click the File tab, click the Print tab, and then click Print at the Backstage view. At the Print Macro Definition dialog box, clear check marks as necessary until only the *Actions and Arguments* check box is checked and then click OK. Close the Macro Builder window.
4. Print the FORMCustOrd macro and the RPTWebSales macro by completing a step similar to Step 3.

Assessment 2

EDIT A MACRO AND ASSIGN MACROS TO COMMAND BUTTONS

1. With the **AL2-C7-VantageVideos.accdb** database open, edit the FORMCustOrd macro to remove the *OpenForm* action. Save and close the revised macro. Rename the FORMCustOrd macro in the Navigation pane to FINDLastName.
2. Create command buttons to run macros as follows:
   a. Open the WebCustOrders form in Design view and create a command button at the right side of the *Form Header* section that runs the FINDLastName macro. You determine appropriate text to display on the face of the button, and a name for the command button. Save and close the form.
   b. Open the WebProducts form in Design view and create two command buttons as follows. Place each button at the bottom of the *Detail* section. You determine appropriate text to display on the face of the button and a name for the command button. Save and close the form.
      - A button at the left side of the form that runs the RPTWebOrders macro.
      - A button at the right side of the form that runs the RPTWebSales macro.
3. Open each form, test the button(s) to make sure the correct form or report displays, and then close each form or report.
4. Open the WebCustOrders form in Form view. Insert a screen image of the database window in a new Microsoft Word document using either Print Screen with Paste or the Windows Snipping tool. Next, switch back to Access and open the WebProducts form. Insert a screen image of the database window below the first image in the Microsoft Word document. Type your name a few lines below the screen images and add any other identifying information as instructed. Save the Microsoft Word document and name it **AL2-C7-A2-FormWindows.docx**. Print **AL2-C7-A2-FormWindows.docx** and then exit Word.
5. Close both forms.

Assessment 3

CREATE A NAVIGATION FORM AND CONFIGURE DATABASE OPTIONS

1. With the **AL2-C7-VantageVideos.accdb** database open, create a Navigation form using the following information.
   a. Use the *Vertical Tabs, Left style*.
   b. Add the WebCustOrders form as the first tab.
   c. Add the WebProducts form as the second tab.
   d. Add the WebOrdersByProd report as the third tab.
   e. Add the WebSalesByDate report as the fourth tab.
   f. Save the form, naming it *MainMenu*.
2. In Layout view or Design view, edit the MainMenu Navigation form as follows:
   a. Delete the logo container object.
   b. Edit the text in the Title control object to *Vantage Classic Videos* and resize the object so that the right edge of the control ends just after the title text. In other words, the width of the control object is only as wide as it needs to be in order to display the title text.
   c. Change the Caption property for the first tab to *Customer Orders*.
   d. Change the Caption property for the second tab to *Classic Products*.
   e. Change the Caption property for the third tab to *Orders by Product*.
   f. Change the Caption property for the fourth tab to *Sales by Month*.

3. Create a new macro named *ExitDB* that will exit Access saving all objects. Assign the macro to a command button positioned in the *Form Header* section of the MainMenu form. You determine appropriate text to display on the face of the button and a name for the command button. Save and close the MainMenu form.
4. Set the MainMenu form as the startup display form.
5. Create an application title for the database with the text **Vantage Classic Videos Web Orders Database**.
6. Hide the Navigation pane.
7. Turn on the *Check for new unassociated labels* error checking option. ***Note: Skip this step if you did not complete Project 3c where this option was turned off.***
8. Close and reopen the database to test your startup options. Click each tab in the MainMenu form to make sure the correct form or report displays.
9. With the database open at the MainMenu form, insert a screen image of the database window in a new Microsoft Word document using either Print Screen with Paste or the Windows Snipping tool. Type your name a few lines below the screen image and add any other identifying information as instructed. Save the Microsoft Word document and name it **AL2-C7-A3-MainMenu.docx**. Print **AL2-C7-A3-MainMenu.docx** and then exit Word.

Assessment 4

SECURE THE DATABASE

1. With the **AL2-C7-VantageVideos.accdb** database open, save a copy of the database in the same folder and using the same name as an ACCDE file.
2. Close the **AL2-C7-VantageVideos.accdb** database.
3. Open the **AL2-C7-VantageVideos7.accde** database.
4. Insert a screen image of the database window in a new Microsoft Word document using either Print Screen with Paste or the Windows Snipping tool. Type your name a few lines below the screen image and add any other identifying information as instructed. Save the Microsoft Word document and name it **AL2-C7-A4-VantageACCDE.docx**. Print **AL2-C7-A4-VantageACCDE.docx** and then exit Word.
5. Use the exit button in the MainMenu form to exit the database.

Visual Benchmark Demonstrate Your Proficiency

AUTOMATE AND CUSTOMIZE RESERVATION DATABASE

1. Open **AL2-C7-PawsParadise.accdb** and enable content.
2. Review the database window shown in Figure 7.11. Create the Navigation form as shown including the command buttons and required macros assigned to the command buttons. Set the required startup and Navigation pane options.
3. Save a copy of the database as an ACCDE file.
4. Close the **AL2-C7-PawsParadise.accdb** database
5. Open the **AL2-C7-PawsParadise.accde** database. Check with your instructor for instructions on whether you need to print the macros and a screen image of the database window.

Figure 7.11 Visual Benchmark

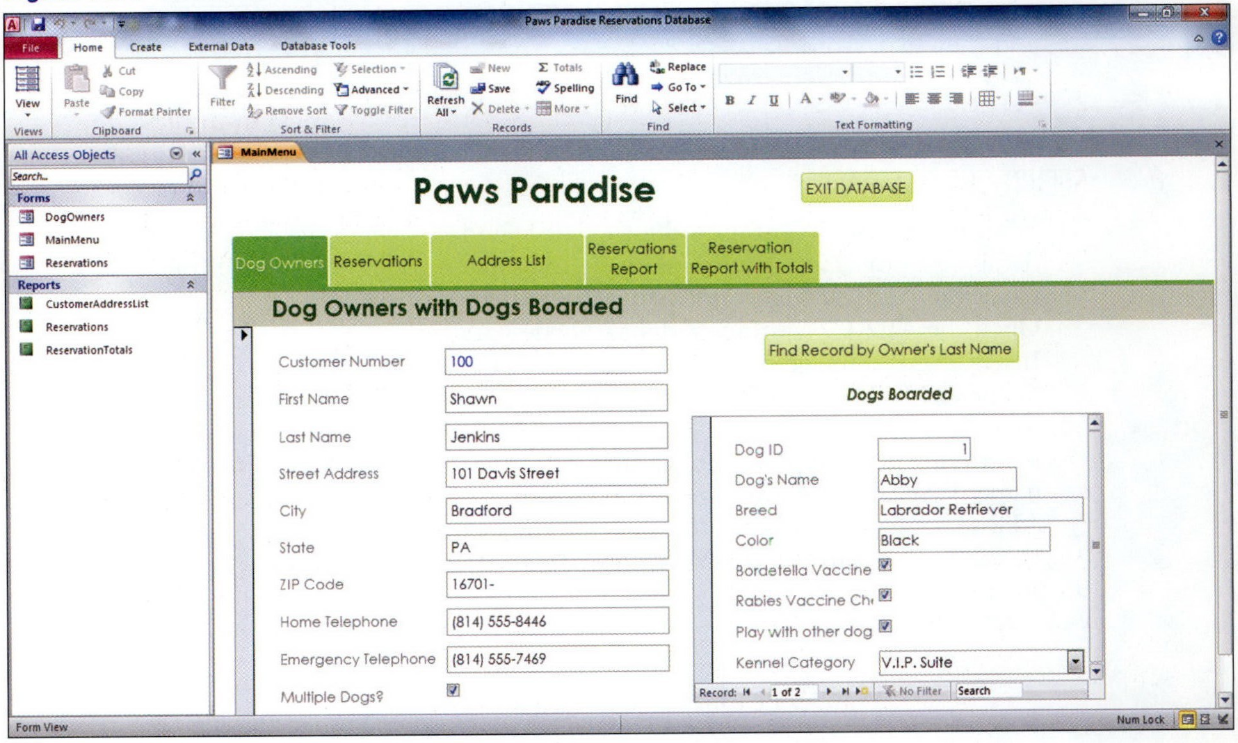

Case Study Apply Your Skills

Part 1

As you near completion of your work as an intern at Hillsdale Realty, you decide to automate the database to make the application easier for the next intern to use. Open **AL2-C7-HillsdaleRealty.accdb** and enable content. Create three macros to accomplish the tasks in the bulleted list. You determine appropriate macro names.

- Move to the *AgentLName* control and open the Find dialog box.
- Move to the *ListingNo* control and open the Find dialog box.
- Exit the database saving all objects.

Assign the first macro as a command button in the Agents form. Assign the second macro as a command button in the ListingsAndSales form. In both forms, you determine where to position the button, the text to display on the button, and the button name. Check with your instructor for instructions on whether you need to print the macros and a screen image of the Agents form and the ListingsAndSales form showing each command button.

Part 2

Create a navigation form to be used as a main menu to display the Agents form, the ListingsAndSales form, and the two reports. Set the form to display automatically when the database is opened. Add an appropriate application title for the database and hide the tables, queries, and macros in the Navigation pane. Assign the macro to exit the database as a button in the main menu form. Edit the main menu form as necessary to show descriptive labels in the tabs and apply other formatting enhancements as necessary. Close and reopen the database to test your startup options. Test each menu tab to make sure each option works. Check with your instructor for instructions on whether you need to print a screen image of the database window with the main menu form displayed.

Part 3

Help

Open a Help window and search for help content using the phrase **access 2010 security** in the Search text box. Click the link to the article titled Introduction to Access 2010 security and then click the link to Package, sign, and distribute an Access 2010 database at the Introduction to Access 2010 security page. Read the information in Help and then compose a memo in your own words addressed to your instructor using Microsoft Word that provides the following answers.

- What is the file extension for an Access Deployment file?
- Why would you package and sign a database file?
- What is applied to the packaged file to indicate that the content has not been altered since the database was packaged?
- Where is the Package and Sign feature located in Microsoft Office Access 2010?
- How many databases can be added to a package?

Save the memo in Word and name it **AL2-C7-CS-P3-PackageMemo.docx**. Print the memo and then exit Word.

Microsoft® Access®

CHAPTER 8

Integrating Access Data

PERFORMANCE OBJECTIVES

Upon successful completion of Chapter 8, you will be able to:

- **Import data from another Access database**
- **Link to a table in another Access database**
- **Determine when to import versus link from external sources**
- **Reset or refresh links using Linked Table Manager**
- **Import data from a text file**
- **Save import specifications**
- **Export data in an Access table or query as a text file**
- **Save and run export specifications**
- **Save an object as an XPS document**
- **Summarize data by using a PivotTable**
- **Summarize data by using a PivotChart**

SNAP Training and Assessment. Simplified.

Tutorials

Integrating data between the applications within the Microsoft Office suite is easily accommodated with buttons in the External Data tab to import from Word and Excel and export to Word and Excel. Data is able to be exchanged between the Microsoft programs with formatting and data structure maintained. In some cases, however, you may need to exchange data between Access and a non-Microsoft program. In this chapter you will learn how to integrate data between individual Access database files and how to import and export in a text file format recognized by nearly all applications. You will also learn how to publish an Access object as an XPS file, which is an XML document format, and summarize data using a PivotTable and PivotChart. Model answers for this chapter's projects appear on the following pages.

Access

Access2010L2C8

Note: Before beginning the projects, copy to your storage medium the Access2010L2C8 subfolder from the Access2010L2 folder on the CD that accompanies this textbook and then make Access2010L2C8 the active folder.

Technician Maintenance

Technician ID	01
SSN	000-45-5368
First Name	Pat
Last Name	Hynes
Street Address	206-31 Woodland Street
City	Detroit
State	MI
ZIP Code	48202-1138
Home Phone	313-555-6874
Cell Phone	313-555-6412
Certifications	Cisco CCNP, CompTIA A+, Microsoft MCTS
Operating Systems	Linux, Unix, Windows 7, Windows XP
Network Specialist?	☑
Design Websites?	☐
Programming?	☑

RSRTechHrsSep2012 11/21/2012

ID	TechID	Date	HoursBilled
1	1	9/7/2012	38.5
2	2	9/7/2012	32.75
3	3	9/7/2012	28.75
4	4	9/7/2012	25
5	5	9/7/2012	39.5
6	6	9/7/2012	41.5
7	7	9/7/2012	36.75
8	8	9/7/2012	32.5
9	9	9/7/2012	30
10	10	9/7/2012	28.5
11	11	9/7/2012	22.5
12	1	9/14/2012	40
13	2	9/14/2012	38.75
14	3	9/14/2012	36
15	4	9/14/2012	34.5
16	5	9/14/2012	38.5
17	6	9/14/2012	32.75
18	7	9/14/2012	31
19	8	9/14/2012	30
20	9	9/14/2012	29
21	10	9/14/2012	28.75
22	11	9/14/2012	25
23	1	9/21/2012	26.75
24	2	9/21/2012	28.75
25	3	9/21/2012	32
26	4	9/21/2012	38.75
27	5	9/21/2012	41
28	6	9/21/2012	44
29	7	9/21/2012	38.5
30	8	9/21/2012	36
31	9	9/21/2012	38.5
32	10	9/21/2012	32.5
33	11	9/21/2012	40
34	1	9/28/2012	41.5
35	2	9/28/2012	38.75
36	3	9/28/2012	36.5
37	4	9/28/2012	40.25
38	5	9/28/2012	40.5
39	6	9/28/2012	38.5
40	7	9/28/2012	36
41	8	9/28/2012	35.5
42	9	9/28/2012	34
43	10	9/28/2012	38.75
44	11	9/28/2012	40

Page 1

Project 1 Import Data from External Sources

Project 1b, Imported TechMaintenance Form

Project 1d, Imported RSRTechHoursSep2012 Table

```
                        TotalWorkOrders.txt
WO,CustID,Descr,ServDate,Total Labor,Parts,Total Work Order
65012,1000,Bi-annual computer maintenance,9/7/2012 0:00:00,37.50,$10.15,$47.65
65013,1000,Replace keyboard,9/10/2012 0:00:00,14.25,$42.75,$57.00
65014,1005,Replace power supply,9/10/2012 0:00:00,52.50,$62.77,$115.27
65015,1008,Restore operating system,9/11/2012 0:00:00,67.50,$0.00,$67.50
65016,1010,Install upgraded video card,9/11/2012 0:00:00,30.00,$48.75,$78.75
65017,1015,Replace DVD drive,9/15/2012 0:00:00,16.87,$55.87,$72.75
65018,1020,Upgrade Office suite,9/15/2012 0:00:00,22.50,$0.00,$22.50
65019,1025,Upgrade to Windows 7,9/17/2012 0:00:00,75.00,$0.00,$75.00
65020,1030,Troubleshoot noisy fan,9/17/2012 0:00:00,33.75,$62.77,$96.52
65021,1035,Customer has blue screen upon boot,9/18/2012 0:00:00,97.50,$0.00,$97.50
65022,1040,Customer reports screen is fuzzy,9/22/2012 0:00:00,45.00,$55.47,$100.47
65023,1045,Upgrade RAM,9/23/2012 0:00:00,37.50,$62.50,$100.00
65024,1005,Install malware protection,9/24/2012 0:00:00,15.50,$75.50,$91.00
65025,1010,Troubleshoot hard drive noise,9/28/2012 0:00:00,45.00,$0.00,$45.00
65026,1025,Upgrade memory,9/29/2012 0:00:00,22.50,$75.75,$98.25
65027,1010,Replace hard drive,10/2/2012 0:00:00,45.00,$375.50,$420.50
65028,1030,Reinstall operating system,10/2/2012 0:00:00,67.50,$0.00,$67.50
65029,1035,Set up automatic backup,10/3/2012 0:00:00,11.25,$0.00,$11.25
65030,1000,Clean malware from system,10/6/2012 0:00:00,15.50,$0.00,$15.50
65031,1045,Customer reports noisy hard drive,10/6/2012 0:00:00,52.50,$0.00,$52.50
65032,1008,Install second hard drive,10/13/2012 0:00:00,60.00,$425.75,$485.75
65033,1000,Install Windows 7,10/13/2012 0:00:00,97.50,$335.75,$433.25
65034,1035,File management training,10/14/2012 0:00:00,45.00,$0.00,$45.00
65035,1020,Office 2010 training,10/15/2012 0:00:00,75.00,$0.00,$75.00
65036,1008,Set up home network,10/16/2012 0:00:00,67.50,$85.22,$152.72
65037,1015,Bi-annual computer maintenance,10/19/2012 0:00:00,37.50,$8.75,$46.25
65038,1010,Install Windows 7,10/19/2012 0:00:00,75.00,$0.00,$75.00
65039,1030,Set up automatic backup,10/19/2012 0:00:00,16.87,$0.00,$16.88
65040,1025,Configure dual monitors,10/20/2012 0:00:00,30.00,$0.00,$30.00
65041,1020,Bi-annual computer maintenance,10/22/2012 0:00:00,37.50,$10.15,$47.65
65042,1030,File management training,10/22/2012 0:00:00,33.75,$0.00,$33.75
65043,1020,Troubleshoot video fuzziness,10/23/2012 0:00:00,15.00,$0.00,$15.00
65044,1008,DVD drive is not working,10/23/2012 0:00:00,30.00,$55.40,$85.40
65045,1025,Set up automatic backup,10/26/2012 0:00:00,11.62,$0.00,$11.63
65046,1010,Windows 7 training,10/26/2012 0:00:00,60.00,$0.00,$60.00
65047,1030,Set up automatic backup,10/29/2012 0:00:00,11.25,$0.00,$11.25
65048,1020,Replace LCD monitor,10/29/2012 0:00:00,15.00,$169.95,$184.95
65049,1040,Set up dual monitor system,10/31/2012 0:00:00,22.50,$0.00,$22.50
65050,1045,Reinstall Windows 7,10/31/2012 0:00:00,45.00,$0.00,$45.00
```

Page 1

```
                                     TotalLabor.txt
WO      ServDate            Hours    Rate     Total Labor
65012   9/7/2012 0:00:00             1.25     $30.00  37.50
65013   9/10/2012 0:00:00            0.50     $28.50  14.25
65014   9/10/2012 0:00:00            1.75     $30.00  52.50
65015   9/11/2012 0:00:00            2.25     $30.00  67.50
65016   9/11/2012 0:00:00            1.00     $30.00  30.00
65017   9/15/2012 0:00:00            0.75     $22.50  16.87
65018   9/15/2012 0:00:00            1.00     $22.50  22.50
65019   9/17/2012 0:00:00            2.50     $30.00  75.00
65020   9/17/2012 0:00:00            1.50     $22.50  33.75
65021   9/18/2012 0:00:00            3.25     $30.00  97.50
65022   9/22/2012 0:00:00            1.50     $30.00  45.00
65023   9/23/2012 0:00:00            1.25     $30.00  37.50
65024   9/24/2012 0:00:00            1.00     $15.50  15.50
65025   9/28/2012 0:00:00            1.50     $30.00  45.00
65026   9/29/2012 0:00:00            0.75     $30.00  22.50
65027   10/2/2012 0:00:00            1.50     $30.00  45.00
65028   10/2/2012 0:00:00            2.25     $30.00  67.50
65029   10/3/2012 0:00:00            0.50     $22.50  11.25
65030   10/6/2012 0:00:00            1.00     $15.50  15.50
65031   10/6/2012 0:00:00            1.75     $30.00  52.50
65032   10/13/2012 0:00:00           2.00     $30.00  60.00
65033   10/13/2012 0:00:00           3.25     $30.00  97.50
65034   10/14/2012 0:00:00           1.50     $30.00  45.00
65035   10/15/2012 0:00:00           2.50     $30.00  75.00
65036   10/16/2012 0:00:00           3.00     $22.50  67.50
65037   10/19/2012 0:00:00           1.25     $30.00  37.50
65038   10/19/2012 0:00:00           2.50     $30.00  75.00
65039   10/19/2012 0:00:00           0.75     $22.50  16.87
65040   10/20/2012 0:00:00           1.00     $30.00  30.00
65041   10/22/2012 0:00:00           1.25     $30.00  37.50
65042   10/22/2012 0:00:00           1.50     $22.50  33.75
65043   10/23/2012 0:00:00           0.50     $30.00  15.00
65044   10/23/2012 0:00:00           1.00     $30.00  30.00
65045   10/26/2012 0:00:00           0.75     $15.50  11.62
65046   10/26/2012 0:00:00           2.00     $30.00  60.00
65047   10/29/2012 0:00:00           0.50     $22.50  11.25
65048   10/29/2012 0:00:00           0.50     $30.00  15.00
65049   10/31/2012 0:00:00           0.75     $30.00  22.50
65050   10/31/2012 0:00:00           1.50     $30.00  45.00
```

Project 2 Export Access Data to a Text File

Project 2a, Exported TotalWorkOrders Query

Project 2b, Exported TotalLabor Query

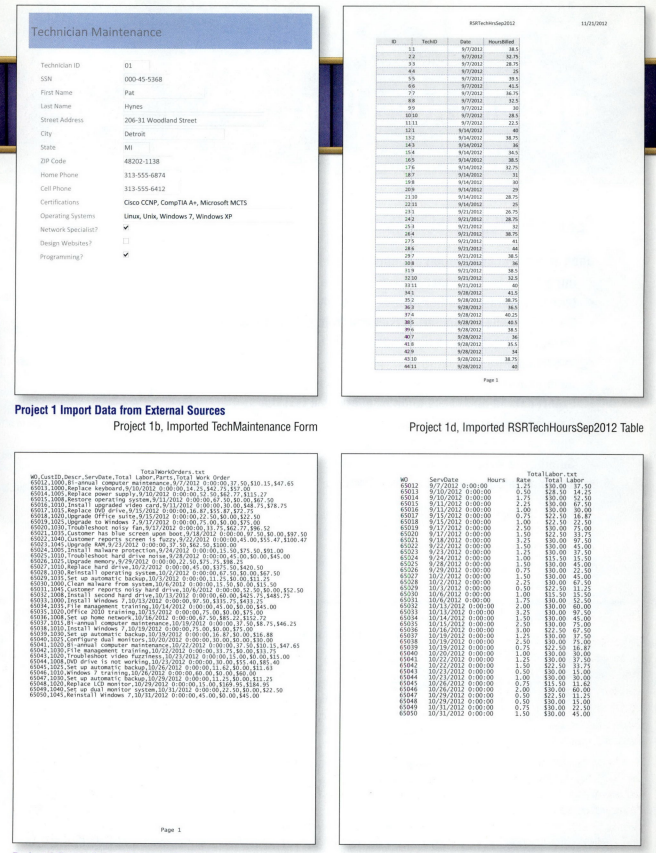

Drop Filter Fields Here

	Months		
	⊞ Sep	⊞ Oct	Grand Total
LName	Sum of Total Work Order	Sum of Total Work Order	Sum of Total Work Order
Bodzek	$173.25	$41.63	$214.88
Carmichael	$67.50	$723.87	$791.37
Cobb	$22.50	$322.60	$345.10
Fahri	$206.27		$206.27
Fennema	$100.00	$97.50	$197.50
Fleming	$104.65	$448.75	$553.40
Friesen	$72.75	$46.25	$119.00
Lemaire	$123.75	$555.50	$679.25
Machado	$100.47	$22.50	$122.97
Pierson	$96.52	$129.38	$225.90
Woodside	$97.50	$56.25	$153.75
Grand Total	$1,165.16	$2,444.22	$3,609.38

Project 4 Summarize Data in a PivotTable and PivotChart

Project 4b, PivotTable for CustomerWorkOrders Query

Project 1 Import Data from External Sources — 4 Parts

You will link and import data from a table in another Access database and from a comma delimited text file. You will also save import specifications for an import routine you expect to repeat often.

Importing Data from Another Access Database

Data stored in another Access database can be integrated into the active database by importing a copy of the source object(s). You can choose to copy multiple objects including duplicating the relationships between tables. When importing, you can specify to import the definition only or the definition and the data. To begin an import operation, click the External Data tab and then click the Import Access database button in the Import group to open the Get External Data - Access Database dialog box shown in Figure 8.1.

Specify the source database containing the object(s) that you want to import by clicking the Browse button to open the File Open dialog box. Navigate to the drive and/or folder containing the source database and double-click the desired Access database file name to insert the database file name in the *File name* text box below *Specify the source of the data*. With *Import tables, queries, forms, reports, macros, and modules into the current database* selected by default, click OK. This opens the Import Objects dialog box shown in Figure 8.2. Select the objects to be imported, change options if necessary, and click OK.

Quick Steps

Import Objects from Access Database

1. Open destination database.
2. Click External Data tab.
3. Click Import Access database button.
4. Click Browse button.
5. If necessary, navigate to drive and/or folder.
6. Double-click source file name.
7. Click OK.
8. Select desired import object(s).
9. Click OK.
10. Click Close.

HINT

If an object with the same name as an imported table already exists in the destination database, Access does not overwrite the existing object. The imported object is named with the number 1 appended.

Access

Figure 8.1 Get External Data - Access Database Dialog Box with Import Option Selected

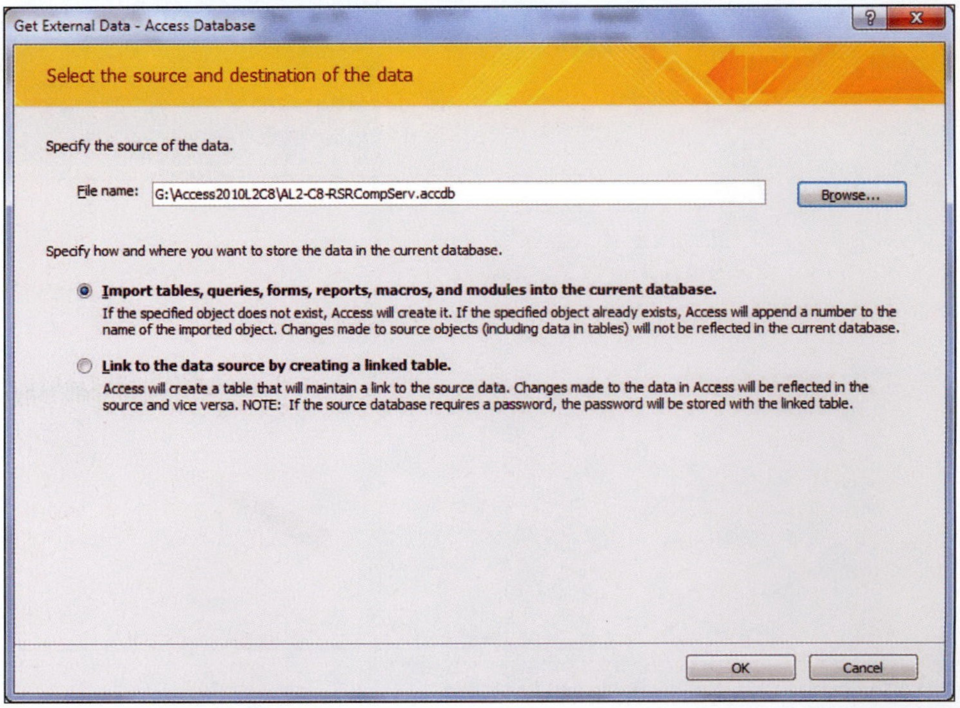

Get External Data - Access Database
Select the source and destination of the data
Specify the source of the data.
File name:
G:\Access2010L2C8\AL2-C8-RSRCompServ.accdb
Browse...
Specify how and where you want to store the data in the current database.
Import tables, queries, forms, reports, macros, and modules into the current database.
If the specified object does not exist, Access will create it. If the specified object already exists, Access will append a number to the name of the imported object. Changes made to source objects (including data in tables) will not be reflected in the current database.
Link to the data source by creating a linked table.
Access will create a table that will maintain a link to the source data. Changes made to the data in Access will be reflected in the source and vice versa. NOTE: If the source database requires a password, the password will be stored with the linked table.
OK
Cancel

Figure 8.2 Import Objects Dialog Box

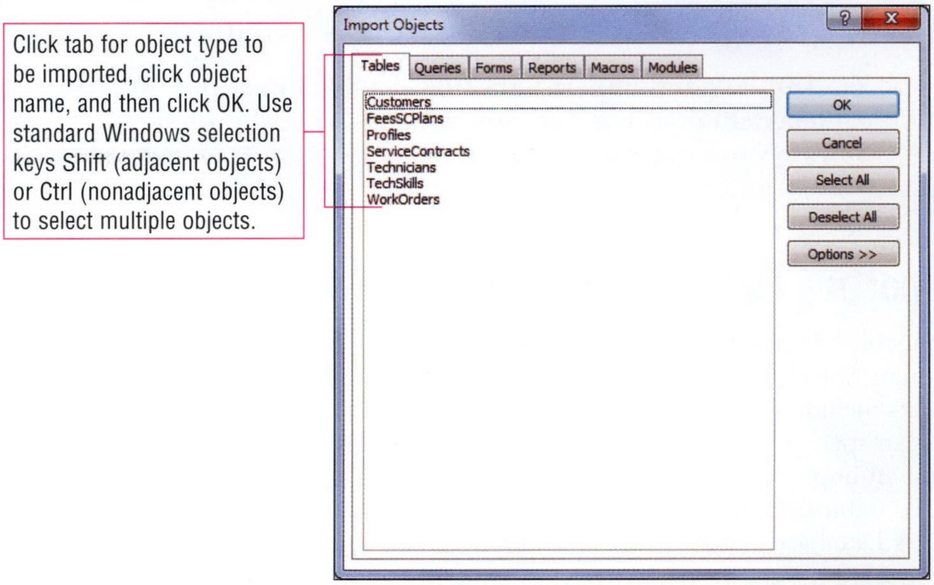

Click tab for object type to be imported, click object name, and then click OK. Use standard Windows selection keys Shift (adjacent objects) or Ctrl (nonadjacent objects) to select multiple objects.
Import Objects
Tables
Queries
Forms
Reports
Macros
Modules
Customers
FeesSCPlans
Profiles
ServiceContracts
Technicians
TechSkills
WorkOrders
OK
Cancel
Select All
Deselect All
Options >>

HINT

If you import a query, form, or report, make sure you also import the underlying tables associated with the object.

Click the Options button to display the *Import*, *Import Tables*, and *Import Queries* options shown in Figure 8.3. By default, Access imports relationships between tables, imports table structure definition and data, and imports a query as a query as opposed to importing the query as a table. Select or clear the options as required before clicking OK to begin the import operation.

Figure 8.3 Import Objects Dialog Box with Options Displayed

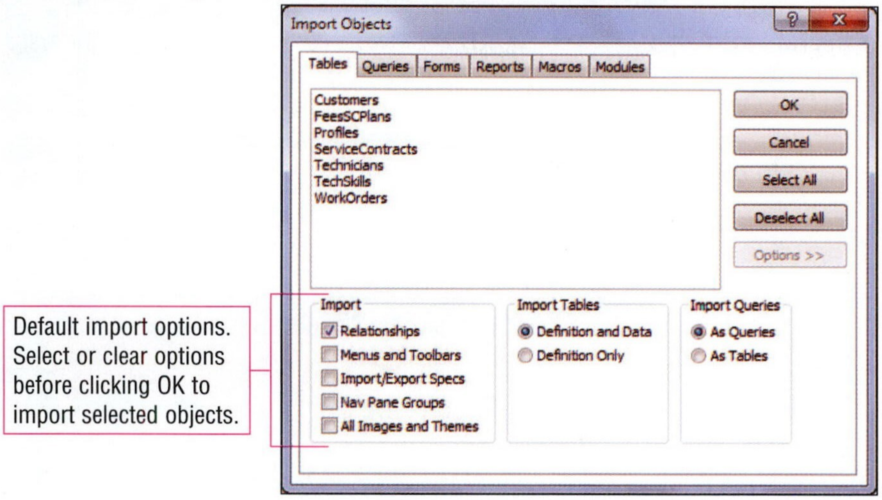
Import Objects
Tables
Queries
Forms
Reports
Macros
Modules
Customers
FeesSCPlans
Profiles
ServiceContracts
Technicians
TechSkills
WorkOrders
OK
Cancel
Select All
Deselect All
Options >>
Import
Relationships
Menus and Toolbars
Import/Export Specs
Nav Pane Groups
All Images and Themes
Import Tables
Definition and Data
Definition Only
Import Queries
As Queries
As Tables
Default import options. Select or clear options before clicking OK to import selected objects.

Project 1a Importing a Form from Another Access Database

Part 1 of 4

1. Open the **AL2-C8-RSRTechPay.accdb** database and enable content.
2. Import the Technicians form from the **AL2-C8-RSRCompServ.accdb** database by completing the following steps:
   a. Click the External Data tab.
   b. Click the Import Access database button in the Import & Link group.
   c. At the Get External Data - Access Database dialog box, click the Browse button.
   d. At the File Open dialog box, double-click the file named ***AL2-C8-RSRCompServ.accdb***. ***Note: Navigate to the Access2010L2C8 folder on your storage medium if necessary.***
   e. With *Import tables, queries, forms, reports, macros, and modules into the current database* already selected, click OK.

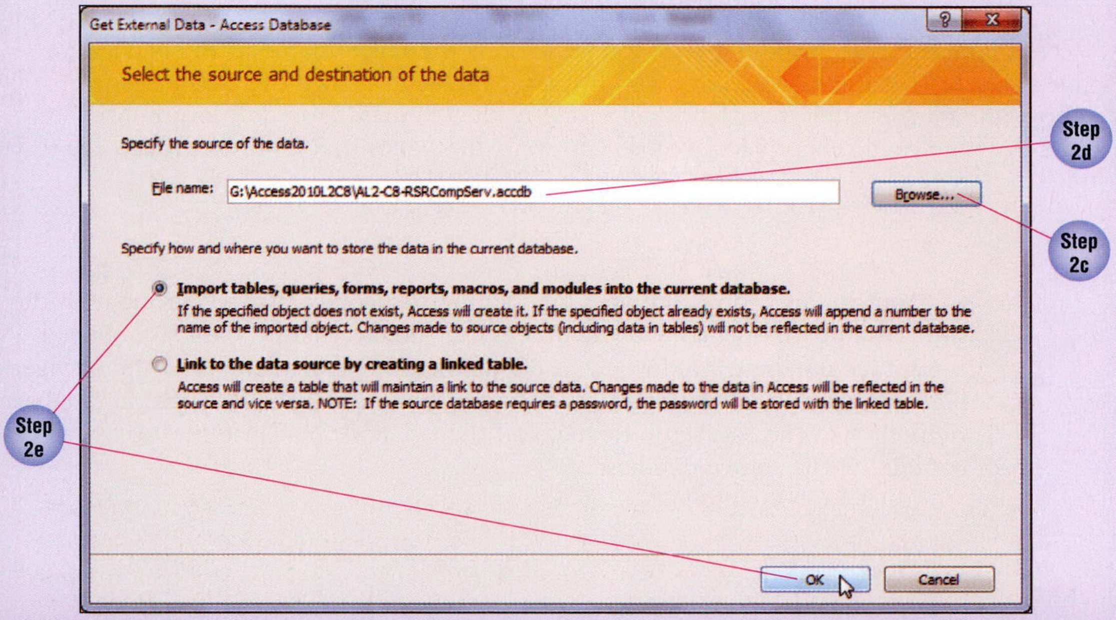
Get External Data - Access Database
Select the source and destination of the data
Specify the source of the data.
File name: G:\Access2010L2C8\AL2-C8-RSRCompServ.accdb
Browse...
Specify how and where you want to store the data in the current database.
Import tables, queries, forms, reports, macros, and modules into the current database.
If the specified object does not exist, Access will create it. If the specified object already exists, Access will append a number to the name of the imported object. Changes made to source objects (including data in tables) will not be reflected in the current database.
Link to the data source by creating a linked table.
Access will create a table that will maintain a link to the source data. Changes made to the data in Access will be reflected in the source and vice versa. NOTE: If the source database requires a password, the password will be stored with the linked table.
OK
Cancel
Step 2d
Step 2c
Step 2e

f. At the Import Objects dialog box, click the Forms tab.

g. Click *TechMaintenance* in the Forms list box and click OK.

h. At the Get External Data - Access Database dialog box with the *Save import steps* check box cleared, click Close.

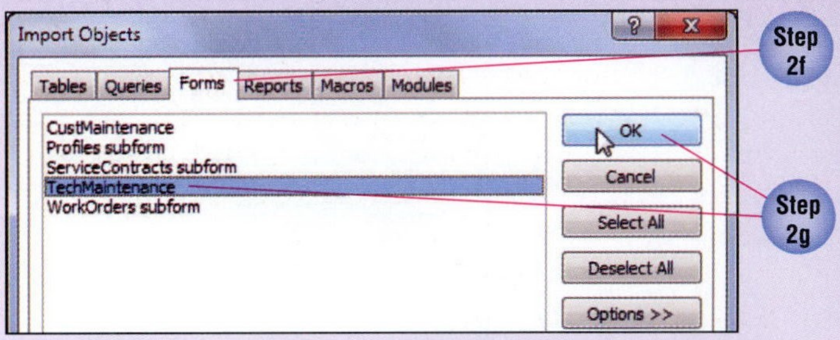

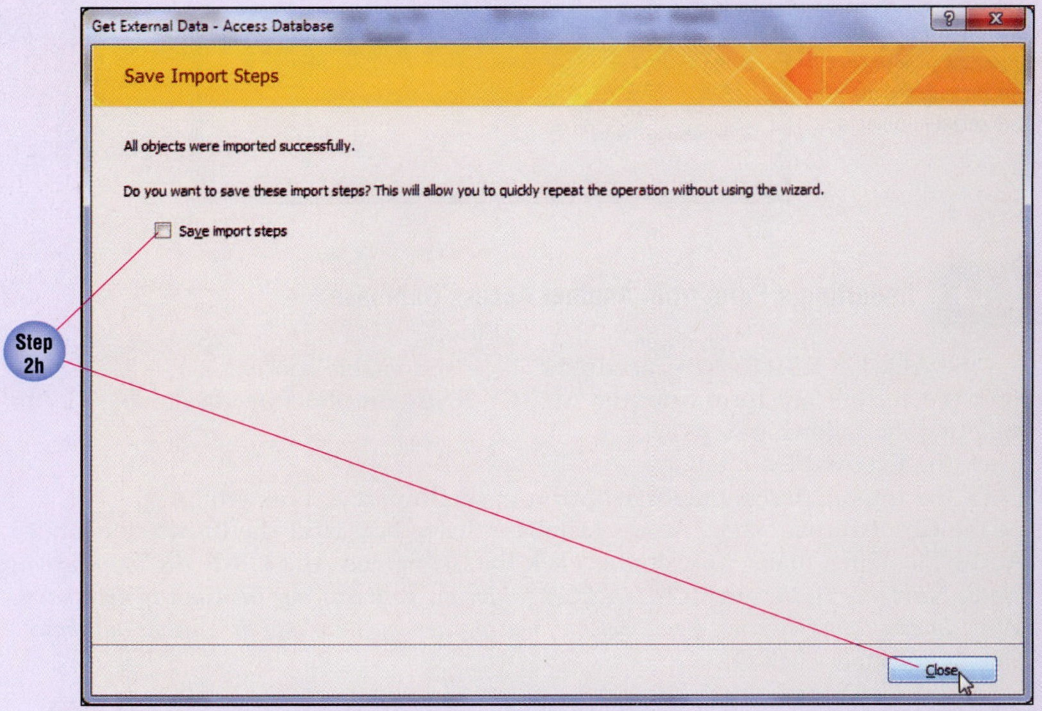

3. Access imports the TechMaintenance form and adds the object name to the Navigation pane. The form will not be operational until after Project 1b since the tables needed to populate data in the form do not yet reside in the database. You did not import the dependent tables in this project because you want the tables that contain the records to be linked.

You can also copy an object by opening two copies of Access, one with the source database opened and the other with the destination database opened. With the source database window active, right-click the source object in the Navigation pane and click *Copy*. Switch to the window containing the destination database, right-click in the Navigation pane, and then click *Paste*. Close the Access window containing the source database.

Linking to a Table in Another Access Database

In Project 1a you imported a form that duplicates the source object from one database to another. If the source object is modified, the imported copy of the object is not altered. Link the data when importing if you want to ensure that the table in the destination database inherits any changes made to the source table. To create a linked table in the destination database, click the External Data tab and then click the Import Access database button. Click the Browse button, navigate to the drive and/or folder in which the source database is stored, and then double-click the source database file name. Click *Link to the data source by creating a linked table* at the Get External Data - Access Database dialog box and then click OK as shown in Figure 8.4.

The Link Tables dialog box shown in Figure 8.5 opens with the *Tables* list box in which you select the tables to be linked. You can use the Shift key or the Ctrl key to select multiple tables to link all in one step. Linked tables are indicated in the Navigation pane with a right-pointing blue arrow.

Quick Steps

Link to Table in Another Database

1. Open destination database.
2. Click External Data tab.
3. Click Import Access database button.
4. Click Browse button.
5. If necessary, navigate to drive and/or folder.
6. Double-click source file name.
7. Click *Link to the data source by creating a linked table.*
8. Click OK.
9. Select desired table(s).
10. Click OK.

Figure 8.4 Get External Data - Access Database Dialog Box with Link Option Selected

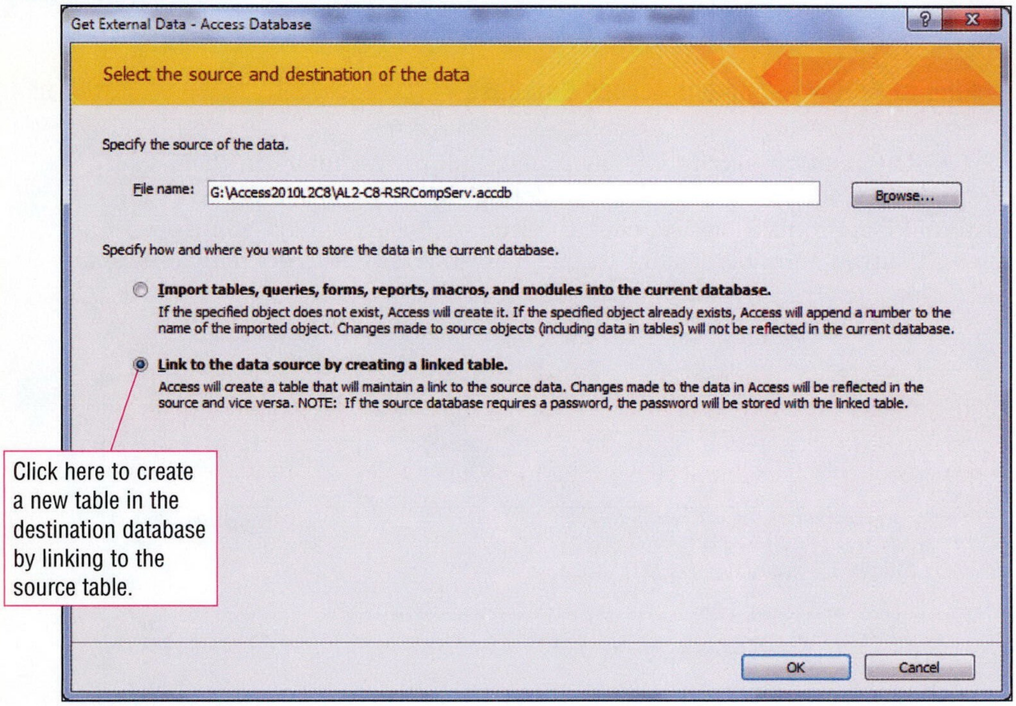
Get External Data - Access Database
Select the source and destination of the data
Specify the source of the data.
File name: G:\Access2010L2C8\AL2-C8-RSRCompServ.accdb
Browse...
Specify how and where you want to store the data in the current database.
Import tables, queries, forms, reports, macros, and modules into the current database.
If the specified object does not exist, Access will create it. If the specified object already exists, Access will append a number to the name of the imported object. Changes made to source objects (including data in tables) will not be reflected in the current database.
Link to the data source by creating a linked table.
Access will create a table that will maintain a link to the source data. Changes made to the data in Access will be reflected in the source and vice versa. NOTE: If the source database requires a password, the password will be stored with the linked table.
Click here to create a new table in the destination database by linking to the source table.
OK
Cancel

Figure 8.5 Link Tables Dialog Box

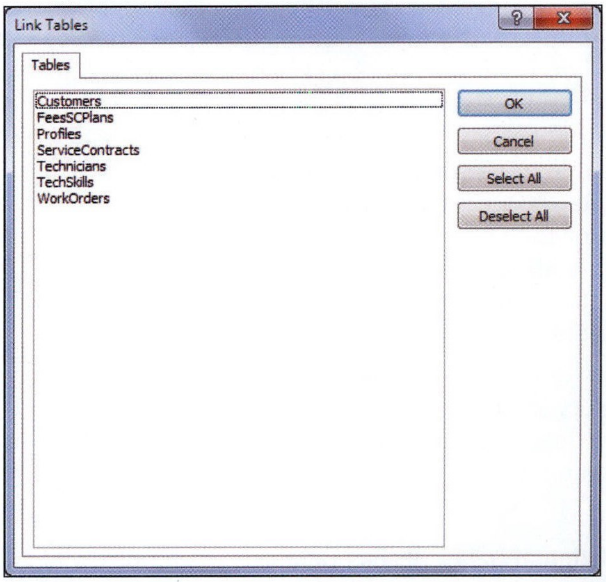
Link Tables
Tables
Customers
FeesSCPlans
Profiles
ServiceContracts
Technicians
TechSkills
WorkOrders
OK
Cancel
Select All
Deselect All

Project 1b Linking to Tables in Another Access Database

Part 2 of 4

1. With the **AL2-C8-RSRTechPay.accdb** database open, link to two tables in the **AL2-C8-RSRCompServ.accdb** database by completing the following steps:
   a. With the External Data tab still active, click the Import Access database button.
   b. Click the Browse button and double-click the file named ***AL2-C8-RSRCompServ.accdb***.
   c. Click *Link to the data source by creating a linked table* and click OK.

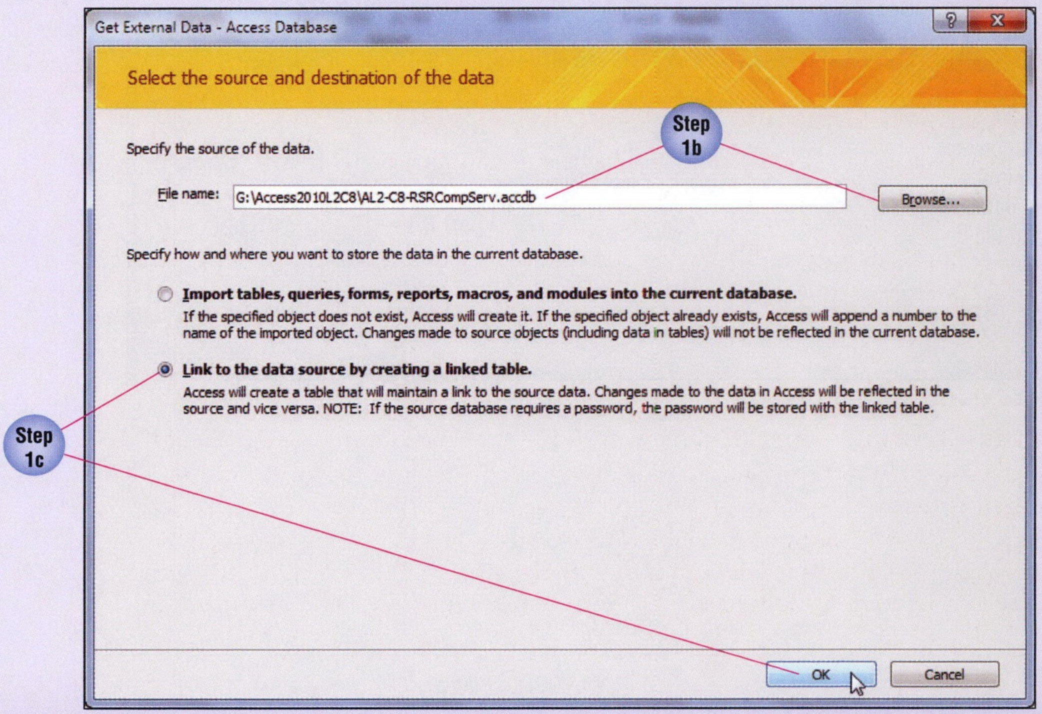
Get External Data - Access Database
Select the source and destination of the data
Specify the source of the data.
File name: G:\Access2010L2C8\AL2-C8-RSRCompServ.accdb
Browse...
Step 1b
Specify how and where you want to store the data in the current database.
Import tables, queries, forms, reports, macros, and modules into the current database.
If the specified object does not exist, Access will create it. If the specified object already exists, Access will append a number to the name of the imported object. Changes made to source objects (including data in tables) will not be reflected in the current database.
Link to the data source by creating a linked table.
Access will create a table that will maintain a link to the source data. Changes made to the data in Access will be reflected in the source and vice versa. NOTE: If the source database requires a password, the password will be stored with the linked table.
Step 1c
OK
Cancel

d. At the Link Tables dialog box, click *Technicians* in the *Tables* list box.

e. Hold down the Shift key and click *TechSkills* in the *Tables* list box.

f. Click OK.

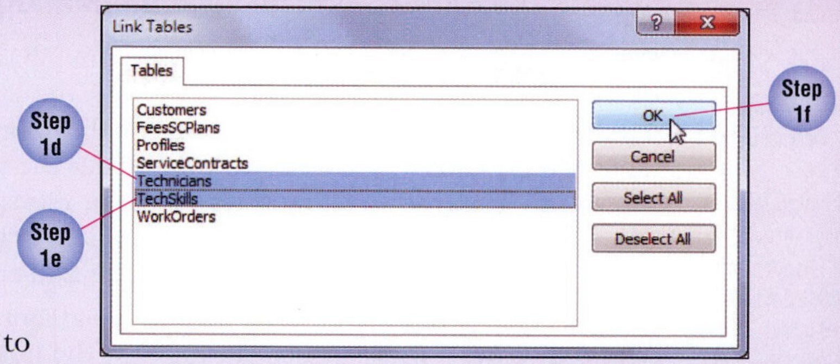

2. Access links the two tables to the source database and adds the table names to the Navigation pane. Linked tables display with a blue right-pointing arrow next to the table icon.
3. Double-click the TechMaintenance form to view the form with the first record displayed. Print the form for the selected record only and then close the form.
4. Double-click the Technicians table to view the table datasheet and then close the datasheet.
5. Double-click the TechSkills table to view the table datasheet and then close the datasheet.

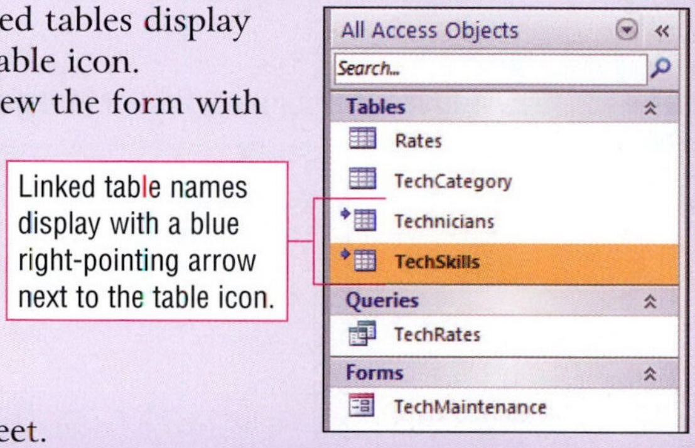

When a table is linked, the source data does not reside in the destination database. Opening a linked table causes Access to dynamically update the datasheet with the information in the source table in the other database. You can edit the source data in either the source database table or the linked table in the destination database.

Deciding between Importing versus Linking to Source Data

In most cases you would import data into Access from another Access database or some other external source if the source data is not likely to be updated. Since importing creates a copy of the data in two locations, changes or updates to the data must be duplicated in both copies. Duplicating the change or update increases the risk of data entry error or missed updates in one or the other location.

If the data is updated frequently, link to the external data source so that all changes are only required to be entered once. Since the data exists only in the source location, the potential for error or missed updates is reduced.

In another situation you may choose to link to the data source when several different databases require a common table such as Inventory. To duplicate the table in each database is inefficient and wastes disk space. The potential for error if individual databases are not refreshed with updated data is also a risk that favors linking over importing. In this scenario a master Inventory table in a separate shared database would be linked to all of the other databases that need to use the data.

Resetting a Link Using Linked Table Manager

Quick Steps

Refresh Link(s)
1. Click External Data tab.
2. Click Linked Table Manager button.
3. Click Select All button or click individual linked table.
4. Click OK.
5. Navigate to drive and/or folder.
6. Double-click source database file name.
7. Click OK.
8. Click Close button.

Linked Table Manager

When a table has been linked to another database, Access stores the full path to the source database file name along with the linked table name. Changing the database file name or folder location for the source database means the linked table will no longer function. Access provides the Linked Table Manager dialog box shown in Figure 8.6 to allow you to reset or refresh a table's link to reconnect to the data source. Click the Linked Table Manager button in the Import & Link group of the External Data tab to open the Linked Table Manager dialog box.

Click the check box next to the link you want to refresh and then click OK. Access displays a message box stating that the link was successfully refreshed or displays a dialog box in which you navigate to the new location for the data source.

Figure 8.6 Linked Table Manager Dialog Box

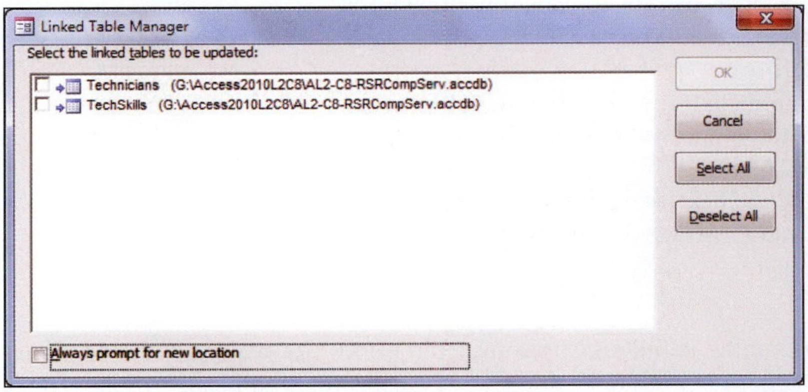

Project 1c **Refreshing a Link** Part 3 of 4

1. With the **AL2-C8-RSRTechPay.accdb** database open, move the location of the **AL2-C8-RSRCompServ.accdb** database by completing the following steps:
   a. Click the File tab and then click Open.
   b. Right-click ***AL2-C8-RSRCompServ.accdb*** in the file list box and then click *Cut* at the shortcut menu.
   c. At the Open dialog box, click the drive representing your storage medium in the *Computer* section of the Navigation pane, for example, *KINGSTON (G:)*, or click the drive letter in the Address bar.
   d. Right-click in a blank area of the file list box and click *Paste*.
   e. Close the Open dialog box. With the location of the source database now moved, the linked tables are no longer connected to the correct location.
2. Refresh the links to the two tables by completing the following steps:
   a. If necessary, click the External Data tab.
   b. Click the Linked Table Manager button in the Import & Link group.

c. At the Linked Table Manager dialog box, click the Select All button to select all linked objects.

d. Click OK. Access attempts to refresh the links. Since the source database has been moved, Access displays a dialog box in which you select the new location.

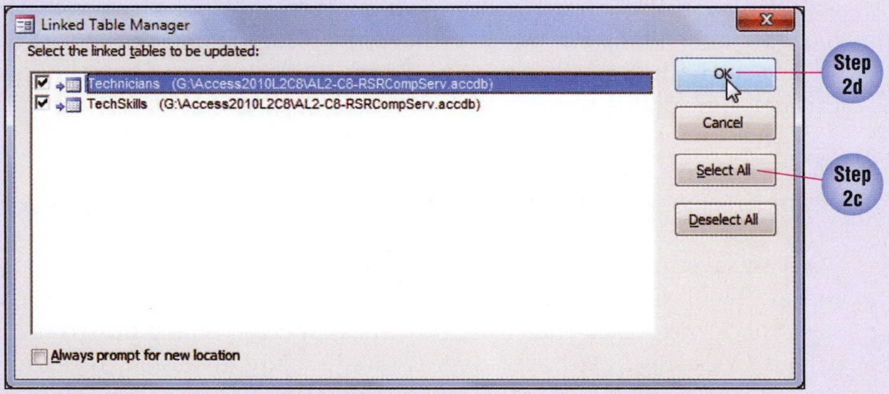

e. At the Select New Location of Technicians dialog box, locate and then double-click ***AL2-C8-RSRCompServ.accdb***.

f. Click OK at the Linked Table Manager message box that indicates all selected links were successfully refreshed.

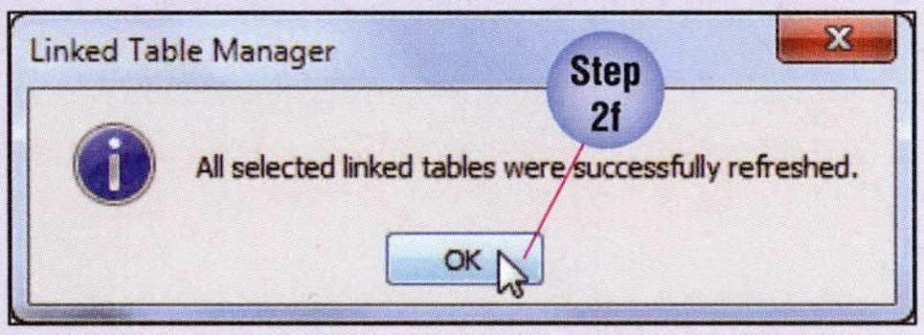

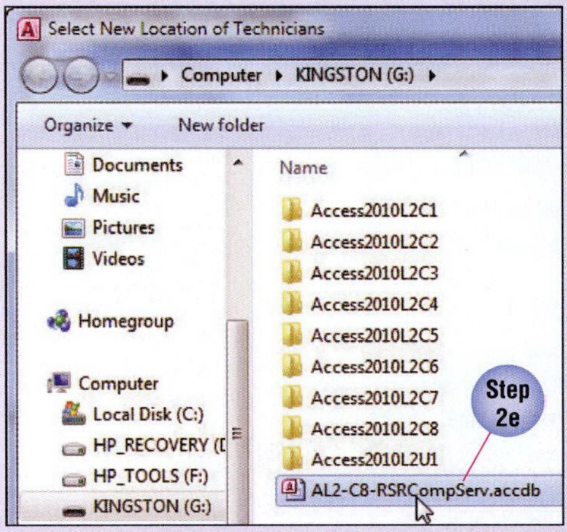

3. Click the Close button at the Linked Table Manager dialog box.

Importing Data to Access from a Text File

A text file is often used to exchange data between dissimilar programs since the file format is recognized by nearly all applications. Text files contain no formatting and consist of letters, numbers, punctuation symbols, and a few control characters only. Two commonly used text file formats separate fields with either a tab character (delimited file format) or a comma (comma separated file format). A partial view of the text file you will use in Project 1d is shown in a Notepad window in Figure 8.7. If necessary, you can view and edit a text file in Notepad prior to importing if the source application inserts characters that you wish to delete.

HINT

Most programs can export data in a text file. If you need to use data from a program that is not compatible with Access, check the source program's export options for a text file format.

Quick Steps

Import Data from Comma Separated Text File

1. Click External Data tab.
2. Click Import text file button.
3. Click Browse button.
4. If necessary, navigate to drive and/or folder.
5. Double-click .csv file name.
6. Click OK.
7. Click Next.
8. If applicable, click *First Row Contains Field Names* check box.
9. Click Next.
10. Choose primary key field.
11. Click Next.
12. Click Finish.

Save Import Specifications

1. At last Get External Data dialog box, click *Save import steps.*
2. If necessary, edit name in *Save as* text box.
3. Type description in *Description* text box.
4. Click Save Import button.

Text File

To import a text file into Access, click the Import text file button in the Import & Link group of the External Data tab. Access opens the Get External Data - Text File dialog box which is similar to the dialog box used to import data from another Access database. When importing a text file, Access adds an append option in addition to the import and link options in the *Specify how and where you want to store the data in the current database* section. Click the Browse button to navigate to the location of the source file and double-click the source file name to launch the Import Text Wizard, which guides you through the import process through four dialog boxes.

Saving and Repeating Import Specifications

You can save import specifications for an import routine that you are likely to repeat. The last step in the Get External Data dialog box displays a *Save import steps* check box. Click the check box to expand the dialog box to display the *Save as* and *Description* text boxes. Type a unique name to assign to the import routine and a brief description that describes the steps. Click the Save Import button to complete the import and store the specifications. Click the *Create Outlook Task* check box if you want to create an Outlook task that you can set up as a recurring item for an import or export operation that is repeated at fixed intervals.

Figure 8.7 Project 1d Partial View of Text File Contents in Notepad

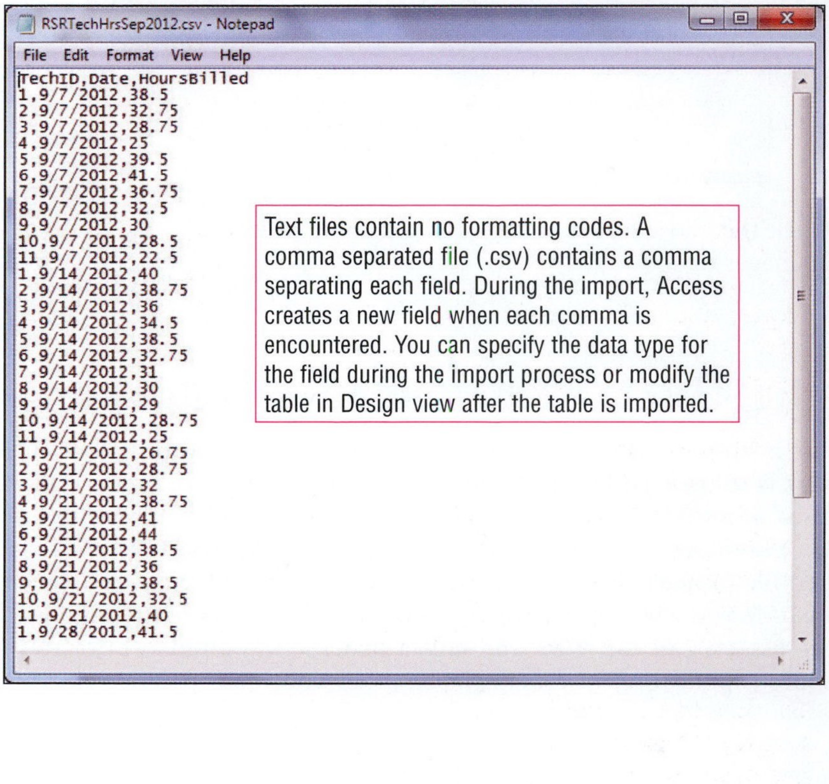

RSRTechHrsSep2012.csv - Notepad
File Edit Format View Help
TechID,Date,HoursBilled
1,9/7/2012,38.5
2,9/7/2012,32.75
3,9/7/2012,28.75
4,9/7/2012,25
5,9/7/2012,39.5
6,9/7/2012,41.5
7,9/7/2012,36.75
8,9/7/2012,32.5
9,9/7/2012,30
10,9/7/2012,28.5
11,9/7/2012,22.5
1,9/14/2012,40
2,9/14/2012,38.75
3,9/14/2012,36
4,9/14/2012,34.5
5,9/14/2012,38.5
6,9/14/2012,32.75
7,9/14/2012,31
8,9/14/2012,30
9,9/14/2012,29
10,9/14/2012,28.75
11,9/14/2012,25
1,9/21/2012,26.75
2,9/21/2012,28.75
3,9/21/2012,32
4,9/21/2012,38.75
5,9/21/2012,41
6,9/21/2012,44
7,9/21/2012,38.5
8,9/21/2012,36
9,9/21/2012,38.5
10,9/21/2012,32.5
11,9/21/2012,40
1,9/28/2012,41.5
Text files contain no formatting codes. A comma separated file (.csv) contains a comma separating each field. During the import, Access creates a new field when each comma is encountered. You can specify the data type for the field during the import process or modify the table in Design view after the table is imported.

Project 1d Importing Data from a Comma Separated Text File and Saving Import Specifications

Part 4 of 4

1. With the **AL2-C8-RSRTechPay.accdb** database open, select a text file to import that contains the weekly hours billed for each technician for the month of September 2012 by completing the following steps:
   a. If necessary, click the External Data tab.
   b. Click the Import text file button in the Import & Link group.
   c. At the Get External Data - Text File dialog box, click the Browse button.
   d. At the File Open dialog box, navigate to the Access2010L2C8 folder on your storage medium if necessary.
   e. Double-click the file named ***RSRTechHrsSep2012.csv***.
   f. With *Import the source data into a new table in the current database* already selected, click OK. This launches the Import Text Wizard.

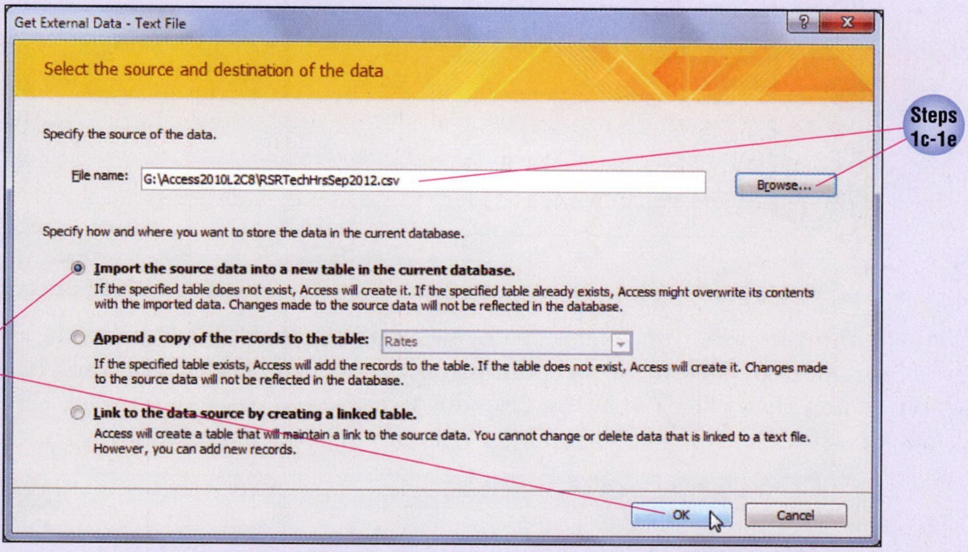

2. Import the comma separated data using the Import Text Wizard by completing the following steps:
   a. At the first Import Text Wizard dialog box, with *Delimited* selected as the format, click Next. Notice the preview window in the lower half of the dialog box displays a sample of the data in the source text file. Delimited files use commas or tabs as separators while fixed width files use spaces.

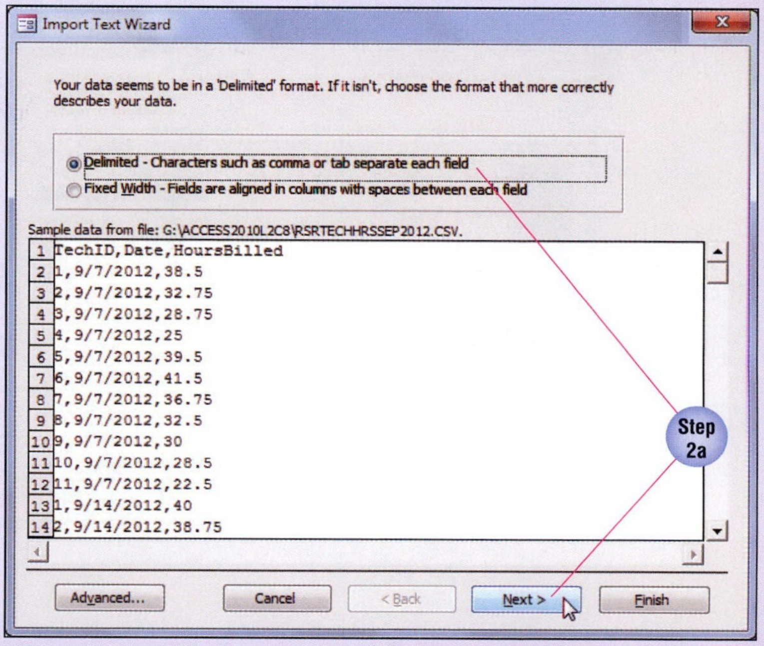

b. At the second Import Text Wizard dialog box with *Comma* already selected as the delimiter, click the *First Row Contains Field Names* check box and then click Next. Notice the preview section already shows the data set in columns similar to a table datasheet.

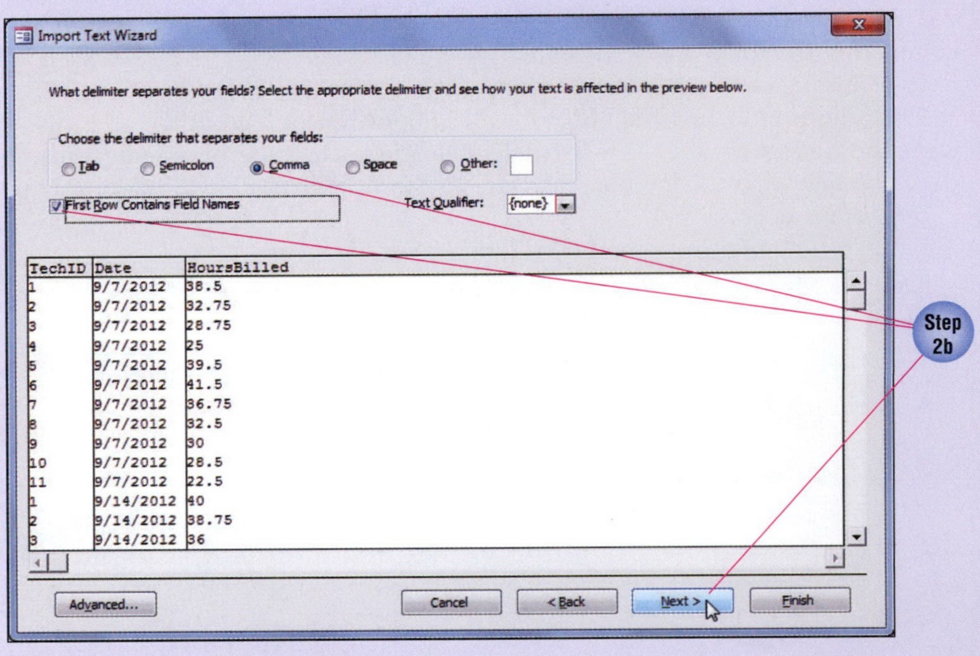

c. At the third Import Text Wizard dialog box with the *TechID* column in the preview section selected, click the down-pointing arrow next to *Data Type* in the *Field Options* section and then click *Text* at the drop-down list.

d. Click Next.

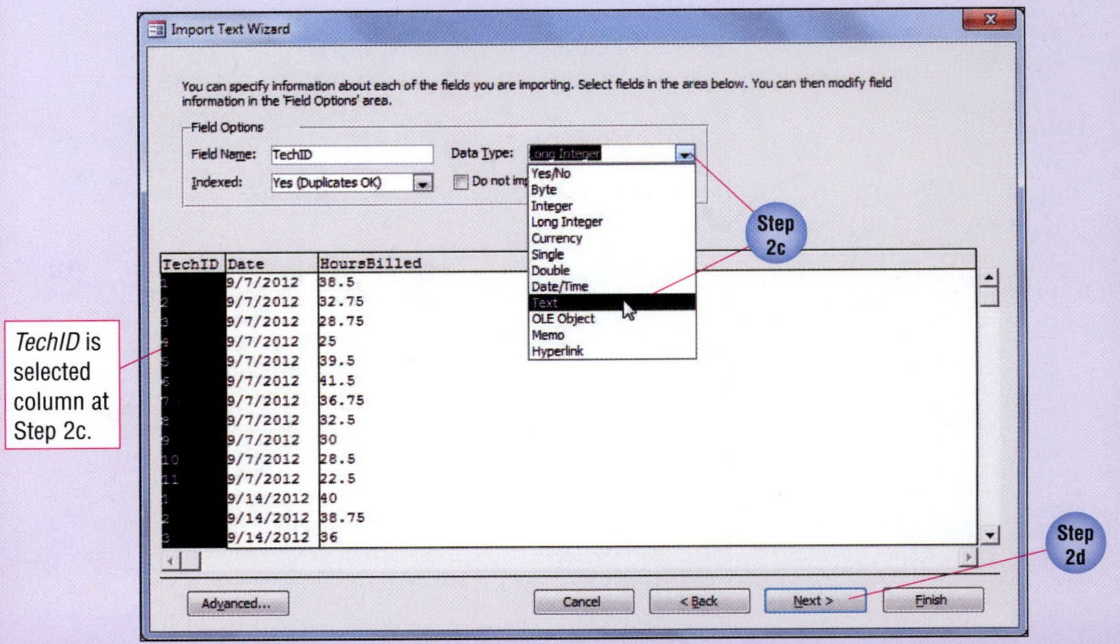

e. At the fourth Import Text Wizard dialog box, with *Let Access add primary key* already selected, click Next. Notice Access has added a column in the preview section with the field title *ID*. The column added by Access is defined as an AutoNumber field where each row in the text file is numbered sequentially to make the row unique.

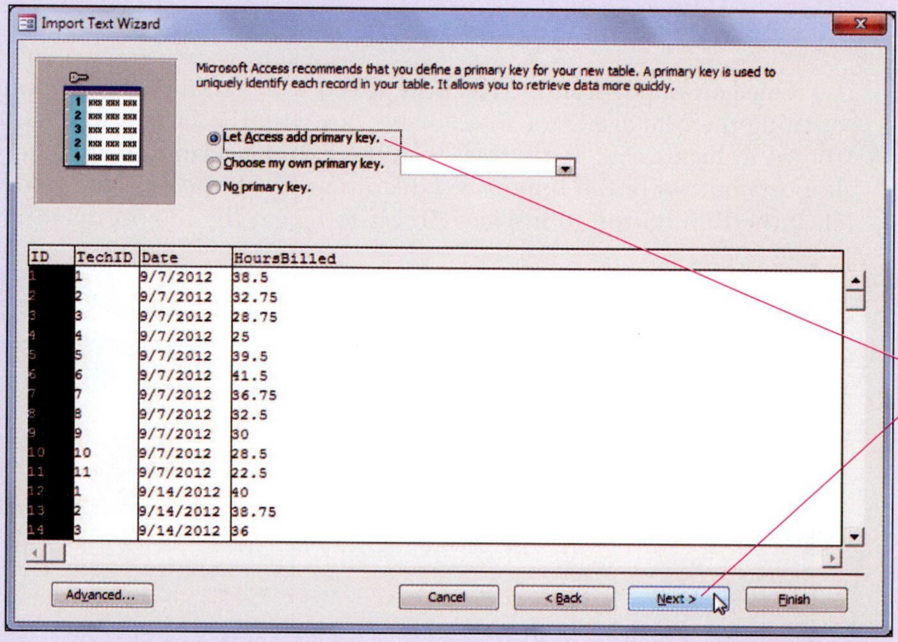

f. At the last Import Text Wizard dialog box, with *RSRTechHrsSep2012* entered in the *Import to Table* text box, click Finish.

3. Save the import specifications in case you want to run this import again at a future date by completing the following steps:
   a. At the Get External Data - Text File dialog box, click the *Save import steps* check box. This causes the *Save as* and *Description* text boxes to appear as well as the *Create an Outlook Task* section. By default Access creates a name in the *Save as* text box with *Import-* preceding the file name containing the imported data.

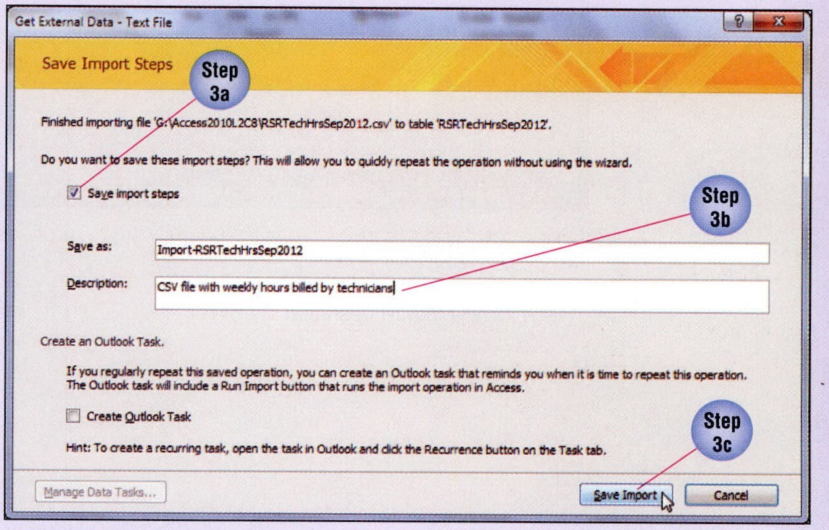

   b. Click in the *Description* text box and type **CSV file with weekly hours billed by technicians**.
   c. Click the Save Import button.

4. Double-click the RSRTechHoursSep2012 table in the Navigation pane to open the table datasheet.
5. Print the datasheet with a bottom margin set to 0.5 inch and then close the datasheet.
6. Close the **AL2-C8-RSRTechPay.accdb** database.

Saved Imports

Once an import routine has been saved, you can repeat the import process by opening the Manage Data Tasks dialog box with the Saved Imports tab selected shown in Figure 8.8. To do this, click the External Data tab and click the Saved Imports button in the Import & Link group. Click the desired import name and click the Run button to instruct Access to repeat the import operation.

Figure 8.8 Manage Data Tasks Dialog Box with Saved Imports Tab Selected

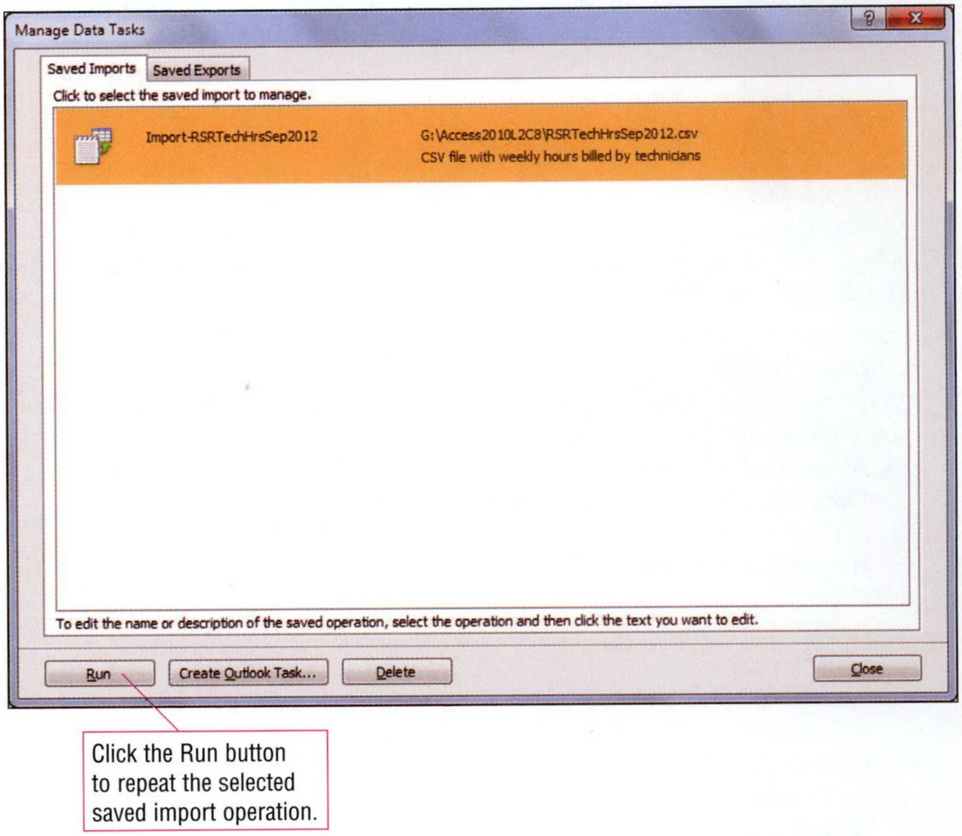

Project 2 Export Access Data to a Text File

2 Parts

You will export a query as a comma delimited text file and another query as a tab delimited text file including saving the second export steps so that you can repeat the export operation.

Exporting Access Data to a Text File

The Export group in the External Data tab contains buttons with which you can export Access data from a table, query, form, or report to other applications such as Excel or Word. If you need to work with data from Access in a program that is not part of the Microsoft Office suite, you can click the More button in the Export group to see if a file format converter exists for the application that you will be using. For example, the More button contains options to export in Word, SharePoint List, ODBC Database, HTML Document, and dBase file formats.

If a file format converter does not exist for the program that you will be using, export the data as a text file since most applications recognize and can import a text data file. Access includes the Export Text Wizard, which is launched after you select an object in the Navigation pane, click the Export to text file button, and then specify the name and location to store the exported text file. The Export Text Wizard uses similar steps to those that you used when you imported a text file in Project 1d.

Quick Steps

Export Data as Text File

1. Select object in Navigation pane.
2. Click External Data tab.
3. Click Export to text file button.
4. Click Browse button.
5. If necessary, navigate to desired drive and/or folder.
6. If necessary, change file name.
7. Click Save button.
8. Click OK.
9. Click Next.
10. Choose delimiter character.
11. If appropriate, click *Include Field Names on First Row* check box.
12. If appropriate, choose *Text Qualifier* character.
13. Click Next.
14. If necessary, change *Export to File* path and/or name.
15. Click Finish.
16. Click Close button.

Text File

Project 2a Exporting a Query as a Text File

Part 1 of 2

1. Display the Open dialog box and move the **AL2-C8-RSRCompServ.accdb** database back to the Access2010L2C8 folder on your storage medium.
2. Open the **AL2-C8-RSRCompServ.accdb** database and enable content.
3. Export the TotalWorkOrders query as a text file by completing the following steps:
   a. Select the query named TotalWorkOrders in the Navigation pane.
   b. Click the External Data tab.
   c. Click the Export to text file button in the Export group.

d. At the Export - Text File dialog box, click the Browse button.
e. At the File Save dialog box, if necessary, navigate to the Access2010L2C8 folder on your storage medium.
f. With the default file name of *TotalWorkOrders.txt* in the *File name* text box, click the Save button.
g. Click OK.

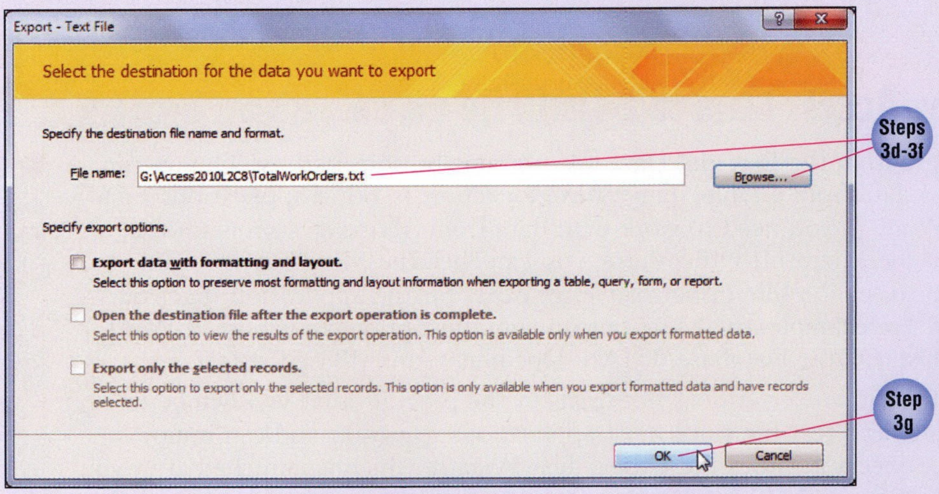

h. At the first Export Text Wizard dialog box with *Delimited* selected as the format, click Next. Notice in the preview section of the dialog box that a comma separates each field and that data in a field defined with the Text data type is encased in quotation symbols.

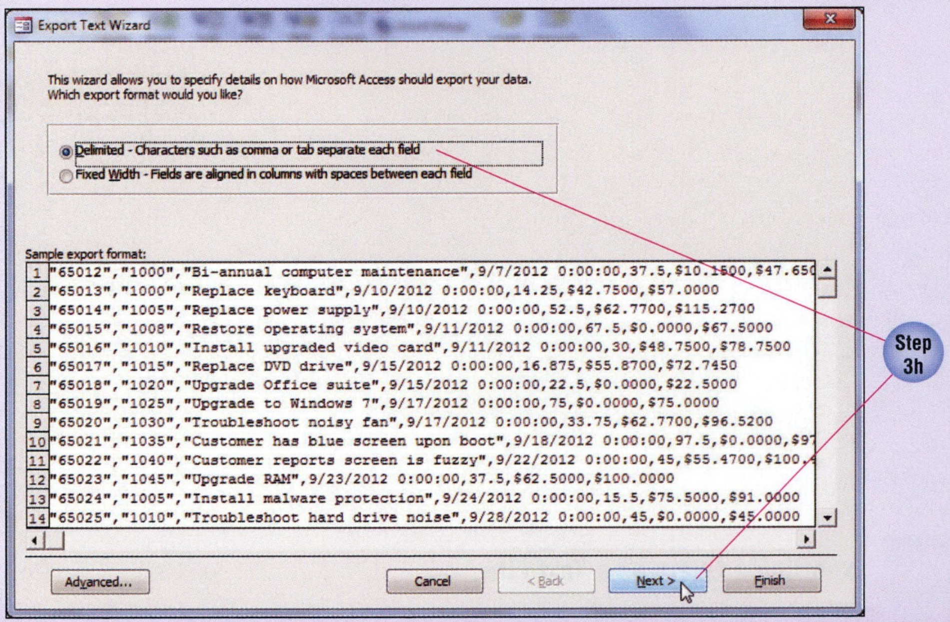

i. At the second Export Text Wizard dialog box, with *Comma* selected as the delimiter character that separates the fields, click the *Include Field Names on First Row* check box. Access adds a row to the top of the data in the preview section with the field names. Each field name is encased in quotation symbols.

j. Click the down-pointing arrow next to the *Text Qualifier* list box and click *{none}* at the drop-down list. Access removes all of the quotation symbols from the text data in the preview section.

k. Click Next.

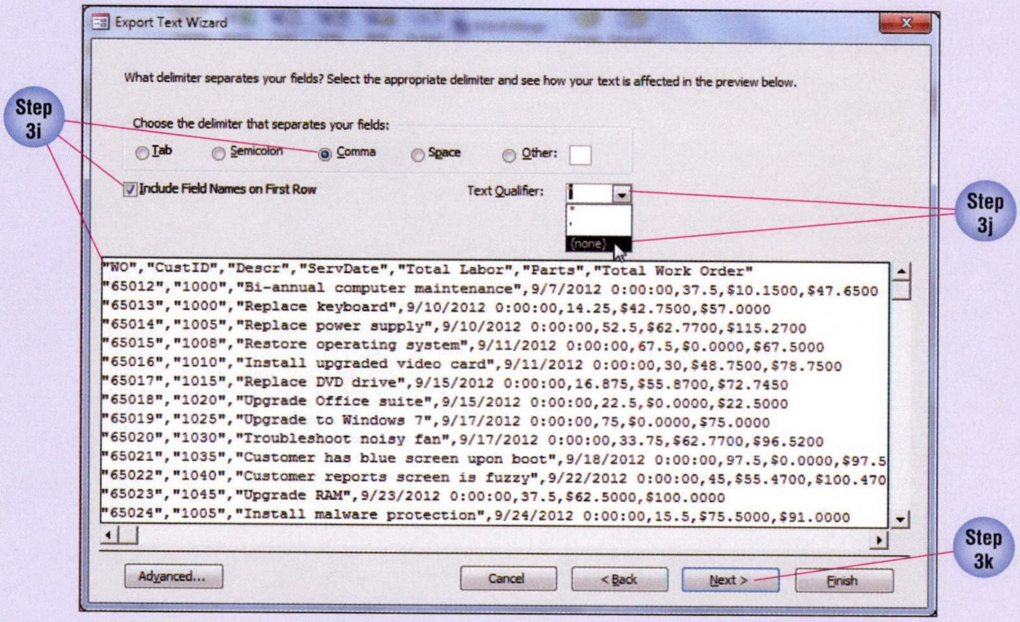

l. At the last Export Text Wizard dialog box, with *[d]:\Access2010L2C8\TotalWorkOrders.txt* (where *[d]* is the drive for your storage medium) entered in the *Export to File* text box, click Finish.

m. Click the Close button at the Export - Text File dialog box to close the dialog box without saving the export steps.

4. Click the Start button, point to *All Programs*, click *Accessories*, and then click *Notepad*.
5. At a blank Notepad window, click File and then click Open. Navigate to the Access2010L2C8 folder on your storage medium and then double-click the exported file named **TotalWorkOrders.txt**.
6. Click File and then click Print to print the exported text file.
7. Exit Notepad.

Saving and Repeating Export Specifications

Access allows you to save export steps similar to how you learned to save import specifications for an import routine that you are likely to repeat. The last step in the Export - Text File dialog box displays a *Save export steps* check box. Click the check box to expand the dialog box options to display the *Save as* and *Description* text boxes. Type a unique name to assign to the export routine and a brief description that describes the steps. Click the Save Export button to complete the export operation and store the specifications for later use.

Quick Steps

Save Export Specifications

1. At last Export - Text File dialog box, click *Save export steps*.
2. If necessary, edit name in *Save as* text box.
3. Type description in *Description* text box.
4. Click Save Export button.

Project 2b Exporting a Query as a Text File and Saving Export Steps Part 2 of 2

1. With the **AL2-C8-RSRCompServ.accdb** database open, export the TotalLabor query as a text file using Tab as the delimiter character by completing the following steps:
   a. Select the query named TotalLabor in the Navigation pane.
   b. Click the Export to text file button in the Export group of the External Data tab.
   c. With *[d]:\Access2010L2C8\TotalLabor.txt* (where *[d]* is the drive for your storage medium) entered in the *File name* text box, click OK.
   d. Complete the steps in the Export Text Wizard as follows:
      1) Click Next at the first dialog box with *Delimited* selected.
      2) Click *Tab* as the delimiter character, click the *Include Field Names on First Row* check box, change the *Text Qualifier* to *{none}*, and then click Next.

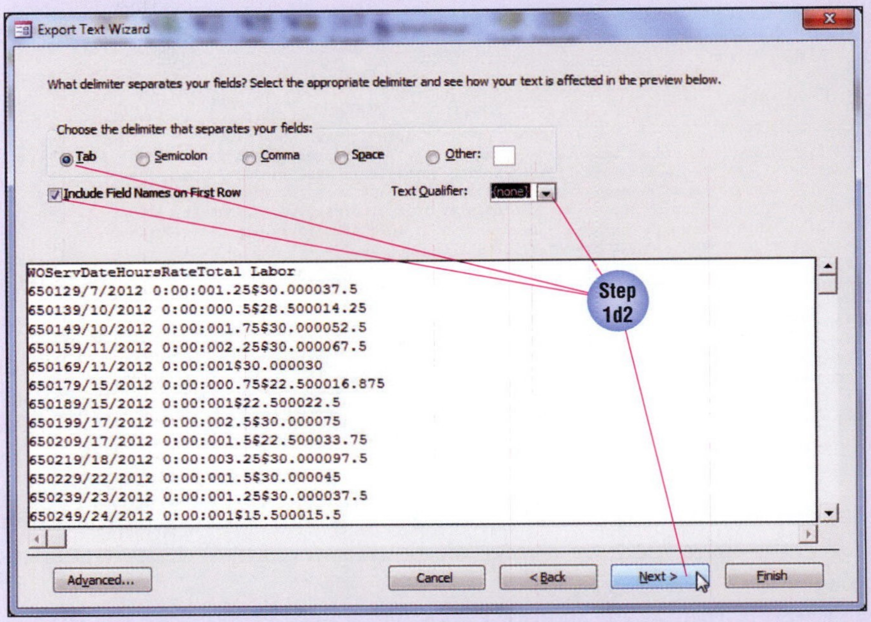

      3) Click Finish.
   e. Click the *Save export steps* check box at the Export - Text File dialog box.
   f. Click in the *Description* text box and type **TotalLabor query for RSR Computer Service work orders as a text file**.
   g. Click the Save Export button.

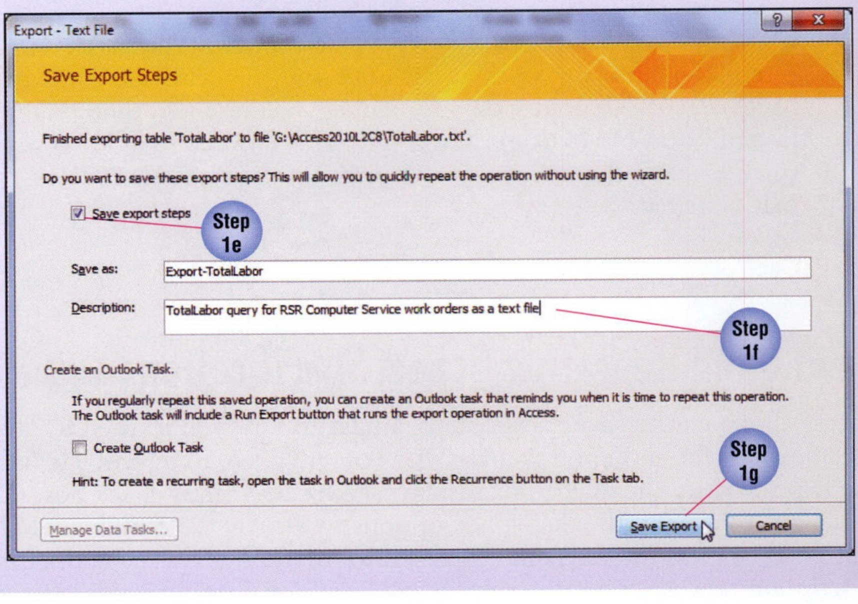

2. Start Notepad.
3. At a blank Notepad window, open the exported file named **TotalLabor.txt**.
4. Print the exported text file and then exit Notepad.

Once an export routine has been saved, you can repeat the export process by opening the Manage Data Tasks dialog box with the Saved Exports tab selected shown in Figure 8.9 by clicking the Saved Exports button in the Export group in the External Data tab. Click the desired export name and click the Run button to instruct Access to repeat the export operation.

Saved Exports

Figure 8.9 Manage Data Tasks Dialog Box with Saved Exports Tab Selected

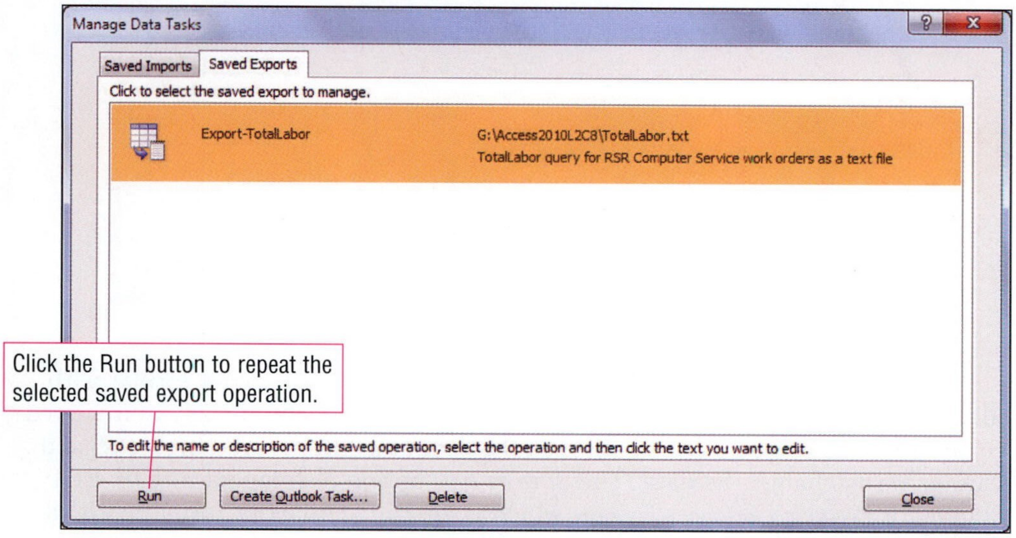

Project 3 Publish a Database Object as an XPS Document — 1 Part

You will publish a report as an XPS file.

Publishing and Viewing Database Objects as XPS Documents

In Level 1, Chapter 7 and Chapter 8, you learned to publish database objects as a PDF document using the Save & Publish tab Backstage view and the PDF or XPS button in the Export group of the External Data tab. Recall that clicking the PDF or XPS button in the Export group of the External Data tab with an object selected in the Navigation pane causes the Publish as PDF or XPS dialog box shown in Figure 8.10 to open.

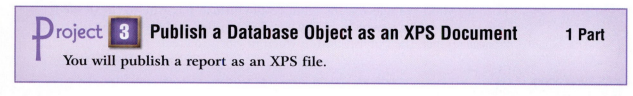

PDF or XPS

Figure 8.10 Publish as PDF or XPS Dialog Box

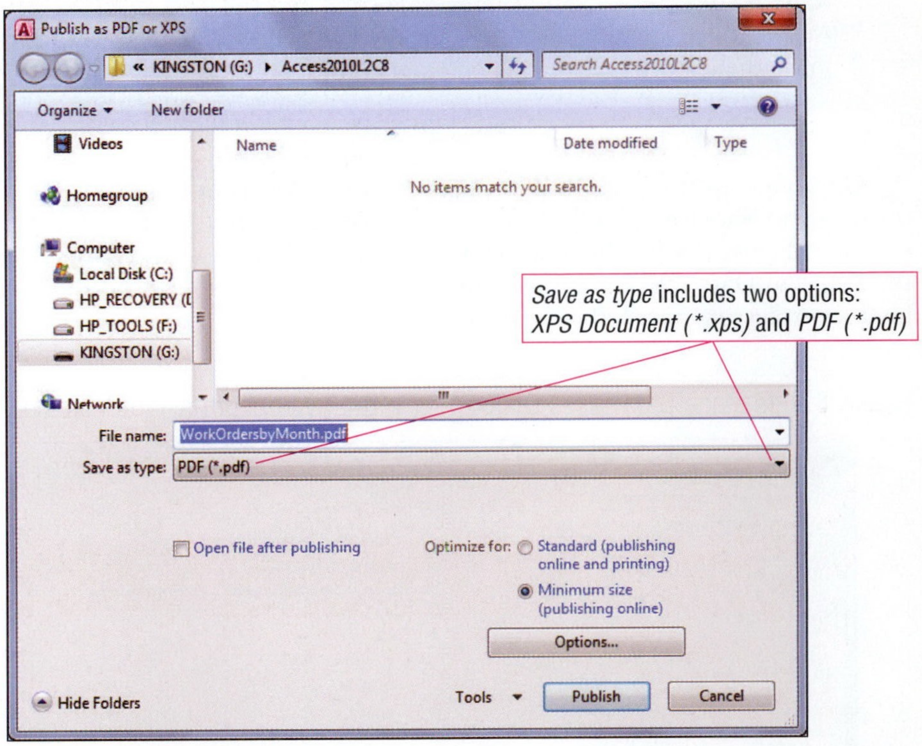

Quick Steps

Publish Object as XPS
1. Select object in Navigation pane.
2. Click External Data tab.
3. Click PDF or XPS button.
4. If necessary, navigate to desired drive and/or folder.
5. If necessary, change file name.
6. Change *Save as type* to *XPS*.
7. Click Publish button.
8. Click Close button.

XPS stands for *XML Paper Specification,* which is a fixed-layout format with all formatting preserved so that when the file is shared electronically and viewed or printed, the recipients of the file see the format as it appeared in Access and cannot easily change the data. The *Save as type* option also includes *PDF*. PDF stands for *Portable Document Format,* which is also a fixed-layout format with all formatting preserved for file sharing purposes.

Once you have selected the required file format, navigate to the desired drive and/or folder in which the file should be stored and change the file name if necessary. Click the Publish button when finished to create the file.

Project 3 **Publishing a Report as an XPS Document** **Part 1 of 1**

1. With the **AL2-C8-RSRCompServ.accdb** database open, export the WorkOrdersbyMonth report as an XPS document by completing the following steps:
   a. Click to select the WorkOrdersbyMonth report in the Navigation pane.
   b. Click the PDF or XPS button in the Export group of the External Data tab.
   c. If necessary, navigate to the Access2010L2C8 folder at the Publish as PDF or XPS dialog box.

d. With *WorkOrdersbyMonth* entered in the *File name* text box, publish the report as an XPS document by completing the following steps:
   1) Click the *Save as type* option and then click *XPS Document (*.xps)*.
   2) If necessary, click the *Open file after publishing* check box to clear the check mark.
   3) Click the Publish button.

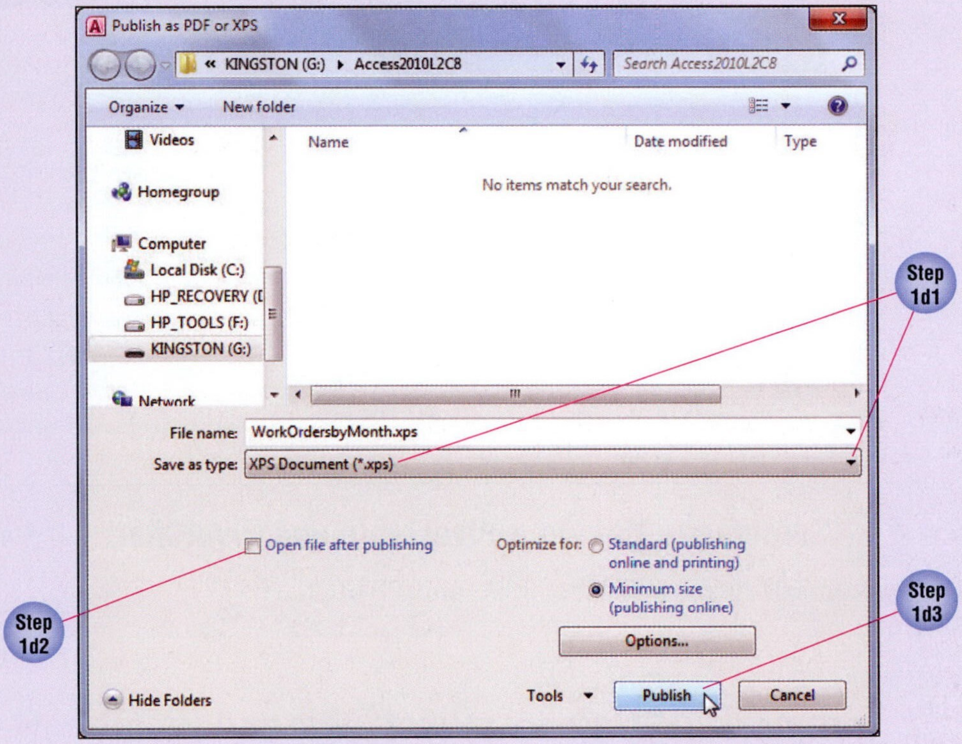

e. Click the Close button at the Export - XPS dialog box to close the dialog box without saving the export steps.

Similar to PDF files that require the Adobe Reader program in which to view documents, you need a viewer in order to read an XPS document. The viewer is provided by Microsoft and is included with Windows Vista and Windows 7.

The WorkOrdersbyMonth.xps document created in Project 3 is shown in an XPS Viewer window in Figure 8.11.

Figure 8.11 WorkOrdersbyMonth.xps Opened in XPS Viewer Window

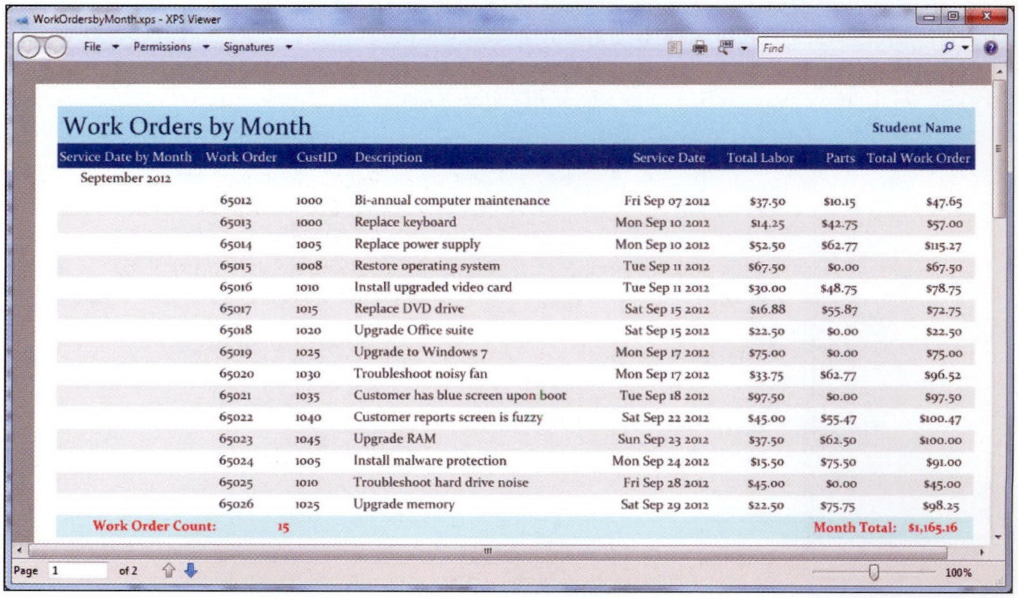

Work Orders by Month — Student Name

Service Date by Month	Work Order	CustID	Description	Service Date	Total Labor	Parts	Total Work Order
September 2012							
	65012	1000	Bi-annual computer maintenance	Fri Sep 07 2012	$37.50	$10.15	$47.65
	65013	1000	Replace keyboard	Mon Sep 10 2012	$14.25	$42.75	$57.00
	65014	1005	Replace power supply	Mon Sep 10 2012	$52.50	$62.77	$115.27
	65015	1008	Restore operating system	Tue Sep 11 2012	$67.50	$0.00	$67.50
	65016	1010	Install upgraded video card	Tue Sep 11 2012	$30.00	$48.75	$78.75
	65017	1015	Replace DVD drive	Sat Sep 15 2012	$16.88	$55.87	$72.75
	65018	1020	Upgrade Office suite	Sat Sep 15 2012	$22.50	$0.00	$22.50
	65019	1025	Upgrade to Windows 7	Mon Sep 17 2012	$75.00	$0.00	$75.00
	65020	1030	Troubleshoot noisy fan	Mon Sep 17 2012	$33.75	$62.77	$96.52
	65021	1035	Customer has blue screen upon boot	Tue Sep 18 2012	$97.50	$0.00	$97.50
	65022	1040	Customer reports screen is fuzzy	Sat Sep 22 2012	$45.00	$55.47	$100.47
	65023	1045	Upgrade RAM	Sun Sep 23 2012	$37.50	$62.50	$100.00
	65024	1005	Install malware protection	Mon Sep 24 2012	$15.50	$75.50	$91.00
	65025	1010	Troubleshoot hard drive noise	Fri Sep 28 2012	$45.00	$0.00	$45.00
	65026	1025	Upgrade memory	Sat Sep 29 2012	$22.50	$75.75	$98.25
Work Order Count:	15					Month Total:	$1,165.16

Project 4 Summarize Data in a PivotTable and PivotChart — 4 Parts

You will summarize data in a PivotTable and PivotChart.

Summarizing Data in a PivotTable and PivotChart

Pivot Table

Access provides additional views in a table and query that you can use to summarize data. Change to the PivotTable view to create a PivotTable, which is an interactive table that organizes and summarizes data. Use the PivotChart view to create a PivotChart that summarizes data in a graph.

Summarizing Data in a PivotTable

Quick Steps

Create PivotTable
1. Open table or query.
2. Click PivotTable View button.
   OR
   Click View button arrow and click *PivotTable View*.
3. Drag fields from *PivotTable Field List* box to desired dimmed text locations.

A PivotTable is an interactive table that organizes and summarizes data based on fields you designate as row headings and column headings. A numeric column you select is then grouped by the row and column field and the data summarized using a function such as Sum, Average, or Count. PivotTables are useful management tools since you can analyze data in a variety of scenarios by filtering a row, a column, or another filter field and instantly see the change in results. The interactivity of a PivotTable allows one to examine a variety of scenarios with just a few mouse clicks.

To create a PivotTable, open a table or query in Datasheet view and then click the PivotTable View button in the view area at the right side of the Status bar, or click the View button arrow in the Views group in the Home tab and then click *PivotTable View* at the drop-down list. This displays the datasheet in PivotTable layout with four sections along with a *PivotTable Field List* box as shown in Figure 8.12. Dimmed text in each section describes the types of fields you should drag and drop.

Figure 8.12 PivotTable View

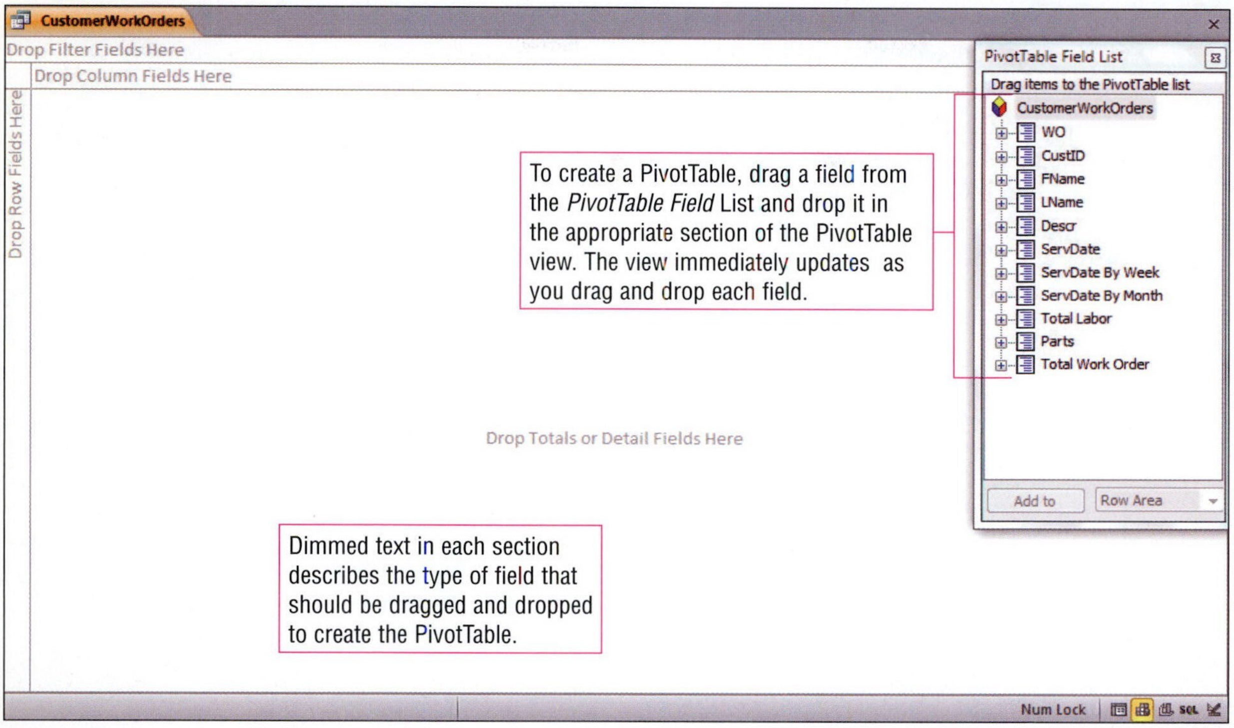

Drag the fields from the *PivotTable Field List* box to the desired locations in the PivotTable layout. The dimmed text in the PivotTable layout identifies the field you should drop in the location. In Project 4a, you will drag the *LName* field to the Row field section, the *ServDate by Month* field to the Column field section, and the *Total Work Order* field to the Totals or Details field section. After adding summary totals and hiding details, the PivotTable will display as shown in Figure 8.13.

Figure 8.13 PivotTable for Project 4a

CustomerWorkOrders

Drop Filter Fields Here

	Months		
	Sep	Oct	Grand Total
LName	Sum of Total Work Order	Sum of Total Work Order	Sum of Total Work Order
Bodzek	$173.25	$41.63	$214.88
Carmichael	$67.50	$723.87	$791.37
Cobb	$22.50	$322.60	$345.10
Fahri	$206.27		$206.27
Fennema	$100.00	$97.50	$197.50
Fleming	$104.65	$448.75	$553.40
Friesen	$72.75	$46.25	$119.00
Lemaire	$123.75	$555.50	$679.25
Machado	$100.47	$22.50	$122.97
Pierson	$96.52	$129.38	$225.90
Woodside	$97.50	$56.25	$153.75
Grand Total	$1,165.16	$2,444.22	$3,609.38

Project 4a Summarizing Data in a PivotTable

Part 1 of 4

1. With the **AL2-C8-RSRCompServ.accdb** database open, modify an existing query to add fields needed for summarizing data in a PivotTable by completing the following steps:
   a. Open the TotalWorkOrders query in Design view.
   b. Click the Show Table button in the Query Setup group. At the Show Table dialog box, double-click *Customers* in the Tables list box and then click the Close button.
   c. Drag *FName* from the Customers field list box to the *Descr* field in the query design grid. The *FName* column is added to the query and the existing *Descr* column and the remaining columns shift right.

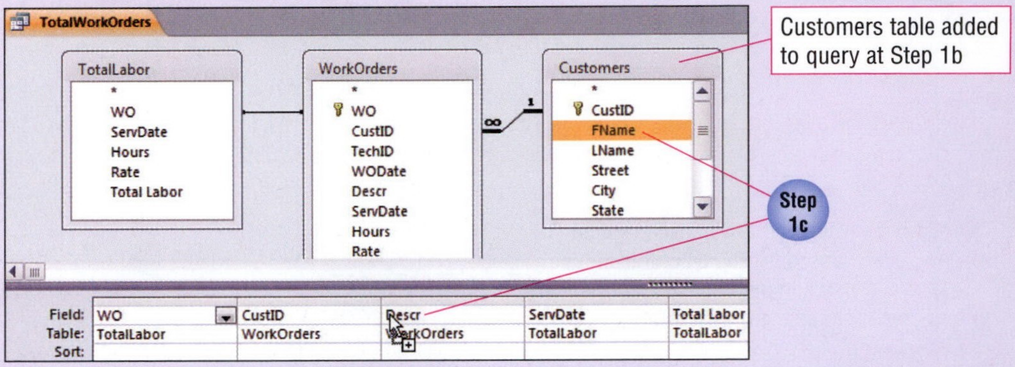

   d. Drag *LName* from the Customers field list box to the *Descr* field in the query design grid.
   e. Run the query.

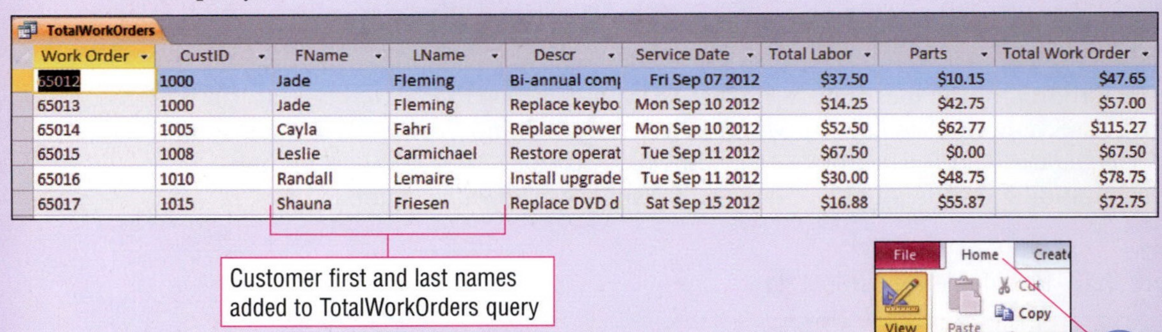

Work Order	CustID	FName	LName	Descr	Service Date	Total Labor	Parts	Total Work Order
65012	1000	Jade	Fleming	Bi-annual com	Fri Sep 07 2012	$37.50	$10.15	$47.65
65013	1000	Jade	Fleming	Replace keybo	Mon Sep 10 2012	$14.25	$42.75	$57.00
65014	1005	Cayla	Fahri	Replace power	Mon Sep 10 2012	$52.50	$62.77	$115.27
65015	1008	Leslie	Carmichael	Restore operat	Tue Sep 11 2012	$67.50	$0.00	$67.50
65016	1010	Randall	Lemaire	Install upgrade	Tue Sep 11 2012	$30.00	$48.75	$78.75
65017	1015	Shauna	Friesen	Replace DVD d	Sat Sep 15 2012	$16.88	$55.87	$72.75

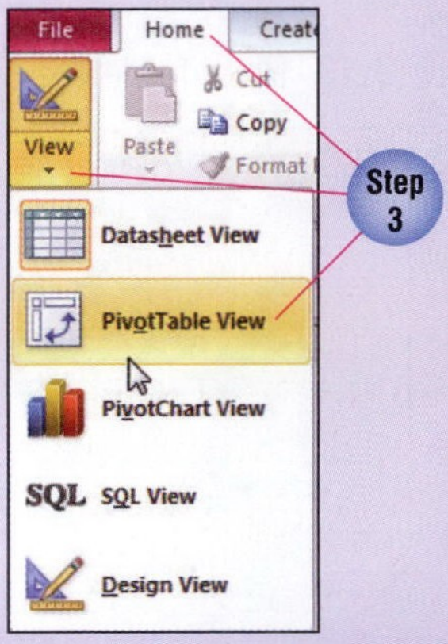

2. Click the File tab, click Save Object As, type **CustomerWorkOrders** at the Save As dialog box, and press Enter or click OK.
3. Click the Home tab, click the View button arrow in the Views group, and then click *PivotTable View* at the drop-down list.
4. At the PivotTable view, drag and drop the *LName* field to the Row field section by completing the following steps:
   a. Position the mouse pointer on the *LName* field in the *PivotTable Field List* box.

b. Hold down the left mouse button, drag to the dimmed text *Drop Row Fields Here* located at the left side of the PivotTable view, and then release the mouse button. Access updates the view to show one row for each unique customer name in the query results datasheet.

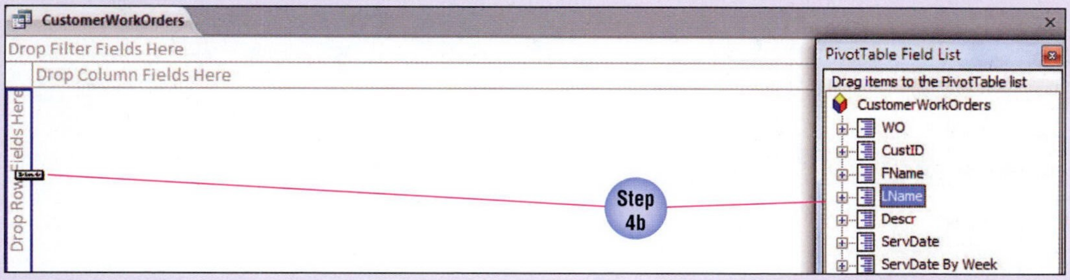

5. Add the column field to summarize the work orders by month by completing the following steps:
   a. Click the expand button (displays as a plus symbol) next to *ServDate by Month* in the *PivotTable Field List* box. This expands the list to show the *ServDate* field in various time intervals such as *Years*, *Quarters*, *Months*, and so on.
   b. Drag the *Months* field in the expanded *ServDate by Month* list from the *PivotTable Field List* box and drop it on the dimmed text *Drop Column Fields Here*. Access updates the view to show one column for each month in the query results datasheet.

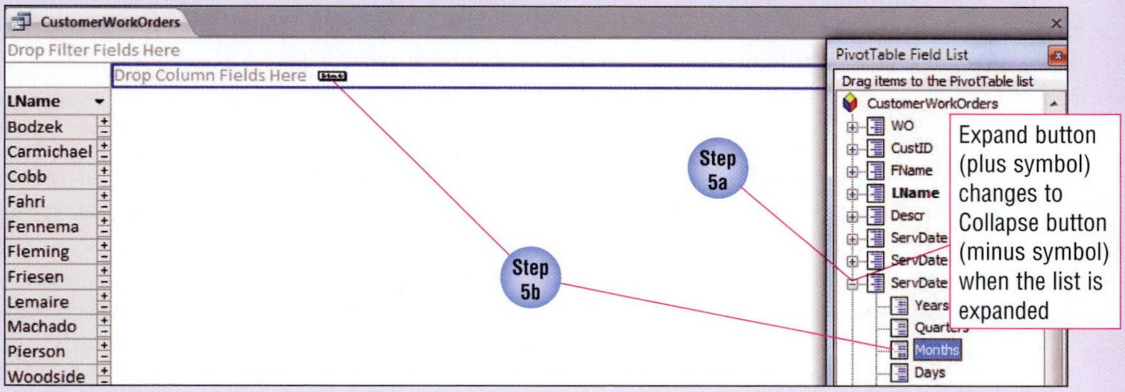

6. Scroll down the *PivotTable Field List* box if necessary and then drag the *Total Work Order* field from the *PivotTable Field List* box and drop it on the dimmed text *Drop Totals or Detail Fields Here*. Access organizes the data and shows the total work order value for each work order by customer by month in the PivotTable.
7. Remove the *PivotTable Field List* box from the screen by clicking the Field List button in the Show/Hide group in the PivotTable Tools Design tab.
8. Add summary totals and hide details by completing the following steps:
   a. Click either one of the *Total Work Order* column headings below *Sep* or *Oct* in the PivotTable. This selects all of the values in the PivotTable.

b. Click the AutoCalc button in the Tools group of the PivotTable Tools Design tab and then click *Sum* at the drop-down list. Access adds a subtotal of the work order values for each customer below each month and a total of all work orders for each customer in the *Grand Total* column at the right.

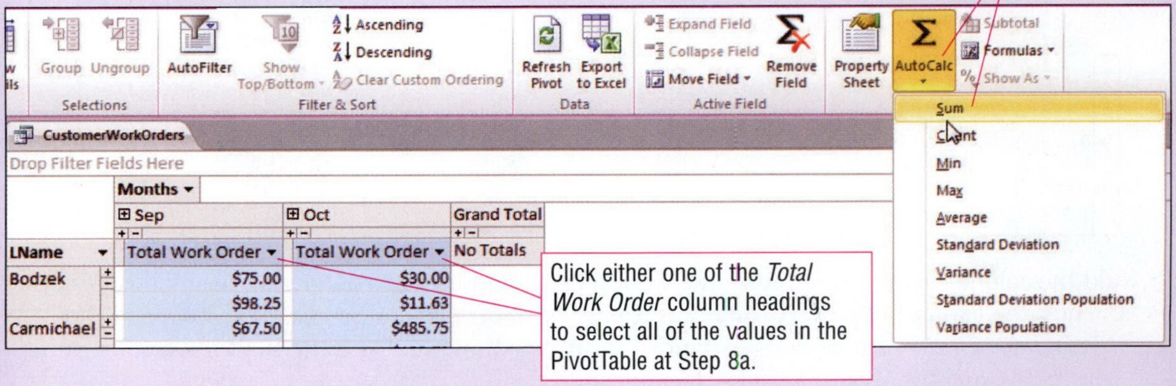

c. Click the Hide Details button in the Show/Hide group of the PivotTable Tools Design tab. Access removes the individual work order values and shows the summary totals only for each customer.

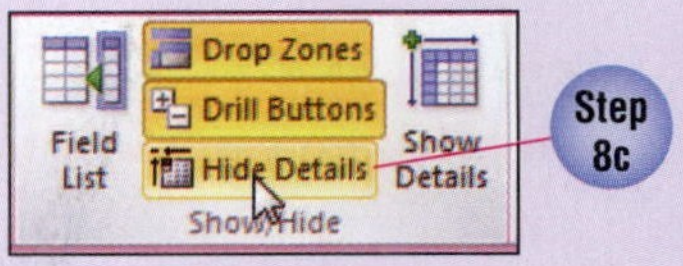

9. Compare your results with Figure 8.13 on page 303.
10. Save and then close the CustomerWorkOrders query.

When you create a PivotTable in a query or table, it becomes a part of and is saved with the table or query. The next time you open the table or query, display the PivotTable by clicking the PivotTable View button in the view area on the Status bar or by clicking the View button arrow in the Views group in the Home tab and then clicking *PivotTable View* at the drop-down list. If you make changes to data in fields that are part of the table or query, the data is automatically updated in the PivotTable.

The power of a PivotTable is the ability to analyze data for numerous scenarios. For example, in the PivotTable you created in Project 4a, you can display work orders for a specific date or a specific customer or group of customers. Use the plus and minus symbols that display in a row or column heading to show (plus symbol) or hide (minus symbol) data. Use the down-pointing arrow (called the ***filter arrow***) that displays next to a field name to filter the PivotTable by one or more values in the field.

Project 4b Analyzing Data in PivotTable View — Part 2 of 4

1. With the **AL2-C8-RSRCompServ.accdb** database open, open the CustomerWorkOrders query.
2. Click the View button arrow in the Views group in the Home tab and then click *PivotTable View* at the drop-down list.

3. Display only those work orders from September by completing the following steps:
   a. Click the filter arrow (down-pointing black arrow) at the right of *Months* (located above the *Sep* and *Oct* columns in the PivotTable).
   b. At the drop-down list that displays, click the *(All)* check box to remove the check mark.
   c. Click the expand button (displays as a plus symbol) next to *2012*.
   d. Click the expand button next to *Qtr3*.
   e. Click the *Sep* check box to insert a check mark.
   f. Click OK. Notice the arrow on the *Months* button changes color to blue to indicate the PivotTable is filtered by the field.

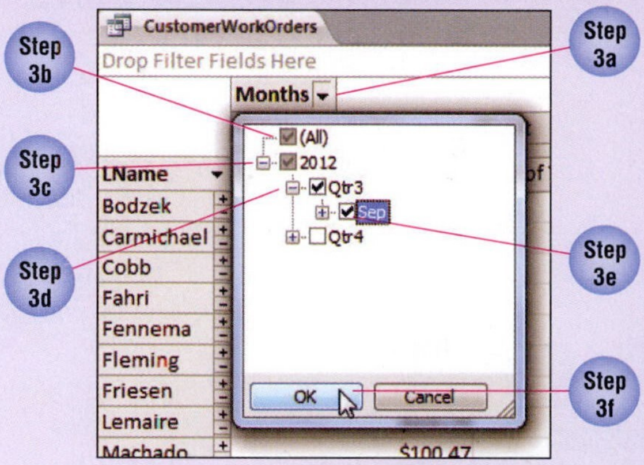

4. Redisplay all months by clicking the *Months* filter arrow, clicking the *(All)* check box, and then clicking OK.

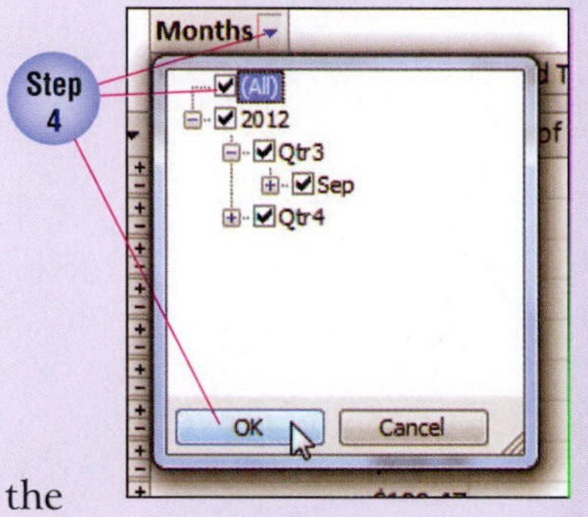

5. Display only those work orders for Fahri, Fennema, and Fleming by completing the following steps:
   a. Click the filter arrow next to the *LName* field.
   b. At the drop-down list, click the *(All)* check box to remove the check mark before each customer name.
   c. Click the check box next to *Fahri*.
   d. Click the check box next to *Fennema*.
   e. Click the check box next to *Fleming*.
   f. Click OK.
6. Redisplay all customers by clicking the *LName* filter arrow, clicking the *(All)* check box, and then clicking OK.
7. Save, print, and then close the PivotTable.

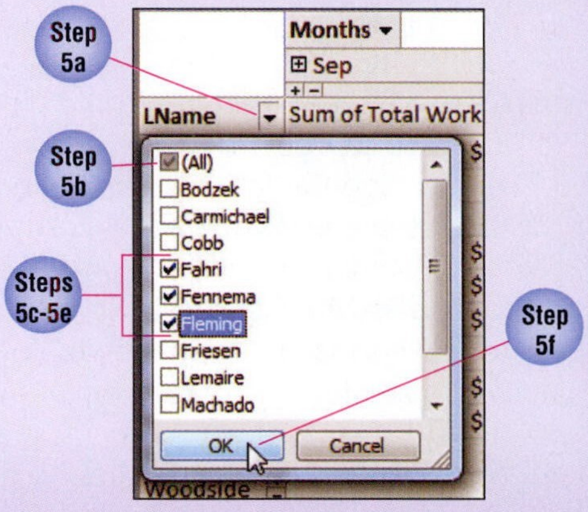

Summarizing Data in a PivotTable Form

When you create a PivotTable in a query or table, the PivotTable settings are saved and become part of the table or query. When you open a table or query in which you have created a PivotTable and then switch to PivotTable view, the table or query displays with the PivotTable settings you created. If you want to view different fields or perform other functions in PivotTable view, you have to edit the last settings. For example, if you created a PivotTable in a Work Orders query that summed the total work order field by customer and by month, and then wanted to sum by quarter, you would have to edit the previous PivotTable. If you want to routinely view data in PivotTable view by different criteria (such as by month and by quarter), consider creating a PivotTable form. A PivotTable form is a separate object from the query or table, so you could create one showing the sum by month and another showing the sum by quarter. This way, you do not have to constantly edit the PivotTable's settings each time you want to change the way the data is summarized.

To create a PivotTable form, click the desired object in the Navigation pane and then click the Create tab. Click the More Forms button in the Forms group and then click *PivotTable* at the drop-down list. This displays the object in PivotTable layout. Click the Field List button in the Show/Hide group to display the *PivotTable Field List* box. (You may need to click the button twice to display the list box.)

Project 4c **Creating a PivotTable Form** Part 3 of 4

1. With the **AL2-C8-RSRCompServ.accdb** database open, save the CustomerWorkOrders query as a form by completing the following steps:
   a. Click to select the CustomerWorkOrders query in the Navigation pane.
   b. Click the File tab and then click *Save Object As* at the Info tab Backstage view.
   c. At the Save As dialog box, type **CustWorkOrders** in the *Save 'CustomerWorkOrders' to* text box.
   d. Click the down-pointing arrow at the right of the *As* list box (currently reads *Query*) and then click *Form* at the drop-down list.
   e. Click OK.
   f. Click the Home tab and then close the CustWorkOrders form.

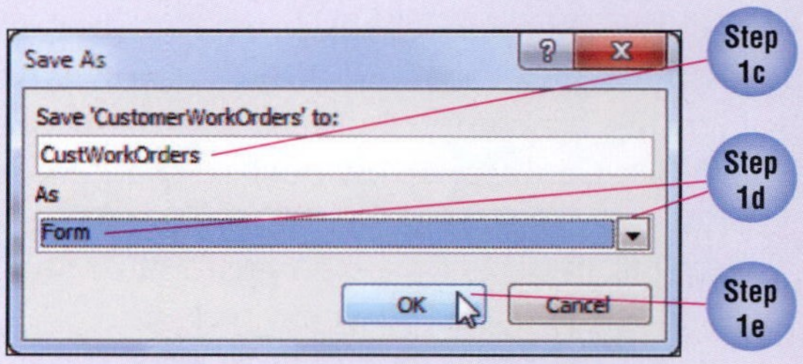

2. Create a PivotTable form by completing the following steps:
   a. Click the CustWorkOrders form in the Navigation pane.
   b. Click the Create tab.
   c. Click the More Forms button in the Forms group and then click *PivotTable* at the drop-down list.
   d. At the PivotTable form, click twice on the Field List button in the Show/Hide group in the PivotTable Tools Design tab.
   e. Drag the *LName* field in the *PivotTable Field List* box and drop it on the dimmed text *Drop Row Fields Here*.
   f. Expand the *ServDate By Month* field in the *PivotTable Field List* box, and then drag the *Months* field to the dimmed text *Drop Column Fields Here*.

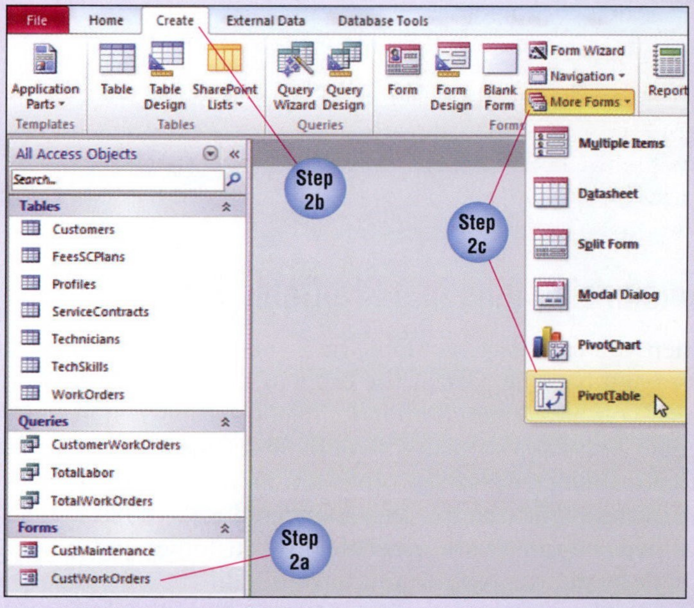

g. Drag the *Total Work Order* field from the *PivotTable Field List* box and drop it on the dimmed text *Drop Totals or Detail Fields Here*.
h. Close the *PivotTable Field List* box.

3. Click to select either one of the *Total Work Order* column headings, click the AutoCalc button in the Tools group of the PivotTable Tools Design tab, and then click *Sum* at the drop-down list.
4. Display only the work orders for Fleming and save the filtered PivotTable in a new form by completing the following steps:
   a. Click the filter arrow at the right of the *LName* field.
   b. Click the *(All)* check box to remove all of the check marks, click the *Fleming* check box to insert a check mark, and then click OK.
   c. Click the Save button on the Quick Access toolbar.
   d. At the Save As dialog box, type **FlemingWorkOrders** and then press Enter or click OK.
5. Close the FlemingWorkOrders PivotTable form.

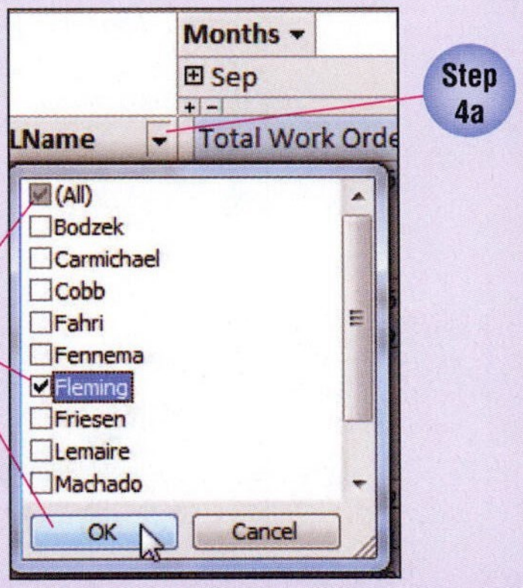

Summarizing Data Using PivotChart View

A PivotChart performs the same function as a PivotTable with the exception that Access displays the source data in a graph instead of a table or query. You create a chart by dragging fields from the *Chart Field List* box to the *Filter, Data, Category,* and *Series* sections of the chart. As with a PivotTable, you can easily alter the PivotChart using the filter arrows.

To create a PivotChart, open a table or query in Datasheet view, click the PivotChart View button in the view area at the right side of the Status bar, or click the View button arrow in the Views group in the Home tab, and then click *PivotChart View* at the drop-down list. This changes the datasheet to PivotChart layout, which contains four sections, and displays the *Chart Field List* box. Dimmed text in each section describes the types of fields that you should drag and drop. If a table or query datasheet has previously had a PivotTable that has been saved with the table or query, PivotChart view automatically graphs the existing PivotTable. For example, Figure 8.14 displays the PivotChart that appears if you open the CustomerWorkOrders query and change the view to PivotChart view. The PivotChart is dynamically linked to the PivotTable you created in Project 4a.

Quick Steps

Create PivotChart
1. Open table or query.
2. Click PivotChart View button.
   OR
   Click View button arrow and click *PivotChart View*.
3. Drag fields from *Chart Field List* box to desired dimmed text locations.

Pivot Chart

Figure 8.14 PivotChart Connected to PivotTable Created in Project 4a

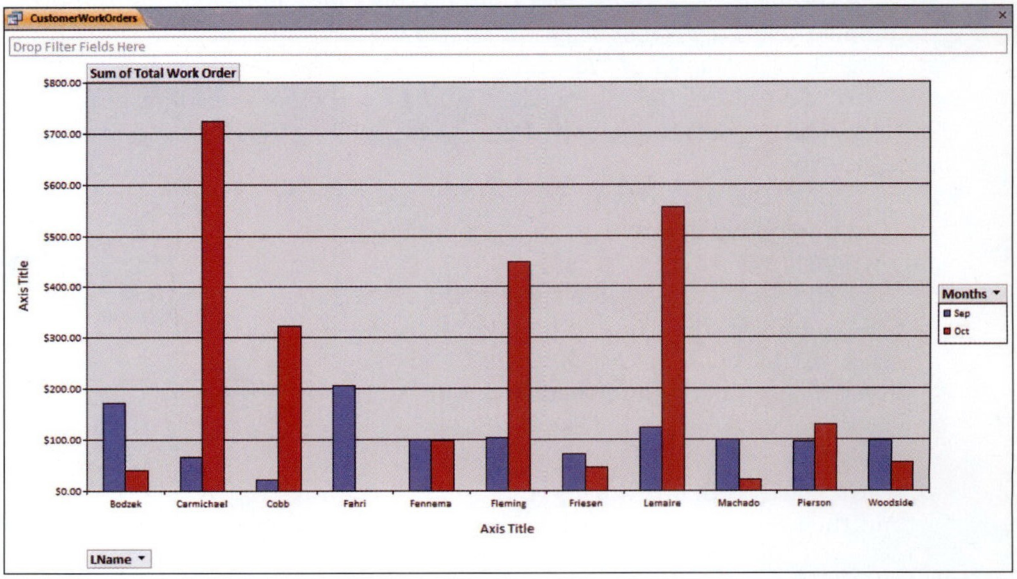

Figure 8.15 illustrates the PivotChart layout for a query or table for which no previous PivotTable exists. Drag the fields from the *Chart Field List* box to the desired locations in the PivotChart layout. The dimmed text in the PivotChart layout identifies the field you should drop in the location. In Project 4d, you will create a new query to summarize the work order values by the technicians who performed the service work. You will begin by creating a new query with the fields from two tables and then change the view to build the PivotChart from scratch.

Figure 8.15 PivotChart View for Table or Query with No Pre-Existing PivotTable

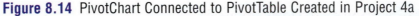

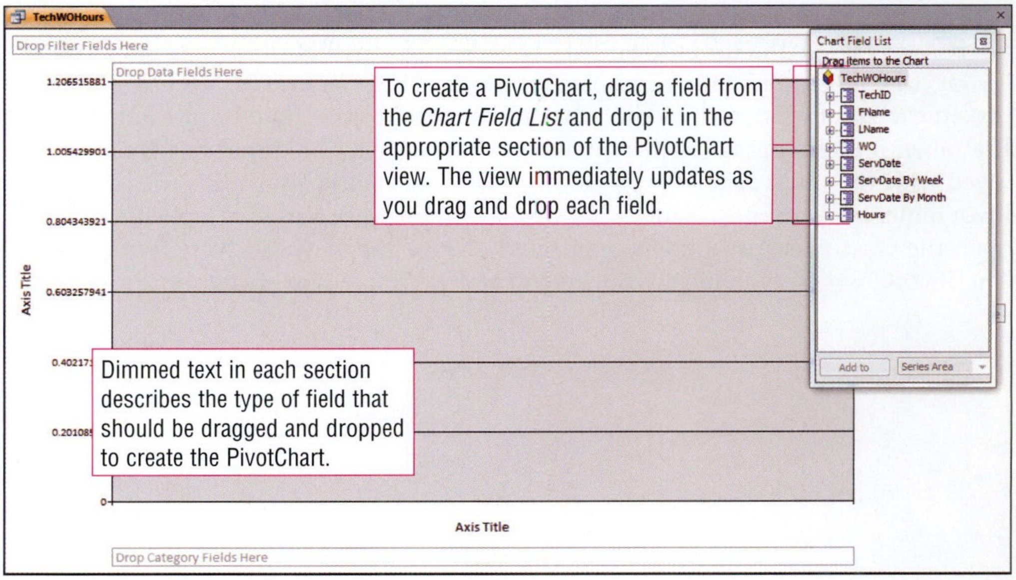

Project 4d Summarizing Data in a PivotChart

Part 4 of 4

1. With the **AL2-C8-RSRCompServ.accdb** database open, create a new query in Design view with the following specifications:
   a. Add the Technicians and WorkOrders tables to the design grid.
   b. Add the following fields from the specified tables:

      TechID = Technicians table
      FName = Technicians table
      LName = Technicians table
      WO = WorkOrders table
      ServDate = WorkOrders table
      Hours = WorkOrders table

   c. Run the query.
   d. Save the query and name it *TechWOHours*.

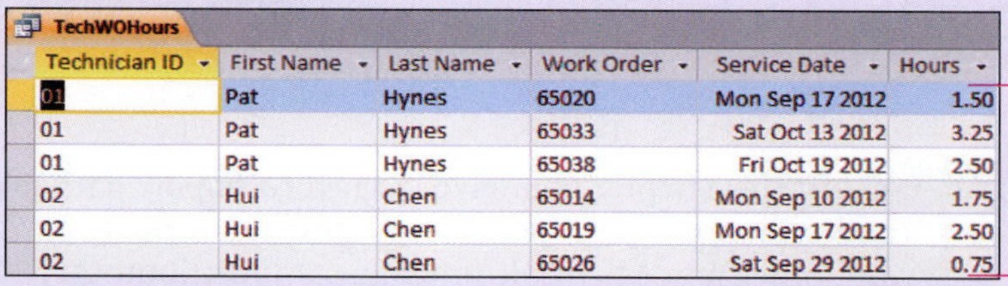

TechWOHours

Technician ID	First Name	Last Name	Work Order	Service Date	Hours
01	Pat	Hynes	65020	Mon Sep 17 2012	1.50
01	Pat	Hynes	65033	Sat Oct 13 2012	3.25
01	Pat	Hynes	65038	Fri Oct 19 2012	2.50
02	Hui	Chen	65014	Mon Sep 10 2012	1.75
02	Hui	Chen	65019	Mon Sep 17 2012	2.50
02	Hui	Chen	65026	Sat Sep 29 2012	0.75

Steps 1a-1d

2. Click the View button arrow in the Views group in the Home tab and then click *PivotChart View* at the drop-down list.
3. At the PivotChart layout, drag and drop the following fields:
   a. Drag the *LName* field from the *Chart Field List* box and drop it on the dimmed text *Drop Category Fields Here*.
   b. Expand the *ServDate By Month* field in the *Chart Field List* box and then drag the *Months* field to the dimmed text *Drop Series Fields* here. ***Hint: You may need to drag the* Chart Field List *box out of the way to see the dimmed text* Drop Series Fields *here.***
   c. Drag the *Hours* field (make sure you drag the *Hours* field name that appears last in the list) from the *Chart Field List* box and drop it on the dimmed text *Drop Data Fields Here*.
4. Remove the *Chart Field List* box from the screen by clicking the Field List button in the Show/Hide group.
5. Click the Legend button in the Show/Hide group of the PivotTable Tools Design tab. A legend appears below the Months field button at the right side of the PivotChart.

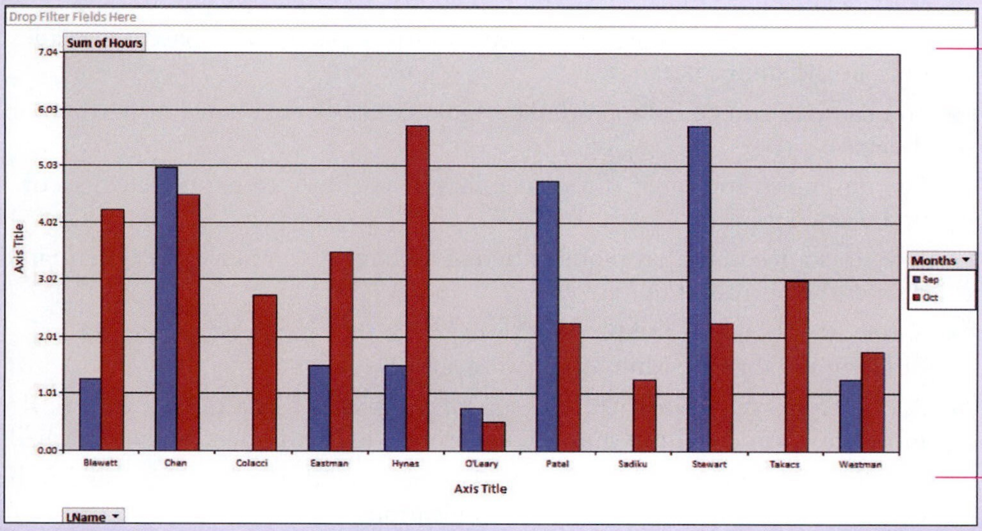

PivotChart created in Steps 3–5

6. Save the PivotChart.
7. Click the View button arrow in the Views group and then click *PivotTable View* at the drop-down list. Notice that Access automatically created a PivotTable behind the scenes as you built the PivotChart.
8. Close the TechWOHours query.

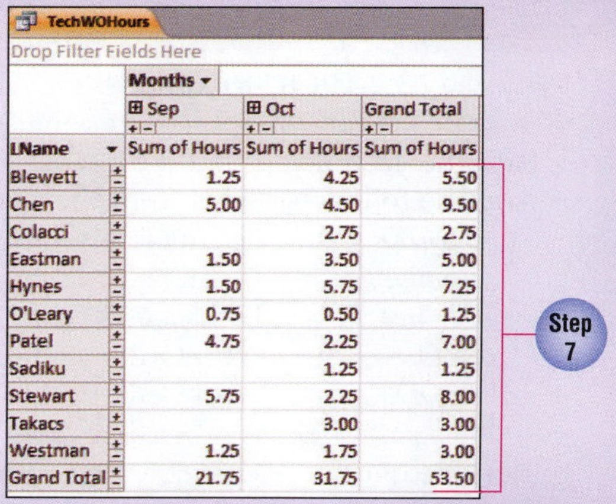

	Months		
	Sep	Oct	Grand Total
LName	Sum of Hours	Sum of Hours	Sum of Hours
Blewett	1.25	4.25	5.50
Chen	5.00	4.50	9.50
Colacci		2.75	2.75
Eastman	1.50	3.50	5.00
Hynes	1.50	5.75	7.25
O'Leary	0.75	0.50	1.25
Patel	4.75	2.25	7.00
Sadiku		1.25	1.25
Stewart	5.75	2.25	8.00
Takacs		3.00	3.00
Westman	1.25	1.75	3.00
Grand Total	21.75	31.75	53.50

In this chapter you have learned to import data from another Access database and to import and export using a text file format to exchange data between Access and other non-Microsoft programs. To distribute Access data with formatting preserved in a non-editable format, publish an object as a PDF or XPS document. Finally, numeric data can be summarized and analyzed by creating a PivotTable and/or a PivotChart.

Chapter Summary

- An object in another Access database can be imported into the active database using the Import Access database button in the Import & Link group of the External Data tab.
- If the source object is a table, you can choose to import or link the source table.
- In a linked table, the data is not copied into the active database but resides only in the source database.
- You can edit source data in a linked table in either the source or destination database.
- Use an import routine if the source data is not likely to require changes or updates.
- Link to source data that requires frequent changes to reduce the potential for data entry or missed update errors.
- You may also decide to link to a source table that is shared among several different databases within an organization.
- Access stores the full path to the source database when a table is linked. If you move the location of the source database the links will need to be refreshed.
- A text file is often used to exchange data between dissimilar programs because a text file is recognized by nearly all applications.

- Import a text file into an Access database by clicking the Import text file button in the Import & Link group of the External Data tab.
- When a text file is selected for import, Access launches the Text Import Wizard, which guides you through the steps to import the text into a table.
- If an import operation is often repeated, consider saving the import steps so that you can run the import routine without having to walk through each step every time you import.
- Open the Manage Data Tasks dialog box to run a saved import by clicking the Saved Imports button in the Import & Link group of the External Data tab.
- Export Access data in a text file format using the Export Text Wizard by clicking the Export to text file button in the Export group of the External Data tab.
- Within the Export Text Wizard you are prompted to choose the text format, delimiter character, field names, text qualifier symbols, and export path and file name.
- You can save export steps at the last Export - Text File dialog box in order to repeat an export operation.
- Click the Saved Exports button in the Export group of the External Data tab to run a saved export routine.
- Access includes a feature that allows you to save an object in XPS or PDF format in order to distribute Access data with formatting preserved in a non-editable format.
- Publish an object by selecting the object name in the Navigation pane and then clicking the PDF or XPS button in the Export group in the External Data tab.
- A PivotTable is an interactive table that organizes and summarizes data which can easily be filtered to display the effects of different scenarios.
- Open a table or query datasheet and change to PivotTable view to build a PivotTable by dragging field names from the *PivotTable Field List* box to the appropriate dimmed text locations in the view.
- Create a PivotTable form by clicking the More Forms button in the Forms group of the Create tab and then clicking *PivotTable* at the drop-down list.
- Create separate PivotTable forms for those situations where you need to routinely view the same data by different filter criteria. Each PivotTable form is a separate object that allows you to maintain individual PivotTable settings.
- A PivotChart allows you to analyze data in a graph format rather than a table format. Change to PivotChart view to view the chart for an existing PivotTable, or create a new chart from scratch.

Commands Review

FEATURE	RIBBON TAB, GROUP	BUTTON
Export data as text file	External Data, Export	
Import or link data from Access database	External Data, Import & Link	
Import data from text file	External Data, Import & Link	
Linked Table Manager	External Data, Import & Link	
PivotTable form	Create, Forms	
PivotTable view	Home, Views	
PivotChart view	Home, Views	
Save object as XPS document	External Data, Export	
Saved exports	External Data, Export	
Saved imports	External Data, Import & Link	

Concepts Check Test Your Knowledge

Completion: In the space provided at the right, indicate the correct term, command, or number.

1. Click this button at the Import Objects dialog box to choose whether or not relationships between tables will be imported. ____________________
2. Click this option at the Get External Data - Access Database dialog box to create a table in which changes to data are automatically updated in either the source or destination databases. ____________________
3. Data that is not likely to be changed should be brought into the active database from another database using this method. ____________________
4. Data that is updated frequently should be brought into the active database from another database using this method. ____________________
5. If the location of a source database has moved, open this dialog box to refresh the link to the source table. ____________________

6. This type of file format is used to exchange data between programs for which an application-specific file format converter is not available. ____________

7. A file in which each field is separated by a comma has this file extension. ____________

8. Click this check box at the last Get External Data dialog box to store the steps used in the import process in order to repeat the import routine at a future date. ____________

9. The Export Text Wizard is launched from this button in the Export group in the External Data tab. ____________

10. XPS is a document format that stands for this type of document specification. ____________

11. Change to this view to create an interactive table that organizes data by fields you specify for row and column headings and calculates a Sum function for each group. ____________

12. This type of form allows you to store an interactive table and is created using the More Forms button in the Forms group of the Create tab. ____________

13. Change to this view to create an interactive chart that graphs data by fields you specify. ____________

Skills Check Assess Your Performance

Assessment 1

IMPORT AND LINK OBJECTS FROM ANOTHER ACCESS DATABASE

1. Open the database named **AL2-C8-VantageStock.accdb** and enable content.
2. Using **AL2-C8-VantageVideos.accdb** as the data source, integrate the following objects into the active database.
   a. Import the form named WebProducts.
   b. Link to the tables named WebProducts, WebOrders, and WebOrderDetails.
3. Display the Relationships window and create a relationship between the WebProducts and WebProductsCost tables using the field named *WebProdID*. Save and close the Relationships window.
4. Modify the WebProducts form as follows:
   a. Open the form in Layout view.
   b. Delete the *Retail Value* label and text box control objects at the bottom of the form. This will leave the form with four fields: *Product ID, Product, In Stock,* and *Selling Price*.
   c. Display the Field List pane and show all tables in the pane. Expand the field list for the WebProductsCost table.
   d. Add the field named *CostPrice* below the *Selling Price* field in the form.

e. Move, resize, and format the field as necessary so that the cost price displays similarly to the selling price.
f. Modify the form title to *Inventory Stock and Pricing*.

5. Save the revised form, print the form for the first record only, and then close the form.
6. Open the WebProdCostsWithSupp query in Design view and modify the query as follows:
   a. Add the WebProducts table to the query.
   b. Add the *SellPrice* field to the query design grid, placing the field between the *Product* and *CostPrice* columns.
   c. Add a calculated column at the right of the *CostPrice* column that subtracts the cost price from the selling price. Display the column heading *Gross Profit*.
7. Save the revised query and then run the query.
8. Print the query in landscape orientation and then close the query.

Assessment 2

IMPORT A TEXT FILE

1. With the **AL2-C8-VantageStock.accdb** database open, append records from a text file using the following information:
   - The data source file is named **WebProducts.csv**.
   - Append a copy of the records to the end of the existing WebProductsCost table.
   - Save the import steps. You determine an appropriate description for the import routine.
2. Open the WebProductsCost table and print the table datasheet.
3. Close the datasheet.
4. Close the **AL2-C8-VantageStock.accdb** database.

Assessment 3

EXPORT AND PUBLISH ACCESS DATA

1. Open the **AL2-C8-VantageVideos.accdb** database and enable content.
2. Export the query named CustWebOrders to a comma delimited text file using the following information:
   - Include the field names and remove the quotation marks.
   - Save the export steps. You determine an appropriate description for the export routine.
3. Open Notepad, open the **CustWebOrders.txt** file, and then print the document.
4. Exit Notepad.
5. Publish the WebSalesByDate report as an XPS document named **WebSalesByDate.xps**.
6. Open the **WebSalesByDate.xps** document in an XPS Viewer window (Windows 7 users) or in an Internet Explorer window (Windows Vista users) and print the document.
7. Exit XPS Viewer or Internet Explorer.

Assessment

4 ANALYZE WEB SALES USING A PIVOTTABLE AND A PIVOTCHART

1. With the **AL2-C8-VantageVideos.accdb** database open, open the WebSalesWithTotal query and then create a PivotTable using the following information:
   - Display the customer last names in rows.
   - Sum the total sale by months in columns.
   - Hide details so that only the total for each month displays next to each customer's last name.
   - Add titles and make any other formatting changes you think improve the appearance of the table.
   - Save and print the PivotTable and then close the query.
2. Open the WebOrdersByProd query and then create a PivotChart using the following information:
   - Display the Months (*DateOrd by Month*) as the category axis labels.
   - Graph the average of the selling price field.
   - Add titles or make any other formatting changes you think improve the appearance of the chart. ***Hint: You can add a title to an axis by right-clicking the axis title, selecting* Properties, *and then typing the desired title in the Caption property of the Format tab.***
   - Save and print the PivotChart and then close the query.
3. Close the **AL2-C8-VantageVideos.accdb** database.

Visual Benchmark Demonstrate Your Proficiency

ANALYZE RESERVATION DATABASE

1. Open **AL2-C8-PawsParadise.accdb** and enable content.
2. Create a PivotTable similar to the one shown in Figure 8.16 using the ReservationTotals query. Note that the table is filtered to show only the V.I.P. Suite data.
3. Save, print, and then close the PivotTable.
4. Open the DaysBoarded query.
5. Create a PivotChart similar to the one shown in Figure 8.17. Note that the chart is filtered to show only the number of days boarded for each dog in week 47. ***Hint: To adjust the scale in the value axis, right-click any value to select the axis, click* Properties *at the shortcut menu and change the major unit to a whole number in the Scale tab.***
6. Save, print, and then close the PivotChart.
7. Close the **AL2-C8-PawsParadise.accdb** database.

Figure 8.16 Visual Benchmark Assessment PivotTable

Type		
V.I.P. Suite		
	Drop Column Fields Here	
LName	Sum of Amount Due	Sum of Days Boarded
Doherty	$192.50	5
Gallagher	$115.50	3
Jenkins	$231.00	6
Murphy	$154.00	4
Rivera	$192.50	5
Torres	$154.00	4
Grand Total	$1,039.50	27

Figure 8.17 Visual Benchmark Assessment PivotChart

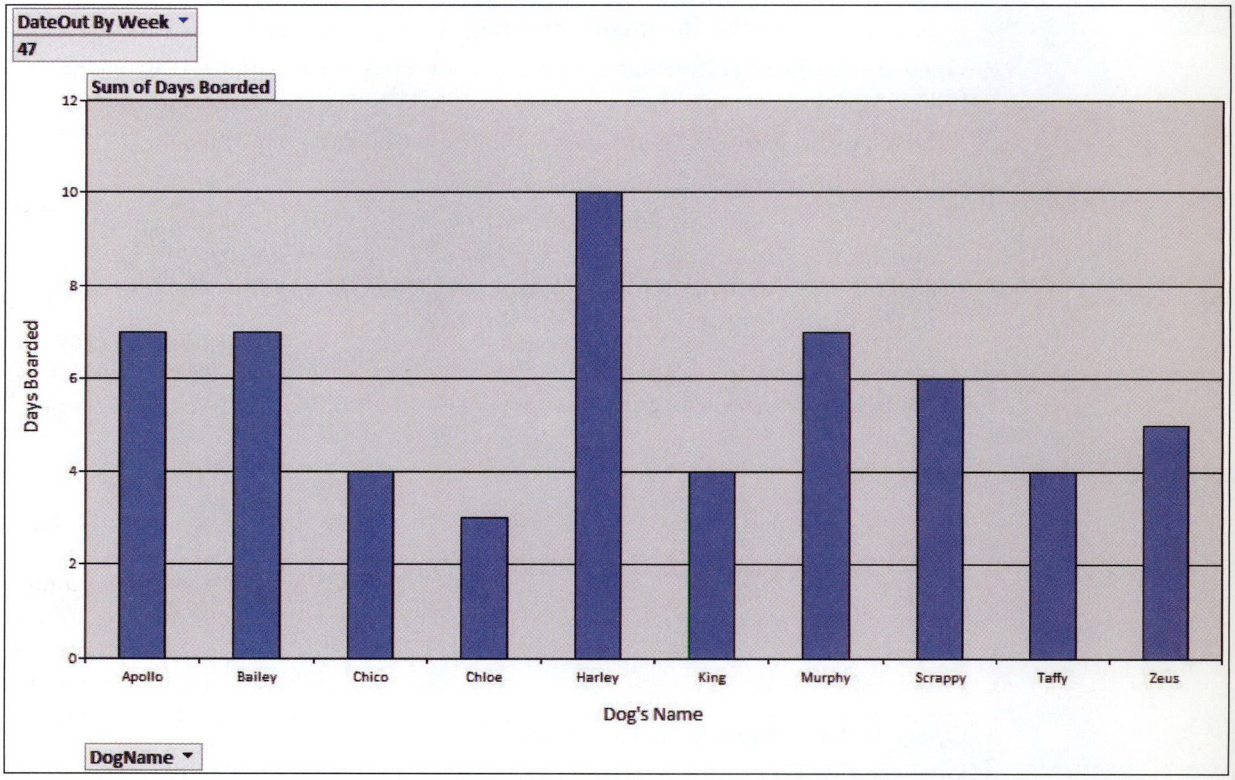

Case Study Apply Your Skills

Part 1

The office manager at Hillsdale Realty has asked you to assist her with summarizing data for the monthly sales meeting. Open the **AL2-C8-HillsdaleRealty.accdb** database and enable content. Using the SalesByAgentWithComm query, create a PivotTable that illustrates for each sales agent, the total sale price and the total commissions earned. Organize the PivotTable so that the sales and commissions are in columns by city. This will enable the office manager to filter the report to view the data by city. Show totals only for each salesperson. Save, print, and then close the PivotTable.

Part 2

The office manager would like the Listings table data exported from the database to use in a custom software package that accepts comma separated data files. Create the text file for the manager including field names and quotations symbols as text qualifiers. Save the export steps since the manager has advised this data exchange file will be required often. Print the text file for your records.

The CEO has requested an electronic copy of the SalesAndCommissions report. The CEO is not familiar with Access and has asked that you send the report with the formatting as displayed in Access but in a file that can be opened on her laptop that does not have Microsoft Office software. Publish the report as an XPS document using the default name and email the report to your professor as an email attachment using an appropriate subject line and message. ***Note: Check with your instructor for alternate instructions before emailing the file in case he or she would prefer you submit the XPS file in a different manner.***

Part 3

Help

You want to find out if Access and Outlook can integrate to collect data using email messages and automatically update tables when replies are received. You decide to research this topic using Access Help. Use the search phrase *collect data using email* to locate a related Help topic. Locate and read an article that describes when to use data collection and the steps that should be completed before starting to ensure a successful data collection process. Compose a memo in your own words addressed to your instructor using Microsoft Word that provides the following information.

- Describe two scenarios in which data collection using Access and Outlook would be appropriate.
- What do you need to create if the data collection will be used to update more than one table in the Access database?
- What software is needed by the recipients of the email message in order to view the form?

Save the memo in Word and name it **AL2-C8-CS-P3-DataCollectionMemo**. Print the memo and then exit Word.

UNIT 2

Microsoft® Access®

Performance Assessment

Access
Access2010L2U2

Note: Before beginning unit assessments, copy to your storage medium the Access2010L2U2 subfolder from the Access2010L2 folder on the CD that accompanies this textbook and then make Access2010L2U2 the active folder.

Assessing Proficiency

In this unit you have learned to design and create reports with grouping, sorting, totals, and subreports; to use Access tools to analyze tables and improve database efficiency; to automate a database using macros and a Navigation form; to configure startup options and customize the database and Navigation pane; to integrate Access data with other programs; and to summarize data using PivotTables and PivotCharts.

Assessment 1 Import Data from Text Files and Create Reports for a Property Management Database

1. Open **AL2-U2-BenchmarkPropMgt.accdb** from the Access2010L2U2 folder on your storage medium and enable content. In this unit you will continue working with the residential property management database started in Unit 1. The database design and objects have been modified since Unit 1 based on feedback from the property manager and the office staff.
2. Import data into tables from two text files as follows. Save each set of import specifications for future use. You determine an appropriate description for each set of import steps.
   a. Append the data in the text file named ***TenantsU2.csv*** to the Tenants table.
   b. Append the data in the text file named ***LeasesU2.csv*** to the Leases table.
3. Design and create reports as follows:
   a. A report based on the LeasesByBldg query with all fields included except the building code field. Group the records by the building name and sort by Unit No within each group. Name the report *BuildingsAndLeases*. Include the current date and page numbering in the page footer. Add your name as the report designer in the report footer. Insert an appropriate clip art image in the report header. You determine the remaining layout and formatting elements including a descriptive report title.

b. A report based on the RentalIncome query with all fields included except the building code field. Group the records by the building name and sort by Unit No within each group. Name the report *IncomeByBuilding*. Sum the rent and annual rent columns and count the unit numbers. Show the statistics in the group footer and as grand totals at the end of the report. Include appropriate labels to describe the statistics and format the values to a suitable numeric format if necessary. Add your name as the report designer in the report footer. Insert an appropriate clip art image in the report header. You determine the remaining layout and formatting elements including a descriptive report title.

4. Print the BuildingAndLeases and IncomeByBuilding reports.

Assessment 2 Use Access Tools to Improve the Property Management Database Design

1. With the **AL2-U2-BenchmarkPropMgt.accdb** database open, use the Performance Analyzer feature to analyze all objects in the database. In the *Analysis Results* list, use the Optimize button to fix each *Suggestion* item (displays with a green question mark).
2. Use the Database Splitter to split the database into two files in order to create a back-end database. Accept the default file name at the Create Back-end Database dialog box.
3. Close the **AL2-U2-BenchmarkPropMgt.accdb** database.
4. Open the **AL2-U2-BenchmarkPropMgt_be.accdb** database and enable content.
5. Use the Database Documenter feature to generate a table definition report for the Leases table with the following options: *Include for Table* set to *Properties* and *Relationships*, *Include for Fields* set to *Names, Data Types, and Sizes* and *Include for Indexes* set to *Nothing*. Print and then close the report.
6. Close the **AL2-U2-BenchmarkPropMgt_be.accdb** database.

Assessment 3 Automate the Property Management Database with Macros and Command Buttons

1. Open the **AL2-U2-BenchmarkPropMgt.accdb** database and enable content.
2. Create the following macros. Run each macro to make sure the macro works properly, print each macro's definition, and then close the macro.
   a. A macro named *QLeasesByTenant* that opens the LeasesByTenant query in Datasheet view and Edit mode. Use the macro action *OpenQuery*.
   b. A macro named *QLeaseTerms* that opens the LeaseTermsAndDeposits query in Datasheet view and Edit mode. Use the macro action *OpenQuery*.
   c. A macro named *RBldgLeases* that opens the BuildingsAndLeases report in report view.
   d. A macro named *RIncome* that opens the IncomeByBuilding report in report view.
3. Open the BldgsAndMgrs form in Design view.

4. Create two command buttons in the Form Header section as follows. You determine the placement of the button within the section, text to display on the face of each button, and a name to assign each button.
   a. A button that runs the RBldgLeases macro.
   b. A button that runs the RIncome macro.
5. Test each button to make sure the macros display the correct report and use Print Screen or the Windows Snipping tool to make a screen capture of the BldgsAndMgrs form with the buttons displayed. Print the screen capture by pasting the image into a blank Word document. Exit Word without saving.
6. Make sure all objects are closed.

Assessment 4 Create a Navigation Form and Configure Startup Options for the Property Management Database

1. With the **AL2-U2-BenchmarkPropMgt.accdb** database open, create a Navigation form named MainMenu using the Horizontal Tabs style with forms and reports in the following tab order.
   - BldgsAndMgrs form
   - TenantsAndLeases form
   - BuildingsAndLeases report
   - IncomeByBuilding report
2. Edit the form title and delete the logo container object. You determine appropriate text to replace *Navigation Form*.
3. Edit the tab captions. You determine appropriate text for each tab.
4. Create a macro named *ExitDB* that quits Access saving all objects and then create a command button placed at the right end of the MainMenu form header section that runs the macro. You determine the text to display on the face of the button and a name for the button.
5. Display the form in Form view and click each tab to make sure the correct form or report displays.
6. Set the MainMenu form to display as the startup form, add an appropriate title as the application title for the database, and hide the Navigation pane.
7. Close and then reopen the **AL2-U2-BenchmarkPropMgt.accdb** database.
8. Use Print Screen or the Windows Snipping tool to capture an image of the database window. Paste the image into a Word document. Print the Word document and then exit Word without saving.

Assessment 5 Configure Security for the Property Management Database

1. With the **AL2-U2-BenchmarkPropMgt.accdb** database open, make an ACCDE file from the database saving the copy in the same folder and using the same file name.
2. Close the **AL2-U2-BenchmarkPropMgt.accdb** database.
3. Open the **AL2-U2-BenchmarkPropMgt.accde** database.
4. Change the database startup option to display the Navigation pane with the Tables and Macros hidden.
5. Close and then reopen **AL2-U2-BenchmarkPropMgt.accde**.
6. Use Print Screen or the Windows Snipping tool to capture an image of the database window. Paste the image into a Word document. Print the Word document and then exit Word without saving.

Assessment 6 Export and Publish Data from the Property Management Database

1. With the **AL2-U2-BenchmarkPropMgt.accde** database open, export the LeaseTermsAndDeposits query as a text file using the default name and making sure the file is saved in the Access2010L2U2 folder on your storage medium. Include the field names in the first row and remove the quotation symbols. Do not save the export steps.
2. Open Notepad, open the **LeaseTermsAndDeposits.txt** file, and then print the document.
3. Exit Notepad.
4. Publish the IncomeByBuilding report as an XPS document named **AL2-U2-BenchmarkRentInc.xps** making sure the file is saved in the Access2010L2U2 folder on your storage medium. Do not save the export steps.
5. Open the **AL2-U2-BenchmarkRentInc.xps** document in an XPS window (Windows 7) or Internet Explorer window (Windows Vista) and print the report.
6. Exit the XPS or Internet Explorer window

Assessment 7 Summarize Rental Income in a PivotTable and PivotChart

1. With the **AL2-U2-BenchmarkPropMgt.accde** database open, open the LeaseTermsAndDeposits query in Design view.
2. Add the *Rent* field from the Tenants table to the design grid placing it between the *EndDate* field and the *SecDep* field.
3. Save the revised query.
4. Create a PivotTable using the following information:
   - Show the names of the buildings in rows.
   - Show the end dates of the leases in months in columns.
   - Add the rent field as the detail field.
   - Add subtotals and grand totals and then hide details.
5. Filter the table to show only those months with end dates in 2013.
6. Save and then print the PivotTable in landscape orientation.
7. Switch to PivotChart view.
8. Filter the chart to display only the data for Mornington Place.
9. Print the PivotChart.
10. Redisplay all of the buildings and then save and close the query.
11. Close the **AL2-U2-BenchmarkPropMgt.accde** database.

Writing Activities

The following activities give you the opportunity to practice your writing skills along with demonstrating an understanding of some of the important Access features you have mastered in this unit. Use correct grammar, appropriate word choices, and clear sentence constructions when required.

Activity 1 Create a New Database for Renovation Contracts by Importing Data

You work for a sole proprietor home renovation contractor. The contractor has an old computer in his basement that he has been using to keep invoice records for renovation contracts. The computer is from the Windows XP operating system era and the software program the contractor used is no longer being sold or updated. The contractor was able to copy data from the old system in a tab-delimited text file named **DavisRenos.txt**. Create a new Access database named **AL2-U2-DavisRenos.accdb** and import the data from the old system into a new table. Modify the table design after importing to change the *Amount* field to Currency. Design and create a form based on the table to be used for entering new records. Design and create a report to print the records including a total of the invoice amount column. The proprietor is not familiar with Access and would like you to create a user-friendly menu that can be used to add new records using the form you designed and view the report. Create the menu using a Navigation form and configure startup options so that the menu is the only object displayed in the work area when the database is opened. Test your menu to make sure each tab functions correctly. Using Microsoft Word, compose a quick reference instruction page for the proprietor that instructs him on how to open the database, add a new record, view and print the report, and exit the database. Save the Word document and name it **AL2-U2-Act1-DavisRenos**. Print the document.

Activity 2 Design and Publish a Report for a Painting Franchise

You are helping a friend who has started a student painting franchise for a summer job. Your friend has asked for your help designing a database to store job information and revenue earned from the jobs over the summer. Create a new database named **AL2-U2-StudentPainters.accdb**. Design and create tables to store the records for painting contract jobs that include the date the job is completed, the invoice number, the homeowner name, address, and telephone number, and the contract price. Enter at least 10 records into the tables. Design a report to print the records in ascending order by date completed. Include statistics at the bottom of the report that provide your friend with the maximum, minimum, average, and total of the contract price field. Include appropriate titles and other report elements. Add your name in the footer as the report designer. Publish and print the report as an XPS document named **AL2-U2-PaintingContracts.xps**.

Internet Research

Buying a Home

Within the next few years you plan on buying a home. While you save money for this investment, you decide to maintain a database of the homes offered for sale within the area where you are interested in buying. Design and create tables and relationships in a new database named **AL2-U2-Homes4Sale.accdb**. Include fields to store data that would be of interest to you such as: the address, asking price, style of home (condominium, ranch, two stories, semi-detached, etc.), number of bedrooms, number of bathrooms, type of heating/cooling system, property taxes, basement, and garage. Design and create a form to be used to enter the information into the tables. Research on the Internet at least five listings within the area that you wish to live and use the form to enter records for each listing. Design and create a report that groups the records by style of home. Calculate the average list price at the end of each group and at the end of the report. Include five hyperlink control objects that will link to the web page from which you retrieved the information for each listing. Include appropriate titles and other report elements. Add your name in the footer as the report designer. Publish and print the report as an XPS document named **AL2-U2-AvgHousePrices.xps**.

Job Study

Meals on Wheels Database

You are a volunteer working in the office of your local Meals on Wheels community organization. Meals on Wheels delivers nutritious, affordable meals to citizens in need of the service such as seniors, convalescents, or people with disabilities. The organization requires volunteers using their own vehicle to drive to the meal depot, pick up meals, and deliver them to clients' homes. The volunteer coordinator has expressed an interest in using an Access database to better organize and plan volunteer delivery routes. Create a new database named **AL2-U2-MealsOnWheels.accdb**. Design and create tables and relationships to store the following information. Remember to apply best practices in database design to minimize data redundancy and validate data whenever possible to ensure accuracy.

- Client name, address, telephone, gender, age, reason for requiring meals (senior, convalescent, or disability), meals required (breakfast, lunch, dinner), date service started, and estimated length of service required.
- Volunteer name, address, telephone, gender, age, date started, availability by day and by meal (breakfast, lunch, dinner), and receipt of police check clearance.
- Incorporate in your design an assignment for both the client and the volunteer to the quadrant of the city or town in which he or she is located. The volunteer coordinator divides the city or town by north, south, east, and west and tries to match drivers with clients in the same quadrant.
- Any other information you think would be important to the volunteer coordinator for this service.

Create a user-defined form template so that each of your forms has a consistent look. Design and create forms to be used to enter the information into the tables and then use the forms to enter at least eight client records and five volunteer records. Make sure you enter records for both clients and volunteers in all four quadrants and for all three meals (breakfast, lunch, dinner).

Design and create queries to extract records of clients and volunteers within the same quadrant. Include in the query results datasheet the information you think would be useful to the volunteer coordinator to set up route schedules. Design and create reports based on the queries. Print the reports.

Create a main menu for the database to provide access to the forms and reports. Configure startup options to display an application title, the main menu form, and hide the tables in the Navigation pane when the database is opened. Close the database and then reopen it. Use Print Screen or the Windows Snipping tool to capture an image of the Access window. Print the image from Word and then exit Word without saving.

A

B

C

D

E

F

G

R

S

T

U

V

W

X

Y

Z

Access 2010 Feature	Ribbon Tab, Group	Button, Option	Shortcut
Advanced Filter Options	Home, Sort & Filter		
Append query	Query Tools Design, Query Type		
Application Parts	Create, Templates		
Copy	Home, Clipboard		Ctrl + C
Create ACCDE file	File, Save & Publish		
Create table	Create, Tables		
Customize Access options or Navigation Pane	File	Options	
Cut	Home, Clipboard		Ctrl + X
Delete query	Query Tools Design, Query Type		
Delete record	Home, Records		Delete key
Design view	Home, Views		
Export as PDF or XPS document	External Data, Export		
Export to Excel worksheet	External Data, Export		
Export to Word document	External Data, Export	, Word	
Filter	Home, Sort & Filter		
Find	Home, Find		
Form	Create, Forms		
Form wizard	Create, Forms		
Import Excel worksheet	External Data, Import & Link		
Import from Access Database	External Data, Import & Link		
Labels	Create, Reports		

Access 2010 Feature	Ribbon Tab, Group	Button, Option	Shortcut
Macro	Create, Macros & Code		
Make Table query	Query Tools Design, Query Type		
Navigation Forms	Create, Forms		
New record	Home, Records		Ctrl + +
Paste	Home, Clipboard		Ctrl + V
Performance Analyzer	Database Tools, Analyze		
Primary Key	Table Tools Design, Tools		
Property Sheet	Form Design Tools Design, Tools or Report Design Tools Design, Tools		F4
Query design	Create, Queries		
Query wizard	Create, Queries		
Relationships	Database Tools, Relationships		
Report	Create, Reports		
Report Design	Create, Reports		
Report wizard	Create, Reports		
Sort ascending	Home, Sort & Filter		
Sort descending	Home, Sort & Filter		
Spelling	Home, Records		F7
Split database	Database Tools, Move Data		
Table Analyzer Wizard	Database Tools, Analyze		
Total row	Home, Records		
Update query	Query Tools Design, Query Type		